XML 1.1 Bible

3rd Edition

XML 1.1 Bible

3rd Edition

Elliotte Rusty Harold

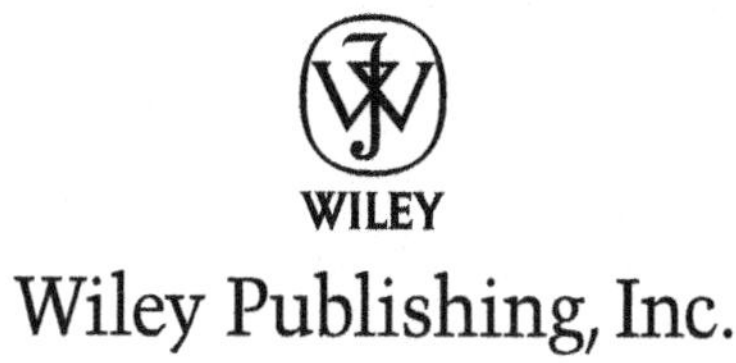

Wiley Publishing, Inc.

XML 1.1 Bible, 3rd Edition

Published by
Wiley Publishing, Inc.
10475 Crosspoint Boulevard
Indianapolis, IN 46256
www.wiley.com

Published simultaneously in Canada

ISBN: 978-0-7645-4986-1

Manufactured in the United States of America

10 9 8 7 6 5 4 3

3O/RT/QS/QU/IN

For general information on our other products and services or to obtain technical support, please contact our Customer Care Department within the U.S. at (800) 762-2974, outside the U.S. at (317) 572-3993 or fax (317) 572-4002.

Wiley also publishes its books in a variety of electronic formats. Some content that appears in print may not be available in electronic books.

Library of Congress Control Number: 2004101453

About the Author

Elliotte Rusty Harold is an internationally respected writer, programmer, and educator, both on the Internet and off. He got his start writing FAQ lists for the Macintosh newsgroups on Usenet and has since branched out into books, Web sites, and newsletters. He's an adjunct professor of computer science at Polytechnic University in Brooklyn, New York. His Cafe con Leche Web site at `http://www.cafeconleche.org/` has become one of the most popular independent XML sites on the Internet.

Elliotte is originally from New Orleans, to which he returns periodically in search of a decent bowl of gumbo. However, he currently resides in the Prospect Heights neighborhood of Brooklyn with his wife Beth, and his cats Charm (named after the quark) and Marjorie (named after his mother-in-law). When not writing books, he enjoys working on genealogy, mathematics, free software, and quantum mechanics. His previous books include *The Java Developer's Resource*, *Java Network Programming*, *Java Secrets*, *JavaBeans*, *Java I/O*, *XML: Extensible Markup Language*, *XML in a Nutshell*, *Processing XML with Java*, and *Effective XML*.

Credits

Acquisitions Editor
Jim Minatel

Development Editor
Marcia Ellett

Technical Editor
David Schultz

Production Editor
Angela Smith

Copy Editor
Joanne Slike

Editorial Manager
Mary Beth Wakefield

Vice President & Executive Group Publisher
Richard Swadley

Vice President and Executive Publisher
Robert Ipsen

Vice President and Publisher
Joseph B. Wikert

Executive Editorial Director
Mary Bednarek

Project Coordinator
Erin Smith

Graphics and Production Specialists
Joyce Haughey
Jennifer Heleine
Kristin McMullan
Heather Ryan
Mary Gillot Virgin

Quality Control Technicians
Laura Albert
Susan Moritz
Carl William Pierce

Permissions Editor
Laura Moss

Media Development Specialist
Greg Stafford

Proofreading and Indexing
TECHBOOKS Production Services

Preface

Welcome to the third edition of the *XML 1.1 Bible*. When the first edition was published about five years ago, XML was a promising technology with a small but growing niche. In the last half decade, it has absolutely exploded. XML no longer needs to be justified as a good idea. In fact, the question developers are asking has changed from "Why XML?" to "Why not XML?" XML has become the data format of choice for fields as diverse as stock trading and graphic design. More new programs today are using XML than aren't. A solid understanding of just what XML is and how to use it has become a *sine qua non* for the computer literate.

The *XML 1.1 Bible,* 3rd Edition is your introduction to the exciting and fast-growing world of XML. With this book, you'll learn how to write documents in XML and how to use style sheets to convert those documents into HTML so that legacy browsers can read them. You'll also learn how to use document type definitions (DTDs) and schemas to describe and validate documents. You'll encounter a variety of XML applications in many domains, ranging from finance to vector graphics to genealogy. And you'll learn how to take advantage of XML for your own unique projects, programs, and web pages.

What's New in the Third Edition

The French philosopher and mathematician Blaise Pascal once wrote in a letter, "I have only made this longer because I have not had the time to make it shorter." I know how he felt. The first edition of the *XML Bible* was written under great time pressure, was finished well after deadline, and totaled more than 1000 pages, the largest book I had written up to that point. My favorite reader comment about that edition was, "It would seem to me that if you asked the author to write 10,000 words about the colour blue, he would be able to do it without breaking into a sweat." While I probably could write 10,000 words about blue, for the third edition, I did try to restrain myself and take the time to write more concisely. I rewrote the book from the ground up; and while I retained the basic flavor and outline that proved so popular with the first edition, I tightened up the writing and cut many examples down to size. With the benefit of five years of hindsight, I have also been able to expand coverage of promising new technologies (schemas, XInclude, XHTML, SVG, XML Base, and RDDL) while eliminating coverage of applications that proved to be less useful than they initially appeared (WML, VML, CDF, HTML+TIME, RDF, and so on). The result is a more concise, approachable volume that covers more of what you need to know and less of what you don't. If you liked the first or second edition, you're going to like the third edition even more. I'm confident you'll find this an even more useful tutorial and reference.

Who You Are

Unlike most other XML books on the market, the *XML 1.1 Bible,* 3rd Edition discusses XML from the perspective of a web page author, not from the perspective of a software developer. I don't spend a lot of time discussing BNF grammars or parsing element trees. Instead, I show you how you can use XML and existing tools today to more efficiently produce attractive, exciting, easy-to-use, easy-to-maintain web sites that keep your readers coming back for more.

This book is aimed directly at web site developers. I assume you want to use XML to produce web sites that are difficult or impossible to create with raw HTML. You'll be amazed to discover that in conjunction with style sheets and a few free tools, XML enables you to do things that previously required either custom software costing thousands of dollars per site or extensive knowledge of programming languages such as Perl. None of the software discussed in this book will cost you more than a few minutes of download time. None of the tricks require any programming.

What You Need to Know

XML does build on top of the underlying infrastructure of the Internet and the Web. Consequently, I will assume you know how to FTP files, send e-mail, and load URLs into your web browser of choice. I will also assume you have a reasonable knowledge of HTML. On the other hand, when I discuss newer aspects of HTML that are not yet in widespread use, such as Cascading Style Sheets, I discuss them in depth.

To be more specific, in this book I assume that you can do the following:

- ✦ Write a basic HTML page, including links, images, and text, using a text editor.
- ✦ Place that page on a web server.

On the other hand, I do not assume that you

- ✦ Know SGML. In fact, this preface is almost the only place in the entire book you'll see the word SGML used. XML is supposed to be simpler and more widespread than SGML. It can't be that if you have to learn SGML first.
- ✦ Are a programmer, whether of Java, Perl, C, or some other language. XML is a markup language, not a programming language. You don't need to be a programmer to write XML documents.

What You'll Learn

This book has one primary goal: to teach you to write XML documents for the Web. Fortunately, XML has a decidedly flat learning curve, much like HTML (and unlike SGML). As you learn a little, you can do a little. As you learn a little more, you can do a little more. Thus, the chapters in this book build steadily on one another. They are meant to be read in sequence. Along the way you'll learn the following:

- How to author XML documents and deliver them to readers
- How semantic tagging makes XML documents easier to maintain and develop than their HTML equivalents
- How to post XML documents on web servers in a form everyone can read
- How to make sure your XML is well formed
- How to write with international characters such as Ж and Æ
- How to validate documents against DTDs and schemas
- How to build large documents from smaller parts using entities and XInclude
- How to merge different XML vocabularies with namespaces
- How to format your documents with CSS and XSL style sheets
- How to connect documents with XLinks and XPointers

In the final part of this book, you'll see several practical examples of XML being used for real-world applications, including the following:

- Web site design
- Schemas
- Vector graphics
- Genealogy

How the Book Is Organized

This book is divided into five parts:

I. Introducing XML

II. Document Type Definitions

III. Style Languages

IV. Supplemental Technologies

V. XML Applications

By the time you finish reading this book, you'll be ready to use XML to create compelling web pages.

Part I: Introducing XML

Part I (Chapters 1 through 6) begins with the history and theory behind XML and the goals XML is trying to achieve. It shows you how the different pieces of the XML equation fit together to enable you to create and deliver documents to readers. You'll see several compelling examples of XML applications to give you some idea of the wide applicability of XML, including Scalable Vector Graphics (SVG), the Open Financial Exchange (OFX), the Mathematical Markup Language (MathML), the Extensible Forms Description Language (XFDL), and many others. Then you'll learn by example how to write XML documents with tags that you define that make sense for your document. You'll learn how to edit them in a text editor, attach style sheets to them, and load them into a web browser such as Internet Explorer 5.0 or Mozilla.

Part II: Document Type Definitions

Part II (Chapters 7 through 11) focuses on document type definitions (DTDs). A DTD specifies which elements are and are not allowed in an XML document, and the exact context and structure of those elements. A validating parser can read a document, compare it to its DTD, and report any mistakes it finds. DTDs enable document authors to ensure that their work meets any necessary criteria.

In Part II, you'll learn how to attach a DTD to a document, how to validate your documents against their DTDs, and how to write new DTDs that solve your own problems. You'll learn the syntax for declaring elements, attributes, entities, and notations. You'll learn how to use entity declarations and entity references to build both a document and its DTD from multiple, independent pieces. This allows you to make long, hard-to-follow documents much simpler by separating them into related modules and components. And you'll learn how to use namespaces to mix together different XML vocabularies in one document.

Part III: Style Languages

Part III (Chapters 12 through 16) teaches you everything you need to know about style sheets. XML markup only specifies what's in a document. Unlike HTML, it does not say anything about what that content should look like. Instead, style shheets provide all necessary information about an XML document's appearance when printed, viewed in a web browser, or otherwise displayed. Different style sheets can be applied to the same document. You might, for example, want to use one style sheet that specifies small fonts for printing, another one with larger fonts for on-screen presentation, and a third with absolutely humongous fonts to project the document on a wall at a seminar. You can change the appearance of an XML document by choosing a different style sheet without touching the document itself.

Part III describes in detail the two style sheet languages in broadest use today, Cascading Style Sheets (CSS) and the Extensible Stylesheet Language (XSL). CSS is a simple style sheet language originally designed for use with HTML. It applies fixed style rules to the contents of particular elements.

XSL, by contrast, is a more complicated and more powerful style language that can apply styles to the contents of elements, as well as rearrange elements, add boilerplate text, and transform documents in almost arbitrary ways. XSL is divided into two parts: a transformation language for converting XML trees to alternative trees, and a formatting language for specifying the appearance of the elements of an XML tree.

Part IV: Supplemental Technologies

Part IV (Chapters 17 through 20) introduces some XML-based languages and syntaxes that layer on top of basic XML to provide additional functionality and features. XLink provides multidirectional hypertext links that are far more powerful than the simple HTML `<A>` tag. XPointers introduce a new syntax you can attach to the end of URLs to link not only to particular documents but also to particular parts of particular documents. XInclude enables you to build large XML documents out of multiple smaller XML documents. XML Schemas provide a more complete validations language that includes data typing and range checking. All of these can be added to your own XML-based markup languages to extend their power and utility.

Part V: XML Applications

Part V (Chapters 21 to 25) demonstrates several practical uses of XML in different domains. XHTML is a reformulation of HTML 4.0 as valid XML. RDDL is an XHTML- and XLink-based language for documents containing meta-information placed at the end of namespace URLs. Scalable Vector Graphics (SVG) is a standard XML format for drawings recommended by the World Wide Web Consortium (W3C). Finally, a completely new application is developed for genealogical data to show you not just how to use XML tags and technologies, but why and when to choose them. Combining all of these different applications, you'll develop a good sense of how XML applications are designed, built, and used in the real world.

What You Need

XML is a platform-independent technology. You'll notice that screen shots in this book have been captured from Windows, Mac OS 9, Mac OS X, and Linux. Almost all the examples work equally well across all common platforms. You will need a web browser that supports XML, such as Mozilla, Netscape 6.0 or later, or Internet Explorer 6.0.

Furthermore, much of the best software for working with XML is written in Java and can run on multiple platforms. Much of this is freely available on the Internet. You will need a Java 1.2 or later virtual machine. (Java 1.1 can do in a pinch.) You won't need to write any programs to use this book. You'll just need it to run programs written in Java.

How to Use This Book

This book is designed to be read more or less cover to cover. Each chapter builds on the material in the previous chapters in a fairly predictable fashion. Of course, you're always welcome to skim over material that's already familiar to you. I also hope you'll stop along the way to try out some of the examples and to write some XML documents of your own. It's important to learn not just by reading, but also by doing. Before you get started, I'd like to make a couple of notes about grammatical conventions used in this book.

Unlike HTML, XML is case-sensitive. `<FATHER>` is not the same as `<Father>` or `<father>`. The `father` element is not the same as the `Father` element or the `FATHER` element. Unfortunately, case-sensitive markup languages have an annoying habit of conflicting with standard English usage. On rare occasion, this means that you may encounter sentences that don't begin with a capital letter. More commonly, you'll see capitalization used in the middle of a sentence where you wouldn't normally expect it. Please don't get too bothered by this. All XML and HTML code used in this book is placed in a `monospaced font`, so most of the time it will be obvious from the context what is meant.

I have also adopted the British convention of placing punctuation inside quote marks only when it belongs with the material quoted. Frankly, although I learned to write in the American educational system, I find the British system far more logical, especially when dealing with source code where the difference between a comma or a period and no punctuation at all can make the difference between perfectly correct and perfectly incorrect code.

What the Icons Mean

Throughout the book, I've used icons in the left margin to call your attention to points that are particularly important.

Note Note icons provide supplemental information about the subject at hand, but generally something that isn't quite the main idea. Notes are often used to elaborate on a detailed technical point.

Tip icons indicate a more efficient way of doing something, or a technique that may not be obvious.

Caution icons warn you of a common misconception or that a procedure doesn't always work quite like it's supposed to. The most common reason for a Caution icon in this book is to point out the difference between what a specification says should happen and what actually does.

The Cross-Reference icon refers you to other chapters that have more to say about a particular subject.

Reach Out

Feedback on past editions has had a significant positive effect on the structure and content of this edition, and I encourage you to let me know what you think of it so I can continue to improve future editions. After you have had a chance to read this book, please take a moment to send me an e-mail at `elharo@metalab.unc.edu`. Be sure to include the title of this book in your e-mail. Please be honest in your evaluation. If you thought a particular chapter didn't tell you enough, let me know. Of course, I would prefer to receive comments such as "This is the best book I've ever read," "Thanks to this book, my web site won Cool Site of the Year," or "Because I was reading this book on the beach, I met a stunning swimsuit model who thought I was the hottest thing on feet," but I'll take any comments I can get. ☺

You should also feel free to send me specific questions regarding the material in this book. I'll do my best to help you out and answer your questions, but I can't guarantee a reply. Generally, more specific questions (How do I change the value of a variable in XSLT?) are more likely to receive timely, useful answers than very generic, broad questions (How is XML used in the legal profession?).

Also, I invite you to visit my Cafe con Leche web site at `http://www.cafeconleche.org`, which contains a lot of XML-related material and is updated almost daily. Despite my persistent efforts to make this book perfect, some errors have doubtless slipped by. Even more certainly, some of the material discussed here will change over time. I'll post any necessary updates and errata on my web site at `http://www.cafeconleche.org/books/bible3/`. Please let me know via e-mail of any errors that you find that aren't already listed.

I hope you enjoy the book. Happy XMLing!

Elliotte Rusty Harold
`elharo@metalab.unc.edu`
`http://www.cafeconleche.org`
New York City, December 11, 2003

Acknowledgments

The folks at Wiley Publishing have all been great. The acquisitions editors, John Osborn, Grace Buechlein on the second edition, and Jim Minatel on this edition deserve special thanks for arranging the unusual scheduling this book required to hit the moving target that XML presents. Marcia Ellett shepherded this book through the development process. She managed the shifting outline and schedule that a book based on unstable specifications and software requires with poise and grace. Angela Smith proved equally adept on shepherding this book through its final production. Terri Varveris edited the first edition and Sharon Nash the second edition. Without them, there could never have been a third edition.

Steven Champeon brought his SGML experience to the book, and provided many insightful comments on the text. My brother, Thomas Harold, put his command of chemistry at my disposal when I was trying to grasp the Chemical Markup Language. Carroll Bellau provided me with the parts of my family tree, which you'll find in Chapter 18. Piroz Mohseni and Heather Williamson served as technical editors on the first edition and corrected many of my errors. Ken Cox performed the same service for the second edition, and B.K. Delong for the Gold edition. David Schultz stepped up to the plate for this edition.

I also greatly appreciate all the comments, questions, and corrections sent in by readers of the first and second editions and *XML: Extensible Markup Language*. I hope that I've managed to address most of those comments in this book. They've definitely helped make the *XML 1.1 Bible,* 3rd Edition a better book. Particular thanks are due to Michael Dyck, Alan Esenther, and Donald Lancon, Jr. for their especially detailed comments.

The agenting talents of David and Sherry Rogelberg of the Studio B Literary Agency (`http://www.studiob.com/`) have made it possible for me to write effectively full-time. I recommend them highly to anyone thinking about writing computer books. And, as always, thanks go to my wife, Beth, for her endless love and understanding.

Contents at a Glance

Contents

Part II: Document Type Definitions 187

Introducing XML

PART I

✦ ✦ ✦ ✦

In This Part

✦ ✦ ✦ ✦

An Eagle's Eye View of XML

✦ ✦ ✦ ✦

In This Chapter

What is XML?

Why are developers excited about XML?

The life of an XML document

Related technologies

✦ ✦ ✦ ✦

This chapter introduces you to XML, the Extensible Markup Language. It explains, in general terms, what XML is and how it is used. It shows you how different XML technologies work together, and how to create an XML document and deliver it to readers.

What Is XML?

XML stands for Extensible Markup Language (often miscapitalized as *eXtensible Markup Language* to justify the acronym). XML is a set of rules for defining semantic tags that break a document into parts and identify the different parts of the document. It is a meta-markup language that defines a syntax in which other domain-specific markup languages can be written.

XML is a meta-markup language

The first thing you need to understand about XML is that it isn't just another markup language like HTML, TeX, or troff. These languages define a fixed set of tags that describe a fixed number of elements. If the markup language you use doesn't contain the tag you need, you're out of luck. You can wait for the next version of the markup language, hoping that it includes the tag you need; but then you're really at the mercy of whatever the vendor chooses to include.

XML, however, is a meta-markup language. It's a language that lets you make up the tags you need as you go along. These tags must be organized according to certain general principles, but they're quite flexible in their meaning. For example, if you're working on genealogy and need to describe family names, personal names, dates, births, adoptions, deaths, burial sites, marriages, divorces, and so on, you can create tags for each of these. You don't have to force your data to fit into paragraphs, list items, table cells, or other very general categories.

You can document the tags you create in a schema written in any of several languages, including document type definitions (DTDs) and the W3C XML Schema Language. You'll learn more about DTDs and schemas in Parts II and IV of this book. For now, think of a schema as a vocabulary and a syntax for certain kinds of documents. For example, the schema for Peter Murray-Rust's Chemical Markup Language (CML) is a DTD that describes a vocabulary and a syntax for the molecular sciences: chemistry, crystallography, solid-state physics, and the like. It includes tags for atoms, molecules, bonds, spectra, and so on. Many different people in the field can share this schema. Other schemas are available for other fields, and you can create your own.

XML defines the meta syntax that domain-specific markup languages such as MusicXML, MathML, and CML must follow. It specifies the rules for the low-level syntax, saying how markup is distinguished from content, how attributes are attached to elements, and so forth, without saying what these tags, elements, and attributes are or what they mean. It gives the patterns that elements must follow without specifying the names of the elements. For example, XML says that tags begin with a < and end with a >. However, XML does not tell you what names must go between the < and the >.

If an application understands this meta syntax, it at least partially understands all the languages built from this meta syntax. A browser does not need to know in advance each and every tag that might be used by thousands of different markup languages. Instead, the browser discovers the tags used by any given document as it reads the document or its schema. The detailed instructions about how to display the content of these tags are provided in a separate style sheet that is attached to the document.

For example, consider the three-dimensional Schrödinger equation:

$$i\hbar \frac{\partial \psi(\mathbf{r}, t)}{\partial t} = -\frac{\hbar^2}{2m}\nabla^2\psi(\mathbf{r}, t) + V(\mathbf{r})\psi(\mathbf{r}, t)$$

XML means you don't have to wait for browser vendors to catch up with your ideas. You can invent the tags you need, when you need them, and tell the browsers how to display these tags.

XML describes structure and semantics, not formatting

XML markup describes a document's structure and meaning. It does not describe the formatting of the elements on the page. You can add formatting to a document with a style sheet. The document itself only contains tags that say what is in the document, not what the document looks like.

By contrast, HTML encompasses formatting, structural, and semantic markup. <B> is a formatting tag that makes its content bold. <STRONG> is a semantic tag that means its contents are especially important. <TD> is a structural tag that indicates that the contents are a cell in a table. In fact, some tags can have all three kinds of meaning. An <H1> tag can simultaneously mean 20-point Helvetica bold, a level 1 heading, and the title of the page.

For example, in HTML, a song might be described using a definition title, definition data, an unordered list, and list items. But none of these elements actually have anything to do with music. The HTML might look something like this:

```
<DT>Hot Cop
<DD> by Jacques Morali, Henri Belolo, and Victor Willis
<UL>
<LI> Jacques Morali
<LI> PolyGram Records
<LI> 6:20
<LI> 1978
<LI> Village People
</UL>
```

In XML, the same data could be marked up like this:

```
<SONG>
  <TITLE>Hot Cop</TITLE>
  <COMPOSER>Jacques Morali</COMPOSER>
  <COMPOSER>Henri Belolo</COMPOSER>
  <COMPOSER>Victor Willis</COMPOSER>
  <PRODUCER>Jacques Morali</PRODUCER>
  <PUBLISHER>PolyGram Records</PUBLISHER>
  <LENGTH>6:20</LENGTH>
  <YEAR>1978</YEAR>
  <ARTIST>Village People</ARTIST>
</SONG>
```

Instead of generic tags such as <DT> and <LI>, this example uses meaningful tags such as <SONG>, <TITLE>, <COMPOSER>, and <YEAR>. These tags didn't come from any preexisting standard or specification. I just made them up on the spot because they fit the information I was describing. Domain-specific tagging has a number of advantages, not the least of which is that it's easier for a human to read the source code to determine what the author intended.

XML markup also makes it easier for nonhuman automated computer software to locate all of the songs in the document. A computer program reading HTML can't tell more than that an element is a `DT`. It cannot determine whether that `DT` represents a song title, a definition, or some designer's favorite means of indenting text. In fact, a single document might well contain `DT` elements with all three meanings.

XML element names can be chosen such that they have extra meaning in additional contexts. For example, they might be the field names of a database. XML is far more flexible and amenable to varied uses than HTML because a limited number of tags don't have to serve many different purposes. XML offers an infinite number of tags to fill an infinite number of needs.

Why Are Developers Excited About XML?

XML makes easy many web-development tasks that are extremely difficult with HTML, and it makes tasks that are impossible with HTML possible. Because XML is extensible, developers like it for many reasons. Which reasons most interest you depends on your individual needs, but once you learn XML, you're likely to discover that it's the solution to more than one problem you're already struggling with. This section investigates some of the generic uses of XML that excite developers. In Chapter 2, you'll see some of the specific applications that have already been developed with XML.

Domain-specific markup languages

XML enables individual professions (for example, music, chemistry, human resources) to develop their own domain-specific markup languages. Domain-specific markup languages enable practitioners in the field to trade notes, data, and information without worrying about whether or not the person on the receiving end has the particular proprietary payware that was used to create the data. They can even send documents to people outside the profession with a reasonable confidence that those who receive them will at least be able to view the documents.

Furthermore, creating separate markup languages for different domains does not lead to bloatware or unnecessary complexity for those outside the profession. You may not be interested in electrical engineering diagrams, but electrical engineers are. You may not need to include sheet music in your web pages, but composers do. XML lets the electrical engineers describe their circuits and the composers notate their scores, mostly without stepping on each other's toes. Neither field needs special support from browser manufacturers or complicated plug-ins, as is true today.

Self-describing data

Much computer data from the last 40 years is lost, not because of natural disaster or decaying backup media (though those are problems too, ones XML doesn't solve), but simply because no one bothered to document how the data formats. A Lotus 1-2-3 file on a 15-year-old 5.25-inch floppy disk might be irretrievable in most corporations today without a huge investment of time and resources. Data in a less-known binary format such as Lotus Jazz may be gone forever.

XML is, at a low level, an incredibly simple data format. It can be written in 100 percent pure ASCII or Unicode text, as well as in a few other well-defined formats. Text is reasonably resistant to corruption. The removal of bytes or even large sequences of bytes does not noticeably corrupt the remaining text. This starkly contrasts with many other formats, such as compressed data or serialized Java objects, in which the corruption or loss of even a single byte can render the rest of the file unreadable.

At a higher level, XML is self-describing. Suppose you're an information archaeologist in the twenty-third century and you encounter this chunk of XML code on an old floppy disk that has survived the ravages of time:

```
<PERSON ID="p1100" SEX="M">
  <NAME>
    <GIVEN>Judson</GIVEN>
    <SURNAME> McDaniel</SURNAME>
  </NAME>
  <BIRTH>
    <DATE>21 Feb 1834</DATE>  </BIRTH>
  <DEATH>
    <DATE>9 Dec 1905</DATE>  </DEATH>
</PERSON>
```

Even if you're not familiar with XML, assuming you speak a reasonable facsimile of twentieth-century English, you've got a pretty good idea that this fragment describes a man named Judson McDaniel, who was born on February 21, 1834 and died on December 9, 1905. In fact, even with gaps in or corruption of the data, you could probably still extract most of this information. The same could not be said for a proprietary, binary spreadsheet or word-processor format.

Furthermore, XML is very well documented. The World Wide Web Consortium (W3C)'s XML specification and numerous books tell you exactly how to read XML data. There are no secrets waiting to trip the unwary.

Interchange of data among applications

Because XML is nonproprietary and easy to read and write, it's an excellent format for the interchange of data among different applications. XML is not encumbered by copyright, patent, trade secret, or any other sort of intellectual property restrictions. It has been designed to be extremely expressive and very well structured while at the same time being easy for both human beings and computer programs to read and write. Thus, it's an obvious choice for exchange languages.

One such format is the Open Financial Exchange 2.0 (OFX, `http://www.ofx.net/`). OFX is designed to let personal finance programs, such as Microsoft Money and Quicken, trade data. The data can be sent back and forth between programs and exchanged with banks, brokerage houses, credit card companies, and the like.

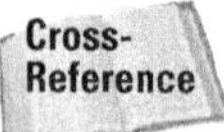

OFX is further discussed in Chapter 2.

By choosing XML instead of a proprietary data format, you can use any tool that understands XML to work with your data. You can even use different tools for different purposes, one program to view and another to edit, for example. XML keeps you from getting locked into a particular program simply because that's what your data is already written in, or because that program's proprietary format is all your correspondent can accept.

For example, many publishers require submissions in Microsoft Word. This means that most authors have to use Word, even if they would rather use OpenOffice.org Writer or WordPerfect. This makes it extremely difficult for any other company to publish a competing word processor unless it can read and write Word files. To do so, the company's programmers must reverse-engineer the binary Word file format, which requires a significant investment of limited time and resources. Most other word processors have a limited ability to read and write Word files, but they generally lose track of graphics, macros, styles, revision marks, and other important features. Word's document format is undocumented, proprietary, and constantly changing, and thus Word tends to end up winning by default, even when writers would prefer to use other, simpler programs. Word 2003 offers the option to save its documents in an XML application called WordML instead of its native binary file format. It is far easier to reverse-engineer an undocumented XML format than a binary format. In the future, Word files will much more easily be exchanged among people using different word processors.

Structured data

XML is ideal for large and complex documents because the data is structured. You specify a vocabulary that defines the elements in the document, and you can specify the relations between elements. For example, if you're putting together a web page of sales contacts, you can require every contact to have a phone number and an e-mail address. If you're inputting data for a database, you can make sure that no fields are missing. You can even provide default values to be used when no data is available.

XML also provides a client-side include mechanism that integrates data from multiple sources and displays it as a single document. (In fact, it provides at least three different ways of doing this, a source of some confusion.) The data can even be rearranged on the fly. Parts of it can be shown or hidden depending on user actions. You'll find this extremely useful when you're working with large information repositories like relational databases.

The Life of an XML Document

XML is, at its root, a document format, a series of rules about what a document looks like. There are two levels of conformity to the XML standard. The first is *well-formedness* and the second is *validity*. Part I of this book shows you how to write well-formed documents. Part II shows you how to write valid documents.

HTML is a document format that is designed for use on the Internet and inside web browsers. XML can certainly be used for that, as this book demonstrates. However, XML is far more broadly applicable. It can be used as a storage format for word processors, as a data interchange format for different programs, as a means of enforcing conformity with intranet templates, and as a way to preserve data in a human-readable fashion.

However, like all data formats, XML needs programs and content before it's useful. It isn't enough to just understand XML itself. That's not much more than a specification for what data should look like. You also need to know how XML documents are edited, how processors read XML documents and pass the information they read on to applications, and what these applications do with that data.

Editors

XML documents are most commonly created with an editor. This might be a basic text editor, such as Notepad or vi, that doesn't really understand XML at all. On the other hand, it might be a completely WYSIWYG editor, such as Adobe FrameMaker, that insulates you almost completely from the details of the underlying XML format. Or it may be a structured editor, such as Visual XML (`http://www.pierlou.com/visxml/`), that displays XML documents as trees. For the most part, the fancy editors aren't very useful as of yet, so this book concentrates on writing raw XML by hand in a text editor.

Other programs can also create XML documents. For example, previous editions of this book included several XML documents whose data came straight out of a FileMaker database. In this case, the data was first entered into the FileMaker database. Next, a FileMaker calculation field converted that data to XML. Finally, an AppleScript program extracted the data from the database and wrote it as an XML file. Similar processes can extract XML from MySQL, Oracle, and other databases by using XML, Perl, Java, PHP, or any convenient language. In general, XML works extremely well with databases.

In any case, the editor or other program creates an XML document. More often than not, this document is an actual file on some computer's hard disk, but it doesn't absolutely have to be. For example, the document might be a record or a field in a database, or it might be a stream of bytes received from a network.

Parsers and processors

An XML parser (also known as an XML processor) reads the document and verifies that the XML it contains is well formed. It may also check that the document is valid, although this test is not required. The exact details of these tests are covered in Part II. If the document passes the tests, the processor converts the document into a tree of elements.

Browsers and other applications

Finally, the parser passes the tree or individual nodes of the tree to the client application. If this application is a web browser such as Mozilla, the browser formats the data and shows it to the user. But other programs may also receive the data. For example, a database might interpret an XML document as input data for new records; a MIDI program might see the document as a sequence of musical notes to play; a spreadsheet program might view the XML as a list of numbers and formulas. XML is extremely flexible and can be used for many different purposes.

The process summarized

To summarize, an XML document is created in an editor. The XML parser reads the document and converts it into a tree of elements. The parser passes the tree to the browser or other application that displays it. Figure 1-1 shows this process.

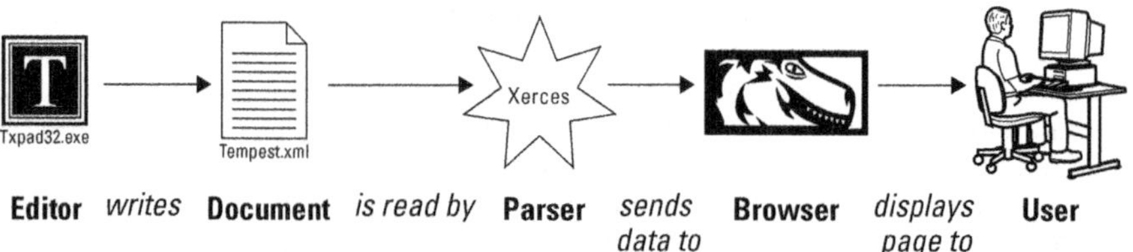

Figure 1-1: XML document life cycle

It's important to note that all of these pieces are independent of and decoupled from each other. The only thing that connects them is the XML document. You can change the editor program independently of the end application. In fact, you may not always know what the end application is. It might be an end user reading your work, it might be a database sucking in data, or it might be something not yet invented. It may even be all of these. The document is independent of the programs that read and write it.

HTML is also somewhat independent of the programs that read and write it, but it's really only suitable for browsing. Other uses, such as database input, are beyond its scope. For example, HTML does not provide a way to force an author to include certain required content such as the ISBN in every book. XML enables you to do this. You can even control the order in which particular elements appear (for example, that level 2 headers must always follow level 1 headers).

Related Technologies

XML doesn't operate in a vacuum. Using XML as more than a data format involves several related technologies and standards, including the following:

- HTML for backward compatibility with legacy browsers
- The CSS and XSL style sheet languages to define the appearance of XML documents
- URLs and URIs to specify the locations of XML documents
- XLinks to connect XML documents to each other
- The Unicode character set to encode the text of an XML document

HTML

Mozilla 1.0, Opera 4.0, Internet Explorer 5.0, and Netscape 6.0 and later provide some (albeit incomplete) support for XML. However, it takes about two years before most users have upgraded to a particular release of the software (in 2004, my wife still uses Netscape 4 on her Mac at work), so you're going to need to convert your XML content into classic HTML for some time to come.

Therefore, before you jump into XML, you should be completely comfortable with HTML. You don't need to be a hotshot graphical designer, but you should know how to link from one page to the next, how to include an image in a document, how to make text bold, and so forth. Because HTML is the most common output format of XML, the more familiar you are with HTML, the easier it will be to create the effects you want.

On the other hand, if you're accustomed to using tables or single-pixel GIFs to arrange objects on a page, or if you begin planning a web site by sketching out its design in Photoshop, you're going to have to unlearn some bad habits. As previously discussed, XML separates the content of a document from the appearance of the document. You develop the content first, and then design a style sheet that formats the content. Separating content from presentation is an extremely effective technique that improves both the content and the appearance of the document. Among other things, it enables authors, programmers, and designers to work more independently of each other. However, it does require a different way of thinking about the design of a web site, and perhaps even the use of different project management techniques when multiple people are involved.

CSS

Because XML allows arbitrary tags in a document, the browser has no way to know in advance how each element should be displayed. When you send a document to a user, you also need to send along a style sheet that tells the browser how to format the tags you've used. One kind of style sheet you can use is a CSS style sheet.

Cascading style sheets, initially invented for HTML, define formatting properties such as font size, font family, font weight, paragraph indentation, paragraph alignment, and other styles that can be applied to particular elements. For example, CSS allows HTML documents to specify that all `H1` elements should be formatted in 32-point, centered, Helvetica bold. Individual styles can be applied to most HTML tags that override the browser's defaults. Multiple style sheets can be applied to a single document, and multiple styles can be applied to a single element. The styles then cascade according to a particular set of rules.

Cross-Reference

CSS rules and properties are explored in more detail in Chapters 12, 13, and 14.

Mozilla, Opera 4.0, Netscape 6.0, and Internet Explorer 5.0 and later can display XML documents with associated CSS style sheets. They differ a little in how many CSS properties they support and how well they support them.

XSL

The Extensible Stylesheet Language (XSL) is a more powerful style language designed specifically for XML documents. XSL style sheets are themselves well-formed XML documents. XSL is actually two different XML applications:

- ✦ XSL Transformations (XSLT)
- ✦ XSL Formatting Objects (XSL-FO)

Generally, an XSLT style sheet describes a transformation from an input XML document in one format to an output XML document in another format. That output format can be XSL-FO, but it can also be any other text format (XML or otherwise), such as HTML, plain text, or TeX.

An XSLT style sheet contains templates that match particular patterns of XML elements. An XSLT processor reads an XML document and an XSLT style sheet and compares the elements it finds in the document to the patterns in the style sheet. When the processor recognizes a pattern from the XSLT style sheet in the input XML document, it instantiates the template and outputs the resulting text. Unlike cascading style sheets, this output text is somewhat arbitrary and is not limited to the input text plus formatting information. It depends on the instructions in the template.

A CSS style sheet can only change the format of a particular element, and it can only do so on an element-wide basis. An XSLT style sheet, on the other hand, can rearrange and reorder elements. It can hide some elements and display others. Furthermore, it can choose the style to use based not just on the element name, but also on the contents and attributes of the element, on the position of the element in the document relative to other elements, and on a variety of other criteria.

Cross-Reference XSLT is introduced in Chapter 5 and explored in detail in Chapter 15.

XSL-FO is an XML application that describes the layout of a page. It specifies where particular text is placed on the page in relation to other items on the page. It also assigns styles, such as italic, or fonts, such as Arial, to individual items on the page. You can think of XSL-FO as a page description language like PostScript (minus PostScript's built-in, Turing-complete programming language).

Cross-Reference XSL-FO is covered in Chapter 16.

Which style sheet language should you choose? CSS has the advantage of broader browser support. However, XSL is far more flexible and powerful, and better suited to XML documents. Furthermore, XML documents with XSLT style sheets can easily be converted to HTML documents with CSS style sheets. XSL-FO is a little past the bleeding edge, however. No browsers support it, and even third-party FO-to-PDF converters such as FOP don't support all of the current formatting object specification.

Which language you pick largely depends on your use case. If you want to serve XML files directly to clients and use their CPU power to format and transform the documents, you really need to be using CSS (and even then, the clients had better have very up-to-date browsers). On the other hand, if you want to support older browsers, you're better off converting documents to HTML on the server using XSLT, and sending the browsers pure HTML. For high-quality printing, you're better off with XSLT plus XSL-FO. An advantage of XML is that it's quite easy to do all of this at the same time. You can change the style sheet and even the style sheet language you use without changing the XML documents that contain your content.

URLs and URIs

XML documents can live on the Web, just like HTML and other documents. When they do, they are referred to by Uniform Resource Locators (URLs). For example, at the URL `http://cafeconleche.org/examples/shakespeare/tempest.xml` you'll find the complete text of Shakespeare's *Tempest* marked up in XML.

Although URLs are well understood and well supported, the XML specification uses the more general Uniform Resource Identifier (URI). URIs are a more general scheme for locating resources; URIs focus a little more on the resource and a little less on the location. Furthermore, they aren't necessarily limited to resources on the Internet. For example, the URI for this book is `urn:isbn:0764549863`. This doesn't refer to the specific copy you're holding in your hands. It refers to the almost-Platonic form of the third edition of the *XML Bible* shared by all individual copies.

In theory, a URI can find the closest copy of a mirrored document or locate a document that has been moved from one site to another. In practice, URIs are still an area of active research, and the only kinds of URIs that current software actually supports are URLs.

XLinks and XPointers

As long as XML documents are posted on the Internet, people will want to link them to each other. Standard HTML link tags can be used in XML documents, and HTML documents can link to XML documents. For example, this HTML link points to the aforementioned copy of the *Tempest* in XML:

```
<A HREF=
"http://cafeconleche.org/examples/shakespeare/tempest.xml">
  The Tempest by Shakespeare
</A>
```

Whether the browser can display this document if you follow the link depends on just how well the browser handles XML files. Fourth-generation and earlier browsers don't handle them very well.

However, XML lets you go further with XLinks for linking to documents and XPointers for addressing individual parts of a document.

XLinks enable any element to become a link, not just an `A` element. For example, in XML, the preceding link might be written like this:

```
<PLAY xlink:type="simple"
      xmlns:xlink="http://www.w3.org/1999/xlink"
      xlink:href=
   "http://cafeconleche.org/examples/shakespeare/tempest.xml">
  <TITLE>The Tempest</TITLE> by <AUTHOR>Shakespeare</AUTHOR>
</PLAY>
```

Furthermore, XLinks can be bidirectional, multidirectional, or even point-to-multiple mirror sites from which the nearest is selected. XLinks use normal URLs to identify the site to which they're linking. As new URI schemes become available, XLinks will be able to use those, too.

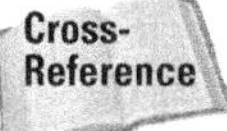

XLinks are discussed in Chapter 17.

XPointers allow links to point not just to a particular document at a particular location, but to a particular part of a particular document. An XPointer can refer to a particular element of a document; to the first, the second, or the seventeenth such element; to the first element that's a child of a given element; and so on. XPointers provide extremely powerful connections between documents that do not require the targeted document to contain additional markup just so its individual pieces can be linked to another document.

Furthermore, unlike HTML anchors, XPointers don't just refer to a point in a document. They can point to ranges or spans. For example, an XPointer might be used to select a particular part of a document so that it can be copied or loaded into a program.

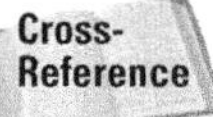

XPointers are discussed in Chapter 18.

Unicode

The Web is international, yet a disproportionate amount of the text you'll find on it is in English. XML is helping to change that. XML provides full support for the Unicode character set. This character set supports almost every character that is commonly used in every modern script on Earth.

Unfortunately, XML and Unicode alone are not enough to enable you to read and write Russian, Arabic, Chinese, and other languages written in non-Roman scripts. To read and write a language on your computer, it needs three things:

1. A character set for the script in which the language is written
2. A font for the character set
3. An operating system and application software that understand the character set

If you want to write in the script as well as read it, you'll also need an input method for the script. However, XML defines character references that allow you to use pure ASCII to encode characters not available in your native character set. This is sufficient for an occasional quote in Greek or Chinese, although you wouldn't want to rely on it to write a novel in another language.

Putting the pieces together

XML defines the syntax for the tags you use to mark up a document. An XML document is marked up with XML tags. The default character set for XML documents is Unicode.

Among other things, an XML document may contain hypertext links to other documents and resources. These links are created according to the XLink specification. XLinks identify the documents that they're linking to with URIs (in theory) or URLs (in practice). An XLink may further specify the individual part of a document it's linking to. These parts are addressed via XPointers.

If an XML document is intended to be read by human beings — and not all XML documents are — a style sheet provides instructions about how individual elements are formatted. The style sheet may be written in any of several style sheet languages. CSS and XSL are the two most popular style sheet languages, and the two best suited to use with XML.

Summary

In this chapter, you've seen a high-level overview of what XML is and what it can do for you. In particular, you learned the following:

✦ XML is a meta-markup language that enables the creation of markup languages for particular documents and domains.

✦ XML tags describe the structure and semantics of a document's content, not the format of the content. The format is described in a separate style sheet.

✦ XML documents are created in an editor, read by a parser, and displayed by a browser.

✦ XML on the Web rests on the foundations provided by HTML, CSS, and URLs.

✦ Numerous supporting technologies layer on top of XML, including XSL style sheets, XLinks, and XPointers. These let you do more than you can accomplish with just CSS and URLs.

The next chapter presents a number of XML applications that demonstrate the ways that XML is being used in the real world. Examples include vector graphics, musical notation, mathematics, chemistry, human resources, and more.

✦ ✦ ✦

XML Applications

This chapter investigates many examples of XML applications: publicly standardized markup languages, XML applications that are used to extend and expand XML itself, and some behind-the-scene uses of XML. It is inspiring to see so many different uses for XML, because it shows just how widely applicable XML is. Many more XML applications are being created or ported from other formats every day.

✦ ✦ ✦ ✦

In This Chapter

What is an XML application?

XML for XML

Behind-the-scene uses of XML

✦ ✦ ✦ ✦

What Is an XML Application?

XML is a meta-markup language for designing domain-specific markup languages. Each specific XML-based markup language is called an *XML application*. This is not an application that uses XML, such as the Mozilla web browser, the Gnumeric spreadsheet, or the XML Spy editor; instead, it is an application of XML to a specific domain, such as Chemical Markup Language (CML) for chemistry or GedML for genealogy.

Each XML application has its own semantics and vocabulary, but the application still uses XML syntax. This is much like human languages, each of which has its own vocabulary and grammar, while adhering to certain fundamental rules imposed by human anatomy and the structure of the brain.

XML is an extremely flexible format for text-based data. The reason XML was chosen as the foundation for the wildly different applications discussed in this chapter (aside from the hype factor) is that XML provides a sensible, well-documented format that's easy to read and write. By using this format for its data, a program can offload a great quantity of detailed processing to a few standard free tools and libraries. Furthermore, it's easy for such a program to layer additional levels of syntax and semantics on top of the basic structure XML provides.

Chemical Markup Language

Peter Murray-Rust's Chemical Markup Language (CML) may have been the first XML application. CML was originally developed as a Standard Generalized Markup Language (SGML) application, and gradually transitioned to XML as the XML standard developed. In its most simplistic form, CML is "HTML plus molecules," but it has applications far beyond the limited confines of the Web.

Molecular documents often contain thousands of different, very detailed objects. For example, a single medium-sized organic molecule might contain hundreds of atoms, each with at least one bond and many with several bonds to other atoms in the molecule. CML seeks to organize these complex chemical objects in a straightforward manner that can be understood, displayed, and searched by a computer. CML can be used for molecular structures and sequences, spectrographic analysis, crystallography, scientific publishing, chemical databases, and more. Its vocabulary includes molecules, atoms, bonds, crystals, formulas, sequences, symmetries, reactions, and other chemistry terms. For example, Listing 2-1 is a basic CML document for water (H_2O).

Listing 2-1: The Water Molecule H_2O Described in CML

```
<?xml version="1.0"?>
<cml xmlns="http://www.xml-cml.org/schema/cml2/core"
     xmlns:xsi="http://www.w3.org/2001/XMLSchema-instance"
     xsi:schemaLocation=
      "http://www.xml-cml.org/schema/cml2/core cmlCore.xsd">
  <molecule title="Water">
    <atomArray>
      <atom id="a1" elementType="H" hydrogenCount="0"/>
      <atom id="a2" elementType="O" hydrogenCount="2"/>
      <atom id="a3" elementType="H" hydrogenCount="0"/>
    </atomArray>
    <bondArray>
      <bond atomRefs2="a1 a2" order="1"/>
      <bond atomRefs2="a2 a3" order="1"/>
    </bondArray>
  </molecule>
</cml>
```

CML has several advantages over more traditional approaches to managing chemical data, such as the Protein Data Bank (PDB) format or MDL Molfiles. First, CML is easier to search, especially for generic tools that don't understand all the intricacies of a particular format. It's also more easily integrated with web sites, a crucial advantage at a time when Internet preprints and discussion groups are rapidly replacing traditional paper journals and scientific meetings. Finally, and most importantly, because the underlying XML is platform-independent, CML avoids the platform-dependency that has plagued the binary formats used by traditional chemical software and document formats. All chemists can read and write CML files, regardless of the hardware and software they've chosen to adopt.

Murray-Rust also created JUMBO, the first general-purpose XML browser. Figure 2-1 shows JUMBO 3 displaying a CML file. JUMBO works by assigning each XML element to a Java class that knows how to render that element. To enable JUMBO to support new elements, you simply write Java classes for those elements. JUMBO is distributed with classes for displaying the basic set of CML elements, including molecules, atoms, and bonds, and is available at `http://www.xml-cml.org/`.

Mathematical Markup Language

Legend claims that Tim Berners-Lee invented the World Wide Web and HTML at CERN, the European Laboratory for Particle Physics, so that high-energy physicists could exchange papers and preprints. Personally, I've never believed that story. I grew up in physics, and while I've wandered back and forth between physics, applied math, astronomy, and computer science over the years, one thing the papers in all of these disciplines had in common was lots and lots of equations. Until XML, there wasn't a good way to include equations in web pages. There were a few hacks — Java applets that parse a custom syntax, converters that turn LaTeX equations into GIF images, custom browsers that read TeX files — but none produced high-quality results, and none caught on with web authors, even in scientific fields. XML is changing this.

The Mathematical Markup Language (MathML) is an XML application for mathematical equations. MathML is sufficiently expressive to handle most math from grammar-school arithmetic through calculus and differential equations. Although there are a few limits to MathML at the high end of pure mathematics and theoretical physics, it is eloquent enough to handle almost all educational, scientific, engineering, business, economics, and statistics needs. And MathML is likely to be expanded in the future, so even the purest of the pure mathematicians and the most theoretical of the theoretical physicists will be able to publish and do research on the Web. MathML completes the development of the Web into a serious tool for scientific research and communication (despite its long digression to make it suitable as a new medium for advertising brochures).

Mozilla is just beginning to support MathML. Figure 2-2 shows Mozilla displaying the covariant form of Maxwell's equations written in MathML. Other common browsers do not support it at all. However, plug-ins and Java applets that add this support are available, such as IBM's Tech Explorer (`http://www.software.ibm.com/techexplorer`) and Design Science's WebEQ (`http://www.dessci.com/en/products/webeq/`).

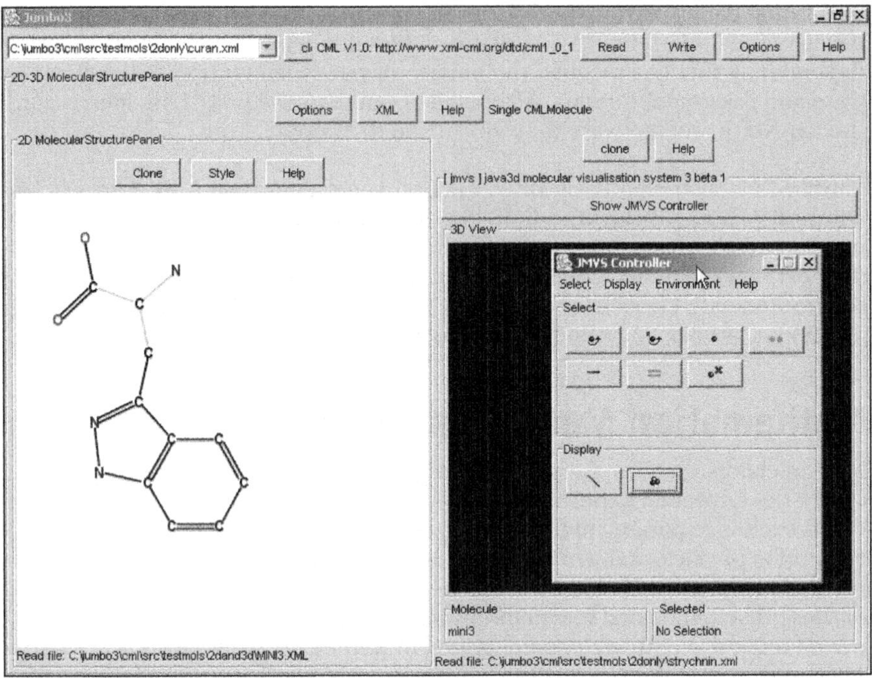

Figure 2-1: The JUMBO browser displaying a CML file

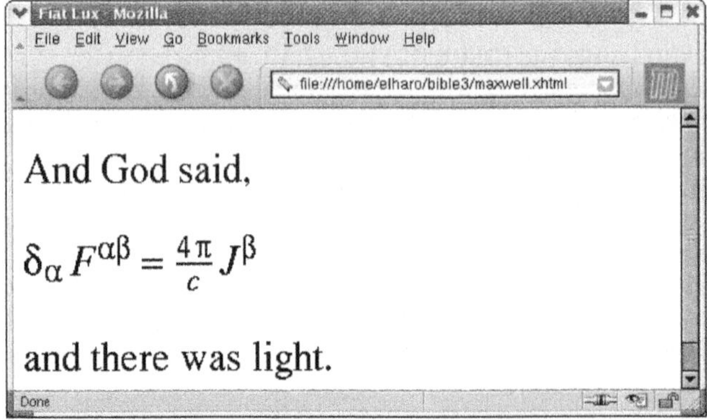

Figure 2-2: Mozilla displaying the covariant form of Maxwell's equations written in MathML

Listing 2-2 contains the document Mozilla is displaying.

Listing 2-2: Maxwell's Equations in MathML

```
<?xml version="1.0"?>
<!DOCTYPE html PUBLIC
  "-//W3C//DTD XHTML 1.1 plus MathML 2.0//EN"
  "http://www.w3.org/TR/MathML2/dtd/xhtml-math11-f.dtd">
<html xmlns="http://www.w3.org/1999/xhtml">
<head>
<title>Fiat Lux</title>
</head>
<body>
<p>And God said,</p>

<math xmlns="http://www.w3.org/1998/Math/MathML">
  <mrow>
    <msub>
      <mi>&delta;</mi>
      <mi>&alpha;</mi>
    </msub>
    <msup>
      <mi>F</mi>
      <mi>&alpha;&beta;</mi>
    </msup>
    <mo>=</mo>
    <mfrac>
      <mrow>
        <mn>4</mn>
        <mi>&pi;</mi>
      </mrow>
      <mi>c</mi>
    </mfrac>
    <msup>
      <mi>J</mi>
      <mrow>
        <mi>&beta;</mi>
      </mrow>
    </msup>
  </mrow>
</math>
<p>and there was light.</p>
</body>
</html>
```

Listing 2-2 is an example of a mixed HTML/MathML page. The headers and paragraphs of text ("Fiat Lux," "Maxwell's Equations," "And God said," "and there was light") are given in HTML. The equation is written in MathML, an XML application.

In general, such mixed pages require special support from the browser, as is the case here, or perhaps plug-ins, ActiveX controls, or JavaScript programs that parse and display the embedded XML data.

RSS

RSS (nobody can agree on exactly what, if anything, the acronym stands for) is a simple XML format used for content syndication by numerous web sites ranging from personal web logs to major newspapers to government agencies. It's useful for any site that wants to provide a continuing feed of new information to interested readers. Until now, it's mostly been used for web logs, but it's beginning to find other uses, including software updates, security bulletins, government regulations, court decisions, art gallery openings, office calendars, and more.

The person or organization providing the information publishes an RSS document at a well-known URL. Interested parties subscribe to this information using any of a variety of clients. Normally, when the user launches the RSS client, it automatically fetches the latest content from all the subscribed sites. Each item in the document includes a headline, perhaps a description, and a link to the full story at the main web site. Users can activate this link to load that site and story into their web browser if they want to know more.

An RSS document is an XML file, separate from the HTML pages it describes. Those pages normally provide a link to the RSS document, and the RSS document links back to pages on the main site. However, users don't read the RSS document in a standard web browser. Instead, they use custom client programs. The RSS client's purpose is to aggregate many different RSS feeds from many different web sites so readers can pick and choose the stories they want to read without having to visit each site individually.

Listing 2-3 shows the RSS document from my Cafe au Lait web site from June 23, 2003. You can see it contains a title, description, and various metadata about the site, such as the copyright notice and the language. This is followed by two items, each of which represents one story. Each item has a title, a longer description of the story, and a link to the full story on the web site. Figure 2-3 shows this feed loaded into NetNewsWire Lite. Also notice the other channels I've subscribed to in the left-hand panel.

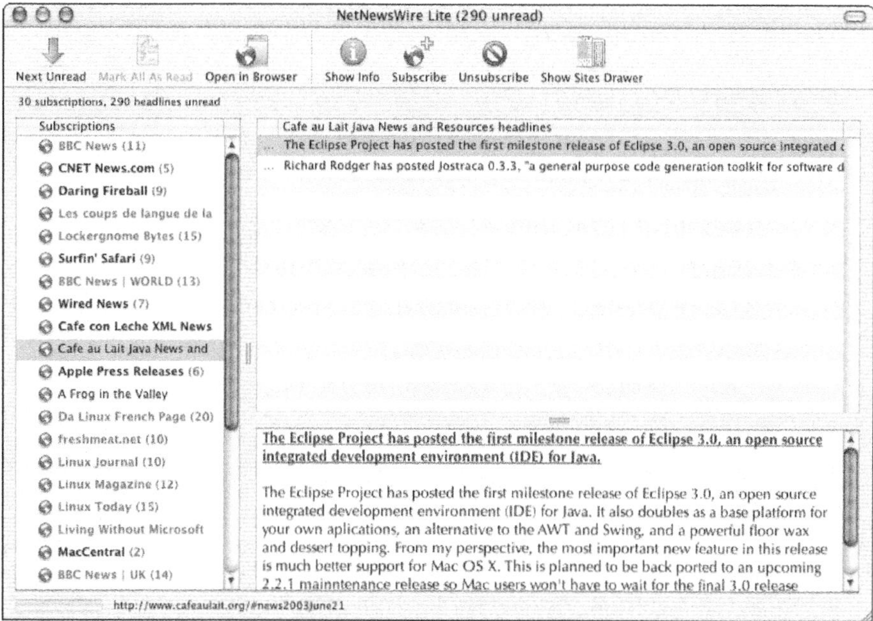

Figure 2-3: The Café au Lait RSS feed in NetNewsWire Lite

Listing 2-3: The RSS Feed from Cafe au Lait

```
<?xml version="1.0"?>
<rss version="0.92">
  <channel>
    <title>Cafe au Lait Java News and Resources</title>
    <link>http://www.cafeaulait.org/</link>
    <description>Cafe au Lait is  the preeminent independent
source of Java information on the net. Unlike many other Java
sites,  Cafe au Lait is neither beholden to specific companies
nor to advertisers. At Cafe au Lait you'll find many resources
to help you develop your Java programming skills here
including daily news summaries, FAQ lists, tutorials, course
notes, examples, exercises, book reviews, user groups and
more.
    </description>
    <language>en-us</language>
    <copyright>(c) 2003 Elliotte Rusty Harold</copyright>
    <webMaster>elharo@metalab.unc.edu</webMaster>
```

Continued

Listing 2-3 *(continued)*

```
    <image>
      <title>Cafe au Lait</title>
      <url>http://www.cafeaulait.org/cup.gif</url>
      <link>http://www.cafeaulait.org/</link>
      <width>89</width>
      <height>67</height>
    </image>
    <item>
      <title>The Eclipse Project has posted the first
milestone release of Eclipse 3.0, an open source integrated
development environment (IDE) for Java.
          </title>
      <description>
The Eclipse Project has posted the first milestone release of
Eclipse 3.0, an open source integrated development environment
(IDE) for Java. It also doubles as a base platform for your
own applications, an alternative to the AWT and Swing, and a
powerful floor wax and dessert topping. From my perspective,
the most important new feature in this release is much better
support for Mac OS X.  This is planned to be back ported to an
upcoming 2.2.1 maintenance release so Mac users won't have to
wait for the final 3.0 release currently scheduled for 2004.
Other new features are mostly minor. Overall this feels more
like a 2.2  than a full version shift.
</description>
      <link>http://www.cafeaulait.org/#news2003June21</link>
    </item>
    <item>
      <title>Richard Rodger has posted Jostraca 0.3.3, "a
general purpose code generation toolkit for software
developers.
          </title>
      <description>
Richard Rodger has posted Jostraca 0.3.3, "a general purpose
code generation toolkit for software developers. Code
generation helps save you time and effort by reducing
redundancy and drudge work. Code generation can be thought of
as programming by example. Show the computer an example of
what you want, and it does the rest. Jostraca generates code
using the Java Server Pages syntax. However this syntax can be
used with any language. Jostraca comes preconfigured for Java,
Perl, Python, Ruby, Rebol and C, with more to come." Jostraca
is published under the GPL. Jostraca is written in Java, and
Java 1.2 or later is required.
</description>
      <link>http://www.cafeaulait.org/#news2003June21</link>
    </item>
  </channel>
</rss>
```

RSS is a good example of XML's contribution to platform and application independence. Thousands of sites now publish RSS data to millions of independent systems. RSS clients are available for pretty much all modern desktop operating systems, written in many different languages. No other format could have been as broadly or as quickly adopted. Choosing XML as the substrate for RSS made it much easier to generate and consume in many different systems ranging from cell phones and Palm Pilots on the low end to traditional PC desktops and big iron servers on the high end. RSS can be generated and processed by simple tools hacked together in a couple of hours out of Perl, and it can be straightforwardly integrated with multi-gigabyte relational databases and six-figure content management systems. RSS is normally sent over HTTP, but it can also be transmitted via e-mail, FTP, or even sneaker net. RSS is architecture-, operating system-, protocol-, software-, and language-independent. It gains all those benefits because XML is architecture-, operating system-, protocol-, software-, and language-independent.

Classic literature

Jon Bosak has translated all of Shakespeare's plays into XML. He includes the complete text of the plays and uses XML markup to distinguish between titles, subtitles, stage directions, speeches, lines, speakers, and more.

What does this offer over a book, or even a plain-text file? To a human reader, not much. But to a computer doing textual analysis, it offers the opportunity to easily distinguish between the different elements into which the plays are divided. For example, it makes it quite simple for the computer to go through the text and extract all of Romeo's lines.

Furthermore, by altering the style sheet with which the document is formatted, an actor could easily print a version of the document in which all of their lines were formatted in boldface, and the lines immediately before and after theirs were italicized. Anything else you might imagine that requires separating a play into the lines uttered by different speakers is much more easily accomplished with the XML-formatted versions than with the raw text.

Bosak has also marked up English translations of the Old and New Testaments, the Koran, and the Book of Mormon in XML. The markup in these is a little different. For example, it doesn't distinguish between speakers. Thus, you couldn't use these particular XML documents to create a red-letter Bible, for example, although a different set of tags might allow you to do that. (A red-letter Bible prints words spoken by Jesus in red.) And because these files are in English rather than the original languages, they are not as useful for scholarly textual analysis. Still, time and resources permitting, those are exactly the sorts of things that XML would enable you to do if you wanted. You'd simply need to invent a different vocabulary and syntax than the one Bosak used.

Synchronized Multimedia Integration Language

The Synchronized Multimedia Integration Language (SMIL, pronounced “smile”) is a W3C-recommended XML application for writing “TV-like” multimedia presentations for the Web. SMIL documents don’t describe the actual multimedia content (that is, the video and sound that are played); instead, the SMIL documents describe when and where the video and sound are played.

For example, a typical SMIL document for a film festival might say that the browser should simultaneously play the sound file beethoven9.mid, show the video file corange.mov, and display the HTML file clockwork.htm. Then, when it’s done, it should play the video file 2001.mov and the audio file zarathustra.mid, and display the HTML file aclarke.htm. This eliminates the need to embed low-bandwidth data such as text in high-bandwidth data such as video just to combine them. Listing 2-4 is a simple SMIL file that does exactly this.

Listing 2-4: A SMIL Film Festival

```
<?xml version="1.0" encoding="ISO-8859-1"?>
<!DOCTYPE smil PUBLIC "-//W3C//DTD SMIL 1.0//EN"
  "http://wgw.w3.org/TR/REC-smil/SMIL10.dtd">
<smil>
  <body>
    <seq id="Kubrick">
      <audio src="beethoven9.mid"/>
      <video src="corange.mov"/>
      <text src="clockwork.htm"/>
      <audio src="zarathustra.mid"/>
      <video src="2001.mov"/>
      <text src="aclarke.htm"/>
    </seq>
  </body>
</smil>
```

Furthermore, as well as specifying the time sequencing of data, a SMIL document can position individual graphic elements on the display and attach links to media objects. For example, at the same time as the movie and sound are playing, the text of the respective novels could be subtitling the presentation.

Open Software Description

The Open Software Description (OSD) format is an XML application that was codeveloped by Marimba and Microsoft to update software automatically. OSD defines XML tags that describe software components. The description of a component includes the version of the component, its underlying structure, and its relationships to and dependencies on other components. This provides enough information to decide whether a user needs a particular update. If the update is needed, it can be pushed automatically to the user without requiring the usual manual download and installation. Listing 2-5 is an example of an OSD file for an update to the fictional product WhizzyWriter 1000.

Listing 2-5: An OSD File for an Update to WhizzyWriter 1000

```
<?xml version="1.0"?>
<CHANNEL HREF="http://updates.whizzy.com/updateChannel.html">
  <TITLE>WhizzyWriter 1000 Update Channel</TITLE>
  <USAGE VALUE="SoftwareUpdate"/>
  <SOFTPKG HREF="http://updates.whizzy.com/updateChannel.html"
           NAME="{46181F7D-1C38-22A1-3329-00415C6A4D54}"
           VERSION="5,2,3,1"
           STYLE="MSAppLogo5"
           PRECACHE="yes">
    <TITLE>WhizzyWriter 1000</TITLE>
    <ABSTRACT>
      Abstract: WhizzyWriter 1000: now with tint control!
    </ABSTRACT>
    <IMPLEMENTATION>
     <CODEBASE HREF="http://updates.whizzy.com/tnupdate.exe"/>
    </IMPLEMENTATION>
  </SOFTPKG>
</CHANNEL>
```

Only information about the update is kept in the OSD file. The actual update files are stored in a separate CAB archive or executable and downloaded when needed. There is considerable controversy about whether this is actually a good thing. Many software companies, Microsoft not least among them, have a long history of releasing updates that cause more problems than they fix. Many users prefer to stay away from new software for a while until other, more adventurous souls have given it a shakedown.

Scalable Vector Graphics

Vector graphics are preferable to bitmaps for many kinds of pictures including flowcharts, cartoons, assembly diagrams, and similar images. However, the PNG, GIF, and JPEG formats currently used on the Web are bitmap only; and most traditional vector graphics formats, such as PDF, PostScript, and EPS, were designed with ink (or toner) on paper in mind rather than electrons on a screen. (This is one reason PDF on the Web is such an inferior substitute for HTML, despite PDF's much larger collection of graphics primitives.) A vector graphics format for the Web should support a lot of features that don't make sense on paper, such as transparency, antialiasing, additive color, hypertext, animation, and hooks to allow search engines and audio renderers to extract text from graphics. None of these features are needed for the ink-on-paper world of PostScript and PDF. The W3C has developed a vector graphics format called Scalable Vector Graphics (SVG) to do for vector drawings what GIF, JPEG, and PNG do for bitmap images.

SVG is an XML application for describing two-dimensional graphics. It defines three basic types of graphics: shapes, images, and text. A shape is defined by its outline, also known as its path, and may have various strokes or fills. An image is a bitmap such as a GIF or a JPEG. Text is defined as a string of characters in a particular font, and may be attached to a path, so it's not restricted to horizontal lines of text as on this page. All three kinds of graphics can be positioned on the page at a particular location, rotated, scaled, skewed, and otherwise manipulated. Listing 2-6 shows a pink triangle in SVG.

Listing 2-6: A Pink Triangle in SVG

```
<?xml version="1.0"?>
<svg xmlns="http://www.w3.org/2000/svg"
     width="12cm" height="8cm">
  <title>Listing 2-6 from the XML Bible, 3rd Edition</title>
  <text x="10" y="15">This is SVG!</text>
  <polygon style="fill: pink" points="0,311 180,0 360,311" />
</svg>
```

Because SVG describes graphics rather than text — unlike most of the other XML applications discussed in this chapter — it requires special display software. All of the proposed style sheet languages assume that they're displaying fundamentally text-based data, and none of them can support the heavy graphics requirements of an application such as SVG. Adobe has published browser plug-ins that support SVG on Windows and the Mac (`http://www.adobe.com/svg/`), and the XML Apache Project has released Batik (`http://xml.apache.org/batik/`), an open source Java program that can display SVG documents and rasterize them to JPEG, GIF, or PNG files. Figure 2-4 shows Listing 2-6 displayed in Batik. Native SVG support might be added to future browsers. Mozilla already includes some preliminary code for rendering SVG, though it's not yet turned on in the release builds (`http://www.mozilla.org/projects/svg/`).

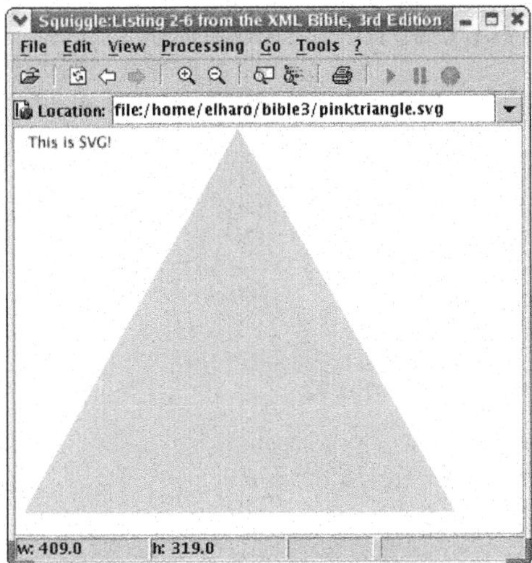

Figure 2-4: The pink triangle displayed in Batik

For authoring, the current versions of many traditional drawing programs, such as Adobe Illustrator and CorelDRAW, can save SVG files just like their native formats. There are also numerous SVG-native programs such as Jasc Software's WebDraw (`http://www.jasc.com/products/webdraw/`).

Because SVG documents are pure text (like all XML documents), the SVG format is easy for programs to generate automatically; and it's easy for software to manipulate. In particular, you can combine SVG with DOM and ECMAScript to make the pictures on a web page animated and responsive to user action. Long term, SVG will probably replace Macromedia's proprietary, binary Flash format.

SVG is discussed in more detail in Chapter 24.

MusicXML

Recordare has created an XML application for musical notation called MusicXML. MusicXML includes notes, beats, clefs, staffs, rows, rests, beams, repeats, dynamics, articulations, slurs, and more. Listing 2-7 shows the first three measures from Beth Anderson's *Flute Swale* in MusicXML. This is a single-part piece for one instrument. The document begins with some metadata about the piece. This is followed by a single part containing the measures. The measures are divided into notes. The first measure also has the usual information about clef, key, and time.

Listing 2-7: The First Three Bars of Beth Anderson's *Flute Swale*

```
<?xml version="1.0" standalone="no"?>
<!DOCTYPE score-partwise PUBLIC
   "-//Recordare//DTD MusicXML 0.7a Partwise//EN"
  "http://www.musicxml.org/dtds/partwise.dtd">
<score-partwise>
  <work><work-title>Flute Swale</work-title></work>
  <identification>
    <creator type="composer">Beth Anderson</creator>
    <rights>© 2003 Beth Anderson</rights>
    <encoding>
      <encoding-date>2003-06-21</encoding-date>
      <encoder>Elliotte Rusty Harold</encoder>
      <software>jEdit</software>
      <encoding-description>
         Listing 2-7 from the XML Bible, 3rd Edition
      </encoding-description>
    </encoding>
  </identification>
  <part-list>
    <score-part id="P1">
      <part-name>flute</part-name>
    </score-part>
  </part-list>
  <part id="P1">
    <measure number="1">
      <attributes>
        <divisions>4</divisions>
        <key><fifths>2</fifths> <mode>major</mode></key>
        <time><beats>4</beats><beat-type>4</beat-type></time>
        <clef><sign>G</sign><line>2</line></clef>
      </attributes>
      <note>
        <pitch><step>A</step></octave>4</octave></pitch>
        <duration>6</duration> <type>sixteenth</type>
       <stem>up</stem>
      </note>
      <note>
        <pitch><step>B</step></octave>4</octave></pitch>
        <duration>6</duration> <type>sixteenth</type>
        <stem>up</stem>
      </note>
      <note>
        <pitch>
          <step>C</step><alter>1</alter><octave>5</octave>
        </pitch>
        <duration>6</duration> <type>sixteenth</type>
        <stem>up</stem>
```

```
    </note>
    <note>
      <pitch><step>A</step></octave>4</octave></pitch>
      <duration>6</duration> <type>sixteenth</type>
      <stem>up</stem>
    </note>
    <note>
      <pitch><step>D</step></octave>5</octave></pitch>
      <duration>12</duration> <type>eighth</type>
      <stem>down</stem>
    </note>
    <note>
      <pitch>
       <step>C</step></alter>1</alter><octave>5</octave>
      </pitch>
      <duration>12</duration> <type>eighth</type>
      <stem>down</stem>
    </note>
    <note>
      <pitch><step>B</step></octave>4</octave></pitch>
      <duration>24</duration> <type>quarter</type>
      <stem>down</stem>
    </note>
    <note>
      <pitch><step>A</step></octave>4</octave></pitch>
      <duration>24</duration> <type>quarter</type>
      <stem>up</stem>
    </note>
  </measure>
  <measure number="2">
    <note>
      <pitch><step>A</step></octave>4</octave></pitch>
      <duration>6</duration> <type>sixteenth</type>
      <stem>up</stem>
    </note>
    <note>
      <pitch><step>B</step></octave>4</octave></pitch>
      <duration>6</duration> <type>sixteenth</type>
      <stem>up</stem>
    </note>
    <note>
      <pitch>
        <step>C</step></alter>1</alter><octave>5</octave>
      </pitch>
      <duration>6</duration> <type>sixteenth</type>
      <stem>up</stem>
    </note>
    <note>
      <pitch><step>A</step></octave>4</octave></pitch>
      <duration>6</duration> <type>sixteenth</type>
      <stem>up</stem>
```

Continued

Listing 2-7 *(continued)*

```
      </note>
      <note>
        <pitch><step>D</step></octave>5</octave></pitch>
        <duration>12</duration> <type>eighth</type>
        <stem>down</stem>
      </note>
      <note>
        <pitch>
          <step>C</step></alter>1</alter><octave>5</octave>
        </pitch>
        <duration>12</duration> <type>eighth</type>
        <stem>down</stem>
      </note>
      <note>
        <pitch><step>B</step></octave>4</octave></pitch>
        <duration>24</duration> <type>quarter</type>
        <stem>down</stem>
      </note>
      <note>
        <pitch><step>A</step></octave>4</octave></pitch>
        <duration>24</duration> <type>quarter</type>
        <stem>up</stem>
      </note>
    </measure>
    <measure number="3">
      <note>
        <pitch><step>A</step></octave>4</octave></pitch>
        <duration>6</duration> <type>sixteenth</type>
        <stem>up</stem>
      </note>
      <note>
        <pitch><step>B</step></octave>4</octave></pitch>
        <duration>6</duration> <type>sixteenth</type>
        <stem>up</stem>
      </note>
      <note>
        <pitch>
          <step>C</step></alter>1</alter><octave>5</octave>
        </pitch>
        <duration>6</duration> <type>sixteenth</type>
        <stem>up</stem>
      </note>
      <note>
        <pitch><step>A</step></octave>4</octave></pitch>
        <duration>6</duration> <type>sixteenth</type>
        <stem>up</stem>
      </note>
```

```
      <note>
        <pitch><step>D</step></octave>5</octave></pitch>
        <duration>12</duration> <type>eighth</type>
        <stem>down</stem>
      </note>
      <note>
        <pitch>
          <step>C</step><alter>1</alter><octave>5</octave>
        </pitch>
        <duration>12</duration> <type>eighth</type>
        <stem>down</stem>
      </note>
      <note>
        <pitch><step>B</step></octave>4</octave></pitch>
        <duration>12</duration> <type>eighth</type>
        <stem>up</stem>
      </note>
      <note>
        <pitch><step>A</step></octave>4</octave></pitch>
        <duration>12</duration> <type>eighth</type>
        <stem>up</stem>
      </note>
      <note>
        <pitch>
          <step>F</step><alter>1</alter><octave>4</octave>
        </pitch>
        <duration>12</duration> <type>eighth</type>
        <stem>up</stem>
      </note>
      <note>
        <pitch><step>E</step></octave>4</octave></pitch>
        <duration>12</duration> <type>eighth</type>
        <stem>up</stem>
      </note>
    </measure>
 </part>
</score-partwise>
```

An increasing number of music programs can import and/or export MusicXML, including music notation editors, MIDI players, sheet music scanners, audio scanners, converters into and out of other music formats, and more. However, in my tests, the several programs I tried all had significant problems handling the above-mentioned MusicXML. None of them could render or play it correctly. MusicXML isn't going to replace Finale anytime soon, but as the bugs are slowly fixed, it should become a more useful, nonproprietary way to exchange and store music on and off the Web.

VoiceXML

VoiceXML (http://www.voicexml.org/) is an XML application for the spoken word. In particular, it's intended for voice mail and automated phone response systems ("If you found a boll weevil in Natural Goodness biscuit dough, please press 1. If you found a cockroach in Natural Goodness biscuit dough, please press 2. If you found an ant in Natural Goodness biscuit dough, please press 3. Otherwise, please stay on the line for the next available entomologist.").

VoiceXML enables the same data that's used on a web site to be served up via telephone. It's particularly useful for information that's created by combining small nuggets of data, such as stock prices, sports scores, weather reports, and test results. JSmart (http://www.jsmart.com/) uses VoiceXML to send games and jokes to phones. In Mexico, Domino's Pizza uses VoiceXML for a restaurant locator application that receives more than 90,000 calls a month. Yahoo! sells a service based on VoiceXML that lets users listen to their e-mail, look up contacts in their address book, and get stock quotes, weather, sports, and news over the phone (1-800-MY-YAHOO).

A small VoiceXML file for a shampoo manufacturer's automated phone response system might look something like that shown in Listing 2-8.

Listing 2-8: A VoiceXML Document

```
<?xml version="1.0"?>
<vxml version="1.0">

  <form>
    <block>
      <prompt bargein="false">
        Welcome to TIC hair products division,
        home of Wonder Shampoo.
      </prompt>
      <goto next="#color_choice"/>
    </block>
  </form>

  <menu id="color_choice">
    <property name="inputmodes" value="dtmf"/>
    <prompt>
    If Wonder Shampoo turned your hair green, please press 1.
    If Wonder Shampoo turned your hair purple, please press 2.
    If Wonder Shampoo made you bald, please press 3.
     </prompt>
    <choice dtmf="1" next="#green.vxml"/>
    <choice dtmf="2" next="#purple.vxml"/>
    <choice dtmf="3" next="#bald.vxml"/>
  </menu>
```

```
    <form id="green">
      <block>
         <prompt>
           If Wonder Shampoo turned your hair green and you wish
           to return it to its natural color, simply shampoo
           seven times with three parts soap, seven parts water,
           four parts kerosene, and two parts iguana bile.
         </prompt>
        <goto next="#bye"/>
      </block>
    </form>

    <form id="purple">
      <block>
         <prompt>
           If Wonder Shampoo turned your hair purple and you
           wish to return it to its natural color, please walk
           widdershins around your local cemetery
           three times while chanting "Surrender Dorothy."
         </prompt>
        <goto next="#bye"/>
      </block>
    </form>

    <form id="bald">
      <block>
         <prompt>
           If you went bald as a result of using Wonder Shampoo,
           please purchase and apply a three-month supply
           of our Magic Hair Growth Formula. Please do not
           consult an attorney as doing so would violate the
           license agreement printed on the inside fold of the
           Wonder Shampoo box in 3-point type. By opening the
           package, you agreed to the license terms.
         </prompt>
         <goto next="#bye"/>
      </block>
    </form>

    <form id="bye">
      <block>
        <prompt>
         Thank you for visiting TIC Corp. Goodbye.
        </prompt>
        <disconnect/>
      </block>
    </form>

  </vxml>
```

I can't show you a screen shot of this example, because it's not intended to be shown in a web browser. Instead, you would listen to it on a telephone.

Open Financial Exchange

Software cannot be changed willy-nilly. The data that software operates on has inertia. The more data you have in a given program's proprietary, undocumented format, the harder it is to change programs. For example, my personal finances for the last eight years are stored in Quicken. How likely is it that I will change to Microsoft Money even if Money has features I need that Quicken doesn't have? Unless Money can read and convert Quicken files with zero loss of data, the answer is "NOT LIKELY!"

The problem can even occur within a single company or a single company's products. When I upgraded from Quicken 5 to Quicken 98, Quicken split one of my retirement accounts into two accounts for no apparent reason. I had to create a new account and manually rekey all the entries for that account. Needless to say, I have not upgraded since and don't plan to again if I can avoid it. The only reason I upgraded then was that Quicken 5 was not Y2K-compliant.

As noted in Chapter 1, the Open Financial Exchange 2.0 (OFX) is an XML application for describing financial data of the type stored in a personal finance product such as Money or Quicken. Any program that understands OFX can read OFX data. Moreover, because OFX is fully documented and nonproprietary (unlike the binary formats of Money, Quicken, and similar programs), it's easy for programmers to write the code to understand OFX.

OFX not only enables Money and Quicken to exchange data with each other; it also enables other programs that use the same format to exchange the data. For example, if a bank wants to deliver statements to customers electronically, it only has to write one program to encode the statements in the OFX format rather than several programs to encode the statement in Quicken's format, Money's format, GnuCash's format, and so forth.

The more programs that use a given format, the greater the savings in development cost and effort. For example, six programs reading and writing their own and each other's proprietary formats require 30 different converters. Six programs reading and writing the same OFX format require only six converters. Effort is reduced to O(n) rather than to O(n^2). Figure 2-5 depicts six programs reading and writing their own and each other's proprietary binary formats. Figure 2-6 depicts the same six programs reading and writing a single, open OFX format. Every arrow represents a converter that has to trade files and data between programs. The XML-based exchange is much simpler and cleaner than the binary-format exchange.

Extensible Forms Description Language

I went to my local bookstore and bought a copy of Armistead Maupin's novel *Sure of You.* I paid for that purchase with a credit card, and when I did so, I signed a piece of paper agreeing to pay the credit card company $14.07 when billed. Eventually they sent me a bill for that purchase, and I paid it. If I had refused to pay it, the credit card company could have taken me to court to collect, and they would have used my signature on that piece of paper to prove to the court that on October 15 I really did agree to pay them $14.07.

The same day I also ordered Anne Rice's *The Vampire Armand* from the online bookstore Amazon.com. Amazon charged me $16.17 plus $3.95 shipping and handling, and again I paid for that purchase with a credit card. The difference is that Amazon.com never got a signature on a piece of paper from me. Eventually the credit card company sent me a bill for that purchase, and I paid it. But if I had refused to pay the bill, they didn't have a piece of paper with my signature on it showing that I agreed to pay $20.12 on October 15. If I had claimed that I never made the purchase, the credit card company would have billed the charges back to Amazon. Before Amazon or any other online or phone-order merchant is allowed to accept credit card purchases without a signature in ink on paper, the merchant has to agree that it will be responsible for all disputed transactions.

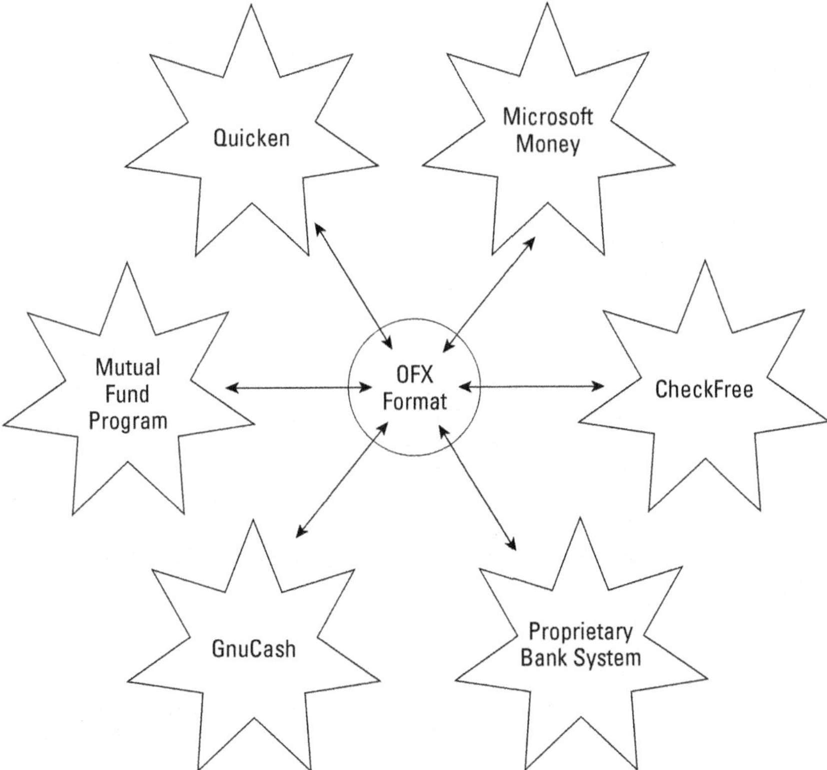

Figure 2-5: Six different programs reading and writing their own and each other's formats

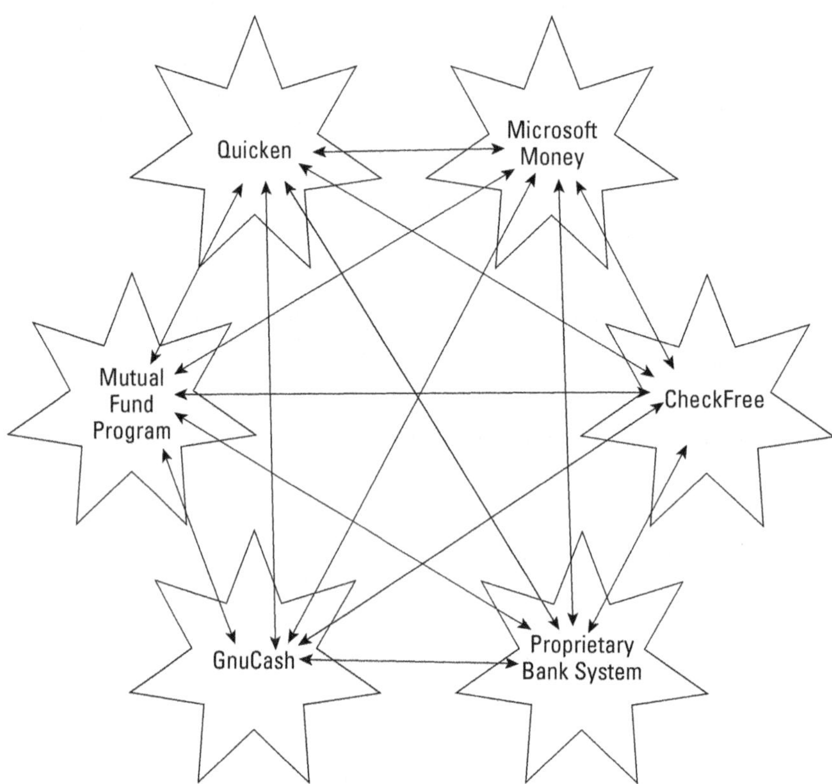

Figure 2-6: Six programs reading and writing the same OFX format

Exact numbers are hard to come by and vary from merchant to merchant, but probably around 2 percent of Internet transactions are billed back to the originating merchant because of credit card fraud or disputes. This is a *huge* amount, especially in an arena where margins are often negative to start with. Consumer businesses such as Amazon simply accept this as a cost of doing business on the Internet and work it into their price structure, but this won't work for six-figure business-to-business transactions. Nobody wants to send out $200,000 of masonry supplies only to have the purchaser claim they never made the order. Before business-to-business transactions can move onto the Internet, a method needs to be developed that can verify that an order was in fact made by a particular person and that this person is who he or she claims to be. Furthermore, this has to be enforceable in court.

Part of the solution to the problem is digital signatures — the electronic equivalent of ink on paper. To digitally sign a document, you calculate a hash code for the document using a known algorithm, encrypt the hash code with your private key, and attach the encrypted hash code to the document. Correspondents can decrypt the hash code using your public key and verify that it matches the document. However, they can't sign documents on your behalf because they don't have your private key. The exact protocol followed is a little more complex in practice, but the bottom line is that your private key is merged with the data you're signing in a verifiable fashion. No one who doesn't know your private key can sign the document.

The scheme isn't foolproof — it's vulnerable to your private key being stolen, for example — but it's probably as hard to forge a digital signature as it is to forge a real ink-on-paper signature. However, a number of less obvious attacks on digital signature protocols exist. One of the most important is changing the data that's signed. Changing the data should invalidate the signature, but it doesn't if the changed data wasn't included in the first place. For example, when you submit an HTML form, the only things sent are the values that you fill into the form's fields and the names of the fields. The rest of the HTML markup is not included. You might agree to pay $1500 for a new 3GHz Pentium 4 PC, but the only thing sent on the form is the $1500. Signing this number signifies what you're paying, but not what you're paying for. The merchant can then send you two gross of flushometers and claim that's what you bought for your $1500. Obviously, if digital signatures are to be useful, all details of the transaction must be included.

The problem gets worse if you're trying to sell to the United States government. Government regulations for purchase orders and requisitions often spell out the contents of forms in minute detail, right down to the font face and type size. Failure to adhere to the exact specifications can lead to your invoice for $20,000,000 worth of depleted uranium artillery shells being rejected. Therefore, you need to establish exactly what was agreed to and that you met all legal requirements for the form. HTML's forms just aren't sophisticated enough to handle these needs.

XML, however, can. It is almost always possible to use XML to develop a markup language with the right combination of power and rigor to meet your needs, and this case is no exception. In particular, UWI.COM has proposed an XML application called the Extensible Forms Description Language (XFDL, `http://www.uwi.com/xfdl/`) for forms with extremely tight legal requirements that are to be signed with digital signatures. XFDL further offers the option to do simple mathematics in the form, for example, to automatically fill in the sales tax and shipping and handling charges, and then to total the price.

UWI.COM has submitted XFDL to the W3C, but it's really overkill for web browsers, and probably won't be adopted there. The real benefit of XFDL, if it becomes widely adopted, is in business-to-business and business-to-government transactions. XFDL can become a key part of electronic commerce, which is not to say that it *will* become a key part of electronic commerce. It's still early, and there are other players in this space.

HR-XML

The HR-XML Consortium (http://www.hr-xml.org/) is a nonprofit organization with over 100 different members from various branches of the human resources industry, including recruiters, temp agencies, large employers, and so on. It's trying to develop standard XML applications that describe resumes, available jobs, candidates, benefits, background checks, payroll instructions, education histories, and other information human resource departments commonly use. Listing 2-9 shows a job listing encoded in HR-XML. This application defines elements matching the parts of a typical classified want ad such as companies, positions, skills, contact information, compensation, experience, and more.

Listing 2-9: A Job Listing in HR-XML

```
<?xml version="1.0"?>
<JobPositionPosting>
  <JobPositionPostingId>25740</JobPositionPostingId>
  <HiringOrg>
    <HiringOrgName>John Wiley &amp; Sons</HiringOrgName>
    <WebSite>http://www.wiley.com</WebSite>
    <Industry><SummaryText>Publishing</SummaryText></Industry>
    <Contact>
      <PersonName>
        <GivenName>Mara</GivenName>
        <FamilyName>Cordal</FamilyName>
      </PersonName>
    </Contact>
  </HiringOrg>

  <JobPositionInformation>
    <JobPositionTitle>Editor</JobPositionTitle>
    <JobPositionDescription>
      <JobPositionPurpose>
        Working in our Scientific, Technical and Medical
        Division as an Editor, you will be responsible for the
        development and implementation of the strategic
        publishing plan for designated market/subject
        category. You will also ensure effective management of
        the program, including the acquisition, development,
        and profitable publication of books.
      </JobPositionPurpose>
      <JobPositionLocation>
        <LocationSummary>
          <Municipality>Hoboken</Municipality>
          <Region>NJ</Region>
        </LocationSummary>
      </JobPositionLocation>
      <Classification>
        <DirectHireOrContract>
          <DirectHire/>
```

```
      </DirectHireOrContract>
      <Duration>
        <Regular/>
      </Duration>
    </Classification>
    <CompensationDescription>
      <Pay>
        <SalaryAnnual currency="USD">60,000</SalaryAnnual>
      </Pay>
    </CompensationDescription>
  </JobPositionDescription>
  <JobPositionRequirements>
    <QualificationsRequired>
      <Qualification type="education">College</Qualification>
      <Qualification type="experience"
                     yearsOfExperience="3-5">
        Book acquisitions
      </Qualification>
      <Qualification type="skill">
         Electrical engineering
      </Qualification>
      <Qualification type="skill">
        Telecommunications
      </Qualification>
    </QualificationsRequired>
    <SummaryText>
      In-depth knowledge of the markets and subject areas
      assigned; Proven expertise in acquiring, developing
      projects and successfully managing and expanding a
      program; Excellent leadership, analytical,
      communication and interpersonal skills.
    </SummaryText>
  </JobPositionRequirements>
</JobPositionInformation>

<HowToApply distribute="external">
  <ApplicationMethods>
    <ByEmail>
      <E-mail>opportunities@wiley.com</E-mail>
      <SummaryText>Please put the job title, department,
      location, and reference number in the subject line.
      Your resume and cover letter must either be contained
      in the body of your e-mail or be in Word or PDF
      format.
      </SummaryText>
    </ByEmail>
    <ByFax>
      <PersonName>
         <GivenName>Attn:</GivenName>
         <FamilyName>Human Resources</FamilyName>
       </PersonName>
```

Continued

Listing 2-9 *(continued)*

```
          <FaxNumber>
            <AreaCode>201</AreaCode>
            <TelNumber>748-6049</TelNumber>
          </FaxNumber>
       </ByFax>
        <ByMail>
          <PostalAddress>
            <CountryCode>US</CountryCode>
            <PostalCode>07030</PostalCode>
            <Region>NJ</Region>
            <Municipality>Hoboken</Municipality>
            <DeliveryAddress>
              <AddressLine>111 River Street</AddressLine>
            </DeliveryAddress>
          </PostalAddress>
        </ByMail>
      </ApplicationMethods>
      <SummaryText>
        Please be sure to indicate the position and job number
        for which you are applying. Please note that any writing
        samples you submit along with your resume will not be
        returned. Once we receive your letter and resume, you
        will receive acknowledgment of receipt. You may be
        contacted if your qualifications match current openings.
        If there is no suitable position, we will retain your
        resume in our files for future consideration.
      </SummaryText>
    </HowToApply>
    <EEOStatement>
      John Wiley &amp; Sons is an equal opportunity employer.
    </EEOStatement>
    <NumberToFill>1</NumberToFill>
  </JobPositionPosting>
```

Although you could certainly define a style sheet for HR-XML documents and use it to place job listings on web pages, that's not its main purpose. Instead, HR-XML is trying to automate the exchange of job information between companies, applicants, recruiters, job boards, and other interested parties. Hundreds of job boards exist on the Internet today, along with numerous Usenet newsgroups and mailing lists. It's impossible for one individual to search them all, and it's hard for a computer to search them all because they all use different formats for salaries, locations, benefits, and the like.

But if many sites adopt HR-XML, it becomes relatively easy for a job seeker to search with criteria such as "all the jobs for Java programmers in New York City paying more than $100,000 a year with full health benefits." The IRS could enter a search for all full-time, onsite, freelance openings so that it would know which companies to go after for failure to withhold tax and to pay unemployment insurance.

In practice, these searches would likely be mediated through an HTML form just like current web searches. The main difference is that such a search would return far more useful results because it could use the structure in the data and semantics of the markup rather than relying on imprecise English text.

XML for XML

XML is an extremely general-purpose format for text data. Some of the things it is used for are further refinements of XML itself. These include the XSL style sheet language, the XLink hypertext vocabulary, and the W3C XML Schema Language.

XSL

XSL, the Extensible Stylesheet Language, is actually two XML applications. The first application is a vocabulary for transforming XML documents called XSL Transformations (XSLT). XSLT defines markup that represents trees, nodes, patterns, templates, and other constructs that can be used to transform XML documents from one markup vocabulary to another (or even to the same vocabulary with different data).

The second application is an XML vocabulary for formatting the transformed XML document produced by the first part. This application is called XSL Formatting Objects (XSL-FO). XSL-FO provides elements that describe the layout of a page, including pagination, blocks, characters, lists, graphics, boxes, fonts, and more. A simple XSLT style sheet that transforms an input document into XSL formatting objects is shown in Listing 2-10.

Listing 2-10: An XSL Style Sheet

```
<?xml version="1.0"?>
<xsl:stylesheet version="1.0"
  xmlns:xsl="http://www.w3.org/1999/XSL/Transform"
  xmlns:fo="http://www.w3.org/1999/XSL/Format">

<xsl:template match="/">
    <fo:root xmlns:fo="http://www.w3.org/1999/XSL/Format">

      <fo:layout-master-set>
        <fo:simple-page-master master-name="only">
          <fo:region-body/>
        </fo:simple-page-master>
      </fo:layout-master-set>

      <fo:page-sequence master-reference="only">
```

Continued

Listing 2-10 (continued)

```
        <fo:flow flow-name="xsl-region-body">
          <xsl:apply-templates select="//ATOM"/>
        </fo:flow>

      </fo:page-sequence>

    </fo:root>
  </xsl:template>

  <xsl:template match="ATOM">
    <fo:block font-size="20pt" font-family="serif"
              line-height="30pt">
      <xsl:value-of select="NAME"/>
    </fo:block>
  </xsl:template>

</xsl:stylesheet>
```

Cross-Reference

Chapters 15 and 16 explore XSL in great detail.

XLinks

XML makes possible a new, more general kind of link called an XLink. XLinks accomplish everything possible with HTML's URL-based hyperlinks and anchors. However, any element can become a link, not just A elements. For example, a footnote element can link directly to the text of the note like this:

```
<footnote xmlns:xlink="http://www.w3.org/1999/xlink"
          xlink:type="simple"
          xlink:href="footnote7.xml">7</footnote>
```

Furthermore, XLinks can do many things that HTML links cannot do. XLinks can be bidirectional so that readers can return to the page they came from. XLinks can link to arbitrary positions in a document. XLinks can embed text or graphic data inside a document rather than requiring the user to activate the link (much like HTML's <IMG> tag but more flexible). In short, XLinks make hypertext even more powerful.

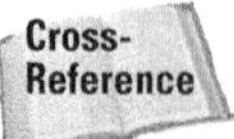

XLinks are discussed in more detail in Chapter 17.

Schemas

XML's facilities for specifying the permissibility of different character data inside elements are weak to nonexistent. For example, suppose as part of a bank statement application you set up ACCOUNT_BALANCE elements like this:

```
<ACCOUNT_BALANCE>$934.12</ACCOUNT_BALANCE>
```

All pure XML 1.0 can say is that the contents of the ACCOUNT_BALANCE element should be character data. It cannot say that the balance should be given as a decimal number with two decimal digits of precision, preceded by a currency sign.

A number of schemes have been proposed to use XML itself to more tightly restrict what can appear in the content of any given element. The W3C has endorsed XML Schema for this purpose. For example, Listing 2-11 shows a schema that declares that ACCOUNT_BALANCE elements must contain a decimal number with two decimal digits of precision, preceded by a currency sign.

Listing 2-11: A Schema for Money

```
<?xml version="1.0"?>
<xsd:schema
targetNS="http://www.cafeconleche.org/namespaces/money"
            version="1.0"
            xmlns:xsd="http://www.w3.org/2001/XMLSchema">

  <xsd:simpleType name="money">
    <xsd:restriction base="xsd:string">
      <xsd:pattern value="\p{Sc}\p{Nd}+(\.\p{Nd}\p{Nd})?"/>
      <!--
         Regular Expression:
         \p{Sc}              Any Unicode currency indicator;
                             e.g., $, &#xA5, &#xA3, &#A4, etc.
         \p{Nd}              A Unicode decimal digit character
         \p{Nd}+             One or more Unicode decimal digits
         \.                  The period character
         (\.\p{Nd}\p{Nd})
         (\.\p{Nd}\p{Nd})?   Zero or one strings like .35
         This works for any decimalized currency.
      -->
    </xsd:restriction>
  </xsd:simpleType>


  <xsd:element name="BALANCE" type="money"/>

</xsd:schema>
```

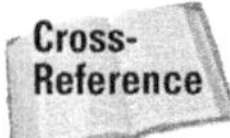

Schemas are discussed in more detail in Chapter 20.

I could show you more examples of XML used for XML, but the ones I've already discussed demonstrate the basic point: XML is powerful enough to describe and extend itself. Among other things, this means that the XML specification can remain small and simple. There may well never be an XML 2.0 because any major additions that are needed can be built *from* XML rather than being built *into* XML. People and programs that need these enhanced features can use them. Others who don't need them can ignore them. You don't need to know about what you don't use. XML provides the bricks and mortar from which you can build simple huts or towering castles.

Behind-the-Scene Uses of XML

Not all XML applications are public, open standards. Many software vendors are moving to XML for their own data simply because it's a well-understood, general-purpose format for structured data that can be manipulated with easily available, cheap, and free tools.

Microsoft Office 2003

Microsoft Office 2003 is the first edition to move away from the traditional undocumented proprietary, closed, binary formats of the past and move forward into the open world of XML. The major Office 2003 applications, including Word, PowerPoint, Excel, and even Visio, can save their documents in XML (though, unfortunately, a binary format is still the default). There are many advantages to this. First among them, XML makes Office files much easier to exchange with other programs. The professional edition of Office can even use custom, user-provided schemas instead of Microsoft's default schema. This is like Word styles and templates on steroids.

Listing 2-12 shows a small Word document containing just the string "Hello XML!" encoded in WordML. I've had to add some line breaks to make this legible, but otherwise the file is just as Word saved it. As ugly as this is, it's still about a thousand times prettier than the old binary format. Unlike files written by previous versions of Word, this document does not have to be read by a word processor. Many different tools can be written in a variety of languages to manipulate it. For instance, for a long time I've wanted a tool that will extract just the outline from a Word file while leaving all the body text behind. This would be very useful for planning the table of contents for a new edition of a book based on the headers in the old version. However, I never wanted that tool badly enough to learn Visual Basic for Applications and the proprietary Word API. Now that Word is saving its data in XML, I can write the tool I need in XSLT, Java, Perl, or some other language. I don't have to use a Microsoft language I don't know to process a Microsoft document.

Listing 2-12: A Simple Word 2003 Document

```
<?xml version="1.0" encoding="UTF-8" standalone="yes"?>
<?mso-application progid="Word.Document"?>
<w:wordDocument xmlns:w=
    "http://schemas.microsoft.com/office/word/2003/2/wordml"
  xmlns:v="urn:schemas-microsoft-com:vml"
  xmlns:w10="urn:schemas-microsoft-com:office:word"
  xmlns:SL=
   "http://schemas.microsoft.com/schemaLibrary/2003/2/core"
  xmlns:aml="http://schemas.microsoft.com/aml/2001/core"
  xmlns:wx=
    "http://schemas.microsoft.com/office/word/2003/2/auxHint"
  xmlns:o="urn:schemas-microsoft-com:office:office"
  xmlns:dt="uuid:C2F41010-65B3-11d1-A29F-00AA00C14882"
  xml:space="preserve">
<o:DocumentProperties>
<o:Title>Hello World</o:Title>
<o:Author>Elliotte Rusty Harold</o:Author>
<o:LastAuthor>Elliotte Rusty Harold</o:LastAuthor>
<o:Revision>1</o:Revision><o:TotalTime>1</o:TotalTime>
<o:Created>2003-06-27T02:38:00Z</o:Created>
<o:LastSaved>2003-06-27T02:39:00Z</o:LastSaved>
<o:Pages>1</o:Pages>
<o:Words>1</o:Words><o:Characters>12</o:Characters>
<o:Company>Cafe au Lait</o:Company>
<o:Lines>1</o:Lines><o:Paragraphs>1</o:Paragraphs>
<o:CharactersWithSpaces>12</o:CharactersWithSpaces>
<o:Version>11.4920</o:Version>
</o:DocumentProperties>
<w:fonts>
  <w:defaultFonts w:ascii="Times New Roman"
     w:fareast="Times New Roman"
     w:h-ansi="Times New Roman" w:cs="Times New Roman"/>
  <w:font w:name="Tahoma">
  <w:panose-1 w:val="020B0604030504040204"/>
  <w:charset w:val="00"/>
  <w:family w:val="Swiss"/>
  <w:pitch w:val="variable"/>
  <w:sig w:usb-0="21007A87" w:usb-1="80000000"
     w:usb-2="00000008" w:usb-3="00000000"
     w:csb-0="000101FF" w:csb-1="00000000"/>
  </w:font>
</w:fonts>
<w:styles>
  <w:versionOfBuiltInStylenames w:val="3"/>
  <w:latentStyles w:defLockedState="off"
w:latentStyleCount="156"/>
  <w:style w:type="paragraph" w:default="on"
           w:styleId="Normal">
```

Continued

Listing 2-12 *(continued)*

```
  <w:name w:val="Normal"/>
  <w:rPr><wx:font wx:val="Times New Roman"/>
  <w:sz w:val="24"/>
  <w:sz-cs w:val="24"/>
  <w:lang w:val="EN-US" w:fareast="EN-US" w:bidi="AR-SA"/>
  </w:rPr></w:style>
  <w:style w:type="character" w:default="on"
   w:styleId="DefaultParagraphFont">
  <w:name w:val="Default Paragraph Font"/>
  <w:semiHidden/></w:style>
  <w:style w:type="table" w:default="on"
w:styleId="TableNormal">
  <w:name w:val="Normal Table"/>
  <wx:uiName wx:val="Table Normal"/>
  <w:semiHidden/>
  <w:rPr><wx:font wx:val="Times New Roman"/></w:rPr>
  <w:tblPr>
  <w:tblInd w:w="0" w:type="dxa"/>
  <w:tblCellMar>
  <w:top w:w="0" w:type="dxa"/>
  <w:left w:w="108" w:type="dxa"/>
  <w:bottom w:w="0" w:type="dxa"/>
  <w:right w:w="108" w:type="dxa"/>
  </w:tblCellMar></w:tblPr></w:style>
  <w:style w:type="list" w:default="on" w:styleId="NoList">
  <w:name w:val="No List"/>
  <w:semiHidden/></w:style>
  <w:style w:type="paragraph" w:styleId="BalloonText">
  <w:name w:val="Balloon Text"/>
  <w:basedOn w:val="Normal"/>
  <w:semiHidden/>
  <w:rsid w:val="A43BDF"/>
  <w:pPr>
  <w:pStyle w:val="BalloonText"/></w:pPr>
  <w:rPr>
  <w:rFonts w:ascii="Tahoma" w:h-ansi="Tahoma" w:cs="Tahoma"/>
  <wx:font wx:val="Tahoma"/>
  <w:sz w:val="16"/>
  <w:sz-cs w:val="16"/></w:rPr></w:style></w:styles>
  <w:docPr>
  <w:view w:val="print"/>
  <w:zoom w:percent="100"/>
  <w:doNotEmbedSystemFonts/>
  <w:attachedTemplate w:val=""/>
```

```
<w:defaultTabStop w:val="720"/>
<w:characterSpacingControl w:val="DontCompress"/>
<w:optimizeForBrowser/>
<w:validateAgainstSchema/>
<w:saveInvalidXML w:val="off"/>
<w:ignoreMixedContent w:val="off"/>
<w:alwaysShowPlaceholderText w:val="off"/>
<w:compat>
<w:dontAllowFieldEndSelect/>
<w:useWord2002TableStyleRules/></w:compat></w:docPr>
<w:body><wx:sect>
<w:p>
<w:r>
<w:t>Hello XML!</w:t></w:r></w:p>
<w:sectPr>
<w:pgSz w:w="12240" w:h="15840"/>
<w:pgMar w:top="1440" w:right="1800" w:bottom="1440"
  w:left="1800" w:header="720" w:footer="720" w:gutter="0"/>
<w:cols w:space="720"/>
<w:docGrid w:line-pitch="360"/>
</w:sectPr></wx:sect></w:body></w:wordDocument>
```

Microsoft is hardly alone in moving its file formats to XML. Other products that use XML as their native format include Sun's StarOffice, Apple's Keynote presentation software, Apple's iTunes music player, Mac OS X properties files, the Apache Project's Ant build tool, the Gnumeric spreadsheet, and the Dia drawing program. Mozilla and Netscape are even storing their GUIs as XML. The common link that unites all these products is that they're all fairly recent programs, with limited if any legacy data. Although legacy formats that predate XML data are likely to be with us through your lifetime and mine, more and more new software is choosing XML as a convenient, efficient format for any data it needs to save.

Netscape's What's Related

Netscape 6.0 and later support direct display of XML in the browser, but Netscape actually started using XML internally as early as version 4.0.6. When you ask Netscape to show you a list of sites related to the current one you're looking at, your browser connects to a CGI program running on a Netscape server (`http://www-r11.netscape.com/wtgn` through `http://www-r17.netscape.com/wtgn`). The data that the server sends back is in XML. Listing 2-13 shows the XML data for sites related to `http://www.wiley.com`. (This data was not designed for human eyes, so I've had to add a few line breaks where they otherwise would not occur.)

Listing 2-13: XML Data for Sites Related to http://www.wiley.com


```
<?xml version="1.0" encoding="UTF-8"?>
<RDF:RDF>
<RelatedLinks>
<child href="http://info.netscape.com/fwd/rlstatic/
http://search.netscape.com/cgi-bin/search?search=wiley"
name="Search on 'wiley'"/>
<child instanceOf="Separator1"/>
<child href="http://info.netscape.com/fwd/rlstatic/
http://directory.netscape.com/Business/Industries/Publishing/
Publishers/Academic_and_Technical"
name="Business: ...Business: Industries: Publishing:
Publishers: Academic and Technical"/>
<child href="http://info.netscape.com/fwd/rlstatic/
http://directory.netscape.com/Business/Major_Companies/Publicly_Traded/J"
name="Business: ...: Publicly Traded: J"/>
<child href="http://info.netscape.com/fwd/rlstatic/
http://directory.netscape.com/Science/Math/Operations_Research
/Commercial_Sites/Book_and_Journal_Publishers"
name="Science: Math: ...Science: Math: Operations Research:
Commercial Sites: Book and Journal Publishers"/>
<child href="http://info.netscape.com/fwd/rlstatic/
http://search.netscape.com/add.html"
name="Submit a site to the Open Directory"/>
<child href="http://info.netscape.com/fwd/rlstatic/
http://home.netscape.com/escapes/search/beditor.html"
name="Become an Open Directory editor"/>
<child instanceOf="Separator1"/>
<child href="http://info.netscape.com/fwd/rlurls/
http://www.oup-usa.org/"
name="Oxford University Press Usa " priority="7"/>
<child href="http://info.netscape.com/fwd/rlurls/
http://www.jefco.com/"
name="Jefferies Internet Site " priority="7"/>
<child href="http://info.netscape.com/fwd/rlurls/
http://www.jriver.com/"
name="J. River, Inc. - Network Gear " priority="7"/>
<child href="http://info.netscape.com/fwd/rlurls/
http://www.jostens.com/"
name="Jostens Inc. " priority="7"/>
<child href="http://info.netscape.com/fwd/rlurls/
http://www.jboxford.com/"
name="Jb Oxford - Online Trading The Way " priority="7"/>
<child href="http://info.netscape.com/fwd/rlurls/
http://www.ibtauris.com/"
name="The I.b.tauris Website " priority="7"/>
```

```
<child href="http://info.netscape.com/fwd/rlurls/
http://www.haworthpressinc.com/"
name="Haworth " priority="7"/>
<child href="http://info.netscape.com/fwd/rlurls/
http://www.duxbury.com/"
name="Duxbury Resource Center " priority="7"/>
<child href="http://info.netscape.com/fwd/rlurls/
http://www.cornellpress.cornell.edu/"
name="Cornell University Press Publishes " priority="7"/>
<child href="http://info.netscape.com/fwd/rlurls/
http://www.arnoldpublishers.com/"
name="Arnold - Academic And Professional " priority="7"/>
<child href="http://editorial.alexa.com/netscape_editor"
name="Suggest related links"/>
<child href="http://info.netscape.com/fwd/rlstatic/
http://home.netscape.com/escapes/related/index.html"
name="Learn more about What's Related" />
<child instanceOf="Separator1"/>
<Topic
name="Site info for www.wiley.com">
<child href="http://info.netscape.com/fwd/rlstatic/
http://home.netscape.com/escapes/related/faq.html"
name="Owner: John Wiley &amp; Sons, Inc."/>
<child href="http://info.netscape.com/fwd/rlstatic/
http://home.netscape.com/escapes/related/faq.html"
name="Date established: 12-Oct-1994"/>
<child href="http://info.netscape.com/fwd/rlstatic/
http://home.netscape.com/escapes/related/faq.html"
name="Popularity: in top 25404 sites on web"/>
<child href="http://info.netscape.com/fwd/rlstatic/
http://home.netscape.com/escapes/related/faq.html"
name="Number of pages on site: 3758"/>
<child href="http://info.netscape.com/fwd/rlstatic/
http://home.netscape.com/escapes/related/faq.html"
name="Number of links to site on web: 17709"/>
</Topic>
<child instanceOf="Separator1"/>
<child href="http://info.netscape.com/fwd/rlstatic/
http://home.netscape.com/escapes/keywords/index.html"
name="Learn more about Internet Keywords"/>
</RelatedLinks>
</RDF:RDF>
```

This all happens completely behind the scenes. The users never know that the data is being transferred in XML. The actual display is a sidebar in Netscape Navigator, shown in Figure 2-7, not an XML or HTML page.

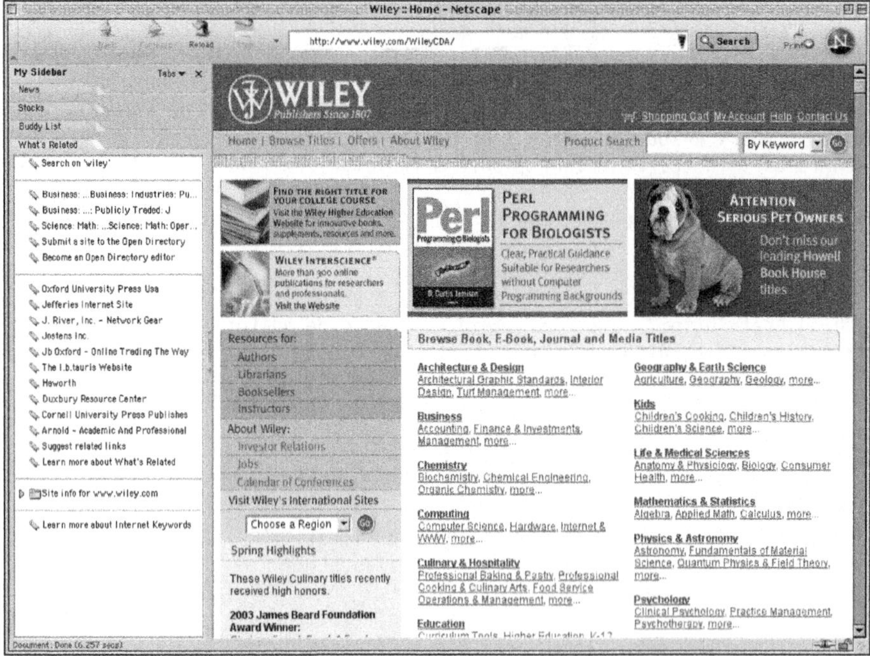

Figure 2-7: Netscape's What's Related sidebar

UPS

The United Parcel Service makes a number of tools available to their customers to track shipments over the Internet, check shipping rates, validate addresses, and more (`http://www.ec.ups.com/ecommerce/solutions`). The content is sent from a UPS server to the customer who requests it. In the earliest versions, the data was sent in HTML so online stores and other shippers could paste it into their web pages. However, the UPS HTML code didn't always mesh very neatly with the site's own code. It could easily look out of place. Then UPS began offering the same information in XML. XML can't be pasted directly into the stores' HTML, but it can be easily manipulated using an XSL style sheet or other tool to take on the form the site needs. It's a much more flexible solution.

That's not all UPS does with XML either. Individual consumers like me that occasionally ship a package can use UPS's web site to track those packages and schedule pickups. However, large organizations that ship dozens to tens of thousands of packages a day don't want to type each tracking number into a form individually. They want to integrate the tracking information and the schedule pickup with their own systems so it can be queried only when necessary and processed automatically. I don't know what kind of servers and systems UPS uses, but I can guarantee you that whatever it is, they have tens of thousands of customers that use something else. They can't rely on any one vendor's format to exchange this information with their customers. Instead, they use XML.

XML is even more important when the process runs in reverse; that is, when customers send information to UPS, to schedule a pickup, for example. UPS lets its customers know what formats it expects to receive the data in, but it can't trust them to actually follow that format. Of the thousands of different programs at different customer sites sending data to UPS, some of them (maybe most of them) are going to have bugs. Some of them are going to send bad data, leave out the shipping address, swap the order of the sender's and recipient's addresses, request pickups at 3:00 A.M. instead of 3:00 P.M., calculate prices in Canadian dollars instead of U.S. dollars, and make a whole slew of other mistakes. Before UPS schedules a pickup or accepts any other request from a potentially unreliable source, it needs to verify that all the required information is present and that it makes sense. XML makes it very straightforward to list most of the relevant constraints in a simple, declarative schema language, and then to validate each request against the expected schema. If the validation succeeds, the request is accepted. If the validation fails, the request can be passed off to a human for further processing or kicked back to the originating system. This protects the integrity of UPS's systems. XML validation can't catch all problems. For example, it probably won't notice an account number that doesn't correspond to a real account. But it is often a very good first step that easily performs about 80 to 90 percent of the checks that need to be made. Whatever checks remain to be done can be coded up more simply against XML than against a more opaque binary format.

This really just scratches the surface of the use of XML for internal data. Many other projects that use XML are just getting started, and many more will be started over the next several years. Most of these won't receive any publicity or write-ups in the trade press, but they nonetheless have the potential to save their companies millions of dollars in development costs over the life of the project. The self-documenting nature of XML can be as useful for a company's internal data as for its external data. For instance, recently many companies were scrambling to try to figure out whether programmers who retired 20 years ago used two-digit or four-digit dates. If that were your job, would you rather be pouring over data that looked like this?

```
3c 79 65 61 72 3e 39 39 3c 2f 79 65 61 72 3e
```

Or data that looked like this?

```
<YEAR>99</YEAR>
```

Binary file formats meant that programmers were stuck trying to clean up data in the first format. XML even makes the mistakes easier to find and fix.

Summary

This chapter has just begun to touch on the many and varied applications for which XML has been and will be used. Some of these applications, such as SVG, MathML, and MusicXML, are clear extensions of HTML for web browsers. Many others, however, such as OFX, XFDL, and HR-XML, go in new directions. And all of these applications have their own semantics and syntax that sits on top of the underlying XML. In some cases, the XML roots are obvious. In other cases, you could easily spend months working with one of theseand only hear of XML tangentially. In this chapter, you explored the following applications in which XML has been put to use:

- ✦ Molecular sciences with CML
- ✦ Science and math with MathML
- ✦ Webcasting with RSS
- ✦ Classic literature
- ✦ Multimedia with SMIL
- ✦ Software updates through OSD
- ✦ Vector graphics with SVG
- ✦ Music notation in MusicXML
- ✦ Automated voice responses with VoiceXML
- ✦ Financial data with OFX 2.0
- ✦ Legally binding forms with XFDL
- ✦ Job listings with HR-XML
- ✦ Extending XML itself with XSL, XLink, and XML Schemas
- ✦ Internal use of XML by various companies, including Microsoft, Netscape, and FederalUPS

In the next chapter, you will begin writing your own XML documents and displaying them in a web browser.

✦ ✦ ✦

CHAPTER 3

Your First XML Document

◆ ◆ ◆ ◆

In This Chapter

Creating a simple XML document

Exploring the simple XML document

Meaning in markup

Writing style sheets for XML documents

Attaching style sheets to XML documents

◆ ◆ ◆ ◆

This chapter teaches you to create simple XML documents with tags that you define that make sense for your document. You learn which tools and software you can use to edit and save an XML document. You also learn to write a style sheet for the document that describes how the content of those tags should be displayed. Finally, you learn to load the document into a web browser so that it can be viewed.

Because this chapter teaches you by example, it will not cross all the t's and dot all the i's. Experienced readers may notice a few exceptions and special cases that aren't discussed here. Don't worry about them; I'll get to them over the course of the next several chapters. For the most part, you don't need to memorize the technical rules up front. As with HTML, you can learn and do a lot by copying a few simple examples that others have prepared and modifying them to fit your needs.

Toward that end, I encourage you to follow along by typing in the examples given in this chapter and loading them into the different programs discussed. This will give you a basic feel for XML that will make the technical details in future chapters easier to grasp in the context of these specific examples.

Hello XML

This section follows an old programmer's tradition of introducing a new language with a program that prints "Hello World" on the console. XML is a markup language, not a programming language; but the basic principle still applies. It's easiest to get started if you begin with a complete, working example that you can expand, instead of starting with more fundamental pieces that by themselves don't do anything. If you do encounter problems with the basic tools, those problems are a lot easier to debug and fix in the context of the short, simple documents used here, than in the context of the more complex documents developed in the rest of the book.

Creating a simple XML document

In this section, you create a simple XML document and save it in a file. Listing 3-1 is about the simplest XML document I can imagine, so start with it. You can type this document in any convenient text editor, such as Notepad, BBEdit, or emacs.

Listing 3-1: Hello XML

```
<?xml version="1.0"?>
<FOO>
Hello XML!
</FOO>
```

Listing 3-1 is not very complicated, but it is a good XML document. To be more precise, it is a *well-formed* XML document. (XML has special terms for documents that it considers "good" depending on exactly which set of rules they satisfy. "Well-formed" is one of those terms, but we'll get to that later.)

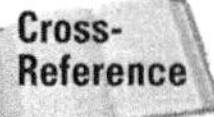

Well-formedness is covered in detail in Chapter 6.

Saving the XML file

After you've typed in Listing 3-1, save it in a file called hello.xml, HelloWorld.xml, MyFirstDocument.xml, or some other name. The three-letter extension .xml is fairly standard. However, do make sure that you save it in plain-text format, and not in the native format of a word processor such as WordPerfect or Microsoft Word.

If you're using Notepad on Windows 95 or 98 to edit your files, be sure to enclose the filename in double quotes when saving the document; for example, "Hello.xml", not merely Hello.xml, as shown in Figure 3-1. Without the quotes, Notepad will append the .txt extension to your filename, naming it Hello.xml.txt, which is not what you want.

The Windows NT version of Notepad gives you the option to save the file in Unicode; and Windows 2000 lets you choose UTF-8 and Unicode big endian, as well. All of these will work equally well for XML.

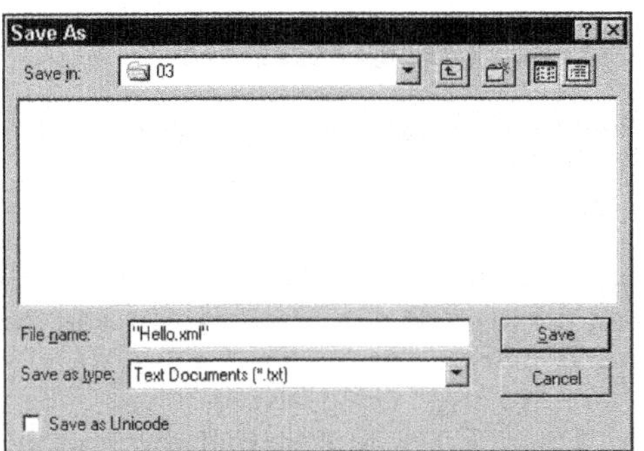

Figure 3-1: An XML document saved in Notepad with the filename in quotes

Loading the XML file into a web browser

Now that you've created your first XML document, you're going to want to look at it. You can open the file directly in a browser that supports XML such as Internet Explorer 5.0 or later. Figure 3-2 shows the result.

What you see will vary from browser to browser. In this case, it's a nicely formatted and syntax-colored view of the document's source code. Opera will simply show you the string "Hello XML!" in the default font. Whatever the browser shows you, it's not likely to be particularly attractive. The problem is that the browser doesn't really know what to do with the `FOO` element. You have to tell the browser how to handle each element by adding a style sheet. You'll learn to do that shortly, but let's first look a little more closely at this XML document.

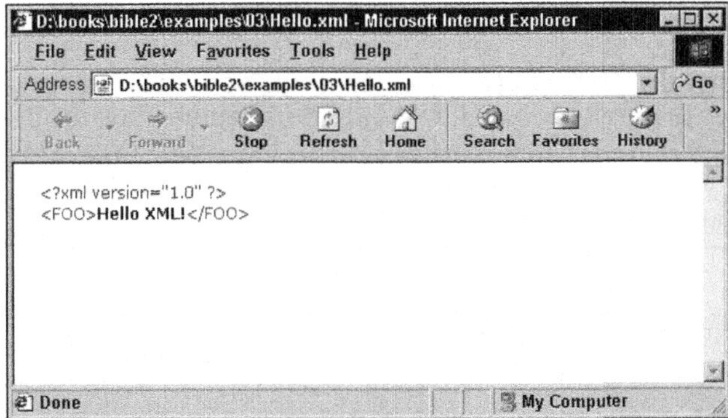

Figure 3-2: Hello.xml displayed in Internet Explorer 6.0

Exploring the Simple XML Document

The first line of the simple XML document in Listing 3-1 is the *XML declaration*:

```
<?xml version="1.0"?>
```

The XML declaration has a `version` attribute. An *attribute* is a name-value pair separated by an equals sign. The name is on the left side of the equals sign, and the value is on the right side between double quote marks.

Every XML document should begin with an XML declaration that specifies the version of XML in use. (Some XML documents will omit this for reasons of backward compatibility, but you should include a version declaration unless you have a specific reason to leave it out.) In the previous example, the `version` attribute says that this document conforms to the XML 1.0 specification.

If you have to ask whether you need XML 1.1, you don't need it. I'll have more to say about this later, but for now, stick to XML 1.0. XML 1.1 gains you absolutely nothing.

Now look at the next three lines of Listing 3-1:

```
<FOO>
Hello XML!
</FOO>
```

Collectively, these three lines form a `FOO` *element*. Separately, `<FOO>` is a *start-tag*; `</FOO>` is an *end-tag*; and `Hello XML!` is the *content* of the `FOO` element. Divided another way, the start-tag, end-tag, and XML declaration are all *markup*. The text `Hello XML!` is *character data*.

You might be asking what the `<FOO>` tag means. The short answer is "whatever you want it to mean." Rather than relying on a few hundred predefined tags, XML lets you create the tags that you need when you need them. The `<FOO>` tag, therefore, has whatever meaning you assign it. The same XML document could have been written with different tag names, as shown in Listings 3-2, 3-3, and 3-4.

Listing 3-2: greeting.xml

```
<?xml version="1.0"?>
<GREETING>
Hello XML!
</GREETING>
```

Listing 3-3: paragraph.xml

```
<?xml version="1.0"?>
<P>
Hello XML!
</P>
```

Listing 3-4: document.xml

```
<?xml version="1.0"?>
<DOCUMENT>
Hello XML!
</DOCUMENT>
```

The four XML documents in Listings 3-1 through 3-4 have tags with different names. However, they are all equivalent because they have the same structure and content.

Meaning in Markup

Markup can indicate three kinds of meaning: structural, semantic, or stylistic. *Structure* specifies the relations between the different elements in the document. *Semantics* relates the individual elements to the real world outside of the document itself. *Style* specifies how an element is displayed.

Structure merely expresses the form of the document, without regard for differences between individual tags and elements. For example, the four XML documents shown in Listings 3-1 through 3-4 are structurally the same. They all specify documents with a single nonempty, root element that contains the same content. The different names of the tags have no structural significance.

Semantic meaning exists outside the document, in the mind of the author or reader, or in some computer program that generates or reads these files. For example, a web browser that understands HTML, but not XML, would assign the meaning "paragraph" to the tags `<P>` and `</P>` but not to the tags `<GREETING>` and `</GREETING>`, `<FOO>` and `</FOO>`, or `<DOCUMENT>` and `</DOCUMENT>`. An English-speaking human would be more likely to understand `<GREETING>` and `</GREETING>` or `<DOCUMENT>` and `</DOCUMENT>` than `<FOO>` and `</FOO>` or `<P>` and `</P>`. Meaning, like beauty, is in the mind of the beholder.

Computers, being relatively dumb machines, can't really be said to understand the meaning of anything. They simply process bits and bytes according to predetermined formulas (albeit very quickly). A computer is just as happy to use <FOO> or <P> as it is to use the more meaningful <GREETING> or <DOCUMENT> tags. Even a web browser can't be said to really understand what a paragraph is. All the browser knows is that when it encounters the end of a paragraph it should place a blank line before the next element.

Naturally, it's better to pick tags that more closely reflect the meaning of the information they contain. Many disciplines, such as math and chemistry, are working on creating industry-standard tag sets. These should be used when appropriate. However, many tags are made up as you need them. Here are some other possible tags with different semantic meanings:

```
<MOLECULE>        <sign>
<INTEGRAL>        <ellipse>
<PERSON>          <AOL>
<SALARY>          <plus/>
<author>          <TimeWarner>
<email>           <equals/>
<planet>          <Bankruptcy>
```

The third kind of meaning that can be associated with a tag is stylistic. Style says how the content of a tag is to be presented on a computer screen or other output device. Style says whether a particular element is bold, italic, green, two inches high, and so on. Computers are better at understanding stylistic than semantic meaning. In XML, style is applied through style sheets.

Writing a Style Sheet for an XML Document

XML allows you to create any tags that you need. Because you have almost complete freedom in creating tags, a generic browser has no way to anticipate your tags and provide rules for displaying them. Therefore, you also need to write a style sheet for the XML document that tells browsers how to display particular tags. Like tag sets, style sheets can be shared between different documents and different people, and the style sheets you create can be integrated with style sheets others have written.

As discussed in Chapter 1, there is more than one style sheet language to choose from. The one introduced in this chapter is cascading style sheets (CSS). CSS has the advantage of being an established W3C standard, being familiar to many people from HTML, and being supported in the first wave of XML-enabled web browsers.

As noted in Chapter 1, another possibility is XSL. XSL is currently the most powerful and flexible style sheet language, and the only one designed specifically for use with XML. However, XSL is more complex than CSS and not yet as well supported in web browsers.

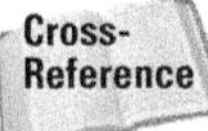

XSL is discussed in Chapters 5, 15, and 16.

The greeting.xml example shown in Listing 3-2 only contains one tag, `<GREETING>`, so all you need to do is define the style for the `GREETING` element. Listing 3-5 is a very simple style sheet that specifies that the contents of the `GREETING` element should be rendered as a block-level element in 24-point bold type.

Listing 3-5: greeting.xsl

```
GREETING {display: block; font-size: 24pt; font-weight: bold}
```

Listing 3-5 should be typed in a text editor and saved in a new file called greeting.css in the same directory as Listing 3-2. The .css extension stands for cascading style sheet. Again, the .css extension is important, although the exact filename is not. However, if a style sheet is to be applied only to a single XML document, it's often convenient to give it the same name as that document with the extension .css instead of .xml.

Attaching a Style Sheet to an XML Document

After you've written an XML document and a style sheet for that document, you need to tell the browser to apply the style sheet to the document. In the long term, there are likely to be a number of different ways to do this, including browser-server negotiation via HTTP headers, naming conventions, and browser-side defaults. However, right now, the only way that works is to include an `<?xml-stylesheet?>` processing instruction in the XML document to specify the style sheet to be used.

The `<?xml-stylesheet?>` processing instruction has two required attributes: `type` and `href`. The `type` attribute specifies the style sheet language used, and the `href` attribute specifies a URL, possibly relative, where the style sheet can be found. In Listing 3-6, the `xml-stylesheet` processing instruction specifies that the style sheet named `greeting.css` written in the CSS language is to be applied to this document.

Listing 3-6: styledgreeting.xml with an xml-stylesheet Processing Instruction

```
<?xml version="1.0"?>
<?xml-stylesheet type="text/css" href="greeting.css"?>
<GREETING>
Hello XML!
</GREETING>
```

Now that you've created your first XML document and style sheet, you will want to look at it. All you have to do is open Listing 3-6 in an XML-enabled web browser such as Mozilla, Safari, Opera 4.0, or Internet Explorer 5.0. Figure 3-3 shows styledgreeting.xml in Safari.

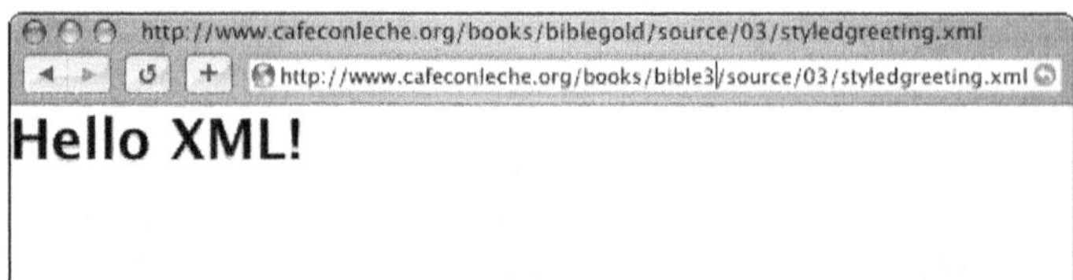

Figure 3-3: styledgreeting.xml in Safari

Summary

In this chapter, you learned how to create a simple XML document. In particular, you learned the following:

- ✦ How to write and save simple XML documents
- ✦ How to assign XML elements three kinds of meaning: structural, semantic, and stylistic
- ✦ How to write a CSS style sheet that tells browsers how to display particular elements
- ✦ How to attach a CSS style sheet to an XML document with an `xml-stylesheet` processing instruction
- ✦ How to load XML documents into a web browser

The next chapter develops a much larger example of an XML document that demonstrates more of the practical considerations involved in choosing XML element names.

✦ ✦ ✦

CHAPTER 4

Structuring Data

✦ ✦ ✦ ✦

In This Chapter

Examining the data

XMLizing the data

The advantages of the XML format

Preparing a style sheet for document display

✦ ✦ ✦ ✦

This chapter develops a longer example that shows how television listings might be stored in XML. By following along with this example, you'll learn many useful techniques that you can apply to all kinds of data-heavy documents.

A document such as this has many potential uses. Most obviously, it can be displayed on a web page. It can also be used to generate printed listings for the daily newspaper. Advertisers can use it to help decide where to buy ads. Digital video recorders like TiVo can use it to decide when and what to record. Nielsen boxes can use it to map the channels viewers are watching to the shows playing on those channels. Hotels can use it to generate custom listings for each reservation they sell that cover just the channels shown at that hotel during a customer's stay. Unions such as the Screen Actors Guild can use it to check which shows are playing how often to determine which producers to bill for an actor's appearances. A web site could send subscribers automatic e-mail notification of their favorite shows and movies. Once the data is in XML, it's very easy to repurpose for a thousand different uses.

Given so many different use cases, this information will almost certainly be processed on a variety of hardware and operating systems, ranging from the mainframes running large television networks to PCs and Macs in local affiliates to operating systems embedded in VCRs in homes. The software running all these devices is written in a plethora of programming languages with different capabilities and characteristics. They need a device-independent format they can all handle, and XML provides it.

As the example is developed, you'll learn, among other things, how to mark up data in XML, the principles for good XML names, and how to prepare a style sheet for a document.

Examining the Data

The first step in developing an XML vocabulary for any domain of interest is to identify the relevant categories. You can probably think of a few obvious ones on the spot: show name, airtime, length of show, and a few others. However, to avoid missing anything essential, it's useful to look at some samples of the existing information, even if it's a noncomputerized form on paper. In this case, the obvious place to look is *TV Guide* or the television listings in the daily newspaper. Table 4-1 shows one such sample that you might find in a typical newspaper.

Looking at this sample, you can immediately pick out some of the obvious information any successful format must provide:

- Station
- Network
- Channel
- Title
- Date
- Start time
- Length or end time
- Description
- Rating
- Whether or not the show is closed captioned
- Year when a movie was made
- Movie type
- Number of stars

The information as shown in Table 4-1 is not necessarily in the same order as it might appear in the XML document. For example, shows could be ordered by time or network or not at all. Different systems might have different information. The documents a network such as ABC sends to local affiliates might contain only the shows broadcast by that network, and may not include channel numbers. The documents generated by a local station and sent to the local newspaper would probably contain all the shows on that station and the channel number. A producer of syndicated programming like King World might not include start times because that can vary from one market to the next, but could include the expected air dates. The documents sent to their members by a media watchdog group such as the American Family Association or the Gay and Lesbian Alliance Against Defamation might contain only the shows they find particularly objectionable or praiseworthy.

Table 4-1
Television Schedule

July 3, 2003	*7:00pm*	*7:30pm*	*8:00pm*	*8:30pm*
CBS 2	Hollywood Squares Repeat, CC	Entertainment Tonight CC American Juniors remaining contestants; Sex and the City preview.	The Amazing Race 4 CC Eight twenty-somethings speed through foreign cultures as quickly as possible in attempt to avoid learning anything.	
NBC 4	EXTRA TVPG, CC	Access Hollywood TVPG, CC	Friends TV14, Repeat, CC Ross does something stupid while Phoebe acts annoying.	Scrubs TV14, Repeat, CC J.D. worries a lot.
FOX 5	The Simpsons TVPG, CC	Seinfeld TVPG, CC	The Hurricane (1999) *** (R) TV14, CC Jailed boxer seeks to be exonerated after imprisonment for murders he did not commit.	
ABC 7	Jeopardy! TVG, CC	Wheel of Fortune TVG, Repeat, CC	The Love Letter (1999) ** (PG13) TV14, CC A bookstore manager in a small town finds an anonymous love letter and searches for the person who wrote it.	
UPN 9	The Steve Harvey Show TVPG, CC	The Jamie Foxx Show CC	WWE SmackDown! TVPG, CC Steroid-enhanced body builders pretend to hit each other while grunting loudly. Referees pretend to care.	
WB 11	Friends TVPG, CC	Everybody Loves Raymond CC	Air Bud: Seventh Inning Fetch (2002) (G) TVG, CC Golden retriever plays baseball.	
PBS 13	The NewsHour With Jim Lehrer CC		Cincinnati Pops: Patriotic Broadway TVG, CC	

Continued

Table 4-1 *(continued)*

July 3, 2003	*7:00pm*	*7:30pm*	*8:00pm*	*8:30pm*
PBS 21	BBC World News	Face-Off	Globe Trekker CC Jamaica; crocodile; Treasure Beach; Bob Marley's mausoleum; Blue Mountain	
PBS 25	Le Journal	The Open Mind	Isadora Duncan: Movement for the Soul The dancer moves to Russia following the revolution. Discovers Bolshevism is boring, and everybody's poor.	
WPXN 31	Supermarket Sweep TVG	Family Feud TVPG, CC	It's a Miracle TVPG, CC Survivors of shark attacks, avalanches, and airport security checkpoints.	
WXTV 41	Las Vias del Amor		Rebeca	
WNJU 47	Sofia Dame Tiempo		Los Teens	
PBS 50	BBC World News CC	NJN News	American Experience CC	
WLNY 55	Oprah Winfrey TVPG, Repeat, CC		Silicon Towers (1999) (PG13)	
HBO 501	Final Fantasy: The Spirits Within *** (PG13), CC		Terminator 3: Rise of the Machines: HBO First Look	Star Wars: Episode II Attack of the Clones *** (PG), CC

Similarly, this one sample might not contain all the information you need to provide. Television networks routinely send out much more information about any one show than can fit in the limited amount of space available. This includes episode titles, cast lists, directors, original air dates, and more. On a web site such as `tv.yahoo.com`, this might be accessible on a separate page accessed through a hyperlink. In a printed version in the daily newspaper, this extra content will probably be omitted entirely. This is not an excuse not to include it, though. Generally, in XML, each party to a transfer of information sends everything it knows and extracts what it wants from what other parties send to it. It's easier to chop out excess information than it is to fill in missing data.

You should look at several independent samples in case one of them contains information the other doesn't contain. It's certainly possible to leave out some of the information some of the time if it isn't relevant or useful in any particular instance. However, you want to make the application flexible enough to handle a range of uses.

XMLizing the Data

XML is based on a containment model. Each XML element can contain text or other XML elements, both of which are called the element's *children*. Some XML elements may contain both text and child elements. However, there's often more than one way to organize the data, depending on your needs. One advantage of XML is that it makes it fairly straightforward to write a program that reorganizes the data in a different form.

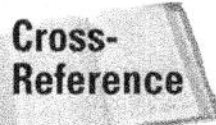

Chapter 16 shows you one way of doing this using XSL transformations.

To get started, the first question you have to address is what contains what, or, another way of putting it, which information is a part of which other information? For instance, it is fairly obvious that a show has a rating and a title. The rating and title belong to the show. Thus, the rating and title elements should be children of the show element, rather than the other way around.

However, does a network contain a show or does a show contain a network? Is the network a characteristic of a show, or is a show part of a network? Both approaches are plausible. Indeed, it might be something else altogether, such as both the network and the show being independent elements that are somehow linked together (although doing so effectively would require some advanced techniques that aren't discussed for several chapters yet). There's no one right answer to these questions, though some approaches are likely to work better than others.

Readers familiar with database theory might recognize XML's model as essentially a hierarchical database, and, consequently, recognize that it shares all the disadvantages (and a few advantages) of that data model. There are times when a table-based relational approach makes more sense. This example certainly looks like one of those times. However, XML doesn't follow a relational model.

On the other hand, it is completely possible to store the actual data in multiple tables in a relational database, and then generate the XML on the fly. This enables one set of data to be presented in multiple formats. Transforming the data with style sheets provides still more possible views of the data.

Because I'm not a network executive, my personal interests lie in the individual shows rather than the networks. Therefore, I'm going to design my application around shows. Most information will be a child of the individual show elements. Different shows can be grouped together as part of a station element. The schedule will contain separate stations. However, this is far from the only way to do it, and different developers might well choose different arrangements for the same data. You, however, might have other interests and can choose to divide the data in some other fashion. There's almost always more than one way to organize data in XML. In fact, several upcoming chapters explore alternative markup vocabularies for this very example.

Let's begin the process of marking up the data. For the sake of the example, I've picked just a few representative channels (CBS, WLNY, and HBO) in New York on July 3, 2003. To keep the example manageably sized, I'm only going to include shows that begin between 7:00 P.M. and 8:30 P.M. However, as you'll soon see, this is easy to extend to much larger chunks of time and many more stations and networks.

Remember that in XML you're allowed to make up the tags as you go along. We've already decided that the root element of this document will be a schedule. Schedules will contain shows. Shows will have titles, start times, run lengths, actors, descriptions, and so forth. Some of these will be optional. For example, the evening newscast might not list actors. The 17,345th repeat of *The Honeymooners* might not include a description. Some of the elements might contain child elements of their own. For example, actors typically have a first name, a last name, and often a middle initial. XML is very flexible. It's easy to vary the exact information provided with any particular element. If you don't know something, it's easy to leave it out. If you have extra information that wasn't planned for, you can easily add an extra element covering that content.

XML documents can be recognized by the XML declaration. This is placed at the start of XML files to identify the version in use. The only version currently understood is 1.0.

```
<?xml version="1.0"?>
```

Version 1.1 is under development now, but offers no benefits to anyone reading this book and is substantially less interoperable than XML 1.0. Version 1.1 is only useful to people who speak Cherokee, Mongolian, Burmese, Amharic, and a few other languages this book is not translated into. This is discussed further in Chapter 6.

Every good XML document (where *good* has a very specific meaning to be discussed in Chapter 6) must have a root element. This is an element that completely contains all other elements of the document. The root element's start-tag comes before all other elements' start-tags, and the root element's end-tag comes after all other element's end-tags. For the root element, I'll pick `SCHEDULE` with a start-tag of `<SCHEDULE>` and an end-tag of `</SCHEDULE>`. The document now looks like this:

```
<?xml version="1.0"?>
<SCHEDULE>
</SCHEDULE>
```

The XML declaration is not an element or a tag. Therefore, it does not need to be contained inside the root element `SCHEDULE`. But every element that you put in this document will go between the `<SCHEDULE>` start-tag and the `</SCHEDULE>` end-tag.

Naming Conventions

Before I go any further, I'd like to say a few words about naming conventions. As you'll see in Chapter 6, XML element names are quite flexible and can contain any number of letters and digits in either upper- or lowercase. You have the option of writing XML tags that look like any of the following:

```
<SCHEDULE>

<Schedule>

<schedule>

<TV_Schedule>

<TV-Schedule>

<TelevisionSchedule>
```

There are several thousand more variations. You can use all uppercase, all lowercase, mixed-case with internal capitalization, or some other convention. However, I do recommend that you choose one convention and stick to it.

On the other hand, it is very important that you use full, unabbreviated names. This makes the documents much more comprehensible, and much easier to process. Throughout this example, I'm following the explicit XML principle that "Terseness in XML markup is of minimal importance." If document size is truly an issue, it's easy to compress the files with gzip or another compression program. However, this can mean that XML documents tend to be quite long and relatively tedious to type by hand.

The next question to ask is whether there's any information in Table 4-1 that applies to the entire table, rather than individual rows or columns. I think there's one key piece: the date the table describes. This may or may not be present in all variations. For instance, it's very important in a monthly or weekly program guide, but not nearly as important in the daily newspaper. Networks and local stations might publish documents containing a week's worth of shows, which a newspaper uses to create a schedule for a single day. Still, whether a single date will be present in every instance of this application, it's at least present here. It's easily included in a DATE child element of the root SCHEDULE element:

```
<?xml version="1.0"?>
<SCHEDULE>
  <DATE>July 3, 2003</DATE>
</SCHEDULE>
```

Following along with Table 4-1, the next obvious division is either the rows or the columns of the table. The columns indicate times. The rows indicate stations. XML does not by its nature lend itself to tabular structures. One or the other of these has to be the next level of the hierarchy. Choosing the rows, that is, the stations, makes sense because the shows don't always line up evenly on column boundaries. On the other hand, picking columns would allow you to sort the data by time instead of station, which might be more useful. But one has to be chosen, so I choose the rows. Still, there's more than one way to do it, and picking the columns instead would not be wrong.

What do you know about a station? Several things:

- The network affiliation
- The call letters
- The channel number

Choosing the most obvious names for each of these elements, the first station looks like this:

```
<STATION>
  <NETWORK>CBS</NETWORK>
  <CALL_LETTERS>WCBS</CALL_LETTERS>
  <CHANNEL>2</CHANNEL>
</STATION>
```

Later you'll add the shows as children of the station that broadcasts them.

Not all stations have all these pieces, however. For example, independent stations aren't affiliated with a network, and cable-only channels don't have call letters. You can include those that apply and leave out those that don't. For example, here are STATION elements for WLNY, an independent channel, and HBO, a cable-only network with no local affiliates:

```
<STATION>
  <CALL_LETTERS>WLNY</CALL_LETTERS>
  <CHANNEL>55</CHANNEL>
</STATION>
<STATION>
  <NETWORK>HBO</NETWORK>
  <CHANNEL>501</CHANNEL>
</STATION>
```

XML makes it very easy to include the information that applies and leave out the information that doesn't. There aren't any special null values, or elements used just to fill an expected slot.

So far, the complete document is as shown in Listing 4-1 (though you could always add more stations, of course).

Listing 4-1: **The Stations in the Schedule**

```
<?xml version="1.0"?>
<SCHEDULE>
  <DATE>July 3, 2003</DATE>
  <STATION>
    <NETWORK>CBS</NETWORK>
    <CALL_LETTERS>WCBS</CALL_LETTERS>
    <CHANNEL>2</CHANNEL>
  </STATION>
  <STATION>
    <CALL_LETTERS>WLNY</CALL_LETTERS>
    <CHANNEL>55</CHANNEL>
  </STATION>
  <STATION>
    <NETWORK>HBO</NETWORK>
    <CHANNEL>501</CHANNEL>
  </STATION>
</SCHEDULE>
```

I've used indentation here and in other examples to make it more obvious that the STATION elements are children of the SCHEDULE elements and that the CHANNEL, NETWORK, and CALL_LETTERS elements are children of the STATION elements. This is good coding style, but it is not required. Parsers do faithfully report all white space in the event that it is necessary, but in most applications white space is not particularly significant, especially boundary white space that occurs solely between two tags. The same example could have been written like this, but with a corresponding loss of clarity:

```
<?xml version="1.0"?><SCHEDULE><DATE>July 3,
2003</DATE><STATION><CHANNEL>2</CHANNEL><NETWORK>CBS
</NETWORK><CALL_LETTERS>WCBS</CALL_LETTERS>
</STATION><STATION><CHANNEL>55</CHANNEL>
<CALL_LETTERS>WLNY</CALL_LETTERS></STATION><STATION>
<CHANNEL>501</CHANNEL><NETWORK>HBO</NETWORK>
</STATION></SCHEDULE>
```

Of course, this version is much harder to read and to understand. The tenth goal listed in the XML specification is "Terseness in XML markup is of minimal importance." It is much more important that documents be legible than that they be terse. The examples in this book reflect this principle throughout.

The key component of the information will be the individual shows. Let's begin with the first one in Table 4-1, *Hollywood Squares*. After examining it, you know the following:

- ✦ The name of the show: *Hollywood Squares*.
- ✦ The start time: 7:00 P.M.
- ✦ The end time: 7:30 P.M.
- ✦ The length of the show: 30 minutes.
- ✦ The channel: 2.
- ✦ The network: CBS.
- ✦ The air date: July 3, 2003.
- ✦ The show is closed captioned.
- ✦ The show is a repeat.

The channel and network will become part of each STATION element. There's no need to duplicate them. The remainder of these items can each be made a child element of a SHOW element like so:

```
<SHOW>
  <NAME>Hollywood Squares</NAME>
  <START_TIME>7:00 P.M.</START_TIME>
```

```
  <END_TIME>7:00 P.M.</END_TIME>
  <LENGTH>30 minutes</LENGTH>
  <AIR_DATE>July 3, 2003</AIR_DATE>
  <CLOSED_CAPTIONED>Yes</CLOSED_CAPTIONED>
  <REPEAT>Yes</REPEAT>
</SHOW>
```

However, some of this information is deceptive and may need to be cleaned up before it can be used:

✦ The start and end times are in the eastern time zone. These are the correct local times for New York. However, it might be useful to indicate the time zone in which these times are stated, typically by giving the offset from Greenwich Mean Time and often using a 24-hour clock. For example, New York is five hours behind Greenwich Mean Time, so the start time could be written as 19:00-0500.

✦ One of the three numbers—start time, end time, and length—is redundant. Given two of these it's possible to calculate the other. It might be wiser not to include all three.

✦ The air date at least seems redundant with date of the entire schedule. However, most television listings prefer to start the day somewhere around 5:00 or 6:00 A.M., rather than at midnight. Thus, it's not uncommon for a show that's broadcast in the early morning one day to appear in the schedule for the previous day.

Accounting for this, the SHOW element becomes something like this:

```
<SHOW>
  <NAME>Hollywood Squares</NAME>
  <START_TIME>19:00-0500</START_TIME>
  <LENGTH>30 minutes</LENGTH>
  <AIR_DATE>July 3, 2003</AIR_DATE>
  <CLOSED_CAPTIONED>Yes</CLOSED_CAPTIONED>
  <REPEAT>Yes</REPEAT>
</SHOW>
```

Furthermore, a lot of information that could be made available doesn't always show up in the daily newspaper but might be used if the show is a pick of the day. This includes the following:

✦ The cast: Don Rickles, Jerry Springer, Richard Simmons, Vicki Lawrence, John Salley, Joanie Laurer, Martin Mull, Jillian Barberie, Kennedy

✦ The Producers: Henry Winkler, Michael Levitt

✦ The original air date: January 16, 2003

Even if this will be omitted from a particular view of the data, it might well be included in the XML. At the minimum, it needs to be able to be included. Adding this content, a SHOW element looks like this:

```
<SHOW>
  <NAME>Hollywood Squares</NAME>
  <TYPE>Series/Game Shows</TYPE>
  <EPISODE_NUMBER>5074</EPISODE_NUMBER>
  <START_TIME>19:00-0500</START_TIME>
  <LENGTH>30 minutes</LENGTH>
  <AIR_DATE>July 3, 2003</AIR_DATE>
  <ORIGINAL_AIR_DATE>January 16, 2003</ORIGINAL_AIR_DATE>
  <CLOSED_CAPTIONED>Yes</CLOSED_CAPTIONED>
  <REPEAT>Yes</REPEAT>
  <CAST>
    Don Rickles, Jerry Springer, Richard Simmons,
    Vicki Lawrence, John Salley, Joanie Laurer,
    Martin Mull, Jillian Barberie, Kennedy
  </CAST>
  <PRODUCER>Henry Winkler</PRODUCER>
  <PRODUCER>Michael Levitt</PRODUCER>
</SHOW>
```

However, the CAST element is less than ideal. It has significant substructure that is not yet reflected in the XML markup. The CAST is composed of individual actors. However, because XML has no limit on the number of elements that may share names, it's easy to expand the markup to more thoroughly annotate this information:

```
<CAST>
   <ACTOR>Don Rickles</ACTOR>
   <ACTOR>Jerry Springer</ACTOR>
   <ACTOR>Richard Simmons</ACTOR>
   <ACTOR>Vicki Lawrence</ACTOR>
   <ACTOR>John Salley</ACTOR>
   <ACTOR>Joanie Laurer</ACTOR>
   <ACTOR>Martin Mull</ACTOR>
   <ACTOR>Jillian Barberie</ACTOR>
   <ACTOR>Kennedy</ACTOR>
</CAST>
```

There's still substructure we haven't captured here, though. Actors (and producers) have both first and last names. Assuming you might want to do something with this data, such as sort by last name, it makes sense to mark that up separately:

```
<CAST>
   <ACTOR>
     <GIVEN_NAME>Don</GIVEN_NAME>
     <SURNAME>Rickles</SURNAME>
   </ACTOR>
   <ACTOR>
```

```
      <GIVEN_NAME>Jerry</GIVEN_NAME>
      <SURNAME>Springer</SURNAME>
    </ACTOR>
    <ACTOR>
      <GIVEN_NAME>Richard</GIVEN_NAME>
      <SURNAME>Simmons</SURNAME>
    </ACTOR>
    <ACTOR>
      <GIVEN_NAME>Vicki</GIVEN_NAME>
      <SURNAME>Lawrence</SURNAME>
    </ACTOR>
    <ACTOR>
       <GIVEN_NAME>John</GIVEN_NAME>
       <SURNAME>Salley</SURNAME>
    </ACTOR>
    <ACTOR>
      <GIVEN_NAME>Joanie</GIVEN_NAME>
      <SURNAME>Laurer</SURNAME>
    </ACTOR>
    <ACTOR>
      <GIVEN_NAME>Martin</GIVEN_NAME>
      <SURNAME>Mull</SURNAME>
    </ACTOR>
    <ACTOR>
      <GIVEN_NAME>Jillian</GIVEN_NAME>
      <SURNAME>Barberie</SURNAME>
    </ACTOR>
    <ACTOR>
       <GIVEN_NAME>Kennedy</GIVEN_NAME>
    </ACTOR>
    <PRODUCER>
      <GIVEN_NAME>Henry</GIVEN_NAME>
      <SURNAME>Winkler</SURNAME>
    </PRODUCER>
    <PRODUCER>
      <GIVEN_NAME>Michael</GIVEN_NAME>
      <SURNAME>Levitt</SURNAME>
    </PRODUCER>
</CAST>
```

Kennedy is the odd one out here. She only uses one name professionally, which is actually her middle name. Fortunately, in XML it's straightforward to leave out any element that doesn't apply in a particular instance. This is much better than including an empty element, N/A, null, or some similar flag. The proper representation of information that doesn't exist is no element at all.

Note

The tags `<GIVEN_NAME>` and `<SURNAME>` are preferable to the more obvious `<FIRST_NAME>` and `<LAST_NAME>` or `<FIRST_NAME>` and `<FAMILY_NAME>`. Whether the family name or the given name comes first or last varies from culture to culture. Furthermore, surnames aren't necessarily family names in all cultures.

When developing a new format, it's important to look at multiple examples. The first one never shows every aspect of the domain. The second show on the schedule is *Entertainment Tonight.* This is a syndicated news show instead of a syndicated game show like *Hollywood Squares*. How well does this structure fit it? In terms of scheduling, they're not that different. The main difference is that it doesn't have a cast, and does include a description, but that's easily handled by removing the CAST element and adding a DESCRIPTION element. Not all elements with the same name have to have exactly the same structure.

```
<SHOW>
  <NAME>Entertainment Tonight</NAME>
  <TYPE>Series/News</TYPE>
  <EPISODE_NUMBER>5689</EPISODE_NUMBER>
  <START_TIME>17:30-0500</START_TIME>
  <LENGTH>30 minutes</LENGTH>
  <AIR_DATE>July 3, 2003</AIR_DATE>
  <ORIGINAL_AIR_DATE>July 3, 2003</ORIGINAL_AIR_DATE>
  <CLOSED_CAPTIONED>Yes</CLOSED_CAPTIONED>
  <REPEAT>No</REPEAT>
  <DESCRIPTION>
    American Juniors remaining contestants;
    Sex and the City preview.
  </DESCRIPTION>
</SHOW>
```

One open question here is whether the DESCRIPTION element has identifiable substructure. It certainly seems to. For example, you could mark it up as two separate segments, each of which also contains a SERIES element:

```
<DESCRIPTION>
  &lt;SEGMENT&gt;
    <SERIES>American Juniors</SERIES> remaining contestants
  &lt;/SEGMENT&gt;
  &lt;SEGMENT&gt;
    <SERIES>Sex and the City</SERIES> preview
  &lt;/SEGMENT&gt;
</DESCRIPTION>
```

The real question is whether this is useful. Will similar content be found in enough different shows to make it worthwhile to call this out individually? I think the answer is yes. It might not be obvious in this small example, but if nothing else, this one show is likely to reappear every night for years. The episode number here is 5689. There've been a lot of instances of this show in the past, and there'll be more in the future. However, looking at other examples of similar shows may indicate this isn't the ideal way to mark up this information. There may well be better, more general ways. A final decision will have to wait until you have more experience with the domain, but when in doubt, it's better to have too much markup than too little, so I'll leave this in.

The next show is a little different. Instead of a half hour syndicated show, it's an hour-long network show. The actors aren't listed, but the producers are. It also adds a couple of new elements lacking in the previous two shows (though not seen in Table 4-1), a title for the individual episode, and a middle name for a person. This is not a problem. XML is the *extensible* markup language. When you encounter new information, you can always invent an element to fit it.

```
<SHOW>
  <NAME>The Amazing Race</NAME>
  <TITLE>I Could Never Have Been Prepared for What
        I'm Looking at Right Now</TITLE>
  <TYPE>Series/Game Shows</TYPE>
  <EPISODE_NUMBER>406</EPISODE_NUMBER>
  <START_TIME>20:00-0500</START_TIME>
  <LENGTH>60 minutes</LENGTH>
  <AIR_DATE>July 3, 2003</AIR_DATE>
  <ORIGINAL_AIR_DATE>July 3, 2003</ORIGINAL_AIR_DATE>
  <CLOSED_CAPTIONED>Yes</CLOSED_CAPTIONED>
  <REPEAT>No</REPEAT>
  <PRODUCER>
     <GIVEN_NAME>Jerry</GIVEN_NAME>
     <SURNAME>Bruckheimer</SURNAME>
  </PRODUCER>
  <PRODUCER>
     <GIVEN_NAME>Bertram</GIVEN_NAME>
     <SURNAME>van Munster</SURNAME>
  </PRODUCER>
  <PRODUCER>
     <GIVEN_NAME>Hayma</GIVEN_NAME>
     <MIDDLE_NAME>Screech</MIDDLE_NAME>
     <SURNAME>Washington</SURNAME>
  </PRODUCER>
  <PRODUCER>
     <GIVEN_NAME>Jon</GIVEN_NAME>
     <SURNAME>Kroll</SURNAME>
  </PRODUCER>
  <DESCRIPTION>
    Eight twenty-somethings speed through foreign cultures
    as quickly as possible in attempt to avoid learning
    anything
  </DESCRIPTION>
</SHOW>
```

So far I've looked only at series, but television also has numerous nonrecurring shows. What would a movie look like, for example? When I checked the detailed listings for the first movie on HBO this particular night, I discovered it had several new pieces that had not been noted before, including a director, the writers, a rating, and a number of stars. The cast was also much larger, and the original air date was omitted.

```
<SHOW>
  <NAME>Final Fantasy: The Spirits Within</NAME>
  <TYPE>Movie/Animated</TYPE>
  <START_TIME>18:30-0500</START_TIME>
  <LENGTH>105 minutes</LENGTH>
  <AIR_DATE>July 3, 2003</AIR_DATE>
  <CLOSED_CAPTIONED>Yes</CLOSED_CAPTIONED>
  <REPEAT>Yes</REPEAT>
  <RATING>PG-13</RATING>
  <STARS>3</STARS>
  <DESCRIPTION>
    The last city on Earth defends itself against alien
    phantoms. The plot has little to no relationship to
    the video games of the same name.
  </DESCRIPTION>
  <DIRECTOR>
     <GIVEN_NAME>Hironobu</GIVEN_NAME>
     <SURNAME>Sakaguchi</SURNAME>
  </DIRECTOR>
  <WRITER>
     <GIVEN_NAME>Al</GIVEN_NAME>
     <SURNAME>Reinart</SURNAME>
  </WRITER>
  <WRITER>
     <GIVEN_NAME>Jeff Vintar</GIVEN_NAME>
     <SURNAME>Sakaguchi</SURNAME>
  </WRITER>
  <PRODUCER>
     <GIVEN_NAME>Hironobu</GIVEN_NAME>
     <SURNAME>Sakaguchi</SURNAME>
  </PRODUCER>
  <PRODUCER>
     <GIVEN_NAME>Jun</GIVEN_NAME>
     <SURNAME>Aida</SURNAME>
  </PRODUCER>
  <PRODUCER>
     <GIVEN_NAME>Chris</GIVEN_NAME>
     <SURNAME>Lee</SURNAME>
  </PRODUCER>
  <CAST>
    <ACTOR>
      <GIVEN_NAME>Ming</GIVEN_NAME>
      <SURNAME>Na</SURNAME>
    </ACTOR>
    <ACTOR>
      <GIVEN_NAME>Alec</GIVEN_NAME>
      <SURNAME>Baldwin</SURNAME>
    </ACTOR>
    <ACTOR>
      <GIVEN_NAME>Ving</GIVEN_NAME>
      <SURNAME>Rhames</SURNAME>
```

```
      </ACTOR>
      <ACTOR>
        <GIVEN_NAME>Steve</GIVEN_NAME>
        <SURNAME>Buscemi</SURNAME>
      </ACTOR>
      <ACTOR>
         <GIVEN_NAME>Peri</GIVEN_NAME>
         <SURNAME>Gilpin</SURNAME>
      </ACTOR>
      <ACTOR>
        <GIVEN_NAME>Donald</GIVEN_NAME>
        <SURNAME>Sutherland</SURNAME>
      </ACTOR>
      <ACTOR>
        <GIVEN_NAME>James</GIVEN_NAME>
        <SURNAME>Woods</SURNAME>
      </ACTOR>
    </CAST>
  </SHOW>
```

Until now, I've been showing the XML document in pieces, element by element. However, it's now time to put all the pieces together and look at the complete document containing the schedule for three New York stations between 7:00 and 8:30 P.M., July 3, 2003. Listing 4-2 demonstrates. Figure 4-1 shows this document loaded into Mozilla 1.4.

Listing 4-2: **tvschedule2003-07-03.xml—The Completed XML Document**

```
<?xml version="1.0"?>
<SCHEDULE>
  <DATE>July 3, 2003</DATE>
  <STATION>
    <NETWORK>CBS</NETWORK>
    <CALL_LETTERS>WCBS</CALL_LETTERS>
    <CHANNEL>2</CHANNEL>

    <SHOW>
      <NAME>Hollywood Squares</NAME>
      <TYPE>Series/Game Shows</TYPE>
      <EPISODE_NUMBER>5074</EPISODE_NUMBER>
      <START_TIME>19:00-0500</START_TIME>
      <LENGTH>30 minutes</LENGTH>
      <AIR_DATE>July 3, 2003</AIR_DATE>
      <ORIGINAL_AIR_DATE>January 16, 2003</ORIGINAL_AIR_DATE>
      <CLOSED_CAPTIONED>Yes</CLOSED_CAPTIONED>
      <REPEAT>Yes</REPEAT>
      <CAST>
```

Continued

Listing 4-2 *(continued)*

```
      <ACTOR>
        <GIVEN_NAME>Don</GIVEN_NAME>
        <SURNAME>Rickles</SURNAME>
      </ACTOR>
      <ACTOR>
        <GIVEN_NAME>Jerry</GIVEN_NAME>
        <SURNAME>Springer</SURNAME>
      </ACTOR>
      <ACTOR>
        <GIVEN_NAME>Richard</GIVEN_NAME>
        <SURNAME>Simmons</SURNAME>
      </ACTOR>
      <ACTOR>
        <GIVEN_NAME>Vicki</GIVEN_NAME>
        <SURNAME>Lawrence</SURNAME>
      </ACTOR>
      <ACTOR>
         <GIVEN_NAME>John</GIVEN_NAME>
         <SURNAME>Salley</SURNAME>
      </ACTOR>
      <ACTOR>
        <GIVEN_NAME>Joanie</GIVEN_NAME>
        <SURNAME>Laurer</SURNAME>
      </ACTOR>
      <ACTOR>
        <GIVEN_NAME>Martin</GIVEN_NAME>
        <SURNAME>Mull</SURNAME>
      </ACTOR>
      <ACTOR>
        <GIVEN_NAME>Jillian</GIVEN_NAME>
        <SURNAME>Barberie</SURNAME>
      </ACTOR>
      <ACTOR>
         <GIVEN_NAME>Kennedy</GIVEN_NAME>
      </ACTOR>
    </CAST>
    <PRODUCER>
      <GIVEN_NAME>Henry</GIVEN_NAME>
      <SURNAME>Winkler</SURNAME>
    </PRODUCER>
    <PRODUCER>
      <GIVEN_NAME>Michael</GIVEN_NAME>
      <SURNAME>Levitt</SURNAME>
    </PRODUCER>
  </SHOW>

  <SHOW>
    <NAME>Entertainment Tonight</NAME>
    <TYPE>Series/News</TYPE>
    <EPISODE_NUMBER>5689</EPISODE_NUMBER>
```

```
    <START_TIME>19:30-0500</START_TIME>
    <LENGTH>30 minutes</LENGTH>
    <AIR_DATE>July 3, 2003</AIR_DATE>
    <ORIGINAL_AIR_DATE>July 3, 2003</ORIGINAL_AIR_DATE>
    <CLOSED_CAPTIONED>Yes</CLOSED_CAPTIONED>
    <REPEAT>No</REPEAT>
    <DESCRIPTION>
      American Juniors remaining contestants;
      Sex and the City preview.
    </DESCRIPTION>
  </SHOW>

  <SHOW>
    <NAME>The Amazing Race</NAME>
    <TITLE>I Could Never Have Been Prepared for What
          I'm Looking at Right Now</TITLE>
    <TYPE>Series/Game Shows</TYPE>
    <EPISODE_NUMBER>406</EPISODE_NUMBER>
    <START_TIME>20:00-0500</START_TIME>
    <LENGTH>60 minutes</LENGTH>
    <AIR_DATE>July 3, 2003</AIR_DATE>
    <ORIGINAL_AIR_DATE>July 3, 2003</ORIGINAL_AIR_DATE>
    <CLOSED_CAPTIONED>Yes</CLOSED_CAPTIONED>
    <REPEAT>No</REPEAT>
    <PRODUCER>
       <GIVEN_NAME>Jerry</GIVEN_NAME>
       <SURNAME>Bruckheimer</SURNAME>
    </PRODUCER>
    <PRODUCER>
       <GIVEN_NAME>Bertram</GIVEN_NAME>
       <SURNAME>van Munster</SURNAME>
    </PRODUCER>
    <PRODUCER>
       <GIVEN_NAME>Hayma</GIVEN_NAME>
       <MIDDLE_NAME>Screech</MIDDLE_NAME>
       <SURNAME>Washington</SURNAME>
    </PRODUCER>
    <PRODUCER>
       <GIVEN_NAME>Jon</GIVEN_NAME>
       <SURNAME>Kroll</SURNAME>
    </PRODUCER>
    <DESCRIPTION>
      Eight twenty-somethings speed through foreign
      cultures as quickly as possible in desperate
      attempt to avoid learning anything.
    </DESCRIPTION>
  </SHOW>

</STATION>

<STATION>
  <CALL_LETTERS>WLNY</CALL_LETTERS>
```

Continued

Listing 4-2 *(continued)*

```
<CHANNEL>55</CHANNEL>

<SHOW>
  <NAME>Oprah Winfrey</NAME>
  <TYPE>Series/Talk</TYPE>
  <START_TIME>19:00-0500</START_TIME>
  <LENGTH>60 minutes</LENGTH>
  <AIR_DATE>July 3, 2003</AIR_DATE>
  <ORIGINAL_AIR_DATE>February 4, 2003</ORIGINAL_AIR_DATE>
  <CLOSED_CAPTIONED>Yes</CLOSED_CAPTIONED>
  <REPEAT>Yes</REPEAT>
  <RATING>TV-PG</RATING>
  <DESCRIPTION>
    Guests gabber; Oprah looks sympathetic.
  </DESCRIPTION>
</SHOW>

<SHOW>
  <NAME>Silicon Towers</NAME>
  <TYPE>Movie</TYPE>
  <START_TIME>20:00-0500</START_TIME>
  <LENGTH>60 minutes</LENGTH>
  <AIR_DATE>July 3, 2003</AIR_DATE>
  <YEAR_MADE>1999</YEAR_MADE>
  <CLOSED_CAPTIONED>Yes</CLOSED_CAPTIONED>
  <REPEAT>Yes</REPEAT>
  <RATING>TV-PG</RATING>
  <CAST>
    <ACTOR>
      <GIVEN_NAME>Brian</GIVEN_NAME>
      <SURNAME>Dennehy</SURNAME>
    </ACTOR>
    <ACTOR>
      <GIVEN_NAME>Daniel</GIVEN_NAME>
      <SURNAME>Baldwin</SURNAME>
    </ACTOR>
    <ACTOR>
      <GIVEN_NAME>Brad</GIVEN_NAME>
      <SURNAME>Dourif</SURNAME>
    </ACTOR>
    <ACTOR>
      <GIVEN_NAME>Gary</GIVEN_NAME>
      <SURNAME>Mosher</SURNAME>
    </ACTOR>
  </CAST>
  <DESCRIPTION>
    A programmer discovers his company manufactures
    chips for cracking bank systems.
  </DESCRIPTION>
</SHOW>
```

```
</STATION>

<STATION>
  <NETWORK>HBO</NETWORK>
  <CHANNEL>501</CHANNEL>

  <SHOW>
    <NAME>Final Fantasy: The Spirits Within</NAME>
    <TYPE>Movie/Animated</TYPE>
    <START_TIME>18:30-0500</START_TIME>
    <LENGTH>105 minutes</LENGTH>
    <AIR_DATE>July 3, 2003</AIR_DATE>
    <CLOSED_CAPTIONED>Yes</CLOSED_CAPTIONED>
    <REPEAT>Yes</REPEAT>
    <DESCRIPTION>
      The last city on Earth defends itself against alien
      phantoms. Little to no relationship to the video
      games of the same name.
    </DESCRIPTION>
    <RATING>PG-13</RATING>
    <STARS>2</STARS>
    <DIRECTOR>
       <GIVEN_NAME>Hironobu</GIVEN_NAME>
       <SURNAME>Sakaguchi</SURNAME>
    </DIRECTOR>
    <WRITER>
       <GIVEN_NAME>Al</GIVEN_NAME>
       <SURNAME>Reinart</SURNAME>
    </WRITER>
    <WRITER>
       <GIVEN_NAME>Jeff</GIVEN_NAME>
       <SURNAME>Vintar</SURNAME>
    </WRITER>
    <PRODUCER>
       <GIVEN_NAME>Hironobu</GIVEN_NAME>
       <SURNAME>Sakaguchi</SURNAME>
    </PRODUCER>
    <PRODUCER>
       <GIVEN_NAME>Jun</GIVEN_NAME>
       <SURNAME>Aida</SURNAME>
    </PRODUCER>
    <PRODUCER>
       <GIVEN_NAME>Chris</GIVEN_NAME>
       <SURNAME>Lee</SURNAME>
    </PRODUCER>
    <CAST>
      <ACTOR>
        <GIVEN_NAME>Ming</GIVEN_NAME>
        <SURNAME>Na</SURNAME>
      </ACTOR>
      <ACTOR>
        <GIVEN_NAME>Alec</GIVEN_NAME>
```

Continued

Listing 4-2 *(continued)*

```
        <SURNAME>Baldwin</SURNAME>
      </ACTOR>
      <ACTOR>
        <GIVEN_NAME>Ving</GIVEN_NAME>
        <SURNAME>Rhames</SURNAME>
      </ACTOR>
      <ACTOR>
        <GIVEN_NAME>Steve</GIVEN_NAME>
        <SURNAME>Buscemi</SURNAME>
      </ACTOR>
      <ACTOR>
         <GIVEN_NAME>Peri</GIVEN_NAME>
         <SURNAME>Gilpin</SURNAME>
      </ACTOR>
      <ACTOR>
        <GIVEN_NAME>Donald</GIVEN_NAME>
        <SURNAME>Sutherland</SURNAME>
      </ACTOR>
      <ACTOR>
        <GIVEN_NAME>James</GIVEN_NAME>
        <SURNAME>Woods</SURNAME>
      </ACTOR>
    </CAST>
  </SHOW>

  <SHOW>
    <NAME>Terminator 3: Rise of the Machines:
          HBO First Look</NAME>
    <TYPE>Special/Documentary</TYPE>
    <START_TIME>20:15-0500</START_TIME>
    <LENGTH>15 minutes</LENGTH>
    <AIR_DATE>July 3, 2003</AIR_DATE>
    <ORIGINAL_AIR_DATE>June 26, 2003</ORIGINAL_AIR_DATE>
    <CLOSED_CAPTIONED>Yes</CLOSED_CAPTIONED>
    <REPEAT>Yes</REPEAT>
    <RATING>TV14</RATING>
  </SHOW>

  <SHOW>
    <NAME>Star Wars: Episode II -- Attack of
          the Clones</NAME>
    <TYPE>Movie</TYPE>
    <START_TIME>20:30-0500</START_TIME>
    <LENGTH>150 minutes</LENGTH>
    <AIR_DATE>July 3, 2003</AIR_DATE>
    <YEAR_MADE>2002</YEAR_MADE>
    <CLOSED_CAPTIONED>Yes</CLOSED_CAPTIONED>
    <REPEAT>Yes</REPEAT>
    <RATING>PG-13</RATING>
    <STARS>3</STARS>
```

```
      <DESCRIPTION>
        Obi-wan Kenobi and Anakin Skywalker battle
        Count Dooku and the Trade Federation.
      </DESCRIPTION>
      <DIRECTOR>
        <GIVEN_NAME>George</GIVEN_NAME>
        <SURNAME>Lucas</SURNAME>
      </DIRECTOR>
      <WRITER>
        <GIVEN_NAME>George</GIVEN_NAME>
        <SURNAME>Lucas</SURNAME>
      </WRITER>
      <WRITER>
        <GIVEN_NAME>Jonathan</GIVEN_NAME>
        <SURNAME>Hales</SURNAME>
      </WRITER>
      <PRODUCER>
        <GIVEN_NAME>George</GIVEN_NAME>
        <SURNAME>Lucas</SURNAME>
      </PRODUCER>
      <PRODUCER>
        <GIVEN_NAME>George</GIVEN_NAME>
        <SURNAME>McCallam</SURNAME>
      </PRODUCER>
      <CAST>
        <ACTOR>
          <GIVEN_NAME>Ewan</GIVEN_NAME>
          <SURNAME>McGregor</SURNAME>
        </ACTOR>
        <ACTOR>
          <GIVEN_NAME>Natalie</GIVEN_NAME>
          <SURNAME>Portman</SURNAME>
        </ACTOR>
        <ACTOR>
          <GIVEN_NAME>Christopher</GIVEN_NAME>
          <SURNAME>Lee</SURNAME>
        </ACTOR>
        <ACTOR>
          <GIVEN_NAME>Samuel</GIVEN_NAME>
          <MIDDLE_INITIAL>L</MIDDLE_INITIAL>
          <SURNAME>Jackson</SURNAME>
        </ACTOR>
        <ACTOR>
           <GIVEN_NAME>Frank</GIVEN_NAME>
           <SURNAME>Oz</SURNAME>
        </ACTOR>
      </CAST>
    </SHOW>
  </STATION>

</SCHEDULE>
```

In general, order matters in XML. Listing 4-2 arranges the three stations in ascending numeric order (2, 55, 501), and within each station it lists the shows in ascending order based on start time. It is possible to reorder the content when processing or displaying it—just as it's possible to sort any other list—but the parser will faithfully report the elements in the order they appear in the input document. You can rely on the order if you want to. On the other hand, you don't have to. You may decide, for example, that you don't care what order the `NAME`, `TITLE`, `TYPE`, `CAST`, and other children of each `SHOW` element appear. However, that's a decision for you to make; XML does not it make for you. Whether or not to treat order as significant depends on whether or not it helps out in your use cases.

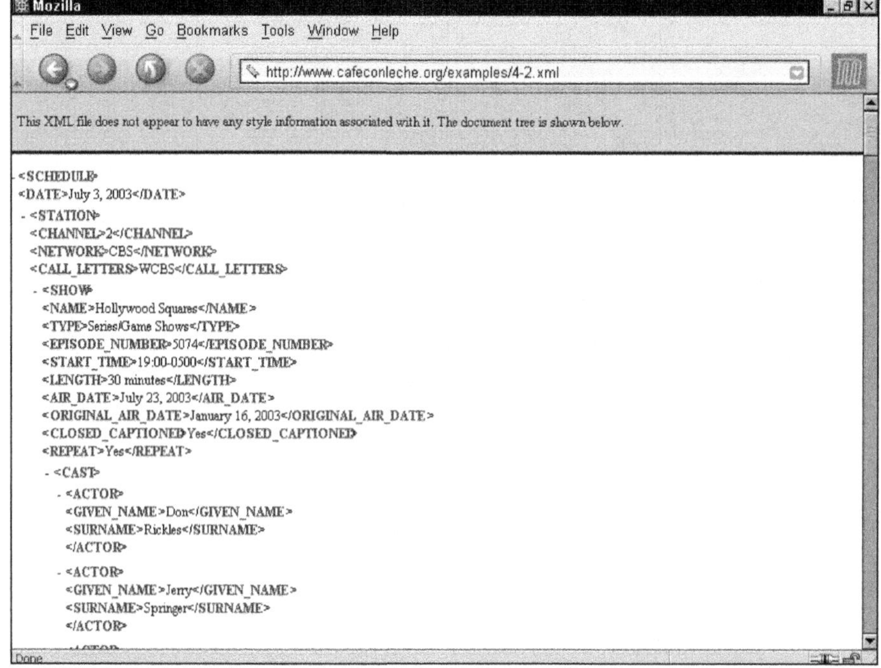

Figure 4-1: The raw TV schedule displayed in Mozilla 1.4

Even as large as it is, this document is incomplete. It contains only a couple of hour's worth of shows from three networks. Showing more than that would make the example too long to include in this book. If you continued to look at more shows, you would discover numerous other relevant pieces of information that deserve to be marked up, including role played by an actor, broadcast language, pay-per-view prices, and more. However, I will stop the XMLization of the data here to move on; first to a brief discussion of why this data format is useful, and then to the techniques that can be used for displaying it more attractively in a web browser.

The Advantages of the XML Format

Table 4-1 does a good job of displaying a daily television schedule in a comprehensible and compact fashion. What has been gained by rewriting that table as the much longer XML document of Listing 4-2? There are several benefits, including the following:

- ✦ The data is self-describing.
- ✦ The data can be manipulated with standard tools.
- ✦ The data can be viewed with standard tools.
- ✦ Different views of the same data are easy to create with style sheets.

The first major benefit of the XML format is that the data is self-describing. The meaning of each item of information is clearly and unambiguously indicated by the markup. For example, one of the more opaque values is the `CLOSED_CAPTION` element. Its value is either Yes or No. In a more traditional, tab- or comma-delimited format, there'd be no evidence of exactly what Yes or No meant. In XML, however, it's obvious that this tells you whether or not the show is closed captioned. Sometimes, it takes several levels of markup to tease out the meaning of a string. For instance, knowing that "Oprah Winfrey" is a name still leaves open the possibility that it may be the name of a person, a show, a book, a play, a high school, or something else. However, the hierarchical nature of the XML document makes it clear that this is indeed the name of a show.

Another common error in less-verbose formats is transposing values; for example, flipping the order of the given name and the surname. More than one database knows me as "Harold Elliotte" instead of "Elliotte Harold." XML lets you transpose with abandon. As long as the markup is transposed along with the content, no information is lost or misunderstood. It doesn't matter whether the first name comes first or the last name comes first. It's still completely obvious which is which.

The second benefit of the XML format is that data can be manipulated in a wide range of XML-enabled tools, from expensive payware such as Adobe FrameMaker to free open source software such as Cocoon and eXist. The data may be bigger, but the extra redundancy allows more tools to process it. If you want to write your own tools, there are parser libraries available in most major programming languages, including C, C#, C++, Java, Perl, Python, Haskell, AppleScript, and many others. You don't have to start from scratch.

The same is true when the time comes to view the data. The XML document can be loaded into Internet Explorer, Mozilla, Adobe FrameMaker, xmlspy, and many other tools, all of which provide unique, useful views of the data. The document can even be loaded into simple, plain-vanilla text editors such as vi, BBEdit, and TextPad. XML is at least marginally viewable on all platforms.

New software isn't the only way to get a different view of the data either. The next section develops a style sheet for television listings that provides a completely different way of looking at the data than what you see in Figure 4-1. Each time you apply a different style sheet to the same document, you see a different picture.

Lastly, you should ask yourself if the size is really that important. Modern hard drives are quite big and can a hold a lot of data, even if it's not stored very efficiently. Furthermore, XML files compress very well. Using gzip or similar algorithms, it's not uncommon to see a reduction in the file size of 90 percent or more. Many current HTTP servers can actually compress the files they send so that network bandwidth used by a document like this is fairly close to its actual information content. Finally, don't assume that binary file formats, especially general-purpose ones, are necessarily more efficient. In practice, relational databases, such as Oracle, and typical office software, such as Microsoft Excel, are quite spendthrift with disk space. Although you can certainly create more efficient file formats to hold this data, in practice, that isn't often necessary.

Preparing a Style Sheet for Document Display

The view of the raw XML document shown in Figure 4-1 is not bad for some uses. For instance, it allows you to collapse and expand individual elements so you see only those parts of the document you want to see. However, most of the time, you'd probably like a more finished look, especially if you're going to display it on the Web. To provide a more polished look, you must write a style sheet for the document.

In this chapter, I use cascading style sheets (CSS). A CSS style sheet associates particular formatting with each element of the document. The complete list of elements used in the XML document of Listing 4-1 follows:

```
ACTOR               LENGTH              SHOW
AIR_DATE            MIDDLE_INITIAL      STARS
CALL_LETTERS        MIDDLE_NAME         START_TIME
CAST                NAME                STATION
CHANNEL             NETWORK             SURNAME
CLOSED_CAPTIONED    ORIGINAL_AIR_DATE   TITLE
DESCRIPTION         PRODUCER            TYPE
DIRECTOR            RATING              WRITER
EPISODE_NUMBER      REPEAT              YEAR_MADE
GIVEN_NAME          SCHEDULE
```

Generally, you'll want to follow an iterative procedure, adding style rules for each of these elements one at a time, checking that they do what you expect, then moving on to the next element. In this example, such an approach also has the advantage of introducing CSS properties one at a time for those who are not familiar with them.

Linking to a style sheet

The style sheet can be named anything you like. If it's only going to apply to one document, it's customary to give it the same name as the document but with the three-letter extension .css instead of .xml. For example, the style sheet for the TV schedule XML documents might be called tvschedule.css.

To attach a style sheet to the document, you simply add an `<?xml-stylesheet?>` processing instruction between the XML declaration and the root element like this:

```
<?xml version="1.0" standalone="yes"?>
<?xml-stylesheet type="text/css" href="tvschedule.css"?>
<SEASON>
...
```

This tells a browser reading the document to apply the CSS style sheet found in the file `tvschedule.css` to this document. This file is assumed to reside in the same directory and on the same server as the XML document itself. In other words, `tvschedule.css` is a relative URL. Absolute URLs may also be used, as in the following code fragment:

```
<?xml version="1.0"?>
<?xml-stylesheet type="text/css"
href="http://cafeconleche.org/styles/tvschedule.css"?>
<SCHEDULE>
...
```

You can begin by simply placing an empty file named `tvschedule.css` in the same directory as the XML document. After you've done this and added the necessary processing instruction to Listing 4-2, the document appears as shown in Figure 4-2. Only the element content is shown. The collapsible outline view of Figure 4-1 is gone. The formatting of the element content uses the browser's defaults—black 12-point Times New Roman on a white background, in this case.

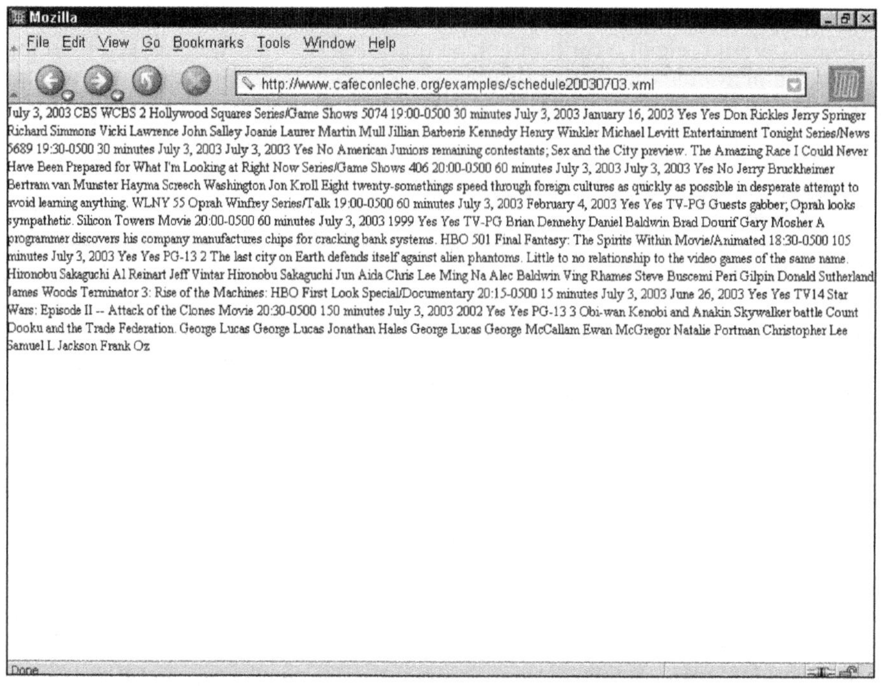

Figure 4-2: The TV schedule after a blank style sheet is applied

Assigning style rules to the root element

You do not have to assign a style rule to each element in the list. Many elements can rely on the styles of their parents cascading down. The most important style, therefore, is the one for the root element — `SCHEDULE` in this example. This defines the default for all the other elements on the page. Computer monitors display at roughly 96 dots per inch (dpi) and don't have as high a resolution as paper at 300 or more dpi. Therefore, web pages should generally use a larger point size than is customary in print. Let's make the default 14-point type, black on a white background, as shown in the following:

```
SCHEDULE {font-size: 14pt; background-color: white;
          color: black; display: block}
```

Place this statement in a text file, save the file with the name tvschedule.css in the same directory as Listing 4-2, tvschedule2003-07-03.xml, and open the XML document in your browser. You should see something similar to Figure 4-3.

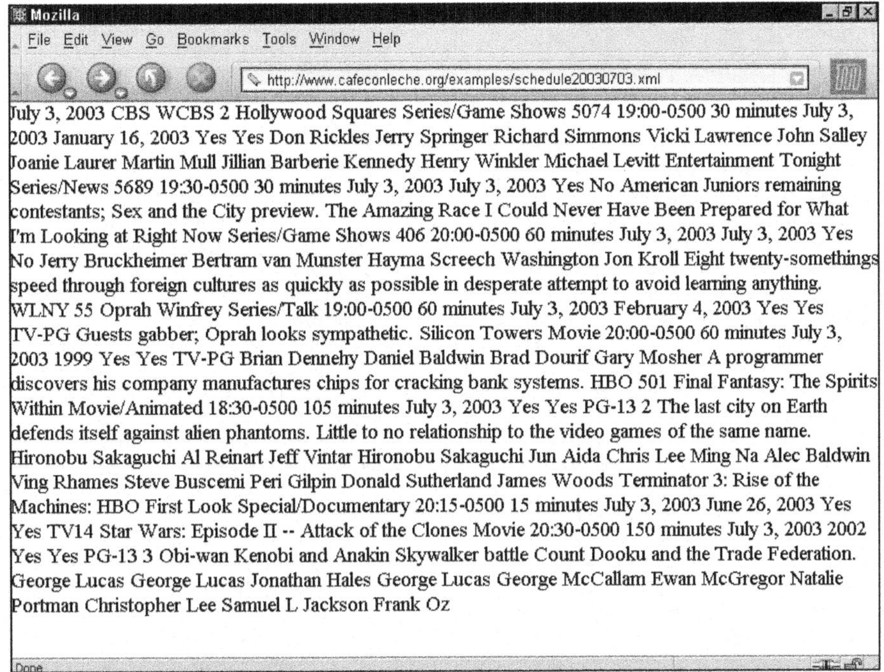

Figure 4-3: A TV schedule in 14-point type with a black on white background

The default font size changed between Figure 4-2 and Figure 4-3. The text color and background color did not. Indeed, it was not absolutely required to set them, because black foreground and white background are the defaults. Nonetheless, nothing is lost by being explicit about what you want.

Assigning style rules to titles

The `DATE` element is more or less the title of the document. Therefore, let's make it appropriately large and bold — 32 points should be big enough. Furthermore, it should stand out from the rest of the document rather than simply running together with the rest of the content, so let's make it a centered block element. All of this can be accomplished by the following style rule:

```
DATE {display: block; font-size: 32pt; font-weight: bold;
      text-align: center}
```

Figure 4-4 shows the document after this rule has been added to the style sheet. Notice in particular the line break after 2003. That's there because `DATE` is now a block-level element. Everything else in the document is an inline element. Only block-level elements can be centered (or left-aligned, right-aligned, or justified).

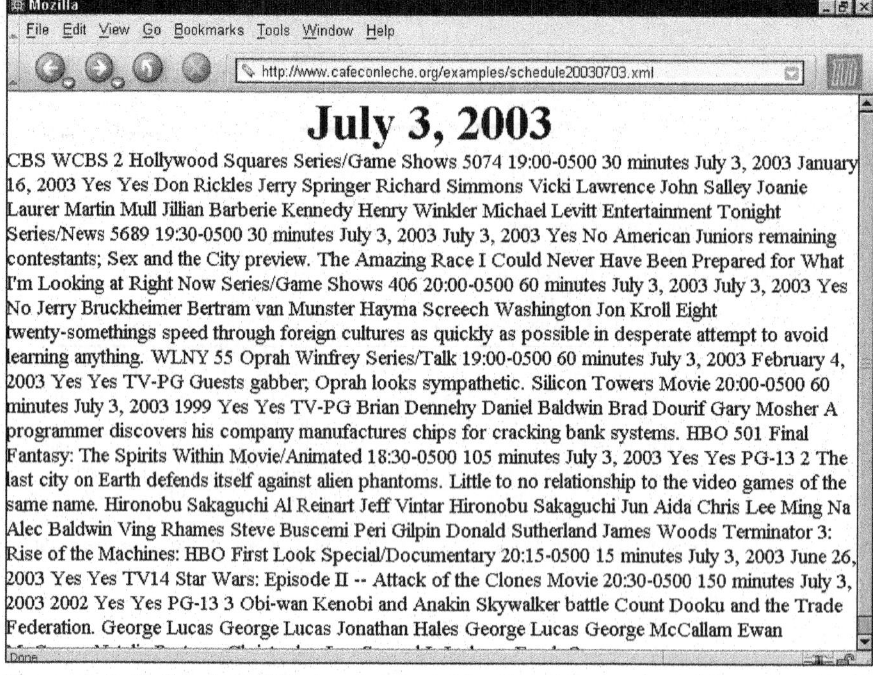

Figure 4-4: Styling the DATE element as a title

"July 3, 2003" isn't the ideal title for this document. "TV Schedule: July 23, 2003" would be better, but the phrase "TV Schedule" isn't included in the XML document. CSS lets you add extra content from the style sheet either before or after particular elements using the `:before` and `:after` pseudoselectors. The text that you want to add is given as a string value of the `content` property. For example, to add the phrase "TV Listings: " to the beginning of the `DATE` element, add this rule to the style sheet:

```
DATE:before {content: "TV Schedule: "}
```

Figure 4-5 shows the document after this rule has been added.

Caution Internet Explorer doesn't support either the `:before` and `:after` pseudoselectors or the `content` property.

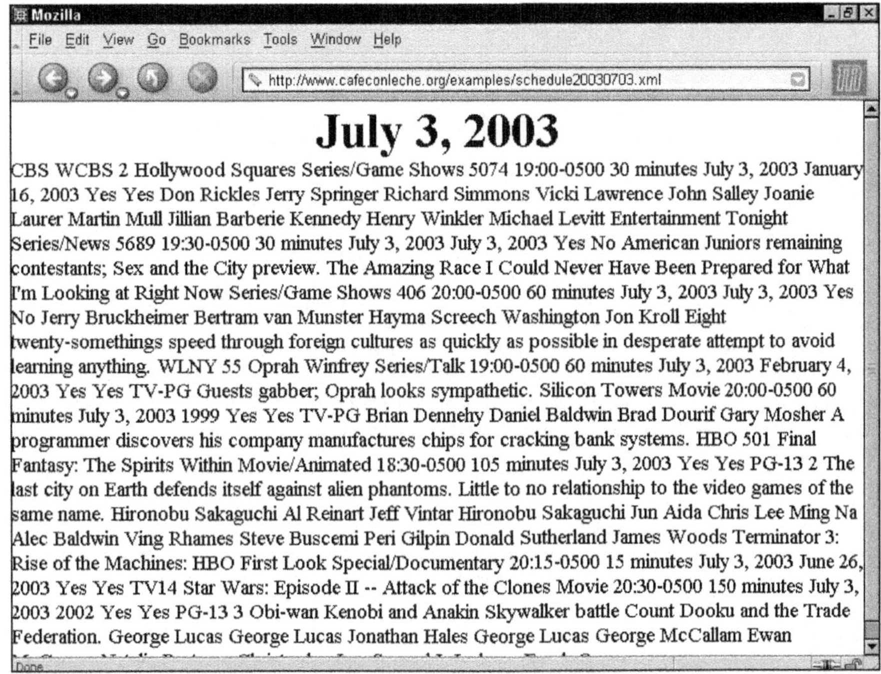

Figure 4-5: Adding content to the YEAR element

In this document, with these style rules, DATE duplicates the functionality of HTML's H1 header element. Because this document is so neatly hierarchical, several other elements serve the role of H2 headers, H3 headers, and so on. These elements can be formatted by similar rules with only a slightly smaller font size. For this document, the name of the network, channel, and call letters makes a nice level 2 division, while each show makes a nice level 3 division. These four rules format them accordingly:

```
STATION {display: block}
SHOW    {display: block}
NETWORK, CHANNEL, CALL_LETTERS {font-size: 28pt;
                                font-weight: bold}
NAME {font-weight: bold}
```

Figure 4-6 shows the resulting document. Because SHOW and STATION are formatted as block-level elements, there are line breaks before and after them.

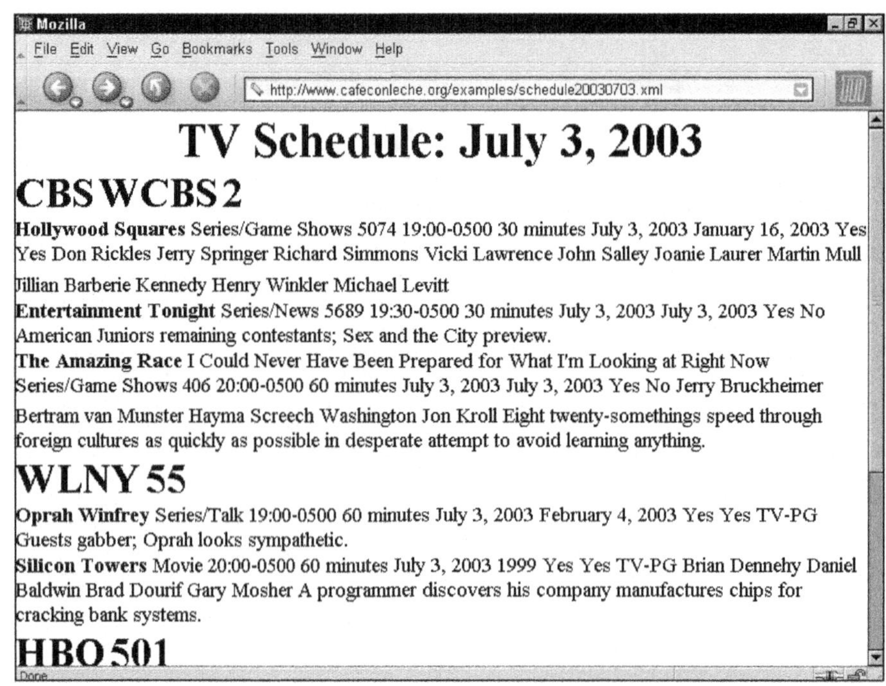

Figure 4-6: Styling CHANNEL, NETWORK, CALL_LETTERS, and NAME as headings

This is beginning to break up the document into more manageable, paragraph-sized chunks. However, is this what you really want? Television listings are formatted as tables for good reason. It makes them easier to scan and read. Could you instead format this document as a table? CSS does allow you to format elements as parts of tables instead of blocks. For example, these rules attempt to duplicate the table structure of Table 4-1:

```
STATION {display: table-row}
NETWORK, CHANNEL, CALL_LETTERS {display: table-cell;
      color: white; background-color: grey}
SHOW {border-width: 1px; border-style: solid;
      display: table-cell}
```

However, CSS assumes that each element occupies a single cell. In the television schedule, this translates into each show being exactly half an hour long. When this isn't the case, the cells rapidly get out of sync with the headings and each other, as shown in Figure 4-7. Adding a caption row at the top for times simply isn't possible. Even within the realm of what CSS can theoretically handle, table support is extremely limited and buggy in most current browsers. Sophisticated table layout that can handle column spans, row spans, styles that depend on row and column, and other advanced features — and that works reasonably well across browsers — will have to wait until the more powerful XSL style sheet language is introduced in the next chapter.

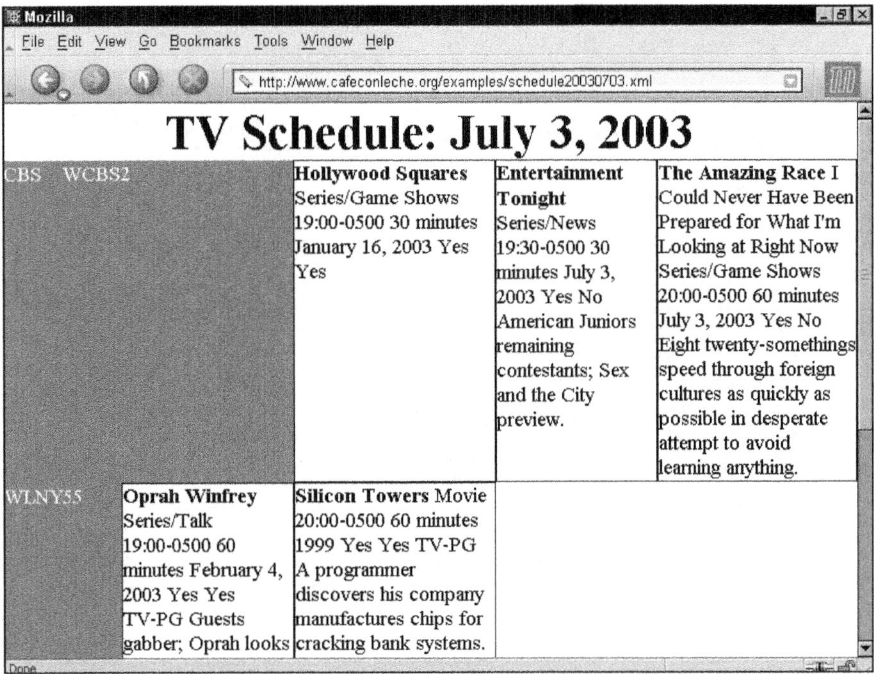

Figure 4-7: CSS table layout

Now it's time to look at styling the individual shows. You've already made the name bold. The next obvious step is to remove the information you don't need. For example, most printed television listings don't bother to list the producer, director, episode number, or current date. I'm also going to omit the complete cast. Sometimes this is included, but most of the time it isn't, and CSS doesn't provide any way to choose when to include it. In CSS, you can set an element's display property to none to hide it from view:

```
CAST {display: none}
AIR_DATE {display: none}
DIRECTOR {display: none}
EPISODE_NUMBER {display: none}
PRODUCER {display: none}
WRITER {display: none}
```

Figure 4-8 shows the result.

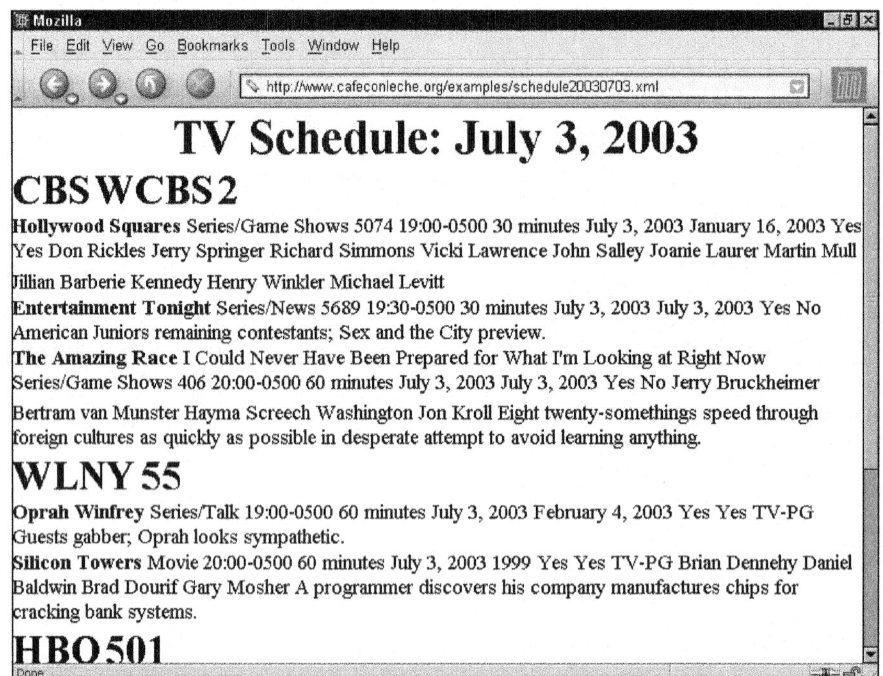

Figure 4-8: Hiding unwanted content

The final step is to choose styles for the remainder of SHOW's child elements. One nice approach is to format everything except the description as a bulleted list. The description can be formatted as a simple block-level element. For the bulleted list, use the list-item value of the display property, a .35-inch indent, and a standard disk bullet.

```
TYPE {display: list-item; list-style-type: disc;
      margin-left: 0.35in }
LENGTH {display: list-item; list-style-type: disc;
        margin-left: 0.35in}
START_TIME {display: list-item; list-style-type: disc;
            margin-left: 0.35in}
ORIGINAL_AIR_DATE {display: list-item; list-style-type: disc;
        margin-left: 0.35in}
REPEAT {display: list-item; list-style-type: disc;
        margin-left: 0.35in}
CLOSED_CAPTIONED {display: list-item; list-style-type: disc;
        margin-left: 0.35in}
ORIGINAL_AIR_DATE {display: list-item; list-style-type: disc;
        margin-left: 0.35in}
RATING {display: list-item; list-style-type: disc;
        margin-left: 0.35in}
```

```
STARS {display: list-item; list-style-type: disc;
      margin-left: 0.35in}
YEAR_MADE {display: list-item; list-style-type: disc;
      margin-left: 0.35in}
```

Figure 4-9 shows the result.

This is beginning to look decent, but it still isn't obvious what each bullet point represents. For example, the last two bullet points for Hollywood Squares are Yes and Yes, but yes what? Once again, you can use the content property and the `:before` pseudo-element to describe what each piece of the information is, with the result shown in Figure 4-10.

```
LENGTH:before {content: "Length: "}
START_TIME:before {content: "Starts at "}
ORIGINAL_AIR_DATE:before {"First aired on "}
REPEAT:before {content: "Repeat: "}
CLOSED_CAPTIONED:before {content: "Closed captioned: "}
RATING:before {content: "Rating: "}
STARS:before {content: "Stars: "}
YEAR_MADE:before {content: "Made in "}
```

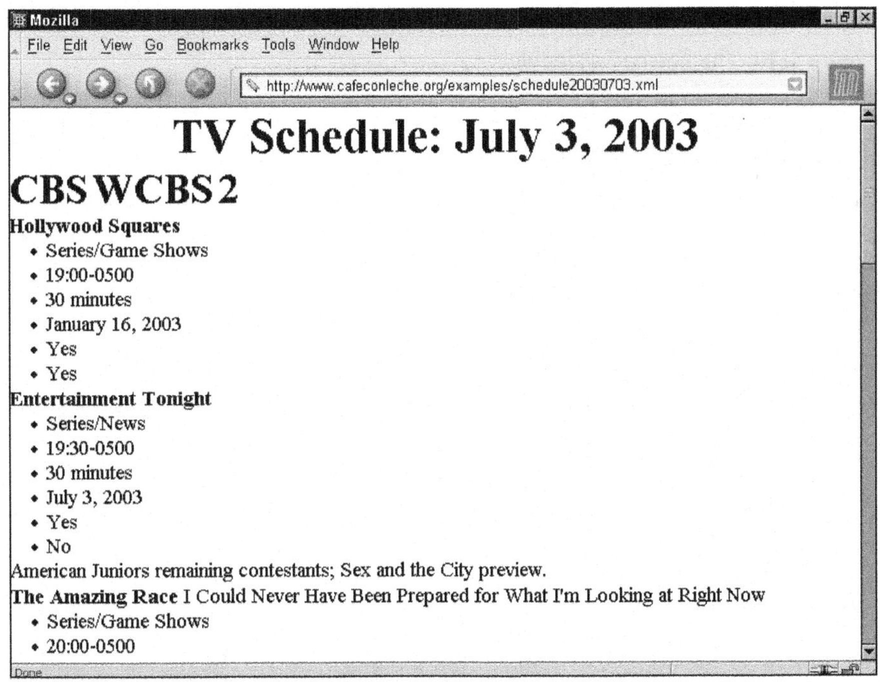

Figure 4-9: Styling the show data as a bulleted list

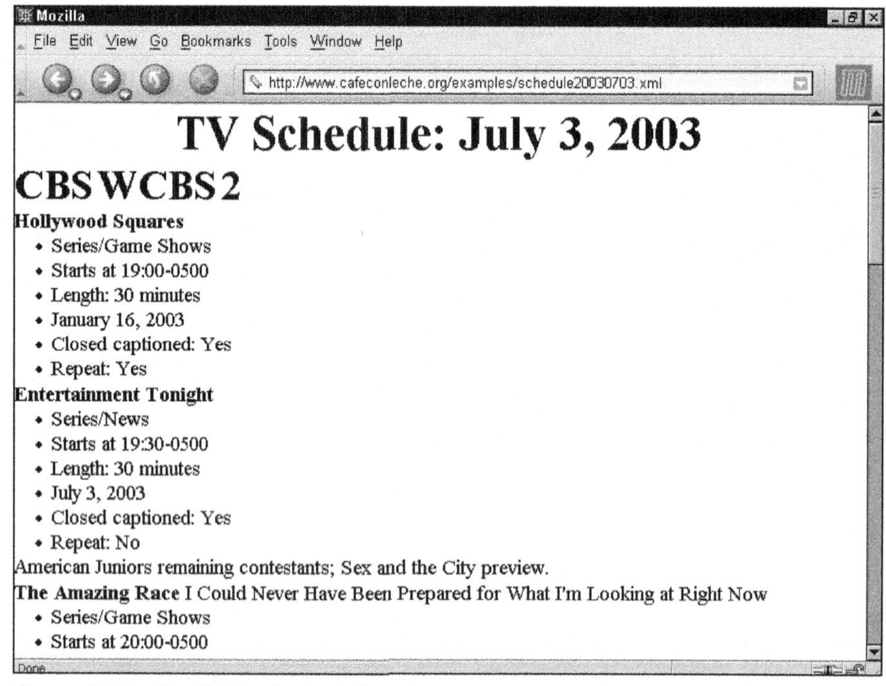

Figure 4-10: The finished schedule

The complete style sheet

Listing 4-3 shows the finished style sheet. CSS style sheets don't have a lot of structure beyond the individual rules. In essence, this is just a list of all the rules that I introduced separately in the preceding material. Reordering them wouldn't make any difference as long as they're all present.

Listing 4-3: tvschedule.css

```
STATION {display: block}
SHOW    {display: block}
NETWORK, CHANNEL, CALL_LETTERS {font-size: 28pt;
                                font-weight: bold}
NAME {font-weight: bold}
DATE:before {content: "TV Schedule: "}
DATE {display: block; font-size: 32pt; font-weight: bold;
      text-align: center}
SCHEDULE {font-size: 14pt; background-color: white;
          color: black; display: block}
```

```
AIR_DATE {display: none}
DIRECTOR  {display: none}
EPISODE_NUMBER  {display: none}
PRODUCER  {display: none}
WRITER  {display: none}
CAST {display: none}

DESCRIPTION {display: block}

TYPE {display: list-item; list-style-type: disc;
    margin-left: 0.35in }
LENGTH {display: list-item; list-style-type: disc;
    margin-left: 0.35in}
START_TIME {display: list-item; list-style-type: disc;
    margin-left: 0.35in}
ORIGINAL_AIR_DATE {display: list-item;
    list-style-type: disc; margin-left: 0.35in}
REPEAT {display: list-item; list-style-type: disc;
    margin-left: 0.35in}
CLOSED_CAPTIONED {display: list-item; list-style-type: disc;
    margin-left: 0.35in}
ORIGINAL_AIR_DATE {display: list-item;
    list-style-type: disc; margin-left: 0.35in}
RATING {display: list-item; list-style-type: disc;
    margin-left: 0.35in}
STARS {display: list-item; list-style-type: disc;
    margin-left: 0.35in}
YEAR_MADE {display: list-item; list-style-type: disc;
    margin-left: 0.35in}

LENGTH:before {content: "Length: "}
START_TIME:before {content: "Starts at "}
ORIGINAL_AIR_DATE:before {"First aired on "}
REPEAT:before {content: "Repeat: "}
CLOSED_CAPTIONED:before {content: "Closed captioned: "}
RATING:before {content: "Rating: "}
STARS:before {content: "Stars: "}
YEAR_MADE:before {content: "Made in "}
```

This completes the basic formatting for the television schedule. However, work clearly remains to be done. Some things that you might want to add include the following:

- ✦ Instead of writing “Closed captioned: yes” or “Repeat: Yes”, it might be nicer to simply write (CC) or (repeat) as in many actual TV schedules.
- ✦ Sort by start time rather than station.
- ✦ The call letters should be included only if the station is independent.

- ✦ The start times could be converted back to a more human-friendly format, such as 7:00 P.M. instead of 19:00-0500.
- ✦ A two-star movie should be listed as ★★ instead of Stars: 2.
- ✦ You might want to include one or two actors, even if not the entire cast.
- ✦ You might want to include descriptions for some of the more important shows, but not all of them.
- ✦ Even if you don't lay out a grid schedule using a table, you might still want to use multiple columns, as is often done in actual newspapers.

What unifies all these goals is that they require changing the information in the document rather than merely annotating it with different styles. You could address some of these points by adding more content to the document or changing the content that's there. For example, the `STARS` element could be written as `<STARS>★★</STARS>` instead of `<STARS>2</STARS>`. (Yes, ★ is a Unicode character, which can be used in an XML document.) The original document could be ordered by start time rather than station. The `CALL_LETTERS` child element of a `STATION` could be present only if the network isn't.

Still, there's something fundamentally troublesome about such tactics. If you organize the document so it's absolutely perfect for this one use (a printed table in a newspaper or a magazine), you may have eliminated information that's critical for other uses. What's flawed here is not XML. XML is robust enough to handle all these needs. However, CSS is a limited style language. It's intended for words in a row that already contain all the document content in the right order and nothing else. A few elements can be hidden by setting `display` to `none`, and a little text can be added using `:before`, `:after`, and the `content` property. However, at its core, CSS just isn't designed to handle complicated document manipulations before displaying the result to the end user.

What's really needed is a different style language that enables you to add certain boilerplate content to elements and to perform transformations on the element content that is present. Such a language exists — the Extensible Stylesheet Language (XSL). CSS is simpler than XSL. CSS works well for basic web pages and reasonably straightforward documents. XSL is considerably more complex, but it is also more powerful. XSL builds on the simple CSS formatting that you learned in this chapter, but it also transforms the source document into various forms that the reader can view. It's often a good idea to make a first pass at a problem using CSS while you're still debugging your XML, and to then move to XSL to achieve greater flexibility.

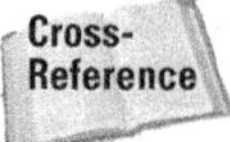

XSL is further discussed in Chapters 5, 16, and 17.

Summary

In this chapter, you saw an example of an XML document being built from scratch. This chapter was full of seat-of-the-pants/back-of-the-envelope coding. The document was written with only minimal concern for details. In particular, you learned the following:

- ✦ How to examine the data to be included in the XML document to identify the elements
- ✦ How to mark up the data with XML tags that you define
- ✦ The advantages of XML formats over traditional formats
- ✦ How to write a CSS style sheet that says how the document should be formatted and displayed

The next chapter explores an alternative way to organize and encode television listings in XML by using attributes. It also introduces another style sheet language, XSLT, which can serve as a supplement or an alternative to CSS.

✦ ✦ ✦

CHAPTER 5

Attributes, Empty-Element Tags, and XSL

✦ ✦ ✦ ✦

In This Chapter

Attributes

Attributes versus elements

Empty-element tags

XSL

✦ ✦ ✦ ✦

There are an infinite number of ways to encode any given set of data in XML. There's no one right way to do it, although some ways are more right than others and some are more appropriate for particular uses. This chapter explores a different solution to the problem of marking up television listings in XML, carrying over the example from the previous chapter. Specifically, you learn to use attributes to store information and to use empty-element tags to define element positions. In addition, because CSS doesn't work well with contentless XML elements of this form, this chapter examines an alternative and more powerful style sheet language called XSL.

Attributes

In Chapter 4, all information was provided either by a tag name or as the text content of an element. This is a straightforward and easy-to-understand approach, but it's not the only one. As in HTML, XML elements may have attributes. An *attribute* is a name-value pair associated with an element. The name and the value are each strings, and no element can contain two attributes with the same name.

You're already familiar with attribute syntax from HTML. For example, consider this `<IMG>` tag:

```
<IMG SRC=cup.gif WIDTH=89 HEIGHT=67 ALT="Cup
of coffee">
```

It has four attributes: the `SRC` attribute whose value is `cup.gif`, the `WIDTH` attribute whose value is `89`, the `HEIGHT` attribute whose value is `67`, and the `ALT` attribute whose value is Cup of coffee. However, in XML — unlike HTML — attribute values must always be quoted, and start-tags must have matching end-tags. Thus, the XML equivalent of this tag is as follows:

```
<IMG SRC="cup.gif" WIDTH="89" HEIGHT="67"
    ALT="Cup of coffee"></IMG>
```

Note

Another difference between HTML and XML is that XML assigns no specific meaning to the IMG element and its attributes. In particular, there's no guarantee that an XML browser will interpret this element as an instruction to load and display the image in the file cup.gif.

Attribute syntax fits the television listings example quite nicely. One advantage is that it makes the markup somewhat more concise. For example, instead of containing a DATE child element, the SCHEDULE element only needs a DATE attribute.

```
<SCHEDULE DATE="July 3, 2003">
</SCHEDULE>
```

On the other hand, STATION should be a child of the SCHEDULE element rather than an attribute. For one thing, there are many stations in a schedule. Anytime there's likely to be more than one of something, child elements are called for. Attribute names must be unique within an element. You cannot, for example, write a SCHEDULE element like this:

```
<SCHEDULE DATE="July 3, 2003" STATION="WPIX" STATION="WCBS">
</SCHEDULE>
```

The second reason STATION is naturally a child element rather than an attribute is that it has substructure; that is, it is divided into NETWORK, CALL_LETTERS, SHOW, and CHANNEL elements. Attribute values are unstructured, flat text. XML elements can conveniently encode structure.

The shows should also be child elements rather than attributes. Like STATION, they have substructure; but there's another reason they should be child elements: The shows are ordered by time. It matters which one comes first. XML parsers preserve element order. However, they do not preserve attribute order. Whenever order matters, you need elements rather than attributes.

However, the network, call letters, and channel of a station are all unstructured, flat text; there's only one of each per station, and their order doesn't matter. Therefore, STATION elements can easily have CALL_LETTERS, SHOW, and CHANNEL attributes instead of CALL_LETTERS, SHOW, and CHANNEL child elements:

```
<STATION NETWORK="CBS" CALL_LETTERS="WCBS" CHANNEL="2">
</STATION>
```

You don't have to store this information in attributes. Child elements still work, but you can use attributes here if you want to.

Shows will have many attributes if you choose to make each nonrepeating, nonstructured item an attribute. For example, here's the listing for *Entertainment Tonight* marked up as attributes:

```
<SHOW NAME="Entertainment Tonight" TYPE="Series/News"
      EPISODE_NUMBER="5689" START_TIME="17:30-0500"
      LENGTH="30 minutes" AIR_DATE="July 3, 2003"
      ORIGINAL_AIR_DATE="July 3, 2003"
      CLOSED_CAPTIONED="Yes" REPEAT="No"
      DESCRIPTION="American Juniors remaining contestants;
       Sex and the City preview.">
</SHOW>
```

However, not all the content can fit into attributes. For example, the `CAST` has substructure. A show may have multiple writers, producers, and directors. Even the `DESCRIPTION` may have substructure in some cases. These should all remain child elements.

Listing 5-1 uses this new attribute style for a complete XML document containing the schedule for three New York stations between 7:00 and 8:30 P.M. on July 3, 2003. It provides all the same information as shown in Listing 4-2 in the previous chapter. It is merely marked up differently.

Listing 5-1: A Complete XML Document Using Attributes to Store Television Listings

```
<?xml version="1.0"?>
<SCHEDULE DATE="July 3, 2003">

  <STATION NETWORK="CBS" CALL_LETTERS="WCBS" CHANNEL="2">
    <SHOW NAME="Hollywood Squares" TYPE="5074"
          START_TIME="19:00-0500" AIR_DATE="July 3, 2003"
          ORIGINAL_AIR_DATE="January 16, 2003"
          LENGTH="30 minutes" REPEAT="Yes"
          CLOSED_CAPTIONED="Yes">
      <CAST>
       <ACTOR GIVEN_NAME="Don" SURNAME="Rickles"></ACTOR>
       <ACTOR GIVEN_NAME="Jerry" SURNAME="Springer"></ACTOR>
       <ACTOR GIVEN_NAME="Richard" SURNAME="Simmons"></ACTOR>
       <ACTOR GIVEN_NAME="Vicki" SURNAME="Lawrence"></ACTOR>
       <ACTOR GIVEN_NAME="John" SURNAME="Salley"></ACTOR>
       <ACTOR GIVEN_NAME="Joanie" SURNAME="Laurer"></ACTOR>
       <ACTOR GIVEN_NAME="Martin" SURNAME="Mull"></ACTOR>
```

Continued

Listing 5-1 *(continued)*

```
      <ACTOR GIVEN_NAME="Jillian" SURNAME="Barberie"></ACTOR>
      <ACTOR MIDDLE_NAME="Kennedy"></ACTOR>
    </CAST>
    <PRODUCER GIVEN_NAME="Henry"
              SURNAME="Winkler"></PRODUCER>
    <PRODUCER GIVEN_NAME="Michael"
              SURNAME="Levitt"></PRODUCER>
  </SHOW>
  <SHOW NAME="Entertainment Tonight" TYPE="5689"
        START_TIME="19:30-0500" AIR_DATE="July 3, 2003"
        ORIGINAL_AIR_DATE="July 3, 2003" LENGTH="30 minutes"
        REPEAT="No" CLOSED_CAPTIONED="Yes" DESCRIPTION="
          American Juniors remaining contestants;
          Sex and the City preview."></SHOW>
  <SHOW NAME="The Amazing Race" TYPE="406"
        START_TIME="20:00-0500" AIR_DATE="July 3, 2003"
        ORIGINAL_AIR_DATE="July 3, 2003" LENGTH="60 minutes"
        REPEAT="No" CLOSED_CAPTIONED="Yes" DESCRIPTION="
        Eight twenty-somethings speed through foreign
        cultures as quickly as possible in desperate
        attempt to avoid learning anything.">
    <PRODUCER GIVEN_NAME="Jerry"
             SURNAME="Bruckheimer"></PRODUCER>
    <PRODUCER GIVEN_NAME="Bertram"
              SURNAME="van Munster"></PRODUCER>
    <PRODUCER GIVEN_NAME="Hayma" MIDDLE_NAME="Screech"
              SURNAME="Washington"></PRODUCER>
    <PRODUCER GIVEN_NAME="Jon" SURNAME="Kroll"></PRODUCER>
  </SHOW>
</STATION>

<STATION NETWORK="" CALL_LETTERS="WLNY" CHANNEL="55">
  <SHOW NAME="Oprah Winfrey" TYPE="Series/Talk"
        START_TIME="19:00-0500" AIR_DATE="July 3, 2003"
        ORIGINAL_AIR_DATE="February 4, 2003"
        LENGTH="60 minutes" REPEAT="Yes"
        CLOSED_CAPTIONED="Yes"
        DESCRIPTION="Guests gabber;
        Oprah looks sympathetic."
        RATING="TV-PG"></SHOW>
  <SHOW NAME="Silicon Towers" TYPE="Movie"
        START_TIME="20:00-0500" AIR_DATE="July 3, 2003"
        LENGTH="60 minutes" REPEAT="Yes"
        CLOSED_CAPTIONED="Yes" DESCRIPTION="A programmer
        discovers his company manufactures chips for
        cracking bank systems." RATING="TV-PG">
    <CAST>
      <ACTOR GIVEN_NAME="Brian" SURNAME="Dennehy"></ACTOR>
      <ACTOR GIVEN_NAME="Daniel" SURNAME="Baldwin"></ACTOR>
      <ACTOR GIVEN_NAME="Brad" SURNAME="Dourif"></ACTOR>
      <ACTOR GIVEN_NAME="Gary" SURNAME="Mosher"></ACTOR>
```

```
      </CAST>
    </SHOW>
  </STATION>

  <STATION NETWORK="HBO" CALL_LETTERS="" CHANNEL="501">
    <SHOW NAME="Final Fantasy: The Spirits Within"
          TYPE="Movie/Animated" START_TIME="18:30-0500"
          AIR_DATE="July 3, 2003" LENGTH="105 minutes"
          REPEAT="Yes" CLOSED_CAPTIONED="Yes"
          DESCRIPTION="The last city on Earth defends itself
          against alien phantoms. Little to no relationship
          to the video games of the same name."
          RATING="PG-13" STARS="2">
      <DIRECTOR GIVEN_NAME="Hironobu"
SURNAME="Sakaguchi"></DIRECTOR>
      <WRITER GIVEN_NAME="Al" SURNAME="Reinart"></WRITER>
      <WRITER GIVEN_NAME="Jeff" SURNAME="Vintar"></WRITER>
      <PRODUCER GIVEN_NAME="Hironobu"
SURNAME="Sakaguchi"></PRODUCER>
      <PRODUCER GIVEN_NAME="Jun" SURNAME="Aida"></PRODUCER>
      <PRODUCER GIVEN_NAME="Chris" SURNAME="Lee"></PRODUCER>
      <CAST>
        <ACTOR GIVEN_NAME="Ming" SURNAME="Na"></ACTOR>
        <ACTOR GIVEN_NAME="Alec" SURNAME="Baldwin"></ACTOR>
        <ACTOR GIVEN_NAME="Ving" SURNAME="Rhames"></ACTOR>
        <ACTOR GIVEN_NAME="Steve" SURNAME="Buscemi"></ACTOR>
        <ACTOR GIVEN_NAME="Peri" SURNAME="Gilpin"></ACTOR>
        <ACTOR GIVEN_NAME="Donald"
SURNAME="Sutherland"></ACTOR>
        <ACTOR GIVEN_NAME="James" SURNAME="Woods"></ACTOR>
      </CAST>
    </SHOW>
    <SHOW NAME="Terminator 3: Rise of the Machines:
       HBO First Look" TYPE="Special/Documentary"
       START_TIME="20:15-0500" AIR_DATE="July 3, 2003"
       ORIGINAL_AIR_DATE="June 26, 2003" LENGTH="15 minutes"
       REPEAT="Yes" CLOSED_CAPTIONED="Yes"
RATING="TV14"></SHOW>
    <SHOW NAME="Star Wars: Episode II --
       Attack of the Clones" TYPE="Movie"
       START_TIME="20:30-0500" AIR_DATE="July 3, 2003"
       LENGTH="150 minutes" REPEAT="Yes"
       CLOSED_CAPTIONED="Yes" DESCRIPTION="Obi-wan Kenobi
       and Anakin Skywalker battle Count Dooku and the
       Trade Federation." RATING="PG-13" STARS="3">
      <DIRECTOR GIVEN_NAME="George" SURNAME="Lucas"></DIRECTOR>
      <WRITER GIVEN_NAME="George" SURNAME="Lucas"></WRITER>
      <WRITER GIVEN_NAME="Jonathan" SURNAME="Hales"></WRITER>
      <PRODUCER GIVEN_NAME="George"
               SURNAME="Lucas"></PRODUCER>
      <PRODUCER GIVEN_NAME="George"
               SURNAME="McCallam"></PRODUCER>
```

Continued

Listing 5-1 *(continued)*

```
      <CAST>
        <ACTOR GIVEN_NAME="Ewan" SURNAME="McGregor"></ACTOR>
        <ACTOR GIVEN_NAME="Natalie" SURNAME="Portman"></ACTOR>
        <ACTOR GIVEN_NAME="Christopher" SURNAME="Lee"></ACTOR>
        <ACTOR GIVEN_NAME="Samuel" MIDDLE_INITIAL="L"
              SURNAME="Jackson"></ACTOR>
        <ACTOR GIVEN_NAME="Frank" SURNAME="Oz"></ACTOR>
      </CAST>
    </SHOW>
  </STATION>

</SCHEDULE>
```

Listing 5-1 uses mostly attributes for text content. Listing 4-2 used only elements. There are intermediate approaches as well. For example, you could make the show name and description part of element content, while leaving the rest of the data as attributes, like this:

```
<SHOW TYPE="Series/News" EPISODE_NUMBER="5689"
      START_TIME="17:30-0500" LENGTH="30 minutes"
      AIR_DATE="July 3, 2003" ORIGINAL_AIR_DATE="July 3, 2003"
      CLOSED_CAPTIONED="Yes" REPEAT="No">
  <NAME>Entertainment Tonight</NAME>
  <DESCRIPTION>
    American Juniors remaining contestants;
    Sex and the City preview.
  </DESCRIPTION>
</SHOW>
```

This would include the show and description name in the text of a page while still making the rest of the data available. With the appropriate style sheet, it could be displayed as a hypertext footnote or as a ToolTip to readers who want to look deeper. The data in the attributes may also be processed in ways other than direct display. For example, a program could use the `AIR_DATE` and `START_TIME` attributes to sort the shows or to line them up in the right columns in a table, without directly showing these times to the user. There's always more than one way to represent the same data. Which one you pick depends on the needs of your specific application.

Attributes versus Elements

Chapter 4's no-attribute approach was an extreme position. It's also possible to swing to the other extreme — storing all the information in the attributes and none in the content. Listing 5-1 does this. In general, I don't recommend this approach. Storing all the information in element content — while equally extreme — is much easier to work with in practice. However, this chapter entertains the possibility of using only attributes for the sake of elucidation.

There are no hard-and-fast rules about when to use child elements and when to use attributes. Generally, you'll use whichever suits your application. With experience, you'll gain a feel for when attributes are easier than child elements and vice versa. Until then, one good rule of thumb is that the data itself should be stored in elements. Information about the data (metadata) should be stored in attributes. When in doubt, put the information in the elements.

To differentiate between data and metadata, ask yourself whether someone reading the document would want to see a particular piece of information. If the answer is yes, the information probably belongs in a child element. If the answer is no, the information probably belongs in an attribute. If all tags were stripped from the document along with all the attributes, the basic information should still be present. Attributes are good places to put ID numbers, URLs, references, and other information not directly or immediately relevant to the reader. However, there are many exceptions to the basic principal of storing metadata as attributes. Reasons for making an exception include the following:

- ✦ Attributes can't hold structure well.
- ✦ Attributes are unordered. Elements are ordered.
- ✦ Elements allow you to include meta-metadata (information about the information about the information).
- ✦ Not everyone always agrees on what is and isn't metadata.
- ✦ Elements are more extensible in the face of future changes.

Structured metadata

Elements can have substructure; attributes can't. This makes elements far more flexible and may convince you to encode metadata as child elements. For example, suppose you're writing an article and you want to include a source for a fact. It might look something like this:

```
<FACT SOURCE="The Biographical History of Baseball,
Donald Dewey and Nicholas Acocella (New York: Carroll &amp;
Graf Publishers, Inc. 1995) p. 169">
```

```
  Josh Gibson is the only person in the history of baseball
  to hit a pitch out of Yankee Stadium.
</FACT>
```

Clearly, the information "The Biographical History of Baseball, Donald Dewey and Nicholas Acocella (New York: Carroll & Graf Publishers, Inc. 1995) p. 169" is metadata. It is not the fact itself. Rather, it is information about the fact. However, the SOURCE attribute contains a lot of implicit substructure. You might find it more useful to organize the information like this:

```
<SOURCE>
  <AUTHOR>Donald Dewey</AUTHOR>
  <AUTHOR>Nicholas Acocella</AUTHOR>
  <BOOK>
    <TITLE>The Biographical History of Baseball</TITLE>
    <PAGES>169</PAGES>
    <YEAR>1995</YEAR>
  </BOOK>
</SOURCE>
```

Furthermore, using elements instead of attributes makes it straightforward to include additional information such as the authors' e-mail addresses, a URL where an electronic copy of the document can be found, the chapter title, and anything else that seems important.

Dates are another example. A common piece of metadata about scholarly articles is the date the article was first received. This is important for establishing priority of discovery and invention. It's easy to include a DATE attribute in an ARTICLE tag:

```
<ARTICLE DATE="06/28/1969">
  Polymerase Reactions in Organic Compounds
</ARTICLE>
```

However, the DATE attribute has substructure signified by the /. Getting that structure out of the attribute value is much more difficult than reading child elements of a DATE element like this one:

```
<DATE>
  <YEAR>1969</YEAR>
  <MONTH>06</MONTH>
  <DAY>28</DAY>
</DATE>
```

For example, with CSS, it's easy to format the day and month invisibly so that only the year appears:

```
YEAR  {display: inline}
MONTH {display: none}
DAY   {display: none}
```

If the DATE is stored as an attribute, however, there's no easy way to access only part of it. You must write a separate program in a programming language such as ECMAScript or Java that can parse your date format. It's easier to use the standard XML tools and child elements.

Furthermore, the attribute syntax is ambiguous. What does the date "10/07/2004" signify? Is it October 7th or July 10th? Readers from different countries will interpret this data differently. Even if your parser understands one format, there's no guarantee the people entering the data will enter it correctly. The XML, by contrast, is unambiguous.

Finally, using DATE children rather than attributes allows more than one date to be associated with an element. For example, scholarly articles are often returned to the author for revisions. In these cases, it can also be important to note when the revised article was received, as in the following example:

```
<ARTICLE>
  <TITLE>
    Maximum Projectile Velocity in an Augmented Railgun
  </TITLE>
  <AUTHOR>Elliotte Harold</AUTHOR>
  <AUTHOR>Bruce Bukiet</AUTHOR>
  <AUTHOR>William Peter</AUTHOR>
  <DATE>
    <YEAR>1992</YEAR>
    <MONTH>10</MONTH>
    <DAY>29</DAY>
  </DATE>
  <DATE>
    <YEAR>1993</YEAR>
    <MONTH>10</MONTH>
    <DAY>26</DAY>
  </DATE>
</ARTICLE>
```

As another example, consider the ALT attribute of an IMG tag in HTML. This is limited to a single string of text. However, given that a picture is worth a thousand words, you might well want to replace an IMG with marked-up text. For instance, consider the pie chart shown in Figure 5-1.

When you use an ALT attribute, the best description of this picture that you can provide is as follows:

```
<IMG SRC="05021.gif"
     ALT="Pie Chart of Positions in Major League Baseball"
     WIDTH="819" HEIGHT="623">
</IMG>
```

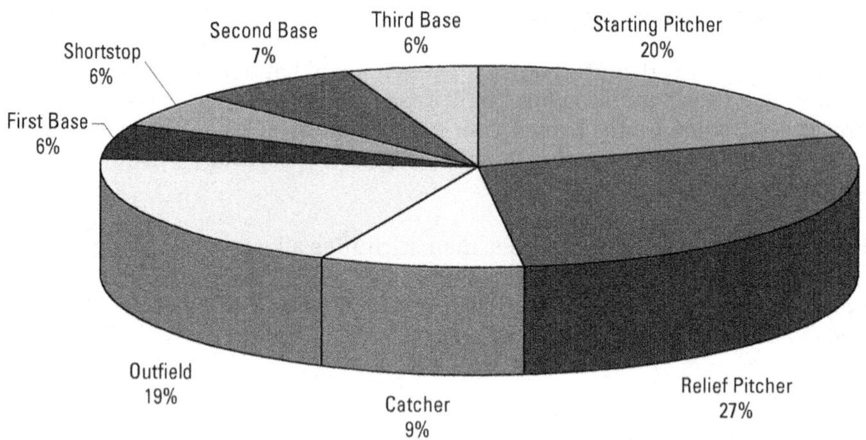

Figure 5-1: Distribution of positions in major league baseball

However, by using an ALT child element, you have more flexibility because you can embed markup. For example, you might provide a table of the relevant numbers instead of a pie chart:

```
<IMG SRC="05021.gif" WIDTH="819" HEIGHT="623">
  <ALT>
    <TABLE>
      <TR>
        <TD>Starting Pitcher</TD> <TD>242</TD> <TD>20%</TD>
      </TR>
      <TR>
        <TD>Relief Pitcher</TD> <TD>336</TD> <TD>27%</TD>
      </TR>
      <TR>
        <TD>Catcher</TD> <TD>104</TD> <TD>9%</TD>
      </TR>
      <TR>
        <TD>Outfield</TD> <TD>235</TD> <TD>19%</TD>
      </TR>
      <TR>
        <TD>First Base</TD> <TD>67</TD> <TD>6%</TD>
      </TR>
      <TR>
        <TD>Shortstop</TD> <TD>67</TD> <TD>6%</TD>
      </TR>
      <TR>
        <TD>Second Base</TD> <TD>88</TD> <TD>7%</TD>
```

```
      </TR>
      <TR>
        <TD>Third Base</TD> <TD>67</TD> <TD>6%</TD>
      </TR>
    </TABLE>
  </ALT>
</IMG>
```

You might even provide the actual PostScript or Scalable Vector Graphics (SVG) code to render the picture in the event that the bitmap image is not available.

Meta-metadata

Using elements for metadata also easily allows for meta-metadata, or information about the information about the information. For example, the author of a poem might be considered to be metadata about the poem. The language in which that author's name is written is data about the metadata about the poem. This isn't a trivial concern, especially for distinctly non-Roman languages. For example, is the author of the *Odyssey* Homer or Ομηρος? Using elements, it's easy to write the following:

```
<POET LANGUAGE="English">Homer</POET>
<POET LANGUAGE="Greek">Ομηρος</POET>
```

However, if POET is an attribute rather than a child element, you're stuck with unwieldy constructs such as this:

```
<POEM POET="Homer" POET_LANGUAGE="English"
 POEM_LANGUAGE="English">
  Tell me, O Muse, of the cunning man...
</POEM>
```

And it's even more bulky if you want to provide both the poet's English and Greek names:

```
<POEM POET_NAME_1="Homer" POET_LANGUAGE_1="English"
 POET_NAME_2="Ομηρος" POET_LANGUAGE_2="Greek"
 POEM_LANGUAGE="English">
  Tell me, O Muse, of the cunning man...
</POEM>
```

What's your metadata is someone else's data

"Meta-ness" is in the mind of the beholder. Who's reading your document and why they're reading it determines what they consider to be data and what they consider to be metadata. For example, if you're simply reading an article in a scholarly journal, the name of the author of the article is tangential to the information it contains. However, if you're sitting on a tenure and promotions committee scanning a journal to see who's publishing and who's not, the names of the authors and the number of articles they've published may be more important to you than what they wrote (sad but true).

In fact, you yourself might change your mind about what's meta and what's data. What's only tangentially relevant today might become crucial next week. You can use style sheets to hide unimportant elements today, and you can change the style sheets to reveal them later. However, it's more difficult to later reveal information that was first stored in an attribute. This may require rewriting the document itself rather than simply changing the style sheet.

Elements are more extensible

Attributes are certainly convenient when you only need to convey one or two words of unstructured information. In these cases, there may genuinely be no current need for a child element. However, this doesn't preclude such a need in the future.

For example, you may only need to store the name of the author of an article now, and you may not need to distinguish between the first and last names. However, in the future you might uncover a need to store first and last names, e-mail addresses, institutions, snail-mail addresses, URLs, and more. If you've stored the author of the article as an element, it's easy to add child elements to include this additional information.

Although any such change will probably require some revision of your documents, style sheets, and associated programs, it's still much easier to change a simple element to a tree of elements than it is to make an attribute a tree of elements. If you used an attribute, it's very difficult to extend attribute syntax beyond the region for which it was originally designed.

Good times to use attributes

Having exhausted all the reasons why you should use elements instead of attributes, I feel compelled to point out that there are times when using attributes makes sense. As previously mentioned, attributes are fully appropriate for very simple data without substructure that the reader is unlikely to want to see. One example is the `HEIGHT` and `WIDTH` attributes of an `IMG` element. Although the values of these attributes may change if the image changes, it's hard to imagine how the data in the attribute could be anything more than a very short string of text. `HEIGHT` and `WIDTH` are one-dimensional quantities (in many ways), so they work well as attributes.

Furthermore, attributes are appropriate for simple information about the document that has nothing to do with the content of the document. For example, it is often useful to assign an ID attribute to each element. The value of an ID attribute is a unique string possessed only by one element in the document. You can then use this string for a variety of tasks including linking to particular elements of the document, even if the elements move around as the document changes over time. For example:

```
<SOURCE ID="S1">
  <AUTHOR ID="A1">Donald Dewey</AUTHOR>
  <AUTHOR ID="A2">Nicholas Acocella</AUTHOR>
  <BOOK ID="B1">
    <TITLE ID="B2">
      The Biographical History of Baseball
    </TITLE>
    <PAGES ID="B3">169</PAGES>
    <YEAR ID="B4">1995</YEAR>
  </BOOK>
</SOURCE>
```

ID attributes make links to particular elements in the document possible. In this way, they can serve the same purpose as the NAME attributes of HTML's A elements. Other data associated with linking — HREFs to link to, SRCs to pull images and binary data from, and so forth — also work well as attributes.

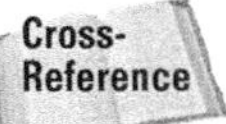

There are more examples of linking via ID attributes in Chapter 17 and Chapter 18.

Attributes are also useful containers for document-specific style information. For example, if TITLE elements are normally rendered as bold text, but you want to make just one TITLE element both bold and italic, you might write something similar to this:

```
<TITLE STYLE="font-style: italic">Significant Others</TITLE>
```

This allows the style information to be embedded without changing the tree structure of the document. Although using a separate element would be ideal, this scheme gives document authors more control when they cannot add elements to the tag set that they're working with. For example, the webmasters of a site might require page authors and designers to use a particular XML vocabulary with a fixed list of elements and attributes. Nonetheless, they might want to allow designers to make minor adjustments to individual pages. Use this scheme with restraint, however, or you'll soon find yourself back in the HTML hell that XML was supposed to save you from, in which formatting is freely intermixed with meaning and documents are no longer maintainable.

The final reason to use attributes is to maintain compatibility with legacy formats such as HTML. To the extent that you're using tags that at least look similar to HTML, such as <IMG>, <P>, and <TD>, you might as well employ the standard HTML attributes for these tags. This has the double advantage of allowing legacy browsers to at least partially parse and display your document, and of being more familiar to the people writing the documents.

Empty Elements and Empty-Element Tags

An element that contains no content, not even white space, is called an *empty element*. For example, this is an empty STATION element:

```
<STATION NETWORK="CBS" CALL_LETTERS="WCBS"
CHANNEL="2"></STATION>
```

The end-tag immediately follows the start-tag. Rather than including both a start-tag and an end-tag, you can include one empty-element tag. Empty-element tags are distinguished from start-tags by a closing /> instead of a closing >. For example, instead of <STATION></STATION>, you would write <STATION/>. The WCBS STATION element can be written with an empty-element tag like this:

```
<STATION NETWORK="CBS" CALL_LETTERS="WCBS" CHANNEL="2"/>
```

Often a space is placed before the closing /> to separate it from the last attribute and make it a little easier to read:

```
<STATION NETWORK="CBS" CALL_LETTERS="WCBS" CHANNEL="2" />
```

XML parsers treat both single-tag forms identically to the two-tag version. This STATION element is precisely equal (though not identical) to the previous STATION element formed with an empty tag. The difference between <STATION></STATION> and <STATION/> is syntax sugar and nothing more. If you don't like the empty-element tag syntax or find it hard to read, don't use it.

Listing 5-2 rewrites Listing 5-1 using empty-element tags where possible. This is a little shorter and perhaps a little clearer than the two-tag version. However, it is exactly the same document. There is no significant difference between Listing 5-1 and 5-2. Parsers will read the same information from both documents, and browsers will display them identically.

Listing 5-2: A Complete XML Document Using Empty-Element Tags to Store Television Listings

```
<?xml version="1.0"?>
<SCHEDULE DATE="July 3, 2003">

  <STATION NETWORK="CBS" CALL_LETTERS="WCBS" CHANNEL="2">
    <SHOW NAME="Hollywood Squares" TYPE="5074"
          START_TIME="19:00-0500" AIR_DATE="July 3, 2003"
          ORIGINAL_AIR_DATE="January 16, 2003"
          LENGTH="30 minutes" REPEAT="Yes"
          CLOSED_CAPTIONED="Yes">
      <CAST>
        <ACTOR GIVEN_NAME="Don" SURNAME="Rickles"/>
        <ACTOR GIVEN_NAME="Jerry" SURNAME="Springer"/>
```

```
      <ACTOR GIVEN_NAME="Richard" SURNAME="Simmons"/>
      <ACTOR GIVEN_NAME="Vicki" SURNAME="Lawrence"/>
      <ACTOR GIVEN_NAME="John" SURNAME="Salley"/>
      <ACTOR GIVEN_NAME="Joanie" SURNAME="Laurer"/>
      <ACTOR GIVEN_NAME="Martin" SURNAME="Mull"/>
      <ACTOR GIVEN_NAME="Jillian" SURNAME="Barberie"/>
      <ACTOR MIDDLE_NAME="Kennedy"/>
    </CAST>
    <PRODUCER GIVEN_NAME="Henry" SURNAME="Winkler"/>
    <PRODUCER GIVEN_NAME="Michael" SURNAME="Levitt"/>
  </SHOW>
  <SHOW NAME="Entertainment Tonight" TYPE="5689"
        START_TIME="19:30-0500" AIR_DATE="July 3, 2003"
        ORIGINAL_AIR_DATE="July 3, 2003" LENGTH="30 minutes"
        REPEAT="No" CLOSED_CAPTIONED="Yes" DESCRIPTION="
          American Juniors remaining contestants;
          Sex and the City preview."/>
  <SHOW NAME="The Amazing Race" TYPE="406"
        START_TIME="20:00-0500" AIR_DATE="July 3, 2003"
        ORIGINAL_AIR_DATE="July 3, 2003" LENGTH="60 minutes"
        REPEAT="No" CLOSED_CAPTIONED="Yes" DESCRIPTION="
        Eight twenty-somethings speed through foreign
        cultures as quickly as possible in desperate
        attempt to avoid learning anything.">
    <PRODUCER GIVEN_NAME="Jerry" SURNAME="Bruckheimer"/>
    <PRODUCER GIVEN_NAME="Bertram" SURNAME="van Munster"/>
    <PRODUCER GIVEN_NAME="Hayma" MIDDLE_NAME="Screech"
              SURNAME="Washington"/>
    <PRODUCER GIVEN_NAME="Jon" SURNAME="Kroll"/>
  </SHOW>
</STATION>

<STATION NETWORK="" CALL_LETTERS="WLNY" CHANNEL="55">
  <SHOW NAME="Oprah Winfrey" TYPE="Series/Talk"
        START_TIME="19:00-0500" AIR_DATE="July 3, 2003"
        ORIGINAL_AIR_DATE="February 4, 2003"
        LENGTH="60 minutes" REPEAT="Yes"
        CLOSED_CAPTIONED="Yes"
        DESCRIPTION="Guests gabber;
        Oprah looks sympathetic."
        RATING="TV-PG"/>
  <SHOW NAME="Silicon Towers" TYPE="Movie"
        START_TIME="20:00-0500" AIR_DATE="July 3, 2003"
        LENGTH="60 minutes" REPEAT="Yes"
        CLOSED_CAPTIONED="Yes" DESCRIPTION="A programmer
        discovers his company manufactures chips for
        cracking bank systems." RATING="TV-PG">
    <CAST>
      <ACTOR GIVEN_NAME="Brian" SURNAME="Dennehy"/>
      <ACTOR GIVEN_NAME="Daniel" SURNAME="Baldwin"/>
      <ACTOR GIVEN_NAME="Brad" SURNAME="Dourif"/>
      <ACTOR GIVEN_NAME="Gary" SURNAME="Mosher"/>
```

Continued

Listing 5-2 *(continued)*

```
    </CAST>
  </SHOW>
</STATION>

<STATION NETWORK="HBO" CALL_LETTERS="" CHANNEL="501">
  <SHOW NAME="Final Fantasy: The Spirits Within"
        TYPE="Movie/Animated" START_TIME="18:30-0500"
        AIR_DATE="July 3, 2003" LENGTH="105 minutes"
        REPEAT="Yes" CLOSED_CAPTIONED="Yes"
        DESCRIPTION="The last city on Earth defends itself
        against alien phantoms. Little to no relationship
        to the video games of the same name."
        RATING="PG-13" STARS="2">
    <DIRECTOR GIVEN_NAME="Hironobu" SURNAME="Sakaguchi"/>
    <WRITER GIVEN_NAME="Al" SURNAME="Reinart"/>
    <WRITER GIVEN_NAME="Jeff" SURNAME="Vintar"/>
    <PRODUCER GIVEN_NAME="Hironobu" SURNAME="Sakaguchi"/>
    <PRODUCER GIVEN_NAME="Jun" SURNAME="Aida"/>
    <PRODUCER GIVEN_NAME="Chris" SURNAME="Lee"/>
    <CAST>
      <ACTOR GIVEN_NAME="Ming" SURNAME="Na"/>
      <ACTOR GIVEN_NAME="Alec" SURNAME="Baldwin"/>
      <ACTOR GIVEN_NAME="Ving" SURNAME="Rhames"/>
      <ACTOR GIVEN_NAME="Steve" SURNAME="Buscemi"/>
      <ACTOR GIVEN_NAME="Peri" SURNAME="Gilpin"/>
      <ACTOR GIVEN_NAME="Donald" SURNAME="Sutherland"/>
      <ACTOR GIVEN_NAME="James" SURNAME="Woods"/>
    </CAST>
  </SHOW>
  <SHOW NAME="Terminator 3: Rise of the Machines:
     HBO First Look" TYPE="Special/Documentary"
     START_TIME="20:15-0500" AIR_DATE="July 3, 2003"
     ORIGINAL_AIR_DATE="June 26, 2003" LENGTH="15 minutes"
     REPEAT="Yes" CLOSED_CAPTIONED="Yes" RATING="TV14"/>
  <SHOW NAME="Star Wars: Episode II --
     Attack of the Clones" TYPE="Movie"
     START_TIME="20:30-0500" AIR_DATE="July 3, 2003"
     LENGTH="150 minutes" REPEAT="Yes"
     CLOSED_CAPTIONED="Yes" DESCRIPTION="Obi-wan Kenobi
     and Anakin Skywalker battle Count Dooku and the
     Trade Federation." RATING="PG-13" STARS="3">
    <DIRECTOR GIVEN_NAME="George" SURNAME="Lucas"/>
    <WRITER GIVEN_NAME="George" SURNAME="Lucas"/>
    <WRITER GIVEN_NAME="Jonathan" SURNAME="Hales"/>
    <PRODUCER GIVEN_NAME="George" SURNAME="Lucas"/>
    <PRODUCER GIVEN_NAME="George" SURNAME="McCallam"/>
    <CAST>
      <ACTOR GIVEN_NAME="Ewan" SURNAME="McGregor"/>
      <ACTOR GIVEN_NAME="Natalie" SURNAME="Portman"/>
```

```
        <ACTOR GIVEN_NAME="Christopher" SURNAME="Lee"/>
        <ACTOR GIVEN_NAME="Samuel" MIDDLE_INITIAL="L"
              SURNAME="Jackson"/>
        <ACTOR GIVEN_NAME="Frank" SURNAME="Oz"/>
      </CAST>
    </SHOW>
  </STATION>
</SCHEDULE>
```

XSL

Figure 5-2 shows Listing 5-1 after the TV schedule style sheet from the previous chapter is applied. It looks like a blank document because CSS styles only apply to element content, not to attributes. If you use CSS, any data that you want to display to the reader should be part of an element's content rather than one of its attributes.

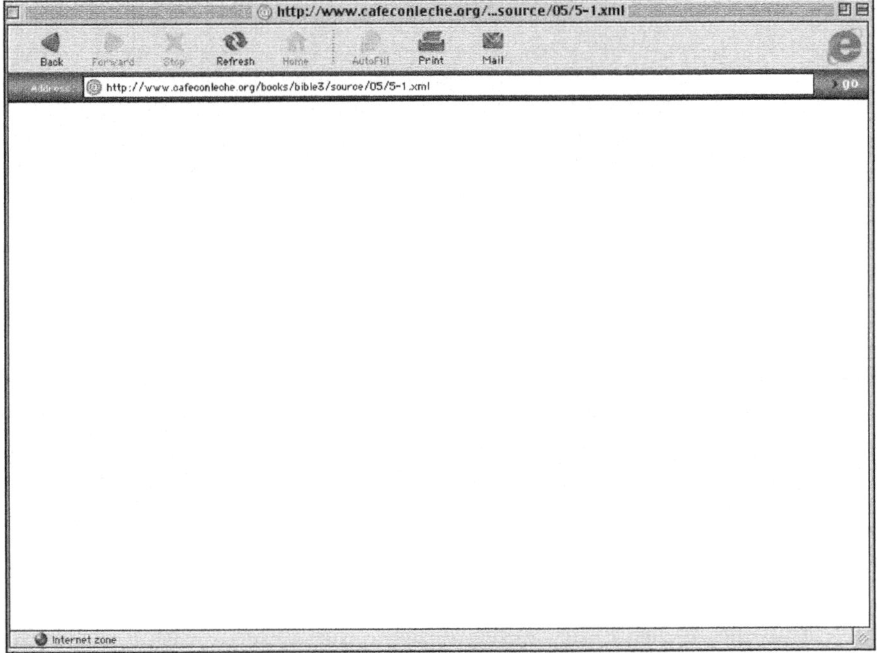

Figure 5-2: A blank document is displayed when CSS is applied to an XML document whose elements do not contain any character data.

However, there is an alternative style sheet language that does allow browsers to display attribute content. This is the Extensible Stylesheet Language (XSL). XSL is divided into two parts, XSL Transformations (XSLT) and XSL Formatting Objects (XSL-FO). XSLT enables you to replace one tag with another. You define rules that map your XML tags to standard HTML tags, or to HTML tags plus CSS attributes. XSLT can reorder elements in the document and even add additional content that was never present in the XML document.

Not all browsers support XSLT. In particular, Opera, Safari, Lynx, OmniWeb, iCab, and Konqueror do not support XSLT. In addition, Internet Explorer has a number of nasty bugs you have to work around that make XSLT development less pleasant than it should be. Mozilla-derived browsers, including Camino, Firebird, and Netscape 6.0 and later, do support XSLT quite well; however, Netscape 4.x and earlier do not.

Chapter 15 introduces some techniques that enable you to use XSLT even with browsers that don't support it directly. In the meantime, however, don't expect any of the examples in the rest of this chapter to work as advertised except in Internet Explorer 5.0 or later, Mozilla 1.0 or later, or Netscape 6.0 or later.

The formatting half of XSL defines an extremely powerful view of documents as pages. XSL-FO enables you to specify the appearance and layout of a page, including multiple columns, text flow around objects, line spacing, widow and orphan control, font faces, styles, sizes, and more. It's designed to be powerful enough to lay out documents for both the Web and print automatically from the same source document. For example, a local newspaper could use two different XSL style sheets to generate both the printed and online editions of the television listings from the same source document automatically. However, no web browsers yet support XSL formatting objects. Thus, I focus on XSL transformations in this section.

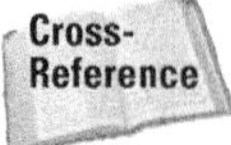

XSL-FO is discussed in Chapter 16.

Templates

An XSLT style sheet contains templates into which data from the XML document is poured. For example, a template might look similar to this:

```
<HTML>
  <HEAD>
    <TITLE>
      XSLT Instructions to get the date
    </TITLE>
  </HEAD>
  <BODY>
    <H1>XSLT Instructions to get the date</H1>
    XSLT Instructions to get the schedule
  </BODY>
</HTML>
```

The italicized sections will be replaced by particular XSLT elements that copy data from the underlying XML document into this template. You can apply this template to many different data sets. For example, if the template is designed to work with the TV schedule, the same style sheet can display schedules for different days.

This may remind you of some server-side include schemes for HTML. In fact, this is very much like server-side includes. However, the actual transformation of the source XML document by the XSLT style sheet takes place on the client rather than on the server. Furthermore, the output document does not have to be HTML. It can be any well-formed XML.

Servers can be configured to perform the transformation on the server side instead. This is how you make XML documents with XSLT style sheets compatible with legacy browsers that don't support XSL.

XSLT instructions can retrieve any data in the XML document. This includes element content, element names, and most importantly for this example, attribute values. Particular elements are chosen by a pattern that considers the element's name, its value, its attributes' names and values, its absolute and relative position in the tree structure of the XML document, and more. Once the data is extracted from an element, it can be moved, copied, and manipulated in a variety of ways. This brief introduction doesn't discuss everything you can do with XSLT. However, you will learn to use XSLT to write some pretty amazing documents that can be immediately viewed on the Web.

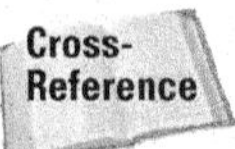

Chapter 15 discusses XSLT in depth.

The body of the document

Let's begin by looking at a simple example and applying it to the TV schedule document of Listing 5-1. Listing 5-3 is an XSLT style sheet. This style sheet provides the HTML mold into which XML data will be poured.

Listing 5-3: An XSLT Style Sheet

```
<?xml version="1.0"?>
<xsl:stylesheet version="1.0"
      xmlns:xsl="http://www.w3.org/1999/XSL/Transform">

  <xsl:template match="SCHEDULE">
    <HTML>
      <HEAD>
        <TITLE>
          TV Listings
        </TITLE>
      </HEAD>
```

Continued

Listing 5-3 *(continued)*

```
      <BODY>
        <H1>TV Listings</H1>

        <HR></HR>
        Copyright 2003
        <A HREF="http://www.elharo.com">
         Elliotte Rusty Harold
        </A>
        <BR />
        <A HREF="mailto:elharo@metalab.unc.edu">
         elharo@metalab.unc.edu
        </A>

      </BODY>
    </HTML>
  </xsl:template>

</xsl:stylesheet>
```

Listing 5-3 resembles an HTML file included inside an `xsl:template` element. In other words, its structure looks like this:

```
<?xml version="1.0"?>
<xsl:stylesheet version="1.0"
       xmlns:xsl="http://www.w3.org/1999/XSL/Transform">

  <xsl:template match="SCHEDULE">
    HTML file goes here
  </xsl:template>

</xsl:stylesheet>
```

Listing 5-3 is not just an XSLT style sheet; it's also an XML document. It begins with an XML declaration. The root element of this document is `xsl:stylesheet`. This style sheet contains a single template for the XML data encoded as an `xsl:template` element. The `xsl:template` element has a `match` attribute with the value `SCHEDULE`, and its content is a well-formed HTML document. It's not a coincidence that the output HTML is well formed. Because the HTML must first be part of an XSLT style sheet, and because XSLT style sheets are well-formed XML documents, all the HTML included in an XSLT style sheet must be well formed.

Attaching the XSLT style sheet of Listing 5-3 to the XML document in Listing 5-1 is straightforward. Simply add an <?xml-stylesheet?> processing instruction with a type attribute with value application/xml and an href attribute that points to the style sheet between the XML declaration and the root element, as in the following example:

```
<?xml version="1.0"?>
<?xml-stylesheet type="application/xml" href="5-2.xsl"?>
<SCHEDULE DATE="July 3, 2003">
...
```

This is the same way that a CSS style sheet is attached to a document. The only difference is that the type attribute has the value application/xml instead of text/css.

Caution Internet Explorer expects the nonstandard and incorrect MIME type text/xsl instead of application/xml. For maximum portability, you might want to include two xml-stylesheet processing instructions pointing to the same style sheet, one instruction with type text/xsl and the second instruction with type application/xml, like this:

```
<?xml version="1.0"?>
<?xml-stylesheet type="application/xml"
                 href="5-2.xsl"?>
<?xml-stylesheet type="text/xsl" href="5-2.xsl"?>
<SCHEDULE DATE="July 3, 2003">
...
```

The browser will pick whichever one it understands.

After the browser loads the XML document, it compares the root to each xsl:template element until it finds one that matches. In this case, the single template matches the root SCHEDULE element. When the browser finds this match, it inserts the content of that template into the output document, producing what you see in Figure 5-3.

The title

Of course, there's something rather obvious missing from Figure 5-3—the data! Although the style sheet in Listing 5-3 displays something (unlike the CSS style sheet of Figure 5-2), it doesn't show any data from the XML document. To add this, you need to use XSLT instruction elements to copy data from the source XML document into the output document. Listing 5-4 adds xsl:value-of instructions that extract the DATE attribute from the SCHEDULE element and insert it into the TITLE and H1 elements of the output document. Figure 5-4 shows the rendered document.

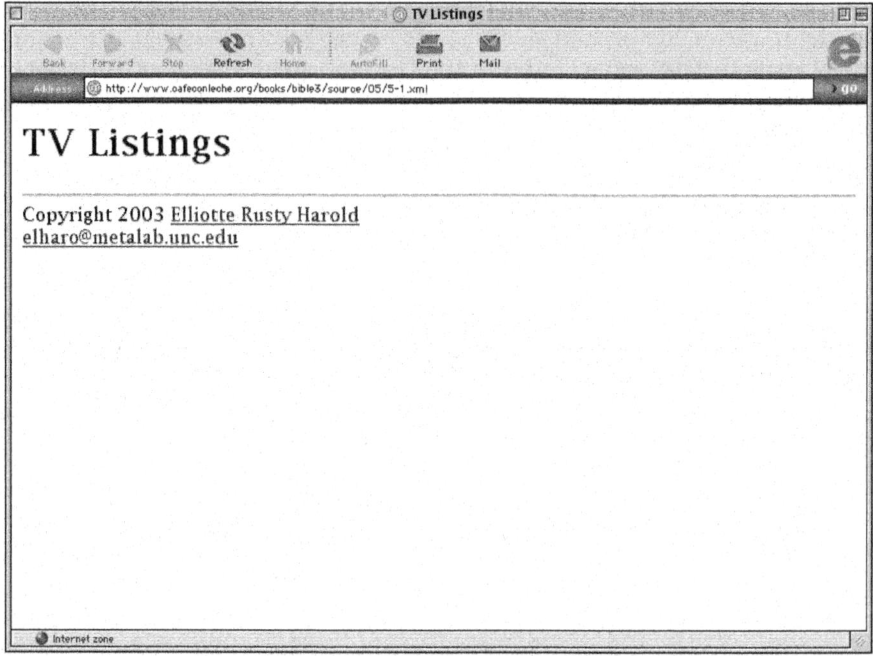

Figure 5-3: TV listings after application of the XSL style sheet in Listing 5-3

Listing 5-4: An XSL Style Sheet with Instructions to Extract the DATE Attribute of the SCHEDULE Element

```
<?xml version="1.0"?>
<xsl:stylesheet version="1.0"
       xmlns:xsl="http://www.w3.org/1999/XSL/Transform">

  <xsl:template match="SCHEDULE">
    <HTML>
      <HEAD>
        <TITLE>
          TV Listings <xsl:value-of select="@DATE"/>
        </TITLE>
      </HEAD>
      <BODY>
        <H1>TV Listings <xsl:value-of select="@DATE"/></H1>

        <HR></HR>
        Copyright 2003
        <A HREF="http://www.elharo.com">
```

```
          Elliotte Rusty Harold
        </A>
        <BR />
        <A HREF="mailto:elharo@metalab.unc.edu">
          elharo@metalab.unc.edu
        </A>

      </BODY>
    </HTML>
  </xsl:template>

</xsl:stylesheet>
```

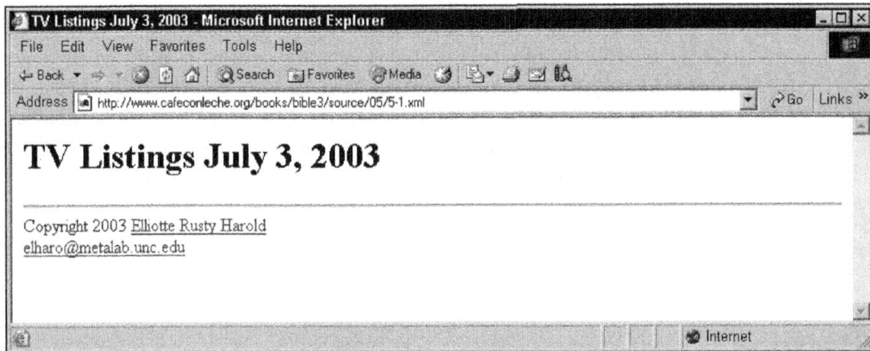

Figure 5-4: Listing 5-1 after application of the XSL style sheet in Listing 5-4

The XSLT instruction that extracts the `DATE` attribute from the `SCHEDULE` element is as follows:

```
<xsl:value-of select="@DATE"/>
```

The `xsl:value-of` element copies the value of a node from the input document into the output document. Here, the @ sign in front of `DATE` means you're asking for the attribute named `DATE`, rather than the child element named `DATE`. This element appears twice because the year should appear twice in the output document — once in the `H1` header and once in the `TITLE`. Each time it appears, this instruction does the same thing: It inserts the value of the `DATE` attribute, the string "July 3, 2003".

XSLT instructions are distinguished from output elements such as `HTML` and `H1` by being placed in the `http://www.w3.org/1999/XSL/Transform` namespace. In most cases, this namespace is associated with the prefix `xsl`. That is, the names of all XSLT elements begin with `xsl:`. The namespace is identified by the `xmlns:xsl` attribute of the root element of the style sheet. In Listings 5-2 and 5-3, and in all other examples in this book, the value of that attribute is `http://www.w3.org/1999/XSL/Transform`.

The prefix can and occasionally does change. However, the URI absolutely must be `http://www.w3.org/1999/XSL/Transform`, nothing else. Various early and outdated drafts of the XSLT specification used different namespace URIs. However, modern, up-to-date, specification-compliant software uses `http://www.w3.org/1999/XSL/Transform` and `http://www.w3.org/1999/XSL/Transform` only! If you use any other namespace URI, or make even a small typo in the URI, the results are likely to be very strange and hard to debug.

You should avoid any software that uses other namespaces because it's likely to be out-of-date and quite buggy. Furthermore, you should be wary of anybody who tries to tell you to use a different namespace. *They are not your friends!* (Yes, I'm talking about Microsoft here. Its trainers and evangelists have been promulgating a nonstandard, Microsoft-only version of XSLT that doesn't work with anything except Internet Explorer. This nonstandard XSLT can be identified by its use of the `http://www.w3.org/TR/WD-xsl` namespace URI. Treat this URI as a warning: Dangerous nonstandard Microsoft extensions ahead!) In this book, I adhere strictly to W3C standard XSLT that works with all XSLT-savvy browsers and platforms.

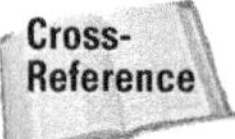

Namespaces are discussed in depth in Chapter 11.

Stations

Next, let's add some XSLT instructions to pull out the `STATION` elements. There's more than one of these, so use the `xsl:for-each` instruction to iterate through them. `xsl:value-of` elements will extract the network, call letters, and channel from the attributes of each `STATION` element. These will all be placed in an `H2` header. Listing 5-5 shows the code. Figure 5-5 shows the document rendered with this style sheet.

Listing 5-5: An XSL Style Sheet with Instructions to Extract STATION Elements

```
<?xml version="1.0"?>
<xsl:stylesheet version="1.0"
      xmlns:xsl="http://www.w3.org/1999/XSL/Transform">

  <xsl:template match="SCHEDULE">
    <HTML>
      <HEAD>
        <TITLE>
          TV Listings <xsl:value-of select="@DATE"/>
```

```
        </TITLE>
      </HEAD>
      <BODY>
        <H1>TV Listings <xsl:value-of select="@DATE"/></H1>

        <xsl:for-each select="STATION">
          <H2>
            <xsl:value-of select="@NETWORK"/>
            <xsl:value-of select="@CALL_LETTERS"/>
            <xsl:value-of select="@CHANNEL"/>
          </H2>
        </xsl:for-each>

        <HR></HR>
        Copyright 2003
        <A HREF="http://www.elharo.com">
         Elliotte Rusty Harold
        </A>
        <BR />
        <A HREF="mailto:elharo@metalab.unc.edu">
         elharo@metalab.unc.edu
        </A>

      </BODY>
    </HTML>
  </xsl:template>

</xsl:stylesheet>
```

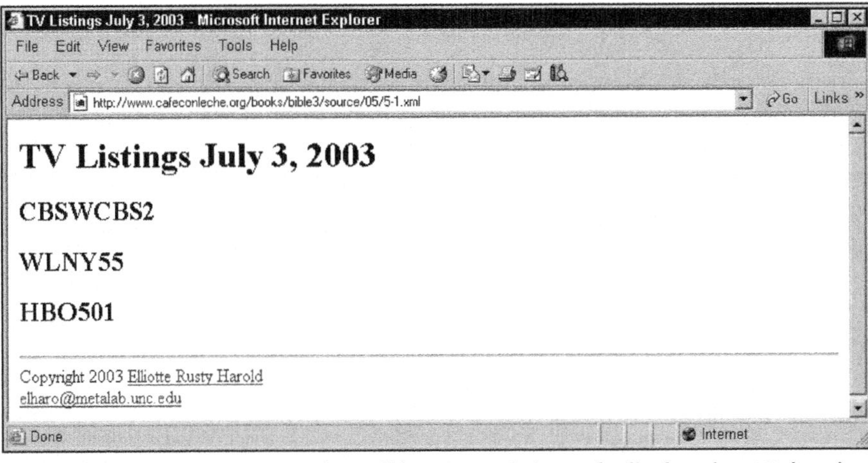

Figure 5-5: The station networks, call letters, and channels displayed as H2 headers when the XSLT style sheet in Listing 5-5 is applied

The key new instruction is the `xsl:for-each` element:

```
<xsl:for-each select="STATION">
  <H2>
    <xsl:value-of select="@NETWORK"/>
    <xsl:value-of select="@CALL_LETTERS"/>
    <xsl:value-of select="@CHANNEL"/>
  </H2>
</xsl:for-each>
```

`xsl:for-each` loops through all the `STATION` elements (more accurately, those `STATION` elements that are children of the previously matched `SCHEDULE` element, although in this document that's all the `STATION` elements). As the XSLT processor visits each `STATION` element, it outputs an `<H2>` start-tag, the value of its `NETWORK`, `CALL_LETTERS`, and `CHANNEL` attributes in that order, and a `</H2>` end-tag.

The first station in Figure 5-5, WCBS, looks a little funny, because as a broadcast network affiliate, it has both a network and call letters. Ideally, you'd include the call letters only if the network is not available, as for WLNY (or perhaps the reverse: include the network only if the station doesn't have call letters). Either is easy with XSLT. You can use an `xsl:if` element to test the value of particular nodes. The contents of the `xsl:if` element are placed in the output only if the test attribute of the `xsl:if` instruction is true. In this case, you test whether the value of the `NETWORK` attribute is an empty string:

```
<H2>
  <xsl:if test="@NETWORK=''">
    <xsl:value-of select="@CALL_LETTERS"/>
  </xsl:if>
  <xsl:value-of select="@NETWORK"/>
  <xsl:value-of select="@CHANNEL"/>
</H2>
```

In other words, you're only including the call letters if there's no network. After this test is added, the call letters for WCBS are omitted from the output, as shown in Figure 5-6.

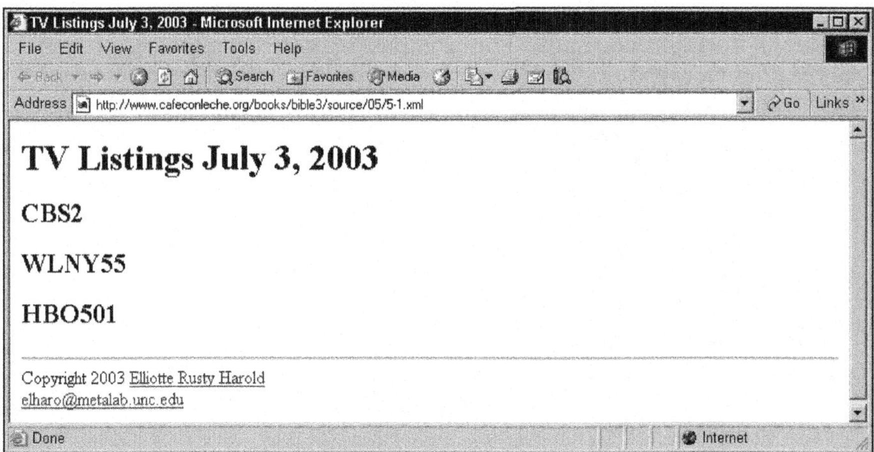

Figure 5-6: The xsl:if instruction omits the call letters for network affiliates.

Shows

The next step is to add the individual shows. A nested `xsl:for-each` loop can select the shows. Let's put each show inside an HTML `DIV` element:

```
<xsl:for-each select="STATION">
  <H2>
    <xsl:if test="@NETWORK=''">
      <xsl:value-of select="@CALL_LETTERS"/>
    </xsl:if>
    <xsl:value-of select="@NETWORK"/>
    <xsl:value-of select="@CHANNEL"/>
  </H2>

  <xsl:for-each select="SHOW">
    <DIV>
      ...
    </DIV>
  </xsl:for-each>

</xsl:for-each>
```

Notice that the nesting of the `xsl:for-each` elements that select stations and shows mirrors the hierarchy of the document itself. This is not a coincidence. While other schemes are possible that don't require matching hierarchies, this is the simplest, especially for highly structured data like the television schedule of Listing 5-1.

Inside the `DIV` element, you find instructions to select and format content from the attributes of each `SHOW` element. One advantage of XSL over CSS is that you can select exactly what you want and leave the rest out. Furthermore, what you do include can appear in exactly the order you want it, even if that's not the order it appears in the input document. For example, if you're trying to create something like the columnar listings in *TV Guide*, as opposed to the show-by-show grid, you might want the following content in this order:

1. The time the show starts
2. The number of stars
3. Show title in bold
4. (CC) if the show is closed captioned
5. The length of the show
6. The description, which normally begins on a new line
7. The primary actors

This can vary a lot from one show to the next, though. In general, the shows deemed the most important get longer listings with more information. Less important shows may be limited to a time, channel, and title. However, for the moment, I'm going to assume all the shows in the list are equally important and include all this information for each one.

The time of the show can be extracted with a simple `xsl:value-of` element, like those you've used several times before:

```
<xsl:value-of select="@START_TIME"/>
```

Applying the formatting is simply a matter of outputting the appropriate HTML tags, perhaps with CSS `STYLE` attributes. For example, to print the channel number in bold, just wrap a `B` element around an `xsl:value-of` instruction that selects `@CHANNEL`, like this:

```
<B><xsl:value-of select="@CHANNEL"/></B>
```

The closed caption information is a little different. Here, the input document has a value that says "Yes" or "No" (or no attribute at all), but what you want to put (or not put) in the output is the completely different string (CC). In this case, you can use another `xsl:if` element to test the value of the `CLOSED_CAPTIONED` attribute:

```
<xsl:if test="@CLOSED_CAPTIONED='Yes'"> (CC) </xsl:if>
```

If and only if the test passes, the processor will output the string (CC). This is an example of completely replacing the input content with the same information in a very different form.

A slightly more complicated example of this is the `STARS` attribute. The value of this attribute is a number, but it's a number you want to replace with a string such as ★. There are several ways to do this, most involving advanced features of XSLT you won't learn about for several chapters yet. However, assuming the STARS attribute always contains an integer between 1 and 5, there is a simple naïve approach. Just list all the possible values inside xsl:if statements like so:

```
<xsl:if test="@STARS=1"> ★ </xsl:if>
<xsl:if test="@STARS=2"> ★★ </xsl:if>
<xsl:if test="@STARS=3"> ★★★ </xsl:if>
<xsl:if test="@STARS=4"> ★★★★ </xsl:if>
<xsl:if test="@STARS=5"> ★★★★★ </xsl:if>
```

Note If your text editor doesn't let you type the ★ character, you can type ★ instead. This is called a *character reference*. I'll explain how this works in Chapter 6.

There's one more piece of information that's often included with the show information in television listings: the primary actors. They are often listed inside parentheses after the description like this: (Ewan McGregor, Natalie Portman, Christopher Lee, Samuel L. Jackson, Frank Oz).

This is tricky because some listings don't include actors at all, others just mention the single most important actor, and still others mention several of the primary actors. There are various ways to handle this, but I'm going to pick the simplest, listing them all. Because the actors are child elements of CAST, which is a child element of SHOW, this is going to require one more nested xsl:for-each element. Since it's really the actors we want, rather than the CAST, this xsl:for-each element will iterate over CAST/ACTOR:

```
(<xsl:for-each select="CAST/ACTOR">
   <xsl:value-of select="@GIVEN_NAME"/>
   <xsl:value-of select="@MIDDLE_INITIAL"/>
   <xsl:value-of select="@MIDDLE_NAME"/>
   <xsl:value-of select="@SURNAME"/>,
 </xsl:for-each>)
```

However, this first approach has a number of problems. First, not all shows list a cast. You should really wrap this in an xsl:if element that tests for the presence of a CAST element, like so:

```
<xsl:if test="CAST">(<xsl:for-each select="CAST/ACTOR">
    <xsl:value-of select="@GIVEN_NAME"/>
    <xsl:value-of select="@MIDDLE_INITIAL"/>
    <xsl:value-of select="@MIDDLE_NAME"/>
    <xsl:value-of select="@SURNAME"/>,
  </xsl:for-each>)</xsl:if>
```

Next, the white space is only preserved in XSLT when there's some non-white-space character next to it. This means the names come out looking like "RichardSimmons" instead of "Richard Simmons." There are several ways to fix this, but the easiest is to add an xml:space="preserve" attribute to the xsl:for-each element like so:

```
<xsl:for-each select="CAST/ACTOR" xml:space="preserve">
  <xsl:value-of select="@GIVEN_NAME"/>
  <xsl:value-of select="@MIDDLE_INITIAL"/>
  <xsl:value-of select="@MIDDLE_NAME"/>
  <xsl:value-of select="@SURNAME"/>,
</xsl:for-each>
```

The final problem is that this template puts a comma after every name, including the last. You actually want to include a comma only if this is not the last element. Once again the `xsl:if` element comes to the rescue. The following code outputs a comma only if the position of the current element (as indicated by the `position()` function) is not the last child element (as indicated by the `last()` function):

```
<xsl:if test="CAST">(<xsl:for-each
   select="CAST/ACTOR" xml:space="preserve">
  <xsl:value-of select="@GIVEN_NAME"/>
  <xsl:value-of select="@MIDDLE_INITIAL"/>
  <xsl:value-of select="@MIDDLE_NAME"/>
  <xsl:value-of select="@SURNAME"/><xsl:if
    test="position() != last()">, </xsl:if></xsl:for-each>)
</xsl:if>
```

The indentation has gotten quite funky here because the `xml:space="preserve"` attribute has made all the white space significant. You can no longer rely on the XSLT processor to throw it away for you. Thus, you can't add any white space you aren't willing to see in the output. On the other hand, the rendered HTML output looks quite pretty, as evidenced by Figure 5-7. Listing 5-6 shows the complete style sheet.

Listing 5-6: **An XSL Style Sheet That Formats Shows**

```
<?xml version="1.0"?>
<xsl:stylesheet version="1.0"
       xmlns:xsl="http://www.w3.org/1999/XSL/Transform">

  <xsl:template match="SCHEDULE">
    <HTML>
      <HEAD>
        <TITLE>
          TV Listings <xsl:value-of select="@DATE"/>
        </TITLE>
      </HEAD>
      <BODY>
        <H1>TV Listings <xsl:value-of select="@DATE"/></H1>

        <xsl:for-each select="STATION">
          <H2>
```

```
          <xsl:if test="@NETWORK=''">
            <xsl:value-of select="@CALL_LETTERS"/>
          </xsl:if>
          <xsl:value-of select="@NETWORK"/>
          <xsl:value-of select="@CHANNEL"/>
        </H2>

        <xsl:for-each select="SHOW">
          <DIV>
            <xsl:value-of select="@START_TIME"/>
            <B><xsl:value-of select="@CHANNEL"/></B>
            <xsl:if test="@STARS=1"> ★ </xsl:if>
            <xsl:if test="@STARS=2"> ★★ </xsl:if>
            <xsl:if test="@STARS=3"> ★★★ </xsl:if>
            <xsl:if test="@STARS=4"> ★★★★ </xsl:if>
            <xsl:if test="@STARS=5"> ★★★★★ </xsl:if>
            <B><xsl:value-of select="@NAME"/></B>
      <xsl:if test="@CLOSED_CAPTIONED='Yes'"> (CC) </xsl:if>
            <xsl:value-of select="@LENGTH"/><BR />
            <xsl:value-of select="@DESCRIPTION"/>

            <xsl:if test="CAST">(<xsl:for-each
                select="CAST/ACTOR"
                xml:space="preserve"><xsl:value-of
                select="@GIVEN_NAME"/>
                <xsl:value-of select="@MIDDLE_INITIAL"/>
                <xsl:value-of select="@MIDDLE_NAME"/>
                <xsl:value-of select="@SURNAME"/><xsl:if
                  test="position() != last()"
                >, </xsl:if></xsl:for-each>)
            </xsl:if>
          </DIV>
        </xsl:for-each>

      </xsl:for-each>

      <HR></HR>
      Copyright 2003
      <A HREF="http://www.elharo.com">
       Elliotte Rusty Harold
      </A>
      <BR />
      <A HREF="mailto:elharo@metalab.unc.edu">
       elharo@metalab.unc.edu
      </A>

    </BODY>
  </HTML>
</xsl:template>

</xsl:stylesheet>
```

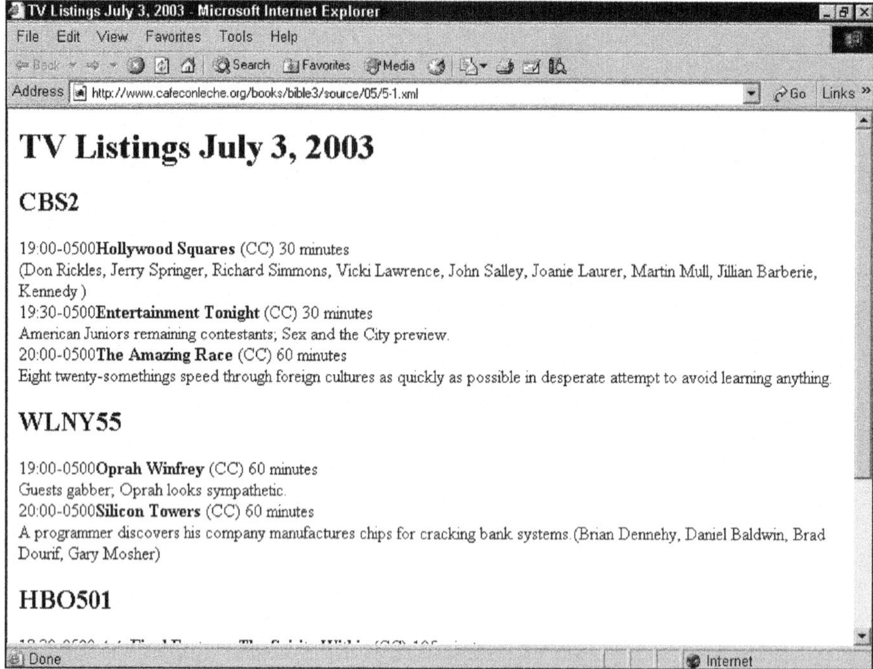

Figure 5-7: Shows formatted by the XSL style sheet in Listing 5-6

Sorting

There's one major problem with the style sheet as designed so far. It arranges shows by station and the order they appear in the input document. This is of little use for a TV schedule. You only rarely want to know what shows are playing on a particular station at all times. You very often want to know what shows are playing on all stations at the same time. The data needs to be sorted by time rather than by station, and the station should be added to the information about the individual shows. This isn't how the data is organized in the input document, but there's no reason the output document can't use a different arrangement.

Fortunately, XSLT makes it easy to sort the data by various criteria. Each `xsl:for-each` element can have an `xsl:sort` child element that specifies a sort key. In this case, you want to sort in ascending order by start time. You also want to adjust the `xsl:for-each` elements so they grab all the shows in the document at once, rather than just those associated with one channel. Finally, you want to add the channel before each show. This is a little tricky because a `SHOW` element doesn't have a `CHANNEL` attribute or child element. However, you can select the `CHANNEL` attribute of the `STATION` parent element by using `../@CHANNEL` in the `select` attribute. In XSLT, the double period means the parent element, just like it means the parent directory in UNIX and DOS. For good measure, I put the channel inside vertical bars to make it more distinct.

Listing 5-7 shows the finished style sheet, and Figure 5-8 shows the document rendered with this style sheet.

Listing 5-7: An XSL Style Sheet That Sorts by Start Time

```
<?xml version="1.0"?>
<xsl:stylesheet version="1.0"
      xmlns:xsl="http://www.w3.org/1999/XSL/Transform">

  <xsl:template match="SCHEDULE">
    <HTML>
      <HEAD>
        <TITLE>
          TV Listings <xsl:value-of select="@DATE"/>
        </TITLE>
      </HEAD>
      <BODY>
        <H1>TV Listings <xsl:value-of select="@DATE"/></H1>

          <xsl:for-each select="STATION/SHOW">
            <xsl:sort select="@START_TIME" />
            <DIV>
              <xsl:value-of select="@START_TIME"/> |
              <B><xsl:value-of select="../@CHANNEL"/></B> |
              <xsl:if test="@STARS=1"> ★ </xsl:if>
              <xsl:if test="@STARS=2"> ★★ </xsl:if>
              <xsl:if test="@STARS=3"> ★★★ </xsl:if>
              <xsl:if test="@STARS=4"> ★★★★ </xsl:if>
              <xsl:if test="@STARS=5"> ★★★★★ </xsl:if>
              <B><xsl:value-of select="@NAME"/></B>
        <xsl:if test="@CLOSED_CAPTIONED='Yes'"> (CC) </xsl:if>
              <xsl:value-of select="@LENGTH"/><BR />
              <xsl:value-of select="@DESCRIPTION"/>

              <xsl:if test="CAST">(<xsl:for-each
                  select="CAST/ACTOR"
                  xml:space="preserve"><xsl:value-of
                  select="@GIVEN_NAME"/>
                  <xsl:value-of select="@MIDDLE_INITIAL"/>
                  <xsl:value-of select="@MIDDLE_NAME"/>
                  <xsl:value-of select="@SURNAME"/><xsl:if
                    test="position() != last()"
                  >, </xsl:if></xsl:for-each>)
              </xsl:if>
            </DIV>
          </xsl:for-each>

        <HR></HR>
        Copyright 2003
```

Continued

Listing 5-7 *(continued)*

```
          <A HREF="http://www.elharo.com">
           Elliotte Rusty Harold
          </A>
          <BR />
          <A HREF="mailto:elharo@metalab.unc.edu">
           elharo@metalab.unc.edu
          </A>

        </BODY>
      </HTML>
    </xsl:template>

  </xsl:stylesheet>
```

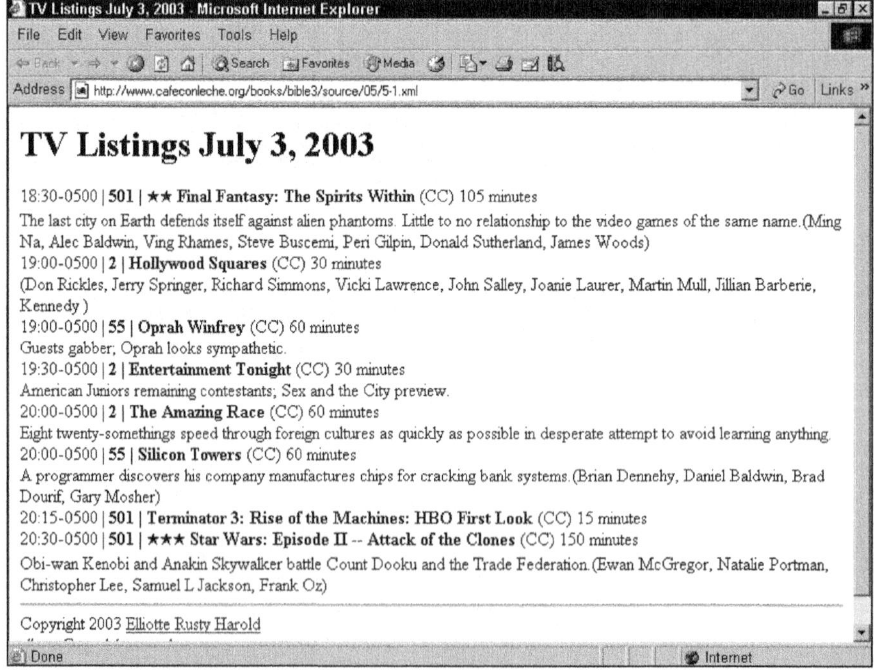

Figure 5-8: Television listings sorted by start time

There's more you could do. You could convert the universal times such as 18:30-0500 into more typical times such as 6:30 P.M. You could group shows that start at the same time together. However, while possible, this would take you into the area sometimes referred to as "XSLT rocket science." For this example, I'm going to stop here with the simple stuff, but in the next section I'll fire off a rocket or two.

Tables

Figure 5-8 is a fairly decent textual television schedule. However, the example began with a grid. Is it possible to reproduce this tabular format with XSLT? Yes. In fact, it's possible to do a considerably better job than with CSS. The task is a little detailed, but not horribly difficult. Listing 5-8 shows an XSLT style sheet that arranges the shows in a table. Time advances to the right. Channel numbers increase down. No new XSLT elements are introduced. The same `xsl:for-each`, `xsl:value-of`, and `xsl:sort` elements are used as before. This time, however, the style sheet produces HTML table tags instead of `DIV`s. Figure 5-9 displays the results.

Listing 5-8: An XSL Style Sheet that Places the Television Schedule in a Table

```
<?xml version="1.0"?>
<xsl:stylesheet version="1.0"
      xmlns:xsl="http://www.w3.org/1999/XSL/Transform">

  <xsl:template match="SCHEDULE">
    <HTML>
      <HEAD>
        <TITLE>
          TV Listings <xsl:value-of select="@DATE"/>
        </TITLE>
      </HEAD>
      <BODY>
        <H1 STYLE="text-align: center">
           TV Listings <xsl:value-of select="@DATE"/>
        </H1>

        <TABLE CELLSPACING="0" RULES="all" FRAME="box">
          <xsl:for-each select="STATION">
            <xsl:sort select="@CHANNEL" />
            <TR>
              <TD>
                <xsl:if test="@NETWORK=''">
                  <xsl:value-of select="@CALL_LETTERS"/>
                </xsl:if>
                <xsl:value-of select="@NETWORK"/>
              </TD>
```

Continued

Listing 5-8 *(continued)*

```
            <TD>
               <xsl:value-of select="@CHANNEL"/>
            </TD>
            <xsl:for-each select="SHOW">
              <TD>
                <B><xsl:value-of select="@NAME"/></B>
      <xsl:if test="@CLOSED_CAPTIONED='Yes'"> (CC) </xsl:if>
                <xsl:value-of select="@DESCRIPTION"/>
              </TD>
            </xsl:for-each>
          </TR>
        </xsl:for-each>
      </TABLE>

      <HR></HR>
      Copyright 2003
      <A HREF="http://www.elharo.com">
       Elliotte Rusty Harold
      </A>
      <BR />
      <A HREF="mailto:elharo@metalab.unc.edu">
       elharo@metalab.unc.edu
      </A>

    </BODY>
  </HTML>
</xsl:template>

</xsl:stylesheet>
```

The hard part is lining up the shows by time, so that shows that start at 7:00 begin in the same column, shows that start at 7:30 begin in the same column, and so forth. Once again, we're heading into the realm of XSLT rocket science, but it is doable. The trick is that you need to divide the main body of the table into the smallest unit of time you're likely to encounter. In this case, five minutes works well. Then, in each row, you need to calculate the start time to the nearest five minutes. This tells you what column the show begins in. Then you need to divide the length of the show by five minutes to get the number of cells the show spans. This will become the value of the COLSPAN attribute. The operation is made trickier because neither the START_TIME attribute nor the LENGTH attribute contains a pure number. You need to do some string manipulation to extract the numbers before you can operate on them. However, arithmetic and string manipulation at this level is within the bounds of what XSLT can do, as Listing 5-9 and Figure 5-10 prove.

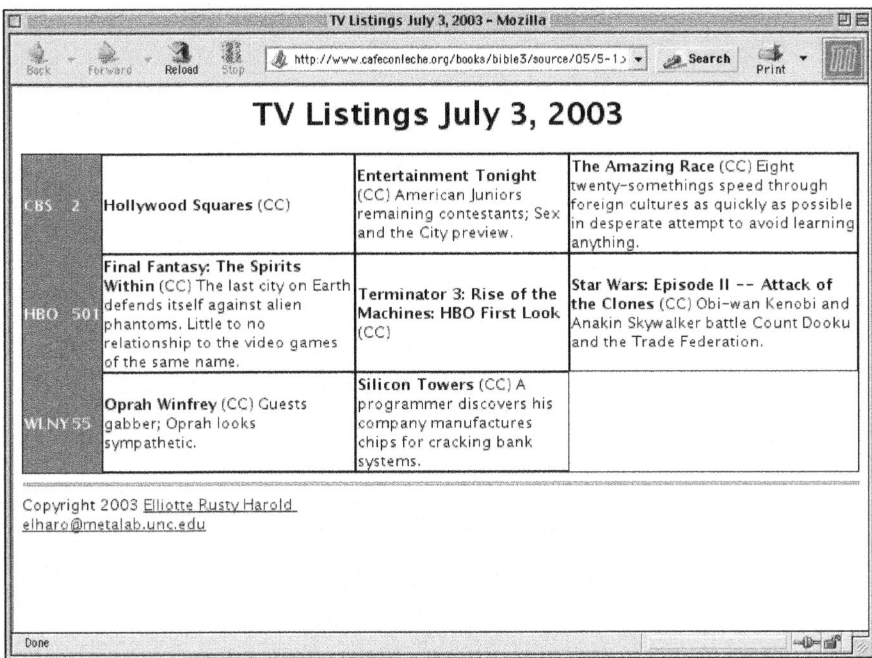

Figure 5-9: Television listings sorted by start time

Listing 5-9: An XSL Style Sheet that Dynamically Calculates Column Spans for the Table

```
<?xml version="1.0"?>
<xsl:stylesheet version="1.0"
  xmlns:xsl="http://www.w3.org/1999/XSL/Transform">

  <!-- count in 5 minute increments
       with 6:00 A.M. as the zero point. Thus this sets
       the start-time to 7:00 PM and the end time to
       9:00 PM. However, these parameters can be
       adjusted when the stylesheet is invoked. -->
  <xsl:param name="start"  select="156"/>
  <xsl:param name="finish" select="180"/>

  <xsl:template match="SCHEDULE">
    <HTML>
      <HEAD>
        <TITLE>
          TV Listings <xsl:value-of select="@DATE"/>
        </TITLE>
```

Continued

Listing 5-9 *(continued)*

```
</HEAD>
<BODY>
  <H1 STYLE="text-align: center">
     TV Listings <xsl:value-of select="@DATE"/>
  </H1>

  <TABLE CELLSPACING="0" RULES="all" FRAME="box">
    <COLGROUP>
       <COL WIDTH="20"/>
       <COL WIDTH="10"/>
    </COLGROUP>
    <COLGROUP SPAN="{$finish - $start}" WIDTH="20"/>
    <THEAD STYLE="text-align: center">
      <TR>
        <TD />
        <TD />
        <xsl:call-template name="fillTableHead"/>
      </TR>
    </THEAD>
    <TBODY>
    <xsl:for-each select="STATION">
      <xsl:sort select="@CHANNEL" data-type="number"/>
      <TR>
        <TD STYLE="color: white; background-color: grey;
                   font-weight: bold">
          <xsl:if test="@NETWORK=''">
            <xsl:value-of select="@CALL_LETTERS"/>
          </xsl:if>
          <xsl:value-of select="@NETWORK"/>
        </TD>
        <TD STYLE="color: white; background-color: grey;
                   font-weight: bold">
           <xsl:value-of select="@CHANNEL"/>
        </TD>

        <xsl:for-each select="SHOW">
          <xsl:variable name="showstart">
            <xsl:call-template name="getLocalTime">
              <xsl:with-param name="input"
                              select="@START_TIME"/>
            </xsl:call-template>
          </xsl:variable>
          <xsl:variable name="showlength" select=
        "number(substring-before(@LENGTH, ' ')) div 5"/>
          <xsl:variable name="realshowlength">
            <xsl:call-template name="getRealShowLength">
              <xsl:with-param name="showstart"
                              select="$showstart"/>
              <xsl:with-param name="showlength"
                              select="$showlength"/>
            </xsl:call-template>
```

```
            </xsl:variable>

            <TD COLSPAN="{$realshowlength}"  valign="top">
              <B><xsl:value-of select="@NAME"/></B>
              <xsl:if test="@CLOSED_CAPTIONED='Yes'">
                (CC)
              </xsl:if>
              <xsl:value-of select="@DESCRIPTION"/>
            </TD>
          </xsl:for-each>

        </TR>
      </xsl:for-each>
      </TBODY>
    </TABLE>

    <HR/>
    Copyright 2003
    <A HREF="http://www.elharo.com">
     Elliotte Rusty Harold
    </A>
    <BR/>
    <A HREF="mailto:elharo@metalab.unc.edu">
     elharo@metalab.unc.edu
    </A>

  </BODY>
</HTML>
</xsl:template>

<xsl:template name="getLocalTime">
   <!-- returns number of five-minute increments
        since 6:00 A.M. -->
  <xsl:param name="input"/> <!-- in form 19:00-0500 -->

  <xsl:variable name="time24"
                select="substring-before($input, '-')"/>
  <xsl:variable name="hour"
                select="substring-before($time24, ':')"/>
  <xsl:variable name="minutes"
                select="substring-after($time24, ':')"/>

  <xsl:value-of
              select="(($hour - 6)*12) + ($minutes div 5)"/>

</xsl:template>

<xsl:template name="getRealShowLength">
  <xsl:param name="showstart"/>
  <xsl:param name="showlength"/>

  <xsl:choose>
```

Continued

Listing 5-9 *(continued)*

```
        <xsl:when test="$showstart &lt; $start">
          <xsl:value-of
            select="$showlength - ($start - $showstart)"/>
        </xsl:when>
        <xsl:otherwise>
          <xsl:value-of select="$showlength"/>
        </xsl:otherwise>
      </xsl:choose>
    </xsl:template>

    <!-- Note use of recursion -->
    <xsl:template name="fillTableHead">
      <xsl:param name="time" select="$start"/>
      <TD COLSPAN="6">
        <xsl:call-template name="formatTime">
          <xsl:with-param name="time" select="$time"/>
        </xsl:call-template>
      </TD>
      <xsl:if test="$time &lt; $finish - 6">
        <xsl:call-template name="fillTableHead">
          <xsl:with-param name="time" select="$time + 6"/>
        </xsl:call-template>
      </xsl:if>
    </xsl:template>

    <xsl:template name="formatTime">
      <xsl:param name="time"/>
      <xsl:variable name="minutes" select="($time * 5) mod 60"/>
      <xsl:variable name="hours"
                    select="(floor(($time div 12) + 6)) mod 12"/>
      <xsl:value-of select="$hours"/>
      <xsl:value-of select="':'"/>
      <xsl:value-of select="format-number($minutes, '00')"/>
    <xsl:if test="$time &lt; 72 or $time &gt;= 216"> AM</xsl:if>
   <xsl:if test="$time &gt;= 72 and $time &lt; 216"> PM</xsl:if>
    </xsl:template>

  </xsl:stylesheet>
```

If it's not immediately obvious to you how this style sheet works, don't worry too much. It definitely uses some of the more advanced features of XSLT, such as named templates, variables, parameters, attribute value templates, functions, and recursion. I'll come back to XSLT and explain all these techniques in Chapter 15. For now, just know that XSLT can perform quite complicated operations on the data in an XML document before ultimately formatting it for display to the end user. It is, in fact, a Turing-complete programming language.

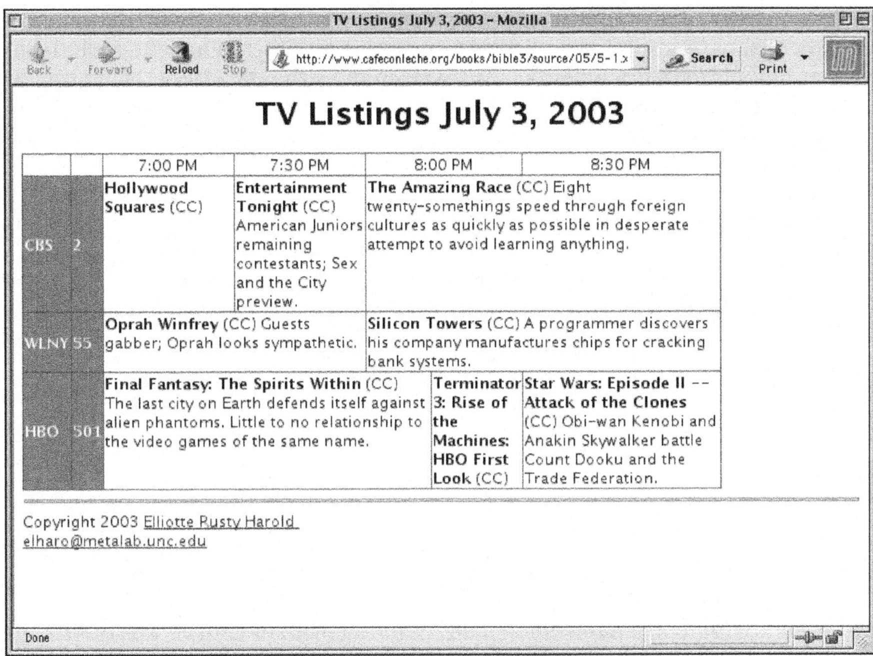

Figure 5-10: Television listings arranged by duration

CSS or XSL?

CSS and XSL overlap to some extent. XSL is certainly more powerful than CSS. This chapter only touched on the basics of XSL. However, XSL's power is matched by its complexity. XSL is definitely harder to learn and use than CSS. So the question is, "When should you use CSS and when should you use XSL?"

CSS is more broadly supported than XSL. Netscape 4 and Internet Explorer 4 support parts of CSS Level 1 for HTML elements (although there are many annoying differences between the two). Furthermore, most of CSS Level 1 and some of CSS Level 2 is supported by Internet Explorer 5.0 and later, Opera 4.0 and later, Netscape 6.0 and later, Safari, Konqueror, and Mozilla. Thus, choosing CSS gives you more compatibility with a broader range of browsers.

However, XSL is definitely more powerful than CSS. CSS only allows you to apply formatting to element content. It does not allow you to change or reorder that content, choose different formatting for elements based on their contents or attributes, or add boilerplate text like a signature block. XSL is far more appropriate when the XML documents contain only the minimum of data and none of the HTML frou-frou that surrounds the data.

XSL lets you separate the crucial data from everything else on the page, such as mastheads, navigation bars, and signatures. With CSS, you have to include all these pieces in your data documents. XML+XSL enables the data documents to live separately from the web page documents. This makes XML+XSL documents more maintainable and easier to work with.

In the long run, XSL should become the preferred choice for data-intensive applications. CSS is more suitable for simple web pages like the ones grandparents write to post pictures of their grandchildren. But for these uses, HTML alone is sufficient. If you've really hit the wall with HTML, XML+CSS doesn't take you much further before you run into another wall. XML+XSL, by contrast, takes you far past the walls of HTML. You still need CSS to work with legacy browsers, but in the long term, XSL is the way to go.

Summary

In this chapter, you saw examples of creating an XML document from scratch. Specifically, you learned the following:

- An attribute is a name-value pair included in an element's start-tag.
- Attributes typically hold meta-information about the element rather than the element's data.
- Attributes are less convenient to work with than the contents of an element.
- Attributes work well for very simple information that's unlikely to change its form as the document evolves. In particular, style and linking information work well as attributes. Structured and ordered information is often better represented as elements.
- Empty-element tags are syntax sugar for elements with no content.
- XSL is a powerful style language that enables you to transform documents from one XML vocabulary to other XML vocabularies or to non-XML vocabularies such as HTML or tab-delimited text.

The next chapter discusses the exact rules to which well-formed XML documents must adhere. It also explores some additional means of embedding information in XML documents, including comments and processing instructions.

✦ ✦ ✦

CHAPTER 6

Well-formedness

In This Chapter

XML documents

Well-formedness rules

Text in XML

Elements and tags

Attributes

Entity references

CDATA sections

Comments

Unicode

XML 1.1

Well-formed HTML

HTML 4.0 has 91 different elements. Most of these elements have 12 or more possible attributes for several thousand different possible variations. Because XML is more powerful than HTML, you might think that you need to learn even more elements, but you don't. XML gets its power through simplicity and extensibility, not through a plethora of elements.

In fact, XML predefines no elements at all. Instead, XML allows you to define your own elements, as needed. However, these elements and the documents built from them are not completely arbitrary. They have to follow a specific set of rules elaborated in this chapter. A *well-formed* document is one that follows these rules. Well-formedness is the minimum criterion necessary for XML processors and browsers to read files. This chapter examines the rules for well-formed documents. It explores the different parts of an XML document — tags, text, attributes, elements, and so on — and discusses the primary rules each part must follow. Particular attention is paid to how XML differs from HTML. Along the way I introduce several new XML constructs including comments, processing instructions, entity references, and CDATA sections. This chapter isn't an exhaustive discussion of well-formedness rules. Some of the rules I present must be adjusted slightly for documents that have a document type definition (DTD), and there are additional well-formedness rules that define the relationship between the document and its DTD, but these will be explored in later chapters.

Well-formedness Rules

Although XML allows you to invent as many different elements and attributes as you need, these elements and attributes, as well as their contents and the documents that contain them, must all follow certain rules in order to be *well-formed.* If a document is not well-formed, any attempts to read it or render it will fail.

The XML specification strictly prohibits XML parsers from trying to fix and understand malformed documents. All a parser can do is signal the error. It is not allowed to fix the error. It cannot make a best-faith effort to render what the author intended. It cannot ignore the offending malformed markup. All it can do is report the error and exit.

The objective here is to avoid the bug-for-bug compatibility wars that have hindered HTML and that have made writing HTML parsers and renderers so difficult. Because web browsers allow malformed HTML, web page designers don't make the extra effort to ensure that their HTML is correct. In fact, they even rely on bugs in individual browsers to achieve special effects. To properly display the huge installed base of HTML pages, every new web browser must support every nuance, every quirk of all the browsers that have come before. The marketplace would ignore any browser that strictly adhered to the HTML standard. It is to avoid this sorry state that XML processors are explicitly required to only accept well-formed XML.

To be well-formed, an XML document must follow more than 100 different rules. However, most of these rules simply forbid things that you're not very likely to do anyway if you follow the examples given in this book. For example, one rule is that the name of the element must immediately follow the < of the element's start-tag. For example, `<TRIANGLE>` is a legal start-tag but `< TRIANGLE>` isn't. On the other hand, the same rule says that it is OK to have extra space before the tag's closing angle bracket. That is, both `<TRIANGLE>` and `<TRIANGLE >` are well-formed start-tags. Another rule says that element names must have at least one character; that is, `<>` is not a legal start-tag and `</>` is not a legal end-tag. Chances are it never would have occurred to you to create an element with a zero-length name, but computers are dumber than human beings and need to have constraints like this spelled out for them. XML's well-formedness rules are designed to be understood by software rather than human beings, so quite a few of them are a little technical and won't present much of a problem in practice. The only source for the complete list of rules is the XML specification itself. However, if you follow the rules given here, and check your work with an XML parser before distributing them, your documents should be fine.

XML Documents

An XML document is made up of text. It is a sequence of characters with a fixed length that adheres to certain constraints. It may or may not be a file. For instance, an XML document could be any of the following:

✦ A CLOB field in an Oracle database

✦ The result of a query against a database that combines several records from different tables

✦ A data structure created in memory by a Java program

✦ A data stream created on the fly by a CGI program written in Perl

✦ Some combination of several different files, each of which is embedded in another

✦ One part of a larger file containing several XML documents

However, nothing essential is lost if you think of an XML document as a file, as long as you keep in the back of your mind that it might not really be a file on a hard drive.

XML documents are made up of storage units called *entities*. Each entity contains a well-formed document fragment. This is a piece of text that meets all of XML's well-formedness rules except for the one about there being a single root element. The various entities that make up a document will be stored in different files, databases, and other locations. The parser combines them all to form the complete document.

The XML declaration

In this and the next several chapters, I treat only simple XML documents that are made up of a single entity, the document itself. Such documents can be understood completely on their own without reading any other files. In other words, they stand alone. Such a document normally contains a `standalone` pseudo-attribute in its XML declaration with the value `yes`, similar to this one:

```
<?xml version="1.0" standalone="yes"?>
```

I call this a *pseudo-attribute* because technically only elements can have attributes. The XML declaration is not an element. Therefore, `standalone` is not an attribute even if it looks like one.

External entities and entity references can be used to combine multiple files and other data sources to create a single XML document. These documents cannot be parsed without reference to other files. Therefore, they normally have a `standalone` pseudo-attribute with the value `no`:

```
<?xml version="1.0" standalone="no"?>
```

If a document does not have an XML declaration, or if a document has an XML declaration but that XML declaration does not have a `standalone` pseudo-attribute, the value `no` is assumed. That is, the document is assumed incapable of standing on its own, and the parser will prepare itself to read external pieces as necessary. If the document can, in fact, stand on its own, nothing is lost by the parser being ready to read an extra piece.

XML documents do not have to include XML declarations, although they generally should. If an XML document does include an XML declaration, this declaration must be the first thing in the file (except possibly for an invisible Unicode byte order mark). XML processors determine which character set is being used (ASCII compatible, EBCDIC compatible, big-endian UTF-16, little-endian UTF-16) by reading the first several bytes of a file and comparing those bytes against various encodings of the string `<?xml` . Nothing should come before this, including white space. For example, the following line is not an acceptable way to start an XML file because of the extra spaces at the front of the line:

```
   <?xml version="1.0" standalone="yes"?>
```

Single root element

An XML document has a root element that completely contains all other elements of the document. This is also sometimes called the *document element*, although this element does not have to have the name `document` or `root`. Just like any other element, root elements are delimited by a start-tag and an end-tag. For example, consider Listing 6-1.

Listing 6-1: greeting.xml

```
<?xml version="1.0"?>
<GREETING>
Hello XML!
</GREETING>
```

In this document, the root element is `GREETING`. The XML declaration is not an element. Therefore, it does not have to be included inside the root element. Similarly, other nonelement data in an XML document, such as an `xml-stylesheet` processing instruction, a `DOCTYPE` declaration, or comments, do not have to be inside the root element. But all other elements (other than the root itself) and all raw character data must be contained in the root element.

Text in XML

An XML document is made up of text. Text is made up of characters. A character is a letter, a digit, a punctuation mark, a space or tab, or some similar thing. XML uses the Unicode character set, which not only includes the usual letters and symbols from English and other Western European alphabets, but also the Cyrillic, Greek, Hebrew, Arabic, and Devanagari alphabets, the Han ideographs for Chinese and Japanese, the Korean Hangul syllabary, and many more writing systems.

A document's text is divided into character data and markup. To a first approximation, markup describes a document's logical structure, while character data is the basic information of the document. For example, in Listing 6-1, `<?xml version="1.0"?>`, `<GREETING>`, and `</GREETING>` are markup. `Hello XML!`, along with its surrounding white space, is the character data. A big advantage of XML over other formats is that it clearly separates the actual data of a document from its markup.

To be more precise, markup includes all tags, processing instructions, DTDs, entity references, character references, comments, CDATA section delimiters, and the XML declaration. Everything else is character data. However, this is tricky because when a document is processed, some of the markup turns into character data. For example, the markup `>` is turned into the greater than sign character (>). The character data that's left after the document is processed, and after all markup that refers to character data has been replaced by the actual character data, is called *parsed character data*, or PCDATA for short.

Elements and Tags

An XML document is a singly rooted hierarchical structure of elements. Each element is delimited by a start-tag and an end-tag or is represented by a single empty-element tag. An XML tag has the same form as an HTML tag; that is, start-tags begin with a `<` followed by the name of the element the tag starts and end with the first `>` after the opening `<` (for example, `<GREETING>`). End-tags begin with a `</` followed by the name of the element the tag finishes and are terminated by a `>` (for example, `</GREETING>`). Empty-element tags begin with a `<` followed by the name of the element and are terminated with a `/>` (for example, `<GREETING/>`).

Element names

Every element has a name made up of one or more characters. This is the name included in the element's start- and end-tags. Element names begin with a letter, such as `y` or `A`, or an underscore `_`. Subsequent characters in the name may include letters, digits, underscores, hyphens, and periods. They cannot include white space. (The underscore often substitutes for white space.) Both lower- and uppercase letters may be used in XML names, and the difference between them is significant. In this book, I mostly follow the convention of making my names uppercase, mainly because this makes them stand out better in the text. However, when I'm using a tag set that was developed by others, it is necessary to adopt their case conventions. For example, the following are legal XML start-tags with legal XML names:

```
<HELP>
<Book>
<volume>
<heading1>
<section.paragraph>
<Mary_Smith>
<_8ball>
```

Colons are also technically legal in tag names. However, these are reserved for use with namespaces. Namespaces allow you to mix and match tag sets that may use the same tag names. Namespaces are discussed in Chapter 11. Until then, you should not use colons in your tag names.

The following are not legal start-tags because they don't contain legal XML names:

```
<Book%7>
<volume control>
<1heading>
<Mary Smith>
<.employee.salary>
```

The rules for element names actually apply to names of many other things as well. The same rules are used for attribute names, ID attribute values, entity names, and a number of other constructs that you encounter over the next several chapters.

Every start-tag must have a corresponding end-tag

Web browsers are relatively forgiving if you forget to close an HTML tag. For example, if you include a `<B>` tag in your document but no corresponding `</B>` tag, the part of the document that follows the `<B>` tag will be made bold. However, the document will still be displayed.

XML is not so forgiving. Every start-tag must be closed with the corresponding end-tag. If a document fails to close an element with the right end-tag, the parser reports an error message and the browser does not display any of the document's content after the error is detected (and possibly not before it either).

End-tags have the same name as the corresponding start-tag but are prefixed with a / after the initial angle bracket. For example, if the start-tag is <FOO>, the end-tag is </FOO>. These are the end-tags for the previous set of legal start-tags.

```
</HELP>
</Book>
</volume>
</heading1>
</section.paragraph>
</Mary_Smith>
</_8ball>
```

XML names are case-sensitive. This is different from HTML in which <P> and <p> are the same tag, and a </p> can close a <P> tag. The following are *not* end-tags for the set of legal start-tags being discussed because the case does not match that of the opening tag.

```
</help>
</book>
</Volume>
```

```
</HEADING1>
</Section.Paragraph>
</MARY_SMITH>
</_8BALL>
```

Empty-element tags

Many HTML elements do not have closing tags. For example, there are no </LI>, </IMG>, </HR>, or </BR> tags in HTML. Some page authors do include </LI> tags after their list items, and some HTML tools also use </LI>. However, the HTML 4.0 standard specifically denies that this is required. Like all unrecognized tags in HTML, the presence of an unnecessary </LI> has no effect on the rendered output.

This is *not* the case in XML. The whole point of XML is to enable new elements and their corresponding tags to be discovered as a document is parsed. Thus, unrecognized tags should not be ignored. Furthermore, an XML processor must be capable of determining on the fly whether a tag it has never seen before does or does not have an end-tag.

XML distinguishes between normal start-tags that must have corresponding end-tags and *empty-element tags*, which are tags that do not have end-tags. Empty-element tags are closed with a slash and a closing angle bracket (/>); for example, <BR/> or <HR/>. From the perspective of XML, these are the same as the equivalent syntax using both start- and end-tags with nothing in between them; for example,
</BR> and <HR></HR>.

However, empty-element tags can only be used when the element is truly empty, not when the end-tag is simply omitted. For example, in HTML you might write an unordered list like this:

```
<UL>
<LI>I've a Feeling We're Not in Kansas Anymore
<LI>Buddies
<LI>Everybody Loves You
</UL>
```

In XML, you cannot simply replace the <LI> tags with <LI/> because the elements are not truly empty. Instead they contain text. In normal HTML the closing </LI> tag is omitted by the editor and implied by the parser. This is not the same thing as the element itself being empty. The first LI element in this example contains the content I've a Feeling We're Not in Kansas Anymore. In XML, you must close these tags like this:

```
<UL>
<LI>I've a Feeling We're Not in Kansas Anymore</LI>
<LI>Buddies</LI>
<LI>Everybody Loves You</LI>
</UL>
```

On the other hand, a BR or HR or IMG element really is empty. It doesn't contain any text or child elements. Thus, in XML, you have two choices for these elements. You can either write them with a start- and an end-tag in which the end-tag immediately follows the start-tag—for example, <HR></HR>—or you can write them with an empty-element tag, as in <HR/>.

Note

Current web browsers deal inconsistently with empty-element tags. For example, some browsers will insert a line break when they see an <HR/> tag and some won't. Furthermore, the problem may arise even without empty-element tags. Some browsers insert two horizontal lines when they see <HR></HR>, and some insert one horizontal line. The most generally compatible scheme is to use an extra attribute before the closing />. The CLASS attribute is often a good choice; for example, <HR CLASS="empty"/>.

Elements may nest but may not overlap

Elements may contain (and indeed often do contain) other elements. However, elements may not overlap. Practically, this means that if an element contains a start-tag for an element, it must also contain the corresponding end-tag. Conversely, an element may not contain an end-tag without its matching start-tag. For example, this is legal XML:

```
<H1><CITE>What the Butler Saw</CITE></H1>
```

However, the following is not legal XML because the closing </CITE> tag comes after the closing </H1> tag:

```
<H1><CITE>What the Butler Saw</H1></CITE>
```

Most HTML browsers can handle this case with ease. However, XML browsers are required to report an error for this construct.

Empty-element tags may appear anywhere, of course. For example,

```
<PLAYWRIGHTS>Oscar Wilde<HR/>Joe Orton</PLAYWRIGHTS>
```

This implies that for all nonroot elements, there is exactly one other element that contains the element, but that does not contain any other element containing the element. This immediate container is called the *parent* of the element. The element is referred to as a *child* of the parent element. Thus, each nonroot element always has exactly one parent, but a single element may have an indefinite number of children or no children at all.

Consider Listing 6-2. The root element is the PLAYS element. This contains two PLAY children. Each PLAY element contains three child elements: TITLE, AUTHOR, and YEAR. Each of these contains character data.

Listing 6-2: Parents and Children

```
<?xml version="1.0" standalone="yes"?>
<PLAYS>
  <PLAY>
    <TITLE>What the Butler Saw</TITLE>
    <AUTHOR>Joe Orton</AUTHOR>
    <YEAR>1969</YEAR>
  </PLAY>
  <PLAY>
    <TITLE>The Ideal Husband</TITLE>
    <AUTHOR>Oscar Wilde</AUTHOR>
    <YEAR>1895</YEAR>
  </PLAY>
</PLAYS>
```

In programmer terms, this means that XML documents form a tree. Figure 6-1 shows why this structure is called a tree. It starts from the root and gradually grows limbs with leaves on their ends. Trees have a number of nice properties that make them congenial to programmatic traversal, although this doesn't matter so much to you as the author of the document.

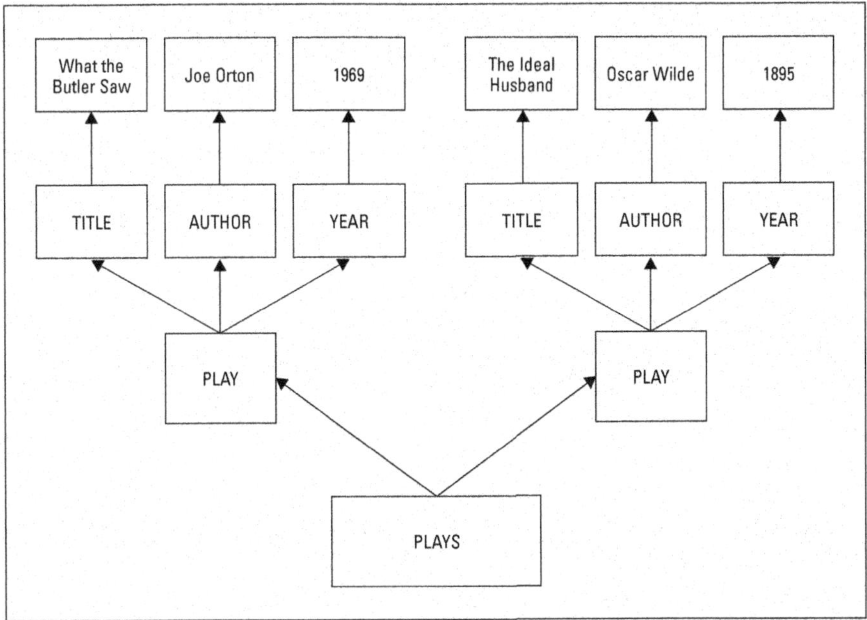

Figure 6-1: Listing 6-2's tree structure

Trees are more commonly drawn from the top down. That is, the root of the tree is shown at the top of the picture rather than the bottom. While this looks less like a real tree, it doesn't affect the topology of the data structure in the least.

Attributes

Elements can have *attributes*. Each attribute of an element is encoded in the start-tag of the element as a name-value pair separated by an equals sign (=) and, optionally, some extra white space. The attribute value is enclosed in either single or double quotes. For example,

```
<GREETING LANGUAGE="English">
  Hello XML!
  <MOVIE SRC = 'WavingHand.mov'/>
</GREETING>
```

Here, the `GREETING` element has a `LANGUAGE` attribute that has the value `English`. The `MOVIE` element has an `SRC` attribute with the value `WavingHand.mov`.

Attribute names

Attribute names are strings that follow the same rules as element names. That is, attribute names must contain one or more characters and the first character must be a letter or the underscore (_). Subsequent characters in the name may include letters, digits, underscores, hyphens, and periods. They may not include white space.

The same element cannot have two attributes with the same name. For example, this is illegal:

```
<RECTANGLE SIDE="8" SIDE="10"/>
```

Attribute names are case-sensitive. The `SIDE` attribute is not the same as the `side` or the `Side` attribute. Therefore, the following is legal:

```
<BOX SIDE="8" side="10" Side="31"/>
```

However, this is extremely confusing, and I strongly urge you not to write markup that depends on case.

Attribute values

Attributes values are strings. Even when the string shows a number, as in the `LENGTH` attribute that follows, that number is the two characters 7 and 2, not the binary number 72.

```
<RULE LENGTH="72"/>
```

If you're writing code to process XML, you'll need to convert the string to a number before performing arithmetic on it.

Unlike attribute names, there are few limits on the content of an attribute value. Attribute values can contain white space, begin with a number, or contain any punctuation characters (except, sometimes, for single and double quotes). The only characters an attribute value cannot contain are the angle brackets < and >, though these can be included using the `<` and `>` entity references (discussed soon).

XML attribute values are delimited by quote marks. Unlike HTML attribute values, XML attribute values *must* be enclosed in quotes whether or not the attribute value includes spaces. For example:

```
<A HREF="http://www.ibiblio.org/">IBiblio</A>
```

Most people choose double quotes. However, you can also use single quotes, which is useful if the attribute value itself contains a double quote. For example:

```
<IMG SRC="sistinechapel.jpg"
     ALT='And God said, "Let there be light,"
          and there was light'/>
```

If the attribute value contains both single and double quotes, the one that's not used to delimit the string must be replaced with the proper entity reference. You can use the entity reference `'` for a single quote (an apostrophe) and `"` for a double quote. I often just replace both, which is always legal. For example:

```
<PARAM NAME="joke" VALUE="The diner said,
   &quot;Waiter, There&apos;s a fly in my soup!&quot;">
```

Predefined attributes

XML assigns special meaning to attributes that begin with `xml:`. Currently three such attributes are defined: `xml:lang`, `xml:space`, and `xml:base`. You should only use these attributes for their intended purposes. The `xml:space` attribute describes how white space is treated in the element. The `xml:lang` attribute describes the language (and, optionally, dialect and country) in which the element is written. The `xml:base` attribute provides the base URL against which relative URLs in the element should be resolved. I'll talk about `xml:space` and `xml:lang` now. `xml:base` is covered in Chapter 17.

xml:space

In HTML, white space is relatively insignificant. Although the difference between one space and no space is significant, the difference between 1 space and 2 spaces, 1 space and a carriage return, or 1 space, 3 carriage returns, and 12 tabs is not important. For text in which white space is significant — computer source code, certain mainframe database reports, or the poetry of e. e. cummings, for example—you can use a PRE element to specify a monospaced font and preservation of white space.

XML, however, preserves white space by default. The XML processor passes all white space characters to the application unchanged. The application usually ignores the extra white space. However, the XML processor can tell the application that certain elements contain significant white space that should be preserved. The page author uses the xml:space attribute to indicate these elements to the application. The value preserve indicates that white space is significant; the value default indicates that it isn't. Listing 6-3 demonstrates.

Listing 6-3: Java Source Code with Significant White Space Encoded in XML

```
<?xml version="1.0"?>
<PROGRAM xml:space="preserve">public class AsciiTable {

  public static void main (String[] args) {

    for (int i = 0; i &lt; 128; i++) {
      System.out.println(i + "   " + (char) i);
    }

  }

}
</PROGRAM>
```

Descendants (child elements and their children, and their children's children, and so on) of an element for which xml:space is defined are assumed to behave similarly to their parent (either preserving or not preserving space), unless they possess an xml:space attribute with a conflicting value.

Note

An XML parser always passes all white space to the application, regardless of whether xml:space's value is default or preserve. With a value of default, however, the application does what it would normally do with extra white space. With a value of preserve, the application treats the extra white space as significant. Significance depends somewhat on the eventual destination of the data. For example, extra white space in Java source code is relevant to a source code editor but not to a compiler.

xml:lang

The `xml:lang` attribute identifies the language in which its element's content is written. Ideally, each of these attribute values should be one of the two-letter language codes defined by the original ISO-639 standard. The complete list of codes can be found on the Web at `http://www.ics.uci.edu/pub/ietf/http/related/iso639.txt`.

For example, consider this sentence from Petronius's *Satyricon* in both Latin and English. A `SENTENCE` element encloses both versions, but the first `SENTENCE` element has an `xml:lang` attribute for Latin, while the second has an `xml:lang` attribute for English.

```
<SENTENCE xml:lang="la">
  Veniebamus in forum deficiente iam die, in quo notavimus
  frequentiam rerum venalium, non quidem pretiosarum sed tamen
  quarum fidem male ambulantem obscuritas temporis
  facillime tegeret.
</SENTENCE>
<SENTENCE xml:lang="en">
  We have come to the marketplace now when the day is failing,
  where we have seen many things for sale, not for the
  valuable goods but rather that the darkness of
  the time may most easily conceal their shoddiness.
</SENTENCE>
```

While an English-speaking reader can easily tell which is the original text and which is the translation, a computer can use the hint provided by the `xml:lang` attribute. This distinction enables a spell checker to determine whether to check a particular element and designate which dictionary to use. Search engines can inspect these language attributes to determine whether to index a page and return matches based on the user's preferences. The language applies to the element and all its content until one of its descendants declares a different language.

Too Many Languages, Not Enough Codes

XML remains a little behind the times in this area. The original ISO-639 standard language codes were formed from two case-insensitive ASCII alphabetic characters. This standard allows no more than 26 × 26, or 676 different codes. Almost 10 times that many different languages are spoken on Earth today (not even counting dead languages such as Etruscan). In practice, the reasonable codes are somewhat fewer than 676 because the language abbreviations should have some relation to the name of the language.

ISO-639, part two, uses three-letter language codes, which should handle all languages spoken on Earth. The XML standard specifically requires two-letter codes, however. On the other hand, because of some very technical details about how the XML specification is written, parsers are not required to enforce this constraint. Unfortunately, some do and some do not, so documents really have to assume that two-letter codes are required.

Country codes

The value of the `xml:lang` attribute may include additional subcode segments, separated from the primary language code by a hyphen. Most often, the first subcode segment is a two-letter country code specified by ISO 3166. You can retrieve the most current list of country codes from `http://www.isi.edu/in-notes/iana/assignments/country-codes`. For example:

```
<P xml:lang="en-US">Put the body in the trunk of the car.</P>
<P xml:lang="en-GB">Put the body in the boot of the car.</P>
```

By convention, language codes are written in lowercase and country codes are written in uppercase. However, this is merely a convention. This is one of the few parts of XML that is case-insensitive, because of its heritage in the case-insensitive ISO standard.

IANA language codes

If no appropriate ISO code is available for the primary language, you can use one of the codes registered with the Internet Assigned Numbers Authority (IANA). You can find the most current list at `http://www.isi.edu/in-notes/iana/assignments/languages`. IANA codes beginning with i-, such as i-navajo, represent new languages not currently included in two-letter form in ISO 639. IANA codes beginning with a two-letter ISO 639 code, such as zh-yue, represent a dialect of the primary language. Thus, zh is the ISO-639 code for Chinese; zh-yue is the IANA code for the Yue dialect of Chinese (more commonly known as Cantonese in English). The criteria for what qualifies as a language and what qualifies as a dialect are not particularly well defined. For instance, Swedish and Norwegian, two different languages, are mutually intelligible; but Cantonese and Mandarin, two different dialects of Chinese, are mutually unintelligible. To be perfectly honest, the best answer is that the people who speak different languages have their own armies and the people who speak different dialects don't.

For example, Listing 6-4 gives the national anthem of Luxembourg in both Letzeburgesh (i-lux) and English (en):

Listing 6-4: The Luxembourg National Anthem in Letzeburgesh and English

```
<?xml version="1.0" encoding="ISO-8859-1"?>
<DOCUMENT>
  <SONG xml:lang="i-lux"
        LYRICIST="Michel Lentz" COMPOSER="J.A. Zinnen">
    <STANZA>
      <VERSE>Wo d'Uelzecht duerch d'Wisen ze't,</VERSE>
      <VERSE>D◇rch d'Fielzen d'Sauer brûcht,</VERSE>
```

```
      <VERSE>Wo' d'Ref lϕnscht d'Musel dofteg ble't,</VERSE>
      <VERSE>Den Himmel Wein ons mûcht:</VERSE>
      <VERSE>Dat ass onst Land, fir dat mer ge'f</VERSE>
      <VERSE>Heinidden alles won,</VERSE>
      <VERSE>Ons Hemeschtsland dat mir so' de'f</VERSE>
      <VERSE>An onsen Hierzer dron.</VERSE>
      <VERSE>Ons Hemeschtsland dat mir so' de'f</VERSE>
      <VERSE>An onsen Hierzer dron.</VERSE>
    </STANZA>
    <STANZA>
      <VERSE>O Du do uewen, dem seng Hand</VERSE>
      <VERSE>Durch d'Welt Natio'ne let,</VERSE>
      <VERSE>Behitt du d'Lûtzeburger Land</VERSE>
      <VERSE>Vum frieme Joch a Led;</VERSE>
      <VERSE>Du hues ons all als Kanner schon</VERSE>
      <VERSE>De freie G—scht jo ginn,</VERSE>
      <VERSE>Loss viru blûnken d'Freihetsonn,</VERSE>
      <VERSE>De' mir so' lϕng gesinn.</VERSE>
      <VERSE>Loss viru blûnken d'Freihetsonn,</VERSE>
      <VERSE>De' mir so' lϕng gesinn.</VERSE>
    </STANZA>
  </SONG>
  <SONG xml:lang="en" TRANSLATOR="Nicholas E. Weydert">
    <STANZA>
      <VERSE>Where slow you see the Alzette flow,</VERSE>
      <VERSE>The Sura play wild pranks,</VERSE>
      <VERSE>Where lovely vineyards amply grow,</VERSE>
      <VERSE>Upon the Moselle's banks,</VERSE>
      <VERSE>There lies the land for which our thanks</VERSE>
      <VERSE>Are owed to God above,</VERSE>
      <VERSE>Our own, our native land which ranks</VERSE>
      <VERSE>Well foremost in our love.</VERSE>
      <VERSE>Our own, our native land which ranks</VERSE>
      <VERSE>Well foremost in our love.</VERSE>
    </STANZA>
    <STANZA>
      <VERSE>Oh Father in Heaven whose powerful hand</VERSE>
      <VERSE>Makes states or lays them low,</VERSE>
      <VERSE>Protect the Luxembourger land</VERSE>
      <VERSE>From foreign yoke and woe.</VERSE>
      <VERSE>God's golden liberty bestow</VERSE>
      <VERSE>On us now as of yore.</VERSE>
      <VERSE>Let Freedom's sun in glory glow</VERSE>
      <VERSE>For now and evermore.</VERSE>
      <VERSE>Let Freedom's sun in glory glow</VERSE>
      <VERSE>For now and evermore.</VERSE>
    </STANZA>
  </SONG>
</DOCUMENT>
```

X-Codes

If neither the ISO nor the IANA has a code for the language you need, which is often the case for many aboriginal languages, you may define new language codes. These *x-codes* must begin with the string `x-` or `X-` to identify them as user-defined, private-use codes, as in the following example:

```
<P xml:lang="x-choctaw">
  Chahta imanumpa ish anumpola hinla ho?
</P>
<P xml:lang="en">Do you speak Choctaw?</P>
```

Entity References

You're probably familiar with a number of entity references from HTML. For example, `©` represents the copyright symbol ©; and `®` stands for the registered trademark symbol ®. XML predefines the five entity references listed in Table 6-1. These predefined entity references are used in XML documents in place of specific characters that would otherwise be interpreted as part of markup. For example, the entity reference `<` stands for the less than sign (<), which would otherwise be interpreted as the beginning of a tag.

Table 6-1
XML Predefined Entity references

Entity Reference	*Character*
`&`	&
`<`	<
`>`	>
`"`	"
`'`	'

Caution: In XML, unlike HTML, entity references must end with a semicolon. `>` is a correct entity reference; `>` is not.

XML assumes that the opening angle bracket always starts a tag, and that the ampersand always starts an entity reference. (This is often true of HTML as well, but most browsers are more forgiving.) For example, consider this line:

```
<H1>A Homage to Ben & Jerry's
    New York Super Fudge Chunk Ice Cream</H1>
```

Web browsers that treat this as HTML will probably display it correctly. However, XML parsers will reject it, and for maximum safety, you should escape the ampersand with `&`, like this:

```
<H1>A Homage to Ben &amp; Jerry's
    New York Super Fudge Chunk Ice Cream</H1>
```

The open angle bracket (<) is similar. Consider this common Java code embedded in HTML:

```
<CODE>     for (int i = 0; i <= args.length; i++ ) { </CODE>
```

Both XML and HTML consider the less than sign in <= to be the start of a tag. The tag continues until the next >. Thus, a web browser treating this fragment as HTML will render this line as

```
        for (int i = 0; i
```

rather than

```
        for (int i = 0; i <= args.length; i++ ) {
```

The `= args.length; i++ ) {` is interpreted as part of an unrecognized tag. Again, an XML parser will reject this line completely because it's malformed.

The less than sign can be included in text in both XML and HTML by writing it as `<`, as in the following example:

```
<CODE>   for (int i = 0; i &lt;= args.length; i++ ) { </CODE>
```

Raw less than signs and ampersands in normal XML text are always interpreted as starting tags and entity references, respectively. (The abnormal text is CDATA sections, described in an upcoming section.) Therefore, less than signs and ampersands that are text rather than markup must always be encoded as `<` and `&`, respectively. Attribute values are text, too, and as you already saw, entity references can be used inside attribute values.

Greater than signs, double quotes, and apostrophes must be encoded when they would otherwise be interpreted as part of markup. However, it's easier just to get in the habit of encoding all of them rather than trying to figure out whether a particular use would or would not be interpreted as markup.

Other than the five entity references already discussed, you can only use an entity reference if you define it in a DTD first. Because you don't know about DTDs yet, if the ampersand character `&` appears anywhere in your document, it must be immediately followed by `amp;`, `lt;`, `gt;`, `apos;`, or `quot;`. All other uses violate well-formedness.

Chapter 10 teaches you how to define new entity references for other characters and longer strings of text using DTDs.

Comments

XML comments are almost exactly like HTML comments. They begin with <!-- and end with --> . All data between the <!-- and --> is ignored by the XML processor. It's as if it weren't there. This can be used to make notes to yourself or your coauthors, or to temporarily comment out sections of the document that aren't ready, as Listing 6-5 demonstrates.

Listing 6-5: An XML Document That Contains a Comment

```
<?xml version="1.0"?>
<!-- This is Listing 6-5 from The XML Bible -->
<GREETING>
Hello XML!
<!--Goodbye XML-->
</GREETING>
```

Because comments aren't elements, they can be placed before or after the root element. However, comments cannot come before the XML declaration, which must be the very first thing in the document. For example, this is not a well-formed XML document:

```
<!-- This is Listing 6-5 from The XML Bible -->
<?xml version="1.0"?>
<GREETING>
Hello XML!
<!--Goodbye XML-->
</GREETING>
```

Comments cannot be placed inside a tag. This document is also illegal:

```
<?xml version="1.0"?>
<GREETING>
Hello XML!
</GREETING <!--Goodbye--> >
```

However, comments may surround and hide tags. In Listing 6-6, the <ANTIGREETING> tag and all its children are commented out. They are not shown when the document is rendered. It's as if they don't exist.

Listing 6-6: A Comment That Comments Out an Element

```
<?xml version="1.0"?>
<DOCUMENT>
  <GREETING>
    Hello XML!
  </GREETING>
 <!--
  <ANTIGREETING>
    Goodbye XML!
  </ANTIGREETING>
 -->
</DOCUMENT>
```

Because comments effectively delete sections of text, you must take care to ensure that the remaining text is still a well-formed XML document. For example, be careful not to comment out essential tags, as in this malformed document:

```
<?xml version="1.0"?>
<GREETING>
Hello XML!
<!--
</GREETING>
-->
```

Once the commented text is removed, what remains is as follows:

```
<?xml version="1.0"?>
<GREETING>
Hello XML!
```

Because the `<GREETING>` tag is no longer matched by a closing `</GREETING>` tag, this is no longer a well-formed XML document.

There is one final constraint on comments. The two-hyphen string `--` cannot occur inside a comment. For example, this is an illegal comment:

```
<!-- The red door--that is, the second one--was left open -->
```

This means, among other things, that you cannot nest comments like this:

```
<?xml version="1.0"?>
<DOCUMENT>
  <GREETING>
    Hello XML!
  </GREETING>
```

```
  <!--
   <ANTIGREETING>
     <!--Goodbye XML!-->
   </ANTIGREETING>
  -->
</DOCUMENT>
```

It also means that you might run into trouble if you're commenting out a lot of C, Java, or JavaScript source code that's full of expressions such as `i--` or `numberLeft--`. Generally, it's not too hard to work around this problem once you recognize it.

Processing Instructions

Processing instructions are like comments that are intended for computer programs reading the document rather than people reading the document. However, XML parsers are required to pass along the contents of processing instructions to the application on whose behalf they're parsing, unlike comments that a parser is allowed to silently discard. However, the application that receives the information is free to ignore any processing instruction it doesn't understand.

Processing instructions begin with `<?` and end with `?>`. The starting `<?` is followed by an XML name called the *target,* which identifies the program that the instruction is intended for, followed by data for that program. For example, you saw this processing instruction in the last chapter:

```
<?xml-stylesheet type="text/xml" href="5-2.xsl"?>
```

The target of this processing instruction is `xml-stylesheet`. This is a standard name that means the data in this processing instruction is intended for any web browser that can apply a style sheet to the document. `type="text/xml" href="5-2.xsl"` is the processing instruction data that will be passed to the application reading the document. If that application happens to be a web browser that understands XSLT, it will apply the style sheet 5-2.xsl to the document and render the result. If that application is anything other than a web browser, it will simply ignore the processing instruction.

Note Appearances to the contrary notwithstanding, the XML declaration is technically not a processing instruction. The difference is academic unless you're writing a program to read an XML document using an XML parser. In that case, the parser's API will provide different methods to get the contents of processing instructions and the contents of the XML declaration.

`xml-stylesheet` processing instructions are always placed in the document's prolog between the XML declaration and the root element start-tag. Other processing instructions may also be placed in the prolog, or at almost any other convenient location in the XML document, either before, after, or inside the root element. For example, PHP processing instructions generally appear wherever you want the PHP processor to place its output. The only place a processing instruction cannot appear is inside a tag or before the XML declaration.

The target of a processing instruction may be the name of the program it is intended for, or it may be a generic identifier such as `xml-stylesheet` that many different programs recognize. Target names that begin with the three letters `xml` (or `XML`, `Xml`, `xMl`, or any other variation) are reserved for use by the World Wide Web Consortium. However, you're free to use any other convenient name for processing instruction targets. Different applications support different processing instructions. Most applications simply ignore any processing instruction whose target they don't recognize.

The `xml-stylesheet` processing instruction uses a very common format for processing instructions in which the data is divided into pseudo-attributes; that is, the data is passed as name-value pairs, and the values are delimited by quotes. However, as with the XML declaration, these are not true attributes because a processing instruction is not a tag. Furthermore, this format is optional. Some processing instructions will use this style; others won't. The only limit on the content of processing instruction data is that it cannot contain the two-character sequence `?>` that signals the end of a processing instruction. Otherwise, it's free to contain any legal character that may appear in XML documents. For example, this is a legal processing instruction:

```
<?php

echo "Abercrombie & Fitch: <<Clothes for White People>>";
?>
```

In this example, the target is `php`. The rest of the processing instruction is data and contains a lot of malformed text that would otherwise be illegal in an XML document. Some programs might read this, recognize the `php` target, execute the little program, and copy the text into the page. Other programs that don't recognize the `php` target will simply ignore it.

CDATA Sections

Suppose your document contains one or more large blocks of text that have a lot of <, >, &, or " characters but no markup. This would be true for a Java or HTML tutorial, for example. It would be inconvenient to have to replace each instance of one of these characters with the equivalent entity reference. Instead, you can include the block of text in a *CDATA section*.

CDATA sections begin with <![CDATA[and end with]]>, as in the following example:

```
<![CDATA[
System.out.print("<");
if (x <= args.length && y > z) {
  System.out.println(args[x - y]);
}
System.out.println(">");
]]>
```

The only text that's not allowed within a CDATA section is the closing CDATA delimiter]]>. Comments may appear in CDATA sections but do not act as comments. That is, both the comment tags and all the text they contain will be displayed.

Most of the time, anything inside a pair of <> angle brackets is markup, and anything that's not is character data. However, in CDATA sections, all text is pure character data. Anything that looks like a tag or an entity reference is really just the text of the tag or the entity reference. The XML processor does not try to interpret it in any way. CDATA sections are used when you want all text to be interpreted as pure character data rather than as markup.

CDATA sections are extremely useful if you're trying to write about HTML or XML in XML. For example, this book contains many small blocks of XML code. The word processor I'm using doesn't care about that. But if I were to convert this book to XML, I'd have to painstakingly replace all the less than signs with < and all the ampersands with &, like this:

```
&lt;?xml version="1.0" standalone="yes"?&gt;
&lt;GREETING&gt;
Hello XML!
&lt;/GREETING&gt;
```

To avoid having to do this, I can instead use a CDATA section to indicate that a block of text is to be presented as is with no translation, as in the following example:

```
<![CDATA[<?xml version="1.0" standalone="yes"?>
<GREETING>
Hello XML!
</GREETING>]]>
```

Note Because the CDATA section end delimiter]]> may not appear in a CDATA section, CDATA sections cannot nest. This makes it relatively difficult to write about CDATA sections in XML. If you need to do this, you just have to bite the bullet and use the < and & escapes.

CDATA sections aren't needed that often, but when they are needed, they're needed badly.

Do not use CDATA sections to hide malformed markup. This is commonly done when embedding HTML in XML, especially in RSS. This practice creates very fragile systems that cannot be processed with off-the-shelf XML tools. CDATA sections are for text, not markup. If you need to embed HTML in XML, make it well formed first, as discussed in the final section of this chapter.

Unicode

All XML documents are read in Unicode. *Unicode* is a platform-independent character set that includes almost all characters from most of the world's living languages and not a few dead ones, including English, German, Russian, Greek, Japanese, Chinese, Arabic, Hebrew, Hindi, French, Cherokee, Thai, Burmese, Cambodian, Korean, Turkish, Danish, Dutch, Gaelic, and many, many more. Unicode has room for over 1 million different characters. In the current version, 4.0, a few more than 90,000 different Unicode characters are actually defined.

Unicode assigns each character a unique integer called its *code point*. For example, the capital letter A is mapped to 65. The Greek letter π is mapped to the number 960. The Cyrillic character Ч is mapped to 1206. The musical symbol 𝄠 is mapped to the number 119,072.

Almost all of these characters are legal in well-formed XML documents. In fact, it's easier to list the characters that aren't allowed than those that are. In brief, the illegal characters are as follows:

✦ The C0 controls with code points from 0 through 31, except for the carriage return, linefeed, and tab. Illegal characters include the bell, form feed, vertical tab, and null.

✦ The surrogate characters with code points from 55,296 to 57,343. The UTF-16 encoding pairs these up to represent characters from outside the Basic Multilingual Plane (the first 65,535 characters of Unicode). However, they are not themselves characters.

Including any of these characters in an XML document makes it malformed. This most commonly happens when legacy text data from a database or other source is blindly copied into an XML document without first scanning it for illegal characters. Null and form feed are especially common problems in practice.

All other Unicode characters are allowed in XML documents, even the private-use characters and characters that haven't been defined yet. Not all characters can appear as part of markup. For instance, ∞ and © are not allowed to be part of element and attribute names. However, they are allowed in PCDATA and attribute values. Characters with special meaning to XML, such as < and &, can also be included in PCDATA and attribute values, provided they are properly escaped first with an entity or character reference.

Character encodings

Unicode code points are abstract numbers. They are not ints, shorts, floats, longs, or any other particular data type, though they might be encoded that way on a particular system. Before these abstract integers can be used in a computer, they have to be encoded as bytes. There's more than one way to do this. For example, a naïve encoding might simply represent each code point as a 4-byte big endian int. Another might represent each code point as a 4-byte little endian int. And still another might represent the numbers as either big endian or little endian ints, but add an initial magic number to the file to determine which is being used.

Several different encodings of Unicode are in general use today. The two most common and important are UTF-8 and UTF-16. These are the only ones all XML parsers support. Both are variable-width encodings that use different numbers of bytes for different character ranges.

UTF-8 only uses a single byte for the most common characters, that is the ASCII characters 0 to 127, at the expense of having to use 3 bytes for the less common characters, particularly the Hangul syllables and Han ideographs. It uses 2 bytes for most other characters. If you're writing in English, UTF-8 can reduce file sizes by as much as 50 percent compared to UTF-16. On the other hand, if you're writing mostly in Chinese, Korean, or Japanese, UTF-8 can *increase* your file size by as much as 50 percent—so use it with caution. UTF-8 has mostly no effect on non-Roman, non-CJK scripts such as Greek, Arabic, Cyrillic, and Hebrew.

UTF-16 is another very common encoding of Unicode, which all XML parsers are required to support. UTF-16 encodes characters 0 through 65,535 (the Basic Multilingual Plane, or BMP for short) directly as 2-byte values. Characters from 65,536 to 1,048,575 are encoded as 4-byte surrogate pairs.

Furthermore, legacy character sets such as ASCII, ISO-8859-1 (Latin-1), SJIS, or MacRoman are treated as encodings of subsets of the Unicode character set. When the parser reads an XML document, it converts all the data into Unicode.

The encoding declaration

XML processors assume text data is in the UTF-8 format unless told otherwise. This means that they can read ASCII files, because ASCII is a strict subset of UTF-8. If you like, you can write in other encodings besides UTF-8, provided the parser recognizes them. Each document written in an alternative character encoding must have an encoding declaration that specifies which character set or encoding is being used. For example, this XML declaration says that the document is written in Latin-1:

```
<?xml version="1.0" encoding="ISO-8859-1"?>
```

This one says the document is written in UTF-16:

```
<?xml version="1.0" encoding="UTF-16"?>
```

Documents that are written in UTF-16 should also have an invisible byte-order mark before the XML declaration. This is normally inserted automatically by the editor when it saves a file in UTF-16. This helps the parser determine whether the UTF-16 is big endian or little endian. UTF-8 documents sometimes also have such a byte-order mark, though it's not required because UTF-8 is completely byte-order-independent.

Numeric character references

Every Unicode character has a code point between 0 and 1,114,111. If the text editor or encoding does not support the character you need, you can use a numeric character reference to insert the character in the XML file instead.

A numeric character reference consists of the two characters `&#` followed by the character code and a semicolon. For instance, the Greek letter π has Unicode value 960 so it can be inserted in an XML file as `π`. The Cyrillic character Ч has Unicode value 1206, so it can be included in an XML file with the character reference `Ҷ`.

Listing 6-7 demonstrates by encoding the first article of the Universal Declaration of Human Rights in Chinese using numeric character references.

Listing 6-7: Decimal Numeric Character References

```
<?xml version="1.0" encoding="ISO-8859-1"?>
<ARTICLE>
&#20154; &#20154; &#29983; &#32780; &#33258; &#30001;,
&#22312; &#23562; &#20005; &#21644; &#26435; &#21033;
&#19978; &#19968; &#24459; &#24179; &#31561;&#12290;
&#20182; &#20204; &#36171; &#26377; &#29702; &#24615;
&#21644; &#33391; &#24515;, &#24182; &#24212; &#20197;
&#20804; &#24351; &#20851; &#31995; &#30340; &#31934;
&#31070; &#30456; &#23545; &#24453;&#12290;.
</ARTICLE>
```

This isn't particularly legible. It may be written in Chinese, but it's all Greek to me. However, if you load the result into a browser, all the references are resolved into the actual Chinese characters, as shown in Figure 6-2. Your system will need a Chinese font installed to display this.

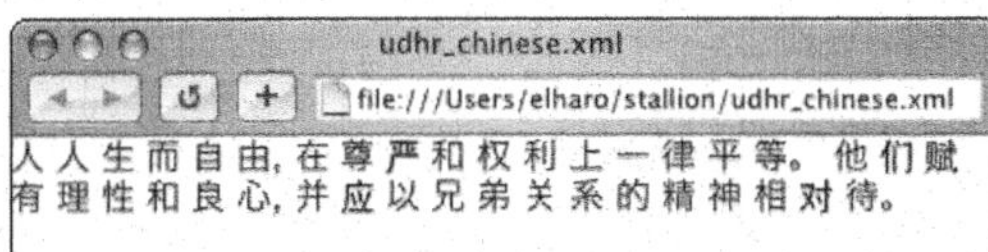

Figure 6-2: Browsers convert numeric character references into the actual characters before displaying them.

Numeric character references can also be specified in hexadecimal (base 16). Although most people are more comfortable with decimal numbers, the Unicode specification gives character values as 2-byte hexadecimal numbers. It's often easier to use hex values directly rather than converting them to decimal.

All you need to do is include an `x` after the `&#` to signify that you're using a hexadecimal value. For example, π has hexadecimal value 3C0, so it can be inserted in an XML file as `π`. The Cyrillic character Ч has hexadecimal value 4B6, so it can be included in an XML file with the escape sequence `Ҷ`. Because 2 bytes always produce exactly four hexadecimal digits, it's customary (although not required) to include leading zeros in hexadecimal character references so they are rounded out to four digits. Listing 6-8 repeats Listing 6-7 with hexadecimal instead of decimal character references.

Listing 6-8: **Hexadecimal Numeric Character References**

```
<?xml version="1.0"?>
<ARTICLE>
&#x4EBA; &#x4EBA; &#x751F; &#x800C; &#x81EA; &#x7531;,
&#x5728; &#x5C0A; &#x4E25; &#x548C; &#x6743; &#x5229;
&#x4E0A; &#x4E00; &#x5F8B; &#x5E73; &#x7B49;&#x3002;
&#x4ED6; &#x4EEC; &#x8D4B; &#x6709; &#x7406; &#x6027;
&#x548C; &#x826F; &#x5FC3;, &#x5E76; &#x5E94; &#x4EE5;
&#x5144; &#x5F1F; &#x5173; &#x7CFB; &#x7684; &#x7CBE;
&#x795E; &#x76F8; &#x5BF9; &#x5F85;&#x3002;
</ARTICLE>
```

Numeric character references, both hexadecimal and decimal, can also be used to embed characters that would otherwise be interpreted as markup. For example, the ampersand (&) is encoded as `&` or `&`. The less than sign (<) is encoded as `<` or `<`.

Numeric character references can only be used in character data and attribute values, however. They cannot be used in element or attribute names. For example, Listing 6-9, which attempts to escape the tag names, is malformed.

Listing 6-9: **A Malformed Document That Tries to Use Character References in Element Names**

```
<?xml version="1.0"?>
<&#x7B2C;&#x6761;>
&#x4EBA; &#x4EBA; &#x751F; &#x800C; &#x81EA; &#x7531;,
&#x5728; &#x5C0A; &#x4E25; &#x548C; &#x6743; &#x5229;
```

```
&#x4E0A; &#x4E00; &#x5F8B; &#x5E73; &#x7B49;&#x3002;
&#x4ED6; &#x4EEC; &#x8D4B; &#x6709; &#x7406; &#x6027;
&#x548C; &#x826F; &#x5FC3;, &#x5E76; &#x5E94; &#x4EE5;
&#x5144; &#x5F1F; &#x5173; &#x7CFB; &#x7684; &#x7CBE;
&#x795E; &#x76F8; &#x5BF9; &#x5F85;&#x3002;
</&#x7B2C;&#x6761;>
```

If you want to use Chinese in an element name or other markup, you must use a character encoding that includes Chinese so you can type the actual characters rather than character references.

Character references may seem to appear inside comments, processing instructions, and CDATA sections. However, in those contexts they are merely interpreted as text. The parser does not convert a string such as `&` into a different character inside CDATA sections, comments, and processing instructions.

XML 1.1

XML 1.0 was based on Unicode 2.0. XML 1.1 is designed to be independent of any particular Unicode version. XML 1.0 explicitly listed all the characters that could be used in XML names (including element names, attribute names, entity names, and processing instruction targets). Characters that weren't defined yet in Unicode 2.0 weren't allowed in names. For example, you can't write XML 1.0 names in Amharic, Burmese, or Cambodian because those scripts weren't added to Unicode until version 3.0. Naturally, this is a bit of a problem for developers whose preferred language is Amharic, Burmese, or Cambodian.

XML 1.1 allows you to use these scripts and others defined after Unicode 2.0 in documents. All you have to do is set the `version` attribute to 1.1 instead of 1.0. Listing 6-10 demonstrates with Article 1 of the Universal Declaration of Human Rights written in Burmese:

Listing 6-10: A Burmese Document in XML 1.1

```
<?xml version="1.1"?>
<အပိုဒ်>
လူတိုင်းသည် တူညီ လွတ်လပ်သော ဂုဏ်သိက□ာဖြင့် လည်းကောင်း?
တူညီလွတ်လပ်သော အခွင့်အရေးများဖြင့် လည်းကောင်း?
မွေးဖွားလာသူများ ဖြစ်သည်၏ ထိုသူတို့□ ပိုင်းခြား
ဝေဖန်တတ်သော ဉာဏ်နှင့် ကျင့်ဝတ် သိတတ်သော စိတ်တို့ရှိက□
ထိုသူတို့သည် အချင်းချင်း မေတ□ာထား□ ဆက်ဆံကျင့်သုံးသင့်၏
</အပိုဒ်>
```

However, this is only important for markup, not for PCDATA. XML 1.0 documents can contain Burmese, Cambodian, Amharic, and other Unicode 4.0 scripts in text content. They just can't use it for markup. Listing 6-11 is a perfectly well-formed XML document that uses the Burmese script for text but English markup.

Listing 6-11: **Burmese Text with English Markup in XML 1.0**

```
<?xml version="1.0"?>
<ARTICLE>
လူတိုင်းသည် တူညီ လွတ်လပ်သော ဂုဏ်သိက□ါဖြင့်၎ လည်းကောင်း?
တူညီလွတ်လပ်သော အခွင့်၎အရေးများဖြင့်၎ လည်းကောင်း?
မွေးဖွားလာသူများ ဖြစ်သည်၏ ထိုသူတို့□ ပိုင်းခြား
ဝေဖန်တတ်သော ဉာဏ်နှင့်၎ ကျင့်၎ဝတ် သိတတ်သော စိတ်တို့၎ရှိက□
ထိုသူတို့၎သည် အချင်းချင်း မေတ□ါထား□ ဆက်ဆံကျင့်၎သုံးသင့်၎ကာ၏
</ARTICLE>
```

The second change XML 1.1 makes is allowing the use of the newline character, Unicode code point 133, NEL, as a substitute for carriage returns and linefeeds. This NEL character is used as a line terminator on some IBM mainframe systems instead of the worldwide standards carriage return and linefeed. There's no excuse for this uninteroperability, and IBM really should have fixed this on their mainframes decades ago. Nonetheless, XML 1.1 does allow NEL to be used as white space in XML documents. However, it never has to be used. It can't do anything a simple carriage return or linefeed can't do, and it's incompatible with existing XML processors and systems as well as plain-vanilla text editors such as emacs and BBEdit. Allowing NEL into XML 1.1 was a bad decision with no real value to anyone.

The third change XML 1.1 makes is forbidding the direct inclusion of the C1 control characters with Unicode code points 128 through 159 in your documents with the single exception of the NEL character. The C1 controls have never achieved broad adoption, and their inclusion in XML 1.0 was an oversight. They should have been banned like the C0 controls from 0 to 31. When you find these characters in a document, what you most often have is a mislabeled Cp1252 document. Cp1252 is the U.S. Windows default encoding. It's mostly identical to ISO-8859-1 (Latin-1) except that it uses the space from 128 to 159 for additional graphic characters such as ‰ and Œ. Other vendor character sets such as MacRoman also use this range. It's rare to find any of these code points used in a genuine Latin-1 or Unicode document. XML 1.1 does allow these characters to be included if they're escaped as numeric character references such as `‡` or `Œ`.

The fourth change XML 1.1 makes is allowing additional C0 control characters such as form feed and bell in XML data. However, these cannot be typed directly. They must always be escaped with numeric character references such as  and . Character 0, the null, is still not allowed whether you escape it or not. The remaining C0 control characters are allowed, though only the three allowed in XML 1.0—carriage return, linefeed, and tab—do not have to be escaped. This may be useful if you have a lot of legacy data with embedded control characters, but these control characters simply aren't needed in new XML documents. Markup is much better for indicating page breaks, beeps, and other control structures than the C0 characters ever were.

Bottom line: If you aren't interested in writing markup in Amharic, Burmese, Cambodian, Yi, Tagalog, Mongolian, or a few other languages only lately added to Unicode, you don't need XML 1.1. Indeed, you should not use XML 1.1, because it merely makes your documents incompatible with the large installed base of XML software for no good reason. If you do want to write markup (not PCDATA but markup) in one of these languages, set the `version` attribute of the XML declaration to 1.1 and then proceed as normal.

The XML 1.1 specification also expends a lot of verbiage on Unicode normalization. Very roughly, this is the act of changing characters like the letter e followed by a combining accent acute into the single character é. However, the rules for normalization are so weak that they have no actual effect on parsers. In brief, the specification suggests that document authors should normalize their text, but forbids parsers from actively text. Parsers are allowed but not required to warn client applications if they encounter unnormalized text. However, they were allowed to warn about this (or anything else they didn't like) in XML 1.0. Nothing has really changed with respect to normalization in XML 1.1.

There is one more change XML 1.1 makes that's potentially relevant to a few more users, but it involves namespaces, so discussion will have to wait until namespaces are introduced in Chapter 11.

Well-formed HTML

You can practice your XML skills even before all web browsers directly support XML by writing well-formed HTML. Well-formed HTML is HTML that adheres to XML's well-formedness constraints but only uses standard HTML tags. Well-formed HTML is easier to read than the sloppy HTML most humans and WYSIWYG tools such as FrontPage write. It's also easier for web robots and automated search engines to understand. It's more robust and less likely to break when you make a change. And it's less likely to be subject to annoying cross-browser and cross-platform differences in rendering. Furthermore, you can then use XML tools to work on your HTML documents while still maintaining backward compatibility with browsers that don't support XML.

Rules for HTML

Real-world web pages are extremely sloppy. Tags aren't closed. Elements overlap. Raw less than signs appear in text. Semicolons are omitted from the ends of entity references. Web pages with these problems are technically incorrect, but most browsers accept them. Nonetheless, your web pages will be cleaner, display faster, and be easier to maintain if you fix these problems.

Some of the common problems that you need to look for in HTML include the following:

1. Start-tags without matching end-tags (unclosed elements)
2. End-tags without start-tags (orphaned tags)
3. Overlapping elements
4. Unquoted attributes
5. Unescaped <, >, and & signs
6. Documents without root elements
7. End-tags in a different case than the corresponding start-tag

I've listed these in rough order of importance. Exact details vary from tag to tag, however. For example, an unclosed `<STRONG>` tag will turn all elements following it bold. However, an unclosed `<LI>` or `<P>` tag causes no problems at all.

Some constructs only apply to XML documents; they might cause problems if you attempt to integrate them into your existing HTML pages. These XML-only constructs include the following:

1. The XML declaration
2. Empty-element tags
3. Entity references besides `&`, `<`, and `>` and numeric character references

Fixing these problems isn't hard, but there are a few pitfalls to trip up the unwary. They are explored in the following section.

Close all elements

Any element that contains content, whether text or other child elements, should have a start-tag and an end-tag. HTML doesn't absolutely require this. For example, `<P>` , `<DT>`, `<DD>`, and `<LI>` are often used in isolation. However, this relies on the web browser to make a good guess at where the element ends, and browsers don't always do quite what authors want or expect. Therefore, it's best to explicitly close all elements.

The biggest change this requires to how you write HTML is thinking of `<P>` as a container rather than a simple paragraph break mark. For example, previously, you would probably have formatted these maxims from Oscar Wilde's *Phrases and Philosophies for the Use of the Young* like this:

```
Wickedness is a myth invented by good people to account
 for the curious attractiveness of others.
<P>
```

```
Those who see any difference between soul and body have
neither.
<P>

Religions die when they are proved to be true. Science is the
record of dead religions.
<P>

The well-bred contradict other people. The wise contradict
themselves.
<P>
```

Now you have to format them like this instead:

```
<P>
Wickedness is a myth invented by good people to account
for the curious attractiveness of others.
</P>

<P>
Those who see any difference between soul and body
have neither.
</P>

<P>
Religions die when they are proved to be true. Science is the
record of dead religions.
</P>

<P>
The well-bred contradict other people. The wise contradict
themselves.
</P>
```

You've probably been taught to think of <P> as ending a paragraph. Now you have to think of it as beginning one. This does provide some advantages, though. For example, you can easily assign a variety of formatting attributes to a paragraph. Here's the original HTML title of House Resolution 581 as seen on http://thomas.loc.gov/home/hres581.html:

```
<center>
<p><h2>House Calendar No. 272</h2>

<p><h1>105TH CONGRESS 2D SESSION H. RES. 581</h1>

<p>[Report No. 106-795]

<p><b>Authorizing and directing the Committee on the
Judiciary to investigate whether sufficient grounds
exist for the impeachment of William Jefferson Clinton,
President of the United States.</b>
</center>
```

Here's the same text, but using well-formed HTML. The `align` attribute now replaces the deprecated `center` element, and a CSS attribute is used instead of the `<b>` tag.

```
<h2 align="center">House Calendar No. 272</h2>

<h1 align="center">105TH CONGRESS 2D SESSION H. RES. 581</h1>

<p align="center">[Report No. 106-795]</p>

<p align="center" style="font-weight: bold">
Authorizing and directing the Committee on the Judiciary to
investigate whether sufficient grounds exist for the
impeachment of William Jefferson Clinton,
President of the United States.
</p>
```

Delete orphaned end-tags; don't let elements overlap

When you are editing pages, it's not uncommon to remove a start-tag and forget to remove its associated end-tag. In HTML, an orphaned end-tag, such as a `</STRONG>` or `</TD>` that doesn't have any matching start-tag, is unlikely to cause problems by itself. However, it does make the file longer than it needs to be, increases the time that it takes to download the document, and has the potential to confuse people or tools that are trying to understand and edit the HTML source. Therefore, you should make sure that each end-tag is properly matched with a start-tag.

More often an end-tag that doesn't match any start-tag means that elements incorrectly overlap. Most elements that overlap on web pages are quite easy to fix. For example, consider this common problem taken from the White House home page (`http://www.whitehouse.gov/`, November 4, 1998).

```
<font size=2><b>
<!-- New Begin -->
<a href="/WH/New/html/19981104-12244.html">Remarks Of The
President Regarding Social Security</a>
<BR>
<!-- New End -->
 </font>
</b>
```

Because the `b` element starts inside the `font` element, it must end inside the `font` element. All that's needed to fix it is to swap the end-tags like this:

```
<font size=2><b>
<!-- New Begin -->
<a href="/WH/New/html/19981104-12244.html">Remarks Of The
President Regarding Social Security</a>
<BR>
<!-- New End -->
</b>
</font>
```

Alternately, you can swap the start-tags instead:

```
<b><font size=2>
<!-- New Begin -->
<a href="/WH/New/html/19981104-12244.html">Remarks Of The
President Regarding Social Security</a>
<BR>
<!-- New End -->
 </font>
</b>
```

Occasionally, you'll have a tougher problem. For example, consider this larger fragment from the same page. I've made the problem tags bold to make it easier to see the mistake:

```
<TD valign=TOP width=85>
<FONT size=+1>
<A HREF="/WH/New"><img border=0
src="/WH/images/pin_calendar.gif"
align=LEFT height=50 width=75 hspace=5 vspace=5></A><br> </TD>
<TD valign=TOP width=225>
<A HREF="/WH/New"><B>What's New:</B></A><br>
</FONT>
What's happening at the White <nobr>House - </nobr><br>
 <font size=2><b>
<!-- New Begin -->
<a href="/WH/New/html/19981104-12244.html">Remarks Of The
President Regarding Social Security</a>
<BR>
<!-- New End -->
 </font>
</b>
</TD>
```

Here the <FONT size=+1> element begins inside the first <TD valign=TOP width=85> element and continues past that element into the <TD valign=TOP width=225> element, where it finishes. The proper solution in this case is to close the FONT element immediately before the first </TD> closing tag, and to then add a new <FONT size=+1> start-tag immediately after the start of the second TD element, like this:

```
<TD valign=TOP width=85>
<FONT size=+1>
<A HREF="/WH/New"><img border=0
src="/WH/images/pin_calendar.gif"
align=LEFT height=50 width=75 hspace=5 vspace=5></A><br>
</FONT></TD>
<TD valign=TOP width=225>
<FONT size=+1>
<A HREF="/WH/New"><B>What's New:</B></A><br>
</FONT>
What's happening at the White <nobr>House - </nobr><br>
```

```
 <b><font size=2>
<!-- New Begin -->
<a href="/WH/New/html/19981104-12244.html">Remarks Of The
President Regarding Social Security</a>
<BR>
<!-- New End -->
 </font>
</b>
</TD>
```

Quote all attributes

HTML attributes only require quote marks if they contain embedded white space. Nonetheless, it doesn't hurt to include them. Furthermore, using quote marks may help in the future, if you later decide to change the attribute value to something that does include white space. It's quite easy to forget to add the quote marks later, especially if the attribute is similar to an ALT in an <IMG> whose malformedness is not immediately apparent when you are viewing the document in a web browser.

For example, consider this <IMG> tag:

```
<IMG SRC=cup.gif WIDTH=89 HEIGHT=67 ALT=Cup>
```

It should be rewritten like this:

```
<IMG SRC="cup.gif" WIDTH="89" HEIGHT="67" ALT="Cup">
```

The previously listed fragment from the White House home page has a lot of attributes that require quoting. When the quote marks are fixed, it looks like this:

```
<TD valign="TOP" width="85">
<FONT size="+1">
<A HREF="/WH/New"><img border="0"
src="/WH/images/pin_calendar.gif" align="LEFT"
height="50" width="75" hspace="5" vspace="5"></A><br>
</FONT></TD>
<TD valign="TOP" width="225">
<FONT size="+1">
<A HREF="/WH/New"><B>What's New:</B></A><br>
</FONT>
What's happening at the White <nobr>House - </nobr><br>
 <b><font size="2">
<!-- New Begin -->
<a href="/WH/New/html/19981104-12244.html">Remarks Of The
President Regarding Social Security</a>
<BR>
<!-- New End -->
 </font>
</b>
</TD>
```

Escape <, >, and & signs

HTML is more forgiving of loose less than signs and ampersands than is XML. Nonetheless, even in pure HTML, they do cause trouble, especially if they're followed immediately by some other character. For example, consider this e-mail address as it might easily be copied and pasted from the From: header in Eudora:

```
Elliotte Rusty Harold <elharo@metalab.unc.edu>
```

Were it to be rendered in HTML, this is all you would see:

```
Elliotte Rusty Harold
```

The e-mail address has been unintentionally hidden by the angle brackets. Anytime you want to include a raw less than sign or ampersand in HTML, you really should use the < and & entity references. The correct HTML for such a line would be as follows:

```
From: Elliotte Rusty Harold &lt;elharo@metalab.unc.edu&gt;
```

You're slightly less likely to see problems with an unescaped greater than sign because this will only be interpreted as markup if it's preceded by an as yet unfinished tag. However, there may be such unfinished tags in a document, and a nearby greater than sign can mask their presence. For example, consider this fragment of Java code:

```
for (int i=0;i<10;i++) {
  for (int j=20;j>10;j--) {
```

It's likely to be rendered as follows:

```
for (int i=0;i10;j--) {
```

If those are only 2 lines in a 100-line program, it's entirely possible you'll miss the omission when casually proofreading. On the other hand, if the greater than sign is escaped, the unescaped less than sign will probably obscure the rest of the program, and the problem will be harder to spot.

Use the same case for all tags

HTML isn't case-sensitive, but XML is. If you open an element with <TD> you can't close it with </td>. When I went back to the White House home page for the second edition of this book, I found that they'd fixed the problems I previously noted. However, this time I found a lot of elements like this:

```
<A href="/WH/Services"><B>Commonly Requested Federal Services:</B></a>
```

The end-tags need to at least match the case of the corresponding start-tags. Thus, in this example, </a> should be </A>, like this:

```
<A href="/WH/Services"><B>Commonly Requested Federal Services:</B></A>
```

However, most of the time I'd go a little further. In particular, I recommend picking a single convention for tag case, either all uppercase, all lowercase, or camel case, and sticking to it throughout the document. This is easier than trying to remember details of each tag. In this book, I'm mostly using all uppercase tags so that the tags will stand out in the text, but for HTML I normally use all lowercase because it's much easier to type and because, eventually, XHTML will require it. Thus, I'd rewrite the preceding fragment like this:

```
<a href="/WH/Services"><b>Commonly Requested Federal Services:</b></a>
```

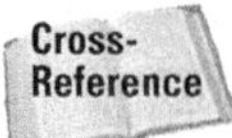

XHTML is discussed in Chapters 21 and 22.

Include a root element

The root element for HTML files is supposed to be html. Most browsers forgive a failure to include this. Nonetheless, it's definitely better to make the very first tag in your document <html> and the very last </html>. If any extra text or tags have gotten in front of <html> or behind </html>, move them between <html> and </html>.

One common manifestation of this problem is simply forgetting to include </html> at the end of the document. I always begin my documents by typing <html> and </html>, then type between them, rather than waiting until I've finished writing the document and hoping that by that point, possibly days later, I still remember that I need to put in a closing </html> tag.

Close empty-element tags with a />

Empty-element tags are the bête noir of converting HTML to well-formed XML. HTML does not formally recognize the XML <elementname/> syntax for empty elements. You can convert <BR> to <BR/>, <HR> to <HR/>, <IMG> to <IMG/>, and so on quite easily. However, it's a tossup whether any given browser will render the transformed tags properly or not.

Do not confuse truly empty elements such as <BR>, <HR>, and <IMG> with elements that do contain content but often only have a start-tag in standard HTML, such as <P>, <LI>, <DT>, and <DD>.

The simplest solution, and the solution approved by the XML specification, is to replace the empty-element tags with start-tag/end-tag pairs with no content. The browser should then ignore the unrecognized end-tag, as in the following example:

```
<BR></BR>
<HR></HR>
<IMG SRC="cup.gif" WIDTH="89" HEIGHT="67" ALT="Cup"></IMG>
```

This seems to work well in practice with one notable exception. Netscape treats </BR> the same as <BR>; that is, as a signal to break the line. Thus, while <br> is a single line break,
</BR> is a double line break, more akin to a paragraph mark in practice. Furthermore, Netscape ignores <BR/> completely. Web sites that must support legacy browsers (essentially all web sites) cannot use either
</BR> or <BR/>. What does seem to work in practice for XML and legacy browsers is this:

```
<BR />
```

Note the space between <BR and />. If the space bothers you, you can add an extra attribute like this:

```
<BR CLASS="empty"/>
```

Use no entity references other than &, <, >, ', and "

Many web pages don't need entity references other than &, <, >, ', and ". However, the HTML 4.0 specification does define many more, including the following:

- ✦ ™, the trademark symbol ™
- ✦ ©, the copyright symbol ©
- ✦ ∞, the infinity symbol ∞
- ✦ π, the lowercase Greek letter π

There are several hundred others. These are just a sample. However, using any of these will make your document malformed. The real solution to this problem is to use a DTD. I discuss the effect that DTDs have on entity references in Chapter 10. In the meantime, there are several short-term solutions.

The simplest is to write the document in a character set that has all the symbols you need, and then use a <META> directive to specify the character set in use. For example, to specify that your document uses UTF-8 encoding, a character set discussed in the next chapter that contains all the characters you're likely to want, you would place this <META> directive in the head of your document:

```
<META http-equiv="Content-Type" content="text/html;
      charset=UTF-8"></META>
```

Alternately, you can simply tell your web server to emit the necessary content type header. However, it's normally easier to use the <META> tag.

```
Content-Type: text/html; charset=UTF-8
```

The problem with this approach is that many browsers are likely not to be capable of displaying the UTF-8 character set. The same is true of most of the other character sets that you're likely to use to provide these special characters.

HTML 4.0 supports character entity references just like XML's; that is, you can replace a character by &# and the decimal or hexadecimal value of the character in Unicode, as in the following examples:

- ™ is the trademark symbol ™
- © is the copyright symbol ©
- ∞ is the infinity symbol ∞
- π is the lowercase Greek letter π

Unfortunately, HTML 3.2 only officially supports the numeric character references between 0 and 255 (ISO Latin-1), and many commonly used web browsers won't recognize character references outside this range.

If you're really desperate for well-formed XML that's backward-compatible with HTML, you can create bitmapped images of each desired character and include them using inline images:

- <img src="tm.gif" width="12" height="12" alt="TM"></img>
- <img src="copyright.gif" width="12" height="12" alt="Copyright"></img>
- img src="infinity.gif" width="12" height="12" alt="infinity"></img>
- <img src="pi.gif" width="12" height="12" alt="pi"></img>

In practice, however, I don't recommend including these characters as inline images. Well-formedness is not nearly so important in HTML that it justifies the added download and rendering time that using characters as inline images imposes on your readers.

Don't include an XML declaration

HTML documents don't need XML declarations. However, they can have them. Web browsers should simply ignore tags they don't recognize. From their perspective, the line

```
<?xml version="1.0" standalone="yes"?>
```

is just another tag. Because browsers that don't understand XML don't understand the `<?xml?>` tag, they quietly ignore it. However, I've encountered strange behaviors when different browsers are presented with an HTML document that includes an XML declaration. When faced with such a file, Internet Explorer 4.0 for the Mac tried to download the file rather than displaying it. Netscape Navigator 3.0 showed the declaration as text at the top of the document. Admittedly, these are older browsers, but they are still used by millions of people. Consequently, because the XML declaration is not required for XML documents and because it doesn't really add a lot to XMLized HTML pages, I've removed it from my web sites.

Tools

It is not particularly difficult to write well-formed XML documents that follow the rules described in this chapter. However, XML browsers are less forgiving of poor syntax than are HTML browsers, so you do need to be careful.

If you violate any well-formedness constraints, XML parsers and browsers will report a syntax error. Thus, the process of writing XML can be a little like the process of writing code in a real programming language. You write it, and then you compile it; when the compilation fails, you note the errors reported and fix them. In the case of XML you parse the document rather than compile it, but the pattern is the same.

Generally, you go through several edit-parse cycles before you get your first look at the finished document in this iterative process. Despite this, there's no question that writing XML is a lot easier than writing C or Java source code. With a little practice, you'll get to the point at which you have relatively few errors, and at which you can write XML almost as quickly as you can type.

There are several tools that will help you clean up your pages, most notably RUWF (Are You Well-Formed?) from XML.COM and Tidy from Dave Raggett of the World Wide Web Consortium.

RUWF

Any tool that can check XML documents for well-formedness can test well-formed HTML documents as well. One of the easiest to use is the RUWF well-formedness checker from XML.COM at `http://www.xml.com/pub/a/tools/ruwf/check.html`. Figure 6-3 shows this tester. Simply type in the URL of the page that you want to check, and RUWF returns the first several dozen errors on the page.

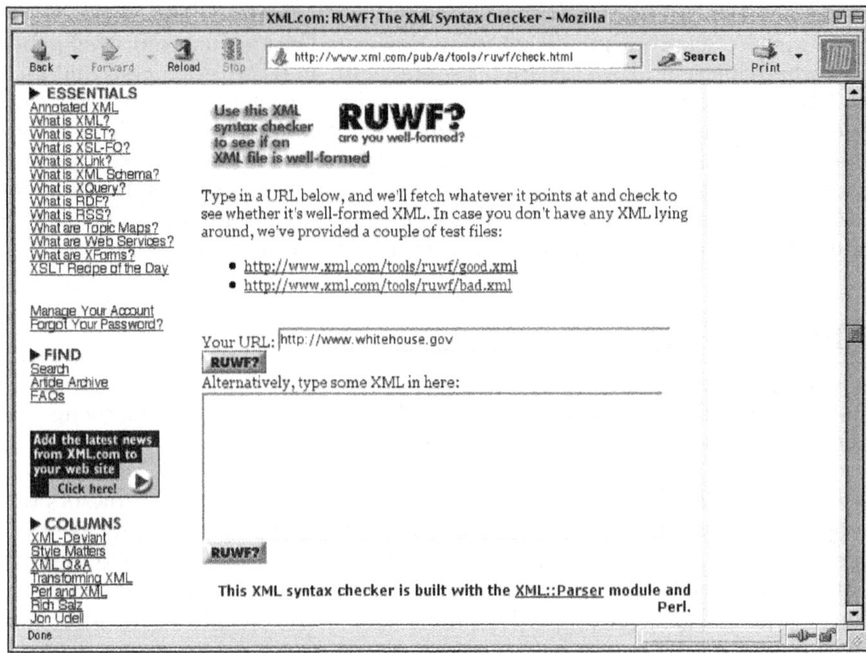

Figure 6-3: The RUWF well-formedness tester

Here's the first batch of errors RUWF found on the White House home page. Most of these errors are malformed XML, but legal (if not necessarily well styled) HTML. However, at least one error ("Line 55, column 30: Encountered </FONT> with no start-tag.") is a problem for both HTML and XML.

```
Line 28, column 7: Encountered </HEAD> expected </META>
...assumed </META> ...assumed </META> ...assumed </META>
...assumed </META>
Line 36, column 12, character '0': after AttrName= in start-tag
Line 37, column 12, character '0': after AttrName= in start-tag
Line 38, column 12, character '0': after AttrName= in start-tag
Line 40, column 12, character '0': after AttrName= in start-tag
Line 41, column 10, character 'A': after AttrName= in start-tag
Line 42, column 12, character '0': after AttrName= in start-tag
Line 43, column 14: Encountered </CENTER> expected </br>
...assumed </br> ...assumed </br>
Line 51, column 11, character '+': after AttrName= in start-tag
Line 52, column 51, character '0': after AttrName= in start-tag
Line 54, column 57: after &
Line 55, column 30: Encountered </FONT> with no start-tag.
Line 57, column 10, character 'A': after AttrName= in start-tag
Line 59, column 15, character '+': after AttrName= in start-tag
```

Tidy

After you've identified the problems, you'll want to fix them. Many common problems — for example, putting quote marks around attribute values — can be fixed automatically. The most convenient tool for doing this is Dave Raggett's command-line program HTML Tidy (`http://tidy.sourceforge.net`). Tidy is a character mode program written in ANSI C that can be compiled and run on most platforms, including Windows, UNIX, BeOS, and the Mac.

Tidy cleans up HTML files in several ways, not all of which are relevant to XML well-formedness. In fact, in its default mode, Tidy tends to remove unnecessary (for HTML, but not for XML) end-tags such as `</LI>` and to make other modifications that break well-formedness. However, you can use the `-asxml` switch to specify that you want well-formed XML output. For example, to convert the file index.html to well-formed XML, you would type this command from a DOS window or shell prompt:

```
C:\> tidy -m -asxml index.html
```

The `-m` flag tells Tidy to convert the file in place. The `-asxml` flag tells Tidy to format the output as XML.

Summary

In this chapter, you learned about XML's well-formedness rules. In particular, you learned the following:

- ✦ XML documents are sequences of characters that meet certain well-formedness criteria.
- ✦ The text of an XML document is divided into character data and markup.
- ✦ An XML document is a tree structure made up of elements.
- ✦ Tags delimit elements.
- ✦ Start-tags and empty-element tags can have attributes, which describe elements.
- ✦ The `xml:space` attribute determines whether white space in an element is significant. The two possible values are `default` and `preserve`.
- ✦ The `xml:lang` attribute specifies the language in which an element's content is written.
- ✦ Entity references allow you to include `<`, `>`, `&`, `"`, and `'` in your document.
- ✦ CDATA sections are useful for embedding text that contains a lot of `<`, `>`, and `&` characters but no markup.

- Comments can document your code for other people who read it, but parsers sometimes fail to report them. Comments can also hide sections of the document that aren't ready.
- Processing instructions allow you to pass application-specific information to particular applications.
- When writing XML in encodings other than UTF-8, include an `encoding` attribute in the XML or text declaration.
- Decimal and hexadecimal numeric character references such as `A` and `σ` enable you to escape characters that do not exist in the document's encoding in PCDATA and attribute values.
- XML 1.1 is unlikely to be useful unless your preferred language is Burmese, Amharic, Mongolian, Cambodian, or one of a few others not encoded in Unicode 2.0.
- HTML documents can also be well formed with a little extra effort.

This chapter concludes your exploration of basic, well-formed XML. The next chapter takes up document type definitions (DTDs) and validity. A DTD defines a structure for a class of XML documents. It specifies what document in that class must, must not, and may contain. By validating documents against DTDs, you can quickly and easily verify that your documents meet various conditions.

✦ ✦ ✦

Document Type Definitions

PART

II

✦ ✦ ✦ ✦

In This Part

✦ ✦ ✦ ✦

CHAPTER 7

Validity

✦ ✦ ✦ ✦

In This Chapter

Document type definitions

DTD files

Document type declarations

Validation against a DTD

The list of elements

Element declarations

Comments in DTDs

✦ ✦ ✦ ✦

XML has been described as a meta-markup language; that is, a language for describing markup languages. In this chapter, you begin to learn how to document and describe the new markup languages that you create. Such markup languages (also known as *vocabularies* or *XML applications*) are defined via a document type definition (DTD). Individual documents can be compared against DTDs in a process known as *validation*. If the document matches the constraints listed in the DTD, the document is said to be *valid*; if the document doesn't match the constraints, the document is said to be *invalid*.

Document Type Definitions

A *document type definition* lists the elements, attributes, entities, and notations that can be used in a document, as well as their possible relationships to one another. A DTD specifies a set of rules for the structure of a document. For example, a DTD may dictate that each `BOOK` element has exactly one `ISBN` child element, exactly one `TITLE` child element, and one or more `AUTHOR` children, and it may or may not contain a single `SUBTITLE`. Each such rule is given in a *declaration*.

Every valid XML document must specify the DTD it's valid with respect to. This DTD can be included in the XML document it describes, or that document can link to it at an external URL. Such external DTDs can be shared by different documents and web sites. If the DTD is not directly included in the document but is linked in from an external source, changes made to the DTD automatically propagate to all documents using that DTD. On the other hand, backward compatibility is not guaranteed when a DTD is modified. Incompatible changes can invalidate documents.

The real power of XML comes from common DTDs that are shared among many documents written by different people. DTDs provide a means for businesses, organizations, and interest groups to agree upon, document, and enforce adherence to markup standards. For example, a publisher may want an author to adhere to a particular format because it makes laying out a book easier. An author may prefer writing words in a row without worrying about matching up each bullet point in the front of the chapter with a subhead inside the chapter. If the author writes in XML, it's easy for the publisher to check whether the author adhered to the predetermined format specified by the DTD, and even to find out exactly where and how the author deviated from the format. This is much easier than reading through the document manually, hoping to spot all the minor deviations based on style alone.

DTDs also help ensure that different people and programs can read each other's files. For example, if chemists agree on a single DTD for basic chemical notation, possibly via the intermediary of an appropriate professional organization such as the American Chemical Society, they can rest assured that they can all read and understand one another's papers. The DTD defines exactly what is and is not allowed to appear inside a document. The DTD establishes a standard for the elements that viewing and editing software must support. Even more importantly, it establishes that extensions beyond those the DTD declares are invalid. This helps prevent software vendors from embracing and extending open protocols to lock users into their proprietary software.

Furthermore, a DTD shows how the different elements of a document are arranged. A DTD shows the generic structure of a document separate from the actual data in the individual document instances. This means that you can slap a lot of fancy styles and formatting onto the underlying structure without destroying it, much as you paint a house without changing its basic architectural plan. The reader of your page may not see or even be aware of the underlying structure, but as long as it's there, human authors and JavaScripts, servlets, databases, and other computer programs can use it.

Element Declarations

Recall Listing 3-2 (greeting.xml) from Chapter 3, repeated here:

```
<?xml version="1.0"?>
<GREETING>
Hello XML!
</GREETING>
```

This XML document contains a single element, `GREETING`. (Remember, `<?xml version="1.0"?>` is the XML declaration, not an element.) A DTD for this document has to declare the `GREETING` element. It may declare other elements, too, including ones that aren't present in this particular document, but it must at least declare the `GREETING` element.

Elements are declared using element declarations. Each element declaration gives the name of the element and lists the elements and text that it can contain. This list is called the *content specification*. For example, this element declaration for the GREETING element says that elements with the name GREETING must contain only parsed character data:

```
<!ELEMENT GREETING (#PCDATA)>
```

Every declaration begins with <!. Element declarations begin with <!ELEMENT (case-sensitive, as most things are in XML). This is followed by some white space and the name of the element being declared, GREETING in this example. Then there's some more white space and the content specification for this element. This content spec (#PCDATA) says that the element must contain parsed character data. Parsed character data is essentially any text that's not markup. This also includes entity references, such as &, that are replaced by text when the document is parsed. In other words, GREETING elements can contain text but no child elements. A valid GREETING element must look like this:

```
<GREETING>
  various random text but no markup
</GREETING>
```

There's no restriction on what text the element can contain. It can be zero or more Unicode characters, with any meaning. DTDs don't let you specify that an element must contain a year such as 2004 or a floating-point number like 3.14152. You can only say whether the element contains text, or child elements, or both. A GREETING element can also look like this:

```
<GREETING>Hello!</GREETING>
```

Or even this:

```
<GREETING></GREETING>
```

However, a valid GREETING element cannot look like this:

```
<GREETING>
  <SOME_TAG>various random text</SOME_TAG>
  <SOME_EMPTY_TAG/>
</GREETING>
```

Nor may it look like this:

```
<GREETING>
  <GREETING>various random text</GREETING>
</GREETING>
```

Each GREETING element must consist of nothing more and nothing less than parsed character data between an opening <GREETING> tag and a closing </GREETING> tag.

DTD Files

Declarations are placed in DTDs. Often a DTD is a single file, separate from the document itself (although as you'll soon see, other storage schemes are possible). Such a DTD can be saved in a text file using any standard text editor. By convention, this file will have the three-letter extension .dtd, although this isn't required. For example, you might save a DTD describing only `GREETING` elements in a file called greeting.dtd, as shown in Listing 7-1.

Listing 7-1: greeting.dtd

```
<!ELEMENT GREETING (#PCDATA)>
```

Of course, DTDs are usually much longer and more complex and contain many more declarations than this trivial example.

Most of the time, DTDs are written in either ASCII or UTF-8. If you use any other encoding, the DTD must have a text declaration identifying the encoding used, as discussed in the last chapter. For example, Listing 7-2 shows a DTD that uses the ISO-8859-5 encoding because it uses the Russian word for *greeting* as an element name:

Listing 7-2: russian_greeting.dtd

```
<?xml encoding="ISO-8859-5"?>
<!ELEMENT ПРИВЕТСТВИЕ (#PCDATA)>
```

Document Type Declarations

A document type declaration is placed in an XML document's prolog to say what DTD that document adheres to. It also specifies which element is the root element of the document. The document type declaration can either specify the DTD directly, by including it inside the document type declaration, or indirectly, by giving the URL where the DTD is found. It may even do both, in which case the DTD has two parts, the internal and external subsets.

Caution

A document type *declaration* is not the same thing as a document type *definition*. Only the document type definition is abbreviated *DTD*. A document type declaration must contain or refer to a document type definition, but a document type definition never contains a document type declaration. I agree that this is unnecessarily confusing. Unfortunately, XML is stuck with this terminology.

A document type declaration begins with `<!DOCTYPE` and ends with a `>`. In between is the name of the root element, followed either by a pair of square brackets containing the DTD itself or by the `SYSTEM` keyword and a URL where the DTD can be found (or, occasionally, both). A document type declaration has this basic form:

```
<!DOCTYPE name_of_root_element
   SYSTEM "URL of the external DTD subset" [
   internal DTD subset
]>
```

Here, *`name_of_root_element`* is simply the name of the root element. The `SYSTEM` keyword indicates that what follows is a URL where the DTD is located. The square brackets enclose the internal subset of the DTD; that is, those declarations included inside the document itself. You can omit either the `SYSTEM` keyword and the URL to the external DTD subset or the square brackets and internal DTD subset, but you must have at least one of them for the document to be valid. For example, this document type declaration only specifies an external DTD that can be found at the URL `http://example.org/greeting.dtd`:

```
<!DOCTYPE GREETING SYSTEM "http://example.org/greeting.dtd">
```

This document type declaration includes the DTD inside itself:

```
<!DOCTYPE GREETING [
  <!ELEMENT GREETING (#PCDATA)>
]>
```

Line breaks and extra white space are not significant in a DTD. The same document type declaration could be written on a single line like this:

```
<!DOCTYPE GREETING [ <!ELEMENT GREETING (#PCDATA)> ]>
```

In all cases, the document type declaration is placed in the document's prolog, after the XML declaration but before the root element. For example, Listing 7-3 adds a document type declaration to the hello.xml document previously listed.

Listing 7-3: Hello XML with DTD

```
<?xml version="1.0"?>
<!DOCTYPE GREETING SYSTEM "greeting.dtd">
<GREETING>
Hello XML!
</GREETING>
```

Listing 7-3 uses a relative URL to locate the DTD so that it will be searched for in the same directory in which the document itself was found. You might also wish to locate DTDs relative to the web server's document root or to the current directory. In general, any reference that forms a URL relative to the location of the document is acceptable. For example, these are all acceptable document type declarations:

```
<!DOCTYPE SEASON SYSTEM "/xml/dtds/greeting.dtd">
<!DOCTYPE SEASON SYSTEM "dtds/greeting.dtd">
<!DOCTYPE SEASON SYSTEM "../greeting.dtd">
```

A document can't have more than one document type declaration, that is, more than one `<!DOCTYPE>`. To use elements declared in more than one external DTD, you need external parameter entity references. These are discussed in Chapter 10.

Internal DTDs

Putting the entire DTD inside the document type declaration isn't as reusable or modular as locating it with a URL, but it sometimes helps when you're developing a new DTD and want to keep your example document and the DTD in sync. Moreover, it will have some important consequences when entities are discussed in a couple of chapters. Listing 7-4 shows a complete greeting document with an internal DTD.

Listing 7-4: Hello XML with an Internal DTD

```
<?xml version="1.0"?>
<!DOCTYPE GREETING [
  <!ELEMENT GREETING (#PCDATA)>
]>
<GREETING>
Hello XML!
</GREETING>
```

You can load this document into an XML browser as usual. Figure 7-1 shows Listing 7-4 in Internet Explorer 5.5. The result is probably what you'd expect, a collapsible outline view of the document source. Internet Explorer indicates that a document type declaration is present by adding the line `<!DOCTYPE GREETING (View Source for full doctype...)>` in blue. However, most web browsers (and all common ones) do not check for validity and are happy to load invalid documents as well.

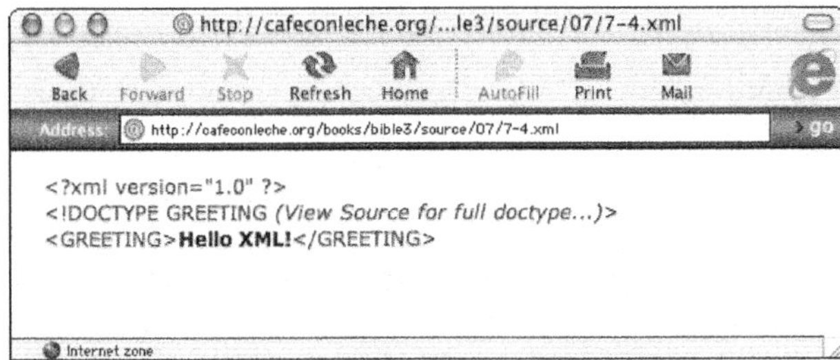

Figure 7-1: Hello XML with DTD displayed in Internet Explorer 5.2

Internal and external DTD subsets

Although most documents consist of easily defined pieces, not all documents use a common template. Many documents may need to use standard DTDs while adding custom elements for their own use. Other documents may use only standard elements but need to reorder them. For example, one page might have a `BODY` that must contain exactly one `H1` header followed by a `DL` definition list, while another may have a `BODY` that contains many different headers, paragraphs, and images in no particular order. If a particular document has a different structure than other pages on the site, it can be useful to define its structure in the document itself rather than in a separate DTD. This approach also makes the document easier to edit.

To this end, a document can use both an internal and an external DTD subset. The internal declarations go in square brackets inside the document type declaration. For example, Listing 7-5 is an XML document whose root element is `DOCUMENT`. The `DOCUMENT` element contains a `GREETING` child element followed by a `DATE` child element. This structure is declared by placing a comma between each element that must appear as a child element like this:

```
<!ELEMENT DOCUMENT (GREETING, DATE)>
```

The `DATE` element is also declared inside Listing 7-5's document type declaration. However, the declaration for the `GREETING` element is pulled from the file greeting.dtd, which forms the external DTD subset.

Listing 7-5: A Document Whose DTD Has Both an Internal and an External Subset

```
<?xml version="1.0"?>
<!DOCTYPE DOCUMENT SYSTEM "greeting.dtd" [
   <!ELEMENT DOCUMENT (GREETING, DATE)>
   <!ELEMENT DATE (#PCDATA)>
]>
<DOCUMENT>
  <GREETING>Hello</GREETING>
  <DATE>January 10, 2004</DATE>
</DOCUMENT>
```

A conflict between elements of the same name in the internal and external DTD subsets is a validity error. The same element cannot be declared twice, whether in the internal or external DTD subsets or both.

Public DTDs

The `SYSTEM` keyword is intended for private DTDs used by a single author or group. Part of the promise of XML, however, is that broader organizations covering an entire industry, such as the ISO or the IEEE, can standardize public DTDs to cover their fields. This standardization saves developers from having to reinvent tag sets for the same items and makes it easier for users to exchange interoperable documents.

DTDs designed for writers outside the creating organization use the `PUBLIC` keyword instead of the `SYSTEM` keyword. Furthermore, the DTD gets a name. The syntax is as follows:

```
<!DOCTYPE name_of_root_element PUBLIC "DTD_name" "DTD_URL">
```

Once again, *`name_of_root_element`* is the name of the root element. `PUBLIC` is an XML keyword that indicates that this DTD is intended for broad use and has a *public identifier*. *`DTD_name`* is the public identifier associated with this DTD. Some XML processors may attempt to use this identifier to retrieve the DTD from a central repository. Finally, *`DTD_URL`* is a relative or absolute URL where the DTD can be found if the public identifier is not recognized.

Public identifiers follow different rules than most XML names. They can only contain the ASCII alphanumeric characters, the space, the carriage return, the linefeed, and these punctuation marks: -'()+,/:=?;!*#@$_%. Furthermore, public identifiers follow a few conventions.

If a DTD is an ISO standard, its public identifier begins with the string ISO. If a non-ISO standards body has approved the DTD, its public identifier begins with a plus sign (+). If no standards body has approved the DTD, its name begins with a hyphen (-). These initial strings are followed by a double slash (//) and the name of the DTD's owner, which is followed by another double slash and the type of document the DTD describes. Then there's another double slash followed by an ISO 639 language identifier, such as EN for English. A complete list of ISO 639 identifiers is available at `http://www.ics.uci.edu/pub/ietf/http/related/iso639.txt`. For example, the greeting DTD can be named as follows:

```
-//Elliotte Rusty Harold//DTD Greetings and salutations//EN
```

This public identifier says that the DTD is not standards-body approved (-), belongs to Elliotte Rusty Harold, describes greetings and salutations, and is written in English. A full document type declaration pointing to this DTD with this name follows:

```
<!DOCTYPE SEASON PUBLIC
 "-//Elliotte Rusty Harold//DTD Greetings and salutations//EN"
 "http://www.cafeconleche.org/dtds/greeting.dtd">
```

You may have noticed that many HTML editors, such as BBEdit, automatically place the following string at the beginning of every HTML file they create:

```
<!DOCTYPE HTML PUBLIC "-//W3C//DTD HTML//EN">
```

Now you know what this string means! It says the document follows a nonstandards-body-approved (-) DTD for HTML produced by the World Wide Web Consortium (W3C) in the English language.

Note

Technically, the W3C is not a standards organization, because its membership is limited to corporations that pay its fees rather than to official government-approved bodies. It only publishes *recommendations* instead of *standards*. In practice, the distinction is irrelevant.

DTDs and style sheets

A valid document with a DTD can be combined with a style sheet just as a well-formed document can be. Simply add the usual `<?xml-stylesheet?>` processing instruction to the prolog, as shown in Listing 7-6.

Listing 7-6: Hello XML with a DTD and Style Sheet

```
<?xml version="1.0"?>
<?xml-stylesheet type="text/css" href="greeting.css"?>
<!DOCTYPE GREETING [
  <!ELEMENT GREETING (#PCDATA)>
]>
<GREETING>
Hello XML!
</GREETING>
```

Figure 7-2 shows the resulting web page. In fact, this gives you *exactly* the same result as did the same document in Chapter 3 without the DTD. Formatting generally does not consider the DTD.

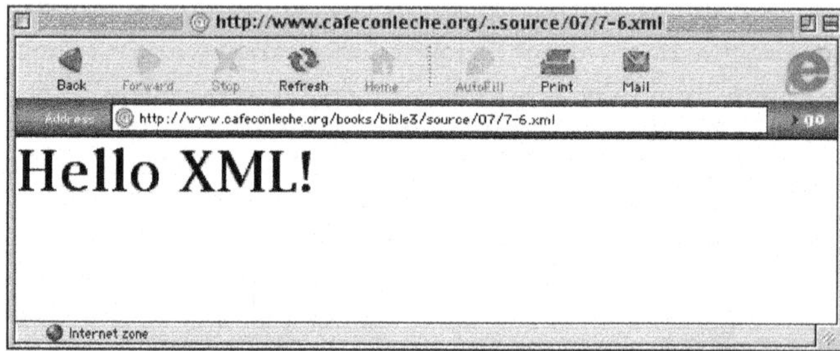

Figure 7-2: Hello XML with a DTD and style sheet displayed in Internet Explorer 5.1

Notice how the three essential parts of the document can be stored in three different files. The data is in the document file, the structure applied to the data is in the DTD file, and the formatting is in the style sheet. This tripartition enables you to inspect or change any or all of these relatively independently.

The DTD and the document are more closely linked than the document and the style sheet. Changing the DTD generally requires revalidating the document and may require edits to the document to bring it back into conformance with the DTD. The necessity of this sequence depends on your edits; adding elements is rarely an issue, although removing elements can be problematic.

Validating against a DTD

To be considered *valid,* an XML document must satisfy four criteria:

1. It must be well formed.
2. It must have a document type declaration.
3. Its root element must be the one specified by the document type declaration.
4. It must satisfy all the constraints of the DTD specified by the document type declaration.

Not all XML documents have to be valid, and not all parsers check documents for validity. Often, it's enough to merely be well formed. In fact, most web browsers, including Internet Explorer, Opera, Safari, Konqueror, Netscape, and Mozilla, do not check documents for validity.

Suppose you make a simple change to the hello.xml example by replacing the `<GREETING>` and `</GREETING>` tags with `<FOO>` and `</FOO>`, as shown in Listing 7-7. Listing 7-7 is *invalid.* It is a well-formed XML document, but it does not meet the constraints specified by the document type declaration and the DTD.

Listing 7-7: This Document Is Invalid because It Does Not Satisfy the DTD's Rules

```
<?xml version="1.0"?>
<!DOCTYPE GREETING SYSTEM "greeting.dtd">
<FOO>
Hello XML!
</FOO>
```

This document has two problems:

1. The root element is not `GREETING` as required by the document type declaration.
2. The `FOO` element has not been declared within the DTD.

Command-line validators

In more complex documents, it's not so easy to just look at a document and its DTD and tell whether or not it's valid. Instead, you'll want to use a validating parser that understands all the DTD rules and makes the checks for you. As a validating parser reads a document, it checks whether the document adheres to the rules specified by the document's DTD. If it does, the parser passes the data along to the XML application (such as a web browser or a database). If the parser finds a mistake, it reports the error. If you're writing XML by hand, you'll want to validate your documents before posting them so that you can be confident that readers won't encounter errors.

Not all XML parsers are validating parsers, but the Gnome Project's libxml2 (`http://xmlsoft.org`) is. libxml2 includes xmllint, a character mode application you can use to validate documents. It was originally developed for Linux, but has been ported to most common UNIXes, Windows, and Mac OS X. It may be installed by default on a few Linux distros, but most users will need to download it from `http://xmlsoft.org/downloads.html` first. Once you've installed libxml2 and made sure xmllint is somewhere in your path, you run xmllint by typing the following at the shell prompt or in a DOS window:

```
C:\>xmllint -valid 7-7.xml
```

You can use a URL instead of a filename, like this:

```
C:\>xmllint -valid
    http://www.cafeconleche.org/books/bible3/source/07/7-1.xml
```

In either case, `xmllint` responds with a list of the errors it found. If the document is well formed, `xmllint` also prints the document:

```
C:\> xmllint -valid 7-7.xml
7-7.xml:3: validity error: Not valid: root and DtD name do
not match 'FOO' and 'GREETING'
<FOO>
    ^
7-7.xml:5: validity error: No declaration for element FOO
</FOO>
      ^
<?xml version="1.0"?>
<!DOCTYPE GREETING SYSTEM "greeting.dtd">
<FOO>
Hello XML!
</FOO>
```

You use `xmllint` or a similar tool first to find your mistakes so that you can fix them, and then to verify that you've written valid XML that other programs can handle. In essence, this is a proofreading or quality assurance phase, not finished output.

Web-based validators

Web-based validators are an alternative for documents that aren't particularly private and that can easily be placed on a public web server. These validators only require you to enter the URL of your document in an HTML form. They have the distinct advantage of not requiring you to muck around with paths, environment variables, and the other arcana required to install a command-line program.

Richard Tobin's web-hosted XML well-formedness checker and validator is shown in Figure 7-3. You'll find it at `http://www.cogsci.ed.ac.uk/%7Erichard/xml-check.html`. Figure 7-4 shows the errors displayed as a result of using this program to validate Listing 7-7.

Brown University's Scholarly Technology Group provides a validator at `http://www.stg.brown.edu/service/xmlvalid/` that's notable for allowing you to upload files from your computer instead of placing them on a public web server. This validator is shown in Figure 7-5. Figure 7-6 shows the results of using this program to validate Listing 7-7.

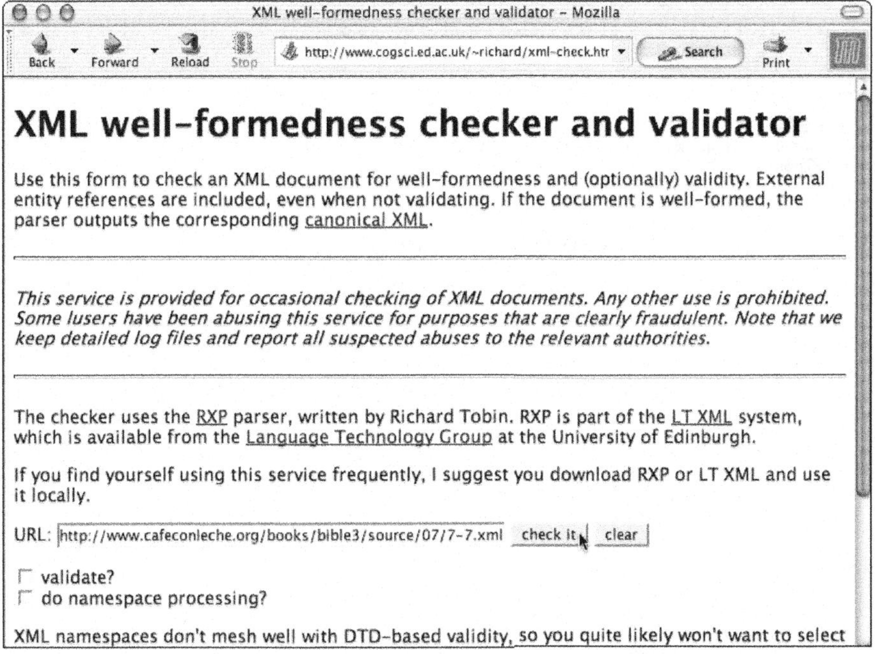

Figure 7-3: Richard Tobin's RXP-based, web-hosted XML well-formedness checker and validator

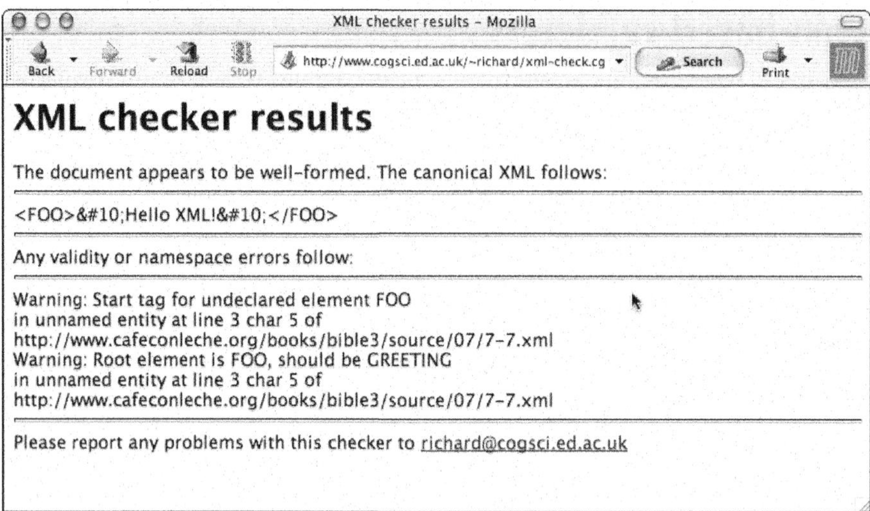

Figure 7-4: The errors in Listing 7-7, as reported by Richard Tobin's XML validator

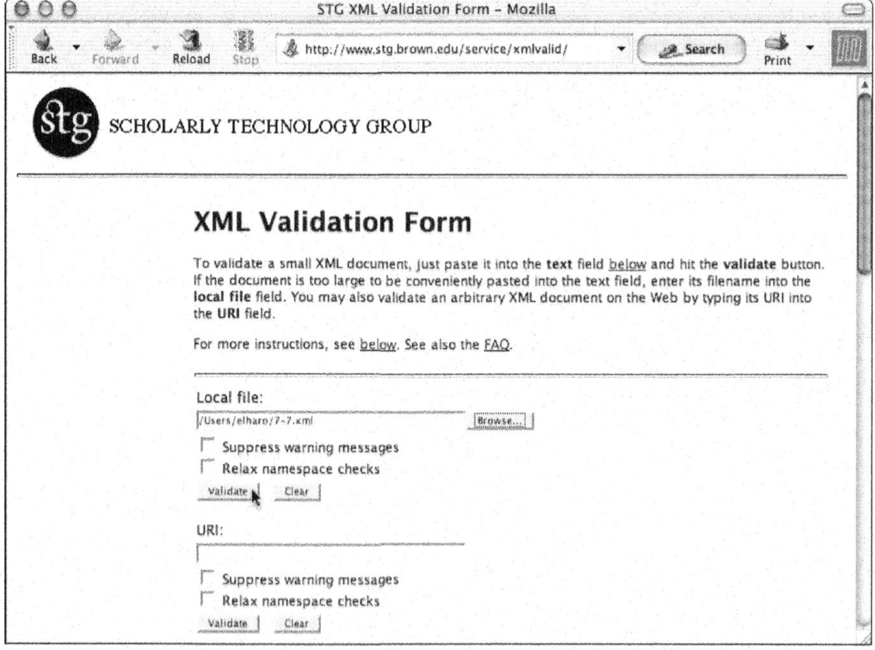

Figure 7-5: Brown University's Scholarly Technology Group's web-hosted XML validator

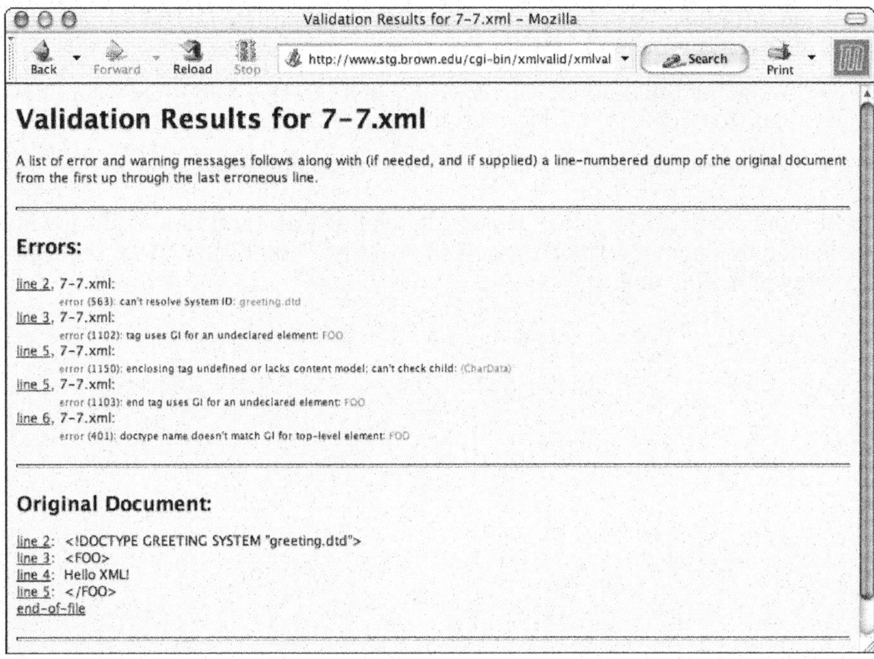

Figure 7-6: The errors in Listing 7-7, as reported by Brown University's Scholarly Technology Group's XML validator

Summary

In this chapter, you learned how to write a simple DTD and how to validate a document against that DTD. In particular, you learned the following:

- ✦ A document type definition (DTD) provides a list of the elements, attributes, entities, and notations that may be used in the document, and their relationships to one another.
- ✦ DTDs lay out the permissible tags and the structure of a document.
- ✦ DTDs help document and enforce markup standards.
- ✦ A document's prolog may contain a document type declaration that specifies the root element and either contains or refers to the DTD.
- ✦ External DTDs can be located using the `SYSTEM` keyword and a URL in the document type declaration.
- ✦ Standard DTDs can be located using the `PUBLIC` keyword in the document type declaration.

- ✦ An internal DTD subset (which may be the complete DTD) can appear in the document type declaration surrounded by square brackets.
- ✦ A document that adheres to the rules of its DTD is said to be valid. A document that does not or that does not have a DTD is said to be invalid.
- ✦ Element declarations declare the name and children of an element.

In the next chapter, you delve deeper into element declarations, exploring how to use different kinds of content models to describe complicated structures applicable to many XML documents.

✦ ✦ ✦

Element Declarations

✦ ✦ ✦ ✦

In This Chapter

Analyzing the document

ANY

#PCDATA

Child elements

Mixed content

Empty elements

Comments in DTD

✦ ✦ ✦ ✦

Elements form the primary structure of an XML document. In valid documents, elements are constrained by element declarations. An element declaration specifies what children in which orders and quantities an element with a particular name can have.

Each element used in a valid XML document must be declared by an element declaration in the document's DTD. Each element declaration gives the name of an element and lists the permissible contents of elements with that name. The list of contents is sometimes called the *content specification*. The content specification uses a simple grammar to precisely specify what is and isn't allowed in a document. This sounds complicated, but all it really means is that you attach punctuation marks such as *, ?, +, |, (, and) to element names to indicate where and how many times an element may appear. In this chapter, you learn the syntax and semantics of element declarations.

Analyzing the Document

The first step to creating a DTD appropriate for a particular document is to understand the structure of the information that you'll encode. Sometimes information is quite structured, as in a contact list. At other times, it is relatively free-form, as in an illustrated short story or a magazine article.

It's often easier to begin if you have a concrete, well-formed example document in mind that uses all the elements you want in your DTD. When designing a new XML application, I recommend writing some actual instance documents first, and only then designing the DTD. This chapter uses a relatively structured document you're already familiar with as an example, the television schedule document first discussed in Chapter 4. You might want to flip back to Example 4-2 to refresh your memory. In fact, you might want to print out a copy from my web site at http://www.cafeconleche.org/books/bible3/source/04/4-2.xml so you can have the example document in hand as you read this chapter, to avoid a lot of flipping back and forth

Adding a DTD to this document enables you to enforce constraints that were previously adhered to only by convention. For example, the DTD can require that a SHOW have exactly one NAME child, and that every STATION have a CHANNEL and at least one CALL_LETTERS or NETWORK. It can require that a SHOW contain exactly one each of NAME, TYPE, START_TIME, and LENGTH but make it optional whether a SHOW has an ORIGINAL_AIR_DATE or a CAST. Furthermore, it can require that the NAME, TYPE, START_TIME, and LENGTH child elements occur in a particular order. A DTD can also require that elements occur in a particular context. For example, the GIVEN_NAME, SURNAME, and MIDDLE_NAME elements may be used only inside ACTOR, PRODUCER, WRITER, and DIRECTOR elements.

Table 8-1 summarizes the different elements in this particular XML application, as well as the conditions each must satisfy. Each element has a list of the elements it must contain and the elements it may contain. In some cases, an element may contain more than one child element of the same type. A SCHEDULE contains one DATE and one or more SHOW elements. A CAST generally contains more than one ACTOR. Some shows are repeated a few hours later on the same station, especially on cable networks. Thus, a single SHOW element might have more than one START_TIME. In the table, the possibility of multiple children is indicated by adding (s) to the end of the element's name, such as ACTOR(s). When you write a DTD to describe this document, you'll need to write one element declaration for each distinct element name that appears in the table. This declaration will list the permissible children of that element, as well as their order and quantity.

Table 8-1
The Elements in the Television Schedule

Element	*Required Children*	*Optional Children*
SCHEDULE	DATE, STATION(s)	
DATE	Text	
STATION	CHANNEL	NETWORK, CALL_LETTERS, SHOW(s)
SHOW	NAME, START_TIME(s), LENGTH	EPISODE_NUMBER, START_TIME, LENGTH, AIR_DATE, ORIGINAL_AIR_DATE, CLOSED_CAPTIONED, REPEAT, DESCRIPTION, TITLE, RATING, YEAR_MADE, STARS, DIRECTOR, WRITER, PRODUCER, CAST

Element	*Required Children*	*Optional Children*
CAST	ACTOR(s)	
ACTOR		GIVEN_NAME, MIDDLE_NAME, MIDDLE_INITIAL, SURNAME
WRITER		GIVEN_NAME, MIDDLE_NAME, MIDDLE_INITIAL, SURNAME
PRODUCER		GIVEN_NAME, MIDDLE_NAME, MIDDLE_INITIAL, SURNAME
DIRECTOR		GIVEN_NAME, MIDDLE_NAME, MIDDLE_INITIAL, SURNAME
NAME	Text	
TYPE	Text	
CALL_LETTERS	Text	
NETWORK	Text	
CHANNEL	Text	
EPISODE_NUMBER	Text	
START_TIME	Text	
LENGTH	Text	
AIR_DATE	Text	
ORIGINAL_AIR_DATE	Text	
COLSED_CAPTIONED	Text	
REPEAT	Text	
GIVEN_NAME	Text	
MIDDLE_NAME	Text	
MIDDLE_INITIAL	Text	
SURNAME	Text	
DESCRIPTION	Text	
STARS	Text	
RATING	Text	
YEAR_MADE	Text	

Now that the information being stored and the optional and required relationships between these elements have been identified, you're ready to build a DTD for the document that concisely—if a bit opaquely—summarizes those relationships.

DTDs are conservative. Everything not explicitly permitted is forbidden. If an element has not been declared, it cannot be used (at least not in a valid document), and this does sometimes make the development of DTDs rather tedious. However, DTD syntax does enable you to compactly specify relationships that are cumbersome to specify in sentences. For example, DTDs make it easy to say that NAME must precede TYPE, which must precede START_TIME, which must precede LENGTH, which must precede AIR_DATE, which must precede ORIGINAL_AIR_DATE, which must precede CLOSED_CAPTIONED, which must precede REPEAT, which must precede RATING, which must precede DESCRIPTION, and that all of these elements can only appear inside a SHOW element.

ANY

It's easiest to build DTDs hierarchically, working from the outside in. This enables you to build a sample document at the same time that you build the DTD so that you can verify that the DTD is itself correct and actually describes the format you want. Thus the root element is probably the first element you'll want to deal with. In the television listings example, SCHEDULE is the root element. The document type declaration in the XML document specifies the name of this element:

```
<!DOCTYPE SCHEDULE SYSTEM "tvschedule.dtd">
```

However, this merely says that the root element is SCHEDULE. It does not say anything about what a SCHEDULE element may or may not contain, which is why you must next declare the SCHEDULE element in an element declaration inside the DTD. That's done with this line of code:

```
<!ELEMENT SCHEDULE ANY>
```

All element declarations begin with <!ELEMENT (case-sensitive) and end with >. They include the name of the element being declared (SCHEDULE in this example) followed by the content specification. In this declaration, the content specification is the keyword ANY (again case-sensitive). This says that all possible elements as well as plain text can be children of the SCHEDULE element.

Because ANY is so unrestrictive, it lets you very quickly create a DTD that will validate a document. Simply list all the element names and give each of them the content specification ANY. Listing 8-1 demonstrates.

Listing 8-1: A Very Loose DTD for Television Listings

```
<!ELEMENT SCHEDULE ANY>
<!ELEMENT DATE ANY>
<!ELEMENT STATION ANY>
<!ELEMENT NETWORK ANY>
<!ELEMENT CALL_LETTERS ANY>
<!ELEMENT CHANNEL ANY>
<!ELEMENT SHOW ANY>
<!ELEMENT NAME ANY>
<!ELEMENT TYPE ANY>
<!ELEMENT EPISODE_NUMBER ANY>
<!ELEMENT START_TIME ANY>
<!ELEMENT LENGTH ANY>
<!ELEMENT AIR_DATE ANY>
<!ELEMENT ORIGINAL_AIR_DATE ANY>
<!ELEMENT CLOSED_CAPTIONED  ANY>
<!ELEMENT REPEAT ANY>
<!ELEMENT CAST ANY>
<!ELEMENT ACTOR ANY>
<!ELEMENT GIVEN_NAME ANY>
<!ELEMENT SURNAME ANY>
<!ELEMENT PRODUCER ANY>
<!ELEMENT DESCRIPTION ANY>
<!ELEMENT TITLE ANY>
<!ELEMENT MIDDLE_NAME ANY>
<!ELEMENT RATING ANY>
<!ELEMENT YEAR_MADE ANY>
<!ELEMENT STARS ANY>
<!ELEMENT DIRECTOR ANY>
<!ELEMENT WRITER ANY>
<!ELEMENT MIDDLE_INITIAL ANY>
```

However, this DTD really doesn't say very much. It provides a complete list of all the possible elements, but it places no restrictions on where they may appear and what they may contain. Given this DTD, it's not just documents like Listing 4-2 that are valid, but essentially any document that contains only the elements declared in Listing 8-1. For example, the document in Listing 8-2 is valid, though ultimately you'll want to forbid documents like this one that omit crucial information and put other information in the wrong place.

Listing 8-2: A Document That's Valid According to the DTD in Listing 8-1

```
<?xml version="1.0"?>
<!DOCTYPE DATE SYSTEM "tvschedule.dtd">
<DATE>
  July 3, 2003
  <CAST>
    <NETWORK>CBS</NETWORK>
    <CALL_LETTERS>WCBS</CALL_LETTERS>
    <CHANNEL>2</CHANNEL>
  </CAST>
  <SHOW>
    Hollywood Squares
    <START_TIME>19:00-0500</START_TIME>
  </SHOW>
</DATE>
```

On the other hand, the document in Listing 8-3 is not valid, because it uses two elements that are not declared in Listing 8-1, `NAME` and `ROLE`. The problem is not that `ACTOR` is not allowed to contain `NAME` and `ROLE` elements, but rather that the `NAME` and `ROLE` elements have not been declared. The `ANY` content model really means any declared element, not any element at all.

Listing 8-3: A Document That's Invalid According to the DTD in Listing 8-1

```
<?xml version="1.0"?>
<!DOCTYPE ACTOR SYSTEM "tvschedule.dtd">
<ACTOR>
  <NAME>
    <GIVEN_NAME>Frank</GIVEN_NAME>
    <SURNAME>Oz</SURNAME>
  </NAME>
  <ROLE>Yoda</ROLE>
  <DATE>May 25, 1944</DATE>
</ACTOR>
```

A loose DTD such as Listing 8-1 is useful to get started, because you can validate documents immediately for testing. Starting with a very loose DTD like this one does allow you to add one constraint at a time, test it, and move on to the next one.

It's easier than trying to write down the complete DTD starting from a blank page. However, you'll want to be more strict about most elements as you develop the DTD.

#PCDATA

Beginning at the top of the document, the first child of the root element is DATE. The DATE element contains a little text, not even a whole line, like so:

```
<DATE>July 3, 2003</DATE>
```

The amount of text or the number of lines the DATE element contains doesn't matter. A validating parser doesn't make any validity checks on the character data of an element. However, that the DATE element can only contain text, and that it cannot contain child elements, does matter. An element that can only contain plain text is declared using the keyword #PCDATA in parentheses, like this:

```
<!ELEMENT YEAR (#PCDATA)>
```

This declaration says that a DATE can contain only parsed character data, that is, text that's not markup. It cannot contain children of its own. Therefore, this DATE element is valid:

```
<DATE>June 20, 2004</DATE>
```

These DATE elements are also valid:

```
<DATE>2003</DATE>
<DATE>July 3</DATE>
<DATE>
 The third day of the seventh month in the year of our Lord
 two thousand and three
</DATE>
```

Even this DATE element is valid because XML does not attempt to validate the contents of PCDATA, only that it is text that doesn't contain markup.

```
<DATE>Delicious, delicious, oh how boring</DATE>
```

However, this DATE element is invalid because it contains child elements:

```
<DATE>
  <MONTH>July</MONTH>
  <DAY>3</DAY>
  <YEAR>2003</YEAR>
</DATE>
```

There are two basic kinds of elements in XML. Simple elements can only contain plain text. They can't have any child elements. Complex elements can contain other elements or both plain text and other elements. There are no integer, floating-point, date, or other data types in standard XML. Thus, you can't use a DTD to say that a channel number must be an integer, or that the call letters must be four uppercase letters beginning with either K or W, even though doing so would match U.S. requirements for call letters. Various other schema languages, including the W3C XML Schema Language, do allow you to make and validate constraints on simple content like these. Schemas are explored in Chapter 20.

There are quite a few more elements in the TV listings example that can only contain character data, no child elements. Each of these is declared in the same way. Adding these declarations, the DTD becomes as shown in Listing 8-4.

Listing 8-4: A Television Listing DTD That Uses Content Models

```
<!ELEMENT SCHEDULE ANY>
<!ELEMENT DATE                (#PCDATA)>
<!ELEMENT SHOW ANY>
<!ELEMENT STATION ANY>
<!ELEMENT NETWORK             (#PCDATA)>
<!ELEMENT CALL_LETTERS        (#PCDATA)>
<!ELEMENT CHANNEL             (#PCDATA)>
<!ELEMENT NAME                (#PCDATA)>
<!ELEMENT TYPE                (#PCDATA)>
<!ELEMENT EPISODE_NUMBER      (#PCDATA)>
<!ELEMENT START_TIME          (#PCDATA)>
<!ELEMENT LENGTH              (#PCDATA)>
<!ELEMENT AIR_DATE            (#PCDATA)>
<!ELEMENT ORIGINAL_AIR_DATE (#PCDATA)>
<!ELEMENT CLOSED_CAPTIONED    (#PCDATA)>
<!ELEMENT REPEAT              (#PCDATA)>
<!ELEMENT GIVEN_NAME          (#PCDATA)>
<!ELEMENT SURNAME             (#PCDATA)>
<!ELEMENT DESCRIPTION         (#PCDATA)>
<!ELEMENT TITLE               (#PCDATA)>
<!ELEMENT MIDDLE_NAME         (#PCDATA)>
<!ELEMENT MIDDLE_INITIAL      (#PCDATA)>
<!ELEMENT RATING              (#PCDATA)>
<!ELEMENT YEAR_MADE           (#PCDATA)>
<!ELEMENT STARS               (#PCDATA)>
<!ELEMENT DIRECTOR ANY>
<!ELEMENT WRITER ANY>
<!ELEMENT PRODUCER ANY>
<!ELEMENT ACTOR ANY>
<!ELEMENT CAST ANY>
```

Using this revised DTD, Listing 8-2 is now invalid because the DATE element is no longer allowed to contain anything except character data. This hasn't yet ruled out all the documents you'd like to prohibit. However, you're well on the way.

Child Elements

Because the SCHEDULE element was declared to accept any element as a child, elements could be tossed in willy-nilly. This is occasionally useful when you have text that's more or less unstructured, such as a magazine article in which paragraphs, sidebars, bulleted lists, numbered lists, graphs, photographs, and subheads may appear pretty much anywhere in the document. However, most of the time you want to exercise more discipline and control over the placement of the data. For example, you can require that every SCHEDULE have a DATE and one or more SHOWs, that every ACTOR have a GIVEN_NAME and a SURNAME, and that the GIVEN_NAME come before the SURNAME. This discipline is provided by a *content model*, a parenthesized list of the possible child elements along with various quantifiers that identify how many of each can appear and other punctuation that indicates whether or not order is significant.

Some developers and books use the term content model to refer to all content specifications, not just choices and sequences, but also mixed content declarations and the EMPTY and ANY keywords. The XML specification only uses the words *content model* to refer to parenthesized lists of child elements, and I follow that usage here. However, not a lot is lost by conflating content model with content specification.

The first child of the SCHEDULE element is DATE. To declare that a SCHEDULE must have a DATE, the content model is simply a pair of parentheses containing the element name DATE, like this:

```
<!ELEMENT SCHEDULE (DATE)>
```

What this says is that each SCHEDULE element should contain exactly one DATE child element, and possibly some boundary white space, but nothing else. Of course, the SCHEDULE in Listing 4-2 doesn't contain just a date. It also has three STATION child elements. You can add additional children in their proper order, separated from each other by commas. Here's a complete declaration for the SCHEDULE element:

```
<!ELEMENT SCHEDULE (DATE, STATION, STATION, STATION)>
```

This form of content model is called a *sequence*. This says that each SCHEDULE element should contain exactly one DATE child element, followed by exactly three STATION elements. Listing 8-5 shows the revised DTD.

Listing 8-5: A Television Listing DTD That Uses ##PCDATA Content Specifications

```
<!ELEMENT SCHEDULE (DATE, STATION, STATION, STATION)>
<!ELEMENT DATE              (#PCDATA)>
<!ELEMENT SHOW ANY>
<!ELEMENT STATION ANY>
<!ELEMENT NETWORK           (#PCDATA)>
<!ELEMENT CALL_LETTERS      (#PCDATA)>
<!ELEMENT CHANNEL           (#PCDATA)>
<!ELEMENT NAME              (#PCDATA)>
<!ELEMENT TYPE              (#PCDATA)>
<!ELEMENT EPISODE_NUMBER    (#PCDATA)>
<!ELEMENT START_TIME        (#PCDATA)>
<!ELEMENT LENGTH            (#PCDATA)>
<!ELEMENT AIR_DATE          (#PCDATA)>
<!ELEMENT ORIGINAL_AIR_DATE (#PCDATA)>
<!ELEMENT CLOSED_CAPTIONED  (#PCDATA)>
<!ELEMENT REPEAT            (#PCDATA)>
<!ELEMENT GIVEN_NAME        (#PCDATA)>
<!ELEMENT SURNAME           (#PCDATA)>
<!ELEMENT DESCRIPTION       (#PCDATA)>
<!ELEMENT TITLE             (#PCDATA)>
<!ELEMENT MIDDLE_NAME       (#PCDATA)>
<!ELEMENT MIDDLE_INITIAL    (#PCDATA)>
<!ELEMENT RATING            (#PCDATA)>
<!ELEMENT YEAR_MADE         (#PCDATA)>
<!ELEMENT STARS             (#PCDATA)>
<!ELEMENT DIRECTOR ANY>
<!ELEMENT WRITER ANY>
<!ELEMENT PRODUCER ANY>
<!ELEMENT ACTOR ANY>
<!ELEMENT CAST ANY>
```

Each element should be declared in its own `<!ELEMENT>` declaration exactly once, even if it appears as a child in other `<!ELEMENT>` declarations. Listing 8-5 places the declaration of `NETWORK` after the declaration of `SCHEDULE` that refers to it, but that doesn't matter. XML allows forward references. It even allows circular references; that is, two elements `A` and `B`, either of which can be the child of the other. The order in which element declarations appear is irrelevant as long as all elements used in any content specification are declared somewhere in the DTD.

Listing 4-2 does adhere to this DTD because its `SCHEDULE` element contains one `DATE` child followed by three `STATION` children, and nothing else. However, if the document included only one or two `STATION` child elements or more than three `STATION` child elements, it would be invalid. Similarly, if the `STATION` came before the `DATE` element instead of after it, or if the document in any other way did not adhere to the DTD, the document would be invalid and validating parsers would reject it. You can loosen the restrictions on the number of child elements by using quantifiers. You can loosen the restrictions on order by using choices.

+ One or More Children

Listing 8-4 validates Listing 4-2. However, it's a little too restrictive. It requires that there be exactly three stations. That's only true because I cut this example down to fit in the book. More common cases would have all the stations broadcast in a particular market, which could range into the hundreds. On the flip side, a document sent out by one network or station might contain data for only a single network.

To indicate that you want one or more of a given element, place a plus sign (+) after the element name in the child list, as in the following example:

```
<!ELEMENT SCHEDULE (DATE, STATION+)>
```

This says that a SCHEDULE element must contain a single DATE element followed by one or more STATION elements.

You can also use the + quantifier to indicate that each cast has one or more actors:

```
<!ELEMENT CAST (ACTOR+)>
```

If a cast had no actors at all, you just wouldn't include that CAST element in the instance document.

? Zero or One Child

In many cases, an element may only appear once or not at all. For example, consider the names of the various person elements in the example: ACTOR, PRODUCER, DIRECTOR, and WRITER. Most, but not all, of these have a GIVEN_NAME and a SURNAME. Some, but not most, have a MIDDLE_NAME. One has a MIDDLE_INITIAL, but none of the others do. None of these child elements appear more than once in any given parent.

You can indicate that a child element is optional in a sequence—that is, that it can appear or not appear—by suffixing its name with a ?. For example, here are better declarations for the ACTOR, PRODUCER, DIRECTOR, and WRITER elements:

```
<!ELEMENT ACTOR    (GIVEN_NAME?, MIDDLE_NAME?,
                    MIDDLE_INITIAL?, SURNAME?)>
<!ELEMENT WRITER   (GIVEN_NAME?, MIDDLE_NAME?,
                    MIDDLE_INITIAL?, SURNAME?)>
<!ELEMENT PRODUCER (GIVEN_NAME?, MIDDLE_NAME?,
                    MIDDLE_INITIAL?, SURNAME?)>
<!ELEMENT DIRECTOR (GIVEN_NAME?, MIDDLE_NAME?,
                    MIDDLE_INITIAL?, SURNAME?)>
```

Different elements in the same content model can have different quantifiers. For example, consider the STATION element. Each STATION contains one CHANNEL, either a NETWORK, CALL_LETTERS, or both, and one or more SHOW elements. It's declaration can be written by making use of both the + and ?, like this:

```
<!ELEMENT STATION (NETWORK?, CALL_LETTERS?, CHANNEL, SHOW+)>
```

* Zero or More Children

The final quantifier used in content models is the asterisk. This indicates a child can appear zero or more times. It can appear once, twice, a thousand times, or not at all. In the example, you might use this for middle names and middle initials, to account for actors such as William Billy Bob Muddle with more than one middle name:

```
<!ELEMENT ACTOR    (GIVEN_NAME?, MIDDLE_NAME*,
                    MIDDLE_INITIAL*, SURNAME?)>
<!ELEMENT WRITER   (GIVEN_NAME?, MIDDLE_NAME?*,
                    MIDDLE_INITIAL*, SURNAME?)>
<!ELEMENT PRODUCER (GIVEN_NAME?, MIDDLE_NAME*,
                    MIDDLE_INITIAL*, SURNAME?)>
<!ELEMENT DIRECTOR (GIVEN_NAME?, MIDDLE_NAME*,
                    MIDDLE_INITIAL*, SURNAME?)>
```

This is also important for the SHOW element. Several potential child elements of SHOW can appear once, several times, or not at all, including PRODUCER, DIRECTOR, and WRITER. Of course, other children of the SHOW element are optional (?) and some must appear (no quantifier). Because each SHOW element can have so many children, its declaration is fairly long:

```
<!ELEMENT SHOW (NAME, TYPE?, EPISODE_NUMBER?, START_TIME+,
    LENGTH, AIR_DATE, ORIGINAL_AIR_DATE? CLOSED_CAPTIONED?,
    REPEAT?, RATING?, STARS?, DIRECTOR*, WRITER*, CAST?,
    PRODUCER*, DESCRIPTION)>
```

Choices

So far, I've assumed that child elements appear or do not appear in a specific order. You, however, might want to make your DTD more flexible, for example, by allowing document authors to choose between different elements in a given place. For example, in a DTD describing a purchase by a customer, each PAYMENT element might have either a CREDIT_CARD child or a CASH child providing information about the method of payment. However, an individual PAYMENT would not have both.

You can indicate that the document author needs to input either one or another element by separating child elements with a vertical bar (|) rather than with a comma (,) in the parent's element declaration. For example, this declaration says that the PAYMENT element must have a single child element of type CASH or CREDIT_CARD:

```
<!ELEMENT PAYMENT (CASH | CREDIT_CARD)>
```

This sort of content specification is called a *choice*. You can separate any number of children with vertical bars when you want exactly one of them to be used. For example, the following says that the PAYMENT element must have a single child of type CASH, CREDIT_CARD, or CHECK.

```
<!ELEMENT PAYMENT (CASH | CREDIT_CARD | CHECK)>
```

Parentheses

Each set of parentheses combines several elements so that the combination is treated as a single unit when validating. This parenthesized unit can then be nested inside other parentheses in place of a single element. Furthermore, you can then affix a plus sign, an asterisk, or a question mark to it. You can group these parenthesized combinations into still larger parenthesized groups to produce quite complex structures. This is a very powerful technique.

For example, consider a list composed of two elements that must alternate with each other. This is essentially how HTML's definition list works. Each DT element should be followed by one DD element. The declaration of such a DL element looks like this:

```
<!ELEMENT DL (DT, DD)*>
```

The parentheses indicate that it's the matched <DT><DD> pair being repeated, not <DD> alone.

Both choices and sequences appear in parentheses. These parentheses can also have +, *, or ? quantifiers suffixed to them, with the expected meaning. For example, this declaration says that an ACTOR element can have one or more of GIVEN_NAME, MIDDLE_NAME, MIDDLE_INITIAL, or SURNAME child elements:

```
<!ELEMENT ACTOR
  (GIVEN_NAME| MIDDLE_NAME | MIDDLE_INITIAL | SURNAME )+ >
```

Because this is a choice, these can appear in any order.

Even more usefully, you can include parenthesized choices and sequences in the place of a single element name inside another choice or sequence. For example, suppose you want to indicate that an ACTOR can have any number of middle names and middle initials in any order. However, they can have at most one GIVEN_NAME and one SURNAME. That constraint can be encoded like this:

```
<!ELEMENT ACTOR (GIVEN_NAME?,
                 (MIDDLE_NAME | MIDDLE_INITIAL)*,
                 SURNAME?)>
```

This still allows an ACTOR to have no names at all. A more complex nesting of parentheses can require that each actor have at least one name, though it doesn't matter whether it's a GIVEN_NAME (Cher), a MIDDLE_NAME (Kennedy), or a SURNAME (Teller):

```
<!ELEMENT ACTOR (
   (GIVEN_NAME, (MIDDLE_NAME | MIDDLE_INITIAL)*, SURNAME?)
  | ((MIDDLE_NAME | MIDDLE_INITIAL)+, SURNAME)
  | SURNAME
)>
```

For a STATION element, ideally, you'd want either a NETWORK or CALL_LETTERS or both. However, at least one must be present, and if both are present, the network must come first. This declaration accomplishes that:

```
<!ELEMENT STATION (
   (NETWORK | CALL_LETTERS | (NETWORK, CALL_LETTERS)),
    CHANNEL, SHOW+)>
```

There's actually a very subtle technical problem with this declaration. Its content model is *ambiguous*. What this means is that when a parser sees an initial NETWORK child element of a STATION, it doesn't know whether it belongs to the first branch of the choice or the third. Some validators can handle ambiguous content models, but not all can. This model needs to be refactored to remove the ambiguity by placing the initial NETWORK child element in a single branch. This rearrangement works nicely:

```
<!ELEMENT STATION (
   ( (NETWORK, CALL_LETTERS?) | CALL_LETTERS ),
    CHANNEL, SHOW+)>
```

Listing 8-6 puts this all together to show the finished DTD for television listings such as those of Listing 4-2.

Listing 8-6: The Finished Television Listing DTD

```
<!ELEMENT SCHEDULE (DATE, STATION+)>
<!ELEMENT DATE              (#PCDATA)>
<!ELEMENT STATION (
   ( (NETWORK, CALL_LETTERS?) | CALL_LETTERS ),
    CHANNEL, SHOW+)>
<!ELEMENT SHOW (NAME, TITLE?, TYPE?, EPISODE_NUMBER?, START_TIME+,
    LENGTH, AIR_DATE, ORIGINAL_AIR_DATE?, YEAR_MADE?,
    CLOSED_CAPTIONED?, REPEAT?, RATING?, STARS?, DIRECTOR*,
    WRITER*, CAST?, PRODUCER*, DESCRIPTION?)>
<!ELEMENT NETWORK           (#PCDATA)>
<!ELEMENT CALL_LETTERS      (#PCDATA)>
<!ELEMENT CHANNEL           (#PCDATA)>
```

```
<!ELEMENT NAME              (#PCDATA)>
<!ELEMENT TITLE             (#PCDATA)>
<!ELEMENT TYPE              (#PCDATA)>
<!ELEMENT EPISODE_NUMBER    (#PCDATA)>
<!ELEMENT START_TIME        (#PCDATA)>
<!ELEMENT LENGTH            (#PCDATA)>
<!ELEMENT AIR_DATE          (#PCDATA)>
<!ELEMENT ORIGINAL_AIR_DATE (#PCDATA)>
<!ELEMENT CLOSED_CAPTIONED  (#PCDATA)>
<!ELEMENT REPEAT            (#PCDATA)>
<!ELEMENT GIVEN_NAME        (#PCDATA)>
<!ELEMENT MIDDLE_NAME       (#PCDATA)>
<!ELEMENT MIDDLE_INITIAL    (#PCDATA)>
<!ELEMENT SURNAME           (#PCDATA)>
<!ELEMENT RATING            (#PCDATA)>
<!ELEMENT YEAR_MADE         (#PCDATA)>
<!ELEMENT STARS             (#PCDATA)>
<!ELEMENT DESCRIPTION       (#PCDATA)>

<!ELEMENT CAST (ACTOR+)>
<!ELEMENT ACTOR (
    (GIVEN_NAME, (MIDDLE_NAME | MIDDLE_INITIAL)*, SURNAME?)
  | ((MIDDLE_NAME | MIDDLE_INITIAL)+, SURNAME)
  | SURNAME
)>
<!ELEMENT WRITER (
    (GIVEN_NAME, (MIDDLE_NAME | MIDDLE_INITIAL)*, SURNAME?)
  | ((MIDDLE_NAME | MIDDLE_INITIAL)+, SURNAME)
  | SURNAME
)>
<!ELEMENT PRODUCER (
    (GIVEN_NAME, (MIDDLE_NAME | MIDDLE_INITIAL)*, SURNAME?)
  | ((MIDDLE_NAME | MIDDLE_INITIAL)+, SURNAME)
  | SURNAME
)>
<!ELEMENT DIRECTOR (
    (GIVEN_NAME, (MIDDLE_NAME | MIDDLE_INITIAL)*, SURNAME?)
  | ((MIDDLE_NAME | MIDDLE_INITIAL)+, SURNAME)
  | SURNAME
)>
```

Once you've finished the DTD, you'll want to test it by validating your instance documents. Just like any reasonably complex program, there are likely to be bugs. The first few variants of this DTD I wrote did have bugs, both syntax and semantic errors. Eventually, I fixed those. However, it still couldn't completely validate Listing 4-2. The problem was order. Listing 8-6 is quite specific about the order of the child elements of `SHOW`. Not all the elements in Listing 4-2 use that particular order. For example, some put the `PRODUCER` before the `CAST`, others after. Some put the `DESCRIPTION` at the end. Some don't. I could loosen up the order by using a choice instead of a sequence. The problem is then I lose the ability to control the number of each child element. If I say that PRODUCER can come before or after CAST, I can't say there's at most one CAST. You're forced to choose between more order than you may want or less control of size than you need. In this case, I decided that since order didn't really matter and the number of child elements did, it wouldn't be as big a problem to impose an arbitrary order as to allow more of some elements than I wanted.

There's more that could be done, with a reasonable investment of effort. For example, you could use a choice to specify different sets of data for different kinds of shows. You might have one set of child elements for movies, a different set for television series, and a different set for news. However, you could not specify that the branch of the choice for movies could be used only if the TYPE element had the value Movie.

Nonetheless, using parentheses to create blocks of elements, either in sequences with a comma or in choices with a vertical bar, and then suffixing the blocks with quantifiers such as * and ? enables you to create complex structures with detailed rules for how different elements follow one another. Try not to go overboard with this, though. Simpler solutions are better solutions. The more complex a DTD is, the harder it is to write valid files that satisfy the DTD, to say nothing of the complexity of maintaining the DTD itself.

Mixed Content

You may have noticed that in most of the examples so far, elements either contained child elements or character data, but not both. You can declare tags that contain both child elements and character data. This is called *mixed content*. You can use this to allow each CAST to include arbitrary text as well as ACTOR child elements, as in the following example:

```
<!ELEMENT CAST (#PCDATA | ACTOR)*>
```

Mixing child elements with parsed character data severely restricts the structure you can impose on your documents. In particular, you can specify only the names of the child elements that can appear. You cannot constrain the order in which they appear, the number of each that appears, or whether they appear at all. In terms of DTDs, think of this as meaning that the child part of the DTD must look like this:

```
<!ELEMENT PARENT (#PCDATA | CHILD1 | CHILD2 | CHILD3 )* >
```

Almost everything else, other than changing the list of permitted child elements, is invalid. You cannot place the #PCDATA after the child elements. You cannot use commas, question marks, or plus signs in an element declaration that includes #PCDATA. A list of elements and #PCDATA separated by vertical bars is valid. Any other use is not. For example, the following is illegal:

```
<!ELEMENT CAST (ACTOR*, #PCDATA)>
```

Thus, once you've said that a CAST element can contain parsed character data, you can no longer say that it must have exactly one ACTOR child, or that the ACTOR children come before or after the plain text.

Mixed content is most common in narrative content such as web pages and newspaper articles. While writing a paragraph, you might want to <EMPHASIZE>emphasize a phrase</EMPHASIZE> or note a <PERSON>person's name</PERSON>. On the other hand, most of the text of the paragraph or sentence that surrounds the emphasized phrase or noted name is just text, with nothing special to distinguish it from all the other text of the paragraph or sentence. This structure is common to both written and spoken narratives.

More recordlike documents such as the television listings example tend to avoid mixed content. Structured documents are easier to work with if all elements contain either other elements or unmarked-up text, but not both. You can always create a new element that holds parsed character data if you find you need it. For example, you can include a block of text at the end of each CAST element by declaring a new BLURB element that holds only #PCDATA and adding it as the last child element of CAST. Here's how this looks:

```
<!ELEMENT CAST (ACTOR*, BLURB)>
<!ELEMENT BLURB (#PCDATA)>
```

This does not significantly change the structure of the document. All it does is add one more optional element to each CAST element. However, human thought is not nearly so structured, and these strict forms of markup don't work as well in that domain. Articles, essays, novels, diaries, travelogues, short stories, speeches, and similar narratives are likely to make much heavier use of mixed content.

Empty Elements

As discussed in earlier chapters, it's occasionally useful to define an element that has no content. Examples in HTML include the image <IMG>, horizontal rule <HR>, and break <BR>. In XML, such empty elements are sometimes denoted by empty-element tags that end with />, such as <IMG/>, <HR/>, and <BR/>.

Valid documents must declare both the empty and nonempty elements they use. Because empty elements by definition don't have children, they're easy to declare. Use an <!ELEMENT> declaration containing the name of the empty element as normal, but use the keyword EMPTY (case-sensitive as all XML tags are) instead of a list of children. For example:

```
<!ELEMENT BR  EMPTY>
<!ELEMENT IMG EMPTY>
<!ELEMENT HR  EMPTY>
```

Listing 8-7 is a valid document that uses both empty and nonempty elements.

Listing 8-7: A Valid Document Using Empty Elements

```
<?xml version="1.0"?>
<!DOCTYPE DOCUMENT [
   <!ELEMENT DOCUMENT (TITLE, SIGNATURE)>
   <!ELEMENT TITLE (#PCDATA)>
   <!ELEMENT COPYRIGHT (#PCDATA)>
   <!ELEMENT EMAIL (#PCDATA)>
   <!ELEMENT BR EMPTY>
   <!ELEMENT HR EMPTY>
   <!ELEMENT LAST_MODIFIED (#PCDATA)>
   <!ELEMENT SIGNATURE (HR, COPYRIGHT, BR, EMAIL,
       BR, LAST_MODIFIED)>
]>
<DOCUMENT>
  <TITLE>Empty-element Tags</TITLE>
  <SIGNATURE>
    <HR/>
    <COPYRIGHT>2003 Elliotte Rusty Harold</COPYRIGHT><BR/>
    <EMAIL>elharo@metalab.unc.edu</EMAIL><BR/>
    <LAST_MODIFIED>Wednesday, December 3, 2003</LAST_MODIFIED>
  </SIGNATURE>
</DOCUMENT>
```

Declaring an element to be EMPTY requires that all instances of it be empty. However, an element that is declared to have PCDATA content or purely optional child elements may also be empty some of the time. For example, Listing 8-12 declares that the TITLE element contains parsed character data. Therefore, these are all valid TITLE elements according to that DTD:

```
<TITLE>Empty-element Tags</TITLE>
<TITLE></TITLE>
<TITLE/>
<TITLE />
```

The empty-element tag syntax used in <TITLE/> is pure syntax sugar for the longer form <TITLE></TITLE>. You can use <TITLE/> anywhere you use <TITLE></TITLE>. The TITLE element does not need to be declared EMPTY before it can be represented by an empty-element tag.

Comments in DTDs

DTDs can contain comments, just like the rest of an XML document. These comments cannot appear inside a declaration, but they can appear outside one. Comments are often used to organize the DTD in different parts, to document the allowed content of particular elements, and to further explain what an element is. For example, the element declaration for the DATE element might have a comment such as this:

```
<!-- A date in the form Month Day, Year
     The year is always written with four digits. -->
<!ELEMENT DATE (#PCDATA)>
```

As with all comments, this is only for the benefit of people reading the source code. XML processors will ignore it.

Besides additional information about the format of character data, DTDs often use comments to indicate:

- ✦ Who wrote the DTD
- ✦ Copyright for the DTD
- ✦ Usage conditions
- ✦ Usage instructions
- ✦ Customary PUBLIC and SYSTEM identifiers

Listing 8-8 is similar to previous television schedule examples but uses comments to more fully explain the DTD.

Listing 8-8: A Commented DTD

```
<!-- Television Listings DTD
     Copyright 2003 Elliotte Rusty Harold

     This DTD was developed as an example for the
     XML Bible, 3rd Edition by Elliotte Rusty Harold
     (John Wiley & Sons, 2003).
     You'll find complete documentation in Chapter 8.
     Feel free to use this DTD in any way you like.
     Address questions and comments to
     elharo@metalab.unc.edu

     This DTD is customarily identified with the following
     PUBLIC and SYSTEM IDs:
```

Continued

Listing 8-8 *(continued)*

```
PUBLIC
  "-//Cafe con Leche//DTD TV Listings 1.0//EN"
SYSTEM
  "http://cafeconleche.org/dtds/tvschedule.dtd"

     However, you can make a local copy and use a different
     SYSTEM ID if you like.

-->

<!-- The schedule for one day. However, the day may start
     after midnight, and finish in the A.M. hours of the
     following day. -->
<!ELEMENT SCHEDULE (DATE, STATION+)>

<!-- Dates are given in a human readable format such as
     "July 23, 2004" -->
<!ELEMENT DATE              (#PCDATA)>

<!-- One distinct show -->
<!ELEMENT SHOW (NAME, TITLE?, TYPE?, EPISODE_NUMBER?,
    START_TIME+, LENGTH, AIR_DATE, ORIGINAL_AIR_DATE?,
    YEAR_MADE?, CLOSED_CAPTIONED?, REPEAT?, RATING?, STARS?,
    DIRECTOR*, WRITER*, CAST?, PRODUCER*, DESCRIPTION?)>

<!-- A broadcast channel, satellite system or cable provider
     in a particular geographic area.  -->
<!ELEMENT STATION (
   ( (NETWORK, CALL_LETTERS?) | CALL_LETTERS ),
    CHANNEL, SHOW+)>

<!-- This is the typical name of the network, such as
     CBS, HBO, or CNN. -->
<!ELEMENT NETWORK           (#PCDATA)>

<!-- These are the call letters assigned by the FCC or foreign
     equivalent in all caps. For example, WPIX, KRGO, WTBS-->
<!ELEMENT CALL_LETTERS      (#PCDATA)>

<!-- A positive integer listing the channel for the station
    in the local market -->
<!ELEMENT CHANNEL           (#PCDATA)>

<!-- The name of the series such as "Friends" or
     "Babylon 5" -->
<!ELEMENT NAME              (#PCDATA)>

<!-- The title of the individual episode such as
     "The One with the Improbably Large Apartment" -->
```

```
<!ELEMENT TITLE             (#PCDATA)>

<!-- The type of the show. This is one of the
     following values:

     Series
     Series/Comedy
     Series/News
     Series/Game Shows
     Series/Talk
     Movie
     Movie/Action
     Movie/Animated
     Movie/Comedy
     Movie/Drama
     Sports
     Sports/Football
     Sports/Baseball
     Sports/Basketball
     Sports/Racing
     Sports/Tennis
     Sports/Golf

 -->
<!ELEMENT TYPE              (#PCDATA)>

<!-- The episode number in the format issued by the
     producers. Not necessarily an integer. -->
<!ELEMENT EPISODE_NUMBER    (#PCDATA)>

<!-- The time the show starts. This is given in
     Universal Coordinated Time using a 24 hour clock.
     For example, 18:30-0500. To get the local time
     remove the time zone offset that follows the hyphen. -->
<!ELEMENT START_TIME        (#PCDATA)>

<!-- The duration of the show in minutes. -->
<!ELEMENT LENGTH            (#PCDATA)>

<!-- The date on which the show begins broadcasting.
     The may not be the same as the date of the schedule
     if the show starts on or after midnight. -->
<!ELEMENT AIR_DATE          (#PCDATA)>

<!-- The date when this show was first broadcast. -->
<!ELEMENT ORIGINAL_AIR_DATE (#PCDATA)>

<!-- Yes if the show is closed captioned, No if it isn't.
     This element is omitted if it is not known whether
     the show is closed captioned. -->
<!ELEMENT CLOSED_CAPTIONED  (#PCDATA)>
```

Continued

Listing 8-8 *(continued)*

```
<!-- Yes if the show is a repeat, No if it isn't.
     This element is omitted if it is not known whether
     the show is a repeat. -->
<!ELEMENT REPEAT            (#PCDATA)>

<!-- A person's first name. -->
<!ELEMENT GIVEN_NAME        (#PCDATA)>

<!-- The family name of a person. May be more than
     one word in cases like "Van Zandt" -->
<!ELEMENT SURNAME           (#PCDATA)>

<!-- A person's middle name. -->
<!ELEMENT MIDDLE_NAME       (#PCDATA)>

<!-- A person's middle initial. -->
<!ELEMENT MIDDLE_INITIAL    (#PCDATA)>

<!-- FCC rating for a show. Possible values are

     TV-Y
     TV-Y7
     TV-G
     TV-PG
     TV-PG14
     TV-MA

     Movies on cable channels may instead carry
     one of these MPAA ratings:

     G
     PG
     PG-13
     R
     NC-17

  -->
<!ELEMENT RATING            (#PCDATA)>

<!-- The year in which a movie was released theatrically -->
<!ELEMENT YEAR_MADE         (#PCDATA)>

<!-- The number of stars to assign to a show.
     The value is a number, typically 1 to 5,
      occasionally including halves like 3.5 -->
<!ELEMENT STARS             (#PCDATA)>
```

```
<!-- Brief description of the show -->
<!ELEMENT DESCRIPTION        (#PCDATA)>

<!ELEMENT CAST (ACTOR+)>
<!ELEMENT ACTOR (
   (GIVEN_NAME, (MIDDLE_NAME | MIDDLE_INITIAL)*, SURNAME?)
 | ((MIDDLE_NAME | MIDDLE_INITIAL)+, SURNAME)
 | SURNAME
)>
<!ELEMENT WRITER (
   (GIVEN_NAME, (MIDDLE_NAME | MIDDLE_INITIAL)*, SURNAME?)
 | ((MIDDLE_NAME | MIDDLE_INITIAL)+, SURNAME)
 | SURNAME
)>
<!ELEMENT PRODUCER (
   (GIVEN_NAME, (MIDDLE_NAME | MIDDLE_INITIAL)*, SURNAME?)
 | ((MIDDLE_NAME | MIDDLE_INITIAL)+, SURNAME)
 | SURNAME
)>
<!ELEMENT DIRECTOR (
   (GIVEN_NAME, (MIDDLE_NAME | MIDDLE_INITIAL)*, SURNAME?)
 | ((MIDDLE_NAME | MIDDLE_INITIAL)*, SURNAME)
 | (MIDDLE_NAME | MIDDLE_INITIAL)+
)>
```

There's no limit to the amount of information that you can or should include in comments. Including more does make your DTDs a little longer (and therefore harder to scan and slower to download). However, the increased clarity provided by using comments far outweighs these disadvantages. I recommend using comments liberally in all of your DTDs, but especially in those intended for public use.

Summary

In this chapter, you learned the complete syntax for element declarations in DTDs. In particular, you learned the following:

- Element declarations declare the name and content specification of an element.
- The content specification determines what an element may and may not contain.
- The keyword ANY is a content specification indicating that there are no restrictions on the content of an element.

- A sequence is a parenthesized list of child elements separated by commas. When a sequence is used as a content specification, child elements in the instance document must appear in the same order as they appear in the sequence.
- A choice is a parenthesized list of child elements separated by vertical bars (|). When a choice is used as a content specification, one of the child elements listed in the choice must appear in the instance document.
- A plus sign (+) means one or more instances of the element, sequence, or choice may appear.
- An asterisk (*) means zero or more instances of the element, sequence, or choice may appear.
- A question mark (?) means zero or one instance of the element, sequence, or choice may appear.
- Parenthesized sequences and choices can be nested to produce more complex content models.
- An element with mixed content contains both child elements and parsed character data. However, declaring mixed content limits the structure that you can impose on the parent element.
- Empty elements are declared with the `EMPTY` keyword.
- Comments make DTDs much more legible.

When a document uses attributes, the attributes must also be declared in the DTD. Chapter 9 shows you how to declare attributes in DTDs, and how you can attach constraints to the attribute values.

✦ ✦ ✦

CHAPTER 9

Attribute Declarations

✦ ✦ ✦ ✦

In This Chapter

What is an attribute?

Declaring attributes

Declaring multiple attributes

Alternatives to default attribute values

Attribute types

A DTD for attribute-based television listings

✦ ✦ ✦ ✦

Some XML elements have attributes, that is, name-value pairs. Attributes are intended for extra information associated with an element (such as an ID number) used only by programs that read and write the file, and not normally for the content of the element that's read and written by humans. In this chapter, you learn about the various attribute types and how to declare attributes in document type definitions (DTDs).

What Is an Attribute?

As first discussed in Chapter 5, start-tags and empty-element tags may contain attributes — name-value pairs separated by an equals sign (=). For example,

```
<GREETING LANGUAGE="English">
  Hello XML!
  <MOVIE SOURCE="WavingHand.mov"/>
</GREETING>
```

In this example, the `GREETING` element has a `LANGUAGE` attribute, which has the value `English`. The `MOVIE` element has a `SOURCE` attribute, which has the value `WavingHand.mov`. The `GREETING` element's content is `Hello XML!`. The language in which the content is written is useful information about the content. The language, however, is not itself part of the content.

Similarly, the `MOVIE` element's content is the binary data stored in the file WavingHand.mov. The name of the file is not the content, although the name tells you where the content can be found. The attribute contains information about the content rather than the content itself.

Elements can possess more than one attribute, as in the following example:

```
<SCRIPT LANGUAGE="javascript" ENCODING="ISO-8859-1">
  ...
</SCRIPT>
<RECTANGLE WIDTH="30" HEIGHT="45"/>
```

In this example, the `SCRIPT` element's `LANGUAGE` attribute has the value `javascript`. The `SCRIPT` element's `ENCODING` attribute has the value `ISO-8859-1`. The `RECTANGLE` element's `WIDTH` attribute has the value `30`. The `RECTANGLE` element's `HEIGHT` attribute has the value `45`. These values are all strings, not numbers.

Declaring Attributes

Like elements, the attributes used in a document must be declared in the DTD for the document to be valid. Attributes are declared by an attribute list in the following form:

```
<!ATTLIST Element_name Attribute_name Type Default_value>
```

`<!` starts all declarations. *`ATTLIST`* is the keyword that indicates this is an attribute list. *`Element_name`* is the name of the element possessing this attribute. *`Attribute_name`* is the name of the attribute. *`Type`* is the kind of attribute—one of the 10 types listed in Table 9-1. Finally, *`Default_value`* is the value the attribute takes on if no value is specified for the attribute.

Table 9-1
Attribute Types

Type	*Meaning*
`CDATA`	Character data – text that is not markup
Enumerated	A list of possible values from which exactly one will be chosen
`ID`	A unique name not shared by any other ID type attribute in the document
`IDREF`	The value of an ID type attribute of an element in the document
`IDREFS`	Multiple IDs of elements separated by white space
`ENTITY`	The name of an unparsed entity declared in the DTD
`ENTITIES`	Multiple names of unparsed entities declared in the DTD, separated by white space
`NMTOKEN`	An XML name token
`NMTOKENS`	Multiple XML name tokens separated by white space
`NOTATION`	One or more names of notations declared in the DTD

For example, consider the following element:

```
<GREETING LANGUAGE="French">
  Salut!
</GREETING>
```

This element might be declared as follows in the DTD:

```
<!ELEMENT GREETING (#PCDATA)>
<!ATTLIST GREETING LANGUAGE CDATA "English">
```

The <!ELEMENT> declaration simply says that a GREETING element contains parsed character data. That's nothing new. The <!ATTLIST> declaration says that GREETING elements have an attribute with the name LANGUAGE and the type CDATA, essentially the same as #PCDATA for element content. The word English in quotation marks is the default value. If you encounter a GREETING element without a LANGUAGE attribute, the value English is used by default.

Not all parsers read external DTD subsets. A parser that doesn't will not see and report any default attribute values declared in the external DTD subset, whereas a parser that does read the external DTD subset will. When attribute values are defaulted in from the DTD, two different parsers can see different information in the same document. For this reason, it's a good idea to include all important information in the instance document, even if it's available from the DTD. For maximum interoperability, avoid relying on default attribute values.

The attribute is declared separately from the element itself. The name of the element to which the attribute belongs is included in the <!ATTLIST> declaration. This attribute declaration applies only to that element, GREETING in the preceding example. If other elements also have LANGUAGE attributes, they require separate <!ATTLIST> declarations.

As with most declarations, the exact order in which attribute declarations appear is not important. They can come before or after the element declaration they're associated with. In fact, you can even declare an attribute more than once (although I don't recommend this practice), in which case the first such declaration takes precedence.

You can even declare attributes for elements that are not declared, although this is uncommon. This is sometimes done to provide default attribute values or assign attribute types in invalid documents.

Declaring Multiple Attributes

Elements often have more than one attribute. HTML's IMG element can have HEIGHT, WIDTH, ALT, BORDER, ALIGN, and several other attributes. In fact, all HTML elements can have multiple attributes. XML tags can also have multiple attributes. For example, a RECTANGLE element naturally needs both a LENGTH and a WIDTH.

```
<RECTANGLE LENGTH="70px" WIDTH="85px"/>
```

You can declare these attributes in several attribute declarations, with one declaration for each attribute, as in the following example:

```
<!ELEMENT RECTANGLE EMPTY>
<!ATTLIST RECTANGLE LENGTH CDATA "0px">
<!ATTLIST RECTANGLE WIDTH  CDATA "0px">
```

The preceding example says that `RECTANGLE` elements possess `LENGTH` and `WIDTH` attributes, each of which has the default value `0px`.

You can combine the two `<!ATTLIST>` declarations into a single declaration like this:

```
<!ATTLIST RECTANGLE LENGTH CDATA "0px"
                    WIDTH  CDATA "0px">
```

This single declaration declares both the `LENGTH` and `WIDTH` attributes, each with type `CDATA`, and each with a default value of `0px`. You can also use this syntax when the attributes have different types or defaults, like this:

```
<!ATTLIST RECTANGLE LENGTH CDATA "15px"
                    WIDTH  CDATA "34pt">
```

Attributes are unordered. Both of the following elements are valid:

```
<RECTANGLE LENGTH="70px" WIDTH="85px"/>
<RECTANGLE WIDTH="85px" LENGTH="70px"/>
```

The parser does not consider attribute order when validating. It won't even tell the client application which one came first. Do not write any code that depends on attribute order. If order matters, use child elements instead.

Alternatives to Default Attribute Values

Instead of specifying an explicit default attribute value such as `0px`, an attribute declaration can require the author to provide a value, allow the value to be omitted completely, or even always use the default value. These requirements are specified with the three keywords `#REQUIRED`, `#IMPLIED`, and `#FIXED`, respectively.

#REQUIRED

You may not always have a good option for a default value. For example, when writing a DTD for use on your intranet, you might want to require that all documents have at least one empty `AUTHOR` element. This element might not be rendered, but it can identify the person who created the document. This element can have NAME, EMAIL, and EXTENSION attributes so that the author can be contacted, as shown in the following example:

```
<AUTHOR NAME="Elliotte Rusty Harold"
  EMAIL="elharo@metalab.unc.edu" EXTENSION="4093"/>
```

Instead of providing default values for these attributes, suppose you want to force everyone posting a document on the intranet to identify themselves Although XML can't prevent someone from attributing authorship to Luke Skywalker, it can at least require that authorship be attributed to someone by using #REQUIRED as the default value. For example:

```
<!ELEMENT AUTHOR EMPTY>
<!ATTLIST AUTHOR NAME      CDATA #REQUIRED>
<!ATTLIST AUTHOR EMAIL     CDATA #REQUIRED>
<!ATTLIST AUTHOR EXTENSION CDATA #REQUIRED>
```

If the parser encounters an AUTHOR element that does not include one or more of these attributes, it signals the error.

You might also want to use #REQUIRED to force authors to give their IMG elements WIDTH, HEIGHT, and ALT attributes, as in the following example:

```
<!ELEMENT IMG EMPTY>
<!ATTLIST IMG ALT    CDATA #REQUIRED>
<!ATTLIST IMG WIDTH  CDATA #REQUIRED>
<!ATTLIST IMG HEIGHT CDATA #REQUIRED>
```

Any attempt to omit these attributes (as all too many web pages do) produces an invalid document. The XML parser notices the error and informs the author of the missing attributes.

#REQUIRED helps you guarantee that the minimum information necessary for processing a document is present. Any attribute that must be in the document should be defaulted to #REQUIRED.

#IMPLIED

Sometimes you may not have a good option for a default value, but you do not want to require the author of the document to include the attribute either. The attribute is optional. For example, suppose some of the people posting documents to your intranet are offsite freelancers who have e-mail addresses but lack phone extensions. You don't want to require them to include an extension attribute in their AUTHOR elements.

```
<AUTHOR NAME="Elliotte Rusty Harold"
        EMAIL="elharo@metalab.unc.edu" />
```

You still don't want to provide a default value for the extension, but you do want to allow authors to include such an attribute. In this case, use #IMPLIED as the default declaration like this:

```
<!ELEMENT AUTHOR EMPTY>
<!ATTLIST AUTHOR EXTENSION CDATA #IMPLIED>
<!ATTLIST AUTHOR NAME      CDATA #REQUIRED>
<!ATTLIST AUTHOR EMAIL     CDATA #REQUIRED>
```

An AUTHOR element without an EXTENSION attribute simply has no such attribute. The application can treat such an element as it chooses. For example, if the application is feeding elements into a SQL database in which the attributes are mapped to fields, the application would probably insert a null into the corresponding database field.

As with elements, attribute values are almost never set to N/A, Not Available, unknown, the empty string, or an illegal flag value such as -1. If the value of an attribute is not known or not available, simply omit it from the instance document, and declare it #IMPLIED in the DTD.

#FIXED

Finally, you may want to provide a default value for the attribute without allowing the author to change it. For example, you might want to specify a common COMPANY attribute of the AUTHOR element for anyone posting documents to your intranet, like this:

```
<AUTHOR NAME="Elliotte Rusty Harold" COMPANY="TIC"
  EMAIL="elharo@metalab.unc.edu" EXTENSION="3459"/>
```

You can require that everyone use this value for the company name by specifying the default value as #FIXED, followed by the actual default, as in the following example:

```
<!ELEMENT AUTHOR EMPTY>
<!ATTLIST AUTHOR COMPANY   CDATA #FIXED "TIC">
<!ATTLIST AUTHOR EXTENSION CDATA #IMPLIED>
<!ATTLIST AUTHOR NAME      CDATA #REQUIRED>
<!ATTLIST AUTHOR EMAIL     CDATA #REQUIRED>
```

Document authors are not required to actually include the fixed attribute in their tags. If they don't include the fixed attribute, a parser that reads the DTD will report the default value. If the fixed attribute is included in the instance document, however, it must have the value indicated in the DTD. Otherwise, the parser will report an error.

As with regular string defaults, if the parser does not read the DTD, it won't see the fixed default value. Thus, some parsers can ignore these attributes completely. For this reason, if you put critical information in a fixed attribute, you should include it in the instance document, too.

Attribute Types

All preceding examples have been `CDATA` type attributes. This is the most general type, but there are nine other types permitted for attributes. Altogether the 10 types are as follows:

- `CDATA`
- `NMTOKEN`
- `NMTOKENS`
- Enumerated
- `ID`
- `IDREF`
- `IDREFS`
- `ENTITY`
- `ENTITIES`
- `NOTATION`

Nine of the preceding types are constants used in the type field. The tenth, an enumerated type, lists all valid values explicitly. Let's investigate each type in depth.

The CDATA attribute type

`CDATA`, the most general attribute type, means the attribute value may be any string of text not containing a less than sign (<) or quotation marks ("). These characters can be inserted using the usual entity references (`<`, and `"`) or by character references (`<`, and `"`). Furthermore, all raw ampersands (&)—that is, ampersands that do not begin a character or entity reference—must also be escaped as `&` or `&`.

In fact, even if the value itself contains double quotes, they do not have to be escaped. Instead, you can use single quotes to delimit the attributes, as in the following example:

```
<RECTANGLE LENGTH='7"' WIDTH='8.5"'/>
```

If the attribute value contains single and double quotes, the one not used to delimit the value must be replaced with the entity reference `'` (apostrophe) or `"` (double quote), as in the following example:

```
<RECTANGLE LENGTH='8&apos;7"' WIDTH="10'6&quot;"/>
```

The NMTOKEN attribute type

The `NMTOKEN` attribute type restricts the value of the attribute to a legal XML name token. As discussed in Chapter 6, XML names must begin with a letter or an underscore (_), and subsequent characters in the name may include letters, digits, underscores, hyphens, and periods. They cannot include white space. (The underscore often substitutes for white space.) Technically, names can contain colons, but you shouldn't use this character because it's reserved for use with namespaces. A name token is the same as an XML name except that it may begin with digits, hyphens, and periods rather than just letters and the underscore. Thus, `73` and `-red` are legal name tokens even though they're not legal names. All names are name tokens, but not all name tokens are names.

The `NMTOKEN` attribute type helps when you need to pick from any large group of names that aren't specifically part of XML but do meet requirements for XML name tokens. The most significant of these requirements is the prohibition of white space. For example, `NMTOKEN` could be used for an attribute whose value had to map to an 8.3 DOS filename. On the other hand, it wouldn't work well for UNIX, Macintosh, or Windows NT filenames, because those names often contain white space.

For example, suppose you want to require a `STATE` attribute in an `ADDRESS` element to be a two-letter abbreviation. You cannot force this characteristic with a DTD, but you can prevent people from entering New York or Puerto Rico with the following `<!ATTLIST>` declaration:

```
<!ATTLIST ADDRESS STATE NMTOKEN #REQUIRED>
```

However, California, Nevada, and other single-word states are still valid values. Of course, you could simply use an enumerated list (to be covered shortly) with several dozen two-letter codes (for example, CA for California), but that approach results in more effort than many developers want to expend. On the other hand, if you define this list once in a parameter entity reference in a DTD file, you can reuse the file many times over.

The NMTOKENS attribute type

The `NMTOKENS` attribute type is the plural form of `NMTOKEN`. It enables the value of the attribute to consist of multiple XML name tokens that are separated from each other by white space. Generally, you use `NMTOKENS` for the same reasons as `NMTOKEN`, but only when multiple tokens are required. For example, if you want to require multiple two-letter state codes for a `STATES` attribute, you can use the following declaration:

```
<!ATTLIST ADDRESS STATES NMTOKENS #REQUIRED>
```

Then, documents could contain an ADDRESS element like this one:

```
<ADDRESS STATES="MI NY LA CA"/>
```

Unfortunately, if you apply this technique, you're no longer ruling out states such as New York, because each individual part of the state name qualifies as an NMTOKEN, as shown here:

```
<ADDRESS STATES="MI New York LA CA"/>
```

The enumerated attribute type

The enumerated type is not an XML keyword, but a list of possible values for the attribute, separated by vertical bars. Each value must be a valid XML name token. The document author can choose any member of the list as the value of the attribute.

For example, suppose you want an element to be visible or invisible. You may want the element to have a VISIBLE attribute, which can only have the values TRUE or FALSE. If that element is the simple P element, the <!ATTLIST> declaration looks like this:

```
<!ATTLIST P VISIBLE (TRUE | FALSE) "TRUE">
```

The preceding declaration says that a P element may or may not have a VISIBLE attribute. If it does have a VISIBLE attribute, the value of that attribute must be either TRUE or FALSE. If it does not have such an attribute, the value TRUE is assumed. For example:

```
<P VISIBLE="FALSE">You can't see me! Nyah! Nyah!</P>
<P VISIBLE="TRUE">You can see me.</P>
<P>You can see me too.</P>
```

By itself, this declaration is not a magic incantation that hides text. It still relies on the application to understand that it shouldn't display invisible elements. Whether the element is shown or hidden would probably be set through a style sheet rule applied to elements with VISIBLE attributes. For example, these XSLT template rules throw away content with a VISIBLE="FALSE" attribute.

```
<xsl:template match="P[@VISIBLE='FALSE']" />

<xsl:template match="P[@VISIBLE='TRUE']">
  <xsl:apply-templates/>
</xsl:template>
```

The ID attribute type

An ID type attribute uniquely identifies an element in the document. Authoring tools and other applications commonly use ID to help identify the elements of a document without concern for their exact meaning or relationship to one another.

An attribute value of type ID must be a valid XML name—that is, it begins with a letter and is composed of alphanumeric characters and the underscore without white space. A particular name may not be used as an ID attribute of more than one element. Using the same ID twice in one document causes the parser to return an error. Furthermore, each element may not have more than one attribute of type ID.

Typically, ID attributes exist solely for the convenience of programs that manipulate the data. In many cases, multiple elements can be effectively identical except for the value of an ID attribute. If you choose IDs in some predictable fashion, a program can enumerate all the different elements or all the different elements of one type in the document.

The ID type is incompatible with #FIXED. An attribute cannot be both fixed and have ID type, because a #FIXED attribute can only have a single value, whereas each ID type attribute must have a different value. Most ID attributes use #REQUIRED, as Listing 9-1 demonstrates.

Listing 9-1: A Required ID Attribute Type

```
<?xml version="1.0"?>
<!DOCTYPE DOCUMENT [
   <!ELEMENT DOCUMENT (P*)>
   <!ELEMENT P (#PCDATA)>
   <!ATTLIST P PNUMBER ID #REQUIRED>
]>
<DOCUMENT>
  <P PNUMBER="p1">The quick brown fox</P>
  <P PNUMBER="p2">The quick brown fox</P>
</DOCUMENT>
```

The IDREF attribute type

The value of an attribute with the IDREF type is the ID of another element in the document. For example, Listing 9-2 shows the IDREF and ID attributes used to connect children to their parents.

Listing 9-2: family.xml

```
<?xml version="1.0"?>
<!DOCTYPE DOCUMENT [
   <!ELEMENT DOCUMENT (PERSON*)>
   <!ELEMENT PERSON   (#PCDATA)>
   <!ATTLIST PERSON PNUMBER ID #REQUIRED>
   <!ATTLIST PERSON FATHER IDREF #IMPLIED>
   <!ATTLIST PERSON MOTHER IDREF #IMPLIED>
]>
<DOCUMENT>
  <PERSON PNUMBER="a1">Susan</PERSON>
  <PERSON PNUMBER="a2">Jack</PERSON>
  <PERSON PNUMBER="a3" MOTHER="a1" FATHER="a2">Chelsea</PERSON>
  <PERSON PNUMBER="a4" MOTHER="a1" FATHER="a2">David</PERSON>
</DOCUMENT>
```

You generally use this uncommon but crucial type when you need to establish connections between elements that aren't reflected in the tree structure of the document. In Listing 9-2, each child is given FATHER and MOTHER attributes containing the ID attributes of its father and mother. However, based on the element structure alone, there are simply four PERSON elements. None is the parent or child of the other elements.

The IDREFS attribute type

You cannot easily and directly use an IDREF to link parents to their children in Listing 9-2 because each parent has an indefinite number of children. As a workaround, you can group all the children of the same parents into a FAMILY element and link to the FAMILY. Even this approach falters in the face of half-siblings who share only one parent. In short, IDREF works for many-to-one relationships, but not for one-to-many or many-to-many relationships.

If one attribute potentially needs to refer to more than one ID in the document, you can declare it to have type IDREFS. The value of such an attribute is a white-space-separated list of XML names. Each name in the list must be the ID of some element somewhere in the same document.

Listing 9-3 uses a single PARENTS attribute of type IDREFS rather than separate FATHER and MOTHER attributes. This is a more realistic approach for a world in which families often don't come in neat packages of one father, one mother, and two children.

Listing 9-3: alternative_family.xml

```
<?xml version="1.0"?>
<!DOCTYPE DOCUMENT [
   <!ELEMENT DOCUMENT (PERSON*)>
   <!ELEMENT PERSON   (#PCDATA)>
   <!ATTLIST PERSON PNUMBER ID      #REQUIRED>
   <!ATTLIST PERSON PARENTS IDREFS #IMPLIED>
]>
<DOCUMENT>
  <PERSON PNUMBER="a1">Susan</PERSON>
  <PERSON PNUMBER="a2">Jack</PERSON>
  <PERSON PNUMBER="a3" PARENTS="a1 a2">Chelsea</PERSON>
  <PERSON PNUMBER="a4" PARENTS="a1 a2">David</PERSON>
</DOCUMENT>
```

The ENTITY attribute type

An ENTITY type attribute enables you to link external binary data—that is, an external, unparsed, general entity—into the document. The value of the ENTITY attribute is the name of an unparsed general entity declared in the DTD, which links to the external data.

The classic example of an ENTITY attribute is an image. The image consists of binary data available from another URL. Provided the XML browser can support it, you can include an image in an XML document with the following declarations in your DTD:

```
<!ELEMENT IMAGE EMPTY>
<!ATTLIST IMAGE SOURCE ENTITY #REQUIRED>
<!ENTITY LOGO SYSTEM "logo.gif" NDATA GIF>
<!NOTATION GIF PUBLIC
   "-//IETF//NONSGML Media Type image/gif//EN">
```

Then, at the desired image location in the document, insert the following IMAGE tag:

```
<IMAGE SOURCE="LOGO"/>
```

This approach is not a magic formula that all XML browsers automatically understand. It is simply one technique that browsers and other applications may or may not adopt to embed non-XML data in documents.

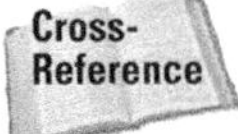

This technique is explored further in Chapter 10.

The ENTITIES attribute type

ENTITIES is a relatively rare plural form of ENTITY. The value of an ENTITIES type attribute consists of multiple unparsed entity names separated by white space. Each entity name refers to an external non-XML data source. One use for this approach is a slide show that rotates different pictures, as in the following example:

```
<!ELEMENT SLIDESHOW EMPTY>
<!ATTLIST SLIDESHOW SOURCES ENTITIES #REQUIRED>
<!ENTITY PIC1 SYSTEM "cat.gif">
<!ENTITY PIC2 SYSTEM "dog.gif">
<!ENTITY PIC3 SYSTEM "cow.gif">
```

Then, at the point in the document where you want the slide show to appear, insert the following tag:

```
<SLIDESHOW SOURCES="PIC1 PIC2 PIC3"/>
```

Again, this is not a universal formula that all (or even any) XML browsers automatically understand; it is simply one method that browsers and other applications might adopt to embed non-XML data in documents.

The NOTATION attribute type

The NOTATION attribute type specifies that an attribute's value is the name of a notation declared in the DTD. The default value of this attribute must also be the name of a notation declared in the DTD. In brief, notations identify the format of data, for instance, by specifying whether length is measured in meters or feet.

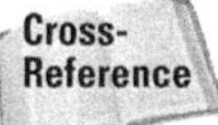

Notations are further discussed in Chapter 10.

For example, there are actually two kinds of ratings in the television listings document, MPAA ratings for movies (G, PG, PG-13, R, and NC-17) and TV parental guidelines for made-for-TV shows (TV-Y, TV-Y7, TV-G, TV-PG, TV-14, TV-MA). A notation attribute can indicate the type of the rating. First, the two notations must be declared:

```
<!NOTATION MOVIE PUBLIC
  "-//Motion Picture Association of America//Movie
     Rating System//EN"
  "http://www.mpaa.org/movieratings">
<!NOTATION TV PUBLIC
  "-//TV Parental Guidelines Board//The TV Parental
     Guidelines//EN"
  "http://www.tvguidelines.org/ratings.asp">
```

Next, specify that the RATING element has a TYPE attribute whose own type is NOTATION. This declaration must list the legal notations for this attribute:

```
<!ATTLIST RATING TYPE NOTATION (MOVIE | TV) #REQUIRED>
```

A valid RATING element must now have a TYPE attribute with one of the two values MOVIE or TV. RATING elements in the instance document now look like this:

```
<RATING TYPE="MOVIE">PG-13</RATING>
<RATING TYPE="TV">TV-PG</RATING>
```

Each element can have at most one NOTATION type attribute. More than one is invalid.

At first glance, this approach may appear inconsistent with the handling of other list attributes, such as ENTITIES and NMTOKENS, but these two approaches are actually quite different. ENTITIES and NMTOKENS have a list of attributes in the actual element in the document but only one value in the attribute declaration in the DTD. NOTATION only has a single value in the attribute of the actual element in the document, however. The list of possible values occurs in the attribute declaration in the DTD.

A DTD for Attribute-Based Television Listings

Chapter 5 developed a well-formed XML document for television listings that used attributes to store the DATE of a SCHEDULE, the NETWORK, CHANNEL, and CALL_LETTERS of a STATION, the NAME, TYPE, START_TIME, and LENGTH of a SHOW, and more. You saw this in Listing 5-1. You may want to print out a copy from my web site at http://www.cafeconleche.org/books/bible3/source/05/5-1.xml so you can have the example document in hand as you read this chapter, to avoid a lot of flipping back and forth.

To make this document valid, you need to provide a DTD. This DTD must declare both the elements and the attributes used in Listing 5-1. The element declarations resemble the ones used in Chapter 8, except that there are fewer of them because most of the information has been moved into attributes:

```
<!ELEMENT SCHEDULE (STATION+)>
<!ELEMENT STATION  (SHOW+)>
<!ELEMENT SHOW     (DIRECTOR*, WRITER*, PRODUCER*, CAST?)>
<!ELEMENT CAST     (ACTOR+)>
<!ELEMENT ACTOR    EMPTY>
<!ELEMENT WRITER   EMPTY>
<!ELEMENT PRODUCER EMPTY>
<!ELEMENT DIRECTOR EMPTY>
```

Declaring SCHEDULE attributes

The SCHEDULE element has a single attribute, DATE. Although some semantic constraints determine what is and is not a date ("July 3, 2003" is a date; "Queen Victoria's underpants" is not), the DTD doesn't enforce these. Thus, the best approach declares that the DATE attribute has the most general attribute type, CDATA. Furthermore, we want all schedules to have a date, so we'll make the DATE attribute required.

```
<!ATTLIST SCHEDULE DATE CDATA #REQUIRED>
```

Although you really can't restrict the form of the text authors enter in DATE attributes, you can at least provide a comment that shows what's expected. For example, it might be a good idea to specify that four-digit years are required.

```
<!-- In the form "July 3, 2003" -->
<!-- DO NOT USE TWO-DIGIT YEARS like 98, 99, 00!! -->
<!ATTLIST SCHEDULE DATE CDATA #REQUIRED>
```

The W3C XML Schema Language uses XML documents to describe information that might traditionally be encoded in a DTD, as well as data type information. Schemas do allow you to express requirements such as "Each DATE element must contain a four-digit year between 1843 and 1902." Schemas are explored in Chapter 20.

Declaring STATION attributes

Next, consider STATION. Each has a CHANNEL attribute, a CALL_LETTERS attribute, and a NETWORK attribute, all of which are optional. The channel is always a positive integer. DTDs don't let you say that the channel is a positive integer, but you can say that it's a name token. Not all name tokens are positive integers, but all positive integers are name tokens.

```
<!ATTLIST STATION CHANNEL NMTOKEN #REQUIRED>
```

This doesn't catch all illegal values, but it at least catches some of them.

Similarly, the call letters are always a legal XML name token. They're composed exclusively of ASCII letters, and, in a few countries, digits. This can also be declared as a name token:

```
<!ATTLIST STATION CALL_LETTERS NMTOKEN #REQUIRED>
```

Traditionally, network names are also name tokens (CBS, NBC, HBO, and so on). However, cable stations are increasingly using longer network names (Oxygen, Home Shopping Network, and so on). These can all be abbreviated as name tokens. However, as the world moves to digital cable and satellite television, it seems increasingly unlikely that new networks will stick to the old conventions. It feels safer to me to allow network names to be more arbitrary, so I'll make them CDATA.

```
<!ATTLIST STATION NETWORK CDATA #REQUIRED>
```

If you prefer, these three separate declarations for attributes of the same element can be combined into one attribute list declaration:

```
<!ATTLIST STATION NETWORK      CDATA    #IMPLIED
                  CALL_LETTERS NMTOKEN #IMPLIED
                  CHANNEL      NMTOKEN #REQUIRED>
```

One disadvantage of using a single attribute list to declare several attributes is that it makes it impossible to include even simple comments next to the individual attributes, because comments cannot appear inside declarations, only outside them.

Given these declarations, in either single or multiple form, all of these STATION start-tags are valid:

```
<STATION NETWORK="HBO" CHANNEL="501">
<STATION NETWORK="CBS" CHANNEL="2" CALL_LETTERS="WCBS">
<STATION CHANNEL="55" CALL_LETTERS="WLNY">
<STATION CHANNEL="882">
```

The last one is a bit of a problem. It has neither a NETWORK nor a CALL_LETTERS attribute, at least one of which you want to require, but without requiring both. You were able to do this when NETWORK and CALL_LETTERS were child elements. However, with attributes, you just can't do this. Attributes are independent of each other. You can't make the presence or absence of one a precondition for the presence or absence of the other.

Declaring SHOW attributes

SHOW has the most attributes of any of the elements in the document. A few of these (NAME, START_TIME, LENGTH) are required, because they are absolutely necessary for processing the document. If they're missing, the style sheet (of Listing 5-8) and other software that reads these documents will fail. The rest of the attributes are optional. None have plausible default values. Most have no constraints that are expressible in a DTD. A couple (STARS, YEAR_MADE) must be numbers and can therefore be set to NMTOKEN. However, there is one notable exception. The RATING attribute has a fixed list of values: TV-Y, TV-Y7, TV-G, TV-PG, TV-PG14, TV-MA, G, PG, PG-13, R, NC-17. This is exactly the situation for an enumerated attribute:

```
<!ATTLIST SHOW RATING
    (TV-Y | TV-Y7 | TV-G | TV-PG | TV-PG14 | TV-MA
          | G | PG | PG-13 | R | NC-17) #IMPLIED>
```

The REPEAT and CLOSED_CAPTIONED attributes are equally well served by an enumeration. In these two cases, the possible values are only two-fold, yes and no:

```
<!ATTLIST SHOW CLOSED_CAPTIONED (Yes | No) #IMPLIED
               REPEAT           (Yes | No) #IMPLIED
```

Like most things in XML, these matches are case-sensitive. If you want to allow upper and mixed case variants, you need to explicitly list them:

```
<!ATTLIST SHOW
    CLOSED_CAPTIONED (Yes | No | yes | no | YES | NO) #IMPLIED
    REPEAT           (Yes | No | yes | no | YES | NO) #IMPLIED
>
```

Here you see something attributes can do better than child elements. In the previous chapter where RATING, REPEAT, and CLOSED_CAPTION were child elements, all you could do was declare them to have a content specification of #PCDATA, document the possible values with a comment, and hope the document authors read the DTD. Attributes can actually enforce the restrictions.

Declaring person attributes

The television listings example has four person elements that differ primarily in element name: ACTOR, PRODUCER, PUBLISHER, and WRITER. Each can have GIVEN_NAME, MIDDLE_NAME, MIDDLE_INITIAL, and SURNAME attributes. There are no particular rules for what characters are allowed in names. For example, surnames can contain white space (de Havilland), apostrophes (d'Abo), and more. Thus, the only really sensible type for these is CDATA. Because any particular person may not have any of these, the only sensible default value is #IMPLIED. Given that, here's the declaration of the ACTOR element:

```
<!ATTLIST ACTOR    GIVEN_NAME     CDATA #IMPLIED
                   MIDDLE_NAME    CDATA #IMPLIED
                   MIDDLE_INITIAL CDATA #IMPLIED
                   SURNAME        CDATA #IMPLIED>
```

Using attributes instead of child elements to hold this information has two distinct disadvantages. First, as with NETWORK and CALL_LETTERS for SHOW, it's not possible to say that an ACTOR must have at least one of GIVEN_NAME, MIDDLE_NAME, MIDDLE_INITIAL, and SURNAME, though all of them are individually optional. <ACTOR/> is now a valid ACTOR element even though it has no names at all. Second, only one of each is allowed for each person. This means you have to force multiple middle names and aliases into a single attribute. Child elements are really a better fit here.

The other three person elements can be declared almost identically:

```
<!ATTLIST PRODUCER GIVEN_NAME     CDATA #IMPLIED
                   MIDDLE_NAME    CDATA #IMPLIED
                   MIDDLE_INITIAL CDATA #IMPLIED
                   SURNAME        CDATA #IMPLIED>
<!ATTLIST DIRECTOR GIVEN_NAME     CDATA #IMPLIED
                   MIDDLE_NAME    CDATA #IMPLIED
                   MIDDLE_INITIAL CDATA #IMPLIED
                   SURNAME        CDATA #IMPLIED>
<!ATTLIST WRITER   GIVEN_NAME     CDATA #IMPLIED
                   MIDDLE_NAME    CDATA #IMPLIED
                   MIDDLE_INITIAL CDATA #IMPLIED
                   SURNAME        CDATA #IMPLIED>
```

Given the similarity between the four declarations for different kinds of people, you might be wondering whether XML has any sort of macro expansion facility that enables you to leverage the similarity. The short answer is yes, it does. That mechanism, parameter entity references, is explored in the next chapter.

The complete DTD for the television listings example

Listing 9-4 shows the complete attribute-based television schedule DTD.

Listing 9-4: The Complete DTD for Television Listings Using Attributes for Most Information

```
<!ELEMENT SCHEDULE (STATION+)>
<!ELEMENT STATION  (SHOW+)>
<!ELEMENT SHOW     (DIRECTOR*, WRITER*, PRODUCER*, CAST?)>
<!ELEMENT CAST     (ACTOR+)>
<!ELEMENT ACTOR    EMPTY>
<!ELEMENT WRITER   EMPTY>
<!ELEMENT PRODUCER EMPTY>
<!ELEMENT DIRECTOR EMPTY>

<!ATTLIST SCHEDULE DATE           CDATA #REQUIRED>

<!ATTLIST STATION NETWORK         CDATA   #IMPLIED
                  CALL_LETTERS    NMTOKEN #IMPLIED
                  CHANNEL         NMTOKEN #REQUIRED>
```

```
<!ATTLIST SHOW NAME              CDATA #REQUIRED
               TITLE             CDATA #IMPLIED
               TYPE              CDATA #IMPLIED
               EPISODE_NUMBER    CDATA #IMPLIED
               START_TIME        CDATA #REQUIRED
               LENGTH            CDATA #REQUIRED
               AIR_DATE          CDATA #IMPLIED
               ORIGINAL_AIR_DATE CDATA #IMPLIED
               CLOSED_CAPTIONED  (Yes | No) #IMPLIED
               REPEAT            (Yes | No) #IMPLIED
               YEAR_MADE         NMTOKEN #IMPLIED
               STARS             NMTOKEN #IMPLIED
               DESCRIPTION       CDATA   #IMPLIED
               RATING   (TV-Y | TV-Y7 | TV-G | TV-PG
 | TV-PG14 | TV-MA | G | PG | PG-13 | R | NC-17) #IMPLIED
 >

<!ATTLIST ACTOR    GIVEN_NAME     CDATA #IMPLIED
                   MIDDLE_NAME    CDATA #IMPLIED
                   MIDDLE_INITIAL CDATA #IMPLIED
                   SURNAME        CDATA #IMPLIED>
<!ATTLIST PRODUCER GIVEN_NAME     CDATA #IMPLIED
                   MIDDLE_NAME    CDATA #IMPLIED
                   MIDDLE_INITIAL CDATA #IMPLIED
                   SURNAME        CDATA #IMPLIED>
<!ATTLIST DIRECTOR GIVEN_NAME     CDATA #IMPLIED
                   MIDDLE_NAME    CDATA #IMPLIED
                   MIDDLE_INITIAL CDATA #IMPLIED
                   SURNAME        CDATA #IMPLIED>
<!ATTLIST WRITER   GIVEN_NAME     CDATA #IMPLIED
                   MIDDLE_NAME    CDATA #IMPLIED
                   MIDDLE_INITIAL CDATA #IMPLIED
                   SURNAME        CDATA #IMPLIED>
```

To attach this DTD to Listing 5-1, you must add a document type declaration to its prolog, assuming of course that Listing 9-4 is stored in a file called tvlistings.dtd:

```
<!DOCTYPE SEASON SYSTEM "tvlistings.dtd">
```

Listing 9-4 does not really use any default attribute values. Instead, each attribute is declared #IMPLIED or #REQUIRED. This is actually quite common and is sometimes a good idea even when reasonable defaults are known. Not all parsers read the external DTD subset of a document, especially those parsers built into web browsers. Explicitly specifying all attribute values in the instance document is safer and more robust than defaulting them in from the DTD.

Summary

In this chapter, you learned how to declare attributes in DTDs. In particular, you learned the following concepts:

- Attributes are declared by an <!ATTLIST> declaration in the DTD.
- One <!ATTLIST> can declare an indefinite number of attributes for a single element.
- Attributes normally have default values, but this condition can be changed by using the keywords #REQUIRED, #IMPLIED, or #FIXED.
- There are 10 attribute types: CDATA, Enumerated, NMTOKEN, NMTOKENS, ID, IDREF, IDREFS, ENTITY, ENTITIES, and NOTATION.
- The CDATA type is the most general. It means an attribute can contain character data. Any well-formed content is valid.
- The NMTOKEN type means a valid attribute contains an XML name token. A name token is like an XML name except that it can start with numbers or a hyphen.
- The NMTOKENS type means a valid attribute contains a list of XML name tokens separated by white space.
- The ID type means a valid attribute contains an XML name that is unique among all ID type attributes in the document. An element can have at most one attribute of ID type.
- The IDREF type means a valid attribute contains an XML name that is also the value of an ID type attribute of some element in this document.
- The IDREFS type means a valid attribute contains a list of ID values separated by white space.
- The ENTITY type means a valid attribute contains the name of an unparsed entity declared in the DTD.
- The ENTITIES type means a valid attribute contains a white-space separated list of unparsed entity names declared in the DTD.
- The NOTATION type means a valid attribute contains the name of a notation declared in the DTD.

In the next chapter, you learn more about DTDs, including how to define new entity references such as `©`, `α`, and `&chapter10;`. You'll see how to use multiple DTDs to describe a single document, and how to divide one large document into many smaller parts. You'll also learn how notations, processing instructions, and unparsed external entities can be used to embed non-XML data in XML documents.

✦ ✦ ✦

Entity Declarations

In This Chapter

What is an entity?

Internal general entities

External general entities

Internal parameter entities

External parameter entities

Building a document from pieces

Unparsed entities

Conditional sections

A single XML document can draw both data and declarations from many different sources in many different files. In fact, some of the data may draw directly from databases, CGI scripts, or other nonfile sources. The items where the pieces of an XML document are stored, in whatever form they take, are called *entities*. Entity references load these entities into the main XML document. General entity references load data into the root element of an XML document. `<`, `>`, `'`, `"e;`, and `&` are predefined general entity references that refer to the text entities <, >, ', ", and &, respectively. Parameter entity references load data into the document's document type definition (DTD). They begin with a `%` instead of an `&`. Unparsed entities point to non-XML, binary data whose type is identified with a notation and are referenced by an `ENTITY` type attribute. All three kinds of entities are declared in the DTD.

What Is an Entity?

Logically speaking, an XML document is composed of a prolog followed by a root element that strictly contains all other elements; but physically the content of an XML document can be spread across multiple files. For example, each `SHOW` element might appear in a separate file even though the root element contains several thousand shows broadcast on one day. The storage units that contain particular parts of an XML document are *entities*. An entity can be a file, a database record, or any other item that contains data. For example, all the complete well-formed XML examples in this book are entities.

The storage unit that contains the XML declaration, the document type declaration, and the root element is called the *document entity*. Thus, every XML document has at least one entity. However, the root element and its descendents may also contain entity references pointing to additional data that should be inserted into the document. A validating XML processor combines all the referenced entities into a single logical document before it passes the document on to the end application or displays the file.

Note Nonvalidating processors may, but do not have to, insert entities defined in the external DTD subset. They must insert entities defined in the internal DTD subset.

Entities hold content: well-formed XML, other forms of text, or binary data. The prolog and the document type declaration are part of the root entity of the document. An XSL style sheet qualifies as an entity, but only because it itself is a well-formed XML document. The entity that makes up the style sheet is not one of the entities that compose the XML document to which the style sheet applies. A CSS style sheet is not an entity at all.

Most entities have names by which you can refer to them. The only exception is the document entity—the main file containing the XML document (although there's no requirement that this has to be a file as opposed to a database record, the output of a CGI program, or something else).

Entities can be either internal or external. *Internal entities* are defined completely within the DTD. *External entities*, by contrast, draw their content from another source located via a URL. The main document only includes a reference to the URL where the actual content resides.

Entities fall into two categories: parsed and unparsed. *Parsed entities* contain well-formed XML text. *Unparsed entities* contain either binary data or non-XML text (such as an e-mail message). Currently, unparsed entities aren't well supported (if at all) by most browsers, editors, and other tools.

Internal General Entities

You can think of an internal general entity reference as an abbreviation for commonly used text or text that's hard to type. An `<!ENTITY>` declaration in the DTD defines an abbreviation and the text that the abbreviation stands for. For example, instead of typing the same footer at the bottom of every page, you can simply define that text as the `FOOTER` entity in the DTD and then type `&FOOTER;` at the bottom of each page. Furthermore, if you decide to change the footer block (perhaps because your e-mail address changes), you only need to make the change once in the DTD instead of on every page that shares the footer.

General entity references begin with an ampersand (&) and end with a semicolon (;), with the entity's name between these two characters. For example, `<` is a general entity reference for the less than sign (<). The name of this entity is `lt`. The replacement text of this entity is the one-character string <. Entity names consist of any set of alphanumeric characters and the underscore. White space and other punctuation characters are prohibited. Like most everything else in XML, entity references are case-sensitive.

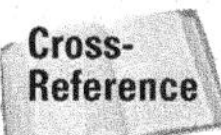

Although the colon (:) is technically permitted in entity names, this character is reserved for use with namespaces, which are discussed in Chapter 11.

Defining an internal general entity reference

Internal general entities are defined in the DTD with an `<!ENTITY>` declaration, which has the following format:

```
<!ENTITY name "replacement text">
```

The *`name`* is the abbreviation for the *`replacement text`*. The replacement text must be enclosed in quotation marks because it can contain white space and XML markup. You type the name of the entity in the document, but the reader sees the replacement text.

For example, my name is the somewhat excessive Elliotte Rusty Harold (blame my parents for that one). Even with years of practice, I still make typos with that phrase. I can define a general entity reference for my name so that every time I type `&ERH;`, the reader will see Elliotte Rusty Harold. That definition is as follows:

```
<!ENTITY ERH "Elliotte Rusty Harold">
```

Listing 10-1 demonstrates the `&ERH;` general entity reference. Figure 10-1 shows this document loaded into Internet Explorer. You see that the `&ERH;` entity reference in the source code is replaced by `Elliotte Rusty Harold` in the output.

Listing 10-1: The ERH Internal General Entity Reference

```
<?xml version="1.0"?>
<!DOCTYPE DOCUMENT [

  <!ENTITY ERH "Elliotte Rusty Harold">

  <!ELEMENT DOCUMENT (TITLE, SIGNATURE)>
  <!ELEMENT TITLE (#PCDATA)>
  <!ELEMENT COPYRIGHT (#PCDATA)>
```

Continued

Listing 10-1 *(continued)*

```
    <!ELEMENT EMAIL (#PCDATA)>
    <!ELEMENT LAST_MODIFIED (#PCDATA)>
    <!ELEMENT SIGNATURE (COPYRIGHT, EMAIL, LAST_MODIFIED)>
]>
<DOCUMENT>
   <TITLE>&ERH;</TITLE>
   <SIGNATURE>
     <COPYRIGHT>2004 &ERH;</COPYRIGHT>
     <EMAIL>elharo@metalab.unc.edu</EMAIL>
     <LAST_MODIFIED>July 30, 2004</LAST_MODIFIED>
   </SIGNATURE>
</DOCUMENT>
```

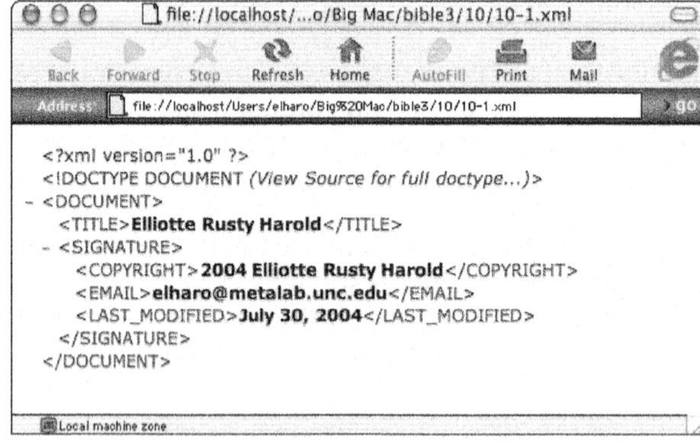

Figure 10-1: Listing 10-1 after the internal general entity reference has been replaced by the actual entity

Notice that the general entity reference, `&ERH;`, appears inside both the `COPYRIGHT` and `TITLE` elements even though these are declared to accept only `#PCDATA` as children. This arrangement is valid because the replacement text of the `&ERH;` entity reference is parsed character data. Validation occurs after the parser replaces the entity references with their values. The same thing happens when you use a style sheet. The styles are applied to the element tree as it exists after entity values replace the entity references.

However, validation is optional, even when the DTD defines entities that the document uses. A parser can read the DTD to find entity definitions but still not check for validity. For example, Listing 10-2 provides the same basic data as Listing 10-1 even though it's invalid, because the DTD doesn't include declarations for every element:

Listing 10-2: An Invalid Document That Uses a DTD Solely to Define a General Entity Reference

```
<?xml version="1.0"?>
<!DOCTYPE DOCUMENT [
   <!ENTITY ERH "Elliotte Rusty Harold">
]>
<DOCUMENT>
  <TITLE>&ERH;</TITLE>
  <SIGNATURE>
    <COPYRIGHT>2004 &ERH;</COPYRIGHT>
    <EMAIL>elharo@metalab.unc.edu</EMAIL>
    <LAST_MODIFIED>July 30, 2004</LAST_MODIFIED>
   </SIGNATURE>
</DOCUMENT>
```

General entity definitions cannot contain the three characters `%`, `&`, and " directly, although you can include them via character references; `&` and `%` may be included if they're starting an entity reference rather than simply representing themselves. An entity value can contain tags and span multiple lines. For example, the following `SIGNATURE` entity is valid:

```
<!ENTITY SIGNATURE
  "<SIGNATURE>
     <COPYRIGHT>2004 Elliotte Rusty Harold</COPYRIGHT>
     <EMAIL>elharo@metalab.unc.edu</EMAIL>
     <LAST_MODIFIED>July 30, 2004</LAST_MODIFIED>
   </SIGNATURE>"
>
```

An entity value can also contain multiple elements, as in the following example:

```
<!ENTITY SIGNATURE
  "<HR/>
   <COPYRIGHT>2004 Elliotte Rusty Harold</COPYRIGHT>
   <EMAIL>elharo@metalab.unc.edu</EMAIL>
   <LAST_MODIFIED>July 30, 2004</LAST_MODIFIED>"
>
```

However, if an entity value contains the start-tag for an element, it must also contain the end-tag for the same element. That is, it cannot contain only part of an element. For example, these are both illegal, even if they're used in such a way that the resulting document would be well formed:

```
<!ENTITY COPYYEAR "<COPYRIGHT>2004 ">
<!ENTITY COPYNAME "Elliotte Rusty Harold</COPYRIGHT>">
```

The same is true for comments, processing instructions, entity references, and anything else you might place inside an entity value. If it starts inside the entity, it must finish inside the entity.

One advantage of using entity references instead of the full text is that it's easier to change the text. This is especially useful when a single DTD is shared between multiple documents. For example, suppose I decide to use the e-mail address `eharold@solar.stanford.edu` instead of `elharo@metalab.unc.edu`. Rather than searching and replacing through multiple files, I simply change one line of the DTD as follows:

```
<!ENTITY SIGNATURE
  "<HR/>
   <COPYRIGHT>2004 Elliotte Rusty Harold</COPYRIGHT>
   <EMAIL>eharold@solar.stanford.edu</EMAIL>
   <LAST_MODIFIED>July 30, 2004</LAST_MODIFIED>"
>
```

Using general entity references in the DTD

The next obvious question is whether it's possible to parameterize entities. For example, could you use the preceding `SIGNATURE` entity but change the date in each separate `LAST_MODIFIED` element on each page? The answer is yes. Entities can contain other entities, and all of these entities can be redefined in a document's internal DTD subset. This enables both modularization and parameterization of DTDs. You can include one general entity reference inside the definition another, like this:

```
<!ENTITY COPY2004 "Copyright 2004 &ERH;">
```

This example is legal because the `ERH` entity appears as part of the `COPY2004` entity that itself will ultimately become part of the instance document. You can also use general entity references in other places in the DTD that ultimately become part of the instance document content (such as a default attribute value), although there are restrictions. The first restriction is that the declaration cannot contain a circular reference such as the following:

```
<!ENTITY ERH "&COPY2004 Elliotte Rusty Harold">
<!ENTITY COPY2004 "Copyright 2004 &ERH;">
```

The second restriction: General entity references cannot insert text that is only part of the DTD and that will not be used as part of the document content. For example, the following attempted shortcut fails:

```
<!ENTITY  PCD     "(#PCDATA)">
<!ELEMENT GIVEN_NAME &PCD;>
<!ELEMENT SURNAME    &PCD;>
```

It's often useful, however, to have entity references merge text into a document's DTD. For this purpose, XML uses the parameter entity reference, which is discussed later in this chapter.

Predefined general entity references

XML predefines the five general entity references listed in Table 10-1. These five entity references appear in XML documents in place of specific characters that would otherwise be interpreted as markup. For example, the entity reference `<` stands for the less than sign (<), which could be interpreted as the beginning of a tag.

Table 10-1
XML Predefined Entity References

Entity Reference	*Character*
`&`	&
`<`	<
`>`	>
`"`	"
`'`	'

For maximum compatibility with older SGML parsers, you should declare these references in your DTD if you plan to use them. Declaration is actually quite tricky, because you must also escape the characters in the DTD without using recursion. To do this, use character references containing the hexadecimal value of each character. Listing 10-3 shows the necessary declarations:

Listing 10-3: Declarations for the Predefined General Entity References

```
<!ENTITY lt   "&#38;#60;">
<!ENTITY gt   "&#62;">
<!ENTITY amp  "&#38;#38;">
<!ENTITY apos "&#39;">
<!ENTITY quot "&#34;">
```

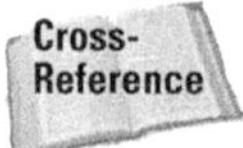

Character references are discussed in Chapter 6.

External General Entities

Documents using only internal entities closely resemble the HTML model. The complete text of the document is available in a single file. Images, applets, sounds, and other non-HTML data may be linked to the file, but at least all the text is present. Of course, the HTML model has some problems. In particular, it's quite difficult to embed dynamic information in the file. CGI scripts, Java applets, fancy database software, server-side includes, ASP, JSP, PHP, and various other technologies can all add this capability to HTML; but HTML alone only provides a static document. You have to go outside HTML to build a document from multiple pieces. Frames are perhaps the simplest HTML solution to this problem, but they are a user interface disaster that consistently confuse and annoy users.

XML allows you to embed both well-formed XML documents and document fragments inside other XML documents. Furthermore, XML defines the syntax whereby an XML parser can build a document out of multiple smaller XML documents and pieces thereof found either on local or remote systems. Documents may contain other documents, which may contain other documents. As long as there's no recursion (an error reported by the processor), the application only sees a single, complete document. In essence, this provides client-side includes.

External entities are data outside the main file containing the root element/document entity. External entity references let you embed these external entities in the parsed character data content of your document (though not in the attribute values) and thus build a single XML document from multiple independent files.

An external general entity reference indicates where in the document the parser should insert the external entity. The text of the entity comes from a document at a given Uniform Resource Identifier (URI). This URI is specified in the entity's declaration in the DTD using this syntax:

```
<!ENTITY name SYSTEM "URI">
```

URIs are similar to Uniform Resource Locators (URLs) but allow for more precise specification of the linked resource. In theory, URIs separate the resource from the location so that a web browser can select the nearest or least congested of several mirrors without requiring an explicit link to that mirror. URIs are an area of active research and heated debate. Therefore, in practice, and certainly in this book, URIs are URLs for all purposes.

For example, you might want to put the same signature block on almost every page of a site. For the sake of definiteness, assume that the signature block is the XML code shown in Listing 10-4. This would be a well-formed XML document except that it doesn't have a root element.

Listing 10-4: An XML External Parsed Entity

```
<COPYRIGHT>2004 Elliotte Rusty Harold</COPYRIGHT>
<EMAIL>elharo@metalab.unc.edu</EMAIL>
<LAST_MODIFIED>July 30, 2004</LAST_MODIFIED>
<HR/>
```

Furthermore, assume that you can retrieve this code from the URL `http://cafeconleche.org/boilerplate/signature.xml`. You associate this file with the entity reference `&SIG;` by adding the following declaration to the DTD:

```
<!ENTITY SIG SYSTEM
  "http://cafeconleche.org/boilerplate/signature.xml">
```

You can also use a relative URL. For example:

```
<!ENTITY SIG SYSTEM "/boilerplate/signature.xml">
```

If the file to be included is in the same directory as the file doing the including, you only need to use the filename, as in the following example:

```
<!ENTITY SIG SYSTEM "signature.xml">
```

With any of these declarations, you can include the contents of the signature file in a document at any point merely by using `&SIG;`, as illustrated with the simple document in Listing 10-5. Figure 10-2 shows the rendered document in Internet Explorer.

Listing 10-5: The SIG External General Entity Reference

```
<?xml version="1.0" standalone="no"?>
<!DOCTYPE DOCUMENT [
   <!ELEMENT DOCUMENT
     (TITLE, COPYRIGHT, EMAIL, LAST_MODIFIED, HR?)>
   <!ELEMENT TITLE (#PCDATA)>
   <!ELEMENT COPYRIGHT (#PCDATA)>
   <!ELEMENT EMAIL (#PCDATA)>
   <!ELEMENT HR EMPTY>
   <!ELEMENT LAST_MODIFIED (#PCDATA)>
   <!ENTITY SIG SYSTEM "signature.xml">
]>
<DOCUMENT>
  <TITLE>Entity references</TITLE>
  &SIG;
</DOCUMENT>
```

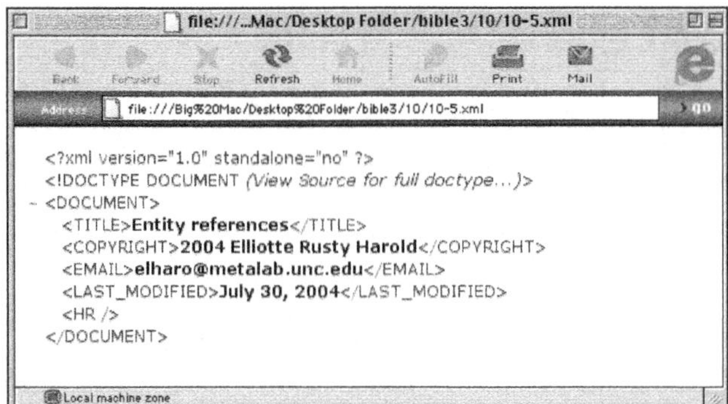

Figure 10-2: A document that uses an external general entity reference

The DTD declares both the internal elements, such as `TITLE`, and the external elements, such as `COPYRIGHT`. Validating parsers are required to resolve all entity references and replace them with their values before checking the document against its DTD.

The `standalone` attribute of the XML declaration now has the value `no` because this file is no longer complete. Parsing the file requires additional data from the external file signature.xml. Technically, though, the standalone declaration isn't required because its default value is `no`.

Text declarations

Because neither Listing 10-4 nor Listing 10-5 has an encoding declaration, the parser assumes both are written in the UTF-8 encoding of Unicode. However, in general, there's no guarantee or requirement that all the external parsed entities a document includes will use the same encoding. Indeed each external parsed entity can have a different encoding. To account for this, each external parsed entity can have its own text declaration. Text declarations look like XML declarations except that the `version` pseudo-attribute is optional, the `encoding` pseudo-attribute is required, and there's no `standalone` pseudo-attribute. These are legal text declarations:

```
<?xml version="1.0" encoding="UTF-8"?>
<?xml encoding="UTF-8"?>
```

However, this is not a legal text declaration because the encoding is omitted:

```
<?xml version="1.0"?>
```

This is not a legal text declaration because it includes a `standalone` declaration:

```
<?xml version="1.0" encoding="UTF-8" standalone="no"?>
```

Listing 10-6 has a text declaration that says the entity is encoded in UTF-16 instead of the default UTF-8.

Listing 10-6: An XML External Parsed Entity with a Text Declaration

```
<?xml encoding="UTF-16"?>
<COPYRIGHT>2004 Elliotte Rusty Harold</COPYRIGHT>
<EMAIL>elharo@metalab.unc.edu</EMAIL>
<LAST_MODIFIED>July 30, 2004</LAST_MODIFIED>
<HR/>
```

If the external parsed entity has a root element, and if it either has a `version` pseudo-attribute in the text declaration or does not have a text declaration at all, then the external parsed entity may itself be a well-formed XML document. For example, it could be the signature block shown in Listing 10-7. However, while sometimes useful, this is not required.

Listing 10-7: An External Parsed Entity That Is Also a Well-Formed XML Document

```
<?xml version="1.0" encoding="ISO-8859-1"?>
<SIGNATURE>
  <COPYRIGHT>2004 Elliotte Rusty Harold</COPYRIGHT>
  <EMAIL>elharo@metalab.unc.edu</EMAIL>
  <LAST_MODIFIED>July 30, 2004</LAST_MODIFIED>
</SIGNATURE>
```

Whether a well-formed XML document or not, an external parsed entity cannot contain a document type declaration. This means an external parsed entity cannot be valid on its own. It can only be validated when it's inserted into a full XML document that does have a document type declaration. A document that uses external parsed entities can be valid as long as it properly declares all the elements and attributes used in both the document entity and all the other entities. Indeed, Listing 10-5 is valid, but it does not have to be. Well-formedness only requires that a document declare all the entities it uses. Listing 10-8 is an invalid but well-formed version of Listing 10-5.

Listing 10-8: An Invalid but Well-Formed Document That Uses an External General Entity Reference

```
<?xml version="1.0" standalone="no"?>
<!DOCTYPE DOCUMENT [
   <!ENTITY SIG SYSTEM "signature.xml">
]>
<DOCUMENT>
  <TITLE>Entity references</TITLE>
  &SIG;
</DOCUMENT>
```

Nonvalidating parsers

All XML parsers resolve internal entity references defined in the internal DTD subset. Nonvalidating processors can resolve external entity references, but they are not required to do so. Expat, the open source XML parser used by Mozilla, for example, does not resolve external entity references. Most other parsers do resolve external entity references.

In the world of web browsers, Mozilla, Netscape, Safari, and Opera do not resolve external entity references. Most recent versions of Internet Explorer do resolve external entity references (though I did have trouble getting this to work on Internet Explorer 5.2 for Mac OS X).

Internal Parameter Entities

General entities become part of the instance document, not the DTD. They can be used in the DTD, but only in places where they will become part of the document content. General entity references cannot insert text that is only part of the DTD and will not be used as part of the document content. It's often useful, however, to have entity references in a DTD. For this purpose, XML provides the *parameter entity reference.*

Parameter entity references are very similar to general entity references except for these two key differences:

1. Parameter entity references begin with a percent sign (%) instead of an ampersand (&).
2. Parameter entity references can only appear in the DTD, not the document content.

Parameter entities are declared in the DTD like general entities with the addition of a percent sign before the name. The syntax looks like this:

```
<!ENTITY % name "replacement text">
```

The name is the abbreviation for the entity. The reader sees the replacement text, which must appear in quotes, as in the following example:

```
<!ENTITY % ERH "Elliotte Rusty Harold">
<!ENTITY COPY2004 "Copyright 2004 %ERH;">
```

Our earlier failed attempt to abbreviate `(#PCDATA)` works when a parameter entity reference replaces the general entity reference:

```
<!ENTITY % PCD "(#PCDATA)">
<!ELEMENT GIVEN_NAME %PCD;>
<!ELEMENT SURNAME    %PCD;>
```

The real value of parameter entity references becomes apparent when you're sharing common lists of children and attributes between elements. The larger the block of text you're replacing and the more times you use it, the more useful parameter entity references become. For example, in the television listing example of the last few chapters, there are four person elements: `ACTOR`, `WRITER`, `PRODUCER`, and `DIRECTOR`. Each had the same content model or attribute list containing a given name, middle name, middle initial, and/or surname. The element declarations looked like this:

```
<!ELEMENT ACTOR (
   (GIVEN_NAME, (MIDDLE_NAME | MIDDLE_INITIAL)*, SURNAME?)
  | ((MIDDLE_NAME | MIDDLE_INITIAL)+, SURNAME)
  | SURNAME
)>
<!ELEMENT WRITER (
   (GIVEN_NAME, (MIDDLE_NAME | MIDDLE_INITIAL)*, SURNAME?)
  | ((MIDDLE_NAME | MIDDLE_INITIAL)+, SURNAME)
  | SURNAME
)>
<!ELEMENT PRODUCER (
   (GIVEN_NAME, (MIDDLE_NAME | MIDDLE_INITIAL)*, SURNAME?)
  | ((MIDDLE_NAME | MIDDLE_INITIAL)+, SURNAME)
  | SURNAME
)>
<!ELEMENT DIRECTOR (
   (GIVEN_NAME, (MIDDLE_NAME | MIDDLE_INITIAL)*, SURNAME?)
  | ((MIDDLE_NAME | MIDDLE_INITIAL)+, SURNAME)
  | SURNAME
)>
```

The person elements all have the same contents. If you invent a new child element, such as TITLE or HONORIFIC, this element must be declared as a possible child of all four person elements. Adding it to three, but forgetting to add it to the fourth element, may cause trouble. Or imagine you discover a bug in the content model. You need to fix it in four different places instead of one. This problem multiplies when you have 40 or 400 parent elements instead of 4.

DTDs are much easier to maintain if you don't give each similar element a separate content model. Instead, make the content model a parameter entity reference; then use that parameter entity reference in each of the container element declarations, as in the following example:

```
<!ENTITY % NAMES_CONTENT
  "((GIVEN_NAME, (MIDDLE_NAME | MIDDLE_INITIAL)*, SURNAME?)
 | ((MIDDLE_NAME | MIDDLE_INITIAL)+, SURNAME)
 | SURNAME)">
<!ELEMENT ACTOR    %NAMES_CONTENT;>
<!ELEMENT DIRECTOR %NAMES_CONTENT;>
<!ELEMENT NAME     %NAMES_CONTENT;>
<!ELEMENT PRODUCER %NAMES_CONTENT;>
```

To add a new element or fix a bug, you only have to change a single parameter entity declaration, rather than 4, 40, or 400 element declarations.

Parameter entity references must be declared before they're used. The following example is malformed because the %NAMES_CONTENT; reference is not declared until it's already been used twice:

```
<!ELEMENT ACTOR    %NAMES_CONTENT;>
<!ELEMENT DIRECTOR %NAMES_CONTENT;>
<!ELEMENT NAME     %NAMES_CONTENT;>
<!ELEMENT PRODUCER %NAMES_CONTENT;>
<!ENTITY % NAMES_CONTENT
  "((GIVEN_NAME, (MIDDLE_NAME | MIDDLE_INITIAL)*, SURNAME?)
 | ((MIDDLE_NAME | MIDDLE_INITIAL)+, SURNAME)
 | SURNAME)">
```

Parameter entities can only be used to define content models, element names, and other *parts* of declarations in the external DTD subset. That is, parameter entity references can only appear inside a declaration in the external DTD subset when their replacement text is something less than a complete declaration. The preceding examples are all illegal if they're used in an internal DTD subset; that is, inside the square brackets in a document type declaration.

Parameter entity references can be used in the internal DTD subset, but only if they provide whole declarations, not simply pieces of them. For example, the following declaration is legal in both the internal and external DTD subsets:

```
<!ENTITY % hr "<!ELEMENT HR EMPTY>">
%hr;
```

Of course, this really isn't any easier than declaring the HR element without parameter entity references:

```
<!ELEMENT HR EMPTY>
```

You'll mainly use parameter entity references in internal DTD subsets when they're referring to external parameter entities; that is, when they're pulling in declarations or parts of declarations from a different file. This is the subject of the next section.

External Parameter Entities

Up to this point, the examples have used monolithic DTDs that defined all the elements used in the document. This technique becomes unwieldy with longer documents, however. Furthermore, you often want to use part of a DTD in many different places. For example, consider a DTD that describes a snail-mail address. The definition of an address is quite general and can easily be used in many different contexts. Similarly, the list of predefined entity references in Listing 10-2 is useful in many XML documents, but you'd rather not copy and paste it all the time.

External parameter entities enable you to build large DTDs from smaller ones; that is, one DTD can link to another and, in so doing, pull in the elements and entities declared in the first. Although cycles are prohibited — DTD 1 cannot refer to DTD 2 if DTD 2 refers to DTD 1 — such nested DTDs can become large and complex.

At the same time, breaking a DTD into smaller, more manageable chunks makes the DTD easier to analyze, modify, and reuse. Many of the examples in Chapter 8 and 9 were unnecessarily large. Both the document and its DTD become much easier to understand when split into separate files.

Furthermore, using smaller, modular DTDs that only describe one set of elements makes it easier to mix and match DTDs created by different people or organizations. For example, if you're writing a technical article about high-temperature superconductivity, you can use a molecular sciences DTD to describe the molecules involved, a math DTD to write down your equations, a vector graphics DTD for the figures, and a basic HTML DTD to handle the explanatory text.

Note

In particular, you can use the mol.dtd DTD from Peter Murray-Rust's Chemical Markup Language, the MathML DTD from the World Wide Web Consortium (W3C)'s Mathematical Markup Language, the SVG DTD from the W3C's Scalable Vector Graphics, and the W3C's XHTML DTD.

You can probably think of more examples where you need to mix and match concepts (and therefore tags) from different fields. Human thought doesn't restrict itself to narrowly defined categories. It tends to wander all over the map. The documents you write will reflect this.

Let's see how to organize the television listings DTD from Chapter 8 as a combination of several different DTDs. This example is extremely hierarchical. One possible division is to write separate DTDs for SHOW, STATION, and SCHEDULE. This is far from the only way to divide the DTD into more manageable chunks, but it will serve as a reasonable example. Listing 10-9 shows a DTD solely for a show that can be stored in a file named show.dtd. Notice that it does not declare the STATION, SCHEDULE, NETWORK, CALL_LETTERS, CHANNEL, or DATE elements.

Listing 10-9: A DTD for the SHOW Element and Its Children (show.dtd)

```
<!ELEMENT SHOW (NAME, TITLE?, TYPE?, EPISODE_NUMBER?,
    START_TIME+, LENGTH, AIR_DATE, ORIGINAL_AIR_DATE?,
    YEAR_MADE?, CLOSED_CAPTIONED?, REPEAT?, RATING?, STARS?,
    DIRECTOR*, WRITER*, CAST?, PRODUCER*, DESCRIPTION?)>
<!ELEMENT NAME              (#PCDATA)>
<!ELEMENT TITLE             (#PCDATA)>
<!ELEMENT TYPE              (#PCDATA)>
<!ELEMENT EPISODE_NUMBER    (#PCDATA)>
<!ELEMENT START_TIME        (#PCDATA)>
<!ELEMENT LENGTH            (#PCDATA)>
<!ELEMENT AIR_DATE          (#PCDATA)>
<!ELEMENT ORIGINAL_AIR_DATE (#PCDATA)>
<!ELEMENT CLOSED_CAPTIONED  (#PCDATA)>
<!ELEMENT REPEAT            (#PCDATA)>
<!ELEMENT GIVEN_NAME        (#PCDATA)>
<!ELEMENT MIDDLE_NAME       (#PCDATA)>
<!ELEMENT MIDDLE_INITIAL    (#PCDATA)>
<!ELEMENT SURNAME           (#PCDATA)>
<!ELEMENT RATING            (#PCDATA)>
<!ELEMENT YEAR_MADE         (#PCDATA)>
<!ELEMENT STARS             (#PCDATA)>
<!ELEMENT DESCRIPTION       (#PCDATA)>

<!ELEMENT CAST (ACTOR+)>
<!ELEMENT ACTOR (
   (GIVEN_NAME, (MIDDLE_NAME | MIDDLE_INITIAL)*, SURNAME?)
  | ((MIDDLE_NAME | MIDDLE_INITIAL)+, SURNAME)
  | SURNAME
)>
<!ELEMENT WRITER (
   (GIVEN_NAME, (MIDDLE_NAME | MIDDLE_INITIAL)*, SURNAME?)
  | ((MIDDLE_NAME | MIDDLE_INITIAL)+, SURNAME)
  | SURNAME
```

```
))>
<!ELEMENT PRODUCER (
    (GIVEN_NAME, (MIDDLE_NAME | MIDDLE_INITIAL)*, SURNAME?)
  | ((MIDDLE_NAME | MIDDLE_INITIAL)+, SURNAME)
  | SURNAME
)>
<!ELEMENT DIRECTOR (
    (GIVEN_NAME, (MIDDLE_NAME | MIDDLE_INITIAL)*, SURNAME?)
  | ((MIDDLE_NAME | MIDDLE_INITIAL)+, SURNAME)
  | SURNAME
)>
```

By itself, this DTD doesn't enable you to create very interesting documents. Listing 10-10 shows a simple valid file that only uses the DTD in Listing 10-9. This simple file is not important for its own sake; however, you can build other, more complex files out of these small parts.

Listing 10-10: A Valid Document Using the SHOW DTD

```
<?xml version="1.0" standalone="no"?>
<!DOCTYPE SHOW SYSTEM "show.dtd">
<SHOW>
  <NAME>Oprah Winfrey</NAME>
  <TYPE>Series/Talk</TYPE>
  <START_TIME>19:00-0500</START_TIME>
  <LENGTH>60 minutes</LENGTH>
  <AIR_DATE>July 3, 2003</AIR_DATE>
  <ORIGINAL_AIR_DATE>February 4, 2003</ORIGINAL_AIR_DATE>
  <CLOSED_CAPTIONED>Yes</CLOSED_CAPTIONED>
  <REPEAT>Yes</REPEAT>
  <RATING>TV-PG</RATING>
  <DESCRIPTION>
    Guests gabber; Oprah looks sympathetic.
  </DESCRIPTION>
</SHOW>
```

What other parts of the document can have their own DTDs? Obviously, a `STATION` is a big part. You could write its DTD as follows:

```
<!ELEMENT STATION (
   ( (NETWORK, CALL_LETTERS?) | CALL_LETTERS ),
    CHANNEL, SHOW+)>
<!ELEMENT NETWORK          (#PCDATA)>
<!ELEMENT CALL_LETTERS     (#PCDATA)>
<!ELEMENT CHANNEL          (#PCDATA)>
```

On closer inspection, however, you should notice that something is missing: the definition of the SHOW element. The definition is in the separate file show.dtd and needs to be connected to this DTD.

You connect DTDs with external parameter entity references. This connection takes the following form:

```
<!ENTITY % name SYSTEM "URI">
%name;
```

For example:

```
<!ENTITY % SHOW SYSTEM "show.dtd">
%SHOW;
```

This example uses a relative URL (show.dtd) and assumes that the file show.dtd will be found in the same place as the linking DTD. If that's not the case, you can use an absolute URL, as follows:

```
<!ENTITY % SHOW SYSTEM
   "http://www.cafeconleche.org/dtds/show.dtd">
%SHOW;
```

Listing 10-11 shows a completed station DTD that includes a reference to the show DTD.

Listing 10-11: **The STATION DTD (station.dtd)**

```
<!ELEMENT STATION (
   ( (NETWORK, CALL_LETTERS?) | CALL_LETTERS ),
    CHANNEL, SHOW+)>
<!ELEMENT NETWORK            (#PCDATA)>
<!ELEMENT CALL_LETTERS       (#PCDATA)>
<!ELEMENT CHANNEL            (#PCDATA)>

<!ENTITY % SHOW SYSTEM
   "http://www.cafeconleche.org/dtds/show.dtd">
%SHOW;
```

By using this DTD, producing a valid document whose root element is STATION is straightforward. Listing 10-12 demonstrates one such valid station document. This document uses both the elements declared in station.dtd and those declared in show.dtd.

Listing 10-12: A Valid Station Document

```
<?xml version="1.0"?>
<!DOCTYPE STATION SYSTEM "station.dtd">
<STATION>
  <CALL_LETTERS>WLNY</CALL_LETTERS>
  <CHANNEL>55</CHANNEL>

  <SHOW>
    <NAME>Oprah Winfrey</NAME>
    <TYPE>Series/Talk</TYPE>
    <START_TIME>19:00-0500</START_TIME>
    <LENGTH>60 minutes</LENGTH>
    <AIR_DATE>July 3, 2003</AIR_DATE>
    <ORIGINAL_AIR_DATE>February 4, 2003</ORIGINAL_AIR_DATE>
    <CLOSED_CAPTIONED>Yes</CLOSED_CAPTIONED>
    <REPEAT>Yes</REPEAT>
    <RATING>TV-PG</RATING>
    <DESCRIPTION>
    Guests gabber; Oprah looks sympathetic.
    </DESCRIPTION>
  </SHOW>

  <SHOW>
    <NAME>Silicon Towers</NAME>
    <TYPE>Movie</TYPE>
    <START_TIME>20:00-0500</START_TIME>
    <LENGTH>60 minutes</LENGTH>
    <AIR_DATE>July 3, 2003</AIR_DATE>
    <YEAR_MADE>1999</YEAR_MADE>
    <CLOSED_CAPTIONED>Yes</CLOSED_CAPTIONED>
    <REPEAT>Yes</REPEAT>
    <RATING>TV-PG</RATING>
    <CAST>
    <ACTOR>
      <GIVEN_NAME>Brian</GIVEN_NAME>
      <SURNAME>Dennehy</SURNAME>
    </ACTOR>
    <ACTOR>
      <GIVEN_NAME>Daniel</GIVEN_NAME>
      <SURNAME>Baldwin</SURNAME>
    </ACTOR>
    <ACTOR>
      <GIVEN_NAME>Brad</GIVEN_NAME>
      <SURNAME>Dourif</SURNAME>
    </ACTOR>
```

Continued

Listing 10-12 *(continued)*

```
    <ACTOR>
      <GIVEN_NAME>Gary</GIVEN_NAME>
      <SURNAME>Mosher</SURNAME>
    </ACTOR>
    </CAST>
    <DESCRIPTION>
    A programmer discovers his company manufactures
    chips for cracking bank systems.
    </DESCRIPTION>
  </SHOW>

</STATION>
```

Besides shows, a SCHEDULE also contains a DATE child element. Although DATE could have its own DTD, it doesn't pay to go overboard with splitting DTDs. Unless you expect you'll have some documents that contain DATE elements that are not part of a SCHEDULE, you might as well include it in the same DTD. Listing 10-13 demonstrates.

Listing 10-13: The SCHEDULE DTD (schedule.dtd)

```
<!ELEMENT SCHEDULE (DATE, STATION+)>
<!ELEMENT DATE     (#PCDATA)>

<!ENTITY % STATION SYSTEM "station.dtd">
%STATION;
```

It's now possible to write a valid document including all the shows and stations in the schedule. This document only refers to the schedule DTD of Listing 10-13 using the following document type declaration:

```
<!DOCTYPE SCHEDULE SYSTEM "schedule.dtd">
```

It does not need to include the station DTD specifically because the schedule DTD will pull it in, and it does not need to include the show DTD because the station DTD will pull that in. DTD inclusion has an indefinite number of levels. Although neither the schedule DTD nor the station DTD it imports declares the SHOW element, you can still use SHOW elements in the right places in a schedule document because the show DTD that the station DTD imports does declare the SHOW element. Only after all parameter entity references are fully resolved is the document checked against the DTD.

Building a Document from Pieces

The television listing examples have been quite large. Although only a truncated version with limited numbers of shows appears in this book, a full document containing all the shows on the hundreds of stations broadcast over 24 hours on a satellite TV or digital cable system could be way too large to comfortably download or search, especially if the reader is only interested in a single show or station. General entity references allow authors to split documents into many different, smaller, more manageable documents, one for each schedule, station, and show. External entity references connect the shows to form stations and the stations to form schedules.

Unfortunately, you cannot embed just any XML document as an external parsed entity. In particular, the documents you embed cannot have document type declarations. Furthermore, they cannot have standalone declarations because they use a text declaration instead of an XML declaration. Consider, for example, Listing 10-14, oprah.xml. This is a revised version of Listing 10-10. However, if you look closely, you'll notice that the prolog is different. Listing 10-10's prolog is as follows:

```
<?xml version="1.0" standalone="no"?>
<!DOCTYPE SHOW SYSTEM "show.dtd">
```

Listing 10-14 modifies Listing 10-10 so it can be embedded into a new document using an entity reference. The prolog has a text declaration instead of an XML declaration. The document type declaration is completely omitted.

Listing 10-14: oprah.xml

```
<?xml encoding="UTF-8"?>
<SHOW>
  <NAME>Oprah Winfrey</NAME>
  <TYPE>Series/Talk</TYPE>
  <START_TIME>19:00-0500</START_TIME>
  <LENGTH>60 minutes</LENGTH>
  <AIR_DATE>July 3, 2003</AIR_DATE>
  <ORIGINAL_AIR_DATE>February 4, 2003</ORIGINAL_AIR_DATE>
  <CLOSED_CAPTIONED>Yes</CLOSED_CAPTIONED>
  <REPEAT>Yes</REPEAT>
  <RATING>TV-PG</RATING>
  <DESCRIPTION>
     Guests gabber; Oprah looks sympathetic.
  </DESCRIPTION>
</SHOW>
```

Listing 10-15, wlny.dtd, and Listing 10-16, wlny.xml, use external parsed entities pointing to Listing 10-14 and a similar document for another show to put together a complete station. The DTD defines external entity references for each show on the station. The XML document loads the DTD using an external parameter entity reference in its internal DTD subset. Then, its document entity resolves many external general entity references that load in the individual shows.

Listing 10-15: The WLNY DTD with Entity References for Show (wlny.dtd)

```
<!ENTITY Oprah SYSTEM "oprah.xml">
<!ENTITY SiliconTowers SYSTEM "silicontowers.xml">
```

Listing 10-16: WLNY with Shows Loaded from External Entities (wlny.xml)

```
<?xml version="1.0"?>
<!DOCTYPE STATION SYSTEM "wlny.dtd">
<STATION>
  <CALL_LETTERS>WLNY</CALL_LETTERS>
  <CHANNEL>55</CHANNEL>

  &Oprah;
  &SiliconTowers;

</STATION>
```

Figure 10-3 shows Listing 10-16 loaded into Internet Explorer. Notice that the data for the shows is present even though the main document only contains references to the entities where the show data resides. Internet Explorer resolves external references — not all XML parsers/browsers do.

It would be nice to continue this procedure — building a cast by combining actors, a person by combining names, and so forth. Unfortunately, if you try this, you rapidly run into a wall. The documents embedded via external entities cannot have their own document type declarations. At most, their prologs can contain text declarations. This means you can only have a single level of document embedding. This contrasts with DTD embedding. DTDs can be nested arbitrarily deeply, but instance documents cannot be.

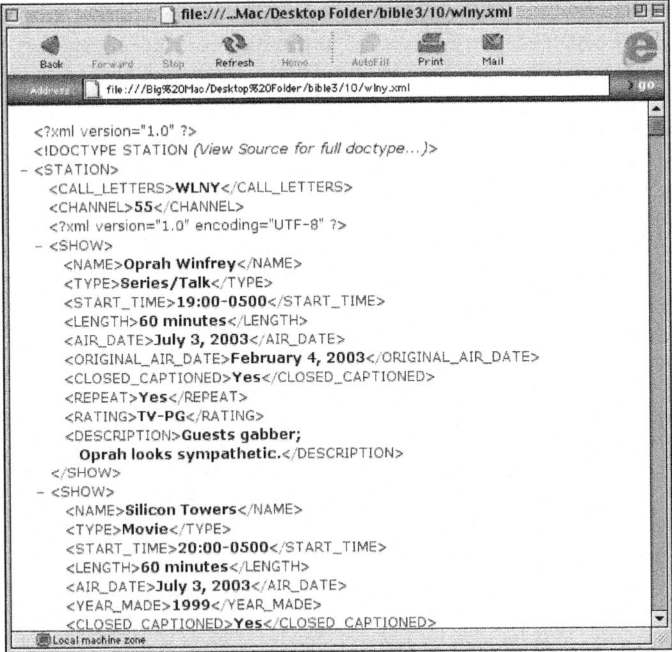

Figure 10-3: The XML document displays all shows on the schedule.

There are two roads around this problem. One is to include all stations in a single document that refers to the many different show documents. This requires one entity declaration for each show. The other is to remove the document type declarations from the individual station files. They can then no longer be parsed on their own. They will only make sense when rendered as part of a document that does define all the various entity references they make use of.

In both cases, you need a DTD that defines entity references for each station. Because there's no limit to how deeply DTDs can nest (unlike instance documents), Listing 10-17 begins with a DTD that pulls in DTDs containing entity definitions for all the stations.

Listing 10-17: **The Station DTD (stations.dtd)**

```
<!ENTITY % wlny SYSTEM "wlny.dtd">
%wlny;
<!ENTITY % wcbs SYSTEM "wcbs.dtd">
%wcbs;
<!ENTITY % hbo SYSTEM "hbo.dtd">
%hbo;
```

You'll notice that in Listing 10-17 and other examples in this chapter, the entity names are often the same or closely related to the names of the files the entities point to. That's occasionally more legible, but it's not in any way required. I could have called the entities foo1, foo2, and foo3 as long as the URLs they dereferenced into were correct.

Listing 10-18 takes the first path. It pulls together all the show subdocuments and then adds the DTDs that define the entities for each show. It includes one entity reference for each show in the schedule. The show entities are defined by Listing 10-19, which is loaded from the internal DTD subset in Listing 10-18. The largest problem with this approach is that if the document is served via HTTP, browsers will need to make over several hundred separate connections to the server (one for each show) before the document can be displayed.

Listing 10-18: Master Television Schedule Document Using External Entity References for Shows

```
<?xml version="1.0" standalone="no"?>
<!DOCTYPE SCHEDULE SYSTEM "schedule.dtd" [
   <!ENTITY % shows SYSTEM "shows.dtd">
   %shows;
]>
<SCHEDULE>
  <DATE>July 3, 2003</DATE>
  <STATION>
    <NETWORK>CBS</NETWORK>
    <CALL_LETTERS>WCBS</CALL_LETTERS>
    <CHANNEL>2</CHANNEL>
    &HollywoodSquares;
    &EntertainmentTonight;
    &AmazingRace;
  </STATION>

  <STATION>
    <CALL_LETTERS>WLNY</CALL_LETTERS>
    <CHANNEL>55</CHANNEL>
    &Oprah;
    &SiliconTowers;
  </STATION>

  <STATION>
    <NETWORK>HBO</NETWORK>
    <CHANNEL>501</CHANNEL>
    &FinalFantasy;
    &Terminator3;
    &StarWars;
  </STATION>

</SCHEDULE>
```

Listing 10-19: DTD That Defines External Entity References for Shows (shows.dtd)

```
<!ENTITY HollywoodSquares SYSTEM "hollywoodsquares.xml">
<!ENTITY EntertainmentTonight SYSTEM
"entertainmenttonight.xml">
<!ENTITY AmazingRace SYSTEM "amazingrace.xml">
<!ENTITY Oprah SYSTEM "oprah.xml">
<!ENTITY SiliconTowers SYSTEM "silicontowers.xml">
<!ENTITY FinalFantasy SYSTEM "finalfantasy.xml">
<!ENTITY Terminator3 SYSTEM "terminator3.xml">
<!ENTITY StarWars SYSTEM "starwars.xml">
```

You do have some flexibility in which levels you choose for the master document and embedded data. For example, one alternative to the structure used by Listing 10-18 places the stations and all their shows in individual documents, then combines those station files into a season with external entities, as shown in Listing 10-20. This has the advantage of using a smaller number of XML files of more even sizes that place less load on the web server and that would download and display more quickly. To be honest, however, the advantage of one approach over the other is minimal. Feel free to use whichever one more closely matches the organization of your data, or simply whichever you feel more comfortable with.

Listing 10-20: A Television Schedule Using External Entity References for Stations

```
<?xml version="1.0" standalone="no"?>
<!DOCTYPE SCHEDULE SYSTEM "schedule.dtd" [
   <!ENTITY % shows SYSTEM "shows.dtd">
   %shows;
   <!ENTITY WLNY SYSTEM "wlny.xml">
   <!ENTITY WCBS SYSTEM "wcbs.xml">
   <!ENTITY HBO  SYSTEM "hbo.xml">
]>
<SCHEDULE>
  <DATE>July 3, 2003</DATE>
  &WCBS:
  &WLNY;
  &HBO;
</SCHEDULE>
```

The individual station files included in this example, such as wlny.xml, contain the data for the shows on those stations. They can either contain the data directly or they can contain the entity references defined by shows.dtd. Listing 10-21 shows what one such station document looks like. This is not by itself a complete or well-formed XML document. It does not define any of the entity references it uses, and it has a text declaration instead of an XML declaration. It can only be parsed when imported into a document that does define these entity references, such as Listing 10-20. It is only a part of an XML document. The station documents are not usable on their own because the entity references they contain are not defined until they're aggregated into the master document.

Listing 10-21: HBO Schedule with Shows Loaded from External Entities

```
<?xml encoding="ISO-8859-1"?>
<STATION>
  <NETWORK>HBO</NETWORK>
  <CHANNEL>501</CHANNEL>
  &FinalFantasy;
  &Terminator3;
  &StarWars;
</STATION>
```

It's unfortunate that only the top-level document is allowed to have a document type declaration. This somewhat limits the utility of external parsed entities.

XInclude is a proposed standard that offers an alternative, non-DTD–based means of building an XML document out of smaller XML documents. However, XInclude is not part of the core XML standard and is not necessarily supported by any validating XML processor and web browser, unlike the techniques of this chapter, which are supported. XInclude is discussed in Chapter 19.

Non-XML Data

Not all data in the world is XML. In fact, I'd venture to say that most of the world's accumulated data isn't XML. A heck of a lot is stored in plain text, HTML, and Microsoft Word, to name just three common non-XML formats. Although most of this data could theoretically be rewritten in XML—interest and resources permitting—not all of the world's data should be in XML. Encoding images in XML, for example, would be extremely inefficient.

XML provides three constructs for working with non-XML data: notations, unparsed entities, and processing instructions. Notations describe the format of non-XML data. Unparsed entities provide links to the actual location of the non-XML data. Processing instructions give information about how to view the data.

The material discussed in this section is controversial. Although everything I describe is part of the XML 1.0 specification, not everyone agrees that it should be. You can certainly write XML documents without using any notations or unparsed entities, and with only a few simple processing instructions.

Notations

The first problem you encounter when working with non-XML data in an XML document is identifying the format of the data so that the application knows how to display the non-XML data. For example, it would be silly to try to draw an MP3 file on the screen.

To a limited extent, you can solve this problem within a single application by using a fixed set of elements for particular kinds of data. For example, if all pictures are embedded through `IMAGE` elements and all sounds via `AUDIO` elements, it's not hard to develop a browser that knows how to handle those two elements. In essence, this is the approach that HTML takes. However, this approach does prevent document authors from creating new tags that more specifically describe their content (for example, a `PERSON` element that happens to have a `HEADSHOT` attribute that points to a JPEG image of that person).

Furthermore, no application understands all possible file formats. Most web browsers can recognize and read GIF, JPEG, PNG, and perhaps a few other kinds of image files, but they fail completely when faced with EPS, TIFF, FITS, or any of the hundreds of other common and uncommon image formats. The dialog box in Figure 10-4 is probably all too familiar.

Ideally, a document should tell the application what format an unparsed entity is in so that you don't have to rely on the application recognizing the file type by a magic number or a potentially unreliable filename extension. Furthermore, you'd like to give the application some hints about what program it can use to display the unparsed entity if it's unable to do so itself.

Notations provide a partial (although not always well supported) solution to this problem. A notation describes one possible format for non-XML data through a `NOTATION` declaration in the DTD. Each notation declaration contains a name and an external identifier in the following syntax:

```
<!NOTATION name SYSTEM "externalID">
```

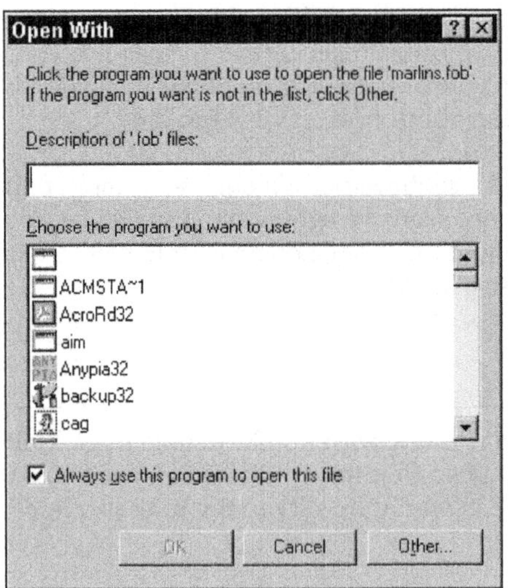

Figure 10-4: What happens when Netscape Navigator doesn't recognize a file type

The *name* is an identifier for this particular format used in the document. The *externalID* contains a human-intelligible string that somehow identifies the notation. For example, you might use MIME types as in this notation for GIF images:

```
<!NOTATION GIF SYSTEM "image/gif">
```

You can also use a `PUBLIC` identifier instead of the `SYSTEM` identifier:

```
<!NOTATION GIF PUBLIC "image/gif">
```

An alternate approach is to use a formal public identifier like those discussed in Chapter 7, along with a URL, as in the following example:

```
<!NOTATION GIF PUBLIC
   "-//IETF//NONSGML Media Type image/gif//EN"
   "http://www.isi.edu/in-notes/iana/assignments/media-
types/image/gif">
```

There is *a lot* of debate about what exactly makes a good external identifier. MIME types, such as image/gif or text/html, are one possibility. Another possibility is to use URLs or other locators for standards documents, such as `http://www.w3.org/TR/REC-html40/`. A third possibility is the name of an official international standard such as ISO 8601 for representing dates and times. In some cases, an ISBN or Library of Congress catalog number for the paper document where the standard is defined might be more appropriate, and there are many more choices.

Which you choose may depend on the expected life span of your document. For example, if you use an unusual format, you don't want to rely on a URL that changes from month to month. If you expect or hope that your document will still spark interest in 100 years, you might want to consider identifiers that are likely to have meaning in 100 years, as opposed to those that are merely this decade's technical ephemera.

You can also use notations to describe data that does fit in an XML document. For example, consider this DATE element:

```
<DATE>05-07-06</DATE>
```

What day, exactly, does 05-07-06 represent? Is it May 7, 2006 C.E.? Or is it July 5, 2006 C.E.? The answer depends on whether you read this in the United States or Europe. Maybe it's even May 7, 1906 C.E. or July 5, 1906 C.E. Or perhaps what's meant is May 7, 6 C.E., during the reign of the Roman emperor Augustus in the West and the Han dynasty in China. It's also possible that this date isn't in the "Common Era" at all, but is given in the traditional Jewish, Muslim, or Chinese calendar. Without more information, you cannot determine the true meaning.

To avoid this type of confusion, ISO standard 8601 defines a precise means of representing dates. In this scheme, July 5, 2006 C.E. is written as 20060705 or, in XML, as follows:

```
<DATE>20060705</DATE>
```

This format doesn't match *anybody's* expectations; it's equally confusing to everybody and is thus more or less culturally neutral (although still biased toward the traditional Western calendar).

Notations are declared in the DTD and then used as the values of NOTATION-type attributes. To continue with the date example, Listing 10-22 defines two possible notations for dates in ISO 8601 and conventional U.S. formats. Then, a required FORMAT attribute of type NOTATION is added to each DATE element to describe the structure of the particular element.

Listing 10-22: **DATE Elements in an ISO 8601 and Conventional U.S. Formats**

```
<?xml version="1.0" standalone="yes"?>
<!DOCTYPE SCHEDULE [

  <!NOTATION ISODATE SYSTEM
    "http://www.iso.ch/cate/d15903.html">
```

Continued

Listing 10-22 *(continued)*

```
    <!NOTATION USDATE SYSTEM
      "http://tf.nist.gov/timefreq/general/enc-d.htm#date">

    <!ELEMENT SCHEDULE (APPOINTMENT*)>
    <!ELEMENT APPOINTMENT (NOTE, DATE, TIME?)>

    <!ELEMENT NOTE (#PCDATA)>
    <!ELEMENT DATE (#PCDATA)>
    <!ELEMENT TIME (#PCDATA)>

    <!ATTLIST DATE FORMAT NOTATION (ISODATE | USDATE) #IMPLIED>

]>
<SCHEDULE>
  <APPOINTMENT>
    <NOTE>Deliver presents</NOTE>
    <DATE FORMAT="USDATE">12-25-1999</DATE>
  </APPOINTMENT>
  <APPOINTMENT>
    <NOTE>Party like it's 1999</NOTE>
    <DATE FORMAT="ISODATE">19991231</DATE>
  </APPOINTMENT>
</SCHEDULE>
```

Notations can't force authors to use the format described by the notation, but it is sufficient for simple uses where you trust authors to correctly describe their data.

Unparsed entities

XML is not an ideal format for all data, particularly nontext data. For example, you could store each pixel of a bitmap image as an XML element like this:

```
<PIXEL X="232" Y="128" COLOR="FF5E32" />
```

This is hardly a good idea, though. Anything remotely like this would cause image files to balloon to obscene proportions. Since you shouldn't encode all data in XML, XML documents must be capable of referring to data that is not currently XML and probably never will be.

A typical web page can include GIF and JPEG images, Java applets, ActiveX controls, various kinds of sounds, and so forth. In XML, any block of non-XML data is called an *unparsed entity* because the XML processor won't attempt to understand it. At most, it informs the application of the entity's existence and provides the application with the entity's name and location.

HTML pages embed non-HTML entities through a variety of tags. Pictures are included with the <IMG> tag whose SRC attribute provides the URL of the image file. Java applets are embedded via the <APPLET> tag whose CLASS and CODEBASE attributes refer to the file and directory where the applet resides. The <OBJECT> tag uses its CODEBASE attribute for a URI from which the object's data is retrieved. In each case, a particular predefined element represents a particular kind of content. A predefined attribute contains the URL for that content.

XML applications can work like this, but they don't have to. Instead, XML applications can use an unparsed entity to refer to the content. Unparsed entities provide links to the actual location of the non-XML data. Then they use an ENTITY-type attribute to associate that entity with a particular element in the document.

Declaring unparsed entities

As seen in previous sections, an external entity declaration looks like this:

```
<!ENTITY SIG SYSTEM
"http://www.cafeconleche.org/signature.xml">
```

However, this form is only acceptable if the external entity that the URL names is well-formed XML. If the external entity is not XML, you have to specify the entity's type using the NDATA keyword. For example, to associate the GIF file logo.gif with the name LOGO, you would place this ENTITY declaration in the DTD:

```
<!ENTITY LOGO SYSTEM "logo.gif" NDATA GIF>
```

The final word in the declaration, GIF in this example, must be the name of a notation declared in the DTD. For example, the notation for GIF might look like this:

```
<!NOTATION GIF PUBLIC "image/gif">
```

As usual, you can use absolute or relative URLs for the external entity as convenience dictates. For example,

```
<!ENTITY LOGO SYSTEM "http://www.cafeconleche.org/logo.gif"
   NDATA GIF>
<!ENTITY LOGO SYSTEM "/xml/logo.gif" NDATA GIF>
<!ENTITY LOGO SYSTEM "../logo.gif" NDATA GIF>
```

Embedding unparsed entities

You cannot simply embed an unparsed entity at an arbitrary location in the document using a general entity reference as you can with parsed entities. For example, Listing 10-23 is malformed because LOGO is an unparsed entity.

Listing 10-23: A Malformed XML Document That Tries to Embed an Unparsed Entity with a General Entity Reference

```
<?xml version="1.0" standalone="no"?>
<!DOCTYPE DOCUMENT [
  <!ELEMENT DOCUMENT ANY>
  <!ENTITY LOGO SYSTEM "http://www.ibiblio.org/xml/logo.gif"
     NDATA GIF>
  <!NOTATION GIF SYSTEM "image/gif">
]>
<DOCUMENT>
  &LOGO;
</DOCUMENT>
```

To embed unparsed entities, rather than using general entity references such as `&LOGO;`, you declare an element that serves as a placeholder for the unparsed entity (`IMAGE`, for example). Then you declare an `ENTITY`-type attribute for the `IMAGE` element (`SOURCE`, for example) that provides only the name of the unparsed entity. Listing 10-24 demonstrates.

Listing 10-24: A Valid XML Document That Correctly Embeds an Unparsed Entity

```
<?xml version="1.0" standalone="no"?>
<!DOCTYPE DOCUMENT [

  <!ELEMENT DOCUMENT ANY>
  <!ENTITY LOGO SYSTEM "http://www.ibiblio.org/xml/logo.gif"
     NDATA GIF>
  <!NOTATION GIF SYSTEM "image/gif">
  <!ELEMENT IMAGE EMPTY>
  <!ATTLIST IMAGE SOURCE ENTITY #REQUIRED>

]>
<DOCUMENT>
  <IMAGE SOURCE="LOGO" />
</DOCUMENT>
```

It is now up to the application reading the XML document to recognize the unparsed entity and display it. Applications may choose not to display the unparsed entity (just as a web browser may choose not to load images when the user has disabled image loading).

These examples show empty elements as the containers for unparsed entities. That's not required, however. For example, imagine an XML-based corporate ID system that a security guard uses to look up people entering a building. The PERSON element might have NAME, PHONE, OFFICE, and EMPLOYEE_ID children and a PHOTO ENTITY attribute. Listing 10-25 demonstrates.

Listing 10-25: A Nonempty PERSON Element with a PHOTO ENTITY Attribute

```
<?xml version="1.0" standalone="no"?>
<!DOCTYPE PERSON [
  <!ELEMENT  PERSON (NAME, EMPLOYEE_ID, PHONE, OFFICE)>
  <!ELEMENT  NAME         (#PCDATA)>
  <!ELEMENT  EMPLOYEE_ID  (#PCDATA)>
  <!ELEMENT  PHONE        (#PCDATA)>
  <!ELEMENT  OFFICE       (#PCDATA)>
  <!NOTATION JPEG SYSTEM "image/jpg">
  <!ENTITY   ROGER SYSTEM "rogers.jpg" NDATA JPEG>

  <!ATTLIST PERSON PHOTO ENTITY #REQUIRED>

]>
<PERSON PHOTO="ROGER">
  <NAME>Jim Rogers</NAME>
  <EMPLOYEE_ID>4534</EMPLOYEE_ID>
  <PHONE>X396</PHONE>
  <OFFICE>RH 415A</OFFICE>
</PERSON>
```

This example might seem a little contrived. In practice, you'd be better advised to make an empty PHOTO element with a SOURCE attribute a child of a PERSON element rather than adding an ENTITY attribute to PERSON. Furthermore, you'd probably separate the DTD into external and internal subsets. The external subset, shown in Listing 10-26, declares the elements, notations, and attributes. These are the parts likely to be shared among many different documents. The entity, however, changes from document to document. Thus, you can better place it in the internal DTD subset of each document, as shown in Listing 10-27.

Listing 10-26: The External DTD Subset person.dtd

```
<!ELEMENT  PERSON (NAME, EMPLOYEE_ID, PHONE, OFFICE, PHOTO)>
<!ELEMENT  NAME          (#PCDATA)>
<!ELEMENT  EMPLOYEE_ID   (#PCDATA)>
<!ELEMENT  PHONE         (#PCDATA)>
<!ELEMENT  OFFICE        (#PCDATA)>
<!ELEMENT  PHOTO         EMPTY>
<!NOTATION JPEG SYSTEM "image/jpeg">
<!ATTLIST  PHOTO SOURCE ENTITY #REQUIRED>
```

Listing 10-27: A Document That Uses an Internal DTD Subset to Locate the Unparsed Entity

```
<?xml version="1.0" standalone="no"?>
<!DOCTYPE PERSON [

  <!ENTITY % PERSON_DTD SYSTEM "person.dtd">
  %PERSON_DTD;
  <!ENTITY ROGER SYSTEM "rogers.jpg" NDATA JPEG>

]>
<PERSON>
  <NAME>Jim Rogers</NAME>
  <EMPLOYEE_ID>4534</EMPLOYEE_ID>
  <PHONE>X396</PHONE>
  <OFFICE>RH 415A</OFFICE>
  <PHOTO SOURCE="ROGER"/>
</PERSON>
```

Embedding multiple unparsed entities

On rare occasions, you may need to refer to more than one unparsed entity in a single attribute, perhaps even an indefinite number. You can do this by declaring an attribute of the entity placeholder to have type `ENTITIES`. An `ENTITIES`-type attribute has a value part that consists of multiple unparsed entity names separated by white space. Each entity name refers to an external non-XML data source and must be declared in the DTD. For example, you might use this to write a slide show element that rotates different pictures. The DTD would require these declarations:

```
<!ELEMENT   SLIDESHOW EMPTY>
<!ATTLIST   SLIDESHOW SOURCES ENTITIES #REQUIRED>
<!NOTATION JPEG      SYSTEM "image/jpeg">
<!ENTITY   CHARM     SYSTEM "charm.jpg"    NDATA JPEG>
<!ENTITY   MARJORIE  SYSTEM "marjorie.jpg" NDATA JPEG>
<!ENTITY   POSSUM    SYSTEM "possum.jpg"   NDATA JPEG>
<!ENTITY   BLUE      SYSTEM "blue.jpg"     NDATA JPEG>
```

Then, at the point in the document where you want the slide show to appear, insert the following element:

```
<SLIDESHOW SOURCES="CHARM MARJORIE POSSUM BLUE"/>
```

Once again, I must emphasize that this is not a magic formula that all (or even any) XML browsers automatically understand. It is simply one technique that browsers and other applications may or may not adopt to embed non-XML data in documents.

Conditional Sections

When developing DTDs or documents, you may need to comment out parts of the DTD not yet reflected in the documents. In addition to using comments directly, you can omit a particular group of declarations in the DTD by wrapping it in an `IGNORE` directive. The syntax follows:

```
<![IGNORE[
  declarations that are ignored
]]>
```

As usual, white space doesn't really affect the syntax, but you should keep the opening `<![IGNORE[` and the closing `]]>` on separate lines for easy viewing.

You can ignore any declaration or combination of declarations — elements, entities, attributes, or even other `IGNORE` blocks — but you must ignore entire declarations. The `IGNORE` construct must completely enclose the entire declarations it removes from the DTD. You cannot ignore a piece of a declaration (such as the `NDATA GIF` in an unparsed entity declaration).

You can also specify that a particular section of declarations is included — that is, not ignored. The syntax for the `INCLUDE` directive is just like the `IGNORE` directive but with the `INCLUDE` keyword:

```
<![INCLUDE[
  declarations that are included
]]>
```

When an `INCLUDE` is inside an `IGNORE`, the `INCLUDE` and its declarations are ignored. When an `IGNORE` is inside an `INCLUDE`, the declarations inside the `IGNORE` block are still ignored. In other words, an `INCLUDE` never overrides an `IGNORE`.

Given these conditions, you might wonder why `INCLUDE` even exists. No DTD would change if all `INCLUDE` blocks were simply removed, leaving only their contents. `INCLUDE` appears to be completely extraneous. However, there is one neat trick with parameter entity references and both `IGNORE` and `INCLUDE` that you can't do with `IGNORE` alone. First, define a parameter entity reference as follows:

```
<!ENTITY % fulldtd "IGNORE">
```

You can ignore elements by wrapping them in the following construct:

```
<![ %fulldtd; [
  declarations
]]>
```

The `%fulldtd;` parameter entity reference evaluates to `IGNORE`, so the declarations are ignored. Now, suppose you make the one-word edit to change `fulldtd` from `IGNORE` to `INCLUDE`, as follows:

```
<!ENTITY % fulldtd "INCLUDE">
```

Immediately, all the `IGNORE` blocks convert to `INCLUDE` blocks. In effect, you have a one-line switch to turn blocks on or off.

In this example, I've only used one switch, `fulldtd`. You can use this switch in multiple `IGNORE/INCLUDE` blocks in the DTD. You can also have different groups of `IGNORE/INCLUDE` blocks that you switch on or off based on different conditions.

You'll find this capability particularly useful when designing DTDs for inclusion in other DTDs. The ultimate DTD can change the behavior of the DTDs it embeds by changing the value of the parameter entity switch.

Summary

In this chapter, you discovered that XML documents are built from both internal and external entities. In particular, you learned the following:

- ✦ Entities are the physical storage units from which an XML document is assembled.
- ✦ An entity holds content: well-formed XML, other forms of text, or binary data.
- ✦ Internal entities are defined completely within the DTD.
- ✦ External entities draw their content from another resource located via a URL.
- ✦ General entity references have the form `&name;` and are used in a document's content.
- ✦ Internal general entity references are replaced by an entity value given in the entity declaration.
- ✦ External general entity references are replaced by the data at a URL specified in the entity declaration after the `SYSTEM` keyword.
- ✦ Parameter entity references have the form `%name;` and are used exclusively in DTDs.
- ✦ You can merge different DTDs with external parameter entity references.
- ✦ External entity references enable you to build large, compound documents out of small parts.
- ✦ Invalid documents can still use DTDs to define entity references.
- ✦ Notations define a data type for non-XML data using a `NOTATION` declaration.
- ✦ Unparsed entities are storage units containing non-XML text or binary data.
- ✦ Unparsed entities are defined in the DTD using an `ENTITY` declaration with an extra `NDATA` declaration identifying the type of data through a notation name.
- ✦ Documents include unparsed entities using `ENTITY` or `ENTITIES` attributes.
- ✦ `INCLUDE` and `IGNORE` blocks specify that the enclosed declarations of the DTD are or are not (respectively) to be considered when parsing the document.

You'll see a lot more examples of documents with DTDs over the next several parts of this book, but as far as basic syntax and usage goes, this chapter concludes the exploration of DTDs. However, there's one more fundamental technology that you need to add to your toolbox before you've got a complete picture of XML itself. That technology is namespaces, a way of attaching prefixes and URIs to element and attribute names so that applications can tell the difference between elements and attributes from different XML vocabularies, even when they have the same names. Chapter 11 explores namespaces.

✦ ✦ ✦

Namespaces

In This Chapter

The need for namespaces

Namespace syntax

Namespaces and validity

While documents that use a single markup vocabulary are useful (witness the television examples of Chapters 4 and 5), documents that mix and match markup from different XML applications are even more functional. For example, imagine you want to include a `BIOGRAPHY` element in each `ACTOR` element. Because the biography consists basically of free-form, formatted text, it's convenient to write it in well-formed HTML without reinventing all the elements for paragraphs, line breaks, list items, bold elements, and so forth from scratch.

However, when mixing and matching elements from different XML applications, you're likely to find the same name used for two different things. Is a `TITLE` the title of a page, the title of a book, or the title of a person? Is an `ADDRESS` the mailing address of a company or the e-mail address of a webmaster? Namespaces disambiguate these cases by associating a Uniform Resource Identifier (URI) with each XML application and attaching a prefix to each element to indicate which application it belongs to. Thus, you can have both `BOOK:TITLE` and `HTML:TITLE` elements or `POSTAL:ADDRESS` and `HTML:ADDRESS` elements instead of just one kind of `TITLE` or `ADDRESS`. This chapter shows you how to use namespaces.

If you're familiar with namespaces as used in C++ and other programming languages, you need to put aside your preconceptions before reading further. XML namespaces are similar to, but not quite the same as, the namespaces used in programming. In particular, XML namespaces do not necessarily form a set (a collection with no duplicates).

The Need for Namespaces

XML enables developers to create their own markup languages for their own projects. These languages can be shared with people working on similar projects all over the world. One specific example of this is Scalable Vector Graphics (SVG). SVG is an XML application that describes line art such as might be produced by Adobe Illustrator or Visio. SVG documents are embedded in HTML or XHTML documents to add vector graphics to web pages. SVG elements include `desc`, `title`, `metadata`, `defs`, `path`, `text`, `rect`, `circle`, `ellipse`, `line`, `polyline`, `polygon`, `use`, `image`, `svg`, `g`, `view`, `switch`, `a`, `altGlyphDef`, `script`, `style`, `symbol`, `marker`, `clipPath`, `mask`, `linearGradient`, `radialGradient`, `pattern`, `filter`, `cursor`, `font`, `animate`, `set`, `animateMotion`, `animateColor`, `animateTransform`, `color-profile`, and `font-face`. Five of these—`title`, `a`, `script`, `style`, and `font`—happen to share names with HTML elements. Several others conflict with other XML vocabularies you might want to embed in an HTML document. For example, MathML uses `set` to mean a mathematical set; the Resource Description Framework (RDF) uses `title` to identify the title of a resource.

How is a browser reading a document that mixes HTML, SVG, and RDF supposed to know whether any given `title` element is an HTML `title`, an SVG `title`, or an RDF `title`? Perhaps the browser could have enough knowledge of where the different kinds of SVG pictures, RDF metadata, MathML equations, and other extra-HTML vocabularies are supposed to appear to be able to tell which is which. But what is the browser supposed to do when it encounters conflicts with nonstandard vocabularies that it hasn't seen before and of which it has no understanding? XML is designed to allow authors and developers to extend it with their own elements in an infinite variety of ways. When authors begin mixing and matching tag sets created by different developers, name conflicts are almost inevitable.

Namespaces are the solution. They allow each element and attribute in a document to be placed in a different namespace mapped to a particular URI. The XML elements that come from SVG are placed in the `http://www.w3.org/2000/svg` namespace. The XML elements that come from XHTML are placed in the `http://www.w3.org/1999/xhtml` namespace. MathML goes in the `http://www.w3.org/1998/Math/MathML` namespace. If you mix in elements from some vocabulary you created yourself, you can place that in another namespace, with a URI somewhere in a domain you own.

Note A Uniform Resource Identifier is an abstraction of a URL. Whereas a URL *locates* a resource, a URI *identifies* a resource. For example, a URI for a person might include that person's social security number. This doesn't mean you can look the person up in a web browser using a person URI. In theory, URIs are a superset of URLs, which also include Uniform Resource Names (URNs). In practice, most URIs used today, including most namespace URIs, are, in fact, URLs.

This URI doesn't even have to point at any particular file. The URI that defines a namespace is purely formal. Its only purpose is to group and disambiguate element and attribute names in the document. It does not necessarily point to anything. In particular, *there is no guarantee that the document at the namespace URI describes the syntax used in the document; or, for that matter, that any document exists at the URI.* Most namespace URIs produce 404 Not Found errors when you attempt to resolve them. Having said that, if there is a canonical URI for a particular XML application, that URI is a good choice for the namespace definition.

Namespaces have been carefully crafted to layer on top of the XML 1.0 specification. Other than reserving the colon character to separate prefixes and local names, namespaces have no direct effect on standard XML syntax. An XML 1.0 processor that knows nothing about namespaces can still read a document that uses namespaces and will not find any errors. Conversely, a document that uses namespaces must still be well formed when read by a processor that knows nothing about namespaces. If the document is validated, it must be validated without specifically considering the namespaces. To an XML processor, a document that uses namespaces is just a document in which some of the element and attribute names have a single colon. Documents that use namespaces do not break existing XML parsers; and users don't have to wait for notoriously unpunctual software companies to release upgrades before using namespaces.

Namespace Syntax

Suppose you're a webmaster at a small agency in Hollywood that represents screenwriters. You want a web page that describes the scripts currently available for auction from the agency's clients. The basic page that provides the list is written in HTML. The information about each client is given in some industry standard DTD for describing people that requires `PERSON` elements to have this form:

```
<PERSON>
  <FIRST>Larry</FIRST>
  <LAST>Smith</LAST>
  <TITLE>Mr.</TITLE>
</PERSON>
```

The information about screenplays is provided in `SCRIPT` elements that look like this:

```
<SCRIPT>
  <TITLE>New York Stories</TITLE>
  <AUTHOR>
    <PERSON>
      <FIRST>Larry</FIRST>
      <LAST>Smith</LAST>
      <TITLE>Mr.</TITLE>
    </PERSON>
  </AUTHOR>
  <SYNOPSIS>
    Six friends with no visible means of support nonetheless
    manage to live in improbably large apartments in
    Manhattan.
  </SYNOPSIS>
</SCRIPT>
```

The entire document might look something like Listing 11-1.

Listing 11-1: A Well-Formed XML Document That Uses HTML and Two Custom XML Applications

```
<HTML>
  <HEAD><TITLE>Screenplays for Auction</TITLE></HEAD>
  <BODY>
    <H1>January 27, 2004 Auction</H1>

    <P>Pilot scripts for the Fall season:</P>

    <SCRIPT>
      <TITLE>Chicken Feathers</TITLE>
      <AUTHOR>
        <PERSON>
          <FIRST>William</FIRST>
          <LAST>Sanders</LAST>
          <TITLE>Col.</TITLE>
        </PERSON>
      </AUTHOR>
      <SYNOPSIS>
        Hijinks in a poultry factory
      </SYNOPSIS>
    </SCRIPT>

    <SCRIPT>
      <TITLE>Soft Copy</TITLE>
      <AUTHOR>
        <PERSON>
          <FIRST>Nora</FIRST>
          <LAST>Lessinger</LAST>
          <TITLE>Dr.</TITLE>
        </PERSON>
      </AUTHOR>
      <SYNOPSIS>Sex lives of the rich and famous</SYNOPSIS>
    </SCRIPT>

    Send inquiries to
    <PERSON>
      <TITLE>Mr.</TITLE>,
      <FIRST>Mikhail</FIRST>
      <LAST>Ovitsky</LAST>
      <COMPANY>Duplicative Artists Mismanagement</COMPANY>,
      <ADDRESS>135 Agents Row, Hollywood, CA 90123</ADDRESS>
    </PERSON>

  </BODY>
</HTML>
```

There are several problems with this document, even though it's well-formed XML. Some of the elements used as part of the custom vocabularies conflict with each other and with standard HTML. The first problem is that the TITLE element is used for three separate things: the title of the page, the title of a script, and the title of a person. The second problem may be even worse in practice. The SCRIPT element conflicts with the HTML SCRIPT element. A web browser reading this document might try to interpret the contents of the SCRIPT element as a JavaScript program. Even though this particular page doesn't use any JavaScript, an HTML renderer, even one that supports XML embedded in HTML documents, is still going to think that a SCRIPT element contains JavaScript. These sorts of problems crop up all the time when you mix and match different XML vocabularies. In this case, the problem is the attempt to merge three different vocabularies — one for persons, one for scripts, and one for web pages — that were designed without much concern for each other.

Even if the names don't conflict, how is an XML browser supposed to be able to distinguish between groups of elements from different vocabularies? For example, a studio robot might want to collect script proposals from various agencies by harvesting all the SCRIPT elements that contain synopses while ignoring all the JavaScript. You can fix all these problems by adding namespaces to the document. Namespaces identify which elements in the document belong to which XML vocabularies.

Defining namespaces with xmlns attributes

The script auction example uses elements from three different vocabularies, so three different namespaces are needed. Each namespace has a URI. You can choose any convenient absolute URI in a domain that you own for the namespace. In this example, I use the URI `http://ns.cafeconleche.org/people/` for the person application because I happen to own the cafeconleche.org domain.

Note

The URI you choose does not have to refer to anything. There does not have to be a DTD or a schema or any other page at all at the location identified by the namespace URI. In fact, there isn't even a host named ns.cafeconleche.org. A namespace URI is nothing more than a formal identifier that helps to distinguish between elements with the same name from different organizations. URIs were chosen for this purpose because they allow developers to choose their own namespace URIs without having to create yet another central registration authority.

However, URIs often contain characters that can't appear in XML element and attribute names. For example, `http://ns.cafeconleche.org/people/first` is not a legal name for an XML element because it contains forward slashes. Therefore, you have to associate the URI with a prefix and put the prefix in the element name instead. The prefixes are generally some abbreviated form of the thing that the XML application describes. For the person application, you might choose the prefix P, p, or PE, or perhaps even person or PEOPLE. In this example, I use P as the prefix for the person vocabulary with the associated URI `http://ns.cafeconleche.org/people/`.

You associate a namespace URI with a prefix by adding an `xmlns:`*`prefix`* attribute to the elements they apply to. *`prefix`* is replaced by the actual prefix used for the namespace. The value of the attribute is the URI of the namespace. For example, this `xmlns:P` attribute associates the prefix `P` with the URI `http://ns.cafeconleche.org/people/`.

```
xmlns:P="http://ns.cafeconleche.org/people/"
```

Once this attribute is added to an element, the `P` prefix can then be attached to that element's name as well as the names of its attributes and descendants. Within that element, the `P` prefix identifies something as belonging to the `http://ns.cafeconleche.org/people/` namespace. The prefix is attached to the local name by a colon. Listing 11-2 demonstrates by adding the `P` prefix to the `PERSON`, `FIRST`, and `LAST` elements, as well as those `TITLE` elements that come from the people application, but not to the `TITLE` elements that come from HTML or the script application.

Listing 11-2: **Placing the Person Application Elements in a Separate Namespace**

```
<HTML>
  <HEAD><TITLE>Screenplays for Auction</TITLE></HEAD>
  <BODY>
    <H1>January 27, 2004 Auction</H1>

    <P>Pilot scripts for the Fall season:</P>

    <SCRIPT>
      <TITLE>Chicken Feathers</TITLE>
      <AUTHOR>
       <P:PERSON xmlns:P="http://ns.cafeconleche.org/people/">
          <P:FIRST>William</P:FIRST>
          <P:LAST>Sanders</P:LAST>
          <P:TITLE>Col.</P:TITLE>
       </P:PERSON>
      </AUTHOR>
      <SYNOPSIS>
        Hijinks in a poultry factory
      </SYNOPSIS>
    </SCRIPT>

    <SCRIPT>
      <TITLE>Soft Copy</TITLE>
      <AUTHOR>
       <P:PERSON xmlns:P="http://ns.cafeconleche.org/people/">
          <P:FIRST>Nora</P:FIRST>
          <P:LAST>Lessinger</P:LAST>
          <P:TITLE>Dr.</P:TITLE>
       </P:PERSON>
```

```
    </AUTHOR>
    <SYNOPSIS>Sex lives of the rich and famous</SYNOPSIS>
  </SCRIPT>

  Send inquiries to
  <P:PERSON xmlns:P="http://ns.cafeconleche.org/people/">
   <P:TITLE>Mr.</P:TITLE>,
   <P:FIRST>Mikhail</P:FIRST>
   <P:LAST>Ovitsky</P:LAST>
   <P:COMPANY>Duplicative Artists Mismanagement</P:COMPANY>,
   <P:ADDRESS>
     135 Agents Row, Hollywood, CA 90123
   </P:ADDRESS>
  </P:PERSON>

 </BODY>
</HTML>
```

It's now quite easy to distinguish between the title of the page and the title of a person. The page's title is represented by a TITLE element, while a person's title is represented by a P:TITLE element.

The elements with the P prefix are said to have *qualified names* beginning with the P prefix:

✦ P:PERSON

✦ P:TITLE

✦ P:FIRST

✦ P:LAST

✦ P:COMPANY

✦ P:ADDRESS

The part of the name after the colon is called the *local name*. These six elements have these six local names:

✦ PERSON

✦ TITLE

✦ FIRST

✦ LAST

✦ COMPANY

✦ ADDRESS

The prefix can change as long as the URI and the local names stay the same. The true names of these elements are based on the URI rather than on the prefix. Thus, the abstract true names of these six elements have a form like this:

- http://ns.cafeconleche.org/people/:PERSON
- http://ns.cafeconleche.org/people/:TITLE
- http://ns.cafeconleche.org/people/:FIRST
- http://ns.cafeconleche.org/people/:LAST
- http://ns.cafeconleche.org/people/:COMPANY
- http://ns.cafeconleche.org/people/:ADDRESS

However, you'll never use a name like this anywhere in an XML document. In essence, the shorter qualified names are mandatory nicknames that are used within the document because URIs often contain characters such as ~, %, and / that aren't legal in XML names.

A namespace prefix can be any legal XML name that does not contain a colon. Recall from Chapter 6 that a legal XML name must begin with a letter or an underscore (_). Subsequent letters in the name may include letters, digits, underscores, hyphens, and periods. They may not include white space.

Two prefixes are specifically disallowed: xml and xmlns. The xml prefix should only be used for the xml:space and xml:lang attributes defined in the XML 1.0 specification and other generic attributes defined later by the W3C such as xml:base. The prefix xml is automatically mapped to the URI http://www.w3.org/XML/1998/namespace. The xmlns prefix is used to bind elements to namespaces and is therefore not available as a prefix to be bound to.

Multiple namespaces

The difference between the title of a page and the title of a script is still up in the air, as is the difference between a screenplay SCRIPT and a JavaScript SCRIPT. To fix this, you must add another namespace to the document. This time, I use the prefix SCR and the URI http://ns.cafeconleche.org/scripts/. Defining this mapping requires adding this attribute to all the SCRIPT elements:

```
xmlns:SCR="http://ns.cafeconleche.org/scripts/"
```

Alternately, instead of placing the declaration of the SCR namespace prefix on all SCRIPT elements, I can put it on one element that contains them all. There are two such elements in the example, HTML and BODY. When the namespace declaration is not placed directly on the start-tag that begins the vocabulary, it's generally put on the root element, as shown in Listing 11-3.

Listing 11-3: Declaring a Namespace on the Root Element

```
<HTML xmlns:SCR="http://ns.cafeconleche.org/scripts/">
  <HEAD><TITLE>Screenplays for Auction</TITLE></HEAD>
  <BODY>
    <H1>January 27, 2004 Auction</H1>

    <P>Pilot scripts for the Fall season:</P>

    <SCR:SCRIPT>
      <SCR:TITLE>Chicken Feathers</SCR:TITLE>
      <SCR:AUTHOR>
       <P:PERSON xmlns:P="http://ns.cafeconleche.org/people/">
          <P:FIRST>William</P:FIRST>
          <P:LAST>Sanders</P:LAST>
          <P:TITLE>Col.</P:TITLE>
       </P:PERSON>
      </SCR:AUTHOR>
      <SCR:SYNOPSIS>
        Hijinks in a poultry factory
      </SCR:SYNOPSIS>
    </SCR:SCRIPT>

    <SCR:SCRIPT>
      <SCR:TITLE>Soft Copy</SCR:TITLE>
      <SCR:AUTHOR>
       <P:PERSON xmlns:P="http://ns.cafeconleche.org/people/">
          <P:FIRST>Nora</P:FIRST>
          <P:LAST>Lessinger</P:LAST>
          <P:TITLE>Dr.</P:TITLE>
       </P:PERSON>
      </SCR:AUTHOR>
      <SCR:SYNOPSIS>Sex lives of the rich and famous
      </SCR:SYNOPSIS>
    </SCR:SCRIPT>

    Send inquiries to
    <P:PERSON xmlns:P="http://ns.cafeconleche.org/people/">
      <P:TITLE>Mr.</P:TITLE> <P:FIRST>Mikhail</P:FIRST>
      <P:LAST>Ovitsky</P:LAST>
      <P:COMPANY>Duplicative Artists Mismanagement</P:COMPANY>
      <P:ADDRESS>
        135 Agents Row, Hollywood, CA 90123
      </P:ADDRESS>
    </P:PERSON>

  </BODY>
</HTML>
```

Whether you choose to declare a namespace on the root element or on some element further down the hierarchy is mostly a matter of personal preference and convenience in the document at hand. Some developers prefer to declare all namespaces on the root element. Others prefer to declare the namespaces closer to where they're actually used. XML doesn't care. For example, Listing 11-3 could have equally well been written as shown in Listing 11-4, with both the SCR and P prefixes declared on the root element.

Listing 11-4: **Declaring All Namespaces on the Root Element**

```
<HTML xmlns:SCR="http://ns.cafeconleche.org/scripts/"
      xmlns:P="http://ns.cafeconleche.org/people/">
  <HEAD><TITLE>Screenplays for Auction</TITLE></HEAD>
  <BODY>
    <H1>January 27, 2004 Auction</H1>

    <P>Pilot scripts for the Fall season:</P>

    <SCR:SCRIPT>
      <SCR:TITLE>Chicken Feathers</SCR:TITLE>
      <SCR:AUTHOR>
        <P:PERSON>
          <P:FIRST>William</P:FIRST>
          <P:LAST>Sanders</P:LAST>
          <P:TITLE>Col.</P:TITLE>
        </P:PERSON>
      </SCR:AUTHOR>
      <SCR:SYNOPSIS>
        Hijinks in a poultry factory
      </SCR:SYNOPSIS>
    </SCR:SCRIPT>

    <SCR:SCRIPT>
      <SCR:TITLE>Soft Copy</SCR:TITLE>
      <SCR:AUTHOR>
        <P:PERSON>
          <P:FIRST>Nora</P:FIRST>
          <P:LAST>Lessinger</P:LAST>
          <P:TITLE>Dr.</P:TITLE>
        </P:PERSON>
      </SCR:AUTHOR>
      <SCR:SYNOPSIS>Sex lives of the rich and famous
      </SCR:SYNOPSIS>
    </SCR:SCRIPT>

    Send inquiries to
    <P:PERSON>
      <P:TITLE>Mr.</P:TITLE>,
      <P:FIRST>Mikhail</P:FIRST>
      <P:LAST>Ovitsky</P:LAST>
```

```
      <P:COMPANY>Duplicative Artists Mismanagement</P:COMPANY>
      <P:ADDRESS>
        135 Agents Row, Hollywood, CA 90123
      </P:ADDRESS>
    </P:PERSON>

  </BODY>
</HTML>
```

In most cases (validation against a DTD being the notable exception), it's the URI that's important, not the prefix. The prefixes can change. As long as the URI stays the same, the meaning of the document is unchanged. For example, Listing 11-5 uses the prefixes PERSON and SCRIPT instead of P and SCR. However, this document has the same meaning and content as Listing 11-4.

Listing 11-5: **Same Document, Different Prefixes**

```
<HTML xmlns:SCRIPT="http://ns.cafeconleche.org/scripts/"
      xmlns:PERSON="http://ns.cafeconleche.org/people/">
  <HEAD><TITLE>Screenplays for Auction</TITLE></HEAD>
  <BODY>
    <H1>January 27, 2004 Auction</H1>

    <P>Pilot scripts for the Fall season:</P>

    <SCRIPT:SCRIPT>
      <SCRIPT:TITLE>Chicken Feathers</SCRIPT:TITLE>
      <SCRIPT:AUTHOR>
        <PERSON:PERSON>
          <PERSON:FIRST>William</PERSON:FIRST>
          <PERSON:LAST>Sanders</PERSON:LAST>
          <PERSON:TITLE>Col.</PERSON:TITLE>
        </PERSON:PERSON>
      </SCRIPT:AUTHOR>
      <SCRIPT:SYNOPSIS>
        Hijinks in a poultry factory
      </SCRIPT:SYNOPSIS>
    </SCRIPT:SCRIPT>

    <SCRIPT:SCRIPT>
      <SCRIPT:TITLE>Soft Copy</SCRIPT:TITLE>
      <SCRIPT:AUTHOR>
        <PERSON:PERSON>
          <PERSON:FIRST>Nora</PERSON:FIRST>
          <PERSON:LAST>Lessinger</PERSON:LAST>
          <PERSON:TITLE>Dr.</PERSON:TITLE>
        </PERSON:PERSON>
```

Continued

Listing 11-5 *(continued)*

```
      </SCRIPT:AUTHOR>
      <SCRIPT:SYNOPSIS>Sex lives of the rich and famous
      </SCRIPT:SYNOPSIS>
    </SCRIPT:SCRIPT>

    Send inquiries to
    <PERSON:PERSON>
      <PERSON:TITLE>Mr.</PERSON:TITLE>,
      <PERSON:FIRST>Mikhail</PERSON:FIRST>
      <PERSON:LAST>Ovitsky</PERSON:LAST>
      <PERSON:COMPANY>Duplicative Artists Mismanagement
      </PERSON:COMPANY>,
      <PERSON:ADDRESS>
        135 Agents Row, Hollywood, CA 90123
      </PERSON:ADDRESS>
    </PERSON:PERSON>

  </BODY>
</HTML>
```

In fact, it's even possible to redeclare prefixes so that one prefix refers to different URIs in different places in the document, or so that two different prefixes refer to the same URI. This is, however, needlessly confusing; I strongly recommend that you avoid it. There are more than enough prefixes to go around, and almost no need to reuse them within the same document. The main reason for this is to allow different documents from different authors that happen to use the same prefix to be combined. This is a good reason to avoid short prefixes such as A, S, and X that are likely to be reused for different purposes.

Attributes

Because attributes belong to particular elements, they're more easily distinguished from similarly named attributes without namespaces. Consequently, it's not nearly as essential to add namespaces to attributes as to elements. For example, the XSLT specification requires that all XSLT elements be in the http://www.w3.org/1999/XSL/Transform namespace. However, it does not require that the attributes of these elements be in any particular namespace. (In fact, it requires that they *not* be in any namespace.) Nonetheless, you can attach namespace prefixes to attributes, if necessary. For example, all the attributes in this SCRIPT element and its children live in the http://namespaces.cafeconleche.org/scripts/ namespace.

```
<SCR:SCRIPT SCR:TYPE="Sitcom"
            SCR:COPYRIGHT="2004 William Sanders"
  xmlns:SCR="http://namespaces.cafeconleche.org/scripts/"
  xmlns:P="http://namespaces.cafeconleche.org/people/">
```

```
    <SCR:TITLE SCR:ALT="NO">Chicken Feathers</SCR:TITLE>
    <SCR:AUTHOR SCR:ID="A67Y">
      <P:PERSON>
        <P:FIRST>William</P:FIRST>
        <P:LAST>Sanders</P:LAST>
        <P:TITLE>Col.</P:TITLE>
      </P:PERSON>
    </SCR:AUTHOR>
    <SCR:SYNOPSIS SCR:LANG="English">
      Hijinks in a poultry factory
    </SCR:SYNOPSIS>
  </SCR:SCRIPT>
```

This might occasionally prove useful if you need to combine attributes from two different XML applications on the same element. XLink uses prefixed attributes to allow any element to become a link.

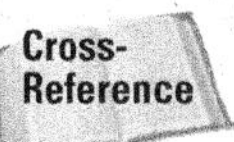

XLinks are discussed in Chapter 17.

It is possible (though mostly pointless) to associate the same namespace URI with two different prefixes. The only reason I bring it up here is simply to warn you that it is the true name of the attribute that must satisfy XML's rules for an element not having more than one attribute with the same name. For example, this code is illegal because SCR:ID and SCRIPT:ID are the same:

```
<SCR:SCRIPT SCR:TYPE="Sitcom"
            SCR:COPYRIGHT="2004 William Sanders"
  xmlns:SCR="http://namespaces.cafeconleche.org/scripts/"
  xmlns:SCRIPT="http://namespaces.cafeconleche.org/scripts/"
  xmlns:P="http://namespaces.cafeconleche.org/people/">
  <SCR:TITLE SCR:ID="A67Y" SCRIPT:ID="Y76A">
    Chicken Feathers
  </SCR:TITLE>
</SCR:SCRIPT>
```

On the other hand, the parser does not actually check the URI to see what it points to. The URIs http://ibiblio.org/xml/ and http://www.ibiblio.org/xml/ point to the same page, but the following code is legal:

```
<SCR:SCRIPT SCR:TYPE="Sitcom"
            SCR:COPYRIGHT="2004 William Sanders"
  xmlns:SCR="http://ibiblio.org/xml/"
  xmlns:SCRIPT="http://www.ibiblio.org/xml/"
  xmlns:P="http://namespaces.cafeconleche.org/people/">
  <SCR:TITLE SCR:ID="A67Y" SCRIPT:ID="Y76A">
    Chicken Feathers
  </SCR:TITLE>
</SCR:SCRIPT>
```

Default namespaces

In long documents with a lot of markup all in the same namespace, it may be inconvenient to add a prefix to each element name. You can attach a default namespace to an element and to its child elements using an `xmlns` attribute with no prefix. The element itself and all its children are considered to be in the defined namespace unless they have an explicit prefix.

For example, you might wish to place the HTML elements in the script auction example in a namespace of their own, but not to give them any prefixes so that legacy browsers will still recognize them. Listing 11-6 does exactly this.

Listing 11-6: Placing the HTML Elements in the Same Namespace

```
<HTML xmlns="http://www.w3.org/1999/xhtml"
     xmlns:SCRIPT="http://ns.cafeconleche.org/scripts/"
     xmlns:PERSON="http://ns.cafeconleche.org/people/">
  <HEAD><TITLE>Screenplays for Auction</TITLE></HEAD>
  <BODY>
    <H1>January 27, 2004 Auction</H1>

    <P>Pilot scripts for the Fall season:</P>

    <SCRIPT:SCRIPT>
      <SCRIPT:TITLE>Chicken Feathers</SCRIPT:TITLE>
      <SCRIPT:AUTHOR>
        <PERSON:PERSON>
          <PERSON:FIRST>William</PERSON:FIRST>
          <PERSON:LAST>Sanders</PERSON:LAST>
          <PERSON:TITLE>Col.</PERSON:TITLE>
        </PERSON:PERSON>
      </SCRIPT:AUTHOR>
      <SCRIPT:SYNOPSIS>
        Hijinks in a poultry factory
      </SCRIPT:SYNOPSIS>
    </SCRIPT:SCRIPT>

    <SCRIPT:SCRIPT>
      <SCRIPT:TITLE>Soft Copy</SCRIPT:TITLE>
      <SCRIPT:AUTHOR>
        <PERSON:PERSON>
          <PERSON:FIRST>Nora</PERSON:FIRST>
          <PERSON:LAST>Lessinger</PERSON:LAST>
          <PERSON:TITLE>Dr.</PERSON:TITLE>
        </PERSON:PERSON>
      </SCRIPT:AUTHOR>
      <SCRIPT:SYNOPSIS>Sex lives of the rich and famous
      </SCRIPT:SYNOPSIS>
    </SCRIPT:SCRIPT>
```

```
    Send inquiries to
    <PERSON:PERSON>
      <PERSON:TITLE>Mr.</PERSON:TITLE>,
      <PERSON:FIRST>Mikhail</PERSON:FIRST>
      <PERSON:LAST>Ovitsky</PERSON:LAST>
      <PERSON:COMPANY>Duplicative Artists Mismanagement
      </PERSON:COMPANY>,
      <PERSON:ADDRESS>
        135 Agents Row, Hollywood, CA 90123
      </PERSON:ADDRESS>
    </PERSON:PERSON>

  </BODY>
</HTML>
```

From the perspective of most XML applications, a document that uses the default namespace is the same as a document that uses prefixes as long as the URIs associated with each element are the same. However, a legacy HTML browser will have a much easier time with the code in Listing 11-6 than with the equivalent version in Listing 11-7 that attaches the prefix `HTML` to all the HTML elements.

Listing 11-7: Prefixing the HTML Elements in the Same Namespace

```
<HTML:HTML xmlns:HTML="http://www.w3.org/1999/xhtml"
     xmlns:SCRIPT="http://ns.cafeconleche.org/scripts/"
     xmlns:PERSON="http://ns.cafeconleche.org/people/">
  <HTML:HEAD>
    <HTML:TITLE>Screenplays for Auction</HTML:TITLE>
  </HTML:HEAD>
  <HTML:BODY>
    <HTML:H1>January 27, 2004 Auction</HTML:H1>

    <HTML:P>Pilot scripts for the Fall season:</HTML:P>

    <SCRIPT:SCRIPT>
      <SCRIPT:TITLE>Chicken Feathers</SCRIPT:TITLE>
      <SCRIPT:AUTHOR>
        <PERSON:PERSON>
          <PERSON:FIRST>William</PERSON:FIRST>
          <PERSON:LAST>Sanders</PERSON:LAST>
          <PERSON:TITLE>Col.</PERSON:TITLE>
        </PERSON:PERSON>
      </SCRIPT:AUTHOR>
      <SCRIPT:SYNOPSIS>
        Hijinks in a poultry factory
```

Continued

Listing 11-7 *(continued)*

```
      </SCRIPT:SYNOPSIS>
    </SCRIPT:SCRIPT>

    <SCRIPT:SCRIPT>
      <SCRIPT:TITLE>Soft Copy</SCRIPT:TITLE>
      <SCRIPT:AUTHOR>
        <PERSON:PERSON>
          <PERSON:FIRST>Nora</PERSON:FIRST>
          <PERSON:LAST>Lessinger</PERSON:LAST>
          <PERSON:TITLE>Dr.</PERSON:TITLE>
        </PERSON:PERSON>
      </SCRIPT:AUTHOR>
      <SCRIPT:SYNOPSIS>Sex lives of the rich and famous
      </SCRIPT:SYNOPSIS>
    </SCRIPT:SCRIPT>

    Send inquiries to
    <PERSON:PERSON>
      <PERSON:TITLE>Mr.</PERSON:TITLE>,
      <PERSON:FIRST>Mikhail</PERSON:FIRST>
      <PERSON:LAST>Ovitsky</PERSON:LAST>
      <PERSON:COMPANY>Duplicative Artists Mismanagement
      </PERSON:COMPANY>,
      <PERSON:ADDRESS>
        135 Agents Row, Hollywood, CA 90123
      </PERSON:ADDRESS>
    </PERSON:PERSON>

  </HTML:BODY>
</HTML:HTML>
```

A good time to use default namespaces is when you need to attach a namespace to every element in an existing document to which you're now going to add elements from a different language. For example, if you place some MathML in an XHTML document, you only have to add prefixes to the MathML elements. You can put all the HTML elements in the XHTML namespace simply by adding an `xmlns` attribute to the start-tag like this:

```
<html xmlns="http://www.w3.org/1999/xhtml">
```

You do not need to edit the rest of the file. The MathML tags you insert still need to be in the proper MathML namespace. However, as long as they aren't mixed up with a lot of HTML markup, you can simply declare an `xmlns` attribute on the MathML's root element. This defines a default namespace for the MathML elements that overrides the default namespace of the document containing the MathML. Listing 11-8 demonstrates.

Listing 11-8: A MathML Math Element Embedded in a Well-Formed HTML Document

```
<?xml version="1.0"?>
<html xmlns="http://www.w3.org/1999/xhtml">
  <head>
    <title>Fiat Lux</title>
    <meta name="GENERATOR" content="amaya V1.3b" />
  </head>
  <body>

    <P>And God said,</P>

    <math xmlns="http://www.w3.org/1998/Math/MathML">
      <mrow>
        <msub>
          <mi>&#x3B4;</mi>
          <mi>&#x3B1;</mi>
        </msub>
        <msup>
          <mi>F</mi>
          <mi>&#x3B1;&#x3B2;</mi>
        </msup>
        <mi></mi>
        <mo>=</mo>
        <mi></mi>
        <mfrac>
          <mrow>
            <mn>4</mn>
            <mi>&#x3C0;</mi>
          </mrow>
          <mi>c</mi>
        </mfrac>
        <mi></mi>
        <msup>
          <mi>J</mi>
          <mrow>
            <mi>&#x3B2;</mi>
            <mo></mo>
          </mrow>
        </msup>
      </mrow>
    </math>

    <P>and there was light</P>

  </body>
</html>
```

Here, `math`, `mrow`, `msub`, `mo`, `mi`, `mfrac`, `mn`, and `msup` are all in the `http://www.w3.org/1998/Math/MathML` namespace, even though the document that contains them uses the `http://www.w3.org/1999/xhtml` namespace.

Attributes are never in a default namespace. They must be explicitly prefixed. An unprefixed attribute is in no namespace at all. Even if the element it is a part of is in some namespace, default or otherwise, the unprefixed attribute is still not in that or any other namespace.

Namespaces and Validity

Namespaces do not get any special exemptions from the normal rules of well-formedness and validity. Well-formedness is generally not a problem, but validity can be. For a document that uses namespaces to be valid, you must declare the `xmlns` attributes in the DTD just like you'd declare any other attribute. Furthermore, you must declare the elements and attributes using the prefixes they use in the document. For example, if a document uses a `PERSON:ADDRESS` element, the DTD must declare a `PERSON:ADDRESS` element, not merely an `ADDRESS` element, like this:

```
<!ELEMENT PERSON:ADDRESS (#PCDATA)>
```

This means that if a DTD was written without namespace prefixes, it must be rewritten using the namespace prefixes before it can be used to validate documents that use prefixed element and attribute names. For example, consider this element declaration:

```
<!ELEMENT SCRIPT (TITLE, AUTHOR, SYNOPSIS)>
```

You have to rewrite it as follows if the elements are all given the `SCR` namespace prefix:

```
<!ELEMENT SCR:SCRIPT (SCR:TITLE, SCR:AUTHOR, SCR:SYNOPSIS)>
```

This means that you cannot easily use the same DTD for both documents with namespaces and documents without, even if they use essentially the same vocabulary. In fact, you can't even use the same DTD for documents that use the same tag sets and namespaces but different prefixes, because DTDs are tied to the actual prefixes rather than the URIs of the namespaces.

If you have a question about whether a document that uses namespaces is well formed or valid, forget everything you know about namespaces. Simply treat the document as a normal XML document that happens to have some element and attribute names that contain colons. The document is as well formed and valid as it is when you don't consider namespaces.

There is one really ugly hack that enables a single DTD to describe documents from the same application that use different namespace prefixes (or no prefix at all). You can define the namespace prefix, the element names, and the namespace declaration attributes as parameter entity references. Then the internal DTD subset can override these entity references to define them as whatever prefix that particular document uses. For example, to parameterize the namespace prefix for the http://ns.cafeconleche.org/people/ namespace used in several previous examples, first declare PREFIX, COLON, and NAMESPACE_DECLARATION parameter entities:

```
<!ENTITY % PREFIX "PERSON">
<!ENTITY % COLON ":">
<!ENTITY % NAMESPACE_DECLARATION "xmlns%COLON;%PREFIX;">
```

Next, declare parameter entities for the element names that depend on these parameter entities. For example, here's the declaration for the ADDRESS element:

```
<!ENTITY % ADDRESS.NAME "%PREFIX;%COLON;ADDRESS">
```

Finally, declare the ADDRESS element using the ADDRESS.NAME entity:

```
<!ELEMENT %ADDRESS.NAME; (#PCDATA)>
```

Do not try to save a step by using the PREFIX and COLON entities directly in the declaration of the PERSON element like this:

```
<!ELEMENT %PREFIX;%COLON;ADDRESS (#PCDATA)>
```

For various technical reasons, this is not well formed and does not work.

Similarly, every other use of a prefixed name, whether in an element declaration, a content model, or an attribute list, should be parameterized. Listing 11-9 shows the completely parameterized DTD.

Listing 11-9: **A Parameterized DTD**

```
<!ENTITY % PREFIX "PERSON">
<!ENTITY % COLON ":">
<!ENTITY % NAMESPACE_DECLARATION "xmlns%COLON;%PREFIX;">

<!ENTITY % PERSON.NAME   "%PREFIX;%COLON;PERSON">
<!ENTITY % TITLE.NAME   "%PREFIX;%COLON;TITLE">
<!ENTITY % FIRST.NAME   "%PREFIX;%COLON;FIRST">
<!ENTITY % LAST.NAME    "%PREFIX;%COLON;LAST">
<!ENTITY % COMPANY.NAME "%PREFIX;%COLON;COMPANY">
<!ENTITY % ADDRESS.NAME "%PREFIX;%COLON;ADDRESS">
```

Continued

Listing 11-9 *(continued)*

```
<!ELEMENT %PERSON.NAME; (%TITLE.NAME;, %FIRST.NAME;,
%LAST.NAME;, %COMPANY.NAME;, %ADDRESS.NAME;)>
<!ATTLIST %PERSON.NAME; %NAMESPACE_DECLARATION; CDATA
                #FIXED "http://ns.cafeconleche.org/people/">

<!ELEMENT %TITLE.NAME;   (#PCDATA)>
<!ELEMENT %FIRST.NAME;   (#PCDATA)>
<!ELEMENT %LAST.NAME;    (#PCDATA)>
<!ELEMENT %COMPANY.NAME; (#PCDATA)>
<!ELEMENT %ADDRESS.NAME; (#PCDATA)>
```

Now you can override the parameter entities in the internal DTD subset of the instance document to choose a different prefix. For example, Listing 11-10 shows a valid document that uses the prefix P instead of PERSON.

Listing 11-10: A Document That Changes the Namespace Prefix

```
<?xml version="1.0"?>
<!DOCTYPE P:PERSON SYSTEM "person.dtd" [
  <!ENTITY % PREFIX "P">
]>
<P:PERSON xmlns:P="http://ns.cafeconleche.org/people/">
  <P:TITLE>Mr.</P:TITLE>
  <P:FIRST>Mikhail</P:FIRST>
  <P:LAST>Ovitsky</P:LAST>
  <P:COMPANY>Duplicative Artists Mismanagement</P:COMPANY>
  <P:ADDRESS>
    135 Agents Row, Hollywood, CA 90123
  </P:ADDRESS>
</P:PERSON>
```

To use the default namespace with no prefix at all, just set both the PREFIX and COLON entities to the empty string, as demonstrated in Listing 11-11.

Listing 11-11: A Document That Removes the Namespace Prefix

```
<?xml version="1.0"?>
<!DOCTYPE PERSON SYSTEM "person.dtd" [
  <!ENTITY % PREFIX "">
  <!ENTITY % COLON "">
]>
<PERSON xmlns="http://ns.cafeconleche.org/people/">
  <TITLE>Mr.</TITLE>
  <FIRST>Mikhail</FIRST>
  <LAST>Ovitsky</LAST>
  <COMPANY>Duplicative Artists Mismanagement</COMPANY>
  <ADDRESS>
    135 Agents Row, Hollywood, CA 90123
  </ADDRESS>
</PERSON>
```

Summary

This chapter explained namespaces. In particular, you learned the following:

✦ Namespaces distinguish between elements and attributes with the same name from different XML applications.

✦ In a document that mixes markup from multiple XML applications, namespaces identify which elements and attributes are part of which XML applications.

✦ Namespaces are declared by an `xmlns` attribute whose value is the URI of the namespace. The document referred to by this URI need not exist.

✦ The prefix associated with a namespace is the part of the name of the `xmlns` attribute that follows the colon; for example, `xmlns:`*`prefix`*.

✦ Prefixes are attached to all element and attribute names that belong to the namespace identified by the prefix.

✦ If an `xmlns` attribute has no prefix, it establishes a default namespace for that element and its child elements (but not for any attributes).

✦ DTDs must be written in such a fashion that a processor that knows nothing about namespaces can still parse and validate the document.

This completes Part II. You now have a solid grasp of XML fundamentals. The next several parts look at a number of supplementary technologies that layer on top of XML, as well as applications built with XML. Many of these applications use namespaces for one purpose or another. In particular, you'll learn how namespaces are used in the Extensible Stylesheet Language (XSL), the XML Linking Language (XLink), Scalable Vector Graphics (SVG), and several other XML applications.

✦ ✦ ✦

P A R T

Style Languages

✦ ✦ ✦ ✦

In This Part

✦ ✦ ✦ ✦

CHAPTER 12

CSS Style Sheets

✦ ✦ ✦ ✦

In This Chapter

What is CSS?

Selecting elements

Inheritance

Cascades

Different rules for different media

Importing style sheets

Character sets

✦ ✦ ✦ ✦

Cascading style sheets (CSS) is a very simple and straightforward language for applying styles to XML documents. Most of the styles CSS supports should be familiar to you from using any word processor. For example, you can choose the font, the font weight, the font size, the background color, the spacing between paragraphs, the borders around elements, and more. However, rather than being stored as part of the document itself, all the style information is placed in a separate document called a style sheet. A single XML document can be formatted in many different ways just by changing the style sheet. Different style sheets can be designed for different purposes — for print, the Web, presentations, and other uses — all with the styles appropriate for the specific medium, and all without changing any of the content in the document itself.

Netscape 6.0 and later, Mozilla, Opera 4.0 and later, Safari, and Internet Explorer 5.0 and later all implement some (but not all) parts of the CSS specification. Earlier versions of the major browsers, while perhaps supporting some form of CSS for HTML documents, do not support it at all for XML documents. To make matters worse, they all implement different subsets of the specification, and sometimes don't implement the same subsets for XML as they do for HTML. I'll try to indicate where one browser or another has a particular problem as it comes up. However, if you find that something in this chapter doesn't work as advertised in your favorite browser (or in any browser), please complain to the browser vendor, not to me.

What Are Cascading Style Sheets?

Cascading style sheets (referred to as CSS from now on) is a declarative language introduced in 1996 as a standard means of adding information about style properties, such as fonts and borders, to HTML documents. However, CSS actually works better with XML than with HTML because HTML is burdened with backward-compatibility issues. For example, properly supporting the CSS `nowrap` property requires eliminating the nonstandard but frequently used `NOWRAP` element in HTML. Because XML elements don't have any predefined formatting, they don't restrict which CSS styles can be applied to which elements.

A simple CSS style sheet

A CSS style sheet contains a list of rules. Each rule gives the names of the elements it applies to and the styles to apply to those elements. Consider Listing 12-1, a CSS style sheet for poems. Listing 12-1 can be typed in any text editor, saved as a text file, and called something like poem.css. The three letter extension .css is conventional, but not required.

Listing 12-1: A CSS Style Sheet for Poems

```
POEM   { display: block }
TITLE  { display: block; font-size: 16pt; font-weight: bold }
POET   { display: block; margin-bottom: 10px }
STANZA { display: block; margin-bottom: 10px }
VERSE  { display: block }
```

This style sheet has five rules. Each rule has a *selector*—in this instance the name of the element to which it applies—and a list of styles to apply to instances of that element. The first rule says that the contents of the `POEM` element should have a line break before and after it (`display: block`). The second rule says that the contents of the `TITLE` element should have a line break before and after it (`display: block`) in 16-point (`font-size: 16pt`) bold type (`font-weight: bold`). The third rule says that the `POET` element should have a line break before and after it (`display: block`) and should be set off from what follows it by 10 pixels (`margin-bottom: 10px`). The fourth rule is the same as the third rule except that it applies to `STANZA` elements. Finally, the fifth rule simply states that each `VERSE` element also has a line break before and after it.

Comments

CSS style sheets can include comments. CSS comments are similar to C's `/* */` comments, but not to the `<!-- -->` XML and HTML comments. Listing 12-2 demonstrates. This style sheet doesn't merely apply style rules to elements. It also describes, in English, the results those style rules are supposed to achieve.

Listing 12-2: A Style Sheet for Poems with Comments

```
/* Work around a Mozilla bug */
POEM { display: block }

/* Make the title look like an H1 header */
TITLE  { display: block; font-size: 16pt; font-weight: bold }
POET   { display: block; margin-bottom: 10px }

/* Put a blank line in-between stanzas,
   only a line break between verses */
STANZA { display: block; margin-bottom: 10px }
VERSE  { display: block }
```

CSS style sheets aren't nearly as convoluted as DTDs, or Java, C, or Perl programs, so comments aren't quite as necessary as they are in other languages. However, it's rarely a bad idea to include comments. They can only help someone who's trying to make sense out of a style sheet you wrote.

Attaching style sheets to documents

To really make sense out of the style sheet in Listing 12-1 or 12-2, you have to give it an XML document to format. Listing 12-3 is a poem from Walt Whitman's *Leaves of Grass* marked up in XML. The second line is the `xml-stylesheet` processing instruction that instructs the web browser loading this document to apply the style sheet found in the file poem.css to this document. Figure 12-1 shows this document loaded into Mozilla.

Listing 12-3: *Darest Thou Now O Soul* Marked Up in XML

```
<?xml version="1.0"?>
<?xml-stylesheet type="text/css" href="poem.css"?>
<POEM>

  <TITLE>Darest Thou Now O Soul</TITLE>
  <POET>Walt Whitman</POET>

  <STANZA>
    <VERSE>Darest thou now O soul,</VERSE>
    <VERSE>Walk out with me toward the unknown region,</VERSE>
    <VERSE>Where neither ground is for the feet nor
           any path to follow?</VERSE>
```

Continued

Listing 12-3 *(continued)*

```
  </STANZA>
  <STANZA>
    <VERSE>No map there, nor guide,</VERSE>
    <VERSE>Nor voice sounding, nor touch of
           human hand,</VERSE>
    <VERSE>Nor face with blooming flesh, nor lips,
           are in that land.</VERSE>
  </STANZA>
  <STANZA>
    <VERSE>I know it not O soul,</VERSE>
    <VERSE>Nor dost thou, all is blank before us,</VERSE>
    <VERSE>All waits undream'd of in that region,
           that inaccessible land.</VERSE>
  </STANZA>
  <STANZA>
    <VERSE>Till when the ties loosen,</VERSE>
    <VERSE>All but the ties eternal, Time and Space,</VERSE>
    <VERSE>Nor darkness, gravitation, sense,
           nor any bounds bounding us.</VERSE>
  </STANZA>
  <STANZA>
    <VERSE>Then we burst forth, we float,</VERSE>
    <VERSE>In Time and Space O soul,
           prepared for them,</VERSE>
    <VERSE>Equal, equipt at last, (O joy! O fruit of all!)
           them to fulfil O soul.</VERSE>
  </STANZA>

</POEM>
```

The `type` pseudo-attribute in the `xml-stylesheet` processing instruction is the MIME media type of the style sheet. Its value is `text/css` for CSS and `application/xml` for XSL.

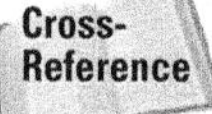

XSL is discussed in Chapters 5, 15, and 16.

The value of the `href` pseudo-attribute in the `xml-stylesheet` processing instruction is the URL, often relative, where the style sheet is located. If the style sheet can't be found, the browser will use its default style sheet instead.

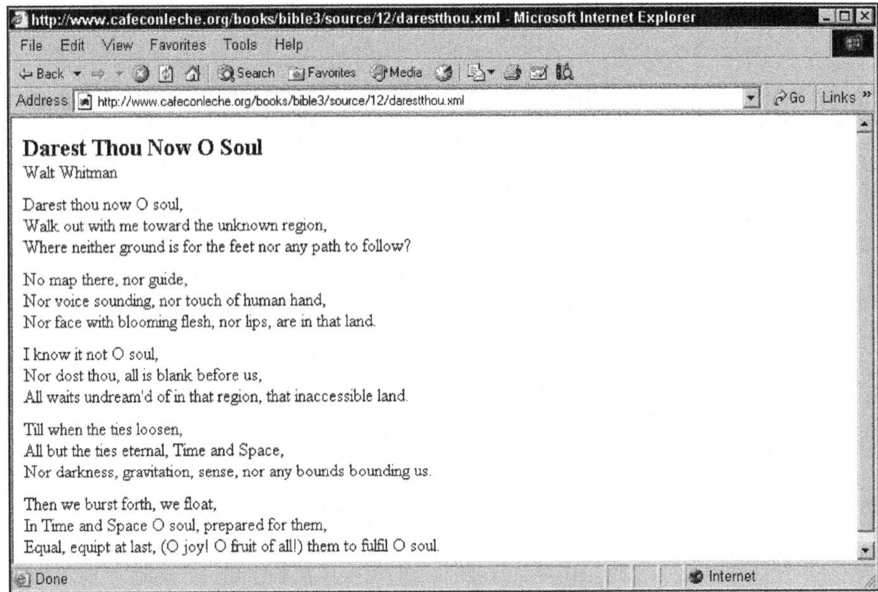

Figure 12-1: *Darest Thou Now O Soul* as rendered by Internet Explorer 6

You can apply the same style sheet to many documents. Indeed, you generally will. Thus, it's common to put your style sheets in some central location on your web server where all of your documents can refer to them; a convenient location is a styles directory in the web server's document root.

```
<?xml-stylesheet type="text/css" href="/styles/poem.css"?>
```

You might even use an absolute URL to a style sheet on another web site, though this does leave your site dependent on the status of the external site.

```
<?xml-stylesheet type="text/css"
      href="http://www.cafeconleche.org/styles/poem.css"?>
```

You can even use multiple `xml-stylesheet` processing instructions to pull in rules from different style sheets, as in the following example:

```
<?xml version="1.0"?>
<?xml-stylesheet type="text/css" href="/styles/poem.css"?>
<?xml-stylesheet type="text/css"
      href="http://www.cafeconleche.org/styles/poem.css"?>
<POEM>
...
```

CSS with HTML versus CSS with XML

Although XML is the focus of this book, CSS style sheets also work with HTML documents. The main differences between CSS with HTML and CSS with XML are as follows:

1. In HTML, the elements you can attach rules to are limited to standard HTML elements, such as `P`, `PRE`, `LI`, `DIV`, and `SPAN`.

2. HTML browsers don't recognize processing instructions, so style sheets are attached to HTML documents using `LINK` tags in the `HEAD` element. Furthermore, per-document style rules can be included in the `HEAD` in a `STYLE` element, as in the following example:

```
<LINK REL=STYLESHEET TYPE="text/css" HREF="/styles/poem.css" >
<STYLE TYPE="text/css">
  PRE { color: red }
</STYLE>
```

3. HTML browsers don't render CSS properties as faithfully as XML browsers because of the legacy formatting of elements. Tables are notoriously problematic in this respect.

DTDs and style sheets

Style sheets are more or less orthogonal to DTDs. A document with a style sheet may or may not have a DTD, and a document with a DTD may or may not have a style sheet. However, DTDs do often serve as convenient lists of the elements that you need to provide style rules for.

In this and the next several chapters, most of the examples use documents that are well formed but not valid. The lack of DTDs will make the examples shorter and the relevant parts more obvious. However, there's absolutely no reason why you can't attach a style sheet to a document that has a DTD. In either case, the style rules only apply to the content of the document, not to the DTD.

CSS1 versus CSS2

The first version of CSS was thrown together rather quickly and left a lot to the imagination. It was quite limited in what it could accomplish. For example, CSS could make an element red but couldn't make it the same color as the desktop. It could make text bold but couldn't make it shadowed. The underlying layout model only really worked for left-to-right languages, such as English and Greek, and fell apart when faced with documents containing right-to-left languages, such as Arabic, or top-to-bottom languages, such as Chinese. Many details were insufficiently specified and open to multiple incompatible interpretations. Most importantly for the purposes of this book, CSS only really considered HTML; it didn't work well for XML. For example, it didn't provide table formatting because that could be done with HTML table tags.

In 1998, the World Wide Web Consortium (W3C) published a revised and expanded specification for CSS called CSS Level 2 (CSS2). At the same time, they renamed the original CSS to CSS Level 1 (CSS1). CSS2 is mostly a superset of CSS1, with a few minor exceptions. CSS2 incorporates many features that web developers and designers have long requested from browser vendors. Of course, CSS2 fights the same backward-compatibility battles with HTML that CSS1 fought. However, with XML, CSS2 can format content on both paper and the Web almost as well as a desktop publishing program such as PageMaker or QuarkXPress can.

All browsers that can display XML documents support CSS Level 2, at least in part. Therefore, this chapter focuses on CSS2 exclusively. The distinction between CSS1 and CSS2 is really only important for older browsers that don't support XML at all.

CSS3

Work is ongoing to produce CSS Level 3 (CSS3). This is currently being developed at the W3C as several independent pieces, including the following:

- ✦ Better page formatting, including running headers and footers, page numbers, and automatically updated cross-references
- ✦ Styles for forms, including input fields, checkboxes, radio buttons, buttons, list boxes, and more
- ✦ Math styles for equations and numbers
- ✦ Behavioral styles for tasks currently accomplished with JavaScript and DHTML
- ✦ More accurate color matching
- ✦ Multicolumn layouts
- ✦ Selectors that operate by element content and relative position in the document

When all of these are done, they'll be rolled together with the existing CSS2 specification to produce CSS Level 3. However, it's unlikely that this will be finished before 2004, and it certainly won't be implemented by browsers in any large way until at least 2005.

Selecting Elements

The part of a CSS rule that specifies which elements it applies to is called a *selector*. The most common kind of selector is simply the name of an element; for example, `TITLE` in this rule:

```
TITLE { display: block; font-size: 16pt; font-weight: bold }
```

However, selectors can also specify multiple elements, elements with a particular ID, and elements that appear in particular contexts relative to other elements. Indeed, a selector can be anything from a simple element name to a complex system of contextual patterns. Table 12-1 summarizes the selector patterns.

Table 12-1
CSS Selector Patterns

Syntax	*Meaning*
`*`	Matches all elements.
`X`	Matches every element with the name `X`; for example, the pattern `STANZA` matches all `STANZA` elements.
`X Y`	Matches every element with the name `Y` that is a descendent of an element with the name `X`; for example, `POEM VERSE` matches all `VERSE` descendents of `POEM` elements.
`X > Y`	Matches every element named `Y` that is a child of an element named `X`; for example, `STANZA > VERSE` matches all `VERSE` children of a `STANZA` element.
`X + Y`	Matches all elements named `Y` whose preceding sibling is an element named `X`. For example, `STANZA + REFRAIN` matches every `REFRAIN` element that is immediately preceded by a `STANZA` element. `VERSE + VERSE` matches every `VERSE` element that is immediately preceded by another `VERSE` element. In Listing 12-3, this matches all verses in each `STANZA` except the first.
`X:first-child`	Matches every element named `X` that is the first child of its parent element; for example, `POEM:first-child` matches the first child element of the `POEM` element. In Listing 12-3, this is the `TITLE` element.
`X[A]`	Matches all elements named `X` that have an `A` attribute, no matter what its value; for example, `AUTHOR[NAME]` matches every `AUTHOR` element with a `NAME` attribute.
`X[A="M"]`	Matches all elements named `X` whose `A` attribute has the value `M`; for example, `AUTHOR[NAME="Walt Whitman"]` matches every `AUTHOR` element whose `NAME` attribute has the value Walt Whitman.
`X[A~="M"]`	Matches all elements named `X` whose `A` attribute contains a space-separated list of names, one of which is `M`; for example, `AUTHOR[NAME= "Walt"]` matches every `AUTHOR` element whose `NAME` attribute has the value Walt Whitman, Walt Smith, Walt Irving, or Irving Walt.
`X[A|="M"]`	Matches all elements named `X` whose `A` attribute contains a space-separated list of names the first of which is `M`; for example, `AUTHOR [NAME|="Walt"]` matches every `AUTHOR` element whose `NAME` attribute has the value Walt Whitman but not those whose `NAME` attribute has the value Irving Walt.

Syntax	*Meaning*
`X#M`	Matches any elements named `X` whose ID is `M`, as identified by an ID type attribute. Unfortunately, this selector does not work properly for XML in most web browsers.
`X:lang(i)`	Matches all elements named `X` that are written in the natural language *i*, as indicated by an `xml:lang` attribute.
`X:link`	Matches all elements named `X` that are inside a link whose target has not yet been visited.
`X:visited`	Matches all elements named `X` that are inside a link whose target has been visited.
`X:active`	Matches all elements named `X` that are currently selected.
`X:hover`	Matches all elements named `X` over which the cursor is currently positioned.
`X:focus`	Matches all elements named `X` that currently have the focus.

Demonstrating these selectors calls for a poem with a slightly more complicated structure. Listing 12-4 shows Shakespeare's twenty-first sonnet. This has both `STANZA` and `REFRAIN` elements, each of which contains `VERSE` elements. The `STANZA` elements have `NUMBER` attributes of ID type, as established by a document type declaration. The `POEM` element has a `TYPE` attribute with the value `SONNET`.

Listing 12-4: **Shakespeare's Twenty-First Sonnet**

```
<?xml version="1.0"?>
<?xml-stylesheet type="text/css" href="sonnet.css"?>
<!DOCTYPE POEM [
  <!ATTLIST STANZA NUMBER ID #IMPLIED>
]>
<POEM TYPE="SONNET">
  <POET>William Shakespeare</POET>
  <TITLE>Sonnet 21</TITLE>
  <STANZA NUMBER="st1">
    <VERSE>So is it not with me as with that Muse</VERSE>
    <VERSE>Stirr'd by a painted beauty to his verse,</VERSE>
    <VERSE>Who heaven itself for ornament doth use</VERSE>
    <VERSE>And every fair with his fair doth rehearse;</VERSE>
  </STANZA>
  <STANZA NUMBER="st2">
    <VERSE>Making a couplement of proud compare</VERSE>
    <VERSE>With sun and moon, with earth and sea's rich
           gems,</VERSE>
```

Continued

Listing 12-4 *(continued)*

```
    <VERSE>With April's first-born flowers, and all things
          rare</VERSE>
    <VERSE>That heaven's air in this huge rondure hems.</VERSE>
  </STANZA>
  <STANZA NUMBER="st3">
    <VERSE>O, let me, true in love, but truly write,</VERSE>
    <VERSE>And then believe me, my love is as fair</VERSE>
    <VERSE>As any mother's child, though not so bright</VERSE>
    <VERSE>As those gold candles fix'd in heaven's air.</VERSE>
  </STANZA>
  <REFRAIN>
    <VERSE>Let them say more that like of hearsay well,</VERSE>
    <VERSE>I will not praise that purpose not to sell.</VERSE>
  </REFRAIN>
</POEM>
```

The universal selector

The * symbol selects all elements in the document. This lets you set default styles for all elements. For example, this rule sets the default font to New York:

```
* { font-family: "New York" }
```

You can use * instead of an element name in other selector patterns to apply styles to all elements with a specific attribute, attribute value, role, and so forth. For example, this rule makes all elements whose `TYPE` attribute has the value `SONNET` italic:

```
*[TYPE="SONNET"] { font-style: italic }
```

There's only one such element in Listing 12-4, but other documents might have more of these, which may or may not be `POEM` elements.

Tip

If you are using the universal selector with just one other property specification, you can leave out the *. For example, the preceding rule could be rewritten as follows:

```
[TYPE="SONNET"] { font-style: italic }
```

Grouping selectors

If you want to apply a set of properties to some but not all elements, list the element names in the selector separated by commas. For example, in Listing 12-1 `POET` and `STANZA` were both styled as block display with a 10-pixel margin. You can combine these two rules like this:

```
POET, STANZA { display: block; margin-bottom: 10px }
```

You can add as many elements as you like. For example, this rule applies style to POET, STANZA, and REFRAIN elements:

```
POET, STANZA, REFRAIN { display: block; margin-bottom: 10px }
```

Furthermore, more than one rule can apply styles to a single element. So you can combine some standard properties into a rule with many selectors, then use more specific rules to apply custom formatting to selected elements. For example, in Listing 12-1 all the elements were listed as block display. This can be combined into one rule while additional formatting for the POET, STANZA, REFRAIN, and TITLE elements is contained in separate rules, as shown in Listing 12-5.

Listing 12-5: sonnet.css

```
POEM, VERSE, TITLE, POET, STANZA, REFRAIN { display: block }
POET, STANZA, REFRAIN { margin-bottom: 10px }
TITLE {font-size: 16pt; font-weight: bold }
```

If the rules conflict, the last one in the style sheet is chosen.

Hierarchy selectors

In XML, as in life, what you look like depends heavily on what your ancestors looked like. You can individually select elements that are children or descendents of a specified type of element with descendant, child, and sibling selectors.

Child selectors

A child selector uses the greater than sign > to select an element if and only if it's an immediate child of a specified parent. For example, to apply a rule to VERSE elements that are children of STANZA elements but not to VERSE elements that are children of REFRAIN elements, you'd use the selector STANZA > VERSE. These rules make stanza verses bold but refrain verses italic:

```
STANZA  > VERSE {font-weight: bold }
REFRAIN > VERSE {font-style:  italic }
```

You can expand this to look at the parent of the parent, the parent of the parent of the parent, and so forth. For example, the following rule says that a VERSE element inside a STANZA element inside a POEM element should be rendered in a monospaced font:

```
POEM > REFRAIN > VERSE { font-family: Courier, monospaced }
```

In practice, this level of specificity is rarely needed. In cases in which it does seem necessary, you can often rewrite the style sheet to rely more on inheritance, cascades, and relative units, and less on the precise specification of formatting.

Descendant selectors

A descendant selector chooses elements that are children, grandchildren, or other descendants of a specified element. For example, you can specify one style for VERSE elements contained in a POEM element and a different style for VERSE elements contained in a BOOK element. To do this, prefix the name of the ancestor element to the name of the styled element separated by a space. The following rules make book verses bold, but poem verses italic:

```
BOOK VERSE {font-weight: bold }
POEM VERSE {font-style:  italic; font-weight: normal }
```

In the event of a conflict between two rules, the closer one takes precedence. For example, if a BOOK contains a POEM that contains VERSE elements, those VERSE elements will be italic and not bold. In case of a conflict between two equally specific rules, the last rule encountered in the style sheet takes precedence.

You can even give VERSE elements inside POEM elements inside BOOK elements a completely different style that is not shared by VERSE elements inside POEM elements that are not inside BOOK elements or VERSE elements that are not inside POEM elements but are inside BOOK elements. For example, this rule makes such elements red:

```
BOOK POEM VERSE {color: red }
```

Not all styles conflict with each other. For example, consider these three rules:

```
BOOK VERSE    {font-weight: bold }
POEM VERSE    {font-style: italic }
CHAPTER VERSE {color: red }
```

Together these say that every VERSE element contained inside a BOOK element will be bold; every VERSE element contained inside a POEM element will be italic; and every VERSE element contained inside a CHAPTER element will be red. A VERSE element that matches all three rules—one that has a BOOK ancestor, a POEM ancestor, and a CHAPTER ancestor—will have all three properties; that is, it will be bold, italic, and red.

In Listings 12-2 and 12-4, all VERSE elements are descendants of POEM elements, but not immediate children. Some VERSE elements are immediate children of STANZA elements, and some are immediate children of the REFRAIN element. A descendant selector of the form POEM VERSE matches a VERSE element that is an arbitrary descendant of a SONNET element. To specify a minimum generation for a descendant, you can use the selector POEM * VERSE, which forces the VERSE element to be at least a grandchild, or lower descendent of the POEM element.

You can combine descendant and child selectors to find specific elements. For example, the following rule italicizes all VERSE elements that are children of a REFRAIN element that is, in turn, a descendant of a POEM element.

```
POEM REFRAIN>VERSE { font-style: italic }
```

Adjacent sibling selectors

A plus sign (+) between two element names signifies that the left-hand element precedes the right-hand element at the same level of the hierarchy. The right-hand element is selected. For example, this rule finds all REFRAIN elements that share a parent with a STANZA element and that immediately follow a STANZA element:

```
STANZA+REFRAIN {color: red}
```

This rule finds all VERSE elements that are preceded by another VERSE element:

```
VERSE+VERSE {color: blue}
```

Applied to Listings 12-2 and 12-4, this has the effect of coloring all verses blue except the first one in the stanza.

Attribute selectors

Attribute selectors identify specific element/attribute combinations. Square brackets surround the name of the attribute being specified. For example, this rule specifies a script font for all <POEM TYPE="*x*"> elements, but not plain <POEM> elements:

```
POEM[TYPE]  { font-family: "Zapf Chancery", cursive }
```

To distinguish between <POEM TYPE="*x*"> and <POEM TYPE="*y*"> elements, you can add an equals sign (=) followed by the quoted attribute value. For example, this rule only applies to sonnets:

```
POEM[TYPE="SONNET"]  { font-style: italic }
```

You can use a ~= to indicate that the attribute value only needs to contain the specified word somewhere within it. For example, this rule italicizes all POEM elements whose TYPE attribute contains the word SONNET:

```
POEM[TYPE~="SONNET"]  { font-style: italic }
```

However, this would not find elements whose TYPE attribute contains the word SONNETS or UNISONNET. CSS only looks for complete words. It does not look for substrings.

You can use a |= to indicate that the attribute value needs to begin with the specified word. For example, this rule italicizes all POEM elements whose TYPE attribute begins with the word SONNET:

```
POEM[TYPE|="SONNET"]  { font-style: italic }
```

This would not find elements whose TYPE attribute had the value "HEXAMETER SONNET", but it would match a POEM with a TYPE attribute having the value "SONNET HEXAMETER".

ID selectors

Sometimes, a unique element needs a unique style. You need a rule that applies to exactly that one element. For example, suppose you want to make one element in a list bold to really emphasize it in contrast to its siblings. In this case, you can write a rule that selects the element by its ID—that is, by the value of its ID type attribute. The selector is the name of the element, followed by a sharp sign (#) and the value of the ID attribute.

For example, this rule makes the first STANZA element, and only the first STANZA element, in Listing 12-4 bold. Other STANZA elements appear with the default weight.

```
STANZA#st1 {font-weight: bold}
```

However, there's a catch. To tell which attributes have ID type and can therefore be selected by an ID selector, the browser must read the DTD. Most browsers, including Safari, Mozilla, and Netscape, do not read the external DTD subset, so if that's where the attribute is declared, they won't know that its type is ID and won't apply the style rule. Internet Explorer does read the external DTD subset, but it's just plain buggy and won't apply this style rule no matter what. Opera also fails to apply this rule even when the attribute is declared in the internal DTD subset. You're better off simply using an attribute selector that picks up the attribute by name, like this:

```
STANZA[NUMBER="st1"] {font-weight: bold}
```

Pseudo-elements

Pseudo-elements are treated as elements in style sheets but are not necessarily particular named elements in the document source code or the document tree. They are abstractions of certain parts of the rendered document after application of the style sheet (for example, the first line of a paragraph). Pseudo-elements address parts of the document that aren't normally identified as separate elements, but nonetheless often need separate styles. These include the following:

- The first line of an element
- The first letter of an element
- The position immediately before an element
- The position immediately after an element

Addressing the first letter

The most common reason to format the first letter of an element separately from the rest of the element is to insert a drop cap, as shown in Figure 12-2. This is accomplished by writing a rule that is addressed with the element name and followed by `:first-letter`, as in the following example:

```
CHAPTER:first-letter {
  font-size: 300%;
  float: left;
  vertical-align: text-top;
  margin-right: 12px
}
```

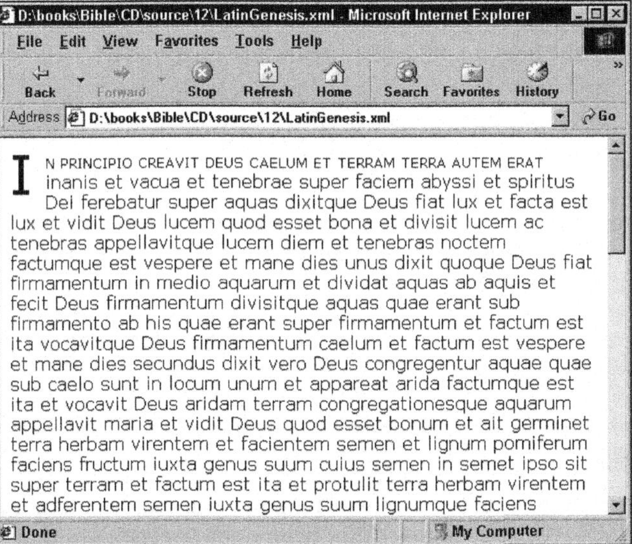

Figure 12-2: A drop cap on the first-letter pseudo-element with small caps used on the first-line pseudo-element

Addressing the first line

The first line of an element is also often formatted differently than subsequent lines. For example, it might be printed in small caps instead of normal body text, as shown in Figure 12-2. You can attach the `:first-line` selector to the name of an element to create a rule that only applies to the first line of the element, as in the following example:

```
CHAPTER:first-line { font-variant: small-caps }
```

Exactly what this pseudo-element selects is relative to the current layout. If the window is larger and there are more words in the first line, more words will be in small caps. If the window is made smaller or the font gets larger so that the text wraps differently and fewer words fit on the first line, the words that are wrapped to the next line are no longer in small caps. The determination of which characters compose the `first-line` pseudo-element is deferred until the document is actually displayed.

Before and after

The `:before` and `:after` pseudo-elements select the location immediately before and after the element that precedes them. The `content` property is used to put data into this location. For example, this rule places the string —— between `STANZA` objects to help separate the stanzas. The line breaks are encoded as `\A` in the string literal:

```
STANZA:after  {content: "\A----------\A"}
STANZA:before {content: "\A----------\A"}
```

`Content` is the only property a `:before` or `:after` selector is allowed to have. In addition to including raw text, this can insert the value of an attribute, various kinds of quotation marks, or a file found at a particular URL.

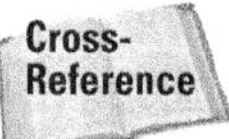

The `content` property is discussed in more depth in the section on generated content in Chapter 14.

Pseudo-classes

Pseudo-classes select elements that have something in common, but do not necessarily have the same type. Pseudo-classes differ from regular classes in that they select elements based on aspects other than the name, attributes, or content of the element. Pseudo-classes differ from pseudo-elements in that they always select an entire element, never just a part of it.

For example, a pseudo-class might be based on the position of the mouse, the object that has the focus, or whether an object is a link. The `:hover` pseudo-class refers to whichever element the cursor is currently over, regardless of the element's type. An element can even change its pseudo-class as the reader interacts with the document. Some pseudo-classes are mutually exclusive, but most can be applied simultaneously to the same element and can be placed anywhere within an element selector. CSS pseudo-classes include the following:

- `:first-child`
- `:hover`
- `:lang`
- `:right`
- `:left`
- `:first`

:first-child

The `:first-child` pseudo-class selects the first child of the named element, regardless of its type. For example, this rule makes the first verse of each stanza bold:

```
STANZA:first-child {font-weight: bold}
```

:hover

The `:hover` pseudo-class refers to elements that the mouse or other pointing device is pointing at, but without the mouse button depressed. For example, this rule emboldens the `STANZA` element the cursor is pointing at:

```
STANZA:hover { font-weight: bold }
```

The `STANZA` element returns to its normal weight when the cursor is no longer positioned over it.

:lang()

The `:lang()` pseudo-class selects elements with a specified language. In XML, the language is specified via the `xml:lang` attribute. The following rule changes the direction of all `VERSE` elements written in Hebrew to read right to left, rather than left to right:

```
VERSE:lang(he) { direction: "rtl" }
```

Inheritance

CSS does not require that you define a rule giving a value for every property to every element. Some properties have default values that are used when no rule is specified. Even more importantly, most elements can simply inherit the value of a property from their parent element. For example, if no rule explicitly specifies the font size of an element, the element has the same font size as its parent. If no rule specifies the color of an element, the element has the same color as its parent. The same is true of most CSS properties. In fact, the only properties that aren't inherited are the background and box properties. For example, consider these rules:

```
P       { font-weight: bold;
          font-size:   24pt;
          font-family: sans-serif}
BOOK    { font-style:  italic; font-family: serif}
```

Now consider this XML fragment:

```
<P>
  According to the American Library Association,
  Michael Willhoite's <BOOK>Daddy's Roommate</BOOK> was
  the #2 most frequently banned book in the U.S. in the 1990s.
</P>
```

Although the BOOK element has not been specifically assigned a font-weight or a font-size, it will be rendered in 24-point bold because it is a child of the P element. It will also be italicized because that is specified in its own rule. BOOK *inherits* the font-weight and font-size of its parent P. If later in the document a BOOK element appears in the context of some other element, it will inherit the font-weight and font-size of that element.

The font-family is a little trickier because both P and BOOK declare conflicting values for this property. Inside the BOOK element, the font-family declared by BOOK takes precedence. Outside the BOOK element, P's font-family is used. So, "Daddy's Roommate" is drawn in a serif font, while "most frequently banned book" is drawn in a sans serif font.

Often, you want the child elements to inherit formatting from their parents, so it's important not to overspecify the formatting of any element. For example, suppose I had declared that BOOK was written in a 12-point font, as follows:

```
BOOK {font-style: italic; font-family: serif; font-size: 12pt}
```

Then the example would be rendered as shown in Figure 12-3, with the BOOK title being much smaller than the body text it's embedded in.

You could fix this with a special rule that uses a contextual selector to pick out BOOK elements inside P elements, but it's easier to simply inherit the parent's font-size.

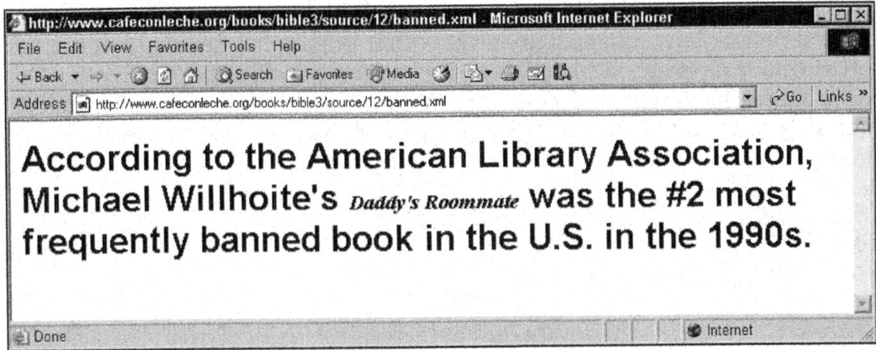

Figure 12-3: The BOOK written in a 12-point font size

One way to avoid problems like this, while retaining some control over the size of individual elements, is to use relative units such as ems and exs instead of absolute units such as points, picas, inches, and centimeters. An em is the width of the letter *m* in the current font. An ex is the height of the letter *x* in the current font. If the font gets bigger, so does everything measured in ems and exs.

A similar option that's available for some properties is to use percentage units. For example, the following rule sets the font size of the `FOOTNOTE_NUMBER` element to 80 percent of the font size of the parent element. If the parent element's font size increases or decreases, `FOOTNOTE_NUMBER`'s font size scales accordingly.

```
FOOTNOTE_NUMBER { font-size: 80% }
```

Exactly what the percentage is a percentage of varies from property to property. In the `vertical-align` property, the percentage is of the line height of the element itself. In a margin property, a percentage is a percentage of the element's width.

Cascades

There are several ways a CSS style sheet can be attached to an XML document:

- ✦ The XML document can include an `<?xml-stylesheet?>` processing instruction in its prolog. In fact, there can be more than one of these.
- ✦ The style sheet itself can import other style sheets.
- ✦ The user can specify a style sheet for the document using mechanisms inside the browser.
- ✦ The browser can provide a default style sheet.

Thus, a single document might have more than one style sheet. For example, a browser might have a default style sheet that is added to the one that the designer provides for the page. In such a case, it's entirely possible that there will be multiple rules that apply to one element, and that these rules may conflict. It's important to determine in which order the rules are applied. This process is called a *cascade*, from which cascading style sheets get their name.

When multiple style rules match a particular element, the most specific one is chosen. For example, these two rules say that verses have a plain font-style but that verses inside a refrain are italicized:

```
VERSE          {font-style: normal }
REFRAIN VERSE {font-style: italic }
```

A verse inside a refrain will be italic because a rule that applies only to verses inside refrains is more specific than one that applies to all verses. In case of a conflict between two equally specific rules, the last rule encountered in the style sheet takes precedence.

Try to avoid depending on cascading order. It's rarely a mistake to specify as little style as possible and to let the browser preferences take control.

If no rule matches a given element, that element inherits its properties from its parent. If there is no value to be inherited from the parent element, the default value is used. You can give most properties the value `inherit` to say explicitly that it inherits the value from its parent. However, because this is normally the default, this isn't done much in practice. Instead, the property is simply left unspecified.

Different Rules for Different Media

XML documents aren't just for web pages. They can be shown on TV screens, printed on paper, bound in books, read by speech synthesizers, beamed to Palm Pilots, and projected onto movie screens. Each media type has its own customary styles and formats. Italics don't make much sense on a dumb terminal. A font that's easily readable on paper at 300 dpi might be illegible when displayed on a low-resolution computer screen.

CSS allows you to vary styles to match the medium in which the content is displayed. For example, text is easier to read onscreen if it uses a sans serif font, while text on paper is generally easiest to read if it is written in a serif font. You can enclose style rules intended for only one medium in an `@media` rule naming that medium. There can be as many `@media` rules in a document as there are media types to specify. For example, Listing 12-6 formats a `POEM` differently depending on whether it's being printed on paper or displayed onscreen.

Listing 12-6: A CSS Style Sheet with Different Styles for Different Media

```
@media print {
  POEM  { font-size: 10pt; font-family: Times, serif }
  TITLE { font-size: larger; font-weight: bold;
          font-family: Helvetica, sans-serif }
}
@media screen {
  POEM { font-size: 12pt;
         font-family: Geneva, Arial, sans-serif }
}
@media screen, print {
  VERSE { line-height: 1.2 }
}
POEM, VERSE, TITLE, POET, STANZA, REFRAIN { display: block }
POET, STANZA, REFRAIN { margin-bottom: 2mm }
TITLE {font-size: larger; font-weight: bold }
```

The first `@media` block defines styles that will only be used if the document is printed on paper. The second `@media` block defines styles that will only be used when the document is displayed on the screen. The screen rules pick a larger font than the print rules do. Because computer displays have much lower resolutions than printers, it's important to make the font larger on the screen than on the printout and to choose a font that's designed for the screen. The third `@media` block provides styles that apply to both of these media types. To designate style instructions for multiple media types simultaneously, simply list them following the `@media` rule designator separated by a comma. The last three rules apply in all media: screen, print, or anything else.

The browser decides which rules make sense in its current context when it knows how it's going to display the document. CSS does not specify an all-inclusive list of media types, although it does provide a list of 10 possible values:

✦ `all`—All devices

✦ `aural` (continuous, aural)—Speech synthesizers

✦ `braille` (continuous, tactile)—Braille tactile feedback devices for the sight impaired

✦ `embossed` (paged, tactile)—Paged Braille printers

✦ `handheld` (visual)—PDAs and other handheld devices, such as Windows CE palmtops, Newtons, and Palm Pilots

✦ print (paged, visual)—All printed, opaque material

✦ projection (paged, visual)—Presentation and slide shows, whether projected directly from a computer or printed on transparencies

✦ screen (continuous, visual)—Bitmapped, color computer displays

✦ tty (continuous, visual)—Dumb terminals and old PC monitors that use a fixed-pitch, monochromatic character grid

✦ tv (aural/visual)—Television-type devices; that is, low-resolution, analog display, color

Some properties are only available with specific media types. For example, the pitch property only makes sense with the aural media type.

Browsing software does not have to support all these types. Indeed, I know of no single device that does support all of these. However, style sheet designers should probably assume that readers will use any or all of these types of devices to view their content.

Importing Style Sheets

The @import rule embeds a different style sheet into an existing style sheet. This allows you to build large style sheets from smaller, easier-to-understand pieces. An absolute or relative URL is used to identify the style sheets. For example, the following rule imports the file poetry.css:

```
@import url(poetry.css);
```

@import rules may specify a media type following the name of the style sheet, in which case the imported style sheet rules will only be used in the specified medium. For example, the following rule imports the file printmedia.css. However, the rules in this style sheet will only be applied to printouts and not to screen displays.

```
@import url(printmedia.css) print;
```

The next rule imports the file continuous.css that will be used for both computer monitors and/or television display:

```
@import url(continuous.css) tv, screen;
```

The @import directives must appear at the beginning of the style sheet, before any rules. Cycles (for example, poem.css imports stanza.css, which imports poem.css) are prohibited.

Style sheets that are imported into other style sheets have lower precedence than the importing style sheet. This means that if sonnet.css imported poem.css and they declared conflicting rules for an element, the rules in sonnet.css would override those in poem.css.

Character Sets

CSS style sheets can be written in a multitude of encodings — ISO 8859-1, SJIS, UTF-8, and so on — just like XML documents. There are three ways to specify the character set in which a style sheet is written, and they take precedence in the following order:

1. The HTTP "charset" parameter in a "Content-Type" field
2. An `@charset` rule in the style sheet itself
3. The `charset` pseudo-attribute of the `xml-stylesheet` processing instruction that links the style sheet to the XML document

Most of the time, the `@charset` rule is the easiest one to use because it lets the person who writes the style sheet choose whatever encoding is convenient for him or her. Each style sheet can contain no more than one of these. If present, it must appear at the very beginning of the document and cannot be preceded by any other characters. It's followed by the name of the character set in double quotes. For example, this rule says that the style sheet is written in the ISO 8859-1 character set, a.k.a. Latin-1:

```
@charset "ISO-8859-1"
```

The character set name specified in this statement must be a name as described in the IANA registry. The complete list can be found at `http://www.iana.org/assignments/character-sets`.

Summary

This chapter showed you how to apply CSS styles to XML elements and documents. In this chapter, you learned the following:

✦ CSS is a straightforward declarative language for applying styles to the contents of elements that works well with HTML and even better with XML.

✦ Browser implementations of CSS are imperfect. Extensive testing is necessary before publishing a document and its style sheet.

✦ One or more processing instructions in the form `<?xml-stylesheet type="text/css" href="url"?>` in the prolog indicates which style sheets a browser should apply to the document.

✦ Selectors are a list of the elements that a rule applies to.

✦ Many (though not all) CSS properties are inherited by the children of the elements they apply to.

✦ If multiple rules apply to a single element, the formatting properties cascade in a sensible way.

✦ You can include C-like `/* */` comments in a CSS style sheet.

✦ One style sheet can import another using an `@import` rule.

✦ An `@media` rule identifies in which media the given styles should be applied.

✦ An `@charset` rule identifies the character set in which the style sheet is encoded.

This chapter focused on how you choose the elements to apply styles to. The next two chapters focus on the styles themselves. You'll learn about all the different CSS properties that let you specify borders, colors, margins, fonts, sizes, positions, and more.

✦ ✦ ✦

CSS Layouts

When a browser renders an XML document, it places the document text on one or more pages. The text on each page is organized into nested boxes. Each paragraph is a box. Each line in the paragraph is a box. And these line boxes can contain still other boxes, which ultimately contain text. As well as paragraphs, there may be tables and lists and other items that are placed in boxes and that are subdivided into smaller boxes. Furthermore, the browser can create boxes to hold images, pull quotes, and other content that isn't part of the normal flow of the page. This chapter shows you how CSS arranges text on the page in boxes with different sizes, borders, margins, padding, and positions. You learn how to create boxes that are a certain size or that fall into a certain range of sizes. You also learn how to position the boxes at particular points on the page, as well as how to let the browser do the hard work for you.

In This Chapter

CSS units

The display property

Box properties

Size

Positioning

Formatting pages

Caution

Netscape 6.0 and 7.0, Mozilla, Opera 4.0 and later, Safari, and Internet Explorer 5.0 and later all implement only some parts of the CSS specification. Earlier versions of the major browsers, while perhaps supporting some form of CSS for HTML documents, do not support it at all for XML documents. To make matters worse, they all implement different subsets of the specification, and sometimes don't implement the same subsets for XML as they do for HTML. I'll note where one browser or another has a particular problem as we go along. However, if you find that something in this chapter doesn't work as advertised in your favorite browser, please complain to the browser vendor, not to me.

CSS Units

CSS properties have names and values. Table 13-1 lists a few of these property names and sample values.

Table 13-1
Sample Property Names and Values

Name	*Value*
display	none
font-style	italic
margin-top	0.5in
font-size	12pt
border-style	solid
color	#CC0033
background-color	white
background-image	url(http://www.idgbooks.com/images/paper.gif)
list-style-image	url(/images/redbullet.png)
line-height	120%

The names are all CSS keywords. However, the values are much more diverse. Some of them are keywords, such as the `none` in `display: none` or the `solid` in `border-style: solid`. Other values are numbers with units, such as the `0.5in` in `margin-top: 0.5in` or the `12pt` in `font-size: 12pt`. Still other values are URLs, such as `url(http://www.idgbooks.com/images/paper.gif)` in `background-image: url(http://www.idgbooks.com/images/paper.gif)`; and still others are RGB colors, such as the `#CC0033` in `color: #CC0033`. Different properties permit different values. However, only five different kinds of values account for almost all properties. These five types are:

- ✦ Length
- ✦ URL
- ✦ Color
- ✦ Keyword
- ✦ String

Keywords vary from property to property, but the other kinds of values are the same from property to property. That is, a length is a length regardless of which property it's the value of. If you know how to specify the length of a border, you also know how to specify the length of a margin, a padding, an image, and a font. This reuse of syntax makes working with different properties much easier.

Length values

In CSS, length is a scalar measure used for width, height, font size, word and letter spacing, text indentation, line height, margins, padding, border widths, and many other properties. Lengths are given as a number followed by the abbreviation for one of these units:

Inches	`in`
Centimeters	`cm`
Millimeters	`mm`
Points	`pt`
Picas	`pc`
Pixels	`px`
Ems	`em`
Exs	`ex`

For example, this rule says that the font used for the `TITLE` element should be exactly 1 centimeter high:

```
TITLE {font-size: 1cm}
```

Although font sizes are normally specified in points rather than centimeters, the browser will perform any necessary conversion between units.

The number may have a decimal point (for example, `margin-top: 0.3in`). Some properties allow negative values, such as `-0.5in`, but not all do; and even those that do often place limits on how negative a length can be. It's best to avoid negative lengths for maximum cross-browser compatibility.

The units of length are divided into three classes:

✦ Absolute units — Inches, centimeters, millimeters, points, and picas

✦ Relative units — Pixels, ems, and exs

✦ Percentages

Absolute units of length

Absolute units of length are something of a misnomer because there's really no such thing as an absolute unit of length on a computer screen. Changing a monitor's resolution from 640×480 to 1600×1200 changes the length of everything on the screen, inches and centimeters included. Nonetheless, CSS supports five "absolute" units of length that at least don't change from one font to the next. These are listed in Table 13-2, along with the conversion factors between them.

Table 13-2
Absolute Units of Length

	Inch (in)	*Centimeters (cm)*	*Millimeters (mm)*	*Points (pt)*	*Picas (pc)*
Inch	1.0	2.54	25.4	72	6
Centimeters	0.3937	1.0	10	28.3464	4.7244
Millimeters	0.03937	0.1	1.0	2.83464	0.47244
Points	0.01389	0.0352806	0.352806	1.0	0.83333
Picas	0.16667	0.4233	4.233	12	1.0

Relative units of length

CSS also supports three relative units for lengths:

- ✦ `em`—The width of the letter *m* in the current font
- ✦ `ex`—The height of the letter *x* in the current font
- ✦ `px`—The size of a pixel (This assumes square pixels. All common modern displays use square pixels, although some older PC monitors, mostly now leaking lead into landfills, did not.)

For example, this rule sets the left and right borders of the `PULLQUOTE` element to twice the width of the letter *m* in the current font and the top and bottom borders to one and a half times the height of the letter *x* in the current font:

```
PULLQUOTE { border-right-width:  2em;
            border-left-width:   2em;
            border-top-width:    1.5ex;
            border-bottom-width: 1.5ex }
```

The normal purpose of ems and exs is to set a width that's appropriate for a given font, without necessarily knowing how big the font is. For example, in the preceding rule, the font size is not known, so the exact width of the borders is not known either. It can be determined at display time by comparison with the *m* and the *x* in the current font. Larger font sizes will have correspondingly larger ems and exs.

Lengths in pixels are relative to the height and width of a (presumably square) pixel on the monitor. Widths and heights of images are often given in pixels.

Pixel measurements are generally not a good idea. First, the size of a pixel varies widely with resolution. Most power users set their monitors at much too high a resolution, which makes the pixels far too small for legibility.

Second, within the next five years, 200-dpi and even 300-dpi monitors will become common, finally breaking away from the rough 72-pixels-per-inch (give or take 28 pixels) de facto standard that's prevailed since the first Macintosh in 1984. Documents that specify measurements in non-screen-based units, such as ems, exs, points, picas, and inches, will be able to make the transition. However, documents that use pixel-level specifications will become illegibly small when viewed on high-resolution monitors.

Percentage units of length

Finally, lengths can be specified as a percentage of something. Generally, this is a percentage of the current value of a property. For example, if the font-size of a `STANZA` element is 12 points, and the font size of the `VERSE` the `STANZA` contains is set to 150 percent, the font size of the `VERSE` will be 18 points. Such a rule would look like this:

```
VERSE {font-size: 150%}
```

The exact size in this case does depend on the size of the font in the parent element. If the parent element font-size is bigger, the font-size of the child element will be bigger. If the parent element font-size is smaller, the font-size of the child element will be smaller.

URL values

Several CSS properties can have URL values, including `background-image`, `content`, and `list-style-image`. Furthermore, as you saw in the last chapter, the `@import` rule uses URL values. Literal URLs are placed inside `url()`. All forms of relative and absolute URLs are allowed. For example:

```
DOC    {background-image: url(http://www.mysite.com/bg.gif) }
LETTER {background-image: url(/images/paper.gif) }
GAME   {background-image: url(currentposition.gif)}
INSTRC {background-image: url(../images/screenshot.gif)}
```

You can enclose the URL in single or double quotes, although nothing is gained by doing so. For example:

```
DOC    {background-image: url("http://www.mysite.com/bg.gif")}
LETTER {background-image: url('/images/paper.gif') }
GAME   {background-image: url("currentposition.gif") }
INSTRC {background-image: url('../images/screenshot.gif') }
```

Any parentheses that appear inside the URL should be escaped as `\(` and `\)` or `%2B` and `%2C`. Otherwise, standard URL escaping rules apply.

Color values

One of the most widely adopted uses of CSS is applying foreground and background colors to elements on the page. Properties that take on color values include `color`, `background-color`, and `border-color`.

CSS provides four ways to specify color: by name, by hexadecimal components, by integer components, and by percentages. Defining color by name is the simplest approach. CSS understands these 16 color names adopted from the Windows VGA palette:

aqua	navy
black	olive
blue	purple
fuchsia	red
gray	silver
green	teal
lime	white
maroon	yellow

Of course, the typical color monitor can display several million more colors. You can create other colors by specifying values for the RGB components of the colors. CSS uses a 24-bit color model. Each primary color is stored in 8 bits. An 8-bit unsigned integer is a number between 0 and 255. This number can be given in either decimal or hexadecimal. Alternately, each component can be given as a percentage between 0 percent (0) and 100 percent (255). Table 13-3 lists some of the possible colors and their decimal, hexadecimal, and percentage RGB values.

Table 13-3
Sample CSS Colors

Color	*Decimal RGB*	*Hexadecimal RGB*	*Percentage RGB*
Pure red	rgb(255,0,0)	#FF0000	rgb(100%, 0%, 0%)
Pure green	rgb(0,255,0)	#00FF00	rgb(0%, 100%, 0%)
Pure blue	rgb(0,0,255)	#0000FF	rgb(0%, 0%, 100%)
White	rgb(255,255,255)	#FFFFFF	rgb(100%, 100%, 100%)
Black	rgb(0,0,0)	#000000	rgb(0%, 0%, 0%)
Light violet	rgb(255,204,255)	#FFCCFF	rgb(100%, 80%, 100%)
Medium gray	rgb(153,153,153)	#999999	rgb(60%, 60%, 60%)

Color	Decimal RGB	Hexadecimal RGB	Percentage RGB
Brown	rgb(153,102,51)	#996633	rgb(60%, 40%, 20%)
Pink	rgb(255,204,204)	#FFCCCC	rgb(100%, 80%, 80%)
Orange	rgb(255,204,204)	#FFCC00	rgb(100%, 80%, 80%)

Tip

Many people still use 256-color displays. Some people even browse the Web in monochrome, especially on handheld devices such as Palm Pilots. Even on more capable systems, some colors are distinctly different on Macs and PCs. The most reliable colors are the 16 named colors.

The next most reliable colors are those formed using only the hexadecimal components 00, 33, 66, 99, CC, and FF (0, 51, 102, 153, 204, 255 in decimal; 0%, 20%, 40%, 60%, 80%, 100% in percentage units). For example, 33FFCC is a "browser-safe" color because the red component is made from two 3s, the green from two Fs, and the blue from two Cs.

If you specify a hexadecimal RGB color using only three digits, CSS duplicates them; for example, #FC0 is really #FFCC00 and #963 is really #996633.

System colors

CSS also allows you to specify colors by copying them from the local graphical user interface (GUI). These system colors can be used with all color-related properties. Style rules based on system colors take into account user preferences, and therefore offer some advantages, including the following:

- ✦ Pages that fit the user's preferred look and feel
- ✦ Greater accessibility for users whose default settings compensate for a disability

Table 13-4 lists system color keywords and their descriptions. Any of the color properties can take on these values.

Table 13-4
Additional System Colors Used with All Color-Related Properties

System Color Keywords	Description
`ActiveBorder`	The color of the border of the currently active window.
`ActiveCaption`	The color of the caption of the currently active window.
`AppWorkspace`	The background color of the multiple-document interface parent window.

Continued

Table 13-4 *(continued)*

System Color Keywords	***Description***
`Background`	Desktop background color.
`ButtonFace`	The foreground color for three-dimensional GUI widgets.
`ButtonHighlight`	The shadow color for three-dimensional widgets (for edges facing away from the light source).
`ButtonShadow`	The shadow color for three-dimensional widgets.
`ButtonText`	Color of the text on push buttons.
`CaptionText`	Color of the text in captions, size boxes, and scroll bar arrow boxes.
`GrayText`	The color of disabled text. This color is set to #000 if the current display driver does not support a solid gray color.
`Highlight`	The color of items selected in a control.
`HighlightText`	The color with which selected text is highlighted.
`InactiveBorder`	The color of an inactive window border.
`InactiveCaption`	The color of an inactive window caption.
`InactiveCaptionText`	The color of the text of a caption of an inactive window.
`InfoBackground`	The background color for ToolTip controls.
`InfoText`	The text color used in ToolTip controls.
`Menu`	The background color of a menu.
`MenuText`	The color of text in menu items.
`Scrollbar`	The color of the scroll bar area.
`ThreeDDarkShadow`	Dark shadow for three-dimensional widgets.
`ThreeDFace`	The face color for three-dimensional widgets.
`ThreeDHighlight`	The highlight color for three-dimensional widgets.
`ThreeDLightShadow`	The light color for three-dimensional widgets (for edges facing the light source).
`ThreeDShadow`	The color of the dark shadow for three-dimensional widgets.
`Window`	The color in the window background.
`WindowFrame`	The color of the window frame.
`WindowText`	The color of the text in the window.

For example, this rule sets the foreground and background colors of a VERSE to the same colors used for the foreground and background of the browser's window:

```
VERSE { color: WindowText; background-color: Window}
```

Keyword values

Keywords are not necessarily the same from property to property, but similar properties generally support similar keywords. For example, the value of border-left-style can be any one of the keywords none, dotted, dashed, solid, double, groove, ridge, inset, or outset. The border-right-style, border-top-style, border-bottom-style, and border-style properties can also assume one of this set of values. The individual keywords are discussed in the sections about the individual properties.

Strings

A few CSS properties, such as font-family and content, have string values. In CSS, a string is a sequence of Unicode characters enclosed in either single or double quotes. If the string contains double quotes, single quotes must be used to enclose the string and vice versa.

You can also use a backslash to escape otherwise illegal characters, typically single or double quotes. For example, you can use \" to include a double quote mark inside a string that's surrounded by double quotes. Strings cannot contain line breaks. However, you can use \A to insert one. You can also include a raw line break if you prefix it by a backslash first. This is sometimes useful in the content property.

You can also use a backslash followed by the hexadecimal value of a Unicode character to insert a character that isn't easy to type. For example, to insert the Greek letter Θ, Unicode value 398 (in hexadecimal), you could simply use \398.

The Display Property

From the perspective of CSS, all elements are block elements, inline elements, table parts, or invisible. The display property specifies which one of these an element is. This property has 19 possible values given by keywords, as shown in Table 13-5.

Table 13-5
Values for the Display Property

Block Level	*Inline Elements*	*Table Parts*	*Invisible*
block	inline	table-column	none
table	inline-table	table-cell	
list-item	marker	table-footer-group	
run-in	run-in	table-column-group	
compact	compact	table-row	
		table-header-group	
		table-row-group	
		table-caption	

Block elements are usually separated from other elements by line breaks before and after each one. Table elements are parts of a grid. Inline elements are placed one after the other in a row. These are like words in a sentence. They move freely as text is added and deleted around them. Block elements are more fixed and, at most, move up and down but not left and right as content is added before and after them. Block elements include tables, lists, and list items. Most display types are just modifications of the main block or inline types.

A browser uses the distinction between these elements to make its first pass at laying out the document. It will place the text of any inline elements on the page moving from left to right, until it fills the line. If necessary, it will continue on the next line down. (The `direction` property lets you reverse the order so that elements are placed from right to left, useful if you're formatting Hebrew or Arabic.) However, when the browser comes to a block-level element, either the start or the end of one, it breaks the line and continues on the next line.

Consider Listing 13-1, which is a synopsis of William Shakespeare's *Twelfth Night*. The root element, `SYNOPSIS`, contains six top-level elements, one `TITLE` and five `ACT` elements. Each `ACT` contains an `ACT_NUMBER` and one or more `SCENE` children. Each `SCENE` contains a `SCENE_NUMBER` and a `LOCATION`. `LOCATION` elements contain mixed content, possibly including one or more `CHARACTER` elements.

Listing 13-1: A Synopsis of Shakespeare's *Twelfth Night* in XML

```
<?xml version="1.0"?>
<?xml-stylesheet type="text/css" href="synopsis.css"?>
<SYNOPSIS>
  <TITLE>Twelfth Night</TITLE>
```

```
<ACT>
  <ACT_NUMBER>Act 1</ACT_NUMBER>
  <SCENE>
    <SCENE_NUMBER>Scene 1</SCENE_NUMBER>
    <LOCATION><CHARACTER>Duke Orsino</CHARACTER>'s palace
    </LOCATION>
  </SCENE>
  <SCENE>
    <SCENE_NUMBER>Scene 2</SCENE_NUMBER>
    <LOCATION>The sea-coast</LOCATION>
  </SCENE>
  <SCENE>
    <SCENE_NUMBER>Scene 3</SCENE_NUMBER>
    <LOCATION><CHARACTER>Olivia</CHARACTER>'s house
    </LOCATION>
  </SCENE>
  <SCENE>
    <SCENE_NUMBER>Scene 4</SCENE_NUMBER>
    <LOCATION><CHARACTER>Duke Orsino</CHARACTER>'s palace.
    </LOCATION>
  </SCENE>
  <SCENE>
    <SCENE_NUMBER>Scene 5</SCENE_NUMBER>
    <LOCATION><CHARACTER>Olivia</CHARACTER>'s house
    </LOCATION>
  </SCENE>
</ACT>

<ACT>
  <ACT_NUMBER>Act 2</ACT_NUMBER>
  <SCENE>
    <SCENE_NUMBER>Scene 1</SCENE_NUMBER>
    <LOCATION>The sea-coast</LOCATION>
  </SCENE>
  <SCENE>
    <SCENE_NUMBER>Scene 2</SCENE_NUMBER>
    <LOCATION>A street</LOCATION>
  </SCENE>
  <SCENE>
    <SCENE_NUMBER>Scene 3</SCENE_NUMBER>
    <LOCATION><CHARACTER>Olivia</CHARACTER>'s house
    </LOCATION>
  </SCENE>
  <SCENE>
    <SCENE_NUMBER>Scene 4</SCENE_NUMBER>
    <LOCATION><CHARACTER>Duke Orsino</CHARACTER>'s palace.
    </LOCATION>
  </SCENE>
  <SCENE>
    <SCENE_NUMBER>Scene 5</SCENE_NUMBER>
    <LOCATION><CHARACTER>Olivia</CHARACTER>'s garden
    </LOCATION>
```

Continued

Listing 13-1 *(continued)*

```
    </SCENE>
  </ACT>

  <ACT>
    <ACT_NUMBER>Act 3</ACT_NUMBER>
    <SCENE>
      <SCENE_NUMBER>Scene 1</SCENE_NUMBER>
      <LOCATION><CHARACTER>Olivia</CHARACTER>'s garden
      </LOCATION>
    </SCENE>
    <SCENE>
      <SCENE_NUMBER>Scene 2</SCENE_NUMBER>
      <LOCATION><CHARACTER>Olivia</CHARACTER>'s house
      </LOCATION>
    </SCENE>
    <SCENE>
      <SCENE_NUMBER>Scene 3</SCENE_NUMBER>
      <LOCATION>A street</LOCATION>
    </SCENE>
    <SCENE>
      <SCENE_NUMBER>Scene 4</SCENE_NUMBER>
      <LOCATION><CHARACTER>Olivia</CHARACTER>'s garden
      </LOCATION>
    </SCENE>
  </ACT>

  <ACT>
    <ACT_NUMBER>Act 4</ACT_NUMBER>
    <SCENE>
      <SCENE_NUMBER>Scene 1</SCENE_NUMBER>
      <LOCATION><CHARACTER>Olivia</CHARACTER>'s front yard
      </LOCATION>
    </SCENE>
    <SCENE>
      <SCENE_NUMBER>Scene 2</SCENE_NUMBER>
      <LOCATION><CHARACTER>Olivia</CHARACTER>'s house
      </LOCATION>
    </SCENE>
    <SCENE>
      <SCENE_NUMBER>Scene 3</SCENE_NUMBER>
      <LOCATION><CHARACTER>Olivia</CHARACTER>'s garden
      </LOCATION>
    </SCENE>
  </ACT>
```

```
  <ACT>
    <ACT_NUMBER>Act 5</ACT_NUMBER>
    <SCENE>
      <SCENE_NUMBER>Scene 1</SCENE_NUMBER>
      <LOCATION><CHARACTER>Olivia</CHARACTER>'s front yard
      </LOCATION>
    </SCENE>
  </ACT>

</SYNOPSIS>
```

You can do a fair job of formatting this document using only display properties. SYNOPSIS, TITLE, ACT, and SCENE are all block-level elements. ACT_NUMBER, SCENE_NUMBER, LOCATION, and CHARACTER can remain inline elements. Listing 13-2 is a very simple style sheet that accomplishes this.

Listing 13-2: A Very Simple Style Sheet for the Synopsis of a Play

```
SYNOPSIS, TITLE, ACT, SCENE { display: block }
```

Figure 13-1 shows the synopsis of *Twelfth Night* loaded into Mozilla with the style sheet of Listing 13-2. Notice that in Listing 13-2 it is not necessary to explicitly specify that ACT_NUMBER, SCENE_NUMBER, LOCATION, and CHARACTER are all inline elements. This is the default unless otherwise specified. Children do not inherit the display property. Thus, just because SCENE is a block-level element does not mean that its children, SCENE_NUMBER and LOCATION, are also block-level elements.

Inline elements

Inline elements are laid out horizontally in a row, starting from the top of the containing box of the surrounding page or block element and moving from left to right. When a row fills up, a new row is started on the next line down. Words can be wrapped, but only as necessary to fit the text on the screen. There are no hard line breaks. In HTML, EM, STRONG, B, I, and A are all inline elements. As another example, you can think of EM, STRONG, B, I, and A in this paragraph as inline code elements. They aren't separated out from the rest of the text. If no value is specified for the display property, the default is to make the element an inline element.

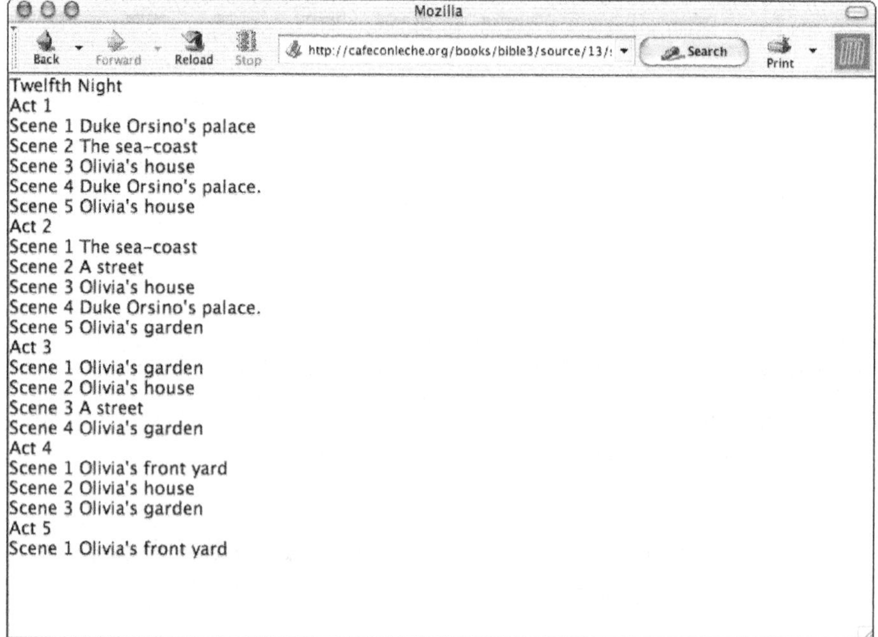

Figure 13-1: The synopsis of *Twelfth Night* as displayed in Mozilla

Block elements

Block-level elements are laid out vertically, one on top of the other. The first block is laid out in the top left corner of the containing block; then the second block is placed below it, also flush against the left edge of the containing block. Each block-level element is separated from its sibling and parent elements, generally by placing a line break before and after it. The vertical distance between each block is defined by the individual block's margin and padding properties. In HTML, `P`, `BLOCKQUOTE`, `H1` through `H6`, and `HR` are all examples of block-level elements. The paragraphs and headings you see on this page are all block-level elements. Block-level elements may contain inline elements and other block-level elements, but inline elements should only contain other inline elements, not block-level elements, although this rule is not strictly enforced.

None

Setting `display` to `none` hides the element. An element whose `display` property is set to `none` is invisible and not rendered on the screen. It does not affect the position of other visible elements on the page. In HTML, `TITLE`, `META`, and `HEAD` would have a `display` property of `none`. In XML, `display: none` is often useful for meta-information in elements.

For example, suppose you wanted to list the locations in the synopsis but drop everything else. You could use the style sheet in Listing 13-3. This hides the `TITLE`, `ACT_NUMBER`, and `SCENE_NUMBER` elements by setting their `display` property to `none`. The `LOCATION` element is displayed as a block. Figure 13-2 shows the result of applying this style sheet to Listing 13-1.

Listing 13-3: A Style Sheet for the Synopsis of a Play That Only Shows the Locations

```
TITLE, ACT_NUMBER, SCENE_NUMBER { display: none }
LOCATION { display: block}
```

Once you've hidden an element by using `display: none`, you cannot then show any of its descendants. For example, consider these rules:

```
SYNOPSIS { display: none }
LOCATION { display: block}
```

Because the `LOCATION` element is contained inside the `SYNOPSIS` element, it is hidden even though its own `display` property is set to `block`.

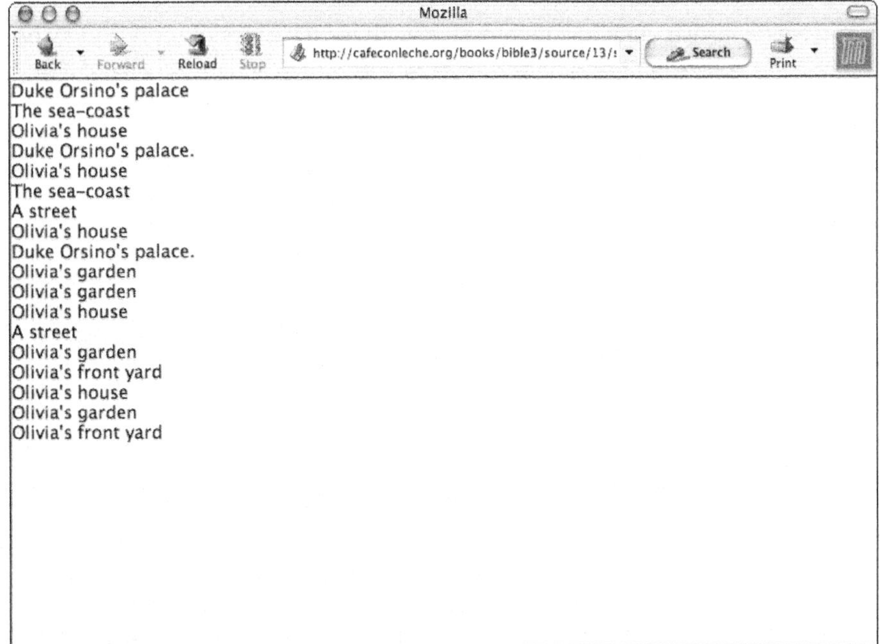

Figure 13-2: The synopsis of *Twelfth Night* showing only locations

Compact and run-in elements

The `compact` and `run-in` values of the `display` property identify an element as either a block or an inline box depending on context. Other properties declared as these types will treat them as either a block or inline element depending on what they eventually become.

A run-in box is a block-level element if the element that follows it is an inline element. It is an inline element if the element that follows it is a block-level element. In other words, it guarantees that there will be a line break before it but not after it. This is sometimes useful for headings.

A compact box will normally be a block-level element. However, if it's followed by a block-level element and it can fit in the margin of that element's box, the browser will put it in the margin rather than making it a separate element.

Marker

Setting the `display` property to `marker` identifies a block that's formed by content generated in the style sheet rather than copied in from the XML document. This value is only used with the `:before` and `:after` pseudo-elements that have been attached to block-level elements.

Tables

CSS lets you format elements in tables using these 10 values of the `display` property:

- `table`
- `inline-table`
- `table-row-group`
- `table-header-group`
- `table-footer-group`
- `table-row`
- `table-column-group`
- `table-column`
- `table-cell`
- `table-caption`

For example, setting the `display` property to `table` indicates that the selected element is a block-level container for various smaller children that will be arranged in a grid. The `inline-table` value forces the table to act as an inline element, allowing text to float along its sides, and allows multiple tables to be placed side by side.

The other eight values in this list identify particular parts of a table, and should only be used when the elements they're applied to are descendants of an element formatted as a table or inline table. The `table-caption` value formats an element as a table caption. The `table-row-group`, `table-header-group`, and `table-footer-group` values create groups of data cells that are formatted as a single row. The `table-column-group` creates a group of data cells that are formatted as a single column that was defined using the `table-column` value. XML elements that appear in table cells have — naturally enough — a `display` property with the value `table-cell`.

For example, if you were to build a table of the scenes and locations in the synopsis, each scene could be a row. Scene numbers and locations could be cells. Each act could be a row group. The title would be a header. Listing 13-4 demonstrates.

Listing 13-4: A Style Sheet That Formats Synopses as Tables

```
SYNOPSIS {display: table}
TITLE {display: table-header}
SCENE { display: table-row}
ACT { display: table-row-group }
LOCATION, SCENE_NUMBER { display: table-cell }
```

Figure 13-3 shows the result of applying this style sheet to the *Twelfth Night* synopsis. By default, there are no grid lines or borders. These could be inserted using the border properties that you'll encounter shortly. It also wouldn't hurt to add a little padding around each cell.

Caution: Internet Explorer 6.0 and earlier does not support table formatting using CSS.

List items

List-item elements are block-level elements with a list-item marker preceding them. In HTML, `LI` is a list-item element. If you simply set the `display` property to `list-item` and don't do anything else, the element is formatted as a block-level element that may or may not have a bullet, called a *marker*, in front of it. However, you can set three additional properties that affect how list items are displayed, as follows:

- `list-style-type`
- `list-style-image`
- `list-style-position`

Figure 13-3: A table-based synopsis layout in Mozilla

There's also a shorthand `list-style` property that lets you set all three in a single rule.

Internet Explorer 6.0 and earlier on Windows does not support `display: list-item`. Internet Explorer 5.1 and 5.2 for Macintosh do support `display: list-item`.

One thing CSS lists do not imply, however, is indentation. If you're accustomed to using lists to indent items from HTML, you need to break yourself of that habit. In CSS, indentation is provided by the margin and padding properties, as well as the `text-indent` property. List items are not automatically indented unless you set the other properties necessary to indent something. However, the list item marker may be indented to the left of the normal text. That is, it may have a negative indent, and this may place the marker off the screen. It's important to set a reasonable positive left margin on the list's parent element.

The list-style-type property

The `list-style-type` property determines the nature of the bullet character in front of each list item. Possibilities include the following:

- `disc`: •
- `circle`: ○

- square: □
- decimal: 1, 2, 3, 4, 5, and so on
- decimal-leading-zero: 01, 02, 03, 04, 05, and so on
- lower-roman: i, ii, iii, iv, and so on
- upper-roman: I, II, III, IV, and so on
- lower-alpha: a, b, c, and so on
- upper-alpha: A, B, C, and so on
- lower-latin: Same as lower-alpha; a, b, c, and so on
- upper-latin: Same as upper-alpha; A, B, C, and so on
- lower-greek: α, β, γ, δ, ε, and so on
- hebrew: ב, ג, ד, ה, and so on
- armenian: Ա2 Բ2 Գ2 Դ2 Ե2 and so on
- georgian: ფ, ა, ე, and so on
- cjk-ideographic: 一, 二, 三, and so on
- hiragana: あ, い, う, え, お, か, and so on
- katakana: ア, イ, ウ, エ, オ, カ, キ, and so on
- hiragana-iroha: い, ろ, は, に, ほ, へ, と, and so on
- katakana-iroha: イ, ロ, ハ, ニ, ホ, ヘ, ト, and so on
- none: No bullet character is used

I would not rely on a typical Western browser being capable of handling the more unusual of these. In that case, it will default to decimal. (European-style numerals have pretty much replaced Hebrew, Han, Roman, and other traditional number systems in most of the world for day-to-day use.) If no value is set, the default is disc. For example, the style sheet in Listing 13-5 defines ACT and SCENE as list items. However, ACT is given no bullet, and SCENE is given a square bullet. Figure 13-4 shows the synopsis in Opera with this style sheet.

Listing 13-5: A Style Sheet for a Play Synopsis That Uses List Items

```
SYNOPSIS { display: block; margin-left: 0.5in }
TITLE { display: block }
ACT { display: list-item; list-style-type: none }
SCENE { display: list-item; list-style-type: square }
```

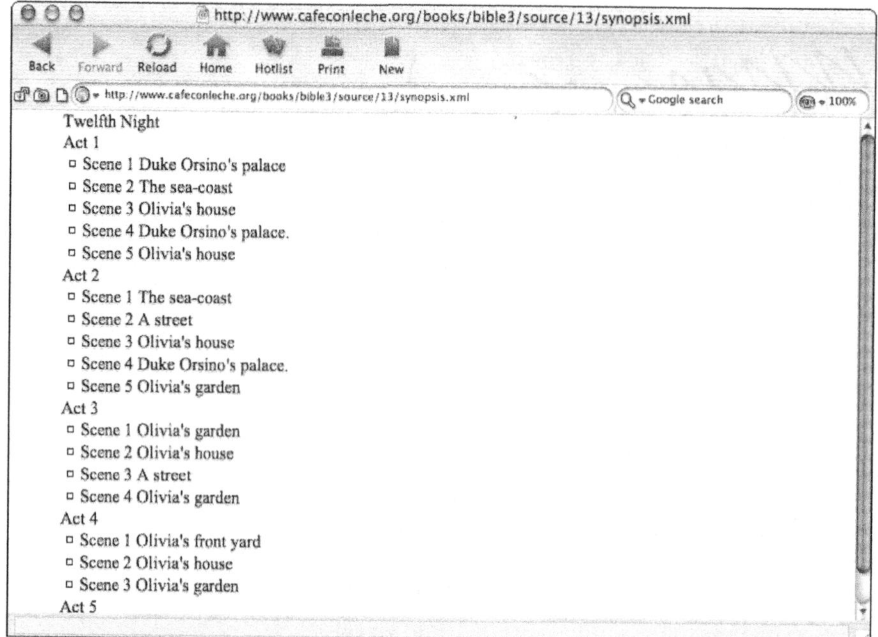

Figure 13-4: A list-based synopsis layout

The list-style-image property

Alternately, you can use a bitmapped image as the bullet. To do this, you set the `list-style-image` property to the URL of the image file. If both `list-style-image` and `list-style-type` are set, the `list-style-image` will be used, unless it can't be found, in which case the bullet specified by `list-style-type` will be used. For example, this rule uses a heart (♥) stored in the file heart.jpg as the bullet before each scene. (After all, *Twelfth Night* is a romantic comedy.) Figure 13-5 shows the result of adding this rule to the synopsis style sheet.

```
SCENE { display: list-item;
        list-style-image: url(heart.jpg);
        list-style-type: square
}
```

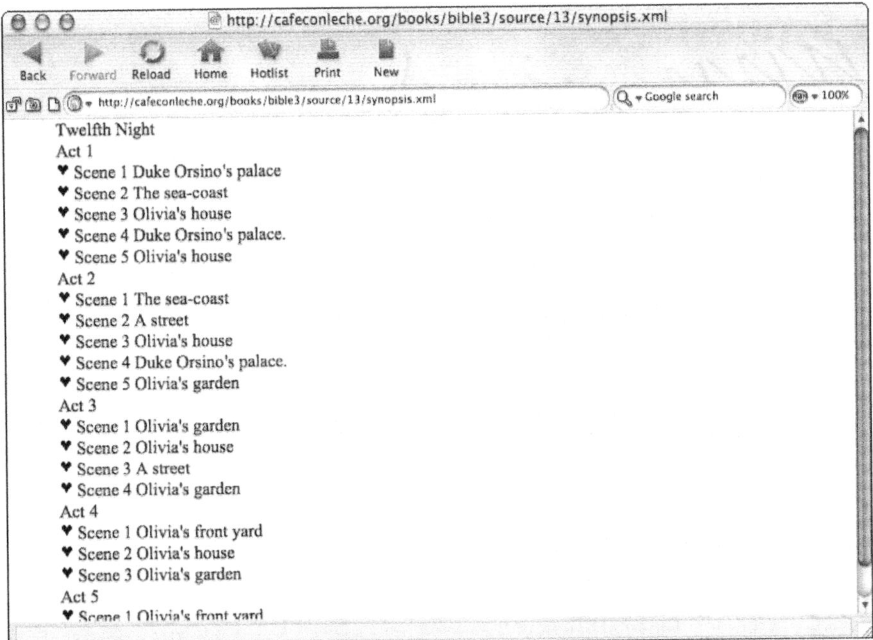

Figure 13-5: A list-based synopsis layout with an image bullet

The list-style-position property

The `list-style-position` property specifies whether the bullet is drawn inside or outside the text of the list item. The legal values are `inside` and `outside`. The default is `outside`. The difference is only obvious when the text wraps onto more than one line. This is inside:

*   If music be the food of love, play on/Give me excess of it, that, surfeiting,/The appetite may sicken, and so die./That strain again! it had a dying fall:

This is outside:

*   If music be the food of love, play on/Give me excess of it, that, surfeiting,/The appetite may sicken, and so die./That strain again! it had a dying fall:

The list-style shorthand property

Finally, the `list-style` property is a shorthand that allows you to set all three of `list-style-image`, `list-style-type`, and `list-style-position` properties simultaneously. For example, this rule says that a `SCENE` is displayed inside with a heart image and no bullet:

```
SCENE { display: list-item;
        list-style: none inside url(heart.jpg) }
```

Box Properties

CSS arranges text on a two-dimensional canvas. The elements drawn on this canvas are laid out in imaginary rectangles called *boxes*. Each box is given a size and a position, as well as margins, borders, and padding. The box edges are always oriented parallel to the edges of the canvas. Box properties control the width, height, margins, padding, and borders of the individual boxes. Figure 13-6 shows how these properties relate to each other.

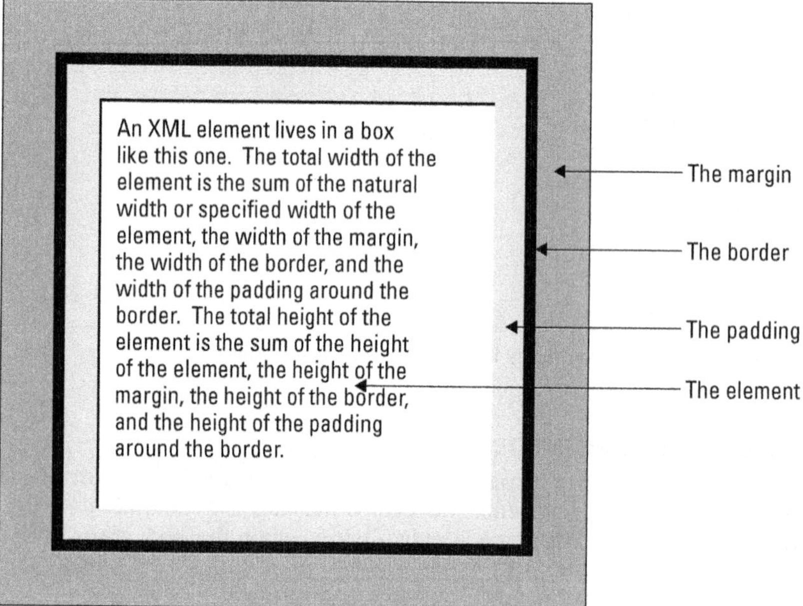

Figure 13-6: A CSS box with margin, border, and padding

These boxes stack together and wrap around each other so that the contents of each element are aligned in an orderly fashion, based upon the rules of the style sheets.

Margin properties

Margin properties control the amount of space added to the box outside its border. This can be set separately for the top, bottom, right and left margins using the `margin-top`, `margin-bottom`, `margin-right`, and `margin-left` properties. Each margin can be specified as an absolute length or as a percentage of the size of the parent element's width. For example, you can add a little extra space between each `ACT` element and the preceding element by setting `ACT`'s `margin-top` property to 3ex, as Listing 13-6 and Figure 13-7 demonstrate.

Listing 13-6: **Extra Space on the Top Margin of Each Act**

```
ACT { margin-top: 3ex }
SYNOPSIS, TITLE, ACT, SCENE { display: block }
```

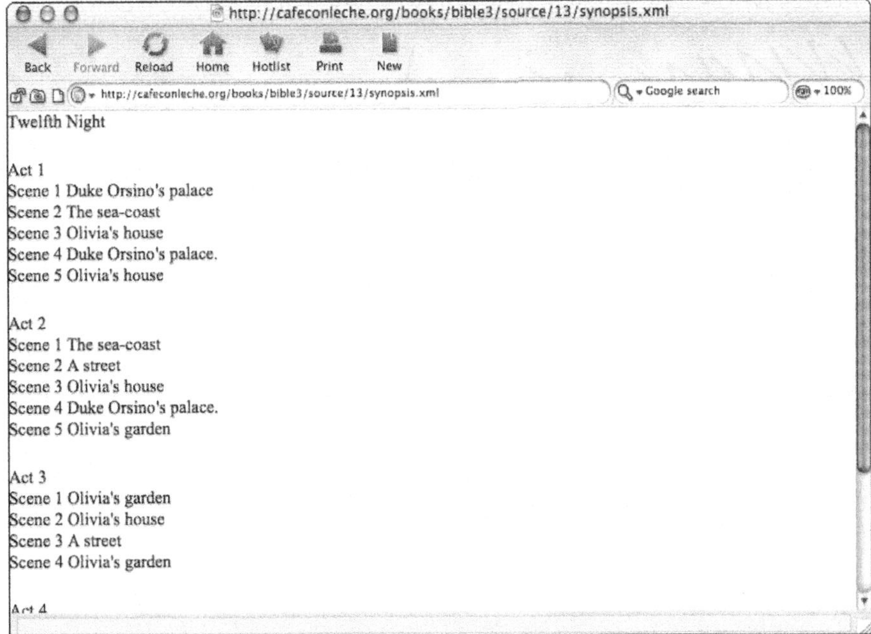

Figure 13-7: The top margin of the ACT element is larger.

You can also set all four margins simultaneously using the shorthand `margin` property. For example, you can add extra white space around the entire *Twelfth Night* document by setting the margin property for the root-level element (`SYNOPSIS` in this example), as shown by the first rule of Listing 13-7 and in Figure 13-8.

Listing 13-7: **Adding a 1-Centimeter Margin on Each Side of the SYNOPSIS**

```
SYNOPSIS { margin: 1.0cm 1.0cm 1.0cm 1.0cm }
SYNOPSIS, TITLE, ACT, SCENE { display: block }
ACT { margin-top: 3ex }
```

Figure 13-8: One centimeter of white space around the entire synopsis

In fact, this is the same as using a single value for margin, which CSS interprets as being applicable to all four sides.

```
SYNOPSIS { margin: 1.0cm }
```

Given two `margin` values, the first applies to top and bottom, the second to right and left. Given three `margin` values, the first applies to the top, the second to the right and left, and the third to the bottom. It's probably easier to just use the separate `margin-top`, `margin-bottom`, `margin-right`, and `margin-left` properties if you want to specify different margins for different sides.

Border properties

Most boxes don't have borders. They are invisible rectangles that affect the layout of their contents, but are not seen as boxes by the readers. However, you can make a box visible by drawing lines around it using the border properties. Border properties let you specify the style, width, and color of the border.

Border style

By default, no border is drawn around boxes regardless of the width and color of the border. To make a border visible, you must change the `border-style` property of the box from its default value of `none` to one of these 10 values:

- `none`—No line
- `hidden`—An invisible line that still takes up space
- `dotted`—A dotted line
- `dashed`—A dashed line
- `solid`—A solid line
- `double`—A double solid line
- `grooved`—A line that appears to be drawn into the page
- `ridge`—A line that appears to be coming out of the page
- `inset`—The entire element (not just the line around the edge) appears pushed into the document
- `outset`—The entire element (not just the line around the edge) appears to be pushed out of the document

The `border-style` property can have between one and four values. As with the `margin` property, a single value applies to all four borders. Two values set the top and bottom borders to the first style, right and left borders to the second style. Three values set the top, right and left, and bottom border styles, in that order. Four values set each border in the order top, right, bottom, and left. For example, Listing 13-8 adds a rule to enclose the entire `SYNOPSIS` in a solid border.

Listing 13-8: Bordering the SYNOPSIS

```
SYNOPSIS { border-style: solid }
SYNOPSIS { margin: 1cm 1cm 1cm 1cm }
SYNOPSIS, TITLE, ACT, SCENE { display: block }
ACT { margin-top: 3ex }
```

Figure 13-9 shows the result in Mozilla. In this case, the border has the secondary effect of making the margin more obvious. (Remember that the margin is outside the border.)

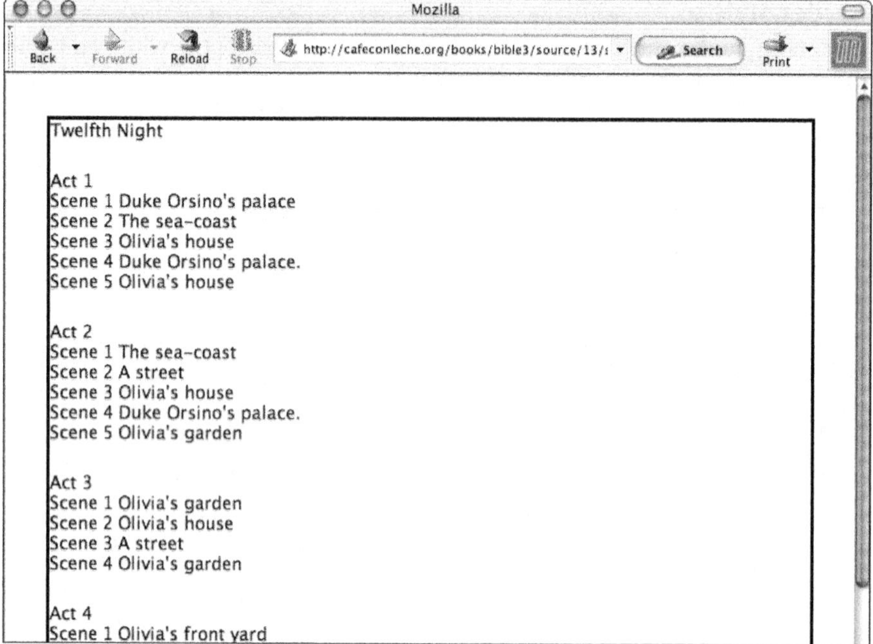

Figure 13-9: A border around the synopsis

Border width

Four border-width properties specify the width of the borderlines along the top, bottom, right, and left edges of the box. These are as follows:

- ✦ `border-top-width`
- ✦ `border-right-width`
- ✦ `border-bottom-width`
- ✦ `border-left-width`

Each may be specified as an absolute length or as one of three keywords: `thin`, `medium`, or `thick`. Border widths cannot be negative but can be zero.

For example, to enclose the `SYNOPSIS` element in a 1-pixel-wide, solid border (the thinnest border any computer monitor can display), use this rule:

```
SYNOPSIS { border-style:        solid;
           border-top-width:    1px;
           border-right-width:  1px;
           border-bottom-width: 1px;
           border-left-width:   1px }
```

If you want to set all or several borders to the same width, it's more convenient to use the `border-width` shorthand property. This property can have between one and four values. One value sets all four border widths. Two values set the top and bottom borders to the first value, right and left borders to the second value. Three values set the top, right and left, and bottom widths in that order. Four values set each border in the order top, right, bottom, and left. For example, the following is equivalent to the previous rule:

```
SYNOPSIS { border-style: solid; border-width: 1px }
```

Border color

Most browsers draw borders in black by default, or possibly in shades of gray if necessary to produce 3D effects for the grooved, ridge, inset, and outset styles. However, you can use the `border-color` properties to change this for one or more sides of the box. These properties are as follows:

- `border-top-color`
- `border-right-color`
- `border-bottom-color`
- `border-left-color`

There's also a `border-color` shorthand property that sets the color of all four borders. A single value sets all four border colors. Two values set the top and bottom borders to the first color, the right and left borders to the second color. Three values set the top, right and left, and bottom border colors in that order. Four values set each border in the order top, right, bottom, and left. The value can be any recognized color name or an RGB triplet. For example, this rule encloses the `SYNOPSIS` element in a 1-pixel-wide, solid red border:

```
SYNOPSIS { border-style: solid;
           border-width: 1px;
           border-color: red }
```

Shorthand border properties

Five shorthand border properties let you set the width, style, and color of a border with one rule. These five properties are:

- `border-top`
- `border-right`
- `border-bottom`
- `border-left`
- `border`

The border-top property provides a width, style, and color for the top border. The border-right, border-bottom, and border-left properties are similar. For example, the first rule of Listing 13-9 produces a 2-pixel groove blue border (a horizontal rule if you will) below each act. Figure 13-10 shows the result.

Listing 13-9: Using Borders to Produce Horizontal Rules

```
ACT { border-bottom: 2px groove blue }
SYNOPSIS { border-style: solid }
SYNOPSIS { margin: 1cm 1cm 1cm 1cm }
SYNOPSIS, TITLE, ACT, SCENE { display: block }
ACT { margin-top: 3ex }
```

The border property sets all four sides to the specified width, style, and height. For example, this rule draws a 3-pixel-wide, solid, red border around a SYNOPSIS element.

```
SYNOPSIS { border: 3pt solid red }
```

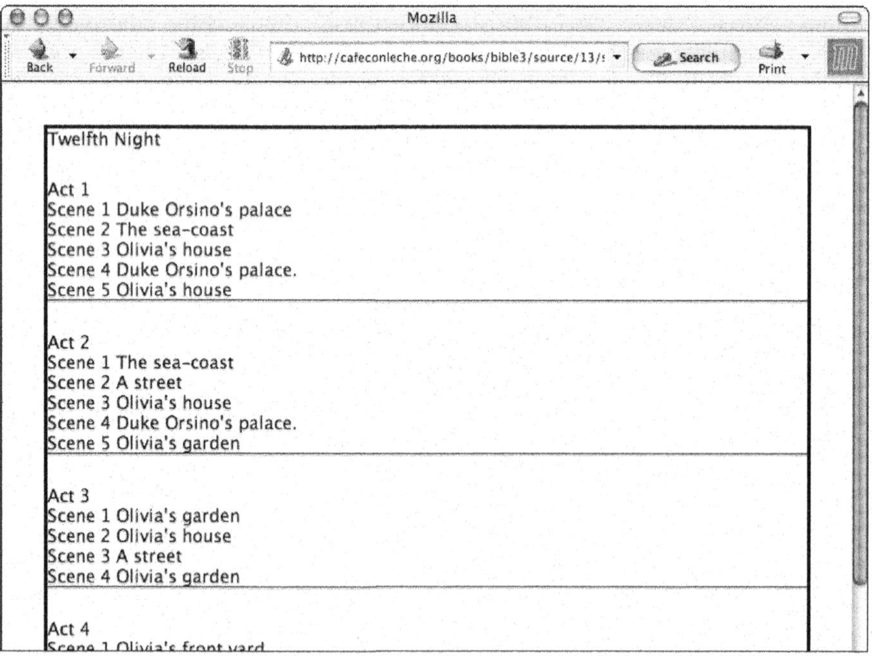

Figure 13-10: A 2-pixel groove bottom border is similar to HTML's HR element.

Padding properties

The padding properties specify the amount of space on the *inside* of the border of the box. The border of the box, if shown, falls between the margin and the padding as shown in Figure 13-6. Padding may be set separately for the top, bottom, right, and left padding using the padding-top, padding-bottom, padding-right, and padding-left properties. Each padding can be given as an absolute length or as a percentage of the element's width. For example, you can set off the SYNOPSIS from its border by setting its padding properties, as shown in this rule:

```
SYNOPSIS { padding-bottom: 1em;
           padding-top:    1em;
           padding-right:  1em;
           padding-left:   1em }
```

You can also set all four at once using the shorthand padding property. For example, this rule is the same as the previous one:

```
SYNOPSIS { padding: 1em 1em 1em 1em }
```

In fact, this is the same as using a single value for the padding property, which CSS interprets as applying to all four sides:

```
SYNOPSIS { padding: 1em }
```

Given two padding values, the first applies to the top and bottom, the second to the right and left. Given three padding values, the first applies to the top, the second to the right and left, and the third to the bottom. It's probably easier to use the separate padding-top, padding-bottom, padding-right, and padding-left properties.

The blue borders below the acts in the synopsis in Figure 13-10 seem a little too close, so let's add an ex of padding between the end of the act and the border with the padding-bottom property, as shown in the first rule of Listing 13-10. Figure 13-11 shows the result. Generally, it's a good idea to use a little padding around borders to make the text easier to read.

Listing 13-10: **Padding the Border**

```
ACT { padding-bottom: 1ex }
ACT { border-bottom: 2px groove blue }
SYNOPSIS { border-style: solid }
SYNOPSIS { margin: 1cm 1cm 1cm 1cm }
SYNOPSIS, TITLE, ACT, SCENE { display: block }
ACT { margin-top: 3ex }
```

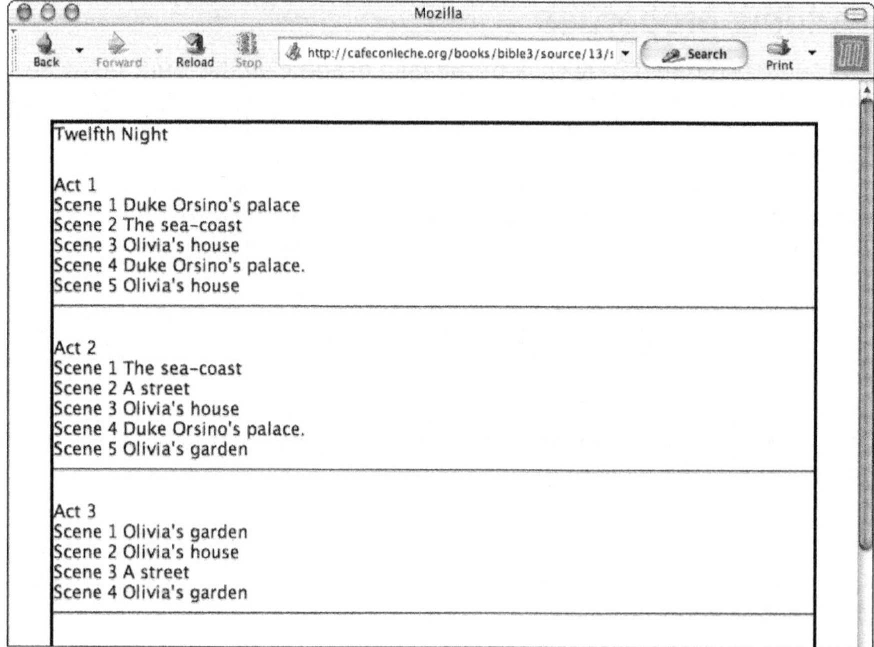

Figure 13-11: Padding makes borders easier on the eye.

Size

CSS lets you choose exactly how big each element's box will be. By default, boxes are just big enough to contain their contents, borders, and padding. Inline and table elements that contain text always have these automatically calculated dimensions. However, you can make block-level elements either bigger or smaller than this default by using these six properties:

✦ `height`

✦ `width`

✦ `min-width`

✦ `max-width`

✦ `min-height`

✦ `max-height`

The width and height properties

Generally, the browser decides how much space each element requires by adding up the total size of its contents, along with the size of any borders and padding; and usually, this is exactly what you want it to do. However, you can force a block-level element to a predetermined size by setting its `width` and `height` properties. Consider Listing 13-11. The first rule says that every `TITLE` element will be exactly 3 inches wide and 2 inches high. Even if it doesn't use up all this space, other elements that follow it will leave the extra space empty.

Listing 13-11: A Style Sheet That Sets a Fixed Size for the TITLE Element

```
TITLE    { width: 3in; height: 2in }
SYNOPSIS, TITLE, ACT, SCENE { display: block }
TITLE    { border-style: solid }
SYNOPSIS { border-style: dotted }
ACT      { border-style: dashed }
SCENE    { border-style: groove }
ACT, SCENE, TITLE, SYNOPSIS { margin: 1ex }
```

Figure 13-12 demonstrates the effect of Listing 13-11. Borders are added to all the block-level elements so you can see where their boxes are placed. All of them except for `TITLE` take up the minimum amount of vertical space they need to hold their contents and the maximum amount of horizontal space. However, because the `TITLE` element's `width` and `height` properties have been set, it's taller than it needs to be and narrower than it could be.

If the box size specified is too small to hold the contents of the box, the contents will not be scaled to fit. By default, the content will spill out of the box and overlap whatever follows. Figure 13-13 demonstrates this with a box that's too small for the actual title. However, you can clip or scroll the overflowed contents using the `overflow` property.

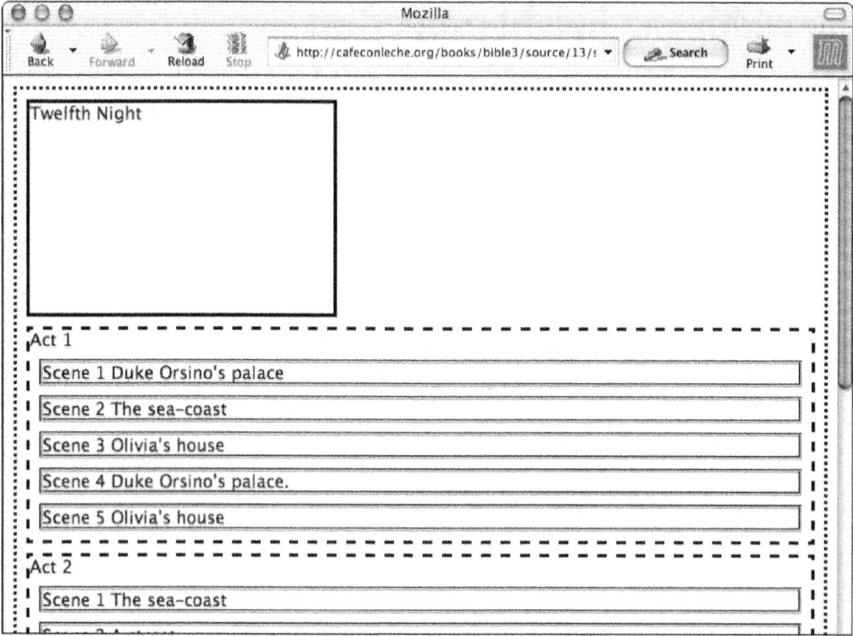

Figure 13-12: This TITLE element is exactly 3 inches wide and 2 inches high.

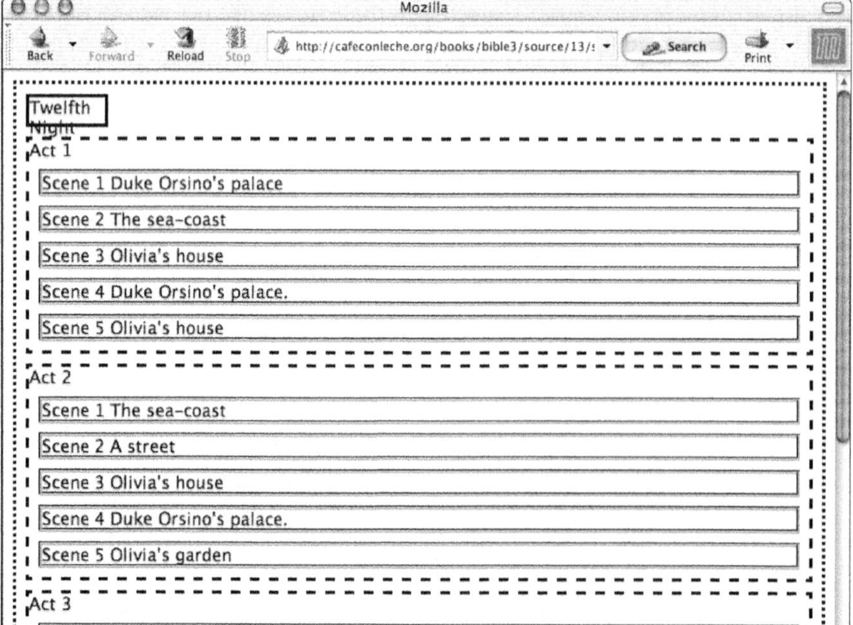

Figure 13-13: This TITLE element is exactly 3 ems wide and 1 em high, too small to hold the entire title.

You do not have to set both width and height. You can set one or the other, or neither. The default setting for both is auto; that is, calculate the necessary size based on the contents and context of the box.

The min-width and min-height properties

If you want an element to take up at least a minimum amount of space, but also want to allow it to grow larger, if necessary, to hold its contents, you can set the min-height and min-width properties. These specify the smallest dimensions that the element will use. For example, this rule says that a TITLE element must be at least 1 inch wide and 1 inch high:

```
TITLE { min-width: 1in; min-height: 1in }
```

If the title needs more space than that, the browser is free to make its box larger. If it takes up less space than that, the browser will leave some empty space. Min-height and min-width should be preferred to height and width because you can never be sure exactly how much space any given string of text is going to occupy from one computer to the next. Using min-height and min-width instead of height and width will give you the same effect most of the time, and look much better in the occasional cases where you do need the extra space.

The min-height and min-width properties override height and width. If height is set to something smaller than min-height, the value of the min-height property determines the height of the box, regardless of the value of height. The same is true for width and min-width.

The max-width and max-height properties

If you want an element to occupy no more than a certain amount of space, but you do want it to be smaller if its contents allow, you can set the max-height and max-width properties. Together, these specify the largest area that an element will occupy. For example, this rule says that a TITLE element must be no more than 3 inches wide and 2 inches high:

```
TITLE { max-width: 3in; max-height: 2in }
```

If the title needs less space than that, the browser is free to shrink its box. However, if it needs more space than that, the browser will let some text fall outside the box, or otherwise handle it as specified by the overflow property. Because max-height and max-width can cause text to overlap other text in an unattractive fashion, just like height and width can, you should use it sparingly.

The max-height and max-width properties override height and width. If height is set to something larger than max-height, the value of the max-height property determines the height of the box, regardless of the value of height. The same is true for width and max-width.

The overflow property

When the size of a box is precisely specified using `width` and `height` or limited by `max-width` and `max-height`, it's entirely possible that its contents may take up more area than the box actually has. The `overflow` property controls how the excess content is dealt with. This property can be set to one of four values:

- `visible`
- `hidden`
- `scroll`
- `auto`

The default is `visible`, which means let the text continue outside the box, on top of the text in other boxes, if necessary. You saw an example of this in Figure 13-13. On the other hand, if `overflow` is set to `hidden`, the visible text will be clipped to its containing box, as shown for the `TITLE` element in Figure 13-14. This rule produces that effect:

```
TITLE { width: 3em; height: 1em; overflow: hidden}
```

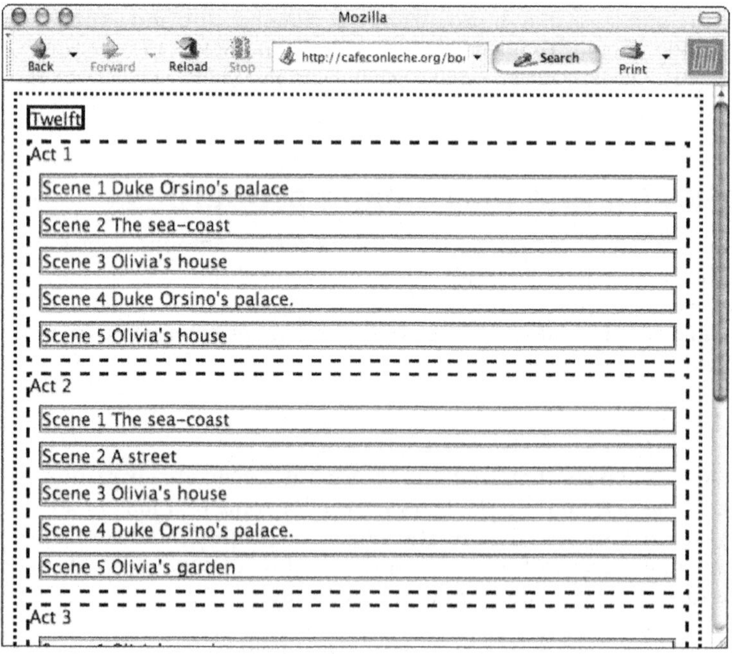

Figure 13-14: This TITLE element is exactly 3 ems wide and 1 em high, too small to hold the entire title, so the overflow is hidden.

Another option that's useful, especially for relatively large blocks that contain still larger amounts of text, is to provide scroll bars. You can request this by setting `overflow` to `scroll`. To specify scroll bars only if they're actually needed — that is, only if the content does indeed overflow — choose the value `auto`.

Positioning

For truly precise layouts, CSS lets you decide exactly where to put each element's box. By default, block-level elements contained inside the same parent element follow each other on the page. They do not line up side by side or wrap around each other. You can change this with judicious use of the `float` and `clear` properties. You can even make elements overlap each other, in which case the `z-index` property determines which element is on top and which is on bottom.

The position property

Element boxes can be positioned automatically by the browser, offset relative to their automatically calculated positions, or placed at a fixed position in the box that contains them or at a fixed position on the page. The `position` property determines which of these options the browser uses to position each element. It can have one of these four keyword values:

- `static` — The default layout
- `relative` — Elements are offset from their static positions
- `absolute` — Elements are placed at a specific position relative to the box they're contained in
- `fixed` — Elements are placed at a specific point in the window or on the page

Relative positioning

As a document is being laid out, the formatter chooses positions for items according to the normal flow of elements and text. This is the default, static formatting used by most documents. After this has been completed, the elements can be shifted relative to their natural, calculated positions. This adjustment in an element's position is known as *relative positioning*. Altering the position of an element in this manner does not affect the positions of other elements. Thus, boxes can overlap because relatively positioned boxes retain all of their normal sizes and spacing.

To relatively position an element, set its `position` property to `relative`. Then specify the length to offset the left edge of the element to the right of its normal position as the value of the `left` attribute and the length to offset the top edge of the element down from its normal position as the value of the `top` attribute. You can use negative numbers to offset to the left and up. For example, Listing 13-12 moves the `TITLE` element 50 pixels to the right and down from where it would normally be placed.

Listing 13-12: A Style Sheet That Adjusts the Position of the TITLE Element

```
TITLE     { position: relative; left: 50px; top: 50px }
SYNOPSIS, TITLE, ACT, SCENE { display: block }
TITLE     { border-style: solid }
SYNOPSIS  { border-style: dotted }
ACT       { border-style: dashed }
SCENE     { border-style: groove }
ACT, SCENE, TITLE, SYNOPSIS { margin: 1ex }
```

Figure 13-15 shows how this makes the `TITLE` element overlap some other elements on the page.

You can use the `right` property to offset the right edge of the element from the right edge of its normal block; that is, to move it to the left. Similarly, you can set the `bottom` property to offset the bottom edge of the element from the bottom edge of its normal position and move it up.

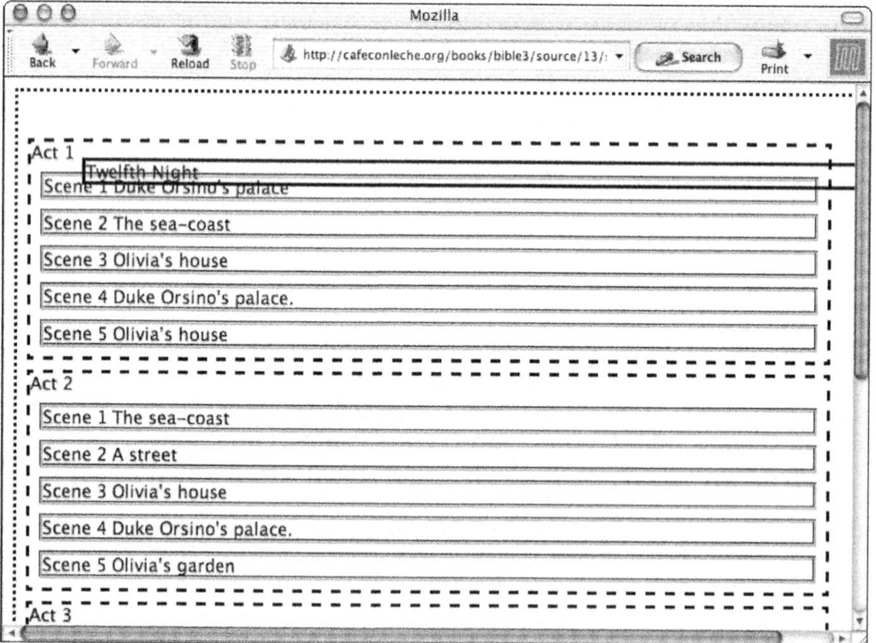

Figure 13-15: A relatively positioned TITLE element

Absolute positioning

An absolutely positioned element is placed at a specific point inside the block that contains it. For example, the coordinates of an absolutely positioned `TITLE` element are relative to the top left corner of the `SYNOPSIS` block. If the `SYNOPSIS` block moves, the `TITLE` element moves with it. However, if a sibling `ACT` element moves, the `TITLE` element won't move to accommodate it. The contents of absolutely positioned elements do not flow around other boxes, so absolute positioning may cause elements to overlap. In fact, absolutely positioned elements have no impact on the flow of their following siblings, so elements that follow the absolutely positioned one act as if it were not there.

The position of the upper left corner of an absolutely positioned element is set by the `top` and `left` properties. The position of the lower right corner of an absolutely positioned element is set by the `bottom` and `right` properties. Specifying all four positions fixes the height and width of the box. If one corner is omitted, the box is sized appropriately for its contents. For example, the following rule places the `TITLE` element exactly one inch down and one inch to the right of the upper left corner of its parent `SYNOPSIS` element:

```
TITLE { position: absolute;
        left: 1.0in; top: 1.0in; width: 3.0in; height: 2.0in}
```

Figure 13-16 shows the result. Notice that unlike a relatively positioned element, an absolutely positioned element does not reserve any space for itself. Unless everything on the page is absolutely positioned, it's almost certain that some elements will overlap each other.

Most of the time, absolute positioning is a bad idea for the same reason that absolute sizes are a bad idea. Although an absolutely positioned element might look okay on your system, it probably won't on some of the systems that people will use to read the document.

Fixed positioning

Elements with fixed positions are placed at coordinates relative to the window in which they're displayed or the piece of paper on which they're printed. A fixed element does not move when the document is scrolled. When printed on paper, a fixed element appears in the same place on each page. This enables you to place a footer or header on a document, or a signature at the end of a series of one-page letters. For example, this rule puts the title near the top center of the window even when the user has scrolled down to the bottom of the synopsis:

```
TITLE  { position: fixed; top: 0.1in; left: 2in}
```

Unfortunately, this isn't as useful as it might sound, because unless you also carefully apply a fixed position to everything else on the page, the elements will overlap, as shown in Figure 13-17.

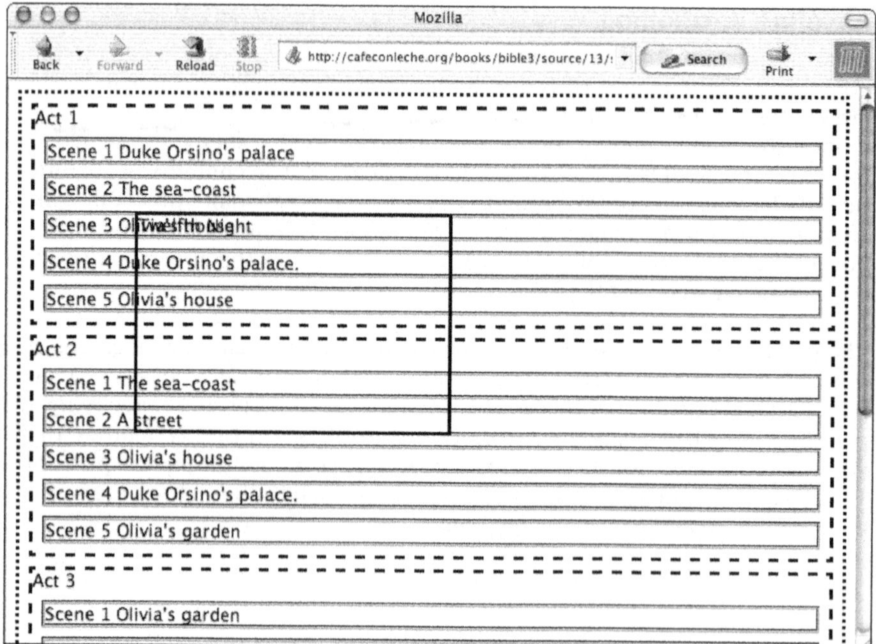

Figure 13-16: An absolutely positioned TITLE element

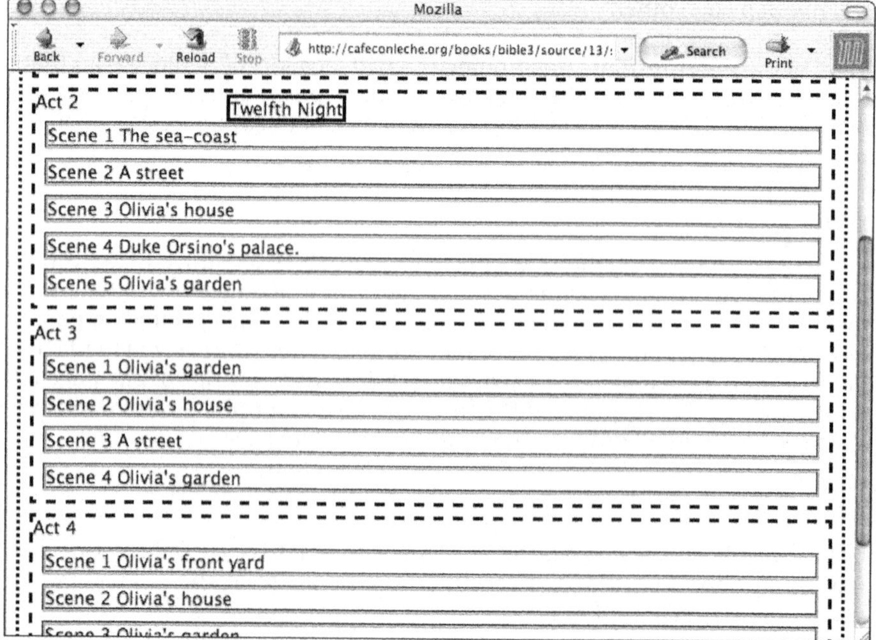

Figure 13-17: A fixed position TITLE element

Stacking elements with the z-index property

When boxes overlap, the `z-index` property determines which boxes are on top of which others. Elements with larger z-indexes are placed on top of elements with smaller z-indexes. Whether the elements on the bottom show through is a function of the background properties of the element on top of them. If the background is transparent, at least some of what's below will probably show through. For example, Figure 13-17 showed the title on top of the synopsis. You can change the z-index to put the title behind the synopsis using these rules:

```
TITLE     { z-index: 1}
SYNOPSIS  { z-index: 2}
```

Internet Explorer does not support the z-index property.

The float property

The `float` property, whose value is `none` by default, can be set to `left` or `right`. If the value is `left`, the element is moved to the left side of the page and the text flows around it on the right. In HTML, this is how an `IMG` with `ALIGN="LEFT"` behaves. If the value is `right`, the element is moved to the right side of the page and the text flows around it on the left. In HTML, this is how an `IMG` with `ALIGN="RIGHT"` behaves. For example, the first rule in Listing 13-13 lets text float to the right of the title, as shown in Figure 13-18.

Listing 13-13: A Floating TITLE

```
TITLE  { float: left }
SYNOPSIS, TITLE, ACT, SCENE { display: block }
TITLE     { border-style: solid }
SYNOPSIS { border-style: dotted }
ACT       { border-style: dashed }
SCENE     { border-style: groove }
ACT, SCENE, TITLE, SYNOPSIS { margin: 1ex }
```

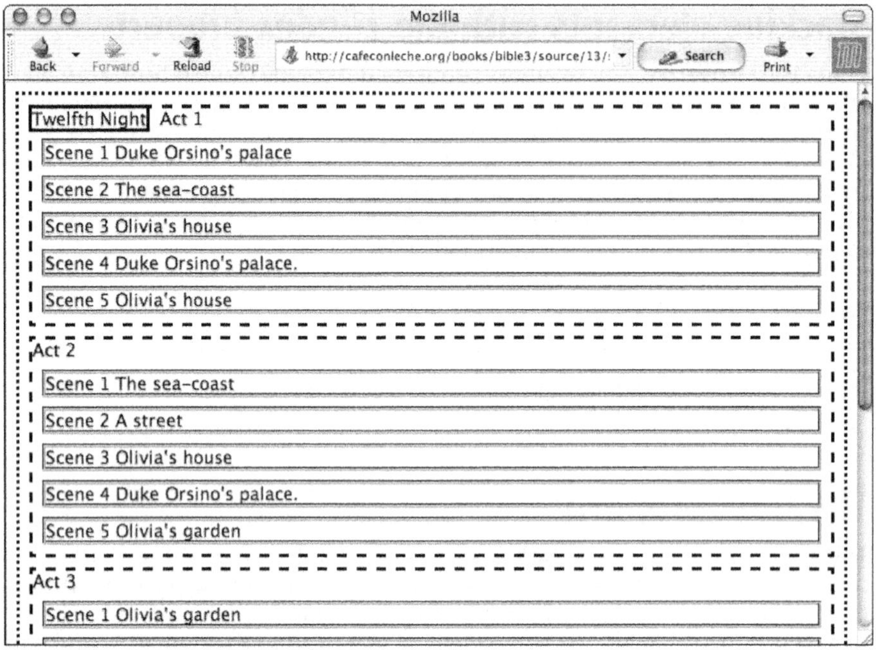

Figure 13-18: The title floating on the left

The clear property

The `clear` property specifies whether an element can have floating elements on its sides. If it cannot, the element will be moved below any floating elements that precede it. It's analogous to the HTML `<BR CLEAR="ALL">` element. There are four possible values:

- `none`
- `left`
- `right`
- `both`

The default value, `none`, causes floating elements to appear on both sides of the element. The value `left` bans floating elements on the left side of the element. The value `right` bans floating elements on the right side of the element. The value `both` bans floating elements on both sides of the element. For example, suppose you add this rule to the style sheet in Listing 13-13:

```
ACT { clear: left }
```

Now, although the TITLE element wants to float on the left of the first ACT, ACT doesn't allow that, as is shown in Figure 13-19. TITLE is still on the left, but now ACT is pushed down below the image.

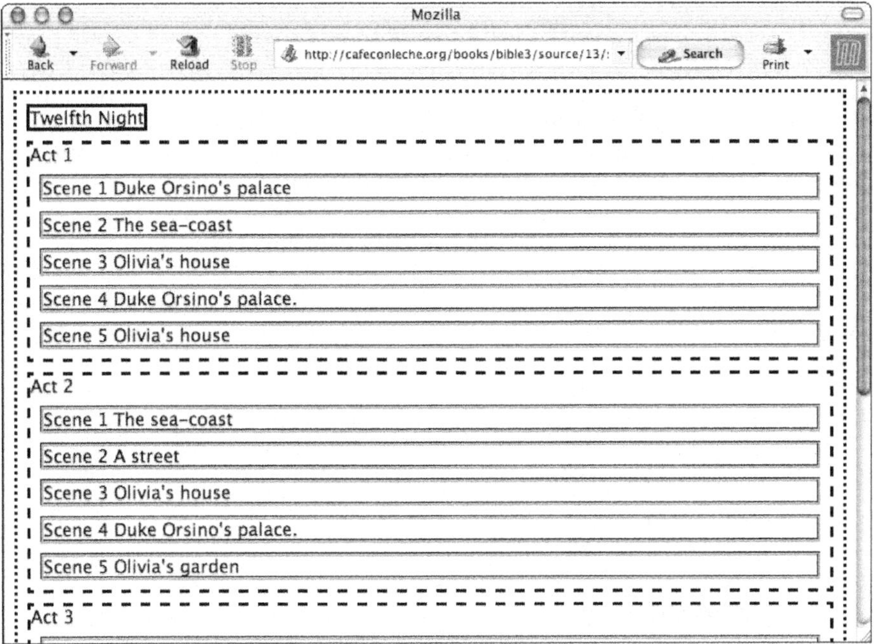

Figure 13-19: The ACT clears the TITLE on the left.

Formatting Pages

CSS makes the reasonable assumption that pages are rectangular. A page can have all the standard box properties, including margins and size, except for borders and padding. However, a page box does not have borders or padding because these would fall off the actual page. The @page selector selects the page so you can set those properties that apply to the page itself rather than XML elements on the page. Pseudo-classes can specify different properties for the first page, right-facing pages, and left-facing pages.

@page

@page is a selector that refers to the page box. This is a rectangular area, roughly the size of a printed page, which contains the page area and the margin block. The page area contains the material to be displayed, and the edges of the box provide a container in which page layout occurs between page breaks. For example, this rule gives the page 1-inch margins on all four sides:

```
@page  { margin-left:   1.0in;
         margin-right:  1.0in;
         margin-top:    1.0in;
         margin-bottom: 1.0in }
```

Because the @page rule is unaware of the page's content, including the fonts it uses, it can't understand measurements in ems and exs. All other units of measurement are acceptable, including percentages. Percentages used on margin settings are a percentage of the total page box size. Page boxes allow negative values for margins, which can place content outside of the area normally accessible by the application or printer. In most of these cases, the content is simply cut.

@page selects every page of a document. You can use one of the page pseudo-class selectors— :first, :left, or :right—to specify different properties for the first page of a document, for the left (generally even numbered) pages of a document, and for the right (generally odd numbered) pages of a document. For example, these rules specify 1-inch outside margins and half-inch inside margins:

```
@page:right  { margin-left: 0.5in; margin-right: 1.0in }
@page:left   { margin-left: 1.0in; margin-right: 0.5in }
@page:first  { margin-left: 0.5in; margin-right: 1.0in }
```

The size property

In an @page rule, the size property specifies the height and width of the page. You can set the size as one or two absolute lengths, or as one of the four keywords auto, portrait, landscape, or inherit. If only one length is given, the page will be a square. When both dimensions are given, the first is the width of the page, and the second is the height, as in this rule:

```
@page { size: 8.5in 11in }
```

The auto setting automatically sizes to the target screen or sheet. landscape forces the document to be formatted to fit the target page, but with long sides horizontal. The portrait setting formats the document to fit the default target page size, but with long sides vertical.

The margin property

The margin property determines the sizes of the margins of the page, the rectangular areas on all four sides in which nothing is printed. This property is used as shorthand for setting the margin-top, margin-bottom, margin-right, and margin-left properties separately. These properties are the same as they are for boxes. For example, this rule describes an 8.5-by-11-inch page with 1-inch margins on all sides:

```
@page { size: 8.5in 11in; margin: 1.0in }
```

The mark property

The mark property places marks on the page delineating where the paper should be cut and/or how pages should be aligned. These marks appear in the margins outside of the page box. The software controls the rendering of the marks, which are only displayed on absolute page boxes. Absolute page boxes cannot be moved and are controlled by the general margins of the page. Relative page boxes are aligned against a target page, in most cases, forcing the marks off the edge of the page. When aligning a relative page box, you are essentially looking at the page in your mind's eye and using margin and padding properties to move the printed area of that page about the physical paper.

The mark property has four possible values — crop, cross, inherit, and none — and can only be used with the @page element. Crop marks identify the cutting edges of paper. Cross marks, also known as registration marks, are used to align pages after printing. If set to none, no marks will be displayed on the document. For example, this rule specifies a page with both crop and cross marks:

```
@page { mark: crop cross}
```

The page property

As well as using the @page selector to specify page properties, you can attach page properties to individual elements by using the page property. To do this, you write an @page rule that specifies the page properties, give that @page rule a name, and then use the name as the value of the page property of a normal element rule. For example, these two rules together say that a SYNOPSIS will be printed in landscape orientation:

```
@page rotated { size: landscape}
SYNOPSIS      { page: rotated}
```

When you are using the page property, it's possible that different sibling elements will specify different page properties. If this happens, a page break will be inserted between the elements. If a child uses a different page layout than its parent, the child's layout takes precedence.

Controlling page breaks

When you are working in paged media, it's often useful to be able to specify that one or more elements are kept on the same page, if possible. Conversely, you might want to suggest a good place to break a page. You can control page breaks with these five CSS properties:

- page-break-before
- page-break-after
- page-break-inside
- orphans
- widows

Generally, these properties are ignored in nonpaged media such as browser windows.

The page-break-before property controls whether pages are allowed, forbidden, or required before the selected element. The page-break-after property controls whether pages are allowed, forbidden, or required after the selected element. The page-break-inside property determines whether pages are allowed, forbidden, or required inside the selected element. These can be used to keep paragraphs of related text, headings and their body text, images and their captions, or complete tables together on the same page. They can also be used to insert page breaks. Page-break-before and page-break-after can have any of these five values:

- auto
- always
- avoid
- left
- right

Page-break-inside is limited to avoid and auto.

The default for all three properties is auto, which means the formatter is free to put page breaks wherever it likes. The value always means that a page break is required in the specified place. The value avoid prevents a page break from occurring where indicated. Finally, the values left and right force either one or two page breaks, whichever is necessary to make the next page either a left or right-hand page. This is useful at the end of a chapter in a book where chapters generally start on right-hand pages, even when that leaves blank pages.

The following rule inserts a page break before and after every SYNOPSIS element in a document but not inside a synopsis, so that each synopsis appears on its own page:

```
SYNOPSIS { page-break-before: always;
           page-break-after:  always;
           page-break-inside: avoid }
```

This rule prevents page breaks inside acts, but allows them between acts:

```
ACT {  page-break-before: auto;
       page-break-after:  auto;
       page-break-inside: avoid }
```

This keeps every act complete on one page. Of course, it is possible that one ACT element will simply be too large to fit on a single page. In this case, the formatter may break the page anyway.

Widows and orphans

Sometimes it's necessary to insert a page break in the middle of an element. For example, a paragraph might begin on one page and continue on the next. This avoids large runs of white space at the ends of pages. However, if too little of a paragraph is left on any one page, the page looks ugly. For example, you would normally prefer to avoid printing just the first line of a paragraph at the end of a page and the rest of the paragraph on the next page. It would be more aesthetic to leave a blank line at the bottom of the page and move the entire paragraph to the next page. Similarly, there should be more than one line of a paragraph at the top of any given page. If the normal line-breaking algorithm only places the last line of a paragraph at the top of the page, the second-to-last line of the paragraph should be removed from the bottom of the previous page and placed at the top of the next page.

Single lines at the bottom of a page are called *orphans*. Single lines at the top of a page are called *widows*. You can set an element's orphans and widows properties to specify the minimum number of lines of a block-level element that the formatter must place before and after each page break. For example, this rule says that if there's a page break in the middle of an ACT, there must be at least two lines of the ACT on both sides of the break:

```
ACT {  orphans: 2; widows: 2 }
```

Summary

This chapter discussed CSS's layout model. In this chapter, you learned the following:

- ✦ Lengths in CSS can be specified in relative or absolute units. Relative units are preferred.
- ✦ Color is given in a 24-bit RGB space in decimal, hexadecimal, or percentages.
- ✦ The display property determines whether an element is a block element, inline element, list item, or table part.
- ✦ The text of XML elements is placed in rectangular boxes on one or more pages when rendered by a browser.

✦ Box properties let you adjust borders, margins, and padding around elements.

✦ Margins are extra white space inside an element's box and can be set separately for each side.

✦ Padding is extra white space inside an element's box and can be set separately for each side.

✦ A border is a line drawn between the margin and padding of a box, and can be set separately for each side in a variety of styles, widths, and colors.

✦ The `height`, `width`, `min-height`, `min-width`, `max-height`, and `max-width` properties adjust the size of element boxes.

✦ The `position`, `left`, `right`, `top`, and `bottom` properties adjust where an element box is placed on the page.

✦ The `@page` rule lets you set the margins, size, and other properties of the pages on which the XML elements will be placed.

The documents in this chapter were rather dry. Elements moved around on the page, but they didn't have any *flare*. They weren't italic or bold or big or small or flashing neon. The next chapter shows you the CSS properties that adjust a variety of text styles, including font weight, font size, alignment, and color.

✦ ✦ ✦

CSS Text Styles

✦ ✦ ✦ ✦

In This Chapter

Fonts

Color

Text

Backgrounds

Visibility

Content

✦ ✦ ✦ ✦

The first part of each CSS rule is a selector that says which elements the rule applies to. The second part is a list of the properties that the rule applies to those elements. This chapter focuses on the properties that you can specify in a CSS rule. You learn how to change the font size, style, and weight; how to align text and order paragraphs; how to control the behavior of speech synthesizers reading the text; and more.

Netscape 6.0 and 7.0, Mozilla, Opera 4.0 and later, Safari, and Internet Explorer 5.0 and later all implement only some parts of the CSS specification. Earlier versions of the major browsers, while perhaps supporting some form of CSS for HTML documents, do not support it at all for XML documents. To make matters worse, they all implement different subsets of the specification, and sometimes don't implement the same subsets for XML as they do for HTML. I'll note where one browser or another has a particular problem as we go along. However, if you find that something in this chapter doesn't work as advertised in your favorite browser, please complain to the browser vendor, not to me.

Fonts

CSS provides several properties that control the font used to draw the text, including the following:

- `font-family`
- `font-size`
- `font-style`
- `font-variant`
- `font-weight`

In addition, there's a `font` shorthand property that can set most of these properties simultaneously.

Choosing the font family

The font family is the font in which the text is drawn. The value of the `font-family` property is a comma-separated list of font names, such as Helvetica, Times, and Palatino. Font names that include white space, such as Times New Roman, should be enclosed in single or double quotes.

Names may also be one of the five generic names: `serif`, `sans-serif`, `cursive`, `fantasy`, and `monospace`. The browser replaces these names with a font of the requested type installed on the local system. Table 14-1 demonstrates these fonts.

Table 14-1
Generic Fonts

Name	*Typical Families*	*Distinguishing Characteristic*	*Example*
Serif	Times, Times New Roman, Palatino	Curlicues on the edges of letters make serif text easier to read in small body type.	The quick brown fox jumped over the lazy dog.
Sans-serif	Geneva, Helvetica, Verdana	Block type, often used in headlines.	The quick brown fox jumped over the lazy dog.
Monospace	Courier, Courier New, Monaco, American Typewriter	A typewriter-like font in which each character has exactly the same width; commonly used for source code and e-mail.	`The quick brown fox jumped over the lazy dog.`
Cursive	ZapfChancery	Script font, a simulation of handwriting.	*The quick brown fox jumped over the lazy dog.*
Fantasy	Western, Critter	Text with special effects; for example, letters on fire, letters formed by tumbling acrobats, and letters made from animals.	THE QUICK BROWN FOX JUMPED OVER THE LAZY DOG.

Because there isn't a guarantee that any given font will be available or appropriate on a particular client system (10-point Times is practically illegible on a Macintosh, much less a Palm Pilot), you should provide a comma-separated list of choices for the font in the order of preference. The last choice in the list should always be one of the generic names. However, even if you don't specify a generic name and the fonts you do specify aren't available, the browser will pick something. It just might not be anything like what you wanted.

For example, Listing 14-1 is a style sheet for play synopses similar to Listing 13-1 of the previous chapter. It has rules that make the TITLE element Helvetica with fallback positions of Verdana and any sans serif font, and the rest of the elements Times with fallback positions of Times New Roman and any serif font.

Listing 14-1: A Style Sheet for the Synopsis of a Play

```
TITLE    { font-family: Helvetica, Verdana, sans-serif }
SYNOPSIS { font-family: Times, "Times New Roman", serif }
SYNOPSIS, TITLE, ACT, SCENE { display: block }
```

Figure 14-1 shows the synopsis loaded into Internet Explorer 6.0 with this style sheet. Not a great deal has changed since Figure 13-1 in the last chapter. Times or something very close to it is commonly the default font. The most obvious difference is that the title is now in Helvetica, a sans serif font.

The `font-family` property is inherited by child elements. Thus, by setting `SYNOPSIS`'s `font-family` to Times, all the child elements are also set to Times except for `TITLE`, whose own `font-family` property overrides the one it inherits.

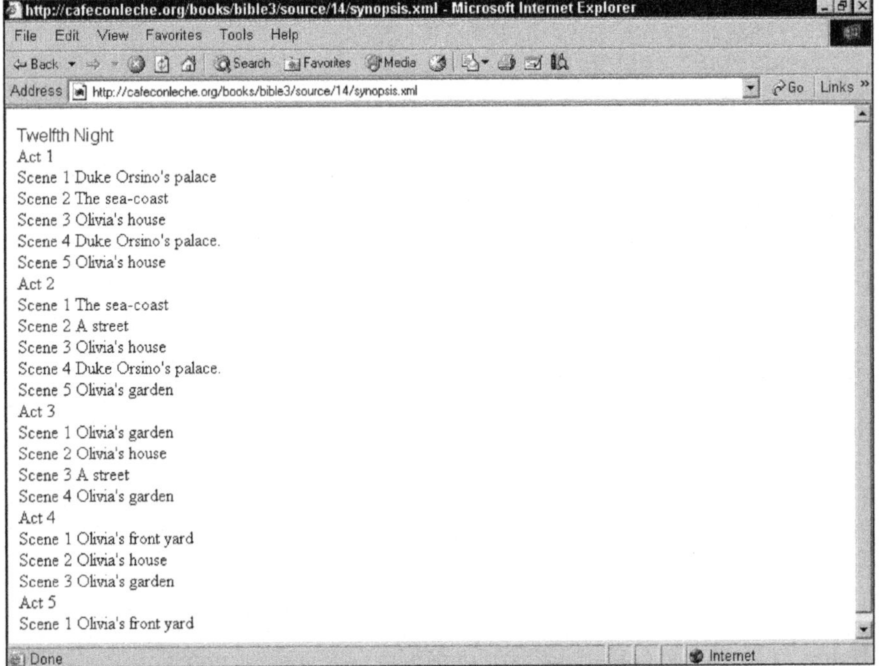

Figure 14-1: The synopsis of *Twelfth Night* with the title in Helvetica

Choosing the font style

The `font-style` property has three possible values: `normal`, `italic`, and `oblique`. The regular text you're reading now is normal. The typical rendering of the HTML `EM` element is *italicized*. Oblique text is very similar to italicized text. However, a computer creates oblique text by algorithmically slanting normal text. A human designer creates italics by carefully handcrafting a font to look good in its slanted form. Listing 14-2 adds a rule to the synopsis style sheet that italicizes scene numbers.

Listing 14-2: A Style Sheet That Italicizes Scene Numbers

```
TITLE    { font-family: Helvetica, Verdana, sans-serif }
SYNOPSIS { font-family: Times, "Times New Roman", serif }
SYNOPSIS, TITLE, ACT, SCENE { display: block }
SCENE_NUMBER { font-style: italic}
```

Figure 14-2 shows the synopsis loaded into Internet Explorer with this style sheet.

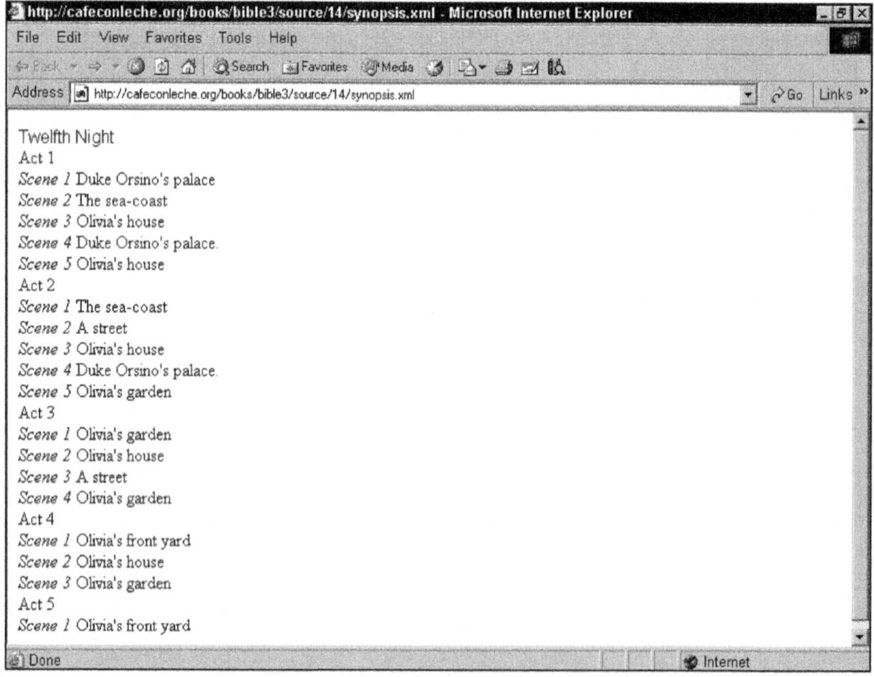

Figure 14-2: The synopsis of *Twelfth Night* with italic scene numbers

Small caps

The `font-variant` property has two possible values: `normal` and `small-caps`. The default is normal. Setting `font-variant` to `small-caps` replaces lowercase letters with capital letters in a smaller font size than the main body text.

You can achieve a very nice effect by combining the `font-variant` property with the `first-letter` pseudo-element. For example, define the `ACT_NUMBER` element to have the `font-variant: small-caps`. Next, define the first letter of `ACT_NUMBER` to have `font-variant: normal`. This produces act numbers that look like this:

Act 1

Here are the rules:

```
ACT_NUMBER              { font-variant: small-caps}
ACT_NUMBER:first-letter { font-variant: normal}
```

The second rule overrides the first, but only for the first letter of the act number.

Setting the font weight

The `font-weight` property determines how dark (bold) or light the text appears. There are 13 possible values for this property:

- `normal`
- `bold`
- `bolder`
- `lighter`
- `100`
- `200`
- `300`
- `400`
- `500`
- `600`
- `700`
- `800`
- `900`

Weights range from 100 (the lightest) to 900 (the darkest). Intermediate, noncentury values such as 850 are not allowed. Normal weight is 400. Bold is 700. The `bolder` value makes an element bolder than its parent. The `lighter` value makes an element less bold than its parent. However, there's no guarantee that a particular font has as many as nine separate levels of boldness.

Here's a simple rule that makes the `TITLE` and `ACT_NUMBER` elements bold:

```
TITLE, ACT_NUMBER { font-weight: bold}
```

Figure 14-3 shows the effect of adding this rule to the synopsis style sheet.

Setting the font size

The `font-size` property determines the height and the width of a typical character in the font. Larger sizes take up more space. The size may be specified as a keyword, a value relative to the font size of the parent, a percentage of the size of the parent element's font size, or an absolute number.

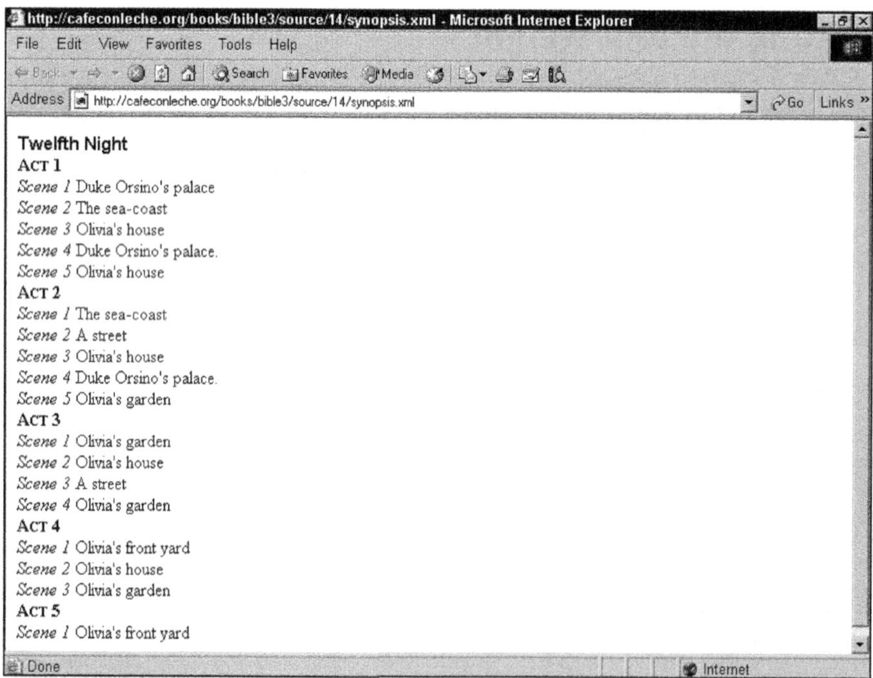

Figure 14-3: The synopsis of *Twelfth Night* with bold title and act numbers

Keyword

Absolute size keywords are as follows:

- xx-small
- x-small
- small
- medium
- large
- x-large
- xx-large

These keywords are the preferred way to set font sizes because they are relative to the base font size of the page. For example, if a nearsighted user has adjusted the default font size to 20 points, a large font will be even larger and a small font will still be pretty large.

Although the exact values are up to the browser's best judgment, in general, each size is 1.2 times larger than the next smallest size. The default is medium, so if a browser's default is 12 points, large type will be 14.4 points, x-large type will be 17.28 points, and xx-large type will be 20.736 points. By contrast, small type will be 10 points, x-small type will be 8.33 points, and xx-small will be a possibly illegible 7 points. A browser might well choose to round these values to the nearest integer. Here's a simple rule that makes the TITLE extra large:

```
TITLE { font-size: x-large }
```

Figure 14-4 shows the results after this rule is added to the synopsis style sheet.

Value relative to parent's font size

You can also specify the size relative to the parent element as either larger or smaller. For example, with the following rule, the SCENE_NUMBER will have a font size that is smaller than the font size of its parent SCENE.

```
SCENE_NUMBER { font-size: smaller }
```

Figure 14-5 shows the result of adding this rule to the synopsis style sheet.

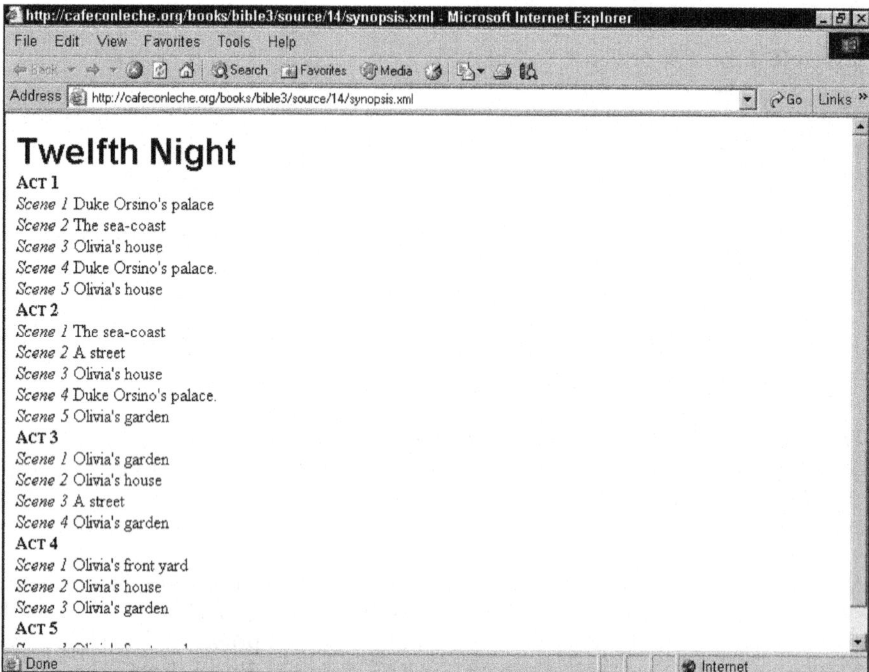

Figure 14-4: The synopsis of *Twelfth Night* with an extra large title

There's no hard-and-fast rule for exactly how much smaller a smaller font will be or how much larger a larger font will be. Generally, the browser will attempt to move from medium to small, from small to x-small, and so forth. The same is true (in the other direction) for larger fonts. Thus, making a font larger should increase its size by about 20 percent, and making a font smaller should decrease its size by about 16.6 percent; but browsers are free to fudge these values to match the available font sizes.

Percentage of parent element's font size

If these options aren't precise enough, you can make finer adjustments by using a percentage of the parent element's font size. For example, this rule says that the font used for a `SCENE_NUMBER` is 50 percent of the size of the font for the `SCENE` (its parent).

```
SCENE_NUMBER { font-size: 50% }
```

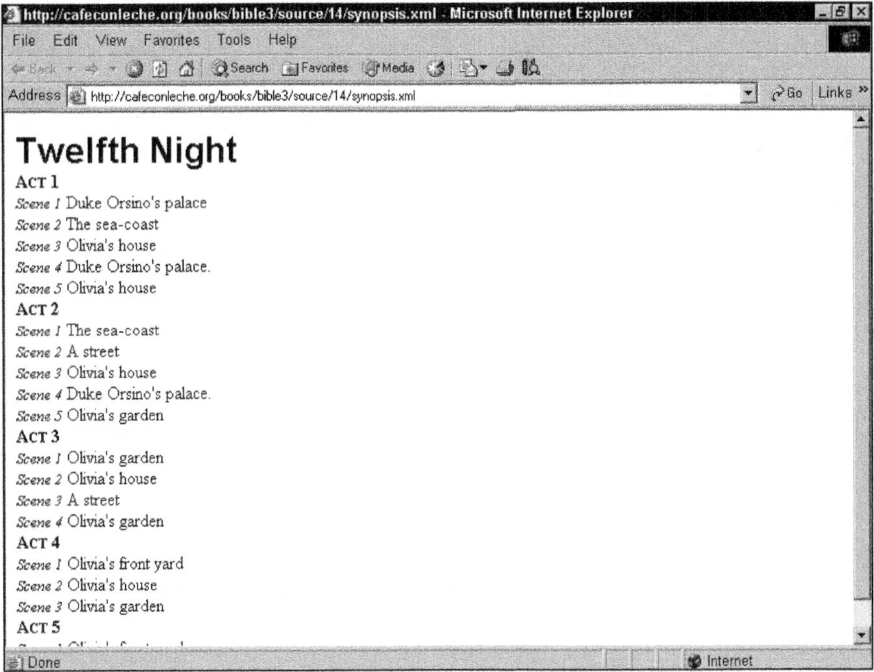

Figure 14-5: The synopsis of *Twelfth Night* with a smaller scene number

Absolute lengths

Finally, you can specify a font size as an absolute length. Although you can use pixels, picas, centimeters, millimeters, or inches, the most common unit when measuring fonts is the point. For example, this rule sets the default `font-size` for the `SYNOPSIS` element and its children to 14 points.

```
SYNOPSIS { font-size: 14pt }
```

I urge you not to use absolute units to describe font sizes. It's extremely difficult (I'd argue impossible) to pick a font size that's legible across all the different platforms on which your page might be viewed, ranging from cell phones to the Sony JumboTron in Times Square. Even when restricting themselves to standard personal computers, most designers usually pick a font that's too small. Any text that's intended to be read on the screen should be at least 12 points, possibly more.

Figure 14-6 shows the results after all these font rules have been added to the synopsis style sheet. The text of the scenes is not really bolder. It's just bigger. In any case, it's a lot easier to read.

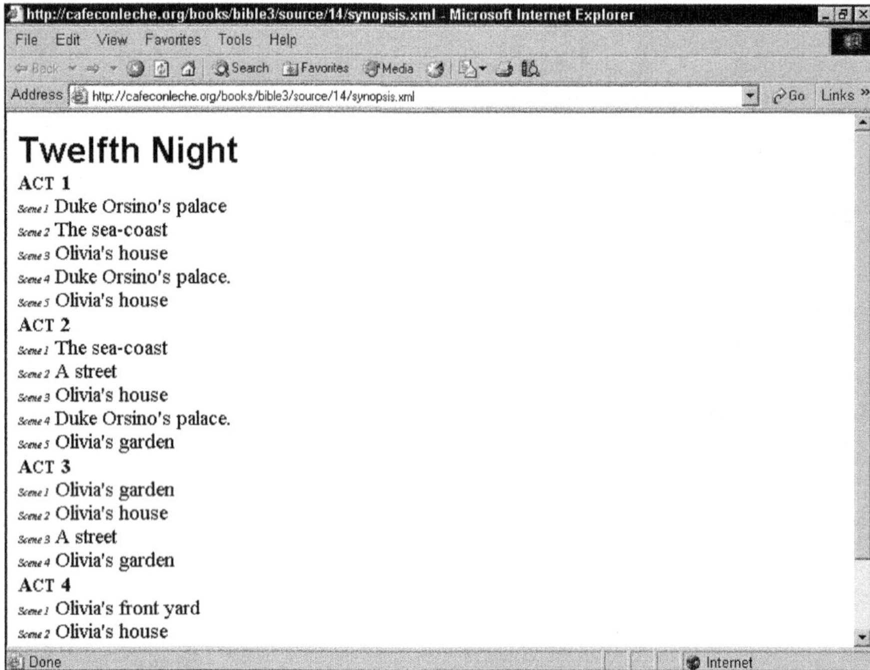

Figure 14-6: The synopsis of *Twelfth Night* in a larger font size

The font shorthand property

`Font` is a shorthand property that sets the font style, variant, weight, size, and family with one rule. For example, here are two rules for the `TITLE` and `SCENE_NUMBER` elements that combine the separate rules of the previous section:

```
TITLE { font: bold x-large Helvetica, sans-serif }
SCENE_NUMBER { font: italic smaller Times, serif }
```

Values must be given in the following order:

1. One each of style, variant, and weight, in any order, any of which can be omitted
2. Size, which cannot be omitted
3. Optionally, a forward slash (/) and a line height
4. Family, which cannot be omitted

If this sounds complicated and hard to remember, that's because it is. I certainly can't remember the exact details for the order of these properties without looking them up. I prefer to just set the individual properties one at a time. It's questionable whether shorthand properties like this really save any time.

Listing 14-3 is the style sheet for the synopsis with all the rules devised so far, using the `font` shorthand properties. However, because a `font` property is exactly equivalent to the sum of the individual properties it represents, there's no change to the rendered document.

Listing 14-3: A Style Sheet for the Synopsis with font Shorthand

```
SYNOPSIS, TITLE, ACT, SCENE { display: block }
ACT_NUMBER { font: bold small-caps}
SYNOPSIS { font: 14pt Times, "Times New Roman", serif }
ACT_NUMBER:first-letter { font-variant: normal}
TITLE {
  font: bold x-large Helvetica, Verdana, Arial, sans-serif
}
SCENE_NUMBER { font: italic smaller Times, serif }
```

The `font` property may also have one of these six keyword values that match all of a font's properties to the properties of particular elements of the browser user interface or the user's system:

- ✦ `caption`—The font used for captioned widgets such as buttons
- ✦ `icon`—The font that labels icons
- ✦ `menu`—The font used for menu items
- ✦ `message-box`—The font used for display text in dialog boxes
- ✦ `small-caption`—The font used for labels on small widgets
- ✦ `status-bar`—The font used in the browser's status bar

For example, this rule says that a `SYNOPSIS` element will be formatted with the same font family, size, weight, and style as the font the browser uses in its status bar:

```
SYNOPSIS { font: status-bar }
```

Color

CSS can specify the color of almost any element on a page with the color property. The value of this color property may be one of 16 named color keywords, or an RGB triple in decimal, hexadecimal, or percentages. Children inherit the color property. For example, the following rules specify that every element in the SYNOPSIS is colored black except the SCENE_NUMBER, which is colored blue:

```
SYNOPSIS     { color: black }
SCENE_NUMBER { color: blue}
```

The following rules are all equivalent to the preceding two. I recommend using named colors, when possible, and browser-safe colors when not.

```
SYNOPSIS     { color: #000000 }
SCENE_NUMBER { color: #0000FF}
SYNOPSIS     { color: rgb(0, 0, 0) }
SCENE_NUMBER { color: rgb(0, 0, 255)}
SYNOPSIS     { color: rgb(0%, 0%, 0%) }
SCENE_NUMBER { color: rgb(0%, 0%, 100%)}
```

The color property specifies the foreground color for the text content of an element. It may be given as a literal color name such as red, or an RGB value such as #CC0000. Color names include aqua, black, blue, fuchsia, gray, green, lime, maroon, navy, olive, purple, red, silver, teal, white, and yellow.

The following style rules apply color to three elements, using three different methods of identifying color. It specifies the RGB hex value #FF0000 for SCENE_NUMBER elements, all TITLE elements to appear in red, and all ACT_NUMBER elements to appear in rgb(255,0,0).

```
SCENE_NUMBER  {  color: #FF0000}
TITLE         {  color: red}
ACT_NUMBER    {  color: rgb(255,0,0) }
```

In fact, these are just three different ways of saying pure red; and all three elements will have the same color.

Text

These properties affect the appearance of text, irrespective of font:

- word-spacing
- letter-spacing

✦ `text-decoration`

✦ `vertical-align`

✦ `text-transform`

✦ `text-align`

✦ `text-indent`

✦ `line-height`

✦ `white-space`

Word spacing

The `word-spacing` property expands text by adding additional space between words. A negative value removes space between words. The only reason I can think of to alter the word spacing on a web page is if you are a student laboring under tight page-count limits who wants to make a paper look bigger or smaller than it is.

Note

Desktop publishers love to spend hours tweaking these details pixel by pixel. The problem is that all the rules they've learned about how and when to adjust spacing are based on ink on paper and really don't work when transferred to the medium of electrons on phosphorus (a typical CRT monitor). You're almost always better off letting the browser make decisions about word and letter spacing for you.

If, on the other hand, your target medium *is* ink on paper, there's a little more to be gained by adjusting these properties. The main difference is that with ink on paper you control the delivery medium. You know exactly how big the fonts are, how wide and high the display is, how many dots per inch are being used, and so forth. On the Web, you simply don't have enough information about the output medium available to control everything at this level of detail.

To change this from the default value of `normal`, you set a length for the property, as in the following example:

```
SYNOPSIS { word-spacing: 1em }
```

Browsers are not required to respect this property, especially if it interferes with other properties such as `align: justified`. Figure 14-7 demonstrates.

Caution

Spacing words requires that the browser be able to figure out where the boundaries between words fall. While this is relatively straightforward in most Western languages—just look for the white space—it's much more complex in some other languages, such as Sanskrit and Japanese. I wouldn't count on most browsers being able to handle this property for the more typographically challenging languages.

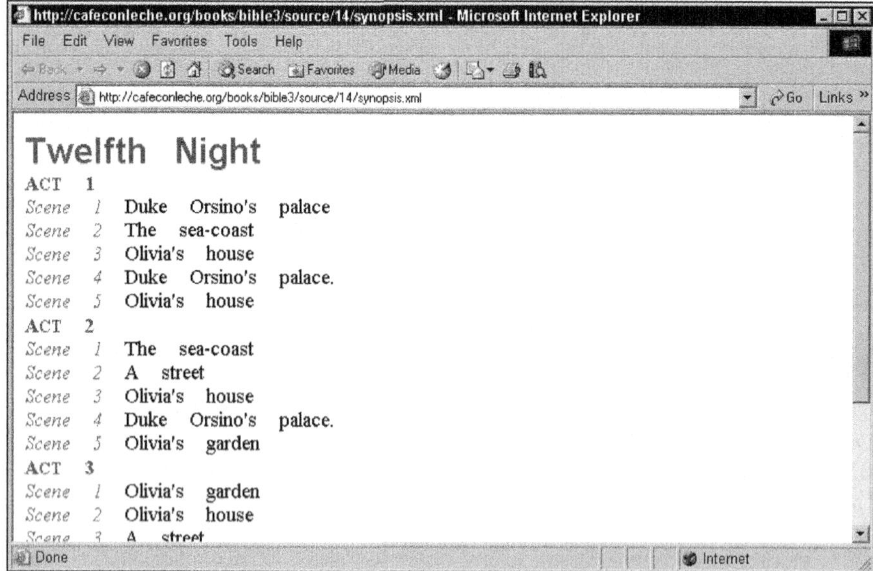

Figure 14-7: The synopsis of *Twelfth Night* with 1 em of word spacing

The letter-spacing property

The `letter-spacing` property expands text by adding additional space between letters. A negative value removes space between letters. Again, the only reason I can think of to do this on a web page is to make a paper look bigger or smaller than it really is to meet a length requirement.

To change this from the default value of `normal`, set a length for the property, as in the following example:

```
SYNOPSIS { letter-spacing: 0.3em }
```

Because justification works by adjusting the amount of space between letters, changing the letter spacing manually can prevent the browser from justifying text. However, browsers are not required to respect this property, especially if it interferes with other properties such as `align: justified`. Nonetheless, most browsers attempt to implement it as best they can within the restrictions of other rules, as shown in Figure 14-8.

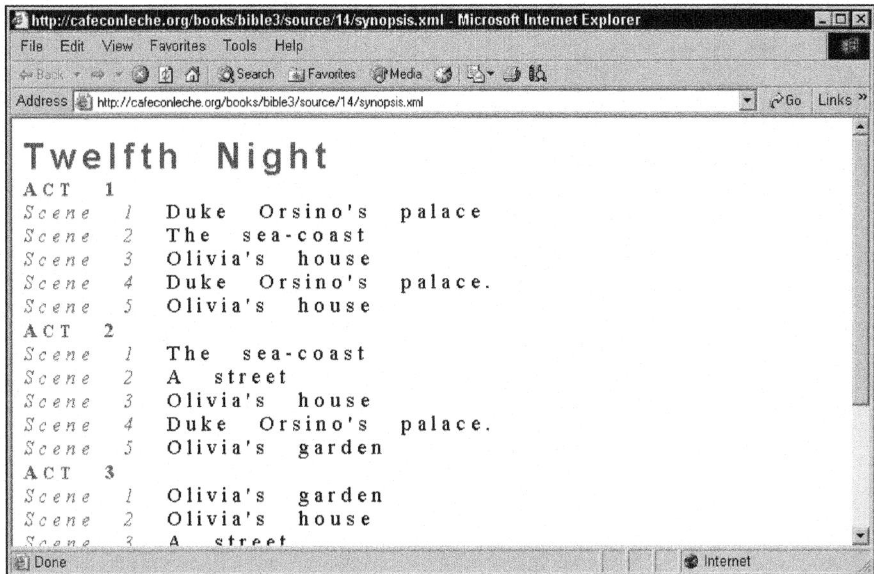

Figure 14-8: The SYNOPSIS element with 0.3 em letter spacing

The text-decoration property

The `text-decoration` property can have one of the following five values:

- `none`
- `underline`
- `overline`
- `line-through`
- `blink`

Except for `none`, which is the default, these values are not mutually exclusive. You may, for example, specify that a paragraph is underlined, overlined, struck through, and blinking. (I do not, however, recommend that you do this.)

> **Note** Browsers, fortunately, are not required to support blinking text.

For example, the next rule specifies that `CHARACTER` elements are underlined. Figure 14-9 shows the result of applying this rule to the synopsis of *Twelfth Night*.

```
CHARACTER { text-decoration: underline }
```

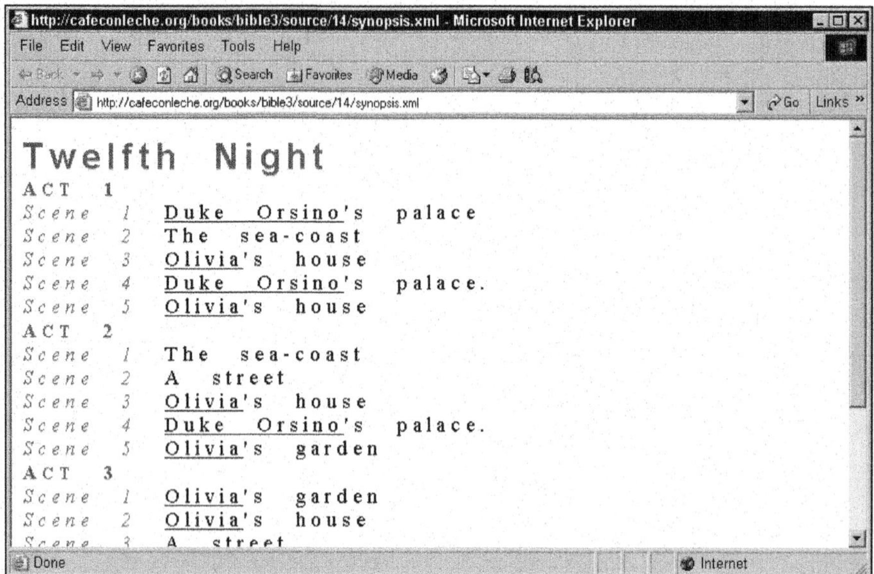

Figure 14-9: The synopsis of *Twelfth Night* with underlined characters

The vertical-align property

The `vertical-align` property controls the vertical alignment of text within an inline box. It specifies how an inline element is positioned relative to the baseline of the text. Valid values are as follows:

- ✦ `baseline`—Align the baseline of the inline box with the baseline of the block box (this is the default)
- ✦ `sub`—Position the inline box as a subscript
- ✦ `super`—Position the inline box as a superscript
- ✦ `top`—Align the top of the inline box with the top of the line
- ✦ `middle`—Align the midpoint of the inline box with the baseline of the block box, plus half of the x-height of the block box
- ✦ `bottom`—Align the bottom of the inline box with the bottom of the line
- ✦ `text-top`—Align the top of the inline box with the top of the parent element's font
- ✦ `text-bottom`—Align the bottom of the inline box with the bottom of the parent element's font

You can also set the vertical-align property to a percentage that raises (positive value) or lowers (negative value) the box by the percentage of the line-height. A value of 0% is the same as the baseline value. Finally, you can set vertical-align to a signed length that will raise or lower the box by the specified distance. A value of 0cm is the same as the baseline value.

The sub value makes the element a subscript. The super value makes the element a superscript. The text-top value aligns the top of the element with the top of the parent element's font. The middle value aligns the vertical midpoint of the element with the baseline of the parent plus half the *x*-height. The text-bottom value aligns the bottom of the element with the bottom of the parent element's font.

The top value aligns the top of the element with the tallest letter or element on the line. The bottom value aligns the bottom of the element with the bottom of the lowest letter or element on the line. The exact alignment changes as the height of the tallest or lowest letter changes.

For example, the rule for a footnote number might look like this one that superscripts the number and decreases its size by 20 percent:

```
FOOTNOTE_NUMBER { vertical-align: super; font-size: 80% }
```

The text-transform property

The text-transform property can specify that text should be rendered in all uppercase, all lowercase, or with initial letters capitalized. This is useful in headlines, for example. The valid values are as follows:

- capitalize
- uppercase
- lowercase
- none

Capitalization Makes Only The First Letter Of Every Word Uppercase Like This Sentence. PLACING THE SENTENCE IN UPPERCASE, HOWEVER, MAKES EVERY LETTER IN THE SENTENCE UPPERCASE. The following rule converts the TITLE element in the *Twelfth Night* synopsis to uppercase:

```
TITLE { text-transform: uppercase }
```

Internet Explorer doesn't support the text-transform property, so Figure 14-10 shows the document in Mozilla.

Mozilla
File Edit View Go Bookmarks Tools Window Help
http://cafeconleche.org/books/bible3/source/14/synopsis.xml

TWELFTH NIGHT
ACT 1
Scene 1 Duke Orsino's palace
Scene 2 The sea-coast
Scene 3 Olivia's house
Scene 4 Duke Orsino's palace.
Scene 5 Olivia's house
ACT 2
Scene 1 The sea-coast
Scene 2 A street
Scene 3 Olivia's house
Scene 4 Duke Orsino's palace.
Scene 5 Olivia's garden
ACT 3
Scene 1 Olivia's garden
Scene 2 Olivia's house
Scene 3 A street
Scene 4 Olivia's garden
ACT 4
Scene 1 Olivia's front yard
Done

Figure 14-10: The synopsis of *Twelfth Night* with an uppercased title

The `text-transform` property is somewhat language-dependent because many languages—Hebrew, modern Georgian, and Chinese, for example—don't have distinct upper and lowercases. Even worse, letters that have the same capital form in two languages might have different lowercase forms or vice versa.

The text-align property

The `text-align` property applies only to block-level elements. It specifies whether the text in the block is aligned with the left side, the right side, centered, or justified. The valid values are as follows:

- ✦ `left`
- ✦ `right`
- ✦ `center`
- ✦ `justify`

The following rules center the TITLE element in the *Twelfth Night* synopsis and justify everything else. Figure 14-11 shows the synopsis after these rules have been applied. I also changed SCENE to `display: inline` so that there'd be enough text in a paragraph to extend across the browser window and show that the text is truly justified.

```
SCENE    { display: inline}
TITLE    { text-align: center }
SYNOPSIS { text-align: justify }
```

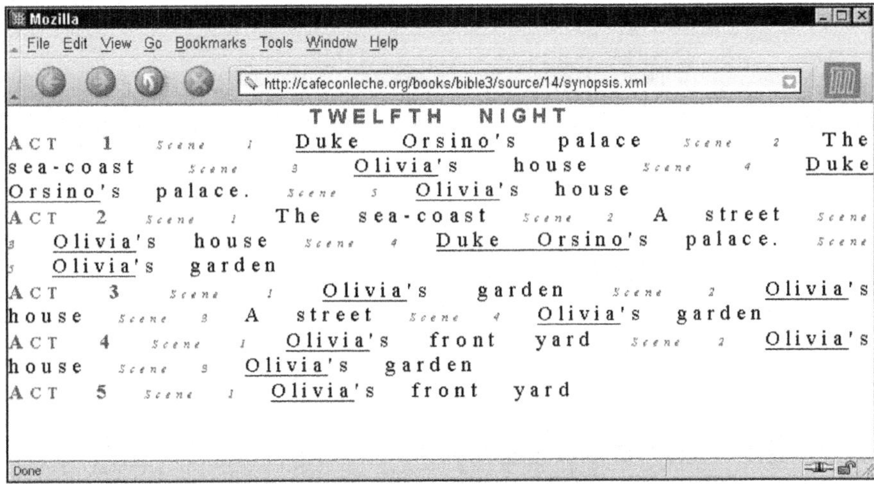

Figure 14-11: The TITLE in the synopsis is centered and the rest of the text is justified.

The text-indent property

The `text-indent` property, which only applies to block-level elements, specifies how far the first line of a block is indented with respect to the remaining lines of the block. It is given either as an absolute length or as a percentage of the width of the parent element. The value can be negative to create a hanging indent.

Tip To indent all the lines of an element, rather than just the first, use the box properties discussed in Chapter 13 to set an extra left margin on the element.

For example, the following rule indents the scenes in the synopsis by half an inch. Figure 14-12 shows the synopsis after this rule has been applied.

```
SCENE { text-indent: 0.5in }
```

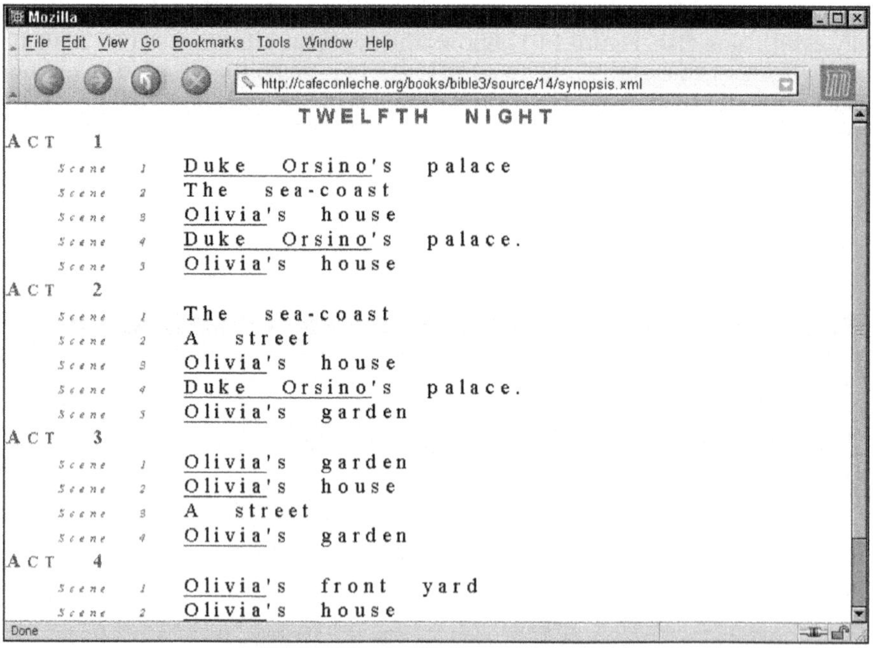

Figure 14-12: Each SCENE and its children in the synopsis are indented half an inch.

The line-height property

The `line-height` property specifies the distance between the baselines of successive lines. It can be given as an absolute number, an absolute length, or a percentage of the font size. For example, the following rule double-spaces the `SYNOPSIS` element. Figure 14-13 shows the *Twelfth Night* synopsis after this rule has been applied.

```
SYNOPSIS { line-height: 200% }
```

Double spacing isn't particularly attractive, though, so I'll remove it. Listing 14-4 summarizes the additions made in this and the previous sections to the synopsis style sheet (minus the double spacing).

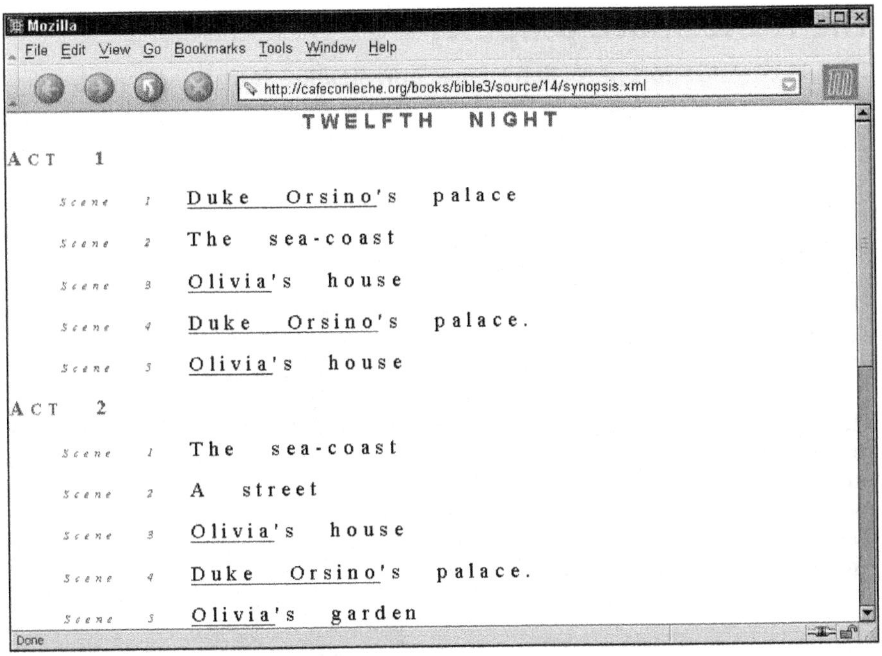

Figure 14-13: A double-spaced synopsis

Listing 14-4: **The Synopsis Style Sheet with Text Properties**

```
SYNOPSIS, TITLE, ACT, SCENE { display: block }
ACT_NUMBER { font-weight: bold}
SYNOPSIS { font-size: 14pt }
SYNOPSIS { word-spacing: 1em }
SYNOPSIS { letter-spacing: 0.3em }
SCENE_NUMBER  {  color: #FF0000}
TITLE         {  color: red}
ACT_NUMBER    {  color: rgb(255,0,0) }
ACT_NUMBER    { font-variant: small-caps}
CHARACTER { text-decoration: underline }
SCENE_NUMBER  {  vertical-align: subscript}
TITLE    { font-size-adjust: ".58";  }
SYNOPSIS { font-size-adjust: ".46"
           font-family: Times, "Times New Roman", serif }
TITLE { font: normal bold x-large Helvetica, Verdana,
                                              Arial, sans-serif
}
SCENE_NUMBER { font: italic smaller Times, serif }
TITLE    { text-align: center }
SYNOPSIS { text-align: justify }
SCENE { text-indent: 0.5in }
```

The white-space property

The `white-space` property determines how significant white space (spaces, tabs, line breaks) is within an element. The allowable values are as follows:

- ✦ `normal`
- ✦ `pre`
- ✦ `nowrap`

The default value, `normal`, simply means that runs of white space are condensed to a single space and words are wrapped to fit on the screen or page. This is the way white space is normally handled in both HTML and XML.

The `pre` value acts like the `PRE` (preformatted) element in HTML. All white space in the input document is considered significant and faithfully reproduced on the output device. It may be accompanied by a shift to a monospaced font. This would be useful for computer source code or concrete poetry. Listing 14-5 is a poem, *The Altar* by George Herbert, in which spacing is important. In this poem, the lines form the shape of the poem's subject.

Listing 14-5: *The Altar* in XML

```
<?xml version="1.0"?>
<?xml-stylesheet type="text/css" href="14-6.css"?>
<POEM>

<TITLE>The Altar</TITLE>
<POET>George Herbert</POET>

<VERSE>   A broken ALTAR, Lord, thy servant rears,</VERSE>
<VERSE>   Made of a heart, and cemented with tears:</VERSE>
<VERSE>    Whose parts are as thy hand did frame;</VERSE>
<VERSE>    No workman's tool hath touched the same.</VERSE>
<VERSE>    No workman's tool hath touched the same.</VERSE>
<VERSE>            A     HEART     alone</VERSE>
<VERSE>            Is    such   a   stone,</VERSE>
<VERSE>            As    nothing     but</VERSE>
<VERSE>            Thy   power  doth  cut.</VERSE>
<VERSE>            Wherefore  each  part</VERSE>
<VERSE>            Of   my    hard   heart</VERSE>
<VERSE>            Meets in  this  frame,</VERSE>
<VERSE>            To  praise  thy  name:</VERSE>
<VERSE>    That  if  I  chance  to  hold  my  peace,</VERSE>
<VERSE>    These stones to praise thee may not cease.</VERSE>
<VERSE>   O  let  thy  blessed  SACRIFICE  be  mine,</VERSE>
<VERSE>   And  sanctify   this   ALTAR  to  be  thine.</VERSE>

</POEM>
```

Listing 14-6 is a style sheet that uses `white-space: pre` to preserve this form. Figure 14-14 shows the result in Mozilla.

Caution Internet Explorer does not correctly implement the `white-space` property. Mozilla, Netscape, Safari, and Opera do.

Listing 14-6: A Style Sheet for White Space-Sensitive Poetry

```
POEM   { display: block }
TITLE  { display: block; font-size: 16pt; font-weight: bold }
POET   { display: block; margin-bottom: 10px }
STANZA { display: block; margin-bottom: 10px }
VERSE  { display: block;
         white-space: pre; font-family: monospace }
```

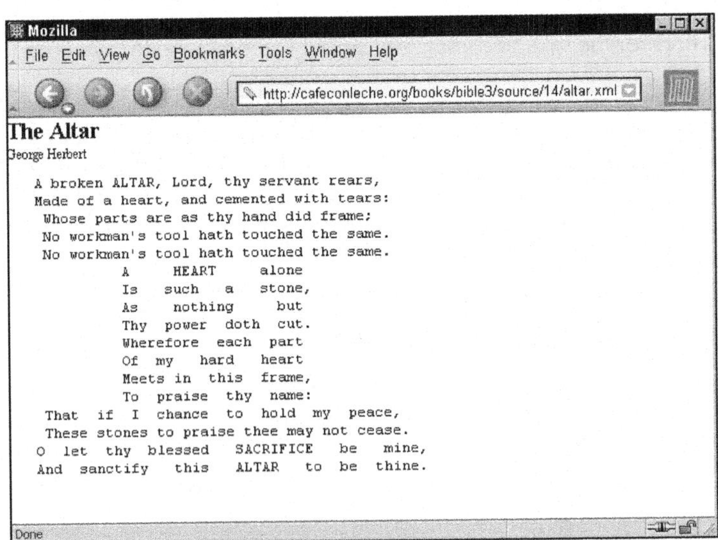

Figure 14-14: *The Altar* by George Herbert with white-space: pre

Finally, the `nowrap` value is a compromise that breaks lines exactly where there's an explicit break in the source text, but condenses other runs of space to a single space. This might be useful when you're trying to faithfully reproduce the line breaks in a classical manuscript or some other poetry where the line breaks are significant but the space between words isn't.

Backgrounds

The background of an element can be set to a color or an image. If it's set to an image, the image can be positioned differently relative to the content of the element. This is accomplished with the following five basic properties:

- `background-color`
- `background-image`
- `background-repeat`
- `background-attachment`
- `background-position`

Finally, there's a `background` shorthand property that allows you to set some or all of these five properties in one rule.

Fancy backgrounds are vastly overused. Anything other than a very light background color only makes your page harder to read and annoys users. I list these properties here for the sake of completeness, but I recommend that you use them sparingly, if at all.

None of the background properties are inherited. Each child element must specify the background it wants. However, it may appear as if background properties are inherited because the default is for the background to be transparent. The background of whatever element is drawn below an element will show through. Most of the time, this is the background of the parent element.

The background-color property

The `background-color` property can be set to the same values as the `color` property. However, rather than changing the color of the element's contents, it changes the color of the element's background on top of which the contents are drawn. For example, to draw a `SIGN` element with yellow text on a blue background, you would use this rule:

```
SIGN { color: yellow; background-color: blue}
```

You can also set the `background-color` to the keyword `transparent` (the default), which simply means that the background takes on the color or image of whatever the element is laying on top of, generally, the parent element.

The background-image property

The `background-image` property is either `none` (the default) or a URL (generally relative) where a bitmapped image file can be found. If it's a URL, the browser will load the image and use it as the background, much like the `BACKGROUND` attribute of the `BODY` element in HTML. For example, the following rule attaches the file shakespeare.jpg (shown in Figure 14-15) as the background for a `SYNOPSIS` element.

```
SYNOPSIS { background-image: url(shakespeare.jpg) }
```

Figure 14-15: The original, untiled, uncropped background image for the synopsis

Internet Explorer does not support fixed background images; Mozilla, Netscape, Safari, and Opera do.

The image referenced by the `background-image` property is drawn underneath the specified element, *not* underneath the browser pane like the `BACKGROUND` attribute of HTML's `BODY` element. Background images will generally not be the exact same size as the contents of the page. If the image is larger than the element's box, the image will be cropped. If the image is smaller than the element's box, it will be tiled vertically and horizontally. Figure 14-16 shows a background image that has tiled exactly far enough to cover the underlying content.

Tiling takes place across the element whose `background-image` property is set, *not* across the browser window. You can set background images for nonroot elements such as the `ACT` or the `SCENE`, if you like.

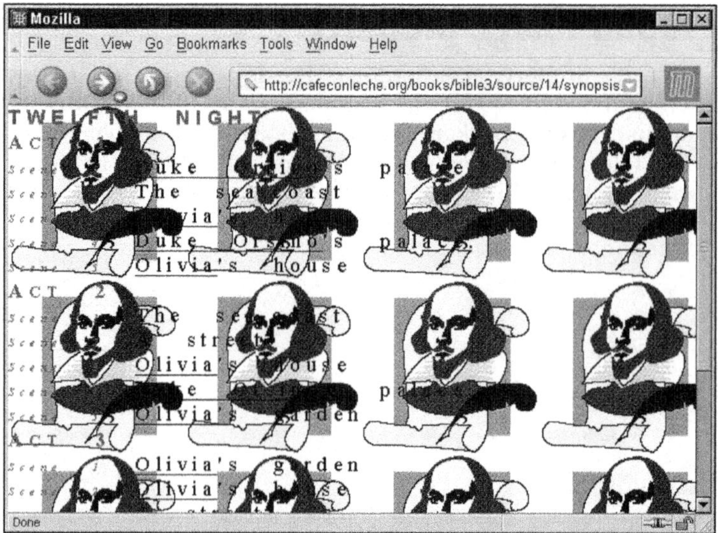

Figure 14-16: A tiled background image

The background-repeat property

The `background-repeat` property adjusts how background images are tiled across the screen. You can specify that background images are not tiled or are only tiled horizontally or vertically. Possible values for this property are as follows:

- `repeat`
- `repeat-x`
- `repeat-y`
- `no-repeat`

For example, to show only a single picture of Shakespeare, you would set the `background-repeat` of the `SYNOPSIS` element to `no-repeat`, like this:

```
SYNOPSIS { background-image:  url(shakespeare.jpg);
           background-repeat: no-repeat }
```

Figure 14-17 shows the result.

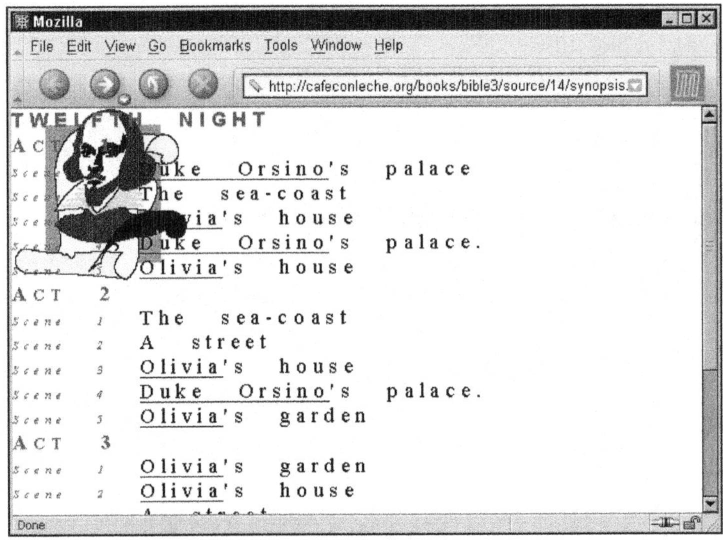

Figure 14-17: An untiled background image

To tile across but not down the page, set `background-repeat` to `repeat-x`, like this:

```
SYNOPSIS { background-image:  url(shakespeare.jpg);
           background-repeat: repeat-x }
```

The result is shown in Figure 14-18:

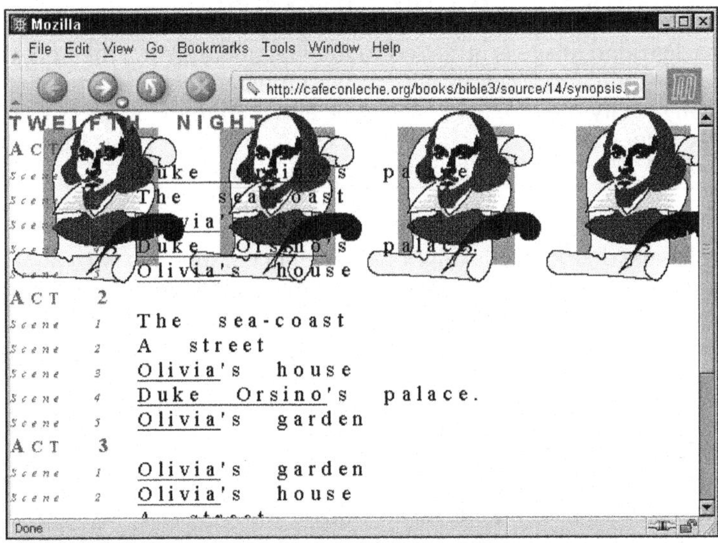

Figure 14-18: A background image tiled across but not down

To tile down but not across the page, as shown in Figure 14-19, set background-repeat to repeat-y, like this:

```
SYNOPSIS { background-image: url(shakespeare.jpg);
           background-repeat: repeat-y }
```

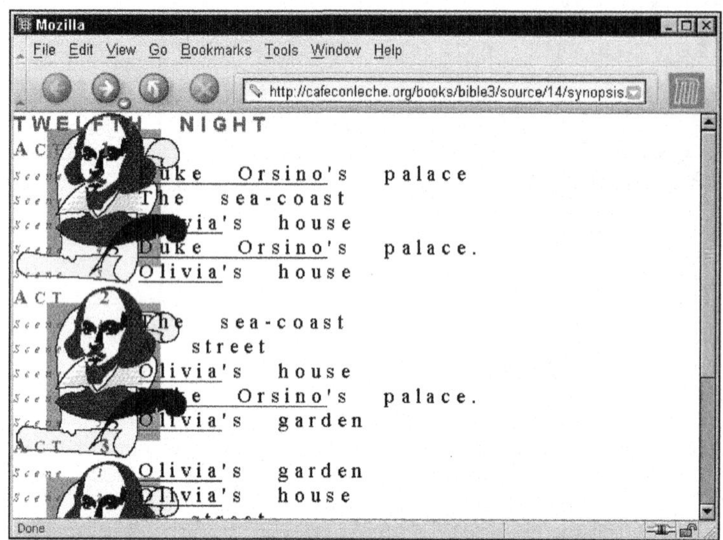

Figure 14-19: A background image tiled down but not across

The background-attachment property

In HTML, the background image is attached to the document. When the document is scrolled, the background image scrolls with it. With the background-attachment property, you can specify that the background be attached to the window or pane instead. Possible values are scroll and fixed. The default is scroll; that is, the background is attached to the document rather than the window.

However, with background-attachment set to fixed, the document scrolls but the background image doesn't. This might be useful in conjunction with an image that's big enough for a typical browser window but not big enough to be a backdrop for a large document when you don't want to tile the image. You would code that request like this:

```
SYNOPSIS { background-image: url(shakespeare.jpg);
           background-attachment: fixed;
           background-repeat: no-repeat }
```

Figure 14-20 shows the effect after a little scrolling.

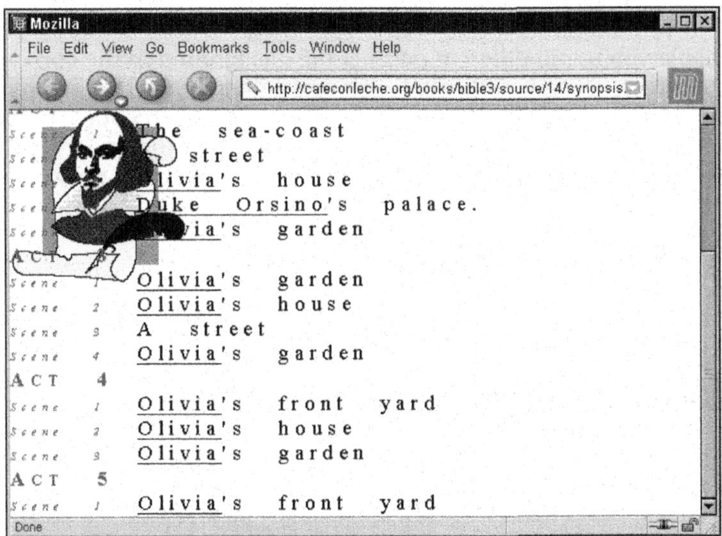

Figure 14-20: A fixed background image stays in the same position in the window even as the document scrolls.

The background-position property

By default, the upper left corner of a background image is aligned with the upper left corner of the element it's attached to. (See Figure 14-17 for an example.) Most of the time, this is exactly what you want. However, for those rare times when you want a different appearance, the `background-position` property allows you to move the background relative to the element.

You can specify the offset by using percentages of the width and height of the parent element, by using absolute lengths, or by using two of the following six keywords:

- `top`
- `center`
- `bottom`
- `left`
- `center`
- `right`

Percentages of parent element's width and height

Percentages enable you to pin different parts of the background to the corresponding part of the element. The *x* coordinate is given as a percentage ranging from 0% (left side) to 100% (right side). The *y* coordinate is given as a percentage ranging from 0% (top) to 100% (bottom). For example, this rule places the upper right corner of the image in the upper right corner of the `SYNOPSIS` element. Figure 14-21 shows the result.

```
SYNOPSIS { background-image: url(shakespeare.jpg);
           background-repeat: no-repeat;
           background-position: 100% 0% }
```

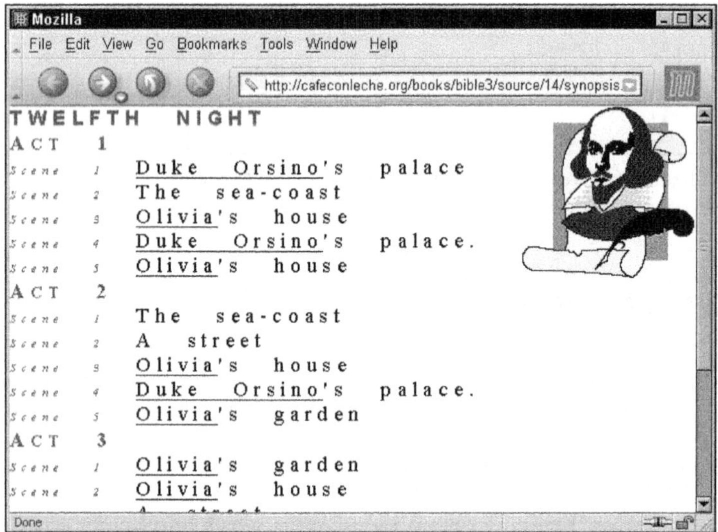

Figure 14-21: A background image aligned with the upper right corner of the content

Absolute lengths

Setting `background-position` to a length fixes the upper left corner of the background at an absolute position in the element. The next rule places the upper left corner of the background image shakespeare.jpg one centimeter to the right and two centimeters below the upper left corner of the element. Figure 14-22 shows the result.

```
SYNOPSIS { background-image: url(shakespeare.jpg);
           background-repeat: no-repeat;
           background-position: 1cm 2cm }
```

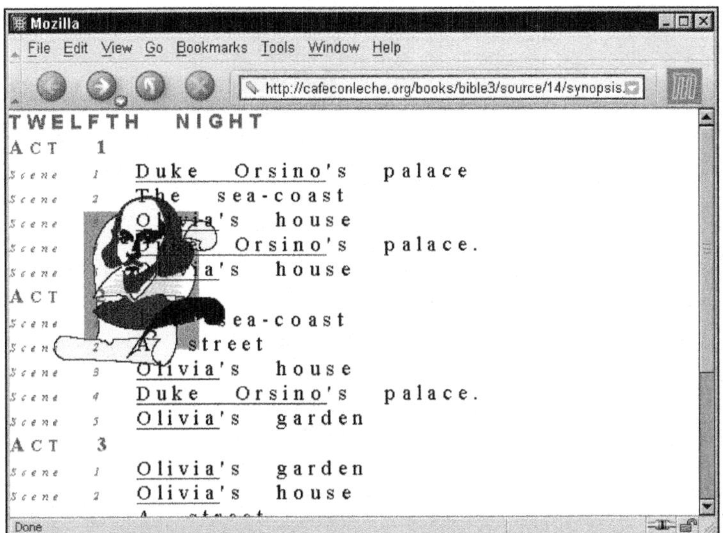

Figure 14-22: A background image positioned one centimeter to the right and two centimeters below the left corner of the element

Keywords

The `top left` and `left top` keywords are the same as 0% 0%. The `top`, `top center`, and `center top` are the same as 50% 0%. The `right top` and `top right` keywords are the same as 100% 0%. The `left`, `left center`, and `center left` keywords are the same as 0% 50%. The `center` and `center center` keywords are the same as 50% 50%. The `right`, `right center`, and `center right` keywords are the same as 100% 50%. The `bottom left` and `left bottom` keywords are the same as 0% 100%. The `bottom`, `bottom center`, and `center bottom` mean the same as 50% 100%. The `bottom right` and `right bottom` keywords are the same as 100% 100%. Figure 14-23 shows the positions for the different values.

For example, this rule positions the image in the top center of the synopsis, as shown in Figure 14-24:

```
SYNOPSIS { background-image: url(shakespeare.jpg);
           background-repeat: no-repeat;
           background-position: center top }
```

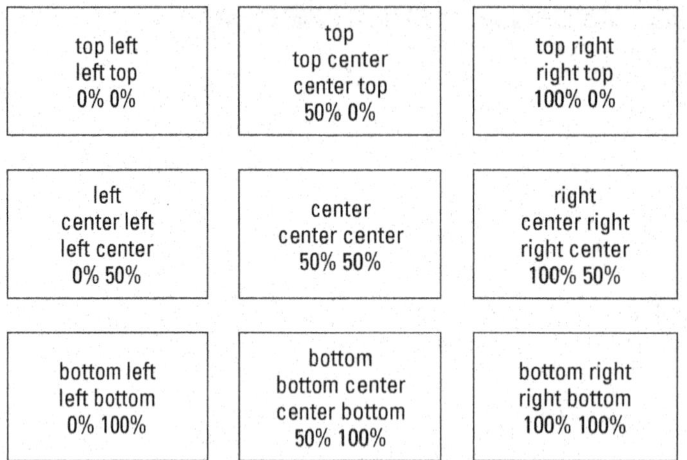

Figure 14-23: Relative positioning of background images

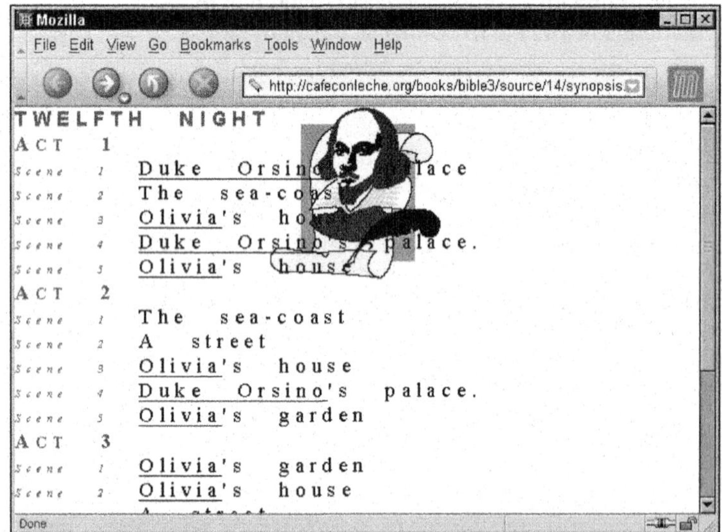

Figure 14-24: An untiled background image pinned to the top center of the SYNOPSIS element

If the `background-attachment` property has the value `fixed`, the image is placed relative to the windowpane instead of the element. This means that as the window is scrolled, the picture does not change its apparent position. It does not scroll with the document.

The background shorthand property

The `background` property is shorthand for setting the `background-color`, `background-image`, `background-repeat`, `background-attachment`, and `background-position` properties in a single rule. For example, to set `background-color` to `white`, `background-image` to shakespeare.jpg, `background-repeat` to `no-repeat`, and `background-attachment` to `fixed` in the `SYNOPSIS` element, you can use this rule:

```
SYNOPSIS {
  background: url(shakespeare.jpg) white no-repeat fixed
}
```

The preceding rule means exactly the same thing as this longer but more legible rule:

```
SYNOPSIS { background-image: url(shakespeare.jpg);
           background-color: white;
           background-repeat: no-repeat;
           background-attachment: fixed }
```

When you are using the `background` shorthand property, values for any or all of the five properties can be given in any order. However, none can occur more than once. For example, the upper right corner alignment rule used for Figure 14-21 could have been written like this instead:

```
SYNOPSIS { background: url(shakespeare.jpg) no-repeat 100% 0% }
```

Visibility

The `visibility` property controls whether the contents of an element are seen. The three possible values of this property are as follows:

- `visible`
- `hidden`
- `collapse`

If `visibility` is set to `visible`, the contents of the box, including all borders, are shown. This is the default. If `visibility` is set to `hidden`, the box's contents and border are not drawn. However, unlike an element whose `display` property is set to `none`, invisible boxes still take up space and affect the layout of the document. Setting `visibility` to `hidden` is not the same as setting `display` to `none`.

The `collapse` value is the same as `hidden` for most elements, except for table rows and columns. For table rows and columns, `collapse` hides the row or column, but it does not otherwise change the layout of the `table` as `hidden` would. That is, it acts almost exactly like `display: none`. However, you can't set `display` to both `none` and `table-row` or `table-column`, so for these elements, you have to use `visibility: collapse` instead.

For example, this rule hides the `SCENE_NUMBER` elements:

```
SCENE_NUMBER {visibility: hidden}
```

Figure 14-25 shows the result. Notice that the locations of each scene are still pushed over to the right in pretty much the same position they were in Figure 14-24. That's because the space on the left is taken up by the invisible `SCENE_NUMBER` elements.

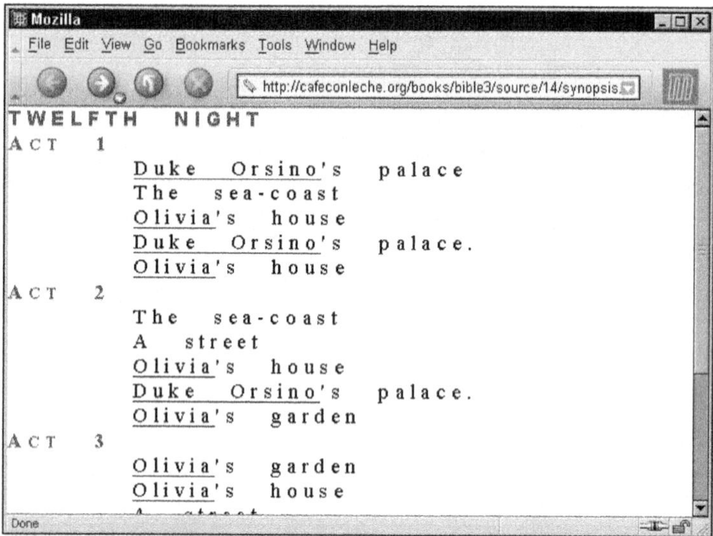

Figure 14-25: Invisible scene numbers

Content

The `content` property places data from the style sheet into the output document at a position indicated by a `:before` or `:after` pseudo-element. The value of the content property may be a string enclosed in quote marks. For example, this rule places an asterisk before and after each `SCENE` element:

```
SCENE:after  { content: "*"}
SCENE:before { content: "*"}
```

Mozilla, Internet Explorer, and Opera currently only support the `content` property on block-level elements. This would not work (although it should) for inline elements such as `SCENE_NUMBER`.

Figure 14-26 shows the result. The asterisks are just part of the display. They do not become part of the XML document itself, so even if you added characters or strings with special meaning to XML, < or &, for example, this would not make the document malformed because the document is never changed.

Mozilla
File Edit View Go Bookmarks Tools Window Help
http://cafeconleche.org/books/bible3/source/14/synopsis

TWELFTH NIGHT
ACT 1
* Scene 1 Duke Orsino's palace *
* Scene 2 The sea-coast *
* Scene 3 Olivia's house *
* Scene 4 Duke Orsino's palace. *
* Scene 5 Olivia's house *
ACT 2
* Scene 1 The sea-coast *
* Scene 2 A street *
* Scene 3 Olivia's house *
* Scene 4 Duke Orsino's palace. *
* Scene 5 Olivia's garden *
ACT 3
* Scene 1 Olivia's garden *
* Scene 2 Olivia's house *
Done

Figure 14-26: Asterisks have been added by the content property.

You can add more than a single character to the content. For example, this rule places a row of asterisks after each act:

```
ACT:after {content: "*****************"}
```

Quotes

Instead of a string literal, the value may be the keyword `open-quote` to insert an opening quote such as “ or `close-quote` to insert a closing quote character such as “. By default, the straight double quote " is used to quote items. However, you can change this with the `quotes` property. The value of this element is the quote pair to be used. For example, this rule says that if a `LOCATION` is quoted, the left quote should be “ and the right quote should be “:

```
LOCATION {quotes: """ """}
```

The quotes can be anything you want. For example, you could use the French guillemets like this:

```
LOCATION {quotes: "«" "»"}
```

You could do e-mail-style quoting by setting the left quote to > and the right quote to nothing at all, like this:

```
LOCATION {quotes: ">" ""}
```

There's not even any requirement that you actually use any sort of quote marks. For example, this rule uses these properties to put a right parenthesis after each SCENE_NUMBER element:

```
SCENE_NUMBER {quotes: "" ")"}
SCENE_NUMBER:before {content: open-quote}
SCENE_NUMBER:after {content: close-quote}
```

If quotes are likely to nest, you can specify multiple quote combinations. For example, this says that a quote inside a quote would be quoted with single quotation marks:

```
LOCATION {quotes: """ """ "'" "'"}
```

You have to match each open quote with a close quote, but if for some reason you don't want to show one or the other, you can use no-open-quote instead of open-quote and no-close-quote where you would normally use close-quote. The no-open-quote and no-close-quote keywords do not insert any characters; they just increment or decrement the level of nesting as if quotes had been used.

Attributes

Normally, the only content the reader sees is character data that came from element content in the XML document. However, you can use the attr() function as the value of the content property to insert an attribute value into the displayed document. For example, this rule inserts the content of the POEM element's TYPE attribute:

```
POEM:before {content: "A " + attr(type)}
```

URIs

One of the most interesting values of the content property is a URI. The URI is given in the same syntax used for the background-image property, and it means much the same thing: Load the document at the specified URI, and display it in the specified location. The browser is allowed to load and embed any kind of document it understands. For example, this rule says that the picture found at the URI `http://www.example.com/shakespeare.jpg` should be inserted before the `TITLE` element:

```
TITLE:before {
  content: uri(http://www.example.com/shakespeare.jpg)
}
```

This can be used for any kind of content that the browser understands: images, text files, PDFs, other XML documents, sound recordings, and more. For example, this rule suggests that a sound file should be played before the `TITLE` element:

```
TITLE:before {
  content: uri(http://www.example.com/12th_night.mp3)
}
```

All of this is subject to the abilities of the browser. For example, if one can't play an MP3 file, it will ignore this rule.

Counters

The final thing you can offer as the value of the `content` property is a *counter*. This is a running total of some type of element from the input document. This enables you to make simple numbered lists, to create outlines that are properly indented with different numbering systems for each level of the outline, to assign numbers to each part, chapter, and section, and more. Numbers can be recalculated on the fly whenever a document changes, rather than having to be painstakingly inserted by hand.

The `counter-increment` property creates and adds to the value of a named counter. The `counter()` function inserts the current value of a specified counter into the output. There's also a `counter-reset property` that returns a counter to its starting point. For example, suppose your XML document did not contain built-in scene numbers or act numbers; that is, suppose it looked like Listing 14-7:

Listing 14-7: A Synopsis of Shakespeare's *Twelfth Night* in XML without Explicit Act or Scene Numbers

```
<?xml version="1.0"?>
<?xml-stylesheet type="text/css" href="counters.css"?>
<SYNOPSIS>
  <TITLE>Twelfth Night</TITLE>

  <ACT>
    <SCENE>
      <LOCATION><CHARACTER>Duke Orsino</CHARACTER>'s palace
      </LOCATION>
```

Continued

Listing 14-7 *(continued)*

```
    </SCENE>
    <SCENE>
      <LOCATION>The sea-coast</LOCATION>
    </SCENE>
    <SCENE>
      <LOCATION><CHARACTER>Olivia</CHARACTER>'s house
      </LOCATION>
    </SCENE>
    <SCENE>
      <LOCATION><CHARACTER>Duke Orsino</CHARACTER>'s palace.
      </LOCATION>
    </SCENE>
    <SCENE>
      <LOCATION><CHARACTER>Olivia</CHARACTER>'s house
      </LOCATION>
    </SCENE>
  </ACT>

  <ACT>
    <SCENE>
      <LOCATION>The sea-coast</LOCATION>
    </SCENE>
    <SCENE>
      <LOCATION>A street</LOCATION>
    </SCENE>
    <SCENE>
      <LOCATION><CHARACTER>Olivia</CHARACTER>'s house
      </LOCATION>
    </SCENE>
    <SCENE>
      <LOCATION><CHARACTER>Duke Orsino</CHARACTER>'s palace.
      </LOCATION>
    </SCENE>
    <SCENE>
      <LOCATION><CHARACTER>Olivia</CHARACTER>'s garden
      </LOCATION>
    </SCENE>
  </ACT>

  <ACT>
    <SCENE>
      <LOCATION><CHARACTER>Olivia</CHARACTER>'s garden
      </LOCATION>
    </SCENE>
    <SCENE>
      <LOCATION><CHARACTER>Olivia</CHARACTER>'s house
      </LOCATION>
    </SCENE>
```

```
    <SCENE>
      <LOCATION>A street</LOCATION>
    </SCENE>
    <SCENE>
      <LOCATION><CHARACTER>Olivia</CHARACTER>'s garden
      </LOCATION>
    </SCENE>
  </ACT>

  <ACT>
    <SCENE>
      <LOCATION><CHARACTER>Olivia</CHARACTER>'s front yard
      </LOCATION>
    </SCENE>
    <SCENE>
      <LOCATION><CHARACTER>Olivia</CHARACTER>'s house
      </LOCATION>
    </SCENE>
    <SCENE>
      <LOCATION><CHARACTER>Olivia</CHARACTER>'s garden
      </LOCATION>
    </SCENE>
  </ACT>

  <ACT>
    <SCENE>
      <LOCATION><CHARACTER>Olivia</CHARACTER>'s front yard
      </LOCATION>
    </SCENE>
  </ACT>

</SYNOPSIS>
```

You can still insert scene numbers using counters. First, add a rule that increments a counter named "scene" by 1 with each SCENE element:

```
SCENE {counter: scene}
```

Next, add a rule that inserts the current value of the scene counter as well as the word "Scene" and a colon before each SCENE element:

```
SCENE:before {content: "Scene " counter(scene) ": "}
```

Finally, reset the scene counter to zero at the beginning of each act so that scenes start over from 1 in each act rather than counting continuously throughout the play:

```
ACT {counter-reset:scene 0}
```

It's not any harder to add an act counter. In fact, it's a little easier, because you don't have to reset it. These two rules suffice:

```
ACT {counter-increment: act}
ACT:before {content: "Act " counter(act) ": "}
```

In my tests, only Opera correctly applied this style sheet and rendered the document with numbered acts and scenes. Various versions of Internet Explorer, Mozilla, and Safari all failed. Regrettably, counters are not very reliable at the present time.

You can increment by a number other than 1 by adding a second value to the `counter-increment` property. For example, this rule increments the act counter by 2 with each act:

```
ACT {counter-increment: act 2}
```

By default, counters are decimal numbers. However, you can provide an optional second argument to the `counter()` function that changes the numbering style. The possible values are the same as for the `list-style-type` property discussed in Chapter 13; that is, `disc`, `circle`, `square`. `decimal`, `lower-roman`, `upper-roman`, `hebrew`, and so on.

If you'd like to use generated content as the list bullet instead of the standard bullet, set the `display` property of the `:before` or `:after` pseudo-element to marker. This must occur inside an element whose `display` property is set to `list-item`. For example, Listing 14-8 uses generated content as a marker for both `ACT` and `SCENE` lists.

Listing 14-8: **Using Scene Numbers as List Bullets**

```
SYNOPSIS, TITLE { display: block }
TITLE { font-family: Helvetica, Verdana, sans-serif;
        font-size: x-large; text-align: center }
SYNOPSIS { font-family: Times, "Times New Roman", serif;
           font-size: 14pt; text-align: justify }
ACT, SCENE, TITLE, SYNOPSIS { margin: 1ex }
SCENE {display: list-item; counter-increment: scene}
ACT {display: list-item; counter-increment: act}
SCENE:before {display: marker;
              content: "Scene " counter(scene) ": "}
ACT {counter-reset: scene 0}
ACT:before {content: "Act " counter(act) ": "}
```

Summary

This chapter discussed CSS's text and character-oriented properties. In this chapter, you learned the following:

- ✦ The `font-family` property specifies the face in which the text is drawn. Its value is a comma-separated list of family names, such as `Helvetica` and `"Times New Roman"`, and generic names, such as `sans-serif`, `serif`, `cursive`, `monospace`, and `fantasy`.
- ✦ The `font-size` property specifies how big text is as either an absolute length such as `12pt`, an absolute keyword such as `small`, a relative keyword such as `smaller`, or a percentage of the parent element's font size such as `80%`.
- ✦ The `font-stretch` property determines how loose or tight a font is; that is, how close the letters are together. Possible values include `normal` (the default), `wider`, `narrower`, `ultra-condensed`, `extra-condensed`, `condensed`, `semi-condensed`, `semi-expanded`, `expanded`, `extra-expanded`, and `ultra-expanded`.
- ✦ The `font-style` property can be set to `normal` (the default), `italic`, or `oblique`.
- ✦ The `font-variant` property can be set to `normal` (the default) or `small-caps`.
- ✦ The `font-weight` property determines how bold a font is. Possible values include the keywords `normal`, `bold`, `bolder`, and `lighter` as well as the numeric levels from `100` (the lightest) to `900` (the darkest).
- ✦ The `color` property can be set to a named color such as `fuchsia`, a hexadecimal triple such as `#FF00FF`, or a decimal triple such as `rgb(255, 0, 255)` to indicate the color of the foreground object.
- ✦ The `word-spacing` property gives a length to be used as extra space between each pair of words.
- ✦ The `letter-spacing` property gives a length to be used as extra space between each pair of characters.
- ✦ The `text-decoration` property can be set to `none` (the default), `underline`, `overline`, `line-through`, and/or `blink`.
- ✦ The `vertical-align` property determines where an object is placed between the top and bottom of its containing box. It can be set to an absolute length, a percentage of the vertical height of the box, or one of the keywords `baseline`, `sub`, `super`, `top`, `text-top`, `middle`, `bottom`, or `text-bottom`.
- ✦ The `text-transform` property can be set to `none` (the default), `capitalize`, `uppercase`, or `lowercase`.

- The text-align property can be set to left, right, center, or justify.
- The text-indent property specifies how far to indent the first line of a paragraph using either an absolute length or a percentage of the width of the paragraph.
- The text-shadow property places a shadow of a specified color, length, width, and blur radius on one corner of an element.
- The line-height property determines the vertical extension of a line box. It can be set to an absolute length or a percentage of the font size.
- The white-space property determines how white space is handled inside the element. Allowed values include normal (the default), pre, and nowrap.
- The background-color property sets the color of an element's background using the same values the color property uses for the foreground color.
- The background of an element can be set to an image using the background-image, background-repeat, background-attachment, and background-position properties.
- The visibility property controls whether the contents of an element are seen. It has three possible values: visible, hidden, and collapse.
- The content property places data from the style sheet into the output document at a position indicated by a :before or :after pseudo-element. The value of the content property can be a literal string, an attribute value loaded with the attr() function, an opening or closing quote mark defined by the quotes property, the value of a counter, or the document at a URI.

Although CSS is quite powerful when fully implemented, there are still some limits to what you can achieve with it. First, CSS can only attach styles to content that already appears in the document. It can only add very limited content to the document, and it cannot transform the content in any way, such as by sorting or reordering it. These needs are addressed by XSL, the Extensible Stylesheet Language. However, a more severe limitation is that you're limited to those parts of CSS that are reliably implemented across multiple browsers, a depressingly small subset of standard CSS. XSL, by contrast, can be implemented on the server side, so you're not restricted to only those parts that browsers actually implement. Chapter 15 explores XSL transformations and shows you how much farther they can take you.

✦ ✦ ✦

CHAPTER 15

XSL Transformations

In This Chapter

The Extensible Stylesheet Language (XSL) includes both a transformation language and a formatting language. Each of these is an XML application. The transformation language provides elements that define rules for how one XML document is transformed into another XML document. The transformed XML document may use the vocabulary of the original document, or it may use a completely different set of elements. In particular, it may use the elements defined by the second part of XSL, the formatting objects. This chapter discusses the transformation language half of XSL.

What Is XSL?

The transformation and formatting halves of XSL can function independently of each other. For instance, the transformation language can transform an XML document into a well-formed HTML file, and completely ignore XSL formatting objects. This is the style of XSL previewed in Chapter 5 and emphasized in this chapter. Furthermore, it's not absolutely required that a document written in XSL formatting objects be produced by using the transformation part of XSL on another XML document. For example, a program written in Java could read TeX or PDF files and translate them into XSL formatting objects.

In essence, XSL is two languages, not one. The first is a transformation language, the second a formatting language. The transformation language is useful independently of the formatting language. Its ability to move data from one XML representation to another makes it an important component of XML-based electronic commerce, electronic data interchange, metadata exchange, and any application that needs to convert between different XML representations of the same information. These uses are also united by their lack of concern with rendering data on a display for humans to read. They are purely about moving data from one computer system or program to another.

Consequently, many implementations of XSL focus exclusively on the transformation part and ignore the formatting objects. These are incomplete implementations, but nonetheless useful. Not all data must ultimately be rendered on a computer monitor or printed on paper.

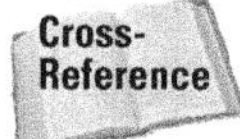

Chapter 16 discusses the XSL formatting language.

XSL is still under development. The language has changed radically in the past, and will almost certainly change again in the future. This chapter is based on the November 16, 1999, XSLT 1.0 Recommendation. Because XSLT is now an official Recommendation of the World Wide Web Consortium (W3C), I'm hopeful that any changes that do occur will simply add to the existing syntax without invalidating style sheets that adhere to the 1.0 spec. Indeed, the W3C has begun work on XSLT 2.0, and it does seem likely that all legal XSLT 1.0 documents will still be legal XSLT 2.0 documents.

Not all software has caught up to the 1.0 Recommendation, however. In particular, Version 5.5 and earlier of Internet Explorer only implement a very old working draft of XSLT that looks almost nothing like the finished standard. You should not expect most of the examples in this chapter to work with these versions of IE, even after substantial tweaking. Internet Explorer 6.0 does implement something close to XSLT 1.0. However, there are still some bugs and areas where Microsoft did not follow the standard.

Overview of XSL Transformations

In an XSL transformation, an XSLT processor reads both an XML document and an XSLT style sheet. The processor applies the instructions in the XSLT style sheet to the data in the input document to generate a new XML document or fragment thereof. Most processors can also output HTML. With some effort, most XSLT processors can also be made to output essentially arbitrary text, though XSLT is designed primarily for XML-to-XML and XML-to-HTML transformations.

Trees

As you learned in Chapter 6, every well-formed XML document forms a tree. A tree is a data structure composed of connected nodes beginning with a top node called the root. The root is connected to its child nodes, each of which is connected to zero or more children of its own, and so forth. A diagram of a tree looks much like a genealogical descendant chart that lists the descendants of a single ancestor. One useful property of a tree is that each node and its children also form a tree. Thus, a tree is a hierarchical structure of trees in which each tree is built out of smaller trees.

For the purposes of XSLT, elements, attributes, namespaces, processing instructions, comments, and parsed character data are counted as nodes. Furthermore, the document itself is the root of the tree. Thus, XSLT processors model an XML document as a tree that contains seven kinds of nodes:

✦ The root

✦ Elements

✦ Text

✦ Attributes

✦ Namespaces

✦ Processing instructions

✦ Comments

The DTD and document type declaration are specifically not included in this tree. However, a DTD may add default attribute values to some elements, which then become additional attribute nodes in the tree. Entity and character references are resolved into their replacement text. They are not counted as separate kinds of nodes themselves. Similarly, CDATA sections merely become part of text nodes. They are not treated differently than any other text.

For example, consider the XML document in Listing 15-1. This shows part of the periodic table of the elements. I'll be using this as an example in this chapter. The root `PERIODIC_TABLE` element contains `ATOM` child elements. Each `ATOM` element contains several child elements providing the atomic number, atomic weight, symbol, boiling point, and so forth. A `UNITS` attribute specifies the units for those elements that have units.

`ELEMENT` would be a more appropriate name here than `ATOM`. However, writing about `ELEMENT` elements and trying to distinguish between chemical elements and XML elements might create confusion. Thus, for the purposes of this chapter, `ATOM` seemed like the more legible option.

Listing 15-1: An XML Periodic Table with Two Atoms: Hydrogen and Helium

```
<?xml version="1.0"?>
<?xml-stylesheet type="application/xml" href="15-2.xsl"?>
<PERIODIC_TABLE>

  <ATOM STATE="GAS">
    <NAME>Hydrogen</NAME>
    <SYMBOL>H</SYMBOL>
    <ATOMIC_NUMBER>1</ATOMIC_NUMBER>
```

Continued

Listing 15-1 *(continued)*

```
    <ATOMIC_WEIGHT>1.00794</ATOMIC_WEIGHT>
    <BOILING_POINT UNITS="Kelvin">20.28</BOILING_POINT>
    <MELTING_POINT UNITS="Kelvin">13.81</MELTING_POINT>
    <DENSITY UNITS="grams/cubic centimeter">
      <!-- At 300K, 1 atm -->
      0.0000899
    </DENSITY>
  </ATOM>

  <ATOM STATE="GAS">
    <NAME>Helium</NAME>
    <SYMBOL>He</SYMBOL>
    <ATOMIC_NUMBER>2</ATOMIC_NUMBER>
    <ATOMIC_WEIGHT>4.0026</ATOMIC_WEIGHT>
    <BOILING_POINT UNITS="Kelvin">4.216</BOILING_POINT>
    <MELTING_POINT UNITS="Kelvin">0.95</MELTING_POINT>
    <DENSITY UNITS="grams/cubic centimeter"><!-- At 300K -->
      0.0001785
    </DENSITY>
  </ATOM>

</PERIODIC_TABLE>
```

You can find a much longer version of Listing 15-1 that includes all elements through atomic number 110 http://www.cafeconleche.org/examples/periodic_table/allelements.xml. This longer version is used in several of the examples in this chapter.

Figure 15-1 displays a tree diagram of this document. It begins at the top with the root node (not the same as the root element), which contains two child nodes, the xml-stylesheet processing instruction and the root element PERIODIC_TABLE. (The XML declaration is not directly visible to the XSLT processor and is not included in the tree the XSLT processor operates on.) The PERIODIC_TABLE element contains five child nodes. Two of them are obvious, the two ATOM elements. The other three are almost invisible. These are the boundary white-space-text nodes between <PERIODIC_TABLE> and <ATOM STATE="GAS">, between </ATOM> and <ATOM STATE="GAS">, and between </ATOM> and </PERIODIC_TABLE>. XSLT can see all the white space between tags. It's up to the style sheet to decide whether or not boundary white space is significant and should be preserved. Figure 15-1 is drawn under the assumption that these nodes aren't important, and thus omits them. However, other applications might treat them as significant.

Each ATOM element has an attribute node for its STATE attribute, text nodes for all the white space between tags, and a variety of child element nodes. Each child element contains a node for its text content, as well as nodes for any attributes, comments, and processing instructions it possesses. Notice, in particular, that many nodes are something other than elements. There are nodes for text, attributes, comments, namespaces, and processing instructions. Unlike CSS, XSL is not limited to working only with whole elements. It has a much more granular view of a document that enables you to base styles on comments, attributes, processing instructions, element content, and more.

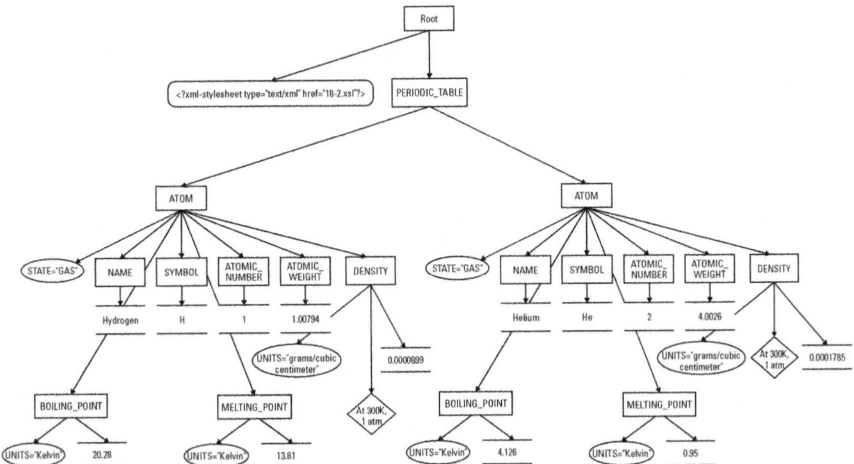

Figure 15-1: Listing 15-1 as a tree diagram

XSLT operates by transforming one XML tree into another XML tree. More precisely, an XSLT processor accepts as input a tree represented as an XML document and produces as output a new tree, also represented as an XML document or document fragment. Consequently, the transformation part of XSL is also called the tree construction part. The XSL transformation language contains operators for selecting nodes from the tree, reordering the nodes, and outputting nodes. If one of these nodes is an element node, it may be an entire tree itself. Remember that all these operators, both for input and output, are designed for operation on a tree.

The input must be an XML document. XSLT cannot transform from non-XML formats such as PDF, TeX, Microsoft Word, PostScript, MIDI, or others. HTML and SGML are borderline cases because they're so close to XML. XSLT can work with HTML and SGML documents that satisfy XML's well-formedness rules. However, XSLT cannot handle the wide variety of non-well-formed HTML and SGML that you encounter on most web sites and document production systems. XSLT is not a general-purpose language for transforming arbitrary data.

Most of the time, the output of an XSLT transformation is also an XML document. However, it can also be a result tree fragment that could be used as an external parsed entity in another XML document. (That is, it would be a well-formed XML document if it were enclosed in a single root element.) In other words, the output may not necessarily be a well-formed XML document, but it will at least be a plausible part of a well-formed XML document.

Tip

The `xsl:output` element and `disable-output-escaping` attribute discussed later in this chapter loosen this restriction somewhat.

Most XSLT processors also support output as HTML and/or raw text, although the specification does not require them to do so. To some extent, this allows you to transform to non-XML formats such as TeX, RTF, or PostScript. However, XSLT is not designed to make these transformations easy. It is designed for XML-to-XML transformations. If you need a non-XML output format, it will probably be easier to use XSLT to transform the XML to an intermediate XML format such as XSL-FO, and then use additional, non-XSLT software to transform that into the format you want.

XSLT style sheet documents

An XSLT document contains *template rules*. A template rule has a pattern specifying the nodes it matches and a template to be instantiated and output when the pattern is matched. When an XSLT processor transforms an XML document under the control of an XSLT style sheet, it walks the XML document tree starting at the root, and following an order defined by the template rules. As the processor visits each node in the XML document, it compares that node with the pattern of each template rule in the style sheet. When it finds a node that matches a template rule's pattern, it outputs the rule's template. This template generally includes some markup, new data, data copied out of the source XML document, as well as some directions about which nodes to process next.

XSLT uses XML to describe these rules, templates, and patterns. The root element of the XSLT document is either a `stylesheet` or a `transform` element in the `http://www.w3.org/1999/XSL/Transform` namespace. By convention, this namespace is mapped to the `xsl` prefix, but you're free to pick another prefix if you prefer. In this chapter, I always use the `xsl` prefix. From this point forward, it should be understood that the prefix `xsl` is mapped to the `http://www.w3.org/1999/XSL/Transform` namespace.

Tip

If you get the namespace URI wrong, either by using a URI from an older draft of the specification, such as `http://www.w3.org/TR/WD-xsl`, or simply by making a typo in the normal URI, the XSLT processor will output the style sheet document itself instead of the transformed input document. This is the result of the interaction between several obscure sections of the XSLT 1.0 specification. The details aren't important. What is important is that this very unusual behavior looks very much like a bug in the processor if you aren't familiar with it. If you are familiar with it, fixing it is trivial; just correct the namespace URI to `http://www.w3.org/1999/XSL/Transform`.

Each template rule is an `xsl:template` element. The pattern of the rule is placed in the `match` attribute of the `xsl:template` element. The output template is the content of the `xsl:template` element. All instructions in the template for doing things, such as selecting parts of the input tree to include in the output tree, are performed by XSLT elements. These are identified by the `xsl:` prefix on the element names. Elements that do not have an `xsl:` prefix are part of the result tree.

Listing 15-2 shows a very simple XSLT style sheet with two template rules. The first template rule matches the root element PERIODIC_TABLE. It replaces this element with an html element. The contents of the html element are the results of applying the other templates in the document to the contents of the PERIODIC_TABLE element.

The second template matches ATOM elements. It converts each ATOM element in the input document into a P element in the output document. The xsl:apply-templates rule inserts the text of the matched source element into the output document. Thus, the contents of a P element will be the text (but not the markup) contained in the corresponding ATOM element.

The xsl:stylesheet root element must have a version attribute with the value 1.0. It will normally also have an xmlns:xsl namespace declaration that binds the prefix xsl to the http://www.w3.org/1999/XSL/Transform namespace URI.

Listing 15-2: An XSLT Style Sheet for the Periodic Table with Two Template Rules

```
<?xml version="1.0"?>
<xsl:stylesheet version="1.0"
         xmlns:xsl="http://www.w3.org/1999/XSL/Transform">

  <xsl:template match="PERIODIC_TABLE">
    <HTML>
      <xsl:apply-templates/>
    </HTML>
  </xsl:template>

  <xsl:template match="ATOM">
    <P>
      <xsl:apply-templates/>
    </P>
  </xsl:template>

</xsl:stylesheet>
```

The xsl:transform element can be used in place of xsl:stylesheet if you prefer. This is an exact synonym with the same syntax, semantics, and attributes, as in this example:

```
<?xml version="1.0"?>
<xsl:transform version="1.0"
        xmlns:xsl="http://www.w3.org/1999/XSL/Transform">
  <!-- templates go here -->
</xsl:transform>
```

In this book, I will stick to xsl:stylesheet.

Where does the XML transformation happen?

There are three primary ways to transform XML documents into other formats, such as HTML, with an XSLT style sheet:

1. The XML document and associated style sheet are both served to the client (web browser), which then transforms the document as specified by the style sheet and presents it to the user.
2. The server applies an XSLT style sheet to an XML document to transform it to some other format (generally HTML) and sends the transformed document to the client (web browser).
3. A third program transforms the original XML document into some other format (often HTML) before the document is placed on the server. Both server and client only deal with the transformed document.

Each of these three approaches uses different software, although they all use the same XML documents and XSLT style sheets. A typical web server sending XML documents to Mozilla is an example of the first approach. A servlet-compatible web server using Apache's Cocoon (`http://cocoon.apache.org`) is an example of the second approach. A human using Michael Kay's command-line Saxon program (`http://saxon.sourceforge.net`) to transform XML documents to HTML documents, then placing the HTML documents on a web server is an example of the third approach. However, these all use the same XSLT language.

In this chapter, I emphasize the third approach, primarily because at the time of this writing, specialized converter programs, such as Michael Kay's Saxon and the Gnome Project's xsltproc (`http://xmlsoft.org/XSLT.html`), provide the most complete and accurate implementations of the XSLT specification. Furthermore, this approach offers the broadest compatibility with legacy web browsers and servers, whereas the first approach requires a more recent browser than many users use, and the second approach requires special web server software. In practice, though, requiring a different server is not nearly as onerous as requiring a particular client. You, yourself, can install your own special server software; but you cannot rely on your visitors to install particular client software.

Using xsltproc

xsltproc is a character mode application written in C. It was originally developed for Linux, but has been ported to most common UNIXes, Windows, and Mac OS X. It may be installed by default on a few Linux distros, but most users will need to download it from `http://xmlsoft.org/XSLT/downloads.html` first. You'll also need to install libxml, the XML parser it depends on. You can download this from `http://www.xmlsoft.org/downloads.html`.

On Windows, you'll also need to install the iconv library, which you can get from the same site. All three libraries are distributed as zip files. When unzipped, these archives each contain a lib and util directory. Simply copy the complete contents of all three lib and util directories to your C:\WINDOWS or C:\WINNT directory.

Although I primarily use xsltproc in this chapter, the examples should work with Saxon, Xalan, or any other XSLT processor that implements the XSLT 1.0 Recommendation. Some processors may produce slightly different output that does not affect the final results, especially when outputting HTML. For example, they may indent the tags a little differently, or add a `META` tag or two to the `HEAD`. Normally these details aren't very relevant, but if they concern you, you can control them using the `xsl:output` instruction discussed toward the end of this chapter.

After everything's installed in the right locations, you run xsltproc by typing the following at the shell prompt or in a DOS window:

```
C:\> xsltproc stylesheet.xsl document.xml
```

The first argument is the style sheet. The second argument is the XML document to transform. You can add additional filenames or URLs to transform more than one document. By default, the output is printed in the same shell prompt/DOS window where you launched the processor. To redirect the output into a file, you can use the `-o` option. For example, this command applies the style sheet in Listing 15-2 to the document in Listing 15-1, and puts the output in the file 15-3.html:

```
C:\> xsltproc -o 15.3.html 15-2.xsl 15-1.xml
```

Listing 15-2 transforms input documents to well-formed HTML files, as discussed in Chapter 6. However, you can transform from any XML application to any other as long as you can write a style sheet to support the transformation. For example, you can imagine a style sheet that transforms from Vector Markup Language (VML) documents to Scalable Vector Graphics (SVG) documents:

```
% xsltproc -o pinktriangle.svg VMLToSVG.xsl pinktriangle.vml
```

Most other command-line XSLT processors behave similarly, though of course they'll have different command-line arguments and options.

Listing 15-3 shows the output of running Listing 15-1 through xsltproc with the XSLT style sheet in Listing 15-2. Notice that xsltproc does not attempt to clean up the HTML it generates, which has a lot of white space. This is not important because ultimately you want to view the file in a web browser that trims white space. Figure 15-2 shows Listing 15-3 loaded into Netscape Navigator 3.0. Because Listing 15-3 is standard HTML, you don't need an XML-capable browser to view it.

Listing 15-3: The HTML Produced by Applying the Style Sheet in Listing 15-2 to the XML in Listing 15-1

```
<HTML>

  <P>
    Hydrogen
    H
    1
    1.00794
    20.28
    13.81


      0.0000899

  </P>

  <P>
    Helium
    He
    2
    4.0026
    4.216
    0.95

      0.0001785

  </P>

</HTML>
```

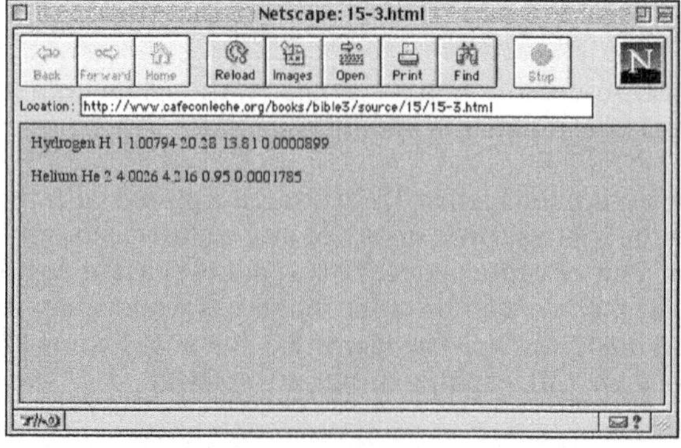

Figure 15-2: The page produced by applying the style sheet in Listing 15-2 to the XML document in Listing 15-1

Browser display of XML files with XSLT style sheets

Instead of preprocessing the XML document, you can send the client both the XML file and the XSLT file that describes how to render it. The client is responsible for applying the style sheet to the document and rendering it accordingly. This is more work for the client, but places much less load on the server. In this case, the XSLT style sheet must transform the document into an XML vocabulary the client understands. HTML is a likely choice, though other XML formats are options as well.

Attaching an XSLT style sheet to an XML document is easy. Simply insert an `xml-stylesheet` processing instruction in the prolog immediately after the XML declaration. This processing instruction should have a `type` attribute with the value `application/xml` and an `href` attribute whose value is a URL pointing to the style sheet, as shown here:

```
<?xml version="1.0"?>
<?xml-stylesheet type="application/xml" href="15-2.xsl"?>
```

This is also how you attach a CSS style sheet to a document. The only difference here is that the `type` attribute has the value `application/xml` instead of `text/css`.

In the not too distant future, the more specific MIME media type `application/xslt+xml` will be available to distinguish XSLT documents from all other XML documents. After browsers are revised to support this, you will be able to write the `xml-stylesheet` processing instruction like this instead:

```
<?xml-stylesheet type="application/xslt+xml"
                 href="15-2.xsl"?>
```

Internet Explorer's XSLT support differs from the XSLT 1.0 Recommendation in several ways. Most importantly, it expects the nonstandard MIME media type `text/xsl` in the `xml-stylesheet` processing instruction rather than `application/xml`. Otherwise, Internet Explorer 6.0 has reasonable, though imperfect, support for XSLT.

Internet Explorer 5.0 and 5.5 do not support XSLT 1.0 out of the box. They support an earlier, beta version of XSLT with some Microsoft extensions. You can tell the difference by looking at the namespace URI. Style sheets written for IE5 use the URI `http://www.w3.org/TR/WD-xsl`. Style sheets written for all other processors use the URI `http://www.w3.org/1999/XSL/Transform`. To work with XML, it really helps to upgrade to Internet Explorer 6.0 or later. If you must stick with IE 5.5 or earlier, you can upgrade the MSXML parser instead. Download MSXML 3.0 from `http://msdn.microsoft.com/library/default.asp?url=/downloads/list/xmlgeneral.asp`. This installer does not automatically replace the earlier, nonstandard-compliant MSXML 2.5 that is bundled. To replace the old version, you also have to download and run a separate program called xmlinst.exe, which you can get from the same page where you found MSXML 3.0. Otherwise, you'll still be stuck with the old, out-of-date beta version of XSLT.

MSXML 4.0 is also available but cannot replace the MSXML 2.5 bundled with Internet Explorer 5.5 and earlier. If you're using Internet Explorer 5.x, you should use MSXML 3.0, not an earlier, nor a later, version.

Even once this is done, there are still some bugs and areas where Microsoft did not follow the specification, so this is not quite a complete implementation of XSLT 1.0. If you find that something in this chapter doesn't work in Internet Explorer, please complain to Microsoft, not to me.

XSL Templates

Template rules defined by `xsl:template` elements are the most important part of an XSLT style sheet. These associate particular output with particular input. Each `xsl:template` element has a `match` attribute that specifies which nodes of the input document the template is instantiated for.

The content of the `xsl:template` element is the template to be instantiated. A template may contain both text, which will appear literally in the output document, and XSLT instructions that copy data from the input XML document to the result. Because all XSLT instructions are in the `http://www.w3.org/1999/XSL/Transform` namespace, it's easy to distinguish between the elements that are literal data to be copied to the output and instructions. For example, here is a template that matches the root node of the input tree:

```
<xsl:template match="/">
  <HTML>
    <HEAD>
    </HEAD>
    <BODY>
    </BODY>
  </HTML>
</xsl:template>
```

When the XSLT processor reads the input document, the first node it sees is the root. This rule matches that root node, and tells the XSLT processor to emit this element:

```
<HTML>
  <HEAD>
  </HEAD>
  <BODY>
  </BODY>
</HTML>
```

This text is well-formed HTML. Because the XSLT document is itself an XML document, its contents — templates included — must be well-formed XML.

If you were to use the preceding rule, and only the preceding rule, in an XSLT style sheet, the output would be limited to the above six tags. That's because no instructions in the rule tell the formatter to move down the tree and look for further matches against the templates in the style sheet.

The xsl:apply-templates element

To get beyond the root, you have to tell the formatting engine to process the children of the root. In general, to include content in the child nodes, you have to recursively process the nodes through the XML document. The element that does this is `xsl:apply-templates`. An `xsl:apply-templates` element tells the processor to compare each child node of the matched source element against the templates in the style sheet and, if a match is found, output the template for the matched node. The template for the matched node may itself contain `xsl:apply-templates` elements to search for matches for its children. When the XSLT engine processes a node, the node is treated as a complete tree. This is the advantage of the tree structure. Each part can be treated the same way as the whole. For example, Listing 15-4 is an XSLT style sheet that uses the `xsl:apply templates` element to process the child nodes.

Listing 15-4: An XSLT Style Sheet That Recursively Processes the Children of the Root

```
<?xml version="1.0"?>
<xsl:stylesheet version="1.0"
  xmlns:xsl="http://www.w3.org/1999/XSL/Transform">

  <xsl:template match="/">
    <HTML>
      <xsl:apply-templates/>
    </HTML>
  </xsl:template>

  <xsl:template match="PERIODIC_TABLE">
    <BODY>
      <xsl:apply-templates/>
    </BODY>
  </xsl:template>

  <xsl:template match="ATOM">
    An Atom
  </xsl:template>

</xsl:stylesheet>
```

When this style sheet is applied to Listing 15-1, here's what happens:

1. The root node is compared with all template rules in the style sheet. It matches the first one.
2. The `<HTML>` tag is written out.
3. The `xsl:apply-templates` element causes the formatting engine to process the child nodes of the root node of the input document.
   A. The first child of the root, the `xml-stylesheet` processing instruction, is compared with the template rules. It doesn't match any of them, so no output is generated.
   B. The second child of the root node of the input document, the root element `PERIODIC_TABLE`, is compared with the template rules. It matches the second template rule.
   C. The `<BODY>` tag is written out.
   D. The `xsl:apply-templates` element in the `body` element causes the XSLT engine to process the child nodes of `PERIODIC_TABLE`.
      a. The first child of the `PERIODIC_TABLE` element, that is the Hydrogen `ATOM` element, is compared with the template rules. It matches the third template rule.
      b. The text "An Atom" is output.
      c. The second child of the `PERIODIC_TABLE` element, that is the Helium `ATOM` element, is compared with the template rules. It matches the third template rule.
      d. The text "An Atom" is output.
   E. The `</BODY>` tag is written out.
4. The `</HTML>` tag is written out.
5. Processing is complete.

The end result is as follows:

```
<HTML>
<BODY>


    An Atom



    An Atom


</BODY>
</HTML>
```

I actually skipped a couple of steps here. The boundary white space text nodes were also processed. Their values were copied by the default template rules, which is why there's so much white space in the output. You'll learn about the default template rules for text nodes shortly.

The select attribute

To replace the text "An Atom" with the name of the ATOM element as given by its NAME child, you need to specify that templates should be applied to the NAME children of the ATOM element. To choose a particular set of children instead of all children, supply xsl:apply-templates with a select attribute designating the children to be selected, as in this template rule:

```
<xsl:template match="ATOM">
  <xsl:apply-templates select="NAME"/>
</xsl:template>
```

The select attribute uses the same kind of patterns as the match attribute of the xsl:template element. For now, I'll stick to simple names of elements; but in the section on patterns for matching and selecting later in this chapter, you'll see many more possibilities for both select and match. If no select attribute is present, all child element, text, comment, and processing instruction nodes are selected. (Attribute and namespace nodes are not selected.)

The result of adding this rule to the style sheet of Listing 15-5 and applying it to Listing 15-1 is this:

```
<HTML>
<BODY>

  Hydrogen

  Helium

</BODY>
</HTML>
```

Computing the Value of a Node with xsl:value-of

The xsl:value-of element computes the string value of something (most of the time, though not always, something in the input document) and copies that plain text value into the output document. The select attribute of the xsl:value-of element specifies exactly which something's value is being computed.

The exact content of the string value depends on the type of the node. The most common type of node is element, and the value of an element node is particularly simple. It's the concatenation of all the character data (but not markup) between the element's start-tag and end-tag. For example, the first ATOM element in Listing 15-1 is as follows:

```
<ATOM STATE="GAS">
  <NAME>Hydrogen</NAME>
  <SYMBOL>H</SYMBOL>
  <ATOMIC_NUMBER>1</ATOMIC_NUMBER>
  <ATOMIC_WEIGHT>1.00794</ATOMIC_WEIGHT>
  <BOILING_POINT UNITS="Kelvin">20.28</BOILING_POINT>
  <MELTING_POINT UNITS="Kelvin">13.81</MELTING_POINT>
  <DENSITY UNITS="grams/cubic centimeter">
    <!-- At 300K, 1 atm -->
    0.0000899
  </DENSITY>
</ATOM>
```

The value of this element is:

```

Hydrogen
H
1
1.00794
1
20.28
13.81


  0.0000899

```

I calculated this value by stripping out all the tags and comments. Everything else including white space was left intact. The values of the other six node types are calculated similarly, mostly in obvious ways. Table 15-1 summarizes.

Table 15-1
Values of Nodes

Node Type	*Value*
Root	The value of the root element
Element	The concatenation of all parsed character data contained in the element, including character data in any of the descendants of the element
Text	The text of the node; essentially the node itself

Node Type	Value
Attribute	The normalized attribute value as specified by Section 3.3.3 of the XML 1.0 Recommendation; basically the attribute value after entities are resolved and leading and trailing white space is stripped; does not include the name of the attribute, the equals sign, or the quotation marks
Namespace	The URI of the namespace
Processing instruction	The data in the processing instruction; does not include the target, <? or ?>
Comment	The text of the comment, <!-- and --> not included

For example, suppose you want to replace the literal text "An Atom" with the name of the ATOM element, as given by the contents of its NAME child. You can replace "An Atom" with `<xsl:value-of select="NAME"/>`, like this:

```
<xsl:template match="ATOM">
  <xsl:value-of select="NAME"/>
</xsl:template>
```

Then, when you apply the style sheet to Listing 15-1, this text is generated:

```
<HTML>
<BODY>

  Hydrogen

  Helium

</BODY>
</HTML>
```

The item whose value is selected, the NAME element in this example, is relative to the current node. The current node is the item matched by the template, the particular ATOM element in this example. Thus, when the Hydrogen ATOM is matched by `<xsl:template match="ATOM">`, the Hydrogen ATOM's NAME is selected by xsl:value-of. When the Helium ATOM is matched by `<xsl:template match="ATOM">`, the Helium ATOM's NAME is selected by xsl:value-of.

Processing Multiple Elements with xsl:for-each

The xsl:value-of element should only be used in contexts where it is obvious which node's value is being taken. If there are multiple possible items that could be selected, only the first one will be chosen. For example, this is a poor rule because a typical PERIODIC_TABLE element contains more than one ATOM:

```
<xsl:template match="PERIODIC_TABLE">
  <xsl:value-of select="ATOM"/>
</xsl:template>
```

There are two ways of processing multiple elements in turn. The first method you've already seen. Simply use `xsl:apply-templates` with a `select` attribute that chooses the particular elements that you want to visit, like this:

```
<xsl:template match="PERIODIC_TABLE">
  <xsl:apply-templates select="ATOM"/>
</xsl:template>

<xsl:template match="ATOM">
  <xsl:value-of select="."/>
</xsl:template>
```

The `select="."` in the second template tells the formatter to take the value of the matched node, `ATOM` in this example.

The second option is `xsl:for-each`. The `xsl:for-each` element processes each element chosen by its `select` attribute in turn. However, no additional template rule is required. Instead, the content of the `xsl:for-each` element serves as a template. For example:

```
<xsl:template match="PERIODIC_TABLE">
  <xsl:for-each select="ATOM">
    <xsl:value-of select="."/>
  </xsl:for-each>
</xsl:template>
```

This is useful when you need to format the same content differently in different places in the style sheet.

Patterns for Matching Nodes

The `match` attribute of the `xsl:template` element supports a complex syntax that allows you to indicate precisely which nodes you do and do not want to match. The `select` attribute of `xsl:apply-templates`, `xsl:value-of`, `xsl:for-each`, `xsl:copy-of`, and `xsl:sort` supports an even more powerful superset of this syntax called XPath that allows you to express exactly which nodes you do and do not want to select. Various patterns for matching and selecting nodes are discussed in following sections.

Matching the root node

In order that the output document be well-formed, the first thing output from an XSL transformation should be the output document's root element. Consequently, XSLT style sheets generally start with a rule that applies to the root node. To specify the root node in a rule, you give its match attribute the value "/", as in the following example:

```
<xsl:template match="/">
  <DOCUMENT>
    <xsl:apply-templates/>
  </DOCUMENT>
</xsl:template>
```

This rule applies to the root node and only the root node of the input tree. When the root node is read, the tag <DOCUMENT> is output, the children of the root node are processed, then the </DOCUMENT> tag is output. This rule overrides the default rule for the root node. Listing 15-5 shows a style sheet with a single rule that applies to the root node.

Listing 15-5: An XSLT Style Sheet with One Rule for the Root Node

```
<?xml version="1.0"?>
<xsl:stylesheet version="1.0"
  xmlns:xsl="http://www.w3.org/1999/XSL/Transform">

    <xsl:template match="/">
      <HTML>
        <HEAD>
          <TITLE>Atomic Number vs. Atomic Weight</TITLE>
        </HEAD>
        <BODY>
          <TABLE>
            Atom data will go here
          </TABLE>
        </BODY>
      </HTML>
    </xsl:template>

</xsl:stylesheet>
```

Because this style sheet only provides a rule for the root node, and because that rule's template does not specify any further processing of child nodes, only literal output that's included in the template is inserted in the resulting document. In other words, the result of applying the style sheet in Listing 15-5 to Listing 15-1 (or any other well-formed XML document) is this:

```
<HTML>
<HEAD>
<TITLE>Atomic Number vs. Atomic Weight</TITLE>
</HEAD>
```

```
<BODY>
<TABLE>
          Atom data will go here
        </TABLE>
<BODY>
</HTML>
```

Matching element names

As previously mentioned, the most basic pattern contains a single element name that matches all elements with that name. For example, this template matches ATOM elements and makes their ATOMIC_NUMBER children bold:

```
<xsl:template match="ATOM">
  <B><xsl:value-of select="ATOMIC_NUMBER"/></B>
</xsl:template>
```

Listing 15-6 demonstrates a style sheet that expands on Listing 15-5. First, an xsl:apply-templates element is included in the template rule for the root node. This element uses a select attribute to ensure that only PERIODIC_TABLE elements are processed.

Second, a rule that only applies to PERIODIC_TABLE elements is created using match="PERIODIC_TABLE". This rule sets up the header for the table, and then applies templates to form the body of the table from ATOM elements.

Finally, the ATOM rule specifically selects the ATOM element's NAME, ATOMIC_NUMBER, and ATOMIC_WEIGHT child elements with <xsl:value-of select="NAME"/>, <xsl:value-of select="ATOMIC_NUMBER"/>, and <xsl:value-of select= "ATOMIC_WEIGHT"/>. These are wrapped up inside HTML's TR and TD elements, so that the end result is a table of atomic numbers matched to atomic weights. Figure 15-3 shows the output of applying the style sheet in Listing 15-6 to the complete periodic table document rendered in Netscape Navigator.

One thing you might want to note about this style sheet: The exact order of the NAME, ATOMIC_NUMBER, and ATOMIC_WEIGHT elements in the input document is irrelevant. They appear in the output in the order they were selected; that is, first number, then weight. Conversely, the individual atoms are sorted in alphabetical order as they appear in the input document. Later, you'll see how to use an xsl:sort element to change that so you can arrange the atoms in the more conventional atomic number order.

Listing 15-6: Templates Applied to Specific Classes of Element with Select

```
<?xml version="1.0"?>
<xsl:stylesheet version="1.0"
  xmlns:xsl="http://www.w3.org/1999/XSL/Transform">

    <xsl:template match="/">
      <HTML>
        <HEAD>
          <TITLE>Atomic Number vs. Atomic Weight</TITLE>
        </HEAD>
        <BODY>
          <xsl:apply-templates select="PERIODIC_TABLE"/>
        </BODY>
      </HTML>
    </xsl:template>

    <xsl:template match="PERIODIC_TABLE">
      <H1>Atomic Number vs. Atomic Weight</H1>
      <TABLE>
        <TH>Element</TH>
        <TH>Atomic Number</TH>
        <TH>Atomic Weight</TH>
          <xsl:apply-templates select="ATOM"/>
      </TABLE>
    </xsl:template>

    <xsl:template match="ATOM">
      <TR>
        <TD><xsl:value-of select="NAME"/></TD>
        <TD><xsl:value-of select="ATOMIC_NUMBER"/></TD>
        <TD><xsl:value-of select="ATOMIC_WEIGHT"/></TD>
      </TR>
    </xsl:template>

</xsl:stylesheet>
```

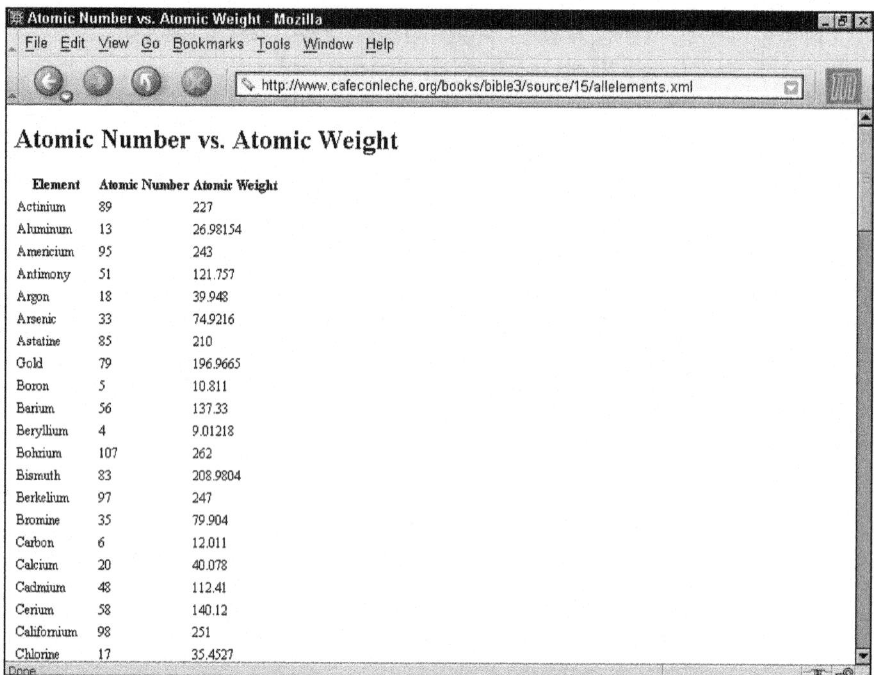

Atomic Number vs. Atomic Weight

Element	Atomic Number	Atomic Weight
Actinium	89	227
Aluminum	13	26.98154
Americium	95	243
Antimony	51	121.757
Argon	18	39.948
Arsenic	33	74.9216
Astatine	85	210
Gold	79	196.9665
Boron	5	10.811
Barium	56	137.33
Beryllium	4	9.01218
Bohrium	107	262
Bismuth	83	208.9804
Berkelium	97	247
Bromine	35	79.904
Carbon	6	12.011
Calcium	20	40.078
Cadmium	48	112.41
Cerium	58	140.12
Californium	98	251
Chlorine	17	35.4527

Figure 15-3: A table showing atomic number versus atomic weight in Netscape Navigator

Wildcards

Sometimes you want a single template to apply to more than one element. You can indicate that a template matches all elements by using the asterisk wildcard (*) in place of an element name in the `match` attribute. For example, this template says that all input elements should be wrapped in a `P` element:

```
<xsl:template match="*">
  <P>
    <xsl:value-of select="."/>
  </P>
</xsl:template>
```

Of course this is probably more than you want. You'd like to use the template rules already defined for `PERIODIC_TABLE` and `ATOM` elements as well as the root node, and only use this rule for the other elements. Fortunately, you can. In the event that two rules both match a single node, by default the more specific one takes precedence. In this case, that means that `ATOM` elements will use the template with `match="ATOM"` instead of a template that merely has `match="*"`. However, `NAME`, `BOILING_POINT`, `ATOMIC_NUMBER` and other elements that don't match a more specific template will cause the `match="*"` template to activate.

You can place a namespace prefix in front of the asterisk to indicate that only elements in a particular namespace should be matched. For example, this template matches all SVG elements, presuming that the prefix `svg` is mapped to the normal SVG URI `http://www.w3.org/2000/svg` in the style sheet.

```
<xsl:template match="svg:*">
  <DIV>
    <xsl:value-of select="."/>
  </DIV>
</xsl:template>
```

Of course in Listing 15-1, there aren't any elements from this namespace, so this template wouldn't produce any output. However, it might when applied to a different document that did include some SVG.

Matching children with /

You're not limited to the children of the current node in `match` attributes. You can use the / symbol to match hierarchies of elements. Alone, the / symbol refers to the root node. However, between two names it indicates that the second is the child of the first. For example, `ATOM/NAME` refers to `NAME` elements that are children of `ATOM` elements.

In `xsl:template` elements, this enables you to match only some of the elements of a given kind. For example, this template rule marks `SYMBOL` elements that are children of `ATOM` elements strong. It does nothing to `SYMBOL` elements that are not direct children of `ATOM` elements.

```
<xsl:template match="ATOM/SYMBOL">
  <STRONG><xsl:value-of select="."/></STRONG>
</xsl:template>
```

Remember that this rule selects `SYMBOL` elements that are children of `ATOM` elements, not `ATOM` elements that have `SYMBOL` children. In other words, the `.` in `<xsl:value-of select="."/>` refers to the `SYMBOL` and not to the `ATOM`.

You can specify deeper matches by stringing patterns together. For example, `PERIODIC_TABLE/ATOM/NAME` selects `NAME` elements whose parent is an `ATOM` element whose parent is a `PERIODIC_TABLE` element.

You can also use the * wildcard to substitute for an arbitrary element name in a hierarchy. For example, this template rule applies to all `SYMBOL` elements that are grandchildren of a `PERIODIC_TABLE` element.

```
<xsl:template match="PERIODIC_TABLE/*/SYMBOL">
  <STRONG><xsl:value-of select="."/></STRONG>
</xsl:template>
```

Finally, as previously described, a / by itself selects the root node of the document. For example, this rule applies to all PERIODIC_TABLE elements that are root elements of the document:

```
<xsl:template match="/PERIODIC_TABLE">
  <HTML><xsl:apply-templates/></HTML>
</xsl:template>
```

While / refers to the root node, /* refers to the root element, whatever it is. For example, this template doesn't care whether the root element is PERIODIC_TABLE, DOCUMENT, or SCHENECTADY. It produces the same output in all cases.

```
<xsl:template match="/*">
  <HTML>
    <HEAD>
      <TITLE>Atomic Number vs. Atomic Weight</TITLE>
    </HEAD>
    <BODY>
      <xsl:apply-templates/>
    </BODY>
  </HTML>
</xsl:template>
```

Matching descendants with //

Sometimes, especially with an uneven hierarchy, you'll find it easier to bypass intermediate nodes and simply select all the elements of a given type, whether they're immediate children, grandchildren, great-grandchildren, or what have you. The double slash, //, refers to a descendant at an arbitrary level. For example, this template rule applies to all NAME descendants of PERIODIC_TABLE, no matter how deep:

```
<xsl:template match="PERIODIC_TABLE//NAME">
  <EM><xsl:value-of select="."/></EM>
</xsl:template>
```

The periodic table example is fairly shallow, but this trick becomes more important in deeper and less predictable hierarchies, especially when an element can contain other elements of its own type (for example, an ATOM contains an ATOM).

The // operator at the beginning of a pattern selects any descendant of the root node. For example, this template rule processes all ATOMIC_NUMBER elements while completely ignoring their location:

```
<xsl:template match="//ATOMIC_NUMBER">
  <EM><xsl:value-of select="."/></EM>
</xsl:template>
```

Matching by ID

You might want to apply a particular style to a particular single element without changing all other elements of that type. The simplest way to do this in XSLT is to attach a style to the element's ID. This is done with the `id()` selector, which contains the ID value in single quotes. For example, this rule makes the element with the ID `e47` bold:

```
<xsl:template match="id('e47')">
  <B><xsl:value-of select="."/></B>
</xsl:template>
```

This assumes, of course, that the elements you want to select in this fashion have an attribute declared as type `ID` in the source document's DTD. This may not be the case, however. For one thing, many documents do not have DTDs. They're merely well-formed, not valid. And even if they have a DTD, there's no guarantee that any element has an `ID` type attribute.

ID-type attributes are not simply attributes with the name `ID`. ID type attributes are discussed in Chapter 9.

Matching attributes with @

As you saw in Chapter 5, the @ sign matches against attributes and selects nodes according to attribute names. Simply prefix the name of the attribute you want to select with the @ sign. For example, this template rule matches `UNITS` attributes, and wraps them in an `I` element:

```
<xsl:template match="@UNITS">
  <I><xsl:value-of select="."/></I>
</xsl:template>
```

However, merely adding this rule to the style sheet will not automatically produce italicized units in the output, because attributes are not children of the elements that contain them. Therefore, by default, when an XSLT processor is walking the tree, it does not see attribute nodes. You have to explicitly process them using `xsl:apply-templates` with an appropriate `select` attribute. Listing 15-7 demonstrates with a style sheet that outputs a table of atomic numbers versus melting points. Not only is the value of the `MELTING_POINT` element written out, so is the value of its `UNITS` attribute. This is selected by `<xsl:apply-templates select="@UNITS"/>` in the template rule for `MELTING_POINT` elements.

Listing 15-7: An XSLT Style Sheet That Selects the UNITS Attribute with @

```
<?xml version="1.0"?>
<xsl:stylesheet version="1.0"
  xmlns:xsl="http://www.w3.org/1999/XSL/Transform">

    <xsl:template match="/PERIODIC_TABLE">
      <HTML>
        <BODY>
          <H1>Atomic Number vs. Melting Point</H1>
          <TABLE>
            <TH>Element</TH>
            <TH>Atomic Number</TH>
            <TH>Melting Point</TH>
            <xsl:apply-templates/>
          </TABLE>
        </BODY>
      </HTML>
    </xsl:template>

    <xsl:template match="ATOM">
       <TR>
        <TD><xsl:value-of select="NAME"/></TD>
        <TD><xsl:value-of select="ATOMIC_NUMBER"/></TD>
        <TD><xsl:apply-templates select="MELTING_POINT"/></TD>
      </TR>
    </xsl:template>

    <xsl:template match="MELTING_POINT">
      <xsl:value-of select="."/>
      <xsl:apply-templates select="@UNITS"/>
    </xsl:template>

    <xsl:template match="@UNITS">
      <I><xsl:value-of select="."/></I>
    </xsl:template>

</xsl:stylesheet>
```

Recall that the value of an attribute node is simply the normalized string value of the attribute. After you apply the style sheet in Listing 15-7, ATOM elements come out formatted like this:

```
    <TR>
<TD>Hydrogen</TD><TD>1</TD><TD>13.81<I>Kelvin</I></TD>
</TR>
```

```
<TR>
<TD>Helium</TD><TD>2</TD><TD>0.95<I>Kelvin</I></TD>
</TR>
```

You can combine attributes with elements using the various hierarchy operators. For example, the pattern BOILING_POINT/@UNITS refers to the UNITS attribute of a BOILING_POINT element. ATOM/*/@UNITS matches any UNITS attribute of a child element of an ATOM element. This is especially helpful when matching against attributes in template rules.

You can also use the @* wildcard to match all attributes of an element, for example BOILING_POINT/@* to match all attributes of BOILING_POINT elements. You can also add a namespace prefix after the @ to match all attributes in a declared namespace. For example, @xlink:* matches all the XLink attributes, such as xlink:show, xlink:type, and xlink:href, assuming the xlink prefix is mapped to the http://www.w3.org/1999/xlink XLink namespace URI.

Matching comments with comment()

Most of the time, you should simply ignore comments in XML documents. Making comments an essential part of a document is a very bad idea. By default, an XSLT style sheet won't do anything with comments. Nonetheless, XSLT does provide a means to match a comment if you absolutely have to.

To match a comment, use the comment() pattern. Although this pattern has functionlike parentheses, it never actually takes any arguments. For example, this template rule italicizes all comments:

```
<xsl:template match="comment()">
  <I><xsl:value-of select="."/></I>
</xsl:template>
```

You can use the hierarchy operators to select particular comments. For example, recall that a DENSITY element looks like this:

```
<DENSITY UNITS="grams/cubic centimeter">
  <!-- At 300K, 1 atm -->
  0.0000899
</DENSITY>
```

This rule only matches comments that occur inside DENSITY elements:

```
<xsl:template match="DENSITY/comment()">
  <I><xsl:value-of select="."/></I>
</xsl:template>
```

The only reason Listing 15-1 uses a comment to specify conditions instead of an attribute or element is precisely for this example. In practice, you should never put important information in comments. The real reason XSLT allows you to select comments is so that a style sheet can transform from one XML application to another while leaving the comments intact. Any other use indicates a poorly designed original document. The following rule matches all comments, and copies them back out again using the `xsl:comment` element.

```
<xsl:template match="comment()">
  <xsl:comment><xsl:value-of select="."/></xsl:comment>
</xsl:template>
```

Matching processing instructions with processing-instruction()

When it comes to writing structured, intelligible, maintainable XML, processing instructions aren't much better than comments. However, there are occasional genuine needs for them, including attaching style sheets to documents.

The `processing-instruction()` function matches processing instructions. The argument to `processing-instruction()` is a quoted string giving the target of the processing instruction to select. If you do not include an argument, all processing instructions are matched. For example, this rule matches the processing instruction children of the root node (most likely the `xml-stylesheet` processing instruction). The `xsl:processing-instruction` element inserts a processing instruction with the specified name and value in the output document. For example, this template rule matches all processing instructions in the document's prolog and epilog and changes each one into a comment containing the processing instruction data:

```
<xsl:template match="/processing-instruction()">
  <xsl:comment>
    <xsl:value-of select="."/>
  </xsl:comment>
</xsl:template>
```

This rule only matches `xml-stylesheet` processing instructions:

```
<xsl:template
  match="processing-instruction('xml-stylesheet')">
  <xsl:comment>
    <xsl:value-of select="."/>
  </xsl:comment>
</xsl:template>
```

In fact, one of the primary reasons for distinguishing between the root element and the root node is so that processing instructions from the prolog can be read and processed. Although the `xml-stylesheet` processing instruction uses a name = value syntax, XSL does not consider these to be attributes because processing instructions are not elements. The value of a processing instruction is simply everything between the white space following its name and the closing `?>`.

Matching text nodes with text()

Text nodes are generally ignored as nodes, although their values are included as part of the value of a selected element. However, the `text()` operator does enable you to specifically select the text child of an element. Despite the parentheses, this operator takes no arguments. For example, this rule emboldens all text:

```
<xsl:template match="text()">
  <B><xsl:value-of select="."/></B>
</xsl:template>
```

The main reason this operator exists is for the default rules. XSLT processors must provide the following default rule whether the author specifies it or not:

```
<xsl:template match="text()">
  <xsl:value-of select="."/>
</xsl:template>
```

This means that whenever a template is applied to a text node, the text of the node is output. If you do not want the default behavior, you can override it. For example, including the following empty template rule in your style sheet will prevent text nodes from being output unless specifically matched by another rule:

```
<xsl:template match="text()" />
```

Using the or operator |

The vertical bar (`|`) allows a template rule to match multiple patterns. If a node matches one pattern or the other, it will activate the template. For example, this template rule matches both `ATOMIC_NUMBER` and `ATOMIC_WEIGHT` elements:

```
<xsl:template match="ATOMIC_NUMBER|ATOMIC_WEIGHT">
  <B><xsl:apply-templates/></B>
</xsl:template>
```

You can include white space around the `|` if that makes the code clearer, as in this template rule:

```
<xsl:template match="ATOMIC_NUMBER | ATOMIC_WEIGHT">
  <B><xsl:apply-templates/></B>
</xsl:template>
```

You can also use more than two patterns in sequence. For example, this template rule applies to `ATOMIC_NUMBER`, `ATOMIC_WEIGHT`, and `SYMBOL` elements (that is, it matches `ATOMIC_NUMBER`, `ATOMIC_WEIGHT` and `SYMBOL` elements):

```
<xsl:template match="ATOMIC_NUMBER | ATOMIC_WEIGHT | SYMBOL">
  <B><xsl:apply-templates/></B>
</xsl:template>
```

The / operator is evaluated before the | operator. Thus, the following template rule matches an ATOMIC_NUMBER child of an ATOM, or an ATOMIC_WEIGHT of unspecified parentage, not an ATOMIC_NUMBER child of an ATOM or an ATOMIC_WEIGHT child of an ATOM.

```
<xsl:template match="ATOM/ATOMIC_NUMBER|ATOMIC_WEIGHT">
  <B><xsl:apply-templates/></B>
</xsl:template>
```

Testing with [ ]

So far, I've merely tested for the presence of various nodes. However, you can test for more details about the nodes that match a pattern using []. You can perform many different tests, including the following:

- ✦ Whether an element contains a given child, attribute, or other node
- ✦ Whether the value of an attribute is a certain string
- ✦ Whether the value of an element contains a string
- ✦ What position a given node occupies in the hierarchy

For example, seaborgium, element 106, has only been created in microscopic quantities. Even its most long-lived isotope has a half-life of only 30 seconds. With such a hard-to-create, short-lived element, it's virtually impossible to measure the density, melting point, and other bulk properties. Consequently, the periodic table document omits the elements describing the bulk properties of seaborgium and similar atoms because the data simply doesn't exist. If you want to create a table of atomic number versus melting point, you should omit those elements with unknown melting points. To do this, you can provide one template for ATOM elements that have MELTING_POINT children and another one for elements that don't, like this:

```
<!-- Include nothing for arbitrary atoms -->
<xsl:template match="ATOM" />

<!-- Include a table row for atoms that do have
     melting points. This rule will override the
     previous one for those atoms that do have
     melting points. -->
<xsl:template match="ATOM[MELTING_POINT]">
  <TR>
    <TD><xsl:value-of select="NAME"/></TD>
    <TD><xsl:value-of select="MELTING_POINT"/></TD>
  </TR>
</xsl:template>
```

Note here that it is the ATOM element being matched, not the MELTING_POINT element as in the case of ATOM/MELTING_POINT.

The test brackets can contain more than simply a child-element name. In fact, they can contain any XPath expression. (XPath expressions are a superset of match patterns that are discussed in the next section.) If the specified element has a child matching that expression, it is considered to match the total pattern. For example, this template rule matches ATOM elements with NAME or SYMBOL children:

```
<xsl:template match="ATOM[NAME | SYMBOL]">
</xsl:template>
```

This template rule matches ATOM elements with a DENSITY child element that has a UNITS attribute:

```
<xsl:template match="ATOM[DENSITY/@UNITS]">
</xsl:template>
```

To find all child elements that have UNITS attributes, use * to find all elements and [@UNITS] to winnow those down to the ones with UNITS attributes, like this:

```
<xsl:template match="ATOM">
  <xsl:apply-templates select="*[@UNITS]"/>
</xsl:template>
```

One type of pattern testing that proves especially useful is string equality. An equals sign (=) can test whether the value of a node identically matches a string. For example, this template finds the ATOM element that contains an ATOMIC_NUMBER element whose content is the string 10 (Neon).

```
<xsl:template match="ATOM[ATOMIC_NUMBER='10']">
  This is Neon!
</xsl:template>
```

Testing against element content may seem extremely tricky because of the need to get the value exactly right, including white space. You may find it easier to test against attribute values because those are less likely to contain insignificant white space. For example, the style sheet in Listing 15-8 applies templates only to those ATOM elements whose STATE attribute value is the three letters GAS.

Listing 15-8: An XSLT Style Sheet That Selects Only Those ATOM Elements Whose STATE Attribute Has the Value GAS

```
<?xml version="1.0"?>
<xsl:stylesheet version="1.0"
  xmlns:xsl="http://www.w3.org/1999/XSL/Transform">

  <xsl:template match="PERIODIC_TABLE">
    <HTML>
```

Continued

Listing 15-8 *(continued)*

```
      <HEAD><TITLE>Gases</TITLE></HEAD>
      <BODY>
        <xsl:apply-templates/>
      </BODY>
    </HTML>
  </xsl:template>

  <xsl:template match="ATOM"/>

  <xsl:template match="ATOM[@STATE='GAS']">
    <P><xsl:value-of select="."/></P>
  </xsl:template>

</xsl:stylesheet>
```

You can use other XPath expressions for more complex matches. For example, you can select all elements whose names begin with "A" or all elements with an atomic number less than 100.

XPath Expressions for Selecting Nodes

The `select` attribute is used in `xsl:apply-templates`, `xsl:value-of`, `xsl:for-each`, `xsl:copy-of`, `xsl:variable`, `xsl:param`, and `xsl:sort` to specify exactly which nodes are operated on. The value of this attribute is an *expression* written in the XPath language. The XPath language provides a means of identifying a particular element, group of elements, text fragment, or other part of an XML document. The XPath syntax is used both for XSLT and XPointer.

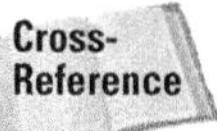

XPointers are discussed in Chapter 18. XPath is discussed further in that chapter as well.

Expressions are a superset of the match patterns discussed in the last section. That is, all match patterns are expressions, but not all expressions are match patterns. Recall that match patterns enable you to match nodes by element name, child elements, descendants, and attributes, as well as by making simple tests on these items. XPath expressions allow you to select nodes through all these criteria, but also by referring to ancestor nodes, parent nodes, sibling nodes, preceding nodes, and following nodes. Furthermore, expressions aren't limited to producing merely a list of nodes, but can also produce booleans, numbers, and strings.

Node axes

Expressions are not limited to specifying the children and descendants of the current node. XPath provides a number of axes that you can use to select from different parts of the tree relative to some particular node in the tree called the context node. In XSLT, the context node is normally initialized to the current node that the template matches, though there are ways to change this. Table 15-2 summarizes the axes and their meanings.

Table 15-2
Expression Axes

Axis	*Selects From*
`ancestor`	The parent of the context node, the parent of the parent of the context node, the parent of the parent of the parent of the context node, and so forth back to the root node
`ancestor-or-self`	The ancestors of the context node and the context node itself
`attribute`	The attributes of the context node
`child`	The immediate children of the context node
`descendant`	The children of the context node, the children of the children of the context node, and so forth
`descendant-or-self`	The context node itself and its descendants
`following`	All nodes that start after the end of the context node, excluding attribute and namespace nodes
`following-sibling`	All nodes that start after the end of the context node and have the same parent as the context node
`namespace`	The namespace of the context node
`parent`	The unique parent node of the context node
`preceding`	All nodes that finish before the beginning of the context node, excluding attribute and namespace nodes
`preceding-sibling`	All nodes that start before the beginning of the context node and have the same parent as the context node
`self`	The context node

Choosing an axis limits the expression so that it only selects from the set of nodes indicated in the second column of Table 15-2. The axis is generally followed by a double colon (: :) and a node test that further winnows down this node-set. For example, a node test may contain the name of the element to be selected, as in the following template rule:

```
<xsl:template match="ATOM">
  <TR>
    <TD>
      <xsl:value-of select="child::NAME"/>
    </TD>
    <TD>
      <xsl:value-of select="child::ATOMIC_NUMBER"/>
    </TD>
    <TD>
      <xsl:value-of select="child::ATOMIC_WEIGHT"/>
    </TD>
  </TR>
</xsl:template>
```

This template rule matches ATOM elements. When an ATOM element is matched, that element becomes the context node. A NAME element, an ATOMIC_NUMBER element, and an ATOMIC_WEIGHT element are all selected from the children of that matched ATOM element and output as table cells. (If there's more than one of these desired elements — for example, three NAME elements — all are selected but only the value of the first one is taken.)

The child axis doesn't let you do anything that you can't do with element names alone. In fact, select="ATOMIC_WEIGHT" is just an abbreviated form of select= "child::ATOMIC_WEIGHT". However, the other axes are a little more interesting.

Referring to the parent element is illegal in match patterns, but not in expressions. To refer to the parent, use the parent axis. For example, this template matches BOILING_POINT elements but outputs the value of the parent ATOM element:

```
<xsl:template match="BOILING_POINT">
  <P><xsl:value-of select="parent::ATOM"/></P>
</xsl:template>
```

Some radioactive atoms, such as polonium, have half-lives so short that bulk properties, such as the boiling point and melting point, can't be measured. Therefore, not all ATOM elements necessarily have BOILING_POINT child elements. The preceding rule enables you to write a template that only outputs those elements that actually have boiling points. Expanding on this example, Listing 15-9 matches the MELTING_POINT elements but actually outputs the parent ATOM element using parent::ATOM.

Listing 15-9: A Style Sheet That Outputs Only Those Elements with Known Melting Points

```
<?xml version="1.0"?>
<xsl:stylesheet version="1.0"
  xmlns:xsl="http://www.w3.org/1999/XSL/Transform">

    <xsl:template match="/">
      <HTML>
        <BODY>
          <xsl:apply-templates select="PERIODIC_TABLE"/>
        </BODY>
      </HTML>
    </xsl:template>

    <xsl:template match="PERIODIC_TABLE">
      <H1>Elements with known Melting Points</H1>
      <xsl:apply-templates select=".//MELTING_POINT"/>
    </xsl:template>

    <xsl:template match="MELTING_POINT">
      <p>
        <xsl:value-of select="parent::ATOM"/>
      </p>
    </xsl:template>

</xsl:stylesheet>
```

Once in awhile, you may need to select from the ancestors of an element. The `ancestor` axis does this. For example, this rule inserts the value of the nearest `PERIODIC_TABLE` element that contains the matched `SYMBOL` element.

```
<xsl:template match="SYMBOL">
  <xsl:value-of select="ancestor::PERIODIC_TABLE"/>
</xsl:template>
```

The `ancestor-or-self` axis behaves like the `ancestor` axis except that if the context node passes the node test, it will be returned as well. For example, this rule matches all elements. If the matched element is a `PERIODIC_TABLE`, that very `PERIODIC_TABLE` is selected in `xsl:value-of`.

```
<xsl:template match="*">
  <xsl:value-of select="ancestor-or-self::PERIODIC_TABLE"/>
</xsl:template>
```

Node tests

Instead of the name of a node, the axis can be followed by one of these four node-type functions:

- comment()
- text()
- processing-instruction()
- node()

The comment() function selects a comment node. The text() function selects a text node. The processing-instruction() function selects a processing instruction node, and the node() function selects any type of node. (The * wildcard only selects element nodes.) The processing-instruction() node type can also contain an optional argument specifying the name of the processing instruction to select.

Hierarchy operators

You can use the / and // operators to string expressions together. For example, Listing 15-10 prints a table of element names, atomic numbers, and melting points for only those elements that have melting points. It does this by selecting the parent of the MELTING_POINT element, then finding that parent's NAME and ATOMIC_NUMBER children with select="parent::*/child::NAME)".

Listing 15-10: A Table of Melting Point versus Atomic Number

```
<?xml version="1.0"?>
<xsl:stylesheet version="1.0"
  xmlns:xsl="http://www.w3.org/1999/XSL/Transform">

    <xsl:template match="/PERIODIC_TABLE">
      <HTML>
        <BODY>
          <H1>Atomic Number vs. Melting Point</H1>
          <TABLE>
            <TH>Element</TH>
            <TH>Atomic Number</TH>
            <TH>Melting Point</TH>
            <xsl:apply-templates select="child::ATOM"/>
          </TABLE>
        </BODY>
      </HTML>
    </xsl:template>

    <xsl:template match="ATOM">
      <xsl:apply-templates
       select="child::MELTING_POINT"/>
    </xsl:template>
```

```
  <xsl:template match="MELTING_POINT">
     <TR>
      <TD>
        <xsl:value-of select="parent::*/child::NAME"/>
      </TD>
      <TD>
        <xsl:value-of
       select="parent::*/child::ATOMIC_NUMBER"/>
      </TD>
      <TD>
        <xsl:value-of select="self::*"/>
        <xsl:value-of select="attribute::UNITS"/>
      </TD>
    </TR>
  </xsl:template>

</xsl:stylesheet>
```

This is not the only way to solve the problem. Another possibility is to use the `preceding-sibling` and `following-sibling` axes, or both if the relative location (preceding or following) is uncertain. The necessary template rule for the `MELTING_POINT` element looks like this:

```
<xsl:template match="MELTING_POINT">
   <TR>
    <TD>
      <xsl:value-of
       select="preceding-sibling::NAME
             | following-sibling::NAME"/>
    </TD>
    <TD>
      <xsl:value-of
       select="preceding-sibling::ATOMIC_NUMBER
             | following-sibling::ATOMIC_NUMBER"/>
    </TD>
    <TD>
      <xsl:value-of select="self::*"/>
      <xsl:value-of select="attribute::UNITS"/>
    </TD>
  </TR>
</xsl:template>
```

Abbreviated syntax

The various axes in Table 15-2 are a bit too wordy for comfortable typing. XPath also defines an abbreviated syntax that can substitute for the most common of these axes and is more commonly used in practice. Table 15-3 shows the full and abbreviated equivalents.

Table 15-3
Abbreviated Syntax for XPath Expressions

Abbreviation	*Full*
`.`	`self::node()`
`..`	`parent::node()`
`name`	`child::`*`name`*
`@`*`name`*	`attribute::`*`name`*
`//`	`/descendant-or-self::node()/`

Listing 15-11 demonstrates by rewriting Listing 15-10 using the abbreviated syntax. The output produced by the two style sheets is exactly the same, however.

Listing 15-11: A Table of Melting Point versus Atomic Number Using the Abbreviated Syntax

```
<?xml version="1.0"?>
<xsl:stylesheet version="1.0"
  xmlns:xsl="http://www.w3.org/1999/XSL/Transform">

    <xsl:template match="/PERIODIC_TABLE">
      <HTML>
        <BODY>
          <H1>Atomic Number vs. Melting Point</H1>
          <TABLE>
            <TH>Element</TH>
            <TH>Atomic Number</TH>
            <TH>Melting Point</TH>
            <xsl:apply-templates select="ATOM"/>
          </TABLE>
        </BODY>
      </HTML>
    </xsl:template>

    <xsl:template match="ATOM">
      <xsl:apply-templates
       select="MELTING_POINT"/>
    </xsl:template>

    <xsl:template match="MELTING_POINT">
       <TR>
        <TD>
          <xsl:value-of
           select="../NAME"/>
```

```
          </TD>
          <TD>
            <xsl:value-of
           select="../ATOMIC_NUMBER"/>
          </TD>
          <TD>
            <xsl:value-of select="."/>
            <xsl:value-of select="@UNITS"/>
          </TD>
        </TR>
      </xsl:template>

    </xsl:stylesheet>
```

Match patterns can only use the abbreviated syntax and the unabbreviated `child` and `attribute` axes. The full syntax using the axes of Table 15-2 is restricted to expressions.

Expression types

Every XPath expression evaluates to a single value. For example, the expression `3 + 2` evaluates to the value `5`. The expressions used so far have all evaluated to node-sets. However, there are four types of expressions in XPath:

- Node-sets
- Booleans
- Numbers
- Strings

In addition, XSLT adds one type to this list, the result tree fragment. This is what an `xsl:template` element creates. However, it is not used by other non-XSLT uses of XPath.

Node-sets

A *node-set* is an unordered group of nodes from the input document. The axes in Table 15-2 all return a node-set containing the nodes they match. Which nodes are in the node-set depends on the context node, the node test, and the axis.

For example, when the context node is the `PERIODIC_TABLE` element of Listing 15-1, the XPath expression `select="child::ATOM"` returns a node-set that contains both `ATOM` elements in that document. The XPath expression `select="child::ATOM/child::NAME"` returns a node-set containing the two element nodes `<NAME>Hydrogen</NAME>` and `<NAME>Helium</NAME>` when the context node is the `PERIODIC_TABLE` element of Listing 15-1.

The context node is a member of the *context node list*. The context node list is that group of elements that all match the same rule at the same time, generally as a result of one `xsl:apply-templates` or `xsl:for-each` instruction. For example, when Listing 15-11 is applied to Listing 15-1, the `ATOM` template is invoked twice, first for the hydrogen atom, then for the helium atom. The first time it's invoked, the context node is the hydrogen `ATOM` element. The second time it's invoked, the context node is the helium `ATOM` element. However, both times the context node list is the set containing both the helium and hydrogen `ATOM` elements.

Table 15-4 lists a number of functions that operate on node-sets, either as arguments or as the context node.

Table 15-4
Functions That Operate on or Return Node-sets

Function	*Return Type*	*Returns*
`position()`	number	The position of the context node in the context node list; the first node in the list has position 1.
`last()`	number	The number of nodes in the context node list; this is the same as the position of the last node in the list.
`count(`*`node-set`*`)`	number	The number of nodes in *`node-set`*.
`id(`*`string1 string2 string3...`*`)`	node-set	A node-set containing all the elements anywhere in the same document that have an ID named in the argument list; the empty set if no element has the specified ID.
`key(`*`string name, Object value`*`)`	node-set	A node-set containing all nodes in this document that have a key with the specified value. Keys are set with the top-level `xsl:key` element.
`document(`*`string URI, string base`*`)`	node-set	A node-set from the document referred to by the URI; the exact subset of nodes are chosen from that document are selected by the XPointer in the URI's fragment identifier. If the URI does not have a fragment identifier, then the root element of the named document is the node-set. Relative URIs are relative to the base URI given in the second argument. If the second argument is omitted, then relative URIs are relative to the URI of the style sheet (not the source document!).

Function	Return Type	Returns
`local-name(node-set)`	string	The local name (everything after the namespace prefix) of the first node in the *node-set* argument; can be used without any arguments to get the local name of the context node.
`namespace-uri (node-set)`	string	The URI of the namespace of the first node in *node-set*; can be used without any arguments to get the URI of the namespace of the context node; returns an empty string if the node is not in a namespace.
`name(node-set)`	string	The qualified name (both prefix and local part) of the first node in *node-set*; can be used without an argument to get the qualified name of the context node.
`generate-id(node-set)`	string	A unique string for the first node in the argument *node-set*; can be used without any argument to generate an ID for the context node.

If an argument of the wrong type is passed to one of these functions, XSLT will attempt to convert that argument to the correct type; for example, by converting the number 12 to the string "12". However, no arguments can be converted to node-sets.

You can use the `position()` function to determine an element's position within a node-set. Listing 15-12 is a style sheet that prefixes the name of each atom's name with its position in the document relative to the other atom names using `<xsl:value-of select="position()"/>`.

Listing 15-12: A Style Sheet That Numbers the Atoms in the Order They Appear in the Document

```
<?xml version="1.0"?>
<xsl:stylesheet version="1.0"
  xmlns:xsl="http://www.w3.org/1999/XSL/Transform">

  <xsl:template match="/PERIODIC_TABLE">
    <HTML>
      <HEAD><TITLE>The Elements</TITLE></HEAD>
```

Continued

Listing 15-12 (continued)

```
      <BODY>
        <xsl:apply-templates select="ATOM"/>
      </BODY>
    </HTML>
  </xsl:template>

  <xsl:template match="ATOM">
    <P>
      <xsl:value-of select="position()"/>.
      <xsl:value-of select="NAME"/>
    </P>
  </xsl:template>

</xsl:stylesheet>
```

When this style sheet is applied to Listing 15-1, the output is this:

```
<HTML>
<HEAD>
<TITLE>The Elements</TITLE>
</HEAD>
<BODY>
<P>1.
      Hydrogen</P>
<P>2.
      Helium</P>
</BODY>
</HTML>
```

Booleans

A *boolean* has one of two values: true or false. XSLT allows any kind of data to be transformed into a boolean. This is often done implicitly when a string or a number or a node-set is used where a boolean is expected, as in the `test` attribute of an `xsl:if` element. These conversions can also be performed by the `boolean()` function, which converts an argument of any type to a boolean according to these rules:

- ✦ A number is false if it's zero or NaN (a special symbol meaning Not a Number, used for the result of dividing by zero and similar illegal operations); true otherwise.
- ✦ An empty node-set is false. All other node-sets are true.
- ✦ An empty result tree fragment is false. All other result tree fragments are true.
- ✦ A zero length string is false. All other strings are true.

Booleans are also produced as the result of expressions involving these operators:

- = Equal to
- != Not equal to
- < Less than (really <)
- > Greater than
- <= Less than or equal to (really <=)
- >= Greater than or equal to

The < sign must be replaced by < even when used as the less-than operator in an XML document such as an XSLT style sheet.

These operators are most commonly used in predicate tests to determine whether a rule should be invoked. An XPath expression can contain not only a pattern that selects certain nodes, but also a predicate that further filters the set of nodes selected. For example, child::ATOM selects all the ATOM children of the context node. However, child::ATOM[position()=1] selects only the first ATOM child of the context node. [position()=1] is a predicate on the node test ATOM that returns a boolean result: true if the position of the ATOM is equal to one; false otherwise. Each node test can have any number of predicates. However, more than one is unusual.

For example, this template rule applies to the first ATOM element in the periodic table, but not to subsequent ones, by testing whether or not the position of the element equals 1.

```
<xsl:template match="PERIODIC_TABLE/ATOM[position()=1]">
  <xsl:value-of select="."/>
</xsl:template>
```

This template rule applies to all ATOM elements that are not the first child element of the PERIODIC_TABLE by testing whether the position is greater than 1:

```
<xsl:template match="PERIODIC_TABLE/ATOM[position()>1]">
  <xsl:value-of select="."/>
</xsl:template>
```

The keywords and and or logically combine two boolean expressions according to the normal rules of logic. For example, suppose you want a template that matches an ATOMIC_NUMBER element that is both the first and last child of its parent element; that is, it is the only element of its parent. This template rule uses and to accomplish that:

```
<xsl:template
 match="ATOMIC_NUMBER[position()=1 and position()=last()]">
  <xsl:value-of select="."/>
</xsl:template>
```

This template matches both the first and last ATOM elements in their parent by matching when the position is 1 or when the position is equal to the number of elements in the set (using the last() function):

```
<xsl:template match="ATOM[position()=1 or position()=last()]">
  <xsl:value-of select="."/>
</xsl:template>
```

This is logical or, so it will also match if both conditions are true. That is, it will match an ATOM that is both the first and last child of its parent (in other words, if the ATOM is the only child of its parent).

The not() function reverses the result of an operation. For example, this template rule matches all ATOM elements that are not the first child of their parents:

```
<xsl:template match="ATOM[not(position()=1)]">
  <xsl:value-of select="."/>
</xsl:template>
```

The same template rule could be written using the not equal operator != instead:

```
<xsl:template match="ATOM[position()!=1]">
  <xsl:value-of select="."/>
</xsl:template>
```

This template rule matches all ATOM elements that are neither the first nor last ATOM child of their parent:

```
<xsl:template match =
 "ATOM[not(position()=1 or position()=last())]">
  <xsl:value-of select="."/>
</xsl:template>
```

XSLT does not have an exclusive or operator. However, one can be formed by judicious use of not(), and, and or. For example, this rule selects those ATOM elements that are either the first or last child, but not both:

```
<xsl:template
 match="ATOM[(position()=1 or position()=last())
             and not(position()=1 and position()=last())]">
  <xsl:value-of select="."/>
</xsl:template>
```

There are three remaining functions that return booleans:

✦ true() always returns true.

✦ false() always returns false.

✦ lang(*code*) returns true if the current node has the same language (as given by the xml:lang attribute) as the *code* argument.

Numbers

XPath numbers are 64-bit IEEE 754 floating-point doubles. Even numbers like 43 or –7000 that look like integers are stored as doubles. Non-number values, such as strings and booleans, are converted to numbers automatically as necessary, or at user request through the `number()` function using these rules:

- Booleans are 1 if true, 0 if false.
- A string is trimmed of leading and trailing white space, then converted to a number in the fashion you would expect; for example, the string "12" is converted to the number 12. If the string cannot be interpreted as a number, it is converted to NaN.
- A node-set is converted to a string; the string is then converted to a number.

For example, this template only outputs the transuranium elements; that is, those elements with atomic numbers greater than 92 (the atomic number of uranium). The node-set produced by `ATOMIC_NUMBER` is implicitly converted to the string value of the current `ATOMIC_NUMBER` node. This string is then converted into a number.

```
<xsl:template match="/PERIODIC_TABLE">
  <HTML>
    <HEAD><TITLE>The Transuranium Elements</TITLE></HEAD>
    <BODY>
      <xsl:apply-templates select="ATOM[ATOMIC_NUMBER>92]"/>
    </BODY>
  </HTML>
</xsl:template>
```

XPath provides the standard four arithmetic operators:

- `+` for addition
- `-` for subtraction
- `*` for multiplication
- `div` for division (the more common / is already used for other purposes in XPath)

For example, `<xsl:value-of select="2+2"/>` inserts the string "4" into the output document. These operations are more commonly used as part of a test. For example, this rule selects those elements whose atomic weight is more than twice their atomic number:

```
<xsl:template match="/PERIODIC_TABLE">
  <HTML>
    <BODY>
      <H1>High Atomic Weight to Atomic Number Ratios</H1>
      <xsl:apply-templates
        select="ATOM[ATOMIC_WEIGHT > 2 * ATOMIC_NUMBER]"/>
```

```
      </BODY>
    </HTML>
  </xsl:template>
```

This template prints the ratio of atomic weight to atomic number:

```
<xsl:template match="ATOM">
  <p>
    <xsl:value-of select="NAME"/>
    <xsl:value-of select="ATOMIC_WEIGHT div ATOMIC_NUMBER"/>
  </p>
</xsl:template>
```

XPath also provides the less familiar mod operator, which takes the remainder of two numbers. When used in conjunction with position(), this operator enables you to perform tasks such as outputting every second ATOM or alternating colors between rows in a table. Just define templates that apply different styles when the position mod two is one and when it's zero. For example, these two rules use different colors for alternate rows of a table:

```
<xsl:template match="ATOM[position() mod 2 = 1]">
    <TR>
     <TD><xsl:value-of select="NAME"/></TD>
     <TD><xsl:value-of select="ATOMIC_NUMBER"/></TD>
     <TD><xsl:apply-templates select="MELTING_POINT"/></TD>
   </TR>
</xsl:template>

<xsl:template match="ATOM[position() mod 2 = 0]">
    <tr style="color: #666666">
     <TD><xsl:value-of select="NAME"/></TD>
     <TD><xsl:value-of select="ATOMIC_NUMBER"/></TD>
     <TD><xsl:apply-templates select="MELTING_POINT"/></TD>
   </TR>
</xsl:template>
```

You can change the divisor to 3 to apply different styles to every third element, to 4 to apply different styles to every fourth element, and so forth.

Finally, XPath includes four functions that operate on numbers:

- ✦ floor() returns the greatest integer less than or equal to the number.
- ✦ ceiling() returns the smallest integer greater than or equal to the number.
- ✦ round() rounds the number to the nearest integer.
- ✦ sum() returns the sum of its arguments.

For example, this template rule estimates the number of neutrons in an atom by subtracting the atomic number (the number of protons) from the atomic weight (the weighted average over the natural distribution of isotopes of the number of neutrons plus the number of protons) and rounding to the nearest integer:

```
<xsl:template match="ATOM">
  <p>
    <xsl:value-of select="NAME"/>
    <xsl:value-of
     select="round(ATOMIC_WEIGHT - ATOMIC_NUMBER)"/>
  </p>
</xsl:template>
```

This rule calculates the average atomic weight of all the atoms in the table by adding all the atomic weights, and then dividing by the number of atoms:

```
<xsl:template match="/PERIODIC_TABLE">
  <HTML>
    <BODY>
    <H1>Average Atomic Weight</H1>
      <xsl:value-of
       select="sum(descendant::ATOMIC_WEIGHT)
               div count(descendant::ATOMIC_WEIGHT)"/>
    </BODY>
  </HTML>
</xsl:template>
```

Strings

A *string* is a sequence of Unicode characters. Other data types can be converted to strings using the `string()` function according to these rules:

✦ Node-sets are converted to strings by taking the value of the first node in the set, as calculated by the `xsl:value-of` element, according to the rules given in Table 15-1.

✦ Result tree fragments are converted by acting as if they're contained in a single element, and then taking the value of that imaginary element. Again, the value of this element is calculated by the `xsl:value-of` element according to the rules given in Table 15-1. That is, all the result tree fragment's text (but not markup) is concatenated.

✦ A number is converted to a European-style number string such as –12 or 3.1415292.

✦ Boolean false is converted to the English word false. Boolean true is converted to the English word true.

Besides `string()`, XSLT contains 10 functions that manipulate strings. These are summarized in Table 15-5.

Table 15-5
XPath String Functions

Function	*Return Type*	*Returns*
`starts-with (main_string, prefix_string)`	Boolean	True if *main_string* starts with *prefix_string*; false otherwise.
`contains (containing_string, contained_string)`	Boolean	True if the *contained_string* is part of the *containing_string*; false otherwise.
`substring(string, offset, length)`	String	*length* characters from the specified *offset* in *string*; or all characters from the *offset* to the end of the *string* if *length* is omitted; *length* and *offset* are rounded to the nearest integer if necessary; the first character in the string is at offset 1.
`substring-before (string, marker-string)`	String	The part of the *string* from the first character up to (but not including) the first occurrence of *marker-string*.
`substring-after (string, marker-string)`	String	The part of the *string* from the point immediately after the first occurrence of *marker-string* to the end of *string*.
`string-length(string)`	Number	The number of characters in *string*.
`normalize-space (string)`	String	The *string* after leading and trailing white space is stripped and runs of white space are replaced with a single space; if the argument is omitted the string value of the context node is normalized.
`translate(string, replaced_text, replacement_text)`	String	Returns *string* with occurrences of characters in *replaced_text* replaced by the corresponding characters from *replacement_text*.
`concat(string1, string2, . . . )`	String	Returns the concatenation of as many strings as are passed as arguments in the order they were passed.

Function	Return Type	Returns
`format-number` (*number*, *format-string*, *locale-string*)	String	Returns the string form of *number* formatted according to the specified *format-string* as if by Java 1.1's `java.text.DecimalFormat` class (see `http://java.sun.com/products/archive/jdk/1.1/index.html`); the *locale-string* is an optional argument that provides the name of the `xsl:decimal-format` element used to interpret the *format-string*.

The Default Template Rules

Having to carefully map the hierarchy of an XML document in an XSLT style sheet may be inconvenient. This is especially true if the document does not follow a stable, predictable order like the periodic table, but rather throws elements together willy-nilly like many web pages. In those cases, you should have general rules that can find an element and apply templates to it regardless of where it appears in the source document.

To make this process easier, XSLT defines several default template rules that are implicitly included in all style sheets. The first default rule matches root and element nodes, and applies templates to all child nodes. The second default rule matches text nodes and attributes, copying their values into the output. Together, these two rules mean that even a blank XSLT style sheet with just one empty `xsl:stylesheet` element will still produce the raw character data of the input XML document as output.

The default rule for elements

The first default rule applies to element nodes and the root node:

```
<xsl:template match="*|/">
  <xsl:apply-templates/>
</xsl:template>
```

`*|/` is XPath shorthand for “any element node or the root node.” The purpose of this rule is to ensure that all elements are recursively processed even if they aren't reached by following the explicit rules. That is, unless another rule overrides this one (especially for the root element), all element nodes will be processed.

However, once an explicit rule for any parent of an element is present, this rule will not be activated for the child elements unless the template rule for the parent has an `xsl:apply-templates` child. For example, you can stop all processing by matching the root element and neither applying templates nor using `xsl:for-each` to process the children, like this:

```
<xsl:template match="/">
</xsl:template>
```

The default rule for text nodes and attributes

Exceptionally observant readers may have noted that several of the examples seem to have output the contents of some elements without actually taking the value of the element they were outputting! These contents were provided by XSLT's default rule for text and attribute nodes. This rule is as follows:

```
<xsl:template match="text()|@*">
  <xsl:value-of select="."/>
</xsl:template>
```

This rule matches all text and attribute nodes (`match="text()|@*"`) and outputs the value of the node (`<xsl:value-of select="."/>`). In other words, it copies the text from the input to the output. This rule ensures that, at the very least, an element's text is output, even if no rule specifically matches it. Another rule can override this one for specific elements where you want either more or less than the text content of an element.

This rule also copies attribute values (but not names). However, they turn from attributes in the input to simple text in the output. Because there's no default rule that ever applies templates to attributes, this rule won't be activated for attributes unless you specifically add a nondefault rule somewhere in the style sheet that does apply templates to attributes of one or more elements.

The default rule for processing instructions and comments

There's also a default rule for processing instructions and comments. It simply says to do nothing; that is, drop the processing instructions and comments from the output as if they didn't exist. It looks like this:

```
<xsl:template match="processing-instruction()|comment()"/>
```

You can, of course, replace this with your own rule for handling processing instructions and comments if you want to.

Implications of the default rules

Together, the default rules imply that applying an empty style sheet with only an `xsl:stylesheet` or `xsl:transform` element but no children (such as Listing 15-13) to an XML document copies all the `#PCDATA` out of the elements in the input to the output. However, this method produces no markup. These are, however, extremely low priority rules. Consequently, any other matches take precedence over the default rules.

Listing 15-13: An Empty XML Style Sheet

```
<?xml version="1.0"?>
<xsl:stylesheet version="1.0"
               xmlns:xsl="http://www.w3.org/1999/XSL/Transform">

</xsl:stylesheet>
```

One of the most common sources of confusion about XSLT in Internet Explorer 5.5 and earlier is that IE does not provide any of these default rules. You have to make sure that you explicitly match any node whose contents (including descendants) you want to output.

Attribute Value Templates

Attribute value templates enable a style sheet to determine the content of an attribute dynamically based on the content of the input document rather than using a literal fixed value in the style sheet. For example, suppose you want to convert the periodic table into empty `ATOM` elements with this attribute-based form:

```
<ATOM NAME="Vanadium"
  ATOMIC_WEIGHT="50.9415"
  ATOMIC_NUMBER="23"
/>
```

To do this, you must extract the contents of elements in the input document and place those in attribute values in the output document. The first thing you're likely to attempt is something similar to this:

```
<xsl:template match="ATOM">
  <ATOM NAME="<xsl:value-of select='NAME'/>"
    ATOMIC_WEIGHT="<xsl:value-of select='ATOMIC_WEIGHT'/>"
    ATOMIC_NUMBER="<xsl:value-of select='ATOMIC_NUMBER'/>"
  />
</xsl:template>
```

But this is malformed XML. The < character is not allowed in an attribute value. Instead, inside attribute values, data enclosed in curly braces {}, takes the place of the `xsl:value-of` element. The correct way to write the preceding template rule is like this:

```
<xsl:template match="ATOM">
  <ATOM NAME="{NAME}"/>
    ATOMIC_WEIGHT="{ATOMIC_WEIGHT}"
    ATOMIC_NUMBER="{ATOMIC_NUMBER}"
  />
</xsl:template>
```

In the output, `{NAME}` is replaced by the value of the `NAME` child element of the matched `ATOM`. `{ATOMIC_WEIGHT}` is replaced by the value of the `ATOMIC_WEIGHT` child element of the matched `ATOM`. `{ATOMIC_NUMBER}` is replaced by the value of the `ATOMIC_NUMBER` child element, and so on.

Attribute value templates can have more complicated patterns than merely an element name. In fact, you can use any XPath expression in an attribute value template. For example, this template rule selects `DENSITY` elements in the form seen in Listing 15-1:

```
<xsl:template match="DENSITY">
  <BULK_PROPERTY
    NAME="DENSITY"
    ATOM="{../NAME}"
    VALUE="{normalize-space(.)}"
    UNITS="{@UNITS}"
  />
</xsl:template>
```

It converts them into `BULK_PROPERTY` elements that look like this:

```
<BULK_PROPERTY NAME="DENSITY" ATOM="Helium"
  VALUE="0.0001785" UNITS="grams/cubic centimeter"/>
```

Attribute values are not limited to a single attribute value template. You can combine an attribute value template with literal data or with other attribute value templates. For example, this template rule matches `ATOM` elements and replaces them with their name formatted as a link to a file in the format H.html, He.html, and so on. The filename is derived from the attribute value template `{SYMBOL}`, while the literal data provides the period and extension.

```
<xsl:template match="ATOM">
  <A HREF="{SYMBOL}.html">
    <xsl:value-of select="NAME"/>
  </A>
</xsl:template>
```

More than one attribute value template can be included in an attribute value. For example, this template rule includes the density units as part of the VALUE attribute rather than making them a separate attribute:

```
<xsl:template match="DENSITY">
  <BULK_PROPERTY
    NAME="DENSITY"
    ATOM="{../NAME}"
    VALUE="{normalize-space(.)} {@UNITS}"
  />
</xsl:template>
```

You can place attribute value templates in many attributes in an XSLT style sheet. This is particularly important in xsl:element, xsl:attribute, and xsl:processing-instruction elements (discussed in the next section), where attribute value templates allow the designer to defer the decision about exactly what element, attribute, or processing instruction appears in the output until the input document is read. You cannot use attribute value templates as the value of a select or match attribute, an xmlns attribute, an attribute that provides the name of another XSLT instruction element, or an attribute of a top-level element (one that's an immediate child of xsl:stylesheet).

Deciding What Output to Include

It's often necessary to defer decisions about what markup to emit until the input document has been read. For example, you might want to change the contents of a FILENAME element into the HREF attribute of an A element, or replace one element type in the input with several different element types in the output depending on the value of an attribute. This is accomplished with xsl:element, xsl:attribute, xsl:processing-instruction, xsl:comment, and xsl:text elements.

Inserting elements into the output with xsl:element

Elements are usually included in the output document simply by including the literal start- and end-tags in template content. For instance, to insert a P element, you merely type <P> and </P> at the appropriate points in the style sheet. However, occasionally, you need to use details from the input document to determine which element to place in the output document. This might happen, for example, when making a transformation from a source vocabulary that uses attributes for information to an output vocabulary that uses elements for the same information.

The xsl:element element inserts an element into the output document. The name of the element is given by an attribute value template in the name attribute of xsl:element. The content of the element derives from the content of the xsl:element element, which may include xsl:attribute, xsl:processing-instruction, and xsl:comment instructions (all discussed shortly) to insert these items.

For example, suppose you want to replace the ATOM elements with GAS, LIQUID, and SOLID elements, depending on the value of the STATE attribute. Using xsl:element, a single rule can do this by converting the value of the STATE attribute to an element name. This is how it is done:

```
<xsl:template match="ATOM">
  <xsl:element name="{@STATE}">
    <NAME><xsl:value-of select="NAME"/></NAME>
    <!-- rules for other children... -->
  </xsl:element>
</xsl:template>
```

By using more complicated attribute value templates, you can perform most of the calculations that you might need.

Inserting attributes into the output with xsl:attribute

You can include attributes in the output document simply by typing the literal attributes themselves. For example, to insert a DIV element with an ALIGN attribute bearing the value CENTER, you merely type <DIV ALIGN="CENTER"> and </DIV> at the appropriate points in the style sheet. However, you frequently have to rely on data that you read from the input document to determine an attribute value and sometimes even to determine the attribute name.

For example, suppose you want a style sheet that selects atom names and formats them as links to files named H.html, He.html, Li.html, and so forth, like this:

```
<LI><A HREF="H.html">Hydrogen</A></LI>
<LI><A HREF="He.html">Helium</A></LI>
<LI><A HREF="Li.html">Lithium</A></LI>
```

Each different element in the input will have a different value for the HREF attribute. The xsl:attribute element calculates an attribute name and value and inserts it into the output. Each xsl:attribute element is a child of either an xsl:element element or a literal result element. The attribute calculated by xsl:attribute will be attached to the element calculated by its parent in the output. The name of the attribute is specified by the name attribute of the xsl:attribute element. The value of the attribute is given by the contents of the xsl:attribute element. For example, this template rule produces the output previously shown:

```
<xsl:template match="ATOM">
  <LI><A>
    <xsl:attribute name="HREF">
      <xsl:value-of select="SYMBOL"/>.html
    </xsl:attribute>
    <xsl:value-of select="NAME"/>
  </A></LI>
</xsl:template>
```

All xsl:attribute elements must come before any other content of their parent element. You can't add an attribute to an element after you've already started writing out its content. For example, this template is illegal:

```
<xsl:template match="ATOM">
  <LI><A>
    <xsl:value-of select="NAME"/>
    <xsl:attribute name="HREF">
      <xsl:value-of select="SYMBOL"/>.html
    </xsl:attribute>
  </A></LI>
</xsl:template>
```

Defining attribute sets

You often need to apply the same group of attributes to many different elements of either the same or different classes. For example, you might want to apply a style attribute to each cell in an HTML table. To make this simpler, you can define one or more attributes as members of an attribute set at the top level of the style sheet with xsl:attribute-set, and then include that attribute set in an element with an xsl:use-attribute-sets attribute.

For example, this xsl:attribute-set element defines an element named CELLSTYLE with a font-family attribute of New York, Times New Roman, Times, serif, and a font-size attribute of 12pt:

```
<xsl:attribute-set name="CELLSTYLE">
  <xsl:attribute name="font-family">
    New York, Times New Roman, Times, serif
  </xsl:attribute>
  <xsl:attribute name="font-size">12pt</xsl:attribute>
</xsl:attribute-set>
```

This template rule then applies those attributes to TD elements in the output:

```
<xsl:template match="ATOM">
  <TR>
    <TD xsl:use-attribute-sets="CELLSTYLE">
      <xsl:value-of select="NAME"/>
    </TD>
    <TD xsl:use-attribute-sets="CELLSTYLE">
      <xsl:value-of select="ATOMIC_NUMBER"/>
    </TD>
  </TR>
</xsl:template>
```

An element can use more than one attribute set by specifying the names of the all the sets in a white-space-separated list in the value of the xsl:use-attribute-sets attribute. All attributes from all the sets are applied to the element. For example, this TD element possesses attributes from both the CELLSTYLE and the NUMBER-STYLE attribute sets:

```
<TD xsl:use-attribute-sets="CELLSTYLE NUMBERSTYLE">
  <xsl:value-of select="ATOMIC_NUMBER"/>
</TD>
```

If more than one attribute set defines the same attribute, the last attribute set mentioned is used. If there is more than one attribute set with the same name, the attributes in the sets are merged.

You can also include attribute sets in particular elements by adding a use-attribute-sets element to an xsl:element, xsl:copy, or xsl:attribute-set element, as in the following example:

```
<xsl:element name="TD" use-attribute-sets="CELLSTYLE">
  <xsl:value-of select="ATOMIC_NUMBER"/>
</xsl:element>
```

The xsl: prefix is unnecessary (and in fact prohibited) when use-attribute-sets is an attribute of an XSLT element rather than a literal result element.

Generating processing instructions with xsl:processing-instruction

The xsl:processing-instruction element places a processing instruction in the output document. The target of the processing instruction is specified by a required name attribute. The contents of the xsl:processing-instruction element become the contents of the processing instruction. For example, this rule replaces PROGRAM elements with a gcc processing instruction:

```
<xsl:template match="PROGRAM">
  <xsl:processing-instruction name="gcc"> -04
  </xsl:processing-instruction>
</xsl:template>
```

PROGRAM elements in the input are replaced by this processing instruction in the output:

```
<?gcc -04
  ?>
```

The contents of the xsl:processing-instruction element can include xsl:value-of elements and xsl:apply-templates elements, provided the result of these instructions is pure text. For example:

```
<xsl:template match="PROGRAM">
  <xsl:processing-instruction name="gcc">-04
```

```
    <xsl:value-of select="NAME"/>
  </xsl:processing-instruction>
</xsl:template>
```

The xsl:processing-instruction element cannot contain xsl:element and other instructions that produce elements and attributes in the result. Furthermore, xsl:processing-instruction cannot include any instructions or literal text that insert a ?> in the output, because that would prematurely end the processing instruction.

Generating comments with xsl:comment

The xsl:comment element inserts a comment in the output document. It has no attributes. Its contents are the text of the comment, as in the following example:

```
<xsl:template match="ATOM">
  <xsl:comment>There was an atom here once.</xsl:comment>
</xsl:template>
```

This rule replaces ATOM nodes with the following comment:

```
<!--There was an atom here once.-->
```

The contents of the xsl:comment element can include xsl:value-of elements and xsl:apply-templates elements, provided the results of these instructions are pure text. It cannot contain xsl:element and other instructions that produce elements and attributes in the result. Furthermore, xsl:comment cannot include any instructions or literal text that inserts a double hyphen in the comment. This would result in a malformed comment in the output.

Generating text with xsl:text

The xsl:text element inserts its contents into the output document as literal text. For example, this rule replaces each ATOM element with the string "There was an atom here once":

```
<xsl:template match="ATOM">
  <xsl:text>There was an atom here once.</xsl:text>
</xsl:template>
```

The xsl:text element isn't often used because most of the time it's easier to simply type the text. However, xsl:text does have a couple of advantages. The first is that it preserves white space exactly, even if the node contains nothing but white space. By default, XSLT processors delete all text nodes from the style sheet that contain only white space. Thus, this element is useful when dealing with concrete poetry, computer source code, or other text in which white space is significant.

The xsl:text element also enables you to insert unescaped < and & into your output document that are not converted to < and &. To do this, place the general entity reference for the symbol (< or &) in an xsl:text element; then set the xsl:text element's disable-output-escaping attribute to yes. This can be useful when you need to include JavaScript source code in the output document, as in the following example:

```
<xsl:template match="SCRIPT">
  <script language="javascript">
    <xsl:text disable-output-escaping="yes">
      &lt;!-- if (
         location.host.tolowercase().indexof("ibiblio")
         &lt; 0) {
           location.href="http://www.ibiblio.org/";
         }
      } // --&gt;
    </xsl:text>
  </script>
</xsl:template>
```

This may produce output that is not well-formed XML. However, if you're trying to write a non-XML format, such as HTML or TeX, this may be what you want. Note, however, that the style sheet and the input document are both still well-formed XML.

Copying the Context Node with xsl:copy

The xsl:copy element copies the source node into the output tree. Child elements, attributes, and other content are not automatically copied. However, the contents of the xsl:copy element are a template that can select these things to be copied as well. This is often useful when transforming a document from one markup vocabulary to the same or a closely related markup vocabulary. For example, this template rule strips the attributes and child elements off an ATOM and replaces it with the value of its contents enclosed in a B element:

```
<xsl:template match="ATOM">
   <xsl:copy>
     <B><xsl:value-of select="."/></B>
   </xsl:copy>
</xsl:template>
```

One useful template xsl:copy makes possible is the identity transformation; that is, a transformation from a document into itself. Such a transformation looks like this:

```
<xsl:template
  match="*|@*|comment()|processing-instruction()|text()">
  <xsl:copy>
    <xsl:apply-templates
```

```
      select="*|@*|comment()|processing-instruction()|text()"/>
  </xsl:copy>
</xsl:template>
```

You can adjust the identity transformation a little to produce similar documents. For example, Listing 15-14 is a style sheet that strips comments from a document, leaving the document otherwise untouched. It simply omits the `comment()` node test from the `match` and `select` attribute values in the identity transformation.

Listing 15-14: An XSLT Style Sheet That Strips Comments from a Document

```
<?xml version="1.0"?>
<xsl:stylesheet version="1.0"
  xmlns:xsl="http://www.w3.org/1999/XSL/Transform">

  <xsl:template
     match="*|@*|processing-instruction()|text()">
    <xsl:copy>
      <xsl:apply-templates
        select="*|@*|processing-instruction()|text()"/>
    </xsl:copy>
  </xsl:template>

</xsl:stylesheet>
```

`xsl:copy` only copies the source node. However, it does not automatically copy the node's attributes, children, or namespaces. In other words, it is a shallow copy. To deep copy the entire node including all its attributes and descendants, use `xsl:copy-of`. The `select` attribute of `xsl:copy-of` chooses the nodes to be copied. For example, Listing 15-15 is a style sheet that uses `xsl:copy-of` to strip out elements without melting points from the periodic table by copying only `ATOM` elements that have `MELTING_POINT` children.

Listing 15-15: A Style Sheet That Copies Only ATOM Elements That Have MELTING_POINT Children

```
<?xml version="1.0"?>
<xsl:stylesheet version="1.0"
  xmlns:xsl="http://www.w3.org/1999/XSL/Transform">

    <xsl:template match="/PERIODIC_TABLE">
      <PERIODIC_TABLE>
```

Continued

Listing 15-15 *(continued)*

```
      <xsl:apply-templates select="ATOM"/>
    </PERIODIC_TABLE>
  </xsl:template>

  <xsl:template match="ATOM">
              <xsl:apply-templates select="MELTING_POINT"/>
  </xsl:template>

 <xsl:template match="MELTING_POINT">
   <xsl:copy-of select=".."/>
 </xsl:template>

</xsl:stylesheet>
```

Listings 15-14 and 15-15 are examples of XSL transformations from a source vocabulary to the same vocabulary. Unlike most of the examples in this chapter, they do not transform to well-formed HTML.

Counting Nodes with xsl:number

The `xsl:number` element inserts a formatted integer into the output document. The value of the integer is given by the `value` attribute. This contains a number, which is rounded to the nearest integer, then formatted according to the value of the `format` attribute. Reasonable defaults are provided for both these attributes. For example, consider the style sheet for the `ATOM` elements in Listing 15-16.

Listing 15-16: An XSLT Style Sheet That Counts Atoms

```
<?xml version="1.0"?>
<xsl:stylesheet version="1.0"
  xmlns:xsl="http://www.w3.org/1999/XSL/Transform">

    <xsl:template match="PERIODIC_TABLE">
      <HTML>
        <HEAD><TITLE>The Elements</TITLE></HEAD>
        <BODY>
          <TABLE>
            <TR><xsl:apply-templates select="ATOM"/></TR>
          </TABLE>
        </BODY>
      </HTML>
    </xsl:template>
```

```
    <xsl:template match="ATOM">
      <TD><xsl:number value="ATOMIC_NUMBER"/></TD>
      <TD><xsl:value-of select="NAME"/></TD>
    </xsl:template>

</xsl:stylesheet>
```

When this style sheet is applied to Listing 15-1, the output appears like this:

```
<HTML>
<HEAD>
<TITLE>The Elements</TITLE>
</HEAD>
<BODY>
<TABLE>
<TR>
<TD>1</TD><TD>Hydrogen</TD><TD>2</TD><TD>Helium</TD>
</TR>
</TABLE>
</BODY>
</HTML>
```

Each element is matched with its atomic number. The `value` attribute can contain any data that XPath knows how to convert to a number. In this case, the `ATOMIC_NUMBER` child element of the matched `ATOM` is converted.

Default numbers

If you use the `value` attribute to calculate the number, that's all you need. However, if the `value` attribute is omitted, the position of the current node in the source tree is used as the number. For example, consider Listing 15-17, which produces a table of atoms that have boiling points less than or equal to the boiling point of nitrogen.

Listing 15-17: An XSLT Style Sheet That Counts Atoms

```
<?xml version="1.0"?>
<xsl:stylesheet version="1.0"
  xmlns:xsl="http://www.w3.org/1999/XSL/Transform">

    <xsl:template match="PERIODIC_TABLE">
      <HTML>
        <HEAD><TITLE>The Elements</TITLE></HEAD>
        <BODY>
          <TABLE>
            <TR>
```

Continued

Listing 15-17 *(continued)*

```
          <TD>Name</TD>
          <TD>Position</TD>
          <TD>Default Number</TD>
          <TD>Boiling Point</TD>
        </TR>
        <xsl:apply-templates
          select="ATOM[BOILING_POINT &lt;= 77.344]"/>
      </TABLE>
    </BODY>
  </HTML>
</xsl:template>

<xsl:template match="ATOM">
  <TR>
    <TD><xsl:value-of select="NAME"/></TD>
    <TD><xsl:number value="position()"/></TD>
    <TD><xsl:number/></TD>
    <TD><xsl:number value="BOILING_POINT"/></TD>
  </TR>
</xsl:template>

</xsl:stylesheet>
```

Figure 15-4 shows the finished table produced by applying this style sheet to the complete periodic table. This shows that the default value calculated by `xsl:number` is the position of the node among other sibling nodes of the same type (`ATOM` elements in this case). This is not the same as the number returned by the `position()` function, which only calculates position relative to other nodes in the context node list (the nodes which the template matched — hydrogen, helium, nitrogen, and neon, in this example). You can change what `xsl:number` counts using these three attributes:

- ✦ `level`
- ✦ `count`
- ✦ `from`

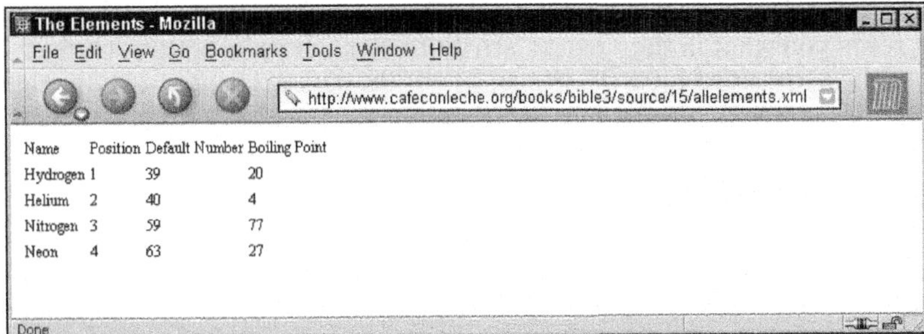

Figure 15-4: Atoms with boiling points less than or equal to nitrogen's

Number to string conversion

Until now, I've implicitly assumed that numbers looked like 1, 2, 3, and so on; that is, a European numeral starting from 1 and counting by 1. However, that's not the only possibility. For example, the page numbers in the preface and other front matter of books often appear in small Roman numerals such as i, ii, iii, iv, and so on. And different countries use different conventions to group the digits, separate the integer and fractional parts of a real number, and represent the symbols for the various digits. These are all adjustable through four attributes of `xsl:number`:

- ✦ `format`
- ✦ `letter-value`
- ✦ `grouping-separator`
- ✦ `grouping-size`

The format attribute

You can adjust the numbering style used by `xsl:number` using the `format` attribute. This attribute generally has one of the following values:

- ✦ `i` — The lowercase Roman numerals i, ii, iii, iv, v, vi, . . .
- ✦ `I` — The uppercase Roman numerals I, II, III, IV, V, VI, . . .
- ✦ `a` — The lowercase letters a, b, c, d, e, f, . . .
- ✦ `A` — The uppercase letters A, B, C, D, E, F, . . .

For example, this rule numbers the atoms with capital Roman numerals:

```
<xsl:template match="ATOM">
  <P>
    <xsl:number value="position()" format="I"/>
    <xsl:value-of select="."/>
  </P>
</xsl:template>
```

You can specify decimal numbering with leading zeros by including the number of leading zeros you want in the `format` attribute. For example, setting `format="01"` produces the sequence 01, 02, 03, 04, 05, 06, 07, 08, 09, 10, 11, 12, ... You might find this useful when lining numbers up in columns.

The letter-value attribute

The `letter-value` attribute distinguishes between letters interpreted as numbers and letters interpreted as letters. For instance, if you want to use `format="I"` to start the sequence I, J, K, L, M, N, . . . instead of I, II, III, IV, V, VI, . . ., you would set the `letter-value` attribute to the keyword `alphabetic`. The keyword `traditional` specifies a numeric sequence, as in the following example:

```
<xsl:template match="ATOM">
  <P>
   <xsl:number value="position()"
               format="I" letter-value="alphabetic"/>
   <xsl:value-of select="."/>
  </P>
</xsl:template>
```

Grouping attributes

In the United States, we tend to write large numbers with commas grouping every three digits; for example, 4,567,302,000. However, in many languages and countries, a period or a space separates the groups instead; for instance, 4.567.302.000 or 4 567 302 000. Furthermore, in some countries, it's customary to group large numbers every four digits instead of every three; for example, 4,5673,0000.

The `grouping-separator` attribute specifies the grouping separator used between groups of digits. The `grouping-size` attribute specifies the number of digits used in a group, as in the following example:

```
<xsl:number grouping-separator=" " grouping-SIZE="3"/>
```

Generally, you'd make these attributes contingent on the language.

Sorting Output

The `xsl:sort` element sorts the output nodes into a different order than they were generated in. An `xsl:sort` element appears as a child of an `xsl:apply-templates` element or `xsl:for-each` element. The `select` attribute of the `xsl:sort` element defines the key used to sort the element's output by `xsl:apply-templates` or `xsl:for-each`.

By default, sorting is performed in alphabetical order of the keys. If more than one `xsl:sort` element is present in a given `xsl:apply-templates` or `xsl:for-each` element, the elements are sorted first by the first key, then by the second key, and so on. If any elements still compare equally, they are output in the order they appear in the source document.

For example, suppose you have a file full of ATOM elements arranged alphabetically. To sort by atomic number, you can use the style sheet in Listing 15-18.

Listing 15-18: An XSLT Style Sheet That Sorts by Atomic Number

```
<?xml version="1.0"?>
<xsl:stylesheet version="1.0"
  xmlns:xsl="http://www.w3.org/1999/XSL/Transform">

    <xsl:template match="PERIODIC_TABLE">
      <HTML>
        <HEAD>
          <TITLE>Atomic Number vs. Atomic Weight</TITLE>
        </HEAD>
        <BODY>
          <H1>Atomic Number vs. Atomic Weight</H1>
          <TABLE>
            <TH>Element</TH>
            <TH>Atomic Number</TH>
            <TH>Atomic Weight</TH>
            <xsl:apply-templates>
              <xsl:sort select="ATOMIC_NUMBER"/>
            </xsl:apply-templates>
          </TABLE>
        </BODY>
      </HTML>
    </xsl:template>

    <xsl:template match="ATOM">
      <TR>
        <TD><xsl:apply-templates select="NAME"/></TD>
        <TD><xsl:apply-templates select="ATOMIC_NUMBER"/></TD>
        <TD><xsl:apply-templates select="ATOMIC_WEIGHT"/></TD>
      </TR>
    </xsl:template>

</xsl:stylesheet>
```

Figure 15-5 shows the limits of alphabetical sorting. Hydrogen, atomic number 1, is the first element. However, the second element is not helium, atomic number 2, but rather neon, atomic number 10. Although 10 sorts after 9 numerically, alphabetically 10 falls before 2.

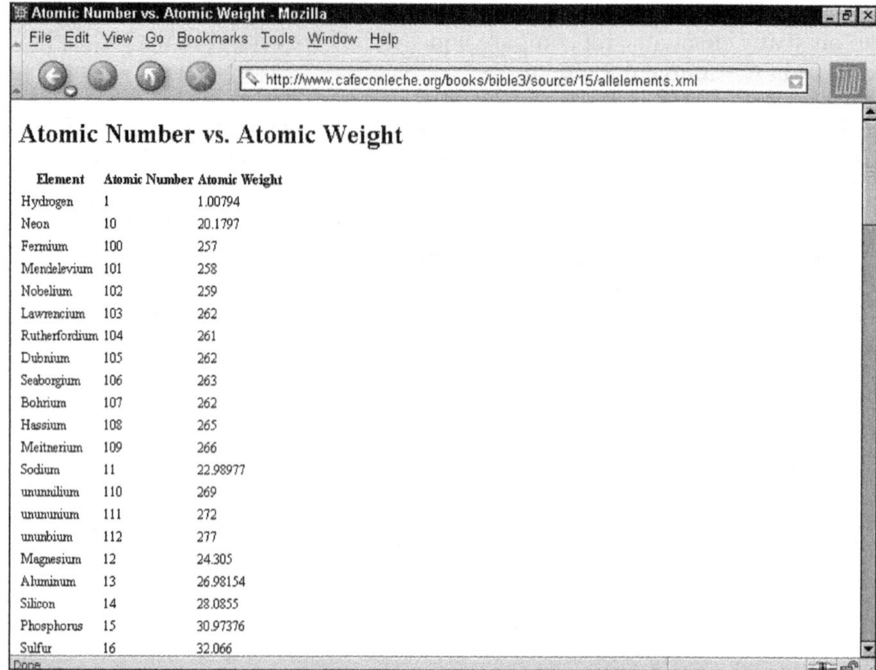

Figure 15-5: Atoms alphabetically sorted by atomic number

You can, however, adjust the order of the sort by setting the optional `data-type` attribute to the value `number`, as in this element:

```
<xsl:sort data-type="number" select="ATOMIC_NUMBER"/>
```

Figure 15-6 shows the elements sorted properly.

You can change the order of the sort from the default ascending order to descending by setting the `order` attribute to `descending`, like this:

```
<xsl:sort order="descending"
          data-type="number"
          select="ATOMIC_NUMBER"/>
```

This sorts the elements from the largest atomic number to the smallest so that hydrogen now appears last in the list.

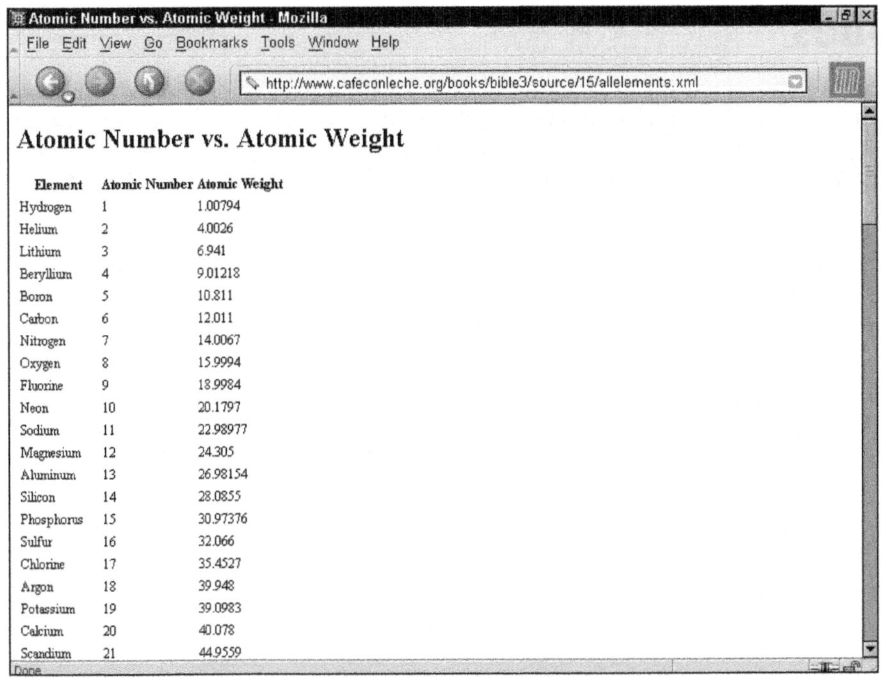

Figure 15-6: Atoms numerically sorted by atomic number

Alphabetical sorting naturally depends on the alphabet. The `lang` attribute can set the language of the keys. The value of this attribute should be an ISO 639 language code such as `en` for English. However, processors are not required to know how to sort in all the different languages that might be encountered in XML. While English sorting is fairly straightforward, many other languages require much more complicated algorithms. Indeed, a few languages actually have multiple standard ways of sorting based on different criteria. The `lang` attribute is ignored if `data-type` is `number`.

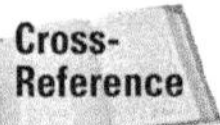

These are the same values supported by the `xml:lang` attribute discussed in Chapter 6.

Finally, you can set the `case-order` attribute to one of the two values, `upper-first` or `lower-first`, to specify whether uppercase letters sort before lowercase letters or vice versa. The default depends on the language.

Modes

Sometimes you want to include the same content from the source document in the output document multiple times. That's easy to do simply by applying templates multiple times, once in each place where you want the data to appear. However, suppose you want the data to be formatted differently in different locations? That's a little trickier.

For example, suppose you want the output of processing the periodic table to be a series of 100 links to more detailed descriptions of the individual atoms. In this case, the output document would start like this:

```
<UL>
<LI><A HREF="#Ac">Actinium</A></LI>
<LI><A HREF="#Al">Aluminum</A></LI>
<LI><A HREF="#Am">Americium</A></LI>
<LI><A HREF="#Sb">Antimony</A></LI>
<LI><A HREF="#Ar">Argon</A></LI>
...
```

Later in the document, the actual atom descriptions would appear, formatted like this:

```
<H3>
<A NAME="H">Hydrogen</A>
</H3>
<P>
    Hydrogen
    H
    1
    1.00794
    20.28
    13.81

      0.0000899

  </P>
```

This sort of application is common anytime you automatically generate a table of contents or an index. The NAME of the atom must be formatted differently in the table of contents than in the body of the document. You need two different rules that both apply to the ATOM element at different places in the document. The solution is to give each of the different rules a mode attribute. Then you can choose which template to apply by setting the mode attribute of the xsl:apply-templates element. Listing 15-19 demonstrates.

Listing 15-19: An XSLT Style Sheet That Uses Modes to Format the Same Data Differently in Two Different Places

```
<?xml version="1.0"?>
<xsl:stylesheet version="1.0"
  xmlns:xsl="http://www.w3.org/1999/XSL/Transform">

  <xsl:template match="/PERIODIC_TABLE">
    <HTML>
      <HEAD><TITLE>The Elements</TITLE></HEAD>
      <BODY>

        <H2>Table of Contents</H2>
        <UL>
          <xsl:apply-templates select="ATOM" mode="toc"/>
        </UL>

        <H2>The Elements</H2>
        <xsl:apply-templates select="ATOM" mode="full"/>

      </BODY>
    </HTML>
  </xsl:template>

  <xsl:template match="ATOM" mode="toc">
    <LI><A>
      <xsl:attribute name="HREF">#<xsl:value-of
        select="SYMBOL"/></xsl:attribute>
      <xsl:value-of select="NAME"/>
    </A></LI>
  </xsl:template>

  <xsl:template match="ATOM" mode="full">
    <H3><A>
      <xsl:attribute name="NAME">
        <xsl:value-of select="SYMBOL"/>
      </xsl:attribute>
      <xsl:value-of select="NAME"/>
    </A></H3>
      <P>
        <xsl:value-of select="."/>
      </P>
  </xsl:template>

</xsl:stylesheet>
```

The default template rule for nodes preserves modes. That is, for every mode *n* you declare in your style sheet, the XSLT processor adds one template rule that applies specifically to that mode and looks like this:

```
<xsl:template match="*|/" mode="n">
  <xsl:apply-templates mode="n"/>
</xsl:template>
```

As usual, you are free to override this default rule with one of your own design.

Defining Constants with xsl:variable

Named constants help clean up code. They can replace commonly used boilerplate text with a simple name and reference. They can also make it easy to adjust boilerplate text that appears in multiple locations by simply changing the constant definition.

The `xsl:variable` element defines a named string for use elsewhere in the style sheet via an attribute value template. It has a single attribute, `name`, which provides a name by which the variable can be referred to. The contents of the `xsl:variable` element provide the replacement text. For example, this `xsl:variable` element defines a variable with the name `copy04` and the value `Copyright 2004 Elliotte Rusty Harold`:

```
<xsl:variable name="copy04">
  Copyright 2004 Elliotte Rusty Harold
</xsl:variable>
```

To access the value of this variable, you prefix a dollar sign to the name of the variable. To insert this in an attribute, use an attribute value template. For example:

```
<BLOCK COPYRIGHT="{$copy04}">
</BLOCK>
```

An `xsl:value-of` element can insert the variable's replacement text into the output document as text:

```
<xsl:value-of select="$copy04"/>
```

The contents of the `xsl:variable` element can contain markup including other XSLT instructions. This means that you can calculate the value of a variable based on other information, including the value of other variables. However, a variable may not refer to itself recursively, either directly or indirectly. For instance, the following example is in error:

```
<xsl:variable name="GNU">
  <xsl:value-of select="$GNU"/>'s not Unix
</xsl:variable>
```

Similarly, two variables may not refer to each other in a circular fashion, like this:

```
<xsl:variable name="Thing1">
  Thing1 loves <xsl:value-of select="$Thing2"/>
</xsl:variable>

<xsl:variable name="Thing2">
  Thing2 loves <xsl:value-of select="$Thing1"/>
</xsl:variable>
```

`xsl:variable` elements can either be top-level children of the `xsl:stylesheet` root element or they can be included inside template rules. A variable present at the top level of a style sheet can be accessed anywhere in the style sheet. It's a global variable. By contrast, a variable that's declared inside a template rule is only accessible by its following sibling elements and their descendants (the *scope* of the variable). It's a *local variable*. That is, it only applies inside that one template rule. It is local to the template. Local variables override global variables with the same name. Local variables can also override other local variables. In the event of a conflict between two variables with the same name, the closest local variable with the same name is used.

Unlike variables in traditional programming languages such as Java, XSLT variables may not be changed. After the value of a variable has been set, it cannot be changed. It can be shadowed by another variable with the same name in a more local scope, but its own value is fixed. An XSLT variable is more like an algebraic variable than a programming language variable.

Named Templates

Variables are limited to basic text and markup. XSLT provides a more powerful macro facility that can wrap standard markup and text around changing data. For example, suppose you want an atom's atomic number, atomic weight, and other key values formatted as a table cell in small, bold Times font in blue. In other words, you want the output to look like this:

```
<TD>
  <FONT FACE="Times, serif" COLOR="blue" SIZE="2">
    <B>52</B>
  </FONT>
</TD>
```

You can certainly include all that in a template rule like this:

```
<xsl:template match="ATOMIC_NUMBER">
  <TD>
    <FONT FACE="Times, serif" COLOR="blue" SIZE="2">
      <B>
        <xsl:value-of select="."/>
```

```
        </B>
      </FONT>
    </TD>
  </xsl:template>
```

This markup can be repeated inside other template rules. When the detailed markup grows more complex, and when it appears in several different places in a style sheet, you may elect to turn it into a named template. Named templates resemble variables. However, they enable you to include data from the place where the template is applied, rather than merely inserting fixed text.

The `xsl:template` element can have a `name` attribute by which it can be explicitly invoked, even when it isn't applied indirectly. For example, this shows a sample named template for the preceding pattern:

```
<xsl:template name="ATOM_CELL">
  <TD>
    <font FACE="Times, serif" COLOR="blue" SIZE="2">
      <B>
        <xsl:value-of select="."/>
      </B>
    </FONT>
  </TD>
</xsl:template>
```

The `<xsl:value-of select="."/>` element in the middle of the named template will be replaced by the value of the current node from which this template was called.

The `xsl:call-template` element appears in the contents of a template rule. It has a required `name` argument that names the template it will call. When processed, the `xsl:call-template` element is replaced by the contents of the `xsl:template` element it names. For example, you can now rewrite the `ATOMIC_NUMBER` rule like this by using the `xsl:call-template` element to call the `ATOM_CELL` named template:

```
<xsl:template match="ATOMIC_NUMBER">
  <xsl:call-template name="ATOM_CELL"/>
</xsl:template>
```

This fairly simple example only saves a few lines of code, but the more complicated the template, and the more times it's reused, the greater the reduction in complexity of the style sheet. Named templates also have the advantage, like variables, of factoring out common patterns in the style sheet so that you can edit them as one. For example, if you decide to change the color of atomic number, atomic weight, and other key values from blue to red, you only need to change it once in the named template. You do not have to change it in each separate template rule. This facilitates greater consistency of style.

Passing Parameters to Templates

Each separate invocation of a template can pass parameters to the template to customize its output. This is done the same way for named templates and unnamed templates. In the `xsl:template` element, the parameters are represented as `xsl:param` child elements. In `xsl:call-template` or `xsl:apply-templates` elements, parameters are represented as `xsl:with-param` child elements.

For example, suppose you also want to include a link to a particular file for each atom cell. The output should look something like this:

```
<TD>
  <FONT FACE="Times, serif" COLOR="blue" SIZE="2">
    <B>
      <A HREF="atomic_number.html">52</A>
    </B>
  </FONT>
</TD>
```

The trick is that the value of the `HREF` attribute has to be passed in from the point where the template is invoked because it changes for each separate invocation of the template. For example, atomic weights will have to be formatted like this:

```
<TD>
  <font FACE="Times, serif" COLOR="blue" SIZE="2">
    <B>
      <A HREF="atomic_weight.html">4.0026</A>
    </B>
  </FONT>
</TD>
```

This template accomplishes that task:

```
<xsl:template name="ATOM_CELL">
  <xsl:param name="file">index.html</xsl:param>
  <TD>
    <font FACE="Times, serif" COLOR="blue" SIZE="2">
      <B>
        <A HREF="{$file}"><xsl:value-of select="."/></A>
      </B>
    </FONT>
  </TD>
</xsl:template>
```

The `name` attribute of the `xsl:param` element gives the parameter a name (important if there are multiple arguments), and the contents of the `xsl:param` element supplies a default value for this parameter to be used if the invocation doesn't provide a value. (This can also be given as a string expression by using a `select` attribute.)

When this template is called, an xsl:with-param child of the xsl:call-template element provides the value of the parameter using its name attribute to identify the parameter and its contents to provide a value for the parameter. For example:

```
<xsl:template match="ATOMIC_NUMBER">
  <xsl:call-template name="ATOM_CELL">
    <xsl:with-param
               name="file">atomic_number.html</xsl:with-param>

  </xsl:call-template>
</xsl:template>
```

Again, this is a simple example. However, much more complex named templates exist. For example, you could define header and footer templates for pages on a web site for importing by many different style sheets, each of which would only have to change a few parameters for the name of the page author, the title of the page, and the copyright date.

Stripping and Preserving White Space

You may have noticed that most of the examples of output have been formatted a little strangely. The reason the examples appeared strange is that the source document needed to break long elements across multiple lines to fit between the margins of this book. Unfortunately, the extra white space added to the input document carried over into the output document. For a computer, the details of insignificant white space aren't important, but for a person they can be distracting.

The default behavior for text nodes read from the input document, such as the content of an ATOMIC_NUMBER or DENSITY element, is to preserve all white space. A typical DENSITY element looks like this:

```
<DENSITY UNITS="grams/cubic centimeter">
  <!-- At 300K, 1 atm -->
  0.0000899
</DENSITY>
```

When its value is taken the leading and trailing white space is included, like this, even though the space is really only there to help fit the example on this printed page and isn't at all significant:

```


  0.0000899


```

You can use the `normalize-space()` function to strip the leading and trailing white space from this or any other string. For example, instead of writing `<xsl:value-of select="DENSITY"/>`, you would write `<xsl:value-of select="normalize-space(DENSITY)"/>`.

You can also automatically delete white-space-only nodes in the input document by using `xsl:strip-space`. The `elements` attribute of this top-level element contains a list of elements from which text nodes that contain nothing but white space should be deleted. For example, this element says that nodes containing only white space should be stripped from `DENSITY`, `NAME`, `SYMBOL`, and `BOILING_POINT` elements:

```
<xsl:strip-space elements="DENSITY NAME SYMBOL BOILING_POINT"/>
```

This is not the same as trimming white space from the ends of text nodes like `normalize-space()` does. This only affects nodes that contain nothing but white space, not nodes that contain white space and other nonspace content.

You can strip space-only nodes in all elements by using the `*` wildcard, like this:

```
<xsl:strip-space elements="*"/>
```

There's also an `xsl:preserve-space` element with a similar syntax but opposite meaning. However, because preserving space is the default, this element isn't much used. Its main purpose is to override `xsl:strip-space` elements imported from other style sheets or to specify a few elements where space is preserved when the default has been reset to stripping by `<xsl:strip-space elements="*"/>`.

White-space-only text nodes in the style sheet, as opposed to the input document, are another matter. They are stripped by default. If you want to preserve one, you attach an `xml:space` attribute with the value `preserve` to its parent element or to another one of its ancestors.

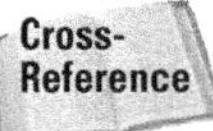

The `xml:space` attribute was discussed in Chapter 6.

Sometimes the easiest way to include significant white space in a style sheet is to wrap it in an `xsl:text` element. Space inside an `xsl:text` element is treated literally and not stripped.

Making Choices

XSLT provides two elements that allow you to choose different output based on the input. The `xsl:if` element either does or does not output a given fragment of XML depending on what patterns are present in the input. The `xsl:choose` element picks one of several possible XML fragments, depending on what patterns are present in the input. Most of what you can do with `xsl:if` and `xsl:choose` can also be done by a suitable application of templates. However, sometimes the solution with `xsl:if` or `xsl:choose` is simpler and more obvious.

xsl:if

The `xsl:if` element provides a simple facility for changing the output based on a pattern. The `test` attribute of `xsl:if` contains an expression that evaluates to a boolean. If the expression is true, the contents of the `xsl:if` element are output. Otherwise, they're not. For example, this template writes out the names of all `ATOM` elements. A comma and a space is added after all except the last element in the list.

```
<xsl:template match="ATOM">
  <xsl:value-of select="NAME"/>
  <xsl:if test="position()!=last()">, </xsl:if>
</xsl:template>
```

This ensures that the list looks like "Hydrogen, Helium" and not "Hydrogen, Helium, "."

There are no `xsl:else` or `xsl:else-if` elements. The `xsl:choose` element provides this functionality.

xsl:choose

The `xsl:choose` element selects one of several possible outputs depending on several possible conditions. Each condition and its associated output template is provided by an `xsl:when` child element. The `test` attribute of the `xsl:when` element is an XPath expression with a boolean value. If multiple conditions are true, only the first true one is instantiated. If none of the `xsl:when` elements are true, the `xsl:otherwise` child element is instantiated. If the `xsl:choose` element does not have an `xsl:otherwise` element, no output created. For example, this rule changes the color of the output based on whether the `STATE` attribute of the `ATOM` element is `SOLID`, `LIQUID`, or `GAS`:

```
<xsl:template match="ATOM">
  <xsl:choose>
    <xsl:when test="@STATE='SOLID'">
      <P style="color: black">
        <xsl:value-of select="."/>
      </P>
    </xsl:when>
    <xsl:when test="@STATE='LIQUID'">
      <P style="color: blue">
        <xsl:value-of select="."/>
      </P>
    </xsl:when>
```

```
      <xsl:when test="@STATE='GAS'">
        <P style="color: red">
          <xsl:value-of select="."/>
        </P>
      </xsl:when>
      <xsl:otherwise>
        <P style="color: green">
          <xsl:value-of select="."/>
        </P>
      </xsl:otherwise>
    </xsl:choose>
  </xsl:template>
```

Merging Multiple Style Sheets

A single XML document may use many different markup vocabularies. You may wish to use different standard style sheets for those different vocabularies. However, you'll also want style rules for particular documents. The `xsl:import` and `xsl:include` elements enable you to merge multiple style sheets so that you can organize and reuse style sheets for different vocabularies and purposes.

Importing with xsl:import

The `xsl:import` element is a top-level element whose `href` attribute provides the URI of a style sheet to import. All `xsl:import` elements must appear before any other top-level element in the `xsl:stylesheet` root element. For example, these `xsl:import` elements import the style sheets genealogy.xsl and standards.xsl.

```
<xsl:stylesheet version="1.0"
  xmlns:xsl="http://www.w3.org/1999/XSL/Transform">
  <xsl:import href="genealogy.xsl"/>
  <xsl:import href="standards.xsl"/>
  <!-- other child elements follow -->
</xsl:stylesheet>
```

Rules in the imported style sheets may conflict with rules in the importing style sheet. If so, rules in the importing style sheet take precedence. If two rules in different imported style sheets conflict, the rule in the last style sheet imported (standards.xsl above) takes precedence.

The `xsl:apply-imports` element is a slight variant of `xsl:apply-templates` that only uses imported rules. It does not use any rules from the importing style sheet. This allows access to imported rules that would otherwise be overridden by rules in the importing style sheet. Other than the name, it has identical syntax to `xsl:apply-templates`. The only behavioral difference is that it only matches template rules in imported style sheets.

Inclusion with xsl:include

The xsl:include element is a top-level element that copies another style sheet into the current style sheet at the point where it occurs. (More precisely, it copies the contents of the xsl-stylesheet or xsl:transform element in the remote document into the current document.) Its href attribute provides the URI of the style sheet to include. An xsl:include element can occur anywhere at the top level after the last xsl:import element.

Unlike rules included by xsl:import elements, rules included by xsl:include elements have the same precedence in the including style sheet that they would have if they were copied and pasted from one style sheet to the other. As far as the XSLT processor is concerned, there is no difference between an included rule and a rule that's physically present.

Output Methods

Most of the examples in this chapter have focused on transforming XML into well-formed HTML. However, most XSLT processors actually support three different output methods:

- XML
- HTML
- Text

The XSLT processor behaves differently depending on which of these output methods it uses. The XML format is the default and in many ways the simplest. The output is mostly exactly what you request in your style sheet. Because well-formed XML does not permit raw less –than signs and ampersands, if you use a character reference such as < or the entity reference < to insert the < character, the formatter will output < or perhaps <. If you use a character reference such as & or the entity reference & to insert the & character, the formatter will insert & or perhaps &.

The HTML output method is designed to output standard HTML 4.0. This is not the well-formed HTML used in this book, but rather traditional HTML in which empty-element tags look like <HR> and <IMG> instead of <HR/> and <IMG/>, processing instructions are terminated with a > instead of ?>, and < signs used in JavaScript are not converted to <. This makes it much easier to output HTML that works across many browsers and platforms without odd effects such as double lines where a single line is expected or other detritus caused by forcing HTML into the XML mold. The HTML output method is automatically selected when the formatter notices that the root output element is html, HTML, HtMl, or any other combination of case that still spells Hypertext Markup Language.

The final output method is pure text. The text output method operates by first forming a full result tree as per the XML output method, but then only outputting the string value of that tree. This is useful for transforming to non-XML formats such as RTF or TeX. The primary benefit of the text output format is that less than signs are not converted to `<` or `<` and ampersands are not converted to `&` or `&`. This allows you to output effectively arbitrary text.

By default, an XSLT processor will use the XML output method, unless it recognizes the output root element as `HTML`, in which case it uses the HTML output method. You can change this by using a top-level `xsl:output` element. The `method` attribute of the `xsl:output` element specifies which output method to use and normally has one of these three values:

- `xml`
- `html`
- `text`

For example, to specify that you want pure well-formed HTML as output, with all the empty-element tags properly indicated, all less than signs escaped, and so forth, you would use this `xsl:output` element at the top level of your style sheet:

```
<xsl:output method="xml"/>
```

To indicate that you want regular HTML output even though you aren't using an `html` root element, you'd put this `xsl:output` element at the top level of your style sheet:

```
<xsl:output method="html"/>
```

The `xsl:output` element also has a number of other allowed attributes that modify how XML is output. These allow you to change the prolog of the document, how the output is indented with insignificant white space, and which elements use `CDATA` sections rather than escaping `<` and `&` characters.

XML Declaration

Four attributes of `xsl:output` format the XML declaration used in your document. This assumes the output method is xml. These attributes are as follows:

- `omit-xml-declaration`
- `version`
- `encoding`
- `standalone`

The omit-xml-declaration attribute has the value yes or no. If yes, an XML declaration is not included in the output document. If no, then it is. For example, to insert a very basic <?xml version="1.0"?> XML declaration in the output document you would use this xsl:output element at the top level of your style sheet:

```
<xsl:output method="xml" omit-xml-declaration="no"/>
```

You could also include it as two separate xsl:output elements, like this:

```
<xsl:output method="xml"/>
<xsl:output omit-xml-declaration="no"/>
```

The default value of the version attribute of the XML declaration is 1.0. Currently, that's the only value allowed. If at some point in the future that changes, the version attribute of xsl:output will allow you to change the version used in the XML declaration, as in the following example:

```
<xsl:output version="1.1"/>
```

You can set the standalone attribute of the XML declaration to the value yes or no using the standalone attribute of the xsl:output element. For example, this xsl:output element would insert the XML declaration <?xml version="1.0" standalone="yes"?>:

```
<xsl:output method="xml"
            omit-xml-declaration="no" standalone="yes"/>
```

The final possible piece of an XML declaration is the encoding declaration. As you probably guessed this can be set with the encoding attribute of the xsl:output element. For example, to insert the XML declaration <?xml version="1.0" encoding="ISO-8859-1"?>, you'd use this xsl:output element:

```
<xsl:output method="xml"
          omit-xml-declaration="no" encoding="ISO-8859-1"/>
```

This also changes the encoding the XSLT processor uses for the output document from its default UTF-8. However, not all processors support all possible encodings. Those written in Java are likely to support the most encodings because Java's rich class library makes it almost trivial to support several dozen popular encodings.

Document Type Declaration

XSLT does not provide any elements for building a DTD for the output document with <!ELEMENT>, <!ATTLIST>, <!ENTITY>, and <!NOTATION> declarations, either as an internal or external DTD subset. However, it does provide two attributes of the xsl:output element you can use to include a DOCTYPE declaration that points to an external DTD. These are doctype-system and doctype-public. The first inserts a `SYSTEM` identifier for the DTD; the second a `PUBLIC` identifier. For example, suppose you want this `DOCTYPE` declaration in your output document:

```
<!DOCTYPE PERIODIC_TABLE SYSTEM "chemistry.dtd">
```

Then you would use this `xsl:output` element at the top level of your style sheet:

```
<xsl:output doctype-system="chemistry.dtd"/>
```

The XSLT processor determines the proper root element for the document type declaration by looking at the root element of the output tree. Using a full URL instead of a relative URL is equally easy:

```
<xsl:output
  doctype-system="http://www.example.com/chemistry.dtd"/>
```

On the other hand, suppose you want this `DOCTYPE` declaration in your output document:

```
<!DOCTYPE html PUBLIC "-//W3C//DTD HTML 4.0 Transitional//EN"
         "http://www.w3.org/TR/REC-html40/loose.dtd">
```

Then you would use both `doctype-system` and `doctype-public` attributes so your `DOCTYPE` declaration will have both a `PUBLIC` and a `SYSTEM` identifier. For example:

```
<xsl:output
  doctype-system="http://www.w3.org/TR/REC-html40/loose.dtd"
  doctype-public="-//W3C//DTD HTML 4.0 Transitional//EN"/>
```

Indentation

The indentation of many of the output examples in this chapter has been more than a little flaky. It's certainly not as neat as the carefully hand-coded indentation of the input documents. However, if white space isn't particularly significant in your output format, you can ask the formatter for "pretty printed" XML with the nesting of different elements indicated by the indentation. This is accomplished by the `indent` attribute of the `xsl:output` element. If this attribute has the value `yes` (the default is `no`), the processor is allowed (but not required) to insert (but not remove) extra white space into the output to try to pretty print the output. This may include indentation and line breaks. For example, this element requests indenting:

```
<xsl:output indent="yes"/>
```

You cannot specify how much you want each level indented (for example, by two spaces or one tab). That's up to the formatter. Nonetheless, the `xsl:strip-space` and the `indent` attribute of the `xsl:output` element allow you to produce output that's almost as attractive as the most painstakingly hand-crafted XML.

CDATA sections

XSLT does not allow you to insert CDATA sections at arbitrary locations in XML documents produced by XSL transformations. However, you can specify that the text contents of a particular element be placed in a `CDATA` section. In this case the < and & symbols are not encoded as `<` and `&` as they would normally be. To do this, place the name of the element whose text contents should be wrapped in CDATA delimiters in the `cdata-section-elements` attribute of the `xsl:output` element. For example, this `xsl:output` element says that the contents of the `SCRIPT` element should be wrapped in a CDATA section:

```
<xsl:output cdata-section-elements="SCRIPT"/>
```

You can enclose multiple names of elements whose text contents should be wrapped in CDATA delimiters in one `cdata-section-elements` attribute simply by separating the names with white space. For example, this `xsl:output` element says that the contents of both the `SCRIPT` and `CODE` elements should be wrapped in a CDATA section:

```
<xsl:output cdata-section-elements="SCRIPT CODE"/>
```

Alternately, you can just use multiple `xsl:output` elements, each naming one element. For example:

```
<xsl:output cdata-section-elements="SCRIPT"/>
<xsl:output cdata-section-elements="CODE"/>
```

Summary

In this chapter, you learned about XSL transformations. In particular, you learned the following:

- ✦ The Extensible Stylesheet Language (XSL) comprises two separate XML applications for transforming and formatting XML documents.
- ✦ An XSL transformation applies rules to a tree read from an XML document to transform it into an output tree written out as an XML document.
- ✦ An XSL template rule is represented as an `xsl:template` element. The `match` attribute determines which nodes the template matches. The contents of the `xsl:template` element are a template that is instantiated when a node is matched.
- ✦ The value of a node is a pure text (no markup) string containing the contents of the node. This can be calculated by the `xsl:value-of` element.
- ✦ You can process multiple elements in two ways: using the `xsl:apply-templates` element and the `xsl:for each` element.

- The value of the match attribute of the xsl:template element is a match pattern specifying which nodes the template matches.
- XPath expressions (or simply expressions) are a superset of match patterns used by the select attribute of xsl:apply-templates, xsl:value-of, xsl:for-each, xsl:copy-of, xsl:variable, xsl:param, xsl:with-param, and xsl:sort elements.
- Default rules apply templates to element nodes and take the value of text nodes and attributes.
- Attribute value templates are braced XPath expressions in certain attributes that are evaluated to create an attribute value.
- The xsl:element, xsl:attribute, xsl:processing-instruction, xsl:comment, and xsl:text elements output elements, attributes, processing instructions, comments, and text calculated from data in the input document.
- The xsl:attribute-set element defines a common group of attributes that can be applied to multiple elements in different templates with the xsl:use-attribute-sets.
- The xsl:copy element shallow copies the current node from the input into the output.
- The xsl:copy-of element deep copies the current node from the input into the output.
- The xsl:number element inserts the number specified by its value attribute into the output using a specified number format given by the format attribute.
- The xsl:sort element can reorder the input nodes before copying them to the output.
- Modes can apply different templates to the same element from different locations in the style sheet.
- The xsl:variable element defines named constants that can clarify your code.
- Named templates help you reuse common template code. Parameters can be defined and passed to templates using the xsl:param and xsl:with-param elements.
- White space in the input document is maintained by default, unless an xsl:strip-space element or xml:space attribute says otherwise.
- The xsl:if element produces output if, and only if, its test attribute is true.
- The xsl:choose element outputs the template of the first one of its xsl:when children whose test attribute is true, or the template of its xsl:otherwise element if no xsl:when element has a true test attribute.

- The `xsl:import` and `xsl:include` elements merge rules from different style sheets.
- The `xsl:stylesheet` element allows you to include a style sheet directly in the document it applies to.
- Various attributes of the `xsl:output` element allow you to specify the output document's format, XML declaration, document type declaration, indentation, encoding, and MIME media type.

The next chapter takes up the second half of XSL: the formatting objects vocabulary. Formatting objects are an extremely powerful way of specifying the precise layout you want your pages to have. XSL transformations are used to transform an XML document into an XSL formatting object document.

✦ ✦ ✦

XSL Formatting Objects

In This Chapter

Formatting objects and their properties

Page layout

Content

Leaders and rules

Graphics

Links

Lists

Tables

Inlines

Footnotes

Floats

Formatting properties

XSL Formatting Objects (XSL-FO) are the second half of the Extensible Stylesheet Language (XSL). XSL-FO is an XML application that describes how pages will look when presented to a reader. A style sheet uses the XSL transformation language to transform an XML document in a semantic vocabulary into a new XML document that uses the XSL-FO presentational vocabulary. While one can hope that web browsers will one day know how to directly display data marked up with XSL formatting objects, for now, an additional step is necessary in which the output document is further transformed into some other format, such as Adobe's PDF.

Formatting Objects and Their Properties

XSL-FO provides a more sophisticated visual layout model than HTML+CSS. Formatting supported by XSL-FO, but not supported by HTML+CSS, includes right-to-left and top-to-bottom text, footnotes, margin notes, page numbers in cross-references, and more. In particular, while cascading style sheets (CSS) is primarily intended for use on the Web, XSL-FO is designed for broader use. You should, for example, be able to write an XSL style sheet that uses formatting objects to lay out an entire printed book. A different style sheet should be able to transform the same XML document into a web site.

Caution

This chapter is based on the October 15, 2001, Recommendation of the XSL specification. However, most software does not implement all of the final Recommendation for XSL. In fact, so far, only a few stand-alone programs convert XSL-FO documents into PDF files. There are no web browsers that can display a document written with XSL formatting objects.

There are exactly 56 XSL formatting object elements. These are placed in the `http://www.w3.org/1999/XSL/Format` namespace. At least 99 percent of the time, the chosen prefix is `fo`. In this chapter, I use the `fo` prefix to indicate this namespace without further comment.

Of the 56 elements, most signify various kinds of rectangular areas. Most of the rest are containers for rectangular areas and spaces. In alphabetical order, these formatting objects are as follows:

- fo:basic-link
- fo:bidi-override
- fo:block
- fo:block-container
- fo:character
- fo:color-profile
- fo:conditional-page-master-reference
- fo:declarations
- fo:external-graphic
- fo:float
- fo:flow
- fo:footnote
- fo:footnote-body
- fo:initial-property-set
- fo:inline
- fo:inline-container
- fo:instream-foreign-object
- fo:layout-master-set
- fo:leader
- fo:list-block
- fo:list-item
- fo:list-item-body
- fo:list-item-label
- fo:marker
- fo:multi-case
- fo:multi-properties
- fo:multi-property-set
- fo:multi-switch
- fo:multi-toggle
- fo:page-number
- fo:page-number-citation
- fo:page-sequence
- fo:page-sequence-master
- fo:region-after
- fo:region-before
- fo:region-body
- fo:region-end
- fo:region-start
- fo:repeatable-page-master-alternatives
- fo:repeatable-page-master-reference
- fo:retrieve-marker
- fo:root
- fo:simple-page-master
- fo:single-page-master-reference
- fo:static-content
- fo:table
- fo:table-and-caption
- fo:table-body
- fo:table-caption
- fo:table-cell
- fo:table-column
- fo:table-footer
- fo:table-header
- fo:table-row
- fo:title
- fo:wrapper

The XSL formatting model is based on rectangular boxes called *areas* that can contain text, empty space, images, or other formatting objects. As with CSS boxes, an area has borders and padding on each of its sides, although CSS's margins are replaced by XSL's space-before and space-after. An XSL formatter reads the formatting objects to determine which areas to place where on the page. Many formatting objects produce single areas (at least most of the time); but because of page breaks, word wrapping, hyphenation, and other details that must be taken into account when fitting an indefinite amount of text into a finite amount of space, some formatting objects do occasionally generate more than one area.

The formatting objects differ primarily in what they represent. For example, the `fo:list-item-label` formatting object is a box that contains a bullet, a number, or another indicator placed in front of a list item. A `fo:list-item-body` formatting object is a box that contains the text, sans label, of the list item. And a `fo:list-item` formatting object is a box that contains both the `fo:list-item-label` and `fo:list-item-body` formatting objects.

When processed, the formatting objects document is broken up into pages. A web browser window will normally be treated as one very long page. A print format will often contain many individual pages. Each page contains a number of areas. There are four primary kinds of areas:

1. Regions
2. Block areas
3. Line areas
4. Inline areas

These form a rough hierarchy. Regions contain block areas. Block areas contain other block areas, line areas, and content. Line areas contain inline areas. Inline areas contain other inline areas and content. More specifically:

✦ A region is the highest-level container in XSL-FO. You can think of a page of this book as containing three regions: the header, the main body of the page, and the footer. Formatting objects that produce regions include `fo:region-body`, `fo:region-before`, `fo:region-after`, `fo:region-start`, and `fo:region-end`.

✦ A block area represents a block-level element, such as a paragraph or a list item. Although block areas may contain other block areas, there should always be a line break before the start and after the end of each block area. A block area, rather than being precisely positioned by coordinates, is placed sequentially in the area that contains it. As other block areas are added and deleted before it or within it, the block area's position shifts as necessary to make room. A block area may contain parsed character data, inline areas, line areas, and other block areas that are sequentially arranged in the containing block area. Formatting objects that produce block areas include `fo:block`, `fo:table-and-caption`, and `fo:list-block`.

- A line area represents a line of text inside a block. For example, each of the lines in this list item is a line area. Line areas can contain inline areas and inline spaces. There are no formatting objects that correspond to line areas. Instead, the formatting engine calculates the line areas as it decides how to wrap lines inside block areas.
- Inline areas are parts of a line such as a single character, a footnote reference, or a mathematical equation. Inline areas can contain other inline areas and raw text. Formatting objects that produce inline areas include `fo:character`, `fo:external-graphic`, `fo:inline`, `fo:instream-foreign-object`, `fo:leader`, and `fo:page-number`.

Formatting properties

When taken as a whole, the various formatting objects in an XSL-FO document specify the order in which content is to be placed on pages. However, *formatting properties* specify the details of formatting, such as size, position, font, color, and a lot more. Formatting properties are represented as attributes on the individual formatting object elements.

The details of many of these properties should be familiar from CSS. Work is ongoing to ensure that CSS and XSL-FO use the same names to mean the same things. For example, the CSS `font-family` property means the same thing as the XSL `font-family` property; and although the syntax for assigning values to properties is different in CSS and XSL-FO, the meaning of the values themselves is the same. To indicate that the `fo:block` element is formatted in some approximation of Times, you might use this CSS rule:

```
fo:block {font-family: 'New York', 'Times New Roman', serif}
```

The XSL-FO equivalent is to include a `font-family` attribute in the `fo:block` start-tag in this way:

```
<fo:block font-family="'New York', 'Times New Roman', serif">
```

Although this is superficially different, the style name (`font-family`) and the style value (`'New York', 'Times New Roman', serif`) are the same. CSS's `font-family` property is specified as a list of font names, separated by commas, in order from first choice to last choice. XSL-FO's `font-family` property is specified as a list of font names, separated by commas, in order from first choice to last choice. Both CSS and XSL-FO quote font names that contain white space. Both CSS and XSL-FO understand the keyword `serif` to mean an arbitrary serif font.

Of course, XSL formatting objects support many properties that have no CSS equivalent, such as `destination-placement-offset`, `block-progression-dimension`, `character`, and `hyphenation-keep`. You need to learn these to take full advantage of XSL. The standard XSL-FO properties follow:

absolute-position
active-state
alignment-adjust
alignment-baseline
auto-restore
azimuth
background
background-attachment
background-color
background-image
background-position
background-position-horizontal
background-position-vertical
background-repeat
baseline-shift
blank-or-not-blank
block-progression-dimension
border
border-after-color
border-after-precedence
border-after-style
border-after-width
border-before-color
border-before-precedence
border-before-style
border-before-width
border-bottom
border-bottom-color
border-bottom-style
border-bottom-width
border-collapse
border-color
border-end-color
border-end-precedence
border-end-style
border-end-width
border-left
border-left-color
border-left-style
border-left-width
border-right
border-right-color
border-right-style
border-right-width
border-separation
border-spacing
border-start-color
border-start-precedence
border-start-style
border-start-width
border-style
border-top
border-top-color
border-top-style
border-top-width
border-width
bottom
break-after
break-before
caption-side
case-name
case-title
character
clear
clip
color
color-profile-name
column-count
column-gap
column-number
column-width
content-height
content-type
content-width
country
cue
cue-after
cue-before
destination-placement-offset
direction
display-align
dominant-baseline
elevation

empty-cells

end-indent

ends-row

extent

external-destination

float

flow-name

font

font-family

font-selection-strategy

font-size

font-size-adjust

font-stretch

font-style

font-variant

font-weight

force-page-count

format

glyph-orientation-horizontal

glyph-orientation-vertical

grouping-separator

grouping-size

height

hyphenate

hyphenation-character

hyphenation-keep

hyphenation-ladder-count

hyphenation-push-character-count

hyphenation-remain-character-count

id

indicate-destination

initial-page-number

inline-progression-dimension

internal-destination

keep-together

keep-with-next

keep-with-previous

language

last-line-end-indent

leader-alignment

leader-length

leader-pattern

leader-pattern-width

left

letter-spacing

letter-value

linefeed-treatment

line-height

line-height-shift-adjustment

line-stacking-strategy

margin

margin-bottom

margin-left

margin-right

margin-top

marker-class-name

master-name

master-reference

max-height

maximum-repeats

max-width

media-usage

min-height

min-width

number-columns-repeated

number-columns-spanned

number-rows-spanned

odd-or-even

orphans

overflow

padding

padding-after

padding-before

padding-bottom

padding-end

padding-left

padding-right

padding-start

padding-top

page-break-after

page-break-before

page-break-inside

page-height

page-position
page-width
pause
pause-after
pause-before
pitch
pitch-range
play-during
position
precedence
provisional-distance-between-starts
provisional-label-separation
reference-orientation
ref-id
region-name
relative-align
relative-position
rendering-intent
retrieve-boundary
retrieve-class-name
retrieve-position
richness
right
role
rule-style
rule-thickness
scaling
scaling-method
score-spaces
script
show-destination
size
source-document
space-after
space-before
space-end
space-start
space-treatment
span
speak
speak-header
speak-numeral
speak-punctuation
speech-rate
src
start-indent
starting-state
starts-row
stress
suppress-at-line-break
switch-to
table-layout
table-omit-footer-at-break
table-omit-header-at-break
target-presentation-context
target-processing-context
target-stylesheet
text-align
text-align-last
text-altitude
text-decoration
text-depth
text-indent
text-shadow
text-transform
top
treat-as-word-space
unicode-bidi
vertical-align
visibility
voice-family
volume
white-space
white-space-collapse
widows
width
word-spacing
wrap-option
writing-mode
xml:lang
z-index

Transforming to formatting objects

XSL-FO is a complete XML vocabulary for laying out text on a page. An XSL-FO document is simply a well-formed XML document that uses this vocabulary. That means it has an XML declaration, a root element, child elements, and so forth. It must adhere to all the well-formedness rules of any XML document, or formatters will not accept it. By convention, a file that contains XSL formatting objects has the three-letter extension .fob or the two-letter extension .fo. However, it might have the suffix .xml because it also is a well-formed XML file.

Listing 16-1 is a simple document marked up using XSL formatting objects. The root of the document is `fo:root`. This element contains a `fo:layout-master-set` and a `fo:page-sequence`. The `fo:layout-master-set` element contains `fo:simple-page-master` child elements. Each `fo:simple-page-master` describes a kind of page on which content will be placed. Here there's only one very simple page, but more complex documents can have different master pages for first, right, and left, body pages, front matter, back matter, and more, each with a potentially different set of margins, page numbering, and other features. The name by which the page master will be referenced is given in the `master-name` attribute.

Content is placed on copies of the master page using a `fo:page-sequence`. The `fo:page-sequence` element has a `master-reference` attribute naming the master page to be used. Its `fo:flow` child element holds the actual content to be placed on the pages. The content is given as two `fo:block` children, each with a `font-size` property of 20 points, a `font-family` property of `serif`, and a line height of 30 points.

Listing 16-1: A Simple XSL-FO Document

```
<?xml version="1.0"?>
<fo:root xmlns:fo="http://www.w3.org/1999/XSL/Format">

  <fo:layout-master-set>
    <fo:simple-page-master master-name="only">
      <fo:region-body/>
    </fo:simple-page-master>
  </fo:layout-master-set>

  <fo:page-sequence master-reference="only">

    <fo:flow flow-name="xsl-region-body">
      <fo:block font-size="20pt" font-family="serif"
                line-height="30pt">
        Hydrogen
      </fo:block>
      <fo:block font-size="20pt" font-family="serif"
                line-height="30pt" >
        Helium
      </fo:block>
    </fo:flow>
```

```
  </fo:page-sequence>

</fo:root>
```

Although you could write a document such as Listing 16-1 by hand, doing so would lose all the benefits of content-format independence achieved by XML. Normally, you write an XSLT style sheet that transforms an XML source document into XSL-FO. Listing 16-2 is the XSLT style sheet that produced Listing 16-1 by transforming the previous chapter's Listing 15-1.

Listing 16-2: A Transformation from a Source Vocabulary to XSL Formatting Objects

```
<?xml version="1.0"?>
<xsl:stylesheet version="1.0"
  xmlns:xsl="http://www.w3.org/1999/XSL/Transform"
  xmlns:fo="http://www.w3.org/1999/XSL/Format">

  <xsl:output indent="yes"/>

  <xsl:template match="/">
    <fo:root xmlns:fo="http://www.w3.org/1999/XSL/Format">

      <fo:layout-master-set>
        <fo:simple-page-master master-name="only">
          <fo:region-body/>
        </fo:simple-page-master>
      </fo:layout-master-set>

      <fo:page-sequence master-reference="only">

        <fo:flow flow-name="xsl-region-body">
          <xsl:apply-templates select="//ATOM"/>
        </fo:flow>

      </fo:page-sequence>

    </fo:root>
  </xsl:template>

  <xsl:template match="ATOM">
    <fo:block font-size="20pt" font-family="serif"
              line-height="30pt">
      <xsl:value-of select="NAME"/>
    </fo:block>
  </xsl:template>

</xsl:stylesheet>
```

Using FOP

At the time of this writing, no web browser can directly display XML documents transformed into XSL formatting objects. However, there are several applications that can convert an XSL-FO document into a viewable format such as PDF or TeX. The one used here is the XML Apache project's open source FOP. FOP is a command-line Java program that converts XSL-FO documents to PDF files as well as several other formats, including PCL, SVG, plain text, and FrameMaker MIF. At the time of this writing, the most recent version of FOP is 0.20.5, which incompletely supports a subset of the formatting objects and properties in the XSL 1.0 Recommendation. You can download the latest version of FOP from `http://xml.apache.org/fop/`.

FOP is a Java program that should run on any platform with a reasonably compatible Java 1.2 or later virtual machine. To install it, just unpack the distribution and add the directory where you put it (I use /usr/local/xml/fop on UNIX and C:\xml\fop on Windows) to your path.

The directory where you installed it contains, among other files, fop.bat and fop.sh. Use fop.bat for Windows and fop.sh for UNIX. Add the appropriate script for your platform to your path environment variable. Then run it from the command line with arguments specifying the input and output files, like this:

```
C:\> fop -fo 16-1.fo -pdf 16-1.pdf
```

The output will look something like this:

```
[INFO] Using org.apache.xerces.parsers.SAXParser as SAX2 Parser
[INFO] FOP 0.20.5
[INFO] Using org.apache.xerces.parsers.SAXParser as SAX2 Parser
[INFO] building formatting object tree
[INFO] setting up fonts
[INFO] [1]
[INFO] Parsing of document complete, stopping renderer
```

Here, 16-1.fo is the input XML file that uses the formatting object vocabulary. 16-1.pdf is the output PDF file that can be displayed and printed by Adobe Acrobat, Preview, GhostView, or other programs that read PDF files.

Although PDF files are themselves ASCII text, this isn't a book about PostScript, so there's nothing to be gained by showing you the exact output of the preceding command. If you're curious, open the PDF file in any text editor. Instead, Figure 16-1 shows the rendered file displayed in Acrobat Reader.

PDF files are not the only destination format for XML documents styled with XSL formatting objects. FOP can also transform XSL-FO documents into PCL, MIF, SVG, and plain-text files. In the near future, it's expected to be able to produce RTF documents, as well. It can also display the file directly in a window, as shown in Figure 16-2. Other XSL-FO tools can produce other formats.

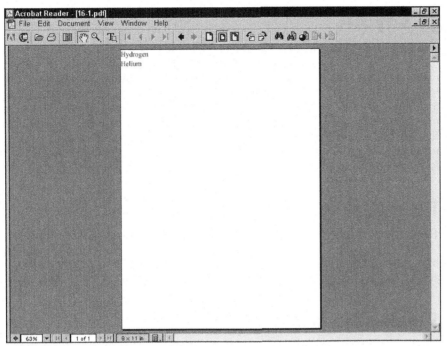

Figure 16-1: The PDF file displayed in Acrobat Reader

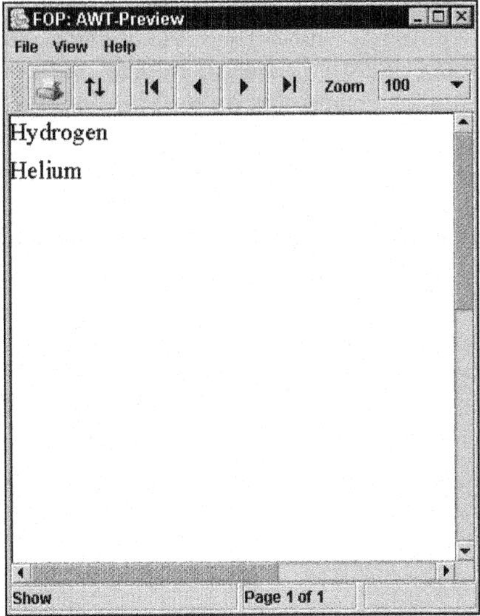

Figure 16-2: FOP rendering the XSL-FO document in a GUI

Page Layout

The root element of a formatting objects document is `fo:root`. This element contains one `fo:layout-master-set` element and one or more `fo:page-sequence` elements. The `fo:page-sequence` elements contain content; that is, text and images to be placed on the pages. The `fo:layout-master-set` contains templates for the pages that will be created. When the formatter reads an XSL-FO document, it creates a page based on the first template in the `fo:layout-master-set`. Then it fills it with content from the `fo:page-sequence`. When it's filled the first page, it instantiates a second page and fills it with content. The process continues until the formatter runs out of content.

The root element

The `fo:root` element generally has an `xmlns:fo` attribute with the value `http://www.w3.org/1999/XSL/Format` and may (though it generally does not) have an `id` attribute. The `fo:root` element exists just to declare the namespace and be the document root. It has no direct effect on page layout or formatting.

Simple page masters

The page templates are called *page masters*. Page masters are similar in purpose to QuarkXPress master pages or PowerPoint slide masters. Each defines a general layout for a page including its margins, the sizes of the header, footer, and body area of the page, and so forth. Each actual page in the rendered document is based on one master page, and inherits certain properties like margins, page numbering, and layout from that master page. XSL-FO 1.0 defines exactly one kind of page master, the `fo:simple-page-master`, which represents a rectangular page. The `fo:layout-master-set` contains one or more `fo:simple-page-master` elements that define master pages.

Note: Future versions of XSL-FO will add other kinds of page masters, possibly including nonrectangular pages.

Each master page is represented by a `fo:simple-page-master` element. A `fo:simple-page-master` element defines a page layout, including the size of its before region, body region, after region, end region, and start region. Figure 16-3 shows the typical layout of these parts. One thing that may not be obvious from this picture is that the body region overlaps the other four regions (though not the page margins); that is, the body is everything inside the thick black line including the start, end, before, and after regions.

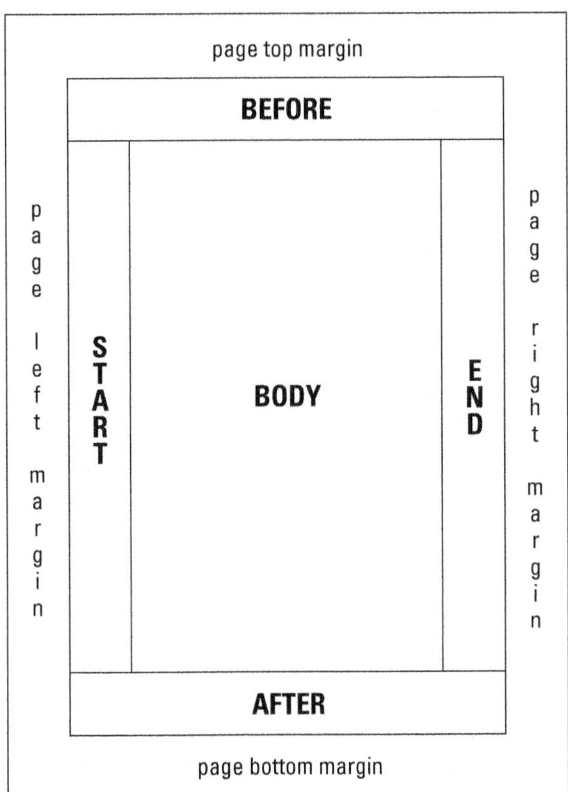

Figure 16-3: The layout of the parts of a simple page of English text

In normal English text, the end region is the right side of the page, and the start region is the left side of the page. This is reversed in Hebrew or Arabic text, because these languages are written from right to left. In most modern languages, the before region is the header and the after region is the footer, but this could be reversed in a language that writes from bottom to top.

Simple page master properties

The `fo:simple-page-master` element has three main attributes:

- `master-name` — The name by which page sequences will reference this master page
- `page-height` — The height of the page
- `page-width` — The width of the page

If the page-height and page-width are not provided, the formatter chooses a reasonable default based on the media in use (for example, 8.5"×11" for paper).

Other attributes commonly applied to page masters include the following:

- ✦ The margin-bottom, margin-left, margin-right, and margin-top attributes, or the shorthand margin attribute
- ✦ The writing-mode attribute that determines which direction text flows on the page, for example, left to right, right to left, or top to bottom
- ✦ The reference-orientation attribute that specifies in 90-degree increments whether and how much the content is rotated

For example, here is a fo:layout-master-set containing one fo:simple-page-master named US-Letter. It specifies an 8.5 × 11-inch page with half-inch margins on each side. It contains a single region, the body, into which all content will be placed.

```
<fo:layout-master-set>
  <fo:simple-page-master  master-name="US-Letter"
     page-height="11in"   page-width="8.5in"
     margin-top="0.5in"   margin-bottom="0.5in"
     margin-left="0.5in"  margin-right="0.5in">
    <fo:region-body/>
  </fo:simple-page-master>
</fo:layout-master-set>
```

Regions

The designer sets the size of the body (center) region, header, footer, end region, and start region, as well as the distances between them, by adding region child elements to the fo:simple-page-master. These are as follows:

- ✦ fo:region-before
- ✦ fo:region-after
- ✦ fo:region-body
- ✦ fo:region-start
- ✦ fo:region-end

The fo:region-before and fo:region-after elements each have an extent attribute that gives the height of these regions. Their width extends from the left side of the page to the right side. The fo:region-start and fo:region-end elements each have an extent attribute that specifies their widths. Their height extends from the bottom of the start region to the top of the end region. (This assumes normal Western text. Details would be rotated in Chinese, Hebrew, or any other non-right-to-left-top-to-bottom script.)

The fo:region-body does not have an extent attribute. Instead, the size of the body is everything inside the page margins. Thus, the region body overlaps the other four regions on the page. If you place text into the body and the other four regions, text will be drawn on top of other content. To avoid this, you must set the left margin of the body to be as large or larger than the extent of the start region, the top margin of the body to be as large or larger than the extent of the before region, and so on.

Each of the five regions of a simple page master may be filled with content when the document is processed. However, the region elements do not contain that content. Instead, they simply give the dimensions of the boxes the formatter will build to put content in. The content is copied from a fo:flow or fo:static-content element elsewhere in the document. The region elements are blueprints for the boxes, not the boxes themselves.

For example, this fo:simple-page-master defines a page with 1 inch before and after regions. The region body extends vertically from the bottom of the before region to the top of the after region. It extends horizontally from the left side of the page to the right side of the page because there is no start or end region.

```
<fo:simple-page-master master-name="table_page">
  <fo:region-before extent="1.0in"/>
  <fo:region-body margin-top="1.0in" margin-bottom="1.0in"/>
  <fo:region-after extent="1.0in"/>
</fo:simple-page-master>
```

For another example, here is a fo:layout-master-set that makes all outer regions 1 inch. Furthermore, the page itself has a half-inch margin on all sides.

```
<fo:layout-master-set>
  <fo:simple-page-master    master-name="only"
       page-width="8.5in"   page-height="11in"
       margin-top="0.5in"   margin-bottom="0.5in"
       margin-left="0.5in"  margin-right="0.5in">
    <fo:region-start  extent="1.0in"/>
    <fo:region-before extent="1.0in"/>
    <fo:region-body   margin="1.0in"/>
    <fo:region-end    extent="1.0in"/>
    <fo:region-after  extent="1.0in"/>
  </fo:simple-page-master>
</fo:layout-master-set>
```

The body regions from pages based on this page master will be 5.5 inches wide and 8 inches high. That's calculated by subtracting the sum of the body region's margins and the page margins from the size of the page.

Page sequences

In addition to a `fo:layout-master-set`, each formatting object document contains one or more `fo:page-sequence` elements. Each page in the sequence has an associated page master that defines how the page will look. The `master-reference` attribute of the `fo:page-sequence` element determines which page master this is. This attribute must match the name of a page master in the `fo:layout-master-set`. Listing 16-1 used a `fo:simple-master-page` named `only` to fill this role, but it is not uncommon to have more than one master page. In this case, the master pages might be grouped as part of a `fo:page-sequence-master` instead. For example, you could have one master page for the first page of each chapter, a different one for all the subsequent left-hand pages, and a third for all the subsequent right-hand pages. Or, there could be one simple page master for a table of contents, another for body text, and a third for the index. In this case, you use one page sequence each for the table of contents, the body text, and the index.

Each page sequence contains up to three kinds of child elements, in this order:

1. An optional `fo:title` element containing inline content that can be used as the title of the document. This would normally be placed in the title bar of the browser window like the `TITLE` element in HTML.
2. Zero or more `fo:static-content` elements containing text to be placed on every page.
3. One `fo:flow` element containing data to be placed on each page in turn.

The main difference between a `fo:flow` and a `fo:static-content` is that text from the flow isn't placed on more than one page, whereas the static content is. For example, the words you're reading now are flow content that only appear on this page, whereas the part and chapter titles at the top of the page are static content that is repeated from page to page throughout the chapter.

The `fo:flow` element contains, in order, the elements to be placed on the page. As each page fills with elements from the flow, a new page is created with the next master page in the page sequence master for the elements that remain in the flow. With a simple page master, the same page will be instantiated repeatedly, as many times as necessary to hold all the content.

The `fo:static-content` element contains information to be placed on each page. For example, it may place the title of a book in the header of each page. Static content can be adjusted depending on the master page. For instance, the part title may be placed on left-hand pages, and the chapter title on right-hand pages. The `fo:static-content` element can also be used for items such as page numbers that have to be calculated from page to page. In other words, what's static is not the text, but the calculation that produces the text.

Flows

The fo:flow object holds the actual content that will be placed on the instances of the master pages. This content is composed of a sequence of fo:block, fo:block-container, fo:table-and-caption, fo:table, and fo:list-block elements. This section sticks to basic fo:block elements, which are roughly equivalent to HTML's DIV elements. Later in this chapter, you learn more block-level elements that a flow can contain.

For example, here is a basic flow containing the names of several atoms, each in its own block:

```
<fo:flow flow-name="xsl-region-body">
  <fo:block>Actinium</fo:block>
  <fo:block>Aluminum</fo:block>
  <fo:block>Americium</fo:block>
</fo:flow>
```

The flow-name attribute of the fo:flow, here with the value xsl-region-body, specifies which of the five regions of the page this flow's content will be placed in. The allowed values are as follows:

- ✦ xsl-region-body
- ✦ xsl-region-before
- ✦ xsl-region-after
- ✦ xsl-region-start
- ✦ xsl-region-end

For example, a flow for the header has a flow-name value of xsl-region-before. A flow for the body has the flow-name of xsl-region-body. There can't be two flows with the same name in the same page sequence. Thus, each fo:page-sequence can contain at most five fo:flow children, one for each of the five regions on the page.

You can now put together a complete style sheet that lays out the entire periodic table. Listing 16-3 demonstrates this with an XSLT style sheet that converts the periodic table into XSL formatting objects. The flow grabs all the atoms and places each one in its own block. A simple page master named only defines an A4-sized master page in landscape mode with half-inch margins on each side.

Listing 16-3: A Basic Style Sheet for the Periodic Table

```
<?xml version="1.0"?>
<xsl:stylesheet version="1.0"
  xmlns:xsl="http://www.w3.org/1999/XSL/Transform"
  xmlns:fo="http://www.w3.org/1999/XSL/Format">

  <xsl:template match="/">
    <fo:root xmlns:fo="http://www.w3.org/1999/XSL/Format">

      <fo:layout-master-set>

        <fo:simple-page-master master-name="A4"
           page-width="297mm"  page-height="210mm"
           margin-top="0.5in"  margin-bottom="0.5in"
           margin-left="0.5in" margin-right="0.5in">
          <fo:region-body/>
        </fo:simple-page-master>

      </fo:layout-master-set>

      <fo:page-sequence master-reference="A4">

        <fo:flow flow-name="xsl-region-body">
          <xsl:apply-templates select="//ATOM"/>
        </fo:flow>

      </fo:page-sequence>

    </fo:root>
  </xsl:template>

  <xsl:template match="ATOM">
    <fo:block><xsl:value-of select="NAME"/></fo:block>
  </xsl:template>

</xsl:stylesheet>
```

Figure 16-4 shows the resulting document after Listing 16-3 has been run through an XSLT processor to produce an XSL-FO document, and that document has been run through FOP to produce a PDF file.

Figure 16-4: The rendered form of Listing 16-3

Static content

Whereas each piece of the content of a `fo:flow` element appears on one page, each piece of the content of a `fo:static-content` element appears on every page. For example, if this book were laid out in XSL-FO, both the header at the top of the page and the footer at the bottom of the page would have been produced by `fo:static-content` elements. You do not have to use `fo:static-content` elements, but if you do use them, they must appear before all the `fo:flow` elements in the page sequence.

`fo:static-content` elements have the same attributes and contents as a `fo:flow`. However, because a `fo:static-content` cannot break its contents across multiple pages if necessary, it generally has less content than a `fo:flow`. For example, Listing 16-4 uses a `fo:static-content` to place the words "The Periodic Table" in the header of each page.

Listing 16-4: **Using fo:static-content to Generate a Header**

```
<?xml version="1.0"?>
<xsl:stylesheet version="1.0"
  xmlns:xsl="http://www.w3.org/1999/XSL/Transform"
  xmlns:fo="http://www.w3.org/1999/XSL/Format">

  <xsl:template match="/">
    <fo:root xmlns:fo="http://www.w3.org/1999/XSL/Format">

      <fo:layout-master-set>

        <fo:simple-page-master master-name="A4"
           page-width="297mm"   page-height="210mm"
           margin-top="0.5in"  margin-bottom="0.5in"
           margin-left="0.5in" margin-right="0.5in">
          <fo:region-before extent="1.0in"/>
          <fo:region-body margin-top="1.0in"/>
        </fo:simple-page-master>

      </fo:layout-master-set>

      <fo:page-sequence master-reference="A4">

        <fo:static-content flow-name="xsl-region-before">
          <fo:block>The Periodic Table</fo:block>
        </fo:static-content>

        <fo:flow flow-name="xsl-region-body">
          <xsl:apply-templates select="//ATOM"/>
        </fo:flow>

      </fo:page-sequence>

    </fo:root>
  </xsl:template>

  <xsl:template match="ATOM">
    <fo:block><xsl:value-of select="NAME"/></fo:block>
  </xsl:template>

</xsl:stylesheet>
```

Figure 16-5 shows the last page of the PDF file ultimately produced from Listing 16-4. The same text, “The Periodic Table,” appears on all four pages of the document.

Figure 16-5: Static content in the header

Page numbering

The `fo:page-sequence` element has eight optional attributes that define page numbers for the sequence:

- `initial-page-number`
- `force-page-count`
- `format`
- `letter-value`
- `country`
- `language`
- `grouping-separator`
- `grouping-size`

The `initial-page-number` attribute gives the number of the first page in this sequence. The most likely value for this attribute is 1, but it could be a larger number if the previous pages are in a different `fo:page-sequence` or even a different document. It can also be set to one of these three key words:

- `auto`—1 unless pages from a preceding `fo:page-sequence` have pushed that up. This is the default.
- `auto-odd`—Same as `auto`, but add 1 if that value is an even number; that is, start on an odd page.
- `auto-even`—Same as `auto`, but add 1 if that value is an odd number; that is, start on an even page.

The `force-page-count` attribute mandates that the document have an even or odd number of pages or ends on an even or odd page. This is sometimes necessary for printed books. The force-page-count attribute can have one of these six keyword values:

- ✦ auto — Make the last page an odd page if the initial-page-number of the next fo:page-sequence is even. Make the last page an even page if the initial-page-number of the next page-sequence is odd. If there is no next fo:page-sequence or if the next fo:page-sequence does not specify an initial-page-number, let the last page fall where it may.
- ✦ even — Require an even number of pages, inserting an extra blank page if necessary to make it so.
- ✦ odd — Require an odd number of pages, inserting an extra blank page if necessary to make it so.
- ✦ end-on-even — Require the last page to have an even page number, inserting an extra blank page if necessary to make it so.
- ✦ end-on-odd — Require the last page to have an odd page number, inserting an extra blank page if necessary to make it so.
- ✦ no-force — Do not require either an even or odd number of pages.

The country attribute should be set to an RFC 1766 country code (http://www.ietf.org/rfc/rfc1766.txt). The language attribute should be set to an RFC 1766 language code. For example, you would use en to indicate English and us to indicate the United States.

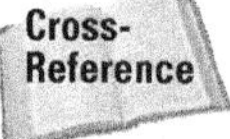

These are essentially the same as the legal values for xml:lang that were discussed in Chapter 6, except that the country code and language codes are placed in two separate attributes rather than in one attribute.

The remaining four attributes have exactly the same syntax and meaning as when used as attributes of the xsl:number element from XSLT, so I won't repeat that discussion here.

The xsl:number element and the format, letter-value, grouping-separator, and grouping-size attributes are discussed in the "Number to String Conversion" section in Chapter 15.

The fo:page-number formatting object is an empty inline element that inserts the number of the current page. The formatter is responsible for determining what that number is. This element can have a variety of formatting attributes common to inline elements such as font-family and text-decoration. For example, Listing 16-5 uses fo:static-content and fo:page-number to put the page number at the bottom of every page.

Listing 16-5: Using fo:page-number to Place the Page Number in the Footer

```
<?xml version="1.0"?>
<xsl:stylesheet version="1.0"
  xmlns:xsl="http://www.w3.org/1999/XSL/Transform"
  xmlns:fo="http://www.w3.org/1999/XSL/Format">

  <xsl:template match="/">
    <fo:root xmlns:fo="http://www.w3.org/1999/XSL/Format">

      <fo:layout-master-set>

        <fo:simple-page-master master-name="A4"
           page-width="297mm"  page-height="210mm"
           margin-top="0.5in"  margin-bottom="0.5in"
           margin-left="0.5in" margin-right="0.5in">
          <fo:region-before extent="1.0in"/>
          <fo:region-body margin-top="1.0in"
                          margin-bottom="1.0in"/>
          <fo:region-after  extent="1.0in"/>
        </fo:simple-page-master>

      </fo:layout-master-set>

      <fo:page-sequence master-reference="A4"
        initial-page-number="1">

        <fo:static-content flow-name="xsl-region-before">
          <fo:block>The Periodic Table</fo:block>
        </fo:static-content>

        <fo:static-content flow-name="xsl-region-after">
          <fo:block>p. <fo:page-number/></fo:block>
        </fo:static-content>

        <fo:flow flow-name="xsl-region-body">
          <xsl:apply-templates select="//ATOM"/>
        </fo:flow>

      </fo:page-sequence>

    </fo:root>
  </xsl:template>

  <xsl:template match="ATOM">
    <fo:block><xsl:value-of select="NAME"/></fo:block>
  </xsl:template>

</xsl:stylesheet>
```

Figure 16-6 shows the second page of the PDF file generated from Listing 16-5. The page number appears at the bottom of this and every other page in the document.

The Periodic Table

Erbium
Einsteinium
Europium
Fluorine
Iron
Fermium
Francium
Gallium
Gadolinium
Germanium
Hydrogen
Helium
Hafnium
Mercury
Holmium
Hassium
Iodine
Indium
Iridium
Potassium
Krypton
Lanthanum
Lithium
Lawrencium
Lutetium
Mendelevium
Magnesium
Manganese
p. 2

Figure 16-6: Automatically generated page numbers in the footer

Page sequence masters

Each page the formatter creates is associated with a master page from the `fo:layout-master-set` that defines how the page will look. The `master-reference` attribute of the `fo:page-sequence` element determines which master page this is. Listings 16-3 through 16-5 used a single `fo:simple-master-page` named `A4` to fill this role, but it is not uncommon to have more than one master page. For example, you could use one master page for the first page of each chapter, a different one for all the subsequent left-hand pages, and a third for all the subsequent right-hand pages. In this case, the master pages might be grouped as part of a `fo:page-sequence-master` instead.

The `fo:page-sequence-master` element is a child of the `fo:layout-master-set` that lists the order in which particular master pages will be instantiated using one or more of these three child elements:

- `fo:single-page-master-reference`
- `fo:repeatable-page-master-reference`
- `fo:repeatable-page-master-alternatives`

The fo:single-page-master-reference and fo:repeatable-page-master-reference elements each have a master-reference attribute that specifies which fo:simple-master-page their pages are based on. The fo:repeatable-page-master-alternatives has child fo:conditional-page-master-reference elements that are instantiated based on various conditions. Each of these child fo:conditional-page-master-reference elements has a master-reference attribute that specifies which fo:simple-master-page to use if its condition is satisfied.

fo:single-page-master-reference

The simplest page master element is fo:single-page-master-reference whose master-reference attribute identifies one master page to be instantiated. For example, this fo:layout-master-set contains a fo:page-sequence-master element named contents that says that all text should be placed on a single instance of the master page named A4:

```
<fo:layout-master-set>

  <fo:simple-page-master master-name="A4"
      page-width="297mm"  page-height="210mm"
      margin-top="0.5in"  margin-bottom="0.5in"
      margin-left="0.5in" margin-right="0.5in">
    <fo:region-body/>
  </fo:simple-page-master>

  <fo:page-sequence-master master-name="contents">
    <fo:single-page-master-reference master-reference="A4"/>
  </fo:page-sequence-master>

</fo:layout-master-set>
```

This page sequence master only allows the creation of a single page. Technically, it's an error if there's more content than can fit on this one page. However, in practice, most formatters simply repeat the last page used until they have enough pages to hold all the content.

Now consider this page sequence master:

```
<fo:page-sequence-master master-name="contents">
  <fo:single-page-master-reference master-name="A4"/>
  <fo:single-page-master-reference master-name="A4"/>
</fo:page-sequence-master>
```

This provides for up to two pages, each based on the master page named A4. If the first page fills up, a second is created. If that page fills up, the formatter may throw an error, or it may create extra pages.

The same technique can be used to apply different master pages. For example, this sequence specification bases the first page on the master page named front and the second on the master page named back:

```
<fo:page-sequence-master master-name="contents">
  <fo:single-page-master-reference master-reference="front"/>
  <fo:single-page-master-reference master-reference="back"/>
</fo:page-sequence-master>
```

The first page the formatter creates will be based on the master page named front. The second page created will be based on the master page named back. If the second page fills up, the formatter may throw an error; or it may create extra pages based on back, the last master page instantiated.

fo:repeatable-page-master-reference

Of course, you usually don't know in advance exactly how many pages there will be. The `fo:repeatable-page-master-reference` element specifies that as many pages as necessary will be used to hold the content, all based on a single master page. The `master-reference` attribute identifies which master page will be repeated. For example, this page sequence master will use as many copies of the master page named `A4` as necessary to hold all the content:

```
<fo:page-sequence-master master-name="contents">
  <fo:repeatable-page-master-reference master-reference="A4"/>
</fo:page-sequence-master>
```

Alternately, you can set the `maximum-repeats` attribute of the `fo:repeatable-page-master-reference` element to limit the number of pages that will be created. For example, this `fo:page-sequence-master` generates at most 10 pages per document:

```
<fo:page-sequence-master master-name="contents">
  <fo:repeatable-page-master-reference master-reference="A4"
                                       maximum-repeats="10"/>
</fo:page-sequence-master>
```

This also lets you do things like using one master for the first 2 pages, another for the next 3 pages, and a third master for the next 10 pages.

fo:repeatable-page-master-alternatives

The `fo:repeatable-page-master-alternatives` element specifies different master pages for the first page, even pages, odd pages, blank pages, last even page, and last odd page. This is more designed for a chapter of a printed book where the first and last pages, as well as the even and odd pages, traditionally have different margins, headers, and footers.

Because a `fo:repeatable-page-master-alternatives` element needs to refer to more than one master page, it can't use a `master-reference` attribute such as `fo:single-page-master-reference` and `fo:repeatable-page-master-reference`. Instead, it has `fo:conditional-page-master-reference` child elements. Each of these has a `master-reference` attribute that identifies the master page to instantiate given that condition. The conditions themselves are determined by three attributes:

✦ page-position — This attribute can be set to first, last, rest, or any to identify it as applying only to the first page, last page, any page except the first, or any page, respectively.

✦ odd-or-even — This attribute can be set to odd, even, or any to identify it as applying only to odd pages, only to even pages, or to all pages, respectively.

✦ blank-or-not-blank — This attribute can be set to blank, not-blank, or any to identify it as applying only to blank pages, only to pages that contain content, or to all pages, respectively.

For example, this page sequence master says that the first page should be based on the master page named letter_first, but that all subsequent pages should use the master page named letter:

```
<fo:page-sequence-master master-name="contents">
  <fo:repeatable-page-master-alternatives>
    <fo:conditional-page-master-reference
      page-position="first" master-reference="letter_first"/>
    <fo:conditional-page-master-reference
      page-position="rest"  master-reference="letter"/>
  </fo:repeatable-page-master-alternatives>
</fo:page-sequence-master master-reference="contents">
```

If the content overflows the first page, the remainder will be placed on a second page. If it overflows the second page, a third page will be created. As many pages as needed to hold all the content will be constructed.

Content

The content (as opposed to markup) of an XSL-FO document is mostly text. Non-XML content such as GIF and JPEG images can be included in a fashion similar to the IMG element of HTML. Other forms of XML content, such as MathML and SVG, can be embedded directly inside the XSL-FO document. This content is stored in several kinds of elements, including the following:

✦ Block-level formatting objects

✦ Inline formatting objects

✦ Table formatting objects

✦ Out-of-line formatting objects

All of these different kinds of elements are descendants of either a fo:flow or a fo:static-content element. They are never placed directly on page masters or page sequences.

Block-level formatting objects

A block-level formatting object is drawn as a rectangular area separated by a line break and possibly extra white space from any content that precedes or follows it. Blocks may contain other blocks, in which case the contained blocks are also separated from the containing block by a line break and perhaps extra white space. Block-level formatting objects include the following:

- `fo:block`
- `fo:block-container`
- `fo:table-and-caption`
- `fo:table`
- `fo:list-block`

The `fo:block` element is the XSL-FO equivalent of `display: block` in CSS or `DIV` in HTML. Blocks may be contained in `fo:flow` elements, other `fo:block` elements, and `fo:static-content` elements. `fo:block` elements may contain other `fo:block` elements, other block-level elements such as `fo:table` and `fo:list-block`, and inline elements such as `fo:inline` and `fo:page-number`. Block-level elements may also contain raw text, as in this example:

```
<fo:block>The Periodic Table, Page <fo:page-number/></fo:block>
```

The block-level elements generally have attributes for both area properties and text-formatting properties. The text-formatting properties are inherited by any child elements of the block unless overridden.

As of version 0.20.5, FOP does not support `fo:block-container` or `fo:table-and-caption`.

Inline formatting objects

An inline formatting object is also drawn as a rectangular area that may contain text or other inline areas. However, inline areas are most commonly arranged in lines running from left to right. When a line fills up, a new line is started below the previous one. The exact order in which inline elements are placed depends on the writing mode. For example, when working in Hebrew or Arabic, inline elements are first placed on the right and fill to the left. Inline formatting objects include the following:

- `fo:bidi-override`
- `fo:character`
- `fo:external-graphic`

- fo:initial-property-set
- fo:instream-foreign-object
- fo:inline
- fo:inline-container
- fo:leader
- fo:page-number
- fo:page-number-citation

As of version 0.20.5, FOP does not support fo:bidi-override, fo:initial-property-set, or fo:inline-container.

Table formatting objects

The table formatting objects are the XSL-FO equivalents of CSS2 table properties. However, tables do work somewhat more naturally in XSL-FO than in CSS. For the most part, an individual table is a block-level object, while the parts of the table aren't really either inline or block level. However, an entire table can be turned into an inline object by wrapping it in a fo:inline-container. There are nine XSL table-formatting objects:

- fo:table-and-caption
- fo:table
- fo:table-caption
- fo:table-column
- fo:table-header
- fo:table-footer
- fo:table-body
- fo:table-row
- fo:table-cell

The root of a table is either a fo:table or a fo:table-and-caption that contains a fo:table and a fo:caption. The fo:table contains a fo:table-header, fo:table-body, and fo:table-footer. The table body contains fo:table-row elements that are divided up into fo:table-cell elements.

FOP 0.20.5 has limited support for the table formatting objects, and none at all for fo:table-and-caption and fo:table-caption.

Out-of-line formatting objects

There are three "out-of-line" formatting objects:

✦ `fo:float`

✦ `fo:footnote`

✦ `fo:footnote-body`

Out-of-line formatting objects "borrow" space from existing inline or block objects. On the page, they do not necessarily appear between the same elements that they appeared between in the input-formatting object XML tree.

FOP 0.20.5 does not support `fo:float`.

Leaders and Rules

A *rule* is a block-level horizontal line inserted into text similar to the line below the chapter title on the first page of this chapter. The `HR` element in HTML produces a rule. A *leader* is a line that extends from the right side of left-aligned text in the middle of a line to the left side of some right-aligned text on the same line. It's most commonly made up of dots, although other characters can be used. Leaders are commonly seen in menus and tables of contents. In fact, if you flip back to the table of contents at the beginning of this book, you'll see leaders between chapter and section titles and the page numbers.

In XSL-FO both leaders and rules are produced by the `fo:leader` element. This is an inline element that represents a leader, although it can easily serve as a rule by placing it inside a `fo:block`.

Six attributes describe the appearance of a leader:

✦ `leader-alignment`—This can be set to `reference-area` or `page` to indicate that the start edge of the leader should be aligned with the start edge of the named item. It can also be set to `none` or `inherit`.

✦ `leader-length`—The length of the leader, such as `12pc` or `5in`.

✦ `leader-pattern`—This can be set to `space`, `rule`, `dots`, `use-content`, or `inherit`. The `use-content` value means that the leader characters should be read from the content of the `fo:leader` element.

✦ `leader-pattern-width`—This property can be set to a specific length such as `2mm` or to `use-font-metrics`, which indicates that the leader should simply be as big as it would naturally be. This is not the length of the entire leader (which is set by `leader-length`); it is the length of each repeating pattern in the leader. If necessary, white space will be added to stretch each pattern out to the requested length.

✦ `rule-style`—This property has the same values as the CSS `border-style` properties; that is, `none`, `dotted`, `dashed`, `solid`, `double`, `groove`, `ridge`, and `inherit`.

✦ `rule-thickness`—This property is the thickness (width) of the rule; 1 point by default.

In addition, a number of other common properties apply to leaders. For instance, you can use the `font-family` property to change the font in which a leader is drawn or the `color` property to change the color in which a leader is drawn. For example, this is a green horizontal line that's 7.5 inches long and 2 points thick:

```
<fo:block>
  <fo:leader leader-length="7.5in" leader-pattern="rule"
             rule-thickness="2pt" color="green"/>
</fo:block>
```

Listing 16-6 uses `fo:leader` to place a rule at the top of each page footer.

Listing 16-6: Using fo:leader to Separate the Footer from the Body with a Horizontal Line

```
<?xml version="1.0"?>
<xsl:stylesheet version="1.0"
  xmlns:xsl="http://www.w3.org/1999/XSL/Transform"
  xmlns:fo="http://www.w3.org/1999/XSL/Format">

  <xsl:template match="/">
    <fo:root xmlns:fo="http://www.w3.org/1999/XSL/Format">

      <fo:layout-master-set>

        <fo:simple-page-master master-name="A4"
           page-width="297mm"  page-height="210mm"
           margin-top="0.5in"  margin-bottom="0.5in"
           margin-left="0.5in" margin-right="0.5in">
          <fo:region-before extent="1.0in"/>
          <fo:region-body margin-top="1.0in"
                          margin-bottom="1.0in"/>
          <fo:region-after  extent="1.0in"/>
        </fo:simple-page-master>
```

Continued

Listing 16-6 *(continued)*

```
        </fo:layout-master-set>

        <fo:page-sequence master-reference="A4"
          initial-page-number="1">

          <fo:static-content flow-name="xsl-region-before">
            <fo:block>The Periodic Table</fo:block>
          </fo:static-content>

          <fo:static-content flow-name="xsl-region-after">
            <fo:block><fo:leader leader-pattern="rule"
                                 leader-length="18cm" />
            </fo:block>
            <fo:block>p. <fo:page-number/></fo:block>
          </fo:static-content>

          <fo:flow flow-name="xsl-region-body">
            <xsl:apply-templates select="//ATOM"/>
          </fo:flow>

        </fo:page-sequence>

      </fo:root>
    </xsl:template>

    <xsl:template match="ATOM">
      <fo:block><xsl:value-of select="NAME"/></fo:block>
    </xsl:template>

  </xsl:stylesheet>
```

Figure 16-7 shows the third page of the PDF file generated from Listing 16-6. The rule appears at the bottom of this and every other page in the document.

The Periodic Table

Molybdenum
Meitnerium
Nitrogen
Sodium
Niobium
Neodymium
Neon
Nickel
Nobelium
Neptunium
Oxygen
Osmium
Phosphorus
Protactinium
Lead
Palladium
Promethium
Polonium
Praseodymium
Platinum
Plutonium
Radium
Rubidium
Rhenium
Rutherfordium
Rhodium
Radon
Ruthenium

p. 3

Figure 16-7: Automatically generated rules in the footer

Graphics

XSL-FO provides two elements for embedding pictures in a rendered document. The `fo:external-graphic` element inserts a non-XML graphic, such as a JPEG image. The `fo:instream-foreign-object` element inserts an XML document that is not an XSL-FO document, such as an SVG picture or a MathML equation.

fo:external-graphic

The `fo:external-graphic` element provides the equivalent of an HTML `IMG` element. That is, it loads an image, probably in a non-XML format, from a URL. `fo:external-graphic` is always an empty element with no children. The `src` attribute contains a URI identifying the location of the image to be embedded. For example, consider this standard HTML `IMG` element:

```
<IMG SRC="cup.gif">
```

The `fo:external-graphic` equivalent looks like this:

```
<fo:external-graphic src="cup.gif"/>
```

Of course, you can use an absolute URL if you like:

```
<fo:external-graphic
     src="http://www.cafeconleche.org/images/cup.gif"/>
```

Just as with web browsers and HTML, there's no guarantee that any particular formatting engine recognizes and supports any particular graphic format. Currently, FOP supports GIF, JPEG, and SVG images. EPS images can be printed but not displayed on-screen. PNG and TIFF are supported if you have Sun's Java Advanced Imaging API library installed. More formats may be added in the future.

`fo:external-graphic` is an inline element. You can make it a block-level picture simply by wrapping it in a `fo:block` element, like this:

```
<fo:block><fo:external-graphic src="cup.gif"/></fo:block>
```

Listing 16-7 shows a style sheet that loads the image at `http://cafeconleche.org/images/atom.jpg` and puts it in the header of all the pages. In this case, the URI of the image is hard-coded in the style sheet. In general, however, it would be read from the input document.

Listing 16-7: An XSL Style Sheet That References an External Graphic

```
<?xml version="1.0"?>
<xsl:stylesheet version="1.0"
  xmlns:xsl="http://www.w3.org/1999/XSL/Transform"
  xmlns:fo="http://www.w3.org/1999/XSL/Format">

  <xsl:template match="/">
    <fo:root xmlns:fo="http://www.w3.org/1999/XSL/Format">

      <fo:layout-master-set>

        <fo:simple-page-master master-name="A4"
           page-width="297mm"  page-height="210mm"
           margin-top="0.5in"  margin-bottom="0.5in"
           margin-left="0.5in" margin-right="0.5in">
          <fo:region-before extent="1.0in"/>
          <fo:region-body margin-top="1.0in"
                          margin-bottom="1.0in"/>
          <fo:region-after  extent="1.0in"/>
        </fo:simple-page-master>

      </fo:layout-master-set>
```

```
      <fo:page-sequence master-reference="A4"
        initial-page-number="1">

        <fo:static-content flow-name="xsl-region-before">
          <fo:block>
            <fo:external-graphic
              src="http://cafeconleche.org/images/atom.jpg"
             />
            The Periodic Table
          </fo:block>
        </fo:static-content>

        <fo:static-content flow-name="xsl-region-after">
          <fo:block>
            <fo:leader leader-pattern="rule"
                       leader-length="18cm"/>
          </fo:block>
          <fo:block>p. <fo:page-number/></fo:block>
        </fo:static-content>

        <fo:flow flow-name="xsl-region-body">
          <xsl:apply-templates select="//ATOM"/>
        </fo:flow>

      </fo:page-sequence>

    </fo:root>
  </xsl:template>

  <xsl:template match="ATOM">
    <fo:block><xsl:value-of select="NAME"/></fo:block>
  </xsl:template>

</xsl:stylesheet>
```

Figure 16-8 shows the first page of the PDF file generated from Listing 16-7. The picture appears at the top of this and every other page in the document.

fo:instream-foreign-object

The `fo:instream-foreign-object` element inserts a graphic that is described in XML and that is included directly in the XSL-FO document. For example, a `fo:instream-foreign-object` element might contain an SVG picture. The formatter would render the picture in the finished document. Listing 16-8 is an XSL-FO document that places the pink triangle SVG example from Chapter 2 on the header of each page.

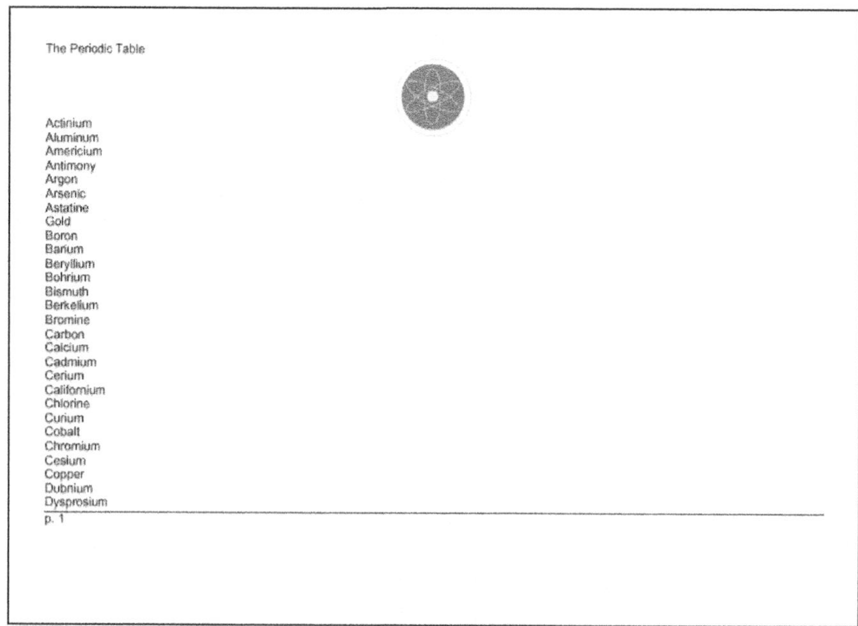

Figure 16-8: Inserting an external graphic in the header

Listing 16-8: An XSL Style Sheet That Contains an Instream SVG Picture

```
<?xml version="1.0"?>
<xsl:stylesheet version="1.0"
  xmlns:xsl="http://www.w3.org/1999/XSL/Transform"
  xmlns:fo="http://www.w3.org/1999/XSL/Format">

  <xsl:template match="/">
    <fo:root xmlns:fo="http://www.w3.org/1999/XSL/Format">

      <fo:layout-master-set>

        <fo:simple-page-master master-name="A4"
           page-width="297mm"  page-height="210mm"
           margin-top="0.5in"  margin-bottom="0.5in"
           margin-left="0.5in" margin-right="0.5in">
          <fo:region-before extent="1.0in"/>
          <fo:region-body   margin-top="1.0in"/>
        </fo:simple-page-master>
```

```
      </fo:layout-master-set>

      <fo:page-sequence master-reference="A4"
        initial-page-number="1">

        <fo:static-content flow-name="xsl-region-before">
          <fo:block> The Periodic Table
            <fo:instream-foreign-object>
              <svg xmlns="http://www.w3.org/2000/svg"
                 width="1.5cm" height="1cm">
       <polygon style="fill:#FFCCCC" points="0,31 18,0 36,31"/>
              </svg>
            </fo:instream-foreign-object>
          </fo:block>
        </fo:static-content>

        <fo:flow flow-name="xsl-region-body">
          <xsl:apply-templates select="//ATOM"/>
        </fo:flow>

      </fo:page-sequence>

    </fo:root>
  </xsl:template>

  <xsl:template match="ATOM">
    <fo:block><xsl:value-of select="NAME"/></fo:block>
  </xsl:template>

</xsl:stylesheet>
```

Figure 16-9 shows the first page of the PDF file generated from Listing 16-8. The triangle appears at the top of this and every other page in the document.

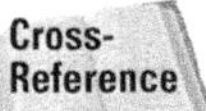

SVG is discussed in depth in Chapter 24.

Not all formatters support all possible XML graphics formats. For example, FOP does not support MathML at all, and only supports a subset of SVG. Still, this is a useful technique, especially when you want XSLT to generate pictures at runtime. For instance, you could write an XSLT style sheet that produced nicely formatted annual reports, including all the charts and graphics, simply by transforming some of the input document into XSL-FO and other parts of the input document into SVG.

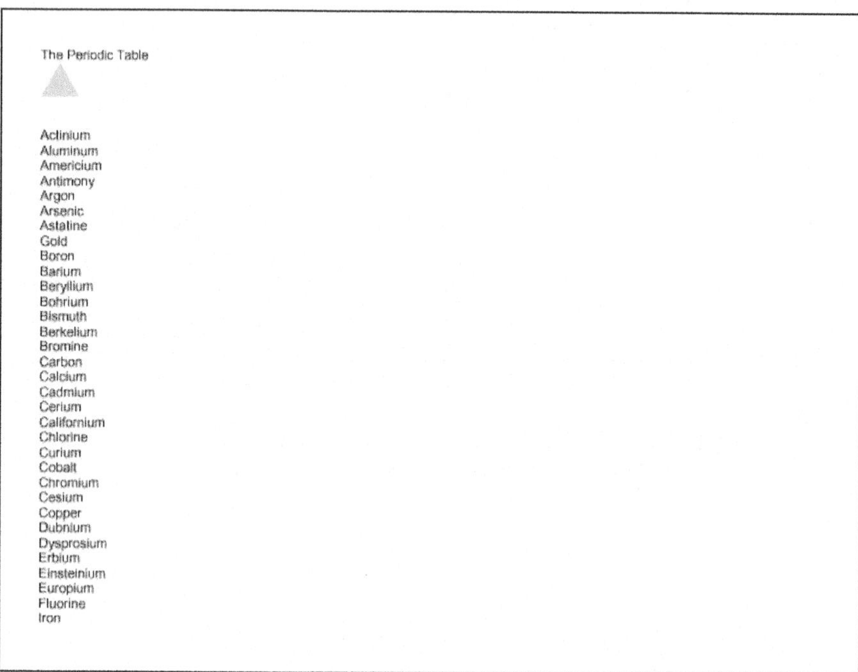

Figure 16-9: Inserting an instream graphic in the header

Graphic properties

`fo:external-graphic` and `fo:instream-foreign-object` share a number of properties designed to scale, position, crop, align, and otherwise adjust the appearance of the image on the page.

Content type

The `content-type` attribute specifies the type of the graphic. You can give this as a MIME media type, such as image/jpg or image/svg+xml, by prefixing the actual type with `content-type:`. For example, to specify that the `fo:external-graphic` element refers to a GIF image, you would write it as follows:

```
<fo:external-graphic content-type="content-type:image/gif"
                     src="cup.gif" />
```

This can also be given in terms of a namespace prefix by using a value in the form `namespace-prefix:`*`prefix`*. For example, to specify that the `fo:instream-foreign-object` includes an SVG picture, you write it as follows:

```
<fo:instream-foreign-object
   xmlns:svg="http://www.w3.org/2000/svg"
   content-type="namespace-prefix:svg">
```

The namespace prefix does not have to be declared on the `fo:instream-foreign-object` element. It simply needs to be declared somewhere in the ancestors of the element.

Size

The `height` and `width` attributes specify the vertical and horizontal size of the rectangle set aside on the page for the image. Either or both of these can be set to the keyword `auto`, rather than to an absolute length, to indicate that the size of the image itself should be used.

The `content-height` and `content-width` attributes specify the vertical and horizontal size of the image itself. If either or both of these is not the same as `height` and `width`, respectively, the image has to be scaled.

Scaling

The `scaling` attribute can be set to either `uniform` or `non-uniform`. Uniform scaling maintains the height-to-width ratio of the image as it's scaled. This is the default. Nonuniform scaling may scale the height and width differently, so that the image is distorted.

You can also choose the algorithm by which scaling occurs by using the `scaling-method` attribute. This can be set to `auto`, `integer-pixels`, or `resample-any-method`. Integer scaling maintains an integral ratio between original and scaled images, such as 2:1 or 3:1, but not 1.5:1 or 3:2. In most cases, integer-scaled images are smaller than images scaled by `resample-any-method`, but won't require dithering. The value `auto` lets the formatter decide what to do.

In addition, you can set a variety of common properties for inline elements. These include the common accessibility, aural, background, border, padding, and margin properties. Because graphics shouldn't be split across multiple pages, they don't support the usual break properties, but they do support `keep-with-next` and `keep-with-previous`.

Links

The `fo:basic-link` element encodes HTML-style hyperlinks in XSL-FO documents. This is an inline formatting object that the user can click on to move to a different document, or to a different place in the same document. This doesn't offer much for print, but it might be useful when and if web browsers support XSL-FO directly. The link behavior is controlled by these eight attributes:

- `external-destination`
- `internal-destination`
- `indicate-destination`

- show-destination
- destination-placement-offset
- target-presentation-context
- target-processing-context
- target-stylesheet

A link to a remote document target specifies the URI through the value of the external-destination attribute. The browser should replace the current document with the document at this URI when the reader activates the link. In most GUI environments, the user activates the link by clicking on its contents. For example:

```
<fo:block> Be sure to visit the
   <fo:basic-link
     external-destination="http://www.cafeconleche.org/">
      Cafe con Leche web site!
   </fo:basic-link>
</fo:block>
```

You can also link to another node in the same document by using the internal-destination attribute. The value of this attribute is not a URI, but rather the ID of the element you're linking to. You can often use XSLT's generate-id() function to produce both the IDs on the output elements and the links to those elements inside the XSL-FO output. You should not specify both an internal and external destination for one link.

The three other destination attributes affect the appearance and behavior of the link. The indicate-destination attribute has a boolean value (true or false; false by default) that specifies whether, when the linked item is loaded, it should somehow be distinguished from nonlinked parts of the same document. For example, if you follow a link to one ATOM element in a table of 100 atoms, the specific atom you were connecting to might be in boldface, while the other atoms are in normal type. The exact details are system-dependent.

The show-destination attribute has two possible values: replace (the default) and new. With a value of replace, when a link is followed, the target document replaces the existing document in the same window. With a value of new, when the user activates a link, the browser opens a new window in which to display the target document.

When a browser follows an HTML link into the middle of a document, generally the specific linked element is positioned at the tip-top of the window. The destination-placement-offset attribute specifies how far down the browser should scroll the linked element in the window. It's given as a length, such as 3in or 156px.

The three target properties describe how the document at the other end of the link will be displayed. The target-presentation-context attribute contains a URI that generally indicates some subset of the external destination that should actually be presented to the user. For example, an XPointer could be used here to say that although an entire book is loaded, only the seventh chapter will be shown.

XPointer is discussed in depth in Chapter 18.

The `target-processing-context` attribute contains the base URI used to resolve relative URIs in the external destination. Without a `target-processing-context` attribute, relative URIs are relative to the current document.

Finally, the `target-stylesheet` attribute contains a URI that points to a style sheet that should be used when the targeted document is rendered. This overrides any style sheet that the targeted document itself specifies, whether through an `xml-stylesheet` processing instruction, a `LINK` element in HTML, or an HTTP header.

In addition, the link may have the usual accessibility, margin, background, border, padding, and aural properties.

Lists

The `fo:list-block` formatting object element describes a block-level list element. (There are no inline lists.) A list may or may not be bulleted, numbered, indented, or otherwise formatted. Each `fo:list-block` element contains either a series of `fo:list-item` elements or `fo:list-item-label` `fo:list-item-body` pairs. (It cannot contain both.) A `fo:list-item` must contain a `fo:list-item-label` and a `fo:list-item-body`. The `fo:list-item-label` contains the bullet, number, or other label for the list item as a block-level element. The `fo:list-item-body` contains block-level elements holding the list item's content. To summarize, a `fo:list-block` contains `fo:list-item` elements. Each `fo:list-item` contains a `fo:list-item-label` and `fo:list-item-body`. However, the `fo:list-item` elements can be omitted. For example:

```
<fo:list-block>
  <fo:list-item>
     <fo:list-item-label><fo:block>*</fo:block>
     </fo:list-item-label>
    <fo:list-item-body>
      <fo:block>Actinium</fo:block>
    </fo:list-item-body>
  </fo:list-item>
  <fo:list-item>
     <fo:list-item-label><fo:block>*</fo:block>
     </fo:list-item-label>
    <fo:list-item-body>
      <fo:block>Aluminum</fo:block>
    </fo:list-item-body>
  </fo:list-item>
</fo:list-block>
```

Or, with the `fo:list-item` tags removed:

```
<fo:list-block>
  <fo:list-item-label>
    <fo:block>*</fo:block>
  </fo:list-item-label>
  <fo:list-item-body>
    <fo:block>Actinium</fo:block>
  </fo:list-item-body>
  <fo:list-item-label>
    <fo:block>*</fo:block>
  </fo:list-item-label>
  <fo:list-item-body>
   <fo:block>Aluminum</fo:block>
  </fo:list-item-body>
</fo:list-block>
```

The `fo:list-block` element has two special attributes that control list formatting:

✦ `provisional-label-separation`—The distance between the list item label and the list item body, given as a triplet of *maximum;minimum;optimum*, such as `2mm;0.5mm;1mm`

✦ `provisional-distance-between-starts`—The distance between the start edge of the list item label and the start edge of the list item body

`fo:list-block` also has the usual accessibility, aural, border, padding, background, margin, and keeps and breaks properties. The `fo:list-item` element has the standard block-level properties for backgrounds, position, aural rendering, borders, padding, margins, and line and page breaking. The `fo:list-item-label` and `fo:list-item-body` elements only have the accessibility properties: `id` and `keep-together`. The rest of their formatting is controlled either by the parent elements (`fo:list-item` and `fo:list-item-block`) or the child elements they contain.

Listing 16-9 formats the periodic table as a list in which the atomic numbers are the list labels and the names of the elements are the list bodies. Figure 16-10 shows the second page of output produced by this style sheet.

Listing 16-9: An XSL Style Sheet That Formats the Periodic Table as a List

```
<?xml version="1.0"?>
<xsl:stylesheet version="1.0"
  xmlns:xsl="http://www.w3.org/1999/XSL/Transform"
  xmlns:fo="http://www.w3.org/1999/XSL/Format">
```

```
  <xsl:template match="/">
    <fo:root xmlns:fo="http://www.w3.org/1999/XSL/Format">

      <fo:layout-master-set>

        <fo:simple-page-master master-name="A4"
           page-width="297mm"  page-height="210mm"
           margin-top="0.5in"  margin-bottom="0.5in"
           margin-left="0.5in" margin-right="0.5in">
          <fo:region-body/>
        </fo:simple-page-master>

      </fo:layout-master-set>

      <fo:page-sequence master-reference="A4">

        <fo:flow flow-name="xsl-region-body">
          <fo:list-block>
            <xsl:apply-templates select="//ATOM">
              <xsl:sort data-type="number"
                        select="ATOMIC_NUMBER"/>
            </xsl:apply-templates>
          </fo:list-block>
        </fo:flow>

      </fo:page-sequence>

    </fo:root>
  </xsl:template>

  <xsl:template match="ATOM">
    <fo:list-item>
      <fo:list-item-label><fo:block>
         <xsl:value-of select="ATOMIC_NUMBER"/>
      </fo:block></fo:list-item-label>
      <fo:list-item-body><fo:block>
        <xsl:value-of select="NAME"/>
      </fo:block></fo:list-item-body>
    </fo:list-item>
  </xsl:template>

</xsl:stylesheet>
```

40 Zirconium
41 Niobium
42 Molybdenum
43 Technetium
44 Ruthenium
45 Rhodium
46 Palladium
47 Silver
48 Cadmium
49 Indium
50 Tin
51 Antimony
52 Tellurium
53 Iodine
54 Xenon
55 Cesium
56 Barium
57 Lanthanum
58 Cerium
59 Praseodymium
60 Neodymium
61 Promethium
62 Samarium
63 Europium
64 Gadolinium
65 Terbium
66 Dysprosium
67 Holmium
68 Erbium
69 Thulium
70 Ytterbium
71 Lutetium
72 Hafnium
73 Tantalum
74 Tungsten
75 Rhenium
76 Osmium
77 Iridium
78 Platinum

Figure 16-10: The periodic table formatted as a list

In HTML, a list item implies a certain level of indenting. However, as you can see in Figure 16-10, no such indenting is implied by any of the XSL-FO list elements. If you want list items to be indented, you can use the `start-indent` and `end-indent` attributes on the `fo:list-item-label` and `fo:list-item-body` elements. Each of these is set to a length. However, because the list item body normally starts on the same line as the list item label, its start indent is often given by the special XSL-FO `body-start()` function. This returns the combined length of the `start-indent` and the `provisional-distance-between-starts`, as in the following example:

```
<xsl:template match="ATOM">
  <fo:list-item>
    <fo:list-item-label start-indent="1.0cm"
                        end-indent="1.0cm">
      <fo:block>
        <xsl:value-of select="ATOMIC_NUMBER"/>
       </fo:block>
    </fo:list-item-label>
    <fo:list-item-body start-indent="body-start()">
      <fo:block>
        <xsl:value-of select="NAME"/>
      </fo:block>
    </fo:list-item-body>
  </fo:list-item>
</xsl:template>
```

Tables

The fundamental table element in XSL is `fo:table-and-caption`. This is a block-level object that contains a `fo:table` and a `fo:caption`. If your table doesn't need a caption, you can just use a raw `fo:table` instead. The XSL-FO table model is quite close to HTML's table model. Table 16-1 shows the mapping between HTML 4.0 table elements and XSL formatting objects.

Table 16-1
HTML Tables versus XSL Formatting Object Tables

HTML Element	*XSL FO Element*
`TABLE`	`fo:table-and-caption`
no equivalent	`fo:table`
`CAPTION`	`fo:table-caption`
`COL`	`fo:table-column`
`COLGROUP`	no equivalent
`THEAD`	`fo:table-header`
`TBODY`	`fo:table-body`
`TFOOT`	`fo:table-footer`
`TD`	`fo:table-cell`
`TR`	`fo:table-row`

Each `fo:table-and-caption` contains an optional `fo:table-caption` element and one `fo:table` element. The caption can contain any block-level elements you care to place in the caption. By default, captions are placed before the table, but this can be adjusted by setting the `caption-side` property of the `table-and-caption` element to one of these eight values:

- ✦ `before`
- ✦ `after`
- ✦ `start`
- ✦ `end`
- ✦ `top`
- ✦ `bottom`
- ✦ `left`
- ✦ `right`

For example, here's a table with a caption on the bottom:

```
<fo:table-and-caption caption-side="bottom">
  <fo:table-caption>
    <fo:block font-weight="bold"
              font-family="Helvetica, Arial, sans"
              font-size="12pt">
      Table 16-1: HTML Tables vs. XSL Formatting Object Tables
    </fo:block>
  </fo:table-caption>
  <fo:table>
    <!-- table contents go here -->
  </fo:table>
</fo:table-and-caption>
```

The `fo:table` element contains `fo:table-column` elements, an optional `fo:table-header`, an optional `fo:table-footer`, and one or more `fo:table-body` elements. The `fo:table-body` is divided into `fo:table-row` elements. Each `fo:table-row` is divided into `fo:table-cell` elements. The `fo:table-header` and `fo:table-footer` can either be divided into `fo:table-cell` or `fo:table-row` elements. For example, here's a simple table that includes the first three rows of Table 16-1:

```
<fo:table>
  <fo:table-header>
    <fo:table-cell>
      <fo:block font-family="Helvetica, Arial, sans"
                font-size="11pt" font-weight="bold">
        HTML Element
      </fo:block>
    </fo:table-cell>
    <fo:table-cell>
      <fo:block font-family="Helvetica, Arial, sans"
                font-size="11pt" font-weight="bold">
        XSL FO Element
      </fo:block>
    </fo:table-cell>
  </fo:table-header>
  <fo:table-body>
    <fo:table-row>
      <fo:table-cell>
        <fo:block font-family="Courier, monospace">
          TABLE
        </fo:block>
      </fo:table-cell>
      <fo:table-cell>
        <fo:block font-family="Courier, monospace">
          fo:table-and-caption
        </fo:block>
      </fo:table-cell>
```

```
      </fo:table-row>
      <fo:table-row>
        <fo:table-cell>
          <fo:block>no equivalent</fo:block>
        </fo:table-cell>
        <fo:table-cell>
          <fo:block font-family="Courier, monospace">
            fo:table
          </fo:block>
        </fo:table-cell>
      </fo:table-row>
    </fo:table-body>
  </fo:table>
```

You can make table cells span multiple rows and columns by setting the number-columns-spanned and/or number-rows-spanned attributes to an integer giving the number of rows or columns to span. The optional column-number attribute can change which column the spanning begins in. The default is the current column.

You can draw borders around table parts using the normal border properties. The empty-cells attribute has the value show or hide; show if borders are to be drawn around cells with no content, hide if not. The default is show.

When a long table extends across multiple pages, sometimes the header and footer are repeated on each page. You can alter this behavior with the table-omit-header-at-break and table-omit-footer-at-break attributes of the fo:table element. The value false indicates that the header or footer is to be repeated from page to page. The value true indicates that it is not. The default is false.

The optional fo:table-column element is an empty element that specifies properties for all cells in a particular column. The cells it applies to are identified by the column-number attribute or by the position of the fo:table-column element itself. fo:table-column does not actually contain any cells. A fo:table-column can apply properties to more than one consecutive column by setting the number-columns-spanned property to an integer greater than one. The most common property to set in a fo:table-column is column-width (a signed length), but the standard border, padding, and background properties (discussed shortly and mostly the same as in CSS) can also be set.

Caution FOP 0.20.5 has limited table support. In particular, it does not support fo:table-caption or fo:table-and-caption. Furthermore, FOP requires you to explicitly specify the column widths using a fo:table-column element. You can't let it choose suitable widths as you might let a web browser do.

For example, Listing 16-10 lays out all the properties of the elements in a table. Figure 16-11 shows the first page of output produced by this style sheet.

Listing 16-10: An XSL Style Sheet That Formats the Elements as a Table

```
<?xml version="1.0"?>
<xsl:stylesheet version="1.0"
  xmlns:xsl="http://www.w3.org/1999/XSL/Transform"
  xmlns:fo="http://www.w3.org/1999/XSL/Format">

  <xsl:template match="/">
    <fo:root xmlns:fo="http://www.w3.org/1999/XSL/Format">

      <fo:layout-master-set>

        <fo:simple-page-master master-name="A4"
           page-width="297mm"  page-height="210mm"
           margin-top="0.5in"  margin-bottom="0.5in"
           margin-left="0.5in" margin-right="0.5in">
          <fo:region-body/>
        </fo:simple-page-master>

      </fo:layout-master-set>

      <fo:page-sequence master-reference="A4">

        <fo:flow flow-name="xsl-region-body">
          <fo:table>
            <fo:table-column column-width="30mm"/>
            <fo:table-column column-width="12mm"/>
            <fo:table-column column-width="12mm"/>
            <fo:table-column column-width="25mm"/>
            <fo:table-column column-width="27mm"/>
            <fo:table-column column-width="18mm"/>
            <fo:table-column column-width="49mm"/>
            <fo:table-column column-width="16mm"/>
            <fo:table-column column-width="16mm"/>
            <fo:table-column column-width="16mm"/>
            <fo:table-column column-width="21mm"/>
            <fo:table-column column-width="21mm"/>
            <fo:table-column column-width="21mm"/>
            <fo:table-body>
              <xsl:apply-templates select="//ATOM">
                <xsl:sort data-type="number"
                  select="ATOMIC_NUMBER"/>
              </xsl:apply-templates>
            </fo:table-body>
          </fo:table>
        </fo:flow>

      </fo:page-sequence>

    </fo:root>
  </xsl:template>
```

```
<xsl:template match="ATOM">
  <fo:table-row>
    <fo:table-cell>
      <fo:block><xsl:value-of select="NAME"/></fo:block>
    </fo:table-cell>
    <fo:table-cell>
      <fo:block><xsl:value-of select="SYMBOL"/></fo:block>
    </fo:table-cell>
    <fo:table-cell>
      <fo:block>
        <xsl:value-of select="ATOMIC_NUMBER"/>
      </fo:block>
    </fo:table-cell>
    <fo:table-cell>
      <fo:block>
        <xsl:value-of select="ATOMIC_WEIGHT"/>
      </fo:block>
    </fo:table-cell>
    <fo:table-cell>
      <fo:block>
        <xsl:value-of select="OXIDATION_STATES"/>
      </fo:block>
    </fo:table-cell>
    <fo:table-cell>
      <fo:block><xsl:value-of select="DENSITY"/></fo:block>
    </fo:table-cell>
    <fo:table-cell>
      <fo:block>
        <xsl:value-of select="ELECTRON_CONFIGURATION"/>
      </fo:block>
    </fo:table-cell>
    <fo:table-cell>
      <fo:block>
        <xsl:value-of select="ELECTRONEGATIVITY"/>
      </fo:block>
    </fo:table-cell>
    <fo:table-cell>
      <fo:block>
        <xsl:value-of select="ATOMIC_RADIUS"/>
      </fo:block>
    </fo:table-cell>
    <fo:table-cell>
      <fo:block>
        <xsl:value-of select="ATOMIC_VOLUME"/>
      </fo:block>
    </fo:table-cell>
    <fo:table-cell>
      <fo:block>
        <xsl:value-of select="SPECIFIC_HEAT_CAPACITY"/>
      </fo:block>
    </fo:table-cell>
    <fo:table-cell>
```

Continued

Listing 16-10 *(continued)*

```
          <fo:block>
            <xsl:value-of select="SPECIFIC_HEAT_CAPACITY"/>
          </fo:block>
        </fo:table-cell>
        <fo:table-cell>
          <fo:block>
            <xsl:value-of select="THERMAL_CONDUCTIVITY"/>
          </fo:block>
        </fo:table-cell>
      </fo:table-row>
    </xsl:template>

</xsl:stylesheet>
```

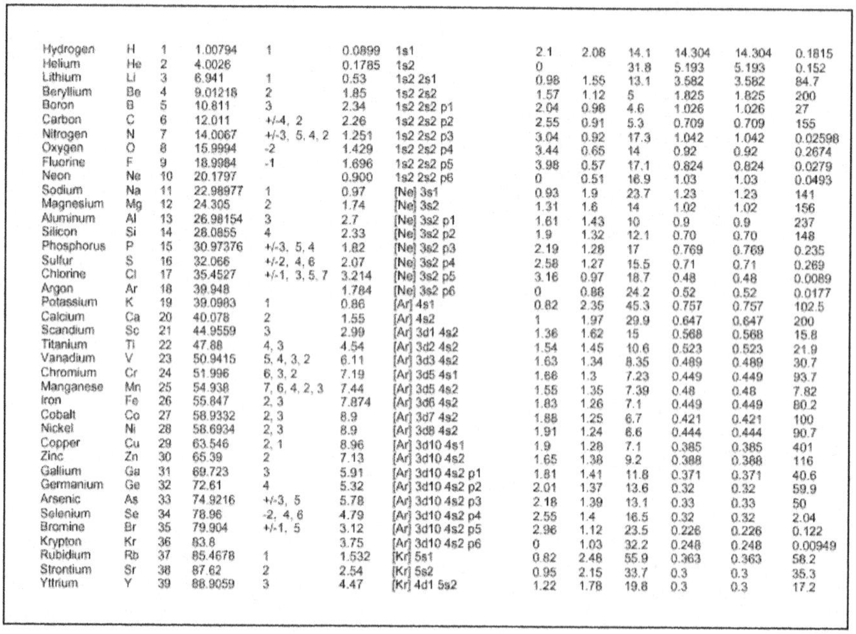

Hydrogen	H	1	1.00794	1	0.0899	1s1	2.1	2.08	14.1	14.304	14.304	0.1815
Helium	He	2	4.0026		0.1785	1s2	0		31.8	5.193	5.193	0.152
Lithium	Li	3	6.941	1	0.53	1s2 2s1	0.98	1.55	13.1	3.582	3.582	84.7
Beryllium	Be	4	9.01218	2	1.85	1s2 2s2	1.57	1.12	5	1.825	1.825	200
Boron	B	5	10.811	3	2.34	1s2 2s2 p1	2.04	0.98	4.6	1.026	1.026	27
Carbon	C	6	12.011	+/-4, 2	2.26	1s2 2s2 p2	2.55	0.91	5.3	0.709	0.709	155
Nitrogen	N	7	14.0067	+/-3, 5, 4, 2	1.251	1s2 2s2 p3	3.04	0.92	17.3	1.042	1.042	0.02598
Oxygen	O	8	15.9994	-2	1.429	1s2 2s2 p4	3.44	0.65	14	0.92	0.92	0.2674
Fluorine	F	9	18.9984	-1	1.696	1s2 2s2 p5	3.98	0.57	17.1	0.824	0.824	0.0279
Neon	Ne	10	20.1797		0.900	1s2 2s2 p6	0	0.51	16.9	1.03	1.03	0.0493
Sodium	Na	11	22.98977	1	0.97	[Ne] 3s1	0.93	1.9	23.7	1.23	1.23	141
Magnesium	Mg	12	24.305	2	1.74	[Ne] 3s2	1.31	1.6	14	1.02	1.02	156
Aluminum	Al	13	26.98154	3	2.7	[Ne] 3s2 p1	1.61	1.43	10	0.9	0.9	237
Silicon	Si	14	28.0855	4	2.33	[Ne] 3s2 p2	1.9	1.32	12.1	0.70	0.70	148
Phosphorus	P	15	30.97376	+/-3, 5, 4	1.82	[Ne] 3s2 p3	2.19	1.28	17	0.769	0.769	0.235
Sulfur	S	16	32.066	+/-2, 4, 6	2.07	[Ne] 3s2 p4	2.58	1.27	15.5	0.71	0.71	0.269
Chlorine	Cl	17	35.4527	+/-1, 3, 5, 7	3.214	[Ne] 3s2 p5	3.16	0.97	18.7	0.48	0.48	0.0089
Argon	Ar	18	39.948		1.784	[Ne] 3s2 p6	0	0.88	24.2	0.52	0.52	0.0177
Potassium	K	19	39.0983	1	0.86	[Ar] 4s1	0.82	2.35	45.3	0.757	0.757	102.5
Calcium	Ca	20	40.078	2	1.55	[Ar] 4s2	1	1.97	29.9	0.647	0.647	200
Scandium	Sc	21	44.9559	3	2.99	[Ar] 3d1 4s2	1.36	1.62	15	0.568	0.568	15.8
Titanium	Ti	22	47.88	4, 3	4.54	[Ar] 3d2 4s2	1.54	1.45	10.6	0.523	0.523	21.9
Vanadium	V	23	50.9415	5, 4, 3, 2	6.11	[Ar] 3d3 4s2	1.63	1.34	8.35	0.489	0.489	30.7
Chromium	Cr	24	51.996	6, 3, 2	7.19	[Ar] 3d5 4s1	1.66	1.3	7.23	0.449	0.449	93.7
Manganese	Mn	25	54.938	7, 6, 4, 2, 3	7.44	[Ar] 3d5 4s2	1.55	1.35	7.39	0.48	0.48	7.82
Iron	Fe	26	55.847	2, 3	7.874	[Ar] 3d6 4s2	1.83	1.26	7.1	0.449	0.449	80.2
Cobalt	Co	27	58.9332	2, 3	8.9	[Ar] 3d7 4s2	1.88	1.25	6.7	0.421	0.421	100
Nickel	Ni	28	58.6934	2, 3	8.9	[Ar] 3d8 4s2	1.91	1.24	6.6	0.444	0.444	90.7
Copper	Cu	29	63.546	2, 1	8.96	[Ar] 3d10 4s1	1.9	1.28	7.1	0.385	0.385	401
Zinc	Zn	30	65.39	2	7.13	[Ar] 3d10 4s2	1.65	1.38	9.2	0.388	0.388	116
Gallium	Ga	31	69.723	3	5.91	[Ar] 3d10 4s2 p1	1.81	1.41	11.8	0.371	0.371	40.6
Germanium	Ge	32	72.61	4	5.32	[Ar] 3d10 4s2 p2	2.01	1.37	13.6	0.32	0.32	59.9
Arsenic	As	33	74.9216	+/-3, 5	5.78	[Ar] 3d10 4s2 p3	2.18	1.39	13.1	0.33	0.33	50
Selenium	Se	34	78.96	-2, 4, 6	4.79	[Ar] 3d10 4s2 p4	2.55	1.4	16.5	0.32	0.32	2.04
Bromine	Br	35	79.904	+/-1, 5	3.12	[Ar] 3d10 4s2 p5	2.96	1.12	23.5	0.226	0.226	0.122
Krypton	Kr	36	83.8		3.75	[Ar] 3d10 4s2 p6	0	1.03	32.2	0.248	0.248	0.00949
Rubidium	Rb	37	85.4678	1	1.532	[Kr] 5s1	0.82	2.48	55.9	0.363	0.363	58.2
Strontium	Sr	38	87.62	2	2.54	[Kr] 5s2	0.95	2.15	33.7	0.3	0.3	35.3
Yttrium	Y	39	88.9059	3	4.47	[Kr] 4d1 5s2	1.22	1.78	19.8	0.3	0.3	17.2

Figure 16-11: The periodic table formatted as a table

Inlines

The `fo:inline` element has no particular effect on the layout of the page. Rather, it's an element on which you can hang formatting attributes, such as `font-style` or `color`, for application to the inline's contents. The `fo:inline` formatting object is a container that groups inline objects together. It cannot contain block-level elements. For example, you can use fo:inline elements to add style to various parts of the footer, like this:

```
<fo:static-content flow-name="xsl-region-after">
  <fo:block font-weight="bold" font-size="10pt"
            font-family="Arial, Helvetica, sans">
     <fo:inline font-style="italic" text-align="start">
       The XML Bible
     </fo:inline>
     <fo:inline text-align="centered">
       Page <fo:page-number/>
     </fo:inline>
     <fo:inline text-align="right">
       Chapter 19: XSL Formatting Objects
     </fo:inline>
  </fo:block>
</fo:static-content>
```

Footnotes

The fo:footnote element creates a footnote. The author places the fo:footnote element in the flow exactly where the footnote reference such as [1] or [*] will occur. The fo:footnote element contains both the reference text and a fo:footnote-body block-level element containing the text of the footnote. However, only the footnote reference is inserted inline. The formatter places the note text in the after region (generally the footer) of the page.

For example, this footnote uses an asterisk as a footnote marker and refers to "*JavaBeans*, Elliotte Rusty Harold (IDG Books, Foster City, 1998), p. 147". Standard properties such as font-size and vertical-align are used to format both the note marker and the text in the customary fashion.

```
<fo:footnote>
  <fo:inline font-size="smaller" vertical-align="super">*
  </fo:inline>
  <fo:footnote-body font-size="smaller">
    <fo:inline font-size="smaller" vertical-align="super">
      *
    </fo:inline>
    <fo:inline font-style="italic">JavaBeans</fo:inline>,
      Elliotte Rusty Harold
      (IDG Books, Foster City, 1998), p. 147
  </fo:footnote-body>
</fo:footnote>
```

Tip

XSL-FO doesn't provide any means of automatically numbering and citing footnotes, but this can be done by judicious use of xsl:number in the transformation style sheet. XSL Transformations make end notes easy as well.

Floats

A `fo:float` produces a floating box anchored to the top of the region where it occurs. A `fo:float` is most commonly used for graphics, charts, tables, or other out-of-line content that needs to appear somewhere on the page, although precisely where it appears is not particularly important. For example, this `fo:block` includes a floating graphic with a caption:

```
<fo:block>
  Although PDF files are themselves ASCII text,
  this isn't a book about PostScript, so there's
  nothing to be gained by showing you the exact
  output of the above command. If you're curious,
  open the PDF file in any text editor.
  Instead, Figure 16-1
  <fo:float float="before">
    <fo:external-graphic src="549863 fg1601.tif"
                         height="485px" width="623px" />
    <fo:block font-family="Helvetica, sans">
      <fo:inline font-weight="bold">
        Figure 16-1:
      </fo:inline>
      The PDF file displayed in Netscape Navigator
    </fo:block>
  </fo:float>
  shows the rendered file displayed in
  Netscape Navigator using the Acrobat plug-in.
</fo:block>
```

The formatter tries to place the graphic somewhere on the same page where the content surrounding the `fo:float` appears. However, it may not always be able to find room on that page. If it can't, it moves the object to a subsequent page.

The value of the `float` attribute indicates on which side of the page the `fo:float` floats. It can be set to `before`, `start`, `end`, `left`, `right`, `none`, or `inherit`.

The `clear` attribute can be set on elements near the floating object to indicate whether they'll flow around the side of the float or whether they'll move below the float. It can have the following values:

- `start` — The start edge of the object must not be adjacent to a floating object.
- `end` — The end edge of the object must not be adjacent to a floating object.
- `left` — The left edge of the object must not be adjacent to a floating object.
- `right` — The right edge of the object must not be adjacent to a floating object.

✦ both — Neither the left nor the right edge of the object may be adjacent to a floating object.

✦ none

Within those limits, the formatter is free to place the graphic anywhere on the page.

FOP 0.20.5 does not support the fo:float formatting object.

Formatting Properties

By themselves, formatting objects say relatively little about how content is formatted. They merely put content in abstract boxes, which are placed in particular parts of a page. Attributes on the various formatting objects determine how the content in those boxes is styled.

As already mentioned, there are more than 200 different formatting properties. Not all properties can be attached to all elements. For instance, there isn't much point to specifying the font-style of a fo:external-graphic. Most properties, however, can be applied to more than one kind of formatting object element. (The few that can't, such as src and provisional-label-separation, were discussed previously with the formatting objects they apply to.) When a property is common to multiple formatting objects, it shares the same syntax and meaning across the objects. For example, you use identical code to format a fo:title in 14-point Times bold as you do to format a fo:block in 14-point Times bold.

Many of the XSL-FO properties are similar to CSS properties. The value of a CSS font-family property is the same as the value of an XSL-FO font-family attribute. If you've read about CSS in Chapters 12 through 14, you're already more than half finished learning XSL-FO properties.

The id property

You can apply the id property to any element. The value of this property must be an XML name that's unique within the style sheet and within the output formatting object document. The last requirement is a little tricky because it's possible that one template rule in the style sheet may generate several hundred elements in the output document. XSLT's generate-id() function can be useful here.

The language property

The language property specifies the language of the content contained in either a fo:block or a fo:character element. Generally, the value of this property is an ISO 639 language code such as en (English) or la (Latin). It may also be the keyword none or use-document. The latter means to simply use the language of the input as specified by the `xml:lang` attribute. For example, consider the first verse of Caesar's *Gallic Wars*:

```
<fo:block id="verse1.1.1" language="la">
  Gallia est omnis divisa in partes tres,
  quarum unam incolunt Belgae, aliam Aquitani,
  tertiam qui ipsorum lingua Celtae, nostra Galli appellantur
</fo:block>
```

Although the `language` property has no direct effect on formatting, it may have an indirect effect if the formatter selects layout algorithms depending on the language. For example, the formatter should use different default writing modes for Arabic and English text. This carries over into determination of the start and end regions and the inline and block progression directions. It can also be used to choose the proper hyphenation dictionary.

Paragraph properties

Paragraph properties are styles that normally are thought of as applying to an entire block of text in a traditional word processor, although perhaps *block-level text properties* is a more appropriate name here. For example, indentation is a paragraph property, because you can indent a paragraph, but you can't indent a single word.

Break properties

The break properties specify where page breaks are and are not allowed. There are five loosely related break properties:

- `keep-with-next`
- `keep-with-previous`
- `keep-together`
- `break-before`
- `break-after`

The `keep-with-next` property determines how much effort the formatter will expend to keep this formatting object on the same page as the following formatting object. The `keep-with-previous` property determines how much effort the formatter will expend to keep this formatting object on the same page as the preceding formatting object. And the `keep-together` property determines how much effort the formatter will expend to keep the contents of this formatting object on one page. These are not hard-and-fast rules because it's always possible that a formatting object is just too big for one page. Each of these properties can be set to an integer giving the strength of the effort to keep the objects on the same page (larger integers are stronger) or to the keywords `always` or `auto`. `always` means maximum effort; `auto` means let the breaks fall where they may.

By contrast, the `break-before` property and `break-after` properties mandate some kind of break. What exactly is broken is determined by the value of the property. This can be one of these five values:

✦ `column`—Break the current column and move to the next column.

✦ `page`—Break the current page and move to the next page.

✦ `even-page`—Break the current page and move to the next even-numbered page, inserting a blank page if the current page is itself an even-numbered page.

✦ `odd-page`—Break the current page and move to the next odd-numbered page, inserting a blank page if the current page is itself an odd-numbered page.

✦ `auto`—Let the formatter decide where to break; the default.

For example, this template rule ensures that each `ATOM` of sufficiently small size is printed on a page of its own:

```
<xsl:template match="ATOM">
  <fo:block break-before="page" break-after="page">
    <xsl:apply-templates/>
  </fo:block>
</xsl:template>
```

Finally, the `inhibit-line-breaks` property is a boolean that can be set to `true` to indicate that not even a line break is allowed, much less a page break.

XSL-FO also defines three shorthand page-break properties: `page-break-after`, `page-break-before`, and `page-break-inside`. These are not absolutely necessary because their effects can be achieved by appropriate combinations of the keep and break properties. For example, to specify a page break after an element, you'd set `break-before` to `page` and `keep-with-previous` to `auto`.

Hyphenation properties

The hyphenation properties determine where hyphenation is allowed and how it should be used. These properties apply only to soft or "optional" hyphens, such as those sometimes used to break long words at the end of a line. They do not apply to hard hyphens, such as the ones in the word *mother-in-law*, although hard hyphens may affect where soft hyphens are allowed. There are six hyphenation properties:

✦ `hyphenate`—Automatic hyphenation is allowed only if this property has the value `true`.

✦ `hyphenation-character`—The Unicode character used to hyphenate words, such as - in English.

✦ `hyphenation-keep`—One of the four keywords (`column`, `none`, `page`, `inherit`) that specify where and whether hyphenation is allowed. The default is not to hyphenate.

✦ `hyphenation-ladder-count`—A nonnegative integer that specifies the maximum number of hyphenated lines that may appear in a row.

✦ `hyphenation-push-character-count`—A nonnegative integer that specifies the minimum number of characters that must follow an automatically inserted hyphen. (Short syllables look bad in isolation.)

✦ `hyphenation-remain-character-count`—A nonnegative integer specifying the minimum number of characters that must precede an automatically inserted hyphen.

For example:

```
<fo:block hyphenate="true"
          hyphenation-character="-"
          hyphenation-keep="none"
          hyphenation-ladder-count="2"
          hyphenation-push-character-count="4"
          hyphenation-remain-character-count="4" >
  some content...
</fo:block>
```

XSL-FO does not specify a word-breaking algorithm to determine where a soft hyphen may be applied. Even when these properties allow hyphenation, it's still completely up to the formatter to figure out how to hyphenate individual words. Indeed, basic formatters may not attempt to hyphenate words at all.

Indent properties

The indent properties specify how far lines are indented from the edge of the text. There are four of these:

✦ `start-indent`

✦ `end-indent`

✦ `text-indent`

✦ `last-line-end-indent`

The `start-indent` property offsets all lines from the start edge (left edge in English). The `end-indent` property offsets all lines from the end edge (right edge in English). The `text-indent` property offsets only the first line from the start edge. The `last-line-end-indent` property offsets only the last line from the start edge. Values are given as a signed length. For example, a standard paragraph with a half-inch, first-line indent might be formatted this way:

```
<fo:block text-indent="0.5in">
  The first line of this paragraph is indented
</fo:block>
```

A block quote with a 1-inch indent on all lines on both sides is formatted like this:

```
<fo:block start-indent="1.0in" end-indent="1.0in">
  This text is offset one inch from both edges.
</fo:block>
```

Because the text-indent is added to the start-indent to get the total indentation of the first line, using a positive value for start-indent and a negative value for text-indent creates hanging indents. For example, all lines except the first in this paragraph are indented by 1 inch. The first line is only indented half an inch:

```
<fo:block text-indent="-0.5in" start-indent="1.0in">
  This paragraph uses a hanging indent.
</fo:block>
```

Character properties

Character properties describe the qualities of individual characters. They are applied to elements that contain characters such as fo:block and fo:list-item-body elements. These include color, font, style, weight, and similar properties.

The color property

The color property sets the foreground color of the contents using the same syntax as the CSS color property. For example, this fo:inline colors the text "Lions and tigers and bears, oh my!" pink:

```
<fo:inline color="#FFCCCC">
  Lions and tigers and bears, oh my!
</fo:inline>
```

Colors are specified in much the same way as they are in CSS; that is, as hexadecimal triples in the form #RRGGBB or as one of the 16 named colors (aqua, black, blue, fuchsia, gray, green, lime, maroon, navy, olive, purple, red, silver, teal, white, and yellow).

Font properties

Any formatting object that holds text can have a wide range of font properties. Most of these are familiar from CSS, including the following:

- font-family—A list of font names in order of preference
- font-size—A signed length
- font-size-adjust—The preferred ratio between the x-height and size of a font, specified as an unsigned real number or as none
- font-stretch—The "width" of a font, given as one of the keywords condensed, expanded, extra-condensed, extra-expanded, narrower, normal, semi-condensed, semi-expanded, ultra-condensed, ultra-expanded, or wider

- font-style—The style of font specified as one of the keywords italic, normal, oblique, reverse-normal, or reverse-oblique
- font-variant—Either normal or small-caps
- font-weight—The thickness of the strokes that draw the font, given as one of the keywords 100, 200, 300, 400, 500, 600, 700, 800, 900, bold, bolder, lighter, or normal

Text properties

The text properties apply styles to text that are more or less independent of the font chosen. These include the following:

- text-transform
- text-shadow
- text-decoration
- score-spaces

The text-transform property defines how text is capitalized, and is identical to the CSS property of the same name. The four possible values are as follows:

- none—Don't change the case (the default)
- capitalize—Make the first letter of each word uppercase and all subsequent letters lowercase
- uppercase—Make all characters uppercase
- lowercase—Make all characters lowercase

This property is somewhat language-specific. (Chinese and Hebrew, for example, don't have separate upper- and lowercases.) Formatters are free to ignore the case recommendations when they're applied to non-Roman text.

The text-shadow property applies a shadow to text. This is similar to a background color but differs in that the shadow is attached to the text itself rather than to the box containing the text. The value of text-shadow can be the keyword none or a named or RGB color. For example:

```
<fo:inline text-shadow="FFFF66">
  This sentence is yellow.
</fo:inline>
```

The text-decoration property is similar to the CSS text-decoration property. Like that property, it has these five possible values:

- none—No decoration, the default
- underline—Underlining
- overline—A line above the text

- `line-through` — ~~Strike through~~
- `blink` — The notorious blinking text introduced by Netscape

In addition to the five values that are familiar from CSS, XSL-FO also adds four values that turn off decoration that is inherited from a parent element:

- `no-underline`
- `no-overline`
- `no-line-through`
- `no-blink`

Scoring is a catchall word for underlining, ~~line through~~, ~~double strike through~~, and so forth. The `score-space` property determines whether white space is scored. For example, if `score-spaces` is `true`, an underlined sentence looks like this. If `score-spaces` is `false`, an underlined sentence looks like this.

Sentence properties

Sentence properties apply to groups of characters, that is, a property that makes sense only for more than one letter at a time, such as how much space to place between letters or words.

Letter spacing properties

Kerning of text is a slippery measure of how much space separates two characters. It's not an absolute number. Most formatters adjust the space between letters based on local necessity, especially in justified text. Furthermore, high-quality fonts use different amounts of space between different glyphs. However, you can make text looser or tighter overall.

The `letter-spacing` property adds additional space between each pair of glyphs, beyond that provided by the kerning. It's given as a signed length specifying the desired amount of extra space to add, as in the following example:

```
<fo:block letter-spacing="2px">
  This is fairly loose text
</fo:block>
```

The length may be negative to tighten up the text. Formatters, however, generally impose limits on how much extra space they allow to be added to or removed from the space between letters.

Word spacing properties

The `word-spacing` property adjusts the amount of space between words. Otherwise, it behaves much like the letter spacing properties. The value is a signed length giving the amount of extra space to add between two words. For example:

```
<fo:block word-spacing="0.3cm">
  This is pretty loose text.
</fo:block>
```

Line spacing properties

An XSL-FO formatting engine divides block areas into line areas. You cannot create line areas directly from XSL-FO. However, with these five properties you can affect how they're vertically spaced:

- `line-height`—The minimum height of a line
- `line-height-shift-adjustment`—`consider-shifts` if subscripts and superscripts should expand the height of a line; `disregard-shifts` if they shouldn't
- `line-stacking-strategy`—`line-height` (the CSS model and the default); `font-height` (make the line as tall as the font height after addition of `text-altitude` and `text-depth`); or `max-height` (distance between the maximum ascender height and maximum descender depth)
- `text-depth`—A signed length specifying additional vertical space added after each line; can also be the keyword `use-font-metrics` (the default) to indicate that this depends on the font
- `text-altitude`—A signed length specifying the minimum additional vertical space added before each line; can also be the keyword `use-font-metrics` (the default) to indicate that this depends on the font

The line height also depends largely on the size of the font in which the line is drawn. Larger font sizes will naturally have taller lines. For example, the following opening paragraph from Mary Wollstonecraft's *A Vindication of the Rights of Woman* is effectively double-spaced:

```
<fo:block font-size="12pt" line-height="24pt">
  In the present state of society it appears necessary to go
  back to first principles in search of the most simple truths,
  and to dispute with some prevailing prejudice every inch of
  ground. To clear my way, I must be allowed to ask some plain
  questions, and the answers will probably appear as
  unequivocal as the axioms on which reasoning is built;
  though, when entangled with various motives of action, they
  are formally contradicted, either by the words or conduct
  of men.
</fo:block>
```

Text alignment properties

The `text-align` and `text-align-last` properties specify how the inline content is horizontally aligned within its box. The eight possible values are as follows:

- `start` — Left-aligned in left-to-right languages such as English
- `center` — Centered
- `end` — Right-aligned in left-to-right scripts
- `justify` — Expanded with extra space as necessary to fill out the line
- `left` — Align with the left side of the page regardless of the writing direction
- `right` — Align with the right side of the page regardless of the writing direction
- `inside` — Align with the inside edge of the page; that is, the right edge on the left page of two facing pages or the left edge on the right page of two facing pages
- `outside` — Align with the outside edge of the page; that is, the left edge on the left page of two facing pages or the right edge on the right page of two facing pages

The `text-align-last` property enables you to specify a different value for the last line in a block. This is especially important for justified text, where the last line often doesn't have enough words to be attractively justified. The possible values are the same as for `text-align` plus `relative`. A relatively aligned last line will line up the same way as all other lines unless `text-align` is `justified`, in which case the last line will align with the start edge instead.

White space properties

The `space-treatment` property specifies what the formatting engine should do with white space that's still present after the original source document is transformed into formatting objects. It can be set to either `preserve` (the default) or `ignore`. If you set it to ignore, leading and trailing white space will be thrown away.

The `white-space-collapse` property can be set to `true` (the default) or `false`. When true, runs of white space are replaced by a single space. When false, they're left unchanged.

The `wrap-option` property determines how text that's too long to fit on a line is handled. This property can be set to `wrap` (the default) or `no-wrap`. When set to `wrap`, this allows the formatter to insert line breaks as necessary to fit the text.

Area properties

Area properties are applied to boxes. These may be either block-level or inline boxes. Each of these boxes has the following:

- A background
- Margins

✦ Borders

✦ Padding

✦ A size

Background properties

The background properties are identical to the CSS background properties. There are five:

✦ The `background-color` property specifies the color of the box's background. Its value is either a color such as `red` or `#FFCCCC` or the keyword `transparent`.

✦ The `background-image` property gives the URI of an image to be used as a background. The value can also be the keyword `none`.

✦ The `background-attachment` property specifies whether the background image is attached to the window or the document. Its value is one of the two keywords `fixed` or `scroll`.

✦ The `background-position` property specifies where the background image is placed in the box. Possible values include `center`, `left`, `right`, `bottom`, `middle`, `top`, or a coordinate.

✦ The `background-repeat` property specifies how and whether a background image is tiled if it is smaller than its box. Possible values include `repeat`, `no-repeat`, `repeat-x`, and `repeat-y`.

The following block shows the use of the `background-image`, `background-position`, `background-repeat`, and `background-color` properties:

```
<fo:block background-image="/bg/paper.gif"
          background-position="0,0"
          background-repeat="repeat"
          background-color="white">
  Two strings walk into a bar...
</fo:block>
```

The only background properties FOP 0.20.5 supports are `background-color` and `background-image`. The others will probably be added in future releases.

Border properties

The border properties describe the appearance of a border around the box. They are mostly the same as the CSS border properties. However, in addition to `border-XXX-bottom`, `border-XXX-top`, `border-XXX-left`, and `border-XXX-right` properties, the XSL versions also have `border-XXX-before`, `border-XXX-after`, `border-XXX-start`, and `border-XXX-end` versions. There are 31 border properties in all:

✦ Color — border-color, border-before-color, border-after-color, border-start-color, border-end-color, border-top-color, border-bottom-color, border-left-color, and border-right-color. The default color is black.

✦ Width — border-width, border-before-width, border-after-width, border-start-width, border-end-width, border-top-width, border-bottom-width, border-left-width, and border-right-width. The default width is medium.

✦ Style — border-style, border-before-style, border-after-style, border-start-style, border-end-style, border-top-style, border-bottom-style, border-left-style, border-right-style. The default style is none.

✦ Shorthand properties — border, border-top, border-bottom, border-left, border-right, border-color, border-style, border-width.

For example, this block has a 2-pixel-wide blue border:

```
<fo:block border-before-color="blue" border-before-width="2px"
          border-after-color="blue"  border-after-width="2px"
          border-start-color="blue"  border-start-width="2px"
          border-end-color="blue"    border-end-width="2px">
  You have been selected for Special High Intensity Training.
</fo:block>
```

Padding properties

The padding properties specify the amount of space between the border of the box and the contents of the box. The border of the box, if shown, falls between the margin and the padding. The padding properties are mostly the same as the CSS padding properties. However, in addition to padding-bottom, padding-top, padding-left, and padding-right, the XSL-FO versions also have padding-before, padding-after, padding-start, and padding-end versions. In total, there are eight padding properties, each of which has a signed length for a value:

✦ padding-after

✦ padding-before

✦ padding-bottom

✦ padding-end

✦ padding-left

✦ padding-start

✦ padding-right

✦ padding-top

For example, this block has half a centimeter of padding on each side:

```
<fo:block padding-before="0.5cm" padding-after="0.5cm"
          padding-start="0.5cm"  padding-end="0.5cm">
  Did you hear the one about the dyslexic agnostic?
</fo:block>
```

Margin properties for blocks

There are five margin properties, each of whose values is given as an unsigned length.

- margin-top
- margin-bottom
- margin-left
- margin-right
- margin

However, these properties are only here for compatibility with CSS. In general, it's recommended that you use these four properties instead, because they fit better in the XSL-FO formatting model:

- space-before
- space-after
- start-indent
- end-indent

The space-before and space-after properties are equivalent to the margin-top and margin-bottom properties, respectively. The start-indent property is equivalent to the sum of padding-left, border-left-width, and margin-left. The end-indent property is equivalent to the sum of padding-right, border-right-width, and margin-right. Figure 16-12 should make this clearer.

For example, this block has a half-centimeter margin at its start and end sides:

```
<fo:block start-indent="0.5cm" end-indent="0.5cm">
  Two strings walk into a bar...
</fo:block>
```

However, unlike margins, space properties are given as space specifiers that contain more than one value. In particular, they contain a preferred value, a minimum value, a maximum value, a conditionality, and a precedence. This allows the formatter somewhat more freedom in laying out the page. The formatter is free to pick any amount of space between the minimum and maximum to fit the constraints of the page.

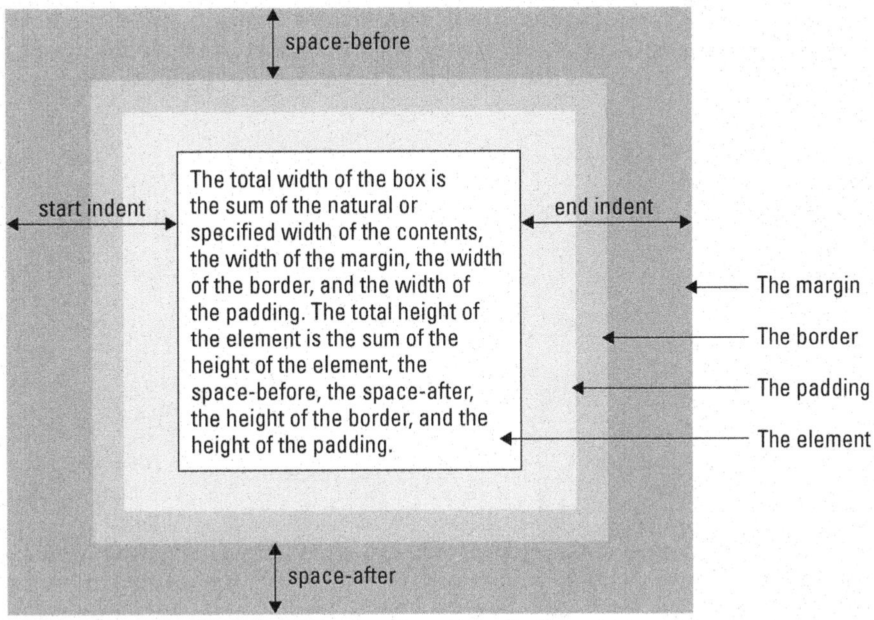

Figure 16-12: Padding, indents, borders, and space before and after for an XSL box

Each of the space values is a length. The conditionality is one of the two keywords `discard` or `retain`. This determines what happens to extra space at the end of a line. The default is to discard it. The precedence can either be an integer or the keyword `force`. The precedence determines what happens when the `space-end` of one inline area conflicts with the `space-start` of the next. The area with higher precedence wins. The default precedence is 0. Semicolons separate all five values.

For example, consider this `fo:block` element:

```
<fo:block space-before="0in;0.5in;0.166in;discard;force">
 It goes to 11.
</fo:block>
```

It says that, ideally, the formatter should add a sixth of an inch of space before this element. However, it can add as little as no space at all and as much as half an inch if necessary. Because the precedence is set to `force`, this will override any other space specifiers that conflict with it. Finally, if there's any extra space that's left over at the end, it will be discarded.

Margin properties for inline boxes

Two margin properties apply only to inline elements:

- ✦ `space-end`
- ✦ `space-start`

Their values are space specifiers that give a range of extra space to be added before and after the element. The actual spaces may be smaller or larger. Because the space is not part of the box itself, one box's end space can be part of the next box's start space.

Size properties

Six properties specify the height and width of the content area of a box:

- height
- width
- max-height
- max-width
- min-height
- min-width

These properties do not specify the total width and height of the box, which also includes the margins, padding, and borders. This is only the width and height of the content area. As well as an unsigned length, the height and width properties may be set to the keyword auto, which chooses the height and width based on the amount of content in the box. However, in no case are the height and width larger than the values specified by the max-height and max-width or smaller than the min-height and min-width. For example:

```
<fo:block height="2in" width="2in">
  Two strings walk into a bar...
</fo:block>
```

The overflow properties

The overflow property determines what happens when there's too much content to fit within a box of a specified size. This may be an explicit specification using the size properties or an implicit specification based on page size or other constraints. There are six possibilities, each of which is represented by a keyword:

- auto—Use scroll bars if there is overflow; don't use them if there isn't. If scroll bars aren't available (for example, on a printed page), add a new page for flow content and generate an error for static content. This is the default.
- hidden—Don't show any content that runs outside the box.
- scroll—Attach scroll bars to the box so the reader can scroll to the additional content.
- visible—The complete contents are shown; if necessary, by overriding the size constraints on the box.

✦ `error-if-overflow`—The formatter should give up and display an error message if content overflows its box.

✦ `paginate`—If the object overflowed is a page, create a new page to hold the excess content.

The `clip` property specifies the shape of the clipping region if the `overflow` property does not have the value `visible`. The default clipping region is simply the box itself. However, you can change this by specifying a particular rectangle, like this:

```
clip=rect(top_offset right_offset bottom_offset left_offset)
```

Here, *`top_offset`*, *`right_offset`*, *`bottom_offset`*, and *`left_offset`* are signed lengths giving the offsets of the clipping region from the top, right, bottom, and left sides of the box. This allows you to make the clipping region larger or smaller than the box itself.

The reference-orientation property

The `reference-orientation` property allows you to specify that the content of a box is rotated relative to its normal orientation. The only valid values are 90-degree increments, which are measured counterclockwise from the orientation of the parent container, that is, `0`, `90`, `180`, and `270`. You can also specify `-90`, `-180`, and `-270`. For example, here's a 90-degree rotation:

```
<fo:block reference-orientation="90">
  Bottom to Top
</fo:block>
```

Writing mode properties

The writing mode specifies the direction of text in the box. This has important implications for the ordering of formatting objects in the box. Most of the time, speakers of English and other Western languages assume a left-to-right, top-to-bottom writing mode, such as this:

```
A B C D E F G
H I J K L M N
O P Q R S T U
V W X Y Z
```

However, in the Hebrew and Arabic-speaking worlds, a right-to-left, top-to-bottom ordering such as this one seems more natural:

```
G F E D C B A
N M L K J I H
U T S R Q P O
Z Y X W V
```

In Taiwan, a top-to-bottom, left-to-right order is conventional:

```
A E I M Q U Y
B F J N R V Z
C G K O S W
D H L P T X
```

In XSL-FO, the writing mode doesn't just affect text. It also affects how objects in a flow or sequence are laid out, how wrapping is performed, and more. You've already noticed that many properties are organized in start, end, before, and after variations instead of left, right, top, and bottom. Specifying style rules in terms of start, end, before, and after, instead of left, right, top, and bottom, produces more robust, localizable style sheets.

The `writing-mode` property specifies the writing mode for an area. This property can have 1 of 13 keyword values. These are as follows:

- `bt-lr`—Bottom-to-top, left-to-right
- `bt-rl`—Bottom-to-top, right-to-left
- `lr-alternating-rl-bt`—Left-to-right lines alternating with right-to-left lines, bottom to top
- `lr-alternating-rl-tb`—Left-to-right lines alternating with right-to-left lines, top to bottom
- `lr-bt`—Left to right, bottom to top
- `lr-inverting-rl-bt`—Left to right, then move up to the next line and go right to left (that is, snake up the page like a backward S)
- `lr-inverting-rl-tb`—Left to right, then move down to the next line and go right to left (that is, snake down the page like a backward S)
- `lr-tb`—Left to right, top to bottom
- `rl-bt`—Right to left, bottom to top
- `rl-tb`—Right to left, top to bottom
- `tb-lr`—Top to bottom, left to right
- `tb-rl`—Top to bottom, right to left
- `tb-rl-in-rl-pairs`—Text is written in two-character, right-to-left pairs; the pairs are then laid out top-to-bottom to form a line; lines are laid out from right to left

Orphans and widows

To a typesetter, an orphan is a single line of a paragraph at the bottom of a page. A widow is a single line of a paragraph at the top of a page. Good typesetters move an extra line from the previous page to the next page or from the next page to the previous page, as necessary, to avoid orphans and widows. You can adjust the number of lines considered an orphan by setting the orphans property to an unsigned integer. You can adjust the number of lines considered a widow by setting the widows property to an unsigned integer. For example, if you want to make sure that every partial paragraph at the end of a page has at least three lines, set the orphans property to 3, as follows:

```
<fo:simple-page-master master-name="even"
    orphans="3" page-height="11in" page-width="8.5in"
/>
```

Summary

In this chapter, you learned about XSL formatting objects. In particular, you learned the following:

- An XSL processor follows the instructions in an XSLT style sheet to transform an XML source document into a new XML document marked up in the XSL formatting object vocabulary.
- Most XSL formatting objects generate one or more rectangular areas. Pages contain regions. Regions contain block areas. Block areas contain block areas and line areas. Line areas contain inline areas. Inline areas contain other inline areas and character areas.
- The root element of a formatting object document is fo:root. This contains fo:layout-master-set elements and fo:page-sequence elements.
- Each fo:layout-master-set element contains one or more fo:simple-page-master elements, each of which defines the layout of a particular kind of page by dividing it into five regions (before, after, start, end, and body) and assigning properties to each one. It may also contain one or more fo:page-sequence-master elements.
- Each fo:page-sequence element contains zero or one fo:title elements, zero or more fo:static-content elements, one or more fo:flow elements, and a master-reference attribute. The contents of the fo:flow are copied onto instances of the master pages in the order specified by the fo:page-sequence-master element identified by the master-reference attribute. The contents of the fo:static-content elements are copied onto every page that's created.
- The fo:external-graphic element loads an image from a URL and displays it inline.
- The fo:instream-foreign-object element displays an image encoded in a non-XSL-FO XML application, such as SVG or MathML. The code is included in the XSL-FO document along with the XSL-FO code.
- The fo:basic-link element creates a hypertext link to a URL.

- A list is a block-level element created by a `fo:list-block` element. It contains block-level `fo:list-item` elements. Each `fo:list-item` contains a `fo:list-item-label` and `fo:list-item-body`, and each of these contains block-level elements.
- The `fo:page-number` element inserts the current page number.
- The `fo:inline` element is a container used to attach properties to the text and areas it contains.
- The `fo:footnote` element inserts an out-of-line footnote and an inline footnote reference into the page.
- The `fo:float` element inserts an out-of-line, block-level element such as a figure or a pull quote onto the page. The `float` property determines which side other elements are allowed to float around it.
- There are more than 200 separate XSL formatting properties, many of which are identical to CSS properties of the same name. These are attached to XSL formatting object elements as attributes.
- The keeps and breaks properties describe where page breaks are required and forbidden. These include `keep-with-next`, `keep-with-previous`, `keep-together`, `break-before`, `break-after`, `widows`, and `orphans`.
- The hyphenation properties describe whether and how to insert soft hyphens. These include `hyphenate`, `hyphenation-character`, `hyphenation-keep`, `hyphenation-ladder-count`, `hyphenation-push-character-count`, and `hyphenation-remain-character-count`.
- The indent properties specify how far lines are indented from the edge of the text. There are four of these: `start-indent`, `end-indent`, `text-indent`, and `last-line-end-indent`.
- Character properties describe attributes of individual characters and include `color`, `font-family`, `font-size`, `font-size-adjust`, `font-stretch`, `font-style`, `font-variant`, `font-weight`, `text-transform`, `text-shadow`, `text-decoration`, and `score-space`.
- Sentence properties describe formatting that only makes sense for groups of letters and words and include `letter-spacing`, `word-spacing`, `line-height`, `line-height-shift-adjustment`, `line-stacking-strategy`, `text-depth`, `text-altitude`, `text-align`, `text-align-last`, `space-treatment`, `white-space-collapse`, and `wrap-option`.
- Area properties describe attributes of boxes produced by various formatting objects, and include the background, border, padding, and margin properties.

The next chapter introduces XLinks, a more powerful linking syntax than the standard HTML `A` element hyperlinks and XSL's `fo:basic-link`.

✦ ✦ ✦

P A R T

IV

Supplemental Technologies

✦ ✦ ✦ ✦

In This Part

✦ ✦ ✦ ✦

CHAPTER 17

XLinks

In This Chapter

XLinks versus HTML links

Linking elements

Descriptions of the remote resource

Link behavior

Extended links

Extended link syntax

Arcs

Out-of-line links

XML Base

Hypertext in XML is divided into multiple parts: XLink, XML Base, XPointer, and XInclude. XLink, the XML Linking Language, defines how one document links to another document. XML Base defines how the base URL of a document (against which relative URLs are resolved) is set. XPointer, the XML Pointer Language, defines how individual parts of a document are addressed. XInclude defines how one document can be built out of different pieces of other documents.

An XLink points to a URI (in practice, a URL) that specifies a particular resource. If this URI is relative, the base URI can be established by an `xml:base` attribute. Relative or not, this URI may have a fragment identifier that more specifically identifies the desired part of the targeted document. When the URI points to an XML document, the fragment identifier is an XPointer. This chapter explores XLink and XML Base. The next two chapters explore XPointer and XInclude.

XLinks versus HTML Links

The Web conquered the more established Gopher protocol for one main reason: HTML made it possible to embed hypertext links in documents. These links could insert images or let the user jump from inside one document to another document or another part of the same document. To the extent that XML is rendered into HTML for viewing, the same syntax that HTML uses for linking can be used in XML documents. Alternate syntaxes can be converted into HTML syntax using XSLT.

XSLT, including several examples of converting XML markup to HTML links, is discussed in Chapter 15.

However, HTML linking has limits. For one thing, URLs are limited to pointing at a single document. More granularity than that, such as linking to the third sentence of the seventeenth paragraph in a document, requires you to manually insert named anchors in the targeted document. It can't be done without write access to the document to which you're linking.

Furthermore, HTML links don't maintain any sense of history or relations between documents. Although browsers may track the path you've followed through a series of documents, such tracking isn't very reliable. From inside the HTML, there's no way to know from where a reader came. Links are purely one-way. The linking document knows to whom it's linking, but the linked document does not know who's linking to it.

XLink supports more powerful links between documents designed especially for use with XML. XLink achieves everything possible with HTML's URL-based hyperlinks and anchors. Beyond this, however, it supports multidirectional links (where the links run in more than one direction). Any element can become a link, not just the A element. Links do not even have to be stored in the same file as the documents they connect. These features make XLinks more suitable not only for new uses, but for things that can be done only with considerable effort in HTML, such as cross-references, footnotes, end notes, and more.

Caution

Only Mozilla and its derivatives (Netscape 6, Netscape 7, Galeon, Camino, Firebird, and so on) have any support for XLinks, and that support is incomplete. Internet Explorer 6.0, Opera 7.0, and Safari 1.0 and earlier have absolutely no support for any kind of XLink. There are no general-purpose applications that support arbitrary XLinks. That's because XLinks have a much broader base of applicability than HTML links. XLinks are not just used for hypertext connections and embedding images in documents. They can be used by any custom application that needs to establish connections between documents and parts of documents, for any reason. Even when XLinks are fully implemented in browsers, they may not always be blue underlined text that you click to jump to another page. They can be that, but they can also be both more and less, depending on your needs.

Linking Elements

In HTML, a link is defined with the `<A>` tag. However, just as XML is more flexible with elements, it is more flexible with links. In XML, any element can be a link or part of a link. XLink elements are identified by an `xlink:type` attribute with one of these seven values:

- `simple`
- `extended`
- `locator`
- `arc`
- `resource`
- `title`
- `none`

The xlink prefix must be bound to the http://www.w3.org/1999/xlink namespace URI. As usual, the prefix can change as long as the URI remains the same. The xlink prefix is customary and should be used unless you've got a good reason to change it. In this chapter, I assume that the prefix xlink has been bound to the http://www.w3.org/1999/xlink URI.

XLinks elements whose xlink:type attribute has the value simple or extended are called *linking elements*. For example, these are three linking elements:

```
<COMPOSER xmlns:xlink="http://www.w3.org/1999/xlink"
          xlink:type="simple"
          xlink:href="http://users.rcn.com/beand/">
    Beth Anderson
</COMPOSER>
<FOOTNOTE xmlns:xlink="http://www.w3.org/1999/xlink"
          xlink:type="simple"
          xlink:href="footnote7.xml">7</FOOTNOTE>
<IMAGE xmlns:xlink="http://www.w3.org/1999/xlink"
       xlink:type="simple" xlink:href="logo.gif"
       xlink:actuate="onLoad" xlink:show="embed"/>
```

Notice that the elements have semantic names that describe the content they contain rather than how the elements behave. The information that these elements are links is included in the attributes, not the element names. Attributes define the linking behavior.

These three examples are simple XLinks. Simple XLinks are similar to standard HTML links and are the only kind of link supported by today's web browsers, so I'll begin with them. Later, I talk about the more complex (and more powerful) extended links.

In the preceding COMPOSER example, the xlink:href attribute defines the target of the link. The value of this attribute is the absolute URL http://users.rcn.com/beand/. This linking element describes a connection from the COMPOSER element in the current document with the content "Beth Anderson" to the remote document at http://users.rcn.com/beand/. If you were to include this element in an XML document and load that document into an XLink-aware web browser, such as Mozilla or Netscape 6, the user could click on it to jump to the page http://users.rcn.com/beand/.

The browser does not necessarily indicate this to the user by underlining it and coloring it blue, however. Visual formatting is still the province of a style sheet. Web documents that use XLinks will normally need CSS rules that use the :link and :visited pseudo-classes to specify how links are formatted. For example, these two rules attempt to duplicate traditional link formatting:

```
*:link {color: blue; text-decoration: underline}
*:visited {color: purple; text-decoration: underline}
```

You're, of course, free to choose other styles, though doing so might cause readers to miss your links. It's best not to change the link colors.

You can also interpret this simple link more abstractly, as simply defining a one-way connection from one resource, the `COMPOSER` element, to another resource, the web page at `http://users.rcn.com/beand/`. Figure 17-1 diagrams this connection. This connection does not really imply any particular semantics or behavior. It's up to the application reading the document to decide what this abstract link means to it.

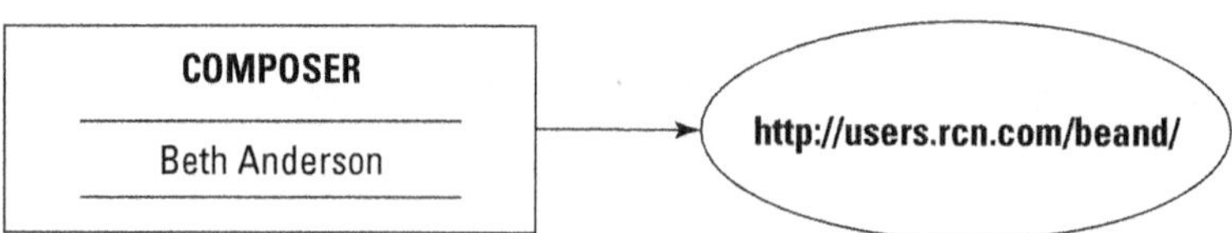

Figure 17-1: A link from the COMPOSER element to http://users.rcn.com/beand/

In the `FOOTNOTE` example, the link target attribute's name is `xlink:href`. Its value is the relative URL `footnote7.xml`. This describes a connection from the `FOOTNOTE` element in the current document with the content "7" to the document named footnote7.xml on the same server in the same directory as the document in which this link appears.

In the third example above, the value of the `xlink:href` attribute is the relative URL `logo.gif`. The scheme, host, and directory of the document are copied from the scheme, host, and directory of the document in which the link appears. However, this element requests slightly different behavior. Instead of waiting for the user to activate the link, the `xlink:actuate` attribute asks that the link be activated automatically as soon as the document is loaded. The `xlink:show` attribute requests that the result be embedded in the current document instead of replacing the current document.

Declaring XLink Attributes in Document Type Definitions

If the document has a document type definition (DTD), these attributes should be declared like any other. For example, declarations of the `FOOTNOTE`, `COMPOSER`, and `IMAGE` elements might look like this:

```
<!ELEMENT FOOTNOTE (#PCDATA)>
<!ATTLIST FOOTNOTE
    xmlns:xlink CDATA  #FIXED "http://www.w3.org/1999/xlink"
    xlink:type  CDATA  #FIXED "simple"
    xlink:href  CDATA  #REQUIRED
>
```

```
<!ELEMENT COMPOSER (#PCDATA)>
<!ATTLIST COMPOSER
    xmlns:xlink CDATA  #FIXED "http://www.w3.org/1999/xlink"
    xlink:type  CDATA  #FIXED "simple"
    xlink:href  CDATA  #REQUIRED
>
<!ELEMENT IMAGE EMPTY>
<!ATTLIST IMAGE
    xmlns:xlink    CDATA  #FIXED "http://www.w3.org/1999/xlink"
    xlink:type     CDATA  #FIXED "simple"
    xlink:href     CDATA  #REQUIRED
    xlink:show     CDATA  #FIXED "onLoad"
    xlink:actuate CDATA  #FIXED "embed"
>
```

With these declarations, the `xlink:type`, `xmlns:xlink`, `xlink:show`, and `xlink:actuate` attributes have fixed values. Therefore, they do not need to be included in the instances of the elements, which you may now write more compactly, like this:

```
<FOOTNOTE xlink:href="footnote7.xml">7</FOOTNOTE>
<COMPOSER xlink:href="http://users.rcn.com/beand/">
  Beth Anderson
</COMPOSER>
<IMAGE xlink:href="logo.gif"/>
```

Making an element a link doesn't impose any restriction on other attributes or contents of the element. An XLink element may contain arbitrary children or other attributes. For example, a more realistic `IMAGE` element would look like this:

```
<IMAGE ALT="Cafe con Leche Logo of a coffee cup"
       WIDTH="89" HEIGHT="67"
       xmlns:xlink="http://www.w3.org/1999/xlink"
       xlink:type="simple" xlink:href="logo.gif"
       xlink:actuate="onLoad" xlink:show="embed"/>
```

Half of the attributes don't have anything to do with linking. The declaration in the DTD would then look like this:

```
<!ELEMENT IMAGE EMPTY>
<!ATTLIST IMAGE
    xmlns:xlink    CDATA  #FIXED "http://www.w3.org/1999/xlink"
    xlink:type     CDATA  #FIXED "simple"
    xlink:href     CDATA  #REQUIRED
    xlink:show     CDATA  #FIXED "onLoad"
    xlink:actuate CDATA  #FIXED "embed"
    ALT            CDATA  #REQUIRED
    ALIGN          CDATA  #IMPLIED
    HEIGHT         CDATA  #REQUIRED
    WIDTH          CDATA  #REQUIRED
>
```

In fact, a linking element might even have children that are themselves linking elements! That is, a linking element may contain another linking element or elements. This doesn't have any special meaning. As far as links go, each linking element is treated in isolation.

Descriptions of the Remote Resource

A linking element can have optional `xlink:role` and `xlink:title` attributes that describe the remote resource; that is, the document or other resource to which the link points. The title contains plain text that describes the resource. The role contains an absolute URI pointing to a document that more fully describes the resource. For example, the title might describe what a page does, and the role might point to a help page for the page:

```
<SEARCH xlink:type="simple"
        xlink:href="http://www.google.com/advanced_search"
        xlink:title="Search with Google"
        xlink:role="http://www.google.com/help.html">
   Search the Web with Google
</SEARCH>
```

Both the role and title describe the remote resource, not the local element. The remote resource in the preceding example is the document at `http://www.google.com/advanced_search`. It's not uncommon, though it's not required, for the value of the `xlink:title` attribute to be the same as the contents of the `TITLE` element of the page to which you are linking.

Another possibility is to have the role point to some form of identifier URL for the format of the data found at the `xlink:href`. This may be a MIME media type, a namespace URI, or the location of a prose specification, DTD, schema, or style sheet. For example, to indicate that the search page is written in HTML you might set the role to the URL of the HTML 4.0 specification:

```
<SEARCH xlink:type="simple"
        xlink:href="http://www.google.com/advanced_search"
        xlink:title="Search with Google"
        xlink:role="http://www.w3.org/TR/html4/">
   Search the Web with Google
</SEARCH>
```

Alternately, you could use the URL for the HTML MIME media type, `http://www.isi.edu/in-notes/iana/assignments/media-types/text/html`, the URL for the XHTML namespace, `http://www.w3.org/1999/xhtml`, or the URL for the HTML 3.2 DTD, `http://www.w3.org/TR/REC-html32#dtd`. You could even use a mailto URL giving the e-mail address of the person who wrote the page. Other values are possible. XLink does not define any rules for how applications should interpret the value of an `xlink:role`, beyond simply stating that it must be an absolute URI.

XLink does not define the user interface by which link roles and titles are presented to users. For example, Mozilla shows the user the title of the link in a ToolTip when the cursor is hovering over the link, and does nothing with the role. A different application might choose to put the title in the status bar of the browser window, or do both, or neither. How or whether any particular application makes use of the role and title is completely up to it.

As with all other attributes, the `xlink:title` and `xlink:role` attributes should be declared in the DTD for all the elements to which they belong. For example, this is a reasonable declaration for the preceding `SEARCH` element:

```
<!ELEMENT SEARCH (#PCDATA)>
<!ATTLIST SEARCH
    xmlns:xlink CDATA  #FIXED "http://www.w3.org/1999/xlink"
    xlink:type  CDATA  #FIXED "simple"
    xlink:href  CDATA  #REQUIRED
    xlink:title CDATA  #IMPLIED
    xlink:role  CDATA  #IMPLIED
>
```

Link Behavior

Linking elements can contain two more optional attributes that suggest to applications how the link behaves when activated. These are:

- `xlink:show`
- `xlink:actuate`

The `xlink:show` attribute suggests *how* the content should be displayed when the link is activated; for example, by opening a new window to hold the remote resource or by loading the remote resource into the current window. The `xlink:actuate` attribute suggests *when* the link should be activated; for instance, as soon as the document is loaded, or only after a specific user request. Behavior is application-dependent, however, and applications are free to ignore the suggestions.

The xlink:show attribute

The `xlink:show` attribute has five possible values:

- `replace`
- `new`
- `embed`
- `other`
- `none`

If the value of xlink:show is replace, then when the link is activated (generally by clicking on it, at least in GUI browsers), the target of the link replaces the current document in the same window. This is the default behavior of HTML links, as in this example:

```
<COMPOSER xlink:type="simple"
          xlink:show="replace"
          xlink:href="http://users.rcn.com/beand/">
    Beth Anderson
</COMPOSER>
```

If the value of xlink:show is new, activating the link opens a new window in which the targeted resource is displayed. This is similar to the behavior of HTML links when the target attribute is set to _blank, as in the following example:

```
<WEBSITE xlink:type="simple"
         xlink:show="new"
         xlink:href="http://www.quackwatch.com/">
  Check this out, but don't leave our site completely!
</WEBSITE>
```

If the value of xlink:show is embed, activating the link inserts the targeted resource into the existing document. Exactly what this means is application-dependent. Mostly, it implies that the application should somehow render the linked content and display it as part of the finished document. This is how the IMG, APPLET, and OBJECT elements behave in HTML. For example, an element like this one might be used to indicate that a JPEG image should be embedded in the document:

```
<PHOTO xlink:type="simple"
       xlink:href="images/nypride.jpg"
       xlink:show="embed"
       ALT="Marchers on 5th Avenue, June 2004"/>
```

If the value of xlink:show is other, the application is supposed to look for other markup in the document that explains what to do. Generally, this would be used when a particular XML application used different, non-XLink elements or attributes to describe the link behavior. For example, many web pages have a LINK element in their header that references a style sheet and looks similar to this:

```
<LINK REL="stylesheet" TYPE="text/css"
      HREF="http://www.w3.org/StyleSheets/TR/W3C-WD.css" />
```

This is a link, but what's at the end of the link does not replace the existing document; it does not embed itself into the existing document; it is not displayed in a new window. In XML documents, you might agree that this behavior was implied whenever a STYLESHEET element was encountered. Because this is not one of the three predetermined link behaviors, you'd set xlink:show to other.

```
<STYLESHEET xlink:show="other"
     xlink:href="http://www.w3.org/StyleSheets/TR/W3C-WD.css"
/>
```

Finally, you can set xlink:show to none to indicate that the document contains no information to help the application decide what, if anything, to do with the link. It's completely up to the application reading the document to make its own choices.

Regardless of what behavior xlink:show suggests, the browser or other application reading the document is free to do whatever it wants when the link is activated, including nothing at all. For example, a browser with "Automatically load images" turned off might well choose to ignore xlink:show="embed".

Like all attributes in valid documents, the xlink:show attribute must be declared in a <!ATTLIST> declaration for the linking element, as in the following example:

```
<!ELEMENT WEBSITE (#PCDATA)>
<!ATTLIST WEBSITE
    xmlns:xlink CDATA  #FIXED "http://www.w3.org/1999/xlink"
    xlink:type  CDATA  #FIXED "simple"
    xlink:href  CDATA  #REQUIRED
    xlink:show (new | replace | embed) #IMPLIED "replace"
>
```

This particular DTD fragment doesn't allow the xlink:show attribute to have the value other or none. That's OK, too. Not all linking elements necessarily support all possible values of xlink:show.

The xlink:actuate attribute

A linking element's xlink:actuate attribute has four possible values:

- onRequest
- onLoad
- other
- none

The value onRequest specifies that the link should be traversed only when and if the user requests it. This is the behavior of a normal HTML link. For example, this link jumps to Powell's bookstore when the user specifically requests that action:

```
<PURCHASE xlink:type="simple" xlink:actuate="onRequest"
          xlink:href="http://www.powells.com/">
  Buy from Powell's
</PURCHASE>
```

On the other hand, if the linking element's xlink:actuate attribute is set to onLoad, the link is traversed as soon as the document containing the link is loaded. For example, you might set the actuate attribute to onLoad for an image or other piece of external content that's to be embedded in the linking document. This way, the user doesn't have to click the link to follow it. The code might look like this:

```
<IMAGE xlink:type="simple" xlink:href="logo.gif"
       xlink:actuate="onLoad" xlink:show="embed"/>
```

If the linking element's xlink:actuate attribute value is other, the application should look at other markup, not defined by XLink, to decide when to traverse the link. For instance, a browser might define a PRELOAD element as indicating that a document or image is not used on this page, but will likely soon be used. For example,

```
<PRELOAD xlink:type="simple"   xlink:href="logo.gif"
         xlink:actuate="other" xlink:show="none"/>
```

Therefore, if the browser has extra bandwidth available while the user is reading the page, it should load the document and cache it. Otherwise, it waits until the user actually actuates the link. Applications that don't recognize the PRELOAD element would simply ignore it. (I should warn you that this is a purely hypothetical example that is not yet and probably never will be implemented by any actual browser.)

Finally, setting xlink:actuate to none leaves it completely up to the application to decide when or if to traverse the link.

Like all attributes in valid documents, the xlink:actuate attribute must be declared in the DTD in an <!ATTLIST> declaration for the linking elements in which it appears, as in the following example:

```
<!ELEMENT IMAGE EMPTY>
<!ATTLIST IMAGE
    xmlns:xlink CDATA  #FIXED "http://www.w3.org/1999/xlink"
    xlink:type  CDATA  #FIXED "simple"
    xlink:href  CDATA  #REQUIRED
    xlink:show    (new | replace | embed) #IMPLIED "embed"
    xlink:actuate (onLoad)                #FIXED "onLoad"
>
```

This particular DTD fragment doesn't allow the xlink:actuate attribute to have the values onRequest, other, or none. That's OK, too. Not all linking elements necessarily support all possible values of xlink:actuate.

A Shortcut for the DTD

Because the attribute names and types are standardized, it's often convenient to make the attribute declarations a parameter entity reference and simply repeat that in the declaration of each linking element if there is more than one linking element in a document. For example:

```
<!ENTITY % link-attributes
"xlink:type     CDATA  #FIXED 'simple'
 xlink:role     CDATA  #IMPLIED
 xlink:title    CDATA  #IMPLIED

 xmlns:xlink    CDATA  #FIXED 'http://www.w3.org/1999/xlink'
 xlink:href     CDATA  #REQUIRED
 xlink:show     (new|replace|embed|other|none) #IMPLIED 'replace'
 xlink:actuate (onRequest|onLoad|other|none) #IMPLIED 'onRequest'
"
>

<!ELEMENT COMPOSER (#PCDATA)>
<!ATTLIST COMPOSER
    %link-attributes;
>
<!ELEMENT AUTHOR (#PCDATA)>
<!ATTLIST AUTHOR
    %link-attributes;
>
<!ELEMENT WEBSITE (#PCDATA)>
<!ATTLIST WEBSITE
    %link-attributes;
>
```

Extended Links

Simple links behave more or less like the old-fashioned links you're accustomed to from HTML. A simple link connects one element in the linking document to one target document. Furthermore, the link is one-way, from the source to the target.

Extended links, however, go substantially beyond HTML links to include multidirectional links between many documents and out-of-line links. An extended link consists of a set of resources and a set of the connections between them. The resources may be local (part of the extended link element) or remote (not part of the extended link element, and generally, though not necessarily, in another document). Each resource may be either a target or a source of a link or both. If a link does not contain any local resources, only remote resources, it's called an *out-of-line link*.

In computer science terms, an extended link is a directed, labeled graph in which the resources are vertices and the links between resources are edges. Thought of abstractly like this, an extended link is really just an XML format for a directed graph. The tricky part comes in deciding exactly what any particular application is supposed to do with such a data structure. For now, I can only speculate about what applications might do with extended links and what sort of user interfaces they might provide.

An extended link is represented in an XML document as an element of some arbitrary type, such as `COMPOSER` or `TEAM`, that has an `xlink:type` attribute with the value `extended`. As usual, the `xlink` prefix is associated with the `http://www.w3.org/1999/xlink` namespace URI. For example:

```
<WEBSITE xmlns:xlink="http://www.w3.org/1999/xlink"
         xlink:type="extended">
  ...
</WEBSITE>
```

Extended Link Syntax

Extended links generally point to more than one target and from more than one source. Both sources and targets are called by the more generic name *resource*. In fact, whether a resource is a source or a target can change depending on which link is being followed and in which direction.

Resources are divided into *remote resources* and *local resources*. A local resource is actually contained inside the extended link element. It is the content of an element of arbitrary type that has an `xlink:type` attribute with the value `resource`.

A remote resource exists outside the extended link element, very possibly in another document. The extended link element contains locator child elements that point to the remote resource. These are elements with any name that have an `xlink:type` attribute with the value `locator`. Each locator element has an `xlink:href` attribute whose value is a URI locating the remote resource.

The terminology is unnecessarily confusing here. Both `xlink:type="locator"` and `xlink:type="resource"` elements locate resources. An `xlink:type="locator"` element locates a remote resource. An `xlink:type="resource"` element locates a local resource. Personally, I think `xlink:type="local"` and `xlink:type="remote"` would be better choices here; but `xlink:type="resource"` and `xlink:type="locator"` are what the standard has given us.

For example, suppose you're writing a page of links to Java sites. One of the sites you want to link to is Cafe au Lait at `http://www.cafeaulait.org/`. However, there are also three mirrors of that site in three other countries. Some people coming to the site will want to access the home site, while others will want to go to one of the mirror sites. With HTML links or simple XLinks, you have to write four different links, one for the home site and one for each mirror, and let the user pick. However, with an extended XLink, you can provide one link that connects all four sites, as well as the page you're linking from. The browser can choose the one closest to the user when the link is activated (though I feel compelled to reiterate here that browser support for this is strictly hypothetical). The four remote sites are identified by locator elements. The text that will be shown to the reader of the page is identified by a resource element. Here's the XML:

```
<WEBSITE xmlns:xlink="http://www.w3.org/1999/xlink"
         xlink:type="extended">
  <NAME xlink:type="resource">Cafe au Lait</NAME>
  <HOMESITE xlink:type="locator"
            xlink:href="http://www.cafeaulait.org/"/>
  <MIRROR xlink:type="locator"
          xlink:href="http://sunsite.kth.se/javafaq"/>
  <MIRROR xlink:type="locator"
          xlink:href="http://ibiblio.org/javafaq/"/>
  <MIRROR xlink:type="locator"
          xlink:href="http://sunsite.cnlab-switch.ch/javafaq"/>
</WEBSITE>
```

This `WEBSITE` element describes an extended link with five resources:

- ✦ The `NAME` element containing the text `Cafe au Lait`, a local resource
- ✦ The document at `http://www.cafeaulait.org/`, a remote resource
- ✦ The document at `http://sunsite.kth.se/javafaq`, a remote resource
- ✦ The document at `http://ibiblio.org/javafaq/`, a remote resource
- ✦ The document at `http://sunsite.cnlab-switch.ch/javafaq`, a remote resource

Figure 17-2 shows the `WEBSITE` extended link element and five resources. The `WEBSITE` element contains one resource and refers to the other four by URLs. However, this just describes these resources. No connections are implied between them.

Both the extended link element itself and the individual locator children may have descriptive attributes, such as `xlink:role` and `xlink:title`. The `xlink:role` and `xlink:title` attributes of the extended link element provide default roles and titles for each of the individual locator child elements. Individual resource and locator elements may override these defaults with `xlink:role` and `xlink:title` attributes of their own. Listing 17-1 demonstrates.

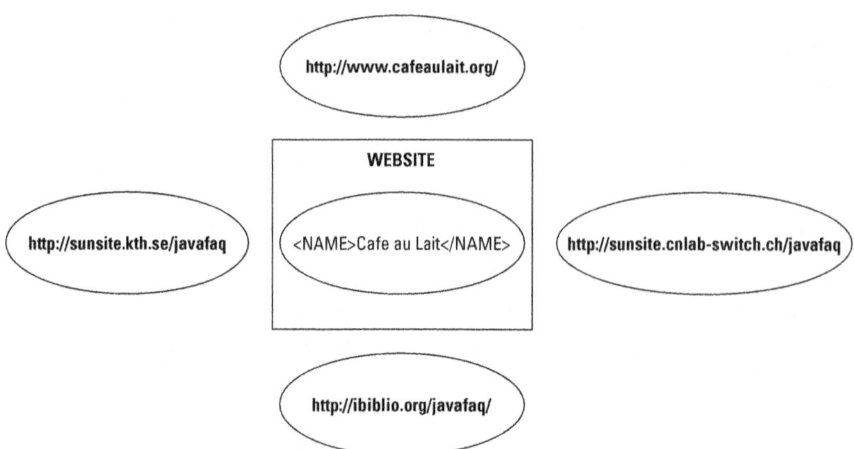

Figure 17-2: An extended link with one local and four remote resources

Listing 17-1: **An Extended Link with One Local and Four Remote Resources**

```
<WEBSITE xmlns:xlink="http://www.w3.org/1999/xlink"
         xlink:type="extended" xlink:title="Cafe au Lait">
  <NAME xlink:type="resource"
        xlink:role="http://www.cafeaulait.org/">
    Cafe au Lait
  </NAME>
  <HOMESITE xlink:type="locator"
            xlink:href="http://www.cafeaulait.org/"
            xlink:role="http://www.cafeaulait.org/"/>
  <MIRROR xlink:type="locator"
         xlink:title="Cafe au Lait Swedish Mirror"
         xlink:role="http://sunsite.kth.se/"
         xlink:href="http://sunsite.kth.se/javafaq"/>
  <MIRROR xlink:type="locator"
         xlink:title="Cafe au Lait U.S. Mirror"
         xlink:role="http://ibiblio.org/"
         xlink:href="http://ibiblio.org/javafaq/"/>
  <MIRROR xlink:type="locator"
         xlink:title="Cafe au Lait Swiss Mirror"
         xlink:role="http://sunsite.cnlab-switch.ch/"
         xlink:href="http://sunsite.cnlab-switch.ch/javafaq"/>
</WEBSITE>
```

As always, in valid documents, the XLink elements and all their possible attributes must be declared in the DTD. For example, Listing 17-2 is a DTD that declares the WEBSITE, HOMESITE, NAME, and MIRROR elements, as used in the preceding example, as well as their attributes.

Listing 17-2: A DTD That Declares the WEBSITE, NAME, HOMESITE, and MIRROR Elements

```
<!ELEMENT WEBSITE (NAME, HOMESITE, MIRROR*) >
<!ATTLIST WEBSITE
  xmlns:xlink  CDATA      #FIXED  "http://www.w3.org/1999/xlink"
  xlink:type  (extended) #FIXED  "extended"
  xlink:title  CDATA      #IMPLIED
  xlink:role   CDATA      #IMPLIED
>

<!ELEMENT NAME (#PCDATA)>
<!ATTLIST NAME
   xlink:type  (resource) #FIXED    "resource"
   xlink:role   CDATA      #IMPLIED
   xlink:title  CDATA      #IMPLIED
>

<!ELEMENT HOMESITE (#PCDATA)>
<!ATTLIST HOMESITE
   xlink:type  (locator)  #FIXED    "locator"
   xlink:href   CDATA      #REQUIRED
   xlink:role   CDATA      #IMPLIED
   xlink:title  CDATA      #IMPLIED
>

<!ELEMENT MIRROR (#PCDATA)>
<!ATTLIST MIRROR
   xlink:type  (locator)  #FIXED    "locator"
   xlink:href   CDATA      #REQUIRED
   xlink:role   CDATA      #IMPLIED
   xlink:title  CDATA      #IMPLIED
>
```

Another Shortcut for the DTD

If you have many extended link, resource, and locator elements, it may be advantageous to define the common attributes in parameter entities in the DTD, which you can reuse in different elements. For example:

```
<!ENTITY % extended.att
  "xlink:type   CDATA    #FIXED 'extended'
   xmlns:xlink  CDATA    #FIXED 'http://www.w3.org/1999/xlink'
   xlink:role   CDATA    #IMPLIED
   xlink:title  CDATA    #IMPLIED"
>

<!ENTITY % resource.att
  "xlink:type (resource) #FIXED  'resource'
   xlink:href    CDATA   #REQUIRED
   xlink:role    CDATA   #IMPLIED
   xlink:title   CDATA   #IMPLIED"
>

<!ENTITY % locator.att
  "xlink:type (locator)  #FIXED  'locator'
   xlink:href    CDATA   #REQUIRED
   xlink:role    CDATA   #IMPLIED
   xlink:title   CDATA   #IMPLIED"
>

<!ELEMENT WEBSITE (HOMESITE, MIRROR*) >
<!ATTLIST WEBSITE
   %extended.att;
>

<!ELEMENT NAME (#PCDATA)>
<!ATTLIST NAME
   %resource.att;
>

<!ELEMENT HOMESITE (#PCDATA)>
<!ATTLIST HOMESITE
   %locator.att;
>

<!ELEMENT MIRROR (#PCDATA)>
<!ATTLIST MIRROR
   %locator.att;
>
```

Arcs

The `xlink:show` and `xlink:actuate` attributes of a simple link define how and when a link is traversed. Extended links are a little more complicated because they provide many different possible traversal paths. For example, in an extended link with three resources, A, B, and C; there are nine different possible traversals:

- A⇨A
- B⇨B
- C⇨C
- A⇨B
- B⇨A
- A⇨C
- C⇨A
- B⇨C
- C⇨B

Each of these possible paths between resources can have different rules for when the link is traversed and what happens when it's traversed. These potential traversals are called *arcs*, and they're represented in XML by elements that have an `xlink:type` attribute with the value `arc`. Traversal rules are specified by attaching `xlink:actuate` and `xlink:show` attributes to arc elements. These attributes have the same values and meanings as they do for simple links. Applications can use arc elements to determine which traversals are and are not allowed and when a link is traversed.

An arc element also has an `xlink:from` attribute and an `xlink:to` attribute. The `xlink:from` attribute says which resource or resources the arc comes from. The `xlink:to` attribute says which resource or resources the arc goes to. They do this by matching the value of the `xlink:label` attributes on the various resources in the extended link. Each `xlink:label` should contain an XML name token. For example, if the `xlink:from` attribute has the value A, and the `xlink:to` attribute has the value B, the arc goes from the resource whose `xlink:label` has the value A to the resource whose `xlink:label` has the value B. Listing 17-3 demonstrates with labels that contain two-letter country codes and state abbreviations mapped to the geographic location of each resource.

Listing 17-3: An Extended Link with Arcs

```
<WEBSITE xmlns:xlink="http://www.w3.org/1999/xlink"
         xlink:type="extended" xlink:title="Cafe au Lait">

  <NAME xlink:type="resource" xlink:label="source">
    Cafe au Lait
  </NAME>

  <HOMESITE xlink:type="locator"
           xlink:href="http://www.cafeaulait.org/"
           xlink:label="ny"/>

  <MIRROR xlink:type="locator"
         xlink:title="Cafe au Lait Swedish Mirror"
         xlink:label="se"
         xlink:href="http://sunsite.kth.se/javafaq"/>

  <MIRROR xlink:type="locator"
         xlink:title="Cafe au Lait U.S. Mirror"
         xlink:label="nc"
         xlink:href="http://ibiblio.org/javafaq/"/>

  <MIRROR xlink:type="locator"
         xlink:title="Cafe au Lait Swiss Mirror"
         xlink:label="ch"
         xlink:href="http://sunsite.cnlab-switch.ch/javafaq"/>

  <CONNECTION xlink:type="arc" xlink:from="source"
              xlink:to="ch"    xlink:show="replace"
              xlink:actuate="onRequest"/>
  <CONNECTION xlink:type="arc" xlink:from="source"
              xlink:to="ny"    xlink:show="replace"
              xlink:actuate="onRequest"/>
  <CONNECTION xlink:type="arc" xlink:from="source"
              xlink:to="se"    xlink:show="replace"
              xlink:actuate="onRequest"/>
  <CONNECTION xlink:type="arc" xlink:from="source"
              xlink:to="nc"    xlink:show="replace"
              xlink:actuate="onRequest"/>

</WEBSITE>
```

The first CONNECTION element in the preceding listing defines an arc from the resource with the label "source" to the resource with the label "ch." The second CONNECTION element defines an arc from the resource with the label "source" to the resource with the label "ny," and so on. Figure 17-3 diagrams this link with ovals representing the resources and arrows representing the arcs. This is the same as Figure 17-2, but now connections have been added between resources, as specified by the arc elements.

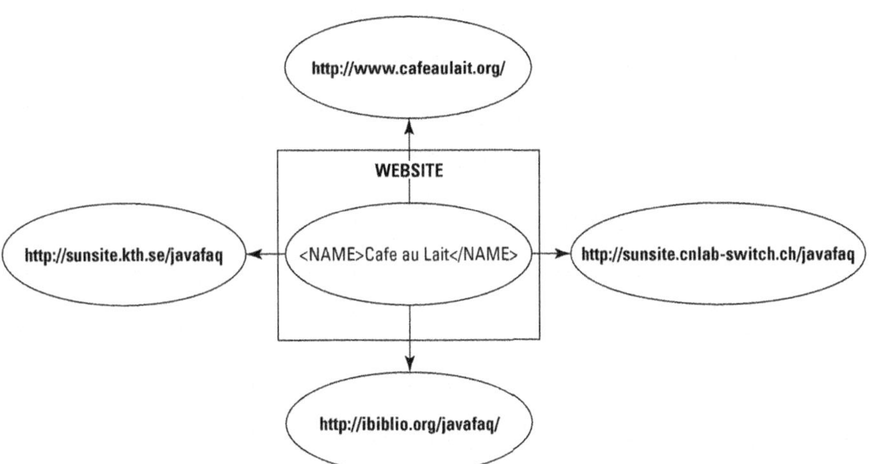

Figure 17-3: An extended link with one local and four remote resources and arcs going from the local resource to each of the remote resources

In this case, each arc element defines exactly one connection, because the target and source labels aren't shared by multiple resources. However, this isn't necessarily the case. Each arc goes from exactly one resource to exactly one other resource. However, a single arc element may actually describe multiple arcs. If more than one resource has the `xlink:label` A, `xlink:from="A"` and `xlink:to="B"` define multiple arcs from all resources with the label A to the resource with label B. If more than one resource has the label B, arcs go from all resources with the label A to all resources with label B. For example, consider the `WEBSITE` element in Listing 17-4.

Listing 17-4: **Labels Can Be Shared between Resources**

```
<WEBSITE xmlns:xlink="http://www.w3.org/1999/xlink"
         xlink:type="extended" xlink:title="Cafe au Lait">

  <NAME xlink:type="resource" xlink:label="source">
    Cafe au Lait
  </NAME>

  <HOMESITE xlink:type="locator"
            xlink:href="http://www.cafeaulait.org/"
            xlink:label="home"/>

  <MIRROR xlink:type="locator"
          xlink:title="Cafe au Lait Swedish Mirror"
          xlink:label="mirror"
          xlink:href="http://sunsite.kth.se/javafaq"/>

  <MIRROR xlink:type="locator"
```

Continued

Listing 17-4 *(continued)*

```
            xlink:title="Cafe au Lait U.S. Mirror"
            xlink:label="mirror"
            xlink:href="http://ibiblio.org/javafaq/"/>

  <MIRROR xlink:type="locator"
          xlink:title="Cafe au Lait Swiss Mirror"
          xlink:label="mirror"
          xlink:href="http://sunsite.cnlab-switch.ch/javafaq"/>

  <CONNECTION xlink:type="arc"  xlink:from="source"
              xlink:to="mirror" xlink:show="replace"
              xlink:actuate="onRequest"/>

</WEBSITE>
```

Here, the "mirror" label is shared by three different elements, and the single arc element defines three arcs: one from the source to the Swedish mirror, one from the source to the Swiss mirror, and one from the source to the U.S. mirror. Figure 17-4 diagrams this. It's very similar to Figure 17-3 except that the link between the NAME element and the home site at http://www.cafeaulait.org/ is missing. Because the HOMESITE has a different label, it isn't connected by the single arc element.

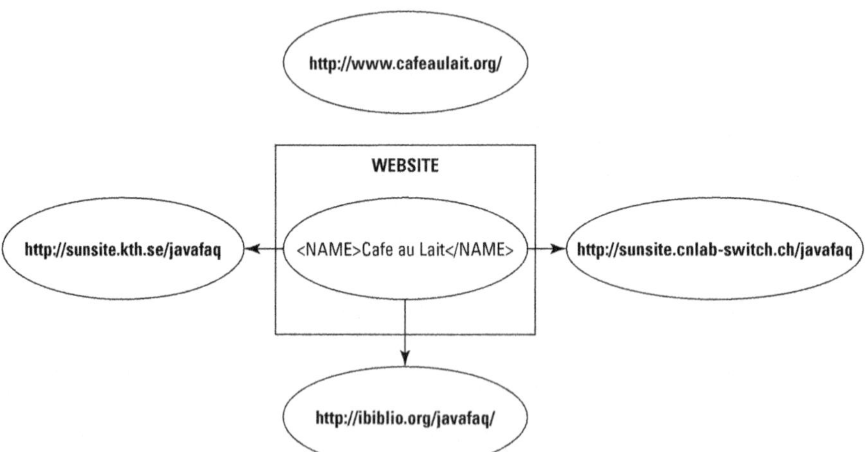

Figure 17-4: An extended link with one local and four remote resources and three arcs going from the local resource to each of the mirror resources

Although I don't recommend it, you can omit either the `xlink:from` attribute, the `xlink:to` attribute, or both from an arc element. In this case, all resources participating in the link, both local and remote, take the place of the missing attribute. For example, consider the `WEBSITE` element in Listing 17-5.

Listing 17-5: An Omitted xlink:to Attribute

```
<WEBSITE xmlns:xlink="http://www.w3.org/1999/xlink"
         xlink:type="extended" xlink:title="Cafe au Lait">

  <NAME xlink:type="resource" xlink:label="source">
    Cafe au Lait
  </NAME>

  <HOMESITE xlink:type="locator"
            xlink:href="http://www.cafeaulait.org/"
            xlink:label="ny"/>

  <MIRROR xlink:type="locator"
          xlink:title="Cafe au Lait Swedish Mirror"
          xlink:label="se"
          xlink:href="http://sunsite.kth.se/javafaq"/>

  <MIRROR xlink:type="locator"
          xlink:title="Cafe au Lait U.S. Mirror"
          xlink:label="nc"
          xlink:href="http://ibiblio.org/javafaq/"/>

  <MIRROR xlink:type="locator"
          xlink:title="Cafe au Lait Swiss Mirror"
          xlink:label="ch"
         xlink:href="http://sunsite.cnlab-switch.ch/javafaq"/>


  <CONNECTION xlink:type="arc" xlink:from="source"
              xlink:show="replace" xlink:actuate="onRequest"/>

</WEBSITE>
```

Its single arc element is missing the `xlink:to` attribute. Consequently, this extended link includes five arcs — one from the source to `us`, three from the source to each of the mirrors, and one from the source to itself. All arcs start at the `NAME` element because the `xlink:from` attribute is present and so specifies. Figure 17-5 diagrams this. It's very similar to Figure 17-3 except that there's now an extra circular arc from the `NAME` element to itself.

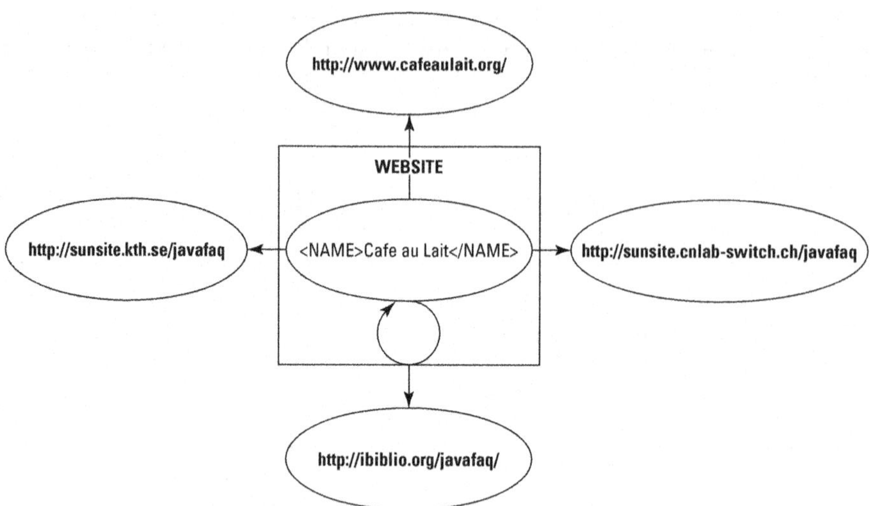

Figure 17-5: An extended link with one local and four remote resources and five arcs going from the local resource to each of the resources, including to itself

As usual, to be valid, all the attributes and elements must be fully declared in the document's DTD. Listing 17-6 is a DTD fragment that describes the preceding `WEBSITE` element.

Listing 17-6: A DTD for the WEBSITE Extended Link

```
<!ELEMENT WEBSITE (HOMESITE, MIRROR*, CONNECTION*) >
<!ATTLIST WEBSITE
  xmlns:xlink  CDATA  #FIXED "http://www.w3.org/1999/xlink"
  xlink:type  (extended) #FIXED  "extended"
  xlink:title  CDATA     #IMPLIED
  xlink:role   CDATA     #IMPLIED
>

<!ELEMENT HOMESITE (#PCDATA)>
<!ATTLIST HOMESITE
   xlink:type     (locator) #FIXED  "locator"
   xlink:href      CDATA    #REQUIRED
   xlink:label     CDATA    #IMPLIED
   xlink:role      CDATA    #REQUIRED
   xlink:title     CDATA    #IMPLIED
>

<!ELEMENT MIRROR (#PCDATA)>
<!ATTLIST MIRROR
   xlink:type     (locator) #FIXED  "locator"
   xlink:href      CDATA    #REQUIRED
```

```
    xlink:label     CDATA    #IMPLIED
    xlink:role      CDATA    #REQUIRED
    xlink:title     CDATA    #IMPLIED
>

<!ELEMENT CONNECTION EMPTY>
<!ATTLIST CONNECTION
  xlink:type     (arc)                  #FIXED   "arc"
  xlink:from      CDATA                 #IMPLIED
  xlink:to        CDATA                 #IMPLIED
  xlink:show     (replace)              #IMPLIED "replace"
  xlink:actuate (onRequest | onLoad) #IMPLIED "onRequest"
>
```

Out-of-Line Links

Inline links, such as the familiar A element from HTML, are themselves part of the source or target of the link. Generally, they link from the document that they're part of to some other document. However, they can also link to a different part of the same document. The source of the link, that is the blue underlined text, is included inside the A element that defines the link. Most simple links are inline.

Extended links can also be out-of-line. An out-of-line link does not contain any part of any of the resources it connects. Instead, the links are stored in a separate document called the *linkbase*. For example, you might use a linkbase to maintain a slide show where each slide requires next and previous links. By changing the order of the slides in the linkbase, you can change the targets of the previous and next links on each page without having to edit the slides themselves.

Out-of-line links also allow you to add links to and from documents that can't be modified, such as a page on someone else's web site. For example, media watchdog groups, such as FAIR (`http://www.fair.org/`) and AIM (`http://www.aim.org/`), could put out-of-line links from the New York Times editorial page to analyses of those editorials. The links would only be visible to users who loaded the right linkbase, however.

Finally, out-of-line links allow you to add links to different parts of non-XML content. For instance, you could link to the third minute of a QuickTime movie, even though the movie doesn't contain any attributes or elements that would normally be used to identify the linked position.

For example, a list of mirror sites for a document, such as Listing 17-5, might be stored in a separate file on a web server in a known location where browsers can find and query it to determine the nearest mirror of a page they're looking for. The out-of-lineness, however, is that this element does not appear in the document from which the link is activated.

This expands the abstraction of style sheets into the linking domain. A style sheet is completely separate from the document it describes, and yet provides rules that modify how the document is presented to the reader. A linkbase containing out-of-line links is separate from the documents it connects, yet it provides the necessary links to the reader. This has several advantages, including keeping more presentation-oriented markup separate from the document and allowing the linking of read-only documents.

I feel compelled to note that application support for out-of-line links is at best hypothetical at the time of this writing. Although I can show you how to create such links, their actual implementation and support is almost certainly some time away. Some of the details remain to be defined and likely will be implemented in vendor-specific fashions, at least initially. Still, they hold the promise of enabling more sophisticated linking than can be achieved with HTML.

For example, I've put the notes for a Java course I teach on my web site. Figure 17-6 shows the introductory page. This particular course consists of 13 classes, each of which contains between 30 and 60 individual pages of notes. A table of contents page for each class is then provided that links to each note page used in that class. Each of the several hundred pages making up the entire site has links to the previous document (Previous link), the next document (Next link), and the table of contents (Top link) for the week, as shown in Figure 17-7. Putting it all together, this amounts to more than a thousand interconnections among this set of documents.

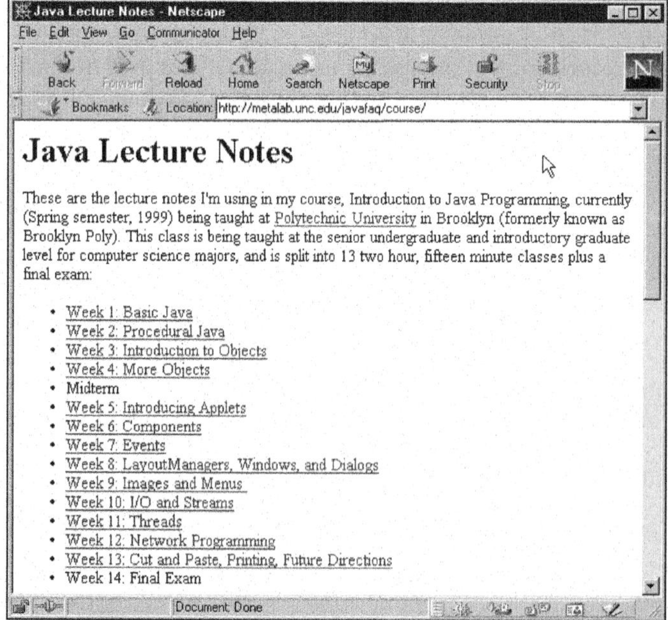

Figure 17-6: The introductory page for my class web site shows 13 weeks of lecture notes.

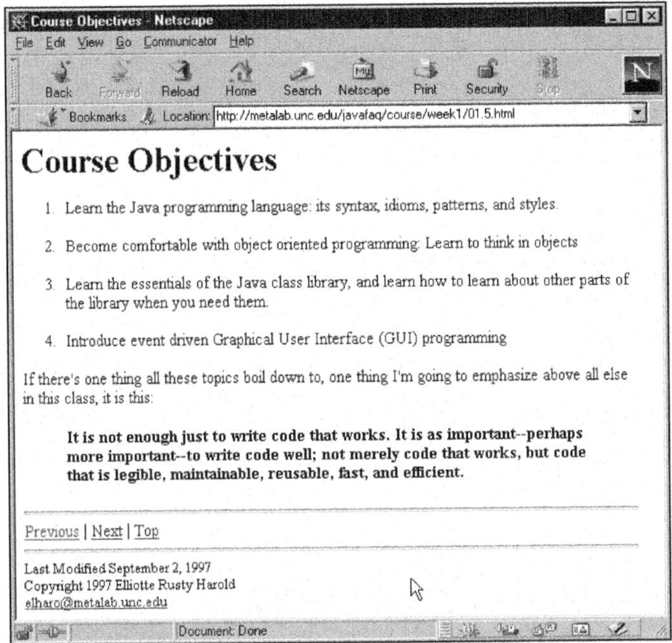

Figure 17-7: One page of lecture notes displaying the Previous, Next, and Top links

The possible interconnections grow exponentially with the number of documents. Every time a document is moved, renamed, or divided into smaller pieces, the links need to be adjusted on that page, on the page before it and after it in the set, and on the table of contents for the week. Quite frankly, this is a lot more work than it should be, and it tends to discourage necessary modifications and updates to the course notes.

The sensible thing to do, if HTML supported it, would be to store the connections in a separate document. Pages could then be reorganized by editing that one document. HTML links don't support this, but extended XLinks do. Listing 17-7 demonstrates one such document. This document describes links from the main index page to the individual classes and vice versa.

Listing 17-7: An Out-of-Line Extended Link

```
<COURSE xmlns:xlink="http://www.w3.org/1999/xlink"
        xlink:type="extended">

  <TOC xlink:type="locator" xlink:href="index.xml"
       xlink:label="index"/>
```

Continued

Listing 17-7 *(continued)*

```
  <CLASS xlink:type="locator" xlink:href="week1.xml"
         xlink:label="class"/>
  <CLASS xlink:type="locator" xlink:href="week2.xml"
         xlink:label="class"/>
  <CLASS xlink:type="locator" xlink:href="week3.xml"
         xlink:label="class"/>
  <CLASS xlink:type="locator" xlink:href="week4.xml"
         xlink:label="class"/>
  <CLASS xlink:type="locator" xlink:href="week5.xml"
         xlink:label="class"/>
  <CLASS xlink:type="locator" xlink:href="week6.xml"
         xlink:label="class"/>
  <CLASS xlink:type="locator" xlink:href="week7.xml"
         xlink:label="class"/>
  <CLASS xlink:type="locator" xlink:href="week8.xml"
         xlink:label="class"/>
  <CLASS xlink:type="locator" xlink:href="week9.xml"
         xlink:label="class"/>
  <CLASS xlink:type="locator" xlink:href="week10.xml"
         xlink:label="class"/>
  <CLASS xlink:type="locator" xlink:href="week11.xml"
         xlink:label="class"/>
  <CLASS xlink:type="locator" xlink:href="week12.xml"
         xlink:label="class"/>
  <CLASS xlink:type="locator" xlink:href="week13.xml"
         xlink:label="class"/>

  <CONNECTION xlink:type="arc" from="index" to="class"/>
  <CONNECTION xlink:type="arc" from="class" to="index"/>

</COURSE>
```

Listing 17-8 demonstrates another possible out-of-line extended link. This one provides previous and next links between the 13 classes.

Listing 17-8: **An Out-of-Line Extended Link**

```
<COURSE xmlns:xlink="http://www.w3.org/1999/xlink"
        xlink:type="extended">

  <CLASS xlink:type="locator" xlink:href="week1.xml"
         xlink:label="1"/>
  <CLASS xlink:type="locator" xlink:href="week2.xml"
         xlink:label="2"/>
  <CLASS xlink:type="locator" xlink:href="week3.xml"
         xlink:label="3"/>
```

```
  <CLASS xlink:type="locator" xlink:href="week4.xml"
         xlink:label="4"/>
  <CLASS xlink:type="locator" xlink:href="week5.xml"
         xlink:label="5"/>
  <CLASS xlink:type="locator" xlink:href="week6.xml"
         xlink:label="6"/>
  <CLASS xlink:type="locator" xlink:href="week7.xml"
         xlink:label="7"/>
  <CLASS xlink:type="locator" xlink:href="week8.xml"
         xlink:label="8"/>
  <CLASS xlink:type="locator" xlink:href="week9.xml"
         xlink:label="9"/>
  <CLASS xlink:type="locator" xlink:href="week10.xml"
         xlink:label="10"/>
  <CLASS xlink:type="locator" xlink:href="week11.xml"
         xlink:label="11"/>
  <CLASS xlink:type="locator" xlink:href="week12.xml"
         xlink:label="12"/>
  <CLASS xlink:type="locator" xlink:href="week13.xml"
         xlink:label="13"/>

  <!-- Previous Links -->
  <CONNECTION xlink:type="arc" xlink:from="2"  xlink:to="1"/>
  <CONNECTION xlink:type="arc" xlink:from="3"  xlink:to="2"/>
  <CONNECTION xlink:type="arc" xlink:from="4"  xlink:to="3"/>
  <CONNECTION xlink:type="arc" xlink:from="5"  xlink:to="4"/>
  <CONNECTION xlink:type="arc" xlink:from="6"  xlink:to="5"/>
  <CONNECTION xlink:type="arc" xlink:from="7"  xlink:to="6"/>
  <CONNECTION xlink:type="arc" xlink:from="8"  xlink:to="7"/>
  <CONNECTION xlink:type="arc" xlink:from="9"  xlink:to="8"/>
  <CONNECTION xlink:type="arc" xlink:from="10" xlink:to="9"/>
  <CONNECTION xlink:type="arc" xlink:from="11" xlink:to="10"/>
  <CONNECTION xlink:type="arc" xlink:from="12" xlink:to="11"/>
  <CONNECTION xlink:type="arc" xlink:from="13" xlink:to="12"/>

  <!-- Next Links -->
  <CONNECTION xlink:type="arc" xlink:from="1"  xlink:to="2"/>
  <CONNECTION xlink:type="arc" xlink:from="2"  xlink:to="3"/>
  <CONNECTION xlink:type="arc" xlink:from="3"  xlink:to="4"/>
  <CONNECTION xlink:type="arc" xlink:from="4"  xlink:to="5"/>
  <CONNECTION xlink:type="arc" xlink:from="5"  xlink:to="6"/>
  <CONNECTION xlink:type="arc" xlink:from="6"  xlink:to="7"/>
  <CONNECTION xlink:type="arc" xlink:from="7"  xlink:to="8"/>
  <CONNECTION xlink:type="arc" xlink:from="8"  xlink:to="9"/>
  <CONNECTION xlink:type="arc" xlink:from="9"  xlink:to="10"/>
  <CONNECTION xlink:type="arc" xlink:from="10" xlink:to="11"/>
  <CONNECTION xlink:type="arc" xlink:from="11" xlink:to="12"/>
  <CONNECTION xlink:type="arc" xlink:from="12" xlink:to="13"/>

</COURSE>
```

Now the topics can be reordered simply by rearranging what's connected to what in the out-of-line extended link. The course notes themselves don't have to be touched. However, a couple of pieces are missing from this puzzle. The first is some notion of how or where in the individual week documents the links will be displayed. It would be easy enough to add `<PREVIOUS/>` and `<NEXT/>` tags to the individual week pages. The XPointers you'll learn about in the next chapter would allow you to select these elements in particular as the sources of outgoing links rather than the entire document.

A single XML document may contain multiple out-of-line extended links. Listings 17-7 and 17-8 could be combined into a single document. However, the XLink specification is relatively silent on exactly what the format of such a compound document should look like. About all it says is that such a document must be a well-formed XML document. An XLink processor would presumably read the entire document and extract and store any extended links it found there.

The final thing that's missing is some way for a browser or other application that's reading the individual pages to be informed that there is a separate linkbase elsewhere that it should read and parse so that it can show the links to the user. This is probably the area in which the specification is weakest. Ideally, it would be handled through some external mechanism such as HTTP headers. However, the only currently defined way to do this (which still isn't supported by any browsers or other software) is to add an extended link inside the documents the out-of-line link connects.

One of the arcs in this extended link has an `xlink:arcrole` attribute with the value `http://www.w3.org/1999/xlink/properties/linkbase`. The `xlink:to` attribute of this arc element should identify a locator element that gives the URL of the linkbase. The `xlink:actuate` attribute of the arc determines whether the links are loaded automatically or whether a user request is required. For example, if Listing 17-7 and Listing 17-8 were found in a file at the URL `http://ibiblio.org/javafaq/course/courselinks.xml`, this element could be included in the main page for the Java course notes:

```
<LINKBASE xlink:type="xlink:extended"
          xmlns:xlink="http://www.w3.org/1999/xlink">
  <SOURCE xlink:type="resource" xlink:label="source"/>
  <LINKS xlink:type="locator" xlink:label="linkbase"
         xlink:href=
         "http://ibiblio.org/javafaq/course/courselinks.xml"/>
  <LOAD  xlink:type="arc"
         xlink:arcrole=
          "http://www.w3.org/1999/xlink/properties/linkbase"
         xlink:from="source" xlink:to="linkbase"
         xlink:actuate="onLoad" />
</LINKBASE>
```

Of course, the problem with this approach is that it requires you to modify the documents before you can link them. At least in this case, however, it might be enough for the browser to load one such document to find the linkbase, so you may not need to modify every document the linkbase connects.

XML Base

Documents on the Web have an annoying tendency to move. Authors edit pages on their local systems or staging servers before uploading them to the server. Readers save copies on their hard drives. Fans make copies of entire sites, both licit and illicit. Google caches almost the entire Web on its servers. Given this, authors really can't assume that readers get documents from the place the authors put them. It's entirely possible that a document will be somewhere else. For example, I used AltaVista to search for a phrase in a document I published on my web site and found it had somehow duplicated itself onto 12 different servers in five different countries, my copyright notices notwithstanding.

Given all this and more, using relative URLs in a web document is a little risky; and that's true whether the URLs are stored in HTML, XML, XHTML, XLinks, XPointers, XInclude, RDF, schemas, RDDL, or any of the other myriad languages that somewhere contain URLs. HTML solves this problem by allowing an empty `BASE` element in the `HEAD` that identifies the base URL via an `HREF` attribute.

For example, Listing 17-9 is a very simple home page for a fictional San Francisco plant nursery called God's Green Earth. This page is normally found at `http://www.geocities.com/godsgreenearthsf/`. Because of the `BASE` element in the `HEAD`, it has the base URL `http://www.geocities.com/godsgreenearthsf/` even if you load it from a copy saved on your local hard drive. The logo image is loaded from GeoCities, even if the page has been moved to a different server. Links that point to relative URLs are relative to `http://www.geocities.com/godsgreenearthsf/`. Indeed, anything in this page that uses a relative URL will be loaded from `http://www.geocities.com`.

Listing 17-9: Setting the Base URL with a BASE Element in HTML

```
<HTML>
  <HEAD>
    <TITLE>God's Green Earth</TITLE>
    <BASE HREF="http://www.geocities.com/godsgreenearthsf/" />
  </HEAD>
  <BODY>
    <H1>God's Green Earth</H1>
    <IMG SRC="/clipart/m/s/appleblossoms.gif" />
    <UL>
      <LI><A HREF="flowers.html">Flowers</A></LI>
      <LI><A HREF="seeds.html">Seeds</A></LI>
      <LI><A HREF="fertilizer.html">Fertilizer</A></LI>
      <LI><A HREF="sod.html">Sod</A></LI>
    </UL>
  </BODY>
</HTML>
```

There are five relative URLs in Listing 17-9, one in an IMG element and four in A elements. When any of these links are activated, the relative URL is combined with the absolute URL in the base before the link is followed. The five URLs in Listing 17-9 become the following:

- http://www.geocities.com/clipart/m/s/appleblossoms.gif
- http://www.geocities.com/godsgreenearthsf/flowers.htm
- http://www.geocities.com/godsgreenearthsf/seeds.html
- http://www.geocities.com/godsgreenearthsf/fertilizer.html
- http://www.geocities.com/godsgreenearthsf/sod.html

The first URL in this list comes from GeoCities, but not from the godsgreenearthsf directory, because the relative URL in the IMG element begins with a forward slash and therefore starts from the root of the web server. It's relative to the host but not the directory. The remaining four URLs do not begin with a forward slash and all are loaded from the godsgreenearthsf directory on www.geocities.com.

Similar approaches work in XHTML, but in most XML-based vocabularies, there's no convenient place to put a BASE element. The BASE element could even be needed for something else entirely, such as the location of a military base or the length of the base of a triangle.

Instead, in XML, you can use an xml:base attribute to establish a base URL. The value of this attribute contains the base URL for that element and all its descendants. For example, Listing 17-10 also has the base URL http://www.geocities.com/godsgreenearthsf/. There are five XLinks in this document. Each XLink contains a relative URL, and each is relative to http://www.geocities.com/godsgreenearthsf/. Again, anything in this page that uses a relative URL will be loaded from http://www.geocities.com no matter where the page itself is found.

Listing 17-10: Setting the Base URL with an xml:base Attribute in XML

```
<?xml version="1.0"?>
<BUSINESS xmlns:xlink="http://www.w3.org/1999/xlink"
    xml:base="http://www.geocities.com/godsgreenearthsf/">
    <NAME>God's Green Earth</NAME>
    <LOGO xlink:type="simple"
          xlink:show="embed"
          xlink:actuate="onLoad"
          xlink:href="/clipart/m/s/appleblossoms.gif" />
    <PRODUCTS>
      <PRODUCT xlink:type="simple"
               xlink:show="replace"
               xlink:actuate="onRequest"
               xlink:href="flowers.html">Flowers</PRODUCT>
```

```
        <PRODUCT xlink:type="simple"
                 xlink:show="replace"
                 xlink:actuate="onRequest"
                 xlink:href="seeds.html">Seeds</PRODUCT>
        <PRODUCT xlink:type="simple"
                 xlink:show="replace"
                 xlink:actuate="onRequest"
                 xlink:href="fertilizer.html">
          Fertilizer
        </PRODUCT>
        <PRODUCT xlink:type="simple"
                 xlink:show="replace"
                 xlink:actuate="onRequest"
                 xlink:href="sod.html">Sod</PRODUCT>
      </PRODUCTS>
  </BUSINESS>
```

When activated, the five XLinks in Listing 17-10 resolve to the same five URLs as before:

- http://www.geocities.com/clipart/m/s/appleblossoms.gif
- http://www.geocities.com/godsgreenearthsf/flowers.htm
- http://www.geocities.com/godsgreenearthsf/seeds.html
- http://www.geocities.com/godsgreenearthsf/fertilizer.html
- http://www.geocities.com/godsgreenearthsf/sod.html

In Listing 17-10, all the URLs the base is attached to are in XLinks. The `xml:base` attribute is more general than that, however. It also applies to URLs found in XInclude `include` elements, processing instructions, W3C Schema Language `schemaLocation` attributes, and more.

The one common kind of URL that `xml:base` does not apply to is the namespace URL. `xml:base` attributes are not considered when processing a namespace URL, even a relative one. However, relative namespace URLs are highly discouraged, and you should not use them in your own work, so this shouldn't be much of an issue in practice.

Listing 17-10 is well formed and namespace well formed, although the latter may be a little surprising because Listing 17-10 appears to be using an undeclared namespace prefix, `xml`. Nowhere do you see an `xmlns:xml` declaration that binds the prefix `xml` to some namespace URI. This is because the prefix `xml` is special. Of all possible namespace prefixes, only this one does not need to be declared. All namespace-aware parsers prebind it to the URI `http://www.w3.org/XML/1998/namespace`. This is a special case accounted for in the namespaces specification to allow namespace-aware parsers to be backwardly compatible with documents that use the `xml:space` and `xml:lang` attributes defined in XML 1.0. You can declare the `xml` prefix if you feel a need to, but if you do it must be set to that URL, like this:

```
<BUSINESS xmlns:xml="http://www.w3.org/XML/1998/namespace"
    xml:base="http://www.geocities.com/godsgreenearthsf/"
    xmlns:xlink="http://www.w3.org/1999/xlink">
```

Most authors don't bother to declare it.

Listing 17-10 is not valid because it doesn't have a document type declaration, but it could be valid if you provided one. The DTD would have to declare the `xml:base` attribute just like any other attribute:

```
<!ATTLIST BUSINESS
      xml:base    CDATA #IMPLIED
      xmlns:xlink CDATA #FIXED  "http://www.w3.org/1999/xlink"
>
```

Most commonly, the `xml:base` attribute is attached to the root element so that it establishes a base URL for the entire document. However, it can be applied to non-root elements, in which case it only applies to the element and its descendants, and not to other elements elsewhere in the tree. For example, Listing 17-11 moves it to the `PRODUCTS` element:

Listing 17-11: An xml:base Attribute on a Nonroot Element

```
<?xml version="1.0"?>
<BUSINESS xmlns:xlink="http://www.w3.org/1999/xlink">
   <NAME>God's Green Earth</NAME>
   <LOGO xlink:type="simple"
         xlink:show="embed"
         xlink:actuate="onLoad"
         xlink:href="/clipart/m/s/appleblossoms.gif" />
   <PRODUCTS
        xml:base="http://www.geocities.com/godsgreenearthsf/">
     <PRODUCT xlink:type="simple"
              xlink:show="replace"
              xlink:actuate="onRequest"
              xlink:href="flowers.html">Flowers</PRODUCT>
     <PRODUCT xlink:type="simple"
              xlink:show="replace"
              xlink:actuate="onRequest"
              xlink:href="seeds.html">Seeds</PRODUCT>
     <PRODUCT xlink:type="simple"
              xlink:show="replace"
              xlink:actuate="onRequest"
              xlink:href="fertilizer.html">
       Fertilizer
     </PRODUCT>
     <PRODUCT xlink:type="simple"
              xlink:show="replace"
```

```
               xlink:actuate="onRequest"
               xlink:href="sod.html">Sod</PRODUCT>
    </PRODUCTS>
  </BUSINESS>
```

In this position, it only applies to the PRODUCT links. It does not apply to the LOGO link. The logo URL /clipart/m/s/appleblossoms.gif is now relative to the physical location of this document. A different image will load if you pull it in from a local drive than from one on a remote web server.

There can even be multiple xml:base attributes on different elements in the document, so that different elements are relative to different URLs. If an element has multiple ancestors with xml:base attributes, the closest one takes precedence. Consider Listing 17-12. Here the root element sets the base URL to http://www.geocities.com/godsgreenearthsf, and the PRODUCTS element sets the base URL to http://www.seedgrow.com.

Listing 17-12: **Multiple xml:base Attributes**

```
<?xml version="1.0"?>
<BUSINESS xmlns:xlink="http://www.w3.org/1999/xlink"
       xml:base="http://www.geocities.com/godsgreenearthsf/">
    <NAME>God's Green Earth</NAME>
    <LOGO xlink:type="simple"
          xlink:show="embed"
          xlink:actuate="onLoad"
          xlink:href="/clipart/m/s/appleblossoms.gif" />
    <PRODUCTS xml:base="http://www.seedgrow.com/">
      <PRODUCT xlink:type="simple"
               xlink:show="replace"
               xlink:actuate="onRequest"
               xlink:href="flowers.html">Flowers</PRODUCT>
      <PRODUCT xlink:type="simple"
               xlink:show="replace"
               xlink:actuate="onRequest"
               xlink:href="seeds.html">Seeds</PRODUCT>
      <PRODUCT xlink:type="simple"
               xlink:show="replace"
               xlink:actuate="onRequest"
               xlink:href="fertilizer.html">
        Fertilizer
      </PRODUCT>
      <PRODUCT xlink:type="simple"
               xlink:show="replace"
               xlink:actuate="onRequest"
               xlink:href="sod.html">Sod</PRODUCT>
    </PRODUCTS>
</BUSINESS>
```

When activated, the five XLinks in Listing 17-12 resolve to these five URLs:

- http://www.geocities.com/clipart/m/s/appleblossoms.gif
- http://www.seedgrow.com/flowers.htm
- http://www.seedgrow.com/seeds.html
- http://www.seedgrow.com/fertilizer.html
- http://www.seedgrow.com/sod.html

On occasion, it might be useful to use relative URLs in `xml:base` attributes. In this case, that URL is itself relative to the URL of the closest ancestor with an `xml:base` attribute. If there is no such ancestor, the URL is relative to the actual URL of the document. For example, Listing 17-13 sets the base URL of the root element to `http://www.geocities.com/godsgreenearthsf/` as before. However, an `xml:base` attribute on the `PRODUCTS` element sets the base URL to `products`.

Listing 17-13: **Relative URLs in xml:base Attributes**

```
<?xml version="1.0"?>
<BUSINESS xmlns:xlink="http://www.w3.org/1999/xlink"
      xml:base="http://www.geocities.com/godsgreenearthsf/">
   <NAME>God's Green Earth</NAME>
   <LOGO xlink:type="simple"
         xlink:show="embed"
         xlink:actuate="onLoad"
         xlink:href="/clipart/m/s/appleblossoms.gif" />
   <PRODUCTS xml:base="products">
     <PRODUCT xlink:type="simple"
              xlink:show="replace"
              xlink:actuate="onRequest"
              xlink:href="flowers.html">Flowers</PRODUCT>
     <PRODUCT xlink:type="simple"
              xlink:show="replace"
              xlink:actuate="onRequest"
              xlink:href="seeds.html">Seeds</PRODUCT>
     <PRODUCT xlink:type="simple"
              xlink:show="replace"
              xlink:actuate="onRequest"
              xlink:href="fertilizer.html">
       Fertilizer
     </PRODUCT>
     <PRODUCT xlink:type="simple"
              xlink:show="replace"
              xlink:actuate="onRequest"
              xlink:href="sod.html">Sod</PRODUCT>
   </PRODUCTS>
</BUSINESS>
```

When activated, the five XLinks in Listing 17-13 resolve to these five URLs:

- `http://www.geocities.com/clipart/m/s/appleblossoms.gif`
- `http://www.geocities.com/godsgreenearthsf/products/flowers.htm`
- `http://www.geocities.com/godsgreenearthsf/products/seeds.html`
- `http://www.geocities.com/godsgreenearthsf/products/fertilizer.html`
- `http://www.geocities.com/godsgreenearthsf/products/sod.html`

The disadvantage to the element-wide scope of `xml:base`, as opposed to the document-wide scope of the `BASE` element in HTML, is that the base URL can never be applied to things outside the root element. Specifically, it does not change the location of a style sheet referenced in an `xml-stylesheet` processing instruction. For example, consider Listing 17-14. The browser will look for the document `business.css` in the same directory in which it found the XML document, regardless of what `xml:base` says.

Listing 17-14: URLs Outside the Root Element

```
<?xml version="1.0"?>
<?xml-stylesheet type="text/css" href="business.css"?>
<BUSINESS xmlns:xlink="http://www.w3.org/1999/xlink"
  xml:base="http://www.geocities.com/godsgreenearthsf/">
   <NAME>God's Green Earth</NAME>
   <LOGO xlink:type="simple"
         xlink:show="embed"
         xlink:actuate="onLoad"
         xlink:href="/clipart/m/s/appleblossoms.gif" />
   <PRODUCTS>
     <PRODUCT xlink:type="simple"
              xlink:show="replace"
              xlink:actuate="onRequest"
              xlink:href="flowers.html">Flowers</PRODUCT>
     <PRODUCT xlink:type="simple"
              xlink:show="replace"
              xlink:actuate="onRequest"
              xlink:href="seeds.html">Seeds</PRODUCT>
     <PRODUCT xlink:type="simple"
              xlink:show="replace"
              xlink:actuate="onRequest"
              xlink:href="fertilizer.html">
       Fertilizer
     </PRODUCT>
     <PRODUCT xlink:type="simple"
              xlink:show="replace"
```

Continued

Listing 17-14 *(continued)*

```
                  xlink:actuate="onRequest"
                  xlink:href="sod.html">Sod</PRODUCT>
   </PRODUCTS>
</BUSINESS>
```

Likewise, `xml:base` has no effect on URIs used inside DTDs and document-type declarations, whether in the internal or external DTD subsets.

Summary

In this chapter, you learned about XLinks and XML Base. In particular, you learned the following:

- XLinks can do everything HTML links can do and quite a bit more, but they aren't well supported by current applications.
- XLink elements are all defined by attributes attached to the existing elements in other XML applications.
- XLink attributes of all types are placed in the `http://www.w3.org/1999/xlink` namespace, normally with the `xlink` prefix.
- Simple links behave much like HTML links, but they are not restricted to a single `<A>` tag.
- XLink elements are identified by `xlink:type` attributes.
- Simple link elements are identified by `xlink:type` attributes with the value `simple`.
- Simple link elements have an `xlink:href` attribute whose value is the URI the link points to.
- Linking elements can describe the resource they're linking to with `xlink:title` and `xlink:role` attributes. The value of the `xlink:role` attribute must be a URI.
- Linking elements can use the `xlink:show` attribute to tell the application how the content should be displayed when the link is activated, for example, by opening a new window.
- Linking elements can use the `xlink:actuate` attribute to tell the application whether the link should be traversed without a specific user request.

- Extended link elements are identified by `xlink:type` attributes with the value `extended`.
- Extended links can contain multiple locators, resources, and arcs.
- Local resource elements are identified by `xlink:type` attributes with the value `resource`. The resource is the content of the resource element.
- Remote resource locator elements are identified by `xlink:type` attributes with the value `locator`.
- A locator element has an `xlink:href` attribute whose value is the URI of the resource it locates.
- Both resource and locator elements have an `xlink:label` attribute that contains an XML name token as a label for the resource.
- Arc elements are identified by `xlink:type` attributes with the value `arc`.
- Arc elements have `xlink:from` and `xlink:to` attributes that identify the resources they connect by their labels.
- Arc elements may have `xlink:show` and `xlink:actuate` attributes to determine when and how traversal of the link occurs.
- An out-of-line link is a link that does not contain any local resources.
- A linkbase is a document containing one or more out-of-line, extended link elements.
- A linkbase is found when a document with an extended link whose `xlink:arcrole` has the value `http://www.w3.org/1999/xlink/properties/linkbase` is read.
- An `xml:base` attribute on any element sets the URL against which relative URLs in that element and its descendants are relative.

In Chapter 18, you learn how you can use XPointers to link not only to remote documents, but also to very specific elements in remote documents.

✦ ✦ ✦

CHAPTER 18

XPointers

◆ ◆ ◆ ◆

In This Chapter

◆ ◆ ◆ ◆

XPointer, the XML Pointer Language, defines an addressing scheme for individual parts of an XML document. These addresses can be used by any application that needs to identify parts of or locations in an XML document. For example, an XML editor could use an XPointer to identify the current position of the insertion point or the range of the selection. An XInclude processor can use an XPointer to determine what part of a document to include. You can also add an XPointer fragment identifier to the URI in an XLink to change it into a URI reference that locates one particular element in the targeted document. XPointers use the same XPath syntax that you're familiar with from XSLT to identify the parts of the document they point to, along with a few additional pieces.

No mainstream browsers have any support for XPointers. You can use URLs with XPointer fragment identifiers in web pages, but browsers will mostly ignore them.

Why XPointers?

Traditional URLs are simple and easy to use, but they're also quite limited. For one thing, a URL only points at a single, complete document. More granularity than that, such as linking to the third sentence of the seventeenth paragraph in a document, requires the author of the targeted document to manually insert named anchors at the targeted location. The author of the document doing the linking can't do this unless he or she also has write access to the document being linked to. Even if the author doing the linking can insert named anchors into the targeted document, it's almost always inconvenient.

It would be more useful to be able to link to a particular element or group of elements on a page without having to change the document you're linking to. For example, given a large document such as the television listings of Chapters 4 and 5, you might want to link to only one station or one show. There are several parts to this problem. The first part is addressing the individual elements. This is the part that XPointers solve. XPointers enable you to target a given element by number, name, type, or relation to other elements in the document.

The second part of the problem is the protocol by which a browser asks a web server to send only part of a document rather than the whole thing. This is an area of active research. More work is needed. XPointers do little to solve this problem, except for providing a foundation on which such systems can build. For example, the best efforts to date are the so-called byte range extensions to HTTP available in HTTP 1.1. So far, these have not achieved widespread adoption, mostly because web authors aren't comfortable specifying a byte range in a document. Furthermore, byte ranges are extremely fragile. Trivial edits to a document, even simple reformatting, can destroy byte range links. HTTP 1.1 does allow other range units besides raw bytes (for example, XML elements), but does not require web servers or browsers to support such units.

For the moment, therefore, an XPointer can be used as an index into a complete document, the whole of which is loaded and then positioned at the location identified by the XPointer, and even this is more than most browsers can handle. In the long term, extensions to XML, XLink, HTTP, and other protocols may allow more sophisticated uses of XPointers. For example, XInclude will let you quote a remote document by using an XPointer to tell browsers where to copy the quote in the original document, rather than retyping the text of the quote. You could include cross-references inside a document that automatically update themselves as the document is revised. These uses, however, will have to wait for the development of several next-generation technologies. For now, you must be content with precisely identifying the part of a document you want to jump to when following an XLink.

XPointer Examples

HTML links generally point to one particular document. Additional granularity—that is, pointing to a particular section, chapter, or paragraph of a particular document—isn't well supported. Provided you control both the linking and the linked document, you can insert a named anchor into an HTML file at the position to which you want to link, as in the following example:

```
<H2><A NAME="xtocid20.2">XPointer Examples</A></H2>
```

You can then link to this position in the file by adding a # and the name of the anchor to the URL. The piece of the URL after the # is called the *fragment identifier*. For example, in this link the fragment identifier is `xtocid20.2`:

```
<A HREF="http://www.cafeconleche.org/bible/20.html#xtocid20.2">
  XPointer Examples
</A>
```

A URL with a fragment identifier is technically a URL reference, not a URL; but outside of specification documents, the distinction is almost never made, nor does it matter.

However, this solution is a kludge. It's not always possible to modify the target document so that the source document can link to it. The target document might be on a different server controlled by someone other than the author of the source document. And the author of the target document might change or move it without notifying the author of the source.

Furthermore, named anchors violate the principle of separating markup from content. Placing a named anchor in a document says nothing about the document or its content. It's just a marker for other documents to refer to. It adds nothing to the document's own content.

XPointers allow much more sophisticated connections between parts of documents. An XPointer can refer to any element of a document; to the first, second, or seventeenth element; to the seventh element named `P`; to the first element that's a child of the second `DIV` element; and so on. XPointers provide precisely targeted addresses of particular parts of documents. They do not require the targeted document to contain additional markup just so its individual pieces can be linked to.

Furthermore, unlike HTML anchors, XPointers don't point to just a single point in a document. They can point to entire elements, to noncontiguous sets of elements, or to a range of text between two points. Thus, you can use an XPointer to select a particular part of a document, perhaps so it can be copied or loaded into a program.

Here are a few examples of XPointers:

```
xpointer(id("ebnf"))
xpointer(descendant::language[position()=2])
ebnf
xpointer(/child::spec/child::body/child::*/child::language[2])
xpointer(/spec/body/*/language[2])
element(/1/14/2)
xpointer(id("ebnf"))xpointer(id("EBNF"))
```

Each of these seven XPointers selects a particular element in a document. The first finds the element with the ID `ebnf`. The second finds the second `language` element in the document. The third is a shorthand form of finding the element with the ID `ebnf`. The fourth and fifth both specify the second `language` child element of any child element of the `body` child elements of the `spec` child of the root node. The sixth finds the second child element of the fourteenth child element of the root element. The final one also points to the element with the ID `ebnf`. However, if no such element is present, it then finds the element with the ID `EBNF`.

The document is not specified by the XPointer; rather, the URI that precedes the XPointer specifies the document. This URI may be contained in an XLink linking element or in anything else that contains a URI pointing at an XML document. The XLinks and URIs you saw in Chapter 17 did not contain XPointers, but it isn't hard to add XPointers to them. Most of the time, you simply append the XPointer to the

URI separated by a #, just as you do with named anchors in HTML. For example, the preceding list of XPointers could be suffixed to URLs and come out looking similar to the following:

```
http://www.w3.org/TR/1998/REC-xml-19980210.xml#xpointer(id("ebnf"))
http://www.w3.org/TR/1998/REC-xml-19980210.xml#xpointer(
descendant::language[position()=2])
http://www.w3.org/TR/1998/REC-xml-19980210.xml#ebnf
http://www.w3.org/TR/1998/REC-xml-19980210.xml#xpointer(
/child::spec/child::body/child::*/child::language[2])
http://www.w3.org/TR/1998/REC-xml-19980210.xml#xpointer(
/spec/body/*/language[2])
http://www.w3.org/TR/1998/REC-xml-19980210.xml#element(/1/14/2)
http://www.w3.org/TR/1998/REC-xml-19980210.xml#xpointer(
id("ebnf"))xpointer(id("EBNF"))
```

In fact, these URIs are just six different ways of pointing to the same element of the document at `http://www.w3.org/TR/1998/REC-xml-19980210.xml`. Often, such URIs are values of the `xlink:href` attribute of a linking element, as in the following example:

```
<SPECIFICATION xmlns:xlink="http://www.w3.org/1999/xlink"
 xlink:type="simple" xlink:href=
  "http://www.w3.org/TR/1998/REC-xml-19980210.xml#xpointer(id('ebnf'))"
 xlink:actuate="onRequest" xlink:show="replace">
  Extensible Markup Language (XML) 1.0
</SPECIFICATION>
```

XPointers don't have any special exemptions from the rules of URIs. In particular, if the XPointer contains characters that are not allowed in URLs such as Ω or ^, these characters must be encoded in UTF-8, and the bytes of the UTF-8 encoding must be hex-escaped using a percent sign. For example, the capital Greek letter omega is Unicode character 3A9 in hexadecimal. When encoded in UTF-8, this character is the two bytes 206 and 169. In hexadecimal, that's CE and A9. Therefore, the XPointer `xpointer(id("Ω"))` would be encoded in a URL as `xpointer(id("%CE%A9"))`.

- ✦ The caret is Unicode character 5E in hexadecimal.
- ✦ The equals sign is Unicode character 3D in hexadecimal.
- ✦ The colon is Unicode character 3A in hexadecimal.

Because these three characters are part of the ASCII character set, their UTF-8 encodings are simply their values. Therefore, `xpointer(descendant::*[.='^'])` would be encoded in a URL as `xpointer(descendant%3A%3A*[.%3D'%5E'])`. Modern web browsers allow the square brackets [and] in URLs. However, some older browsers do not, so for maximum compatibility you should escape these characters as %5B and %5D, respectively. Thus, the preceding XPointer would become `xpointer(descendant%3A%3A*%5B.%3D'%5E'%5D)`.

A Concrete Example

To demonstrate the different types of XPointers, it's useful to have a concrete example in mind. Listing 18-1 is a simple, valid document that should be self-explanatory. It contains information about two related families and their members. The root element is FAMILYTREE. A FAMILYTREE can contain PERSON and FAMILY elements. Each PERSON and FAMILY element has a required ID attribute. Persons contain a name, birth date, death date, and spouse. Families contain a husband, a wife, and zero or more children. The individual persons are referred to from the family by reference to their IDs.

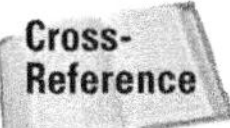

This XML application is revisited in Chapter 25.

Listing 18-1: A Family Tree

```
<?xml version="1.0"?>
<!DOCTYPE FAMILYTREE [

  <!ELEMENT FAMILYTREE (PERSON | FAMILY)*>

  <!-- PERSON elements -->
  <!ELEMENT PERSON (NAME*, BORN*, DIED*, SPOUSE*)>
  <!ATTLIST PERSON
    ID      ID     #REQUIRED
    FATHER  CDATA  #IMPLIED
    MOTHER  CDATA  #IMPLIED
  >
  <!ELEMENT NAME (#PCDATA)>
  <!ELEMENT BORN (#PCDATA)>
  <!ELEMENT DIED  (#PCDATA)>
  <!ELEMENT SPOUSE EMPTY>
  <!ATTLIST SPOUSE IDREF IDREF #REQUIRED>

  <!--FAMILY-->
  <!ELEMENT FAMILY (HUSBAND?, WIFE?, CHILD*) >
  <!ATTLIST FAMILY ID ID #REQUIRED>

  <!ELEMENT HUSBAND EMPTY>
  <!ATTLIST HUSBAND IDREF IDREF #REQUIRED>
  <!ELEMENT WIFE EMPTY>
  <!ATTLIST WIFE IDREF IDREF #REQUIRED>
  <!ELEMENT CHILD EMPTY>
  <!ATTLIST CHILD IDREF IDREF #REQUIRED>

]>
<FAMILYTREE>

  <PERSON ID="p1">
```

Continued

Listing 18-1 *(continued)*

```
    <NAME>Domeniquette Celeste Baudean</NAME>
    <BORN>21 Apr 1836</BORN>
    <DIED>Unknown</DIED>
    <SPOUSE IDREF="p2"/>
  </PERSON>

  <PERSON ID="p2">
    <NAME>Jean Francois Bellau</NAME>
    <SPOUSE IDREF="p1"/>
  </PERSON>

  <PERSON ID="p3" FATHER="p2" MOTHER="p1">
    <NAME>Elodie Bellau</NAME>
    <BORN>11 Feb 1858</BORN>
    <DIED>12 Apr 1898</DIED>
    <SPOUSE IDREF="p4"/>
  </PERSON>

  <PERSON ID="p4">
    <NAME>John P. Muller</NAME>
    <SPOUSE IDREF="p3"/>
  </PERSON>

  <PERSON ID="p7">
    <NAME>Adolf Eno</NAME>
    <SPOUSE IDREF="p6"/>
  </PERSON>

  <PERSON ID="p6" FATHER="p2" MOTHER="p1">
    <NAME>Maria Bellau</NAME>
    <SPOUSE IDREF="p7"/>
  </PERSON>

  <PERSON ID="p5" FATHER="p2" MOTHER="p1">
    <NAME>Eugene Bellau</NAME>
  </PERSON>

  <PERSON ID="p8" FATHER="p2" MOTHER="p1">
    <NAME>Louise Pauline Bellau</NAME>
    <BORN>29 Oct 1868</BORN>
    <DIED>3 May 1938</DIED>
    <SPOUSE IDREF="p9"/>
  </PERSON>

  <PERSON ID="p9">
    <NAME>Charles Walter Harold</NAME>
    <BORN>about 1861</BORN>
    <DIED>about 1938</DIED>
```

```
    <SPOUSE IDREF="p8"/>
  </PERSON>

  <PERSON ID="p10" FATHER="p2" MOTHER="p1">
    <NAME>Victor Joseph Bellau</NAME>
    <SPOUSE IDREF="p11"/>
  </PERSON>

  <PERSON ID="p11">
    <NAME>Ellen Gilmore</NAME>
    <SPOUSE IDREF="p10"/>
  </PERSON>

  <PERSON ID="p12" FATHER="p2" MOTHER="p1">
    <NAME>Honore Bellau</NAME>
  </PERSON>

  <FAMILY ID="f1">
    <HUSBAND IDREF="p2"/>
    <WIFE IDREF="p1"/>
    <CHILD IDREF="p3"/>
    <CHILD IDREF="p5"/>
    <CHILD IDREF="p6"/>
    <CHILD IDREF="p8"/>
    <CHILD IDREF="p10"/>
    <CHILD IDREF="p12"/>
  </FAMILY>

  <FAMILY ID="f2">
    <HUSBAND IDREF="p7"/>
    <WIFE IDREF="p6"/>
  </FAMILY>

</FAMILYTREE>
```

In the sections that follow, this document is assumed to be present at the URL `http://www.theharolds.com/genealogy.xml`. This isn't a real URL, but the emphasis here is on selecting individual parts of a document rather than a document as a whole.

Location Paths, Steps, and Sets

Many (though not all) XPointers are *location paths*. These are the same location paths used by XSLT and discussed in Chapter 15. Consequently, much of the syntax should already be familiar to you.

Location paths are built from *location steps*. Each location step specifies a point in the targeted document, always relative to some other well-known point such as the start of the document or the previous location step. This well-known point is called the *context node*. In general, a location step has three parts: the *axis*, the *node test*, and an optional *predicate*. These are combined in this form:

```
axis::node-test[predicate]
```

For example, in the location step `child::PERSON[position()=2]`, the axis is `child`, the node-test is `PERSON`, and the predicate is `[position()=2]`. This location step selects the second `PERSON` element along the child axis, starting from the context node or, less formally, the second `PERSON` child element of the context node. Of course, which element this actually is depends on what the context node is. Consequently, this is what's referred to as a *relative location step*. It's relative to the context node. There are also absolute location steps that do not depend on the context node.

The axis specifies the direction to search from the context node. For example, an axis can say to look at things that follow the context node, things that precede the context node, things that are children of the context node, things that are attributes of the context node, and so forth.

The node test indicates which nodes to consider along the axis. The most common node test is simply an element name. However, the node test can also be the asterisk (*) wildcard to indicate that any element is to be matched, or one of several functions for selecting comments, text, attributes, processing instructions, points, and ranges. The group of nodes along the given axis that satisfy the node test forms a *location set*.

The predicate is a boolean XPath expression (exactly like the XPath expressions you learned about in XSLT) that tests each node in that set. If that expression returns false, the node is removed from the set.

Often, after the entire location step—axis, node test, and predicate—has been evaluated, what's left is a single, unique node. However, not all location steps select exactly one node. In some cases, there may be multiple nodes in the final location set. On occasion, there might be no nodes in the location set; in other words, the location set is the empty set.

A single location step is often not enough to identify the node you want. Commonly, location steps are strung together, separated by slashes, to form a *location path*. Each location step's location set becomes the context node-set for the next step in the path. For example, consider this XPointer:

```
xpointer(/child::FAMILYTREE/child::PERSON[position()=3])
```

The location path of this XPointer is `/child::FAMILYTREE/child::PERSON[position()=3]`. It is built from two location steps:

- `/child::FAMILYTREE`
- `child::PERSON[position()=3]`

The first location step is an absolute step that selects all child elements of the root node whose name is FAMILYTREE. When applied to Listing 18-1, there's exactly one such element. The second location step is then applied relative to the FAMILYTREE element returned by the first location step. All of its child nodes are considered. Those that satisfy the node test — that is, elements whose name is PERSON — are returned. There are 12 of these nodes. Each of these 12 nodes is then compared against the predicate to see if its position is equal to 3. This turns out to be true for only one node, Elodie Bellau's PERSON element, so that is the single node this XPointer points to.

It is not always the case, however, that an XPointer points to exactly one node. For example, consider this XPointer:

```
xpointer(/child::FAMILYTREE/child::PERSON[position()>3])
```

This is exactly the same as before except that the equals sign has been changed to a greater than sign. Now when each of the 12 PERSON elements are compared, the predicate returns true for 9 of them. Each of these nine is included in the location set that this XPointer returns. This XPointer points to nine nodes, not to one.

The Root Node

Although Listing 18-1 includes ID attributes for most elements, and although they are convenient, they are not required for linking into the document. You can select any element in the document simply by working your way down from the root node. An initial / indicates the root node.

The root node is not the same as the root element. Rather, it is an abstract node that contains the entire document, including any comments or processing instructions that come before or after the root element, such as xml-stylesheet, and the root element itself. For example, to select the root node of the XML 1.0 specification at http://www.w3.org/TR/REC-xml you can use this URI:

```
http://www.w3.org/TR/REC-xml#xpointer(/)
```

For another example, Domeniquette Celeste Baudean is the first person in Listing 18-1. Therefore, to point at her name, you can get the first element child of the root node (that is, the root element of the document, FAMILYTREE), then count one PERSON down from the root element, and then count one NAME down from that, like this:

```
/child::*/child::PERSON[position()=1]/child::NAME
```

This location path says to find the root node, then find all element children of the root node (which, in a well-formed XML document, will be exactly the root element), then find the first PERSON element that's an immediate child of that element, and then find its NAME child elements.

Axes

XPath defines 13 axes along which an XPointer can search for nodes, all from the same XPath syntax used for XSLT. These depend on context to determine exactly what they point to. For example, consider this location path:

```
id("p6")/child::NAME
```

It begins with the id() function that returns a node-set containing the element with the ID type attribute whose value is p6. This provides a context node for the following location step along the relative child axis. Other axes include ancestor, descendant, self, ancestor-or-self, descendant-or-self, attribute, and more. Each serves to select a particular subset of the elements in the document. For example, the following axis selects from nodes that come after the context node. The preceding axis selects from nodes that come before the context node. Table 18-1 summarizes the 13 axes.

Table 18-1
Location Step Axes

Axis	*Selects From*
child	All nodes contained in the context node, but not contained in any other nodes the context node contains
parent	The unique node that contains the context node but that does not contain any other nodes that also contain the context node
self	The context node
ancestor	The parent of the context node, the parent of the parent of the context node, the parent of the parent of the parent of the context node, and so forth, back to the root node
ancestor-or-self	The ancestors of the context node and the context node itself
attribute	The attributes of the context node
descendant	The children of the context node, the children of the children of the context node, and so forth
descendant-or-self	The context node and its descendants
following	All nodes that start after the end of the context node, excluding attribute and namespace nodes

Axis	Selects From
`following-sibling`	All nodes that start after the end of the context node and have the same parent as the context node, excluding attribute and namespace nodes
`preceding`	All nodes that finish before the beginning of the context node, excluding attribute and namespace nodes
`preceding-sibling`	All nodes that start before the beginning of the context node and have the same parent as the context node, excluding attribute and namespace nodes

The child axis

The `child` axis selects from the children of the context node. For example, consider this XPointer:

```
xpointer(/child::FAMILYTREE/child::PERSON[position()=3]/child::NAME)
```

Reading from right to left, it selects the `NAME` child elements of the third `PERSON` element that's a child of the `FAMILYTREE` element that's a child of the root of the document. In this example, there's only one such element; but if there are more than one, all are returned. For instance, consider this XPointer:

```
xpointer(/child::FAMILYTREE/child::PERSON/child::NAME)
```

This selects all `NAME` children of `PERSON` elements that are children of `FAMILYTREE` elements that are children of the root. There are a dozen of these in Listing 18-1.

It's important to note that the `child` axis only selects from the *immediate* children of the context node. For example, consider this URI:

```
http://www.theharolds.com/genealogy.xml#xpointer(/child::NAME)
```

This points nowhere because there are no `NAME` elements in the document that are direct, immediate children of the root node. There are a dozen `NAME` elements that are indirect children. If you'd like to refer to these, you should use the `descendant` axis instead of `child`.

As in XSLT, the `child` axis is implied if no explicit axis name is present. For example, the preceding three XPointers would more likely be written in this abbreviated form:

```
xpointer(/FAMILYTREE/PERSON[position()=3]/NAME)
xpointer(/FAMILYTREE/PERSON/NAME)
xpointer(/NAME)
```

The descendant axis

The `descendant` axis searches through all the descendants of the context node, not just the immediate children. For example, `/descendant::BORN` selects all the `BORN` elements in the document. `/descendant::BORN[position()=3]` selects the third `BORN` element encountered in a depth-first search of the document tree. (Depth first is the order you get if you simply read through the XML document from beginning to end.) In Listing 18-1, that selects Louise Pauline Bellau's birthday, `<BORN>29 Oct 1868</BORN>`. There is no abbreviation for `descendant` axis.

The descendant-or-self axis

The `descendant-or-self` axis searches through all the descendants of the context node and the context node itself. For example, `id("p11")/descendant-or-self::PERSON` refers to all `PERSON` children of the element with ID `p11` as well as that element itself, because it is of type `PERSON`. There is no abbreviation for `descendant-or-self`.

The `descendant-or-self` axis can be abbreviated by using a double slash in place of a single slash. For example, `//BORN[position()=3]` also selects the third `BORN` element encountered in a depth-first search of the document tree. `//NAME` selects all `NAME` elements in the document. `//PERSON/NAME` selects all `NAME` children of `PERSON` elements.

The parent axis

The `parent` axis refers to the node that's the immediate parent of the context node. For example, `/descendant::HUSBAND[position()=1]/parent::*` refers to the parent element of the first `HUSBAND` element in the document. In Listing 18-1, this is the `FAMILY` element with ID `f1`.

Without a node test, the parent axis can be abbreviated by a `..` as in `//HUSBAND[position()=1]/..`.

The self axis

The `self` axis selects the context node. It's sometimes useful when making relative links. For example, `/self::node()` selects the root node of the document (which is not the same as the root element of the document; that would be selected by `/child::*` or, in this example, `/child::FAMILYTREE`.) It can be abbreviated by a single period. However, this axis is rarely used in XPointers. It's more useful for XSLT select expressions.

The ancestor axis

The `ancestor` axis selects all nodes that contain the context node, starting with its parent. For example, `/descendant::BORN[position()=2]/ancestor::*[position()=1]` selects the element that contains the second `BORN` element. Applied to Listing 18-1, it selects Elodie Bellau's `PERSON` element. There's no abbreviation for the `ancestor` axis.

The ancestor-or-self axis

The `ancestor-or-self` axis selects the context node and all nodes that contain it. For example, `id("p1")/ancestor-or-self::*` identifies a node-set that includes Domeniquette Celeste Baudean's `PERSON` element, that has ID `p1`, and its parent, the `FAMILYTREE` element, and its parent, the root node. There's also no abbreviation for the `ancestor-or-self` axis.

The preceding axis

The `preceding` axis selects all nodes that finish before the context node. The first time it encounters an element's start-tag or empty-element tag, moving backwards from the start of the context node, it counts that element. For example, consider this rule:

```
/descendant::BORN[position()=3]/preceding::*[position()=6]
```

This says go to the third `BORN` element from the root, Louise Pauline Bellau's birthday, `<BORN>29 Oct 1868</BORN>`, and then move back six elements. This lands on Maria Bellau's `NAME` element. There's no abbreviation for the `preceding` axis.

The following axis

The `following` axis selects all elements that occur after the context node's closing tag. The first time it encounters an element's start-tag or empty-element tag, it counts that element. For example, consider this location path:

```
/descendant::BORN[position()=2]/following::*[position()=5]
```

This says go to Elodie Bellau's birthday, `<BORN>11 Feb 1858</BORN>`, and then move forward five elements. This lands on John P. Muller's `SPOUSE` element, `<SPOUSE IDREF="p3" />`, after passing through Elodie Bellau's `DIED` element, Elodie Bellau's `SPOUSE` element, John P. Muller's `PERSON` element, and John P. Muller's `NAME` element, in this order. There's no abbreviation for the `following` axis.

The preceding-sibling axis

The `preceding-sibling` axis selects elements that precede the context node in the same parent element. For example, `/descendant::BORN[position()=2]/preceding-sibling::*[position()=1]` selects Elodie Bellau's `NAME` element, `<NAME>Elodie Bellau</NAME>`. `/descendant::BORN[position()=2]/preceding-sibling::*[position()=2]` doesn't point to anything, because there's only one sibling of Elodie Bellau's `BORN` element before it. There's no abbreviation for the `preceding-sibling` axis.

The following-sibling axis

The `following-sibling` axis selects elements that follow the context node in the same parent element. For example, `/descendant::BORN[position()=2]/following-sibling::*[position()=1]` selects Elodie Bellau's `DIED` element, `<DIED>12 Apr 1898</DIED>`. `/descendant::BORN[position()=2]/following-sibling::*[position()=3]` doesn't point to anything, because there are only two sibling elements following Elodie Bellau's `BORN` element. There's no abbreviation for the `following-sibling` axis.

The attribute axis

The `attribute` axis selects attributes of the context node. For example, the location path `/descendant::SPOUSE/attribute::IDREF` selects all `IDREF` attributes of all `SPOUSE` elements in the document. The `attribute` axis can be abbreviated by an @ sign. Thus, `//SPOUSE/@IDREF` also selects all `IDREF` attributes of all `SPOUSE` elements in the document. `@*` is a general abbreviation for an attribute with any name. So, `//SPOUSE/@*` indicates all attributes of all `SPOUSE` elements.

For another example, to find all `PERSON` elements in the document `http://www.theharolds.com/genealogy.xml` whose `FATHER` attribute is Jean Francois Bellau (ID p2), you could write `//PERSON[@FATHER="p2"]`.

The `xmlns` and `xmlns:`*`prefix`* attributes used to declare namespaces are not attribute nodes. To get information about namespaces, you have to use the `namespace` axis instead.

The namespace axis

The `namespace` axis contains the namespaces in scope on the context node. It only applies to element nodes. There is one namespace node for each prefix that is mapped to a URI on that element (whether the prefix is used or not, and whether the `xmlns:`*`prefix`* attribute that created the mapping is on the element itself or one of its ancestors). Furthermore, if the element is in a default, nonprefixed namespace, there is also a namespace node for the default namespace.

Although the element is the parent of the namespace node, the namespace node is not the child of the element. A simple walk of the tree or asking for the children of the element will not find namespaces. Instead, you have to walk the `namespace` axis explicitly. The only node tests that apply to namespace nodes are `node()` and `*`.

Fortunately, there's very little reason to point to a namespace node with an XPointer. This axis is more useful for XSLT and not much used in XPointer.

Node Tests

Most of the time, the node test part of a location step is simply an element or attribute name such as `PERSON` or `IDREF`. However, there are nine other possibilities:

- `*`
- *`prefix:*`*
- `node()`
- `text()`
- `comment()`
- `processing-instruction()`
- `point()`
- `range()`

An asterisk stands for any element, except on the attribute axis, where it stands for any attribute, and along the namespace axis, where it stands for any namespace. For example, `id("p1")/child::*` selects all the child elements of the element with the ID `p1`, regardless of their type. This does, however, select only element nodes. It omits comment nodes, text nodes, processing instruction nodes, and attribute nodes. If you want to select absolutely any kind of node, use the `node()` node test instead.

A prefix followed by an asterisk selects all elements in the namespace that match the prefix. For example, if the `svg` prefix is mapped to the `http://www.w3.org/2000/svg` URI, `svg:*` matches all SVG elements. Similarly, `@`*`prefix`*`:*` matches all attributes in the specified namespace. For example, if `xlink` is mapped to the URI `http://www.w3.org/1999/xlink`, `@xlink:*` matches all XLink attributes in the document, such as `xlink:type`, `xlink:show`, `xlink:actuate`, `xlink:href`, `xlink:role`, and so forth.

The `xmlns:prefix` attributes in the document where the XPointer is found do not apply to XPointers in that document (if indeed, the XPointer is even in an XML document and not in an HTML document, painted on the side of a building, or something else). Instead, you prefix the `xpointer()` part with one or more `xmlns(`*`prefix=URI`*`)` parts that establish a prefix mapping.

For example, suppose you want to point at the MathML math element in the document at http://www.example.com/equations.xml. You know that this element is in the http://www.w3.org/1998/Math/MathML namespace, but you don't know what prefix is used in the document. Regardless of what prefix the target document uses, you can use the prefix mml as long as you use an xmlns(mml=http://www.w3.org/1998/Math/MathML) part to associate it with the right URI, as in the following example:

```
xmlns(mml=http://www.w3.org/1998/Math/MathML)xpointer(//mml:math[1])
```

The text() node test specifically refers to the parsed character data content of an element. It's most commonly used with mixed content. Despite the parentheses, the text() node test does not actually take any arguments. For example, /descendant::text() refers to all of the text but none of the markup of a document. For another example, consider this CITATION element:

```
<CITATION CLASS="TURING" ID="C2">
  <AUTHOR>Turing, Alan M.</AUTHOR>
  "<TITLE>On Computable Numbers,
    With an Application to the Entscheidungs-problem</TITLE>"
  <JOURNAL>
    Proceedings of the London Mathematical Society</JOURNAL>,
  <SERIES>Series 2</SERIES>,
  <VOLUME>42</VOLUME>
  (<YEAR>1936</YEAR>):
  <PAGES>230-65</PAGES>.
</CITATION>
```

The following location path refers to the quotation mark before the TITLE element:

```
id("C2")/child::text()[position()=2]
```

The first text node in this fragment is the white space between <CITATION CLASS="TURING" ID="C2"> and <AUTHOR>. Technically, this location path refers to all text between </AUTHOR> and <TITLE>, including the white space and not just the quotation mark.

Because character data does not contain any child nodes, you cannot add an additional child, descendant, or attribute relative location step after the first term that selects a text node.

The comment() node test specifically refers to comments. For example, this XPointer points to the third comment in the document:

```
xpointer(/descendant::comment()[position()=3])
```

Because comments do not contain attributes or elements, you cannot add an additional child, descendant, or attribute relative location step after the first term that selects a comment. Despite the parentheses, the comment() node test does not actually take any arguments.

Finally, the `processing-instruction()` node test selects any processing instructions that occur along the chosen axis. You can use it without any arguments to select all processing instructions, or with an argument to specify the targets of the particular processing instructions you want to select. For example, `/descendant::processing-instruction()` selects all processing instructions in the document, whereas `/descendant::processing-instruction('xml-stylesheet')` only finds processing instructions that begin `<?xml-stylesheet`. `/descendant::processing-instruction("php")` only finds processing instructions intended for PHP. As with comments, because processing instructions do not contain attributes or elements, you cannot add an additional child, descendant, or attribute relative location step after the first step that selects a processing instruction.

The `point()` and `range()` node tests refer to new ways of dividing an XML document that only work in XPointer, not in other standards that use XPath, such as XSLT. They are discussed later in the chapter.

Predicates

Each location step can contain zero or more predicates that further restrict which nodes an XPointer points to. In many cases, a predicate is necessary to pick the one node from a node-set that you want. This uses the same syntax you learned from XSLT in Chapter 15. Each predicate contains an expression in square brackets (`[]`). This allows an XPointer to select nodes according to many different criteria, such as the following:

- ✦ All elements that have a `color` attribute
- ✦ All elements that have a `width` attribute with the value `100`
- ✦ The first element in the document that contains a `LIMIT` element
- ✦ The second element whose text content includes the word "Gale"
- ✦ All elements that are not the first or last children of their parents
- ✦ All elements whose value is 42
- ✦ All elements whose value is a number greater than 100

These are just a small sampling of the selections that predicates make possible.

The result of a predicate expression is ultimately converted to a boolean after all calculations are finished. Nonboolean results are converted as follows:

- ✦ A number is compared against the position of the node in the context node list. If it matches, the result is true; otherwise, the result is false. (More about this shortly.)
- ✦ An empty node-set is false; all other node-sets are true.
- ✦ A zero-length string is false; all other strings are true (including the string "false").

The predicate expression is evaluated for each node in the context node list. Each node for which the expression ultimately evaluates to false is removed from the list. Thus, only those nodes that satisfy the predicate remain. I will not repeat the discussion of the operators and functions available to use expressions here. However, I will show you a few examples of predicates using the expression syntax as it's likely to be used in XPointers.

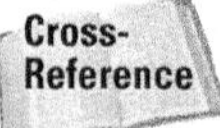

Expression syntax is covered in Chapter 15.

Probably the most frequently used function in XPointer predicates is `position()`. This returns the index of the node in the context node list. This enables you to find the first, second, third, or other indexed node. You can compare positions using the relational operators `<`, `>`, `=`, `!=`, `>=`, and `<=`.

For example, in Listing 18-1 the root `FAMILYTREE` element has 14 immediate children, 12 `PERSON` elements, and 2 `FAMILY` elements. In order, they are:

```
xpointer(/child::FAMILYTREE/child::*[position()=1])
xpointer(/child::FAMILYTREE/child::*[position()=2])
xpointer(/child::FAMILYTREE/child::*[position()=3])
xpointer(/child::FAMILYTREE/child::*[position()=4])
xpointer(/child::FAMILYTREE/child::*[position()=5])
xpointer(/child::FAMILYTREE/child::*[position()=6])
xpointer(/child::FAMILYTREE/child::*[position()=7])
xpointer(/child::FAMILYTREE/child::*[position()=8])
xpointer(/child::FAMILYTREE/child::*[position()=9])
xpointer(/child::FAMILYTREE/child::*[position()=10])
xpointer(/child::FAMILYTREE/child::*[position()=11])
xpointer(/child::FAMILYTREE/child::*[position()=12])
xpointer(/child::FAMILYTREE/child::*[position()=13])
xpointer(/child::FAMILYTREE/child::*[position()=14])
```

In fact, this test is so common that XPath offers a shorthand notation for it. Instead of writing `[position=X]` where X is a number, you can simply enclose the number or an XPath expression that returns the number in the square brackets, like this:

```
xpointer(/child::FAMILYTREE/child::*[1])
xpointer(/child::FAMILYTREE/child::*[2])
xpointer(/child::FAMILYTREE/child::*[3])
xpointer(/child::FAMILYTREE/child::*[4])
xpointer(/child::FAMILYTREE/child::*[5])
xpointer(/child::FAMILYTREE/child::*[6])
xpointer(/child::FAMILYTREE/child::*[7])
xpointer(/child::FAMILYTREE/child::*[8])
xpointer(/child::FAMILYTREE/child::*[9])
xpointer(/child::FAMILYTREE/child::*[10])
xpointer(/child::FAMILYTREE/child::*[11])
xpointer(/child::FAMILYTREE/child::*[12])
xpointer(/child::FAMILYTREE/child::*[13])
xpointer(/child::FAMILYTREE/child::*[14])
```

Greater numbers, such as /child::FAMILYTREE/child::*[15], don't point to anything.

To count all elements in the document, not just the immediate children of the root, you can use the descendant axis instead of child. Table 18-2 shows the first four descendant XPointers for the document element FAMILYTREE of Listing 18-1, and what they point to. Note especially that /child::FAMILYTREE/descendant::*[position()=1] points to the entire first PERSON element, including its children, and not just the <PERSON> start-tag.

Table 18-2
The First Four Descendants of the Document Element

XPointer	*Points To*
/child::FAMILYTREE/ descendant::*[position()=1]	<PERSON ID="p1"> <NAME>Domeniquette Celeste Baudean</NAME> <BORN>11 Feb 1858</BORN> <DIED>12 Apr 1898</DIED> <SPOUSE IDREF="p2"/> </PERSON>
/child::FAMILYTREE/ descendant::*[position()=2]	<NAME>Domeniquette Celeste Baudean</NAME>
/child::FAMILYTREE/ descendant::*[position()=3]	<BORN>21 Apr 1836</BORN>
/child::FAMILYTREE/ descendant::*[position()=4]	<DIED>Unknown</DIED>

Functions That Return Node-Sets

XPointers are not limited to location paths. In fact, they can use any expression that returns a node-set. In particular, they can use functions that return node-sets. There are three of these:

- id()
- here()
- origin()

The last two, here() and origin(), are XPointer extensions to XPath that are not available in XSLT.

id()

The `id()` function is one of the simplest and most robust means of identifying an element node. It selects the element in the document that has an ID type attribute with a specified value. For example, consider this URI:

```
http://www.theharolds.com/genealogy.xml#xpointer(id("p12"))
```

If you look at Listing 18-1, you find this element:

```
<PERSON ID="p12" FATHER="p2" MOTHER="p1">
  <NAME>Honore Bellau</NAME>
</PERSON>
```

Because ID type attributes are unique in valid documents, there shouldn't be any other elements that match this XPointer. Therefore, `http://www.theharolds.com/genealogy.xml#xpointer(id("p12"))` should refer to Honore Bellau's `PERSON` element. Note that the XPointer points to the entire element to which it refers, including all its children, not just the start-tag.

If the document is invalid and more than one element has the same ID, only the first one in the document is selected.

Because ID pointers are so common and so useful, there's also a shortcut for this. If all you want to do is point to a particular element with a particular ID, you can skip all the `xpointer(id(""))` frou-frou and just use the bare ID after the `#`, like this:

```
http://www.theharolds.com/genealogy.xml#p12
```

This is called a *shorthand pointer*. You can only use a shorthand pointer if all you want is the particular element with the particular ID. You cannot add additional relative location steps to a URI that uses this shortcut to select children of the element with ID p12 or the third attribute of the element with ID p12. If you want to do that, you have to use the full `xpointer(id("p12"))` syntax.

The disadvantage of the `id()` function and shorthand pointers is that they require assistance from the targeted document. If the element you want to point to does not have an ID type attribute, you're out of luck. If other elements in the document have ID type attributes, you might be able to point to one of them and use a relative location step to point to the one you really want. Nonetheless, ID type attributes work best when you control both the targeted document and the linking document, so that you can ensure that the IDs match the links even as the documents evolve and change over time.

If the document does not have a DTD, it cannot have any ID type attributes, although it may have attributes named `ID`. In this case, you can't point at anything using the `id()` function or a shorthand pointer.

One possibility is to first use an `id()`-based XPointer, but back it up with an XPointer that looks for the attribute with the specific name anywhere in the document, `ID` in this example. Simply append the second XPointer to the first, like this:

```
xpointer(id("p12"))xpointer(//*[@ID="p12"])
```

XPointers are evaluated from left to right. The first match found is returned, so the backup is only used if an ID type attribute with the value `p12` can't be found.

here()

The second node-set returning function is `here()`. However, it's only useful when used in conjunction with one or more relative location steps. In intradocument links, that is, links from one point in a document to another point in the same document, it's often necessary to refer to "the next element after this one," or "the parent element of this element." The `here()` function refers to the node that contains the XPointer so that such references are possible.

Consider Listing 18-2, a simple slide show. In this example, `here()/../following::SLIDE[1]` refers to the next slide in the show. `here()/../preceding::SLIDE[1]` refers to the previous slide in the show. Presumably, this would be used in conjunction with a style sheet that showed one slide at a time.

Listing 18-2: A Slide Show

```
<?xml version="1.0"?>
<SLIDESHOW xmlns:xlink="http://www.w3.org/1999/xlink">
  <SLIDE>
    <H1>Welcome to the slide show!</H1>
    <BUTTON xlink:type="simple"
            xlink:href="here()/../following::SLIDE[1]">
      Next
    </BUTTON>
  </SLIDE>
  <SLIDE>
    <H1>This is the second slide</H1>
    <BUTTON xlink:type="simple"
            xlink:href="here()/../preceding::SLIDE[1]">
      Previous
    </BUTTON>
    <BUTTON xlink:type="simple"
            xlink:href="here()/../following::SLIDE[1]">
      Next
    </BUTTON>
  </SLIDE>
  <SLIDE>
```

Continued

Listing 18-2 (continued)

```
    <H1>This is the third slide</H1>
    <BUTTON xlink:type="simple"
            xlink:href="here()/../preceding::SLIDE[1]">
      Previous
    </BUTTON>
    <BUTTON xlink:type="simple"
            xlink:href="here()/../following::SLIDE[1]">
      Next
    </BUTTON>
  </SLIDE>
  ...
  <SLIDE>
    <H1>This is the last slide</H1>
    <BUTTON xlink:type="simple"
            xlink:href="here()/../preceding::SLIDE[1]">
      Previous
    </BUTTON>
  </SLIDE>

</SLIDESHOW>
```

Generally, the `here()` function is only used in XLinks where the `href` attribute contains a relative URI pointing to the same document. If any URI part is included, it must be the same as the URI of the current document.

origin()

The `origin()` function is much the same as `here()`; that is, it refers to the source of a link. However, `origin()` is used in out-of-line links where the link is not actually present in the source document. It points to the element in the source document from which the user activated the link.

Points

Selecting a particular element or node is almost always good enough for pointing into well-formed XML documents. However, on occasion, you might need to point into XML data in which large chunks of non-XML text are embedded via CDATA sections, comments, processing instructions, or some other means. In these cases, you might need to refer to particular ranges of text in the document that don't map onto any particular markup element. Or, you might need to point into non-XML substructure in the text content of particular elements; for example, the month in a `BORN` element that looks like this:

```
<BORN>11 Feb 1858</BORN>
```

An XPath expression can identify an element node, an attribute node, a text node, a comment node, or a processing instruction node. However, it can't indicate the first two characters of the `BORN` element (the date) or the substring of text between the first space and the last space in the `BORN` element (the month).

XPointer generalizes XPath to allow identifiers like this. An XPointer can address points in the document and ranges between points. These may not correspond to any one node. For example, the place between the *X* and the *P* in the word *XPointer* at the beginning of this paragraph is a point. The place between the *t* and the *h* in the word *this* at the end of the first sentence of this paragraph is another point. The text fragment "Pointer generalizes XPath to allow pointers like t" between those two points is a range.

Every point is either between two nodes or between two characters in the parsed character data of a document. To make sense of this, you have to remember that parsed character data is part of a text node. For example, consider this very simple but well-formed XML document:

```
<GREETING>
Hello
</GREETING>
```

There are exactly 3 nodes and 14 distinct points in this document. The nodes are the root node, which contains the `GREETING` element node, which contains a text node. In order, the points are as follows:

1. The point before the root node
2. The point before the `GREETING` element node
3. The point before the text node containing the text "Hello" (as well as assorted white space)
4. The point before the line break between `<GREETING>` and `Hello`
5. The point before the first *H* in `Hello`
6. The point between the *H* and the *e* in `Hello`
7. The point between the *e* and the *l* in `Hello`
8. The point between the *l* and the *l* in `Hello`
9. The point between the *l* and the *o* in `Hello`
10. The point after the *o* in `Hello`
11. The point after the line break between `Hello` and `</GREETING>`
12. The point after the text node containing the text "Hello"
13. The point after the `GREETING` element
14. The point after the root node

Points allow XPointers to indicate arbitrary positions in the parsed character data of a document. They do not, however, enable pointing at a position in the middle of a tag. In essence, what points add is the ability to break up the text content into smaller nodes, one for each character.

A point is selected by using the `string-range()` function to select a range, then using the `start-point ()` or `end-point()` function to extract the first or last point from the range. For example, this XPointer selects the point immediately before the *D* in Domeniquette Celeste Baudean's `NAME` element:

```
xpointer(start-point(string-range (id('p1')/NAME,"Domeniquette")))
```

This XPointer selects the point after the last *e* in *Domeniquette*:

```
xpointer(end-point(string-range(id('p1')/NAME,"Domeniquette")))
```

You can also take the `start-point ()` or `end-point ()` of an element, text, comment, processing instruction, or root node to get the first or last point in that node.

Ranges

Some applications need to specify a range across a document rather than a particular point in the document. For example, the selection a user makes with a mouse is not necessarily going to match up with any one element or node. It might start in the middle of one paragraph, extend across a heading and a picture, and then end in the middle of another paragraph two pages down.

Any such contiguous area of a document can be described with a *range*. A range begins at one point and continues until another point. The start point and endpoint are each identified by a location path. If the starting path points to a node-set rather than a point, `range-to()` will return multiple ranges, one starting from the first point of each node in the set.

To specify a range, you append `/range-to(end-point)` to a location path specifying the start point of the range. The parentheses contain a location path specifying the endpoint of the range. For example, suppose you want to select everything between the first `<PERSON>` start-tag and the last`</PERSON>` end-tag in Listing 18-1. The following XPointer accomplishes that:

```
xpointer(/child::FAMILYTREE/child::PERSON[position()=1]/range-to(/child::
FAMILYTREE/child::PERSON[position()=last()]))
```

Range functions

XPointer includes several functions specifically for working with ranges. Most of these operate on *location sets*. A location set is just a node-set that can also contain points and ranges, as well as nodes.

The `range(location-set)` function returns a location set containing one range for each location in the argument. The range is the minimum range necessary to cover the entire location. In essence, this function converts locations to ranges.

The `range-inside(location-set)` function returns a location set containing the interiors of each of the locations in the input. That is, if one of the locations is an element, the location returned is the content of the element (but not including the start- and end-tags). However, if the input location is a range or point, the interior of the location is just the same as the range or point.

The `start-point(location-set)` function returns a location set that contains the first point of each location in the input location set. For example, `start-point(//PERSON[1])` returns the point immediately after the first `<PERSON>` start-tag in the document. `start-point(//PERSON)` returns the set of points immediately after each `<PERSON>` start-tag.

The `end-point(location-set)` function acts the same as `start-point()` except that it returns the points immediately after each location in its input.

String ranges

XPointer provides some very basic string-matching capabilities through the `string-range()` function. This function takes as an argument a location set to search and a substring to search for. It returns a location set containing one range for each nonoverlapping, matching substring. You can also provide optional `index` and `length` arguments indicating how many characters after the match the range should start and how many characters after the start the range should continue. The basic syntax is as follows:

```
string-range(location-set, substring, index, length)
```

The first argument is an XPath expression that returns a location set specifying which part of the document to search for a matching string. The second substring, argument is the actual string to search for. By default, the range returned starts before the first matched character and encompasses all the matched characters. However, the `index` argument can give a positive number to start after the beginning of the match. For example, setting it to 2 indicates that the range starts with the second character after the first matched character. The `length` argument can specify how many characters to include in the range.

A string range points to an occurrence of a specified string, or a substring of a given string in the text (not markup) of the document. For example, this XPointer finds all occurrences of the string "Harold":

```
xpointer(string-range(/,"Harold"))
```

You can change the first argument to specify what nodes you want to look in. For example, this XPointer finds all occurrences of the string "Harold" in NAME elements:

```
xpointer(string-range(//NAME,"Harold"))
```

String ranges can have predicates. For example, this XPointer finds only the first occurrence of the string "Harold" in the document:

```
xpointer(string-range(/,"Harold")[position()=1])
```

This targets the position immediately preceding the word Harold in Charles Walter Harold's NAME element. This is not the same as pointing at the entire NAME element as an element-based selector would do.

A third numeric argument targets a particular position in the string. For example, this targets the point between the *l* and *d* in the first occurrence of the string "Harold" because *d* is the sixth letter:

```
xpointer(string-range(/,"Harold",6)[position()=1])
```

An optional fourth argument specifies the number of characters to select. For example, this URI selects the *old* from the first occurrence of the entire string "Harold":

```
xpointer(string-range(/,"Harold",4,3)[position()=1])
```

If the first string argument in the node test is the empty string, matching positions in the context node's text contents are selected. For example, the following XPointer targets the first six characters of the document's parsed character data:

```
xpointer(string-range(/,""1,6)[position()=1])
```

For another example, suppose that you want to find the year of birth for all people born in the nineteenth century. The following will accomplish that:

```
xpointer(string-range(//BORN, " 18", 2, 4))
```

This says to look in all BORN elements for the string " 18". (The initial space is important to avoid accidentally matching someone born in 1918 or on the 18th day of the month.) When it's found, move one character ahead (to skip the space) and return a range covering the next four characters.

When you are matching strings, case is considered. Markup characters are ignored.

Child Sequences

The two most common ways to identify an element in an XML document are by ID and by location. Identifying an element by ID is accomplished through the `id()` function or a shorthand pointer. Identifying an element by location is generally accomplished by counting children down from the root. For example, the following XPointers both point to John P. Muller's `PERSON` element when applied to Listing 18-1:

```
xpointer(id("p4"))
xpointer(/child::*[position()=1]/child::*[position()=4])
```

A *child sequence* is a shortcut for XPointers like the second example above—that is, an XPointer that consists of nothing but a series of child location steps counting down from the root node, each of which selects a particular child by position only. The shortcut is to use only the position number and the slashes that separate individual elements from each other, like this:

```
element(/1/4)
```

As with the `xpointer()` scheme, this becomes the fragment identifier in a URI reference:

```
http://www.theharolds.com/genealogy.xml#element(/1/4)
```

`/1/4` is a child sequence that selects the fourth child element of the first child element of the root. This syntax can be extended for any depth of child elements. For example, these two URIs point to John P. Muller's `NAME` and `SPOUSE` elements, respectively:

```
http://www.theharolds.com/genealogy.xml#element(/1/4/1)
http://www.theharolds.com/genealogy.xml#element(/1/4/2)
```

Child sequences might include an initial ID. In that case, the counting begins from the element with that ID rather than from the root. For example, John P. Muller's `PERSON` element has an `ID` attribute with the value `p4`. Consequently, `element(p4/1)` points to his `NAME` element and `element(p4/2)` points to his `SPOUSE` element.

Each child sequence always points to a single element. You cannot use child sequences with any other relative location steps. You cannot use them to select elements of a particular type. You cannot use them to select attributes or strings. You can only use them to select a single element by its relative location in the tree.

Summary

In this chapter, you learned about XPointers. In particular, you learned the following:

- ✦ XPointers refer to particular parts of, or locations in, XML documents.
- ✦ An XPointer is used as a fragment identifier for URLs that identify XML documents.
- ✦ An XPointer is composed of one or more XPointer parts, each of which has the form scheme (scheme data)
- ✦ The most expressive XPointer scheme is `xpointer`. The scheme data for the xpointer scheme is an XPath expression that returns a node-set.
- ✦ A shorthand pointer is just the ID of an element. It selects the element with that ID.
- ✦ Each location step contains an axis, a node test, and zero or more predicates.
- ✦ Location steps can be chained to make location paths.
- ✦ Relative location steps select nodes in a document based on their relationship to a context node.
- ✦ The `self` axis points to the context node. It can be abbreviated as a period (`.`).
- ✦ The `parent` axis points to the node that contains the context node. It can be abbreviated as a double period (`..`).
- ✦ The `child` axis includes the immediate children of the context node. It can be abbreviated simply by a node test.
- ✦ The `descendant` axis includes all nodes contained in the context node. It can effectively be abbreviated as a double slash (`//`).
- ✦ The `descendant-or-self` axis includes all nodes contained in the context node, as well as the context node itself.
- ✦ The `ancestor` axis includes all element nodes that contain the context node, as well as the root node.
- ✦ The `ancestor-or-self` axis includes all nodes that contain the context node, as well as the context node itself.
- ✦ The `preceding` axis includes all nodes that finish before the context node.
- ✦ The `following` axis includes all nodes that start after the context node.
- ✦ The `preceding-sibling` axis selects from nodes that precede the context node with the same parent node as the context node.
- ✦ The `following-sibling` axis selects from nodes that follow the context node with the same parent node as the context node.

- The `attribute` axis points to attributes of the context node. It can be abbreviated as an @ sign.
- The node test of a relative location step is normally an element or attribute name, but can also be the * wildcard to select all elements or one of the keywords `comment()`, `text()`, `processing-instruction()`, `node()`, `point()`, or `range()`.
- The optional predicate of a relative location step is a boolean XPath expression enclosed in square brackets that further narrows the node-set to which the XPointer refers.
- The `xmlns(`*`prefix=URI`*`)` scheme is used to declare a namespace prefix for use inside an XPointer.
- A point indicates a position preceding or following a node or a character.
- A range identifies the XML text between two points.
- The `string-range()` function points to a specified block of text.
- A child sequence points to an element by counting children from the root using the `element` scheme.

In this chapter, you saw XPointers used in XLinks. In Chapter 19, you'll see them used in XInclude, the third leg in the XML hypertext tripod. XInclude is an element-based syntax for building large XML documents out of smaller XML documents that are themselves complete, well-formed, possibly valid XML documents. The individual pieces out of which the complete document is built are located via URLs. These URLs can have XPointer parts to indicate that only part of a targeted document should be included in the master document.

✦ ✦ ✦

CHAPTER 19

XInclude

✦ ✦ ✦ ✦

In This Chapter

Use cases for XInclude

Nonsolutions

The xinclude:include element

Validating documents that use XInclude

XPointers in XInclude

Unparsed text

Fallbacks

XML documents can grow extremely large. Some real-world examples have already crossed the gigabyte threshold and are much bigger than can comfortably be stored in a normal file system. These documents need to be broken up into multiple separate files. In other cases, it's simply more useful to store a document in multiple pieces. For example, coauthors of a book would like to be able to work on different chapters of a book or different sections of a chapter simultaneously. This isn't possible if the entire book is stored in a single file.

XInclude is an element-based syntax for building large XML documents out of smaller XML documents that are themselves complete, well-formed, possibly valid XML documents. For example, a book might be built from chapters, which are themselves built from sections. Each chapter and section can also be a complete, well-formed XML document.

XInclude uses URIs (in practice, URLs) to locate the individual parts that make up the complete document. The URIs can have XPointer fragment identifiers to indicate that only one fragment of a document will be included in the composed document. The individual part documents can be used in multiple different composed documents, or even multiple times in the same document. And the individual part documents can stand on their own and remain well-formed and valid as well.

Caution

At the time of this writing (December 2003), XInclude is still bleeding-edge technology. The specification is still undergoing significant development and modification. libxml, xmllint, and xsltproc implement it, but few other parsers and no browsers do. This chapter is based on the November 10, 2003, second last call working draft of the XInclude specification. By the time you're reading this, the exact syntax might have changed, perhaps a little, perhaps a lot. This chapter should give you a pretty good idea of when, where, and how you can use XInclude; but it is not a final description of the exact syntax.

Use Cases for XInclude

Consider this book. It's made up of more than 20 chapters, a preface, a table of contents and other front matter, an index, front and back covers, and more. Each chapter is divided into sections. Some of the sections have subsections. Almost all the chapters have numerous code listings showing actual examples of XML documents. Not surprisingly, this book was not written as a single flowing stream of text starting with the first word on the front cover and finishing with the last word on the back cover. Instead, individual chapters were written in a very roughly beginning-to-end fashion. However, I didn't hesitate to jump from one chapter to the next; nor did I always write in a linear order. As I type these words, I've already finished Chapters 1 through 14 and the appendixes. I've barely begun Chapter 15. Chapters 16 through 18 are mostly done, but a couple of sections in those chapters remain to be written. Chapters 22 through 25 are in varying stages of completion. The preface hasn't been started and is probably the very last thing I will write.

When I complete a chapter, I e-mail it to the development editor. She makes her comments and passes it on to both the technical and copy editors for review. The technical editor checks it for factual mistakes. The copy editor checks the spelling and grammar as well as tightens up the prose. When they're done, each sends their comments back to her. She merges all the comments into a single manuscript and sends the document back to me for author review. When I've reviewed the manuscript, I e-mail the document back to the editor who gives it to Wiley's layout department for conversion to QuarkXPress. This process can be going on in parallel for multiple chapters, each of which can be in a different stage of development. One chapter can be in layout while two chapters are in copyedit, seven more are in technical review, three are being author reviewed, and several are in early incomplete draft stages on my hard drive.

The only reason this all works is that the chapters reside in single files that can be written, reviewed, edited, and laid out more or less independently of each other. Nonetheless, before the finished book you hold in your hands can be printed, all these diverse files must be integrated into a single unit to which page numbers can be applied and from which cross-references can be resolved. Depending on which part of the process we're in, we need different views of the entire document. When the technical editor is checking my code examples, he just wants to see the actual XML source code files and ignore the rest of the text completely. When the copy editor is checking my spelling, grammar, and usage, she needs to see a complete chapter with all text in place. When the indexing service is generating the index, it needs to see the complete book with all page numbers in place.

This book was actually written in Microsoft Word and laid out in QuarkXPress. These tools are a little too weak to make the process as seamless as it should be. For instance, the source code examples have to be manually copied and pasted from the source text files into the manuscript Word document. If I later discover a bug in an example, I have to remember to change both the source document and the chapter manuscript. Needless to say, sometimes a change gets made in one place and not the other, and consequently the examples tend to get out of sync.

Note

Yes, I know there are features in Word that are supposed to allow you to do all of these things. Trust me when I tell you that these are notoriously buggy and unusable for 800-page books. Authors and publishers have long since learned from brutal experience to avoid master documents, linked files, cross-references, autonumbering, and other Word features that are supposed to allow you to build documents from their component parts.

Recordlike documents need to be built out of multiple pieces just as frequently, perhaps more frequently, than narrative documents like this book do. For example, consider the television listing examples in Chapters 4, 5, 8, 9, and 10. Here, a rather large document covering an entire schedule was built out of pieces containing individual stations. Each station contained individual shows. It would be nice if each of those pieces could be a well-formed, valid XML document on its own. Something close to this was achieved in Chapter 10 with external entities. However, not all the pieces could stand on their own. The shows were only well-formed when considered in the context of the entire document, not when considered in isolation. The show documents were individually well-formed, but not valid.

The problem begins with show documents such as the one in Listing 19-1. I want to combine these into a station document like that shown in Listing 19-2. Then I want to combine the station documents into a complete schedule. Maybe I even want to combine the schedules for all days into one humongous document listing all the shows in a week, month, or year.

Listing 19-1: A Valid Document Describing a Single Show

```
<?xml version="1.0" encoding="UTF-8"?>
<!DOCTYPE SHOW SYSTEM "show.dtd">
<SHOW>
  <NAME>Oprah Winfrey</NAME>
  <TYPE>Series/Talk</TYPE>
  <START_TIME>19:00-0500</START_TIME>
  <LENGTH>60 minutes</LENGTH>
  <AIR_DATE>July 3, 2003</AIR_DATE>
  <ORIGINAL_AIR_DATE>February 4, 2003</ORIGINAL_AIR_DATE>
  <CLOSED_CAPTIONED>Yes</CLOSED_CAPTIONED>
  <REPEAT>Yes</REPEAT>
  <RATING>TV-PG</RATING>
  <DESCRIPTION>
     Guests gabber; Oprah looks sympathetic.
  </DESCRIPTION>
</SHOW>
```

Listing 19-2: A Valid Station Document

```
<?xml version="1.0"?>
<!DOCTYPE STATION SYSTEM "station.dtd">
<STATION>
  <CALL_LETTERS>WLNY</CALL_LETTERS>
  <CHANNEL>55</CHANNEL>

  <SHOW>
    <NAME>Oprah Winfrey</NAME>
    <TYPE>Series/Talk</TYPE>
    <START_TIME>19:00-0500</START_TIME>
    <LENGTH>60 minutes</LENGTH>
    <AIR_DATE>July 3, 2003</AIR_DATE>
    <ORIGINAL_AIR_DATE>February 4, 2003</ORIGINAL_AIR_DATE>
    <CLOSED_CAPTIONED>Yes</CLOSED_CAPTIONED>
    <REPEAT>Yes</REPEAT>
    <RATING>TV-PG</RATING>
    <DESCRIPTION>
    Guests gabber; Oprah looks sympathetic.
    </DESCRIPTION>
  </SHOW>

  <SHOW>
    <NAME>Silicon Towers</NAME>
    <TYPE>Movie</TYPE>
    <START_TIME>20:00-0500</START_TIME>
    <LENGTH>60 minutes</LENGTH>
    <AIR_DATE>July 3, 2003</AIR_DATE>
    <YEAR_MADE>1999</YEAR_MADE>
    <CLOSED_CAPTIONED>Yes</CLOSED_CAPTIONED>
    <REPEAT>Yes</REPEAT>
    <RATING>TV-PG</RATING>
    <CAST>
    <ACTOR>
      <GIVEN_NAME>Brian</GIVEN_NAME>
      <SURNAME>Dennehy</SURNAME>
    </ACTOR>
    <ACTOR>
      <GIVEN_NAME>Daniel</GIVEN_NAME>
      <SURNAME>Baldwin</SURNAME>
    </ACTOR>
    <ACTOR>
      <GIVEN_NAME>Brad</GIVEN_NAME>
      <SURNAME>Dourif</SURNAME>
    </ACTOR>
    <ACTOR>
      <GIVEN_NAME>Gary</GIVEN_NAME>
      <SURNAME>Mosher</SURNAME>
    </ACTOR>
```

```
    </CAST>
    <DESCRIPTION>
    A programmer discovers his company manufactures
    chips for cracking bank systems.
    </DESCRIPTION>
  </SHOW>

  </STATION>
```

The most straightforward solution is to copy and paste each file into the next level up in the hierarchy. However, it's always a bad idea to store the same information in multiple places. If you later discover a mistake, for example, that the last name of an actor is spelled "Denehhy" instead of "Dennehy," you need to correct the mistake in multiple places. Quite often you'll miss a place, and the information will get out of sync. Instead, it's better to store each unit of information in exactly one physical storage location (one file) and then reference that information from all the other documents that need it.

Non-Solutions

There are several half-solutions that almost solve the problem. These solutions include:

- ✦ External parsed entities
- ✦ Simple XLinks with `xlink:show="embed"`
- ✦ Server-side includes

However, none of these do everything you need; and you can't mix and match them to get full functionality. What's needed is a fourth option that operates at the parser level and that's orthogonal to validation.

DTDs

Referring to each show document as an external parsed entity is probably the closest XML 1.0 comes to the desired functionality. External parsed entities do allow you to build one document out of multiple smaller parts, do allow you to validate the merged document, and do allow you to treat the merged document as a unit. This approach was demonstrated in Chapter 10, as Listing 19-3 recalls.

Listing 19-3: WLNY with Shows Loaded from External Entities

```
<?xml version="1.0" standalone="no"?>
<!DOCTYPE STATION SYSTEM "station.dtd" [
  <!ENTITY % shows SYSTEM "wlny.dtd">
  %shows;
]>
<STATION>
  <CALL_LETTERS>WLNY</CALL_LETTERS>
  <CHANNEL>55</CHANNEL>

  &Oprah;
  &SiliconTowers;

</STATION>
```

However, there are some strict and inconvenient rules about what can and cannot appear in the external parsed entity files themselves. For example, these files can have a text declaration but not an XML declaration. They can have a root element, so they can be well-formed, but they cannot have a document type declaration, so they cannot be valid. If the station documents look like Listing 19-3, you can't combine them into a schedule document. The document type declaration gets in the way. If you go the other direction and take out the document type declaration so you can combine the station documents, each station document is no longer well-formed on its own, because the entity references that point to shows such as `&Oprah;` are no longer defined. External parsed entities only really work for single-level hierarchies where only the topmost level needs to be valid. Deeper hierarchies than that require another approach.

Embedded XLinks

XLinks allow you to embed one XML document inside another by setting the `xlink:show` attribute to `embed`. For example, Listing 19-4 tries to create a full station document by linking to the individual show documents.

Listing 19-4: WLNY with Shows Loaded from XLinks

```
<?xml version="1.0" standalone="no"?>
<!DOCTYPE STATION SYSTEM "station.dtd">
<STATION xmlns:xlink="http://www.w3.org/1999/xlink">
  <CALL_LETTERS>WLNY</CALL_LETTERS>
  <CHANNEL>55</CHANNEL>
  <SHOW xlink:type="simple" xlink:show="embed"
```

```
    xlink:href="Oprah.xml"/>
  <SHOW xlink:type="simple" xlink:show="embed"
    xlink:href="SiliconTowers.xml"/>
</STATION>
```

However, `xlink:show="embed"` does something a little different than is needed here. It does not actually combine the XML documents the links point to. Instead, when a browser loads Listing 19-4, it sets aside space in the window for each of the individual show documents, such as Oprah.xml. It then loads each of these documents separately, figures out how to render it, and embeds the *graphical representation* of the show document inside the *graphical representation* of the station document. Only the pictures are combined, not the documents themselves.

This has a number of implications. First among them is that Listing 19-4 is invalid, because a validator will see empty `SHOW` elements with XLink attributes instead of `SHOW` elements with child elements, as declared in the DTD. Second, a style sheet processor needs to operate on each of the three documents separately. It can't take advantage of the relationships between information in the individual documents. The information in the show documents is not conveniently available to a program reading the station document. It has to resolve the URLs in the XLinks and parse those documents separately. It has no information to help it determine the relationship between the show documents and the station document that contains them.

Server-side includes

Even before XML, many web servers let authors build HTML documents out of multiple component parts using server-side includes. Typically, when the web server receives a request for a document that contains server-side includes (normally such documents are identified by a .shtml filename extension), it first reads the document looking for special comments that look something like this:

```
<!--#include file="Oprah.html" -->
```

It builds a new document that replaces these comments with the contents of the referenced files.

The biggest problem with this approach is that it ties your pages to one vendor's software. While server-side include syntax is similar on most web servers, both syntax and functionality do change somewhat from server to server, even when you're doing something as simple as including files in different directories. If you switch web servers, you need to change all your server-side includes, too. For example, if you're using Apache, a document that uses server-side includes looks something like Listing 19-5. However, if you use a different web server, it might be some other syntax.

Listing 19-5: WLNY with Shows Loaded via Server-Side Includes

```
<HTML>
  <HEAD>
    <TITLE>WLNY</TITLE>
  </HEAD>
  <BODY>
    <H1>WLNY</H1>

  <!--#include file="Oprah.html" -->
  <!--#include file="SiliconTowers.html" -->

  </BODY>
</HTML>
```

The second disadvantage of this approach should be obvious from Listing 19-5: It's HTML-only, at least on most servers. Web servers can't process an XML document that uses an arbitrary, non-HTML vocabulary. And, of course, this approach assumes you're using a web server. That's not always the case. For example, an XML document containing a book made up of multiple chapters might be meant to be printed after application of an appropriate style sheet. There's no web server anywhere in sight.

There are some other disadvantages even if you're using a web server and serving XHTML. Notice that the document to include is identified by a `file` attribute, not an `href` attribute. Most web servers can only include local documents from the local file system. They can't include a document served by a different web server at a different URL. They often can't include a document served by the same web server if that document is produced dynamically by a CGI or a servlet instead of being read from a static file on a hard drive.

Furthermore, even when the included document is a local file, it's included in its entirety almost as if by copy and paste. You can't include just the contents of the root element, but not the root element itself. In the HTML and XHTML world, where every document has exactly one `html` root element that might not contain other `html` elements, this means an included document can't be served à la carte without first being merged with some other master document. Similarly, you can't say that you just want to include the second section of a document or all sections that have the word Barbara in their title. Inclusion is an all-or-nothing operation.

The next issue can be either an advantage or a disadvantage depending on your point of view. Supporting server-side includes is a lot of work. Typically, the server does that work, leaving the client with a lot less work to do. Sometimes this is what you want, especially if the server is a raging beast of Pentium-fueled power and the clients are 98MHz weaklings. However, in practice, it's much more common that the clients have CPU cycles to spare, while the server is maxed out. In particular, if you're on a local network in an intranet environment where bandwidth isn't much of an issue, it might make more sense to just burst all the documents to the clients and let them do the work of parsing and merging.

Still, despite all these issues, server-side includes are actually the approach that is closest in spirit to the XInclude solution I discuss next. The syntax, environment, and tools, however, are quite different.

The xinclude:include Element

XInclude enables you to include one document in another by using a single `xinclude:include` element. This element has an `href` attribute whose value is a URL pointing to the document to be included. The `xinclude` prefix is mapped to the URI `http://www.w3.org/2003/XInclude`. The shorter prefix `xi` is also commonly used instead of `xinclude`. As always, the prefix can change as long as the URI remains the same.

At the time of this writing (December, 2003) a lot of the available XInclude software, including some I've published myself, only supports an older working draft of the XInclude specification that uses the namespace `http://www.w3.org/2001/XInclude` instead.

Listing 19-6 demonstrates the syntax by building the WLNY station document using `xinclude:include` elements. Each `href` attribute of such an element contains a relative URL pointing to the location of each show document. An XInclude processor will remove the XML declaration and document type declaration from each of the show documents and insert what remains into the including document.

Listing 19-6: WLNY with Shows Included by XInclude

```
<?xml version="1.0" standalone="no"?>
<!DOCTYPE STATION SYSTEM "station.dtd">
<STATION xmlns:xinclude="http://www.w3.org/2003/XInclude">
  <CALL_LETTERS>WLNY</CALL_LETTERS>
  <CHANNEL>55</CHANNEL>
  <xinclude:include href="Oprah.xml"/>
  <xinclude:include href="SiliconTowers.xml"/>
</STATION>
```

Recent versions of libxml, xmllint, and xsltproc support XInclude. To resolve the include elements, simply use the `--xinclude` option when processing a file. xmllint reads an XML document that uses `xinclude:include` elements, replaces all those elements with the things they refer to, and then writes the merged document back out again onto stdout. You just run it from a shell or DOS prompt, like this:

```
$ xmllint --xinclude wlny.xml
<?xml version="1.0" standalone="no"?>
<!DOCTYPE STATION SYSTEM "station.dtd">
<STATION xmlns:xinclude="http://www.w3.org/2003/XInclude">
  <CALL_LETTERS>WLNY</CALL_LETTERS>
  <CHANNEL>55</CHANNEL>
  <SHOW>
  <NAME>Oprah Winfrey</NAME>
  <TYPE>Series/Talk</TYPE>
  <START_TIME>19:00-0500</START_TIME>
...
```

If you prefer, you can use the shell redirection operator > to put the output in a different file rather than printing it on stdout. As well as this simple command-line user interface, you can integrate the library with your own programs.

When processed, each of the `xinclude:include` elements in Listing 19-6 is replaced by the referenced show document. However, the XML declaration and document type declaration of the show documents, if any, are not included in the merged document. This means that both the show and station documents can be valid because both can contain document type declarations. This is not the case when you are using external entity references to connect the files.

On occasion, one of the document type declarations in an included document might affect the content of the root element. In particular, the document type declaration might reference a DTD that defines entity references used in the document instance, or it might provide default values for certain attributes. In this case, these entity references are resolved and the default attribute values are added to the elements to which they apply before the document is included, even though the document type declaration that includes these things is not carried over into the included document. Ninety-nine percent of the time this is exactly the behavior you want. It means you can include documents based solely on their logical structure, without worrying about the details of the physical structure. The only time this is likely to surprise you is when one of the included documents contains an entity reference such as `©`. In this case, the XInclude processor will probably replace it with the actual character, such as ©, or a numeric character reference, such as `©`. Differences like this are only relevant when you're viewing a document as a text file in an editor without parsing it. An XML parser treats all these structures as the same single character.

Note Technically, this behavior comes about because XInclude merges the infosets of the various documents rather than copying and pasting text strings.

When you're building a document out of multiple files like this, it's always possible there'll be a problem with one of the files. For example, somebody might have deleted, renamed, or moved Oprah.xml. Or perhaps you edited one of the included documents and made a mistake so it's no longer well-formed. In these cases, the XInclude processor reports an error when it detects the problem.

In Listing 19-6, relative URLs such as `Oprah.xml` locate the show documents. However, absolute URLs are equally acceptable. For example, Listing 19-7 uses absolute URLs. Notice that this means you can build one document out of multiple documents stored on many different web sites. This is something server-side includes cannot do.

Listing 19-7: **WLNY with Shows Referenced by Absolute URLs**

```
<?xml version="1.0" standalone="no"?>
<!DOCTYPE STATION SYSTEM "station.dtd">
<STATION xmlns:xinclude="http://www.w3.org/2003/XInclude">
  <CALL_LETTERS>WLNY</CALL_LETTERS>
  <CHANNEL>55</CHANNEL>
  <xinclude:include href=
    "http://cafeconleche.org/examples/shows/oprah.xml"/>
  <xinclude:include href=
  "http://cafeconleche.org/examples/shows/silicontowers.xml"/>
</STATION>
```

Other forms of relative URLS, such as `shows/Oprah.xml` or `../shows/Oprah.xml`, are also OK. If an `xml:base` attribute is present on the `xinclude:include` element or one of its ancestors, the relative URL is resolved relative to that base URL. Otherwise, it's resolved relative to the actual URL of the document.

Included documents can themselves include other documents. In other words, includes can nest. There's no limit to the depth. For example, Listing 19-8 builds a schedule by including stations, which themselves include the shows. The only restriction is that includes cannot be circular. Document A cannot include document B if document B includes document A, directly or indirectly.

Listing 19-8: **A Schedule Includes Stations**

```
<?xml version="1.0"?>
<!DOCTYPE SCHEDULE SYSTEM "schedule.dtd">
<SCHEDULE xmlns:xinclude="http://www.w3.org/2003/XInclude">
  <DATE>July 3, 2003</DATE>
  <xinclude:include href="wlny.xml"/>
  <xinclude:include href="wcbs.xml"/>
  <xinclude:include href="hbo.xml"/>
</SCHEDULE>
```

Validating Documents That Use XInclude

Listings 19-6 through 19-8 had document type declarations that denoted the root element for that document and located a DTD against which the instance document could be validated. This is allowed but is certainly not required. XInclude works equally well in well-formed but invalid documents. However, if a DTD is referenced, XInclude processors are allowed to read it to resolve external entity references and supply default attribute values.

If a processor wants to take the next step and actually validate the document, it can. XInclude is deliberately orthogonal to validation. Validation can happen before or after the `xinclude:include` elements are replaced by the documents they refer to. Depending on when you want the validation to happen, you would structure your DTD in one of two ways. If you want to validate before inclusion, your DTD must declare the `xinclude:include` element in the appropriate place. Listing 19-9 demonstrates with a station DTD for pre-inclusion validation.

Listing 19-9: A DTD for Pre-Inclusion STATION Documents

```
<!ELEMENT STATION (
   ( (NETWORK, CALL_LETTERS?) | CALL_LETTERS ),
    CHANNEL, xinclude:include+)>
<!ATTLIST STATION xmlns:xinclude CDATA #FIXED
                  "http://www.w3.org/2003/XInclude">

<!ELEMENT NETWORK (#PCDATA)>
<!ELEMENT CALL_LETTERS (#PCDATA)>
<!ELEMENT CHANNEL (#PCDATA)>

<!ELEMENT xinclude:include EMPTY>
<!ATTLIST xinclude:include href CDATA #REQUIRED>
```

On the other hand, if you want to validate the document after all inclusions are resolved, you have to write a DTD that fits the merged document. XInclude can only be used in instance documents, not DTDs; but you can use parameter entity references to split DTDs into multiple parts. This allows you to match the DTD modularity to the document modularity. For example, assuming that a document called show.dtd contains a proper DTD for `SHOW` elements, Listing 19-10 is an acceptable DTD for post-inclusion validation.

Listing 19-10: A DTD for Post-Inclusion STATION Documents

```
<!ENTITY % show.dtd SYSTEM "show.dtd">
%show.dtd;

<!ELEMENT STATION (
   ( (NETWORK, CALL_LETTERS?) | CALL_LETTERS ),
    CHANNEL, SHOW+))>
<!ATTLIST STATION xmlns:xinclude CDATA #FIXED
                  "http://www.w3.org/2003/XInclude">

<!ELEMENT NETWORK      (#PCDATA)>
<!ELEMENT CALL_LETTERS (#PCDATA)>
<!ELEMENT CHANNEL      (#PCDATA)>
```

With a little effort, it isn't even hard to define a DTD that can validate both the pre- and post-inclusion versions. Just put a choice in the content model that allows either `SHOW` or `xinclude:include` elements. Listing 19-11 demonstrates.

Listing 19-11: A DTD for Both Pre- and Post-Inclusion Station Documents

```
<!ELEMENT STATION (
   ( (NETWORK, CALL_LETTERS?) | CALL_LETTERS ),
    CHANNEL, (xinclude:include | SHOW)+))>
<!ATTLIST STATION xmlns:xinclude CDATA #FIXED
                  "http://www.w3.org/2003/XInclude">

<!ELEMENT NETWORK      (#PCDATA)>
<!ELEMENT CALL_LETTERS (#PCDATA)>
<!ELEMENT CHANNEL      (#PCDATA)>


<!ELEMENT xinclude:include EMPTY>
<!ATTLIST xinclude:include href CDATA #REQUIRED>

<!ENTITY % show.dtd SYSTEM "show.dtd">
%show.dtd;
```

In fact, the DTD in Listing 19-11 actually allows a `STATION` element to contain both `SHOW` and `xinclude:include` elements so that some shows can be linked in from other files, while others are typed directly into the station document.

XPointers in XInclude

In the examples so far, the URLs in the xinclude:include elements have all pointed to complete documents. URLs in XInclude href attributes should not have fragment identifiers, and if one does have a fragment identifier it is ignored. However, each xinclude:include element may have an xpointer attribute in addition to or instead of its href attribute. The xpointer attribute contains, as the name indicates, an XPointer that selects a subset of the document located by the href attribute for inclusion. For example, it might select only the name of a show rather than all the show's info. It might select all NAME elements in the document. It might even select something that isn't an element at all, such as a text node.

The W3C XML Core Working Group radically changed how XPointers were handled in XInclude as this book was in the final stages of editing. However, I am not at all convinced that it changed for the better, and I would not be surprised if it changes again before the final XInclude Recommendation is published. This section reflects the latest working draft available in 2003, but this material seems especially like to change again. Caveat lector.

For example, suppose you just want to list the names of the shows. Then from each show document you'd extract just the NAME elements. The XPointer that does this looks like this:

```
xpointer(/SHOW/NAME)
```

You can use xpointer attributes in the xinclude:include elements. Listing 19-12 demonstrates.

Listing 19-12: The Names of WLNY Shows Referenced by Relative URLs with XPointers

```
<?xml version="1.0" standalone="no"?>
<!DOCTYPE STATION SYSTEM "station.dtd">
<STATION xmlns:xinclude="http://www.w3.org/2003/XInclude">
  <CALL_LETTERS>WLNY</CALL_LETTERS>
  <CHANNEL>55</CHANNEL>
  <xinclude:include href="oprah.xml"
                    xpointer="xpointer(/SHOW/NAME)"/>
  <xinclude:include href="silicontowers.xml"
                    xpointer="xpointer(/SHOW/NAME)"/>
</STATION>
```

After the `xinclude:include` elements are replaced, this document becomes Listing 19-13.

Listing 19-13: **The Names of Shows on WLNY**

```
<?xml version="1.0" standalone="no"?>
<!DOCTYPE STATION SYSTEM "station.dtd">
<STATION xmlns:xinclude="http://www.w3.org/2003/XInclude">
  <CALL_LETTERS>WLNY</CALL_LETTERS>
  <CHANNEL>55</CHANNEL>
  <NAME>Oprah Winfrey</NAME>
  <NAME>Silicon Towers</NAME>
</STATION>
```

By using more complicated XPath expressions, along with XPointers that point to text nodes, it's possible to put together still more complex documents. For example, suppose you want `SHOW` elements that look like this:

```
<SHOW>Oprah Winfrey</SHOW>
```

You'd need to point to the text nodes inside the `NAME` elements of each `SHOW` element, like this:

```
xpointer(/SHOW/NAME/text())
```

Furthermore, you'd need to include the `SHOW` start- and end-tags in the master document and give it an `xinclude:include` child element, as demonstrated in Listing 19-14.

Listing 19-14: **WLNY Shows with Names Only**

```
<?xml version="1.0" standalone="no"?>
<!DOCTYPE STATION SYSTEM "station.dtd">
<STATION xmlns:xinclude="http://www.w3.org/2003/XInclude">
  <CALL_LETTERS>WLNY</CALL_LETTERS>
  <CHANNEL>55</CHANNEL>
  <SHOW><xinclude:include href="oprah.xml"
          xpointer="xpointer(/SHOW/NAME)/text()"/></SHOW>
  <SHOW><xinclude:include href="silicontowers.xml"
          xpointer="xpointer(/SHOW/NAME/text())"/></SHOW>
</STATION>
```

An XPointer that selects a point or a group of points has no effect when included. Points are nondimensional, so including a point doesn't really change the document at all. Ranges are a different matter. If an XPointer selects a range, the complete contents of the range are included. Furthermore, if a range partially selects an element (for example, it covers the start-tag but not the end-tag, or vice versa), the entire element that is only partially selected is included, not just the fraction of the element that is pointed to.

There are, however, some limits on what the XPointer can point to. In particular, it is not allowed to point to anything that, when included, would make the including document malformed. For example, an `xinclude:include` element can be the root element of a document; but, if so, it must be replaced by a node-set containing exactly one element that can serve as the new root. It can't be replaced by a text node or two element nodes. Similarly, the XPointer in an `xinclude:include` element should never point to an attribute or a namespace node, because replacing an element with an attribute or namespace makes no sense. If an XPointer does point to any of these items, the XInclude processor will signal an error and give up.

Unparsed Text

The examples up to this point have all included other well-formed XML documents or pieces thereof. If an included document is not well-formed, the XInclude processor stops processing and reports the error. However, it would be useful to be able to include documents that aren't XML documents, and that aren't well-formed. For example, you might want to include a plain-text document such as an e-mail message. If you were writing a tutorial about Python programming, you'd like to be able to include the text of your example programs. Perhaps the URL you're including actually points to a CGI query against a database that returns a SQL result set as ASCII text. However, in all these and many more cases, the text documents you want to include may contain characters that would make an XML document malformed, such as `<` and `&`. Such characters can be represented in XML documents using entity references, character references, or CDATA sections. However, you still need some way of telling the XInclude processor that it should escape these characters when it reads them in a referenced document, rather than treating them as malformed markup and throwing an error.

To indicate that the included document is plain text that should not be parsed, rather than another XML document, you add a `parse="text"` attribute to the `xinclude:include` element that includes it. For example, this `xinclude:include` element references a Java source code file named HelloWorld.java:

```
<xinclude:include href="HelloWorld.java" parse="text"/>
```

You can also set the value of parse to xml to indicate that the referenced document is XML and should be parsed. For example, the previous television examples could easily have been written like this:

```
<xinclude:include href="Oprah.xml" parse="xml"/>
```

However, since parse="xml" is the default, this is rarely done explicitly.

I often use parse="text" when I want to include an XML document as an example in a larger document. That way, the unresolved markup is shown. For example, if this very chapter were written in XML, it might be marked up like this:

```
<PARA>
Included documents may themselves include other documents. In
other words, includes can nest. There's no limit to the depth.
For example, Listing 19-8 builds a schedule by including
stations which themselves include the shows. The only
restriction is that includes may not be circular. Document A
may not include document B if document B includes, directly
orindirectly, document A.
</PARA>
<LISTING>
  <NUMBER>19-8</NUMBER>
  <CAPTION>A schedule includes stations</CAPTION>
  <BODY>
  <xinclude:include href="source/19/19-8.xml" parse="text"/>
  </BODY>
</LISTING>
```

If the unparsed text contains any reserved characters, such as & or <, they will be escaped using entity references or character references when the result is serialized.

Fallbacks

When you are including documents from remote sites you don't control, it's not uncommon for those documents to disappear. This might be temporary (a server crashed, or a T1 connection was severed) or permanent (a document moved to a new URL or was deleted entirely). In this case, the master document cannot be processed because pieces it needs are missing.

To help alleviate this, each xinclude:include element can contain a single xinclude:fallback child element. The contents of this element are used if the remote resource that would normally be included cannot be found. For example, Listing 19-15 is similar to Listing 19-7. However, if either of the remote documents are not available when this is processed, this example will replace them with the text "N/A". With Listing 19-7, the whole document would simply be dropped with an error.

Listing 19-15: Include Elements with Fallbacks

```
<?xml version="1.0" standalone="no"?>
<!DOCTYPE STATION SYSTEM "station.dtd">
<STATION xmlns:xinclude="http://www.w3.org/2003/XInclude">
  <CALL_LETTERS>WLNY</CALL_LETTERS>
  <CHANNEL>55</CHANNEL>
  <xinclude:include href=
    "http://cafeconleche.org/examples/shows/Oprah.xml">
    <xinclude:fallback>N/A</xinclude:fallback>
  </xinclude:include>
  <xinclude:include href=
   "http://cafeconleche.org/examples/shows/SiliconTowers.xml">
    <xinclude:fallback>N/A</xinclude:fallback>
  </xinclude:include>
</STATION>
```

The `xinclude:fallback` element can include markup as well as plain text. For example, Listing 19-16 replaces missing documents with markup that's filled with N/A values. This might be useful to make sure the result document remains valid.

Listing 19-16: Fallbacks with Child Elements

```
<?xml version="1.0" standalone="no"?>
<!DOCTYPE STATION SYSTEM "station.dtd">
<STATION xmlns:xinclude="http://www.w3.org/2003/XInclude">
  <CALL_LETTERS>WLNY</CALL_LETTERS>
  <CHANNEL>55</CHANNEL>
  <xinclude:include href=
    "http://cafeconleche.org/examples/shows/Oprah.xml">
    <xinclude:fallback>
      <SHOW>
        <NAME>N/A</NAME>
        <START_TIME>N/A</START_TIME>
        <LENGTH>N/A</LENGTH>
        <AIR_DATE>N/A</AIR_DATE>
      </SHOW>
    </xinclude:fallback>
  </xinclude:include>
  <xinclude:include href=
   "http://cafeconleche.org/examples/shows/SiliconTowers.xml">
    <xinclude:fallback>
      <SHOW>
        <NAME>N/A</NAME>
        <START_TIME>N/A</START_TIME>
        <LENGTH>N/A</LENGTH>
        <AIR_DATE>N/A</AIR_DATE>
```

```
    </SHOW>
  </xinclude:fallback>
 </xinclude:include>
</STATION>
```

The xinclude:fallback element might even include other xinclude:include elements, which are resolved only if the top-level include fails. And, of course, these descendant xinclude:include elements may have fallbacks of their own, ad infinitum. For example, you might use this capability to load a document from one of several mirror sites:

```
<xinclude:include href="http://www.example.com/data.xml">
  <xinclude:fallback>
    <xinclude:include href="http://www.example.net/data.xml">
      <xinclude:fallback>
        <xinclude:include href="file:///usr/data/data.xml"/>
      </xinclude:fallback>
    </xinclude:include>
   </xinclude:fallback>
</xinclude:include>
```

As always, if any of these examples are to be validated, the DTD must declare all the elements present in the document when validation takes place. If validation is performed before XInclusion, the xinclude:fallback elements and their children must be declared. If validation is performed after XInclusion, the content that results from resolving the xinclude:include elements and xinclude:fallback elements must be declared.

An xinclude:include element cannot contain more than one xinclude:fallback element. This is forbidden. Similarly, xinclude:fallback elements cannot appear outside an xinclude:include element.

Summary

In this chapter, you learned about XInclude, a W3C standard for building large XML documents out of smaller, more manageable XML documents that are themselves complete, well-formed, possibly valid XML documents. In particular, you learned the following:

- ✦ Previous means of building large documents out of smaller parts, including external general entities, server-side includes, and XLinks, all have significant limitations.
- ✦ An XInclude processor or an XInclude-aware XML parser replaces each xinclude:include element with the document identified by the xinclude:include element's href attribute.

- This `href` attribute contains a relative or absolute URL identifying the document to be included.
- An optional `xpointer` attribute contains an XPointer that indicates which part of the remote document should be included. If this is omitted, the entire remote document is included.
- The `xinclude:include` element can have an optional `parse="text"` attribute to indicate that the document at the remote URL should be treated as plain text rather than a parsed XML document.
- Each `xinclude:include` element can have a single `xinclude:fallback` child element whose contents are included if the remote resource pointed to be the `xinclude:include` element cannot be found.

This chapter addressed modular XML document instances. Chapter 20 explores the W3C XML Schema Language, which, among other advantages, offers modular XML content models. The W3C XML Schema Language is an XML application for defining the permissible contents of documents adhering to a particular XML application. Schemas let you specify element and attribute structures, much as DTDs do, but they do it using an XML instance document syntax. Furthermore, schemas let you impose constraints on the text content of XML elements and attributes, such as specifying that a `SHOE_SIZE` element must contain a number between 1 and 15, or that an `ABSTRACT` element must contain between 100 and 512 characters.

✦ ✦ ✦

Schemas

CHAPTER 20

✦ ✦ ✦ ✦

In This Chapter

What's wrong with DTDs?

What is a schema?

The W3C XML Schema Language

Hello schemas

Complex types

Grouping

Simple types

Deriving simple types

Empty elements

Attributes

Namespaces

Annotations

✦ ✦ ✦ ✦

Schemas are documents that define the valid contents of particular classes of XML documents. The schema language discussed in this chapter, the W3C XML Schema Language, has a number of useful characteristics, most notably the ability to specify data types for text content and attribute values. For example, a schema can state that a `PRICE` element has type double or that a `YEAR` attribute contains a number between 1966 and 2012. However, schemas have a number of other useful characteristics including namespace awareness and the ability to validate complex structures built up out of many different elements of many types.

What's Wrong with DTDs?

Document type definitions (DTDs) are an outgrowth of XML's heritage in the Standardized General Markup Language (SGML). SGML was always intended for narrative-style documents: books, reports, technical manuals, brochures, web pages, and the like. DTDs were designed to serve the needs of these sorts of documents, and indeed they serve them very well. DTDs let you state very simply and straightforwardly that every book must have one or more authors, that every song has exactly one title, that every `PERSON` element has an `ID` attribute, and so forth. Indeed, for narrative documents that are intended for human beings to read from start to finish, that are more or less composed of words in a row, there's really no need for anything beyond a DTD. However, XML has gone well beyond the uses envisioned for SGML. XML is being used for object serialization, stock trading, remote procedure calls, vector graphics, and many more things that look nothing like traditional narrative documents; and it is in these new arenas that DTDs are showing some limits.

The limitation most developers notice first is the almost complete lack of data typing, especially for element content. DTDs can't say that a `PRICE` element must contain a number, much less a number that's greater than zero with two decimal digits of precision and a dollar sign. There's no way to say that a

MONTH element must be an integer between 1 and 12. There's no way to indicate that a TITLE must contain between 1 and 255 characters. None of these are particularly important things to do for the narrative documents SGML was aimed at; but they're very common things to want to do with data formats intended for computer-to-computer exchange of information rather than computer-to-human communication. Humans are very good at handling fuzzy systems where expected data is missing, or perhaps is not in quite the right format; computers are not. Computers need to know that when they expect an element to contain an integer between 1 and 12, the element really contains an integer in that range and nothing else.

The second problem is that DTDs have an unusual non-XML syntax. The same parrsers and APIs that read an XML document can't read a DTD. For example, consider this common element declaration:

```
<!ELEMENT TITLE (#PCDATA)>
```

This is not a legal XML element. You can't begin an element name with an exclamation point. TITLE is not an attribute. Neither is (#PCDATA). This is a very different way of describing information than is used in XML document instances. One would expect that if XML were really powerful enough to live up to all its hype, it would be powerful enough to describe itself. You shouldn't need two different syntaxes: one for the information and one for the meta-information detailing the structure of the information. XML element and attribute syntax should suffice for both info and meta-info.

The third problem is that DTDs are only marginally extensible and don't scale very well. It's difficult to combine independent DTDs together in a sensible way. You can do this with parameter entity references. Indeed, SMIL 2.0 and modular XHTML are based on this idea. However, the modularized DTDs are very messy and very hard to follow. The largest DTDs in use today are in the ballpark of 10,000 lines of code, and it's questionable whether much larger XML applications can be defined before the entire DTD becomes completely unmanageable and incomprehensible. By contrast, the largest computer programs in existence today, which are much more intrinsically complex than even the most ambitious DTDs, easily reach sizes of 1,000,000 lines of code or more.

Perhaps most annoyingly, DTDs are only marginally compatible with namespaces. The first principle of namespaces is that only the URI matters. The prefix does not. The prefix can change as long as the URI remains the same. However, validation of documents that use namespace prefixes works only if the DTD declares the prefixed names. You cannot use namespace URIs in a DTD. You must use the actual prefixes. If you change the prefixes in the document but don't change the DTD, the document immediately ceases to be valid. There are some tricks that you can perform with parameter entity references to make DTDs less dependent on the actual prefix, but they're complicated and not well understood in the XML community. And even when they are understood, these tricks simply feel far too much like a dirty hack rather than a clean, maintainable solution.

Finally, there are a number of annoying minor limitations where DTDs don't allow you to do things that it really feels like you ought to be able to do. For example, DTDs cannot enforce the order or number of child elements in mixed content. That is, you can't enforce constraints such as each `PARAGRAPH` element must begin with exactly one `SUMMARY` element that is followed by plain text. Similarly, you can't enforce the number of child elements without also enforcing their order. For example, you cannot easily say that a `PERSON` element must contain a `FIRST_NAME` child, a `MIDDLE_NAME` child, and a `LAST_NAME` child, but that you don't care what order they appear in. Again, there are workarounds, but they grow combinatorially complex with the number of possible child elements.

Schemas are an attempt to solve all these problems by defining a new XML-based syntax for describing the permissible contents of XML documents that includes the following:

- Powerful data typing including range checking
- Namespace-aware validation based on namespace URIs rather than on prefixes
- Extensibility and scalability

However, schemas are not a be-all and end-all solution. In particular, *schemas do not replace DTDs*! You can use both schemas and DTDs in the same document. DTDs can do several things that schemas cannot do, most importantly declaring entities. And DTDs still work very well for the classic sort of narrative documents they were originally designed for. Indeed, for these types of documents, a DTD is often considerably easier to write than an equivalent schema. Parsers and other software will continue to support DTDs for as long as they support XML.

What Is a Schema?

The word *schema* derives from the Greek word σχημα, meaning form or shape. It was first popularized in the Western world by Immanuel Kant in the late 1700s. According to the 1933 edition of the *Oxford English Dictionary*, Kant used the word *schema* to mean, "Any one of certain forms or rules of the 'productive imagination' through which the understanding is able to apply its 'categories' to the manifold of sense-perception in the process of realizing knowledge or experience." (And you thought computer science was full of unintelligible technical jargon!)

Schemas remained the province of philosophers for the next 200 years until the word schema entered computer science, probably through database theory. Here, schema originally meant any document that described the permissible content of a database. More specifically, a schema was a description of all the tables in a database and the fields in the table. A schema also described what type of data each field could contain: CHAR, INT, CHAR[32], BLOB, DATE, and so on.

You say schemas, I say schemata

Probably no single topic has been more controversial in the schema world than the proper plural form of the word *schema*. The original Greek plural is σχηματα, *schemata* in Latin transliteration; and this is the form which Kant used and which you'll find in most dictionaries. This was fine for the 200 years when only people with Ph.D.s in philosophy actually used the word. However, as often happens when words from other languages are adopted into popular English, its plural changed to something that sounds more natural to an anglophone ear. In this case, the plural form, *schemata,* seems to be rapidly dying out in favor of the simpler *schemas*. In fact, the three World Wide Web Consortium (W3C) schema specifications all use the plural form *schemas*. I follow this convention in this book.

The word schema has grown from that source definition to a more generic meaning of any document that describes the permissible contents of other documents, especially if data typing is involved. Thus, you'll hear about different kinds of schemas from different technologies, including vocabulary schemas, RDF schemas, organizational schemas, X.500 schemas, and of course, XML schemas.

Because schemas is such a generic term, it shouldn't come as any surprise that there's more than one schema language for XML. In fact, there are many, each with its own unique advantages and disadvantages. These include Murata Makoto and James Clark's RELAX NG (`http://relaxng.org/`), Rick Jelliffe's Schematron (`http://www.ascc.net/xml/resource/schematron/schematron.html`), and the W3C's misleadingly, generically titled XML Schema Language. In addition, traditional XML DTDs can be considered to be simply another schema language.

This chapter focuses almost exclusively on the W3C XML Schema Language. Nonetheless, RELAX NG and Schematron are definitely worthy of your attention as well. In particular, if you find W3C schemas to be excessively complex (and many people do) and if you want a simpler schema language that still offers a complete set of extensible data types, you should consider RELAX NG. RELAX NG adopts the less controversial data types half of the W3C XML Schema Recommendation, but replaces the much more complex and much less popular structures half with a much simpler language.

Note There are also several dead XML schema languages that have been abandoned by their manufacturers in favor of other languages. These include Document Content Description (DCD), Commerce One's Schema for Object-Oriented XML (SOX), and Microsoft's XML-Data Reduced (XDR). None of these is worth your time or investment at this point. They never achieved broad adoption, and their vendors are now moving to the W3C XML Schema Language instead.

Most schema languages, including W3C schemas, RELAX NG, and DTDs, take the approach that you must carefully specify what is allowed in the document. They are conservative: Everything not permitted is forbidden. If, on the other hand, you're looking for a less-restrictive schema language in which everything not forbidden is permitted, you should consider Schematron. Schematron is based on XPath, which allows it to make statements none of the other major schema languages can, such as "An a element cannot have another a element as a descendant, even though an a element can contain a strong element that can contain an a element if it itself is not a descendant of an a element." This isn't a theoretical example. This is a real restriction in XHTML that has to be made in the prose of the specification because neither DTDs nor the W3C XML Schema Language are powerful enough to say it. What it means is that links can't nest; that is, a link cannot contain another link.

From this point forward, I will use the unqualified word *schema* to refer to the W3C's XML Schema Language; but please keep in mind that alternatives that are equally deserving of the appellation do exist.

The W3C XML Schema Language

The W3C XML Schema Language was created by the W3C XML Schema Working Group based on many different submissions from a variety of companies and individuals. It is a very large specification designed to handle a broad range of use cases. In fact, the schema specification is considerably larger and more complex than the XML 1.0 specification. It is an open standard, free to be implemented by any interested party. There are no known patent, trademark, or other intellectual property restrictions that would prevent you from doing anything you might reasonably want to do with schemas. (This, unfortunately, is not quite the same thing as saying that there are no known patent, trademark, or other intellectual property restrictions that would prevent you from doing anything you might reasonably want to do. The U.S. Patent Office has been a little out of control lately, granting patents left and right for inventions that really don't deserve it, including a lot of software and business processes. I would not be surprised to learn of an as yet unnoticed patent that at least claims to cover some or all of the W3C XML Schema Language.)

Hello Schemas

Let's begin our exploration of schemas with the ubiquitous Hello World example. Recall, once again, the code from Listing 3-2 (greeting.xml) in Chapter 3. It is shown here:

```
<?xml version="1.0"?>
<GREETING>
Hello XML!
</GREETING>
```

This XML document contains a single element, GREETING. (Remember that <?xml version="1.0"?> is the XML declaration, not an element.) This element contains parsed character data. A schema for this document has to declare the GREETING element. It may declare other elements too, including ones that aren't present in this particular document, but it must at least declare the GREETING element.

The greeting schema

Listing 20-1 is a very simple schema for GREETING elements. By convention it would be stored in a file with the three-letter extension .xsd — greeting.xsd, for example — but that's not required. It is an XML document, so it has an XML declaration. It can be written and saved in any text editor that knows how to save Unicode files. As always, you can use a different character set if you declare it in an encoding declaration. Schema documents are XML documents and have all the privileges and responsibilities of other XML documents. They can even have DTDs, DOCTYPE declarations, and style sheets if that seems useful to you, although in practice most do not.

Listing 20-1: greeting.xsd

```
<?xml version="1.0"?>
<xsd:schema xmlns:xsd="http://www.w3.org/2001/XMLSchema">

  <xsd:element name="GREETING" type="xsd:string"/>

</xsd:schema>
```

The root element of this and all other schemas is schema. This must be in the http://www.w3.org/2001/XMLSchema namespace. Normally, this namespace is bound to the prefix xsd or xs, although this can change as long as the URI stays the same. The other common approach is to make this URI the default namespace, although that generally requires a few extra attributes to help separate out the names from the XML application the schema describes from the names of the schema elements themselves. You'll see this when namespaces are discussed at the end of this chapter.

Elements are declared using xsd:element elements. Listing 20-1 includes a single such element declaring the GREETING element. The name attribute specifies which element is being declared, GREETING in this example. This xsd:element element also has a type attribute whose value is the data type of the element. In this case the type is xsd:string, a standard type for elements that can contain any amount of text in any form but not child elements. It's equivalent to a DTD content model of #PCDATA. That is, this xsd:element says that a valid GREETING element must look like this:

```
<GREETING>
  various random text but no markup
</GREETING>
```

There's no restriction on what text the element can contain. It can be zero or more Unicode characters with any meaning. Thus, a GREETING element can also look like this:

```
<GREETING>Hello!</GREETING>
```

Or even this:

```
<GREETING></GREETING>
```

However, a valid GREETING element may not look like this:

```
<GREETING>
  <SOME_TAG>various random text</SOME_TAG>
  <SOME_EMPTY_TAG/>
</GREETING>
```

Nor may it look like this:

```
<GREETING>
  <GREETING>various random text</GREETING>
</GREETING>
```

Each GREETING element must consist of nothing more and nothing less than parsed character data between a <GREETING> start-tag and a </GREETING> end-tag.

Validating the document against the schema

Before a document can be validated against a DTD, the document itself must contain a document type declaration pointing to the DTD it should be validated against. You cannot easily receive a document from a third party and validate it against your own DTD. You have to validate it against the DTD that the document's author specified. This is excessively limiting.

For example, imagine you're running an e-commerce business that accepts orders for products using SOAP or XML-RPC. Each order comes to you over the Internet as an XML document. Before accepting that order, the first thing you want to do is check that it's valid against a DTD you've defined to make sure that it contains all the necessary information. However, if DTDs are all you have to validate with, there's nothing to prevent a hacker from sending you a document whose DOCTYPE declaration points to a different DTD. Then your system may report that the document is valid according to the hacked DTD, even though it would be invalid when compared to the correct DTD. If your system accepts the invalid document, it could introduce corrupt data that crashes the system or lets the hacker order goods they haven't paid for, all because the person authoring the document got to choose which DTD to validate against rather than the person validating the document.

Schemas are more flexible. The schema specification specifically allows for a variety of different means for associating documents with schemas. For example, one possibility is that both the name of the document to validate and the name of the schema to validate it against could be passed to the validator program on the command line, like this:

```
C:\>validator greeting.xml greeting.xsd
```

Parsers could also let you choose the schema by setting a SAX property or an environment variable. Many other approaches are possible. The schema specification does not mandate any one way of doing this. However, it does define one particular way to associate a document with a schema. As with `DOCTYPE` declarations and DTDs, this requires modifying the instance document to point to the schema. The difference is that with schemas, unlike with DTDs, this is not the only way to do it. Parser vendors are free to develop other mechanisms if they want to.

To attach a schema to a document, add an `xsi:noNamespaceSchemaLocation` attribute to the document's root element. (You can also add it to the first element in the document that the schema applies to, but most of the time adding it to the root element is simplest.) The `xsi` prefix is mapped to the `http://www.w3.org/2001/XMLSchema-instance` URI. As always, the prefix can change as long as the URI stays the same. Listing 20-2 demonstrates.

Listing 20-2: **valid_greeting.xml**

```
<?xml version="1.0"?>
<GREETING xsi:noNamespaceSchemaLocation="greeting.xsd"
  xmlns:xsi="http://www.w3.org/2001/XMLSchema-instance">
Hello XML!
</GREETING>
```

You can now run the document through any parser that supports schema validation. One such parser is Xerces Java from the XML Apache Project (`http://xml.apache.org/xerces2-j/`). It includes a simple command line program named sax.Counter that can validate against schemas as well as DTDs. When you set the `-v` and `-s` flags, sax.Counter validates the documents against its schema as specified by the `xsi:noNamespaceSchemaLocation` attribute. Assuming sax.Counter finds no errors, it simply returns the amount of time that was required to parse the document, as in the following example:

```
C:\XML>java sax.Counter -v -s valid_greeting.xml
valid_greeting.xml: 701 ms (1 elems, 1 attrs, 0 spaces, 12
chars)
```

To install sax.Counter, copy the JAR archives bundled with the Xerces distribution into your jre/lib/ext directory. With the latest versions of the JDK, this may actually be named something like j2re1.4.2/lib/ext instead. On Windows with a default installation, you'll find the appropriate directory in C:\Program Files\Java or perhaps C:\Program Files\Javasoft. (The exact names tend to change from one version of Java to the next.) You will need to have Java 1.2 or later installed. If necessary, you can download the latest version from `http://java.sun.com/`.

Now, suppose you have a document that's not valid, such as Listing 20-3. This document uses a P element that hasn't been declared in the schema.

Listing 20-3: invalid_greeting.xml

```
<?xml version="1.0"?>
<GREETING
  xmlns:xsi="http://www.w3.org/2001/XMLSchema-instance"
  xsi:noNamespaceSchemaLocation="greeting.xsd">
  <P>Hello XML!</P>
</GREETING>
```

Running it through sax.Counter, you now get this output showing you what the problems are:

```
$ java sax.Counter -s -v invalid_greeting.xml
[Error] invalid_greeting.xml:11:12: cvc-type.3.1.2:
Element 'GREETING' is a simple type, so it must have no
element information item [children].
invalid_greeting.xml: 907 ms (2 elems, 1 attrs, 0 spaces,
16 chars)
```

The problem is that the GREETING element is declared to have type xsd:string, one of several "simple" types that cannot have any child elements. However, in this case, the GREETING element does contain a child element: the P element.

Complex Types

The W3C XML Schema Language divides elements into complex and simple types. A simple type element is one such as GREETING that can only contain text and does not have any attributes. It cannot contain any child elements. It may, however, be more limited in the kind of text it can contain. For example, a schema can say that a simple element contains an integer, a date, or a decimal value between 3.76 and 98.24. Complex type elements can have attributes and can have child elements.

Most documents need a mix of both complex and simple elements. For example, consider Listing 20-4. This document describes the song "Yes I Am" by Melissa Etheridge. The root element is SONG. This element has a number of child elements giving the title of the song, the composer, the producer, the publisher, the duration of the song, the year it was released, the price, and the artist who sang it. Except for SONG itself, these are all simple elements that can have type xsd:string. You might see documents like this used in CD databases, MP3 players, Gnutella clients, or anything else that needs to store information about songs.

Listing 20-4: yesiam.xml

```
<?xml version="1.0"?>
<SONG xmlns:xsi="http://www.w3.org/2001/XMLSchema-instance"
      xsi:noNamespaceSchemaLocation="song.xsd">
  <TITLE>Yes I Am</TITLE>
  <COMPOSER>Melissa Etheridge</COMPOSER>
  <PRODUCER>Hugh Padgham</PRODUCER>
  <PUBLISHER>Island Records</PUBLISHER>
  <LENGTH>4:24</LENGTH>
  <YEAR>1993</YEAR>
  <ARTIST>Melissa Etheridge</ARTIST>
  <PRICE>$1.25</PRICE>
</SONG>
```

Now you need a schema that describes this and all other reasonable song documents. Listing 20-5 is the first attempt at such a schema.

Listing 20-5: song.xsd

```
<?xml version="1.0"?>
<xsd:schema xmlns:xsd="http://www.w3.org/2001/XMLSchema">

  <xsd:element name="SONG" type="SongType"/>

  <xsd:complexType name="SongType">
    <xsd:sequence>
      <xsd:element name="TITLE"     type="xsd:string"/>
      <xsd:element name="COMPOSER"  type="xsd:string"/>
      <xsd:element name="PRODUCER"  type="xsd:string"/>
      <xsd:element name="PUBLISHER" type="xsd:string"/>
      <xsd:element name="LENGTH"    type="xsd:string"/>
      <xsd:element name="YEAR"      type="xsd:string"/>
      <xsd:element name="ARTIST"    type="xsd:string"/>
      <xsd:element name="PRICE"     type="xsd:string"/>
    </xsd:sequence>
  </xsd:complexType>

</xsd:schema>
```

The root element of this schema is once again `xsd:schema`, and once again the prefix `xsd` is mapped to the namespace URI `http://www.w3.org/2001/XMLSchema`. This will be the case for all schemas in this chapter, and indeed all schemas that you write.

This schema declares a single *top-level element*. That is, there is exactly one element declared in an `xsd:element` declaration that is an immediate child of the root `xsd:schema` element. This is the `SONG` element. Only top-level elements can be the root elements of documents described by this schema, though in general they do not have to be the root element.

The `SONG` element is declared to have type `SongType`. The W3C Schema Working Group wasn't prescient. They built a lot of common types into the language, but they didn't know that I was going to need a song type, and they didn't provide one. Indeed, they could not reasonably have been expected to predict and provide for the numerous types that schema designers around the world were ever going to need. Instead, they provided facilities to allow users to define their own types. `SongType` is one such user-defined type. In fact, you can tell it's not a built-in type because it doesn't begin with the prefix `xsd`. All built-in types are in the `http://www.w3.org/2001/XMLSchema` namespace.

The `xsd:complexType` element defines a new type. The `name` attribute of this element names the type being defined. Here that name is `SongType`, which matches the type previously assigned to the `SONG` element. Forward references (for example, `xsd:element` using the `SongType` type before it's been defined) are perfectly acceptable in schemas. Circular references are okay, too. Type A can depend on type B, which depends on type A. Schema processors sort all this out without any difficulty.

The contents of the `xsd:complexType` element specify what content a `SongType` element must contain. In this example, the schema says that every `SongType` element contains a sequence of eight child elements: `TITLE`, `COMPOSER`, `PRODUCER`, `PUBLISHER`, `LENGTH`, `YEAR`, `PRICEARTIST`, and `PRICE`. Each of these is declared to have the built-in type `xsd:string`. Each `SongType` element must contain exactly one of each of these in exactly that order. The only other content it may contain is insignificant white space between the tags.

minOccurs and maxOccurs

You can validate Listing 20-4, yesiam.xml, against the song schema, and it does indeed prove valid. Are you done? Is song.xsd now an adequate description of legal song documents? Suppose you instead wanted to validate Listing 20-6, a song document that describes *Hot Cop* by the Village People. Is it valid according to the schema in Listing 20-5?

Listing 20-6: hotcop.xml

```
<?xml version="1.0"?>
<SONG xmlns:xsi="http://www.w3.org/2001/XMLSchema-instance"
      xsi:noNamespaceSchemaLocation="song.xsd">
  <TITLE>Hot Cop</TITLE>
  <COMPOSER>Jacques Morali</COMPOSER>
  <COMPOSER>Henri Belolo</COMPOSER>
  <COMPOSER>Victor Willis</COMPOSER>
  <PRODUCER>Jacques Morali</PRODUCER>
  <PUBLISHER>PolyGram Records</PUBLISHER>
  <LENGTH>6:20</LENGTH>
  <YEAR>1978</YEAR>
  <ARTIST>Village People</ARTIST>
</SONG>
```

The answer is no, it is not. The reason is that this song was a collaboration between three different composers and the existing schema only allows a single composer. Furthermore, the price is missing. If you looked at other songs, you'd find similar problems with the other child elements. *Under Pressure* has two artists, David Bowie and Queen. *We Are the World* has dozens of artists. Many songs have multiple producers. A garage band without a publisher might record a song and post it on Gnutella in the hope of finding one.

The song schema needs to be adjusted to allow for varying numbers of particular elements. This is done by attaching `minOccurs` and `maxOccurs` attributes to each `xsd:element` element. These attributes specify the minimum and maximum number of instances of the element that may appear at that point in the document. The value of each attribute is an integer greater than or equal to zero. The `maxOccurs` attribute can also have the value `unbounded` to indicate that an unlimited number of the particular element may appear. Listing 20-7 demonstrates.

Listing 20-7: minOccurs and maxOccurs

```
<?xml version="1.0"?>
<xsd:schema xmlns:xsd="http://www.w3.org/2001/XMLSchema">

  <xsd:element name="SONG" type="SongType"/>

  <xsd:complexType name="SongType">
    <xsd:sequence>
      <xsd:element name="TITLE"     type="xsd:string"
                   minOccurs="1"    maxOccurs="1"/>
      <xsd:element name="COMPOSER"  type="xsd:string"
                   minOccurs="1"    maxOccurs="unbounded"/>
```

```
      <xsd:element name="PRODUCER"  type="xsd:string"
                   minOccurs="0"    maxOccurs="unbounded"/>
      <xsd:element name="PUBLISHER" type="xsd:string"
                   minOccurs="0"    maxOccurs="1"/>
      <xsd:element name="LENGTH"    type="xsd:string"
                   minOccurs="1"    maxOccurs="1"/>
      <xsd:element name="YEAR"      type="xsd:string"
                   minOccurs="1"    maxOccurs="1"/>
      <xsd:element name="ARTIST"    type="xsd:string"
                   minOccurs="1"    maxOccurs="unbounded"/>
      <xsd:element name="PRICE"     type="xsd:string"
                   minOccurs="0"    maxOccurs="1"/>
    </xsd:sequence>
  </xsd:complexType>

</xsd:schema>
```

This schema says that every `SongType` element must have, in order:

1. Exactly one `TITLE` (`minOccurs="1" maxOccurs="1"`)
2. At least one, and possibly a great many, `COMPOSER`s (`minOccurs="1" maxOccurs="unbounded"`)
3. Any number of `PRODUCER`s, although possibly no producer at all (`minOccurs="0" maxOccurs="unbounded"`)
4. Either one `PUBLISHER` or no `PUBLISHER` at all (`minOccurs="0" maxOccurs="1"`)
5. Exactly one `LENGTH` (`minOccurs="1" maxOccurs="1"`)
6. Exactly one `YEAR` (`minOccurs="1" maxOccurs="1"`)
7. At least one `ARTIST`, possibly more (`minOccurs="1" maxOccurs="unbounded"`)
8. An optional `PRICE`, (`minOccurs="0" maxOccurs="1"`)

This is much more flexible and easier to use than the limited ?, *, and + that are available in DTDs. It is very straightforward to say, for example, that you want between four and seven of a given element. Just set `minOccurs` to 4 and `maxOccurs` to 7.

If `minOccurs` and `maxOccurs` are not present, the default value of each is 1. Taking advantage of this, the song schema can be written a little more compactly, as shown in Listing 20-8.

Listing 20-8: Taking Advantage of the Default Values of minOccurs and maxOccurs

```
<?xml version="1.0"?>
<xsd:schema xmlns:xsd="http://www.w3.org/2001/XMLSchema">

  <xsd:element name="SONG" type="SongType"/>

  <xsd:complexType name="SongType">
    <xsd:sequence>
      <xsd:element name="TITLE"     type="xsd:string"/>
      <xsd:element name="COMPOSER"  type="xsd:string"
                   maxOccurs="unbounded"/>
      <xsd:element name="PRODUCER"  type="xsd:string"
                   minOccurs="0"    maxOccurs="unbounded"/>
      <xsd:element name="PUBLISHER" type="xsd:string"
                   minOccurs="0"/>
      <xsd:element name="LENGTH"    type="xsd:string"/>
      <xsd:element name="YEAR"      type="xsd:string"/>
      <xsd:element name="ARTIST"    type="xsd:string"
                   maxOccurs="unbounded"/>
      <xsd:element name="PRICE"     type="xsd:string"
                   minOccurs="0"/>
    </xsd:sequence>
  </xsd:complexType>

</xsd:schema>
```

Element content

The examples so far have all been relatively flat. That is, a SONG element contained other elements; but those elements only contained character data, not child elements of their own. Suppose, however, that some child elements do contain other elements, as in Listing 20-9. Here the COMPOSER and PRODUCER elements each contain NAME elements.

Listing 20-9: A Deeper Hierarchy

```
<?xml version="1.0"?>
<SONG xmlns:xsi="http://www.w3.org/2001/XMLSchema-instance"
      xsi:noNamespaceSchemaLocation="20-10.xsd">
  <TITLE>Hot Cop</TITLE>
  <COMPOSER>
    <NAME>Jacques Morali</NAME>
  </COMPOSER>
```

```
  <COMPOSER>
    <NAME>Henri Belolo</NAME>
  </COMPOSER>
  <COMPOSER>
    <NAME>Victor Willis</NAME>
  </COMPOSER>
  <PRODUCER>
    <NAME>Jacques Morali</NAME>
  </PRODUCER>
  <PUBLISHER>PolyGram Records</PUBLISHER>
  <LENGTH>6:20</LENGTH>
  <YEAR>1978</YEAR>
  <ARTIST>Village People</ARTIST>
</SONG>
```

Because the COMPOSER and PRODUCER elements now have complex content, you can no longer use one of the built-in types such as xsd:string to declare them. Instead, you have to define a new ComposerType and ProducerType using top-level xsd:complexType elements. Listing 20-10 demonstrates.

Listing 20-10: Defining Separate ComposerType and ProducerType Types

```
<?xml version="1.0"?>
<xsd:schema xmlns:xsd="http://www.w3.org/2001/XMLSchema">

  <xsd:element name="SONG" type="SongType"/>

  <xsd:complexType name="ComposerType">
    <xsd:sequence>
      <xsd:element name="NAME" type="xsd:string"/>
    </xsd:sequence>
  </xsd:complexType>

  <xsd:complexType name="ProducerType">
    <xsd:sequence>
      <xsd:element name="NAME" type="xsd:string"/>
    </xsd:sequence>
  </xsd:complexType>

  <xsd:complexType name="SongType">
    <xsd:sequence>
      <xsd:element name="TITLE"     type="xsd:string"/>
      <xsd:element name="COMPOSER"  type="ComposerType"
                   maxOccurs="unbounded"/>
      <xsd:element name="PRODUCER"  type="ProducerType"
                   minOccurs="0" maxOccurs="unbounded"/>
```

Continued

Listing 20-10 *(continued)*

```
      <xsd:element name="PUBLISHER" type="xsd:string"
                   minOccurs="0"/>
      <xsd:element name="LENGTH" type="xsd:string"/>
      <xsd:element name="YEAR"   type="xsd:string"/>
      <xsd:element name="ARTIST" type="xsd:string"
                   maxOccurs="unbounded"/>
      <xsd:element name="PRICE" type="xsd:string"
                   minOccurs="0"/>
    </xsd:sequence>
  </xsd:complexType>

</xsd:schema>
```

Sharing content models

You may have noticed that PRODUCER and COMPOSER are very similar. Each contains a single NAME child element and nothing else. In a DTD, you'd take advantage of this shared content model via a parameter entity reference. In a schema, it's much easier. Simply give them the same type. While you could declare that the PRODUCER has ComposerType or vice versa, it's better to declare that both have a more generic PersonType. Listing 20-11 demonstrates.

Listing 20-11: Using a Single PersonType for Both COMPOSER and PRODUCER

```
<?xml version="1.0"?>
<xsd:schema xmlns:xsd="http://www.w3.org/2001/XMLSchema">

  <xsd:element name="SONG" type="SongType"/>

  <xsd:complexType name="PersonType">
    <xsd:sequence>
      <xsd:element name="NAME" type="xsd:string"/>
    </xsd:sequence>
  </xsd:complexType>

  <xsd:complexType name="SongType">
    <xsd:sequence>
      <xsd:element name="TITLE"     type="xsd:string"/>
      <xsd:element name="COMPOSER"  type="PersonType"
                   maxOccurs="unbounded"/>
      <xsd:element name="PRODUCER"  type="PersonType"
                   minOccurs="0" maxOccurs="unbounded"/>
      <xsd:element name="PUBLISHER" type="xsd:string"
                   minOccurs="0"/>
```

```
      <xsd:element name="LENGTH" type="xsd:string"/>
      <xsd:element name="YEAR"   type="xsd:string"/>
      <xsd:element name="ARTIST" type="xsd:string"
                   maxOccurs="unbounded"/>
      <xsd:element name="PRICE" type="xsd:string"
                   minOccurs="0"/>
    </xsd:sequence>
  </xsd:complexType>

</xsd:schema>
```

Anonymous types

Suppose you wanted to divide the NAME elements into separate GIVEN and FAMILY elements like this:

```
<NAME>
  <GIVEN>Victor</GIVEN>
  <FAMILY>Willis</FAMILY>
</NAME>
<NAME>
  <GIVEN>Jacques</GIVEN>
  <FAMILY>Morali</FAMILY>
</NAME>
```

To declare this, you could use an xsd:complexType element to define a new NameType element, like this:

```
<xsd:complexType name="NameType">
  <xsd:sequence>
    <xsd:element name="GIVEN"  type="xsd:string"/>
    <xsd:element name="FAMILY" type="xsd:string"/>
  </xsd:sequence>
</xsd:complexType>
```

Then the PersonType would be defined like this:

```
<xsd:complexType name="PersonType">
  <xsd:sequence>
    <xsd:element name="NAME" type="NameType"/>
  </xsd:sequence>
</xsd:complexType>
```

However, the NAME element is only used inside PersonType elements. Perhaps it shouldn't be a top-level definition. For example, you might not want to allow NAME elements to be used as root elements, or to be children of things that aren't PersonType elements. You can prevent this by defining a name with an *anonymous type*. To do this, instead of assigning the NAME element a type with a type attribute on the corresponding xsd:element element, you give it an xsd:complexType child element to define its type. Listing 20-12 demonstrates.

Listing 20-12: Anonymous Types

```
<?xml version="1.0"?>
<xsd:schema xmlns:xsd="http://www.w3.org/2001/XMLSchema">

  <xsd:element name="SONG" type="SongType"/>

  <xsd:complexType name="PersonType">
    <xsd:sequence>
      <xsd:element name="NAME">
        <xsd:complexType>
          <xsd:sequence>
            <xsd:element name="GIVEN"  type="xsd:string"/>
            <xsd:element name="FAMILY" type="xsd:string"/>
          </xsd:sequence>
        </xsd:complexType>
      </xsd:element>
    </xsd:sequence>
  </xsd:complexType>

  <xsd:complexType name="SongType">
    <xsd:sequence>
      <xsd:element name="TITLE"     type="xsd:string"/>
      <xsd:element name="COMPOSER"  type="PersonType"
                   maxOccurs="unbounded"/>
      <xsd:element name="PRODUCER"  type="PersonType"
                   minOccurs="0" maxOccurs="unbounded"/>
      <xsd:element name="PUBLISHER" type="xsd:string"
                   minOccurs="0"/>
      <xsd:element name="LENGTH" type="xsd:string"/>
      <xsd:element name="YEAR"   type="xsd:string"/>
      <xsd:element name="ARTIST" type="xsd:string"
                   maxOccurs="unbounded"/>
      <xsd:element name="PRICE" type="xsd:string"
                   minOccurs="0"/>
    </xsd:sequence>
  </xsd:complexType>

</xsd:schema>
```

Defining the element types inside the `xsd:element` elements that are themselves children of `xsd:complexType` elements is a very powerful technique. Among other things, it enables you to give elements with the same name different types when used in different elements. For example, you can say that the `NAME` of a `PERSON` contains `GIVEN` and `FAMILY` child elements, while the `NAME` of a `MOVIE` contains an `xsd:string`, and the `NAME` of a `VARIABLE` contains a string containing only alphanumeric characters from the ASCII character set.

Mixed content

Schemas offer much greater control over mixed content than DTDs do. In particular, schemas let you enforce the order and number of elements appearing in mixed content. For example, suppose you wanted to allow extra text to be mixed in with the names to provide middle initials, titles, and the like as shown in Listing 20-13.

The format used here is purely for illustrative purposes. In practice, I'd recommend that you make the middle names and titles separate elements as well.

Listing 20-13: Mixed Content

```
<?xml version="1.0"?>
<SONG xmlns:xsi="http://www.w3.org/2001/XMLSchema-instance"
      xsi:noNamespaceSchemaLocation="20-14.xsd">
  <TITLE>Hot Cop</TITLE>
  <COMPOSER>
    <NAME>
     Mr. <GIVEN>Jacques</GIVEN> <FAMILY>Morali</FAMILY> Esq.
    </NAME>
  </COMPOSER>
  <COMPOSER>
    <NAME>
     Mr. <GIVEN>Henri</GIVEN> L. <FAMILY>Belolo</FAMILY>, M.D.
    </NAME>
  </COMPOSER>
  <COMPOSER>
    <NAME>
     Mr. <GIVEN>Victor</GIVEN> C. <FAMILY>Willis</FAMILY>
    </NAME>
  </COMPOSER>
  <PRODUCER>
    <NAME>
     Mr. <GIVEN>Jacques</GIVEN> S. <FAMILY>Morali</FAMILY>
    </NAME>
  </PRODUCER>
  <PUBLISHER>PolyGram Records</PUBLISHER>
  <LENGTH>6:20</LENGTH>
  <YEAR>1978</YEAR>
  <ARTIST>Village People</ARTIST>
</SONG>
```

It's very easy to declare that an element has mixed content in schemas. First, set up the `xsd:complexType` exactly as you would if the element only contained child elements. Then add a `mixed` attribute to it with the value `true`. Listing 20-14 demonstrates. It is almost identical to Listing 20-12 except for the addition of the `mixed="true"` attribute.

Listing 20-14: Declaring Mixed Content in a Schema

```
<?xml version="1.0"?>
<xsd:schema xmlns:xsd="http://www.w3.org/2001/XMLSchema">

  <xsd:element name="SONG" type="SongType"/>

  <xsd:complexType name="PersonType">
    <xsd:sequence>
      <xsd:element name="NAME">
        <xsd:complexType mixed="true">
          <xsd:sequence>
            <xsd:element name="GIVEN"  type="xsd:string"/>
            <xsd:element name="FAMILY" type="xsd:string"/>
          </xsd:sequence>
        </xsd:complexType>
    </xsd:element>
  </xsd:sequence>
</xsd:complexType>

  <xsd:complexType name="SongType">
    <xsd:sequence>
     <xsd:element name="TITLE"     type="xsd:string"/>
      <xsd:element name="COMPOSER"  type="PersonType"
                   maxOccurs="unbounded"/>
      <xsd:element name="PRODUCER"  type="PersonType"
                   minOccurs="0" maxOccurs="unbounded"/>
      <xsd:element name="PUBLISHER" type="xsd:string"
                   minOccurs="0"/>
      <xsd:element name="LENGTH" type="xsd:string"/>
      <xsd:element name="YEAR"   type="xsd:string"/>
      <xsd:element name="ARTIST" type="xsd:string"/>
                   maxOccurs="unbounded"/>
      <xsd:element name="PRICE" type="xsd:string"
                   minOccurs="0"/>
    </xsd:sequence>
  </xsd:complexType>

</xsd:schema>
```

Grouping

So far, all the schemas you've seen have held that order mattered; for example, that it would be wrong to put the COMPOSER before the TITLE or the PRODUCER after the ARTIST. Given these schemas, the document shown in Listing 20-15 is clearly invalid. But should it be? Element order often does matter in narrative documents such as books and web pages. However, it's not nearly as important in record-like documents such as the examples in this chapter. Do you really care whether the

TITLE comes first or not, as long as there is a TITLE? After all, if the document's going to be shown to a human being, it will probably first be transformed with an XSLT style sheet that can easily place the contents in any order it likes.

Listing 20-15: A Song Document That Places the Elements in a Different Order

```
<?xml version="1.0"?>
<SONG xmlns:xsi="http://www.w3.org/2001/XMLSchema-instance"
      xsi:noNamespaceSchemaLocation="song.xsd">
  <ARTIST>Village People</ARTIST>
  <TITLE>Hot Cop</TITLE>
  <COMPOSER>
   <NAME><GIVEN>Jacques</GIVEN> <FAMILY>Morali</FAMILY></NAME>
  </COMPOSER>
  <PUBLISHER>PolyGram Records</PUBLISHER>
  <COMPOSER>
   <NAME><FAMILY>Belolo</FAMILY> <GIVEN>Henri</GIVEN></NAME>
  </COMPOSER>
  <YEAR>1978</YEAR>
  <COMPOSER>
   <NAME><FAMILY>Willis</FAMILY> <GIVEN>Victor</GIVEN></NAME>
  </COMPOSER>
  <PRODUCER>
   <NAME><GIVEN>Jacques</GIVEN> <FAMILY>Morali</FAMILY></NAME>
  </PRODUCER>
  <PRICE>$1.25</PRICE>
</SONG>
```

The W3C XML Schema Language provides three grouping constructs that specify whether and how ordering of individual elements is important:

- ✦ The xsd:all group requires that each element in the group must occur at most once, but that order is not important.
- ✦ The xsd:choice group specifies that any one element from the group should appear. It can also be used to say that between N and M elements from the group should appear in any order.
- ✦ The xsd:sequence group requires that each element in the group appear exactly once, in the specified order.

Unfortunately, these constructs are not everything you might desire. In particular, you can't specify constraints such as those that would be required to really handle Listing 20-14. In particular, you can't specify that you want a SONG to have exactly one TITLE, one or more COMPOSERs, zero or more PRODUCERs, and one or more ARTISTs, but that you don't care in what order the individual elements occur.

The xsd:all Group

You can specify that you want each `NAME` element to have exactly one `GIVEN` child and one `FAMILY` child, but that you don't care what order they appear in. The `xsd:all` group accomplishes this, as in the following example:

```
<xsd:complexType name="PersonType">
  <xsd:sequence>
    <xsd:element name="NAME">
      <xsd:complexType>
        <xsd:all>
          <xsd:element name="GIVEN" type="xsd:string"
                       minOccurs="1" maxOccurs="1"/>
          <xsd:element name="FAMILY" type="xsd:string"
                       minOccurs="1" maxOccurs="1"/>
        </xsd:all>
      </xsd:complexType>
    </xsd:element>
  </xsd:sequence>
</xsd:complexType>
```

The extension to handle what you want for Listing 20-15 seems obvious. It would look like this:

```
<xsd:complexType name="SongType">
  <xsd:all>
    <xsd:element name="TITLE" type="xsd:string"
                 minOccurs="1" maxOccurs="1"/>
    <xsd:element name="COMPOSER" type="PersonType"
                 minOccurs="1" maxOccurs="unbounded"/>
    <xsd:element name="PRODUCER" type="PersonType"
                 minOccurs="0" maxOccurs="unbounded"/>
    <xsd:element name="PUBLISHER" type="xsd:string"
                 minOccurs="0" maxOccurs="1"/>
    <xsd:element name="LENGTH" type="xsd:string"
                 minOccurs="1" maxOccurs="1"/>
    <xsd:element name="YEAR" type="xsd:string"
                 minOccurs="1" maxOccurs="1"/>
    <xsd:element name="ARTIST" type="xsd:string"
                 minOccurs="1" maxOccurs="unbounded"/>
    <xsd:element name="PRICE" type="xsd:string"
                 minOccurs="0"/>
  </xsd:all>
</xsd:complexType>
```

Unfortunately, the W3C XML Schema Language restricts the use of `minOccurs` and `maxOccurs` inside `xsd:all` elements. In particular, each one's value must be `0` or `1`. You cannot set it to `4` or `7` or `unbounded`. Therefore, the preceding type definition is invalid. Furthermore, `xsd:all` can only contain individual element declarations. It cannot contain `xsd:choice` or `xsd:sequence` elements. `xsd:all` offers somewhat more expressiveness than DTDs do, but probably not as much as you want.

Choices

The xsd:choice element is the schema equivalent of the | in DTDs. When xsd:element elements are combined inside an xsd:choice, exactly one of those elements must appear in instance documents. For example, the choice in this xsd:complexType requires either a PRODUCER or a COMPOSER, but not both.

```
<xsd:complexType name="SongType">
  <xsd:sequence>
   <xsd:element name="TITLE" type="xsd:string"/>
   <xsd:choice>
     <xsd:element name="COMPOSER" type="PersonType"/>
     <xsd:element name="PRODUCER" type="PersonType"/>
   </xsd:choice>
   <xsd:element name="PUBLISHER" type="xsd:string"
                minOccurs="0"/>
   <xsd:element name="LENGTH" type="xsd:string"/>
   <xsd:element name="YEAR"   type="xsd:string"/>
   <xsd:element name="ARTIST" type="xsd:string"
                maxOccurs="unbounded"/>
   <xsd:element name="PRICE" type="xsd:string" minOccurs="0"/>
  </xsd:sequence>
</xsd:complexType>
```

The xsd:choice element itself can have minOccurs and maxOccurs attributes that establish exactly how many selections may be made from the choice. For example, setting minOccurs to 1 and maxOccurs to 6 would indicate that between one and six elements listed in the xsd:choice should appear. Each of these can be any of the elements in the xsd:choice. For example, you could have six different elements, three of the same element and three of another, or up to six of the same element. This next xsd:choice allows for any number of artists, composers, and producers. However, in order to require that there be at least one ARTIST element and at least one COMPOSER element, rather than allowing all spaces to be filled by PRODUCER elements, it's necessary to place xsd:element declarations for these two outside the choice. This has the unfortunate side effect of locking in more order than is really needed.

```
<xsd:complexType name="SongType">
  <xsd:sequence>
    <xsd:element name="TITLE" type="xsd:string"/>
    <xsd:element name="COMPOSER" type="PersonType"/>
    <xsd:choice minOccurs="0" maxOccurs="unbounded">
      <xsd:element name="PRODUCER" type="PersonType"/>
      <xsd:element name="COMPOSER" type="PersonType"/>
      <xsd:element name="ARTIST"   type="xsd:string"/>
    </xsd:choice>
    <xsd:element name="ARTIST" type="xsd:string"/>
    <xsd:element name="PUBLISHER" type="xsd:string"
                 minOccurs="0"/>
    <xsd:element name="LENGTH" type="xsd:string"/>
    <xsd:element name="YEAR"   type="xsd:string"/>
```

```
    <xsd:element name="PRICE"  type="xsd:string"
                 minOccurs="0"/>
  </xsd:sequence>
</xsd:complexType>
```

Sequences

An xsd:sequence element requires each member of the sequence to appear in the same order in the instance document as in the xsd:sequence element. I've used this frequently as the basic group for xsd:complexType elements in this chapter so far. The number of times each element is allowed to appear can be controlled by the xsd:element's minOccurs and maxOccurs attributes. You can add minOccurs and maxOccurs attributes to the xsd:sequence element to specify the number of times the sequence should repeat.

Simple Types

Until now I've focused on writing schemas that validate the element structures in an XML document. However, there's also a lot of non-XML structure in the song documents. The YEAR element isn't just a string. It's an integer, and maybe not just any integer either, but a positive integer with four digits. The PRICE element is some sort of money. The LENGTH element is a duration of time. DTDs have absolutely nothing to say about such non-XML structures that are inside the parsed character data content of elements and attributes. Schemas, however, do let you make all sorts of statements about what forms the text inside elements may take and what it means. Schemas provide much more sophisticated semantics for documents than DTDs do.

Listing 20-16 is a new schema for song documents. It's based on Listing 20-8, but read closely and you should notice that a few things have changed.

Listing 20-16: A Schema with Simple Data Types

```
<?xml version="1.0"?>
<xsd:schema xmlns:xsd="http://www.w3.org/2001/XMLSchema">

  <xsd:element name="SONG" type="SongType"/>

  <xsd:complexType name="SongType">
    <xsd:sequence>
      <xsd:element name="TITLE"     type="xsd:string"/>
      <xsd:element name="COMPOSER"  type="xsd:string"
                   maxOccurs="unbounded"/>
      <xsd:element name="PRODUCER"  type="xsd:string"
                   minOccurs="0"    maxOccurs="unbounded"/>
      <xsd:element name="PUBLISHER" type="xsd:string"
                   minOccurs="0"/>
```

```
      <xsd:element name="LENGTH"    type="xsd:duration"/>
      <xsd:element name="YEAR"      type="xsd:gYear"/>
      <xsd:element name="ARTIST"    type="xsd:string"
                   maxOccurs="unbounded"/>
      <xsd:element name="PRICE"     type="xsd:string"
                   minOccurs="0"/>
    </xsd:sequence>
  </xsd:complexType>

</xsd:schema>
```

Did you spot the changes? The values of the `type` attributes of the `LENGTH` and `YEAR` declarations are no longer `xsd:string`. Instead, `LENGTH` has the type `xsd:duration` and `YEAR` has the type `xsd:gYear`. These declarations say that it's no longer okay for the `YEAR` and `LENGTH` elements to contain just any old string of text. Instead, they must contain strings in particular formats. In particular, the `YEAR` element must contain a year; and the `LENGTH` element must contain a recognizable length of time. When you check a document against this schema, the validator will check that these elements contain the proper data. It's not just looking at the elements. It's looking at the content inside the elements!

Let's actually validate hotcop.xml against this schema and see what we get:

```
$ java sax.Counter -s -v hotcop.xml
[Error] hotcop.xml:10:24: cvc-datatype-valid.1.2.1: '6:20'
is not a valid value for 'duration'.
[Error] hotcop.xml:10:24: cvc-type.3.1.3: The value '6:20'
of element 'LENGTH' is not valid.
hotcop.xml: 897 ms (10 elems, 1 attrs, 0 spaces, 126 chars)
```

That's unexpected! The problem is that 6:20 is not in the proper format for time durations, at least not the format that the W3C XML Schema Language uses and that schema validators know how to check. Schema validators expect that time types are expressed in the format defined in ISO standard 8601, *Representations of dates and times* (`http://www.iso.ch/iso/en/prods-services/popstds/datesandtime.html`). This standard says that time durations should have the form PnYnMnDTnHnMdS, where *n* is an integer and *d* is a decimal number. *P* stands for "period." *nY* gives the number of years; the first *nM* gives the number of months; and *nD* gives the number of days. *T* separates the date from the time. Following the T, *nH* gives the number of hours; the second *nM* gives the number of minutes; and *dS* gives the number of seconds. If *d* has a fraction part, the duration can be specified to an arbitrary level of precision.

In this format, a duration of 6 minutes and 20 seconds should be written as P0Y0M0DT0H6M20S. If you prefer, the zero pieces can be left out, so you can write this more compactly as PT6M20S. Listing 20-17 shows the fixed version of hotcop.xml with the `LENGTH` in the right format.

Listing 20-17: fixed hotcop.xml

```
<?xml version="1.0"?>
<SONG xmlns:xsi="http://www.w3.org/2001/XMLSchema-instance"
      xsi:noNamespaceSchemaLocation="20-16.xsd">
  <TITLE>Hot Cop</TITLE>
  <COMPOSER>Jacques Morali</COMPOSER>
  <COMPOSER>Henri Belolo</COMPOSER>
  <COMPOSER>Victor Willis</COMPOSER>
  <PRODUCER>Jacques Morali</PRODUCER>
  <PUBLISHER>PolyGram Records</PUBLISHER>
  <LENGTH>P0YT6M20S</LENGTH>
  <YEAR>1978</YEAR>
  <ARTIST>Village People</ARTIST>
</SONG>
```

Admittedly the ISO 8601 format for time durations is a little obtuse, if precise. You may well be asking whether there's a type that you can specify for the `LENGTH` that would make lengths such as 6:20 and 4:24 legal. In fact, there's no such type built in to the W3C XML Schema Language, but you can define one yourself. You'll learn how to do that soon, but first let's explore some of the other data types that are built in to the W3C XML Schema Language.

There are 44 built-in simple types in the W3C XML Schema Language. These can be unofficially divided into seven groups:

- Numeric types
- Time types
- XML types
- String types
- The boolean type
- The URI reference type
- The binary types

Numeric data types

The most obvious data types, and the ones most familiar to programmers, are the numeric data types. Among computer scientists, there's quite a bit of disagreement about how numbers should be represented in computer systems. The W3C XML

Schema Language tries to make everyone happy by providing almost every numeric type imaginable, including the following:

- ✦ Integer and floating point numbers
- ✦ Finite size numbers similar to those in Java and C and infinitely precise, unlimited-size numbers similar to those in Eiffel and Java's `java.math` package
- ✦ Signed and unsigned numbers

You'll probably only use a subset of these. For example, you wouldn't use both the arbitrarily large `xsd:integer` type and the four-byte-limited `xsd:int` type. Table 20-1 summarizes the different numeric types.

Table 20-1
Schema Numeric Types

Name	*Type*	*Examples*
`xsd:float`	IEEE 754 32-bit floating point number, or as close as you can get using a base 10 representation; same as Java's `float` type	-INF, -1E4, -0, 0, 12.78E-2, 12, INF, NaN
`xsd:double`	IEEE 754 64-bit floating-point number, or as close as you can get using a base 10 representation; same as Java's `double` type	-INF, 1.401E-90, -1E4, -0, 0, 12.78E-2, 12, INF, NaN, 3.4E42
`xsd:decimal`	Arbitrary precision, decimal numbers; same as `java.math.BigDecimal`	-2.7E400, 5.7E-444, -3.1415292, 0, 7.8, 90200.76, 3.4E1024
`xsd:integer`	An arbitrarily large or small integer; same as `java.math.BigInteger`	-500000000000000000000000, -9223372036854775809, -126789, -1, 0, 1, 5, 23, 42, 126789, 9223372036854775808, 456734987324983264987362495 8
`xsd:nonPositiveInteger`	An integer less than or equal to zero	0, -1, -2, -3, -4, -5, -6, -7, -8, -9, . . .
`xsd:negativeInteger`	An integer strictly less than zero	-1, -2, -3, -4, -5, -6, -7, -8, -9, . . .

Continued

Table 20-1 (continued)

Name	*Type*	*Examples*
`xsd:long`	An eight-byte, two's complement integer, such as Java's `long` type	-9223372036854775808, -9223372036854775807, . . . -6, -5, -4, -3, -2, -1, 0, 1, 2, 3, 4, 5, 6, 7, 8, 9, 10, 11, 12, 13, 14, . . ., 2147483645, 2147483646, 2147483647, 2147483648, . . . 9223372036854775806, 9223372036854775807
`xsd:int`	An integer that can be represented as a four-byte, two's complement number, such as Java's `int` type	-2147483648, -2147483647, -2147483646, 2147483645, . . . -6, -5, -4, -3, -2, -1, 0, 1, 2, 3, 4, 5, 6, 7, 8, 9, 10, 11, 12, 13, 14, . . ., 2147483645, 2147483646, 2147483647
`xsd:short`	An integer that can be represented as a two-byte, two's complement number, such as Java's `short` type	-32768, -32767, -32766, . . ., -6, -5, -4, -3, -2, -1, 0, 1, 2, 3, 4, 5, 6, 7, 8, 9, 10, 11, 12, 13, 14, 15, . . . 32765, 32766, 32767
`xsd:byte`	An integer that can be represented as a one-byte, two's complement number such as Java's `byte` type	-128, -127, -126, -125, . . ., -3, -2, -1, 0, 1, 2, 3, 4, 5, 6, 7, 8, 9, 10, 11, 12, 13, 14, 15, 16, . . .121, 122, 123, 124, 125, 126, 127
`xsd: nonNegativeInteger`	An integer greater than or equal to zero	0, 1, 2, 3, 4, 5, 6, 7, 8, 9, 10, 11, 12, 13, 14, 15, ...
`xsd:unsignedLong`	An eight-byte unsigned integer	0, 1, 2, 3, 4, 5, 6, 7, 8, 9, 10, 11, 12, . . .18446744073709551614, 18446744073709551615
`xsd:unsignedInt`	A four-byte unsigned integer	0, 1, 2, 3, 4, 5, . . .4294967294, 4294967295
`xsd:unsignedShort`	A two-byte unsigned integer	0, 1, 2, 3, 4, 5, 6, 7, 8, 9, 10, 11, 12, 13, 14, . . .65533, 65534, 65535
`xsd:unsignedByte`	A one-byte unsigned integer	0, 1, 2, 3, 4, 5, 6, 7, 8, 9, 10, 11, 12, 13, 14, . . . 252, 253, 254, 255
`xsd:positiveInteger`	An integer strictly greater than zero	1, 2, 3, 4, 5, 6, 7, 8, 9, 10, 11, 12, 13, 14, . . .

Time data types

The next set of simple types the W3C XML Schema Language provides are more familiar to database designers than to procedural programmers; these are the time types. These can represent times of day, dates, or durations of time. The formats, shown in Table 20-2, are all based on the ISO standard 8601, *Representations of Dates and Time.* Time zones are given as offsets from Coordinated Universal Time (Greenwich Mean Time to lay people) or as the letter Z to indicate Coordinated Universal Time.

Table 20-2
XML Schema Time Types

Name	*Type*	*Examples*
`xsd:dateTime`	A particular moment in Coordinated Universal Time, up to an arbitrarily small fraction of a second	1999-05-31T13:20:00.000-05:00, 1999-05-31T18:20:00.000Z, 1999-05-31T13:20:00.000, 1999-05-31T13:20:00.000-05:00.321
`xsd:date`	A specific day in history	-0044-03-15, 0001-01-01, 1969-06-27, 2000-10-31, 2001-11-17
`xsd:time`	A specific time of day that recurs every day	14:30:00.000, 09:30:00.000-05:00, 14:30:00.000Z
`xsd:gDay`	A day in no particular month, or rather in every month	--01, --02, . . . –09, --10, --11, --12, . . ., --28, --29, --30, --31
`xsd:gMonth`	A month in no particular year	--01--, --02--, --03--, ---04--, . . . --09--, --10--, --11--, --12--
`xsd:gYear`	A given year	. . . -0002, -0001, 0001, 0002, 0003, . . .1998, 1999, 2000, 2001, 2002, . . .9997, 9998, 9999
`xsd:gYearMonth`	A specific month in a specific year	1999-12, 2001-04, 1968-07
`xsd:gMonthDay`	A date in no particular year, or rather in every year	--10-31, --02-28, --02-29
`xsd:duration`	A length of time, without fixed endpoints, to an arbitrary fraction of a second	P2000Y10M31DT09H32M7.4312S

Notice, in particular, that in all the date formats the year comes first, followed by the month, the day, the hour, and so on. The largest unit of time is on the left, and the smallest unit is on the right. This helps avoid questions such as whether 2004–02–11 is February 11, 2004, or November 2, 2004.

XML data types

The next batch of schema data types should be quite familiar. These are the types related to XML constructs themselves. Most of these types match attribute types in DTDs such as `NMTOKENS` or `IDREF`. The difference is that with schemas these types can be applied to both elements and attributes. These also include four new types related to other XML constructs: `xsd:language`, `xsd:Name`, `xsd:QName`, and `xsd:NCName`. Table 20-3 summarizes the different types.

Table 20-3
XML Schema XML Types

Name	*Type*	*Examples*
`xsd:ID`	XML 1.0 `ID` attribute type; any XML name that's unique among ID type attributes and elements	`p1`, `p2`, `ss120-45-6789`, `_92`, `red`, `green`, `NT-Decl`, `seventeen`
`xsd:IDREF`	XML 1.0 `IDREF` attribute type; any XML name that's used as the value of an ID type attribute or element elsewhere in the document	`p1`, `p2`, `ss120-45-6789`, `_92`, `p1`, `p2`, `red`, `green`, `NT-Decl`, `seventeen`
`xsd:ENTITY`	XML 1.0 `ENTITY` attribute type; any XML name that's declared as an unparsed entity in the DTD	`PIC1`, `PIC2`, `PIC3`, `cow_movie`, `MonaLisa`, `Warhol`
`xsd:NOTATION`	XML 1.0 `NOTATION` attribute type; any XML name that's declared as a notation name in the schema using `xsd:notation`	`GIF`, `jpeg`, `TIF`, `pdf`, `TeX`

Name	Type	Examples
xsd:IDREFS	XML 1.0 IDREFS attribute type; a white space-separated list of XML names that are used as values of ID type attributes or elements elsewhere in the document	p1 p2, ss120-45-6789 _92, red green NT-Decl seventeen
xsd:ENTITIES	XML 1.0 ENTITIES attribute type; a white space-separated list of ENTITY names	PIC1 PIC2 PIC3
xsd:NMTOKEN	XML 1.0 NMTOKEN attribute type	12 are you ready 199
xsd:NMTOKENS	XML 1.0 NMTOKENS attribute type, a white space-separated list of name tokens	MI NY LA CA p1 p2 p3 p4 p5 p6 1 2 3 4 5 6
xsd:language	Valid values for xml:lang as defined in XML 1.0	en, en-GB, en-US, fr, i-lux, ama, ara, ara-EG, x-choctaw
xsd:Name	An XML 1.0 Name, with or without colons	set, title, rdf, math, math123, xlink:href, song:title
xsd:QName	A prefixed name	song:title, math:set, xsd:element
xsd:NCName	A local name without any colons	set, title, rdf, math, tei.2, href

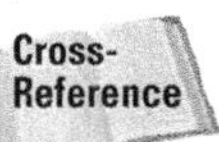

For more details on the permissible values for elements and attributes declared to have these types, see Chapters 9 and 11.

String data types

You've already encountered the xsd:string type. It's the most generic simple type. It requires a sequence of Unicode characters of any length, but this is what all XML element content and attribute values are. There are also two very closely related types: xsd:token and xsd:normalizedString. These are the same as xsd:string, except that a schema aware processor may eliminate some white space from the value before reporting it to the client application. Table 20-4 summarizes the string data types.

Table 20-4
XML Schema String Types

Name	Type	Examples
xsd:string	A sequence of zero or more Unicode characters that are allowed in an XML document; essentially the only forbidden characters are most of the C0 controls, surrogates, and the byte-order mark	p1, p2, 123 45 6789, ^*&^*&_92, red green blue, NT-Decl, seventeen; Mary had a little lamb, The love of money is the root of all Evil., Would you paint the lily? Would you gild gold?
xsd:normalizedString	A string in which all tabs, carriage returns, and linefeeds are replaced by spaces	PIC1, PIC2, PIC3, cow_movie, MonaLisa, Hello World , Warhol, red green
xsd:token	A string in which all tabs, carriage returns, and linefeeds are replaced by spaces, consecutive spaces are compressed to a single space, and leading and trailing white space is trimmed	p1 p2, ss123 45 6789, _92, red, green, NT Decl, seventeenp1, p2, 123 45 6789, ^*&^*&_92, red green blue, NT-Decl, seventeen; Mary had a little lamb, The love of money is the root of all Evil.

It's important to note that none of these three types impose any limits on what values may appear in the instance document. Elements with type `xsd:strring`, `xsd:normalizedString`, and `xsd:token` can all contain tabs, linefeeds, consecutive spaces, and so on. The difference is that for `xsd:normalizedString` and `xsd:token` the parser may throw away some of this white space, while it won't for an `xsd:string`,.

Binary types

It's impossible to include arbitrary binary files in XML documents, because they might contain illegal characters such as a form feed or a null that would make the XML document malformed. Therefore, any such data must first be encoded in legal characters. The W3C XML Schema Language supports two such encodings, `xsd:base64Binary` and `xsd:hexBinary`.

Hexadecimal binary encodes each byte of the input as two hexadecimal digits—00, 01, 02, 03, 04, 05, 06, 07, 08, 09, 0A, 0B, 0C, 0D, 0E, 0F, 10, 11, 12, and so on. Thus, an entire file can be encoded using only the digits 0 through 9 and the letters A through F. (Lowercase letters are also allowed, but uppercase letters are customary.) On the other hand, each byte is replaced by at least two bytes, so this encoding at least doubles the size of the data. UTF-16 uses two bytes for each character so it quadruples the size of the data. Clearly, this is not a very efficient encoding. Hexadecimal binary encoded data tends to look like this:

```
A4E345EC54CC8D52198000FFEA6C807F41F332127323432147A89979EEF3
```

Base 64 encoding uses a more complex algorithm and a larger character set, 65 ASCII characters chosen for their ability to pass through almost all gateways, mail relays, and terminal servers intact, as well as their existence with the same code points in ASCII, EBCDIC, and most other common character sets. Base 64 encodes every three bytes as four characters, typically only increasing file size by a third in a character set such as UTF-8, so it's somewhat more efficient than `xsd:hexBinary`. Base-64-encoded data tends to look something like this:

```
6jKpNnmkkWeArsn50eeg2njcz+nXdk0f9kZI892dd1R8Lg1aMhPeFTYuoq3I6n
BjWzuktNZKiXYBfKsSTB8U09dTiJo2ir3HJuY7eW/p89osKMfixPQsp9vQMgzph
6Qa 1Y7j4MB7y5ROJYsTr1/fFwmj/yhkHwpbpzed1LE=
```

XML Digital Signatures use Base 64 encoding to encode the binary signatures before wrapping them in an XML element.

I really discourage you from using either of these if at all possible. If you have binary data, it's much more efficient and much less obtuse to link to it using XLink or unparsed entities rather than encoding it in Base 64 or hexadecimal binary.

Miscellaneous data types

There are two types left over that don't fit neatly into the previous categories: `xsd:boolean` and `xsd:anyURI`. The `xsd:boolean` type represents something similar to C++'s `bool` data type. It has four legal values: `0`, `1`, `true`, and `false`. `0` is considered to be the same as `false`, and `1` is considered the same as `true`.

The final schema simple type is `xsd:anyURI`. An element of this type contains a relative or absolute URI, possibly a URL, such as `urn:isbn:0764547607`, `http://www.w3.org/TR/2000/WD-xmlschema-2-20000407/#timeDuration`, `/javafaq/reports/JCE1.2.1.htm`, `/TR/2000/WD-xmlschema-2-20000407/`, or `../index.html`.

Deriving Simple Types

You're not limited to the 44 simple types that the W3C XML Schema Language defines. As in object-oriented programming languages, you can create new data types by deriving from the existing types. The most common such derivation is to restrict a type to a subset of its normal values. For example, you can define an integer type that only holds numbers between 1 and 20 by deriving from `xsd:positiveInteger`. You can create enumerated types that only allow a finite list of fixed values. You can create new types that join together the ranges of existing types through a union. For example, you can derive a type that can hold either an `xsd:date` or an `xsd:int`.

New simple types are created by `xsd:simpleType` elements, just as new complex types are created by `xsd:complexType` elements. The `name` attribute of `xsd:simpleType` assigns a name to the new type by which it can be referred to in `xsd:element type` attributes. The allowed content of elements and attributes with the new type can be specified by one of three child elements:

- `xsd:restriction` to select a subset of the values allowed by the base type
- `xsd:union` to combine multiple types
- `xsd:list` to specify a list of elements of an existing simple type

Deriving by restriction

To create a new type by restricting from an existing type, give the `xsd:simpleType` element an `xsd:restriction` child element. The `base` attribute of this element specifies what type you're restricting. For example, this `xsd:simpleType` element creates a new type named `phonoYear` that's derived from `xsd:gYear`:

```
<xsd:simpleType name="phonoYear">
  <xsd:restriction base="xsd:gYear">
  </xsd:restriction>
</xsd:simpleType>
```

With this declaration, any legal `xsd:gYear` is also a legal `phonoYear`, and any illegal year is also an illegal `phonoYear`. You can limit `phonoYear` to a subset of the normal year values by using *facets* to specify which values are and are not allowed. For example, the `minInclusive` facet defines the minimum legal value for a type. This facet is added to a restriction as an `xsd:minInclusive` child element. The `value` attribute of the `xsd:minInclusive` element sets the minimum allowed value for the year:

```
<xsd:simpleType name="phonoYear">
  <xsd:restriction base="xsd:gYear">
    <xsd:minInclusive value="1877"/>
  </xsd:restriction>
</xsd:simpleType>
```

Here the `value` of `xsd:minInclusive` is set to 1877, the year Thomas Edison invented the phonograph. Thus, 1877 is a legal `phonoYear`, 1878 is a legal `phonoYear`, 2001 is a legal `phonoYear`, and 3005 is a legal `phonoYear`. However, 1876, 1875, 1874, and earlier years are not legal `phonoYear`s, even though they are legal `xsd:gYear`s.

After the `phonoYear` type has been defined, you can use it just like one of the built-in types. For example, in the `SONG` schema, you'd declare that the `year` element has the type `phonoYear`, like this:

```
<xsd:element type="phonoYear"/>
```

`minInclusive` is not the only facet you can apply to `xsd:gYear`. Other facets of `xsd:gYear` are as follows:

- `xsd:minExclusive`—The minimum value that all instances must be strictly greater than
- `xsd:maxInclusive`—The maximum value that all instances must be less than or equal to
- `xsd:maxExclusive`—The maximum value that all instances must be strictly less than
- `xsd:enumeration`—A list of all legal values
- `xsd:whiteSpace`—How white space is treated within the element
- `xsd:pattern`—A regular expression to which the instance is compared

Each facet is represented as an empty element inside an `xsd:restriction` element. Each facet has a `value` attribute giving the value of that facet. One restriction can contain more than one facet. For example, this `xsd:simpleType` element defines a `phonoYear` as any year between 1877 and 2100, inclusive:

```
<xsd:simpleType name="phonoYear">
  <xsd:restriction base="xsd:gYear">
    <xsd:minInclusive value="1877"/>
    <xsd:maxInclusive value="2100"/>
  </xsd:restriction>
</xsd:simpleType>
```

It's possible that multiple facets may conflict. For example, the `minInclusive` value could be 2100 and the `maxInclusive` value could be 1877. While this is probably a design mistake, it is syntactically legal. It would just mean that the set of `phonoYear`s was the empty set, and `phonoYear` type elements could not actually be used in instance documents.

Facets

Facets are shared among many types. For example, the minInclusive facet can constrain essentially any well-ordered type, including not only xsd:gYear, but also xsd:byte, xsd:unsignedByte, xsd:integer, xsd:positiveInteger, xsd:negativeInteger, xsd:nonNegativeInteger, xsd:nonPositiveInteger, xsd:int, xsd:unsignedInt, xsd:long, xsd:unsignedLong, xsd:short, xsd:unsignedShort, xsd:decimal, xsd:float, xsd:double, xsd:time, xsd:dateTime, xsd:duration, xsd:date, xsd:gMonth, xsd:gYearMonth, and xsd:gMonthDay. The complete list of constraining facets that can be applied to different types is as follows:

- ✦ xsd:minInclusive—The value that all instances must be greater than or equal to
- ✦ xsd:minExclusive—The value that all instances must be strictly greater than
- ✦ xsd:maxInclusive—The value that all instances must be less than or equal to
- ✦ xsd:maxExclusive—The value that all instances must be strictly less than
- ✦ xsd:enumeration—A list of all legal values
- ✦ xsd:whiteSpace—How white space is treated within the element
- ✦ xsd:pattern—A regular expression to which the instance is compared
- ✦ xsd:length—The exact number of characters in a string, items in a list, or bytes in binary data
- ✦ xsd:minLength—The minimum length
- ✦ xsd:maxLength—The maximum length
- ✦ xsd:totalDigits—The maximum number of digits allowed in the element
- ✦ xsd:fractionDigits—The maximum number of digits allowed in the fractional part of the element

Not all facets apply to all types. For example, it doesn't make much sense to talk about the minimum value of an xsd:NMTOKEN or the number of fraction digits in an xsd:gYear. However, when the same facet is shared by different types, it has the same syntax and basic meaning for all the types.

Facets for strings: length, minLength, maxLength

The three length facets—xsd:length, xsd:minLength, and xsd:maxLength—specify the number of units allowed in a value. For xsd:string and its subtypes—xsd:normalizedString, xsd:token, xsd:hexBinary, xsd:base64Binary, xsd:QName, xsd:NCName, xsd:ID, xsd:IDREF, xsd:IDREFS, xsd:language, xsd:anyURI, xsd:ENTITY, xsd:NOTATION, xsd:NOTATIONS, xsd:NMTOKEN, and xsd:NMTOKENS—the units are characters and these facets specify the number of characters allowed in the element or attribute value. For list types—xsd:ENTITIES, xsd:NOTATIONS, and xsd:NMTOKENS—these facets control the number of instances in the list. And finally for the two binary types—xsd:base64Binary and xsd:hexBinary—these control the number of bytes in the decoded value. The value attribute of each of these facets must contain a nonnegative integer. xsd:length sets the exact number of units in the value, whereas xsd:minLength sets the minimum length and xsd:maxLength sets the maximum length.

For example, the schema in Listing 20-18 uses the xsd:minLength and xsd:maxLength facets to derive a new Str255 data type from xsd:string. Whereas xsd:string allows strings of any length from zero on up, Str255 requires each string to have a minimum length of 1 and a maximum length of 255. The schema then assigns this data type to all the names and titles to indicate that each must contain between 1 and 255 characters.

Listing 20-18: A Schema That Derives a Str255 Data Type from xsd:string

```
<?xml version="1.0"?>
<xsd:schema xmlns:xsd="http://www.w3.org/2001/XMLSchema">

  <xsd:simpleType name="Str255">
    <xsd:restriction base="xsd:string">
      <xsd:minLength value="1"/>
      <xsd:maxLength value="255"/>
    </xsd:restriction>
  </xsd:simpleType>

  <xsd:element name="SONG" type="SongType"/>

  <xsd:complexType name="SongType">
    <xsd:sequence>
      <xsd:element name="TITLE"     type="Str255"/>
      <xsd:element name="COMPOSER"  type="Str255"
                   maxOccurs="unbounded"/>
      <xsd:element name="PRODUCER"  type="Str255"
                   minOccurs="0"    maxOccurs="unbounded"/>
      <xsd:element name="PUBLISHER" type="Str255"
                   minOccurs="0"/>
      <xsd:element name="LENGTH"    type="xsd:duration"/>
      <xsd:element name="YEAR"      type="xsd:gYear"/>
      <xsd:element name="ARTIST"    type="Str255"
                   maxOccurs="unbounded"/>
      <xsd:element name="PRICE"     type="xsd:string"
                   minOccurs="0"/>
    </xsd:sequence>
  </xsd:complexType>

</xsd:schema>
```

The whiteSpace facet

The `whiteSpace` facet is unusual. Unlike the other 11 facets, `xsd:whiteSpace` does not in any way constrain the allowed content of elements. Instead, it suggests what the application should do with any white space that it finds in the instance document. It says how significant that white space is. However, it does not say that any particular kind of white space is legal or illegal.

The `xsd:whiteSpace` facet has three possible values:

- `preserve`—The white space in the input document is unchanged.
- `replace`—Each tab, carriage return, and linefeed is replaced with a single space.
- `collapse`—Each tab, carriage return, and linefeed is replaced with a single space. Furthermore, after this replacement is performed, all runs of multiple spaces are condensed to a single space. Leading and trailing white space is deleted.

Again, these are all just hints to the application. None of them have any effect on validation.

The `whiteSpace` facet can only be applied to `xsd:string`, `xsd:normalizedString`, and `xsd:token` types. Furthermore, it only fully applies to elements. XML 1.0 requires that parsers replace all white space in attributes, and collapse white space in attributes whose DTD type is anything other than CDATA, regardless of what the schema says.

The schema in Listing 20-19 uses the `xsd:whiteSpace` facets to derive a new `CollapsedString` data type from `xsd:string`. Then it assigns this data type to all the names and titles to indicate that white space should be collapsed in these elements.

Listing 20-19: A Schema That Suggests Collapsing White Space in Elements

```
<?xml version="1.0"?>
<xsd:schema xmlns:xsd="http://www.w3.org/2001/XMLSchema">

  <xsd:element name="SONG" type="SongType"/>

  <xsd:simpleType name="CollapsedString">
    <xsd:restriction base="xsd:string">
       <xsd:whiteSpace value="collapse"/>
    </xsd:restriction>
  </xsd:simpleType>

  <xsd:complexType name="SongType">
    <xsd:sequence>
```

```
      <xsd:element name="TITLE"     type="CollapsedString"/>
      <xsd:element name="COMPOSER"  type="CollapsedString"
        maxOccurs="unbounded"/>
      <xsd:element name="PRODUCER"  type="CollapsedString"
        minOccurs="0" maxOccurs="unbounded"/>
      <xsd:element name="PUBLISHER" type="CollapsedString"
        minOccurs="0"/>
      <xsd:element name="LENGTH"    type="xsd:duration"/>
      <xsd:element name="YEAR"      type="xsd:gYear"/>
      <xsd:element name="ARTIST"    type="CollapsedString"
        maxOccurs="unbounded"/>
      <xsd:element name="PRICE"     type="xsd:string"
                   minOccurs="0"/>
    </xsd:sequence>
  </xsd:complexType>

</xsd:schema>
```

Facets for decimal numbers: totalDigits and fractionDigits

When you are formatting numbers, it's useful to be able to specify how many digits should be used in the entire number, the integer parts, and the fraction parts. Schemas don't go as far in this regard as the `printf()` function in C or the `java.text.DecimalFormat` class in Java, but they do offer you some control.

The `xsd:totalDigits` facet specifies the maximum number of decimal digits in a number. It applies to most numeric types including `xsd:byte`, `xsd:unsignedByte`, `xsd:integer`, `xsd:positiveInteger`, `xsd:negativeInteger`, `xsd:nonNegativeInteger`, `xsd:nonPositiveInteger`, `xsd:int`, `xsd:unsignedInt`, `xsd:long`, `xsd:unsignedLong`, `xsd:short`, `xsd:unsignedShort`, and `xsd:decimal`. The only exceptions are the IEEE 754 types that occupy a fixed number of bytes; that is, `xsd:float` and `xsd:double`. The value of this facet must be a positive integer.

The `xsd:fractionDigits` facet specifies the maximum number of decimal digits to the right of the decimal point. (There is no facet that allows you to specify the minimum number of digits or fraction digits.) This only really applies to `xsd:decimal`. Technically, it applies to all the integer types too, but for those types it's fixed to the value zero; that is, no fraction digits at all. You're only allowed to change it for `xsd:decimal`. The value of this facet must be a nonnegative integer.

The enumeration facet

Rather than setting some sort of range on legal values, the `xsd:enumeration` facet simply lists all allowed values. It applies to every simple type except `xsd:boolean`. The syntax is a little unusual. Each possible value gets its own `xsd:enumeration` element as a child of the `xsd:restriction` element.

Listing 20-20 uses an enumeration to derive a `PublisherType` from `xsd:string`. It requires that the publisher be one of the oligopoly that controls 90 percent of all U.S. music (Warner-Elektra-Atlantic, Universal Music Group, Sony Music Entertainment, Inc., Capitol Records, Inc., and BMG Music).

Listing 20-20: A Schema That Uses an Enumeration to Derive a Type from xsd:string

```
<?xml version="1.0"?>
<xsd:schema xmlns:xsd="http://www.w3.org/2001/XMLSchema">

  <xsd:element name="SONG" type="songType"/>

  <xsd:simpleType name="PublisherType">
    <xsd:restriction base="xsd:string">
     <xsd:enumeration value="Warner-Elektra-Atlantic"/>
     <xsd:enumeration value="Universal Music Group"/>
     <xsd:enumeration value="Sony Music Entertainment, Inc."/>
     <xsd:enumeration value="Capitol Records, Inc."/>
     <xsd:enumeration value="BMG Music"/>
    </xsd:restriction>
  </xsd:simpleType>

  <xsd:complexType name="songType">
    <xsd:sequence>
      <xsd:element name="TITLE"     type="xsd:string"/>
      <xsd:element name="COMPOSER"  type="xsd:string"
        maxOccurs="unbounded"/>
      <xsd:element name="PRODUCER"  type="xsd:string"
        minOccurs="0" maxOccurs="unbounded"/>
      <xsd:element name="PUBLISHER" type="PublisherType"
        minOccurs="0"/>
      <xsd:element name="LENGTH"    type="xsd:duration"/>
      <xsd:element name="YEAR"      type="xsd:gYear"/>
      <xsd:element name="ARTIST"    type="xsd:string"
        maxOccurs="unbounded"/>
      <xsd:element name="PRICE"     type="xsd:string"
                   minOccurs="0"/>
    </xsd:sequence>
  </xsd:complexType>

</xsd:schema>
```

`xsd:string` is far from the only type you can derive from via enumeration. You can derive from `xsd:int`, `xsd:NMTOKEN`, `xsd:date`, and, indeed, from all simple types except `xsd:boolean`. Of course, the enumerated values all have to be legal instances of the base type.

The pattern facet

There's one element in the song examples that clearly deserves a data type, but so far doesn't have one — PRICE. However none of the built-in data types really match the format for prices. Recall that PRICE elements look like this:

```
<PRICE>$1.25</PRICE>
```

This isn't an integer of any kind, because it has a decimal point. It could be a floating-point number, but that wouldn't account for the currency sign. You could drop off the currency sign, like this:

```
<PRICE>1.25</PRICE>
```

However, then you'd have to assume you were working in dollars. What if you wanted to sell songs priced in pounds or yen or euros? Perhaps you could make the currency sign part of a separate element, like this:

```
<PRICE>
  <CURRENCY>$</CURRENCY>
  <AMOUNT>1.25</AMOUNT>
</PRICE>
```

AMOUNT could be an xsd:float, and CURRENCY could be an xsd:string. However, this still isn't perfect. You want to limit the CURRENCY to exactly one character, and that character must be a currency sign. You don't want to allow it to contain any arbitrary string. Furthermore, you'd like to limit the precision of the AMOUNT to exactly two decimal places. You probably don't want to sell songs that cost $1.1 or $1.99999.

The solution to this problem, and to many similar problems where the values you want to allow don't quite fit any of the existing types, is to use the xsd:pattern facet whose value attribute contains a regular expression that matches all legal values and doesn't match any illegal values.

The regular expressions used in schemas are similar to the regular expressions you might be familiar with from Perl, grep, or other languages. You use statements like [A-Z]+ to mean "a string containing one more of the capital letters from A to Z" or (club)* to mean "a string composed of zero or more repetitions of the word club."

Table 20-5 summarizes the grammar of XML schema regular expressions. In this table *A* and *B* represent some string or another regular expression particle from elsewhere in the table; that is, they will be replaced by something else when actually used in a regular expression. *n* and *m* represent some integer that will be replaced by a specific number.

Table 20-5
Regular Expression Symbols for XML Schema

<table>
<tr><th>Symbol</th><th>Meaning</th></tr>
<tr><td>A?</td><td>Zero or one occurrences of A</td></tr>
<tr><td>A*</td><td>Zero or more occurrences of A</td></tr>
<tr><td>A+</td><td>One or more occurrences of A</td></tr>
<tr><td>A{n,m}</td><td>Between n and m occurrences of A</td></tr>
<tr><td>A{n}</td><td>Exactly n occurrences of A</td></tr>
<tr><td>A{n,}</td><td>At least n occurrences of A</td></tr>
<tr><td>A|B</td><td>Either A or B</td></tr>
<tr><td>AB</td><td>A followed by B</td></tr>
<tr><td>.</td><td>Any one character</td></tr>
<tr><td>\p{A}</td><td>One character from Unicode character class A</td></tr>
<tr><td>[abcdefg]</td><td>A single occurrence of any of the characters contained in the brackets</td></tr>
<tr><td>[^abcdefg]</td><td>A single occurrence of any of the characters not contained in the brackets</td></tr>
<tr><td>[a-z]</td><td>A single occurrence of any character from a to z inclusive</td></tr>
<tr><td>[^a-z]</td><td>A single occurrence of any of character except those from a to z inclusive</td></tr>
<tr><td>\n</td><td>Linefeed</td></tr>
<tr><td>\r</td><td>Carriage return</td></tr>
<tr><td>\t</td><td>Tab</td></tr>
<tr><td>\\</td><td>Backward slash \</td></tr>
<tr><td>\|</td><td>Vertical bar |</td></tr>
<tr><td>\.</td><td>Period .</td></tr>
<tr><td>\-</td><td>Hyphen -</td></tr>
<tr><td>\^</td><td>Caret ^</td></tr>
<tr><td>\?</td><td>Question mark ?</td></tr>
<tr><td>*</td><td>Asterisk *</td></tr>
<tr><td>\+</td><td>Plus sign +</td></tr>
<tr><td>\{</td><td>Open brace {</td></tr>
<tr><td>\}</td><td>Closing brace }</td></tr>
</table>

Symbol	*Meaning*
`\(`	Open parenthesis (
`\)`	Closing parenthesis)
`\[`	Open bracket [
`\]`	Closing bracket]

For the most part, these symbols have exactly the same meanings that they have in Perl. The schema regular expression syntax is somewhat weaker than Perl's, but then whose isn't? In any case, this should be sufficient power to meet any reasonable needs that schemas have.

Schema regular expressions do have one important feature that isn't available prior to Perl 5.6 and is unfamiliar to most developers—you can use `\p{}` to stand in for a character in a particular Unicode character class. For example, `N` is the Unicode character class for numbers. This doesn't just include the European digits 0 through 9, but also the Arabic-Indic digits, the Devanagari digits, the Thai digits, and many more besides. Therefore, `\p{N}` represents any digit defined anywhere in Unicode. `\p{N}+` represents a string consisting of one or more Unicode digits. Table 20-6 lists the various Unicode character classes you can take advantage of in regular expressions. For the money regular expression, you need the `Sc` class for currency indicators and the `Nd` class for decimal digits. This is a little more restrictive than the N class, which includes nondecimal digits, such as the Roman numerals and the Han ideograph representing 100,000,000.

Table 20-6
Unicode Character Classes

Abbreviation	*Includes*	*Examples*
Letters		
L	All letters	a, b, c, A, B, C, ü, Ü, ç, Ç, ζ, θ, Z, Θ, а, б, в, А, Б, В, א, ב, ג, dz, Dz, DZ
Lu	Uppercase letters	A, B, C, Ü, Ç, Z, Θ, А, Б, В, DZ
Ll	Lowercase letters	a, b, c, ü, ç, ζ, θ, а, б, в, dz
Lt	Title case letters	Dz
Lm	Modifier letters; letters that are attached to the previous characters somehow	ʰ, ʲ, ʳ, ʷ
Lo	Other letters; typically ones from languages that don't distinguish upper- and lowercase	א, ב, ג, Japanese Katakana and Hiragana, most Han ideographs

Continued

Table 20-6 *(continued)*

Abbreviation	*Includes*	*Examples*
Marks		
M	All marks	
Mn	Nonspacing marks; mostly accent marks that are attached to the previous character on the top or bottom, and thus do not change the amount of space the character occupies	̀, ́, ̈, ̄
Mc	Spacing combining marks; accent marks that are attached to the previous character on the left or right, and thus do change the amount of space the character occupies	ਾ, Gurmukhi vowel sign AA
Me	Enclosing marks that completely surround a character	The Cyrillic hundred-thousands and millions signs
Numbers		
N	All numbers	0, 1, 2, 3, ¼, ½, ², ³, ٠, ٩, I, II, III, IV, V, Ⅰ, Ⅱ, Ⅲ, Ⅹ
Nd	Decimal digits; characters that represent one of the numbers 0 through 9	0, 1, 2, 3, ٠, ٩
Nl	Numbers based on letters	I, II, III, IV, Ⅰ, Ⅱ, Ⅲ, Ⅹ
No	Other numbers	¼, ½, ², ³
Punctuation		
P	All punctuation	-, _, ‿, (, [, {,),], }, ', ", «, ', ", », !, ?, @, *, ¡, ¿, ·
Pc	Connectors	_, ‿
Pd	Dashes	Hyphens, soft hyphens, em dashes, en dashes, etc.
Ps	Opening punctuation	(, [, {
Pe	Closing punctuation	),], }
Pi	Initial quote marks	', ", «
Pf	Final quote marks	', ", »
Po	Other punctuation marks	!, ?, @, *, ¡, ¿, ·

Abbreviation	*Includes*	*Examples*
Separators		
Z	All separators	
Zs	Space	Space, nonbreaking space, en space, em space
Zl	Line separators	Unicode character 2028, the line separator
Zp	Paragraph separators	Unicode character 2029, the paragraph separator
Symbols		
S	All symbols	∂, ∅ ∏, $, ¥, £, ~, ¯, ¨, *i*, ©, ®, °, ▲, ☺
Sm	Mathematical symbols	∂, ∅ π, ∑, √, ≠, ≤, ≥, ≈
Sc	Currency signs	$, ¥, £, ¤, €, ₣, ₤, ₧, ₪, ₫
Sk	Modifier symbols	~, ¯, ¨
So	Other symbols	©, ®, °, §, ¶, ↔, ℅, ℓ, ╓, ╖, ╟▲, ☺, ♀, ♂, ♠, ♪, Braille, Han radicals
Other		
C	All others	
Cc	Control characters	Carriage return, linefeed, tab and the C1 controls
Cf	Format characters	The left-to-right and right-to-left marks used to indicate change of direction in bidirectional text
Co	Private use characters; code points that may be used for a program's internal purposes	
Cn	Unassigned; code points that, while legal in XML, the Unicode specification has not yet assigned a character to	

You're now ready to put together a regular expression that describes money strings such as $1.25. What you want to say is that each such string contains the following:

You're now ready to put together a regular expression that describes money strings such as $1.25. What you want to say is that each such string contains the following:

1. A currency symbol
2. One or more decimal digits
3. An optional fractional part, which, if present at all, consists of a decimal point and two decimal digits

Here's the regular expression that says that

```
\p{Sc}\p{Nd}+(\.\p{Nd}\p{Nd})?
```

It begins with `\p{Sc}` to indicate a currency symbol such as $, ¥, £, or €.

This is followed by `\p{Nd}+`. `\p{Nd}` represents any decimal digit character. The + indicates one or more of these characters.

Next there's a parenthesized expression followed by a question mark, `(\.\p{Nd}\p{Nd})?`. The question mark indicates the parenthesized expression is optional. However, if it does appear, its entire contents must be present, not just part. In other words, the question mark stands for zero or one, just as it does in DTDs. The contents of the parentheses are `\.\p{Nd}\p{Nd}`, which represents a period followed by two decimal digits, for example .35. Normally a period in a regular expression means any character at all, so here it's escaped with a preceding backslash to indicate that we really do want the actual period character.

Now that you have a regular expression that represents money, you're ready to define a money type. As for the other facets, this is done with the `xsd:simpleType` and `xsd:restriction` elements. Putting these together with the regular expression produces this type definition:

```
<xsd:simpleType name="money">
  <xsd:restriction base="xsd:string">
    <xsd:pattern value="\p{Sc}\p{Nd}+(\.\p{Nd}\p{Nd})?"/>
  </xsd:restriction>
</xsd:simpleType>
```

Listing 20-21 provides the complete song schema, including this type definition. Take special note of the XML comment used to elucidate the regular expression. Regular expressions can be quite opaque, and a comment like this one can go a long way toward making the schema more comprehensible.

Listing 20-21: A Schema That Defines a Custom Money Type

```
<?xml version="1.0"?>
<xsd:schema xmlns:xsd="http://www.w3.org/2001/XMLSchema">

  <xsd:element name="SONG" type="SongType"/>

  <xsd:simpleType name="money">
    <xsd:restriction base="xsd:string">
      <xsd:pattern value="\p{Sc}\p{Nd}+(\.\p{Nd}\p{Nd})?"/>
      <!--
         Regular Expression:
         \p{Sc}              Any Unicode currency indicator;
                             e.g., $, &#xA5, &#xA3, &#A4, etc.
         \p{Nd}              A Unicode decimal digit character
         \p{Nd}+             One or more Unicode decimal digits
         \.                  The period character
         (\.\p{Nd}\p{Nd})
         (\.\p{Nd}\p{Nd})? Zero or one strings of the form .35

         This works for any decimalized currency.

      -->
    </xsd:restriction>
  </xsd:simpleType>

  <xsd:complexType name="SongType">
    <xsd:sequence>
      <xsd:element name="TITLE"     type="xsd:string"/>
      <xsd:element name="COMPOSER"  type="PersonType"
                   maxOccurs="unbounded"/>
      <xsd:element name="PRODUCER"  type="PersonType"
                   minOccurs="0" maxOccurs="unbounded"/>
      <xsd:element name="PUBLISHER" type="xsd:string"
                   minOccurs="0"/>
      <xsd:element name="LENGTH"    type="xsd:duration"/>
      <xsd:element name="YEAR"      type="xsd:gYear"/>
      <xsd:element name="ARTIST"    type="xsd:string"
                   maxOccurs="unbounded"/>
      <xsd:element name="PRICE" type="money" maxOccurs="1"/>
    </xsd:sequence>
  </xsd:complexType>

  <xsd:complexType name="PersonType">
    <xsd:sequence>
      <xsd:element name="NAME">
        <xsd:complexType>
          <xsd:all>
            <xsd:element name="GIVEN"  type="xsd:string"/>
```

Continued

Listing 20-21 *(continued)*

```
            <xsd:element name="FAMILY" type="xsd:string"/>
          </xsd:all>
        </xsd:complexType>
      </xsd:element>
    </xsd:sequence>
  </xsd:complexType>

</xsd:schema>
```

Unions

Restriction is not the only way to create a new simple type, although it is the most common way. You can also combine types using unions. For example, you could combine the built-in `xsd:decimal` type with the `money` type just defined to create a type that could contain either a decimal or a money value. To do this, give the `xsd:simpleType` element an `xsd:union` child element instead of an `xsd:restriction` child element. The `xsd:union` element contains more `xsd:simpleType` elements identifying the types you're combining in the union. For example, this is the previously described `money/xsd:decimal` combined type:

```
<xsd:simpleType name="MoneyOrDecimal">
  <xsd:union>
    <xsd:simpleType>
      <xsd:restriction base="xsd:decimal">
      </xsd:restriction>
    </xsd:simpleType>
    <xsd:simpleType>
      <xsd:restriction base="xsd:string">
        <xsd:pattern value="\p{Sc}\p{Nd}+(\.\p{Nd}\p{Nd})?"/>
      </xsd:restriction>
    </xsd:simpleType>
  </xsd:union>
</xsd:simpleType>
```

Lists

Schemas can also specify that an element or attribute contains a list of a particular simple type. For example, this `YEARS` element contains a list of years:

```
<YEARS>1987 1999 1992   2002</YEARS>
```

Elements such as this can be specified using an `xsd:list` in the `xsd:simpleType`. The `itemType` attribute says what type of strings may appear in the list, as in the following example:

```
<xsd:simpleType name="YearList">
  <xsd:list itemType="xsd:gYear"/>
</xsd:simpleType>
```

This requires that elements with type `YearList` contain a white space-separated list of legal `xsd:gYear` values.

I must admit that I'm not very fond of list types, especially for elements. It seems to me that if you're going to have a list of different items, each of those items should be a separate element, possibly a child element of some parent element, but still its own element. Lists make a little more sense for attributes, but if there's a lot of substructure in the text, you should probably be using an element instead of an attribute anyway.

You can derive another list type from an existing list type. When so doing, you can restrict it according to the `length`, `minLength`, `maxLength`, and `enumeration` facets. In this case, the values of the three length facets refer to the number of items in the list rather than the number of characters in the content. For example, this `xsd:simpleType` element derives a `DoubleYear` list type that must hold exactly two years from the `YearList` type previously defined:

```
<xsd:simpleType name="DoubleYear">
  <xsd:restriction base="YearList">
    <xsd:length value="2"/>
  </xsd:restriction>
</xsd:simpleType>
```

Empty Elements

Empty elements are those that cannot contain any child elements or parsed character data. This is the same as using the `EMPTY` content model in a DTD. As an example of this technique, I'll define an empty `PHOTO` element. This will be used in the next section when attributes are introduced.

To create an empty element, you define it as a type but don't give it an `xsd:sequence`, `xsd:all`, or `xsd:choice` child. Thus, you don't actually provide any child elements. For example:

```
<!-- An empty element -->
<xsd:complexType name="PhotoType">
</xsd:complexType>
```

This does not require the PHOTO element to be defined with an empty-element tag such as <PHOTO/>. The start-tag-end-tag pair <PHOTO></PHOTO> is also acceptable. In fact, the XML 1.0 specification says these two forms are equivalent. Schemas change nothing about XML 1.0. An XML 1.0 parser that knows nothing about schemas will have no trouble reading a document that uses schemas.

Attributes

In the examples so far, two XML constructs have been conspicuous by their absence: entities and attributes. The omission of entities was quite deliberate. Schemas cannot declare entities. If you need entities, you must use a DTD. (Of course, you can use a schema as well as the DTD.) However, schemas are fully capable of declaring attributes. Indeed, they do a much better job of it than DTDs do because schemas can use the full set of data types like xsd:float and xsd:anyURI.

You may not have noticed my avoidance of attributes, because the examples all used xmlns:xsi and xsi:noNamespaceSchemaLocation attributes on the root element. However, as far as a schema validator is concerned, attributes used to declare namespaces, or to attach documents to schemas, "don't count." You do not have to, and indeed should not, declare these attributes. However, you do have to declare all the other attributes you use.

As a concrete example, let's consider how you might add an empty PHOTO element to the SONG documents. This element would be similar to the IMG element in HTML and would have an SRC attribute that contained a URL pointing to the photo's location, an ALT attribute containing some text in the event that the PHOTO can't be displayed, and WIDTH and HEIGHT attributes that together give the size of the image in pixels. Listing 20-22 demonstrates.

Listing 20-22: The PHOTO Element Has Several Attributes of Different Types

```
<?xml version="1.0"?>
<SONG xmlns:xsi="http://www.w3.org/2001/XMLSchema-instance"
      xsi:noNamespaceSchemaLocation="20-23.xsd">
  <TITLE>Yes I Am</TITLE>
  <PHOTO ALT="Melissa Etheridge holding a guitar"
         WIDTH="100" HEIGHT="300"
         SRC="guitar.jpg"/>
  <COMPOSER>
    <NAME>
      <GIVEN>Melissa</GIVEN>
      <FAMILY>Etheridge</FAMILY>
    </NAME>
```

```
    </COMPOSER>
    <PRODUCER>
      <NAME>
        <GIVEN>Hugh</GIVEN>
        <FAMILY>Padgham</FAMILY>
      </NAME>
    </PRODUCER>
    <PRODUCER>
      <NAME>
        <GIVEN>Melissa</GIVEN>
        <FAMILY>Etheridge</FAMILY>
      </NAME>
    </PRODUCER>
    <PUBLISHER>Island Records</PUBLISHER>
    <LENGTH>P0YT4M24S</LENGTH>
    <YEAR>1993</YEAR>
    <ARTIST>Melissa Etheridge</ARTIST>
    <PRICE>$1.25</PRICE>
  </SONG>
```

Even though the PHOTO element is empty, because it has attributes, it has a complex type. You define a PhotoType just as you previously defined a PersonType and a SongType. However, where those types used xsd:element to declare child elements, this type will use xsd:attribute to declare attributes.

```
<xsd:complexType name="PhotoType">
  <xsd:attribute name="SRC"    type="xsd:anyURI"/>
  <xsd:attribute name="WIDTH"  type="xsd:positiveInteger"/>
  <xsd:attribute name="HEIGHT" type="xsd:positiveInteger"/>
  <xsd:attribute name="ALT"    type="xsd:string"/>
</xsd:complexType>
```

Because the SRC attribute should contain a URL, it's been given the type xsd:anyURI. Because the HEIGHT and WIDTH attributes should each be an integer greater than zero, they're given the type xsd:positiveInteger. Finally, because the ALT attribute can contain essentially any string of text of any length, it's set to the most general type, xsd:string.

In this particular example, all the elements either have child elements or attributes, not both. However, that's certainly not required. In general, elements can have both child elements and attributes. Just use both xsd:element and xsd:attribute in the same xsd:complexType element. The xsd:attribute elements must come after the xsd:sequence, xsd:choice, or xsd:all group that forms the body of the element. For example, this xsd:element says that a PERSON element can have an optional attribute named ID with type ID:

```
<xsd:complexType name="PersonType">
  <xsd:sequence>
    <xsd:element name="NAME">
      <xsd:complexType>
```

```
          <xsd:all>
            <xsd:element name="GIVEN"  type="xsd:string"/>
            <xsd:element name="FAMILY" type="xsd:string"/>
          </xsd:all>
        </xsd:complexType>
      </xsd:element>
    </xsd:sequence>
    <xsd:attribute name="ID" type="xsd:ID"/>
  </xsd:complexType>
```

Attributes can also be attached to elements that can only contain text such as an xsd:string or an xsd:gYear. The details are a little more complex, because an element with attributes by definition has a complex type. To make this work, you derive a new complex type from a simple type by giving the xsd:complexType element an xsd:simpleContent child element instead of an xsd:sequence, xsd:choice, or xsd:all. The xsd:simpleContent element itself has an xsd:extension child element whose base attribute identifies the simple type to extend such as xsd:string. The xsd:attribute elements are placed inside the xsd:extension element.

For example, suppose you want to allow the TITLE elements to have ID attributes, like this:

```
<TITLE ID="test">Yes I Am</TITLE>
```

Previously, TITLE was defined with type xsd:string. Instead, let's derive a new type called StringWithID from xsd:string, like this:

```
<xsd:complexType name="StringWithID">
  <xsd:simpleContent>
    <xsd:extension base="xsd:string">
      <xsd:attribute name="ID" type="xsd:ID"/>
    </xsd:extension>
  </xsd:simpleContent>
</xsd:complexType>
```

The StringWithID type can then be applied to the TITLE element in the usual way, like this:

```
<xsd:element name="TITLE" type="StringWithID"/>
```

By default, attributes declared in schemas are optional (#IMPLIED in DTD terminology). However, an xsd:attribute can have a use attribute with the value required to indicate that the element must occur. In this case, you probably do want to insist that each of the four attributes be present. Therefore, the declaration of PhotoType becomes this:

```
  <xsd:complexType name="PhotoType">
    <xsd:attribute name="SRC"    type="xsd:anyURI"
                   use="required" />
    <xsd:attribute name="WIDTH"  type="xsd:positiveInteger"
```

```
                      use="required" />
    <xsd:attribute name="HEIGHT" type="xsd:positiveInteger"
                      use="required" />
    <xsd:attribute name="ALT"    type="xsd:string"
                      use="required" />
  </xsd:complexType>
```

The use attribute can also have the value optional to indicate that it may or may not be present. (This is also the default if there is no use attribute.) If optional, xsd:attribute may also have a default attribute giving the value the parser will provide if it doesn't find one in the instance document. If there is no default attribute, this is the same as #IMPLIED in ATTLIST declarations in DTDs. Instead of a use attribute, xsd:attribute can have a fixed attribute whose value is the constant value for the attribute, whether present in the instance document or not. This has the same effect as #FIXED in DTDs. Listing 20-23 puts this all together in a complete schema for songs, including a PHOTO element with several required attributes.

Listing 20-23: A SONG Schema That Declares Attributes

```
<?xml version="1.0"?>
<xsd:schema xmlns:xsd="http://www.w3.org/2001/XMLSchema">

  <xsd:element name="SONG" type="SongType"/>

  <xsd:complexType name="PhotoType">
    <xsd:attribute name="SRC"    type="xsd:anyURI"
                      use="required" />
    <xsd:attribute name="WIDTH"  type="xsd:positiveInteger"
                      use="required" />
    <xsd:attribute name="HEIGHT" type="xsd:positiveInteger"
                      use="required" />
    <xsd:attribute name="ALT"    type="xsd:string"
                      use="required" />
  </xsd:complexType>

  <xsd:complexType name="SongType">
    <xsd:sequence>
      <xsd:element name="TITLE"     type="xsd:string"/>
      <xsd:element name="PHOTO"     type="PhotoType"/>
      <xsd:element name="COMPOSER"  type="PersonType"
                   maxOccurs="unbounded"/>
      <xsd:element name="PRODUCER"  type="PersonType"
                   minOccurs="0" maxOccurs="unbounded"/>
      <xsd:element name="PUBLISHER" type="xsd:string"
                   minOccurs="0"/>
      <xsd:element name="LENGTH"    type="xsd:duration"/>
      <xsd:element name="YEAR"      type="xsd:gYear"/>
      <xsd:element name="ARTIST"    type="xsd:string"
                   maxOccurs="unbounded"/>
```

Continued

Listing 20-23 (continued)

```
        <xsd:element name="PRICE" type="money"/>
      </xsd:sequence>
    </xsd:complexType>

    <xsd:simpleType name="money">
      <xsd:restriction base="xsd:string">
        <xsd:pattern value="\p{Sc}\p{Nd}+(\.\p{Nd}\p{Nd})?"/>
        <!--
           Regular Expression:
           \p{Sc}              Any Unicode currency indicator;
                               e.g., $, &#xA5, &#xA3, &#A4, etc.
           \p{Nd}              A Unicode decimal digit character
           \p{Nd}+             One or more Unicode decimal digits
           \.                  The period character
           (\.\p{Nd}\p{Nd})
           (\.\p{Nd}\p{Nd})?   Zero or one strings of the form .35

           This works for any decimalized currency.

        -->
      </xsd:restriction>
    </xsd:simpleType>

    <xsd:complexType name="PersonType">
      <xsd:sequence>
        <xsd:element name="NAME">
          <xsd:complexType>
            <xsd:all>
              <xsd:element name="GIVEN"  type="xsd:string"/>
              <xsd:element name="FAMILY" type="xsd:string"/>
            </xsd:all>
          </xsd:complexType>
        </xsd:element>
      </xsd:sequence>
    </xsd:complexType>

  </xsd:schema>
```

Namespaces

So far, the example song documents have been blissfully namespace-free. Adding namespaces to the documents and designing a schema that applies to the namespace-qualified documents is not particularly difficult. Namespaces add some important features, such as the ability to write schemas and validate documents that use elements and attributes from multiple XML applications. However, the terminology is a little confusing. Some words, such as *qualified*, don't mean quite the same thing in schemas as they do in other XML technologies, so you do need to pay close attention and read what follows carefully.

Schemas for default namespaces

Let's begin with a simple example in which the XML application described by the schema uses a single default, nonprefixed namespace. Most of the time each namespace URI maps to exactly one schema (though later you'll learn several techniques to break large schemas into parts using `xsd:import` and `xsd:include`).

The schema for elements that are not in any namespace is identified by an `xsi:noNamespaceSchemaLocation` attribute. The schemas for elements that are in namespaces are identified by an `xsi:schemaLocation` attribute. This attribute contains a list of namespace URI/schema URI pairs. Each namespace URI is followed by one schema URI. The namespace URI is almost always absolute, but the schema URI is almost always a URL and often a relative URL.

Listing 20-24 demonstrates. This is the familiar hotcop.xml document that you've seen several times already, though it's been simplified a bit to keep the examples smaller. All the elements in this document are in the `http://ns.cafeconleche.org/song` namespace defined by the `xmlns` attribute on the root element. The attributes in this document are not in any namespace because they don't have prefixes. There are two things you need to remember here:

1. Attributes without prefixes are never in any namespace, no matter what namespace their parent element is in, and no matter what default namespace the document uses.
2. For purposes of schema validation, namespace declaration attributes, such as `xmlns` and `xmlns:xsi`, and schema attachment attributes, such as `xsi:schemaLocation`, don't count. You do not need to declare these in your schema.

In this case, all the elements are in the `http://ns.cafeconleche.org/song` namespace, so an `xsi:schemaLocation` attribute is needed to associate this namespace with a URL where the schema can be found, `namespace_song.xsd` for this example.

Listing 20-24: A SONG Document in the http://ns.cafeconleche.org/song Namespace

```
<?xml version="1.0" encoding="UTF-8" standalone="no"?>
<SONG xmlns="http://ns.cafeconleche.org/song"
      xmlns:xsi="http://www.w3.org/2001/XMLSchema-instance"
      xsi:schemaLocation =
       "http://ns.cafeconleche.org/song
```

Continued

Listing 20-24 *(continued)*

```
        namespace_song.xsd"
>
  <TITLE>Hot Cop</TITLE>
  <!-- I've temporarily dropped the SRC attribute on this
       element. I'm going to replace it with XLinks shortly.
    -->
  <PHOTO ALT="Victor Willis in Cop Outfit" WIDTH="100"
        HEIGHT="200"/>
  <COMPOSER>Jacques Morali</COMPOSER>
  <COMPOSER>Henri Belolo</COMPOSER>
  <COMPOSER>Victor Willis</COMPOSER>
  <PRODUCER>Jacques Morali</PRODUCER>
  <PUBLISHER>PolyGram Records</PUBLISHER>
  <LENGTH>P0YT6M20S</LENGTH>
  <YEAR>1978</YEAR>
  <ARTIST>Village People</ARTIST>
</SONG>
```

What does namespace_song.xsd look like? Listing 20-25 shows you. It's much the same schema as before, although I've dropped the `MoneyType` and `PersonType` to save a little room.

Listing 20-25: A Schema for SONG Documents in the http://ns.cafeconleche.org/song Namespace

```
<?xml version="1.0"?>
<xsd:schema xmlns:xsd="http://www.w3.org/2001/XMLSchema"
  xmlns="http://ns.cafeconleche.org/song"
  targetNamespace="http://ns.cafeconleche.org/song"
  elementFormDefault="qualified"
  attributeFormDefault="unqualified"
>

  <xsd:element name="SONG" type="SongType"/>

  <xsd:complexType name="PhotoType">
    <xsd:attribute name="WIDTH"  type="xsd:positiveInteger"
                   use="required" />
    <xsd:attribute name="HEIGHT" type="xsd:positiveInteger"
                   use="required" />
    <xsd:attribute name="ALT"    type="xsd:string"
                   use="required" />
  </xsd:complexType>

  <xsd:complexType name="SongType">
    <xsd:sequence>
```

```
      <xsd:element name="TITLE"     type="xsd:string"/>
      <xsd:element name="PHOTO"     type="PhotoType"/>
      <xsd:element name="COMPOSER"  type="xsd:string"
                   maxOccurs="unbounded"/>
      <xsd:element name="PRODUCER"  type="xsd:string"
                   minOccurs="0" maxOccurs="unbounded"/>
      <xsd:element name="PUBLISHER" type="xsd:string"
                   minOccurs="0"/>
      <xsd:element name="LENGTH"    type="xsd:duration"/>
      <xsd:element name="YEAR"      type="xsd:gYear"/>
      <xsd:element name="ARTIST"    type="xsd:string"
                   maxOccurs="unbounded"/>
    </xsd:sequence>
  </xsd:complexType>

</xsd:schema>
```

The main body of the schema is much the same as before. However, the `xsd:schema` start-tag has several new attributes. It looks like this:

```
<xsd:schema xmlns:xsd="http://www.w3.org/2001/XMLSchema"
  xmlns="http://ns.cafeconleche.org/song"
  targetNamespace="http://ns.cafeconleche.org/song"
  elementFormDefault="qualified"
  attributeFormDefault="unqualified"
>
```

The first `xmlns` attribute establishes the default namespace for this schema, which is, after all, an XML document itself. It sets the namespace to `http://ns.cafeconleche.org/song`, the same as in the instance documents you're trying to model. This says that the unprefixed element names used in this schema such as `PhotoType` are in the `http://ns.cafeconleche.org/song` namespace.

The second attribute says that this schema applies to documents in the `http://ns.cafeconleche.org/song` namespace; that is, the elements identified by `name` attributes such as `SONG`, `PHOTO`, and `TITLE` are in the `http://ns.cafeconleche.org/song` namespace.

The third attribute, `elementFormDefault`, has the value `qualified`. This means that the elements being described in this document are in fact in a namespace; specifically, they're in the target namespace given by the `targetNamespace` attribute. This does not mean that the elements being modeled necessarily have prefixes, merely that they are in some namespace.

Finally, the fourth attribute, `attributeFormDefault`, has the value `unqualified`. This means that the attributes described by this schema are not in a namespace.

Schemas have one major advantage over DTDs when you are working with documents with namespaces. They validate against the local name and the namespace URIs of the elements and attributes, not the prefix and the local name like DTDs do. This means the prefixes do not have to match in the schema and in the instance documents. Indeed, one might use prefixes and the other might use the default namespace.

For example, consider Listing 20-26. This is the same as Listing 20-24 except that it uses the `song` prefix rather than the default namespace to indicate the `http://ns.cafeconleche.org/song` namespace. However, it can use the *exact same schema*! The schema does not need to change just because the prefix (or lack thereof) has changed. As long as the namespace URI stays the same, the schema is happy.

Listing 20-26: A SONG Document in the http://ns.cafeconleche.org/song Namespace with Prefixes

```
<?xml version="1.0" encoding="UTF-8" standalone="no"?>
<song:SONG
      xmlns:song="http://ns.cafeconleche.org/song"
      xmlns:xsi="http://www.w3.org/2001/XMLSchema-instance"
      xsi:schemaLocation =
       "http://ns.cafeconleche.org/song
        namespace_song.xsd"
>
  <song:TITLE>Hot Cop</song:TITLE>
  <!-- I've temporarily dropped the SRC attribute on this
       element. I'm going to replace it with XLinks shortly.
    -->
  <song:PHOTO ALT="Victor Willis in Cop Outfit" WIDTH="100"
        HEIGHT="200"/>
  <song:COMPOSER>Jacques Morali</song:COMPOSER>
  <song:COMPOSER>Henri Belolo</song:COMPOSER>
  <song:COMPOSER>Victor Willis</song:COMPOSER>
  <song:PRODUCER>Jacques Morali</song:PRODUCER>
  <song:PUBLISHER>PolyGram Records</song:PUBLISHER>
  <song:LENGTH>P0YT6M20S</song:LENGTH>
  <song:YEAR>1978</song:YEAR>
  <song:ARTIST>Village People</song:ARTIST>
</song:SONG>
```

Multiple namespaces, multiple schemas

Now, consider the case in which one document mixes markup from different vocabularies. In particular, suppose that you want to use XLink to connect the `PHOTO` element to the actual JPEG image rather than application-specific markup such as `SRC`.

You need to set `xlink:type`, `xlink:href`, `xlink:show`, and `xlink:actuate` attributes on the `PHOTO` element to give it the proper meaning and behavior, like this:

```
<PHOTO xlink:type="simple" xlink:href="hotcop.jpg"
       xlink:show="embed"  xlink:actuate="onLoad"
       ALT="Victor Willis in Cop Outfit"
       WIDTH="100" HEIGHT="200"/>
```

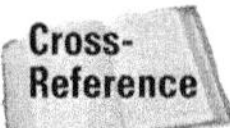

XLinks are discussed in Chapter 17.

Now the document uses two main namespaces, the `http://ns.cafeconleche.org/song` namespace for songs and the `http://www.w3.org/1999/xlink` namespace for XLinks. Thus, it needs two schemas. However, because the root element can have only one `xsi:schemaLocation` attribute, it has to serve double duty and declare both. Listing 20-27 demonstrates.

Listing 20-27: A SONG Document That Uses XLink to Embed Photos

```
<?xml version="1.0" encoding="UTF-8" standalone="no"?>
<SONG xmlns="http://ns.cafeconleche.org/song"
      xmlns:xlink="http://www.w3.org/1999/xlink"
      xmlns:xsi="http://www.w3.org/2001/XMLSchema-instance"
      xsi:schemaLocation =
      "http://ns.cafeconleche.org/song 20-29.xsd
       http://www.w3.org/1999/xlink xlink.xsd"
>
  <TITLE>Hot Cop</TITLE>
  <PHOTO xlink:type="simple" xlink:href="hotcop.jpg"
         xlink:show="embed"  xlink:actuate="onLoad"
         ALT="Victor Willis in Cop Outfit"
         WIDTH="100" HEIGHT="200"/>
  <COMPOSER>Jacques Morali</COMPOSER>
  <COMPOSER>Henri Belolo</COMPOSER>
  <COMPOSER>Victor Willis</COMPOSER>
  <PRODUCER>Jacques Morali</PRODUCER>
  <PUBLISHER>PolyGram Records</PUBLISHER>
  <LENGTH>P0YT6M20S</LENGTH>
  <YEAR>1978</YEAR>
  <ARTIST>Village People</ARTIST>
</SONG>
```

Listing 20-28 shows the XLink schema. It only declares attributes, no elements at all. You haven't seen an example of this yet, but it's not hard. Just use `xsd:attribute` elements at the top level, that is, as direct children of the `xsd:schema` element. The other difference between these top-level xsd:attribute elements and the ones you've seen before is that three of the attributes have fixed values and don't even need to be explicitly included in the instance document. Only the xlink:href attribute asks the author to supply a value. However, this is rather specific to this particular use of XLink. Almost anything else you'd do with an XLink other than embedding an image or other non-XML content into the document would require a different schema that used different defaults.

Listing 20-28: xlink.xsd: An XLink Schema

```
<?xml version="1.0" encoding="UTF-8" standalone="no"?>
<xsd:schema xmlns:xsd="http://www.w3.org/2001/XMLSchema"
  xmlns="http://www.w3.org/1999/xlink"
  targetNamespace="http://www.w3.org/1999/xlink"
  attributeFormDefault="unqualified"
>

  <xsd:attribute name="type"    type="xsd:string"
                 fixed="simple"/>
  <xsd:attribute name="href"    type="xsd:anyURI"/>
  <xsd:attribute name="actuate" type="xsd:string"
                 fixed="onLoad"/>
  <xsd:attribute name="show"    type="xsd:string"
                 fixed="embed"/>

</xsd:schema>
```

This schema doesn't actually apply these attributes to any elements. Therefore, the schema that does describe the PHOTO element needs to import xlink.xsd in order to reference these declarations. This is done with an xsd:import element. The xsd:import's schemaLocation attribute tells the processor where to find the schema to import. The namespace attribute says which elements and attributes the schema declares. After this schema has been imported, you can add those attributes to any xsd:complexType by giving it an xsd:attribute child whose ref attribute identifies the attribute to be attached. Listing 20-29 demonstrates.

Listing 20-29: A SONG Schema That Imports the XLink Schema

```
<?xml version="1.0"?>
<xsd:schema xmlns:xsd="http://www.w3.org/2001/XMLSchema"
  xmlns="http://ns.cafeconleche.org/song"
  xmlns:xlink="http://www.w3.org/1999/xlink"
  targetNamespace="http://ns.cafeconleche.org/song"
  elementFormDefault="qualified"
```

```
    attributeFormDefault="unqualified"
  >

    <xsd:import namespace="http://www.w3.org/1999/xlink"
                schemaLocation="xlink.xsd"/>

    <xsd:element name="SONG" type="SongType"/>

    <xsd:complexType name="PhotoType">
      <xsd:attribute name="WIDTH"  type="xsd:positiveInteger"
                     use="required" />
      <xsd:attribute name="HEIGHT" type="xsd:positiveInteger"
                     use="required" />
      <xsd:attribute name="ALT"    type="xsd:string"
                     use="required" />
      <xsd:attribute ref="xlink:type"/>
      <xsd:attribute ref="xlink:href" use="required"/>
      <xsd:attribute ref="xlink:actuate"/>
      <xsd:attribute ref="xlink:show"/>
    </xsd:complexType>

    <xsd:complexType name="SongType">
      <xsd:sequence>
        <xsd:element name="TITLE"     type="xsd:string"/>
        <xsd:element name="PHOTO"     type="PhotoType"/>
        <xsd:element name="COMPOSER"  type="xsd:string"
                     maxOccurs="unbounded"/>
        <xsd:element name="PRODUCER"  type="xsd:string"
                     minOccurs="0" maxOccurs="unbounded"/>
        <xsd:element name="PUBLISHER" type="xsd:string"
                     minOccurs="0"/>
        <xsd:element name="LENGTH"    type="xsd:duration"/>
        <xsd:element name="YEAR"      type="xsd:gYear"/>
        <xsd:element name="ARTIST"    type="xsd:string"
                     maxOccurs="unbounded"/>
      </xsd:sequence>
    </xsd:complexType>

  </xsd:schema>
```

Annotations

At some point in this chapter, it's likely to have occurred to you that schemas can get rather large and complex. If that hasn't occurred to you yet, just imagine a schema not for the very small and simple song documents demonstrated in this chapter, but for much larger XML applications such as Scalable Vector Graphics or XHTML.

You can certainly use regular XML comments to describe schemas, and I encourage you to do so, especially when you're doing something less than obvious in the schema. The W3C XML Schema Language also provides a more formal mechanism for annotating schemas. Both the top-level `xsd:schema` element itself and the various other schema elements (`xsd:complexType`, `xsd:all`, `xsd:element`, `xsd:attribute`, and so on) can contain `xsd:annotation` child elements that describe that part of the schema for human readers or for other computer programs. This element has two kinds of child elements:

✦ The `xsd:documentation` child element describes the schema for human readers. It often contains copyright and similar information.

✦ The `xsd:appInfo` child element describes the schema for computer programs. For example, it might contain instructions about what style sheets to apply to the schema.

Each `xsd:annotation` element can contain any number of either of these. However, no special syntax has been defined for the content of these elements. You can put anything in there you find convenient, including other XML markup, subject only to the usual well-formedness constraints. Thus, an `xsd:documentation` element might contain XHTML, and an `xsd:appInfo` element might contain XSLT. Then again, either or both might simply contain plain, unmarked-up text. For example, this annotation could be added to the song schemas developed in this chapter:

```
<xsd:annotation>
 <xsd:documentation>
  Song schema for Chapter 20 of the XML Bible, 3rd Edition
  Copyright 2004 Elliotte Rusty Harold.
  elharo@metalab.unc.edu
 </xsd:documentation>
</xsd:annotation>
```

Summary

In this chapter, you learned the following:

✦ Schemas address a number of perceived limitations of DTDs, including a strange, non-XML syntax, namespace incompatibility, lack of data typing, and limited extensibility and scalability.

✦ There are multiple XML schema languages, including RELAX NG and the W3C XML Schema Language (described in this chapter).

✦ An XML document can indicate the schema that applies to its non-namespace-qualified elements via an `xsi:noNamespaceSchemaLocation` attribute, which is normally placed on the root element.

- An XML document can indicate the schema that applies to its namespace qualified elements via an `xsi:schemaLocation` attribute, which is normally placed on the root element.
- Schemas declare elements with `xsd:element` elements.
- The `type` attribute of `xsd:element` specifies the data type of that element.
- Elements with complex types can have attributes and child elements.
- Elements with simple types only contain character data.
- The `xsd:complexType` element defines a new type for an element that can contain child elements, attributes, and/or mixed content.
- The `xsd:group`, `xsd:all`, `xsd:choice`, and `xsd:sequence` elements let you specify particular combinations of elements in an element's content model.
- The `minOccurs` and `maxOccurs` attributes of `xsd:element` determine how many of a given element are allowed in the instance document at that point. The default for each is 1. `maxOccurs` can be set to `unbounded` to indicate that any number of the element may appear.
- There are 44 built-in simple types, including many numeric, string, time, binary, URI, and XML types.
- The `xsd:simpleType` element defines a new type for an element or attribute that can only contain character data.
- You can define your own simple types by restricting an existing type such as `xsd:string` with the `xsd:restriction` element. The `base` attribute of the `xsd:restriction` child specifies what type you're deriving from.
- Each `xsd:restriction` element contains one or more child elements representing facets: `xsd:minInclusive`, `xsd:minExclusive`, `xsd:maxInclusive`, `xsd:maxExclusive`, `xsd:enumeration`, `xsd:whiteSpace`, `xsd:pattern`, `xsd:length`, `xsd:minLength`, `xsd:maxLength`, `xsd:totalDigits`, and/or `xsd:fractionDigits`.
- An `xsd:simpleType` element can create a new type by unifying the value spaces of existing types. Each existing type combined into the new type is identified by an `xsd:union` child element.
- A list type can hold one or more white-space-separated instances of an existing type. Such a type is defined by the `xsd:list` child of an `xsd:simpleType` element.
- Schemas declare attributes with `xsd:attribute` elements.
- The `xsd:import` element imports declarations for elements and attributes in a different namespace from another schema document.
- The `xsd:include` element imports declarations for elements and attributes in the same namespace from another schema document.

- Adding `xsd:annotation` elements helps make your schemas more readable.
- The `xsd:documentation` child of an `xsd:annotation` element provides information for human readers.
- The `xsd:appInfo` child of an `xsd:annotation` element provides information for software programs reading the schema, though schema validators ignore it.

This completes your training in core XML technologies. The next part begins several case studies of different XML applications in different vertical domains. First out of the gate is the Extensible Hypertext Markup Language (XHTML). XHTML 1.0 is an XMLized form of HTML. XHTML 1.1 is a modularized form of XHTML 1.0 that can be mixed with other XML applications.

✦ ✦ ✦

XML Applications

P A R T

V

✦ ✦ ✦ ✦

In This Part

✦ ✦ ✦ ✦

XHTML

✦ ✦ ✦ ✦

In This Chapter

Why validate HTML?

Moving to XHTML

What's new in XHTML

✦ ✦ ✦ ✦

XHTML, the Extensible Hypertext Markup Language, is the W3C's effort to redefine HTML based on XML rather than SGML. This requires tightening up a lot of the looseness of traditional HTML. End-tags must be added to elements that don't normally have them, such as `p` and `dt`. Empty-element tags, such as `hr` and `img`, must end in `/>` instead of just `>`. Attribute values must be quoted. The names of all HTML elements and attributes are standardized in lowercase. But XHTML goes one step further than merely requiring HTML documents to be well-formed XML. It actually provides a document type definition (DTD) that can validate XHTML documents. In fact, it provides three:

- The XHTML strict DTD for new documents: `http://www.w3.org/TR/xhtml1/DTD/xhtml1-strict.dtd`
- The XHTML transitional DTD for legacy documents that still use deprecated tags such as `applet`: `http://www.w3.org/TR/xhtml1/DTD/xhtml1-transitional.dtd`
- The XHTML frameset DTD for documents that use frames: `http://www.w3.org/TR/xhtml1/DTD/xhtml1-frameset.dtd`

You can choose the one that best fits your site.

Why Validate HTML?

XHTML, the Extensible Hypertext Markup Language, is a reformulation of HTML 4.0 as well-formed and valid XML. XHTML documents must adhere to all the rules of XML. For example, all start-tags must have matching end-tags. Elements can nest but cannot overlap. Attribute values must be quoted. The ampersand and less than characters can only be used to start entity references and tags, respectively; and so on.

Valid documents aren't required for HTML, but validity does make it much easier for browsers to understand documents. A valid XHTML document is far more likely to render correctly and predictably across many different browsers than an invalid HTML document. Until recently, too much of the competition among browser vendors revolved around just how much broken HTML they could make sense of. For example, Internet Explorer fills in a missing `</table>` end-tag, whereas Netscape Navigator does not. For some time, many pages on Microsoft's web site contained missing `</table>` tags and could not be viewed in Netscape Navigator. (I'll leave it to the reader to decide whether this was unfortunate happenstance or deliberate sabotage.) In either case, if Microsoft had required valid HTML on its web site, this would not have happened.

It is extremely difficult for even the largest web shops to test their pages against even a small fraction of the browsers that people actually use. Even testing the latest versions of both Netscape and Internet Explorer is more than some designers manage. While I certainly won't argue that you shouldn't test your pages in as many versions of as many browsers as possible, the reality is that time and resources are finite. Validating HTML goes a long way toward ensuring that your pages render reasonably in a broad spectrum of browsers.

In addition, validating HTML helps you find your mistakes. There are a surprising number of HTML documents on the Web today with truly mistaken HTML. I've seen pages where authors have placed attributes on the wrong elements, misspelled element and attribute names, left off the closing " on an attribute or > on a tag, and more. These problems don't just cause problems in some browsers; they cause major problems in all browsers! Yet you'll find mistakes like these on some of the largest and most popular sites on the Web. All of these common problems can be easily detected if you validate your documents before publishing them.

There are also advantages to XHTML beyond the realm of browser display. First, when your documents are XHTML rather than HTML, you get to use the myriad of XML-aware tools to process your HTML documents. For example, you can use XSLT to transform XHTML documents into XSL formatting objects for high-quality printing.

Second, because XML is much more carefully defined and stricter in what it does and doesn't allow than classic HTML, it's much easier for your own custom programs to process XHTML than HTML. Web spiders, indexing tools, link checkers, and other programs are all much easier to write for XHTML than for HTML. My Cafe au Lait and Cafe con Leche web sites use XSLT to generate the RSS feeds.

Third, it's much easier to mix other XML applications like Scalable Vector Graphics (SVG) or MathML into an XHTML document than an HTML document. XHTML's well-formedness and validity rules make it really obvious where other, non-XHTML content can be placed. Furthermore, XML namespaces make it easy for browsers to determine which parts of a page come from which XML vocabulary, so that it knows what to pass to the MathML plug-in, what to display as an SVG picture, and what to format in a normal HTML fashion.

And while it may be marginally more difficult to write XHTML by hand than traditional HTML, it's not significantly more difficult for editors such as Dreamweaver or Microsoft Word to produce XHTML than HTML. The most recent versions of these and many other tools have options to generate valid XHTML without any extra effort on the user's part.

Moving to XHTML

The XHTML 1.0 specification defines a Strictly Conforming XHTML Document as one that meets the following criteria:

1. The root element of the document must be `html`.
2. The root element of the document must set the default namespace to `http://www.w3.org/1999/xhtml`.
3. The document must have a `DOCTYPE` declaration that references the strict, transitional, or frameset DTD using one of these three Formal Public Identifiers:
   - `-//W3C//DTD XHTML 1.0 Strict//EN`
   - `-//W3C//DTD XHTML 1.0 Transitional//EN`
   - `-//W3C//DTD XHTML 1.0 Frameset//EN`
4. The document must be valid.

These requirements have certain implications. For instance, well-formedness is a prerequisite for validity. Therefore, requirement 4 implies that the document must be well-formed. And, of course, requirement 3 has all sorts of implications based on the rules found in those three DTDs. For the most part, these rules match your expectations about what an HTML document should look like. However, there are some exceptions, especially for the strict DTD. For example, all element and attribute names must be lowercase. Nonstandard elements such as `marquee` and `layer` and nonstandard attributes such as `datafld` are strictly forbidden.

Let's explore the process you'll have to go through to convert an existing HTML document to XHTML. I'll choose as an example a page I found in December 2000 on *Project FREEDOM*, the web site of U.S. Representative Ron Paul (`http://www.house.gov/paul/mobileo.htm`). I chose this page because it's a particularly egregious example of malformed, invalid, ugly, and just-plain-wrong HTML. According to the site information at `http://www.house.gov/paul/siteman.htm`, "The site is stored on the main House of Representative [*sic*] secure server and is generally created using a combination of web-design software applications and direct HTML coding. The site operates equally well on the most recent versions of Netscape and Microsoft Internet Explorer-compatible platforms, working best with a frames-enabled browser." In fact, I'd be surprised if it works well in any browser. The most common problem on web sites today is that they've been designed to look good on only one particular browser or platform. However, this one seemed especially unsightly on every browser I tried, including IE5.5 for Windows (shown in Figure 21-1).

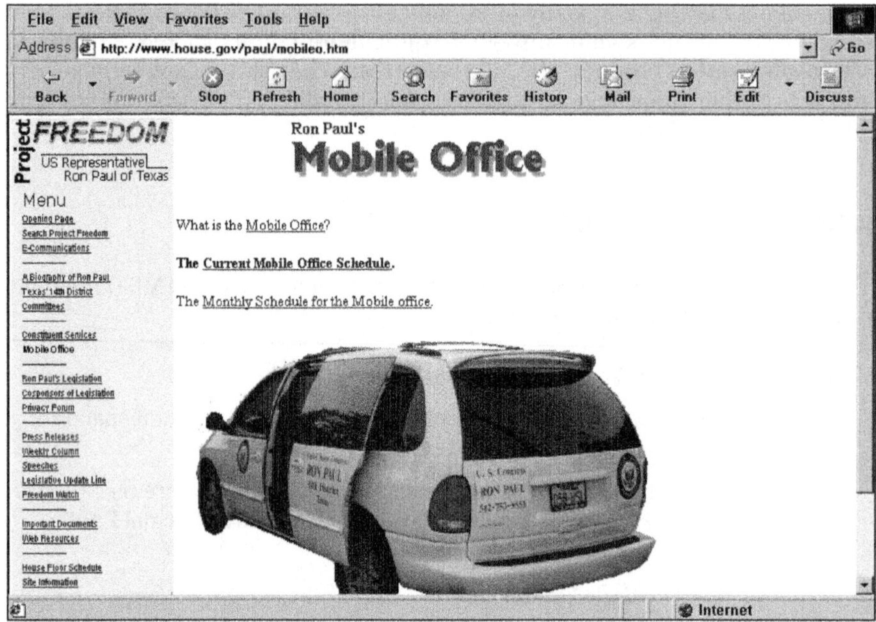

Figure 21-1: Ron Paul's Mobile Office web page

The HTML source code is given in Listing 21-1. This is shown exactly as it appeared on the site on December 1, 2000, aside from adding a few line breaks to fit it on the printed page. (The page has since been deleted from his site.) Read through it carefully and see how many problems you can find.

Listing 21-1: http://www.house.gov/paul/mobileo.htm

```
<head><title>Mobile Office

</title></head>
<!--INSERT TITLE, INSERT TEXT-->

<body bgcolor=#ffffff text=black link=#000080 vlink=#000080
alink=#000080  leftmargin=0 topmargin=0 marginwidth=0
marginheight=0  >
<basefont size=2 face="Times New Roman">
<table border=0 valign=top align=left>
<tr><td bgcolor=#EFEFCE valign=top>
<a href=http://www.house.gov/paul/><IMG
SRC="images/pflogosm.gif" BORDER=0></a><br>
<table border=0><tr><td width=2></td><td border=1>
<font size=+1 face="MS Sans Serif, Geneva,
Verdana">Menu</font><br>
```

```
<font size=-2 face="Arial Narrow">
    <a href=display.htm>Opening Page</a><br>
<a href=search.htm>Search Project Freedom</a><br>
<a href=mail/welcome.htm>E-Communications</a><br>
--------------------<br>
<a href=bio.htm>A Biography of Ron Paul</a><br>
<a href=about14.htm>Texas' 14th District</a><br>
<a href=committeework/welcome.htm>Committees</a><br>
--------------------<br>
<a href=services14.htm>Constituent Services</a><br>
<B>Mobile Office<br></B>
--------------------<br>
<a href=legis/welcome.htm>Ron Paul's Legislation</a><br>
<a href=legis/106/cospon.htm>Cosponsors of Legislation</a><br>
<a href=privacy/display.htm>Privacy Forum</a><br>
--------------------<br>
<a href=press/welcome.htm>Press Releases</a><br>
<a href=tst/welcome.htm>Weekly Column</a><br>
<a href=congrec/welcome.htm>Speeches</a><br>
<a href=tst/lu.htm>Legislative Update Line</a><br>
<a href=fwu/welcome.htm>Freedom Watch</a><br>
--------------------<br>
<a href=impdoc.htm>Important Documents</a><br>
<a href=links.htm>Web Resources</a><br>
--------------------<br>
<a href=http://majoritywhip.house.gov/whipnotice.htm>House
Floor Schedule</a><br>
<a href=siteman.htm>Site Information<br>
</td></tr></table>
<table align=right border=1><tr><td>
<font size=1 face="Arial Narrow">
<P>
The Office of U.S. Rep. Ron Paul<br>
203 Cannon HOB<br>
Washington, DC 20515<br>
(202) 225-2831<p>
</td></tr></table>

</td>

<td valign=top align=left>
<!--PAGE TEXT INSERT HERE-->



<CENTER><img src="images/mo.gif" alt="The Mobile
Office"></CENTER>
<P>
What is the <A HREF="mobilewhatis.htm" >Mobile Office</a>?
<P>
<b>The <A HREF="mosched.htm" target=new>Current Mobile Office
Schedule</A>.</b>
```

Continued

Listing 21-1 *(continued)*

```
<P>
<P>
The <a href=moset.htm>Monthly Schedule for the Mobile
office</a>.<P>
<P>

<IMG SRC="images/mobileoffice.gif" BORDER=0>









<!--END OF PAGE-->
</td></tr>
</table>
<P>
```

In fact, there are more than 25 separate errors in this document, the exact number depending on how you count. Since this document is so completely broken, let's divide the task of converting it to XHTML into three parts:

1. Convert it to well-formed XML.
2. Make it valid XHTML according to the transitional XHTML DTD.
3. Upgrade it to full conformance with the XHTML strict DTD.

Making the document well-formed XML

Listing 21-1 contains numerous well-formedness errors. Let's address them in order. The first one you should have noted is that there's no root element! The `html` element that should enclose all HTML and XHTML documents is missing. The document starts with a `head`. This is followed by a `body` element. All well-formed XML documents must have exactly one root element. Therefore, the first thing you need to do is add an `html` root element, like this:

```
<html>
  <head><title>Mobile Office</title></head>
  <body>
   ...
</html>
```

However, the `html` root element isn't the only element with problems in this document. Many, many elements in this document, the `body` element being just the first one, have start-tags but no corresponding end-tags. You have to fix all these too. For example, near the bottom of the document, you'll find these six paragraphs:

```
<P>
What is the <A HREF="mobilewhatis.htm" >Mobile Office</a>?
<P>
<b>The <A HREF="mosched.htm" target=new>Current Mobile Office
Schedule</A>.</b>
<P>
<P>
The <a href=moset.htm>Monthly Schedule for the Mobile
office</a>.<P>
<P>
```

However, these paragraphs are identified by six <P> start-tags that are all unmatched by </P> end-tags. This needs to be fixed wherever it occurs. For example, that section should be rewritten like this:

```
<P>
What is the <A HREF="mobilewhatis.htm" >Mobile Office</a>?
</P>
<P>
<b>The <A HREF="mosched.htm" target=new>Current Mobile Office
Schedule</A>.</b>
</P>
<P></P>
<P>
The <a href=moset.htm>Monthly Schedule for the Mobile
office</a>.
</P>
<P></P>
<P></P>
```

When you are matching start-tags to end-tags, it's also important to make sure that their cases match. A <P> start-tag cannot be closed with a </p> end-tag. This mistake is made in the first paragraph of this sample:

```
What is the <A HREF="mobilewhatis.htm" >Mobile Office</a>?
```

The opening uppercase <A> tag is closed by a lowercase </a> tag. The easiest way to fix mismatched case problems is to adopt a single case for all tags. The XHTML DTDs actually specify that all tags be written in lowercase, so you should change the preceding fragment to this:

```
<p>
What is the <a href="mobilewhatis.htm" >Mobile Office</a>?
</p>
<p>
<b>The <a HREF="mosched.htm" target=new>Current Mobile Office
Schedule</a>.</b>
```

```
</p>
<p></p>
<p>
The <a href=moset.htm>Monthly Schedule for the Mobile
office</a>.
</p>
<p></p>
<p></p>
```

Another frequent problem with elements, one of the few this document doesn't really exhibit, is overlapping elements. This occurs when a start-tag appears inside an element but the corresponding end-tag appears outside that element. This problem looks like this:

```
<b>The <a HREF="mosched.htm" target=new>Current Mobile Office
Schedule</b>.</a>
```

There are a couple of instances of this in Listing 21-1, but they're all results of omitted end-tags.

The final common problem with elements is an empty element that does not use an empty-element tag. This is extremely prevalent because HTML includes many empty elements such as `br`, `img`, and `hr`. However, HTML browsers don't always recognize XML's empty-element tags, such as `<br/>` and `<hr/>`, and consequently won't always include the line break or horizontal rule you were aiming for. They seem to think that these tags represent an element named `br/` or `hr/` rather than an empty element named `br` or `hr`.

You could use start-tag/end-tag pairs, such as `<br></br>` and `<hr></hr>`, instead. However, these also cause problems for some browsers. In particular, the browser may display two line breaks or horizontal lines where you only wanted one. The solution that seems to work best in practice is to add an attribute to the empty-element tag. This pushes the / away from the element name and eliminates problems with most browsers. Conveniently, XHTML allows all elements to have a `class` attribute with any convenient value. It's normally used as a hook off which to hang CSS style rules. However, it can also be used for any purpose you like, including simply moving the /> away from the element name. For example, consider this fragment with four empty elements from Listing 21-1:

```
--------------------<br>
<a href=impdoc.htm>Important Documents</a><br>
<a href=links.htm>Web Resources</a><br>
--------------------<br>
```

You can easily make the `br` elements well-formed by adding `class="empty"` attributes to their tags like this:

```
--------------------<br class="empty"/>
<a href=impdoc.htm>Important Documents</a><br class="empty"/>
<a href=links.htm>Web Resources</a><br class="empty"/>
--------------------<br class="empty"/>
```

The value of the `class` attribute doesn't have any particular significance here. It does not have to be the word `empty`. If you need to place a different value in the `class` attribute for some other purpose, you can. All that's required to make the empty-element tags work is that some attribute be present with some value. For this function, it doesn't really matter what the attribute is or what value it has.

The final thing that you need to do to make Listing 21-1 well-formed is to quote all the attribute values. Right now, more attribute values are unquoted than quoted. For example, here's the `body` start-tag:

```
<body bgcolor=#ffffff text=black link=#000080 vlink=#000080
alink=#000080  leftmargin=0 topmargin=0 marginwidth=0
marginheight=0  >
```

You can place either single or double quotes around the attribute values, whichever you prefer. Most web browsers will accept either one, but some third-party tools, such as web spiders, work better with double quotes. For example:

```
<body bgcolor="#ffffff" text="black" link="#000080"
      vlink="#000080" alink="#000080" leftmargin="0"
      topmargin="0" marginwidth="0" marginheight="0">
```

After all these changes are made, you now have a fully well-formed document. Listing 21-2 demonstrates. I cleaned up the white space a little, too.

Listing 21-2: A Well-Formed Version of the Mobile Office Page

```
<html>
  <head><title>Mobile Office</title></head>
<!--INSERT TITLE, INSERT TEXT-->

  <body bgcolor="#ffffff" text="black" link="#000080"
      vlink="#000080" alink="#000080" leftmargin="0"
      topmargin="0" marginwidth="0" marginheight="0">
  <basefont size="2" face="Times New Roman"/>
  <table border="0" valign="top" align="left">
    <tr><td bgcolor="#EFEFCE" valign="top">
    <a href="http://www.house.gov/paul/">
    <img SRC="images/pflogosm.gif" border="0"/></a>
    <br class="empty"/>
    <table border="0"><tr><td width="2"></td><td border="1">
      <font size="+1" face="MS Sans Serif, Geneva, Verdana">
        Menu</font><br class="empty"/>
      <font size="-2" face="Arial Narrow">
    <a href="display.htm">Opening Page</a><br class="empty"/>
    <a href="search.htm">Search Project Freedom</a>
    <br class="empty"/>
    <a href="mail/welcome.htm">E-Communications</a>
```

Continued

Listing 21-2 (continued)

```
    <br class="empty"/>
    --------------------<br class="empty"/>
    <a href="bio.htm">A Biography of Ron Paul</a>
    <br class="empty"/>
    <a href="about14.htm">Texas' 14th District</a>
    <br class="empty"/>
    <a href="committeework/welcome.htm">Committees</a>
    <br class="empty"/>
    --------------------<br class="empty"/>
    <a href="services14.htm">Constituent Services</a>
    <br class="empty"/>
    <b>Mobile Office<br class="empty"/></b>
    --------------------<br class="empty"/>
    <a href="legis/welcome.htm">Ron Paul's Legislation</a>
    <br class="empty"/>
  <a href="legis/106/cospon.htm">Cosponsors of Legislation</a>
    <br class="empty"/>
    <a href="privacy/display.htm">Privacy Forum</a>
    <br class="empty"/>
    --------------------<br class="empty"/>
    <a href="press/welcome.htm">Press Releases</a>
    <br class="empty"/>
    <a href="tst/welcome.htm">Weekly Column</a>
    <br class="empty"/>
    <a href="congrec/welcome.htm">Speeches</a>
    <br class="empty"/>
    <a href="tst/lu.htm">Legislative Update Line</a>
    <br class="empty"/>
    <a href="fwu/welcome.htm">Freedom Watch</a>
    <br class="empty"/>
    --------------------<br class="empty"/>
    <a href="impdoc.htm">Important Documents</a>
    <br class="empty"/>
    <a href="links.htm">Web Resources</a><br class="empty"/>
    --------------------<br class="empty"/>
    <a href="http://majoritywhip.house.gov/whipnotice.htm">
    House Floor Schedule</a><br class="empty"/>
    <a href="siteman.htm">Site Information</a>
    <br class="empty"/>
  </font>
</td></tr></table>
<table align="right" border="1"><tr><td>
<font size="1" face="Arial Narrow">
<p></p>
The Office of U.S. Rep. Ron Paul<br class="empty"/>
203 Cannon HOB<br class="empty"/>
Washington, DC 20515<br class="empty"/>
```

```
(202) 225-2831<p></p>
</font>
</td></tr></table>

</td>

<td valign="top" align="left">
<!--PAGE TEXT INSERT HERE-->

<center><img src="images/mo.gif" alt="The Mobile
Office"/></center>
<p>
What is the <a href="mobilewhatis.htm" >Mobile Office</a>?
</p>
<p>
<b>The <a href="mosched.htm" target="new">
Current Mobile Office Schedule</a>.</b>
</p>
<p></p>
<p>
The <a href="moset.htm">Monthly Schedule for the Mobile
office</a>.
</p>
<p></p>

<img src="images/mobileoffice.gif" border="0"/>

<!--END OF PAGE-->
</td></tr>
</table>
<p></p>
</body>
</html>
```

Well-formedness is a very picky criterion for documents to satisfy. I would never trust myself to merely eyeball the well-formedness of a document without checking it. Because XHTML is XML, and a well-formed XHTML document is a well-formed XML document, you can use all the tools you use to check the well-formedness of an XML document, such as xmllint, to check the well-formedness of an XHTML document.

For example, here are the last couple of checks I made using an early version of the Xerces-J parser while I was converting Listing 21-1 into Listing 21-2. The first one found an error where an opening `<A>` tag was closed by `</a>` tag, that is, a case mismatch. The last check was naturally error-free. (Otherwise, it wouldn't have been the last check.)

```
D:\books\bible2\examples\21>java sax.SAXCount 21-2.html
[Fatal Error] 21-2.html:63:57: The element type "A" must be
terminated by the matching end-tag "</A>".
org.xml.sax.SAXException: Stopping after fatal error: The
element type "A" must be terminated by the matching end-tag
"</A>".
        at
org.apache.xerces.framework.XMLParser.
reportError(XMLParser.java:1040)
        at
org.apache.xerces.framework.XMLDocumentScanner.
reportFatalXMLError(XMLDocumentScanner.java:634)
        at org.apache.xerces.framework.XMLDocumentScanner
.abortMarkup(XMLDocumentScanner.java:683)
        at org.apache.xerces.framework.XMLDocumentScanner$
ContentDispatcher.dispatch(XMLDocumentScanner.java:1187)
        at
org.apache.xerces.framework.XMLDocumentScanner.parseSome(
XMLDocumentScanner.java:380)
        at
org.apache.xerces.framework.XMLParser.parse(XMLParser.java:900)
        at
org.apache.xerces.framework.XMLParser.parse(XMLParser.java:939)
        at sax.SAXCount.print(SAXCount.java:152)
        at sax.SAXCount.main(SAXCount.java:372)

D:\books\bible2\examples\27>java sax.SAXCount 21-2.html
21-2.html: 240 ms (87 elems, 90 attrs, 0 spaces, 758 chars)
```

The one thing you cannot do with an XHTML document that you can do with a normal XML document is just load it into an XML-savvy browser such as Mozilla to see whether or not it's well-formed. If you give a web browser a malformed XHTML document, it will probably treat it as a normal HTML document and try to quietly fix any problems it finds rather than reporting the mistakes. This may depend on the details of the MIME media type or filename extension. However, in any case, it's not a reliable way to check XHTML documents for well-formedness.

Another common change that's required to make many documents well-formed, though not this particular one, is to define your entity references. HTML predefines and authors use numerous entity references, including ` `, `©`, `&tm;`, and more. None of these are allowed in an XML document unless they're first declared in a DTD. Fortunately, the XHTML DTD predefines all the usual HTML entity references, as well as a few new ones besides, so as soon as you add a `DOCTYPE` declaration pointing to one of the three XHTML DTDs, these entity references are no longer a problem.

Making the document valid

A well-formed HTML document is only halfway to being a valid XHTML document. Recall that there are four conditions for XHTML validity:

1. The root element of the document must be `html`.
2. The root element of the document must set the default namespace to `http://www.w3.org/1999/xhtml`.
3. It must have a `DOCTYPE` declaration that references the strict, transitional, or frameset DTD using one of these three public identifiers:
   - `-//W3C//DTD XHTML 1.0 Strict//EN`
   - `-//W3C//DTD XHTML 1.0 Transitional//EN`
   - `-//W3C//DTD XHTML 1.0 Frameset//EN`
4. It must be valid.

The document has improved a great deal from its original form, but still only the first of these four conditions and the prerequisite for the fourth condition have been met.

Meeting the second condition is straightforward. Just add the necessary namespace declaration to the `html` root element start-tag like this:

```
<html xmlns="http://www.w3.org/1999/xhtml">
```

Adding the `DOCTYPE` declaration is no harder. Attaching that, the beginning of the document now looks like this:

```
<!DOCTYPE html PUBLIC "-//W3C//DTD XHTML 1.0 Transitional//EN"
    "http://www.w3.org/TR/xhtml1/DTD/xhtml1-transitional.dtd">
<html xmlns="http://www.w3.org/1999/xhtml">
```

I've chosen the transitional DTD because it's the simplest one to move an existing document to. New documents should use the strict DTD instead. It would probably also be a good idea to store a local copy of the DTD on your own site rather than referencing the one on the W3C site. If you did that, the `DOCTYPE` declaration would look similar to this:

```
<!DOCTYPE html PUBLIC "-//W3C//DTD XHTML 1.0 Transitional//EN"
                      "xhtml1-transitional.dtd">
```

If you wanted to, you could also add an XML declaration to the prolog. However, that's not absolutely required. Because a few older web browsers attempt to display the XML declaration as plain text at the start of the document, I prefer not to include it in XHTML documents.

After you've added the `DOCTYPE` declaration, you can attempt to validate the document using xmllint or some other program. The W3C provides an online validation service at `http://validator.w3.org/`, shown in Figure 21-2. This can check XHTML documents against the DTD they specify, as well as check normal HTML documents against the SGML DTD for HTML 4.0.

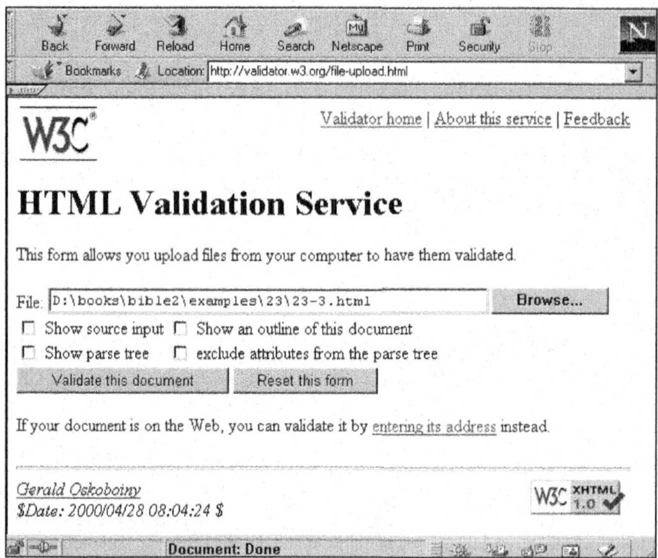

Figure 21-2: The W3C HTML Validation Service

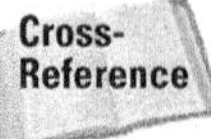

Various tools that you can use to validate XML documents are described in Chapter 7.

Here are the results of my first attempt to validate the XHTMLized Mobile Office page using the W3C validator:

✦ Line 8, column 49:

```
vlink="#000080" alink="#000080" leftmargin="0"
```

Error: there is no attribute "leftmargin"

✦ Line 9, column 16:

```
topmargin="0" marginwidth="0" marginheight="0">
         ^
```

Error: there is no attribute "topmargin"

✦ Line 9, column 32:

```
topmargin="0" marginwidth="0" marginheight="0">
                          ^
```

Error: there is no attribute “marginwidth”

✦ Line 9, column 49:

```
topmargin="0" marginwidth="0" marginheight="0">
                                            ^
```

Error: there is no attribute “marginheight”

✦ Line 11, column 27:

```
<table border="0" valign="top" align="left">
                         ^
```

Error: there is no attribute “valign”

✦ Line 14, column 13:

```
<img SRC="images/pflogosm.gif" border="0"/></a>
         ^
```

Error: there is no attribute “SRC”

✦ Line 14, column 46:

```
<img SRC="images/pflogosm.gif" border="0"/></a>
                                           ^
```

Error: required attribute “src” not specified

✦ Line 14, column 46:

```
<img SRC="images/pflogosm.gif" border="0"/></a>
                                           ^
```

Error: required attribute “alt” not specified

✦ Line 16, column 56:

```
<table border="0"><tr><td width="2"></td><td border="1">
                                                       ^
```

Error: there is no attribute “border”

✦ Line 67, column 2:

```
<p></p>
 ^
```

Error: document type does not allow element “p” here; missing one of “object”, “applet”, “”map””, “iframe”, “button”, “ins”, “del”, “noscript” start-tag

✦ Line 71, column 16:

```
(202) 225-2831<p></p>

                   ^
```

Error: document type does not allow element “p” here; missing one of “object”, “”applet”, “map”, “iframe”, “button”, “ins”, “del”, “noscript” start-tag

✦ Line 94, column 46:

```
<img src="images/mobileoffice.gif" border="0"/>
                                             ^
```

Error: required attribute “alt” not specified

That’s 12 separate errors that need to be dealt with. Some of them have obvious solutions; some of them don’t.

The first two problems reported are of similar provenance. The DTD does not declare `leftmargin` and `topmargin` attributes for the `body` element. In fact, these are Microsoft extensions to HTML that were never supported in standard HTML or Netscape. They should be replaced by a CSS `style` attribute that sets those properties. For example:

```
<body style="leftmargin: 0; topmargin: 0"
      bgcolor="#ffffff" text="black" link="#000080"
      vlink="#000080" alink="#000080"
      marginwidth="0" marginheight="0">
```

This should work in all browsers that `leftmargin` and `topmargin` work in and quite a few more besides. This demonstrates one of the advantages of validating your XHTML: The pages you produce are much more cross-browser-compatible.

The next two problems are the `marginwidth` and `marginheight` attributes on the `body` element. These are nonstandard Netscape extensions to HTML that were never supported in standard HTML or Internet Explorer. They have the same effect in Netscape that `leftmargin` and `topmargin` do in Internet Explorer. However, to achieve XHTML conformance, you must delete them:

```
<body style="leftmargin: 0; topmargin: 0"
      bgcolor="#ffffff" text="black" link="#000080"
      vlink="#000080" alink="#000080">
```

The next error is of a similar nature. The page author placed the `valign` attribute on the `table` element. However, a `table` element isn’t allowed to have a `valign` attribute, so this doesn’t mean anything to a browser. It’s possible that the author meant this to be an `align` attribute, which a `table` is allowed to have; but given the value of `top`, it’s more likely that they were trying to set the default vertical alignment for cells within the table. It’s reasonable to guess that HTML might let you do this, but in fact it doesn't. Instead, you have to place the valign attribute on the tr or td elements. Fortunately, it's fairly easy to fix this here because the table in question only contains a single row. You just move the attribute from the table start-tag to the tr start-tag like this:

```
<table border="0" align="left">
  <tr valign="top">
```

If the table contained multiple rows, you'd just copy the valign attribute to each <tr> start-tag.

This demonstrates another benefit of validating your XHTML—it catches your mistakes. These can be cases in which you misremembered the name of the attribute, or they can be simple typos—gbcolor instead of bgcolor, for example. Whichever they are, these are real problems that cause real trouble for web browsers today, not just anal-retentive rules about how code is supposed to be written. Finding and fixing these sorts of mistakes is important, even if you don't really care whether or not your document is valid.

The next two errors are related, and both stem from this element:

```
<img SRC="images/pflogosm.gif" border="0"/>
```

The first error says, "there is no attribute 'SRC'." The second error says, "required attribute 'src' not specified." In both cases, the problem is XML's case sensitivity. In XHTML, the SRC attribute is not the same as the src attribute, although they are the same in traditional HTML. XHTML requires all attribute and element names to be typed in lowercase. This fix is easy to make. Just change the attribute names to lowercase:

```
<img src="images/pflogosm.gif" border="0"/>
```

The next error also refers to this img element. It says, "required attribute 'alt' not specified." In most cases, the transitional DTD lets most common, but improper, forms of HTML slip through with only a little tweaking to require well-formedness. However, in this case, the W3C has decided to put its foot down in defense of accessibility. In XHTML, unlike in HTML, all images must be supplied with alternate text. This means you have to add content to this element as an alt attribute. For example, this alt attribute suffices:

```
<img src="images/pflogosm.gif" border="0"
     alt="Project Freedom Logo"/>
```

The next problem is a familiar one: "there is no attribute 'border'" for the td element. Again, the attribute was placed on the wrong element. It belongs on the table element, not the td element. However, this table element already has a border attribute with a different value. Because, as written, the border attribute on the td element has no effect, I'll assume that it was just a fluke and delete it completely. That will keep us as close to the original page as possible.

The tenth and eleventh errors are the nastiest. These are the long ones that state, “Error: document type does not allow element ‘p’ here; missing one of ‘object’, ‘applet’, ‘map’, ‘iframe’, ‘button’, ‘ins’, ‘del’, ‘noscript’ start-tag.” This isn’t very clear, and the validator doesn’t tell you which one is missing or how it should be inserted. These sorts of errors, when an element doesn’t match its content model, can be some of the hardest to track down.

A different validator (`sax.SAXCount`) gave the different but equally unhelpful message, “The content of element type ‘font’ must match ‘(#PCDATA|a|br|span|bdo|object|applet| img|map|iframe|tt|i|b|big|small|u|s|strike|font|basefont|em|strong|dfn|code|q|sub|sup|samp| kbd|var|cite|abbr| acronym|input|select|textarea|label|button|ins|del|script|noscript)*’.”

These are two different ways of looking at the same problem. The specific problem is that there’s an element A inside an element B when elements of type B are not allowed to contain elements of type A. The W3C validator reports that as a problem with A, while Xerces’ `sax.SAXCount` reports it as a problem with B. However, in both cases the problem is the same. Neither validator tells you the whole problem, but by putting them together, you see that the problem is that there’s a `p` element inside a `font` element.

Looking at the content model that’s violated, you should notice that, as long as it is, it does not include every element defined in XHTML. In particular, it just includes the inline elements like `a` and `strong`. It does not include any of the block-level elements like `p` or `table`. Therefore, chances are that’s exactly what you’re looking for: a block-level element that’s a child of a `font` element. With that information in hand, it’s not hard to locate the offender. It’s this `font` element:

```
<font size="1" face="Arial Narrow">
  <p>
    The Office of U.S. Rep. Ron Paul<br class="empty"/>
    203 Cannon HOB<br class="empty"/>
    Washington, DC 20515<br class="empty"/>
    (202) 225-2831
  </p>
</font>
```

The solution is straightforward: Move the `font` tags inside the `p` element like this:

```
<p>
  <font size="1" face="Arial Narrow">
    The Office of U.S. Rep. Ron Paul<br class="empty"/>
    203 Cannon HOB<br class="empty"/>
    Washington, DC 20515<br class="empty"/>
    (202) 225-2831
  </font>
</p>
```

There's one final problem to be fixed, but this is one you've seen before. The `img` element in line 94 does not have an `alt` attribute. This particular image is a picture of the mobile office, so fill it in like this:

```
<img src="images/mobileoffice.gif" border="0"
     alt="Mobile Office Minivan"/>
```

Now you're done. The document validates, at least against the transitional DTD. Listing 21-3 shows the finished XHTML document.

Listing 21-3: A Valid XHTML Document

```
<!DOCTYPE html PUBLIC "-//W3C//DTD XHTML 1.0 Transitional//EN"
                      "xhtml1-transitional.dtd">
<html xmlns="http://www.w3.org/1999/xhtml">
  <head><title>Mobile Office</title></head>
<!--INSERT TITLE, INSERT TEXT-->

  <body bgcolor="#ffffff" text="black" link="#000080"
      vlink="#000080" alink="#000080"
      style="leftmargin: 0; topmargin: 0">
    <basefont size="2" face="Times New Roman"/>
    <table border="0" align="left">
      <tr valign="top"><td bgcolor="#EFEFCE" valign="top">
        <a href="http://www.house.gov/paul/">
          <img src="images/pflogosm.gif" border="0"
               alt="Project Freedom Logo"/>
        </a>
        <br class="empty"/>
        <table border="0">
          <tr>
            <td width="2"></td>
            <td>
         <font size="+1" face="MS Sans Serif, Geneva, Verdana">
                Menu
         </font><br class="empty"/>
      <font size="-2" face="Arial Narrow">
      <a href="display.htm">Opening Page</a><br class="empty"/>
      <a href="search.htm">Search Project Freedom</a>
      <br class="empty"/>
      <a href="mail/welcome.htm">E-Communications</a>
      <br class="empty"/>
      --------------------<br class="empty"/>
      <a href="bio.htm">A Biography of Ron Paul</a>
      <br class="empty"/>
      <a href="about14.htm">Texas' 14th District</a>
      <br class="empty"/>
      <a href="committeework/welcome.htm">Committees</a>
```

Continued

Listing 21-3 *(continued)*

```
      <br class="empty"/>
      --------------------<br class="empty"/>
      <a href="services14.htm">Constituent Services</a>
      <br class="empty"/>
      <b>Mobile Office<br class="empty"/></b>
      --------------------<br class="empty"/>
      <a href="legis/welcome.htm">Ron Paul's Legislation</a>
      <br class="empty"/>
  <a href="legis/106/cospon.htm">Cosponsors of Legislation</a>
      <br class="empty"/>
      <a href="privacy/display.htm">Privacy Forum</a>
      <br class="empty"/>
      --------------------<br class="empty"/>
      <a href="press/welcome.htm">Press Releases</a>
      <br class="empty"/>
      <a href="tst/welcome.htm">Weekly Column</a>
      <br class="empty"/>
      <a href="congrec/welcome.htm">Speeches</a>
      <br class="empty"/>
      <a href="tst/lu.htm">Legislative Update Line</a>
      <br class="empty"/>
      <a href="fwu/welcome.htm">Freedom Watch</a>
      <br class="empty"/>
      --------------------<br class="empty"/>
      <a href="impdoc.htm">Important Documents</a>
      <br class="empty"/>
      <a href="links.htm">Web Resources</a><br class="empty"/>
      --------------------<br class="empty"/>
      <a href="http://majoritywhip.house.gov/whipnotice.htm">
      House Floor Schedule</a><br class="empty"/>
      <a href="siteman.htm">Site Information</a>
           <br class="empty"/>
         </font>
       </td></tr>
       </table>
       <table align="right" border="1">
         <tr><td>
           <p><font size="1" face="Arial Narrow">
            The Office of U.S. Rep. Ron Paul<br class="empty"/>
            203 Cannon HOB<br class="empty"/>
            Washington, DC 20515<br class="empty"/>
            (202) 225-2831
           </font></p>
         </td></tr>
       </table>
     </td>

     <td valign="top" align="left">
```

```
          <!--PAGE TEXT INSERT HERE-->

          <center>
            <img src="images/mo.gif" alt="The Mobile Office"/>
          </center>
          <p>
          What is the
          <a href="mobilewhatis.htm">Mobile Office</a>?
          </p>
          <p>
          <b>The <a href="mosched.htm" target="new">
          Current Mobile Office Schedule</a>.</b>
          </p>
          <p></p>
          <p>
            The <a href="moset.htm">Monthly Schedule
            for the Mobile office</a>.
          </p>
          <p></p>

           <img src="images/mobileoffice.gif" border="0"
                alt="Mobile Office Minivan"/>

    <!--END OF PAGE-->
          </td></tr>
        </table>
        <p></p>
      </body>
    </html>
```

The strict DTD

Moving to the transitional DTD is a good first step, and the easiest one to take; but new documents should use the strict DTD instead. Time and resources permitting, you should try to transition your HTML documents and XHTML transitional documents to the strict DTD as well. The very name *transitional* implies that it's not going to be around forever, and that possibly starting with XHTML 2.0 or perhaps some later version, the strict DTD will be the only option for valid, future-looking web pages.

The biggest difference between the strict DTD and the transitional DTD is that the strict DTD almost completely eliminates presentational elements such as `font` and `center` and presentational attributes such as `bgcolor` and `width`. Instead, these should all be replaced by CSS styles. The goal here is to return to the original plan for HTML as a semantic rather than presentational markup language.

To indicate that you want to use the strict DTD, just change the DOCTYPE declaration of the document as follows:

```
<!DOCTYPE html PUBLIC "-//W3C//DTD XHTML 1.0 Strict//EN"
                      "xhtml1-strict.dtd">
```

Then run it through your validation tool of choice. When I changed the document type declaration of Listing 21-3 to point to the strict DTD and passed it through the W3C validator, 19 more problems were uncovered:

✦ Line 7, column 16:

```
<body bgcolor="#ffffff" text="black" link="#000080"
               ^
```

Error: there is no attribute "bgcolor"

✦ Line 7, column 31:

```
<body bgcolor="#ffffff" text="black" link="#000080"
                              ^
```

Error: there is no attribute "text"

✦ Line 7, column 44:

```
<body bgcolor="#ffffff" text="black" link="#000080"
                                           ^
```

Error: there is no attribute "link"

✦ Line 8, column 12:

```
vlink="#000080" alink="#000080"
      ^
```

Error: there is no attribute "vlink"

✦ Line 8, column 28:

```
vlink="#000080" alink="#000080"
                      ^
```

Error: there is no attribute "alink"

✦ Line 10, column 19:

```
<basefont size="2" face="Times New Roman"/>
               ^
```

Error: there is no attribute "size"

✦ Line 10, column 28:

```
<basefont size="2" face="Times New Roman"/>
                        ^
```

Error: there is no attribute "face"

✦ Line 10, column 46:

```
<basefont size="2" face="Times New Roman"/>
 ^
```

Error: element "basefont" undefined

✦ Line 11, column 28:

```
<table border="0" align="left">
                        ^
```

Error: there is no attribute "align"

✦ Line 12, column 35:

```
<tr valign="top"><td bgcolor="#EFEFCE" valign="top">
                              ^
```

Error: there is no attribute "bgcolor"

✦ Line 14, column 48:

```
<img src="images/pflogosm.gif" border="0"
                                       ^
```

Error: there is no attribute "border"

✦ Line 20, column 22:

```
<td width="2"></td>
          ^
```

Error: there is no attribute "width"

✦ Line 22, column 20:

```
<font size="+1" face="MS Sans Serif, Geneva, Verdana">
           ^
```

Error: there is no attribute "size"

✦ Line 22, column 30:

```
<font size="+1" face="MS Sans Serif, Geneva, Verdana">
                     ^
```

Error: there is no attribute "face"

✦ Line 22, column 62:

```
<font size="+1" face="MS Sans Serif, Geneva, Verdana">
                                                     ^
```

Error: element "font" undefined

✦ Line 25, column 41:

```
<font size="-2" face="Arial Narrow">
                                   ^
```

Error: element "font" undefined

✦ Line 74, column 48:

```
<p><font size="1" face="Arial Narrow">
                                     ^
```

Error: element "font" undefined

✦ Line 87, column 14:

```
<center>
       ^
```

Error: element "center" undefined

✦ Line 95, column 43:

```
<b>The <a href="mosched.htm" target="new">
                                   ^
```

Error: there is no attribute "target"

Each of these problems is either an element or attribute that is not available in the strict DTD. An element that's not available in the DTD will produce several error messages — one for the element itself and one for each attribute that element possesses. In every case, the forbidden item provides presentational information that can be replaced with a CSS style. For example, the first five problems all relate to color attributes on the body start-tag:

```
<body bgcolor="#ffffff" text="black" link="#000080"
    vlink="#000080" alink="#000080"
    style="leftmargin: 0; topmargin: 0">
```

You can move the bgcolor and text values inside the allowed style attribute like this:

```
<body style="background-color: #ffffff; color: black;
             leftmargin: 0; topmargin: 0">
```

When moving to CSS, the bgcolor attribute becomes the background-color property and the text attribute becomes the (foreground) color property.

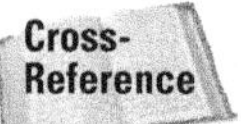

Background-color, color, and the other CSS properties used in this section are discussed in Chapter 14.

The three link colors are trickier. CSS doesn't provide any properties that are exact equivalents for the link, vlink, and alink attributes. Instead, you have to provide

CSS rules that use the appropriate selectors to choose links, visited links, and active links, and assign the desired colors to each one. These rules can be placed in a style element in the document's head like this:

```
<head>
  <title>Mobile Office</title>
  <style type="text/css">
    a:link    {color: #000080}
    a:visited {color: #000080}
    a:active  {color: #000080}
  </style>
</head>
```

Caution

In HTML, it's customary to enclose the CSS rules in the content of the style element in a comment like this:

```
<style type="text/css">
  <!-- a:link    {color: #000080}
       a:visited {color: #000080}
       a:active  {color: #000080} -->
</style>
```

This hides the style rules from older browsers that don't recognize CSS, and that might try to display the contents of the style element as part of the document. However, most browsers that understand strict XHTML can handle CSS, and all of them at least recognize the style element. Furthermore, XML rules dictate that XHTML browsers should not pay any attention to the contents of comments. (In practice some do and some don't.) The XML parser built-in to the browser may not even provide the text of the comments to the rendering engine for display. If you do need to write pages that work well in older browsers, you should use the transitional XHTML DTD instead of the strict one.

Tip

Changing link colors is a very bad thing to do to your readers. Browsing a page that uses nonstandard link colors is a little like driving in a country where the stop signs are blue, the warning signs are green, and the directional signs are red. While the default link colors (blue, purple, and red) are hardly the ideal choices, they are the ones standardized in today's browsers, and they are the colors readers have learned to expect. If you change the link colors, many readers won't realize where the links are on the page. They certainly won't be able to tell the difference between visited and unvisited links.

The next three errors stem from the basefont element:

```
<basefont size="2" face="Times New Roman"/>
```

This is a standard HTML element for setting the default font on the page. The first two errors say that the size and face attributes of this element aren't defined, while the last error says that the basefont element itself isn't defined. It has been deleted from strict XHTML. Instead, you set default font properties for the document by attaching CSS style properties to the body element of the document. The basefont's size attribute can be replaced by a CSS font-size property. In HTML, the size attribute of the basefont is given as a number between 1 and 7, where 3 is the browser's default font size. The CSS equivalent is using smaller on font-size. The basefont's face attribute can be replaced by a CSS font-family property. This makes the body start-tag look like this:

```
<body style="font-size: smaller;
            font-family: 'Times New Roman';
            background-color: #ffffff; color: black;
            leftmargin: 0; topmargin: 0">
```

The next problem is the align attribute on the first table. Because this already has the default value left, you can just drop it out. There's no need to replace it with a CSS style.

The tenth problem is straightforward and easy to fix: The bgcolor attribute is not allowed on table cells (td elements) any more than it's allowed on the body element. Again, you can replace it with a CSS background-color property, like this:

```
<td style="background-color: #EFEFCE" valign="top">
```

Perhaps a little surprisingly, the valign presentational attribute is allowed here. That's because it has a special meaning for table cells that no generic CSS property can really match.

The next problem is similar. In strict XHTML, the img element can't have a border attribute. Instead, it should have a border-width CSS style property. Furthermore, this property can't be an absolute number such as 0 or 2; it must have units. Thus, you change this:

```
<img src="images/pflogosm.gif" border="0"
     alt="Project Freedom Logo"/>
```

to this:

```
<img src="images/pflogosm.gif" style="border-width: 0px"
     alt="Project Freedom Logo"/>
```

The next problem arises in line 20. The td element can't have a width attribute. This must be replaced by a CSS width property. Again, the HTML width is given in pixels, so the equivalent CSS property must specify units of pixels like this:

```
<td style="width: 2px"></td>
```

Next comes one of the most common problems with documents being converted from old-style HTML to XHTML — the font element. Fortunately, this is easy to change to CSS. The font element attributes map to CSS font properties just as they did for the basefont element earlier. The size attribute is replaced by a font-size property and the face attribute is replaced by a font-family property. Of course, because the font element itself is illegal, you need an element to hang this style on. A lot of times there's a fortuitous `p` or `td` or some other element in the right place to fill this need; but if there's not, you can add a `span` or `div` element instead. Use `span` for inline runs of style and `div` for styles that surround one or more block-level elements such as `p` and `blockquote`. For example, in this case you can change the offending `font` element to this `span` element:

```
<span style="font-size: +1;
             font-family: 'MS Sans Serif', Geneva, Verdana">
    Menu
</span>
```

The next problem element is also a `font` element, and it is changed to another `span` element:

```
<span style="font-size: -2; font-family: 'Arial Narrow'">
```

The penultimate problem is the `center` element used to center the picture of the mobile office minivan within its table cell. The `center` element has been completely removed. Instead, you should use a `div` element with a CSS `text-align` property; for example:

```
<div style="text-align: center">
  <img src="images/mo.gif" alt="The Mobile Office"/>
</div>
```

Although this property is named `text-align`, it will align anything contained in the `div` element, including, as in this case, images.

The final problem is an unusual one: The `target` attribute of the `a` element is forbidden. There's no CSS equivalent for this attribute. It's simply gone. Consequently, you have to delete the `target` attribute from your strict XHTML documents, and suffer the corresponding loss in functionality.

```
<a href="mosched.htm">Current Mobile Office Schedule</a>
```

Note The reason the W3C removed `target` from strict XHTML was that it's used to control link behavior. In particular, `target` determines which window or frame the document is displayed in. For example, by setting `target` to `_blank` you can specify that the document will open in a new window rather than the current one. The W3C feels that link behavior is outside the scope of HTML. This is, in my opinion, a flaw in strict XHTML. Link behavior is not presentational information, and I certainly don't see any reason for it to be ruled out of bounds for a *Hypertext* Markup Language. XLink does provide equivalent functionality through the `xlink:show` attribute, but XHTML 1.0 doesn't support XLink.

Cross-Reference XLinks and the `xlink:show` attribute are discussed in Chapter 17.

That's the last error the validator reported. Listing 21-4 is the complete, fixed document with all the changes previously described.

Listing 21-4: The Fixed XHTML Document

```
<!DOCTYPE html PUBLIC "-//W3C//DTD XHTML 1.0 Strict//EN"
                      "xhtml1-strict.dtd">
<html xmlns="http://www.w3.org/1999/xhtml">
  <head>
    <title>Mobile Office</title>
    <style type="text/css">
      a:link    {color: #000080}
      a:visited {color: #000080}
      a:active  {color: #000080}
   </style>
  </head>
<!--INSERT TITLE, INSERT TEXT-->

  <body style="font-size: smaller;
               font-family: 'Times New Roman';
               background-color: #ffffff; color: black;
               leftmargin: 0; topmargin: 0">
    <table border="0">
      <tr valign="top">
        <td style="background-color: #EFEFCE" valign="top">
          <a href="http://www.house.gov/paul/">
      <img src="images/pflogosm.gif" style="border-width: 0px"
               alt="Project Freedom Logo"/>
        </a>
        <br class="empty"/>
        <table border="0">
          <tr>
            <td style="width: 2px"></td>
            <td>
         <span style="font-size: +1;
               font-family: 'MS Sans Serif', Geneva, Verdana">
                Menu
         </span><br class="empty"/>
         <span style="font-size: -2;
                      font-family: 'Arial Narrow'">
     <a href="display.htm">Opening Page</a><br class="empty"/>
      <a href="search.htm">Search Project Freedom</a>
      <br class="empty"/>
      <a href="mail/welcome.htm">E-Communications</a>
      <br class="empty"/>
      --------------------<br class="empty"/>
      <a href="bio.htm">A Biography of Ron Paul</a>
      <br class="empty"/>
      <a href="about14.htm">Texas' 14th District</a>
      <br class="empty"/>
      <a href="committeework/welcome.htm">Committees</a>
      <br class="empty"/>
      --------------------<br class="empty"/>
      <a href="services14.htm">Constituent Services</a>
```

```
    <br class="empty"/>
    <b>Mobile Office<br class="empty"/></b>
    --------------------<br class="empty"/>
    <a href="legis/welcome.htm">Ron Paul's Legislation</a>
    <br class="empty"/>
<a href="legis/106/cospon.htm">Cosponsors of Legislation</a>
    <br class="empty"/>
    <a href="privacy/display.htm">Privacy Forum</a>
    <br class="empty"/>
    --------------------<br class="empty"/>
    <a href="press/welcome.htm">Press Releases</a>
    <br class="empty"/>
    <a href="tst/welcome.htm">Weekly Column</a>
    <br class="empty"/>
    <a href="congrec/welcome.htm">Speeches</a>
    <br class="empty"/>
    <a href="tst/lu.htm">Legislative Update Line</a>
    <br class="empty"/>
    <a href="fwu/welcome.htm">Freedom Watch</a>
    <br class="empty"/>
    --------------------<br class="empty"/>
    <a href="impdoc.htm">Important Documents</a>
    <br class="empty"/>
    <a href="links.htm">Web Resources</a><br class="empty"/>
    --------------------<br class="empty"/>
    <a href="http://majoritywhip.house.gov/whipnotice.htm">
    House Floor Schedule</a><br class="empty"/>
    <a href="siteman.htm">Site Information</a>
         <br class="empty"/>
       </span>
     </td></tr>
     </table>
     <table align="right" border="1">
       <tr><td>
         <p><font size="1" face="Arial Narrow">
         The Office of U.S. Rep. Ron Paul<br class="empty"/>
         203 Cannon HOB<br class="empty"/>
         Washington, DC 20515<br class="empty"/>
         (202) 225-2831
         </font></p>
       </td></tr>
     </table>
   </td>

   <td valign="top" align="left">
     <!--PAGE TEXT INSERT HERE-->

     <div style="text-align: center">
       <img src="images/mo.gif" alt="The Mobile Office"/>
     </div>
     <p>
     What is the
```

Continued

Listing 21-4 *(continued)*

```
        <a href="mobilewhatis.htm">Mobile Office</a>?
        </p>
        <p>
        <b>The <a href="mosched.htm">
        Current Mobile Office Schedule</a>.</b>
        </p>
        <p></p>
        <p>
          The <a href="moset.htm">Monthly Schedule
          for the Mobile office</a>.
        </p>
        <p></p>

         <img src="images/mobileoffice.gif" border="0"
              alt="Mobile Office Minivan"/>

<!--END OF PAGE-->
      </td></tr>
    </table>
    <p></p>
  </body>
</html>
```

Listing 21-4 fixes all the errors that the validator found. Is this now a valid XHTML document? Unfortunately, the answer is still no. If you read Listing 21-4, you should have noticed that it still contains a number of illegal presentational elements, such as `font`, and presentational attributes, such as `border`. In fact, if you rerun Listing 21-4 through the W3C validator, it spits out these five additional error messages:

✦ Line 79, column 20:

```
<table align="right" border="1">
             ^
```

Error: there is no attribute "align"

✦ Line 81, column 25:

```
<p><font size="1" face="Arial Narrow">
                ^
```

Error: there is no attribute "size"

✦ Line 81, column 34:

```
<p><font size="1" face="Arial Narrow">
                       ^
```

Error: there is no attribute "face"

✦ Line 81, column 48:

```
<p><font size="1" face="Arial Narrow">
                                     ^
```

Error: element “font” undefined

✦ Line 112, column 50:

```
<img src="images/mobileoffice.gif" border="0"
                                            ^
```

Error: there is no attribute “border”

Fortunately, all these errors are ones you've seen before, and they're relatively easy to fix. Listing 21-5 makes the necessary corrections. Still, there's a deeper question. Why didn't the validator detect these problems the first time through? The reason is that some problems can mask other problems. In particular, the validator will not check anything inside an undefined element. For example, if a `font` element contains a `center` element, the validator will only report the `font` element as being a problem. It does not look inside the `font` element, so it won't find the `center` element or any other illegal elements or attributes that might be hidden there. Therefore, when you think you're done, you need to run the finished document through the validator to make sure that no hidden problems have been revealed (or even created) by your edits. In some cases, you may even need to make four or five or more passes through the validator before you have finally eliminated all the problems. This, however, is not one of those times. It turns out that Listing 21-5 is indeed valid strict XHTML, and no further edits are required.

Listing 21-5: **The Valid XHTML Document**

```
<!DOCTYPE html PUBLIC "-//W3C//DTD XHTML 1.0 Strict//EN"
                      "xhtml1-strict.dtd">
<html xmlns="http://www.w3.org/1999/xhtml">
  <head>
    <title>Mobile Office</title>
    <style type="text/css">
      a:link    {color: #000080}
      a:visited {color: #000080}
      a:active  {color: #000080}
   </style>
  </head>
<!--INSERT TITLE, INSERT TEXT-->

  <body style="font-size: smaller;
               font-family: 'Times New Roman';
```

Continued

Listing 21-5 *(continued)*

```
               background-color: #ffffff; color: black;
               leftmargin: 0; topmargin: 0">
    <table border="0">
      <tr valign="top">
        <td style="background-color: #EFEFCE" valign="top">
          <a href="http://www.house.gov/paul/">
      <img src="images/pflogosm.gif" style="border-width: 0px"
               alt="Project Freedom Logo"/>
          </a>
          <br class="empty"/>
          <table border="0">
            <tr>
              <td style="width: 2px"></td>
              <td>
         <span style="font-size: +1;
               font-family: 'MS Sans Serif', Geneva, Verdana">
                Menu
         </span><br class="empty"/>
     <span style="font-size: -2; font-family: 'Arial Narrow'">
     <a href="display.htm">Opening Page</a><br class="empty"/>
      <a href="search.htm">Search Project Freedom</a>
      <br class="empty"/>
      <a href="mail/welcome.htm">E-Communications</a>
      <br class="empty"/>
      --------------------<br class="empty"/>
      <a href="bio.htm">A Biography of Ron Paul</a>
      <br class="empty"/>
      <a href="about14.htm">Texas' 14th District</a>
      <br class="empty"/>
      <a href="committeework/welcome.htm">Committees</a>
      <br class="empty"/>
      --------------------<br class="empty"/>
      <a href="services14.htm">Constituent Services</a>
      <br class="empty"/>
      <b>Mobile Office<br class="empty"/></b>
      --------------------<br class="empty"/>
      <a href="legis/welcome.htm">Ron Paul's Legislation</a>
      <br class="empty"/>
  <a href="legis/106/cospon.htm">Cosponsors of Legislation</a>
      <br class="empty"/>
      <a href="privacy/display.htm">Privacy Forum</a>
      <br class="empty"/>
      --------------------<br class="empty"/>
      <a href="press/welcome.htm">Press Releases</a>
      <br class="empty"/>
      <a href="tst/welcome.htm">Weekly Column</a>
      <br class="empty"/>
      <a href="congrec/welcome.htm">Speeches</a>
      <br class="empty"/>
      <a href="tst/lu.htm">Legislative Update Line</a>
      <br class="empty"/>
```

```
 <a href="fwu/welcome.htm">Freedom Watch</a>
 <br class="empty"/>
 --------------------<br class="empty"/>
 <a href="impdoc.htm">Important Documents</a>
 <br class="empty"/>
 <a href="links.htm">Web Resources</a><br class="empty"/>
 --------------------<br class="empty"/>
 <a href="http://majoritywhip.house.gov/whipnotice.htm">
 House Floor Schedule</a><br class="empty"/>
 <a href="siteman.htm">Site Information</a>
      <br class="empty"/>
    </span>
  </td></tr>
  </table>
  <table border="1">
    <tr><td>
   <p style="font-size: -2; font-family: 'Arial Narrow'">
      The Office of U.S. Rep. Ron Paul<br class="empty"/>
      203 Cannon HOB<br class="empty"/>
      Washington, DC 20515<br class="empty"/>
      (202) 225-2831
     </p>
    </td></tr>
  </table>
</td>

<td valign="top" align="left">
  <!--PAGE TEXT INSERT HERE-->

  <div style="text-align: center">
    <img src="images/mo.gif" alt="The Mobile Office"/>
  </div>
  <p>
  What is the
  <a href="mobilewhatis.htm">Mobile Office</a>?
  </p>
  <p>
  <b>The <a href="mosched.htm">
  Current Mobile Office Schedule</a>.</b>
  </p>
  <p></p>
  <p>
    The <a href="moset.htm">Monthly Schedule
    for the Mobile office</a>.
  </p>
  <p></p>

   <img src="images/mobileoffice.gif"
   <img src="images/mobileoffice.gif"
        style="border-width: 0"
        alt="Mobile Office Minivan"/>
```

Continued

Listing 21-5 *(continued)*

```
<!--END OF PAGE-->
        </td></tr>
      </table>
      <p></p>
    </body>
</html>
```

The disadvantage of this approach is that many older browsers don't support all of the CSS style properties used here, although they do support the equivalent presentational elements and attributes. For example, when I loaded Listing 21-5 into Netscape Navigator 4.7.5, as shown in Figure 21-3, the picture of the Mobile Office minivan had moved to the top of the page for no apparent reason. However, Internet Explorer 5.5 for Windows did place the picture in the right place on the page. Because of problems such as this, it may be advisable to stick with the transitional DTD and the presentational attributes for a while longer until all your users have upgraded to browsers that fully support CSS and XHTML. Even in late 2003, the few pure XHTML web pages I've published elicit frequent complaints from readers with older browsers such as Internet Explorer 5.5.

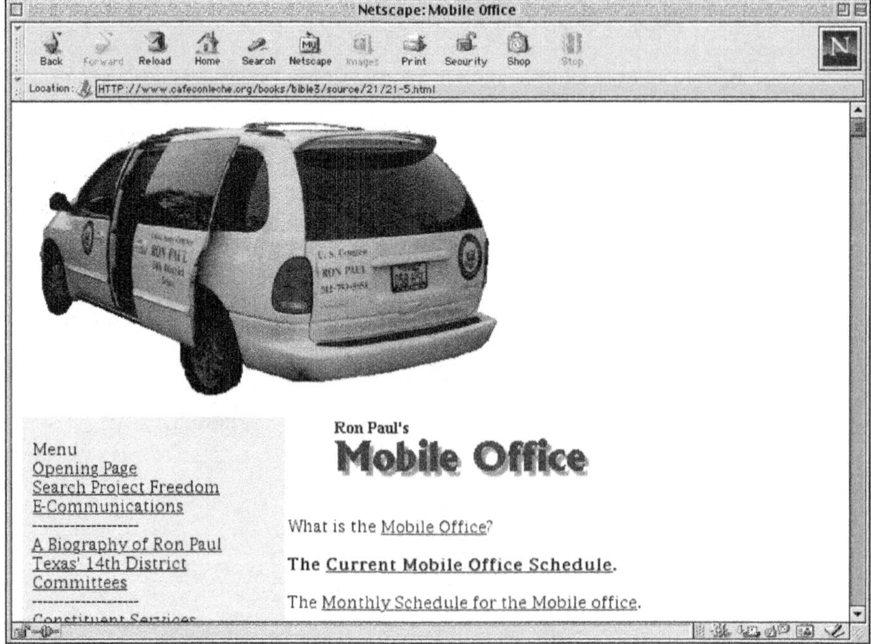

Figure 21-3: A browser exhibiting incorrect and unexplained rendering of an XHTML plus CSS document

The frameset DTD

The transitional DTD omits one popular feature of HTML — frames. The W3C has never liked frames, and with good reason — they're a user interface disaster that consistently irritate and bewilder readers. Nonetheless, many web designers like them, and many existing web sites use them.

Although I agree with the W3C and suggest that you avoid frames on all new pages you create, there are times when an existing site design makes that impossible, at least without an excessive investment of resources. Consequently, if you must use frames but you still want to move to XHTML and validate your documents, you can use the frameset DTD. This is very close to the transitional DTD, but adds all the necessary declarations for `frame`, `iframe`, `frameset`, and other frame-related elements and attributes. The document type declaration for a page built on top of the frame set DTD looks like this:

```
<!DOCTYPE html PUBLIC "-//W3C//DTD XHTML 1.0 Frameset//EN"
   "http://www.w3.org/TR/xhtml1/DTD/xhtml1-frameset.dtd">
```

As with the other two XHTML DTDs, it's probably a good idea to store a local copy of the frameset DTD and identify it by a relative URL rather than relying on the official copy at the W3C. Then the document type declaration would look like this instead:

```
<!DOCTYPE html PUBLIC "-//W3C//DTD XHTML 1.0 Frameset//EN"
                      "xhtml1-frameset.dtd">
```

HTML Tidy

Converting malformed HTML documents to valid XHTML by hand, as I've done in this chapter, can be a tedious and time-consuming job. Fortunately, Dave Raggett of the W3C has published HTML Tidy, an open source tool that can do much of the work for you. Tidy is a character-mode program written in ANSI C that can be compiled and run on most platforms, including Windows, UNIX, BeOS, and the Mac. The latest version is available from `http://tidy.sourceforge.net/`.

In its default mode Tidy tends to remove unnecessary (for HTML, but not for XML) end-tags such as `</li>` and to make other modifications that break well-formedness. However, you can use the `--output-xhtml` switch to specify that you want valid XHTML output. For example, to convert the file mobile_office.html to valid XHTML, you would type this command from a DOS window or shell prompt:

```
C:\> tidy --output-xhtml true mobile_office.html
```

By default, Tidy just prints its output on stdout (the console or DOS window from which you ran it), as well as messages about any problems it couldn't fix. You'll probably want to redirect the corrected document into a file using the > redirection operator, like this:

```
C:\>tidy --output-xhtml true mobile_office.html>21-6.html

Tidy (vers 30th April 2000) Parsing "mobile_office.html"
line 9 column 30 - Warning: <img> lacks "alt" attribute
line 68 column 4 - Warning: <img> lacks "alt" attribute

"mobile_office.html" appears to be HTML 3.2
2 warnings/errors were found!

The alt attribute should be used to give a short description
of an image; longer descriptions should be given with the
longdesc attribute which takes a URL linked to the description.
These measures are needed for people using non-graphical
browsers.

For further advice on how to make your pages accessible
see "http://www.w3.org/WAI/GL". You may also want to try
"http://www.cast.org/bobby/" which is a free Web-based
service for checking URLs for accessibility.

You are recommended to use CSS to specify the font and
properties such as its size and color. This will reduce
the size of HTML files and make them easier maintain
compared with using <FONT> elements.

HTML & CSS specifications are available from http://www.w3.org/
To learn more about Tidy see
http://www.w3.org/People/Raggett/tidy/
Please send bug reports to Dave Raggett care of
<html-tidy@w3.org>
Lobby your company to join W3C, see
http://www.w3.org/Consortium
```

Listing 21-6 shows the XHTML document Tidy produced. As the preceding message indicates, it's not actually a valid XHTML document. In this case, the problem is that two `img` elements are missing `alt` attributes. While Tidy could insert an empty `alt` attribute, that wouldn't really serve any purpose. It has to rely on a human being (you) to fill in a reasonable value for the alternate text. Otherwise, the document is well-formed. Most of the time, the problems Tidy fails to fix are not too difficult to fix by hand.

Listing 21-6: The Well-Formed, Almost-Valid XHTML Document Produced by Tidy

```
<!DOCTYPE html PUBLIC "-//W3C//DTD XHTML 1.0 Transitional//EN"
    "http://www.w3.org/TR/xhtml1/DTD/xhtml1-transitional.dtd">
<html xmlns="http://www.w3.org/1999/xhtml">
<head>
<meta name="generator" content="HTML Tidy, see www.w3.org" />
<title>Mobile Office</title>
<!--INSERT TITLE, INSERT TEXT-->
</head>
<body>
<basefont size="2" face="Times New Roman" />
<table border="0" valign="top" align="left">
<tr>
<td bgcolor="#EFEFCE" valign="top"><a
href="http://www.house.gov/paul/"><img
src="images/pflogosm.gif border="0" /></a><br />
<table border="0">
<tr>
<td width="2"></td>
<td border="1"><font size="+1"
face="MS Sans Serif, Geneva, Verdana">Menu</font><br />
 <font size="-2" face="Arial Narrow"><a
href="display.htm">Opening
Page</a><br />
<a href="search.htm">Search Project Freedom</a><br />
<a href="mail/welcome.htm">E-Communications</a><br />
--------------------<br />
<a href="bio.htm">A Biography of Ron Paul</a><br />
<a href="about14.htm">Texas' 14th District</a><br />
<a href="committeework/welcome.htm">Committees</a><br />
--------------------<br />
<a href="services14.htm">Constituent Services</a><br />
<b>Mobile Office<br />
</b> --------------------<br />
<a href="legis/welcome.htm">Ron Paul's Legislation</a><br />
<a href="legis/106/cospon.htm">Cosponsors of Legislation</a>
<br />
<a href="privacy/display.htm">Privacy Forum</a><br />
--------------------<br />
<a href="press/welcome.htm">Press Releases</a><br />
<a href="tst/welcome.htm">Weekly Column</a><br />
<a href="congrec/welcome.htm">Speeches</a><br />
<a href="tst/lu.htm">Legislative Update Line</a><br />
<a href="fwu/welcome.htm">Freedom Watch</a><br />
--------------------<br />
```

Continued

Listing 21-6 *(continued)*

```
<a href="impdoc.htm">Important Documents</a><br />
<a href="links.htm">Web Resources</a><br />
--------------------<br />
<a href="http://majoritywhip.house.gov/whipnotice.htm">House
Floor Schedule</a><br />
<a href="siteman.htm">Site Information<br />
</a></font> </td>
</tr>
</table>

<table align="right" border="1">
<tr>
<td><font size="1" face="Arial Narrow"></font>

<p><font size="1" face="Arial Narrow">The Office of U.S. Rep.
Ron Paul<br />
203 Cannon HOB<br />
Washington, DC 20515<br />
(202) 225-2831</font></p>

<p><font size="1" face="Arial Narrow"></font></p>
</td>
</tr>
</table>
</td>
<td valign="top" align="left"><!--PAGE TEXT INSERT HERE-->
<center><img src="images/mo.gif" alt="The Mobile Office" />
</center>

<p>What is the <a href="mobilewhatis.htm">Mobile Office</a>?
</p>

<p><b>The <a href="mosched.htm" target="new">Current Mobile
Office Schedule</a>.</b></p>

<p>The <a href="moset.htm">Monthly Schedule for the Mobile
office</a>.</p>

<p><img src="images/mobileoffice.gif" border="0" />
<!--END OF PAGE--></p>
</td>
</tr>
</table>
</body>
</html>
```

Tidy also missed a couple of problems as well. When I ran this document through the W3C validator, in addition to the aforementioned missing `alt` attributes, these two problems were found:

✦ Line 11, column 25:

```
<table border="0" valign="top" align="left">
                         ^
```

Error: there is no attribute "valign"

✦ Line 19, column 11:

```
<td border="1"><font size="+1"
           ^
```

Error: there is no attribute "border"

Still, all of these issues are easy enough to resolve once they're noticed. Tidy may not do everything for you, but it does do a lot.

Setting the MIME media type

There's one final step before you're ready to serve XHTML. You need to make sure browsers recognize your documents as XHTML instead of plain-vanilla HTML. Most browsers will treat a document quite differently depending on whether they think it's HTML or XHTML.

The first step is the filename extension. This should normally be .xhtml instead of .html or .htm. For a file loaded from the file system instead of a server, this is probably all you need to do.

The second step is to make sure the server assigns the MIME media type application/xhtml+xml to the file, not text/html like most HTML documents. If your web server comes configured to recognize XHTML documents, all you need to do is use the .xhtml file extension. Otherwise, you'll need to map the file extension to the MIME type.

The exact instructions for doing this vary from one server to the next. For Apache, you can add the following line to the server's mime.types file, which normally resides somewhere like /etc/mime.types:

```
application/xml+xhtml    xhtml
```

If you don't have access to that directory you can put this line in the .htaccess file for the directory where the XHTML files reside:

```
AddType application/xml+xhtml   xhtml
```

If Microsoft IIS is your web server of choice, you'll need to use the server GUI to add a MIME type. The details vary a little depending on the version of Windows and IIS, but it's roughly like this:

1. In the Start Menu, select Settings ➪ Control Panel.
2. Open the Administrative Tools control panel.
3. Open the Computer Management icon.
4. Select the HTTP Headers tab.
5. Click File Types to show a File Types dialog box.
6. Click New Type in this dialog box, and another dialog box pops up.
7. In this dialog box, enter the filename extension (.xhtml) and the media type associated with it (application/xhtml+xml).
8. Close everything in the reverse order that you opened it.

For other servers, please consult the server's documentation.

What's New in XHTML

For the most part, XHTML just tightens up existing HTML syntax. In the strict version, it even throws out some familiar elements and attributes, such as `font` and `bgcolor`. However, besides the stick of validity, XHTML proffers a few carrots as well. Browsers that understand XHTML can use the full panoply of XML syntax that isn't available in classic HTML. This includes the following:

✦ Character references

✦ Custom entity references defined in the DTD

✦ CDATA sections

✦ Encoding declarations

✦ The `xml:lang` attribute

On the other hand, these constructs are quite near the bleeding edge, because almost all of them cause problems for many browsers people are still using. Nonetheless, they can be viable in certain controlled environments and will become more useful as time passes and more people upgrade their browsers to full XHTML support. This section explores a few of the advantages of using fully XHTML-aware browsers.

Character references

XML documents are Unicode. By implication, that means XHTML documents are Unicode, too. You can present an XHTML browser with a document containing mixed English, Greek, Arabic, and Japanese and expect it to do something reasonable with it. The browser may not have the necessary fonts to render the non-Latin text, but at least it should not try to pretend that Arabic, Japanese, or Greek is just a funny form of Latin-1, as many browsers do now.

Even if the browser can display text written in unusual character sets, it may still not be easy to write such a document using existing editors. However, when writing XHTML, you can use decimal or hexadecimal character references to produce the full range of Unicode characters. A Unicode decimal character reference consists of the two characters `&#` followed by the character code, followed by a semicolon. For example, the capital Greek letter Σ has Unicode value 931, so it can be inserted in an XML file as `Σ`. To use hexadecimal instead, just put an `x` after the `#`. For example, Σ has hexadecimal value 3A3, so it may be inserted in an XML file as `Σ`. Because two bytes always produce exactly four hexadecimal digits and because most current Unicode characters occupy two bytes, it's customary (though not required) to include leading zeros in hexadecimal character references so that they are rounded out to four digits. Listing 21-7 shows an XHTML document containing a few lines from Plato's *Gorgias* that uses a mix of ASCII characters and decimal and hexadecimal character references.

Listing 21-7: An XHTML Document That Uses Character References

```
<!DOCTYPE html PUBLIC "-//W3C//DTD XHTML 1.0 Strict//EN"
                      "xhtml1-strict.dtd">
<html xmlns="http://www.w3.org/1999/xhtml">
<head>
  <title>Gorgias 447a from Plato</title>
</head>
<body>
<h1>Plato, <cite>Gorgias 447a</cite></h1>
<p>
<span style="font-weight: bold">
&#922;&#945;&#955;&#955;&#953;&#x301;&#954;&#955;&#951;&#962;
</span>:
&#960;&#959;&#955;&#949;&#x301;&#956;&#959;&#965;
&#954;&#945;&#953;&#x300;
&#956;&#945;&#x301;&#967;&#951;&#962;
&#966;&#945;&#963;&#953;&#x300;
&#967;&#961;&#951;&#x302;&#957;&#945;&#953;,
&#969;&#x313;&#x302;
&#931;&#969;&#x301;&#954;&#961;&#945;&#964;&#949;&#962;,
&#959;&#965;&#x314;&#x301;&#964;&#969;
&#956;&#949;&#964;&#945;&#955;&#945;&#947;&#967;&#945;&#x301;
&#957;&#949;&#953;&#957;.
</p>
<p>
<span style="font-weight: bold">
```

Continued

Listing 21-7 (continued)

```
&#931;&#969;&#954;&#961;&#945;&#x301;&#964;&#951;&#962;</span>:
&#945;&#x313;&#955;&#955;'
&#951;&#x313;&#x302;, &#964;&#959;&#x300;
&#955;&#949;&#947;&#959;&#x301;&#956;&#949;&#957;&#959;&#957;,
&#954;&#945;&#964;&#959;&#x301;&#960;&#953;&#957;
&#949;&#x314;&#959;&#961;&#964;&#951;&#x302;&#962;
&#951;&#x314;&#x301;&#954;&#959;&#956;&#949;&#957;
&#954;&#945;&#953;&#x300;
&#965;&#x314;&#963;&#964;&#949;&#961;&#959;&#965;&#x302;&#956;
&#949;&#957;;
</p>
<p>
<span style="font-weight: bold">
&#922;&#945;&#955;&#955;&#953;&#x301;&#954;&#955;&#951;&#962;
</span>:
&#954;&#945;&#953;&#x300; &#956;&#945;&#x301;&#955;&#945;
&#947;&#949;
&#945;&#x313;&#963;&#964;&#949;&#953;&#x301;&#945;&#962;
&#949;&#x314;&#959;&#961;&#964;&#951;&#x302;&#962;:
&#960;&#959;&#955;&#955;&#945;&#x300;
&#947;&#945;&#x300;&#961; &#954;&#945;&#953;&#x300;
&#954;&#945;&#955;&#945;&#x300;
&#915;&#959;&#961;&#947;&#953;&#x301;&#945;&#962;
&#951;&#x314;&#956;&#953;&#x302;&#957;&#959;&#x313;&#955;&#953;
&#x301;&#947;&#959;&#957;
&#960;&#961;&#959;&#x301;&#964;&#949;&#961;&#959;&#957;&#949;
&#x313;&#960;&#949;&#948;&#949;&#953;&#x301;&#958;&#945;&#964;
&#959;.
</p>
<p><span style="font-weight: bold">
&#931;&#969;&#954;&#961;&#945;&#x301;&#964;&#951;&#962;</span>:
&#964;&#959;&#965;&#x301;&#964;&#969;&#957;
&#956;&#949;&#x301;&#957;&#964;&#959;&#953;,
&#969;&#x313;&#x302;
&#922;&#945;&#955;&#955;&#953;&#x301;&#954;&#955;&#949;&#953;
&#962;,
&#945;&#953;&#x313;&#x301;&#964;&#953;&#959;&#962;
&#967;&#945;&#953;&#961;&#949;&#966;&#969;&#x302;&#957;
&#959;&#x314;&#x301;&#948;&#949;,
&#949;&#x313;&#957;
&#945;&#x313;&#947;&#959;&#961;&#945;&#x302;&#x345;
&#945;&#x313;&#957;&#945;&#947;&#954;&#945;&#x301;&#963;&#945;
&#962;
&#951;&#x314;&#956;&#945;&#x302;&#962;
&#948;&#953;&#945;&#964;&#961;&#953;&#x302;&psi;&#945;&#953;
</p>
</body>
</html>
```

Figure 21-4 shows this document loaded into the XHTML-savvy Mozilla. However, this document doesn't work nearly so well in older, non-XHTML-aware browsers, as Figure 21-5 shows.

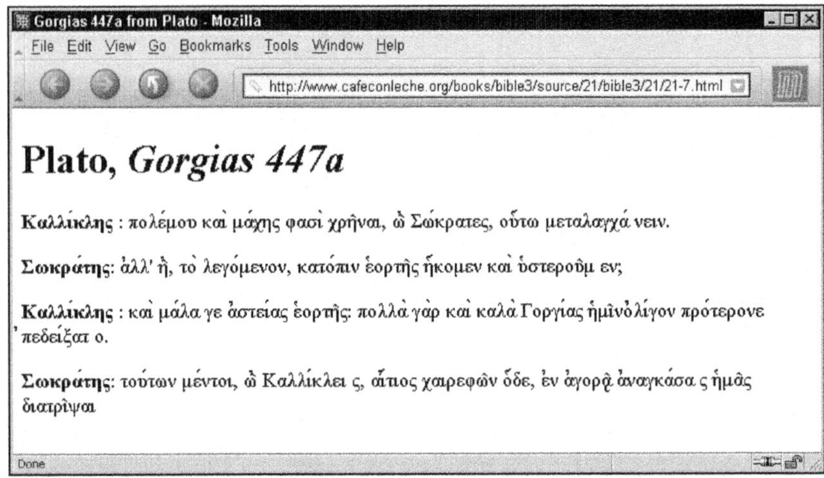

Figure 21-4: Mozilla can display Greek text typed with character references.

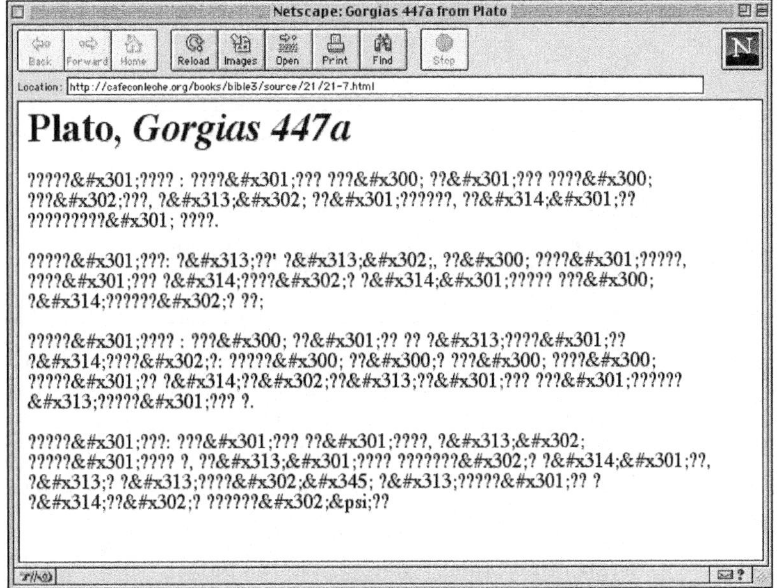

Figure 21-5: Legacy browsers don't know what to do with character references.

There's also a middle ground. Some browsers understand character references but either don't have or don't know how to use the fonts needed to display those characters. Mozilla 1.2 on Mac OS 9 just displayed question marks for most of the characters in Listing 21-7, as shown in Figure 21-6. Internet Explorer 6.0 can handle the Greek letters and some of the accents, but is thrown by the breathing marks, as shown in Figure 21-7.

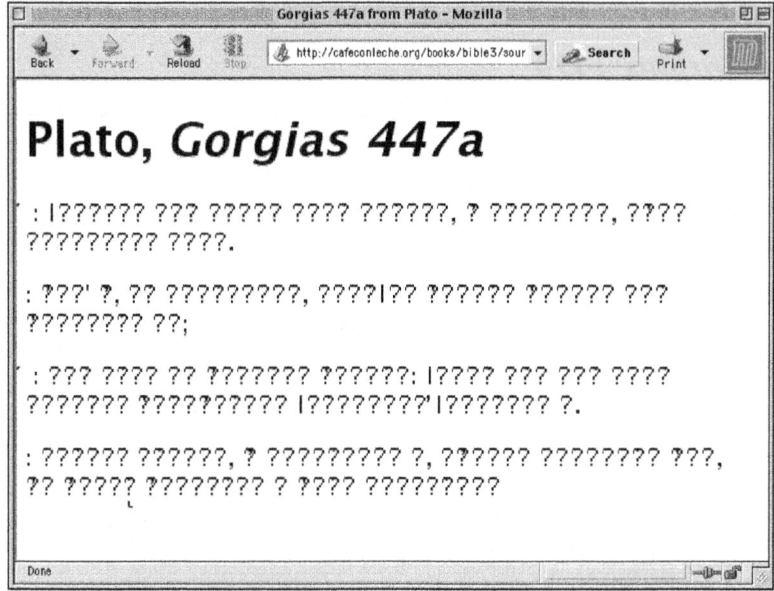

Figure 21-6: Mozilla 1.2 recognizes that the character references are not Roman letters, but can't display them.

Custom entity references defined in DTD

Most web browsers understand a very basic set of predefined entity references, including `<`, `&`, `©`, ` `, and so on. HTML 4.0 expanded this set to several hundred entity references, including characters from the upper half of the Latin-1 character set such as ñ (`ñ`) and Ü (`Ü`), mathematical symbols such as ∂ (`∂`) and √ (`√`), Greek letters such as Θ (`θ`) and Ω (`Ω`), and a few others besides. All of these are available in XHTML documents as well. All three XHTML DTDs define these entities so that you can use them.

In addition, you can define other entity references in the internal or external DTD subsets of your document, just as you might for any XML document. These can either point to individual characters, to text strings, to elements, or to groups of elements. For example, Listing 21-8 is a DTD fragment that defines several combining diacritical marks frequently used in classical Greek.

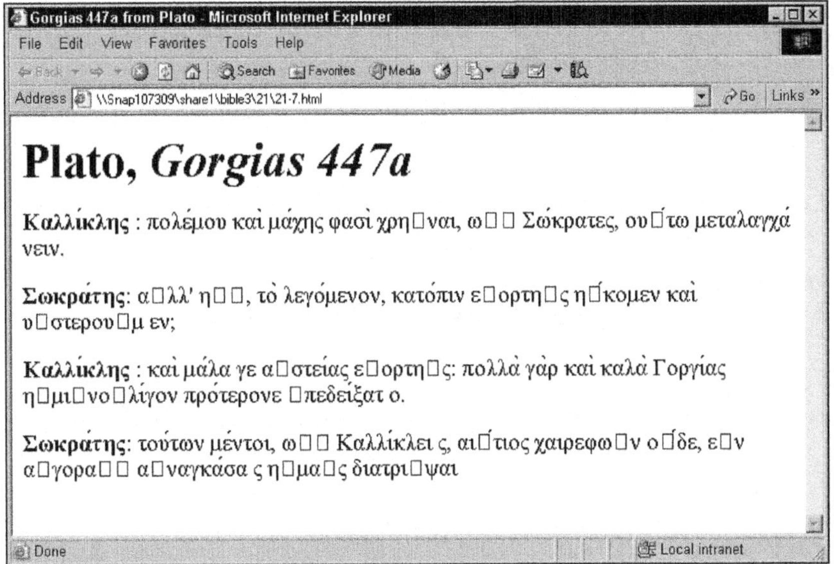

Figure 21-7: Internet Explorer 6.0 can handle the Greek letters but not the breathing marks.

Listing 21-8: greek_accents.ent: A DTD Subset Defining Greek Diacritical Marks

```
<!ENTITY varia          "&#x300;"> <!-- grave accent -->
<!ENTITY oxia           "&#x301;"> <!-- acute accent -->
<!ENTITY circumflex     "&#x302;">
<!ENTITY psili          "&#x313;"> <!-- smooth breathing -->
<!ENTITY dasia          "&#x314;"> <!-- rough breathing -->
<!ENTITY iota_subscript "&#x345;">
```

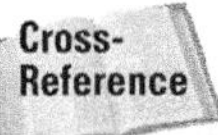

Entity references are discussed in more detail in Chapter 10.

Listing 21-9 is a more intelligible version of Listing 21-7. It imports this entity set and uses the five general entities found there for the accent and breathing marks instead of numeric character references. For the Greek letters, it uses general entity references defined in the XHTML strict DTD. Finally, it defines three general entities in the internal DTD subset for the names of Socrates, Gorgias, and Kallikles.

Listing 21-9: An XHTML Document That Uses Entity References

```
<!DOCTYPE html PUBLIC "-//W3C//DTD XHTML 1.0 Strict//EN"
                      "xhtml1-strict.dtd" [

  <!ENTITY % greek_accents SYSTEM "greek_accents.ent">
  %greek_accents;

  <!ENTITY Socrates
   "&Sigma;&omega;&kappa;&rho;&alpha;&oxia;&tau;&eta;&sigmaf;">
  <!ENTITY Gorgias
   "&Gamma;&omicron;&rho;&gamma;&iota;&oxia;&alpha;&sigmaf;">
  <!ENTITY Kallikles
"&Kappa;&alpha;&lambda;&lambda;&iota;&oxia;&kappa;&lambda;&eta;&sigmaf;"
>

]>
<html xmlns="http://www.w3.org/1999/xhtml">
<head>
  <title>Gorgias 447a from Plato</title>
</head>
<body>
<h1>Plato, <cite>Gorgias 447a</cite></h1>
<p>
<span style="font-weight: bold">&Kallikles;</span>:
&pi;&omicron;&lambda;&epsilon;&oxia;&mu;&omicron;&upsilon;
&kappa;&alpha;&iota;&varia;
&mu;&alpha;&oxia;&chi;&eta;&sigmaf;
&phi;&alpha;&sigma;&iota;&varia;
&chi;&rho;&eta;&circumflex;&nu;&alpha;&iota;,
&omega;&psili;&circumflex;
&Sigma;&omega;&oxia;&kappa;&rho;&alpha;&tau;&epsilon;&sigmaf;,
&omicron;&upsilon;&dasia;&oxia;&tau;&omega;
&mu;&epsilon;&tau;&alpha;&lambda;&alpha;&gamma;&chi;
&alpha;&oxia;&nu;&epsilon;&iota;&nu;.
</p>
<p>
<span style="font-weight: bold">&Socrates;</span>:
&alpha;&psili;&lambda;&lambda;'
&eta;&psili;&circumflex;, &tau;&omicron;&varia;
&lambda;&epsilon;&gamma;&omicron;&oxia;&mu;&epsilon;&nu;
&omicron;&nu;,
&kappa;&alpha;&tau;&omicron;&oxia;&pi;&iota;&nu;
&epsilon;&dasia;&omicron;&rho;&tau;&eta;&circumflex;&sigmaf;
&eta;&dasia;&oxia;&kappa;&omicron;&mu;&epsilon;&nu;
&kappa;&alpha;&iota;&varia;
&upsilon;&dasia;&sigma;&tau;&epsilon;&rho;&omicron;
```

```
&upsilon;&circumflex;&mu;&epsilon;&nu;;
</p>
<p>
<span style="font-weight: bold">
&Kallikles;</span>:
&kappa;&alpha;&iota;&varia;
&mu;&alpha;&oxia;&lambda;&alpha;
&gamma;&epsilon;
&alpha;&psili;&sigma;&tau;&epsilon;&iota;&oxia;&alpha;&sigmaf;
&epsilon;&dasia;&omicron;&rho;&tau;&eta;&circumflex;&sigmaf;:
&pi;&omicron;&lambda;&lambda;&alpha;&varia;
&gamma;&alpha;&varia;&rho; &kappa;&alpha;&iota;&varia;
&kappa;&alpha;&lambda;&alpha;&varia; &Gorgias;
&eta;&dasia;&mu;&iota;&circumflex;&nu;&omicron;&psili;&lambda;
&iota;&oxia;&gamma;&omicron;&nu;
&pi;&rho;&omicron;&oxia;&tau;&epsilon;&rho;&omicron;&nu;
&epsilon;&psili;&pi;&epsilon;&delta;&epsilon;&iota;&oxia;&xi;
&alpha;&tau;&omicron;.
</p>
<p><span style="font-weight: bold">
&Socrates;</span>:
&tau;&omicron;&upsilon;&oxia;&tau;&omega;&nu;
&mu;&epsilon;&oxia;&nu;&tau;&omicron;&iota;,
&omega;&psili;&circumflex;
&Kappa;&alpha;&lambda;&lambda;&iota;&oxia;&kappa;&lambda;
&epsilon;&iota;&sigmaf;,
&alpha;&iota;&psili;&oxia;&tau;&iota;&omicron;&sigmaf;
&Chi;&alpha;&iota;&rho;&epsilon;&phi;&omega;&circumflex;&nu;
&omicron;&dasia;&oxia;&delta;&epsilon;, &epsilon;&psili;&nu;
&alpha;&psili;&gamma;&omicron;&rho;
&alpha;&circumflex;&iota_subscript;
&alpha;&psili;&nu;&alpha;&gamma;&kappa;&alpha;&oxia;&sigma;
&alpha;&sigmaf;
&eta;&dasia;&mu;&alpha;&circumflex;&sigmaf;
&delta;&iota;&alpha;&tau;&rho;&iota;&circumflex;&psi;&alpha;
&iota;
</p>
</body>
</html>
```

Unfortunately, this document requires a level of XHTML savvy that none of the browsers I was able to test possessed. None of them recognized the nonpredefined entities from either the internal or external DTD subsets. They all either displayed something more or less like Figure 21-8 or Figure 21-9, the former if they thought the file was HTML, and the latter if they thought it was XHTML. The use of author-defined entity references in XHTML documents is likely to remain theoretical for some time to come.

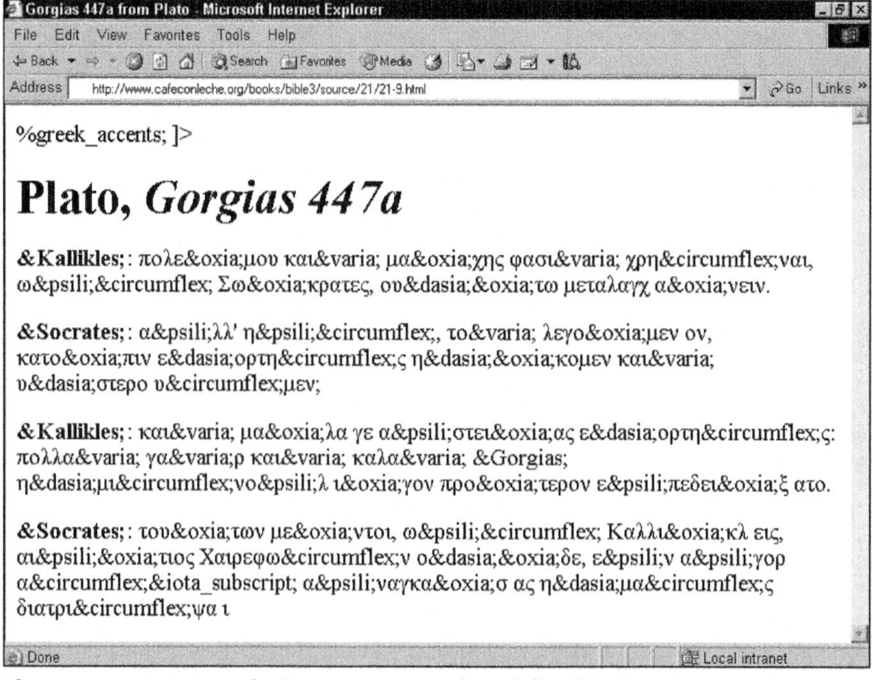

Figure 21-8: Browsers don't yet support author-defined entity references in HTML.

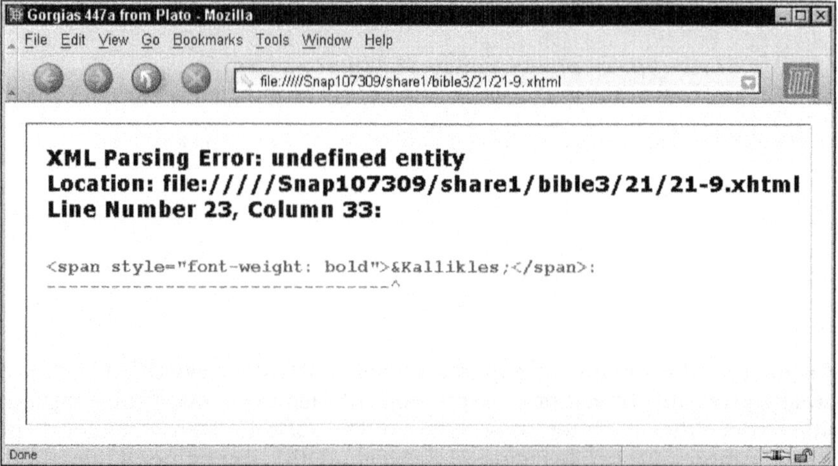

Figure 21-9: Browsers don't yet support author-defined entity references in XHTML.

Encoding declarations

Web servers are supposed to identify the character set and encoding of documents they send in the Content-type field of the HTTP header they prefix to each document. For example, this HTTP header specifies the UTF-8 encoding of the Unicode character set:

```
HTTP/1.1 200 OK
Date: Thu, 07 Dec 2000 21:09:53 GMT
Server: Apache/1.3.6 Ben-SSL/1.36 (Unix)
Last-Modified: Tue, 21 Dec 1999 03:04:51 GMT
Content-Length: 5201
Content-Type: text/html; charset=utf-8
```

In practice, however, most servers fail to do this. Furthermore, it's difficult to configure a web server to understand that particular documents are in some encoding other than the most common one on that particular system. Therefore, HTML authors who use a character set that goes beyond simple ASCII normally identify the set they're using with a `meta` element and an `http-equiv` attribute in the HTML `head`, like this:

```
<meta
  http-equiv="Content-Type" content="text/html; charset=UTF-8"
/>
```

To make matters worse, whereas most web browsers assume a document uses Latin-1 when faced with an unidentified character set, XML processors are required to assume that documents are written in UTF-8 unless they're told otherwise. While some browsers (though not all) will recognize a `charset` parameter passed in an HTTP header, none will notice a `meta` element similar to this one.

Of course, XML documents have a different means of specifying character sets using an encoding declaration inside the XML declaration, as in the following example:

```
<?xml version="1.0" encoding="UTF-8"?>
```

Unfortunately, some browsers that don't recognize this construct as an XML declaration or explicitly support XHTML will try to display it, so you want to avoid including it if possible. The most broadly compatible option is to author your documents in UTF-8 so that you can omit the XML declaration, and use a `meta` element to tell HTML browsers what they're dealing with. If UTF-8 is too sophisticated for your installed base of browsers, you should stick to pure ASCII (a subset of UTF-8) and the predefined entity references.

The xml:lang attribute

The `xml:lang` attribute contains a code identifying which language the content of that element is written in. For example, these opening lines from Marcel Proust's *Du côté de chez Swann* are written in French, *naturellement*:

```
<q xml:lang="fr-FR"
 cite="ftp://movie0.archive.org/pub/etext/etext01/swann10h.htm"
>
Longtemps, je me suis couchà de bonne heure. Parfois, σ peine
ma bougie àteinte, mes yeux se fermaient si vite que je
n'avais pas le temps de me dire: "Je m'endors."
</q>
```

In HTML, language identification is normally handled by the `lang` attribute instead, but otherwise the syntax is the same as in this `q` element:

```
<q lang="fr-FR"
 cite="ftp://movie0.archive.org/pub/etext/etext01/swann10h.htm"
>
Longtemps, je me suis couchà de bonne heure. Parfois, σ peine
ma bougie àteinte, mes yeux se fermaient si vite que je
n'avais pas le temps de me dire: "Je m'endors."
</q>
```

For XHTML 1.0, the W3C recommends using both the `lang` and `xml:lang` attributes, like this:

```
<q lang="fr-FR" xml:lang="fr-FR"
 cite="ftp://movie0.archive.org/pub/etext/etext01/swann10h.htm"
>
Longtemps, je me suis couchà de bonne heure. Parfois, σ peine
ma bougie àteinte, mes yeux se fermaient si vite que je
n'avais pas le temps de me dire: "Je m'endors."
</q>
```

HTML-aware tools will use the `lang` attribute to determine the language. XML-aware tools will use the `xml:lang` attribute. In the event of a conflict between the two, the value of the `xml:lang` attribute should take precedence, though this may depend more on which attribute the tool in question expects to read than on the official rules for disambiguation.

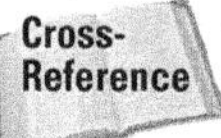

The `xml:lang` attribute was first introduced in Chapter 6.

CDATA sections

Before there were any books about HTML, many people, the author of this book included, learned HTML from the NCSA's *A Beginner's Guide to HTML*, which is itself written in HTML and published on the Web at `http://www.ncsa.uiuc.edu/General/Internet/WWW/HTMLPrimer.html`. Over the years, many other online tutorials about HTML and other new markup languages have been written in HTML and published on the Web. Today, many people are writing and reading online tutorials about SVG, MathML, schemas, XHTML, and other cutting-edge topics. Indeed, I read a few of these while preparing to write the book you're reading now.

Of course, if you've ever written such a tutorial, you've noticed a problem. It's extremely inconvenient to write about HTML or anything that looks remotely like HTML in HTML. The problem is that all the examples of markup are interpreted by the browser as markup and disappear from the rendered document. For example, if I were writing about the `pre` element in HTML, I might write something like this:

```
<p>
HTML normally answers the question of whether white space is
significant or not by predefining the meaning of white space
in particular elements. For instance, white space is
significant inside <code><pre></code> and <code></pre></code>
tags. It's not significant almost everywhere else. This means
that if you want to preserve line breaks without using a
monospaced font, you need to insert a lot of <code><br></code>
tags as in this first stanza from William Blake's poem
<cite>The Tyger</cite>:
</p>
<pre><code><p>
Tyger! Tyger! burning bright<br class="empty"/>
In the forests of the night<br class="empty"/>
What immortal hand or eye<br class="empty"/>
Could frame thy fearful symmetry?<br class="empty"/>
</p></code></pre>
```

Of course, when this was displayed in a browser, you'd see something like this:

> HTML normally answers the question of whether white space is significant or not by predefining the meaning of white space in particular elements. For instance, white space is significant inside and tags. It's not significant almost everywhere else. This means that if you want to preserve line breaks without using a monospaced font, you need to insert a lot of tags, as in this first stanza from William Blake's poem *The Tyger*:
>
> ```
> Tyger! Tyger! burning bright
>
> In the forests of the night
> ```

```
What immortal hand or eye

Could frame thy fearful symmetry?
```

This is not what you wanted at all! Of course, you know the solution. I should have escaped all the less than signs from the markup I wanted to appear in the rendered document using entity references such as `<`, and if there were any raw ampersands in this sample, they'd need to be escaped too. The result looks like this:

```
<p>
HTML normally answers the question of whether white space is
significant or not by predefining the meaning of white space
in particular elements. For instance, white space is
significant inside <code>&lt;pre></code> and
<code>&lt;/pre></code> tags. It's not significant almost
everywhere else. This means that if you want to preserve line
breaks without using a monospaced font, you need to insert a
lot of <code>&lt;br></code> tags as in this first stanza from
William Blake's poem <cite>The Tyger</cite>:
</p>
<pre><code>&lt;p>
Tyger! Tyger! burning bright&lt;br class="empty"/>
In the forests of the night&lt;br class="empty"/>
What immortal hand or eye&lt;br class="empty"/>
Could frame thy fearful symmetry?&lt;br class="empty"/>
&lt;/p></code></pre>
```

While adequate for occasional illegal characters, this is very tedious to do for large examples. XML, by contrast, offers a very neat solution: Just wrap the entire example in a CDATA section and then use the markup as you normally would. You can still use `<` and `&` for the smaller pieces where the example markup is intermingled with real markup, as in the following example:

```
<p>
HTML normally answers the question of whether white space is
significant or not by predefining the meaning of white space
in particular elements. For instance, white space is
significant inside <code><pre></code> and <code></pre></code>
tags. It's not significant almost everywhere else. This means
that if you want to preserve line breaks without using a
monospaced font, you need to insert a lot of <code><br></code>
tags as in this first stanza from William Blake's poem
<cite>The Tyger</cite>:
</p>
<pre><code><![CDATA[<p>
Tyger! Tyger! burning bright<br class="empty"/>
In the forests of the night<br class="empty"/>
What immortal hand or eye<br class="empty"/>
Could frame thy fearful symmetry?<br class="empty"/>
</p>]]></code></pre>
```

CDATA sections are discussed in more detail in Chapter 6.

This is much easier to write, much easier to debug, and much easier to read. Most XML-aware browsers I tested rendered this example correctly, including Mozilla, Opera 7, and Safari, as shown in Figure 21-10. However, several versions of Internet Explorer on three different platforms were all incapable of showing the content inside the CDATA section. CDATA sections are unfortunately still on the wrong side of the bleeding edge. Once Microsoft gets its act together, however, this will make writing online tutorials for the next generation of markup languages much easier.

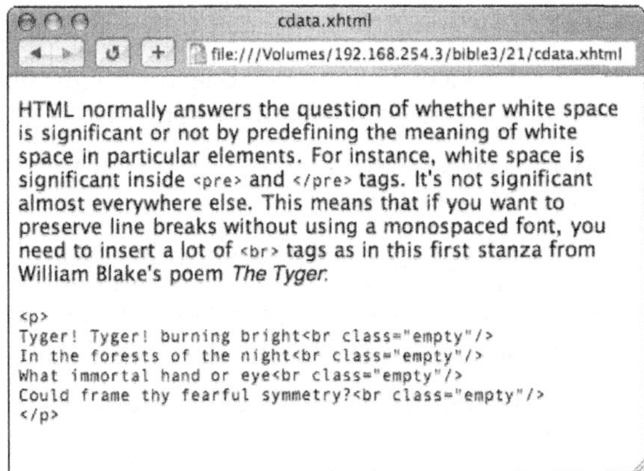

Figure 21-10: Safari recognizes CDATA sections in XHTML documents.

Summary

In this chapter, you learned the following:

- ✦ XHTML is a reformulation of HTML as an XML application. Among other changes, this requires making your HTML documents well-formed.
- ✦ When converting an existing HTML document into well-formed XML, you have to make sure all attribute values are quoted, all entity references are declared, all start-tags have matching end-tags, that there is a single root element, and that elements do not overlap.
- ✦ XHTML documents must be valid according to one of three DTDs.
- ✦ The XHTML transitional DTD allows most standard HTML and XHTML elements and attributes defined in HTML 4.0 and earlier except for frames.

✦ The XHTML frameset DTD allows everything the transitional DTD allows, and adds the elements and attributes needed to work with frames.

✦ The XHTML strict DTD disallows frame elements such as `frame`, presentational elements such as `center` and `bgcolor`, and deprecated elements such as `applet`. The eliminated presentational attributes and elements are replaced by CSS styles.

✦ When converting an existing HTML document into valid XHTML, you have to repeatedly use a validation tool to make sure you're only using allowed elements and attributes and only in the ways the DTD allows them to be used.

✦ Dave Raggett's HTML Tidy is a very useful tool for automating the grunt work involved in converting existing HTML documents to XHTML; but you'll probably need to do some work by hand when Tidy is through with a document.

✦ XHTML lets you use character references in your web pages, though the browser still needs a font it can use to draw those characters.

✦ XHTML lets you define entity references in the DTD to use in your web pages, but current browsers often don't recognize these.

✦ XML parsers determine the character set from an encoding declaration. HTML parsers determine the character set from the `charset` parameter of the Content-type field of an HTTP header. XHTML documents use the encoding declaration, but only if the browser specifically knows about XHTML.

✦ XML's `xml:lang` attribute and HTML's `lang` attribute should both be used to identify the language of an element.

✦ Theoretically, XHTML allows you to use CDATA sections in your web pages, but Internet Explorer 6.0 and later can't handle this.

This chapter described XHTML 1.0. Chapter 22 takes up Modular XHTML and XHTML 1.1. While the basic vocabulary is the same between XHTML 1.0 and 1.1, Modular XHTML divides the XHTML DTD into many separate parts that can be mixed and matched with other applications, such as MathML and SVG, to create unique combinations of functionality. Different profiles of XHTML offer different combinations of functionality suitable for different needs.

✦ ✦ ✦

Modular XHTML

✦ ✦ ✦ ✦

In This Chapter

The modules of XHTML

A sample DTD module

The framework

The driver DTD

The document model

A sample schema module

✦ ✦ ✦ ✦

XHTML 1.0 is still, by and large, HTML. The syntax has changed a little, but the same elements and attributes are present, and they mean essentially the same things in XHTML that they mean in HTML 4.0. You can do pretty much the same things with XHTML 1.0 that you're already doing with HTML. Officially, the acronym XHTML stands for *Extensible Hypertext Markup Language*, but in truth its extensibility is limited. You get to pick the transitional, strict, or frameset DTDs, but that's the limit of your freedom. You can't mix in Scalable Vector Graphics (SVG) or MathML or take out tables without violating the DTDs, and thus producing invalid XHTML.

XHTML 1.1, by contrast, is much more practically extensible. It is divided into abstract modules, each covering a specific area of functionality, such as tables, forms, images, structure, and text. The individual modules are instantiated as particular DTD or schema components. The DTD components are connected by parameter entity references. By overriding particular parameter entity references, you can pick and choose which modules you want to include in your own applications. Furthermore, you can mix in DTD modules from other XML applications such as SVG or the Resource Directory Description Language (RDDL). As well as the full XHTML 1.1 profile, the W3C has published a stripped-down version called XHTML Basic and duded-up versions that add Synchronized Multimedia Integration Language (SMIL) and MathML. Alternately, you can embed XHTML or particular parts of it into your own XML applications.

The Modules of XHTML

Modular XHTML does not define any new elements or attributes not already present in HTML 4.0 and XHTML 1.0. However, it does organize all the elements and attributes of standard HTML into 28 *modules*, each of which defines a different subset of the elements and attributes used in XHTML. Most of these subsets are disjoint, though there are a few places where they overlap. Table 22-1 lists the 28 modules and specifies which elements each declares.

Table 22-1
XHTML Modules

Module	*Purpose*	*Defines*
Structure	Organization of the XML document	body, head, html, and title
Text	Basic text markup	abbr, acronym, address, blockquote, br, cite, code, dfn, div, em, h1, h2, h3, h4, h5, h6, kbd, p, pre, q, samp, span, strong, and var
Hypertext	Linking	The a element and its unique attributes: accesskey, charset, href, hreflang, rel, rev, tabindex, and type
List	Three different kinds of lists	dl, dt, dd, ul, ol, and li.
Applet	Java applets	The applet and param elements, as well as their unique attributes
Presentation	Elements that are solely about appearance rather than meaning	b, big, hr, i, small, sub, sup, and tt
Edit	Revision tracking	del and ins, as well as their unique attributes, cite and datetime
Bi-directional Text	Elements used to indicate a shift from left-to-right to right-to-left text and vice versa	The bdo element and its dir attribute
Basic Forms	Forms as defined in HTML 3.2 and earlier	form, input, label, select, option, and textarea elements
Forms	Forms as defined in HTML 4.0 and later	form, input, label, select, option, textarea, button, fieldset, label, legend, and optgroup
Basic Tables	A limited group of table elements	table, td, th, tr, and caption
Tables	All the table elements	table, td, th, tr, col, colgroup, tbody, thead, tfoot, and caption
Image	Images	The img element and its unique attributes alt, width, height, longdesc, and src

Module	*Purpose*	*Defines*
Client-Side Image Map	Image maps resolved by the client	`area` and `map`; also adds some attributes to the `a`, `img`, `input`, and `object` elements to support their use in image maps
Server-Side Image Map	Image maps interpreted by the server	The `ismap` attribute of the `img` and `input` elements
Object	Embedded non-HTML content like Flash pictures and Shockwave animations	`object` and `param`
Frames	Frame-related elements and attributes	`frame`, `frameset`, and `noframes`
Iframe	Internal frames	`iframe`
Target	Which frame to load a selection in	The `target` attribute of the `a`, `area`, `base`, `link`, and `form` elements
Intrinsic Events	JavaScript event handlers	`onblur`, `onfocus`, `onload`, `onunload`, `onreset`, `onsubmit`, `onchange`, and `onselect` attributes
Scripting	Scripts	The `script` and `noscript` elements
Meta-information	Information about the document	The `meta` element along with its `content`, `http-equiv`, `name`, and `scheme` attributes
Style Sheet	Elements used for CSS styles	The `style` element and its `media`, `title`, and `type` attributes
Style Attribute	Attributes used for CSS styles	The `style` attribute
Link	Related resources	The `link` element used in HTML headers, along with its `charset`, `href`, `hreflang`, `media`, `rel`, `rev`, and `type` attributes
Base	Used to identify the URL against which relative URLs in the document should be resolved	The `base` element and its `href` attribute
Name Identification	Intradocument linking	The deprecated `name` attribute of the `a`, `applet`, `form`, `frame`, `iframe`, `img` and `map` elements
Legacy	Very deprecated presentational elements and attributes you really don't need to use in 2004	`basefont`, `center`, `dir`, `font`, `isindex`, `menu`, `s`, `strike`, and `u`, as well as deprecated presentational attributes like `bgcolor` and `align`

Within some limits you can use these modules independently of each other and pick and choose those you want. For example, if you just want to add simple lists to an application, you only have to load the list module, the modules that define what a list item can contain (mostly the text module), and the framework modules on which all the other XHTML modules depend. (I'll get to these shortly.) However, you don't have to use tables, frames, applets, and all the other complicated parts of HTML if you don't need them.

Some modules are used in almost all variations of XHTML. For example, the structure, text, hypertext, and list modules are the core on which XHTML documents are built. To some extent they correspond to the functionality that's been present since HTML 1.0. Other modules are used quite rarely. For instance, the legacy module declares deprecated elements such as `font`, `center`, and `dir` that you shouldn't use in new documents but might need to validate in older ones. In a few cases, modules are alternatives to each other. For example, you can choose either the Basic Tables module, which includes only the `table`, `caption`, `th`, `td`, and `tr` elements, or the full tables module, which includes `col`, `colgroup`, `tbody`, `thead`, and `tfoot` as well. However, you wouldn't choose both.

For the most part, however, standard HTML pages require most of the modules. It's when you begin mixing XHTML into your own XML applications that you can take advantage of smaller subsets of functionality. For example, in a collection of movie reviews, each review might contain elements for the title of the movie, the year, the actors in the movie, and so forth. However, because the review itself is a more or less free-form narrative text with no particular structure, each review could also contain a `description` element that contained XHTML. If you wanted only simple reviews you might choose to leave out the forms and tables and applet modules, and indeed omit everything except the core modules.

A Sample DTD Module

Listing 22-1 shows the List module, one of the four core modules required for a minimal implementation of XHTML. This defines the definition, unordered and ordered lists represented by the `dl`, `dt`, `dd`, `ul`, `ol`, and `li` elements. You can download this and the other XHTML modules from `http://www.w3.org/TR/xhtml-modularization/`. They're bundled with the zip version of the XHTML modularization specification.

Like all modules in XHTML, it has a standard public identifier, `-//W3C//ELEMENTS XHTML Lists 1.0//EN`. It also has a suggested system identifier, `http://www.w3.org/TR/xhtml-modularization/DTD/xhtml-list-1.mod`. However, this can be changed if you want to point to a different copy of the DTD in a different location; for example, if you wanted to store a copy on your local hard drive rather than relying on the official version at the W3C Web site.

Listing 22-1: xhtml-list-1.mod: The List Module DTD

```
<!-- ...................................................... -->
<!-- XHTML Lists Module  ................................. -->
<!-- file: xhtml-list-1.mod

    This is XHTML, a reformulation of HTML as a modular XML application.
    Copyright 1998-2001 W3C (MIT, INRIA, Keio), All Rights Reserved.
    Revision: $Id: xhtml-list-1.mod,v 4.0 2001/04/02 22:42:49 altheim Exp $ SMI

     This DTD module is identified by the PUBLIC and SYSTEM identifiers:

PUBLIC "-//W3C//ELEMENTS XHTML Lists 1.0//EN"
SYSTEM "http://www.w3.org/TR/xhtml-modularization/DTD/xhtml-list-1.mod"

     Revisions:
     (none)
     ...................................................... -->

<!-- Lists

        dl, dt, dd, ol, ul, li

     This module declares the list-oriented element types
     and their attributes.
-->

<!ENTITY % dl.qname  "dl" >
<!ENTITY % dt.qname  "dt" >
<!ENTITY % dd.qname  "dd" >
<!ENTITY % ol.qname  "ol" >
<!ENTITY % ul.qname  "ul" >
<!ENTITY % li.qname  "li" >

<!-- dl: Definition List ............................... -->

<!ENTITY % dl.element  "INCLUDE" >
<![%dl.element;[
<!ENTITY % dl.content  "( %dt.qname; | %dd.qname; )+" >
<!ELEMENT %dl.qname;  %dl.content; >
<!-- end of dl.element -->]]>

<!ENTITY % dl.attlist  "INCLUDE" >
<![%dl.attlist;[
<!ATTLIST %dl.qname;
      %Common.attrib;
>
<!-- end of dl.attlist -->]]>

<!-- dt: Definition Term ............................... -->
```

Continued

Listing 22-1 *(continued)*

```
<!ENTITY % dt.element  "INCLUDE" >
<![%dt.element;[
<!ENTITY % dt.content
     "( #PCDATA | %Inline.mix; )*"
>
<!ELEMENT %dt.qname;  %dt.content; >
<!-- end of dt.element -->]]>

<!ENTITY % dt.attlist  "INCLUDE" >
<![%dt.attlist;[
<!ATTLIST %dt.qname;
      %Common.attrib;
>
<!-- end of dt.attlist -->]]>

<!-- dd: Definition Description ........................ -->

<!ENTITY % dd.element  "INCLUDE" >
<![%dd.element;[
<!ENTITY % dd.content
     "( #PCDATA | %Flow.mix; )*"
>
<!ELEMENT %dd.qname;  %dd.content; >
<!-- end of dd.element -->]]>

<!ENTITY % dd.attlist  "INCLUDE" >
<![%dd.attlist;[
<!ATTLIST %dd.qname;
      %Common.attrib;
>
<!-- end of dd.attlist -->]]>

<!-- ol: Ordered List (numbered styles) ................ -->

<!ENTITY % ol.element  "INCLUDE" >
<![%ol.element;[
<!ENTITY % ol.content  "( %li.qname; )+" >
<!ELEMENT %ol.qname;  %ol.content; >
<!-- end of ol.element -->]]>

<!ENTITY % ol.attlist  "INCLUDE" >
<![%ol.attlist;[
<!ATTLIST %ol.qname;
      %Common.attrib;
>
<!-- end of ol.attlist -->]]>

<!-- ul: Unordered List (bullet styles) ................ -->
```

```
<!ENTITY % ul.element  "INCLUDE" >
<![%ul.element;[
<!ENTITY % ul.content  "( %li.qname; )+" >
<!ELEMENT %ul.qname;  %ul.content; >
<!-- end of ul.element -->]]>

<!ENTITY % ul.attlist  "INCLUDE" >
<![%ul.attlist;[
<!ATTLIST %ul.qname;
      %Common.attrib;
>
<!-- end of ul.attlist -->]]>

<!-- li: List Item ..................................... -->

<!ENTITY % li.element  "INCLUDE" >
<![%li.element;[
<!ENTITY % li.content
     "( #PCDATA | %Flow.mix; )*"
>
<!ELEMENT %li.qname;  %li.content; >
<!-- end of li.element -->]]>

<!ENTITY % li.attlist  "INCLUDE" >
<![%li.attlist;[
<!ATTLIST %li.qname;
      %Common.attrib;
>
<!-- end of li.attlist -->]]>

<!-- end of xhtml-list-1.mod -->
```

Entity references are used throughout the module for element and attribute names, for content models, and for conditional section markers that allow you to turn particular declarations on or off. This is a common pattern in modular DTDs that allows a great deal of customizability. The key idea is that entity declarations can be overridden by an earlier declaration, especially one in the internal DTD subset of document.

Element names

The names of the elements are all defined by parameter entities that follow the pattern `elementName.qname`. Thus, the name of the `dl` element is defined by the parameter entity reference `%dl.qname;`. The name of the `dt` element is defined by the parameter entity reference `%dt.qname;`. The name of the `dd` element is defined by the parameter entity reference `%dd.qname;`, and so on. Suppose for some reason you wanted to change these to uppercase. To do this, you'd place the following declarations in your internal DTD subset:

```
<!ENTITY % dl.qname   "DL" >
<!ENTITY % dt.qname   "DT" >
<!ENTITY % dd.qname   "DD" >
<!ENTITY % ol.qname   "OL" >
<!ENTITY % ul.qname   "UL" >
<!ENTITY % li.qname   "LI" >
```

Because other modules also use these parameter entity references to define the content models of elements that can contain lists, these changes also change the definitions used in the other modules. Thus, all the elements that contain lists are redefined to contain `DL`, `UL`, and `OL` elements instead of `dl`, `ol`, and `ul` elements. In fact, direct element names are used almost nowhere. This indirection through parameter entity references is used throughout the modular XHTML DTDs.

Element-specific content models

Content models are also defined by parameter entity references. It is easy enough to say that a `dl` element must contain matched `dt dd` pairs, or that a `%dl.qname;` element must contain matched `%dt.qname; %dd.qname;` pairs. Instead, however, a `dl.content` parameter entity is first defined liked this:

```
<!ENTITY % dl.content   "( %dt.qname; | %dd.qname; )+" >
```

The `%dl.content;` parameter entity reference is then used to define the `dl` element like this:

```
<!ELEMENT %dl.qname;  %dl.content; >
```

If for some reason you decide that you want `dl` elements to contain `definition` elements, each of which contains a `dt dd` pair, rather than having the `dl` element contain the `dt dd` pair directly, you simply define the new `definition` element and override the declaration of the `dl.content` entity, like this:

```
<!ELEMENT definition  "( %dt.qname;, %dd.qname; )" >
<!ENTITY % dl.content   "( definition )+" >
```

Of course, if you do change the name or content models of the `dl` element, or of any other element, you should not expect off-the-shelf web browsers to understand your revised elements.

Generic content models

The default content models for dl, ul, and ol elements are defined completely in terms of other elements defined in Listing 22-1. However, that isn't true for the elements they contain: dt, dd, and li. These are defined like this:

```
<!-- dt: Definition Term ............................... -->

<!ENTITY % dt.element  "INCLUDE" >
<![%dt.element;[
<!ENTITY % dt.content
     "( #PCDATA | %Inline.mix; )*"
>
<!ELEMENT %dt.qname;  %dt.content; >
<!-- end of dt.element -->]]>

<!-- dd: Definition Description ........................ -->

<!ENTITY % dd.element  "INCLUDE" >
<![%dd.element;[
<!ENTITY % dd.content
     "( #PCDATA | %Flow.mix; )*"
>
<!ELEMENT %dd.qname;  %dd.content; >
<!-- end of dd.element -->]]>

<!-- li: List Item ..................................... -->

<!ENTITY % li.element  "INCLUDE" >
<![%li.element;[
<!ENTITY % li.content
     "( #PCDATA | %Flow.mix; )*"
>
<!ELEMENT %li.qname;  %li.content; >
<!-- end of li.element -->]]>
```

This can be simplified by resolving the local parameter entity references (assuming that no previously loaded module is redefining any of these parameter entity references), deleting the comments, and including everything that can be included. The result looks like this:

```
<!ELEMENT dt  ( #PCDATA | %Inline.mix; )* >
<!ELEMENT dd  ( #PCDATA | %Flow.mix; )* >
<!ELEMENT li  ( #PCDATA | %Flow.mix; )* >
```

Perhaps surprisingly, there are still three parameter entity references for two different parameter entities left: %Inline.mix; and %Flow.mix;. These are not defined anywhere in Listing 22-1. Instead they must be defined before Listing 22-1 is loaded. Although you could define them in your own DTDs, they are normally defined in the document model module. I will get to this later. In the meantime, what you need to know is that there are three main parameter entity references used to define common content models shared among many different types of elements:

✦ Inline.mix—A choice containing all inline elements such as a, abbr, acronym, br, img, kbd, object, span, em, strong, dfn, cite, code, q, samp, strong, var, input, select, textarea, and label

✦ Block.mix—A choice containing all block-level elements such as p, div, h1, h2, h3, h4, h5, h6, ul, ol, dl, table, form, pre, blockquote, and address

✦ Flow.mix—A choice containing all of the preceding inline and block-level elements

Generic attribute models

The document model also defines a number of common attribute sets that can be applied to most elements. For example, the li element is declared to possess the common attributes:

```
<!ATTLIST %li.qname;
      %Common.attrib;
>
```

Common.attrib is a parameter entity defined in another part of the framework, the common attributes module, xhtml-attribs-1.mod. I discuss it in Table 22-5. For now, what you need to know is that %Common.attrib; has the necessary replacement text so that the id, class, title, and other attributes that apply to almost all HTML elements get applied to this element.

INCLUDE and IGNORE blocks

Another use of parameter entity references is to remove particular elements from content models. For example, let's suppose you just don't like definition lists and want to forbid the dl, dt, and dd elements completely. All the declarations for these elements and their attributes are enclosed in blocks like these:

```
<!ENTITY % dl.element  "INCLUDE" >
<![%dl.element;[
<!ENTITY % dl.content  "( %dt.qname; | %dd.qname; )+" >
<!ELEMENT %dl.qname;  %dl.content; >
<!-- end of dl.element -->]]>

<!ENTITY % dl.attlist  "INCLUDE" >
<![%dl.attlist;[
<!ATTLIST %dl.qname;
      %Common.attrib;
>
<!-- end of dl.attlist -->]]>
```

Normally, %dl.element; and %dl.attlist; have the replacement text INCLUDE. Consequently, the preceding fragment resolves to this, and the dl element is included:

```
<![INCLUDE[
<!ENTITY % dl.content  "( %dt.qname; | %dd.qname; )+" >
<!ELEMENT %dl.qname;  %dl.content; >
<!-- end of dl.element -->]]>

<![INCLUDE[
<!ATTLIST %dl.qname;
      %Common.attrib;
>
<!-- end of dl.attlist -->]]>
```

However, if you redefine dl.element and dl.attlist to IGNORE, those declarations are omitted, and the dl element is effectively forbidden. The same trick can be used for any element and attribute in XHTML. For example, to drop out the blockquote element, define blockquote.element and blockquote.attlist as IGNORE, like this:

```
<!ENTITY % blockquote.element  "IGNORE" >
<!ENTITY % blockquote.attlist  "IGNORE" >
```

To omit the cite element, define cite.element and cite.attlist as IGNORE, like this:

```
<!ENTITY % cite.element  "IGNORE" >
<!ENTITY % cite.attlist  "IGNORE" >
```

Actually, because XML permits declarations of attributes for elements that don't exist, all you absolutely have to do is redeclare *elementName*.content as IGNORE. However, I find it more aesthetically complete to drop both out.

Using XHTML entities in other applications

You can also use the entity references defined here in your own XML applications. For example, suppose you have a DICTIONARY element that you want to allow to contain a definition list, but not all the other XHTML elements. You would simply import the XHTML DTD and then declare your element as possessing a content model of %dl.qname;, like this:

```
<!ENTITY % xhtml SYSTEM "xhtml-basic10.dtd">
%xhtml;
<!ELEMENT DICTIONARY (%dl.qname;)>
```

Even though you aren't using the whole of XHTML in your own application, you still need to import it all because the lists module you are using relies on it.

Or suppose you want to say that in your definition list the dt and dd elements can only contain parsed character data, no child elements. Then, before you imported it, you'd redefine the dt and dd content models as #PCDATA, like this:

```
<!ENTITY % dt.content "(#PCDATA)">
<!ENTITY % dd.content "(#PCDATA)">
<!ENTITY % xhtml SYSTEM "xhtml-basic10.dtd">
%xhtml;
<!ELEMENT DICTIONARY (%dl.qname;)>
```

Another useful trick is to declare that one of your elements contains the same content as one of the standard XHTML elements. For example, suppose your XML application contains a LIST element, and you want to say that this has the same content as XHTML's ul element. Simply import the XHTML DTD and use the %ul.content; parameter entity reference, like this:

```
<!ELEMENT LIST %ul.content;>
```

Depending on context, the most useful parameter entity references are as follows:

✦ %span.content; — For inline elements

✦ %div.content; — For block-level elements that can contain other block-level elements

✦ %p.content; — For block-level elements that cannot contain other block-level elements

The Framework

By themselves the 28 modules are incomplete. They rely on a number of parameter entity references such as %Common.attrib; and %Flow.mix; that must be defined before the modules can be used. These are defined by a driver DTD. More specifically, they are defined by other framework modules that the driver DTD imports.

The framework is provided by the XHTML Modular Framework Module, xhtml-framework-1.mod, shown in Listing 22-2. This module loads the other modules that lay the foundation for the 28 XHTML modules by defining notations, data types, namespaces, common attributes, the document model, and character entities. Until the framework module is loaded, none of the other modules can be used.

The framework module does not declare any elements or attributes itself. It just gathers together all the pieces of the framework and loads them. None of these pieces declare any elements or attributes either. They all just define entity references that will be used to actually declare elements and attributes in the 28 modules.

Listing 22-2: xhtml-framework-1.mod: The XHTML Framework Module DTD

```
<!-- ...................................................... -->
<!-- XHTML Modular Framework Module  ..................... -->
<!-- file: xhtml-framework-1.mod

     This is XHTML, a reformulation of HTML as a modular XML application.
     Copyright 1998-2001 W3C (MIT, INRIA, Keio), All Rights Reserved.
     Revision: $Id: xhtml-framework-1.mod,v 4.0 2001/04/02 22:42:49 altheim Exp
$

     SMI

     This DTD module is identified by the PUBLIC and SYSTEM
     identifiers:

  PUBLIC "-//W3C//ENTITIES XHTML Modular Framework 1.0//EN"
  SYSTEM "http://www.w3.org/TR/xhtml-modularization/DTD/xhtml-framework-1.mod"

     Revisions:
     (none)
     ...................................................... -->

<!-- Modular Framework

     This required module instantiates the modules needed
     to support the XHTML modularization model, including:

        +  notations
        +  datatypes
        +  namespace-qualified names
        +  common attributes
        +  document model
        +  character entities

     The Intrinsic Events module is ignored by default but
     occurs in this module because it must be instantiated
     prior to Attributes but after Datatypes.
-->

<!ENTITY % xhtml-arch.module "IGNORE" >
<![%xhtml-arch.module;[
<!ENTITY % xhtml-arch.mod
     PUBLIC "-//W3C//ELEMENTS XHTML Base Architecture 1.0//EN"
            "xhtml-arch-1.mod" >
%xhtml-arch.mod;]]>

<!ENTITY % xhtml-notations.module "INCLUDE" >
<![%xhtml-notations.module;[
```

Continued

Listing 22-2 *(continued)*

```
<!ENTITY % xhtml-notations.mod
     PUBLIC "-//W3C//NOTATIONS XHTML Notations 1.0//EN"
            "xhtml-notations-1.mod" >
%xhtml-notations.mod;]]>

<!ENTITY % xhtml-datatypes.module "INCLUDE" >
<![%xhtml-datatypes.module;[
<!ENTITY % xhtml-datatypes.mod
     PUBLIC "-//W3C//ENTITIES XHTML Datatypes 1.0//EN"
            "xhtml-datatypes-1.mod" >
%xhtml-datatypes.mod;]]>

<!-- placeholder for XLink support module -->
<!ENTITY % xhtml-xlink.mod "" >
%xhtml-xlink.mod;

<!ENTITY % xhtml-qname.module "INCLUDE" >
<![%xhtml-qname.module;[
<!ENTITY % xhtml-qname.mod
     PUBLIC "-//W3C//ENTITIES XHTML Qualified Names 1.0//EN"
            "xhtml-qname-1.mod" >
%xhtml-qname.mod;]]>

<!ENTITY % xhtml-events.module "IGNORE" >
<![%xhtml-events.module;[
<!ENTITY % xhtml-events.mod
     PUBLIC "-//W3C//ENTITIES XHTML Intrinsic Events 1.0//EN"
            "xhtml-events-1.mod" >
%xhtml-events.mod;]]>

<!ENTITY % xhtml-attribs.module "INCLUDE" >
<![%xhtml-attribs.module;[
<!ENTITY % xhtml-attribs.mod
     PUBLIC "-//W3C//ENTITIES XHTML Common Attributes 1.0//EN"
            "xhtml-attribs-1.mod" >
%xhtml-attribs.mod;]]>

<!-- placeholder for content model redeclarations -->
<!ENTITY % xhtml-model.redecl "" >
%xhtml-model.redecl;

<!ENTITY % xhtml-model.module "INCLUDE" >
<![%xhtml-model.module;[
<!-- instantiate the Document Model module declared in the DTD
driver
-->
%xhtml-model.mod;]]>
```

```
<!ENTITY % xhtml-charent.module "INCLUDE" >
<![%xhtml-charent.module;[
<!ENTITY % xhtml-charent.mod
     PUBLIC "-//W3C//ENTITIES XHTML Character Entities 1.0//EN"
            "xhtml-charent-1.mod" >
%xhtml-charent.mod;]]>

<!-- end of xhtml-framework-1.mod -->
```

This module potentially loads as many as 10 other modules:

✦ The architecture module is ignored by default, but if `xhtml-arch.module` is redefined to `INCLUDE`, it adds declarations that allow XHTML to become an architectural forms base architecture.

✦ The notations module declares a number of notations that can be used to type unparsed entities and element content.

✦ The data types module defines parameter entities that can be used as aliases for attribute types that would otherwise have type `CDATA`, `NMTOKEN`, or `NMTOKENS`.

✦ The XLink module doesn't exist yet, but `xhtml-xlink.mod` holds its place for a future addition or extension.

✦ The qualified names module defines the namespace URIs and prefixes used in XHTML.

✦ The events module declares entities that can be used in attribute declarations for attributes such as `onfocus`, `onblur`, and `onclick`. It is ignored by default because the definitions of these events are expected to change in the future as a result of work on the Document Object Model. However, if `xhtml-events.module` is defined as `INCLUDE` instead, this module is included.

✦ The common attributes module defines entities that can be used in attribute declarations for attributes shared by many XHTML elements such as `id`, `xml:lang`, and `class`.

✦ The content model module defines entities such as `Inline.mix` that can be used inside element declaration content models for many elements.

✦ The redeclaration module is loaded before the normal content model module. You define entities here before they get defined in the content model module to adjust the normal rules of XHTML.

✦ The character entities module defines general entities such as `α` and `©` that can be used in XHTML instance documents.

In 9 of the 10 cases, the framework module defines the location of the module it's loading and then loads it. The tenth case is the document model. It merely loads this from the parameter entity reference `%xhtml-model.mod;`. However, it does not define that parameter entity. It assumes that `%xhtml-model.mod;` has already been defined in the DTD that loaded the framework module. The framework module itself depends on the document model. The document model is defined in the driver DTD. The driver DTD is the one file that is referenced from the instance document's `DOCTYPE` declaration. The driver DTD defines the document model and loads the framework, which then loads the document model and the individual modules.

The notations framework module

The notations module, `xhtml-notations.module`, defines a number of XML notations for unparsed data. For example, this declaration from the notations module defines a notation for dates and times:

```
<!-- date and time information. ISO date format -->
<!NOTATION datetime
    PUBLIC "-//W3C//NOTATION XHTML Datatype: Datetime//EN" >
```

Table 22-2 summarizes the notations declared here, but overall this module doesn't have a lot of practical impact on HTML documents.

Table 22-2
Notations Declared in Modular XHTML

Name	*Public Identifier*	*Type*
`w3c-xml`	ISO 8879//NOTATION Extensible Markup Language (XML) 1.0//EN	XML document
`cdata`	-//W3C//NOTATION XML 1.0: CDATA//EN	XML CDATA
`fpi`	ISO 8879:1986//NOTATION Formal Public Identifier//EN	SGML Formal Public Identifier
`pixels`	-//W3C//NOTATION XHTML Datatype: Pixels//EN	Integer representing length in pixels
`length`	-//W3C//NOTATION XHTML Datatype: Length//EN	nn for pixels or nn% for percentage length
`multiLength`	-//W3C//NOTATION XHTML Datatype: MultiLength//EN	Pixel, percentage, or relative length
`linkTypes`	-//W3C//NOTATION XHTML Datatype: LinkTypes//EN	A space-separated list of link types

Name	*Public Identifier*	*Type*
`mediaDesc`	-//W3C//NOTATION XHTML Datatype: MediaDesc//EN	Single or comma-separated list of media descriptors
`number`	-//W3C//NOTATION XHTML Datatype: Number//EN	One or more digits
`script`	-//W3C//NOTATION XHTML Datatype: Script//EN	Script expression
`text`	-//W3C//NOTATION XHTML Datatype: Text//EN	Textual content
`character`	-//W3C//NOTATION XHTML Datatype: Character//EN	A single Unicode character
`charset`	-//W3C//NOTATION XHTML Datatype: Charset//EN	A MIME character encoding
`charsets`	-//W3C//NOTATION XHTML Datatype: Charsets//EN	A space separated list of MIME character encodings
`contentType`	-//W3C//NOTATION XHTML Datatype: ContentType//EN	A MIME media type
`contentTypes`	-//W3C//NOTATION XHTML Datatype: ContentTypes//EN	A comma-separated list of MIME media types
`datetime`	-//W3C//NOTATION XHTML Datatype: Datetime//EN	ISO 8601 date and time
`languageCode`	-//W3C//NOTATION XHTML Datatype: LanguageCode//EN	An RFC 3066 language code
`uri`	-//W3C//NOTATION XHTML Datatype: URI//EN	A Uniform Resource Identifier (URI)
`uris`	-//W3C//NOTATION XHTML Datatype: URIs//EN	A space-separated list of URIs

Notations are discussed in Chapter 10.

The data types framework module

The data types module defines parameter entity references that can be used as alternate names for attribute types that would otherwise have type CDATA, NMTOKEN, or NMTOKENS. For example, this declaration defines a number type:

```
<!-- one or more digits (NUMBER) -->
<!ENTITY % Number.datatype "CDATA" >
```

Most XML parsers can't enforce these types, but they do make the DTD a little clearer about what kind of data is expected where. Table 22-3 lists the data types defined in modular XHTML. You'll notice there's a considerable amount of overlap with the notations in Table 22-2. That's not an accident. These are for attribute types and those are for unparsed entities, but the basic types are the same.

Table 22-3
Data Types Defined by Modular XHTML

Parameter Entity Reference	*Required Type*	*XML Type*
%Length.datatype;	nn for pixels or nn% for percentage length	CDATA
%LinkTypes.datatype;	A space-separated list of link types	NMTOKENS
%MediaDesc.datatype;	A comma-separated list of media descriptors	CDATA
%MultiLength.datatype;	Pixel, percentage, or relative length	CDATA
%Number.datatype;	One or more digits	CDATA
%Pixels.datatype;	An integer representing a length in pixels	CDATA
%Script.datatype;	A script expression	CDATA
%Text.datatype;	A Unicode string	CDATA
%Character.datatype;	A single Unicode character	CDATA
%Charset.datatype;	A MIME character encoding	CDATA
%Charsets.datatype;	A space separated list of MIME character encodings	CDATA
%Color.datatype;	Color specification using color name or sRGB (#RRGGBB) values	CDATA
%ContentType.datatype;	A MIME media type	CDATA
%ContentTypes.datatype;	A comma-separated list of MIME media types	CDATA
%Datetime.datatype;	An ISO 8601 format date and time	CDATA

Parameter Entity Reference	Required Type	XML Type
`%FPI.datatype;`	An ISO 8879 formal public identifier	`CDATA`
`%LanguageCode.datatype;`	An RFC 3066 language code	`NMTOKEN`
`%URI.datatype;`	A Uniform Resource Identifier (URI)	`CDATA`
`%URIs.datatype;`	A space-separated list of URIs	`CDATA`

Schema-aware parsers can enforce these data types, which makes schema-validated XHTML somewhat stricter and more robust than DTD-validated XML.

The namespace-qualified names module

The namespace-qualified names module, `xhtml-qname-1.mod`, is divided into two sections. Section A declares the namespace URIs and prefixes used for XHTML. By redefining the entities in this part of the module, you can choose which namespace prefix to use or to use no prefix at all (the default). This is normally done in the driver DTD, as you'll see shortly.

Table 22-4 lists the various parameter entity references declared in Section A, their default values, and their purposes. The two most important entities are `%XHTML.prefixed;` and `%XHTML.prefix`. To use namespace prefixes on all elements, define `%XHTML.prefixed;` as `INCLUDE` and `%XHTML.prefix` as the prefix you want to use, such as `html`.

Table 22-4
Parameter Entities Defined in the Qualified Names Module

Parameter Entity Reference	Purpose	Default Value
`%NS.prefixed;`	Whether or not to use namespace prefixes, as inherited from the driver DTD	`IGNORE`
`%XHTML.prefixed;`	Whether or not to use namespace prefixes	`%NS.prefixed;`
`%XHTML.xmlns;`	The namespace for all XHTML elements	`http://www.w3.org/1999/xhtml`
`%XHTML.prefix`	The namespace prefix	The empty string (i.e., no prefix)
`%XHTML.pfx;`	The prefix used when prefixing is active	The empty string (i.e., no prefix)

Continued

Table 22-4 (continued)

Parameter Entity Reference	Purpose	Default Value
`%xhtml-qname-extra.mod;`	The name of the module from which to load additional qualified names	The empty string (no such module is loaded)
`%XHTML.xmlns.extra.attrib;`	Namespace declaration attributes for non-XHTML applications that are embedded in XHTML such as MathML or SVG	The empty string (only XHTML elements are included)
`%NS.decl.attrib;`	All namespace declarations used in the DTD, including the namespace declaration for XHTML	`xmlns:%XHTML.prefix; %URI.datatype; #FIXED '%XHTML.xmlns;' %XHTML.xmlns.extra.attrib;`
`%XLINK.xmlns.attrib;`	A placeholder for future XLink support	The empty string (XLink is not supported yet)
`%XHTML.xmlns.attrib;`	All namespace declarations used in the DTD, including the namespace declarations for XHTML and XLink	`xmlns %URI.datatype; #FIXED '%XHTML.xmlns;' %XLINK.xmlns.attrib;`
`% xhtml-qname.redecl;`	The module from which to load replacements for the standard qualified names	The empty string (do not change the normal names of XHTML elements)

Section B of the qualified names module declares the prefixed names for all the different elements used in XHTML. The actual name of each element is the lowercase name of the element followed by `.qname`. For example, this section defines the names of the block structural elements:

```
<!-- module:  xhtml-blkstruct-1.mod -->
<!ENTITY % div.qname      "%XHTML.pfx;div" >
<!ENTITY % p.qname        "%XHTML.pfx;p" >
```

There are declarations like this for all the hundred plus standard HTML elements.

The common attributes module

The common attributes module, `xhtml-attribs-1.mod`, declares parameter entities that represent parts of `ATTLIST` declarations for attributes that apply to all or most HTML elements such as `id`, `class`, and `lang`. For example, this is the entity declaration for the `title` attribute:

```
<!ENTITY % title.attrib
     "title         %Text.datatype;           #IMPLIED"
>
```

These are then grouped into collections of attributes. For example, this is the declaration for the core attributes entity:

```
<!ENTITY % Core.attrib
     "%XHTML.xmlns.attrib;
      %id.attrib;
      %class.attrib;
      %title.attrib;
      %Core.extra.attrib;"
>
```

Finally, all the different collections are grouped into one master collection called `%Common.attrib;` that includes all of them. Table 22-5 summarizes the different parameter entities defined in this module and the attributes they represent.

Table 22-5
Common Attributes and Attribute Groups Defined in Modular XHTML

Parameter Entity Reference	*Attributes Included*
`%id.attrib;`	`id`
`%class.attrib;`	`class`
`%title.attrib;`	`title`
`%Core.extra.attrib;`	
`%Core.attrib;`	`xmlns, id, class, title`
`%lang.attrib;`	`xml:lang`
`%dir.attrib;`	`dir`
`%I18n.attrib;`	`dir, xml:lang`
`%Common.extra.attrib;`	
`%Events.attrib;`	
`%Common.attrib;`	`xmlns, id, class, title, dir, xml:lang`

This table is not the final word on what attributes belong to which parameter entities. Many of these can be redefined. For example, three of them, Core.extra.attrib, Common.extra.attrib, and Events.attrib, are empty by default. They only exist so that other modules can redefine them.

Furthermore, some of these attributes can be controlled by other parameter entities that determine whether to INCLUDE or IGNORE a particular set. For example, the internationalization attributes are controlled by the definition of %XHTML.bidi;.

```
<![%XHTML.bidi;[
<!ENTITY % dir.attrib
     "dir          ( ltr | rtl )           #IMPLIED"
>

<!ENTITY % I18n.attrib
     "%dir.attrib;
      %lang.attrib;"
>

]]>
<!ENTITY % I18n.attrib
     "%lang.attrib;"
>
```

If %XHTML.bidi; is set to INCLUDE, I18n.attrib includes the dir attribute. If %XHTML.bidi; resolves to IGNORE, I18n.attrib includes only the xml:lang attribute.

The character entity modules

The character entities module, xhtml-charent-1.mod, loads the three entity set modules that define all of HTML's standard entities such as © for the copyright sign © or Ω for the capital Greek letter omega, Ω. There are three of these entity sets modules, each containing a different collection of characters:

✦ xhtml-lat1.ent — Characters 160 through 255 of Latin-1, mostly Western European accented characters and punctuation marks, such as é, ü, £, and ©

✦ xhtml-special.ent — Assorted useful characters and punctuation marks from outside the Latin-1 set, such as the Euro sign and the em dash

✦ xhtml-symbol.ent — The Greek alphabet and assorted symbols commonly used for math, such as ∞ and ∫

The filenames of the entity modules are distinguished from the usual modules because they all end in .ent rather than in .mod.

For example, these are the lines from `xhtml-symbol.ent` that declare the `∞` and `∠` entities:

```
<!ENTITY infin     "&#8734;" ><!-- infinity, U+221E ISOtech -->
<!ENTITY ang       "&#8736;" ><!-- angle, U+2220 ISOamso -->
```

The Driver DTD

The modules discussed so far all provide parts of XHTML, but none of them are suitable for use as the DTD of an actual XHTML document. None of them can be referenced from a document type declaration like this:

```
<!DOCTYPE html SYSTEM "xhtml-framework-1.mod">
```

The DTD that puts them all together so that it can be referenced in a document type declaration is called the *driver DTD*, and in fact there's more than one. One of the advantages of modular XHTML is that you can easily customize a driver DTD to meet the needs of your own documents. Sometimes this means deleting modules that you don't use, such as the table module. At other times it might mean adding in extra pieces, such as MathML equations, that aren't part of standard HTML.

Driver DTDs are customized by redefining the parameter entity references that control particular modules. Each driver DTD is responsible for the following:

✦ Deciding whether to use namespace prefixes or the default namespace by setting the `NS.prefixed` entity to `IGNORE` (no prefixes) or `INCLUDE` (use prefixes).

✦ Specifying what namespace prefix to use by setting the `XHTML.prefix` entity.

✦ Locating the document model by setting the `xhtml-model.mod` entity.

✦ Loading all the modules the instance documents will use.

In addition, the driver DTD may choose to predefine some of the entity references used in the modules to customize the content or attributes of various elements. Alternately, this can be done in a custom document model module or in a redeclaration module.

For example, Listing 22-3 contains the XHTML Basic driver DTD. This is a simple DTD suitable for uncomplicated Web pages. It does not use namespace prefixes (`NS.prefixed` is set to `IGNORE`), and thus the `XHTML.prefix` entity is set to the empty string. It uses the document model found at the relative URL `xhtml-basic10-model-1.mod`. It loads the structural, text, hypertext, list, image, tables, forms, link, meta-information, base, object, and param element modules, and ignores the rest.

Listing 22-3: xhtml-basic10.dtd: The XHTML Basic Driver DTD

```
<!-- XHTML Basic 1.0 DTD  ................................... -->
<!-- file: xhtml-basic10.dtd -->

<!-- XHTML Basic 1.0 DTD

     This is XHTML Basic, a proper subset of XHTML.

 The Extensible HyperText Markup Language (XHTML)
 Copyright 1998-2000 World Wide Web Consortium
 (Massachusetts Institute of Technology, Institut National de
 Recherche en Informatique et en Automatique, Keio University).
 All Rights Reserved.

 Permission to use, copy, modify and distribute the XHTML Basic
 DTD and its accompanying documentation for any purpose and
 without fee is hereby granted in perpetuity, provided that the
 above copyright notice and this paragraph appear in all
 copies.  The copyright holders make no representation about
 the suitability of the DTD for any purpose.

 It is provided "as is" without expressed or implied warranty.

 Editors: Murray M. Altheim <mailto:altheim@eng.sun.com>
          Peter Stark      <mailto:Peter.Stark@ecs.ericsson.se>
        Revision:   $Id: xhtml-basic10.dtd,v 2.13 2000/12/18
                    12:56:23 mimasa Exp $ SMI

-->
<!-- This is the driver file for version 1.0 of the XHTML Basic
     DTD.

  This DTD is identified by the PUBLIC and SYSTEM identifiers:

PUBLIC: "-//W3C//DTD XHTML Basic 1.0//EN"
SYSTEM: "http://www.w3.org/TR/xhtml-basic/xhtml-basic10.dtd"
-->
<!ENTITY % XHTML.version  "-//W3C//DTD XHTML Basic 1.0//EN" >

<!-- Use this URI to identify the default namespace:

         "http://www.w3.org/1999/xhtml"

     See the Qualified Names module for information
     on the use of namespace prefixes in the DTD.
-->
<!ENTITY % NS.prefixed "IGNORE" >
<!ENTITY % XHTML.prefix  "" >

<!-- Reserved for use with the XLink namespace:
-->
```

```
<!ENTITY % XLINK.xmlns "" >
<!ENTITY % XLINK.xmlns.attrib "" >

<!-- For example, if you are using XHTML Basic 1.0 directly,
     use the FPI in the DOCTYPE declaration, with the xmlns
     attribute on the document element to identify the default
     namespace:

       <?xml version="1.0"?>
       <!DOCTYPE html PUBLIC "-//W3C//DTD XHTML Basic 1.0//EN"
        "http://www.w3.org/TR/xhtml-basic/xhtml-basic10.dtd" >
       <html xmlns="http://www.w3.org/1999/xhtml"
             xml:lang="en" >
        ...
        </html>
-->

<!-- reserved for future use with document profiles -->
<!ENTITY % XHTML.profile  "" >

<!-- Bidirectional Text features
     This feature-test entity is used to declare elements
     and attributes used for bidirectional text support.
-->
<!ENTITY % XHTML.bidi  "IGNORE" >

<?doc type="doctype" role="title" { XHTML Basic 1.0 } ?>

<!-- :::::::::::::::::::::::::::::::::::::::::::::::::::: -->

<!ENTITY % xhtml-events.module   "IGNORE" >
<!ENTITY % xhtml-bdo.module      "%XHTML.bidi;" >

<!ENTITY % xhtml-model.mod
    PUBLIC
     "-//W3C//ENTITIES XHTML Basic 1.0 Document Model 1.0//EN"
     "xhtml-basic10-model-1.mod" >

<!ENTITY % xhtml-framework.mod
     PUBLIC "-//W3C//ENTITIES XHTML Modular Framework 1.0//EN"
            "xhtml-framework-1.mod" >
%xhtml-framework.mod;

<!ENTITY % pre.content
     "( #PCDATA
      | %InlStruct.class;
      %InlPhras.class;
      %Anchor.class;
      %Inline.extra; )*"
>

<!ENTITY % xhtml-text.mod
```

Continued

Listing 22-3 *(continued)*

```
     PUBLIC "-//W3C//ELEMENTS XHTML Text 1.0//EN"
            "xhtml-text-1.mod" >
%xhtml-text.mod;

<!ENTITY % xhtml-hypertext.mod
     PUBLIC "-//W3C//ELEMENTS XHTML Hypertext 1.0//EN"
            "xhtml-hypertext-1.mod" >
%xhtml-hypertext.mod;

<!ENTITY % xhtml-list.mod
     PUBLIC "-//W3C//ELEMENTS XHTML Lists 1.0//EN"
            "xhtml-list-1.mod" >
%xhtml-list.mod;

<!-- :::::::::::::::::::::::::::::::::::::::::::::::::::: -->

<!-- Image Module  .................................... -->
<!ENTITY % xhtml-image.module "INCLUDE" >
<![%xhtml-image.module;[
<!ENTITY % xhtml-image.mod
     PUBLIC "-//W3C//ELEMENTS XHTML Images 1.0//EN"
            "xhtml-image-1.mod" >
%xhtml-image.mod;]]>

<!-- Tables Module
............................................. -->
<!ENTITY % xhtml-table.module "INCLUDE" >
<![%xhtml-table.module;[
<!ENTITY % xhtml-table.mod
     PUBLIC "-//W3C//ELEMENTS XHTML Basic Tables 1.0//EN"
            "xhtml-basic-table-1.mod" >
%xhtml-table.mod;]]>

<!-- Forms Module  .................................... -->
<!ENTITY % xhtml-form.module "INCLUDE" >
<![%xhtml-form.module;[
<!ENTITY % xhtml-form.mod
     PUBLIC "-//W3C//ELEMENTS XHTML Basic Forms 1.0//EN"
            "xhtml-basic-form-1.mod" >
%xhtml-form.mod;]]>

<!-- Link Element Module
.................................... -->
<!ENTITY % xhtml-link.module "INCLUDE" >
<![%xhtml-link.module;[
<!ENTITY % xhtml-link.mod
     PUBLIC "-//W3C//ELEMENTS XHTML Link Element 1.0//EN"
            "xhtml-link-1.mod" >
%xhtml-link.mod;]]>
```

```
<!-- Document Metainformation Module
.............................. -->
<!ENTITY % xhtml-meta.module "INCLUDE" >
<![%xhtml-meta.module;[
<!ENTITY % xhtml-meta.mod
     PUBLIC "-//W3C//ELEMENTS XHTML Metainformation 1.0//EN"
            "xhtml-meta-1.mod" >
%xhtml-meta.mod;]]>

<!-- Base Element Module
........................................ -->
<!ENTITY % xhtml-base.module "INCLUDE" >
<![%xhtml-base.module;[
<!ENTITY % xhtml-base.mod
     PUBLIC "-//W3C//ELEMENTS XHTML Base Element 1.0//EN"
            "xhtml-base-1.mod" >
%xhtml-base.mod;]]>

<!-- Param Element Module
....................................... -->
<!ENTITY % xhtml-param.module "INCLUDE" >
<![%xhtml-param.module;[
<!ENTITY % xhtml-param.mod
     PUBLIC "-//W3C//ELEMENTS XHTML Param Element 1.0//EN"
            "xhtml-param-1.mod" >
%xhtml-param.mod;]]>

<!-- Embedded Object Module
..................................... -->
<!ENTITY % xhtml-object.module "INCLUDE" >
<![%xhtml-object.module;[
<!ENTITY % xhtml-object.mod
     PUBLIC "-//W3C//ELEMENTS XHTML Embedded Object 1.0//EN"
            "xhtml-object-1.mod" >
%xhtml-object.mod;]]>

<!ENTITY % xhtml-struct.mod
    PUBLIC "-//W3C//ELEMENTS XHTML Document Structure 1.0//EN"
           "xhtml-struct-1.mod" >
%xhtml-struct.mod;

<!-- end of XHTML Basic 1.0 DTD  ......................... -->
```

However, this is not the only possible DTD for modular XHTML. There are others, and you can create your own as well. For example, Listing 22-4 is a minimal driver DTD that does use the namespace prefix `html`. It refers to the document model `xhtml-minimal-model.mod`, and it loads only the framework, structural, and text modules. It omits links, tables, forms, images, and a lot more. An HTML variant like this might be suitable for embedding a little marked-up narrative text inside a larger, non-HTML application. This is not part of any W3C specification. It's just something I created for this book because it seemed useful to me. You're equally free to make your own drivers to meet your needs.

Listing 22-4: xhtml-minimal.dtd: A Minimal XHTML Driver DTD

```
<!-- XHTML Minimal DTD  ................................ -->
<!-- file: xhtml-minimal.dtd -->

<!-- XHTML Minimal DTD

 This is XHTML Minimal, a proper subset of XHTML.

 The Extensible HyperText Markup Language (XHTML)
 Copyright 1998-2000 World Wide Web Consortium
 (Massachusetts Institute of Technology, Institut National
 de Recherche en Informatique et en Automatique,
 Keio University). All Rights Reserved.

 Permission to use, copy, modify and distribute the XHTML
 Basic DTD and its accompanying documentation for any purpose
 and without fee is hereby granted in perpetuity, provided that
 the above copyright notice and this paragraph appear in all
 copies.  The copyright holders make no representation about
 the suitability of the DTD for any purpose.

 This is an even smaller version of the XHTML Basic DTD
 developed by Elliotte Rusty Harold for the XML Bible,
 Gold Edition.

 It is provided "as is" without expressed or implied warranty.

 Editors: Elliotte Harold <mailto:elharo@metalab.unc.edu>
 Revision:   2001/05/14

-->
<!ENTITY % NS.prefixed "INCLUDE" >
<!ENTITY % XHTML.prefix  "html" >

<!-- Reserved for use with the XLink namespace:
-->
<!ENTITY % XLINK.xmlns "" >
<!ENTITY % XLINK.xmlns.attrib "" >

<!-- reserved for future use with document profiles -->
<!ENTITY % XHTML.profile  "" >
```

```
<!-- Bidirectional Text features
     This feature-test entity is used to declare elements
     and attributes used for bidirectional text support.
-->
<!ENTITY % XHTML.bidi  "IGNORE" >

<!-- ::::::::::::::::::::::::::::::::::::::::::::::::::::: -->

<!ENTITY % xhtml-events.module   "IGNORE" >
<!ENTITY % xhtml-bdo.module      "%XHTML.bidi;" >

<!ENTITY % xhtml-model.mod
     PUBLIC
      "-//ERH//ENTITIES XHTML Minimal Document Model 1.0//EN"
      "xhtml-minimal-model.mod" >

<!ENTITY % xhtml-framework.mod
     PUBLIC "-//W3C//ENTITIES XHTML Modular Framework 1.0//EN"
            "xhtml-framework-1.mod" >
%xhtml-framework.mod;

<!ENTITY % xhtml-text.mod
     PUBLIC "-//W3C//ELEMENTS XHTML Text 1.0//EN"
            "xhtml-text-1.mod" >
%xhtml-text.mod;

<!ENTITY % xhtml-struct.mod
     PUBLIC "-//W3C//ELEMENTS XHTML Document Structure 1.0//EN"
            "xhtml-struct-1.mod" >
%xhtml-struct.mod;

<!-- end of XHTML Minimal 1.0 DTD ...................... -->
```

You can also add things to the driver DTD. For example, if you wanted to add MathML to XHTML Basic, you could simply put this at the end of the normal XHTML Basic DTD:

```
<!ENTITY % mathml.dtd
     PUBLIC "-//W3C//DTD MathML 2.0//EN"
            "http://www.w3.org/TR/MathML2/dtd/mathml2.dtd" >
%mathml.dtd;
```

However, you'd also have to change the document model to enable MathML `math` elements to appear where you wanted them. I take this up in the next section.

The Document Model

In XHTML, the document model is primarily responsible for defining the permissible contents of elements. It accomplishes this by defining three parameter entity references:

- `%Block.mix;`
- `%Flow.mix;`
- `%Inline.mix;`

Many XHTML elements have content models specified almost completely by one of these content models. For example, the inline `code` element defined in the text module declares its content model like this:

```
<!ENTITY % code.element  "INCLUDE" >
<![%code.element;[
<!ENTITY % code.content
     "( #PCDATA | %Inline.mix; )*"
>
<!ENTITY % code.qname  "code" >
<!ELEMENT %code.qname;  %code.content; >
<!-- end of code.element -->]]>
```

When most of the entities and `INCLUDE` blocks are resolved, what's left is this:

```
<!ELEMENT code ( #PCDATA | %Inline.mix; )* >
```

In fact, more than a dozen elements use exactly this content model. The innards of a `code` element are pretty much the same as the innards of an `em` element, a `strong` element, a `kbd` element, and more.

This isn't true of all elements, though. Some elements have unique content models. For example, a `table` can only contain `caption`, `col`, `colgroup`, `thead`, `tbody`, `tr`, and `tfoot` elements. Because this content model is unique to tables, it is defined completely within the tables module, like this:

```
<!ENTITY % table.element  "INCLUDE" >
<![%table.element;[
<!ENTITY % table.content
    "( %caption.qname;?, ( %col.qname;* | %colgroup.qname;* ),
      (( %thead.qname;?, %tfoot.qname;?, %tbody.qname;+ ) |
       ( %tr.qname;+ )))"
>
<!ELEMENT %table.qname;  %table.content; >
<!-- end of table.element -->]]>
```

It is still written using parameter entity references, and these could be predefined in the document model. However, that would be rare. Most of the time, only the cross-module parameter entity references like `%Block.mix;` are predefined in the document model.

The `td` element, by contrast, can contain almost any nonstructural HTML element, and thus its content model is specified using the common content model `%Flow.mix;` like this:

```
<!ENTITY % td.element  "INCLUDE" >
<![%td.element;[
<!ENTITY % td.content
     "( #PCDATA | %Flow.mix; )*"
>
<!ELEMENT %td.qname;  %td.content; >
<!-- end of td.element -->]]>
```

The XHTML Basic document model

Listing 22-5 shows the XHTML Basic document model module, `xhtml-basic10-model-1.mod`. This is a straightforward and simple model that supports most of the nondeprecated features of HTML.

Listing 22-5: xhtml-basic10-model-1.mod: The XHTML Basic Document Model DTD

```
<!-- ...................................................... -->
<!-- XHTML Basic 1.0 Document Model Module
.................................... -->
<!-- file: xhtml-basic10-model-1.mod

     This is XHTML Basic, a proper subset of XHTML.
     Copyright 1998-2000 W3C (MIT, INRIA, Keio), All Rights
     Reserved.
     Revision: $Id: xhtml-basic10-model-1.mod,v 2.8 2000/11/03
     14:28:25 mimasa Exp $ SMI

     This DTD module is identified by the PUBLIC and SYSTEM
     identifiers:

PUBLIC
   "-//W3C//ENTITIES XHTML Basic 1.0 Document Model 1.0//EN"
SYSTEM
   "http://www.w3.org/TR/xhtml-basic/xhtml-basic10-model-1.mod"
```

Continued

Listing 22-5 (continued)

```
     Revisions:
     (none)
     ........................................................ -->

<!-- XHTML Basic Document Model

     This module describes the groupings of elements that make
     up common content models for XHTML elements.
-->

<!-- Optional Elements in head  .............. -->

<!ENTITY % HeadOpts.mix
     "( %meta.qname; | %link.qname; | %object.qname; )*" >

<!-- Miscellaneous Elements  ................. -->

<!ENTITY % Misc.class "" >

<!-- Inline Elements  ........................ -->

<!ENTITY % InlStruct.class "%br.qname; | %span.qname;" >

<!ENTITY % InlPhras.class
    "| %em.qname; | %strong.qname; | %dfn.qname; | %code.qname;
     | %samp.qname; | %kbd.qname; | %var.qname; | %cite.qname;
     | %abbr.qname; | %acronym.qname; | %q.qname;" >

<!ENTITY % InlPres.class "" >

<!ENTITY % I18n.class "" >

<!ENTITY % Anchor.class "| %a.qname;" >

<!ENTITY % InlSpecial.class "| %img.qname; | %object.qname;" >

<!ENTITY % InlForm.class
     "| %input.qname; | %select.qname; | %textarea.qname;
      | %label.qname;"
>

<!ENTITY % Inline.extra "" >

<!ENTITY % Inline.class
     "%InlStruct.class;
      %InlPhras.class;
      %Anchor.class;
      %InlSpecial.class;
      %InlForm.class;
      %Inline.extra;"
>
```

```
<!ENTITY % InlNoAnchor.class
     "%InlStruct.class;
      %InlPhras.class;
      %InlSpecial.class;
      %InlForm.class;
      %Inline.extra;"
>

<!ENTITY % InlNoAnchor.mix
     "%InlNoAnchor.class;
      %Misc.class;"
>

<!ENTITY % Inline.mix
     "%Inline.class;
      %Misc.class;"
>

<!-- Block Elements  ........................ -->

<!ENTITY % Heading.class
     "%h1.qname; | %h2.qname; | %h3.qname;
      | %h4.qname; | %h5.qname; | %h6.qname;"
>
<!ENTITY % List.class  "%ul.qname; | %ol.qname; | %dl.qname;">

<!ENTITY % Table.class "| %table.qname;" >

<!ENTITY % Form.class  "| %form.qname;" >

<!ENTITY % BlkStruct.class "%p.qname; | %div.qname;" >

<!ENTITY % BlkPhras.class
     "| %pre.qname; | %blockquote.qname; | %address.qname;"
>

<!ENTITY % BlkPres.class "" >

<!ENTITY % BlkSpecial.class
     "%Table.class;
      %Form.class;"
>

<!ENTITY % Block.extra "" >

<!ENTITY % Block.class
     "%BlkStruct.class;
      %BlkPhras.class;
      %BlkSpecial.class;
      %Block.extra;"
>
```

Continued

Listing 22-5 *(continued)*

```
<!ENTITY % Block.mix
     "%Heading.class;
      | %List.class;
      | %Block.class;
      %Misc.class;"
>

<!-- All Content Elements  .................. -->

<!-- declares all content except tables
-->
<!ENTITY % FlowNoTable.mix
     "%Heading.class;
      | %List.class;
      | %BlkStruct.class;
      %BlkPhras.class;
      %Form.class;
      %Block.extra;
      | %Inline.class;
      %Misc.class;"
>

<!ENTITY % Flow.mix
     "%Heading.class;
      | %List.class;
      | %Block.class;
      | %Inline.class;
      %Misc.class;"
>

<!-- end of xhtml-basic10-model-1.mod -->
```

This module progressively builds larger collections out of smaller pieces. For example, the `Flow.mix` entity comprises five other entities: `Heading.class`, `List.class`, `Block.class`, `Inline.class`, and `Misc.class`. Each of these entities is built from still other pieces. Table 22-6 lists the parameter entities and their customary replacement text as given in XHTML Basic, assuming the standard element names are used without namespace prefixes. You'll find these same parameter entities in the document models for XHTML 1.1 and XHTML 1.1 plus MathML. However, in those cases, the replacement text will be a little larger and contain a few more elements.

Table 22-6
Document Model Parameter Entities Defined in XHTML Basic

Parameter Entity	*Replacement Text*
%HeadOpts.mix;	(meta | link | object)*
%Misc.class;	
%InlStruct.class;	Br | span
%InlPhras.class;	| em | strong | dfn | code | samp | kbd | var | cite | abbr | acronym | q
%InlPres.class;	
%I18n.class;	
%Anchor.class;	| a
%InlSpecial.class;	| img | object
%InlForm.class;	| input | select | textarea | label
%Inline.extra ;	
%Inline.class;	br | span | em | strong | dfn | code | samp | kbd | var | cite | abbr | acronym | q | a | img | object | input | select | textarea | label
%InlNoAnchor.class;	br | span | em | strong | dfn | code | samp | kbd | var | cite | abbr | acronym | q | img | object | input | select | textarea | label
%InlNoAnchor.mix;	br | span | em | strong | dfn | code | samp | kbd | var | cite | abbr | acronym | q | img | object | input | select | textarea | label
%Inline.mix;	br | span | em | strong | dfn | code | samp | kbd | var | cite | abbr | acronym | q | a | img | object | input | select | textarea | label
%Heading.class;	h1 | h2 | h3 | h4 | h5 | h6
%List.class;	Ul | ol | dl
%Table.class;	| table
%Form.class;	| form
%BlkStruct.class;	p | div
%BlkPhras.class;	| pre | blockquote | address
%BlkPres.class;	

Continued

Table 22-6 (continued)

Parameter Entity	*Replacement Text*
`%BlkSpecial.class;`	`| table | form`
`%Block.extra;`	
`%Block.class;`	`p | div | pre | blockquote | address | table | form`
`%Block.mix;`	`h1 | h2 | h3 | h4 | h5 | h6 | ul | ol | dl | p | div | pre | blockquote | address | table | form`
`%FlowNoTable.mix;`	`h1 | h2 | h3 | h4 | h5 | h6 | ul | ol | dl | p | div | pre | blockquote | address | form | br | span | em | strong | dfn | code | samp | kbd | var | cite | abbr | acronym | q | a | img | object | input | select | textarea | label`
`%Flow.mix;`	`h1 | h2 | h3 | h4 | h5 | h6 | ul | ol | dl | p | div | pre | blockquote | address | table | form | br | span | em | strong | dfn | code | samp | kbd | var | cite | abbr | acronym | q | a | img | object | input | select | textarea | label`

A number of the entities in Table 22-6 are empty by default. There are two reasons for this. Some of them, such as `%InlPres.class;` and `%Blockpres.class;`, hold elements XHTML Basic does not allow. For example, `InlPres.class` represents inline presentational elements such as `i` and `b`. These are included in XHTML 1.1 but not in XHTML Basic. In XHTML 1.1, `%InlPres.class;` and `%Blockpres.class;` are not empty.

The other category of empty parameter entities are the extra entities such as `%Inline.extra;` and `%Block.extra;`. By redefining these, you can add elements to the content models of many elements. For example, to allow the MathML `math` element to appear wherever a block level element can appear, you simply redefine `%Block.extra;`, like this:

```
<!ENTITY % Block.extra "| math" >
```

Of course, you also have to load the MathML DTD that defines the `math` element.

When you're mixing XHTML markup into your own applications, you might want to use these parameter entity references to define the content models for your own elements. For example, a NOTE element in a PATIENT_RECORD might be allowed to contain essentially any XHTML block-level elements. In this case, you'd import the XHTML Basic DTD into your own DTD and then declare the NOTE element, like this:

```
<!ENTITY % xhtml-basic SYSTEM "xhtml-basic10.dtd">
%xhtml_basic;
<!ELEMENT NOTE ((%Block.mix;)*)>
```

Because of interdependencies among the different XHTML modules, it is necessary to pull in the full XHTML Basic DTD rather than just the document model or the block-level elements you actually want. Still, the extra elements won't get in your way. They're defined, but they're not allowed anywhere inside the DTD for the PATIENT_RECORD.

This is a case in which you might want to use a prefix for the XHTML elements rather than rely on the default namespace, especially if the NOTE and PATIENT_RECORD elements themselves use the default namespace. In this case, you'd just predefine the NS.prefixed and XHTML.prefix entities somewhere in the patient record DTD before you load the XHTML driver DTD. For example:

```
<!ENTITY % NS.prefixed "INCLUDE" >
<!ENTITY % XHTML.prefix  "html" >
<!ENTITY % xhtml-basic SYSTEM "xhtml-basic10.dtd">
%xhtml_basic;
<!ELEMENT NOTE ((%Block.mix)*)>
```

Now all the NOTE elements will contain prefixed HTML. You'll still need to declare the XHTML namespace with an xmlns:html attribute on each NOTE element or one of its ancestors in the PATIENT_RECORD documents. One possibility is to make the declaration a fixed attribute of the root PATIENT_RECORD element in its DTD, like this:

```
<!ATTLIST PATIENT_RECORD
      xmlns:html CDATA #FIXED "http://www.w3.org/1999/xhtml">
```

A minimal document model

If you define your own subsets of XHTML, you'll probably need to define your own document models as well. Listing 22-6 is a minimal XHTML document for use with the minimal XHTML driver DTD seen previously in Listing 22-4. It's based on the XHTML Basic document model module, but it removes forms, tables, images, lists, and more from the entity references defined here. The end result is a very Spartan vocabulary.

Listing 22-6: xhtml-minimal-model.mod: A Minimal XHTML Document Model DTD

```
<!-- ...................................................... -->
<!-- XHTML Minimal Document Model Module  ................ -->
<!-- file: xhtml-minimal-model.mod

     This is XHTML Minimal, a proper subset of XHTML, derived
     from XHTML Basic for the XML Bible Gold Edition.

     This DTD module is identified by the PUBLIC and SYSTEM
     identifiers:

     PUBLIC
     "-//ERH//ENTITIES XHTML Basic 1.0 Document Model 1.0//EN"
     SYSTEM "xhtml-minimal-model.mod"

     ...................................................... -->

<!-- XHTML Minimal Document Model

     This module describes the groupings of elements that make
     up common content models for XHTML elements.
-->

<!-- Optional Elements in head  .............. -->

<!ENTITY % HeadOpts.mix "( )*" >

<!-- Miscellaneous Elements  ................. -->

<!ENTITY % Misc.class "" >

<!-- Inline Elements  ........................ -->

<!ENTITY % InlStruct.class "%br.qname; | %span.qname;" >

<!ENTITY % InlPhras.class
    "| %em.qname; | %strong.qname; | %dfn.qname; | %code.qname;
     | %samp.qname; | %kbd.qname; | %var.qname; | %cite.qname;
     | %abbr.qname; | %acronym.qname; | %q.qname;" >

<!ENTITY % InlPres.class "" >

<!ENTITY % I18n.class "" >

<!ENTITY % Anchor.class "" >

<!ENTITY % InlSpecial.class "" >
```

```
<!ENTITY % InlForm.class "" >

<!ENTITY % Inline.extra "" >

<!ENTITY % Inline.class
     "%InlStruct.class;
      %InlPhras.class;
      %Anchor.class;
      %InlSpecial.class;
      %InlForm.class;
      %Inline.extra;"
>

<!ENTITY % InlNoAnchor.class
     "%InlStruct.class;
      %InlPhras.class;
      %InlSpecial.class;
      %InlForm.class;
      %Inline.extra;"
>

<!ENTITY % InlNoAnchor.mix
     "%InlNoAnchor.class;
      %Misc.class;"
>

<!ENTITY % Inline.mix
     "%Inline.class;
      %Misc.class;"
>

<!-- Block Elements  ......................... -->

<!ENTITY % Heading.class
     "%h1.qname; | %h2.qname; | %h3.qname;
      | %h4.qname; | %h5.qname; | %h6.qname;"
>
<!ENTITY % List.class  "" >

<!ENTITY % Table.class "" >

<!ENTITY % Form.class  "" >

<!ENTITY % BlkStruct.class "%p.qname; | %div.qname;" >

<!ENTITY % BlkPhras.class
     "| %pre.qname; | %blockquote.qname; | %address.qname;"
>

<!ENTITY % BlkPres.class "" >
```

Continued

Listing 22-6 *(continued)*

```
<!ENTITY % BlkSpecial.class
     "%Table.class;
      %Form.class;"
>

<!ENTITY % Block.extra "" >

<!ENTITY % Block.class
     "%BlkStruct.class;
      %BlkPhras.class;
      %BlkSpecial.class;
      %Block.extra;"
>

<!ENTITY % Block.mix
     "%Heading.class;
      | %List.class;
      | %Block.class;
      %Misc.class;"
>

<!-- All Content Elements  ................... -->

<!-- declares all content except tables
-->
<!ENTITY % FlowNoTable.mix
     "%Heading.class;
      | %List.class;
      | %BlkStruct.class;
      %BlkPhras.class;
      %Form.class;
      %Block.extra;
      | %Inline.class;
      %Misc.class;"
>

<!ENTITY % Flow.mix
     "%Heading.class;
      | %List.class;
      | %Block.class;
      | %Inline.class;
      %Misc.class;"
>

<!-- end of xhtml-minimal-model.mod -->
```

An alternate approach is to keep the normal XHTML Basic document model, but to add a new module that predefines the various entity references that you want to change. To do this, you'd point the parameter entity reference `%xhtml-model.redecl;` at your module containing the redeclarations, as shown in Listing 22-7.

Listing 22-7: xhtml-minimal-redecl.mod: A Content Model Redeclaration Module for Minimal XHTML

```
<!-- ...................................................... -->
<!-- XHTML Minimal Redeclarations Module  ................ -->
<!-- file: xhtml-minimal-redecl.mod

     This is XHTML Minimal, a proper subset of XHTML, derived
     from XHTML Basic for the XML Bible Gold Edition.

     This DTD module is identified by the PUBLIC and SYSTEM
     identifiers:

    PUBLIC
    "-//ERH//ENTITIES XHTML Minimal 1.0 Redeclarations 1.0//EN"
   SYSTEM "xhtml-minimal-redecl.mod"

     ...................................................... -->

<!-- XHTML Minimal Document Model

     This module describes the groupings of elements that make
     up common content models for XHTML elements.
-->

<!-- Optional Elements in head  .............. -->

<!ENTITY % HeadOpts.mix "( )*" >

<!ENTITY % I18n.class "" >

<!ENTITY % Anchor.class "" >

<!ENTITY % InlSpecial.class "" >

<!ENTITY % InlForm.class "" >

<!-- Block Elements  ........................ -->

<!ENTITY % List.class  "" >

<!ENTITY % Table.class "" >

<!ENTITY % Form.class  "" >

<!-- end of xhtml-minimal-redecl.mod -->
```

This module is much smaller than the module in Listing 22-6 because it only has to change a few entity references. In many cases, it can just accept the defaults.

A Sample Schema Module

The schema implementation of XHTML modularization is not nearly as complete as the DTD implementation, mostly because the W3C XML Schema Language took a lot longer to finish than was expected. Nonetheless, version 1.0 is now more or less complete, and work has begun on schema implementations of the various XHTML modules. Listing 22-8 demonstrates the schema version of the list module, as defined in the October 3, 2003, second Last Call Working Draft of *Modularization of XHTML in XML Schema*.

Listing 22-8: **The List Module Schema**

```
<?xml version="1.0" encoding="UTF-8"?>
<xs:schema xmlns:xs="http://www.w3.org/2001/XMLSchema"
           targetNamespace="http://www.w3.org/1999/xhtml"
           xmlns="http://www.w3.org/1999/xhtml">

  <xs:annotation>
    <xs:documentation>
      List Module
      This is the XML Schema Lists module for XHTML
      List Module Elements

        * dl, dt, dd, ol, ul, li

      This module declares the list-oriented element types
      and their attributes.
      $Id: xhtml-list-1.xsd,v 1.2 2003/09/20 01:41:37 speruvem
       Exp $
    </xs:documentation>
    <xs:documentation source="xhtml-copyright-1.xsd"/>
    <xs:documentation
      source="http://www.w3.org/TR/2001/REC-xhtml-
modularization-20010410/abstract_modules.html#s_listmodule"/>
</xs:annotation>

  <xs:attributeGroup name="dt.attlist">
    <xs:attributeGroup ref="Common.attrib"/>
  </xs:attributeGroup>
    <xs:group name="dt.content">
    <xs:sequence>
      <xs:group ref="Inline.mix" minOccurs="0"
                                   maxOccurs="unbounded"/>
    </xs:sequence>
  </xs:group>
```

```
  <xs:complexType name="dt.type" mixed="true">
    <xs:group ref="dt.content"/>
    <xs:attributeGroup ref="dt.attlist"/>
  </xs:complexType>

  <xs:element name="dt" type="dt.type"/>

  <xs:attributeGroup name="dd.attlist">
    <xs:attributeGroup ref="Common.attrib"/>
  </xs:attributeGroup>
    <xs:group name="dd.content">
    <xs:sequence>
      <xs:group ref="Flow.mix" minOccurs="0"
maxOccurs="unbounded"/>      </xs:sequence>
  </xs:group>

  <xs:complexType name="dd.type" mixed="true">
    <xs:group ref="dd.content"/>
    <xs:attributeGroup ref="dd.attlist"/>
  </xs:complexType>

  <xs:element name="dd" type="dd.type"/>

  <xs:attributeGroup name="dl.attlist">
    <xs:attributeGroup ref="Common.attrib"/>
  </xs:attributeGroup>

  <xs:group name="dl.content">
    <xs:sequence>
      <xs:choice maxOccurs="unbounded">
        <xs:element ref="dt"/>
        <xs:element ref="dd"/>
      </xs:choice>
    </xs:sequence>
  </xs:group>

  <xs:complexType name="dl.type">
    <xs:group ref="dl.content"/>
    <xs:attributeGroup ref="dl.attlist"/>
  </xs:complexType>

  <xs:element name="dl" type="dl.type"/>

  <xs:attributeGroup name="li.attlist">
    <xs:attributeGroup ref="Common.attrib"/>
  </xs:attributeGroup>
    <xs:group name="li.content">
    <xs:sequence>
      <xs:group ref="Flow.mix" minOccurs="0"
maxOccurs="unbounded"/>
    </xs:sequence>        </xs:group>
```

Continued

Listing 22-8 *(continued)*

```
  <xs:complexType name="li.type" mixed="true">
    <xs:group ref="li.content"/>
    <xs:attributeGroup ref="li.attlist"/>
  </xs:complexType>

  <xs:element name="li" type="li.type"/>

  <xs:attributeGroup name="ol.attlist">
    <xs:attributeGroup ref="Common.attrib"/>
  </xs:attributeGroup>

  <xs:group name="ol.content">
    <xs:sequence>
      <xs:element ref="li" maxOccurs="unbounded"/>
    </xs:sequence>
  </xs:group>

  <xs:complexType name="ol.type">
    <xs:group ref="ol.content"/>
    <xs:attributeGroup ref="ol.attlist"/>
  </xs:complexType>

  <xs:element name="ol" type="ol.type"/>

  <xs:attributeGroup name="ul.attlist">
    <xs:attributeGroup ref="Common.attrib"/>
  </xs:attributeGroup>
    <xs:group name="ul.content">
    <xs:sequence>
      <xs:element ref="li" maxOccurs="unbounded"/>
    </xs:sequence>
  </xs:group>

  <xs:complexType name="ul.type">
    <xs:group ref="ul.content"/>
    <xs:attributeGroup ref="ul.attlist"/>
  </xs:complexType>

  <xs:element name="ul" type="ul.type"/>

</xs:schema>
```

A complete schema implementation of modular XHTML also requires schema versions of all the underlying framework modules, such as the common attributes module and the data types module, as well as schemas for the document model.

Instead of a driver DTD, the schema implementation of XHTML 1.1 uses a hub document. All of these are currently under development and may be available by the time you're reading this. Consult `http://www.w3.org/TR/xhtml-m12n-schema` for the latest information.

Summary

In this chapter, you learned about modular XHTML, a W3C Recommendation for organizing XHTML as a set of semi-independent DTDs that are easy to mix and match with other XML applications. In particular, you learned the following:

✦ Modular XHTML divides the different parts of HTML into 28 modules, each defining a related group of elements.

✦ These 28 modules depend on a framework module that defines entities all the modules use to specify element names, namespace URIs and prefixes, content models, and attribute types.

✦ A driver module integrates all the different parts of both the framework and the abstract modules.

✦ A document model module defines the common content models shared among the different modules.

✦ The abstract modules have concrete implementations as both DTDs and schemas.

✦ You can use your own driver modules and document model modules to integrate your own XML applications into XHTML or to subsume XHTML into your own applications.

Chapter 23 investigates an application that's built on top of XHTML Basic and modular XHTML—the Resource Directory Description Language (RDDL). RDDL adds a single `resource` element to XHTML Basic. The `resource` element is an XLink that can locate a resource associated with a particular namespace URI.

✦ ✦ ✦

The Resource Directory Description Language

✦ ✦ ✦ ✦

In This Chapter

What does a namespace URL locate?

The solution

The resource element

Natures

Purposes

✦ ✦ ✦ ✦

If you've read Chapter 11, you know that there isn't a DTD or schema at the end of a namespace URI. In fact, there may well be no page there at all. Even though almost all namespace URIs are URLs, they do not actually locate anything. Namespace URLs are simply formal identifiers. This has proven to be completely counterintuitive and has led to many repetitions of the frequently asked question, "What's at the end of a namespace URL?" on xml-dev and other XML mailing lists and newsgroups.

After answering this question for about the three hundredth time, Tim Bray and Jonathan Borden decided to turn the problem on its head. If they couldn't convince developers that a namespace URL didn't actually locate anything, maybe they should convince document authors to use namespace URLs that did locate things instead. To this end, they invented a new XML application for documents located at the end of a namespace URL. This application is called the Resource Directory Description Language (RDDL, pronounced "riddle"). RDDL is a combination of XHTML Basic, XLink, and one new `resource` element. A RDDL document lists various documents that are related to an XML application identified by a particular namespace URL, including but not limited to schemas, DTDs, specifications, style sheet, logos, software, and more. RDDL was carefully designed to be easily viewed in existing web browsers by humans and to be straightforwardly machine-readable to enable automated resource lookup by software.

What Does a Namespace URL Locate?

XSLT 1.0 is identified by the namespace URL `http://www.w3.org/1999/XSL/Transform`. After teaching numerous XSLT classes, I've learned that as soon as I introduce this, a student—almost inevitably—asks, "Does this mean I need to be connected to the Internet to use XSLT?" In other words, does an XSLT processor actually need to load the page at the URL `http://www.w3.org/1999/XSL/Transform`? The short answer to this question is no, the namespace URL is just a formal identifier that's built into all XSLT 1.0 processors. An XSLT 1.0 processor looks for that URL in the style sheets it processes, but it does not at any time connect to `www.w3.org`.

Nonetheless, it's quite natural to look at a URL such as `http://www.w3.org/1999/XSL/Transform` and expect that there must be something there. Novice developers routinely type these URLs into their browsers just to see what might be there. For a long time, when loading `http://www.w3.org/1999/XSL/Transform` and other official W3C namespace URLs into their browsers, developers simply got a 404 Not Found error. Error logs at the W3C were filling up with the failed requests from people who typed in namespace URLs to see what they would get. In some cases, DNS servers were overloaded with attempts to resolve nonexistent hostnames that were nonetheless used inside namespace URLs. Eventually, the W3C got tired of all the extra messages these URLs added to their error logs and began putting up pages similar to the one shown in Figure 23-1.

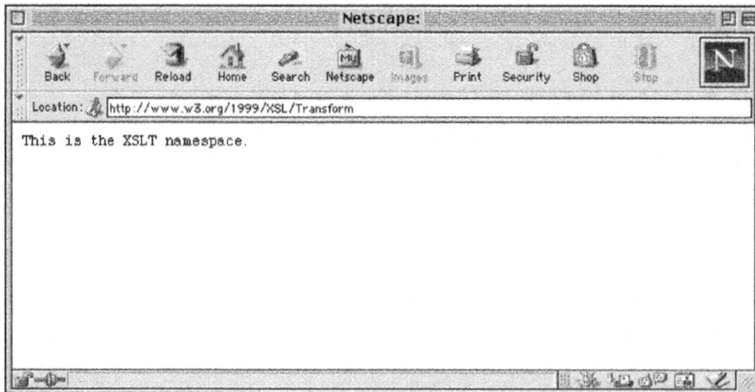

Figure 23-1: The HTML page at the XSLT namespace URL

However, this page was just a quick hack to avoid unnecessarily confusing developers. It was never intended as more than that, or as a suggestion that pages like this should be put at the end of namespace URLs. In fact, the namespaces specification specifically disavows the notion that a namespace URI can be resolved: "The namespace name, to serve its intended purpose, should have the characteristics of uniqueness and persistence. It is not a goal that it be directly usable for retrieval of a schema (if any exists)." Nonetheless, many developers expect that they can find some sort of schema, whether a DTD, a W3C XML Schema Language schema, a Resource Description Framework (RDF) schema, or some other kind of schema at the end of a namespace URL.

The reason the inventors of namespaces decided not to require namespace URLs to be resolved was manyfold. However, it really boils down to the fact that there was no obvious and unique choice of what to put at the end of a namespace URL. For instance, they could have required a DTD, but that would have caused problems for XML applications that used schemas. They could have required a schema or a DTD and used MIME media types to tell which one was there, but that would have required parsers to be able to read both DTDs and schemas. More importantly, it wouldn't have handled at all well the common case where the document using the namespace is merely well formed and not valid. For example, all XSLT style sheets use namespaces, but almost none of them use DTDs.

Another possibility was to put a specification for the XML application at the namespace URL. However, not all XML applications have formal specifications identifiable with a URL. For instance, the television listings example used in the early chapters of this book was developed ad hoc and is not formally documented anywhere. That's a perfectly legal use of XML. Another problem with placing specifications at the namespace URLs is that the specifications often change faster than the namespace URL does. For example, XSLT 1.0, XSLT 2.0, and a now withdrawn proposal for XSLT 1.1 all use the same `http://www.w3.org/1999/XSL/Transform` namespace URL, even though they have three different specification documents.

Because the W3C couldn't decide what to place at the end of a namespace URL, they decided not to require anything to be there. However, they also decided not to forbid documents from being there either, or to make any restrictions on what sort of documents could be there. They deliberately chose not to decide. This allowed specific XML applications to add additional requirements beyond the minimal set mandated by *Namespaces in XML*. For example, the Resource Description Framework requires that an RDF schema be found at the end of a namespace URI for an RDF property.

The Solution

By the time Tim Bray, Jonathan Borden, and the xml-dev mailing list revisited the problem of what to put at the end of a namespace URL in late 2000, it had become obvious that the W3C's nondecision was confusing many developers, and that a solution was needed. Clearly, putting nothing there wasn't working, and leaving the decision about what to put there to individual XML application developers wasn't much better.

Bray and Borden attacked the problem using an old programmer's adage: Every problem can be solved by adding an additional level of indirection. Instead of choosing one possible thing to put at a namespace URL, such as a DTD, a schema, a specification document, or something else, they decided to put a list of pointers to all different kinds of related resources. For any given namespace URL, a single document could provide a pointer to a DTD, a pointer to a schema, a pointer to a specification, a pointer to a style sheet, a pointer to software to process the XML, and more. In fact, it could even have pointers to more than one of each. As this was the Web, the pointers would be URLs. Because this was XML, the URLs would be embedded in XLinks. And because the document containing the list would have to make sense to a human being loading the URL in a traditional, non-XML-aware web browser, the XLinks would be placed in an XHTML Basic document.

The resource Element

A RDDL document is a well-formed XHTML document with one extra element— `resource`. This element may appear anywhere a `div` element can appear, and it can contain anything a `div` element can contain. To distinguish this from XHTML elements, it is placed in the `http://www.rddl.org/` namespace. The prefix `rddl` is customary, but as always, this can be changed as long as the URI remains the same. Naturally, if you actually try to resolve that URL, you'll see a RDDL document describing RDDL itself, as shown in Figure 23-2. To a casual user this looks just like any other Web page, which is the beauty of RDDL. If a developer types a namespace URL into a web browser location bar to see what's there, the developer should see something he or she can read.

Each `rddl:resource` element identifies one resource that is somehow related to the XML application denoted by a particular namespace URL. This related resource can be a DTD, a schema, a style sheet, a specification, software that can read documents written in that XML vocabulary, or something else. For example, here's a typical `rddl:resource` element for the URL `http://www.cafeconleche.org/namespaces/tv/` that says a DTD for the XML application identified by that namespace URI can be found at the URL `http://ibiblio.org/xml/dtds/tv.dtd`:

```
<rddl:resource xmlns:rddl="http://www.rddl.org/"
  xlink:type="simple"
  xlink:href="http://ibiblio.org/xml/dtds/tv.dtd"
  xlink:role=
"http://www.isi.edu/in-notes/iana/assignments/media-types/application/xml-dtd"
>
  XHTML can go here...
</rddl:resource>
```

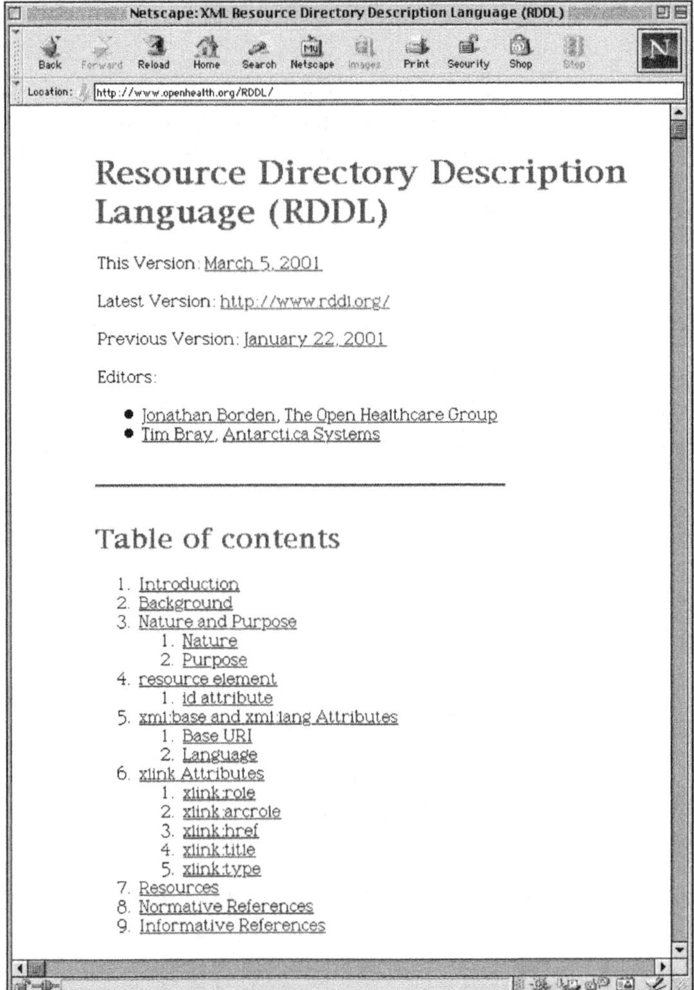

Figure 23-2: The RDDL document at the RDDL namespace URL

`rddl:resource` elements are simple XLinks, as indicated by the `xlink:type="simple"` attribute. The `xlink:href` attribute contains a URL pointing to the location of the related resource. The `xlink:role` attribute contains a URL identifying exactly what the related resource is. In this case, that URL indicates the specific MIME media type registered for DTDs by pointing to the official registration page for the DTD MIME type at the Institute for Information Sciences at the University of Southern California. XLink requires that the value of an `xlink:role` attribute contain an absolute URL, not just a simple MIME media type such as `application/xml-dtd`. The `rddl:resource` element does not specify the namespace URL of the resource that this resource is related to. That's provided by the URL of the page containing the `rddl:resource` element.

The RDDL DTD declares the rddl:resource element like this:

```
<!ELEMENT rddl:resource (#PCDATA | %Flow.mix;)*>
```

If you recall the %Flow.mix; parameter entity reference from the last chapter, you realize that this means a rddl:resource element can contain essentially anything the HTML body element can contain: block-level elements such as p and div, inline elements such as span and em, unmarked-up text, or mixed content. Well-written RDDL documents take advantage of this by putting a full description of the resource being linked to inside each rddl:resource element, as in the following example:

```
<rddl:resource xmlns:rddl="http://www.rddl.org/"
  xlink:type="simple"
  xlink:href="http://ibiblio.org/xml/dtds/tv.dtd"
  xlink:role=
"http://www.isi.edu/in-notes/iana/assignments/media-types/application/xml-dtd" >

    <p>
      A <a href="http://ibiblio.org/xml/dtds/tv.dtd">
      Document Type Definition (<abbr>DTD</abbr>)
      for television listings</a> is available.
      This DTD is developed and described in Chapters 8, 9,
      and 10 of the <cite>XML Bible, 3rd Edition</cite>
      by <a href="mailto:elharo@metalab.unc.edu">Elliotte
      Rusty Harold</a>.
    </p>

</rddl:resource>
```

The rest of a RDDL document is just XHTML. Listing 23-1 demonstrates. Notice how this page is designed to provide a human-readable description of the resource. Novices who naively type namespace URLs into the location bars of their web browsers will no longer find themselves staring at 404 Not Found errors.

Listing 23-1: A Simple RDDL Document that Points to the DTD for the http://www.cafeconleche.org namespaces/tv/ XML Application

```
<!DOCTYPE html PUBLIC "-//XML-DEV//DTD XHTML RDDL 1.0//EN"
                      "http://www.rddl.org/rddl-xhtml.dtd">
<html xmlns="http://www.w3.org/1999/xhtml"
      xmlns:xlink="http://www.w3.org/1999/xlink"
      xmlns:rddl="http://www.rddl.org/">
<head>
  <title>An XML Application for TV Schedules</title>
</head>
```

```
<body>
<h1>An XML Application for TV Schedules</h1>

<div class="head">
<p>This Version:
<a href="http://www.cafeconleche.org/namespaces/tv/200300821/">
  August 21, 2003</a></p>
<p>Latest Version: <a href="http://www.cafeconleche.org/namespaces/tv/">
  http://www.cafeconleche.org/namespaces/tv/
</a></p>
<p>Previous Version:
<a href="http://www.cafeconleche.org/namespaces/tv/20010505/">
  May 5, 2001
</a></p>
<p>Authors:</p>
<ul>
<li><a href="mailto:elharo@metalab.unc.edu">Elliotte
    Rusty Harold</a></li>
</ul>
</div>

<p>
This document describes the an XML application for television
schedules used as an example in the 3rd edition of the <cite>XML Bible</cite> \
by <a href="mailto:elharo@metalab.unc.edu">Elliotte Rusty Harold</a>.
</p>

<p>This document has no official standing and has not been
considered or approved by any organization.</p>

<rddl:resource xmlns:rddl="http://www.rddl.org/"
  xlink:type="simple"
  xlink:href="http://ibiblio.org/xml/dtds/tv.dtd"
  xlink:role=
"http://www.isi.edu/in-notes/iana/assignments/media-types/application/xml-dtd"
>

    <p>
      A <a href="http://ibiblio.org/xml/dtds/tv.dtd">Document Type
      Definition (<abbr>DTD</abbr>) for TV Schedules</a> is available.
      This DTD is developed and described in Chapters 9, 10, and 11 of the
      <cite>XML Bible, 3rd Edition</cite>.
    </p>

</rddl:resource>

</body>
</html>
```

Figure 23-3 shows this document loaded into Netscape Navigator 4. As far as Netscape knows, this is just an HTML document, and Netscape can display it. Netscape does not recognize the <rddl:resource> tags or xmlns attributes, so it ignores them. In all other respects, it treats this as a regular HTML document.

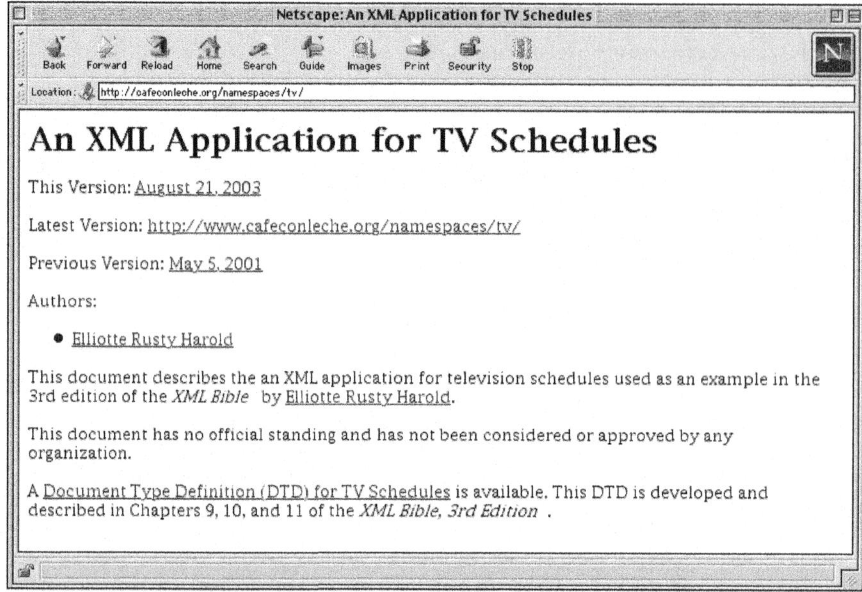

Figure 23-3: Listing 23-1 displayed in an XML-unaware web browser

RDDL documents are free to use any part of XHTML Basic that seems useful, including tables, forms, links, and CSS style sheets. The only major things missing are deprecated presentational elements such as i and b, frames, and bidirectional text.

You can write anything that seems appropriate in the XHTML parts of your document. In Listing 23-1, I placed information about the version at the top of the document, but if I preferred to put it at the bottom, I could. I can make the document as long or short as it needs to be. I could even include the complete text of Chapters 4, 5, 8, 9, and 10 if that seemed useful. There are no more limits on a RDDL document than on any other HTML document. You are free to let your imagination and creativity run wild.

That having been said, don't forget the ultimate purpose of a RDDL page. It's technical documentation for a specific XML application. It should be clear, concise, and straightforward. It should not include extraneous fluff or be overdesigned. For the most part, a simple, top-to-bottom presentation of just the facts is what users will appreciate most. You're not trying to win a Webby with this page. You're just explaining to curious users what the application is and where they can learn more about it.

Software that reads the page will ignore the XHTML markup completely. It can quickly search the page for `rddl:resource` elements and extract all the information it needs from those elements' start-tags.

Of course, one motivation for RDDL is that there's often more than one resource related to any given XML application. Thus, a RDDL document can contain as many `rddl:resource` elements as there are related resources. Listing 23-2 adds `rddl:resource` elements that point to the CSS style sheets and XSLT style sheets developed for baseball earlier in this book.

Listing 23-2: A RDDL Document That Locates Multiple Related Resources for the http://www.cafeconleche.org/namespaces/tv/ XML Application

```
<!DOCTYPE html PUBLIC "-//XML-DEV//DTD XHTML RDDL 1.0//EN"
                      "http://www.rddl.org/rddl-xhtml.dtd">
<html xmlns="http://www.w3.org/1999/xhtml"
      xmlns:xlink="http://www.w3.org/1999/xlink"
      xmlns:rddl="http://www.rddl.org/">
<head>
  <title>An XML Application for TV Schedules</title>
</head>
<body>
<h1>An XML Application for TV Schedules</h1>

<div class="head">
<p>This Version:
<a href="http://www.cafeconleche.org/namespaces/tv/200300821/">August
21, 2003</a></p>
<p>Latest Version: <a href="http://www.cafeconleche.org/namespaces/tv/">
http://www.cafeconleche.org/namespaces/tv/</a></p>
<p>Previous Version:
<a href="http://www.cafeconleche.org/namespaces/tv/20010505/">May 5, 2001</a>
</p>
<p>Authors:</p>
<ul>
<li><a href="mailto:elharo@metalab.unc.edu">Elliotte Rusty Harold</a></li>
</ul>
</div>

<p>
This document describes the an XML application for television schedules used
as an example in the 3rd edition of the <cite>XML Bible</cite> by
<a href="mailto:elharo@metalab.unc.edu">Elliotte Rusty Harold</a>.
</p>
```

Continued

Listing 23-2 *(continued)*

```
<p>This document has no official standing and has not been
considered or approved by any organization.</p>

<h2>Document Type Definition</h2>

<rddl:resource xmlns:rddl="http://www.rddl.org/"
  xlink:type="simple"
  xlink:href="http://ibiblio.org/xml/dtds/tv.dtd"
  xlink:role="http://www.isi.edu/in-notes/iana/assignments/media-
types/application/xml-dtd" >

    <p>
       A <a href="http://ibiblio.org/xml/dtds/tv.dtd">Document Type
       Definition (<abbr>DTD</abbr>) for TV Schedules</a> is available.
       This DTD is developed and described in Chapters 9, 10, and 11 of the
       <cite>XML Bible, 3rd Edition</cite>.
    </p>

</rddl:resource>

<h2>CSS Style Sheet</h2>

<rddl:resource xmlns:rddl="http://www.rddl.org/"
  xlink:type="simple"
  xlink:href="http://ibiblio.org/xml/styles/tvschedule.css"
  xlink:role="http://www.isi.edu/in-notes/iana/assignments/media-types/text/css"
>

    <p>
       A <a href="http://ibiblio.org/xml/styles/baseball.css">CSS style sheet
       for TV Schedules</a> is available. This style sheet was developed and
       described in Chapter 4 of the <cite>XML Bible, 3rd Edition</cite>.
    </p>

</rddl:resource>

<h2>XSLT Style Sheet</h2>

<rddl:resource xmlns:rddl="http://www.rddl.org/"
  xlink:type="simple"
  xlink:href="http://ibiblio.org/xml/styles/baseball.xsl"
  xlink:role=
"http://www.isi.edu/in-notes/iana/assignments/media-types/application/xml+xslt"
>
```

```
  <p>
    An <a href="http://ibiblio.org/xml/styles/tv.xsl">XSLT style sheet for
    TV Schedules</a> is also available. This style sheet was developed and
    described in Chapter 5 of the <cite>XML Bible, 3rd Edition</cite>.
  </p>

</rddl:resource>

</body>
</html>
```

Natures

In a `rddl:resource` element, the `xlink:role` attribute defines the *nature* of the related resource. The nature tells you what kind of document you'll find on the other end of the `xlink:href` attribute for that resource. Examples of natures include CSS style sheets, W3C Schema Language schemas, Schematron schemas, HTML specification documents, Java applets, and more. RDDL does not place any limits on what kinds of resources a RDDL document can point to. If it's useful to you, you can refer to it from a RDDL document.

However, RDDL does specify that certain URLs identify particular natures. For example, the URL `http://www.isi.edu/in-notes/iana/assignments/media-types/application/xml-dtd` always means that the nature is an XML DTD. The URL `http://www.w3.org/TR/xhtml1/DTD/xhtml1-strict` always means that the nature is strict XHTML 1.0.

Using standard URLs for standard natures allows software to find and apply style sheets, schemas, DTDs, and other useful resources without human intervention. For example, suppose a browser reads an XML document using a vocabulary it's never seen before, and it doesn't immediately know how to display it. It needs to find a style sheet that can display documents using that vocabulary. It sees that the namespace URL for the document's root element is `http://www.cafeconleche.org/namespaces/tv/`, so it silently loads that URL. (The browser would not show the page it loaded to the reader in this scenario.) The browser then scans the RDDL document at `http://www.cafeconleche.org/namespaces/ttv/` looking for a `rddl:resource` element whose nature indicates that it's a CSS style sheet. According to the RDDL specification, this is indicated by the URL `http://www.isi.edu/in-notes/iana/assignments/media-types/text/css`, so that's the URL the browser looks for. When it finds a `rddl:resource` with this nature, it loads the URL in the `xlink:href` attribute of that element to get the style sheet. It can then apply the newly found style sheet to the original document.

The same technique can be used anytime a browser or other tool needs to find a resource that's somehow related to the current document. By searching for different natures, it can locate different kinds of related resources. Well-known natures in RDDL include the following:

✦ `http://www.isi.edu/in-notes/iana/assignments/media-types/text/css`—A CSS style sheet

✦ `http://www.isi.edu/in-notes/iana/assignments/media-types/application/xml-dtd`—A document type definition (DTD)

✦ `http://www.rddl.org/natures#mailbox`—A UNIX mailbox

✦ `http://www.isi.edu/in-notes/iana/assignments/media-types/text/html`—An HTML document

✦ `http://www.w3.org/TR/html4/`—An HTML 4.0 document

✦ `http://www.w3.org/TR/html4/strict`—An HTML 4 strict document

✦ `http://www.w3.org/TR/html4/transitional`—An HTML 4 transitional document

✦ `http://www.w3.org/TR/html4/frameset`—An HTML 4 frameset document

✦ `http://www.w3.org/1999/xhtml`—An XHTML document

✦ `http://www.w3.org/TR/xhtml1/DTD/xhtml1-strict`—An XHTML 1.0 strict document

✦ `http://www.w3.org/TR/xhtml1/DTD/xhtml1-transitional`—An XHTML 1.0 transitional document

✦ `http://www.w3.org/2000/01/rdf-schema#`—An RDF schema

✦ `http://www.ascc.net/xml/schematron`—A Schematron schema

✦ `http://www.rddl.org/natures#SOCAT`—An OASIS Open Catalog

✦ `http://www.w3.org/2000/10/XMLSchema`—A W3C XML Schema Language schema

✦ `http://www.w3.org/TR/REC-xml.html#dt-chardata`—Character data

✦ `http://www.w3.org/TR/REC-xml.html#dt-escape`—Character data in which left angle brackets, ampersands, and possibly other characters have been escaped with general entity or character references such as `&` and `&`

✦ `http://www.w3.org/TR/REC-xml.html#dt-unparsed`—An unparsed entity

✦ `http://www.rddl.org/natures/software#language`—Software written in an unspecified programming language

✦ `http://www.rddl.org/natures/software#python`—Software written in Python

✦ `http://www.rddl.org/natures/software#java`—Software written in Java

✦ `http://www.ietf.org/rfc/rfc2026.txt`—An IETF Request for Comments (RFC)

✦ `http://www.iso.ch/`—An ISO standard

This is not a definitive list, and these are not the only allowed natures. In the future, more may be published at `http://www.rddl.org/natures/`. Most importantly, you can use any reasonable URL to identify new kinds of natures that you choose for your own needs. There are some conventional ways to pick these nature URIs, as demonstrated by the preceding list:

✦ A nature with a standard MIME media type can be identified by a URL to the official registration for the type at the Internet Assigned Numbers Authority (IANA) registry at `http://www.isi.edu/in-notes/iana/assignments/media-types/`.

✦ A nature that is an XML document written in a standard vocabulary can be identified by that vocabulary's namespace URI.

✦ Standard, well-known natures that don't have namespace URIs or registered MIME media types can be identified by pointing to a part of a page on the RDDL site at `http://www.rddl.org/`.

However, if none of these feel right for your resources, you're free to identify natures with some other kind of URL. Just make sure that the URL is actually resolvable.

Natures alone are not enough. For example, you may know that an HTML 4.0 document is somehow related to a particular application, but you might not know how. Is it the specification for the application? A tutorial for the vocabulary? The biography of the person who invented it? Something else? Indeed, there may be multiple related HTML 4.0 resources, one for each of these possibilities. To further expand on the relationship between the original XML application and the related resource, you can add a purpose in an `xlink:arcrole` attribute.

Purposes

There's often more than one resource of a given nature associated with an XML application. For example, separate CSS style sheets might be provided for the different environments such as aural, Braille, handheld, print, projection, screen, and television. XHTML 1.0 has one namespace URL but three different DTDs depending on whether you want to use strict, transitional, or frameset XHTML. XHTML 1.1 adds several more possible variations on the DTD while keeping the namespace URL the same.

In cases like this, it's clear that the RDDL document needs to provide more than one resource for each given nature. The different *purposes* of these resources with the same *natures* can be distinguished by an optional `xlink:arcrole` attribute. As with `xlink:role`, the XLink specification requires that the value of the `xlink:arcrole` attribute be a URI.

Once again, the RDDL specification defines a number of URIs for well-known purposes. For example, the URL `http://www.rddl.org/purposes#entities` would be used on a document with the nature `http://www.isi.edu/in-notes/iana/assignments/media-types/application/xml-dtd` to signify that the purpose of this DTD is to define entities. Here's the complete list of well-known purposes as of October 2003:

- `http://www.rddl.org/purposes#validation`—This resource should be used for classic XML or SGML DTD validation before the document is parsed.
- `http://www.rddl.org/purposes#schema-validation`—This resource should be used for validation via some sort of schema after the document is parsed; the type of schema would normally be identified by the nature.
- `http://www.rddl.org/purposes#module`—A file that is only part of a complete DTD and that is typically used in modularized DTDs such as XHTML 1.1 and SMIL 2.0.
- `http://www.rddl.org/purposes#schema-module`—A module used in a schema.
- `http://www.rddl.org/purposes#entities`—A DTD fragment containing only entity definitions such as `xhtml-special.ent` in modular XHTML.
- `http://www.rddl.org/purposes#notations`—A DTD fragment containing only notation declarations such as `xhtml-notations-1.mod` in modular XHTML.
- `http://www.rddl.org/purposes/software#xslt-extension`—Software implementing an extension function or element for XSLT.
- `http://www.rddl.org/purposes/software#software-package`—A grouping of software resources.
- `http://www.rddl.org/purposes/software#software-project`—A collection of resources related to a software package.
- `http://www.rddl.org/purposes#JAR`—A ZIP file with the extension `.jar` containing Java classes.
- `http://www.rddl.org/purposes/software#reference`—Documentation for the resource.
- `http://www.rddl.org/purposes/software#normative-reference`—The definitive specification of the resource's syntax and semantics.

- `http://www.rddl.org/purposes/software#non-normative-reference`— A useful but nonauthoritative description of the resource's syntax and semantics.
- `http://www.rddl.org/purposes#prior-version`—Documentation for a previous version of the resource's vocabulary; for example, the XHTML 1.0 specification relative to XHTML 1.1.
- `http://www.rddl.org/purposes#definition`—The definition of a term.
- `http://www.rddl.org/purposes#icon`—An image that represents the resource.
- `http://www.rddl.org/purposes#directory`—Another RDDL document whose resources should be merged with this document's resources.
- `http://www.rddl.org/purposes#alternate`—An alternative for a resource with the same nature as this one.
- `http://www.rddl.org/purposes#canonicalization`—The canonical form of a resource.
- `http://www.rddl.org/purposes#target`—The namespace that this RDDL document describes.

Currently, all well-known purpose URLs begin with `http://www.rddl.org/purposes#`. However, this may change in the future, and you are allowed to add to this list to create new purposes that suit your applications.

Summary

In this chapter, you learned about RDDL, the Resource Directory Description Language. In particular, you learned the following:

- RDDL documents are placed at the end of namespace URLs to allow both human readers and automated software to locate resources associated with the XML application identified by the namespace URL.
- RDDL documents are essentially XHTML Basic documents with one extra element—`rddl:resource`.
- The `rddl:resource` element is a simple XLink. The `xlink:href` attribute of each `rddl:resource` element points to the related resource.
- The `xlink:role` attribute of the `rddl:resource` element identifies the nature of the related resource. Natures are identified by well-known URLs.
- The `xlink:arcrole` attribute of the `rddl:resource` element identifies the purpose of the related resource. Purposes are also identified by well-known URLs.

The next chapter explores a standard XML application from the W3C — Scalable Vector Graphics (SVG). SVG is a W3C Recommendation for an XML format for line art. Unlike most XML applications that describe text of some kind or another, or perhaps numeric data, SVG documents describe pictures. SVG goes a long way toward proving just how versatile XML really is.

✦ ✦ ✦

Scalable Vector Graphics

✦ ✦ ✦ ✦

In This Chapter

What is SVG?

A simple SVG document

Embedding SVG pictures in web pages

Simple shapes

Paths

Text

Bitmapped images

Coordinate systems and viewports

Grouping shapes

Referencing shapes

Transformations

Linking

Metadata

SVG editors

✦ ✦ ✦ ✦

The world has several well-understood, well-supported, open formats for photographs, painted art, and other bitmapped graphics including TIFF, GIF, JPEG, and, most recently, PNG. These have all achieved broad adoption on the Web and elsewhere. However, a standard format for line art, such as flowcharts, blueprints, technical diagrams, and other sorts of drawings, has been sorely lacking. Scalable Vector Graphics (SVG) is the first realistic candidate to fill this hole.

SVG is a W3C-endorsed XML application for line art. It defines elements that represent polygons, rectangles, ellipses, lines, curves, and more. New shapes can be defined using a simple path language. Color schemes and patterns can be applied to shapes through clipping, masking, compositing, fills, and gradients. Furthermore, the shapes on the page can move. JavaScript can make shapes respond to user input. SVG is a complete format for detailed descriptions of dynamic vector graphics. For static graphics, SVG is almost on a par with Adobe's EPS (Encapsulated PostScript) format, and considerably more powerful than CGM (Computer Graphics Metafile). For animated pictures, it's as powerful as the proprietary SWF format used by Macromedia Flash.

SVG documents can be embedded in web pages. Browser plug-ins exist that enable Netscape and Internet Explorer to display SVG graphics. Eventually, SVG support will be built directly into browsers so that you can include SVG drawings in your web pages with no more effort than you expend today to add a GIF or JPEG picture to a page. However, SVG's significance extends far past the limited domain of Web sites. SVG will eventually become the standard exchange medium for drawings produced by all sorts of vector graphics software on any platform.

At the time of this writing, no software implements the complete SVG 1.0 specification. In fact, so far there are only a few standalone programs and browser plug-ins that can understand SVG documents. None of the major web browsers (Netscape, IE, Opera, Mozilla) know how to interpret and display an SVG picture embedded in an HTML page without a plug-in. Amaya has implemented direct support for SVG, and the Mozilla Project is working on it, though that work has yet to be merged with the main Mozilla code base.

What Is SVG?

Computer graphics come in two primary formats, bitmapped and vector. A bitmapped graphic lists the colors of individual pixels in a usually rectangular area. Examples include the GIF, JPEG, and PNG images used on most web pages. If a bitmapped graphic is 3 inches by 4 inches and has a resolution of 72 pixels per inch, it contains 72×3×72 ×4 pixels, that is, 62,208 pixels. If the image is stored in 24-bit color, each pixel occupies 3 bytes, so this image uses 1,492,992 bits, or about 486K of memory. The actual file may use a variety of lossy and nonlossy compression algorithms to reduce this size somewhat, but bitmapped images still get very big very quickly. This is why web pages with lots of pictures are so slow to load.

By contrast, a vector graphic does not store several bytes of data for each pixel in the image. Instead, it stores a list of instructions for drawing the image. These instructions might say to draw a black line between the upper left corner and the lower right corner of the page, place a purple circle with a 2-inch radius in the middle of the page, and draw the text "Delicious, delicious. Oh how boring!" 12 points high in the Palatino font on top of the circle. As a general rule, the space required for these instructions is much less than the space required for a bitmapped equivalent. Vector graphics are much smaller and more efficient than bitmapped images. Vector formats aren't suitable for all graphics — for example, they don't work well for photographs — but they are much better for graphics that were drawn on a computer by a human being rather than being copied from nature using a camera, digital or otherwise.

There are many vector graphics formats in the world today, including PICT, EPS, and CGM; but for historical and political reasons, there really hasn't been a standard format everyone could use. PICT files are based on the Macintosh's native QuickDraw software and algorithms. They are mostly limited to the Macintosh and don't port well to other platforms. EPS documents require a full-blown PostScript interpreter, which, while potentially cross-platform, is too big a task for a lot of graphic software vendors. CGM was probably the closest to a vendor-neutral, standard, vector graphics format, especially in its WebCGM incarnation; but CGM lacks complex fills, image clipping, image manipulation, detailed color control, and other high-end features that graphic designers need. Furthermore, CGM is a binary file format, with all the concurrent disadvantages of binary file formats. In fact, all three of these formats are so difficult to implement that few web browsers (and none of the major ones) have included built-in support for them. It seems probable that

SVG will be the first successful effort to define a truly open, cross-platform standard for vector graphics.

SVG is an XML application for describing drawings. SVG elements represent two-dimensional shapes: rectangles, ovals, circles, triangles, clouds, spirals, trapezoids, and so forth. Each shape is described as a path formed from a series of lines and curves. SVG uses elements and attributes to describe the position, size, and outline of each shape. CSS styles are used to attach colors, fonts, and other details to the abstract geometric shapes.

XSL also integrates very nicely with SVG. Because SVG documents are well-formed XML documents, an XSLT processor can convert SVG documents into other SVG documents or into other XML applications. More commonly, an existing XML document can be converted into SVG. For example, a file full of numbers might be converted into a bar graph, a pie chart, or even a bar code. The resulting SVG document might then be embedded in an XSL Formatting Objects document. SVG merges very nicely with XSL-FO. XSL-FO can describe the general text-based page layout, while SVG describes all the graphics.

Most SVG documents are drawn using a GUI and only saved into SVG form. Consequently, you don't need to know the detailed syntax of each and every SVG element and attribute. However, if you know a little, you can sometimes do some surprising tricks with the SVG file that might prove impossible with a graphical editor. For example, you can search for all the blue elements and change them to red. SVG is also a much easier graphics format to generate from programs you write than binary formats such as TIFF, PICT, or CGM.

Scalability

The *S* in SVG stands for *Scalable*. That means a given SVG picture is not tied to a single resolution or size. The same picture can be expanded or compressed. The same SVG document can become a very small picture on a Palm Pilot, a medium-sized picture on a web page, or a very large picture projected on a movie screen. An SVG picture can even be zoomed in or out at full resolution on the same display. SVG pictures do not have absolute sizes.

Scalable also means that the same picture can be displayed at different resolutions. I can print a full-page picture on my HP LaserJet 2200, and the picture will be printed at the printer's full resolution of 1200 dots per inch. I can show the same picture on my Silicon Graphics 1600SW flat-panel monitor, and it will use the monitor's lesser resolution of 110 dots per inch. If I used a higher-resolution printer or a lower-resolution monitor, the picture would adjust accordingly. Unlike bitmapped formats such as TIFF, JPEG, and GIF, SVG pictures don't require you to choose between size and resolution.

Scalable also means that SVG can scale to very large projects where documents are built up out of thousands of individual pictures. For example, an architectural diagram for a new campus of a large corporation might include separate SVG documents representing each room. Floor documents would be built up by combining the room documents. Buildings would be created by combining the floor documents. The campus would be created by combining the individual building documents and adding a few pieces to represent the tunnels and roads and green spaces that connected them. Similar buildings and floors might be described by annotating small changes on top of basic templates. Different architects could work on different parts of the campus at the same time, then combine all the pieces together.

In my opinion, this definition of scalability isn't well met by SVG. The problem is that SVG documents don't carry any notion of the real-world sizes of what they describe, just a scalable local coordinate space. This means that there's no standard way of making sure that the water fountain I design will fit through the door of the building you design.

Vector versus bitmapped graphics

Since the demise of daisy-wheel printers, all modern computer-rendering devices have used bitmapped graphics. That is, they divide the canvas on which they draw into a grid of pixels of varying colors. The basic algorithms for rendering raster graphics are the same whether you're talking about a 72-dpi color CRT monitor or a 1200-dpi black-and-white printer. This means that when a vector document such as an SVG picture is drawn, it must first be converted into a bitmap. The real difference, therefore, between finite precision bitmapped pictures and infinitely precise vector graphics is in where the conversion to the bitmap, and subsequent loss of information, takes place. With a bitmapped image, the information is lost when the document is first created at a particular resolution. With a vector image, all information is maintained perfectly until the document is actually drawn on the screen or printed on paper.

Because SVG graphics will eventually be rendered as bitmaps, the W3C Scalable Vector Graphics Working Group decided they might as well take advantage of that fact. Consequently, they added a number of fundamentally bitmapped features to SVG that are applied to SVG pictures on the client side when the document is rendered. For example, you can place bitmapped JPEG and PNG images in an SVG document using the `image` element. For another example, infinitely precise vector text doesn't need antialiasing, but bitmapped text does. SVG renderers can apply a variety of antialiasing algorithms to both text and lines before drawing them on the screen. SVG documents can also request bitmap filter effects such as blurring and drop shadows.

A Simple SVG Document

Listing 24-1 is an SVG document that describes a red circle. This document should be saved in a file named something similar to circle.svg or 24-1.svg. The three-letter extension .svg is customary, although not required. This is an XML document, so it could be saved as circle.xml or as circle.txt. The MIME media type of this document should be set to image/svg+xml in environments that support MIME types.

Figure 24-1 shows the document displayed in Squiggle, the SVG viewer bundled with the Apache XML Project's Batik. The most recent version can be downloaded from `http://xml.apache.org/batik/`. Batik requires Java 1.2 or later. After you've unzipped the zip file, you can run Squiggle at the command line like this:

```
C:\>java -jar C:\batik-1.5\batik-squiggle.jar
```

Of course, you need to have Java installed somewhere in your path, and if you've unzipped Batik anywhere other than C:\batik-1.5, adjust the preceding command accordingly.

As well as providing a way to view files in a GUI, Squiggle can also export SVG images as TIF, JPEG, and PNG bitmapped images, a function that I used to produce many of the figures in this chapter.

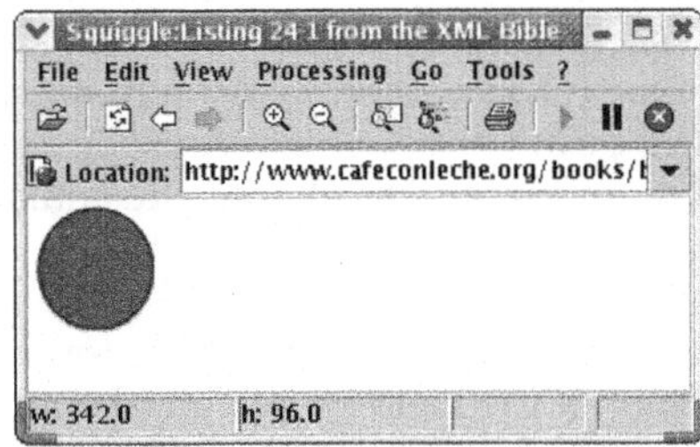

Figure 24-1: An SVG document displayed in Squiggle

Listing 24-1: An SVG Document That Represents a Red Circle with a Blue Outline

```
<?xml version="1.0" encoding="UTF-8" standalone="yes"?>
<svg xmlns="http://www.w3.org/2000/svg"
     width="3.5in" height="1in">
  <title>Listing 24-1 from the XML Bible</title>
  <circle  r="30" cx="34" cy="34"
           style="fill: red; stroke: blue; stroke-width: 2" />
</svg>
```

This is an XML document, so it begins with an XML declaration like all good XML documents should. This particular document doesn't have a document type declaration, so it's only well formed, not valid. However, the SVG specification does include a DTD that you can use to validate SVG documents, and you could reference it if it seemed useful to do so. You could even provide an xml-stylesheet processing instruction that connected this document to a CSS or XSL style sheet.

The root element of this and all SVG documents is svg. This element is in the http://www.w3.org/2000/svg namespace. Sometimes, as here, this is the default namespace. Other times, it's mapped to a prefix. The prefix svg is customary. As usual, the specific prefix (or lack thereof) doesn't matter as long as the URI is correct.

The svg element has width and height attributes that specify the size of the canvas on which the picture is drawn. Here it's a 3.5-inch-wide-by-1-inch-high rectangle. These attributes aren't required, but it's a good idea to include them. Viewers can use this to set window sizes, and it's a useful reminder of how much space there is to draw in.

The root svg element also contains two child elements: a title and a circle. The title contains a string of text that's displayed in the title bar of the SVG browser. The circle is a shape to be drawn. This circle has a radius of 30. But 30 what? Is that 30 pixels? 30 inches? 30 parsecs? It's actually 30 units in the nondimensional local coordinate space. Remember that SVG graphics are scalable. The real size of a radius 30 circle can change from one environment to another. By default, it maps to 30 pixels on the local display, so the circle will be smaller on higher-resolution monitors. However, you can use transforms and other markup to change the actual size, as you'll see soon.

The center of the circle is placed at position x=34, y=34. This is 34 units down from and 34 units to the right of the upper left corner of the window. Standard computer graphics coordinates are used. That is, the upper left corner of this rectangle is point 0, 0. X coordinates increase to the right; Y coordinates increase down. Figure 24-2 diagrams this coordinate system. You can use floating-point numbers such as 7.5 to place shapes anywhere on this grid. You are not limited to placing shapes at the actual pixels of the display. An SVG document represents an abstract, infinitely precise, almost platonic ideal of a two-dimensional plane.

The style attribute assigns CSS properties to this circle. In particular, it sets the fill color to red and the stroke color to blue. Furthermore, it makes the stroke two units wide.

In my opinion, this is one of the flakier aspects of SVG. CSS defines a color property, but it doesn't define any fill, stroke, or stroke-width properties. SVG has adopted the CSS syntax as an optional feature, but applied it to its own set of properties. The same circle could equally well have been written like this:

```
<circle r="30" cx="34" cy="34"
        fill="red" stroke="blue" stroke-width="2" />
```

For inline styles, I prefer to use the more explicit attributes. However, you can also attach external CSS style sheets to SVG documents that set various properties for different elements. This is perhaps a little more useful.

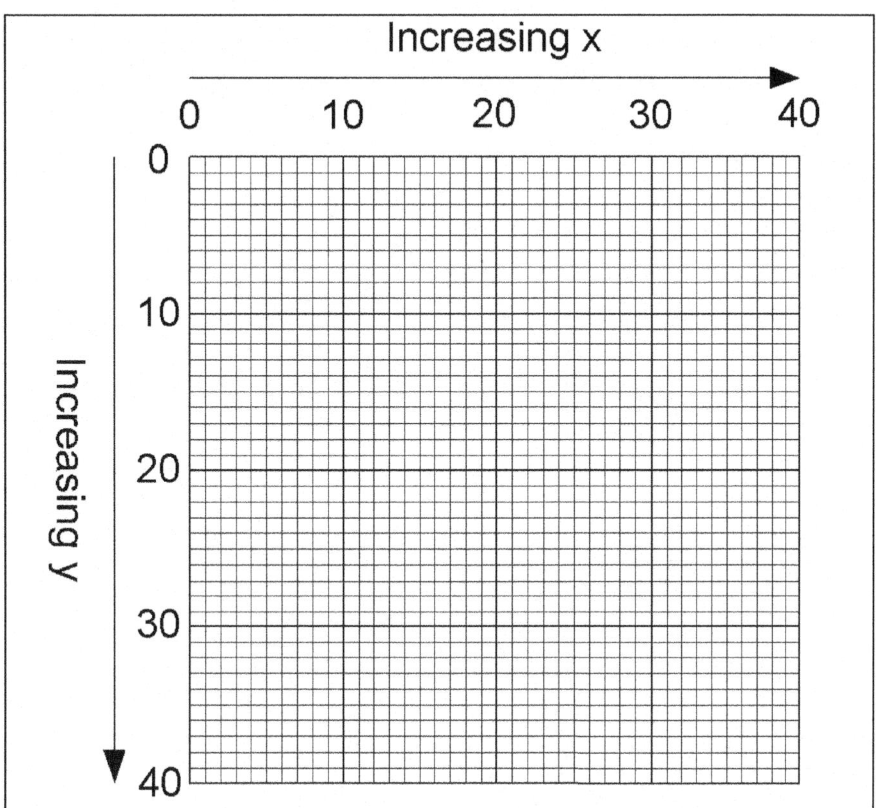

Figure 24-2: SVG coordinate system

SVG element and attribute names only use the ASCII character set, so any normal text editor can produce and save an SVG document. However, if the drawing content itself contains non-ASCII text (for example, a Russian billboard), you'd have to save it in some other character set and use the appropriate encoding declaration to identify it. Of course, as you'll see at the end of this chapter, you don't have to use a text editor to create or save an SVG document at all. In fact, most of the time, you'll probably use a graphics program such as Adobe Illustrator that offers a standard user interface for drawing pictures. You'll just save the finished result as SVG.

Embedding SVG Pictures in Web Pages

It's very easy to include SVG pictures in web pages for browsers that natively understand SVG. You don't even have to use valid XHTML. Just paste the SVG source code into the HTML document where you want the picture to appear. Listing 24-2 demonstrates by embedding Listing 24-1 in a simple HTML document.

Listing 24-2: An HTML Document in Which Listing 24-1 Is Embedded

```
<HTML>
  <HEAD>
    <TITLE>Circles are my friends</TITLE>
  </HEAD>
  <BODY>
  <H1>Rectangles are the Enemy!</H1>

  <svg xmlns="http://www.w3.org/2000/svg"
       style="width: 3.5in; height: 1in">
    <title>Listing 24-1 from the XML Bible</title>
    <circle r="30" cx="34" cy="34"
            style="fill: red; stroke: blue; stroke-width: 2"/>
  </svg>

  <HR>
  Last Modified August 22, 2004<BR>
  Copyright 2004
  <A HREF="mailto:elharo@metalab.unc.edu">
    Elliotte Rusty Harold
  </A>

  </BODY>
</HTML>
```

At the time of this writing, only the Amaya browser from the W3C natively supports SVG included in this fashion. Figure 24-3 shows Amaya displaying Listing 24-2. You can download the latest version from `http://www.w3.org/Amaya/`. This chapter was written using Amaya 8.1a.

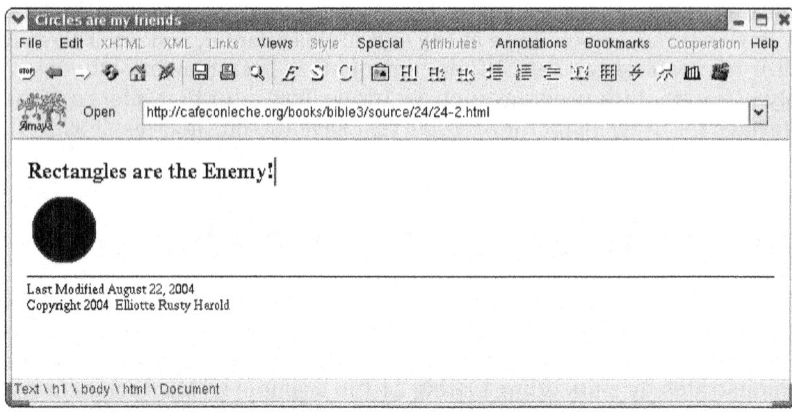

Figure 24-3: An SVG document included in a web page

Although they're text, SVG documents are no more part of HTML than are the binary GIF, JPEG, and PNG formats. Therefore, most browsers don't support SVG pictures that are pasted into HTML source code, as in Listing 24-2. Instead, you have to save the picture in a separate document and link to it from the HTML by using the EMBED element. This is very much like the normal IMG element you're familiar with from HTML. It has WIDTH, HEIGHT, ALT, ALIGN, and SRC attributes that mean more or less the same as they mean for IMG. The only difference is that IMG is used for image formats the browser natively supports, while EMBED is used for data formats that require a separate plug-in. Most EMBED elements also have a PLUGINSPAGE attribute whose value is a URL where the browser can download the plug-in it needs to display the embedded content. I recommend the Adobe SVG Viewer plug-in, which is available for Netscape and Internet Explorer on both Windows and Mac OS. For example, this EMBED element could be used to place Listing 24-1 in 100-pixel-by-100-pixel rectangle on the page:

```
<EMBED WIDTH="100" HEIGHT="100" SRC="24-1.svg"
       ALT="A red circle with a blue border"
       ALIGN="LEFT"
       PLUGINSPAGE="http://www.adobe.com/svg/viewer/install/">
```

The SVG picture will be left-aligned so that text flows around it on the right. If the browser can't handle this type of content, it will display the alternate text "A red circle with a blue border" instead. And if the user does not have the necessary plug-in to load this document, it will ask the user if they want to go to the Adobe web site to get it. Figure 24-4 shows the final result after the plug-in is installed and Listing 24-3 is loaded into Netscape Navigator.

Listing 24-3: An HTML Document in Which Listing 24-1 Is Embedded

```
<HTML>
  <HEAD>
    <TITLE>Circles are my friends</TITLE>
  </HEAD>
  <BODY>
  <H1>Rectangles are the Enemy!</H1>

  <EMBED WIDTH="100" HEIGHT="100" SRC="24-1.svg"
       ALT="A red circle with a blue border"
       ALIGN="LEFT"
       PLUGINSPAGE="http://www.adobe.com/svg/viewer/install/">

  <P>
    You need version 3.0 or later of the Adobe SVG plug-in
    for this to work. Earlier versions support older,
    out-of-date beta drafts of SVG. This chapter describes
    SVG 1.0.
```

Continued

Listing 24-3 *(continued)*

```
  </P>


  <HR>
  Last Modified August 21, 2004<BR>
  Copyright 2004
  <A HREF="mailto:elharo@metalab.unc.edu">
    Elliotte Rusty Harold
  </A>

  </BODY>
</HTML>
```

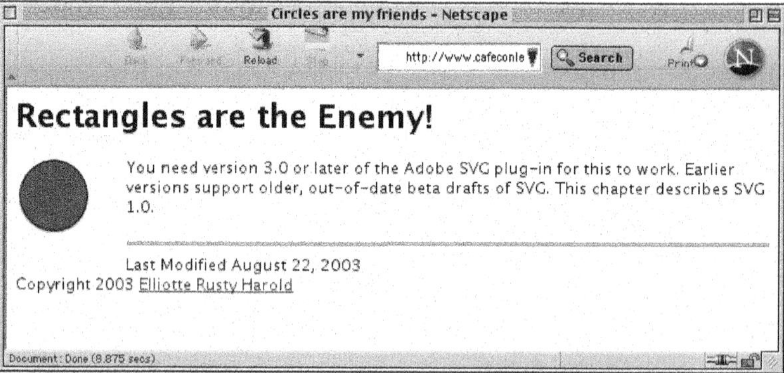

Figure 24-4: An SVG document embedded in a web page

Simple Shapes

SVG defines six simple shape elements that you can use to place particular kinds of shapes on the page:

- ✦ `rect`
- ✦ `circle`
- ✦ `ellipse`
- ✦ `line`
- ✦ `polygon`
- ✦ `polyline`

You're not limited to these shapes, however. You can also define arbitrary one- and two-dimensional shapes using paths. But let's begin with the basic shapes.

The rect element

The `rect` element represents a rectangle aligned with the two coordinate axes. In other words, it represents rectangles like the one on the left side of Figure 24-5 but not the one on the right side.

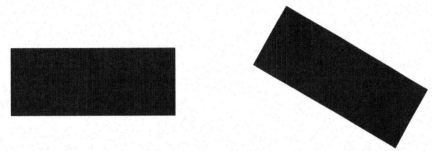

Figure 24-5: SVG rect elements represent rectangles like the one on the left, not the one on the right.

Given the constraint of axis alignment, each rectangle can be fully specified by the coordinates of its upper left corner, its width, and its height. These are given by four attributes on the `rect` element:

- `x` — The x coordinate of the upper left corner of the rectangle
- `y` — The y coordinate of the upper left corner of the rectangle
- `width` — The extent of the rectangle parallel to the x-axis
- `height` — The extent of the rectangle parallel to the y-axis

For example, this `rect` element represents a 10 by 10 square whose upper left corner is aligned with the upper left corner of the picture:

```
<rect x="0" y ="0" width="10" height="10"/>
```

Listing 24-4 draws part of a checkerboard by alternating red and black squares, each 25 units square. Figure 24-6 shows the rendered document.

Listing 24-4: A Partial Checkerboard Made Up out of rects

```
<?xml version="1.0" encoding="UTF-8" standalone="yes"?>
<svg xmlns="http://www.w3.org/2000/svg"
     width="3.5in" height="1.0in">
  <title>Listing 24-4 from the XML Bible</title>
  <rect x="0"  y="0"  width="25" height="25" fill="red"/>
  <rect x="25" y="0"  width="25" height="25" fill="black"/>
  <rect x="50" y="0"  width="25" height="25" fill="red" />
  <rect x="0"  y="25" width="25" height="25" fill="black"/>
  <rect x="25" y="25" width="25" height="25" fill="red" />
  <rect x="50" y="25" width="25" height="25" fill="black"/>
  <rect x="0"  y="50" width="25" height="25" fill="red" />
  <rect x="25" y="50" width="25" height="25" fill="black"/>
  <rect x="50" y="50" width="25" height="25" fill="red" />
</svg>
```

Figure 24-6: A piece of a checkerboard arranged with nine rect elements

You can make rounded rectangles by setting the `rx` and `ry` attributes of the rectangle to a positive length. The larger this number, the more rounded the corners will be. The maximum rounding is half the width of the rectangle for `rx` and half the length of the rectangle for `ry`. This much rounding turns the rectangle into an ellipse. Anything beyond that is ignored. For example, Listing 24-5 adds five units of rounding to each of the rectangles from Listing 24-4. Figure 24-7 shows the results of adding this rounding.

Listing 24-5: A Pattern of Nine Rounded rects

```
<?xml version="1.0" encoding="UTF-8" standalone="yes"?>
<svg xmlns="http://www.w3.org/2000/svg"
     width="3.5in" height="1.0in">
  <title>Listing 24-5 from the XML Bible</title>
  <rect x="0"  y="0"  width="25" height="25" rx="5" ry="5"
        fill="red"/>
  <rect x="25" y="0"  width="25" height="25" rx="5" ry="5"
        fill="black"/>
  <rect x="50" y="0"  width="25" height="25" rx="5" ry="5"
        fill="red" />
```

```
  <rect x="0"  y="25" width="25" height="25" rx="5" ry="5"
        fill="black"/>
  <rect x="25" y="25" width="25" height="25" rx="5" ry="5"
        fill="red" />
  <rect x="50" y="25" width="25" height="25" rx="5" ry="5"
        fill="black"/>
  <rect x="0"  y="50" width="25" height="25" rx="5" ry="5"
        fill="red" />
  <rect x="25" y="50" width="25" height="25" rx="5" ry="5"
        fill="black"/>
  <rect x="50" y="50" width="25" height="25" rx="5" ry="5"
        fill="red" />
</svg>
```

Figure 24-7: A pattern of rounded rects

The circle element

The `circle` element represents a circle. The position of the circle is determined by the coordinates of its center. The size of the circle is determined by its radius. These are specified by three attributes of the `circle` element:

- `cx` — The x coordinate of the center of the circle
- `cy` — The y coordinate of the center of the circle
- `r` — The length of the radius

For example, this `circle` element has a 24-unit radius. Its center is positioned at the upper left corner of the picture. Thus, only the lower right quarter (fourth quadrant) of the circle will be shown. The other three quarters of the circle are off the screen.

```
<circle cx="0" cy="0" r="25" />
```

Listing 24-6 uses `circle` elements to draw a bull's-eye on the screen. The circles in a bull's-eye are concentric, so that the center coordinates are the same for each circle. Only the radius changes. This example takes advantage of the implicit z-ordering of SVG shapes. Each shape is drawn on top of its previous sibling. That is, the first `circle` element is drawn first, the second `circle` element is drawn on top of the first, the third `circle` is drawn on top of the second, and so forth. Without this ordering, the largest circle might be drawn on top of all the others, obscuring them. Figure 24-8 shows the result.

Listing 24-6: An SVG Bull's-eye

```
<?xml version="1.0" encoding="UTF-8" standalone="yes"?>
<svg xmlns="http://www.w3.org/2000/svg"
     width="3.5in" height="2.0in">
  <title>Listing 24-6 from the XML Bible</title>
  <circle cx="90" cy="90" r="70"
       fill="red" stroke="black" stroke-width="2" />
  <circle cx="90" cy="90" r="60"
       fill="white" stroke="black" stroke-width="2" />
  <circle cx="90" cy="90" r="50"
       fill="red" stroke="black" stroke-width="2" />
  <circle cx="90" cy="90" r="40"
       fill="white" stroke="black" stroke-width="2" />
  <circle cx="90" cy="90" r="30"
       fill="red" stroke="black" stroke-width="2" />
  <circle cx="90" cy="90" r="20"
       fill="white" stroke="black" stroke-width="2"/>
  <circle cx="90" cy="90" r="10"
       fill="red" stroke="black" stroke-width="2" />
</svg>
```

Figure 24-8: An SVG bull's-eye

The ellipse element

Ellipses are a little like squashed circles, or, reversing the perspective, circles are degenerate ellipses. Whereas circles have perfect rotational symmetry, ellipses do have definite x and y axes. Like SVG rectangles, SVG ellipses line up their axes parallel to the coordinate axes. Thus, like rectangles, you only need four numbers to specify an ellipse:

- `cx` — The x coordinate of the center of the ellipse
- `cy` — The y coordinate of the center of the ellipse

✦ rx — The length of the radius of the ellipse parallel to the x-axis

✦ ry — The length of the radius of the ellipse parallel to the y-axis

For example, this ellipse is four times as long as it is high:

```
<ellipse cx="45" cy="20" rx="40" ry="10" />
```

Listing 24-7 places two very eccentric ellipses more or less perpendicular to each other to form a simple four-pointed star. These use the default fill color (black) and stroke (none). Figure 24-9 shows the result.

Listing 24-7: Two Ellipses Perpendicular to Each Other

```
<?xml version="1.0" encoding="UTF-8" standalone="yes"?>
<svg xmlns="http://www.w3.org/2000/svg"
     width="3.5in" height="1.0in">
  <title>Listing 24-7 from the XML Bible</title>
  <ellipse cx="45" cy="45" rx="40" ry="10" />
  <ellipse cx="45" cy="45" rx="10" ry="40" />
</svg>
```

Figure 24-9: Two ellipses perpendicular to each other

The line element

The line element represents a straight-line segment between two points. It is identified by the x and y coordinates of its endpoints, as specified in these attributes:

✦ x1 — The x coordinate of the start point

✦ y1 — The y coordinate of the start point

✦ x2 — The x coordinate of the endpoint

✦ y2 — The y coordinate of the endpoint

For example, this is a 100-unit horizontal line:

```
<line x1="0" y1="100" x2="100" y2="100"/>
```

This is a 100-unit vertical line:

```
<line x1="0" y1="100" x2="0" y2="0"/>
```

This line runs at a 45-degree angle between the endpoints of the two previous lines:

```
<line x1="0" y1="0" x2="100" y2="100"/>
```

Listing 24-8 puts them all together to form a right triangle. However, as currently written, these lines won't actually be visible. To display them, you need to set the stroke color to something other than white. Listing 24-8 also expands the stroke width to two pixels. Figure 24-10 shows the result.

Listing 24-8: A Right Triangle Formed from Three Lines

```
<?xml version="1.0" encoding="UTF-8" standalone="yes"?>
<svg xmlns="http://www.w3.org/2000/svg"
     width="3.5in" height="2.0in">
  <title>Listing 24-8 from the XML Bible</title>
  <line x1="0" y1="100" x2="100" y2="100"
        stroke-width="2px" stroke="black"/>
  <line x1="0" y1="100" x2="0" y2="0"
        stroke-width="2px" stroke="black"/>
  <line x1="0" y1="0" x2="100" y2="100"
        stroke-width="2px" stroke="black"/>
</svg>
```

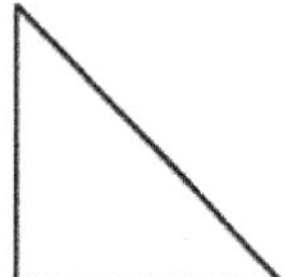

Figure 24-10: A right triangle formed from three lines

Polygons and polylines

A polygon is a closed curve formed by straight-line segments between each consecutive pair of a sequence of three or more points. The first point is connected to the second point, the second to the third, the third to the fourth, and so on, until the last point, which is connected back to the first point. Thus, a polygon with N points has N line segments. A polyline is similar except that the last point is not connected back to the first point. A polyline with N points has only N-1 line segments. SVG polygons include not only the usual convex polygons like triangles and concave polygons like stars, but also considerably stranger items, such as polygons with self-intersecting edges. Figure 24-11 shows the three major kinds. Rectangles are special cases of polygons, but circles are not because they don't use straight lines.

Figure 24-11: A convex polygon, a concave polygon, and a complex polygon, each formed from eight points

The points forming a polygon are listed in order in the `polygon` element's `points` attribute. The first point is connected to the second point, the second point is connected to the third point, the third point is connected to the fourth point, and so on. The last point is connected back to the first point. All points are given as pairs of dimensionless numbers in the local coordinate space separated by a comma. Points are separated from each other by white space. For example, the right triangle of Listing 24-8 could instead be written as this polygon:

```
<polygon points="0,100 100,100 0,0"/>
```

Figure 24-11 was actually created using `polygon` elements in the SVG document shown in Listing 24-9.

Listing 24-9: **Three Polygons**

```
<?xml version="1.0" encoding="UTF-8" standalone="yes"?>
<svg xmlns="http://www.w3.org/2000/svg"
     width="3.5in" height="1.5in">
  <title>Listing 24-9 from the XML Bible</title>
  <polygon points="0,30 30,0 80,0 110,30 110,80 80,110
                   30,110 0,80"/>
  <polygon points="120,55 160,40 180,0 200,40 240,55 200,80
                   180,120 160,80"/>
  <polygon points="240,30 270,45 312,80 270,110 268,82
                   272,23 267,71 311,17 "/>
</svg>
```

The polyline element is almost identical to the polygon element, except that the last point listed in the points attribute is *not* connected back to the first point. However, the last point can repeat the first point, so that the path is connected. For example, the right triangle of Listing 24-8 could instead be written as this polyline:

```
<polyline points="0,100 100,100 0,0 0,100"/>
```

It's necessary to repeat the first point as the last point to get the polyline to close up. On the other hand, polylines are filled by default, so adding the last point is only really necessary if you turn the fill off using style="fill: none".

Paths

The path element represents an arbitrary two-dimensional curve. Paths can be stroked so that they look like lines. They can be filled so they appear as solid shapes. They can even be used as masks or clipping regions. You can think of a path as the curve a pen draws as it moves across the paper. Often paths are connected, but occasionally the artist will pick up the pen and put it down at a different point on the page and continue drawing from there. However, the pen draws in single-color ink (possibly invisible), and the tip of the pen has a fixed thickness. To change the color or size of the line, the artist must change pens.

There are 10 basic operations the artist can perform with a pen:

- **Move to**—Pick the pen up and put it down at a specified point on the paper.
- **Line to**—Draw a straight line from the current pen position to a specified point.
- **Horizontal line to**—Draw a straight line from the current pen position across to a specified x coordinate, keeping the y coordinate the same.
- **Vertical line to**—Draw a straight line from the current pen position up or down to a specified y coordinate, keeping the x coordinate the same.
- **Arc**—Draw an elliptical or circular arc from the current pen position to a specified point.
- **Curve to**—Draw a cubic Bézier curve from the current pen position to a specified point.
- **Smooth curve to**—Draw a "smooth" cubic Bézier curve from the current pen position to a specified point.
- **Quadratic curve to**—Draw a quadratic Bézier curve from the current pen position to a specified point.

- **Smooth quadratic curve to** — Draw a "smooth" quadratic Bézier curve from the current pen position to a specified point.
- **Close path** — Draw a straight line from the current pen position back to the first point in the path.

An SVG document represents a path with a `path` element. The `d` (for data) attribute of the path contains the instructions for drawing the path. The instructions are each represented by single letters:

- `M` and `m` for move to
- `L` and `l` for line to
- `H` and `h` for draw a horizontal line to
- `V` and `v` for draw a vertical line to
- `A` and `a` for draw an elliptical arc to
- `C` and `c` for draw a cubic Bézier curve to
- `S` and `s` for draw a smooth cubic Bézier curve to
- `Q` and `q` for draw a quadratic Bézier curve to
- `T` and `t` for draw a smooth quadratic Bézier curve to
- `Z` and `z` for close path

The uppercase letters give the points as absolute coordinates. The lowercase letters give the points as positive or negative offsets from the current pen position.

Every path begins with an `M` or `m` to set the initial point. Paths must end with a `Z` or `z`. Each `M` and `L` instruction is followed by the coordinates of the point to go to. For example, here's a `path` element that draws an isosceles triangle:

```
<path d="M 0,200 L 100,0 L 200,200 Z" />
```

Don't worry if it isn't obvious to you that this is an isosceles triangle. In fact, I'd be surprised if it were even obvious that this is a triangle. Here's how this `path` attribute is interpreted:

1. `M 0,200` — Move the pen to the point x=0, y=200. This is where the path begins.
2. `L 100,0` — Draw a line from the current pen location (x=0, y=200) to x=100, y=0.
3. `L 200,200` — Draw a line from the current pen location (x=100, y=0) to x=200, y=200.
4. `Z` — Close the path; that is, draw a line from the last point (x=200, y=200) back to the first point (x=0, y=200).

There's often more than one way to define a given path. For example, this `path` element represents that same triangle but uses lowercase, relative units after establishing the initial point:

```
<path d="m 0,200 l 100,-200 l 100,200 z" />
```

Here's how this `path` attribute is interpreted:

1. `m 0,200`—Because this move-to command is the first point in the path, the relative coordinates are treated as absolute coordinates, and the pen is moved to the point x=0, y=200. This is where the path begins.
2. `l 100,-200`—Draw a line from the current pen location (x=0, y=200) that goes 100 pixels to the right and 200 pixels down; that is, draw a line to (x=100, y=0).
3. `l 100,200`—Draw a line from the current pen location (x=100, y=0) that goes 100 pixels to the right and 200 pixels down; that is, draw a line to (x=200, y=200).
4. `z`—Close the shape; that is, draw a line from the current point (x=200, y=200) back to the first point (x=0, y=200).

There are a variety of other forms path data can take, although the meaning is the same. For example, you can use a space to separate the x and y coordinates in a point rather than a comma, and you can provide several coordinates after a line-to command to indicate that you want multiple lines drawn. For example, the preceding path could equally easily have been written like this:

```
<path d="m0 200l100 -200 100 200z" />
```

One reason not to write coordinates this way is that, although this form is equally easy to write, it is far from equally easy to read. For example, is it obvious to you where the second command is in the preceding path? (Hint: Be sure to distinguish between the letter *l* and the digit *1*.)

Listing 24-10 shows a tic-tac-toe board drawn as one single, long, self-intersecting path. Because a tic-tac-toe grid is made up exclusively of horizontal and vertical lines, this document uses the `V` and `H` operators heavily. Also note the use of the `M` command to move the pen around the board without drawing a line. Finally, because paths are filled by default, CSS styles are used to turn off filling and to turn on stroking. Figure 24-12 shows the finished board.

Listing 24-10: **Tic-Tac-Toe**

```
<?xml version="1.0" encoding="UTF-8" standalone="yes"?>
<svg xmlns="http://www.w3.org/2000/svg"
     width="3.6in" height="3.4in">
```

```
  <title>Listing 24-10 from the XML Bible</title>
  <path d="M 100,0 V 300
           M 200,0 V 300
           M 0,100 H 300
           M 0,200 H 300 Z"
           fill="none" stroke="black" stroke-width="2px" />
</svg>
```

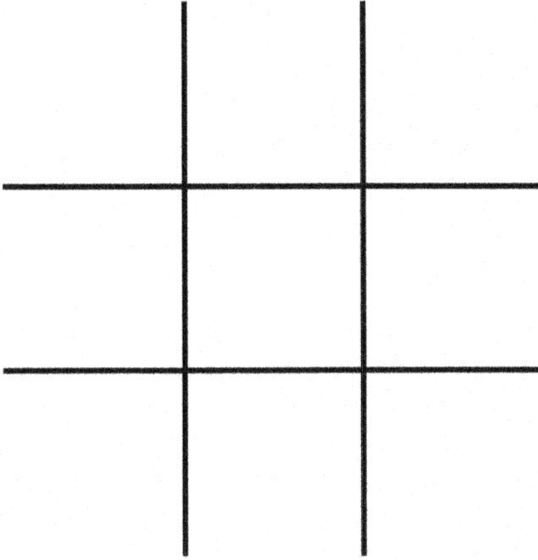

Figure 24-12: A tic-tac-toe board formed from a single path element

Arcs

Arcs are more complex than straight lines. You must specify seven separate numbers to determine which arc will be drawn from the current point:

1. The radius of the arc along the x-axis; the larger the radius, the less curved the arc will be.
2. The radius of the arc along the y-axis; equal x and y radii produce a circular arc.
3. The orientation of the ellipse with respect to the x-axis, in clockwise degrees
4. Whether the arc should subtend an angle greater than or less than 180 degrees; 1 for more than 180 degrees, 0 for less than 180 degrees
5. Whether the arc should be drawn with an increasing (counterclockwise) or decreasing (clockwise) angle; 1 for an increasing angle, 0 for a decreasing angle

6. The x coordinate of the point to draw the arc to
7. The y coordinate of the point to draw the arc to

Here's a `path` that uses an arc to draw a piece of pie with a 30-degree arc centered on the y axis:

```
<path d="M 100,100
         L 74.11809548975, 3.40741737109
         A 100 100 0 0 1 125.8819045103 3.40741737109
         L 100, 100 Z"
      style="fill: none; stroke: black; stroke-width: 1px" />
```

Determining the correct coordinates for the preceding path required trigonometry, a hand calculator, and some experimentation. The endpoints of the arc were calculated like this:

1. Make the radius of the circle 100 units.
2. Place the center of the circle at x=100, y=100.
3. Start the arc at the position x = 100 – 100 sin (30/2), y = 100 – 100 cos (30/2).
4. Finish the arc at the position x = 100 + 100 sin (30/2), y = 100 – 100 cos (30/2).

If that seems a little involved, that's because it is. And this example is simpler than many because only circular arcs were used, not elliptical ones, and the coordinates and radius were deliberately chosen to make the math as simple as possible.

Many arcs will be considerably worse than this. Arcs are really beginning to hit the limit of what you can plausibly work with by hand. Listing 24-11 draws a complete pie with eight 45-degree pieces. Figure 24-13 shows the result. Forty-five-degree increments are marginally easier to work with than 30-degree increments, but the coordinates were still quite burdensome to calculate. The bottom line is that arc paths are really intended for computers to calculate. Humans should use some sort of reasonable GUI to describe them.

Listing 24-11: **A Pie Formed by Eight Arc Paths**

```
<?xml version="1.0" encoding="UTF-8" standalone="yes"?>
<svg xmlns="http://www.w3.org/2000/svg"
     width="3.6in" height="2.4in">
  <title>Listing 24-11 from the XML Bible</title>
  <path d="M 100,100
           L 100, 0
           A 100 100 0 0 1 170.7106781187 29.28932188135
           L 100, 100 Z"
           fill="brown" stroke="black" stroke-width="1px" />
```

```
  <path d="M 100,100
        L 170.7106781187 29.28932188135
        A 100 100 0 0 1 200 100
        L 100, 100 Z"
        fill="brown" stroke="black" stroke-width="1px" />
  <path d="M 100,100
        L 200, 100
        A 100 100 0 0 1 170.7106781187  170.7106781187
        L 100, 100 Z"
        fill="brown" stroke="black" stroke-width="1px" />
  <path d="M 100,100
        L 170.7106781187,170.7106781187
        A 100 100 0 0 1 100 200
        L 100, 100 Z"
        fill="brown" stroke="black" stroke-width="1px" />
  <path d="M 100,100
        L 100,200
        A 100 100 0 0 1 29.28932188135 170.7106781187
        L 100, 100 Z"
        fill="brown" stroke="black" stroke-width="1px" />
  <path d="M 100,100
        L 29.28932188135 170.7106781187
        A 100 100 0 0 1 0 100
        L 100, 100 Z"
        fill="brown" stroke="black" stroke-width="1px" />
  <path d="M 100,100
        L 0, 100
        A 100 100 0 0 1 29.28932188135 29.28932188135
        L 100, 100 Z"
        fill="brown" stroke="black" stroke-width="1px" />
  <path d="M 100,100
        L 29.28932188135 29.28932188135
        A 100 100 0 0 1 100 0
        L 100, 100 Z"
        fill="brown" stroke="black" stroke-width="1px" />
</svg>
```

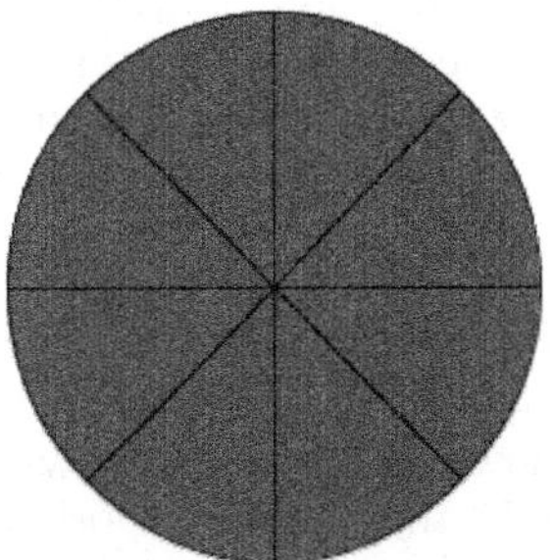

Figure 24-13: A pie formed by eight arc paths

Curves

You now have the tools needed to produce essentially any two-dimensional shape that can be formed from straight lines, as well as circles, ellipses, and pieces thereof. But that still leaves a lot unaccounted for. Figure 24-14 shows just a few of the things that you can't really describe with the shapes and paths discussed so far.

Figure 24-14: Figures drawn with Bézier curves

Paths such as those in Figure 24-14, and many more, can be modeled by *Bézier curves*. A Bézier curve is defined by a start point and an endpoint, as well as one or more control points that define lines tangent to the curve through the start and endpoints. One control point produces a quadratic Bézier curve. Two control points produce a cubic Bézier curve. Smooth Bézier curves mirror one coordinate point off the preceding coordinate point.

If you thought arcs were bad, Bézier curves are even worse. Where trigonometry sufficed for arcs, Bézier curves require differential calculus. Fortunately, no one expects you to calculate the coordinates for Bézier curves by hand. In a few cases, a computer program might calculate them. For example, the spiral in Figure 24-14 is straightforward to generate algorithmically. However, most Bézier curves are produced by a human artist in conjunction with a graphics program like Adobe Illustrator. Indeed, that is exactly how Figure 24-14 was drawn. Thus, I'll spare you all the details of exactly how Bézier coordinates are specified in SVG. Instead, in Listing 24-12, I'll merely show you the SVG source code for the first shape in Figure 24-14. This was produced by Adobe Illustrator and cleaned up a little by hand for printing in the book. The SVG source code for the last three pictures in Figure 24-14 would take too much space to show here, but it is on the web site at `http://www.cafeconleche.org/books/bible3/source/24/24-12.svg`. I suggest that you use a drawing program that can export SVG when you need to draw complicated paths like these.

Listing 24-12: Bézier Curves

```
<?xml version="1.0" encoding="utf-8"?>
<!-- Generator: Adobe Illustrator 9.0, SVG Export Plug-In  -->
<svg xml:space="preserve" xmlns="http://www.w3.org/2000/svg">
 <g id="Layer_x0020_1"
    style="fill-rule:nonzero; clip-rule:nonzero; fill:#FFFFFF;
           stroke:#000000; stroke-width:0.25;
           stroke-miterlimit:4;">
  <path style="stroke-width:1;"
        d="M99.233,22.5c0,27.614-22.386,50-50,50c-22.091,
           0-40-17.909-40-40c0-17.673,14.327-32,
           32-32c14.139,0,25.6,11.461,25.6,25.6c0,
           11.311-9.169,20.48-20.48,20.48c-9.049,
           0-16.384-7.335-16.384-16.384 c0-7.239,
           5.869-13.107,13.107-13.107c5.791,0,10.486,4.694,
           10.486,10.486c0,4.633-3.756,8.389-8.389,
           8.389c-3.707,0-6.711-3.005-6.711-6.711"/>
 </g>
</svg>
```

Bézier curves can also handle the simpler cases of straight lines, arcs, circles, and more. Adobe Illustrator is a Bézier-based program, and consequently uses Bézier curves like the ones shown here for almost all shapes when it exports an SVG document, even for straighter shapes that could have been encoded as rectangles, polygons, or lines.

Text

Picture books are fine for three-year-olds, but most vector graphics meant for adults include text. Sometimes this text can be part of the web page or an XSL-FO document in which the SVG is embedded. However, it's also useful to be able to make text part of the picture. Sometimes you want a single line of text placed at a particular position, and other times you want to wrap text around a curving path. SVG provides all of these features; and, of course, it lets you choose the font family, weight, and style. Furthermore, you can treat text as just another shape or path. This means that you can apply coordinate transformations to skew or rotate text, paint the text, clip and mask it, and do anything else to text that you could do to a circle or a rectangle or a polygon. Finally, because XML documents are Unicode, you aren't just limited to standard Latin text. If the necessary fonts are installed, SVG can handle text in right-to-left languages such as Arabic and ideographic languages such as Chinese.

The one thing that SVG really can't do with text is wrap it. There's no `textBox` element in SVG. You can't define a rectangle, assign some text to the rectangle, and expect it to wrap every time a line reaches the right edge of the box. All line breaks have to be inserted manually. The reason is that many languages, such as Tibetan, Arabic, and Chinese, have relatively complex, context-sensitive rules about how and where to break lines, and SVG implementers couldn't be expected to be familiar with all of them.

Strings

The `text` element places a single line of text on the canvas at the position indicated by its `x` and `y` attributes. These are the coordinates of the lower left corner of the string. The text to place is simply the content of the `text` element. For example, this `text` element places the string Hello SVG! at the coordinates x=50, y=50 in the default font and size:

```
<text x="50" y="50">Hello SVG!</text>
```

Listing 24-13 is a nursery rhyme in SVG. Figure 24-15 shows the displayed text.

Listing 24-13: Four Text Elements, One for Each Line of a Poem

```
<?xml version="1.0" encoding="utf-8"?>
<svg xmlns="http://www.w3.org/2000/svg"
     width="3.6in" height="1.0in">
  <title>Listing 24-13 from the XML Bible</title>
  <text x="50" y="20">Mary had a little lamb</text>
  <text x="50" y="40">whose fleece was white as snow</text>
  <text x="50" y="60">and everywhere that Mary went</text>
  <text x="50" y="80">the lamb was sure to go</text>
</svg>
```

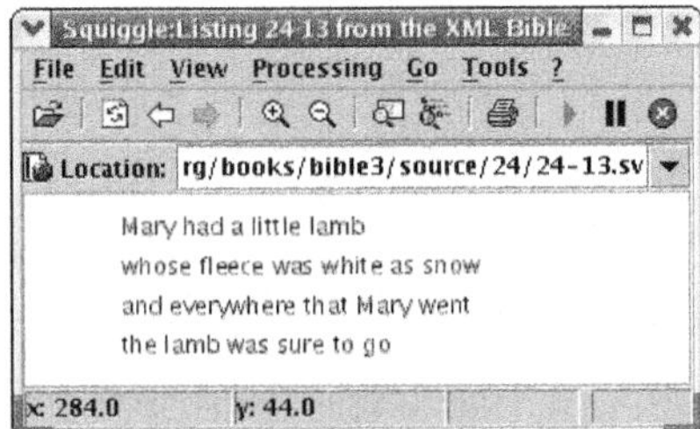

Figure 24-15: Four text strings

Notice that the poem begins on the line with y=20. Y coordinates increase down. The y attribute of the text element specifies the position of the baseline of the string; that is, the bottom of the string. Therefore, if you set y to 0, most of the string, aside from the descenders in letters like *y* and *g*, would be positioned at negative coordinates, outside the visible range.

The text element does not consider line breaks. Each line should be a separate text element with a different y coordinate. For example, suppose you were to use this single text element instead of the four in Listing 24-13:

```
<text x="50" y="20">
  Mary had a little lamb
  whose fleece was white as snow
  and everywhere that Mary went
  the lamb was sure to go
</text>
```

Then SVG would just place all four verses on the same line as shown in Figure 24-16, even if that means some of the text runs off the right-hand side of the visible area and gets truncated.

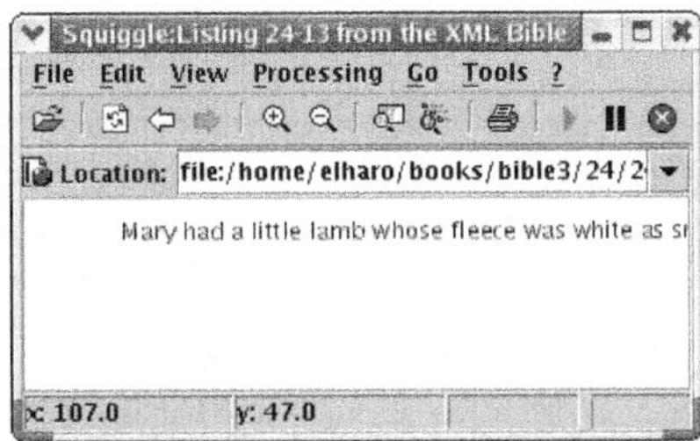

Figure 24-16: One text string

Normally, the SVG renderer compresses all runs of white space to a single space. You can change this behavior by adding an `xml:space` attribute with the value `preserve` to the text element, like this:

```
<text x="50" y="20" xml:space="preserve">
  Mary had a little lamb
  whose fleece was white as snow
  and everywhere that Mary went
  the lamb was sure to go
</text>
```

However, while this will add some extra space between words at the ends of the verses like *lamb* and *whose*, it still won't preserve the line breaks.

Text on a path

Suppose instead of a nursery rhyme that neatly divides into small lines with well-defined line breaks, you have a much larger run of prose, like the text of this paragraph, for example. You normally want to place that inside a box of fixed width and fixed position, but unlimited height, and allow the formatter to decide where to break the lines. SVG can't quite do that, but it can get close.

Note SVG 1.2 will finally add the ability to automatically wrap text inside a shape. However, this is not available in SVG 1.0 or 1.1 and is not yet supported by any SVG tools.

SVG allows you to place text along a path other than a straight line. You can wrap text along a triangle, a spiral, a cloud, Abraham Lincoln's beard, or just about any other path you can imagine. This is accomplished by placing a `textpath` element inside a `text` element. The `textpath` element contains the text to draw and an `xlink:href` attribute pointing to the path along which to draw it.

For example, to wrap the prose of a paragraph along five parallel lines, you first need a `path` element that describes five parallel lines. This one will do:

```
<path id="para5"
      d="M 10,20 L 200,20 M 10,40 L 200,40
         M 10,60 L 200,60 M 10,80 L 200,80
         M 10,100 L 200,100
         M 10, 20 Z"
      fill="none" stroke="none"/>
```

Notice the use of the `M` commands to jump from one line to the next without including the jumps in the path. In particular, notice the last one that moves the pen back to the beginning of the path. Without this, the last line of text might get drawn across a diagonal line connecting the last point to the first point. Also notice that this `path` element has an `id` attribute so that it can be linked to.

The `text` element that writes along this path is given like this:

```
<text>
  <textPath xlink:href="#para5"
            xmlns:xlink="http://www.w3.org/1999/xlink">
    The text to be wrapped along the path goes here
  </textPath>
</text>
```

Don't forget to map the `xlink` prefix to the `http://www.w3.org/1999/xlink` URI. If you use this in multiple places in the document, it might be more convenient to declare it on the root `svg` element.

Listing 24-14 is a complete SVG document that wraps a paragraph of text around a path composed of horizontal lines.

Listing 24-14: Text on a Path

```
<?xml version="1.0" encoding="utf-8"?>
<svg xmlns="http://www.w3.org/2000/svg"
     width="4.0in" height="1.5in">

  <title>Listing 24-14 from the XML Bible</title>

  <path id="para5"
        d="M 10,20 L 360,20 M 10,40 L 360,40
           M 10,60 L 360,60 M 10,80 L 360,80
           M 10,100 L 360,100 M 10, 120 L 360, 120
           M 10,20 Z"
        fill="none" stroke="black"/>/>

  <text>
    <textPath xlink:href="#para5"
              xmlns:xlink="http://www.w3.org/1999/xlink">
      Suppose instead of a nursery rhyme that neatly divides
      into small lines with well-defined line breaks, you have
      a much larger run of prose, like the text of this
      paragraph for example. You normally want to place that
      inside a box of fixed width and fixed position, but
      unlimited height, and allow the formatter to decide
      where to break the lines. SVG can't quite do that yet,
      but it can get close.
    </textPath>
  </text>

</svg>
```

Figure 24-17 shows this example in Squiggle. You'll notice that SVG is not very smart about deciding where to break lines. In fact, it doesn't even try. It just fills up to the end of the line with text and then starts at the next point on the path. Part of the problem here is that SVG needs to be internationalizable. A good line-breaking algorithm is highly language-dependent. Hebrew and Chinese, for example, break very differently than English and French.

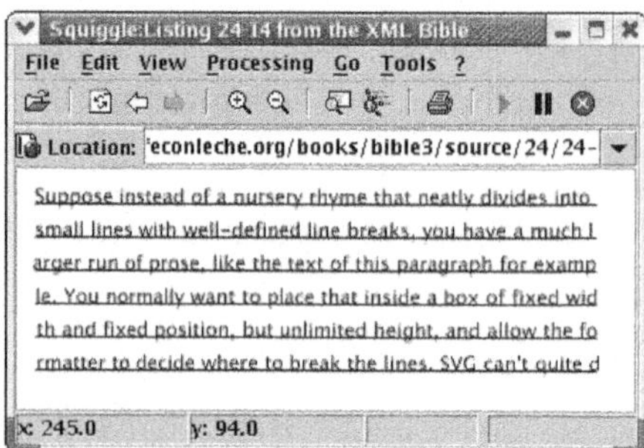

Figure 24-17: Text on a path

Fonts and text styles

SVG adopts CSS text and font properties more or less in toto. You set the font family, font weight, font style, font size, text decoration, color, and so forth by using CSS Level 2 text properties. For example, this paragraph is written in 10-point Times New Roman. If you were to encode it in SVG, it would look something like this:

```
<text x="20" y="20" font-size="10pt;
  font-family="Times, 'Times New Roman', 'New York', serif">
  SVG adopts CSS text and font properties more or less in
  toto. You set the font family, font weight, font style,
  font size, ...
</text>
```

If you prefer, you can use the `text` element's `style` attribute, like this:

```
<text x="20" y="20"
  style="font-size: 10pt;
   font-family: Times, 'Times New Roman', 'New York', serif">
  SVG adopts CSS text and font properties more or less in
  toto. You set the font family, font weight, font style,
  font size, ...
</text>
```

CSS text and font properties are covered in great detail in Chapter 14. A big advantage to SVG adopting CSS for such properties is that you don't need to learn, and I don't have to write about, two different syntaxes that describe pretty much the same thing. As large as this book is, it would have been even larger without such economical reuse of syntax.

Text spans

The `tspan` element lets you apply styles to pieces of a `text` element. It's similar to the `span` element in HTML, that is, a convenient hook off of which to hang CSS styles or other properties. For example, `tspan` enables you to format the first sentence of this paragraph with only the word *tspan* and *text* in Courier. Here's how:

```
<text x="20" y="20" font-size="10pt"
      font-family="Times, 'Times New Roman', serif">
  The <tspan font-family="Courier, monospace">tspan</tspan>
  element lets you apply styles to pieces of a
  <tspan font-family="Courier, monospace">text</tspan>
  element.
</text>
```

Bitmapped Images

SVG is a format for vector graphics. Nonetheless, it's very often useful or necessary to place bitmapped images in line art. For example, you might want to start with a photograph and then overlay text and arrows on that photograph that call out individual parts. Or perhaps a calendar includes both vector graphics for functionality and a photograph of a nature scene to make the calendar pretty to look at. In fact, almost anywhere you look in printed matter, you're likely to find art that combines bitmapped images and vector graphics.

SVG allows you to place bitmapped images in documents in a straightforward fashion. As with the `IMG` element in HTML, the actual bitmap data is not included in the SVG document. Instead, it is linked in from a URL. Also as in HTML, exactly which bitmapped graphic formats are supported depends on what software you're using. All SVG processors can handle JPEG and PNG. GIF is problematical because of patent problems.

The `image` element contains a link to the file containing the bitmapped data. The URL where the image data can be found is read from the `xlink:href` attribute, where the `xlink` prefix is mapped to the standard XLink URI, `http://www.w3.org/1999/xlink`. The `x` and `y` attributes specify where in the local coordinate system the upper left-hand corner of the image should be placed. As with any SVG shape, the chosen position might cause the image to lay on top of or beneath other items on the canvas. The width and height attributes determine the size of the box in which the image is placed. If the actual image is too large or too small for the box, it will be scaled as necessary to fit the box, perhaps even disproportionately exactly like the IMG element in HTML. For example, Listing 24-15 is a complete SVG document that contains a picture of one of my cats, Marjorie. SVG text elements layer the phrases "This is my cat Marjorie." and "She likes to have her picture taken." on top of the picture. Figure 24-18 shows the results.

Listing 24-15: **Placing a JPEG Image in an SVG Picture**

```
<?xml version="1.0" encoding="UTF-8" standalone="yes"?>
<svg xmlns="http://www.w3.org/2000/svg"
     xmlns:xlink="http://www.w3.org/1999/xlink"
     width="360px" height="310px">
  <title>Listing 24-15 from the XML Bible</title>

  <image xlink:href="marjorie.jpg"

  x="20px" y="5px" width="260px" height="297px"/>

  <text x="25px" y="240px"
        font-size="14pt" font-weight="bold"
        font-family="Helvetica, Arial, sans">
    This is my cat Marjorie.
  </text>
  <text x="25px" y="255px"
        font-size="14pt" font-weight="bold"
        font-family="Helvetica, Arial, sans">
    She likes to have her picture taken.
  </text>

</svg>
```

You can also use the image element to load another SVG document into the current one. The XML for the loaded SVG document is not merged into the existing document, as it might be with XInclude. Instead, it's treated as another picture with a certain size at a certain set of coordinates, possibly with some filters applied to it.

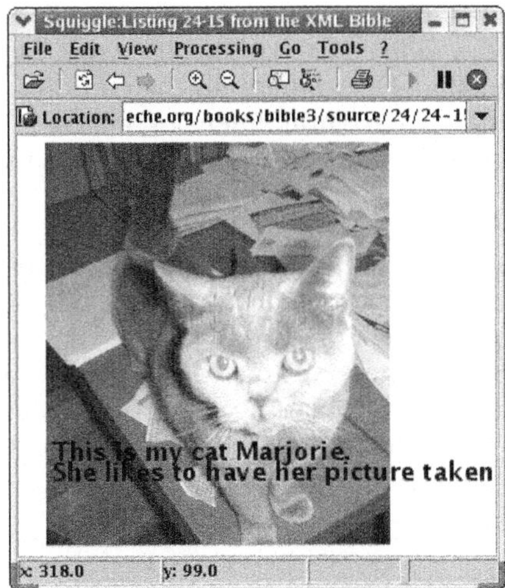

Figure 24-18: Text laid on top of an image

Coordinate Systems and Viewports

So far, we've worked in nondimensional units that map to screen pixels. However, SVG supports all the units of length defined in CSS, including inches, centimeters, millimeters, points, picas, pixels, and even percentages. For example, you can say that a rectangle is 2 inches wide by 3 inches high like this:

```
<rect x="0in" y="0in" width="2in" height="3in"/>
```

When an SVG renderer such as Squiggle displays this rectangle, it will ask its environment how many pixels there are in an inch. On most computer displays, it would get an answer back that is somewhere between 68 and 200 pixels per inch. It would then convert the requested length in inches to the equivalent length in pixels before drawing the picture on the screen. Depending on the resolution of the monitor and the capabilities of both the renderer and the host operating system, the actual sizes might be a little more or a little less than what you asked for. For example, if you draw a circle with a 10-inch radius on your display, then measure it with a ruler (not an on-screen ruler, but a real physical ruler made out of wood), it should be approximately 10 inches — maybe 8, maybe 12, depending on the resolution of the monitor, but something in the ballpark of 10 inches. And if the circle is 20 percent off of its expected size, all the other shapes drawn on that display will also be 20 percent off.

Not all SVG lengths can be specified in real-world units like inches and points. In particular, only rectangles, circles, ellipses, and lines can be specified this way. Polygons and polylines must use nondimensional local units for the coordinates given in their `points` attributes. Paths must also use nondimensional local units for the coordinates given in their `d` attributes. This makes real-world units less useful than they might otherwise be.

However, if you prefer to design your drawings in inches or feet or centimeters rather than pixels, there is a workaround. You can assign a width and a height to your `svg` element to specify how much space it occupies on the page. Then you can set the `viewBox` attribute to define a local coordinate system within that `svg` element. The combination of the actual, on-screen width and height with the view box can define a mapping between the actual pixels and any units of length you desire, from nanometers to parsecs.

The viewport

SVG pictures are drawn on an infinite, two-dimensional plane with infinitely precise coordinates. Of course, when such a picture is actually shown on the screen, you only see a finite rectangular region of limited precision called the *viewport*. This viewport has a certain width and height that can be determined in several ways.

The first possibility applies when an SVG document is included in an HTML page using an `EMBED` element as in Listing 24-3. In this case, the `WIDTH` and `HEIGHT` attributes of the `EMBED` element establish the size of the canvas. Alternately, if the `svg` element is pasted right into the HTML document, as in Listing 24-2, it can have CSS height and width properties that set its size, even if this results in the image being clipped. Listing 24-16 demonstrates.

Listing 24-16: Using CSS Properties to Set the Size of an Embedded SVG Picture

```
<HTML>
  <HEAD>
    <TITLE>Circles are my friends</TITLE>
  </HEAD>
  <BODY>
  <H1>Rectangles are the Enemy!</H1>

  <svg xmlns="http://www.w3.org/2000/svg"
       style="width: 100px; height: 100px">
    <title>Listing 24-16 from the XML Bible</title>
    <circle  r="30" cx="34" cy="34"
             fill="red" stroke="blue" stroke-width="2"/>
  </svg>
```

```
  <HR />
  Last Modified November 10, 2004<BR />
  Copyright 2004
  <A HREF="mailto:elharo@metalab.unc.edu">
    Elliotte Rusty Harold
  </A>

  </BODY>
</HTML>
```

If the svg element is not embedded in HTML in one fashion or another, or if the external document in which it is embedded does not set its width and height, the height is set by the width and height attributes of the svg element itself. For example, this svg element has a viewport that's 10 inches by 5 inches:

```
<svg xmlns="http://www.w3.org/2000/svg"
     width="10in" height="5in">
  <circle r="30" cx="34" cy="34"/>
</svg>
```

Alternately, the width and the height can be given in user coordinates, in which case the real units are pixels. This svg element has a viewport that's 144 pixels by 72 pixels:

```
<svg xmlns="http://www.w3.org/2000/svg"
     width="144" height="72">
  <circle r="30" cx="34" cy="34"/>
</svg>
```

Remember that this only changes the size of the viewport on the screen. It has no effect on the size of the shapes that the svg element contains. If the shapes are too big for the viewport, they'll be truncated; but the plane on which the shapes are rendered is still infinitely large.

Coordinate systems

There are many reasons why you might want to adjust the local coordinate system. For example, if you were drawing a map, it might be convenient to have each local coordinate unit represent a mile. Furthermore, you'd like 1 mile to map to 1 inch, approximately 72 pixels. Or perhaps you want to draw a blueprint of a house on which the local coordinate units reflect the actual size of the rooms in feet. For example, the room in which I'm typing this is 10 feet by 12 feet, so I might represent it as this rect element:

```
<rect x="0" y="0" width="10" height="12"/>
```

However, I do want the room to appear larger than 10 pixels by 12 pixels on the display. So I need to use a local coordinate system that is not so tightly locked to the size of a pixel.

You can both scale and translate the local coordinate system by attaching a `viewBox` attribute to the `svg` element. This changes the local coordinate system inside the viewport by specifying four characteristics of the local coordinate system:

1. The x coordinate of the upper left corner of the viewport
2. The y coordinate of the upper left corner of the viewport
3. The width of the viewport in local coordinates
4. The height of the viewport in local coordinates

These four numbers are given in this order in the `viewBox` attribute of the SVG element. For example, let's suppose you have a 4-inch-by-4-inch space to work with on the screen. However, your arithmetic would be simplified if you could use a 1000-by-1000-unit square. Then you would set up your `svg` element like this:

```
<svg xmlns="http://www.w3.org/2000/svg"
     width="4in" height="4in" viewBox="0 0 1000 1000">
  <!-- SVG shapes -->
</svg>
```

The upper left corner is still at point x=0, y=0. The width and height in the local coordinate space are now 1000 each. Dividing 1000 units by 4 inches, you find that 250 local units equal 1 inch on the screen. For example, consider the `svg` element in Listing 24-17. This is 100 pixels by 100 pixels square. A large (radius=500) circle is placed at x=400, y=400. Figure 24-19 shows the result. Most of the circle is cut off both below and to the right, because most of the circle is outside the viewport. You only see a small part of the upper left quadrant of the circle.

Listing 24-17: **A Circle That Doesn't Fit in Its Viewport**

```
<?xml version="1.0" encoding="UTF-8" standalone="yes"?>
<svg xmlns="http://www.w3.org/2000/svg"
     width="100px" height="100px">
  <title>Listing 24-17 from the XML Bible</title>
  <circle cx="400" cy="400" r="500" />
</svg>
```

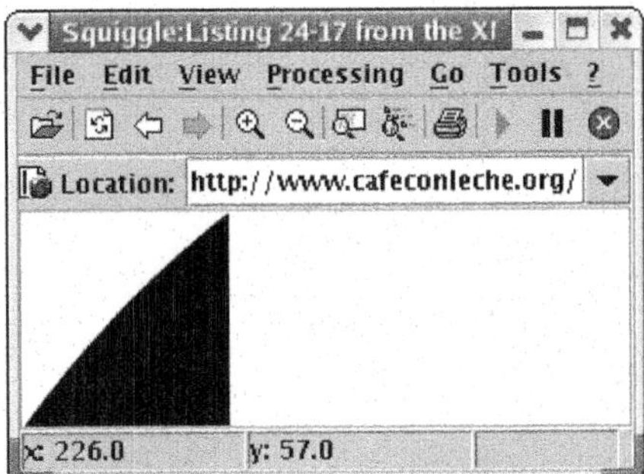

Figure 24-19: A radius 500 circle at 400,400 displayed in a 100-pixel square viewport.

Now suppose you add a `viewBox` attribute to this `svg` element that sets the width of the viewport to 1000 pixels by 1000 pixels. This is shown in Listing 24-18. This effectively shrinks the circle by a factor of 10 to 1, as shown in Figure 24-20. However, because the radius of the circle is 500 and the circle's center is positioned at x=400, y=400, the leftmost and topmost parts of the circle extend into the negative coordinate space and are truncated.

Listing 24-18: Using a viewBox Attribute to Adjust the Local Coordinate System

```
<?xml version="1.0" encoding="UTF-8" standalone="yes"?>
<svg xmlns="http://www.w3.org/2000/svg"
     width="100px" height="100px"
     viewBox="0 0 1000 1000">
  <title>Listing 24-18 from the XML Bible</title>
  <circle cx="400" cy="400" r="500" />
</svg>
```

You can fix the truncation by using the view box to shift the coordinate system 100 units left and up. To do this, set the first two numbers in the `viewBox` attribute to –100. Then the local coordinate system extends from –100 to 899 instead of 0 to 999. Listing 24-19 demonstrates, and Figure 24-21 shows the result.

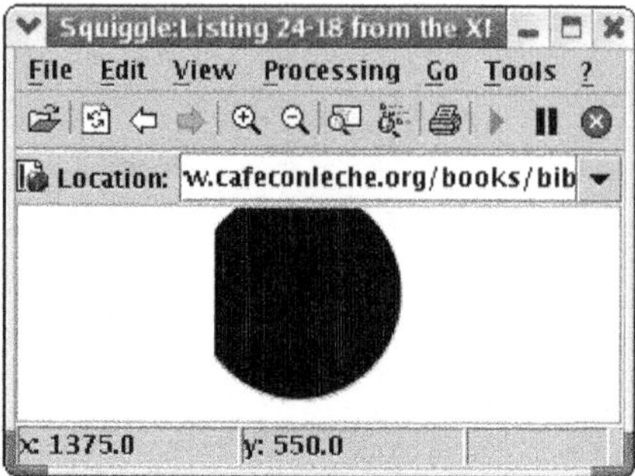

Figure 24-20: A radius 500 circle at 400,400 displayed in a 100-pixel square viewport and a 1000-unit square view box.

Listing 24-19: Using a viewBox Attribute to Adjust the Local Coordinate System

```
<?xml version="1.0" encoding="UTF-8" standalone="yes"?>
<svg xmlns="http://www.w3.org/2000/svg"
     width="100px" height="100px"
     viewBox="-100 -100 1000 1000">
  <title>Listing 24-19 from the XML Bible</title>
  <circle cx="400" cy="400" r="500" />
</svg>
```

Figure 24-21: A radius 500 circle at 400,400 displayed in a 100-pixel square viewport and a 1000-unit square view box shifted down and to the right by 100 units.

Suppose the viewport is 3 inches wide by 4 inches high, and you want 100 local units to equal 1 inch on the screen. You'd multiply the actual width and height by 100/inch to get a 300 width and a 400 height. Then you'd use this `svg` element:

```
<svg xmlns="http://www.w3.org/2000/svg"
     width="3in" height="4in" viewBox="0 0 300 400">
  <!-- SVG shapes -->
</svg>
```

You can even scale the x and y axes independently. For example, suppose you want 100-units-per-inch resolution on the y-axis, but 300 units per inch resolution on the x-axis, and the viewport is 4 inches square. You could use this `svg` element:

```
<svg xmlns="http://www.w3.org/2000/svg"
     width="4in" height="4in" viewBox="0 0 1200 400">
  <!-- SVG shapes -->
</svg>
```

However, by default SVG will attempt to maintain the aspect ratio of the picture. In this case, it will expand the y coordinate to fit the x coordinates. You can change this behavior by setting the `preserveAspectRatio` attribute of the `svg` element to `none`, in which case, different scale factors on the x and y axes can lead to pictures that seem squeezed along the more precise dimension. For example, you'd normally think this `rect` element was a square:

```
<rect x="200" y="200" width="100" height="100"/>
```

However, if you place this `rect` element in the preceding nonuniform coordinate system and set `preserveAspectRatio` to `none`, as shown in Listing 24-20, you get the rectangle shown in Figure 24-22.

Listing 24-20: Nonuniform Coordinate Systems Squeeze Shapes If the Aspect Ratio Isn't Preserved

```
<?xml version="1.0" encoding="UTF-8" standalone="yes"?>
<svg xmlns="http://www.w3.org/2000/svg"
     width="4in" height="4in" viewBox="0 0 1200 400"
     preserveAspectRatio="none">
  <title>Listing 24-20 from the XML Bible</title>
  <rect x="200" y="200" width="100" height="100"/>
</svg>
```

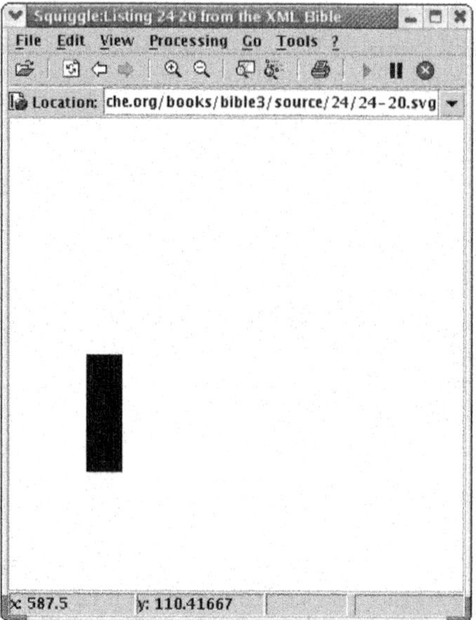

Figure 24-22: Nonuniform coordinate systems squeeze shapes

Grouping Shapes

The g (for group) element combines shapes so they can be treated as a single entity. Each g can have its own local coordinate space in which its child shapes are placed. This entire collection of shapes can then be moved, positioned, styled, and copied as a unit. For example, suppose you need a shape that is a star inside a circle. You can create it by combining a circle with a polygon in a g element, like this:

```
<g width="6cm" height="6cm" viewBox="0 0 250 250">
  <circle cx="115" cy="115" r="100" fill="red" />
  <polygon fill="blue"
    points="33,90 97,90 117,36 137,90 199,90 147,125
            167,180 117,146 67,180 85,125">
  </polygon>
</g>
```

The width and height attributes define the dimensions of the containing block. The viewBox attribute defines the local coordinate system of the elements contained in the group. This is an abstract system, not one based on any sort of physical units such as inches, pixels, or ems. The conversion between the local units and the global units depends on the height and the width of the group. For instance, in the preceding example the group's actual height and width is 6 cm by 6 cm, but its local width and height is 250 by 250. Thus, each local unit is 0.024 cm (6 cm/250). As the height and width of the group change, the sizes of the contents of the group scale proportionately. Furthermore, as you'll see in the next section, the group can be copied by use elements that can adjust the actual height and width. In this case, the contents scale proportionately.

Referencing Shapes

Almost any shape, path, or group in an SVG document can be copied into multiple different places in the document. The use element refers to an element defined elsewhere in the document. For example, suppose you defined red and white squares, like this:

```
<rect id="RedSquare"
      width="1in" height="1in"
      fill="red"/>
<rect id="WhiteSquare"
      width="1in" height="1in"
      fill="white"/>
```

Now suppose you want to place a copy of the red square at coordinates x=3in, y=3in. This use element does that:

```
<use x="3in" y="3in" xlink:href="#RedSquare"/>
```

For this to work, the xlink prefix has to be mapped to the standard XLink namespace URI, http://www.w3.org/1999/xlink. This is normally done on the root element.

It's customary to put the referenced elements inside a defs element. This hides them so they won't be drawn until they're referenced by a use element, as in the following example:

```
<defs>
  <rect id="RedSquare"
        width="1in" height="1in"
        fill="red"/>
  <rect id="WhiteSquare"
        width="1in" height="1in"
        fill="white"/>
</defs>
```

Referencing elements is especially useful if you have many different copies of the same styled element at different positions. For example, designing a checkerboard in SVG would normally require 64 different shapes, one for each square on the board. However, with use and g, you can reduce that to just 2 rectangles, 2 groups of rectangles, and 24 use elements. Listing 24-21 demonstrates. Note especially the nesting of the references. That is, the board uses the rows that use the squares. Figure 24-23 shows the result of Listing 24-21.

Listing 24-21: A Checkerboard

```
<?xml version="1.0" encoding="utf-8"?>
<svg xmlns="http://www.w3.org/2000/svg"
     xmlns:xlink="http://www.w3.org/1999/xlink"
     width="8in" height="8in">

  <title>Listing 24-21 from the XML Bible</title>

  <defs>

    <rect id="RedSquare"
          width="1in" height="1in"
          fill="red"/>
    <rect id="BlackSquare"
          width="1in" height="1in"
          fill="black"/>

    <g id="RowA">
      <use x="0in" xlink:href="#RedSquare"/>
      <use x="1in" xlink:href="#BlackSquare"/>
      <use x="2in" xlink:href="#RedSquare"/>
      <use x="3in" xlink:href="#BlackSquare"/>
      <use x="4in" xlink:href="#RedSquare"/>
      <use x="5in" xlink:href="#BlackSquare"/>
      <use x="6in" xlink:href="#RedSquare"/>
      <use x="7in" xlink:href="#BlackSquare"/>
    </g>

    <g id="RowB">
      <use x="0in" xlink:href="#BlackSquare"/>
      <use x="1in" xlink:href="#RedSquare"/>
      <use x="2in" xlink:href="#BlackSquare"/>
      <use x="3in" xlink:href="#RedSquare"/>
      <use x="4in" xlink:href="#BlackSquare"/>
      <use x="5in" xlink:href="#RedSquare"/>
      <use x="6in" xlink:href="#BlackSquare"/>
      <use x="7in" xlink:href="#RedSquare"/>
    </g>

  </defs>
```

```
    <use y="0in" xlink:href="#RowA"/>
    <use y="1in" xlink:href="#RowB"/>
    <use y="2in" xlink:href="#RowA"/>
    <use y="3in" xlink:href="#RowB"/>
    <use y="4in" xlink:href="#RowA"/>
    <use y="5in" xlink:href="#RowB"/>
    <use y="6in" xlink:href="#RowA"/>
    <use y="7in" xlink:href="#RowB"/>

</svg>
```

Figure 24-23: A checkerboard

This is actually not the most compact solution possible. You could build double rows of two rows each, and then quadruple rows of two double rows each. However, this is the most straightforward solution.

Note

One thing SVG does not give you, which would be very useful in cases such as this, is any sort of iterative structure that would let you simply say, "Give me eight rows of four black squares each spaced two inches apart." Tasks like this can sometimes be accomplished with JavaScript and the SVG Document Object Model (DOM).

Transformations

There are two ways to travel to Jupiter. The first is to get in a rocket ship and fly yourself there. The second is to pick up the entire universe and drag everything in the universe except yourself a few hundred million miles so that Jupiter arrives where you are, with everything else having moved the same amount in the same direction. Needless to say, one of these solutions is considerably easier to accomplish than the other. However, in the abstract, massless world of SVG, that's not true. It is just as easy, sometimes even easier, to move the entire universe to where you want it to be as it is to move a shape or path or group to where it needs to go. The process of moving the SVG universe is called a *coordinate system transformation*, and the engine that powers the move is the `transform` attribute of the `g` element.

The coordinate system transformation that moves the universe so that you end up on Jupiter is called a *translation*, but this is not the only kind of transformation available in SVG. In fact, there are six kinds of transformation, each represented by a different function that can be used in the value of a `transform` attribute:

✦ `translate(dx dy)`—Add `dx` to all x coordinates and `dy` to all y coordinates.

✦ `rotate(θ x y)`—Rotate the coordinate system by θ degrees around a z-axis passing through the point x, y.

✦ `scale(sx sy)`—Multiply the x coordinates by `sx` and the y coordinates by `sy`.

✦ `skewX(θ)`—Skew the y-axis relative to the x-axis by θ degrees.

✦ `skewY(θ)`—Skew the x-axis relative to the y-axis by θ degrees.

✦ `matrix(a b c d e f)`—Multiply all coordinate vectors (x, y, 1) by this translation matrix:

$$\begin{bmatrix} a & c & e \\ b & d & f \\ 0 & 0 & 0 \end{bmatrix}$$

Translations and rotations are *rigid transformations*; that is, they preserve the distance between points. If a line is 70 units long before a translation or a rotation, it is still 70 units long after a translation or rotation. For that matter, it is still 70 units long after any combination of translations and rotations. A scaling, by contrast, might change the sizes of various objects, though their relative sizes will be the same. A skew can change both objects' absolute and relative sizes. Finally, a matrix is a fairly arbitrary transformation that can combine any or all of the other four transforms, as well as adding a few things those can't do, such as a flip.

Coordinate transforms are important tools in SVG and allow you to easily perform tasks that are otherwise quite difficult; particularly because you don't have to make these transformations on the entire canvas at once. Instead, you make it one group at a time. In each group you use the coordinate space that's most appropriate for it. The change from the original coordinate space to the new coordinate space is defined by the `g` element's `transform` attribute.

For example, consider the pie made up of 45-degree arcs from Listing 24-11. It was relatively difficult to do all the trigonometry to calculate the proper endpoints of each of the eight arcs. However, some arcs are easier than others. And once you've got one arc, you can copy it to different positions and rotate each copy. Listing 24-22 is exactly the same pie as Listing 24-11, but it only required one bout with the calculator and is a smaller document over all.

Listing 24-22: A Pie Formed by Eight Rotated Copies of One Wedge

```
<?xml version="1.0" encoding="UTF-8" standalone="yes"?>
<svg xmlns="http://www.w3.org/2000/svg"
     xmlns:xlink="http://www.w3.org/1999/xlink">
  <title>Listing 24-22 from the XML Bible</title>
  <defs>
    <path id="piece"
          d="M 100,100
             L 100, 0
             A 100 100 0 0 1 170.7106781187 29.28932188135
             L 100, 100 Z"
          fill="brown" stroke="black" stroke-width="1px" />
  </defs>

  <g transform="rotate(0 100 100)">
    <use xlink:href="#piece"/>
  </g>
  <g transform="rotate(45 100 100)">
    <use xlink:href="#piece"/>
  </g>
  <g transform="rotate(90 100 100)">
    <use xlink:href="#piece"/>
  </g>
  <g transform="rotate(135 100 100)">
    <use xlink:href="#piece"/>
  </g>
  <g transform="rotate(180 100 100)">
    <use xlink:href="#piece"/>
  </g>
  <g transform="rotate(225 100 100)">
    <use xlink:href="#piece"/>
```

Continued

Listing 24-22 *(continued)*

```
  </g>
  <g transform="rotate(270 100 100)">
    <use xlink:href="#piece"/>
  </g>
  <g transform="rotate(315 100 100)">
    <use xlink:href="#piece"/>
  </g>

</svg>
```

Suppose you want to split the pie apart so that there are gaps between the pieces, as in an exploded drawing. This is relatively difficult to do by manually calculating the coordinates of each piece. However, it's very straightforward to do with a translation. First, you translate the entire picture down and to the right, because as originally written, it butts up against the top and left edges. Then you rotate each piece and translate it 4 units to the right and 10 up. Listing 24-23 demonstrates. Figure 24-24 shows the result.

Listing 24-23: An Exploded Pie

```
<?xml version="1.0" encoding="UTF-8" standalone="yes"?>
<svg xmlns="http://www.w3.org/2000/svg"
     xmlns:xlink="http://www.w3.org/1999/xlink"
     width="3.6in" height="2.8in">
  <title>Listing 24-23 from the XML Bible</title>
  <defs>
    <path id="piece"
          d="M 100,100
             L 100, 0
             A 100 100 0 0 1 170.7106781187 29.28932188135
             L 100, 100 Z"
          fill="brown" stroke="black" stroke-width="1px" />
  </defs>

  <g transform="translate(50 50)">
    <g transform="rotate(0 100 100) translate(4 -10)">
      <use xlink:href="#piece"/>
    </g>
    <g transform="rotate(45 100 100) translate(4 -10)">
      <use xlink:href="#piece"/>
    </g>
    <g transform="rotate(90 100 100) translate(4 -10)">
      <use xlink:href="#piece"/>
```

```
    </g>
    <g transform="rotate(135 100 100) translate(4 -10)">
      <use xlink:href="#piece"/>
    </g>
    <g transform="rotate(180 100 100) translate(4 -10)">
      <use xlink:href="#piece"/>
    </g>
    <g transform="rotate(225 100 100) translate(4 -10)">
      <use xlink:href="#piece"/>
    </g>
    <g transform="rotate(270 100 100) translate(4 -10)">
      <use xlink:href="#piece"/>
    </g>
    <g transform="rotate(315 100 100) translate(4 -10)">
      <use xlink:href="#piece"/>
    </g>
  </g>

</svg>
```

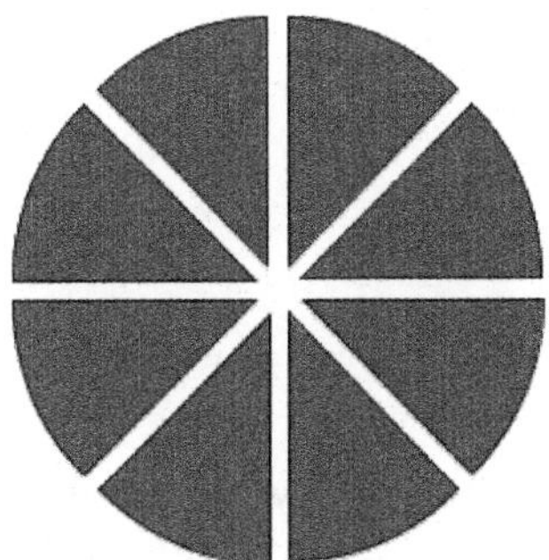

Figure 24-24: An exploded diagram of a pie

In this case each transformation consists of a rotation followed by a translation. You can string as many of these together as you like. However, transformations are not always commutative. Order matters in transformations.

Scaling is a very straightforward operation in which the size of everything is multiplied by a fixed factor. You can provide different scales for the x and y axes, or just one scale for both. For example, Listing 24-24 defines several pie pieces, each one and a half times the size of the previous one. In this example, notice how the coordinate system of the largest piece is actually the product of the multiple groups it's enclosed in and the transformations each imposes. Figure 24-25 shows the result.

Listing 24-24: Scaled Pie

```
<?xml version="1.0" encoding="UTF-8" standalone="yes"?>
<svg xmlns="http://www.w3.org/2000/svg"
     xmlns:xlink="http://www.w3.org/1999/xlink">
  <title>Listing 24-24 from the XML Bible</title>
  <defs>
    <path id="piece"
          d="M 100,100
             L 100, 0
             A 100 100 0 0 1 170.7106781187 29.28932188135
             L 100, 100 Z"
          fill="brown" stroke="black" stroke-width="1px" />
  </defs>

    <g transform="translate(-100 0)">
      <use xlink:href="#piece"/>
      <g transform="translate(0 50) scale(1.5)">
        <use xlink:href="#piece"/>
        <g transform="translate(0 50) scale(1.5)">
          <use xlink:href="#piece"/>
          <g transform="translate(0 50) scale(1.5)">
            <use xlink:href="#piece"/>
          </g>
        </g>
      </g>
    </g>

</svg>
```

Skewing rotates one axis of the coordinate system, either x or y, but not both. Lines that appear perpendicular to each other before skewing no longer appear so after skewing. Figures tend to get squashed and pushed over in one direction or another.

You can skew either the x-axis relative to the y-axis with `skewY()` or the y-axis relative to the x-axis with `skewX()`. Each takes as an argument the number of degrees to skew the axis by. This is sometimes used for text effects, as demonstrated in Listing 24-25 and shown in Figure 24-26. The text normally runs along the x-axis, whereas the letters are oriented parallel to the y-axis. Thus, skewing with respect to the x axis (`skewX()`) merely slants the text within a line. However, skewing with respect to the y-axis (`skewY()`) changes the baseline of the text but keeps all nonitalic text pretty much perpendicular to the baseline.

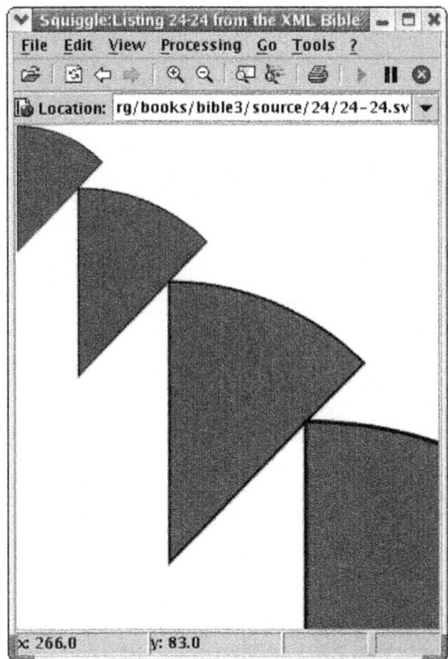

Figure 24-25: Scaled pieces of pie

Listing 24-25: **Skewed Text**

```
<?xml version="1.0" encoding="UTF-8" standalone="yes"?>
<svg xmlns="http://www.w3.org/2000/svg"
     width="4.6in" height="4.6in">
  <title>Listing 24-25 from the XML Bible</title>

    <g transform="skewX(45)">
      <text x="10" y="72"
            font-size="24pt" font-weight="bold"
            font-family="Helvetica, Arial, sans">
        X Skewed 45 Degrees
      </text>
    </g>

    <g transform="skewY(45)">
      <text x="10" y="72"
            font-size="24pt" font-weight="bold"
            font-family="Helvetica, Arial, sans">
        Y Skewed 45 Degrees
      </text>
    </g>

</svg>
```

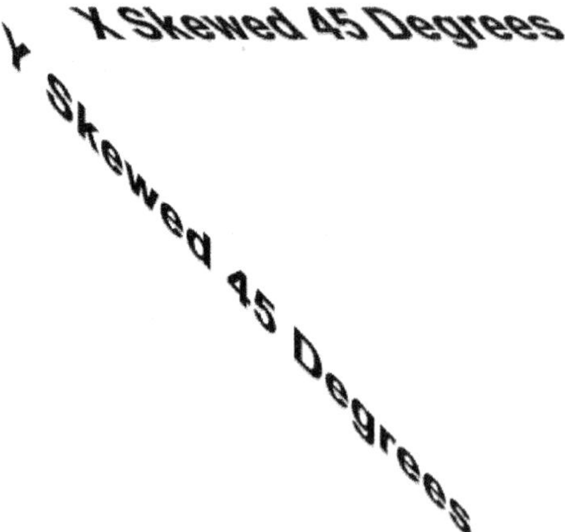

Figure 24-26: Skewed text

All of these transformations — translations, skews, and rotations — are defined mathematically as multiplications of vectors by matrixes. An arbitrary two-dimensional rigid transformation, as well as the nonrigid scales and skews, can be defined in terms of multiplying the coordinate vector by a particular matrix. Furthermore, any combinations of translations, scales, skews, and rotations can be defined as multiplication by a matrix that is the product of the matrixes for each of the individual transformations. However, the reverse is not true. Not all matrix transformations can be decomposed into sequences of rotations, translations, scales, and skews. In particular, a matrix multiplication can flip the coordinate system; that is, map negative coordinates into positive coordinates and vice versa, or, another way of thinking about it, flip the entire plane over through the third dimension. The matrix for flipping the coordinate system around the y-axis looks like this:

$$\begin{bmatrix} -1 & 0 & 0 \\ 0 & 1 & 0 \\ 0 & 0 & 1 \end{bmatrix}$$

If you're familiar with linear algebra, it should be obvious that this simple diagonal matrix multiplies the x coordinates by –1 and leaves the y coordinates untouched. In other words, it transforms vectors such as [x y 1] to [–x y 1]. If you're not familiar with linear algebra, just take my word for it. In SVG, this matrix is written as [–1 0 0 1 0 0]. (The last row of the transformation matrix is always (0 0 1) in SVG.) Thus, to flip the coordinate system, you can use this transform:

```
<g transform="matrix(-1 0 0 1 0 0)">
  <!-- SVG elements here -->
</g>
```

To flip the y-axis around the x-axis, and thus get a coordinate system in which increasing y is up, you'd use this transform:

```
<g transform="matrix(1 0 0 -1 0 0)">
  <!-- SVG elements here -->
</g>
```

There are also matrixes for flips about other axes, but they can all be formed as a flip about the y-axis followed by a translation.

Linking

Because SVG graphics are meant to be used on the Web, it shouldn't come as any great surprise that they can contain simple hypertext links. This allows SVG pictures to be used as image maps on web pages without separate map files.

The `a` element indicates that its contents are a link. This is very similar to the `a` element in HTML and XHTML, and behaves almost identically. However, instead of using an `href` attribute, it uses an `xlink:href` attribute in which the `xlink` prefix is mapped to the `http://www.w3.org/1999/xlink` URI. For example, Listing 24-26 draws nine circles in a 3 by 3 grid. Each `circle` element is enclosed in an element that links to a news site such as CNN or the New York Times. When the user clicks on a circle, the user is transported to the home page of a different news site.

Listing 24-26: Nine Circles Linked to Different Sites

```
<?xml version="1.0" encoding="UTF-8" standalone="yes"?>
<svg xmlns="http://www.w3.org/2000/svg"
     xmlns:xlink="http://www.w3.org/1999/xlink"
     width="3.6in" height="3.6in"
     viewBox="0 0 300 300">
  <title>Listing 24-26 from the XML Bible</title>

  <a xlink:href="http://www.foxnews.com/">
   <circle r="20" cx="25"  cy="25" fill="yellow"/>
  </a>
  <a xlink:href="http://www.msnbc.com/">
   <circle r="20" cx="75"  cy="25" fill="blue"/>
  </a>
  <a xlink:href="http://www.news.com/">
    <circle r="20" cx="125" cy="25" fill="green"/>
  </a>
  <a xlink:href="http://www.cnn.com/">
    <circle r="20" cx="25"  cy="75" fill="red"/>
  </a>
```

Continued

Listing 24-26 *(continued)*

```
  <a xlink:href="http://www.indymedia.org/">
    <circle r="20" cx="75"  cy="75" fill="orange"/>
  </a>
  <a xlink:href="http://www.nytimes.com/">
    <circle r="20" cx="125" cy="75" fill="violet"/>
  </a>
  <a xlink:href="http://www.guardian.co.uk/">
    <circle r="20" cx="25"  cy="125" fill="indigo"/>
  </a>
  <a xlink:href="http://www.csmonitor.com/">
    <circle r="20" cx="75"  cy="125" fill="pink"/>
  </a>
  <a xlink:href="http://news.bbc.co.uk/">
    <circle r="20" cx="125" cy="125" fill="purple"/>
  </a>

</svg>
```

The a element can also have all the other attributes of a simple XLink, including xlink:role, xlink:arcrole, xlink:title, xlink:type, xlink:show, and xlink:actuate. xlink:type must have the value simple. xlink:actuate is limited to onRequest. xlink:show is limited to new and replace. (To embed content in an SVG document, you have to use image rather than a.) These attributes have the same meaning and behavior as for any other XLink.

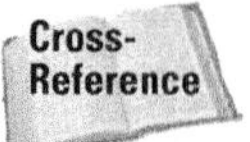

XLinks are discussed in Chapter 17.

Metadata

Graphics, even ones written in XML, can be rather opaque to anyone who can't see very well. This class of users includes not only visually impaired people, but also computer programs such as web spiders, indexers, spell checkers, and so forth. To make the information normally encoded in graphics more accessible to this class of users, most of the elements in an SVG document can contain title, desc, and metadata elements. SVG places no restrictions on the contents of these elements, except the following:

1. The content must be well-formed XML.
2. The content can use any XML vocabulary, provided a namespace distinguishes its elements from SVG's elements.

The main difference between these three elements (`title`, `desc`, and `metadata`) is the rough semantic meaning they imply:

- ✦ The `title` element is a short string of generally unmarked-up text. It can be placed in the title bar of the window showing the picture, as Squiggle does, or in a ToolTip when the user places the mouse over the titled element.
- ✦ The `metadata` element often contains indexing information in some formal vocabulary such as the Resource Description Framework (RDF), topic maps, and/or the Dublin Core.
- ✦ The `desc` element often contains marked-up text intended for humans to read, particularly well-formed HTML.

However, in practice they're pretty much equivalent. Feel free to use whichever elements seem right to you. For example, a `metadata` element might contain XHTML or RDF. The information in the `metadata` element is intended for non-SVG processors that need to try to make sense out of the picture. Listing 24-27 adds some metadata describing the picture of my cat Marjorie originally seen in Listing 24-15. The `title` element says this is Listing 24-27 from the XML Bible. The `desc` element describes Marjorie with a little HTML. The `metadata` element contains an RDF description of this picture. However, when loaded into a browser, the picture hasn't changed at all. Metadata is for almost anything except an SVG renderer.

Listing 24-27: RDF and XHTML Metadata Embedded in an SVG Document

```
<?xml version="1.0" encoding="UTF-8" standalone="yes"?>
<svg xmlns="http://www.w3.org/2000/svg"
     xmlns:xlink="http://www.w3.org/1999/xlink"
     width="300px" height="320px">
  <title>Listing 24-27 from the XML Bible</title>

  <desc>
    <body xmlns="http://www.w3.org/1999/xhtml">
      <p>
        <i>Marjorie</i> is a 9-pound blue British shorthair.
        She's about three years old, loves cameras,
        and hates people. She tolerates Beth and me,
        <em>barely</em>, but hides in the back of the
        bedroom closet anytime company comes over.
      </p>

      <p>
        She's definitely something of a wimp.
        The other cat in our household, <i>Charm</i>, is
        constantly attacking her; and, even though she's a
        couple of pounds heavier than him, her only real
```

Continued

Listing 24-27 *(continued)*

```
         defense is to lay down and wait until he gets bored
         and runs away. When we got her, we hoped she'd bite
         back and teach Charm that biting hurts, but no such
         luck. Charm still bites anything and anyone he can
         catch: mice, cats, dogs, people, furniture, paper,
         computers, household appliances, etc.
         If he can catch it, he will bite it.
       </p>
     </body>
   </desc>

   <metadata>
     <rdf:RDF
        xmlns:rdf="http://www.w3.org/1999/02/22-rdf-syntax-ns#"
        xmlns:dc="http://purl.org/dc/elements/1.1/">

         <rdf:Description about="#marjorie picture">
           <dc:title>Marjorie the Kitten</dc:title>
           <dc:creator
             rdf:resource="mailto:elharo@metalab.unc.edu"/>
           <dc:description>
             A photo of a grey cat standing on a table
             looking into the camera.
           </dc:description>
           <dc:date>2000-12-21</dc:date>
           <dc:type>Photograph</dc:type>
           <dc:format>image/jpeg</dc:format>
           <dc:rights>
             Copyright 2000 Elliotte Rusty Harold
           </dc:rights>
         </rdf:Description>

         <rdf:Description about="mailto:elharo@metalab.unc.edu">
           <dc:title>Elliotte Rusty Harold</dc:title>
         </rdf:Description>

     </rdf:RDF>
   </metadata>

   <image id="marjorie_picture" xlink:href="marjorie.jpg"
     x="20px" y="5px" width="260px" height="297px"/>

   <text x="25px" y="240px"
         font-size="14pt" font-weight="bold"
         font-family="Helvetica, Arial, sans">
     This is my cat Marjorie.
   </text>
```

```
  <text x="25px" y="255px"
        font-size="14pt" font-weight="bold"
        font-family="Helvetica, Arial, sans">
    She likes to have her picture taken.
  </text>

</svg>
```

Although the most common place to put `title`, `desc`, and `metadata` elements is at the top level, as immediate children of the root `svg` element, they can appear essentially anywhere in the SVG document. For example, if one SVG document contained multiple `image` elements, you could give each `image` element a `metadata` child to describe the element.

SVG Editors

Drawing pictures with a keyboard is more than a little like hammering a nail with a sponge. A keyboard simply isn't the right tool with which to draw. A mouse is better, and a graphics tablet is best of all. Fortunately, you can use more traditional graphics tools such as Adobe Illustrator and CorelDRAW to produce SVG documents. Graphics programs that support SVG to some extent include the following:

- ✦ Adobe Illustrator 9.0 can export graphics as SVG. Version 10.0 can also open and edit documents saved as SVG. It's available as payware for both Macintosh and Windows.
- ✦ The W3C's open source Amaya web browser and editor has a very rudimentary drawing tool that produces SVG. However, it's really little more than a proof of concept, and thoroughly inadequate for real work.
- ✦ Jasc Software, best known for Paint Shop Pro, also publishes WebDraw, a native SVG editor for Windows 95/98/Me/NT4/2000.
- ✦ CorelDRAW 10 and later for Windows can both import and export SVG documents.

As time passes, many other traditional graphics tools will add SVG to their repertoire, and programs that already support it will improve their support. Soon SVG will be as ubiquitous in vector drawing programs as GIF and JPEG are today in bitmapped paint programs.

Summary

In this chapter, you learned about SVG, an XML application for vector graphics recommended by the W3C. In particular, you learned the following:

- ✦ SVG provides a standard XML format for vector drawings.
- ✦ SVG pictures can be included directly in HTML documents for browsers that understand SVG natively, such as Amaya.
- ✦ For browsers that don't understand SVG natively, you can link to SVG pictures from HTML using `EMBED` elements and render them with the Adobe SVG Plug-in.
- ✦ All SVG elements are in the `http://www.w3.org/2000/svg` namespace.
- ✦ The root element of an SVG picture is `svg`.
- ✦ Rectangles are defined by their upper left corner, width, and height. They are parallel to the coordinate axes, and are represented by `rect` elements.
- ✦ Circles are defined by their center point and radius. They are represented by `circle` elements.
- ✦ Ellipses are defined by their center point, x radius, and y radius. They are parallel to the coordinate axes and are represented by `ellipse` elements.
- ✦ Line segments are defined by their endpoints. They are represented by `line` elements.
- ✦ Polygons are defined by a list of the points of the corners of the polygon. This list is stored in a `polygon` element's `points` attribute.
- ✦ Polylines are just like polygons except that the last point is not automatically connected back to the first point.
- ✦ Paths are defined by a path element. The `d` attribute of a `path` element contains a list of commands for the path and coordinates for those commands including move to, line to, arc to, curve to, and close path.
- ✦ Each path command is represented by a single letter; uppercase if the coordinates are absolute, lowercase if the coordinates are relative.
- ✦ Shapes and paths can be combined into a single unit called a group and represented by a `g` element.
- ✦ The `use` element copies a shape, path, or group defined elsewhere in the document. An `xlink:href` attribute containing an XPointer identifies the shape to draw.
- ✦ The `defs` element prevents its contents from being drawn until they're referenced by a `use` element.

- CSS styles specify the colors, fonts, and other details of the abstract geometric shapes defined by the SVG elements. These are attached to shapes, paths, and groups using a `style` attribute.
- The `viewBox` attribute of the `svg` element maps a local coordinate space onto the actual rectangular canvas where the picture will be drawn.
- The `transform` attribute of the `g` element can rotate, translate, scale, skew, and flip SVG shapes.
- You can annotate SVG documents and elements with non-SVG information using `title`, `metadata`, and `desc` elements.
- Graphics programs such as Adobe Illustrator are often a better way to produce SVG documents than typing raw code in a text editor.

This and the last several chapters, looked at a variety of XML applications designed by third parties that are ready for you to use today. Chapter 25 changes gears and explains how to design a new XML application from scratch that covers genealogy.

✦ ✦ ✦

Designing a New XML Application

◆ ◆ ◆ ◆

In This Chapter

Organization of the data

Choosing a namespace

Persons

Families

Sources

The family tree

Modularizing the DTDs

A style sheet for family trees

A RDDL document for family trees

◆ ◆ ◆ ◆

The last several chapters discussed XML applications that were already invented by other people and showed you how to use them. This chapter shows you how to develop an XML application from scratch. This chapter builds an XML application and associated document type definitions (DTDs) for genealogical data from the ground up.

Organization of the Data

When developing a new XML application, you need to organize, either in your head or on paper, the data you're describing. There are three basic steps in this process:

1. List the elements.
2. Identify the fundamental elements.
3. Relate the elements to each other.

An easy way to start the process is to explore the forms and reports that are already available from other formats that describe this data. Genealogy is a fairly well established discipline, and genealogists have a fairly good idea of what information is and is not useful and how it should be arranged. This is often included in a family group sheet, a sample of which is shown in Figure 25-1.

Family Group Sheet Page 1 of 1

Name	**Samuel English Anderson**	
Birth	25 Aug 1871	Sideview
Death	10 Nov 1919	Mt. Sterling, KY
Father	Thomas Corwin Anderson (1845-1889)	
Mother	LeAnah (Lee Anna, Annie) DeMint English (1843-1898)	
Other spouses: Cavanaugh		
Misc. Notes		
Samuel English Anderson was known in Montgomery County for his red hair and the temper that went with it. He did once kill a man, but the court found that it was in self-defense. He was shot by a farm worker whom he had fired the day before for smoking in a tobacco barn. Hamp says this may have been self-defense, because he threatened to kill the workers for smoking in the barn. He also says old-time rumors say they mashed his head with a fencepost. Beth heard he was cut to death with machetes in the field, but Hamp says they wouldn't be cutting tobacco in Nov., only stripping it in the barn.		
Marriage	15 Jul 1892	Cincinnati, Ohio, Central Christian Church
Spouse	**Cora Rucker (Blevins?) McDaniel**	
Birth	1 Aug 1873	
Death	21 Jul 1909	Sideview, bronchial trouble TB
Burial		Machpelah Cemetery, Mt. Sterling KY , Sideview
Father	Judson McDaniel (1834-1905)	
Mother	Mary E. Blevins (1847-1886)	
Misc. Notes		
She was engaged to General Hood of the Confederacy, but she was seeing Mr. Anderson on the side. A servant was posted to keep Mr. Anderson away. However the girl fell asleep, and Cora eloped with Mr. Anderson.		
Children		
1 M	**Judson McDaniel Anderson**	
Birth	19 Jul 1894	Montgomery County, KY, 1893
Death	27 Apr 1941	Mt. Sterling, KY
Spouse	Mary Elizabeth Hart	
Marriage	16 Dec 1914	
Spouse	Zelda (Zorah?) Mefford	
2 M	**Thomas Corwin Anderson**	
Birth	16 Jan 1898	
Death		Probably Australia
3 M	**Rodger French Anderson**	
Birth	26 Nov 1899	
Death		Birmingham, AL
Spouse	Ruby McDaniel	
4 F	**Mary English Anderson**	
Birth	8 Apr 1902	August 4, 1902? , Sideview, KY
Death	19 Dec 1972	Mt. Sterling, KY
Spouse	Clark Hagan (Hazen?) Mitchell Major	
Marriage	4 Dec 1939	Fort Knox, KY
Spouse	Carl Edwin (Cully) Berg	
Marriage	1921	
Spouse	Burton Prewitt	

Figure 25-1: A family group sheet

You'll need to duplicate and organize the fields from the standard reports in your DTD to the extent that they match what you want to do. You can, of course, supplement or modify them to fit your specific needs.

Note

Object-oriented programmers will note many similarities between what's described in this section and the techniques they use to gather user requirements. This is partly the result of my own experience and prejudices as an object-oriented programmer, but more of it is due to the similarity of the tasks involved. Gathering user requirements for software is not that different from gathering user requirements for markup languages. Database designers may also notice a lot of similarity between what's done here and what they do when designing a new database.

Listing the elements

The first step in developing an XML application for a domain is to decide what the elements are. This isn't hard. It mostly involves brainstorming to determine what may appear in the domain. As an exercise, write down everything you can think of that may be genealogical information. To keep the problem manageable, include only genealogical data. Assume you can use XHTML for standard text information such as paragraphs, page titles, and so forth. Again, include only elements that specifically apply to genealogy.

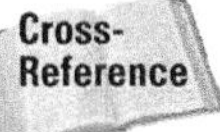

XHTML is discussed in Chapters 21 and 22.

Don't be stingy. It's easy to remove information later if there's too much of it or something doesn't prove useful. At this stage, expect to have redundant elements or elements that you'll throw away after further thought.

Here's the list I came up with. Your list will be at least a little different. Of course, you may have used different names for the same things. That's okay. There's no one right answer (which is not to say that all answers are created equal or that some answers aren't better than others).

Father
Parent
Baptism
Note
Aunt
Mother
Child
Adoption
Gravesite
Niece
Person
Baby
Gender
Source
Grandparent
Family
Birthday
Burial
Surname
Grandmother
Son
Death date
Grandfather
Given name
Uncle
Daughter
Marriage
Date
Middle name
Nephew
Husband
Wife
Spouse
Ancestor
Descendant

Identifying the fundamental elements

The list in the last section has some effective duplicates and some elements that aren't really necessary. It's probably missing a few elements as well, which you'll discover as you continue. This is normal. Developing an XML application is an iterative process that takes some time before you feel comfortable with the result.

What you really need to do at this stage is determine the fundamental elements of the domain. These are likely to be those elements that appear as immediate children of the root, rather than contained in some other element. There are two real possibilities here: family and person. Most of the other items in the list are either characteristics of a person or family (occupation, birthday, marriage) or they're a kind of family or person (uncle, parent, baby).

At this stage, most people's instinct is to say that family is the only fundamental element, and that families contain people. This is certainly consistent with the usage of the terms *parent* and *child* to describe the relationships of XML elements (a usage I eschew in this chapter to avoid confusion with the human parents and children being modeled). For example, you might imagine that a family looks like this:

```
<FAMILY>
  <HUSBAND>Samuel English Anderson</HUSBAND>
  <WIFE>Cora Rucker McDaniel</WIFE>
  <CHILD>Judson McDaniel Anderson</CHILD>
  <CHILD>Thomas Corwin Anderson</CHILD>
  <CHILD>Rodger French Anderson</CHILD>
  <CHILD>Mary English Anderson</CHILD>
</FAMILY>
```

However, there's a problem with this approach. A single person likely belongs to more than one family. I am both the child of my parents and the husband of my wife. That's two different families. Perhaps you can think of this as one extended family, but how far back does this go? Are my grandparents part of the same family? My great-grandparents? My in-laws? Genealogists generally agree that for the purposes of keeping records, a family is a mother, a father, and their children.

Of course, the real world isn't that simple. Some people have both adoptive and biological parents. Many people have more than one spouse over a lifetime. My father-in-law, Sidney Hart Anderson, was married 15 separate times to 12 different women. Admittedly, Sidney is an extreme case. When he died, he was only four marriages away from tying the world record for serial marriage. (Since then, former Baptist minister Glynn Wolfe pushed the record to 29 consecutive marriages, but he lived almost 40 years longer than Sidney did.) Nonetheless, you do need to account for the likelihood that the same people belong to different families.

The standard family group sheets used by the Mormons, a variation of which was shown in Figure 25-1, account for this by repeating the same people and data on different sheets. But for computer applications it's better not to store the same information more than once. Among other things, this avoids problems where data stored in one place is updated while data stored in another is not. Instead, you can make connections between different elements by using `ID` and `IDREF` attributes.

Thus, it is not enough to have only a single fundamental family element. There must be at least one other fundamental element — the person. Each person is unique.

Each has a single birthday, a single death date, most of the time (though not always) a single name, and various other data. Families are composed of different collections of persons. By defining the persons who make up a family, as well as their roles inside the family, you define the family.

Note

We often think of our family as an extended family including grandparents, daughters-in-law, uncles, aunts, and cousins, and perhaps biologically unrelated individuals who happen to live in the same house. However, in the context of genealogy, a family is a single pair of parents and their children. In some cases, the names of these people may be unknown, and in many cases there may be no children or no husband or wife (a single individual qualifies as a family of one). However, a family does not include more distant relationships. A large part of genealogy is the establishment of the actual biological or adoptive relationships between people. It's not uncommon to discover in the course of one's research that the Cousin Puss or Aunt Moot referred to in old letters was in fact no relation at all! Such people should certainly be included in your records, but failure to keep their actual connections straight can only lead to confusion farther down the road.

There's one more key element that may or may not be a direct child of the root. That's the source for information. A source is like a bibliographical footnote, specifying where each piece of information came from. The source may be a magazine article such as "Blaise Pradel, Man At Arms, May/June 1987, pp. 26–31"; a book such as "*A Sesquicentennial History of Kentucky* by Frederik A. Wallis & Hambleon Tapp, 1945, The Historical Record Association, Hopkinsville, KY"; a family Bible such as "English-Demint Anderson Bible, currently held by Beth Anderson in Brooklyn"; or simply word of mouth such as "Anne Sandusky, interview, 6-12-1995".

Tracking the source for a particular datum is important because different sources often disagree. It's not uncommon to see birth and death dates that differ by a day or a year, plus or minus. Less common, but still too frequent, are confusions between parents and grandparents, aunts and cousins, names of particular people, and more. When you uncover information that disputes information you've already collected, it's important to make a reasonable judgment about whether the new information is more reliable than the old. Not all sources are equally reliable. In my own research I've found a document claiming to trace my wife's lineage back to Adam and Eve through assorted biblical figures and various English royalty from the Middle Ages. Needless to say, I don't take this particular source very seriously.

I can think of plausible reasons to make the source a child of the individual elements it documents, but ultimately I think the source is not part of a person or a family in the same way that a birth date or marriage date belongs to a particular person. Rather, it is associated information that should be stored separately and referenced through an ID. The main reason is that a single source, such as an old family Bible, may well contain data about many different people and families. In keeping with principles of data normalization, I'd prefer not to repeat the information about the source more than once in the document. If you like, think of this as akin to using endnotes rather than footnotes.

Establishing relationships among the elements

The third and final step before actually designing the application and writing the DTD is to identify how the different pieces of information you want to track are connected and what they contain. You've determined that the three fundamental elements are the person, the family, and the source. Now you must decide what you want to include in these fundamental elements.

Family

A family is generally composed of a husband, a wife, and zero or more children. Either the husband or the wife is optional. If you wish to account for same-sex marriages (something most genealogy software couldn't do until recently), simply require one or two parents or spouses without specifying gender. Gender can then be included as an attribute of a person, which is where it probably belongs anyway.

There's some question about the proper names for these elements. Husband and wife may not be exactly the right words for unmarried couples, or for single people who never married. Many genealogists prefer father and mother instead, although, again, that's not really accurate when describing either couples or single people who never had children. You could be excessively clinical and call them the male and the female, or perhaps man and woman, but that doesn't really identify the relationship. For purposes of this book, I'm going to choose husband and wife; but you should be aware that the proper choice of names can be somewhat fraught and highly emotional.

Is there other information associated with a family, as opposed to individuals in the family? I can think of one thing that is important to genealogists: marriage information. The date and place a couple was married (if any) and the date and place a couple was divorced (again, if any) are important information. Although you could include such dates as part of each married individual, it really makes sense to make it part of the family. Given that, a family looks something like this:

```
<FAMILY>
  <MARRIAGE>
    <DATE>...</DATE>
    <PLACE>...</PLACE>
  </MARRIAGE>
  <DIVORCE>
    <DATE>...</DATE>
    <PLACE>...</PLACE>
  </DIVORCE>
  <HUSBAND>...</HUSBAND>
  <WIFE>...</WIFE>
  <CHILD>...</CHILD>
  <CHILD>...</CHILD>
  <CHILD>...</CHILD>
</FAMILY>
```

Information can be omitted if it isn't relevant (for example, you wouldn't include a DIVORCE element for a couple that never divorced) or if you don't know it.

Person

The PERSON element is likely to be more complex. Let's review the standard information you'd want to store about a person:

- Name
- Gender
- Birth date
- Baptism date
- Death date
- Burial date and place
- Father
- Mother

Of these, name, birth, baptism, death, and burial are likely to be elements contained inside a person. Gender is probably best modeled as an optional attribute with a fixed-value list. Father and mother are likely to be attributes of the person that refer back to the person elements for those people. Furthermore, a person needs an ID attribute so he or she can be referred to by family and other person elements.

Caution

Father and mother seem to be borderline cases where you might get away with using attributes, but there is the potential to run into trouble. Although everyone has exactly one biological mother and one biological father, many people have adoptive parents that may also need to be connected to the person.

Names are generally divided into family name and given name. This allows you to do things such as write a style sheet that boldfaces all people with the last name Harold.

Birth, death, burial (and possibly baptism — sometimes a baptismal record is all that's available for an individual) can all be divided into a date (possibly including a time) and a place. Again, the place may simply be CDATA, or it can even be a full address element. However, in practice, full street addresses that the post office could deliver mail to are rarely available. Much more common are partial addresses such as Mount Sterling, Kentucky, or the name of an old family farm.

Dates can either be stored as text or broken up into day, month, and year. In general, it's easier to break them into day, month, and year than to stick to a common format for dates. On the other hand, allowing arbitrary text inside a date element also allows for imprecise dates such as 1919-20, before 1753, or about 1800.

That may seem like everything, but one of the most interesting and important pieces of all has been omitted — notes. A note about a person may contain simple data, such as "first Eagle Scout in Louisiana," or it may contain a complete story, such as how Sam Anderson was killed in the field. This may be personal information, such as religious affiliation, or it may be medical information, such as which ancestors died of stomach cancer. If you've got a special interest in particular information such as religion or medical history, you can make that a separate element of its own, but you should still include some element that can hold arbitrary information of interest that you dig up during your research.

There are other things that you could include in a `PERSON` element — photographs, for example — but I'll stop here so that this chapter remains manageable. Let's move on to the `SOURCE` element.

Source

The third and final top-level element is `SOURCE`. A source is bibliographic information that says where you learned a particular fact. It can be a standard citation to a published article or book such as *Collin's History of Kentucky*, Volume II, p. 325, 1840, 1875. Sources such as this have a lot of internal structure that could be captured with elements such as `BOOK`, `AUTHOR`, `VOLUME`, `PAGE_RANGE`, `YEAR`, and so forth.

Several efforts are currently underway to produce DTDs for generic bibliographies. The one that seems furthest along is BiblioML (`http://www.biblioml.org/`) from France's Ministère de la culture et de la communication, Mission de la recherche et de la technologie. BiblioML is based on the international standard Unimarc Bibliographic Format. Unfortunately, this isn't finished as of late 2003.

Furthermore, sources in genealogy tend to be lot messier than in the typical term paper. For instance, one of the most important sources in genealogy can be the family Bible, with records of births, dates, and marriages. In such a case, it's not the edition, translation, or the publisher of the Bible that's important; it's the individual copy that resides in Aunt Doodie's house. For another example, exactly how do you cite an obituary you found in a 50-year-old newspaper clipping in a deceased relative's purse? Chances are the information in the obituary is accurate, but it's not easy to figure out exactly what page of what newspaper on what date it came from.

Because developing an XML application for bibliographies could easily be more than a chapter of its own and is a task best left to professional informaticians, I will satisfy myself with making the `SOURCE` element contain only character data. It will also have an `ID` attribute in the form `s1`, `s2`, `s3`, and so forth, so that each source can be referred to by different elements. Let's move on to writing the DTD that documents this XML application.

Choosing a Namespace

Although not all XML applications need to use namespaces, most public ones should probably use them. Namespaces are the standard way to identify which elements belong with which software when multiple XML vocabularies get mixed together. Even if you plan to keep your documents simple and not mix them with any outside vocabulary, there's no guarantee that other people who use your application will not mix them. For example, even though you think of a genealogy document as an indivisible whole, somebody else might make it a part of a SOAP request.

The namespace URI you pick should be a URL and should be resolvable, because you're eventually going to want to put a RDDL document there. It should probably use the HTTP protocol unless you've got a really good reason to pick something else. Most importantly, the URL should be persistent. It needs to be in a domain name that will remain stable. Thus, it really needs to be in a domain you own. You should not use URLs at free hosts such as GeoCities or ISP user accounts. If you change your ISP for any reason, the namespace URL should still be usable. I have an account at IBiblio so I could use the namespace URL `http://www.ibiblio.org/xml/namespaces/genealogy/`. However, IBiblio has changed its name several times since I started there. It used to be metalab.unc.edu, and before that, it was sunsite.unc.edu. This sort of instability is not acceptable in a host responsible for namespace resolution. Consequently, I will pick a host in a domain I own, cafeconleche.org. Furthermore I'm going to dedicate a specific host just to namespaces, ns.cafeconleche.org, so that the namespace URI will begin `http://ns.cafeconleche.org/`. However, it's equally feasible, and indeed more common, just to set up a special directory on my main web server; for example, `http://www.cafeconleche.org/namespaces/`.

For the sake of convenience, the namespace URL should probably point to a directory rather than to a specific file. You can put the RDDL document in the index file for this directory. The name of this directory should reflect the name of the application you're developing. I'm writing about genealogy, so my full namespace URL will be `http://ns.cafeconleche.org/genealogy/`.

If I wanted to, I could pick a standard prefix at this point, but I'm not going to do that. I expect that most of my genealogy documents will reside in their own files, so I'm not going to need any prefix. The default namespace will do fine. However, I will be careful to design the application in such a way that if someone else wants to add a prefix at a later point, it's straightforward for them to do so.

Persons

By using external entity references or XInclude, it's possible to store individual people in separate files, and then pull them together into families and family trees later. So, let's begin by working on an XML application for a single person. The next sections will merge this into a larger XML application for families and family trees.

A sample person

To develop a DTD or schema, it's often useful to work backwards — that is, first write out the XML markup you'd like to see using a real example or two, then write the DTD that matches the data. I'm going to use my great-grandfather-in-law Samuel English Anderson as an example, because I have enough information about him to serve as a good example, and also because he's been dead long enough that no one should get upset over anything I say about him. (You'd be amazed at the scandals and gossip you dig up when doing genealogical research.) Here's the information I have about Samuel English Anderson, more or less as it appears in a standard genealogy database:

Name: Samuel English Anderson[29, 43]

Birth: 25 Aug 1871 Sideview

Death: 10 Nov 1919 Mt. Sterling, KY

Father: Thomas Corwin Anderson (1845–1889)

Mother: LeAnah (Lee Anna, Annie) DeMint English (1843–1898)

Misc. Notes[219]

Samuel English Anderson was known in Montgomery County for his red hair and the temper that went with it. He did once *kill a man*, but the court found that it was in self-defense.

He was shot by a farm worker whom he had fired the day before for smoking in a tobacco barn. Hamp says this may have been self-defense, because he threatened to kill the workers for smoking in the barn. Hamp also claims that old-time rumors say they mashed his head with a fence post. Beth heard he was cut to death with machetes in the field, but Hamp says they wouldn't be cutting tobacco in November, only stripping it in the barn.

Now let's reformat this into XML as shown in Listing 25-1.

Listing 25-1: An XML Document for Samuel English Anderson

```
<?xml version="1.0"?>
<PERSON ID="p37" SEX="M"
   xmlns="http://ns.cafeconleche.org/genealogy/">
  <REFERENCE SOURCE="s29"/>
  <REFERENCE SOURCE="s43"/>
  <NAME>
    <GIVEN>Samuel English</GIVEN>
    <SURNAME>Anderson</SURNAME>
  </NAME>
  <BIRTH>
    <PLACE>Sideview</PLACE>
    <DATE>25 Aug 1871</DATE>
  </BIRTH>
```

```
    <DEATH>
      <PLACE>Mt. Sterling, KY</PLACE>
      <DATE>10 Nov 1919</DATE>
    </DEATH>
    <SPOUSE PERSON="p1099"/>
    <SPOUSE PERSON="p2660"/>
    <FATHER PERSON="p1035"/>
    <MOTHER PERSON="p1098"/>
    <NOTE>
      <REFERENCE SOURCE="s219"/>
      <body xmlns="http://www.w3.org/1999/xhtml">
        <p>
          Samuel English Anderson was known in Montgomery County
          for his red hair and the temper that went with it. He
          did once <strong>kill a man</strong>, but the court
          found that it was in self-defense.
        </p>

        <p>
          He was shot by a farm worker whom he had
          fired the day before for smoking in a tobacco barn.
          Hamp says this may have been self-defense, because he
          threatened to kill the workers for smoking in the
          barn. Hamp also says old-time rumors say they mashed
          his head with a fence post. Beth heard he was cut to
          death with machetes in the field, but Hamp says they
          wouldn't  be cutting tobacco in November, only
          stripping  it in  the barn.
        </p>
      </body>
    </NOTE>
  </PERSON>
```

The information about other people has been removed and replaced with references to them. The ID numbers are provided by the database I use to store this information (Reunion 5.0 from Leister Productions, `http://www.leisterpro.com`). The endnote numbers become `SOURCE` attributes of `REFERENCE` elements. HTML tags are used to mark up the note.

Eventually you might need to add a document type declaration, schema location attributes, and `xml-stylesheet` processing instructions to this document. However, that can wait. For now, you just need a basic example from which you can work when writing the DTD. Exactly what you put in the document type declaration and/or the schema location attributes will depend on exactly what you come up with when you write the DTD, schema, and style sheet.

The person DTD

Now let's see what a DTD for Listing 25-1 would look like. I'm going to begin with the simplest DTD just to get started. However, once the DTD is finished, I'll parameterize it so users can adjust the namespace prefix. But it's certainly easier to begin with a less indirect approach until the basic application is debugged.

The first element is PERSON. This element may contain names, references, births, deaths, burials, baptisms, notes, spouses, fathers, and mothers. I'm going to allow zero or more of each in any order.

```
<!ELEMENT PERSON (NAME | REFERENCE | BIRTH | DEATH | BURIAL
   | BAPTISM | NOTE | SPOUSE | FATHER | MOTHER )*>
```

At first glance it may seem strange not to require a BIRTH or some of the other elements. After all, everybody has exactly one birthday. However, keep in mind that what's being described here is more your knowledge of the person than the person him- or herself. You often know about a person without knowing the exact day or even year they were born. Similarly, you may sometimes have conflicting sources that give different values for birthdays or other information. Therefore, it may be necessary to include extra data.

The PERSON element has three attributes: xmlns, which I'll make fixed; ID, which I'll require; and a SEX, which I'll make optional. (Old records often contain children of unspecified gender, sometimes named, sometimes not. Even photographs can be unclear about gender, especially when children who died very young are involved.)

```
<!ATTLIST PERSON
  xmlns  CDATA  #FIXED "http://ns.cafeconleche.org/genealogy/"
  ID     ID     #REQUIRED
  SEX    (M | F) #IMPLIED>
```

Next, the child elements must be declared. Four of them — BIRTH, DEATH, BURIAL, and BAPTISM — consist of a place and a date, and are otherwise the same. This is a good place for a parameter entity reference:

```
<!ENTITY % event   "(REFERENCE*, PLACE?, DATE?)*">
<!ELEMENT  BIRTH   %event;>
<!ELEMENT  BAPTISM %event;>
<!ELEMENT  DEATH   %event;>
<!ELEMENT  BURIAL  %event;>
```

I've also added one or more optional REFERENCE elements at the start, even though this example doesn't have a SOURCE for any event information. Sometimes you'll have different sources for different pieces of information about a person. In fact, I'll add REFERENCE elements as potential children of almost every element in the DTD. I declare REFERENCE like this, along with a comment in case it isn't obvious from glancing over the DTD exactly what's supposed to be found in the reference:

```
<!-- The ID number of a SOURCE element
     that documents this entry -->
<!ELEMENT  REFERENCE EMPTY>
<!ATTLIST  REFERENCE SOURCE NMTOKEN #REQUIRED>
```

Here the SOURCE attribute merely contains the number of the corresponding source. When actual SOURCE elements are added to the DTD, this can become the ID of the SOURCE element.

A PLACE contains only text. A DATE contains a date string. I decided against requiring a separate year, date, and month to allow for less-certain dates that are common in genealogy, such as "about 1876" or "sometime before 1920".

```
<!ELEMENT  PLACE (#PCDATA)>
<!ELEMENT  DATE  (#PCDATA)>
```

The SPOUSE, FATHER, and MOTHER attributes each contain a link to the ID of a PERSON element via a PERSON attribute. Again, this is a good opportunity to use a parameter entity reference:

```
<!ENTITY % personref "PERSON NMTOKEN #REQUIRED">
<!ELEMENT  SPOUSE  EMPTY>
<!ATTLIST  SPOUSE  %personref;>
<!ELEMENT  FATHER  EMPTY>
<!ATTLIST  FATHER  %personref;>
<!ELEMENT  MOTHER  EMPTY>
<!ATTLIST  MOTHER  %personref;>
```

Ideally, the PERSON attribute would have type IDREF. However, as long as the person being identified may reside in another file, the best you can do is require a name token type.

The NAME element may contain any number of REFERENCE elements and zero or one SURNAME and GIVEN elements. Each of these may contain text.

```
<!ELEMENT  NAME    (REFERENCE*, GIVEN?, SURNAME?)>
<!ELEMENT  GIVEN   (#PCDATA)>
<!ELEMENT  SURNAME (#PCDATA)>
```

The NOTE element may contain an arbitrary amount of text. Some standard markup would be useful here. The easiest solution is to adopt XHTML Basic. Simply use a parameter entity reference to import the XHTML Basic DTD. I'll allow each NOTE to contain zero or more REFERENCE elements and a single body element:

```
<!ENTITY % xhtml PUBLIC "-//W3C//DTD XHTML Basic 1.0//EN"
                        "xhtml-basic10.dtd">
%xhtml;
<!ELEMENT  NOTE   (REFERENCE*, body)>
```

Those three little lines get you all the markup you need for simple narratives. There's no need to invent your own. You can use the already familiar and well-supported HTML tags. I chose to use only `body` because adding a header here seemed a little superfluous, but if you want to include complete HTML documents, it's easy to do—just replace `body` with `html` in the above. This does assume that the file xhtml-basic10.dtd and all the files it depends on can be found in the same directory as this DTD, although that's easy to adjust if you want to put it somewhere else. You could even use the absolute URL at the W3C web site, `http://www.w3.org/TR/xhtml-basic/xhtml-basic10.dtd`, although I prefer not to make my documents dependent on the availability of a web site I don't control. Listing 25-2 shows the complete person DTD.

Listing 25-2: person.dtd: The Complete PERSON DTD

```
<!ELEMENT PERSON ( NAME | REFERENCE | BIRTH | DEATH | BURIAL
                | BAPTISM | NOTE | FATHER | MOTHER | SPOUSE )* >
<!ATTLIST PERSON
   xmlns  CDATA  #FIXED "http://ns.cafeconleche.org/genealogy/"
   ID     ID     #REQUIRED>

<!ATTLIST PERSON SEX (M | F) #IMPLIED>

<!-- The ID number of a SOURCE element that documents
     this entry -->
<!ELEMENT  REFERENCE  EMPTY>
<!ENTITY % sourceref "SOURCE NMTOKEN #REQUIRED">
<!ATTLIST  REFERENCE %sourceref;>

<!ENTITY % event   "(REFERENCE*, PLACE?, DATE?)">
<!ELEMENT  BIRTH   %event;>
<!ELEMENT  BAPTISM %event;>
<!ELEMENT  DEATH   %event;>
<!ELEMENT  BURIAL  %event;>

<!ELEMENT  PLACE   (#PCDATA)>
<!ELEMENT  DATE    (#PCDATA)>

<!ENTITY % personref "PERSON NMTOKEN #REQUIRED">
<!ELEMENT  SPOUSE  EMPTY>
<!ATTLIST  SPOUSE  %personref;>
<!ELEMENT  FATHER  EMPTY>
<!ATTLIST  FATHER  %personref;>
<!ELEMENT  MOTHER  EMPTY>
<!ATTLIST  MOTHER  %personref;>

<!ELEMENT  NAME    (GIVEN?, SURNAME?)>
<!ELEMENT  GIVEN   (#PCDATA)>
<!ELEMENT  SURNAME (#PCDATA)>
```

```
<!ENTITY % xhtml PUBLIC "-//W3C//DTD XHTML Basic 1.0//EN"
                        "xhtml-basic10.dtd">
%xhtml;

<!ELEMENT  NOTE   (REFERENCE*, body)>
```

Listing 25-2 is a complete DTD for PERSON elements. It's straightforward and reasonably easy to understand. Or is it? Perhaps it only seems so to me because I wrote it. If it's obvious to you, that may only be because you were treated to several pages of exposition and development before you looked at Listing 25-2. What will it look like to someone just staring at the DTD cold? In general, I haven't overly commented the examples in this book because the prose text explains what's going on. However, most real-world DTDs don't come attached to a 800+ page printed book. Thus, actual DTDs need a lot more exposition inside the DTD itself. This normally takes the form of XML comments. Listing 25-3 demonstrates. The DTD is almost twice as long, but correspondingly much easier to understand.

Listing 25-3: commented_person.dtd: The PERSON DTD with Comments

```
<!-- ..................................................... -->
<!-- Genealogy Person DTD  .............................. -->
<!-- file: person.dtd

     This DTD describes a PERSON element intended for use
     in family tree documents. It was developed as an example
     for Chapter 25 of the XML Bible, 3rd Edition, by
     Elliotte Rusty Harold (elharo@metalab.unc.edu)
     Published by Wiley 2004. ISBN 0-7645-4986-3.

     This schema is placed in the public domain. Please
     feel free to use it or adapt it in any way you like.

     This DTD is identified by the PUBLIC and SYSTEM
     identifiers:

     PUBLIC "-//ERH//Genealogy Person DTD 1.0//EN"
     SYSTEM "person.dtd"

     All the elements declared in this DTD are in the
     http://ns.cafeconleche.org/genealogy/ namespace.
     No prefix is used. The attributes are in no namespace.
```

Continued

Listing 25-3 (continued)

```
     It is not a formal standard, and has not been considered
     or approved by any standards body.

     ............................................................ -->

<!-- PERSON is the root element of documents that use this
     DTD. However, it is more intended to be used as a part
     of larger XML applications which would contain multiple
     PERSON elements in a single document. -->
<!ELEMENT PERSON ( NAME | REFERENCE | BIRTH | DEATH | BURIAL
              | BAPTISM | NOTE | FATHER | MOTHER | SPOUSE )* >
<!ATTLIST PERSON
   xmlns  CDATA #FIXED "http://ns.cafeconleche.org/genealogy/"
   ID     ID    #REQUIRED>

<!ATTLIST PERSON
   xmlns:xsi CDATA #FIXED
                    "http://www.w3.org/2001/XMLSchema-instance"
   xsi:schemaLocation CDATA #IMPLIED
>

<!--M means male, F means female -->
<!ATTLIST PERSON SEX (M | F) #IMPLIED>

<!-- The ID number of a SOURCE element that documents
     this entry -->
<!ELEMENT  REFERENCE  EMPTY>
<!ENTITY % sourceref "SOURCE NMTOKEN #REQUIRED">
<!ATTLIST  REFERENCE %sourceref;>

<!-- Events are occurrences at a certain
     time and place, though the exact time and place may
     not be known for certain. Events include marriages,
     births, deaths, baptisms, and burials.  -->
<!ENTITY % event   "(REFERENCE*, PLACE?, DATE?)">
<!ELEMENT  BIRTH   %event;>
<!ELEMENT  BAPTISM %event;>
<!ELEMENT  DEATH   %event;>
<!ELEMENT  BURIAL  %event;>

<!ELEMENT  PLACE   (#PCDATA)>
<!ELEMENT  DATE    (#PCDATA)>

<!-- A person reference is a pointer to another person
     encoded in a PERSON element. The pointer is the ID
     of the PERSON pointed to. -->
```

```
<!ENTITY % personref "PERSON NMTOKEN #REQUIRED">
<!ELEMENT  SPOUSE  EMPTY>
<!ATTLIST  SPOUSE  %personref;>
<!ELEMENT  FATHER  EMPTY>
<!ATTLIST  FATHER  %personref;>
<!ELEMENT  MOTHER  EMPTY>
<!ATTLIST  MOTHER  %personref;>

<!-- Middle names should be encoded as part of the
     given name; e.g.
     <NAME>
       <GIVEN>Elliotte Rusty</GIVEN>
       <SURNAME>Harold</SURNAME>
     </NAME>
 -->
<!ELEMENT  NAME    (GIVEN?, SURNAME?)>
<!ELEMENT  GIVEN   (#PCDATA)>
<!ELEMENT  SURNAME (#PCDATA)>

<!-- The NOTE element contains an XHTML Basic body element
     holding the text of the note. This allows you to write
     essentially anything you care to write in a note.
 -->
<!ENTITY % xhtml PUBLIC "-//W3C//DTD XHTML Basic 1.0//EN"
                        "xhtml-basic10.dtd">
%xhtml;

<!ELEMENT  NOTE   (REFERENCE*, body)>
```

There are a number of useful bits of information in the comments that are not found in the element and attribute declarations:

- ✦ Copyright information so that users know how and where they can use it (any way they please in this case)
- ✦ An e-mail address to write to if the user has questions
- ✦ The public identifier and the suggested filename and system identifier
- ✦ What abbreviations stand for
- ✦ What the text content of some elements should look like

This isn't the limit, either. You could certainly add a lot more detail in the comments, up to and including the complete prose specification for the application. Validators can easily skip over the comments. Human readers may find well-written comments more useful than the declarations.

The person schema

Now that the DTD is finished, let's see what a W3C XML Schema Language schema for Listing 25-1 would look like. The key element is PERSON. This is an element with complex content, and it is the root element of the document. Therefore, it must be declared with a top-level xsd:element element. The big question for this, and other elements with author-defined types, is whether it should be declared with a named type or an anonymous type. Generally, a named type should be used if you expect the element or the type to be used in many different contexts and you want to reuse the type. Although the PERSON element and type are only used in one context in Listing 25-1, it's clear it will be used as a nonroot element in the full family tree document. Thus, it's best to define it as a type of its own.

The application is the same as it was in the DTD, so you don't need to revisit all the questions about what makes up a person. You can just translate the existing declaration of the PERSON element in the DTD into a schema. In the DTD, this declaration is:

```
<!ELEMENT PERSON (NAME | REFERENCE | BIRTH | DEATH | BURIAL
   | BAPTISM | NOTE | SPOUSE | FATHER | MOTHER )*>
```

Translating into an xsd:complexType element, this becomes

```
<xsd:complexType name="PersonType">
  <xsd:choice minOccurs="0" maxOccurs="unbounded">
    <xsd:element name="NAME"      type="NameType"/>
    <xsd:element name="REFERENCE" type="ReferenceType"/>
    <xsd:element name="BIRTH"     type="BirthType"/>
    <xsd:element name="DEATH"     type="DeathType"/>
    <xsd:element name="BURIAL"    type="BurialType"/>
    <xsd:element name="BAPTISM"   type="BaptismType"/>
    <xsd:element name="NOTE"      type="NoteType"/>
    <xsd:element name="SPOUSE"    type="SpouseType"/>
    <xsd:element name="FATHER"    type="FatherType"/>
    <xsd:element name="MOTHER"    type="MotherType"/>
  </xsd:choice>
</xsd:complexType>
```

However, this does raise some new questions about the type of each of the child elements of the PERSON that the DTD does not answer. All of these elements, at least potentially, have either child elements or attributes, so they're all complex types. However, is each of them really a different type? The answer is no. For example, BURIAL, BAPTISM, BIRTH, and DEATH all contain the same child elements and should share a content model. In the DTD, this was indicated by parameter entity references. In a schema, the same effect is achieved by defining one EventType and assigning it to all the elements that share that type:

```
<xsd:complexType name="EventType">
  <xsd:sequence>
```

```
    <xsd:element name="REFERENCE" type="ReferenceType"
                 minOccurs="0"    maxOccurs="unbounded"/>
    <xsd:element name="PLACE" type="xsd:string" minOccurs="0"/>
    <xsd:element name="DATE"  type="xsd:string" minOccurs="0"/>
  </xsd:sequence>
</xsd:complexType>
```

I chose to make PLACE and DATE strings rather than dates for the same reasons they were made #PCDATA in the DTD. In this particular application, dates tend to be quite fuzzy.

Similarly FATHER, MOTHER, and SPOUSE are all just instances of some kind of PersonRefType, an empty element with a PERSON NMTOKEN attribute:

```
<xsd:complexType name="PersonRefType">
  <xsd:attribute name="PERSON" type="xsd:NMTOKEN"/>
</xsd:complexType>
```

Eventually, of course, you'll want to change the type of the PERSON attribute from xsd:NMTOKEN to xsd:IDREF when you build the full family tree schema by overriding the definition of PersonRefType given here.

This still leaves NameType, ReferenceType, and NoteType. These do need their own declarations. The NAME element is only used here, so it might as well use an anonymous type declaration:

```
<xsd:element name="NAME">
  <xsd:complexType>
    <xsd:sequence>
      <xsd:element name="REFERENCE" type="ReferenceType"
                   minOccurs="0" maxOccurs="unbounded"/>
      <xsd:element name="GIVEN" type="xsd:string"
                   minOccurs="0" />
      <xsd:element name="SURNAME" type="xsd:string"
                   minOccurs="0" />
    </xsd:sequence>
  </xsd:complexType>
</xsd:element>
```

The reference type will be used in many places in the schema, so it should have a named type:

```
  <xsd:complexType name="ReferenceType">
    <xsd:attribute name="SOURCE" type="xsd:NMTOKEN"/>
  </xsd:complexType>
```

The note type will also be used in multiple places, so it too has a named type. However, its declaration is much trickier because one of the elements it contains, body, comes from a different namespace. Thus, you first have to import the schema for XHTML to retrieve the necessary declarations for that namespace:

```
<xsd:import namespace="http://www.w3.org/1999/xhtml"
            schemaLocation="xhtml1.1.xsd"/>
```

I'm using the full schema for XHTML here only because a schema for XHTML Basic wasn't available at the time of this writing. It would be easy enough to adjust this when one does become available. The relative URL used here assumes that the file xhtml1.1.xsd and all the files it depends on can be found in the same directory as this schema.

Because the body element is declared in a different schema, I declare it here by reference rather than by name and type. Because the default namespace in this schema is already mapped to http://ns.cafeconleche.org/genealogy/, I also have to put a prefix on the body element and declare that prefix with an xmlns:html attribute:

```
<xsd:complexType name="NoteType"
                 xmlns:html="http://www.w3.org/1999/xhtml">
  <xsd:sequence>
    <xsd:element name="REFERENCE" type="ReferenceType"
                 minOccurs="0" />
    <xsd:element ref="html:body"/>
  </xsd:sequence>
</xsd:complexType>
```

However, none of this means that you have to use such prefixes in your instance documents. Schemas validate against namespace URIs, not prefixes. The prefixes used here are chosen purely for convenience inside the schema. They do not apply in the instance documents.

The PERSON element also has three attributes: xmlns, which doesn't have to be declared in a schema, ID, which I'll require, and SEX, which I'll make optional:

```
<xsd:attribute name="ID"  xsd:type="ID" use="required"/>
<xsd:attribute name="SEX">
  <xsd:simpleType>
    <xsd:restriction base="xsd:string">
      <xsd:enumeration value="M"/>
      <xsd:enumeration value="F"/>
    </xsd:restriction>
  </xsd:simpleType>
</xsd:attribute>
```

After adding all these pieces and putting them together, the completed person schema is shown in Listing 25-4:

Listing 25-4: person.xsd: The Complete PERSON Schema

```
<?xml version="1.0"?>
<xsd:schema xmlns:xsd="http://www.w3.org/2001/XMLSchema"
  xmlns="http://ns.cafeconleche.org/genealogy/"
  xmlns:html="http://www.w3.org/1999/xhtml"
  targetNamespace="http://ns.cafeconleche.org/genealogy/"
  elementFormDefault="qualified"
  attributeFormDefault="unqualified"
>

  <xsd:import namespace="http://www.w3.org/1999/xhtml"
              schemaLocation="xhtml1.1.xsd"/>

  <xsd:complexType name="EventType">
    <xsd:sequence>
      <xsd:element name="REFERENCE" type="ReferenceType"
                   minOccurs="0" maxOccurs="unbounded"/>
      <xsd:element name="PLACE" type="xsd:string"
                   minOccurs="0"/>
      <xsd:element name="DATE"  type="xsd:string"
                   minOccurs="0"/>
    </xsd:sequence>
  </xsd:complexType>

  <xsd:complexType name="PersonRefType">
    <xsd:attribute name="PERSON" type="xsd:NMTOKEN"/>
  </xsd:complexType>

  <xsd:complexType name="ReferenceType">
    <xsd:attribute name="SOURCE" type="xsd:NMTOKEN"/>
  </xsd:complexType>

  <xsd:complexType name="NoteType"
                   xmlns:html="http://www.w3.org/1999/xhtml">
    <xsd:sequence>
      <xsd:element name="REFERENCE" type="ReferenceType"
                   minOccurs="0" />
      <xsd:element ref="html:body"/>
    </xsd:sequence>
  </xsd:complexType>


  <xsd:complexType name="PersonType">
    <xsd:choice minOccurs="0" maxOccurs="unbounded">
      <xsd:element name="NAME">
        <xsd:complexType>
          <xsd:sequence>
            <xsd:element name="REFERENCE" type="ReferenceType"
                         minOccurs="0"  maxOccurs="unbounded"/>
```

Continued

Listing 25-4 *(continued)*

```
            <xsd:element name="GIVEN"      type="xsd:string"
                         minOccurs="0" />
            <xsd:element name="SURNAME"    type="xsd:string"
                         minOccurs="0" />
          </xsd:sequence>
        </xsd:complexType>
      </xsd:element>
      <xsd:element name="REFERENCE" type="ReferenceType"/>
      <xsd:element name="BIRTH"     type="EventType"/>
      <xsd:element name="DEATH"     type="EventType"/>
      <xsd:element name="BURIAL"    type="EventType"/>
      <xsd:element name="BAPTISM"   type="EventType"/>
      <xsd:element name="NOTE"      type="NoteType"/>
      <xsd:element name="SPOUSE"    type="PersonRefType"/>
      <xsd:element name="FATHER"    type="PersonRefType"/>
      <xsd:element name="MOTHER"    type="PersonRefType"/>
    </xsd:choice>
    <xsd:attribute name="ID"  type="xsd:ID" use="required"/>
    <xsd:attribute name="SEX">
      <xsd:simpleType>
        <xsd:restriction base="xsd:string">
          <xsd:enumeration value="M"/>
          <xsd:enumeration value="F"/>
        </xsd:restriction>
      </xsd:simpleType>
    </xsd:attribute>
  </xsd:complexType>

  <xsd:element name="PERSON" type="PersonType"/>

</xsd:schema>
```

Before you can validate the sample document against this schema, you must add the necessary schema location and namespace declaration attributes to the root element of the instance document, like this:

```
<xsd:schema xmlns:xsd="http://www.w3.org/2001/XMLSchema"
  xmlns="http://ns.cafeconleche.org/genealogy/"
  targetNamespace="http://ns.cafeconleche.org/genealogy/"
  elementFormDefault="qualified"
  attributeFormDefault="unqualified"
>
```

Having done that, if you still want to be able to validate against the DTD, you need to add declarations for those attributes to the DTD, like this:

```
<!ATTLIST PERSON
   xmlns:xsi CDATA #FIXED
             "http://www.w3.org/2001/XMLSchema-instance"
   xsi:schemaLocation CDATA #IMPLIED
>
```

Listing 25-4 does provide a complete content model for PERSON elements. It's short, simple, fairly straightforward, and reasonably easy to follow. Or is it? I think it is because I wrote it, and one's own code always seems more obvious to one's self than to anyone else. Furthermore, as I type these words I just wrote that code, so it's very fresh in my mind. It's probably also fairly obvious to you, too, because before you looked at Listing 25-4, you were treated to several pages of exposition and development. Nonetheless, it's almost certain that this schema won't be nearly as clear to anyone who's just picking it up without reading this book. Most schemas can be improved substantially by adding numerous comments and annotations that describe exactly what is going on in the schema and why. Listing 25-5 does exactly this. The schema is longer but much clearer to someone reading this schema for the first time.

Listing 25-5: **annotated_person.xsd: The Annotated PERSON Schema**

```
<?xml version="1.0"?>
<xsd:schema xmlns:xsd="http://www.w3.org/2001/XMLSchema"
  xmlns="http://ns.cafeconleche.org/genealogy/"
  xmlns:html="http://www.w3.org/1999/xhtml"
  targetNamespace="http://ns.cafeconleche.org/genealogy/"
  elementFormDefault="qualified"
  attributeFormDefault="unqualified"
>

  <xsd:annotation>
    <xsd:documentation>

      This schema describes a PERSON element intended for use
      in family tree documents. It was developed as an example
      for Chapter 25 of the XML Bible, 3rd Edition, by
      Elliotte Rusty Harold (elharo@metalab.unc.edu)
      Published by Wiley 2004. ISBN 0-7645-4986-3.

      This schema is placed in the public domain. Please
      feel free to use it or adapt it in any way you like.

      It is not a formal standard, and has not been considered
      or approved by any standards body.
```

Continued

Listing 25-5 *(continued)*

```
    </xsd:documentation>
  </xsd:annotation>

  <xsd:import namespace="http://www.w3.org/1999/xhtml"
              schemaLocation="xhtml1.1.xsd"/>

  <xsd:complexType name="EventType">
    <xsd:annotation>
      <xsd:documentation>
        The EventType describes occurrences at a certain
        time and place, though the exact time and place may
        not be known for certain. Events include marriages,
        births, deaths, baptisms, and burials.
      </xsd:documentation>
    </xsd:annotation>
    <xsd:sequence>
      <xsd:element name="REFERENCE" type="ReferenceType"
                   minOccurs="0" maxOccurs="unbounded"/>
      <xsd:element name="PLACE" type="xsd:string"
                   minOccurs="0"/>
      <xsd:element name="DATE"  type="xsd:string"
                   minOccurs="0"/>
    </xsd:sequence>
  </xsd:complexType>

  <xsd:complexType name="PersonRefType">
    <xsd:annotation>
      <xsd:documentation>
       The PersonRefType contains a pointer to a person
       encoded in a PERSON element somewhere in this document.
       The pointer is the ID of the PERSON pointed to.
      </xsd:documentation>
    </xsd:annotation>
    <xsd:attribute name="PERSON" type="xsd:NMTOKEN"/>
  </xsd:complexType>

  <xsd:complexType name="ReferenceType">
    <xsd:annotation>
      <xsd:documentation>
        The ReferenceType contains a pointer to a SOURCE
        element somewhere in this document. The pointer
        is the ID of the SOURCE element pointed to.
      </xsd:documentation>
    </xsd:annotation>
    <xsd:attribute name="SOURCE" type="xsd:NMTOKEN"/>
  </xsd:complexType>

  <xsd:complexType name="NoteType"
                   xmlns:html="http://www.w3.org/1999/xhtml">
    <xsd:annotation>
      <xsd:documentation>
```

```
        The NoteType is used for NOTE elements that contain
        mostly narrative text discussing whatever seems
        interesting about or relevant to a particular element.
        The contents of the note are marked up in XHTML Basic.
        (http://www.w3.org/TR/xhtml-basic)
      </xsd:documentation>
    </xsd:annotation>
    <xsd:sequence>
      <xsd:element name="REFERENCE" type="ReferenceType"
                   minOccurs="0" />
      <xsd:element ref="html:body"/>
    </xsd:sequence>
  </xsd:complexType>

  <xsd:complexType name="PersonType">
    <xsd:annotation>
      <xsd:documentation>
        The PersonType is used for PERSON elements. It
        describes one unique individual, with a name,
        a birthday, and so on. However, some or all of the
        information about this individual may be unknown
        and hence omitted.
      </xsd:documentation>
    </xsd:annotation>
    <xsd:choice minOccurs="0" maxOccurs="unbounded">
      <xsd:element name="NAME">
        <xsd:complexType>
          <xsd:sequence>
            <xsd:element name="REFERENCE" type="ReferenceType"
                         minOccurs="0" maxOccurs="unbounded"/>
            <xsd:element name="GIVEN"     type="xsd:string"
                         minOccurs="0" />
            <xsd:element name="SURNAME"   type="xsd:string"
                         minOccurs="0" />
          </xsd:sequence>
        </xsd:complexType>
      </xsd:element>
      <xsd:element name="REFERENCE" type="ReferenceType"/>
      <xsd:element name="BIRTH"     type="EventType"/>
      <xsd:element name="DEATH"     type="EventType"/>
      <xsd:element name="BURIAL"    type="EventType"/>
      <xsd:element name="BAPTISM"   type="EventType"/>
      <xsd:element name="NOTE"      type="NoteType"/>
      <xsd:element name="SPOUSE"    type="PersonRefType"/>
      <xsd:element name="FATHER"    type="PersonRefType"/>
      <xsd:element name="MOTHER"    type="PersonRefType"/>
    </xsd:choice>
    <xsd:attribute name="ID"  type="xsd:ID" use="required"/>
    <xsd:attribute name="SEX">
      <xsd:simpleType>
        <xsd:restriction base="xsd:string">
          <xsd:enumeration value="M"/>
```

Continued

Listing 25-5 *(continued)*

```
          <xsd:enumeration value="F"/>
        </xsd:restriction>
      </xsd:simpleType>
    </xsd:attribute>
  </xsd:complexType>

  <xsd:element name="PERSON" type="PersonType">
    <xsd:annotation>
      <xsd:documentation>
        PERSON elements may be used as the root element
        of a document. No other element declared in this
        schema may be so used.
      </xsd:documentation>
    </xsd:annotation>
  </xsd:element>

</xsd:schema>
```

Here I've used mostly `xsd:annotation` elements to describe what's happening. You could also use XML comments. Generally, I prefer annotations for larger blocks of text that describe an entire type or schema, whereas I use comments for smaller notes about individual lines of code or something below the level of an entire schema or top-level element. Listing 25-5 does this when explaining about the values of a particular enumeration that M represents male and F represents female.

Using `xsd:annotation` elements also makes it easier to automatically generate documentation for a schema using XSLT or other XML tools. All the processor needs to do is extract the contents of all the `xsd:documentation` elements. Although here I've only placed plain text in those elements, they are allowed to contain any well-formed markup. For example, each `xsd:documentation` element could contain one or more complete XHTML documents or parts of a whole document that would be assembled automatically when the documentation was desired.

Families

Now that you know what a person looks like, the next step is to design a family. Let's begin with a sample family XML document, as shown in Listing 25-6.

Listing 25-6: An XML Document for Samuel English Anderson's Family

```
<?xml version="1.0" standalone="no"?>
<FAMILY ID="f25"
        xmlns="http://ns.cafeconleche.org/genealogy/">
  <HUSBAND PERSON="p37"/>
  <WIFE    PERSON="p1099"/>
  <CHILD   PERSON="p23"/>
  <CHILD   PERSON="p36"/>
  <CHILD   PERSON="p1033"/>
  <CHILD   PERSON="p1034"/>
  <MARRIAGE>
    <PLACE>Cincinnati, OH</PLACE>
    <DATE>15 Jul 1892</DATE>
  </MARRIAGE>
</FAMILY>
```

All that's needed here are references to the members of the family, not the actual family members themselves. The reference `PERSON` IDs are again provided from the database where this information is stored. Their exact values aren't important as long as they're reliably unique and stable.

The family DTD

Now that you've got a sample family, you have to prepare the DTD for all families, similar to the one shown in Listing 25-7. Don't forget to include items that are needed for some families — even if not for this example — such as a divorce. A parameter entity reference will pull in the declarations from the person DTD of Listing 25-3. You'll need this to define the `%personref;` and `%event;` entity references.

Listing 25-7: family.dtd: A DTD That Describes a Family

```
<!-- ..................................................... -->
<!-- Genealogy Family DTD  ............................... -->
<!-- file: family.dtd

     This DTD describes a FAMILY element intended for use
     in family tree documents. It was developed as an example
     for Chapter 25 of the XML Bible, 3rd Edition, by
     Elliotte Rusty Harold (elharo@metalab.unc.edu)
     Published by Wiley 2004. ISBN 0-7645-4986-3.
```

Continued

Listing 25-7 *(continued)*

```
     This DTD is placed in the public domain. Please
     feel free to use it or adapt it in any way you like.

     This DTD is identified by the PUBLIC and SYSTEM
     identifiers:

     PUBLIC "-//ERH//Genealogy Family DTD 1.0//EN"
     SYSTEM "family.dtd"

     All the elements declared in this DTD are in the
     http://ns.cafeconleche.org/genealogy/ namespace.
     No prefix is used. The attributes are in no namespace.

     It is not a formal standard, and has not been considered
     or approved by any standards body.

     ...................................................... -->

<!-- FAMILY is the root element of documents that use this
     DTD. However, it is more intended to be used as a part
     of larger XML applications which would contain multiple
     FAMILY elements in a single document. -->

<!-- The person DTD defines the %personref; and %event;
     parameter entity references used here -->

<!ENTITY % person SYSTEM "person.dtd">
%person;

<!-- A FAMILY can consist of as little as one person  -->
<!ELEMENT FAMILY (REFERENCE*, HUSBAND?, WIFE?, CHILD*,
                  MARRIAGE*, DIVORCE*, NOTE*)>
<!ATTLIST FAMILY ID ID #REQUIRED>

<!-- HUSBAND and WIFE are used here for legacy reasons.
     They should not be taken to imply anything about
     marital state of the parties.  -->
<!-- HUSBAND, WIFE, and CHILD are all EMPTY elements that
     point to a PERSON element by matching its ID.  -->
<!ELEMENT  HUSBAND  EMPTY>
<!ATTLIST  HUSBAND  %personref;>
<!ELEMENT  WIFE     EMPTY>
<!ATTLIST  WIFE     %personref;>
<!ELEMENT  CHILD    EMPTY>
<!ATTLIST  CHILD    %personref;>
<!ELEMENT  DIVORCE  %event;>
<!ELEMENT  MARRIAGE %event;>
```

I'm assuming no more than one HUSBAND or WIFE per FAMILY element. This is a fairly standard assumption in genealogy, even in cultures where plural marriages are common, because it helps to keep the children sorted out. When you are documenting genealogy in a polygamous society, the same HUSBAND may appear in multiple FAMILY elements. When you are documenting genealogy in a polyandrous society, the same WIFE may appear in multiple FAMILY elements. Aside from overlapping dates, this is essentially the same procedure that's followed when documenting serial marriages. Of course, there's nothing in the DTD that actually requires people to be married in order to have children, any more than there's anything in biology that requires it.

Overall, this scheme is very flexible, much more so than if a FAMILY element had to contain individual PERSON elements rather than merely pointers to them. That would almost certainly require duplication of data across many different elements and files. The only thing this DTD doesn't handle well are same-sex marriages, and that could easily be fixed by changing the FAMILY declaration to the following:

```
<!ELEMENT FAMILY (((HUSBAND, WIFE) | (HUSBAND, HUSBAND?)
                | (WIFE, WIFE?)), MARRIAGE*, DIVORCE*, CHILD*)>
```

Allowing multiple marriages and divorces in a single family may seem a little strange, but it does happen. My mother-in-law married and divorced my father-in-law three separate times. Remarriages to the same person aren't common, but they do happen.

The Family Schema

The schema for families is not much more complicated than the DTD. It declares a top-level FAMILY element with a family type. All the other types defined here can be anonymous because they only appear inside FAMILY elements. There's no reason to pollute the type space with extraneous definitions. Keeping everything as local as possible is a standard principle of good design. Listing 25-8 demonstrates.

Listing 25-8: family.xsd: A Schema That Describes a Family

```
<?xml version="1.0"?>
<xsd:schema xmlns:xsd="http://www.w3.org/2001/XMLSchema"
  xmlns="http://ns.cafeconleche.org/genealogy/"
  targetNamespace="http://ns.cafeconleche.org/genealogy/"
  elementFormDefault="qualified"
  attributeFormDefault="unqualified"
>

  <xsd:annotation>
    <xsd:documentation>
```

Continued

Listing 25-8 *(continued)*

```
    This schema describes a FAMILY element intended for use
    in family tree documents. It was developed as an example
    for Chapter 25 of the XML Bible, 3rd Edition, by
    Elliotte Rusty Harold (elharo@metalab.unc.edu)
    Published by Wiley 2004. ISBN 0-7645-4986-3.

    This schema is placed in the public domain. Please
    feel free to use it or adapt it in any way you like.
  </xsd:documentation>
</xsd:annotation>

<xsd:include schemaLocation="person.xsd"/>

<xsd:complexType name="FamilyType">
  <xsd:annotation>
    <xsd:documentation>
      The FamilyType is used exclusively for FAMILY
      elements. Each such element can contains one father
      (represented by a HUSBAND element for legacy reasons,
      although no marriage is implied), one mother
      (represented by a WIFE element for legacy reasons,
      although no marriage is implied), and any number of
      children represented by CHILD elements. All of these
      elements reference PERSON elements elsewhere in the
      document and any or all of them may be omitted.

      Family membership is not exclusive. A single person
      may be a member of multiple families.
    </xsd:documentation>
  </xsd:annotation>
  <xsd:sequence>
    <xsd:element name="REFERENCE" type="ReferenceType"
                 minOccurs="0" maxOccurs="unbounded"/>
    <xsd:element name="HUSBAND" type="PersonRefType"
                 minOccurs="0" />
    <xsd:element name="WIFE"    type="PersonRefType"
                 minOccurs="0" />
    <xsd:element name="CHILD"   type="PersonRefType"
                 minOccurs="0"  maxOccurs="unbounded"/>
    <xsd:element name="MARRIAGE" type="EventType"
                 minOccurs="0"  maxOccurs="unbounded"/>
    <xsd:element name="DIVORCE" type="EventType"
                 minOccurs="0"  maxOccurs="unbounded"/>
    <xsd:element name="NOTE"   type="NoteType"
                 minOccurs="0" maxOccurs="unbounded"/>
  </xsd:sequence>
  <xsd:attribute name="ID"  xsd:type="ID" use="required"/>
</xsd:complexType>
```

```
  <xsd:element name="FAMILY" type="FamilyType"/>

</xsd:schema>
```

This schema uses the PersonRefType, EventType, and NoteType types defined in Listing 25-4. To get access to them, simply include person.xsd using xsd:include. This element differs from xsd:import in that the included schema covers the same namespace. If you're using two different namespaces (such as HTML), use xsd:import; if you're using the same namespace, use xsd:include.

Sources

The third and final top-level element is SOURCE. I'm using a watered-down SOURCE element with little internal structure. However, storing the DTD in a separate file makes it easy to add structure to it later. Some typical SOURCE elements look like this:

```
<SOURCE ID="s218">Hamp Hoskins interview, 11-38-1996</SOURCE>
<SOURCE ID="s29">English-Demint Anderson Bible</SOURCE>
<SOURCE ID="s43">Anderson Bible</SOURCE>
<SOURCE ID="s43">
  Letter from R. Foster Adams to Beth Anderson, 1972
</SOURCE>
<SOURCE ID="s66">
  Collin's History of Kentucky, Volume II, p. 325, 1840, 1875
</SOURCE>
```

A SOURCE element has a lot of internal structure. Work is ongoing in several places to produce a generic DTD for bibliographic information with elements for articles, authors, pages, publication dates, and more. However, this is quite a complex topic when considered in its full generality; and, as previously mentioned, it doesn't work quite the same for genealogy as it does for most fields. The individual copy of a family Bible or newspaper clipping with handwritten annotations may be more significant than the more generic, standard author, title, publisher data used in most bibliographies.

Because developing an XML application for bibliographies could easily be more than a chapter of its own and is a task best left to experts in the field, I will satisfy myself with making the SOURCE element contain only character data. It will also have an ID attribute in the form s1, s2, s3, and so forth, so that each source can be referred to by different elements. Listing 25-9 shows the extremely simple DTD for sources.

Listing 25-9: source.dtd: A Simple SOURCE DTD

```
<!-- ..................................................... -->
<!-- Genealogy Source DTD  ................................ -->
<!-- file: source.dtd

     This DTD describes a SOURCE element intended for use
     in family tree documents. It was developed as an example
     for Chapter 25 of the XML Bible, 3rd Edition, by
     Elliotte Rusty Harold (elharo@metalab.unc.edu)
     Published by Wiley 2004. ISBN 0-7645-4986-3.

     This schema is placed in the public domain. Please
     feel free to use it or adapt it in any way you like.

     This DTD is identified by the PUBLIC and SYSTEM
     identifiers:

     PUBLIC "-//ERH//Genealogy Source DTD 1.0//EN"
     SYSTEM "source.dtd"

     All the elements declared in this DTD are in the
     http://ns.cafeconleche.org/genealogy/ namespace.
     No prefix is used. The attributes are in no namespace.

     It is not a formal standard, and has not been considered
     or approved by any standards body.

     ..................................................... -->

<!-- SOURCE is the root element of documents that use this
     DTD. However, it is more intended to be used as a part
     of larger XML applications which would contain multiple
     SOURCE elements in a single document. -->

<!-- The character data of the DTD contains a bibliographic
     citation for the source -->
<!ELEMENT  SOURCE  (#PCDATA)>
<!ATTLIST  SOURCE ID ID #REQUIRED>
```

Listing 25-10 shows the almost equally simple source schema. This is an example of a schema that only defines types. It does not actually declare any elements and cannot be used on its own to validate a document. However, it can be included in another schema that does declare elements of type `SourceType`.

Listing 25-10: source.xsd: A Simple SOURCE Schema

```
<?xml version="1.0"?>
<xsd:schema xmlns:xsd="http://www.w3.org/2001/XMLSchema"
  xmlns="http://ns.cafeconleche.org/genealogy/"
  targetNamespace="http://ns.cafeconleche.org/genealogy/"
  elementFormDefault="qualified"
  attributeFormDefault="unqualified"
>

  <xsd:annotation>
    <xsd:documentation>
      This schema describes a REFERENCE element intended for
      use in family tree documents. It was developed as an
      example for Chapter 25 of the XML Bible, 3rd Edition, by
      Elliotte Rusty Harold (elharo@metalab.unc.edu)
      Published by Wiley 2004. ISBN 0-7645-4986-3.

      This schema is placed in the public domain. Please
      feel free to use it or adapt it in any way you like.
    </xsd:documentation>
  </xsd:annotation>

  <xsd:complexType name="SourceType">
    <xsd:annotation>
      <xsd:documentation>
        The SourceType is used exclusively for REFERENCE
        elements. Each such element has a unique ID attribute
        by which it can be referred to, and PCDATA content
        identifying the source of the information; e.g.,
        a document, an interview, personal recollection, etc.
      </xsd:documentation>
    </xsd:annotation>
    <xsd:simpleContent>
      <xsd:extension base="xsd:string">
       <xsd:attribute name="ID" type="xsd:ID" use="required"/>
      </xsd:extension>
    </xsd:simpleContent>
  </xsd:complexType>

  <xsd:element name="SOURCE" type="SourceType"/>

</xsd:schema>
```

The Family Tree

It's now possible to combine the various people, families, and sources into a single grouping that includes everyone. I'll call the root element of this document FAMILY_TREE. It will include PERSON, FAMILY, and SOURCE elements in no particular order. Listing 25-11 shows a complete family tree document that includes 11 people, 3 families, and 7 sources. The necessary document type declaration and schema location attributes have been attached in the right places.

Listing 25-11: An XML Document of a Complete Family Tree

```
<?xml version="1.0" standalone="no"?>
<!DOCTYPE FAMILY_TREE SYSTEM "familytree.dtd">
<FAMILY_TREE xmlns="http://ns.cafeconleche.org/genealogy/"
   xmlns:xsi="http://www.w3.org/2001/XMLSchema-instance"
   xsi:schemaLocation =
       "http://ns.cafeconleche.org/genealogy/ family_tree.xsd
        http://www.w3.org/1999/xhtml xhtml1.1.xsd">

  <PERSON ID="p23" SEX="M">
    <REFERENCE SOURCE="s44"/>
    <FATHER PERSON="p37"/>
    <MOTHER PERSON="p1099"/>
    <NAME>
      <GIVEN>Judson McDaniel</GIVEN>
      <SURNAME>Anderson</SURNAME>
    </NAME>
    <BIRTH>
      <PLACE>Montgomery County, KY, 1893</PLACE>
      <DATE>19 Jul 1894</DATE>
    </BIRTH>
    <DEATH>
      <PLACE>Mt. Sterling, KY</PLACE>
      <DATE>27 Apr 1941</DATE>
    </DEATH>
    <NOTE>
      <body xmlns="http://www.w3.org/1999/xhtml">
      <p>Agriculture College in Iowa</p>
      <p>Farmer</p>
      <p>32nd degree Mason</p>
      <p>
        He shot himself in the pond in the back of Sideview
        when he found that he was terminally ill. It has also
        been claimed that he was having money and wife
        troubles. (He and Zelda did not get along and he was
        embarrassed to have married her.) It has further been
        claimed that this was part of the Anderson family
        curse.
      </p>
    </body>
```

```
  </NOTE>
</PERSON>

<PERSON ID="p36" SEX="F">
  <REFERENCE SOURCE="s43"/>
  <FATHER PERSON="p37"/>
  <MOTHER PERSON="p1099"/>
  <NAME>
    <GIVEN>Mary English</GIVEN>
    <SURNAME>Anderson</SURNAME>
  </NAME>
  <BIRTH>
    <PLACE>August 4, 1902?, Sideview, KY</PLACE>
    <DATE>8 Apr 1902</DATE>
  </BIRTH>
  <DEATH>
    <PLACE>Mt. Sterling, KY</PLACE>
    <DATE>19 Dec 1972</DATE>
  </DEATH>
</PERSON>

<PERSON ID="p37" SEX="M">
  <REFERENCE SOURCE="s29"/>
  <REFERENCE SOURCE="s43"/>
  <FATHER PERSON="p1035"/>
  <MOTHER PERSON="p1098"/>
  <NAME>
    <GIVEN>Samuel English</GIVEN>
    <SURNAME>Anderson</SURNAME>
  </NAME>
  <BIRTH>
    <PLACE>Sideview</PLACE>
    <DATE>25 Aug 1871</DATE>
  </BIRTH>
  <DEATH>
    <PLACE>Mt. Sterling, KY</PLACE>
    <DATE>10 Nov 1919</DATE>
  </DEATH>
  <NOTE>
    <body xmlns="http://www.w3.org/1999/xhtml">
      <p>
        Samuel English Anderson was known in Montgomery
        County for his red hair and the temper that went
        with it. He did once <strong>kill a man</strong>,
        but the court found that it was in self-defense.
      </p>

      <p>
        He was shot by a farm worker whom he had
        fired the day before for smoking in a tobacco barn.
        Hamp says this may have been self-defense, because
```

Continued

Listing 25-11 *(continued)*

```
            He threatened to kill the workers for smoking in the
            barn. Hamp also says old-time rumors say they mashed
            his head with a fence post. Beth heard he was cut to
            death with machetes in the field, but Hamp says they
            wouldn't be cutting tobacco in November, only
            stripping it in the barn.
          </p>
        </body>
      </NOTE>

    </PERSON>

    <PERSON ID="p1033" SEX="M">
      <REFERENCE SOURCE="s43"/>
      <FATHER PERSON="p37"/>
      <MOTHER PERSON="p1099"/>
      <NAME>
        <GIVEN>Thomas Corwin</GIVEN>
        <SURNAME>Anderson</SURNAME>
      </NAME>
      <BIRTH>
        <DATE>16 Jan 1898</DATE>
      </BIRTH>
      <DEATH>
        <PLACE>Probably Australia</PLACE>
      </DEATH>
      <NOTE>
        <body xmlns="http://www.w3.org/1999/xhtml">
           <p>
           Corwin fought with his father and then left home.
           His last letter was from Australia.
           </p>
         </body>
       </NOTE>
    </PERSON>

    <PERSON ID="p1034" SEX="M">
      <REFERENCE SOURCE="s43"/>
       <FATHER PERSON="p37"/>
      <MOTHER PERSON="p1099"/>
      <NAME>
        <GIVEN>Rodger French</GIVEN>
        <SURNAME>Anderson</SURNAME>
      </NAME>
      <BIRTH>
        <DATE>26 Nov 1899</DATE>
      </BIRTH>
      <DEATH>
        <PLACE>Birmingham, AL</PLACE>
      </DEATH>
      <NOTE>
```

```
    <body xmlns="http://www.w3.org/1999/xhtml">
      <p>
      Killed when the car he was driving hit a pig in the
      road. Despite the many suicides in the family, this is
      the only known sowicide.
      </p>
    </body>
  </NOTE>
</PERSON>

<PERSON ID="p1035" SEX="M">
  <NAME>
    <GIVEN>Thomas Corwin</GIVEN>
    <SURNAME>Anderson</SURNAME>
  </NAME>
  <BIRTH>
    <DATE>24 Aug 1845</DATE>
  </BIRTH>
  <DEATH>
    <PLACE>Mt. Sterling, KY</PLACE>
    <DATE>18 Sep 1889</DATE>
  </DEATH>
  <NOTE>
    <body xmlns="http://www.w3.org/1999/xhtml">
      <p>Yale 1869 (did not graduate)</p>
      <p>Breeder of short horn cattle</p>
      <p>He was named after an Ohio senator. The name Corwin
        is from the Latin <span xml:lang="la">corvinus</span>
        which means raven and is akin
        to <em>corbin</em>/<em>corbet</em>.
       In old French it was <span xml:lang="la">cord</span>
       and in Middle English <em>Corse</em> which meant
       raven or cow.
      </p>
      <p>Attended Annapolis for one year, possibly to
        avoid service in the Civil War.</p>
      <p>
        He farmed the old Mitchell farm
        and became known as a leading short horn breeder.
        He suffered from asthma and wanted to move to
        Colorado in 1876 to avoid the Kentucky weather, but
        he didn't.
      </p>
     </body>
  </NOTE>
</PERSON>

<PERSON ID="p1098" SEX="F">
  <REFERENCE SOURCE="s29"/>
  <NAME>
    <GIVEN>LeAnah (Lee Anna, Annie) DeMint</GIVEN>
    <SURNAME>English</SURNAME>
```

Continued

Listing 25-11 *(continued)*

```
    </NAME>
    <BIRTH>
      <PLACE>Louisville, KY</PLACE>
      <DATE>1 Mar 1843</DATE>
    </BIRTH>
    <DEATH>
      <REFERENCE SOURCE="s16"/>
      <PLACE>acute Bright's disease, 504 E. Broadway</PLACE>
      <DATE>31 Oct 1898</DATE>
    </DEATH>
    <NOTE>
      <body xmlns="http://www.w3.org/1999/xhtml">
        <p>Writer (pseudonymously) for Louisville Herald</p>
        <p>Ann or Annie was from Louisville. She wrote under
           an assumed name for the Louisville Herald.</p>
      </body>
    </NOTE>
  </PERSON>

  <PERSON ID="p1099" SEX="F">
    <REFERENCE SOURCE="s39"/>
    <FATHER PERSON="p1100"/>
    <MOTHER PERSON="p1101"/>
    <NAME>
      <GIVEN>Cora Rucker (Blevins?)</GIVEN>
      <SURNAME>McDaniel</SURNAME>
    </NAME>
    <BIRTH>
      <DATE>1 Aug 1873</DATE>
    </BIRTH>
    <DEATH>
      <REFERENCE SOURCE="s41"/>
      <REFERENCE SOURCE="s60"/>
      <PLACE>Sideview, bronchial trouble TB</PLACE>
      <DATE>21 Jul 1909</DATE>
    </DEATH>
    <NOTE>
      <body xmlns="http://www.w3.org/1999/xhtml">
        <p>She was engaged to General Hood of the Confederacy,
        but she was seeing Mr. Anderson on the side. A servant
        was posted to keep Mr. Anderson away. However the girl
        fell asleep, and Cora eloped with Mr. Anderson.</p>
       </body>
    </NOTE>
  </PERSON>

  <PERSON ID="p1100" SEX="M">
    <NAME>
      <GIVEN>Judson</GIVEN>
      <SURNAME>McDaniel</SURNAME>
    </NAME>
```

```
  <BIRTH>
    <DATE>21 Feb 1834</DATE>
  </BIRTH>
  <DEATH>
    <DATE>9 Dec 1905</DATE>
  </DEATH>
</PERSON>

<PERSON ID="p1101" SEX="F">
  <NAME>
    <GIVEN>Mary E.</GIVEN>
    <SURNAME>Blevins</SURNAME>
  </NAME>
  <BIRTH>
    <DATE>1847</DATE>
  </BIRTH>
  <DEATH>
    <DATE>1886</DATE>
  </DEATH>
  <BURIAL>
    <PLACE>Machpelah Cemetery, Mt. Sterling KY</PLACE>
  </BURIAL>
</PERSON>

<PERSON ID="p1102" SEX="M">
  <REFERENCE SOURCE="s29"/>
  <NAME>
    <GIVEN>John Jay (Robin Adair )</GIVEN>
    <SURNAME>Anderson</SURNAME>
  </NAME>
  <BIRTH>
    <REFERENCE SOURCE="s43"/>
    <PLACE>Sideview</PLACE>
    <DATE>13 May 1873</DATE>
  </BIRTH>
  <DEATH>
    <DATE>18 Sep 1889</DATE>
  </DEATH>
  <NOTE>
    <body xmlns="http://www.w3.org/1999/xhtml">
      <p>
        Died of flux. Rumored to have been killed by his
        brother.
      </p>
    </body>
  </NOTE>
</PERSON>

<FAMILY ID="f25">
  <HUSBAND PERSON="p37"/>
  <WIFE PERSON="p1099"/>
  <CHILD PERSON="p23"/>
```

Continued

Listing 25-11 *(continued)*

```
    <CHILD PERSON="p36"/>
    <CHILD PERSON="p1033"/>
    <CHILD PERSON="p1034"/>
  </FAMILY>

  <FAMILY ID="f732">
    <HUSBAND PERSON="p1035"/>
    <WIFE PERSON="p1098"/>
    <CHILD PERSON="p1102"/>
    <CHILD PERSON="p37"/>
  </FAMILY>

  <FAMILY ID="f779">
    <HUSBAND PERSON="p1102"/>
  </FAMILY>

  <SOURCE ID="s16">newspaper death notice in purse</SOURCE>
  <SOURCE ID="s29">English-Demint Anderson Bible</SOURCE>
  <SOURCE ID="s39">
    Judson McDaniel &amp; Mary E. Blevins Bible
  </SOURCE>
  <SOURCE ID="s41">
    Cora McDaniel obituary, clipping from unknown newspaper
  </SOURCE>
  <SOURCE ID="s43">Anderson Bible</SOURCE>
  <SOURCE ID="s44">
    A Sesquicentennial History of Kentucky
    Frederik A. Wallis &amp; Hambleon Tapp, 1945,
    The Historical Record Association, Hopkinsville, KY
  </SOURCE>
  <SOURCE ID="s60">
    Interview with Ann Sandusky, May 1996
  </SOURCE>

</FAMILY_TREE>
```

The Family Tree DTD

FAMILY_TREE is the one new element in Listing 25-11. It can contain any number of PERSON, FAMILY, and SOURCE elements in any order. This is indicated with a choice:

```
<!ELEMENT FAMILY_TREE (PERSON | FAMILY | SOURCE)*>
```

It's not necessary to redeclare the PERSON, FAMILY, and SOURCE elements and their children. Instead, these can be imported by importing the family and source DTDs with external parameter entity references. The family DTD then imports the person DTD:

```
<!ENTITY % family SYSTEM "family.dtd">
%family;
<!ENTITY % source SYSTEM "source.dtd">
%source;
```

One thing you want to do at this point is switch from using NMTOKEN types for spouses, parents, and references to actual ID types. This is because a FAMILY element that's part of a FAMILY_TREE should include all necessary PERSON elements. You can do that by overriding the personref and sourceref parameter entity declarations in the DTD for the family tree:

```
<!ENTITY % personref "PERSON IDREF #REQUIRED">
<!ENTITY % sourceref "SOURCE IDREF #REQUIRED">
```

That's all you need. Everything else is contained in the imported person and family DTDs. Listing 25-12 shows the family tree DTD.

Listing 25-12: **family_tree.dtd: The Family Tree DTD**

```
<!-- ..................................................... -->
<!-- Genealogy Family Tree DTD  ......................... -->
<!-- file: family_tree.dtd

     This DTD describes a FAMILY_TREE element intended for use
     as the root element in family tree documents. It was
     developed as an example for Chapter 25 of the
     XML Bible, 3rd Edition,
     by Elliotte Rusty Harold (elharo@metalab.unc.edu)
     Published by Wiley 2004. ISBN 0-7645-4986-3.

     This DTD is placed in the public domain. Please
     feel free to use it or adapt it in any way you like.

     This DTD is identified by the PUBLIC and SYSTEM
     identifiers:

     PUBLIC "-//ERH//Genealogy Family Tree DTD 1.0//EN"
     SYSTEM "family_tree.dtd"

     All the elements declared in this DTD are in the
     http://ns.cafeconleche.org/genealogy/ namespace.
     No prefix is used. The attributes are in no namespace.
```

Continued

Listing 25-12 *(continued)*

```
     It is not a formal standard, and has not been considered
     or approved by any standards body.

     ............................................................. -->

<!-- Predefine the %personref; and %sourceref; parameter
     entity references so that they'll have type IDREF instead
     of NMTOKEN -->
<!ENTITY % personref "PERSON IDREF #REQUIRED">
<!ENTITY % sourceref "SOURCE IDREF #REQUIRED">

<!-- Import the family and source DTDs. The family DTD imports
     the person DTD. -->
<!ENTITY % family SYSTEM "family.dtd">
%family;

<!ENTITY % source SYSTEM "source.dtd">
%source;

<!-- A family tree consists of any number of SOURCE, PERSON,
     and FAMILY elements in any order. These are all top-level
     elements that refer to each other by ID attributes
     and references. None of them contain any of the others.
-->
<!ELEMENT FAMILY_TREE (SOURCE | PERSON | FAMILY )*>
```

The family tree schema

The family tree schema is similar in general structure to the family tree DTD. It defines one new element, FAMILY_TREE, and uses most of the existing definitions of the other elements. However, now that all the FAMILY, PERSON, and SOURCE elements are in one document, it would be good to change the various reference attributes from type NMTOKEN to type IDREF. In the DTD, this was done by predefining certain parameter entity references. In the schema, use the xsd:redefine element instead. This behaves like the xsd:include element except that you can place type definitions inside xsd:redefine that override the type definitions made in the included schemas. For example, this xsd:redefine element imports most of the family schema (which itself includes the person schema) but overrides the definitions of PersonRefType and SourceRefType:

```
<xsd:redefine schemaLocation="person.xsd">
  <!-- Because all referenced persons will now be included
       in this document, we can switch the pointer
       attributes from name tokens to ID references. -->
```

```
    <xsd:complexType name="PersonRefType">
      <xsd:complexContent>
        <xsd:restriction base="PersonRefType">
          <xsd:attribute name="PERSON" type="xsd:IDREF"/>
        </xsd:restriction>
      </xsd:complexContent>
    </xsd:complexType>

    <xsd:complexType name="ReferenceType">
      <xsd:complexContent>
        <xsd:restriction base="ReferenceType">
          <xsd:attribute name="SOURCE" type="xsd:IDREF"/>
        </xsd:restriction>
      </xsd:complexContent>
    </xsd:complexType>

  </xsd:redefine>
```

Listing 25-13 shows the complete family tree schema.

Listing 25-13: **familytree.xsd: The Family Tree Schema**

```
<?xml version="1.0"?>
<xsd:schema xmlns:xsd="http://www.w3.org/2001/XMLSchema"
  xmlns="http://ns.cafeconleche.org/genealogy/"
  targetNamespace="http://ns.cafeconleche.org/genealogy/"
  elementFormDefault="qualified"
  attributeFormDefault="unqualified"
>

  <xsd:annotation>
    <xsd:documentation>
      This schema describes a FAMILY_TREE element intended for
      as the root element genealogy documents. It was
      developed as an example for Chapter 25 of the XML Bible,
      3rd Edition, by Elliotte Rusty Harold
      (elharo@metalab.unc.edu)
      Published by Wiley 2004. ISBN 0-7645-4986-3.

      This schema is placed in the public domain. Please
      use it or adapt it in any way you like.
    </xsd:documentation>
  </xsd:annotation>

  <xsd:include schemaLocation="source.xsd"/>

  <xsd:include schemaLocation="family.xsd"/>
```

Continued

Listing 25-13 *(continued)*

```
  <xsd:redefine schemaLocation="person.xsd">
    <!-- Because all referenced persons will now be included
         in this document, we can switch the pointer
         attributes from name tokens to ID references. -->

    <xsd:complexType name="PersonRefType">
      <xsd:complexContent>
        <xsd:restriction base="PersonRefType">
          <xsd:attribute name="PERSON" type="xsd:IDREF"/>
        </xsd:restriction>
      </xsd:complexContent>
    </xsd:complexType>

    <xsd:complexType name="ReferenceType">
      <xsd:complexContent>
        <xsd:restriction base="ReferenceType">
          <xsd:attribute name="SOURCE" type="xsd:IDREF"/>
        </xsd:restriction>
      </xsd:complexContent>
    </xsd:complexType>

  </xsd:redefine>

  <xsd:complexType name="FamilyTreeType">
    <xsd:choice minOccurs="0" maxOccurs="unbounded">
      <xsd:element ref="PERSON"/>
      <xsd:element ref="FAMILY"/>
      <xsd:element ref="SOURCE"/>
    </xsd:choice>
  </xsd:complexType>

  <xsd:element name="FAMILY_TREE" type="FamilyTreeType"/>

</xsd:schema>
```

Modularizing the DTDs

As written, the genealogy DTD is already partially modular. It is divided into separate files for the PERSON, FAMILY, SOURCE, and FAMILYTREE elements. It does use parameter entity references for some content models and attribute lists. It does use the DTDs for Modular XHTML and XHTML Basic. However, it's not nearly as modular as the modular XHTML DTD explored in Chapter 22.

This is not unusual at this point. Modular DTDs can be hard to read and hard to follow as compared to monolithic DTDs. When you are designing a new XML application, it's easiest to make everything explicit, at least at the start. However, after the basic application is designed, it's time to ask yourself if there are any ways in which you can restructure the DTD to make it more extensible in the future without changing what is and is not allowed now.

I'm not sure you really need that much modularity here. For one thing, in a record-like application such as this, you may well want to limit the permissible content models and attributes of elements and not allow them to be so easily modified. However, at the very least, you should allow the author to choose whether and which namespace prefix the author wants to use. To do this, you have to define the prefix and all element names as parameter entity references rather than directly. Let's begin by creating a new DTD module that does nothing but define parameter entity references for the namespace URI and prefix. Listing 25-14 demonstrates.

Listing 25-14: genealogy-namespace.mod: The Namespace DTD Module

```
<!-- ...................................................... -->
<!-- Genealogy Namespace Module  ......................... -->
<!-- file: genealogy-namespace.mod

     Copyright 2004 Elliotte Rusty Harold,
     All Rights Reserved.

     This DTD module is identified by the PUBLIC and SYSTEM
     identifiers:

    PUBLIC "-//ERH//Genealogy Namespace Parts 1.0//EN"
    SYSTEM "genealogy-namespace.mod"

    ...................................................... -->

<!-- Genealogy Namespace

     This module declares parameter entities to support
     namespace-qualified names, namespace declarations, and
     name prefixing for the genealogy application developed
     in Chapter 25 of the XML Bible.

-->

<!-- 1. Declare the parameter entity containing
        the namespace URI for the genealogy namespace: -->
```

Continued

Listing 25-14 *(continued)*

```
<!ENTITY % GENEALOGY.xmlns
"http://ns.cafeconleche.org/genealogy/" >

<!-- 2. Declare the parameter entity containing
        the default namespace prefix string to use when
        prefixing is enabled. This may be overridden. -->

<!ENTITY % SMIL.prefix  "" >

<!-- 3. Declare a %GENEALOGY.prefixed; conditional section
        keyword, used to activate namespace prefixing. The
        default is not to use prefixing. -->
<!ENTITY % GENEALOGY.prefixed "IGNORE" >

<!-- 4. Declare parameter entities containing the
        prefix used when prefixing is active, an empty
        string when it is not.
-->
<![%GENEALOGY.prefixed;[
<!ENTITY % GENEALOGY.pfx  "%GENEALOGY.prefix;:" >
]]>
<!ENTITY % GENEALOGY.pfx  "" >
```

Next, you need a DTD that declares the qualified names of all the elements in terms of these parameter entity references. Listing 25-15 is this module. The double indirection of parameter entity references for the element names is really necessary here only to prevent parsers from inserting extra white space into the middle of element names, but it does make this DTD a little more adaptable.

Listing 25-15: genealogy-qname.mod: The Namespace DTD Module

```
<!-- ...................................................... -->
<!-- Genealogy Qualified Names Module  .................. -->
<!-- file: genealogy-qname.mod

     Copyright 2004 Elliotte Rusty Harold

This DTD module is identified by the PUBLIC and SYSTEM
identifiers:
```

```
    PUBLIC "-//ERH//Genealogy Qualified Names 1.0//EN"
    SYSTEM "genealogy-qname.mod"

     ..................................................... -->

<!-- Genealogy Qualified Names

     This module declares parameter entities to support
     namespace-qualified names for the genealogy application
     developed in Chapter 25 of the XML Bible.

-->

<!-- module: person.mod -->
<!ENTITY % PERSON.qname    "%GENEALOGY.pfx;PERSON" >
<!ENTITY % REFERENCE.qname "%GENEALOGY.pfx;REFERENCE" >
<!ENTITY % BIRTH.qname     "%GENEALOGY.pfx;BIRTH" >
<!ENTITY % BAPTISM.qname   "%GENEALOGY.pfx;BAPTISM" >
<!ENTITY % DEATH.qname     "%GENEALOGY.pfx;DEATH" >
<!ENTITY % PLACE.qname     "%GENEALOGY.pfx;PLACE" >
<!ENTITY % DATE.qname      "%GENEALOGY.pfx;DATE" >
<!ENTITY % SPOUSE.qname    "%GENEALOGY.pfx;SPOUSE" >
<!ENTITY % FATHER.qname    "%GENEALOGY.pfx;FATHER" >
<!ENTITY % MOTHER.qname    "%GENEALOGY.pfx;MOTHER" >
<!ENTITY % NAME.qname      "%GENEALOGY.pfx;NAME" >
<!ENTITY % GIVEN.qname     "%GENEALOGY.pfx;GIVEN" >
<!ENTITY % SURNAME.qname   "%GENEALOGY.pfx;SURNAME" >
<!ENTITY % NOTE.qname      "%GENEALOGY.pfx;NOTE" >

<!-- module: family.mod -->
<!ENTITY % HUSBAND.qname   "%GENEALOGY.pfx;HUSBAND" >
<!ENTITY % WIFE.qname      "%GENEALOGY.pfx;WIFE" >
<!ENTITY % CHILD.qname     "%GENEALOGY.pfx;CHILD" >
<!ENTITY % DIVORCE.qname   "%GENEALOGY.pfx;DIVORCE" >
<!ENTITY % MARRIAGE.qname  "%GENEALOGY.pfx;MARRIAGE" >

<!-- module: source.mod -->
<!ENTITY % SOURCE.qname    "%GENEALOGY.pfx;SOURCE" >

<!-- module: family_tree.mod -->
<!ENTITY % FAMILY_TREE.qname "%GENEALOGY.pfx;FAMILY_TREE" >

<!-- end of genealogy-qname-1.mod -->
```

Next, you rewrite the person, source, and family DTDs to use the parameter entities defined in Listing 25-15. These DTDs are shown in Listings 25-16 through 25-19.

Listing 25-16: person.mod: The Person Module

```
<!-- ....................................................... -->
<!-- Genealogy Person DTD module ........................... -->
<!-- file: person.mod

     This DTD module describes a PERSON element intended for
     use in family tree documents. It was developed as part of
     a genealogy example in Chapter 25 of the
     XML Bible, 3rd Edition, by
     Elliotte Rusty Harold (elharo@metalab.unc.edu)
     Published by Wiley 2004. ISBN 0-7645-4986-3.

     This schema is placed in the public domain. Please
     feel free to use it or adapt it in any way you like.

     This DTD is identified by the PUBLIC and SYSTEM
     identifiers:

     PUBLIC "-//ERH//Genealogy Person Module 1.0//EN"
     SYSTEM "person.mod"

     It is not a formal standard, and has not been considered
     or approved by any standards body.

     ....................................................... -->

<!ELEMENT %PERSON.qname; ( %NAME.qname;     | %REFERENCE.qname;|
                           %BIRTH.qname;    | %DEATH.qname;  |
                           %BURIAL.qname;   | %BAPTISM.qname; |
                           %NOTE.qname;     | %FATHER.qname; |
                           %MOTHER.qname;   | %SPOUSE )* >

<!ATTLIST %PERSON.qname;
   xmlns  CDATA #FIXED "http://ns.cafeconleche.org/genealogy/"
   ID     ID    #REQUIRED>

<!ATTLIST %PERSON.qname;
   xmlns:xsi CDATA #FIXED
                   "http://www.w3.org/2001/XMLSchema-instance"
   xsi:schemaLocation CDATA #IMPLIED
>

<!--M means male, F means female -->
<!ATTLIST %PERSON.qname; SEX (M | F) #IMPLIED>

<!-- The ID number of a SOURCE element that documents
     this entry -->
<!ELEMENT  %REFERENCE.qname;  EMPTY>
<!ENTITY % sourceref "SOURCE NMTOKEN #REQUIRED">
<!ATTLIST  %REFERENCE.qname; %sourceref;>
```

```
<!-- Events are occurrences at a certain
     time and place, though the exact time and place may
     not be known for certain. Events include marriages,
     births, deaths, baptisms, and burials.  -->
<!ENTITY % event   "(%REFERENCE.qname;*, %PLACE.qname;?,
%DATE.qname;?)">
<!ELEMENT  %BIRTH.qname;   %event;>
<!ELEMENT  %BAPTISM.qname; %event;>
<!ELEMENT  %DEATH.qname;   %event;>
<!ELEMENT  %BURIAL.qname;  %event;>

<!ELEMENT  %PLACE.qname;   (#PCDATA)>
<!ELEMENT  %DATE.qname;    (#PCDATA)>

<!-- A person reference is a pointer to another person
     encoded in a PERSON element. The pointer is the ID
     of the PERSON pointed to. -->
<!ENTITY % personref "PERSON NMTOKEN #REQUIRED">
<!ELEMENT  %SPOUSE.qname;  EMPTY>
<!ATTLIST  %SPOUSE.qname;  %personref;>
<!ELEMENT  %FATHER.qname;  EMPTY>
<!ATTLIST  %FATHER.qname;  %personref;>
<!ELEMENT  %MOTHER.qname;  EMPTY>
<!ATTLIST  %MOTHER.qname;  %personref;>

<!-- Middle names should be encoded as part of the
     given name; e.g.,
     <NAME>
       <GIVEN>Elliotte Rusty</GIVEN>
       <SURNAME>Harold</SURNAME>
     </NAME>
  -->
<!ELEMENT  %NAME.qname;    (%GIVEN.qname;?, %SURNAME.qname;?)>
<!ELEMENT  %GIVEN.qname;   (#PCDATA)>
<!ELEMENT  %SURNAME.qname; (#PCDATA)>

<!ELEMENT  NOTE   (REFERENCE*, body)>
```

Listing 25-17: **family.mod: The Family Module**

```
<!-- ...................................................... -->
<!-- Genealogy Family DTD  ............................... -->
<!-- file: family.mod

     This DTD module describes a FAMILY element intended for
     use in family tree documents. It was developed as an
     example for Chapter 25 of the XML Bible, 3rd Edition, by
```

Continued

Listing 25-17 *(continued)*

```
     Elliotte Rusty Harold (elharo@metalab.unc.edu)
     Published by Wiley 2004. ISBN 0-7645-4986-3.

     This DTD is placed in the public domain. Please
     feel free to use it or adapt it in any way you like.

     This DTD is identified by the PUBLIC and SYSTEM
     identifiers:

     PUBLIC "-//ERH//Genealogy Family Module 1.0//EN"
     SYSTEM "family.mod"

     All the elements declared in this DTD are in the
     http://ns.cafeconleche.org/genealogy/ namespace.
     No prefix is used. The attributes are in no namespace.

     It is not a formal standard, and has not been considered
     or approved by any standards body.

     ..................................................... -->

<!-- FAMILY is the root element of documents that use this
     DTD. However, it is more intended to be used as a part
     of larger XML applications which would contain multiple
     FAMILY elements in a single document. -->

<!-- A FAMILY can consist of as little as one person  -->
<!ELEMENT %FAMILY.qname; (%REFERENCE.qname;*, %HUSBAND.qname;?,
   %WIFE.qname;?, %CHILD.qname;*, MARRIAGE.qname;*,
   %DIVORCE.qname;*, %NOTE.qname;*)>
<!ATTLIST  %FAMILY.qname; ID ID #REQUIRED>

<!-- HUSBAND and WIFE are used here for legacy reasons.
     They should not be taken to imply anything about
     marital state of the parties.  -->
<!-- HUSBAND, WIFE, and CHILD are all EMPTY elements that
     point to a PERSON element by matching its ID.  -->
<!ELEMENT  %HUSBAND.qname;  EMPTY>
<!ATTLIST  %HUSBAND.qname;  %personref;>
<!ELEMENT  %WIFE.qname;     EMPTY>
<!ATTLIST  %WIFE.qname;     %personref;>
<!ELEMENT  %CHILD.qname;    EMPTY>
<!ATTLIST  %CHILD.qname;    %personref;>
<!ELEMENT  %DIVORCE.qname;  %event;>
<!ELEMENT  %MARRIAGE.qname; %event;>
```

Listing 25-18: source.mod: The Source Module

```
<!-- ....................................................... -->
<!-- Genealogy Source Module  ............................... -->
<!-- file: source.mod

     This DTD describes a SOURCE element intended for use
     in family tree documents. It was developed as an example
     for Chapter 25 of the XML Bible, 3rd Edition, by
     Elliotte Rusty Harold (elharo@metalab.unc.edu)
     Published by Wiley 2004. ISBN 0-7645-4986-3.

     This schema is placed in the public domain. Please
     feel free to use it or adapt it in any way you like.

     This DTD is identified by the PUBLIC and SYSTEM
     identifiers:

     PUBLIC "-//ERH//Genealogy Source Module 1.0//EN"
     SYSTEM "source.mod"

     It is not a formal standard, and has not been considered
     or approved by any standards body.

     ....................................................... -->

<!-- SOURCE is the root element of documents that use this
     DTD. However, it is more intended to be used as a part
     of larger XML applications, which would contain multiple
     SOURCE elements in a single document. -->

<!-- The character data of the DTD contains a bibliographic
     citation for the source -->
<!ELEMENT  %SOURCE.qname; (#PCDATA)>
<!ATTLIST  %SOURCE.qname; ID ID #REQUIRED>
```

Listing 25-19: family_tree.mod: The Family Tree Module

```
<!-- ....................................................... -->
<!-- Genealogy Family Tree Module  .......................... -->
<!-- file: family_tree.mod

     This DTD describes a FAMILY_TREE element intended for use
     as the root element in family tree documents. It was
     developed as an example for Chapter 25 of the
```

Continued

Listing 25-19 *(continued)*

```
     XML Bible, 3rd Edition,
     by Elliotte Rusty Harold (elharo@metalab.unc.edu)
     Published by Wiley 2004. ISBN 0-7645-4986-3.

     This schema is placed in the public domain. Please
     feel free to use it or adapt it in any way you like.

     This DTD is identified by the PUBLIC and SYSTEM
     identifiers:

     PUBLIC "-//ERH//Genealogy Family Tree Module 1.0//EN"
            "family_tree.mod"

     SYSTEM "family_tree.mod"

     It is not a formal standard, and has not been considered
     or approved by any standards body.

     ..................................................... -->

<!-- A family tree consists of any number of SOURCE, PERSON,
     and FAMILY elements in any order. These are all top-level
     elements that refer to each other by ID attributes
     and references. None of them contain any of the others.
-->
<!ELEMENT %FAMILY_TREE.qname; (
   %SOURCE.qname; | %PERSON.qname; | %FAMILY.qname;
   )*
>
```

Finally, you write the complete driver DTD for family trees that imports all five DTDs, as well as XHTML Basic. Listing 25-20 demonstrates.

Listing 25-20: FamilyTree_driver.dtd: The Driver DTD

```
<!-- ..................................................... -->
<!-- Genealogy Family Tree Driver DTD  ................... -->
<!-- file: FamilyTree_driver.dtd

     This DTD describes a FAMILY_TREE element intended for use
     as the root element in family tree documents. It was
     developed as an example for Chapter 25 of the
     XML Bible, 3rd Edition,
     by Elliotte Rusty Harold (elharo@metalab.unc.edu)
     Published by Wiley 2004. ISBN 0-7645-4986-3.
```

```
     This DTD is placed in the public domain. Please
     feel free to use it or adapt it in any way you like.

     This DTD is identified by the PUBLIC and SYSTEM
     identifiers:

     PUBLIC "-//ERH//Genealogy Family Tree DTD 1.0//EN"
            "family_tree.dtd"

     SYSTEM "family_tree.dtd"

     It is not a formal standard, and has not been considered
     or approved by any standards body.

     ....................................................... -->

<!-- Define namespaces and qualified names -->
<!ENTITY % namespaces SYSTEM "genealogy-namespaces.mod">
%namespaces;
<!ENTITY % qnames SYSTEM "genealogy-qname.mod">
%qnames;

<!-- Import XHTML Basic -->
<!ENTITY % xhtml PUBLIC "-//W3C//DTD XHTML Basic 1.0//EN"
                        "xhtml-basic10.dtd">
%xhtml;

<!ENTITY % personref "PERSON IDREF #REQUIRED">
<!ENTITY % sourceref "SOURCE IDREF #REQUIRED">

<!ENTITY % source PUBLIC
    "-//ERH//Genealogy Source Module 1.0//EN"
    "source.mod">
%source;

<!ENTITY % person PUBLIC
    "-//ERH//Genealogy Person Module 1.0//EN"
    "person.mod"
>
%person;

<!ENTITY % family PUBLIC
    "-//ERH//Genealogy Family Module 1.0//EN"
    "family.mod"
>
%family;

<!ENTITY % family_tree PUBLIC
    "-//ERH//Genealogy Family Tree Module 1.0//EN"
    "family_tree.mod">
%family_tree;
```

As written, Listings 25-16 through 25-19 can only be used in conjunction with Listing 25-20 because they don't import the namespace and qualified names modules that declare the parameter entities that they use. However, if it were important that they be able to be used independently, it would not be hard to import the namespace and qualified names modules in a different driver DTD.

No further work is necessary to modularize the schemas. The schemas are already as modular as they need to be. Because schemas only consider namespace URIs and not prefixes, no special tricks are needed to allow authors to change the prefix. Furthermore, schemas allow new types to be derived from existing types, and allow existing types to be redefined in new schemas by using `xsd:redefine` in place of `xsd:include`. All the modularity and extensibility that takes so much work to set up in a DTD comes almost for free with schemas. That's one of the big advantages schemas have over DTDs.

Designing a Style Sheet for Family Trees

The family tree document is organized as records rather than as a narrative. To get a reasonably pleasing view of the document, you need to reorder and reorganize the contents before displaying them. CSS really isn't powerful enough for this task. Consequently, an XSLT style sheet is called for.

The input document uses multiple namespaces, `http://ns.cafeconleche.org/genealogy/` and `http://www.w3.org/1999/xhtml`. In the input document, both of these are the default namespace on their respective sections. I want to output regular HTML instead of XHTML for better compatibility with legacy browsers, so I need to make sure my output elements are not in any namespace at all. And, of course, there's the XSLT namespace, too. Thus, the style sheet itself needs to distinguish between four different namespaces. This would be far too difficult to do if I had to use the same prefix (or lack thereof) in the style sheet as in the input document. Fortunately, I don't. Instead, I can choose to use prefixes in my style sheet even where I didn't in the input document. Specifically, I will choose the following:

- `xsl` for `http://www.w3.org/1999/XSL/Transform`
- `gen` for `http://ns.cafeconleche.org/genealogy/`
- `xhtml` for http://www.w3.org/1999/xhtml

The resulting `xsl:stylesheet` root element will declare all these namespaces, like this:

```
<xsl:stylesheet version="1.0"
  xmlns:xsl="http://www.w3.org/1999/XSL/Transform"
  xmlns:gen="http://ns.cafeconleche.org/genealogy/"
  xmlns:html="http://www.w3.org/1999/xhtml">
```

The default namespace is not explicitly mapped, so any element names without prefixes will be in no namespace at all.

Now you're ready to start writing template rules that match the nodes in the input document. It's best to begin with the root node. That way you can apply the style sheet to the document after you write each template to make sure you're getting what you expect. Here the root node is merely replaced by the standard `html`, `head`, and `body` elements. Templates are applied to the `FAMILY_TREE` root element to continue processing. Note, however, that I have to use the `gen` namespace prefix on `FAMILY_TREE` to make sure that I'm selecting the `FAMILY_TREE` element in the `http://ns.cafeconleche.org/genealogy/` namespace and not the `FAMILY_TREE` element in no namespace.

```
<xsl:template match="/">
  <html>
    <head>
      <title>Family Tree</title>
    </head>
    <body>
      <xsl:apply-templates select="gen:FAMILY_TREE"/>
    </body>
  </html>
</xsl:template>
```

The template rule for the `FAMILY_TREE` element divides the document into three parts, one each for the families, people, and sources. Templates are applied to each separately. Again, prefixes are used to sort the different elements into the right namespaces.

```
<xsl:template match="gen:FAMILY_TREE">

  <h1>Family Tree</h1>

  <h2>Families</h2>
  <xsl:apply-templates select="gen:FAMILY"/>

  <h2>People</h2>
  <xsl:apply-templates select="gen:PERSON"/>

  <h2>Sources</h2>
  <ul>
   <xsl:apply-templates select="gen:SOURCE"/>
  </ul>

</xsl:template>
```

The SOURCE rule is quite simple. Each source is wrapped in a li element. Furthermore, its ID is attached using the name attribute of the HTML a element. This allows for cross-references directly to the source, as shown here:

```
<xsl:template match="gen:SOURCE">

  <li>
    <xsl:element name="a">
      <xsl:attribute name="name">
        <xsl:value-of select="@ID"/>
      </xsl:attribute>
      <xsl:value-of select="."/>
    </xsl:element>
  </li>

</xsl:template>
```

The PERSON element is much more complex, so I'll break it up into several template rules. The PERSON template rule selects the individual parts and formats those that aren't too complex. It applies templates to the rest. The name is placed in an h3 header. This is surrounded with an HTML anchor whose name is the person's ID. The BIRTH, DEATH, BAPTISM, and BURIAL elements are formatted as list items, as demonstrated here:

```
<xsl:template match="gen:PERSON">

    <h3>
      <xsl:element name="a">
        <xsl:attribute name="name">
          <xsl:value-of select="@ID"/>
        </xsl:attribute>
      <xsl:value-of select="gen:NAME"/>
      </xsl:element>
    </h3>

    <ul>
      <xsl:if test="gen:BIRTH">
        <li>Born: <xsl:value-of select="gen:BIRTH"/></li>
      </xsl:if>
      <xsl:if test="gen:DEATH">
        <li>Died: <xsl:value-of select="gen:DEATH"/></li>
      </xsl:if>
      <xsl:if test="gen:BAPTISM">
        <li>Baptism: <xsl:value-of select="gen:BAPTISM"/></li>
      </xsl:if>
      <xsl:if test="gen:BURIAL">
        <li>Burial: <xsl:value-of select="gen:BURIAL"/></li>
      </xsl:if>
      <xsl:apply-templates select="gen:FATHER"/>
      <xsl:apply-templates select="gen:MOTHER"/>
    </ul>
```

```
    <xsl:apply-templates select="gen:NOTE"/>

  </xsl:template>
```

The FATHER and MOTHER elements are also list items, but they need to be linked to their respective people. These two template rules do that:

```
  <xsl:template match="gen:FATHER">
    <li>
      <xsl:element name="a">
        <xsl:attribute name="href">#<xsl:value-of
          select="@PERSON"/></xsl:attribute>
        Father
      </xsl:element>
    </li>
  </xsl:template>

  <xsl:template match="gen:MOTHER">
    <li>
      <xsl:element name="a">
        <xsl:attribute name="href">#<xsl:value-of
          select="@PERSON"/></xsl:attribute>
        </xsl:attribute>
        Mother
      </xsl:element>
    </li>
  </xsl:template>
```

A couple of elements are indented in an unusual fashion — the xsl:attribute elements. These were originally written in a more standard form, like this:

```
<xsl:attribute name="href">
  #<xsl:value-of select="@PERSON"/></xsl:attribute>
</xsl:attribute>
```

The problem with this approach is that the XSLT processor will consider the extra white space between <xsl:attribute name="href"> and # to be significant and include it, encoded line breaks and all, in the attribute values it produces. The attributes come out looking like this:

```
<a href="&#x0A;          #p1099">
  Mother
</a>
```

However, what I want is this:

```
<a href="#p1099">
  Mother
</a>
```

XSLT processors normally strip nodes that contain nothing but boundary white space. However, they do not trim nodes of leading and trailing white space if the node contains something other than white space — the sharp sign in this example. The solution is straightforward — simply trim the extra white space yourself — but it does tend to leave the style sheet looking less than pretty.

The final thing you need to do to format `PERSON` elements is to copy the contents of the `NOTE` into the finished document. This requires replacing the `body` element with a `div` element, because a genealogy document may contain multiple `body` elements but an HTML document may not. However, all the contents should be moved over verbatim. This rule does that by using `xsl:for-each` to iterate through the children and attributes of the `body`, copying each one using `xsl:copy-of`:

```
<xsl:template match="xhtml:body">
  <div>
    <xsl:for-each select="node()|@*">
      <xsl:copy-of select="."/>
    </xsl:for-each>
  </div>
</xsl:template>
```

The template rule for `FAMILY` elements will list the name and role of each member of the family as a list item in an unordered list. Each member element will be linked to the description of that individual. The rules to do this look like the following:

```
<xsl:template match="FAMILY">
  <ul>
    <xsl:apply-templates select="HUSBAND"/>
    <xsl:apply-templates select="WIFE"/>
    <xsl:apply-templates select="CHILD"/>
  </ul>
</xsl:template>

<xsl:template match="HUSBAND">
  <li>Husband: <a href="#{@PERSON}">
    <xsl:value-of select="id(@PERSON)/NAME"/>
  </a></li>
</xsl:template>

<xsl:template match="WIFE">
  <li>Wife: <a href="#{@PERSON}">
    <xsl:value-of select="id(@PERSON)/NAME"/>
  </a></li>
</xsl:template>

<xsl:template match="CHILD">
  <li>Child: <a href="#{@PERSON}">
    <xsl:value-of select="id(@PERSON)/NAME"/>
  </a></li>
</xsl:template>
```

The trickiest thing about these rules is the insertion of data from one element (the PERSON) in a template that matches a different element (HUSBAND, WIFE, CHILD). The ID of the PERSON stored in the HUSBAND/WIFE/CHILD's PERSON attribute is used to locate the right PERSON element; then its NAME child is selected.

Listing 25-21 is the finished family tree style sheet. Figure 25-2 shows the beginning of the document after it's been converted into HTML and loaded into Netscape Navigator.

Listing 25-21: The Complete Family Tree Style Sheet

```
<?xml version="1.0"?>
<xsl:stylesheet version="1.0"
  xmlns:xsl="http://www.w3.org/1999/XSL/Transform"
  xmlns:gen="http://ns.cafeconleche.org/genealogy/"
  xmlns:xhtml="http://www.w3.org/1999/xhtml">

  <xsl:template match="/">
    <html>
      <head>
        <title>Family Tree</title>
      </head>
      <body>
        <xsl:apply-templates select="gen:FAMILY_TREE"/>
      </body>
    </html>
  </xsl:template>

  <xsl:template match="gen:FAMILY_TREE">

    <h1>Family Tree</h1>

    <h2>Families</h2>
    <xsl:apply-templates select="gen:FAMILY"/>

    <h2>People</h2>
    <xsl:apply-templates select="gen:PERSON"/>

    <h2>Sources</h2>
    <ul>
     <xsl:apply-templates select="gen:SOURCE"/>
    </ul>

  </xsl:template>

  <xsl:template match="gen:PERSON">

    <h3>
      <xsl:element name="a">
```

Continued

Listing 25-21 *(continued)*

```
        <xsl:attribute name="name">
          <xsl:value-of select="@ID"/>
        </xsl:attribute>
      <xsl:value-of select="gen:NAME"/>
      </xsl:element>
    </h3>

    <ul>
      <xsl:if test="gen:BIRTH">
        <li>Born: <xsl:value-of select="gen:BIRTH"/></li>
      </xsl:if>
      <xsl:if test="gen:DEATH">
        <li>Died: <xsl:value-of select="gen:DEATH"/></li>
      </xsl:if>
      <xsl:if test="gen:BAPTISM">
        <li>Baptism: <xsl:value-of select="gen:BAPTISM"/></li>
      </xsl:if>
      <xsl:if test="BURIAL">
        <li>Burial: <xsl:value-of select="gen:BURIAL"/></li>
      </xsl:if>
      <xsl:apply-templates select="gen:FATHER"/>
      <xsl:apply-templates select="gen:MOTHER"/>
    </ul>

    <xsl:apply-templates select="gen:NOTE"/>

  </xsl:template>

  <xsl:template match="gen:FATHER">
    <li>
      <xsl:element name="a">
        <xsl:attribute name="href">#<xsl:value-of
          select="@PERSON"/></xsl:attribute>
        Father
      </xsl:element>
    </li>
  </xsl:template>

  <xsl:template match="gen:MOTHER">
    <li>
      <xsl:element name="a">
        <xsl:attribute name="href">#<xsl:value-of
          select="@PERSON"/></xsl:attribute>
        Mother
      </xsl:element>
    </li>
  </xsl:template>
```

```
  <xsl:template match="xhtml:body">
    <div>
      <xsl:for-each select="node()|@*">
        <xsl:copy-of select="."/>
      </xsl:for-each>
    </div>
  </xsl:template>

  <xsl:template match="gen:SOURCE">

    <li>
      <xsl:element name="a">
        <xsl:attribute name="name">
          <xsl:value-of select="@ID"/>
        </xsl:attribute>
        <xsl:value-of select="."/>
      </xsl:element>
    </li>

  </xsl:template>

  <xsl:template match="gen:FAMILY">
    <ul>
      <xsl:apply-templates select="gen:HUSBAND"/>
      <xsl:apply-templates select="gen:WIFE"/>
      <xsl:apply-templates select="gen:CHILD"/>
    </ul>
  </xsl:template>

  <xsl:template match="gen:HUSBAND">
    <li>Husband: <a href="#{@PERSON}">
      <xsl:value-of select="id(@PERSON)/gen:NAME"/>
    </a></li>
  </xsl:template>

  <xsl:template match="gen:WIFE">
    <li>Wife: <a href="#{@PERSON}">
      <xsl:value-of select="id(@PERSON)/gen:NAME"/>
    </a></li>
  </xsl:template>

  <xsl:template match="gen:CHILD">
    <li>Child: <a href="#{@PERSON}">
      <xsl:value-of select="id(@PERSON)/gen:NAME"/>
    </a></li>
  </xsl:template>

</xsl:stylesheet>
```

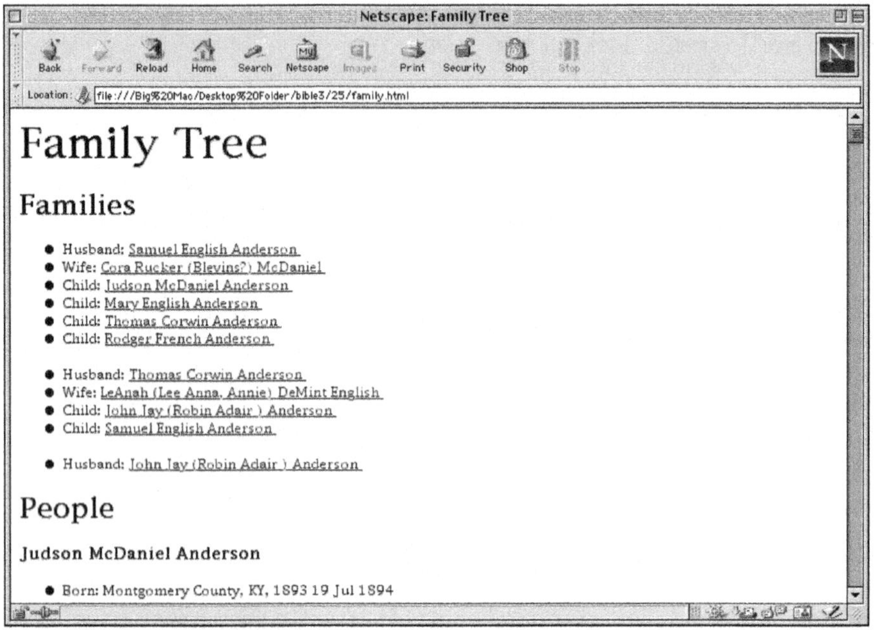

Figure 25-2: The family tree after conversion to HTML

A RDDL document for family trees

The XML application and its style sheet, DTDs, and schemas are now complete. However, one more thing needs to be done before I can say that I'm finished. I've been using the namespace URL `http://ns.cafeconleche.org/genealogy/`. Now I should put something there. Specifically, I should put a RDDL document listing all the related resources for this application. The related resources described in this chapter are as follows:

- ✦ A DTD
- ✦ A modularized DTD
- ✦ A schema
- ✦ An XSLT style sheet

A DTD resource has the nature `http://www.isi.edu/in-notes/iana/assignments/media-types/application/xml-dtd`. This chapter actually developed multiple DTDs: one for the `PERSON`, one for the `FAMILY`, one for the `SOURCE`, and one for the `FAMILY_TREE`. The driver DTD has the validation purpose identified by the well-known URL `http://www.rddl.org/purposes#validation`. The other three DTDs have the DTD module purpose identified by the well-known URL http://www.rddl.org/purposes#module. The family tree DTD depends on the source and family DTDs. The family DTD depends on the person DTD. When I wrote the RDDL document, this dependency seemed to naturally point to embedding one RDDL resource element inside another, which is perfectly OK.

```
<rddl:resource xmlns:rddl="http://www.rddl.org/"
  xlink:type="simple"
  xlink:href="http://cafeconleche.org/dtds/family_tree.dtd"
  xlink:role=
   "http://www.isi.edu/in-notes/iana/assignments/media-
types/application/xml-dtd"
  xlink:arcrole="http://www.rddl.org/purposes#validation"
>
   <p>
   The
   <a href="http://cafeconleche.org/dtds/family_tree.dtd">
      family tree DTD
   </a> describes an XML application for basic
   genealogical data. It's designed to validate documents
   with the root element <code>FAMILY_TREE</code> in the
   http://ns.cafeconleche.org/genealogy/ namespace.
   It depends on two DTD modules:
   </p>

   <ul>
     <li>
       <rddl:resource xlink:type="simple"
           xlink:href="http://cafeconleche.org/dtds/source.dtd"
           xlink:role="http://www.isi.edu/in-
notes/iana/assignments/media-types/application/xml-dtd"
            xlink:arcrole="http://www.rddl.org/purposes#module"
       >
         <p>
          The source DTD describes <code>REFERENCE</code>
          elements in the http://ns.cafeconleche.org/genealogy/
          namespace.
         </p>
       </rddl:resource>
     </li>
     <li>
       <rddl:resource xlink:type="simple"
           xlink:href="http://cafeconleche.org/dtds/family.dtd"
           xlink:role="http://www.isi.edu/in-
notes/iana/assignments/media-types/application/xml-dtd"
           xlink:arcrole="http://www.rddl.org/purposes#module"
       >
          <p>
            The family DTD describes <code>FAMILY</code>
            elements in the http://ns.cafeconleche.org/genealogy/
namespace.
```

```
              This in turn depends on the
              <rddl:resource xlink:type="simple"
              xlink:href="http://cafeconleche.org/dtds/person.dtd"
              xlink:role="http://www.isi.edu/in-
notes/iana/assignments/media-types/application/xml-dtd"
              xlink:arcrole="http://www.rddl.org/purposes#module"
              >
                person DTD. This DTD describes a single
                <code>PERSON</code> element in the
                http://ns.cafeconleche.org/genealogy/ namespace.
              </rddl:resource>
            </p>
          </rddl:resource>
      </li>
    </ul>

  </rddl:resource>
```

The resource describing the modularized DTD is similar, although a little longer because it needs to point to a few more DTD fragments. You can see it in Listing 25-22 later in this chapter.

A schema resource has the nature `http://www.w3.org/2001/XMLSchema`. There are several schema files here, each of which can be thought of as a separate resource. The `FAMILY_TREE` schema has the purpose `http://www.rddl.org/purposes#schema-validation`. The other three schema documents have the purpose `http://www.rddl.org/purposes#schema-module`. The modular structure of these schemas is the same, so it isn't surprising that nesting the `rddl:resource` elements seemed the most natural way to describe them. This `rddl:resource` elements describes all four schemas:

```
  <rddl:resource xmlns:rddl="http://www.rddl.org/"
    xlink:type="simple"
    xlink:href="http://cafeconleche.org/dtds/family_tree.xsd"
    xlink:role="http://www.w3.org/2001/XMLSchema"
   xlink:arcrole="http://www.rddl.org/purposes#schema-validation"
  >
    <p>
    The
    <a href="http://cafeconleche.org/dtds/family_tree.xsd">
       family tree W3C XML Schema Language schema
    </a> describes an XML application for basic
    genealogical data. It's designed to validate documents with
    the root element <code>FAMILY_TREE</code> in the
    http://ns.cafeconleche.org/genealogy/ namespace. It
    depends on two DTD modules:
    </p>

    <ul>
```

```
      <li>
        <rddl:resource xlink:type="simple"
           xlink:href="http://cafeconleche.org/dtds/source.xsd"
           xlink:role="http://www.w3.org/2001/XMLSchema"
     xlink:arcrole="http://www.rddl.org/purposes#schema-module"
        >
          <p>
             The source W3C XML Schema Language schema
             describes <code>REFERENCE</code> elements
             in the http://ns.cafeconleche.org/genealogy/
             namespace.
          </p>
          </rddl:resource>
      </li>
      <li>
        <rddl:resource xlink:type="simple"
           xlink:href="http://cafeconleche.org/dtds/family.xsd"
           xlink:role="http://www.w3.org/2001/XMLSchema"
     xlink:arcrole="http://www.rddl.org/purposes#schema-module"
        >
           <p>
             The family W3C XML Schema Language schema
             describes FAMILY elements in the
             http://ns.cafeconleche.org/genealogy/ namespace.
             This in turn depends on the
            <rddl:resource xlink:type="simple"
            xlink:href="http://cafeconleche.org/dtds/person.xsd"
            xlink:role="http://www.w3.org/2001/XMLSchema"
     xlink:arcrole="http://www.rddl.org/purposes#schema-module"
             >
               person schema. This schema describes a single
               PERSON element in the
               http://ns.cafeconleche.org/genealogy/ namespace.
             </rddl:resource>
           </p>
         </rddl:resource>
      </li>
    </ul>

  </rddl:resource>
```

It's not necessary to include `rddl:resource` elements here that describe the XHTML schemas or DTDs. Those are part of a different namespace and should be described by a RDDL document at that URL, `http://www.w3.org/1999/xhtml`. There isn't one there yet, but that's the W3C's responsibility, not mine.

The next resource is the XSLT style sheet. This has the nature `http://www.isi.edu/in-notes/iana/assignments/media-types/application/xml+xslt` based on its MIME media type. There's only one, so a purpose isn't needed. The `rddl:resource` element describing it is straightforward:

```
<rddl:resource xmlns:rddl="http://www.rddl.org/"
  xlink:type="simple"
  xlink:href="http://cafeconleche.org/styles/familytree.xsl"
  xlink:role="http://www.isi.edu/in-
notes/iana/assignments/media-types/application/xml+xslt"
>
<p>An <a href="http://cafeconleche.org/styles/familytree.xsl">
XSLT 1.0 style sheet for genealogy data</a> is available.
This does not work with Internet Explorer 5.5 and earlier
because of Microsoft's nonconforming implementation of
XSLT.</p>
</rddl:resource>
```

Is there anything else? I can think of one more thing: this book itself. After all, where else are you going to find the complete description of the genealogy application? The problem is that this book isn't easily resolvable because it doesn't live on the Internet anywhere. Nonetheless, it does have a URI based on its ISBN number, if not a URL. This URI is `urn:isbn:0764549863`. You can use this to set up one more `rddl:resource` element identifying a reference for this application (purpose `http://www.rddl.org/purposes/software#reference`).

```
<rddl:resource xmlns:rddl="http://www.rddl.org/"
  xlink:type="simple"
  xlink:href="urn:isbn:0764549863" xlink:arcrole=
           "http://www.rddl.org/purposes/software#reference"
>
  <p>
     Chapter 25 of the XML Bible, 3rd Edition, describes and
     explains this XML application in much greater detail. You
     should be able to find it in any bookstore that stocks
     computer books including <a href=
     "http://www.bookpool.com/">Bookpool</a> and
     <a href="http://www.powells.com/">Powells</a>.
     The list price is $39.99, but it's often discounted.
     If you need to special order it, the
     ISBN number is 0-7645-4986-3 and the author is
     <a href="http://www.elharo.com/">Elliotte
     Rusty Harold</a>
  </p>
</rddl:resource>
```

Listing 25-22 shows the completed RDDL document for the family tree application for the namespace URI, `http://ns.cafeconleche.org/genealogy/`.

Listing 25-22: The RDDL Document for the Family Tree XML Application Developed in This Chapter

```
<!DOCTYPE html PUBLIC "-//XML-DEV//DTD XHTML RDDL 1.0//EN"
                      "http://www.rddl.org/rddl-xhtml.dtd">
<html xmlns="http://www.w3.org/1999/xhtml"
      xmlns:xlink="http://www.w3.org/1999/xlink"
      xmlns:rddl="http://www.rddl.org/">
<head>
  <title>An XML Application for Genealogy</title>
</head>
<body>
<h1>An XML Application for Genealogy</h1>

<div class="head">
<p>This Version:
<a href="http://ns.cafeconleche.org/genealogy/20030824/">August
24, 2003</a></p>
<p>Latest Version: <a
href="http://ns.cafeconleche.org/genealogy/">
  http://ns.cafeconleche.org/genealogy/</a></p>
<p>Previous Version: <a
href="http://ns.cafeconleche.org/genealogy/200100505/">May 25,
  2001</a></p>
<p>Authors:</p>
<ul>
<li><a href="mailto:elharo@metalab.unc.edu">Elliotte
Rusty Harold</a></li>
</ul>
</div>

<p>
This document describes the an XML application for genealogy
statistics used as an example in the 3rd edition of the
<cite>XML Bible</cite>.
</p>

<p>Available related resource include:</p>

<ul>
  <li><a href="#DTD">A DTD</a></li>
  <li><a href="#Modularized">A Modularized DTD</a></li>
  <li><a href="#schema">A schema</a></li>
  <li><a href="#xslt">An XSLT stylesheet</a></li>
</ul>

<rddl:resource xmlns:rddl="http://www.rddl.org/"
  xlink:type="simple"
  xlink:href="urn:isbn:0764549863"
```

Continued

Listing 25-22 (continued)

```
xlink:arcrole="http://www.rddl.org/purposes/software#reference"
>
  <p>
     Chapter 25 of the XML Bible, 3rd Edition, describes and
     explains this XML application in much greater detail. You
     should be able to find it in any bookstore that stocks
     computer books including <a href=
     "http://www.bookpool.com/">Bookpool</a> and
     <a href="http://www.powells.com/">Powells</a>.
     The list price is $39.99, but it's often discounted.
     If you need to special order it, the
     ISBN number is 0-7645-4986-3 and the author is
     <a href="http://www.elharo.com/">Elliotte
     Rusty Harold</a>
  </p>
</rddl:resource>


<p>This document has no official standing and has not been
considered or approved by any organization.</p>

<h2 id="DTD">Document Type Definition</h2>

<rddl:resource xmlns:rddl="http://www.rddl.org/"
  xlink:type="simple"
  xlink:href="http://cafeconleche.org/dtds/family_tree.dtd"
  xlink:role=
   "http://www.isi.edu/in-notes/iana/assignments/media-
types/application/xml-dtd"
  xlink:arcrole="http://www.rddl.org/purposes#validation"
>
   <p>
   The
   <a href="http://cafeconleche.org/dtds/family_tree.dtd">
     family tree DTD
   </a> describes an XML application for basic
   genealogical data. It's designed to validate documents
   with the root element <code>FAMILY_TREE</code> in the
   http://ns.cafeconleche.org/genealogy/ namespace.
   It depends on two DTD modules:
   </p>

   <ul>
     <li>
       <rddl:resource xlink:type="simple"
          xlink:href="http://cafeconleche.org/dtds/source.dtd"
          xlink:role="http://www.isi.edu/in-
notes/iana/assignments/media-types/application/xml-dtd"
          xlink:arcrole="http://www.rddl.org/purposes#module"
       >
```

```
        The
        <a
href="http://cafeconleche.org/dtds/source.dtd">source
        DTD</a> describes <code>SOURCE</code> elements in the
        http://ns.cafeconleche.org/genealogy/ namespace.
       </rddl:resource>
     </li>
     <li>
       <rddl:resource xlink:type="simple"
           xlink:href="http://cafeconleche.org/dtds/family.dtd"
           xlink:role="http://www.isi.edu/in-
notes/iana/assignments/media-types/application/xml-dtd"
           xlink:arcrole="http://www.rddl.org/purposes#module"
       >
          The <a
href="http://cafeconleche.org/dtds/family.dtd">
          family DTD</a> describes <code>FAMILY</code>
          elements in the http://ns.cafeconleche.org/genealogy/
          namespace. This in turn depends on the
          <rddl:resource xlink:type="simple"
           xlink:href="http://cafeconleche.org/dtds/person.dtd"
           xlink:role="http://www.isi.edu/in-
notes/iana/assignments/media-types/application/xml-dtd"
           xlink:arcrole="http://www.rddl.org/purposes#module"
            >
            <a href="http://cafeconleche.org/dtds/person.dtd">
            person DTD</a>. This DTD describes a single
            <code>PERSON</code> element in the
            http://ns.cafeconleche.org/genealogy/ namespace.
           </rddl:resource>
        </rddl:resource>
     </li>
   </ul>

</rddl:resource>


<h2 id="Modularized">A Modularized DTD</h2>

<rddl:resource xmlns:rddl="http://www.rddl.org/"
  xlink:type="simple" xlink:href=
  "http://cafeconleche.org/dtds/FamilyTree_driver.dtd"
  xlink:role=
   "http://www.isi.edu/in-notes/iana/assignments/media-
types/application/xml-dtd"
  xlink:arcrole="http://www.rddl.org/purposes#validation"
>
   <p>
   The
 <a href="http://cafeconleche.org/dtds/FamilyTree_driver.dtd">
      modularized family tree DTD
```

Continued

Listing 25-22 *(continued)*

```
  </a> describes the same XML application for basic
  genealogical data as the previous DTD. However, it's
  designed to allow document authors to modify the namespace
  prefix by overriding the <code>%GENEALOGY.prefix;</code> and
  <code>%GENEALOGY.prefixed;</code> parameter entity
  references.
  If you wish to turn on prefixing, set
  <code>%GENEALOGY.prefixed;</code> to <code>INCLUDE</code>
  and <code>%GENEALOGY.prefix;</code> to the prefix you want
  to use.
  </p>

  <p>
    It is composed of six modules and one driver DTD:
  </p>

  <ul>
    <li>
      <rddl:resource xlink:type="simple"
         xlink:href="http://cafeconleche.org/dtds/source.dtd"
         xlink:role="http://www.isi.edu/in-
notes/iana/assignments/media-types/application/xml-dtd"
         xlink:arcrole="http://www.rddl.org/purposes#module"
      >
       The <a href="http://cafeconleche.org/dtds/source.mod">
       source module</a> describes <code>SOURCE</code>
       elements in the http://ns.cafeconleche.org/genealogy/
       namespace.
      </rddl:resource>
    </li>
    <li>
      <rddl:resource xlink:type="simple"
         xlink:href="http://cafeconleche.org/dtds/family.mod"
         xlink:role="http://www.isi.edu/in-
notes/iana/assignments/media-types/application/xml-dtd"
         xlink:arcrole="http://www.rddl.org/purposes#module"
      >
       The <a href="http://cafeconleche.org/dtds/family.mod">
       family module</a> describes <code>FAMILY</code>
       elements in the http://ns.cafeconleche.org/genealogy/
       namespace.
      </rddl:resource>
    </li>
    <li>
      <rddl:resource xlink:type="simple"
          xlink:href="http://cafeconleche.org/dtds/person.mod"
          xlink:role="http://www.isi.edu/in-notes/iana/
assignments/media-types/application/xml-dtd"
          xlink:arcrole="http://www.rddl.org/purposes#module"
      >
```

```
          The <a href="http://cafeconleche.org/dtds/person.mod">
          person module</a> describes <code>PERSON</code>
          elements in the http://ns.cafeconleche.org/genealogy/
          namespace.
         </rddl:resource>
      </li>
      <li>
        <rddl:resource xlink:type="simple"
           xlink:href="http://cafeconleche.org/dtds/person.mod"
           xlink:role="http://www.isi.edu/in-
notes/iana/assignments/media-types/application/xml-dtd"
           xlink:arcrole="http://www.rddl.org/purposes#module"
        >
           The <a href=
           "http://cafeconleche.org/dtds/family_tree.mod">
           family tree module</a> describes
           <code>FAMILY_TREE</code> elements in the
           http://ns.cafeconleche.org/genealogy/ namespace.
        </rddl:resource>
      </li>
      <li>
        <rddl:resource xlink:type="simple"
            xlink:href=
         "http://cafeconleche.org/dtds/genealogy-namespace.mod"
            xlink:role="http://www.isi.edu/in-
notes/iana/assignments/media-types/application/xml-dtd"
            xlink:arcrole="http://www.rddl.org/purposes#module"
        >
        The <a href=
        "http://cafeconleche.org/dtds/genealogy-namespace.mod">
        namespaces module</a> defines the namespace URI
        and prefix used in this application.
        </rddl:resource>
      </li>
      <li>
        <rddl:resource xlink:type="simple"
 xlink:href="http://cafeconleche.org/dtds/genealogy-qname.mod"
            xlink:role="http://www.isi.edu/in-
notes/iana/assignments/media-types/application/xml-dtd"
            xlink:arcrole="http://www.rddl.org/purposes#module"
        >
           The <a href=
           "http://cafeconleche.org/dtds/genealogy-qname.mod">
           qualified names module</a> defines parameter entity
           references that resolve to the prefixed names of the
           different elements in this application.
         </rddl:resource>
      </li>
      <li>
        <rddl:resource xlink:type="simple" xlink:href=
          "http://cafeconleche.org/dtds/FamilyTree_driver.dtd"
```

Continued

Listing 25-22 *(continued)*

```
            xlink:role="http://www.isi.edu/in-
notes/iana/assignments/media-types/application/xml-dtd"
            xlink:arcrole="http://www.rddl.org/purposes#module"
        >
          The <a href=
          "http://cafeconleche.org/dtds/FamilyTree_driver.dtd">
          driver DTD</a> loads all the modules in the correct
          order.
        </rddl:resource>
      </li>
    </ul>

</rddl:resource>

<h2 id="schema">Schema</h2>

<rddl:resource xmlns:rddl="http://www.rddl.org/"
 xlink:type="simple"
 xlink:href="http://cafeconleche.org/dtds/family_tree.xsd"
 xlink:role="http://www.w3.org/2001/XMLSchema"
xlink:arcrole="http://www.rddl.org/purposes#schema-validation"
>
   <p>
   The
   <a href="http://cafeconleche.org/dtds/family_tree.xsd">
      family tree W3C XML Schema Language schema
   </a> describes an XML application for basic
   genealogical data. It's designed to validate documents with
   the root element <code>FAMILY_TREE</code> in the
   http://ns.cafeconleche.org/genealogy/ namespace. It
   depends on two DTD modules:
   </p>

   <ul>
     <li>
       <rddl:resource xlink:type="simple"
           xlink:href="http://cafeconleche.org/dtds/source.xsd"
           xlink:role="http://www.w3.org/2001/XMLSchema"
     xlink:arcrole="http://www.rddl.org/purposes#schema-module"
       >
        The <a href="http://cafeconleche.org/dtds/source.xsd">
        source W3C XML Schema Language schema</a>
        describes <code>SOURCE</code> elements
        in the http://ns.cafeconleche.org/genealogy/
        namespace.
       </rddl:resource>
```

```
    </li>
    <li>
      <rddl:resource xlink:type="simple"
         xlink:href="http://cafeconleche.org/dtds/family.xsd"
         xlink:role="http://www.w3.org/2001/XMLSchema"
   xlink:arcrole="http://www.rddl.org/purposes#schema-module"
      >
      The <a href="http://cafeconleche.org/dtds/family.xsd">
      family W3C XML Schema Language schema</a>
      describes <code>FAMILY</code> elements in the
      http://ns.cafeconleche.org/genealogy/ namespace.
      This in turn depends on the
      <rddl:resource xlink:type="simple"
         xlink:href="http://cafeconleche.org/dtds/person.xsd"
         xlink:role="http://www.w3.org/2001/XMLSchema"
   xlink:arcrole="http://www.rddl.org/purposes#schema-module"
        >
          <a href="http://cafeconleche.org/dtds/person.xsd">
          person schema</a>. This schema describes a single
          <code>PERSON</code> element in the
          http://ns.cafeconleche.org/genealogy/ namespace.
        </rddl:resource>
      </rddl:resource>
    </li>
  </ul>

</rddl:resource>


<h2 id="xslt">XSLT Style Sheet</h2>

<rddl:resource xmlns:rddl="http://www.rddl.org/"
  xlink:type="simple"
  xlink:href="http://cafeconleche.org/styles/familytree.xsl"
  xlink:role="http://www.isi.edu/in-
notes/iana/assignments/media-types/application/xml+xslt"
>
<p>An <a href="http://cafeconleche.org/styles/familytree.xsl">
XSLT 1.0 style sheet for genealogy data</a> is available.
This does not work with Internet Explorer 5.5 and earlier
because of Microsoft's nonconforming implementation of
XSLT.</p>
</rddl:resource>

</body>
</html>
```

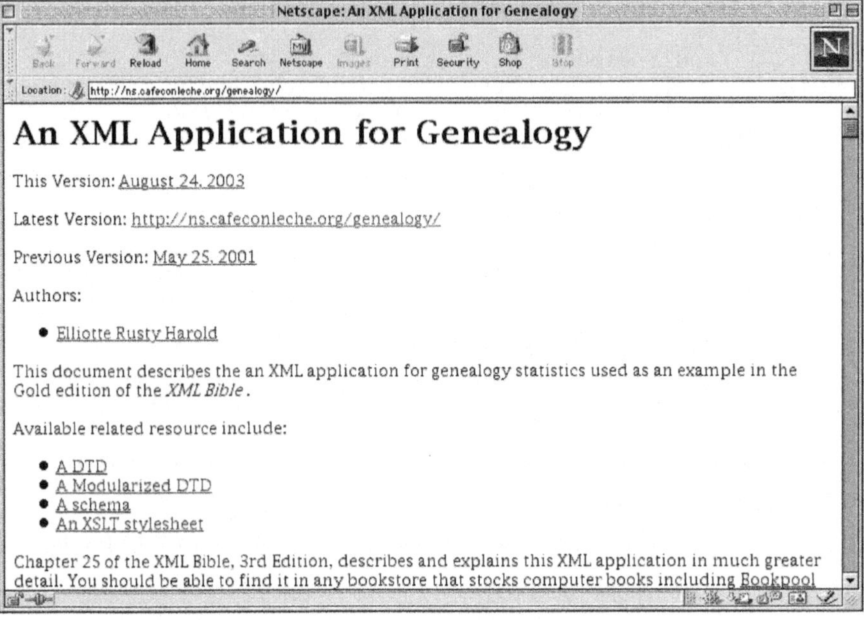

Figure 25-3: The RDDL document for the genealogy application

Summary

In this chapter, you saw an XML application for genealogy developed from scratch. Along the way you learned to

✦ Always begin a new XML application by considering the domain you're describing.

✦ Try to identify the fundamental elements of the domain. Everything else is likely to either be contained in or to be an attribute of one of these.

✦ Try to avoid including the same data in more than one place. Instead, use `ID` and `IDREF` attributes to establish pointers from one element to another.

✦ Be sure to consider special cases. Don't base your entire design on the most obvious cases.

✦ Use parameter entities to merge the DTDs for each piece of the XML application into one complete DTD.

✦ Use `xsd:include` and `xsd:import` to merge the schemas for each piece of the XML application into one complete schema.

- Don't get hung up on what your data will look like when you're designing the application. You can always reorganize it with XSLT.
- Make your namespace URIs resolvable URLs, and place a RDDL document at the end of each namespace URL.

This concludes the *XML Bible*. Go forth now and write your own XML applications!

✦ ✦ ✦

Index

SYMBOLS AND NUMERICS

D

Continued

F

Continued

J

K

L

Continued

N

O

P

Continued

S

Continued

T

U

V

W

X

Continued

Continued

Z

CPSIA information can be obtained at www.ICGtesting.com
Printed in the USA
BVOW08n1610060115

381589BV00014B/24/P